Encyclopedia of Modern China

Encyclopedia of Modern China

VOLUME 3
N–T

David Pong

EDITOR IN CHIEF

CHARLES SCRIBNER'S SONS
A part of Gale, Cengage Learning

GALE
CENGAGE Learning™

Detroit • New York • San Francisco • New Haven, Conn • Waterville, Maine • London

Encyclopedia of Modern China
David Pong, Editor in Chief

For product information and technology assistance, contact us at
Gale Customer Support, 1-800-877-4253.
For permission to use material from this text or product,
submit all requests online at **www.cengage.com/permissions.**
Further permissions questions can be emailed to
permissionrequest@cengage.com

While every effort has been made to ensure the reliability of the information presented in this publication, Gale, a part of Cengage Learning, does not guarantee the accuracy of the data contained herein. Gale accepts no payment for listing; and inclusion in the publication of any organization, agency, institution, publication, service, or individual does not imply endorsement of the editors or publisher. Errors brought to the attention of the publisher and verified to the satisfaction of the publisher will be corrected in future editions.

Library of Congress Cataloging-in-Publication Data

Encyclopedia of modern China / David Pong, editor in chief.
   p. cm. --
   Includes bibliographical references and index.
   ISBN 978-0-684-31566-9 (set : alk. paper) -- ISBN 978-0-684-31567-6 (v. 1 : alk. paper) -- ISBN 978-0-684-31568-3 (v. 2 : alk. paper) -- ISBN 978-0-684-31569-0 (v. 3 : alk. paper) -- ISBN 978-0-684-31570-6 (v. 4 : alk. paper) -- ISBN 978-0-684-31571-3 (e-book)
   1. China--Civilization--1644-1912--Encyclopedias. 2. China--Civilization--1912-1949--Encyclopedias. 3. China--Civilization--1949---Encyclopedias. I. Pong, David, 1939–.

DS755.E63 2009
951.003--dc22
                  2009003279

Gale
27500 Drake Rd.
Farmington Hills, MI 48331-3535

ISBN-13: 978-0-684-31566-9 (set)   ISBN-10: 0-684-31566-1 (set)
ISBN-13: 978-0-684-31567-6 (vol. 1)   ISBN-10: 0-684-31567-X (vol. 1)
ISBN-13: 978-0-684-31568-3 (vol. 2)   ISBN-10: 0-684-31568-8 (vol. 2)
ISBN-13: 978-0-684-31569-0 (vol. 3)   ISBN-10: 0-684-31569-6 (vol. 3)
ISBN-13: 978-0-684-31570-6 (vol. 4)   ISBN-10: 0-684-31570-X (vol. 4)

This title is also available as an e-book.
ISBN-13: 978-0-684-31571-3 ISBN-10: 0-684-31571-8
Contact your Gale sales representative for ordering information.

Printed in the United States of America
1 2 3 4 5 6 7 13 12 11 10 09

Editorial Board

Contents

List of Maps

N

NANJING (NANKING)

Located on the lower bank of the Yangzi River as it makes it first great turn southward, Nanjing links the wealth of Jiangnan to the north by land and China's interior via waterway. Its setting in a mountain-edged basin suits defense but also enhances the summer heat for which it is notorious. Smaller hills ring the city proper, which is punctuated by Mochou and Xuanwu lakes and threaded with the remnants of once numerous canals fed by the Qinhuai River. The city ten times served as imperial capital, most notably at the founding of the Ming. Substantial portions of the massive Ming city wall and its later reconstructions remain today.

In 1800 Nanjing, then known by its classical name Jinling, served as both a prefectural and regional seat. The city had a substantial bannerman community, massive imperial silk works, and one of the largest examination halls in the country; its image of faded refinement was burnished in novels such as Wu Jingzi's *Rulin waishi* (*The Scholars*, 1803).

THE OPIUM WAR AND THE TAIPING UPRISING

Nanjing's economy declined during the early nineteenth century, but its strategic importance remained such that the threat of British naval attack on the city during the Opium War prompted Qing surrender. The 1842 Treaty of Nanjing was signed in the Jinghai Temple, now marked by a museum.

The forces of Hong Xiuquan's Taiping Uprising arrived in Nanjing in March 1853, laying waste to the Manchu quarter and declaring the city the "Heavenly Capital." The Taiping transformed urban life, destroying Buddhist and Daoist temples, enforcing gender and occupational segregation, and exhorting the public to follow the Taiping faith. Many residents fled, especially after the Taiping lost control of the Yangzi in 1857. Zeng Guofan's recapture of Nanjing in July 1864 caused further suffering.

Zeng was given responsibility for rebuilding the devastated city, and he sponsored projects such as the Nanjing Arsenal, but Nanjing remained damaged for decades. The influential lay Buddhist Yang Wenhui (1837–1911), one of the officials charged with reconstruction, founded the Jinling Sutra Publishing House to recover texts destroyed by the Taipings. The 1899 opening of Xiaguan, the port area north of Nanjing, to foreign trade spurred the development of new steamship and rail routes. The Shanghai-Nanjing Railway was opened in 1908 and the Tianjin-Pukou line in 1912. The latter's terminus across the river from Nanjing proper required passengers to complete their journey by ferry; after the line was continued south, railcars were transported this way as well, up until 1968, when the Nanjing Yangzi Bridge was completed.

NANJING AS REPUBLICAN CAPITAL

Nanjing again became an object of physical and symbolic contestation during the 1911 revolution. Although it was the Han official Zhang Xun (1854–1923) who resisted the revolutionaries, when the city finally fell on December 2 the Republican side exacted revenge among the Manchu population. Sun Yat-sen chose the city as his capital in a conscious effort to contest the authority of Qing Beijing. On January 1, 1912, he was sworn in as provisional president in the West Garden Pavilion, the sole Western-style building in the yamen of the Liangjiang governor-general. On February 15, having relinquished the presidency to Yuan Shikai, Sun attempted to cement Nanjing's resurgence by visiting the tomb of Ming Taizu (1328–1398), informing the Ming founder that the revolutionaries had "recovered" China. Yuan, however, reneged on his agreement to retain Nanjing as capital.

The Nationalists' return to Nanjing in March 1927 spurred controversy when forces of their Northern Expedition clashed with Westerners in what came to be known as the "Nanjing Incident." Chiang Kai-shek parlayed his ability to conciliate the United States and Britain into ascendancy against his political rivals in Wuhan and Shanghai. His wish to restore Nanjing as capital was supported by those who wanted to avoid Beijing's associations of failed republicanism. Nanjing's supporters consolidated their moral claim by jump-starting construction of a mausoleum for Sun Yat-sen, delayed since 1925. The tomb, sited grandly above Ming Taizu's on Zijinshan (the Purple Mountains), became the focal point of the Nationalist capital. Zhongshan Road was built as a new artery leading to the mausoleum, along which Sun's body was carried to its final resting place on July 1, 1929.

Historians refer to 1927 to 1937 as the "Nanjing decade," to denote both the location of the national government and the Nationalists' policies during that period. During this decade the government sought to remake the city into a symbol of its nativist modernity. It hired the American architect Henry K. Murphy (1877–1954), who had designed Nanjing's Ginling College (now Nanjing Normal University), to collaborate with Chinese planners on a grand urban design. Fiscal limitations and popular resistance kept much of the plan from coming to fruition. Key elements did emerge, however, such as the "neo-ethnic" style that added Chinese decorative elements to modernist structures, and the tree-lined main boulevards, influenced by the "City Beautiful" movement. Also adopted was the concentration of banking and business around the Xinjiekou intersection in the geographic center of the city, away from the Qing population centers at the Xiaguan port and along the Qinhuai River in the city's south. Nanjing's population nearly tripled during the ten years of prewar Nationalist rule, topping one million in 1935; the annual growth rate during this time exceeded that of China's other major cities by two to five times, as migrants came for government jobs and to escape poverty in nearby regions. Major national cultural institutions developed at this time, including the National Central University, formally established in August 1928 on existing institutional foundations, and the National Central Museum, the preparatory office for which was established in 1933.

In late 1937 the threat of Japanese invasion sent the Nationalist leadership to Wuhan, and eventually to Chongqing. Once the Battle of Shanghai was won on November 26, the Japanese rush to capture the capital was disorderly. They arrived in Nanjing on December 13, launching a month's assault on both civilians and military that became one of the most notorious emblems of war: the Nanjing massacre.

In March 1938 the Japanese installed the Reformed Government in Nanjing as the ostensible national regime; two years later this was replaced by the Wang Jingwei puppet government. The Nationalists reclaimed Nanjing in January 1946 and remained there until April 1949, when the People's Liberation Army took the city.

NANJING DURING THE MAOIST ERA

The loss of Nanjing's bureaucratic population with the Nationalist flight and the subsequent return of the capital to Beijing created substantial employment problems in a city that had developed a service and learning economy during the previous two decades. This as well as nationwide industrialization policies prompted government planners to shift Nanjing's economy to heavy industry during the 1950s and 1960s. By 1997 Nanjing had become China's seventh-largest industrial city. The emblem of such planning was the double-decker auto-rail Yangzi River Bridge, constructed in 1960 to 1968 and hailed as a feat of Chinese engineering and steelmaking.

The bridge had not yet been completed when the Cultural Revolution erupted in 1966. As elsewhere in China, in Nanjing this led to the closing of the city's universities, and after the formal end of the Cultural Revolution in 1969, to the exodus of large numbers of students and cultural workers and their families, many of whom were "sent down" to northern Jiangsu. The universities reopened in the early 1970s and played a key role in the 1976 Nanjing Incident, which was sparked by the death of Zhou Enlai on January 8 that year. In late March mourning for Zhou Enlai, combined with outrage at purported media criticism of him in Shanghai, led to a student march and a poster campaign criticizing Zhou's enemies. The movement culminated in more than 600,000 people visiting Yuhuatai Revolutionary Martyrs cemetery by Qingming Day (April 4), and it inspired action elsewhere, most notably in Beijing.

NANJING IN THE REFORM ERA

During economic reforms, Nanjing lagged behind its coastal neighbors, receiving designation as a special economic zone only in 1988. Priority shifted to the service and technology sectors, which displaced a large percentage of the workforce as state-owned enterprises were restructured

View of the Yangzi River Bridge, Nanjing, October, 2003. *Throughout different periods of China's history, the city of Nanjing has served as the country's capital, including twice during Chiang Kai-shek's tenure leading the Republic of China. Becoming heavily industrialized after the 1950s, the economy of Nanjing shifted to service and technology in the late 1990s.* © **MIKE MCQUEEN/CORBIS**

in the late 1990s. The city established economic technology development zones in its Pukou and Jiangning suburbs (with the former attracting satellite campuses of Nanjing University and other schools), and residents as well as manufacturing facilities relocated outside the city walls. Universities reclaimed the prominent role they once played in the city's identity, with the student population reaching 679,900 in 2007 according to the National Bureau of Statistics. In addition to Nanjing and Nanjing Normal Universities, the city is home to Southeast University (on the site of the Nationalists' Central University), Nanjing Art Institute, and universities of agriculture, aeronautics and astronautics, and traditional Chinese medicine.

Nanjing's historical legacy features more prominently in its current identity than in many Chinese cities of similar size and standing (the city's official population stood at 6.17 million in 2007, but the Nanjing Statistical Bureau put unofficial residents that year at 7.4 million) and has been deliberately exploited during the Reform Era. In 1985 the municipal government opened a memorial hall to the Nanjing massacre, fixing the official Chi-

nese number of 300,000 victims in the public mind by inscribing it on the structure, even though scholars continue to debate the number of fatalities. The museum, which contrasts solemn gardens and historic documentation with the mass graves upon which it is constructed, has been renovated and expanded twice. Also in 1985 the city targeted the Fuzimiao area as a place to link local and international tourism to Nanjing's scholarly culture. The site of the Confucius Temple and the remnants of the Qing examination hall, Fuzimiao had long been a significant cultural and commercial quarter in the city. Lastly, renovations also began on the sites surrounding the Sun Yat-sen mausoleum in Zijinshan, many of which date to the Nanjing decade. These include Murphy's Monument to Fallen Officers and Soldiers, an open-air auditorium and stadium, botanical gardens, an observatory, the Sutra Repository, and the tombs of several revolutionary heroes.

Restoration of key Republican buildings began during the early 1990s, and beginning in 2001 the most important sites were designated national-level protected antiquities. Nanjing is still subject to the pressures of commercial expansion, however, especially in areas such as Xinjiekou; particularly controversial have been street-widening projects that threaten the city's famous trees. In 2003 the Nanjing Urban Planning Institute worked with local government and city residents to mark 134 buildings for preservation.

Local officials thus promote Nanjing's history even as they launch ambitious new infrastructure and building projects. The latter include a subway system (the first line opened in 2005), a new municipal library (2005), and the Nanjing Museum of Art and Architecture slated for completion in 2009. The renovated Nanjing Museum emphasizes recent archaeological findings and the area's distinctive imperial history. City officials and academics threw themselves into the 2005 commemoration of the six hundredth anniversary of the first voyage of the navigator Zheng He (1371–1433), opening the Treasure Boat Factory Ruins Park on a Ming shipyard site. Finally, a major museum of modern history opened at the Presidential Palace in 2003, covering Qing, Taiping, and Republican history.

Nanjing has sustained its strategic importance. It is the base of the PLA Nanjing Military Region, one of the most important of seven such commands because it oversees the offense against Taiwan. Nanjing's military district sits in the northeastern part of the city between Xuanwu Lake and the Ming Palace.

SEE ALSO *Jiangsu; Nanjing Massacre; Special Economic Zones; Taiping Uprising; Treaty Ports; Urban China.*

BIBLIOGRAPHY

PRIMARY WORKS

All China Data Center. 2007. China City Statistics Database. China Data Online. http://chinadataonline.org.

Jinling Wanbao. 07 niandi Nanjing changzhu renkou 741.3 wan; 2020 nian da 962.54 wan [Nanjing residential population 7.413 million at the end of 2007; will reach 9.6254 million in 2020]. April 15, 2008. http://js.xhby.net/system/2008/04/15/010239258.shtml.

Wu Ching-tzu (Wu Jingzi). *The Scholars* [*Rulin waishi*]. Trans. Yang Hsien-yi and Gladys Yang. New York: Columbia University Press, 1992.

SECONDARY WORKS

Fogel, Joshua A., ed. *The Nanjing Massacre in History and Historiography.* Berkeley: University of California Press, 2000.

Harrison, Henrietta. *The Making of the Republican Citizen: Political Ceremonies and Symbols in China, 1911–1929.* Oxford, U.K.: Oxford University Press, 2000.

Lipkin, Zwia. *Useless to the State: "Social Problems" and Social Engineering in Nationalist Nanjing, 1927–1937.* Cambridge, MA: Harvard University Asia Center, 2006.

Lu Haiming and Yang Xinhua, comps. *Nanjing Minguo jianzhu* [Republican architecture in Nanjing]. Nanjing, China: Nanjing Daxue, 2001.

Musgrove, Charles D. Building a Dream: Constructing a National Capital in Nanjing, 1927–1937. In *Remaking the Chinese City: Modernity and National Identity, 1900–1950,* ed. Joseph W. Esherick, 139–157. Honolulu: University of Hawaii Press, 2000.

Spence, Jonathan. *God's Chinese Son: The Taiping Heavenly Kingdom of Hong Xiuquan.* New York: W. W. Norton, 1996.

Wang, Liping. Creating a National Symbol: The Sun Yatsen Memorial in Nanjing. *Republican China* 21, 2 (April 1996): 23–63.

Yamamoto, Masahiro. *Nanking: Anatomy of an Atrocity.* Westport, CT: Praeger, 2000.

Rebecca Nedostup

NANJING MASSACRE

Japan invaded China in 1937 with the intention of forcing the Republic of China into its political and economic orbit. When Chinese forces around Shanghai resisted the invasion and Chiang Kai-shek (Jiang Jieshi) refused to bow to this demand, Japan decided that it had no choice but to destroy Chiang's regime by occupying his capital, Nanjing (Nanking). On December 13, 1937, four months after invading Shanghai, the Japanese army under the command of General Matsui Iwane captured Nanjing through a combination of aerial bombardment, which struck civilian zones as heavily as military installations, and a subsequent massive infantry attack. Resistance was meager, as the Nationalist government had decided to abandon the capital the night before. Japanese soldiers swept into the city, and for the next two months subjected residents to waves of murder, rape, looting, arson, and displacement. They also rounded up Chinese soldiers, deceiving them into believing their lives would be spared, and then executed some 80,000 of them en masse.

Atrocious Japanese troop conduct has been attributed variously to battle weariness, frustration at the scale of resistance, inadequate troop supervision, and an indoctrinated contempt for Chinese, yet this conduct was not unique to Nanjing. Japanese soldiers had already used such tactics in taking other cities. What distinguished Nanjing was the scale of the devastation, Nanjing having a population of roughly 200,000 inhabitants, and also the presence of two dozen foreigners, who organized an International Safety Zone and recorded the devastation for posterity. The foreign press called the takeover the Rape of Nanking. The Chinese remember it as the Nanjing Massacre (Nanjing Datusha).

The massacre was cited in the indictment against Japan's leaders at the International Military Tribunal for the Far East, which sentenced Matsui Iwane and Foreign Minister Hirota Kōki to death for their responsibility. The massacre dwindled to a fading war memory until the passing of the generation that had lived through the

Japanese troops using Chinese prisoners as bayonet targets, Nanjing, 1938. *In December of 1937, Japanese troops entered the Nationalist Chinese capital of Nanjing, beginning a series of war atrocities known as the Nanjing Massacre. In addition to the widespread rape and murder of the civilian population, Japanese soldiers executed an estimated 80,000 Chinese troops, leaving enduring resentment for many citizens.* © BETTMANN/CORBIS

war, when a new generation in the diaspora rediscovered the massacre and sought to refigure China's modern identity from perpetrator of human-rights abuses to victim. What ignited this rediscovery was a proposal in 1982 to remove references to Japan's wartime invasion of China as aggression from some high school textbooks in Japan. Controversy raged through the 1990s. Japan was called on to acknowledge its war record and issue new official apologies, particularly for what happened in Nanjing.

There has been recurring disagreement over the number killed. The official Chinese estimate of 300,000 is enshrined at the Massacre Memorial Hall in Nanjing. Among many Japanese researchers, the estimate is closer to 40,000. The actual total lies in between these two figures. This difference, like the gap between those who feel that the perpetrators have gone unpunished and unrepentant and those who would bury the memory of the atrocity and reestablish the Japan-China relationship on other grounds, is unlikely to be soon bridged. The event still commands too large a role in Chinese

national identity, and imposes too great a burden of guilt for Japanese, for fact finding alone to resolve.

SEE ALSO *Nanjing (Nanking).*

BIBLIOGRAPHY

Brook, Timothy, ed. *Documents on the Rape of Nanking.* Ann Arbor: University of Michigan Press, 1999.

Fogel, Joshua A., ed. *The Nanking Massacre in History and Historiography.* Berkeley: University of California Press, 2000.

Wakabayashi, Bob Tadashi, ed. *The Nanking Atrocity, 1937–38: Complicating the Picture.* Oxford: Berghahn Books, 2007.

Timothy Brook

NANJING ROAD

SEE *Shanghai.*

NATIONAL FLAGS AND NATIONAL ANTHEMS

The history of Chinese national flags and national anthems can be traced to the late Qing. The national flag issued in 1862 was a yellow triangular flag with a blue dragon holding a red ball in its mouth at the center. The dragon is the hallowed Chinese totem and also symbolizes the emperor. The color yellow represents earth in traditional Chinese five-element theory, and it is also the color of the Qing dynasty. This flag also was used as the Qing navy's flag. In 1889 the triangle shape was changed to rectangle.

On October 4, 1911 the Qing government issued the first national anthem, "Gong Jin Ou" ("To consolidate our country"). The lyrics were written by the famous scholar Yan Fu. The music was nominally composed by Aixinjueluo Putong (Aisin Gioro Putong, 1871–1952), but actually based on palace music composed in the Kangxi reign and used from that time as the ceremonial music for an emperor's enthronement.

REPUBLIC OF CHINA

During the 1911 Revolution, in the process of establishing a provisional constitution of the Republic of China in Nanjing, representatives from seventeen provinces together selected the "five-colored flag" as the national flag. This flag was used as the flag of the revolutionary army in Shanghai and northern China. It had five horizontal stripes in different colors—red, yellow, blue, white, and black, from top to bottom—signifying the unity of five major nationalities of China (Han, Manchu, Mongol, Hui, and Tibetan). Though discontented with the design, the provisional president Sun Yat-sen unveiled it in 1912 and soon it was adopted nationwide. It served as the national flag from January 11, 1912 to October 22, 1915.

Accompanying the national flag was a national anthem, "Wu Qi Gonghe Ge" ("Five-colored flag republic song"), composed by Shen Pengnian with lyrics by Shen Enfu (1864–1944). Another national anthem used during the Republican period was "Qingyun ge" ("Clouds of hope"). There were two versions of this song, the words of which are drawn from the biography of Yuxia in the classical work the *Book of History* (*Shangshu Dazhuan Yuxia zhuan*). It was purportedly played at the ceremony when Emperor Yao passed his throne to Shun about 4,000 years ago. Set to music by Jean Hautstont, with two lines added to the original words, this song was first used in the opening ceremony of the first Republican congress on April 8, 1913. As a manifestation of the reformist spirit of the Republic, this song with classical Chinese words and rhythm was played by a Western modern orchestra.

Between October 22, 1915 and March 22, 1916, during the short period of Yuan Shikai's revival of the monarchy, a

Qing dynasty flag, 1862–1890

Republic of China flag, 1912–1928

national flag and national anthem for the restored empire were proclaimed. The national flag preserved the five colors but in a radically different design, so that instead of five stripes, there were now four triangles of yellow, blue, white, and black divided by a red saltire (transverse cross). The national anthem was "Zhonghua Xiongli Yuzhou Jian" ("China stands strong in the universe").

In 1920 the Beiyang government restored the five-colored flag as the national flag and "Qingyun ge" as the national anthem, although this second version retained only the first sixteen words of the first. The adoption of the anthem was announced on March 31, 1921, by the Beiyang government, and it also was used by a number of warlords.

In 1928, following the success of the Northern Expedition and the establishment of the Nationalist government in Nanjing, the anthem was replaced by "San Min Zhuyi" ("The three principles of the people"), which celebrated the three principles central to Sun Yat-sen's political manifesto: nationalism, democracy, and people's

Republic of China flag

People's Republic of China flag

livelihood. The words were written by four Guomindang (GMD) members—Hu Hanmin (1879–1936), Dai Jitao (1890–1949), Liao Zhongkai (1877–1925), and Shao Yuanchong (1890–1936)—in honor of the opening ceremony of the Huangpu (Whampoa) Military Academy on July 16, 1924. They read:

> Three Principles of the People,
> The fundamentals of our party.
> Using this, we establish the Republic;
> Using this, we advance into a state of total peace.
> Oh, you, warriors,
> For the people, be the vanguard.
> Without resting day or night,
> Follow the principles.
> Swear to be diligent; swear to be courageous.
> Obliged to be trustworthy; obliged to be loyal.
> With one heart and one virtue,
> We carry through until the very end.

In 1928 the GMD publicly solicited compositions for the music, and music by Cheng Maoyun (1900–1957) was selected. On February 1, 1929, "Three Principles of the People" was adopted as the party anthem of the Guomindang. In 1930 it was proposed as the national anthem and was provisionally used in this role for twelve years before the Central Standing Committee finally approved the proposal in 1943. Even before official confirmation, it was selected as the world's best national anthem at the 1936 Olympics in Berlin.

The five-colored flag was also replaced by the GMD. The new national flag featured a blue sky and white sun (the GMD party emblem) on a "wholly red earth," a design predating the 1911 Revolution. The "blue sky and white sun" had been designed in 1895 by Lu Haodong (1868–1895), a martyr of the 1911 Revolution. Sun Yat-sen contributed the "wholly red earth" concept. The colors symbolize particular

values: blue for brightness, purity, nation, and freedom; white for honesty, selflessness, democratic rights, and equality; and red for the courage of self-sacrifice, people's livelihood, and humanity. The twelve rays of light of the white sun signify twelve months in a year, and twelve Chinese hours (equal to two hours) in a day. This flag is still used by Taiwan, but it cannot be flown in circumstances where the People's Republic of China is represented; instead, a flag designed for the occasion to represent Chinese Taipei is used. Likewise, the "Three Principles of the People" anthem is avoided on such occasions, replaced by the almost equally historic "Guoqi ge" ("National flag song"), composed by Huang Zi (1904–1938) with lyrics in classical Chinese by Dai Jitao.

PEOPLE'S REPUBLIC OF CHINA

With the birth of the People's Republic of China (PRC), new national emblems were needed. A competition to design the new flag was won by Zeng Liansong (1917–1999), a company manager in Shanghai, whose *wuxing hongqi* (five stars red flag) was adopted at the First Plenary Session of the Chinese People's Political Consultative Conference in September 1949. On October 1, 1949, the new flag was raised in Tiananmen Square for the first time, marking the formal establishment of the People's Republic of China.

The PRC flag is red, symbolizing the spirit of the revolution. The canton (upper left corner) features one large and four smaller yellow stars. The large star signifies the Chinese Communist Party and the five stars together signify the unity of the people of China under the leadership of the Chinese Communist Party.

The national anthem of the People's Republic of China was the theme song of a 1930s film, *Fengyun ernü* (Sons and daughters in times of turmoil), which depicted Chinese resistance to the Japanese during World War II.

The film was inspiring, and the popularity of the theme song "Yiyongjun Jinxing Qu" ("The march of the volunteers") was the basis for its adoption as the provisional national anthem in 1949. The lyrics, in vernacular Chinese, were written by the dramatist and poet Tian Han (1898–1968), and the music was composed by Nie Er (1912–1935) in 1935. The anthem's lyrics are:

> Arise, you who refuse to be slaves;
> With our very flesh and blood
> Let us build our new Great Wall!
> The Peoples of China are in the most critical
>   time,
> Everybody must roar his defiance.
> Arise! Arise! Arise!
> Millions of hearts with one mind,
> Brave the enemy's gunfire,
> March on!
> Brave the enemy's gunfire,
> March on! March on! March on, on!

Tian Han came under attack during the Cultural Revolution (1966–1969) and died in jail. The words to the anthem were no longer sung, and even the tune threatened to be eclipsed by Maoist and revolutionary songs. After the Cultural Revolution new lyrics briefly were used, but in 1982 the original song was confirmed as the official anthem of China. In the same year, new protocols were developed to mark the raising and lowering of the flag in Tiananmen Square, a ceremony now regularly attended by thousands of tourists.

SEE ALSO *Nationalism.*

BIBLIOGRAPHY

Di, Yongjun. *Zhongguo lishi shang de guoqi yu guoge* 中国历史上的国旗与国歌 [National flags and national anthems in Chinese history]. Institute of Ethnology and Anthropology, Chinese Academy of Social Sciences Web site, September 2007. http://iea.cass.cn/ygtd/html/mzs_2007090614224444283.htm

Liang Luo. From Lovers to Volunteers: Tian Han and the National Anthem. *China Beat*, July 16, 2008. http://thechinabeat.blogspot.com/2008/07/from-lovers-to-volunteers-tian-han-and.html

Reed, W. L., and Michael J. Bristow, eds. *National Anthems of the World*. 10th ed. London: Cassell, 2002.

Yiran Zheng

NATIONAL PRODUCTS MOVEMENT

By the early twentieth century, China had begun to import and manufacture thousands of new consumer goods. These commodities created a nascent consumer culture and changed the everyday life of millions. At the center of this new culture were imports and attitudes toward them. Patriotic students, opportunistic businesspeople, and leading politicians feared the loss of sovereignty implicit in the growing foreign dominance of the commercial economy and a burgeoning trade deficit. They began to link this consumer culture with modern ideas of the nation-state, applying the labels *foreign* and *Chinese* to all commodities. In this environment of economic nationalism, heightened by such imperialist outrages as the Twenty-One Demands (1915), Chinese nationalists tried to turn consumers into traitors and patriots with such slogans as "Chinese people should consume Chinese products."

Convincing Chinese to buy domestic products was difficult. The series of unequal treaties imposed on China following its defeat in the Opium War (1839–1842) had denied the Chinese the ability to restrict imports by raising tariffs. Only when China recovered tariff autonomy in 1928 could it use internationally accepted means of nationalizing consumer culture, and it did so by imposing tariffs. But before the establishment of the People's Republic of China in 1949, its autonomy was limited. Throughout the first half of the twentieth century, then, China saw itself as inundated with imports and powerless to stem their inflow. China's semicolonized status made it difficult for foreign powers and their Chinese warlord allies to suppress popular sentiments (as the Japanese colonial authorities attempted in Korea), and its lack of tariff autonomy made it difficult for sympathetic Chinese governments to address the issue through higher tariffs (as Japan did after 1900).

THE NATIONAL PRODUCTS MOVEMENT

Chinese nationalists countered ignorance and apathy by trying to establish cultural constraints on consumption through a multidimensional but diffuse social movement known at the time as the National Products movement (*guohuo yundong*, c. 1905–1949). The problem was that most Chinese either did not hear or did not heed the call to buy Chinese. Indeed, in the early days of Chinese nationalism, the message to interpret objects by nationality was probably incomprehensible. The National Products movement included diverse efforts to create nationalistic consumers. But, as with any social movement, there was never one centrally controlled movement. Silk manufacturers, student protestors, women's organizations, business enterprises, government officials, and ordinary citizens alike invoked the term *national products*. Participants ranged from men leading recognized movement organizations, to women organizing movement events as a way to take part in public life. Other participants included entrepreneurs who were hurt by imports and jumped on the movement bandwagon to sell products, gangsters manipulating movement discourse to extort merchants, and consumers consciously or unconsciously acting on nationalistic categories of consumption.

As the movement grew, its name, its slogans, and the categories of nationalistic consumption it created became ubiquitous in cities and appeared even in the countryside. Its primary manifestations included sumptuary laws mandating the use of Chinese-made fabrics in clothing (the Clothing Law of 1912); frequent anti-imperialist boycotts (especially in 1905, 1911, 1915, 1919, 1925, 1927); *Guohuo yuekan* (National Products monthly) and many other magazines; the government-sponsored national-products campaign of the late 1920s; official National Products Years in the 1930s (Women's in 1934, Children's in 1935, and Citizens' in 1936); weekly supplements published in a major national newspaper (*Shenbao*) in the mid-1930s; thousands of advertisements; regular national-products fashion shows; and specially organized venues (visited by millions) for displaying and selling domestic products, including museums, fixed and traveling exhibitions, and a chain of retail stores. The movement survived the war and formed the backbone of renewed efforts to promote economic nationalism and anti-imperialism. The Nationalist government and the National Chamber of Commerce promoted a "Buy Chinese" campaign. In the winter of 1947 an alleged rape by a U.S. Marine of a Beijing University female led to a new anti-American boycott.

OUTCOMES

The National Products movement popularized a vocabulary that underwrote the idea of nationalistic consumption. The most important terms were *guohuo* (national product) and *yanghuo* (foreign product). The creation and application of positive and negative nationalized social labels led to further elaborations of the movement's vocabulary. In movement literature, an "authentic Chinese woman" did not consume imports, lest she "betray her nation." Moreover, decades before Chinese historians in the People's Republic contrasted the patriotic "national capitalist" (*minzu zibenjia*), whose work aided the nation, and the treasonous "comprador capitalist" (*maiban zibenjia*), whose work benefited foreign companies, the movement sought to create a marketplace that automatically distinguished genuinely patriotic Chinese capitalists from the traitorous agents of foreign interests. Without relying on foreign assistance, the authentic Chinese capitalist produced goods that defended the domestic market by displacing imports.

Complete success was impossible because the movement faced too many obstacles. China's lack of genuine sovereignty allowed imports to pour into the country. Moreover, the powerful associations between imports and modernity, the lower prices, and the mechanized quality of imports heightened demand. Above all, a weak sense of national identity among the vast majority of Chinese consumers (who evaluated their interests in terms of themselves, their families, lineages, communities, and regions) made sacrificing on behalf of the nation unlikely and even unthinkable. But on subtler grounds the movement was much more successful. The movement introduced modern nationalism into countless aspects of China's nascent consumer culture. Such nationalism was visible throughout China, from the growing hostility toward and negative perception of imports in the nineteenth century, through the establishment of a nationalistic male appearance in the late Qing, to the repeated anti-imperialist boycotts and the development of nationalistic commodity spectacles such as advertising and exhibitions in the Republic, to the proliferation of gendered representations of unpatriotic consumption and patriotic producers. This nationalized consumer culture influenced Chinese life from elite discussions of political economy to individual students' decisions of what to wear to school. The movement had an immediate impact on fashion, business, appearance, and language. Its legacies include the representations of unpatriotic consumption and patriotic production that still persist in China. This pervasive cultural influence is the movement's chief success. The general principle, if not the individual practice, of nationalistic consumption is deeply rooted.

SEE ALSO *Imperialism; Industrialization, 1860–1949; Nationalism.*

BIBLIOGRAPHY

Cochran, Sherman. *Big Business in China: Sino-foreign Rivalry in the Cigarette Industry, 1890–1930.* Cambridge, MA: Harvard University Press, 1980.

Fewsmith, Joseph. *Party, State, and Local Elites in Republican China: Merchant Organizations and Politics in Shanghai, 1890–1930.* Honolulu: University of Hawaii Press, 1985.

Gamble, Jos. *Shanghai in Transition: Changing Perspectives and Social Contours of a Chinese Metropolis.* London: RoutledgeCurzon, 2003.

Gerth, Karl. *China Made: Consumer Culture and the Creation of the Nation.* Cambridge, MA: Harvard University Press, 2003.

Remer, Charles F. *A Study of Chinese Boycotts, with Special Reference to Their Economic Effectiveness.* Baltimore, MD: Johns Hopkins Press, 1933.

Karl Gerth

NATIONALISM

From the late nineteenth century, nationalism has been a major political force in China. Nationalism developed in China as a response to the humiliations heaped upon the country by foreign imperialism in the nineteenth and twentieth centuries. It inspired the Republican revolutionaries who overthrew the Qing dynasty (1644–1912), the iconoclasts of the May Fourth movement of 1919, and the labor movement of the 1920s. Both the Guomindang and the Chinese Communist leaders were profoundly influenced by nationalism, as were some warlords. Nationalism helped the Guomindang rally support when it established a national government in 1928, and it inspired resistance during the Japanese occupation. Nationalism also played a role in the Communist Party's rise to power in 1949. Both the Guomindang and the Chinese Communist Party (CCP) sought to legitimize their rule on the basis of nationalism by promoting identity between the nation and the party-state. Since the death of Mao Zedong in 1976, the decline of socialist ideology has led the party-state to rely more heavily on nationalism. Throughout the history of Chinese nationalism, fierce debate has raged on whether Chinese traditional culture should be preserved or whether modernization demands that China model itself on more developed countries.

THE EMERGENCE OF CHINESE NATIONALISM

European imperialism in China in the nineteenth century inspired anger, resistance, and antiforeign movements. Such reactions were visible in the Taiping Uprising (1851–1864) and in the Boxer Uprising of 1900, as well as in many smaller-scale movements. However these movements were not nationalist in the sense of professing their primary loyalty to a nation-state. Such modern nationalism developed only in the late nineteenth century among the elite. The series of defeats inflicted on China first by the expansionist empires of Europe and, then, most traumatically, by a rapidly modernizing Japan in 1895, forced educated Chinese to reassess their view of China as the center of the world possessing a uniquely superior civilization.

In the new understanding, the world consisted of a system of nation-states engaged in a competition for power and dominance that China was losing. Reformers began to move from what historians of China have called *culturalism* to nationalism. Under culturalism, loyalty was inspired by culture. All those who understood and lived by Confucian moral principles and accepted the authority of the emperor and his officials could be part of the Chinese cultural community. Such a perspective allowed non-Han ethnic groups, such as Manchus, Mongols, Tibetans, or Turks, to function as insiders within the Chinese empire, so long as they subscribed to the dominant culture. Nationalism, by contrast, involved loyalty to the nation-state.

The invention of China as a modern nation-state can be seen as part of China's response to imperialism. Repeated military defeats forced China to recognize the existence of other countries that were more advanced, at least in military, scientific, and technical terms. In time, Chinese modernizers began to argue not only that China needed foreign science and technology, but also that foreign political and economic thought and institutions would have to be studied and aspects of China's traditional culture abandoned. Social Darwinist ideas, derived from Yan Fu's 1898 translation of the British biologist Thomas Huxley's (1825–1895) work on evolution, had a profound influence. Reformers such as Liang Qichao argued that nationalism (*minzuzhuyi*) had made Europe preeminent. Applying the concept of the survival of the fittest to the relations between nations, they reasoned that if China could not change and strengthen itself, it would not survive. These arguments provided the rationale for the rejection of traditional culture and institutions and for the construction of a new culture to transform China into a strong modern nation-state.

Even the Qing government eventually accepted the need for change. In the early 1900s, it introduced a program that focused on reform of the military and of education. However, the reforms did not save the dynasty and may even have hastened its downfall by promoting the spread of nationalism in the army and among students.

Based on acceptance of a shared culture, albeit one that was Han in origin, the Qing empire had governed people and territories of quite varied ethnicities, and the ruling dynasty itself was Manchu. The new discourse of nationalism often defined the nation as a community sharing ties of blood, race, and language, as well as customs and territory. Its language and imagery were increasingly racialized as it sought to construct an idea of China as the country of the Han and to reject Manchu rule. Republican thinkers blamed the weakness of China on the claimed racial inferiority of its Manchu rulers.

In 1911 revolutionary forces buoyed by nationalism finally overthrew the moribund Qing government, and the Chinese Republic was born. Early Republican nationalists had envisioned revolution as a struggle between the Han and the Manchu. In the longer term, ethnicity posed different problems to Chinese governments. The Chinese nation had to be defined in such a way that it could attract the loyalty of all the people within the borders of the former Chinese empire. This was to prove an enduring problem in both the twentieth and twenty-first centuries.

NATIONALISM IN THE CHINESE REPUBLIC

After the 1911 revolution, overtly ethnic nationalism subsided. China was called a republic of five nations. The five stripes of its new flag were said to symbolize the Han (red), the Manchus (yellow), the Mongols (blue), the Hui or Muslims (white), and the Tibetans (black). Significantly, the red stripe was on top.

Sun Yat-sen (Sun Yixian), the most respected Republican leader, based his revolutionary appeal strongly on nationalism, which he claimed derived not from a foreign source but from the remote forefathers of the Chinese. Like other Republicans of his era, Sun at first employed strongly anti-Manchu rhetoric and presented the 1911 revolution as having ended centuries of oppression of the Han by the Manchu. However, in 1922, he redefined nationalism as meaning that all races within China's national borders should live on an equal footing.

Nationalism in the early Republic was used by a new urban elite to consolidate its superior social status. The growth of nationalism gave urban dwellers a new identity as citizens (*min*) to whom the new Republic (*minguo* or citizens' country) belonged. The proper citizen was modern. To be modern one must be educated, informed through reading the modern press, and scientific about all aspects of life from family affairs to hygiene. Footbinding for women and the wearing of the queue by men were abjured. The citizen wore distinctive styles of clothing drawn largely but not exclusively from Western dress. Women of the educated classes could be citizens and partake in this new urban culture, whereas peasants were excluded by their lack of education and their traditionalism.

Nationalism began to gain the support of ordinary people in the May Fourth movement of 1919. Japan's "Twenty-one Demands" of 1915—an attempt to increase its political and economic influence in China—inspired patriotic anger. This reached fever pitch when it was found that the Treaty of Versailles allowed the Japanese to retain former German concessions in China seized during World War I (1914–1918). The ensuing student protest against Yuan Shikai's Republican government in Beijing, which had secretly accepted these provisions, grew into a major anti-imperialist movement with support from workers, merchants, traders, and intellectuals. The closely associated New Culture movement sought to inspire a sense of Chinese nationhood through literature, to create a new written language based on the vernacular, to spread literacy, and to establish a standard national spoken language.

Nationalism was also important in the 1920s labor movement based in Shanghai, the largest of the treaty ports. The city, with its foreign-controlled International Concession and many foreign-owned factories, was a natural breeding ground for nationalism. The labor movement was concerned with wages and working conditions, but also organized protests over abuses by foreign bosses. In 1925 a Chinese worker was shot by factory guards when he and other workers broke into a Japanese-owned mill during a lockout. Sympathy strikes and demonstrations followed. At one large demonstration on May 20, the British-officered police of the International Concession opened fire on the crowd, killing ten and wounding fifty people. There followed a citywide strike that lasted until August.

NATIONALISM AND THE GUOMINDANG

Despite Sun Yat-sen's death in 1925, the Guomindang increased its influence and membership as a result of the Shanghai strikes. In 1926 the National Revolutionary Army, a partnership between the Guomindang and the much-smaller Communist Party, launched the Northern Expedition from its base in Guangzhou in support of national unification. By 1928, despite the break with the Communist Party and with the left wing of its own membership, the Guomindang was strong enough to establish a national government in Nanjing under the leadership of Chiang Kai-shek (Jiang Jieshi). Various accommodations had to be made with the warlords who still controlled much of China, but for the next decade the Guomindang gradually expanded its control and the influence of its political and educational institutions and achieved recognition as the government of China by the outside world.

The ideology of the new government was an anti-imperialist and anti-Communist nationalism. In its propaganda, the Guomindang now embodied the nation. The new national flag, a white sun on a blue sky, was that of the Guomindang. Sun Yat-sen, the "father of the nation," became the object of a nationalist cult. Along with the flag, his portrait hung in every school and government office. Sun's political ideas, as expressed in the Three People's Principles (Sanminzhuyi) become part of the new nationalist creed to be studied by every schoolchild in the Republic of China. The impact of foreign imperialism, the unequal treaties, the loss of Korea and Taiwan, the concessions, and the principle of extraterritoriality were also included in the curriculum of patriotic education.

NATIONALISM AND WAR

Chinese nationalism achieved even greater influence and importance as a result of Japanese aggression during the 1930s and 1940s. The Japanese occupied China's Northeast on September 18, 1931. Chiang Kai-shek's decision that the invasion should not be resisted was bitterly resented by exiles from the Northeast and began a long, slow undermining of his reputation as the national leader, exacerbated later that year by his order to the Chinese army to withdraw in the face of a Japanese attack on Shanghai.

Chiang Kai-shek's determination to deal with internal enemies, such as hostile warlords and the Communists, before facing the superior might of the Japanese armies continued until 1936. The policy was deeply unpopular with many of his own supporters. Nationalism found expression in massive campaigns to boycott Japanese goods and in the National Salvation Association (Jiuguohui). Founded in 1935, the association campaigned for greater resistance to the Japanese and criticized Guomindang appeasement policy. By 1936 it had branches in every city in China. Nationalist indignation also found expression in the press, in fiction, and in songs such as "Jiuyiba ge" (September 18 song), still widely sung in China.

War between China and Japan was finally declared in summer 1937, a few months after the formation of a United Front between the Guomindang and the CCP against the Japanese. The Japanese quickly occupied most of northern and southeastern China. The Guomindang government was forced to retreat, first to Wuhan and then to Chongqing far in the west. Japanese atrocities, most notably the Nanjing massacre, sparked mass resistance. Rural nationalism became an important force as peasant resistance grew in reaction to looting, pillaging, and burning by the occupying Japanese and puppet troops. Chiang enjoyed prestige as the national war leader, but the appeasement of the 1930s was not forgotten. The CCP, increasingly seen as organizing serious and successful resistance to the Japanese, was able to expand its support, and by the end of the war many Chinese believed it represented true patriotism. The Guomindang's reluctance to reach a negotiated settlement with the CCP was unpopular and no doubt contributed to its defeat in the civil war of 1946 to 1949.

NATIONALISM IN MAOIST CHINA

Like the Guomindang, the CCP aspired to make China a modern unified nation-state strong enough to safeguard its territorial integrity and command respect from the rest of the world. It did not wholly achieve these aims, but was to be more successful than the Guomindang had been. Like the Guomindang, it presented the interests of the party as identical to those of the nation. "The Chinese people have stood up," intoned Mao as he announced the establishment of the People's Republic of China (PRC) to a vast crowd in Tiananmen Square on October 1—a date thereafter celebrated as National Day. In the new China, children were taught to "love China, love the people, and love the Party."

The new government rapidly extended its power over the whole of the Chinese mainland. China was more unified than it had been since the fall of the Qing dynasty. The power of government was effective even at the village level. A sense of nationhood was promoted through the use of Mandarin or the "common language" in education, broadcasting, film, and stage. Foreigners resident in China lost many of the privileges that they had long enjoyed and, in a gesture of symbolic importance, were required to use the Chinese language in dealing with officialdom.

Internally, the Maoist regime's reliance on socialist and revolutionary ideas, as well as a rhetoric of internationalism, to some extent eclipsed nationalism. There was a perceptible difference between internal propaganda, which focused on socialism, revolution, class struggle, and Mao Zedong

Thought, and the patriotic (*aiguo*) propaganda targeting Hong Kong and Chinese overseas.

Foreign affairs were important to the cultivation of nationalism. The PRC could plausibly continue the narrative of China's victimhood. In the past, the country had been bullied by foreign imperialism. Now that it was internally strong, the United States and many other powers denied it diplomatic recognition, excluded it from the United Nations, and subjected it to a trade embargo. But the PRC was more assertive than its predecessors had been. China's entry into the Korean War (1950–1953) (portrayed as a struggle against American imperialism) was used both to affirm the identity between patriotism and support for the party and to show that the new China could stand up for its interests even against the might of the United States.

In early agreements with the Soviet Union, China had been too weak to resist making the economic concessions demanded by Joseph Stalin (1879–1953). In the early 1960s, when the Sino-Soviet dispute became public, letters from the CCP to the Soviet party make it clear how bitterly the concessions had been resented by the Chinese leadership. The determination of the Chinese government to be seen as an effective guardian of China's national territory and dignity was reflected in many other episodes, such as the armed border conflicts with India (1961–1962), the Soviet Union (1969), and Vietnam (1979). Similarly, its resolve to maintain, as far as possible, the historic frontiers of the Qing empire is evident in its "one-China policy" in relation to Taiwan and its assertion of sovereignty over Tibet. On the other hand, diplomatic recognition by growing numbers of countries from the 1960s despite U.S. opposition, the restoration of China's United Nations seat in 1971, and even U.S. diplomatic recognition in 1979 could all be presented as triumphs for the new power and the tenacity of the Chinese nation-state.

NATIONALISM IN POST-MAO CHINA

After the death of Mao in 1976, the economic reforms involved considerable privatization of the economy and were accompanied by a rapid decline in ideological education and faith in socialism. The state derived some legitimacy from rising living standards and from China's astonishing economic growth rates, but an ideological vacuum remained, giving rise to an increase in popular interest in various belief systems, including Christianity, Islam, and Buddhism and the Falun Gong from the 1980s. The Chinese government attempted to revive popular nationalism as an alternative. Patriotic education in schools was intensified, commemorations of China's wartime sufferings were stepped up, and museum displays were reorganized to promote nationalism. A museum dedicated to the victims of the Nanjing massacre, built in 1985, regularly receives national publicity. The 1997 handover of Hong Kong, ceded to Britain at the end of the First Opium War (1839–1842), was presented as a historic righting of China's national wrongs. Many other events, from minor sporting victories to China's accession in 2001 to the World Trade Organization and the hosting of the 2008 Olympic Games, have been presented as triumphs for China's struggle to achieve proper international recognition.

Chinese nationalism continues to be reflected in extreme sensitivity in foreign affairs. Relations with Japan have long been clouded by the "textbook controversy," that is the disputes about Japan's failure to present a sufficiently critical portrayal of its aggression against China in school textbooks, and other instances of Japan's insufficient contrition for its terrible war record in China. The disputed Diaoyutai (Senkaku) Islands claimed by both Japan and Taiwan are another irritant. China regards them as part of Taiwan and therefore Chinese territory. There have been many minor incidents around the islands when Japanese patrol boats have threatened or opened fire on Chinese or Taiwanese vessels

Incidents such as the accidental bombing of China's embassy in Belgrade by NATO in 1999 have provoked furious government protests and demonstrations against foreign embassies in Beijing that the Chinese police have shown little inclination to control. Support for Taiwan's independence by Taiwanese politicians or by foreign powers is guaranteed to provoke Beijing's wrath. The Chinese government is also extremely sensitive to criticism of its handling of internal affairs. Foreign criticism of China's treatment of Tibet or other human rights issues is met with indignation because it is seen as an infringement of China's sovereignty.

Although the Chinese government promoted the revival of nationalism in the 1980s and 1990s, it has not always been able to control the direction taken by nationalist discourse. In 1988 a much-discussed television series, *River Elegy*, was interpreted as suggesting that it was Chinese tradition rather than imperialism that had held China back. This prompted intense public debate in which official policy was both attacked and defended. In the 1989 student movement, some protesters raised the allegation that the official policy of encouraging foreign investment amounted to selling the country. In the late 1990s, the authors of the best-selling *Zhongguo keyi shuobu* (China can say no) were among the many unofficial voices of Chinese nationalism criticizing Chinese who they claimed had too easily jettisoned their heritage in favor of Western values.

Meanwhile, political relaxation and the increasing wealth of southern and southeastern China led to the rise of new regional challenges to state nationalism. Cantonese-speaking people have attempted to revise the use of Cantonese in official contexts. Some scholars have suggested that

there has been a rise of southern commercial nationalism, which is inevitably in conflict with northern official nationalism. The rise of ethnic nationalism, especially in Tibet and among the Xinjiang Uygurs, poses a threat to the narrative of a multiethnic country united by loyalty to the nation-state. Nationalism remains an important source of legitimacy for the Chinese government. But it can be a two-edged sword. It has been used by dissenters to legitimize their disagreements with government policy and by ethnic minorities demanding greater autonomy.

Reformers of the early twentieth century debated whether traditional culture was an obstacle to China's modernization and whether China should adopt foreign values and customs. These remained key questions for Chinese nationalism a century later.

SEE ALSO *May Fourth Movement; National Flags and National Anthems; Student Organizations and Activism, 1900–1949; Zhongguo.*

BIBLIOGRAPHY

Gries, Peter Hays. *China's New Nationalism: Pride, Politics, and Diplomacy.* Berkeley: University of California Press, 2004.

Harrison, Henrietta. *The Making of the Republican Citizen: Political Ceremonies and Symbols in China, 1911–1929.* Oxford, U.K.: Oxford University Press, 2000.

Harrison, Henrietta. *Inventing the Nation: China.* London: Arnold, 2001.

Smith, S. A. *Like Cattle and Horses: Nationalism and Labor in Shanghai, 1895–1927.* Durham, NC: Duke University Press, 2002.

Song Qiang, Zhang Zangzang, and Qiao Bian. *Zhongguo keyi shuobu* [China can say no]. Beijing: Zhonghua Gongshang Lianhe Chubanshe, 1996.

Unger, Jonathan, ed. *Chinese Nationalism.* Armonk, NY: Sharpe, 1996.

Delia Davin

NATIONALIST GOVERNMENT, 1927–1949

The Nationalist government was founded by the Guomindang in April 1927 with its capital city at Nanjing and lasted until 1949, when the Guomindang was driven out of mainland China. For much of this period, China was under threat or actual occupation by Japan. Mainland and Western historians alike have generally depicted the government as corrupt and ineffectual, but new historical research has tended to pay more attention to its achievements, and mainland Chinese historians are increasingly recognizing its resistance efforts during the Second Sino-Japanese War (1937–1945).

The Nationalist government was built on the organizational and ideological foundation laid by Sun Yat-sen. After Sun's death in March 1925, a period of jostling for power ensued, and Chiang Kai-shek, commander of the Northern Expedition, eventually emerged as his political successor.

Chiang's proclamation of a new government was accompanied by much bloodshed, as he broke away from the United Front with the Communist Party and purged thousands of Communist members and sympathizers. Not all of the Guomindang veterans agreed with his approach, and some were reluctant to accept his rapid ascendancy. He initially faced many leadership challenges, but was able to overcome most of them by the early 1930s. This historical context, along with Chiang's personality, resulted in one-party and one-man dictatorial governance. The Nationalist government's ideological core consisted of the doctrines of Sun Yat-sen (especially the Three Principles of the People), and its cornerstone was anti-Communism. It briefly flirted with European fascism, but this flirtation was short-lived and highly selective, confined mostly to methods of mass mobilization. Ideologically, the government also departed from radical ideals of the May Fourth movement and returned to the Confucian foundations of Chinese society. It shackled student political activism, encouraged the reading of the classics, promoted the New Life movement, and organized commemorations of Confucius.

CHOICE OF CAPITAL AND GOVERNING STRUCTURE

The choice of Nanjing as the capital for the Nationalist government was partly justified by Sun Yat-sen's preference for this site in 1912, at the founding of the Republic, a preference ritually confirmed by the choice of his final resting place. Located in Jiangsu Province, a short distance upstream from the Yangzi River Delta, Nanjing was also viewed as economically vibrant and strategically important, its central location making it a suitable base for the conduct of military and foreign affairs. The capital was briefly moved to Luoyang in 1932 when Shanghai came under Japanese attack, and later to Chongqing, which served as the wartime capital during the Second Sino-Japanese War. Afterward, the Nationalist government returned to Nanjing and governed from there until the latter part of 1949, when it was forced by the raging civil war to move south and then west in rapid succession to Guangzhou, Chongqing, Chengdu, and finally Taibei.

The structure of the government, adopted in 1928, was in accordance with Sun Yat-sen's schema of a division among five branches: an Executive Yuan to run daily operations through various ministries and committees, a Legislative Yuan (Lifa Yuan) to pass laws, a Judicial Yuan

(Sifa Yuan) for adjudication, a Supervisory Yuan (Jiancha Yuan) to oversee governance, and an Examination Yuan (Kaoshi Yuan) to screen public servants. Moreover, in accordance with Sun's idea of having full constitutional governance only after the two preparatory stages of military rule and party tutelage, the Guomindang apparatus held sway over the five-*yuan* state system during most of Nationalist rule, even though conflicts in overlapping party-state relations often proved problematic.

The issue of transitioning from party tutelage to constitutional rule and instituting a national constitution and multiparty national assembly was a major bone of contention. After several rounds of debate and political maneuvering in the early 1930s, a draft national constitution was agreed upon on May 5, 1936. The outbreak of the Second Sino-Japanese War, as well as procrastination by the Guomindang, greatly delayed the process. It was not until November 1946, in the midst of civil war, that a formal national constitution, based primarily on the 1936 draft, was proclaimed. Toward the end of 1947, elections were held for a national assembly, with multiparty credentials being weakly justified by the participation of a few minor non-Guomindang. In early 1948 this was followed by elections for the Legislative Yuan as well as for the presidency and vice presidency of the constitutional republic. Yet by then these constitutional steps had little substantive meaning, apart from placating public opinion and American demands for democratic reforms, because emergency rule to suppress the ongoing Communist rebellion was simultaneously declared, with several constitutional provisions being immediately suspended and the president being granted broad emergency powers. In short, the Nationalist government throughout its twenty-two-year rule was overseen by Guomindang rule and Chiang's leadership.

SOCIAL SUPPORT BASE

Ever suspicious of mass mobilization and the United Front infiltration tactics of the Communist Party, the Nationalist government never seriously attempted to cultivate an organized social base, particularly among the peasants, workers, and intelligentsia. Its governing structure did not enable it to penetrate the rural counties, towns, and villages, and it generally neglected the rural economy. Basically, it did not regard the Chinese peasantry as a support base. Its limited rural Rent Reduction Program to cap land rental rates at 75 percent of income was not successfully implemented even in the Yangzi Delta provinces under its control. The rural cooperative movement, developed to make credit more easily available, was extensive on paper but was hijacked by rural elites and effected little improvement in the lives of poor peasants. Wartime conscription and heavy taxation through direct grain acquisition aggravated the plight of peasants. The new county system implemented from September 1939 had aimed at strengthening the government's grip on rural politics, finance, education, and militia training, but by late 1940s local governance of the rural population remained ineffective and abusive, according to internal-agency assessments.

While the small, modern, urban sector of the economy received greater attention from the Nationalist government prior to the Second Sino-Japanese War, the working class remained underdeveloped, and the emphasis in industrial relations was on proscribing independent trade-union activities. Much of this modern coastal segment was lost when the war forced the government to withdraw deep into the rural hinterland. With the general student population and adult intellectuals in urban centers, there was a great divide, because they had been awakened by May Fourth activism and were angered by the government's adoption of an accommodation policy toward Japanese intrusions and its conservative and dictatorial governance. The two-pronged Nationalist approach of depoliticizing students through school regulations and the cultivation of a small group of loyalist cadres failed to prevent waves of student political protests in the pre-1937 period and again during the civil war years.

The city-based capitalist class was also not well cultivated as a social base, since the prewar Nationalist government focused on squeezing financial resources from them and transferring their business assets and privileges into the hands of central bureaucrats. The limited collection of national income through custom duties, salt taxes, and miscellaneous levies was insufficient to meet expenditure needs, especially in the face of escalating military expenses, even with supplementary borrowing through domestic bonds and foreign loans. The forced creation of a centralized banking system facilitated the easy printing of money to meet the deficit, but it laid the foundation for the hyperinflation of the war years and ultimately destroyed the bourgeois capacity for industrial production and financial services, and it sapped the general morale of the entire society.

RELATIONS WITH THE WARLORDS

The military establishment also failed to provide significant sociopolitical support for the Nationalist government. Far from uniting with the government, it repeatedly challenged Chiang Kai-shek and his central government's authority, especially in the late 1920s and 1930s. The Northern Expedition of 1926–1928 against the warlords attained only superficial national unification, as many of them merely succumbed to monetary enticement or political expediency and kept their armies intact. Apart from numerous small and localized militarists, there were several prominent residual warlord groups scattered throughout China—including

those based in Guangxi (led by Li Zongren and Bai Chongxi), Guangdong (Li Jishen, Zhang Fakui, and Chen Jitang), Henan (Feng Yuxiang), Shanxi (Yan Xishan), and Manchuria (Zhang Xueliang). These warlords had a profound impact on national politics. Whenever the government attempted to reorganize or downsize their armies, they would rise up in rebellion either individually or in concert, and at times in complex entanglement with intra-Guomindang leadership struggles among Chiang and his two party veterans Wang Jingwei and Hu Hanmin. The most intensive battles were fought from 1929 to 1932, but the Nationalist government also had to cope with a 1933 rebellion in Fujian and a 1936 anti-Chiang uprising in Guangxi and Guangdong.

While the outbreak of the Second Sino-Japanese War brought about a greater degree of unity, tension between Chiang's central army and the regional military forces remained high, especially concerning the allocation of resources and conflicting lines of command. Chiang's position was in fact weakened, as a significant portion of his best commanding officers and troops were lost during the initial three months of intensive fighting in the autumn of 1937. Preservation of strength by each military group soon became the order of the day, and this contributed to the increasing stagnation of the war effort. During the civil war period, Chiang's lack of success in executing battle plans and massive defections to the Communist Party can also be partly traced to this residual warlordism.

CONFLICT AND RECONCILIATION WITH THE COMMUNIST PARTY

Part of the process of establishing the Nationalist government was the ouster of Communists and their sympathizers. Yet the Communist Party survived, and after failing to make a comeback by two rounds of urban-based uprisings, it adopted a rural strategy, operating from a Jiangxi Soviet base area. Chiang launched five military campaigns against this base from 1930 to 1934, succeeding only in the last with the help of German military advisors and a change in tactics. The Communist Party fled and embarked on its Long March, suffering heavy casualties and retreating to a new base area, Yan'an, in Northwest China.

Recognizing its depleted strength, the rising tide of anti-Japanese nationalism in Chinese cities, and the need to neutralize the firepower and resources of the urban-based Guomindang, the Communist Party from its new rural base began to send out peace overtures to the Nationalist government and its military units, calling for unity against Japan. Zhang Xueliang and his Manchurian army, having lost their homeland to the Japanese and now being dispatched to blockade and exterminate the Communist Party, responded to the Communist overtures and kidnapped Chiang Kai-shek during the Xi'an Incident in

December 1936 as an act of military remonstrance to force him to negotiate with the Communist Party. Chiang was freed after an understanding of cooperation was reached. With the outbreak of the Second Sino-Japanese War in July 1937, the second United Front between the Guomindang and the Communist Party was put into operation. The Communist Party committed itself to the wartime leadership of Chiang, Sun Yat-sen's Three Principles of the People, representation in the wartime advisory body of the People's Political Council (based first in Wuhan and later in Chongqing), and the reorganization of Communist Party military forces as the Eighth Route Army to fight against Japan.

RESPONSES TO JAPANESE INCURSIONS

The tenure of the Nationalist government coincided with the rise of militarism in Japan. Concerned that a newly unified China under the Guomindang would damage its economic interests in China, Japanese troops briefly disrupted the advancement of the Northern Expedition in May 1927 and May 1928. Japanese militarists also killed the warlord Zhang Zuolin, Zhang Xueliang's father, and attempted to prevent the Manchurian army from declaring allegiance to the new Guomindang government. In autumn of 1931, Japan invaded the entire three provinces of Manchuria, and the fighting briefly spilled over to Shanghai in January 1932.

Despite these Japanese incursions, Chiang judged the Communist Party to be a greater threat to his regime and insisted on a policy of pacifying within to resist without, preferring to do little more than seek help from the League of Nations to restrain the Japanese and thus stirring up waves of urban protests against Japan and the Guomindang's policy of accommodation. From 1933 to 1935, Japan extended its military and political influence in the northern belt of Chinese provinces and struck agreements with the Guomindang to create a buffer zone independent of Chinese control.

However, troop clashes at Marco Polo Bridge on the outskirts of Beijing in July 1937 proved to be the straw that broke the camel's back. By then Chiang's resolve had hardened, and he issued orders to resist, beginning with an intense three-month battle in the vicinity of Shanghai. In addition to Shanghai, he lost the capital city of Nanjing by December 1937, as well as Guangzhou and Wuhan in October 1938. By early 1939 the Nationalist government had settled into its wartime capital at Chongqing, which was safe from direct ground attacks but subjected to air bombardment, especially before the entry of the United States into the war.

WARTIME RELATIONS WITH THE UNITED STATES AND SOVIET UNION

Chiang had written directly to U.S. President Franklin Roosevelt appealing for help as early as January 1938, but the U.S. response was guarded, and the first substantive military-aid package arrived only in April 1941. It was the Japanese bombing of Pearl Harbor and its invasion of Southeast Asia that dragged the United States directly into the wars in Europe and Asia and gave an enormous boost to the Guomindang war effort. By January 1942 the United States and its allies had set up the China-Burma-India war theater, with Chiang Kai-shek as the supreme allied commander in China and U.S. General Joseph Stilwell as his chief of staff. In the following month Roosevelt gave China the first huge loan of US$500 million. Claire Chennault and his band of American volunteer pilots, the Flying Tigers, were reorganized and incorporated as the Fourteenth U.S. Air Force and began to launch air raids on Japanese cities from airfields in China by April 1942. In another gesture of support, the United States and its major allied partner Britain, in October 1942, renounced past unequal treaties signed with China.

However, there was tension in the relationship, as U.S. policy makers increasingly had doubts about the Nationalist government's military capability and governing skills and judged it necessary to share resources with the Communist Party and include them in the Second Sino-Japanese War. There was also the intractable personality clash between Chiang and Joseph Stilwell. Eventually, Roosevelt had to give in to Chiang's demands and remove Stilwell from his command in October 1944. U.S. support for China continued under Harry Truman, who took over the presidency in April 1945, and he brought about the end of the war by dropping two atomic bombs on Japan in August. As part of the surrender and repossession process, Truman airlifted Nationalist government personnel and troops back to several strategic coastal cities and announced further military aid to the Nationalist government to help Chiang maintain peace and security within China, while instructing his American envoys to try to bring about a truce and reconciliation between the Guomindang and Communist Party.

Unlike the United States, the Soviet Union was much less involved with China's affairs, since it was economically weaker and was confronted on its western border with an invasion by Nazi Germany. In an act of self-preservation to maintain the status quo on its eastern flank, the Soviet Union signed the Sino-Soviet Nonaggression Pact with the Nationalist government in August 1937 and the Soviet-Japanese Neutrality Treaty in April 1941. Despite the rhetoric of international communism, the Soviet Union had few links with Mao Zedong's Communist Party after the 1930s. The Nationalist government recognized this fact and had no difficulties in maintaining a working Sino-Soviet diplomatic relationship. It was only on the eve of Japan's surrender that the Soviet Union joined the war against Japan and moved its troops into Northeast China. Its military entry somewhat obstructed the Guomindang's quick return to the strategic Northeast, but it did not give the Communist Party any significant advantage, nor was that the Soviet Union's intention. There was no conspiratorial Soviet master plan to assist the Communist Party to seize power from the Guomindang, as was later claimed by some Cold War warriors. The unfolding civil war was decided by domestic forces, with the United States playing a brief mediating role.

NEGOTIATIONS AND CIVIL WAR

Major clashes between the Guomindang and Communist Party forces broke out as soon as Japan surrendered. Yet owing partly to the pressure of public sentiment, political posturing, and the need for war preparations, there were two major rounds of peace negotiations coordinated by the United States. For the first round, Ambassador Patrick Hurley escorted Mao Zedong by flight from Yan'an to Chongqing to hold talks with the Guomindang and to work out a tentative agreement for a multiparty Political Consultative Conference. The U.S. special presidential envoy George Marshall then took over the mediation baton and was able to convene the proposed Political Consultative Conference, arrange for a cease fire, and draw up a military reorganization and integration plan.

However, the truce did not last, and full-scale civil war broke out from mid-1946. In the first year, the Nationalist government used its military superiority and went on an offensive, attacking many Communist Party areas, even capturing Yan'an. By the following year the Nationalist troops had become overstretched, and from mid-1947 to mid-1948 it was the Communist Party's turn to switch to an offensive mode, with two major battle groups crossing the Yellow River into central China and with the Guomindang being forced to withdraw from Yan'an after holding it for barely a year. In the final stage of the war, the Communist Party had attained military parity in terms of troops and arms and could shift to large-scale frontal assaults. The war was finally decided by the Guomindang's defeat in two large battles: the Liaoshen campaign of September to November 1948 and the Huaihai campaign from November 1948 to January 1949. Chiang Kai-shek decided to withdraw temporarily from politics in January 1949, and it was left to his acting president Li Zongren to negotiate in April 1949 for a possible peace settlement, with China divided into two governed halves by the Yangzi River. The attempt failed, and the Communist Party forces easily crossed the river and quickly swept south, proclaiming the founding of the People's Republic of China on October 1, 1949, and driving the remnant Nationalist-government personnel and military forces to the island of Taiwan by the end of the year.

RETREAT TO TAIWAN AND CONTINUATION OF NATIONALIST RULE

Taiwan was given up as a Chinese territory after China's defeat in the Sino-Japanese War of 1894–1895. It was officially returned to the Nationalist government fifty years later on October 25, 1945, after the surrender of Japan. In the process of takeover and reassertion of control over the island, an antigovernment uprising broke out on February 28, 1947, and it was harshly suppressed by the Guomindang military, an event later taken to symbolize ruthless Nationalist rule. As the civil war turned increasingly unfavorable, the Nationalist government hurriedly transferred the bulk of its remaining financial and military resources over to Taiwan with the intention of turning it into an anti-Communist fortress.

On this island it continued to govern in the name of the Republic of China. Drawing lessons from its past failure, it reformed its government and party apparatus, harboring hopes of an eventual reconquest of the mainland until the dynamics of domestic Taiwan politics took a sudden turn from the 1990s and forced the Guomindang to adopt a new mind-set and agenda.

SEE ALSO *Anti-Japanese War, 1937–1945; Chiang Kai-shek (Jiang Jieshi); Northern Expedition; Sun Yat-sen (Sun Yixian); Three Principles of the People (Sanmin zhuyi).*

BIBLIOGRAPHY

Eastman, Lloyd E. *The Abortive Revolution: China under Nationalist Rule, 1927–1937.* Cambridge, MA: Harvard University Press, 1974.

Eastman, Lloyd E. *Seeds of Destruction: Nationalist China in War and Revolution, 1937–1949.* Stanford, CA: Stanford University Press, 1984.

Fairbank, John K., et al., eds. *The Cambridge History of China.* Vols. 12–13, *Republican China, 1912–1949*, parts 1–2. Cambridge, U.K.: Cambridge University Press, 1983.

Kong Qingtai. *Guomindang zhengfu zhengzhi zhidu shi* [A history of the political institutions of the Guomindang government]. Hefei: Anhui Renmin Chubanshe, 1998.

Pepper, Suzanne. *Civil War in China: The Political Struggle, 1945–1949.* Berkeley: University of California Press, 1978.

Sheridan, James E. *China in Disintegration: The Republican Era in Chinese History, 1912–1949.* New York: Free Press, 1975.

Van de Ven, Hans J. *War and Nationalism in China, 1925–1945.* London: RoutledgeCurzon, 2003.

Zarrow, Peter. *China in War and Revolution, 1895–1949.* London: Routledge, 2005.

Zhang Xianwen et al. *Zhonghua Minguo shi* [A history of the Republic of China]. Nanjing: Nanjing Daxue Chubanshe, 2005.

Zhang Yufa. *Zhongguo jindai xiandai shi* [A history of modern and contemporary China]. Taibei: Taiwan Donghua Shuju, 1989.

Zhu Hanguo, ed. *Nanjing Guomin zhengfu jishi* [A chronological record of the Nanjing Nationalist government]. Hefei: Anhui Renmin Chubanshe, 1993.

Huang Jianli

NATIONALIST PARTY

The Nationalist Party (officially, the Chinese Nationalist Party, Zhongguo Guomindang, or GMD) is the political party founded by Sun Yat-sen (Sun Yixian) that claims his Three Principles of the People as its guiding ideology. A history of the GMD cannot be told without referring to the lives of the four leaders who have dominated its history—Sun Yat-sen (Sun Yixian), Chiang Kai-shek (Jiang Jieshi), Chiang Ching-kuo (Jiang Jingguo), and Lee Tenghui (Li Denghui)—as well as the general history of the Republic of China.

THE REVOLUTIONARY MOVEMENT, 1905–1927

Official GMD history dates back to Sun's first revolutionary group in Honolulu in 1895, one of several he founded during twenty years of unsuccessful uprisings. But the beginning of the GMD as a party was in Japan in 1905 with the joining of several anti-Manchu groups into the Tongmenghui (Revolutionary Alliance), which united revolutionaries with diverse views under the personal leadership of Sun. The Revolutionary Alliance had ethnonationalist goals of overthrowing the Manchus and modernizing China as a republic, and a vague idea of social revolution and equal land ownership modeled on the theories of the American political economist Henry George (1839–1897). Sun was a charismatic and idealistic leader but not a strong organizer or systematic thinker. His Three Principles of the People (nationalism, democracy, and people's livelihood) went through numerous revisions according to the needs of the day. Membership in the alliance grew to more than 10,000 (Sun claimed 30,000) by 1911, consisting mainly of intellectuals, soldiers, and overseas Chinese. Overseas Chinese members were the financial base of the party, and the system of overseas GMD branches continues to this day.

After the 1911 revolution, the Revolutionary Alliance was reorganized into a political party, the Guomindang, to contest the 1912 parliamentary election. The GMD gained the largest number of seats in what is still the only free and fair national election ever held in China. The chief GMD organizer, Song Jiaoren (1882–1913), was assassinated before the parliament convened, and Sun failed to make the GMD caucus an effective force. Yuan Shikai soon banned the GMD. Sun fled to Japan, reinventing the GMD as a secretive revolutionary party, the Gemingdang, united under a personal oath of allegiance to himself. In 1919 he returned to the name *Guomindang*, and a year later he replaced the personal oath with an oath of loyalty to the party. After two unsuccessful attempts, Sun finally established his party as the government of Guangzhou in 1922. The official headquarters of the Guomindang continued in Shanghai, but usually it was ignored by Sun.

In 1923 Sun made an alliance with the small Chinese Communist Party that allowed Communists to join the GMD, but they agreed that a revolution based on class struggle was not appropriate for China. Russian advisers and arms arrived to build the GMD into a disciplined revolutionary party to carry out an anti-imperialist, democratic revolution in China through military power and ideological persuasion. In the next year Sun made a final statement of his ideology: Nationalism was redefined as anti-imperialism, and democracy as a long-term goal to be achieved in the future, after two preliminary stages—military unification, then a period of political tutelage in which the party would rule while educating the people into democratic citizenship. Land reform, without class struggle, was incorporated into the principle of people's livelihood.

The January 1924 First GMD Congress in Guangzhou adopted a party constitution and new party structure—a Leninist party-state, with Sun as leader. Among other new departments, a party military school was established, Huangpu (Whampoa), with Chiang Kai-shek as commander and Zhou Enlai as political commissar. By that time there already was unease over the intentions of the Communists and their growing influence with the GMD. Among the senior associates of Sun, Hu Hanmin (1879–1936) represented the concerned moderates, and Wang Jingwei and Liao Zhongkai (1877–1925) led leftist supporters of the alliance.

Sun Yat-sen died in Beijing on March 12, 1925. With the departure of Sun, who had moderated internal conflict, a struggle for the future of the GMD began. On August 20, 1925, his presumptive heir, Liao Zhongkai, was assassinated, and under a cloud of suspicion, Hu Hanmin withdrew from political activity. Leftists turned the instrument of party discipline against conservatives; the Central Propaganda Bureau (which was headed by Mao Zedong from October 1925 to May 1926) called for class struggle and purge of "counterrevolutionary" members.

On March 20, 1926, claiming a Communist attack on his Huangpu headquarters, Chiang Kai-shek imposed martial law on Guangzhou, sending troops to occupy government buildings. On May 2, the GMD Central Executive Committee adopted Chiang's motion to bar Communists from senior posts in the GMD. Mikhail Borodin (1884–1951), Comintern's representative to the GMD, agreed to limitations on Communist activity, and differences were papered over. On July 1 the GMD declared war on the northern warlords, and the Northern Expedition to unite China began under the command of Chiang.

On October 10, 1926, the GMD conquered Wuhan, and in February 1927 a new provisional GMD government was formed there under the leadership of the Left. In the meantime, Chiang Kai-shek was making other plans in cooperation with merchant and underground circles in Shanghai. On March 21 leftist unions organized an uprising in Shanghai, which quickly was occupied by the GMD army. On April 12 police, gangsters, and troops launched attacks on leftist organizations, killing and arresting thousands. On April 18 Chiang organized a second GMD government, in Shanghai. In Wuhan the Communists attempted to organize peasant rebellions. Wuhan GMD leader Wang Jingwei responded by purging the Communists from the Wuhan government, then reconciled with Chiang. In this process, the GMD lost most of its talented organizers and activists. By 1928 all of the remaining warlords had declared their support for the GMD, and the period of political tutelage officially began.

THE PARTY OF CHIANG KAI-SHEK, 1927–1949

From 1928 to 1932, in a chaotic progression of party meetings, rebellions, and shifting alliances between militarists and GMD factions (usually involving either Hu Hanmin or Wang Jingwei), Chiang's supremacy was challenged frequently. He twice retired (in 1929 and 1931), but in his absence financial and military support also disappeared, and so he returned each time with greater power. Party congresses were postponed, manipulated, or lacked quorums. Debate raged over the merits of political tutelage versus constitutional government, but in reality, regardless of formal structures, Chiang controlled party, military, and state, and the state was officially a one-party dictatorship.

The success of the Northern Expedition and Chiang's clientelist alliances with militarists created an influx of new GMD members more interested in the spoils of power than the ideals of Sun (regardless of how these were understood). GMD members ceased to be an elite dedicated to awakening China. Chiang's reliance on Shanghai capital and military power, coupled with his focus defeating the Communists and uniting China through military effort, meant that little attention and fewer resources were given to party work. To the extent that the GMD functioned, it was as Chiang's clientelist political machine or intelligence apparatus, epitomized by the Blue Shirts Society (Lanyi She), his secret militarized force within the party to carry out special operations and enforce loyalty to him.

Nonetheless, there were efforts to build the party. One of the first bodies established in Nanking in 1928 was the Central Political Institute, to train senior GMD cadres. The skillful organizational work of the brothers Chen Guofu (1892–1951) and Chen Lifu (1900–2001) resulted in the shaping of the GMD into a conservative political machine loyal to Chiang. The Chens developed their own faction, the CC Clique, and constantly worked to supplant other GMD factions. They established a GMD publishing house and party enterprises, and began small efforts at land reform and promoting rural cooperatives. The policies of the Chen brothers can be seen as the mainstream GMD ideology, continued by Chiang Ching-kuo in Taiwan. The other major vein was Chiang Kai-Shek's Confucian reinterpretation of Sun's thought, expressed in his 1934 New Life movement.

GMD membership was overwhelmingly urban, with little penetration among workers or in rural areas beyond the gentry (who resisted any ideas of land reform). Membership was highly concentrated in Guangdong (more than 25% of all members in 1933) and the lower Yangzi Valley, which was the limit of effective direct GMD control over the Republic of China.

The Japanese invasion in 1937 was a disaster for China, and ultimately for the GMD, but in the short term it inspired patriotic support for the GMD inside and outside China. GMD membership soared. Chiang's popularity, ironically strengthened by the 1936 Xi'an Incident, soared with his resistance, against immense odds, to Japan's aggression. In 1938 Chiang was named supreme leader of the GMD, confirming him as the true successor of Sun Yat-sen. The defection of Wang Jingwei to the Japanese in 1939 showed that there was still opposition to Chiang within the GMD, but also discredited Wang within the party.

In 1937 Chiang's son Chiang Ching-kuo was released after twelve years in Russia as the hostage of Joseph Stalin (1879–1953). Chiang Ching-kuo still held the ideals of the revolutionary GMD, but now was an anti-Communist who understood how to use a Leninist party and a Stalinist police-state to implement those ideals. By 1941 he was his father's closest adviser.

Two initiatives to revitalize the GMD were introduced in 1938 to 1939. The first was a training program to build party cells, which would be established in every public organization, and would meet every two weeks. The second was the establishment of the GMD Youth Corps (Sanminzhuyi Qingnian Tuan) under the leadership of General Chen Cheng (1897–1965), who had taught artillery at Huangpu. Chen's appointment demonstrated Chiang's new reliance on trusted loyalists to build a GMD not controlled by the CC Clique. In 1944 Chiang Ching-kuo became dean of the Youth Cadre Training School (Qingniantuan Ganbu Xunlianban).

The Sixth GMD Congress (1945) made some moves toward constitutional rule and possible peaceful competition with the Communist Party. Party branches in the military and schools (the commissar system) were dissolved. Special efforts were made to recruit workers, women, and educated youth into the party. Although these steps and popular enthusiasm generated by the victory over Japan produced 420,856 new party members by 1946, the GMD was damaged by the years of neglect of party work, loss of credibility, corruption, and growing Communist penetration.

THE IDEAL LENINIST PARTY, 1950–1980

The GMD's defeat in China and its retreat to Taiwan in 1949 led to its reinvention as a Leninist party under the leadership of Chiang Ching-kuo (who controlled the security apparatus and headed the Taiwan provincial GMD) and Chen Cheng (who led the government). In 1950 the Central Committee was dismissed and a Central Reorganization Commission (Zhongyang Gaizao Weiyuan) led by Chen and Chiang Ching-kuo replaced it. A reregistration of all members reduced the GMD to about 50,000 members in Taiwan (two-thirds of them military), eliminated Communist agents, removed corrupt and incompetent officials, and marginalized the CC Clique. The system of party cells was thoroughly implemented, extending direct party control to every corner of state and society. The commissar system was restored in the military, and Chiang Ching-kuo headed a new National Defense Political Warfare Department (Guofangbu Zong Zhengzhibu). A system of cadre training was set up, with the Revolutionary Practice Institute (Geming Shijian Yanjiuyuan) at its apex and Chiang as its dean.

In 1952 the Seventh GMD Congress restored the Central Committee, which had been suspended during the period of reorganization. The revitalized GMD by 1952 counted more than 280,000 members in Taiwan. Another 280,000 overseas members gave the GMD legitimacy as representative of the Chinese nation. In the same year, Chiang Ching-kuo founded the China Youth Corps (Jiu Guo Tuan) outside of formal party structures; he remained its director until 1973, naming a Taiwanese, Xie Dongmin (1908–2001) as his deputy. Through this group Chiang began to develop a new generation of Taiwanese (and Taiwan-raised Mainlander) GMD members who would share his ideals.

In Taiwan, growth in party membership, land reform, enforced stability, and the institution of local elections gave the GMD a legitimacy it had never known in China.

GMD membership

Year	Total members	Of which overseas	Of which military	Comment
1910	30,000	majority	NA	Sun's claim
1924	—	—	—	—
1933	1,271,707	101,144	784,195	Includes probationary
1941	5,100,793	79,042	3,590,416	—
1945	8,061,744	91,314	4,855,822	—
1950	Est. 50,000	—	—	Re-registration
1952	282,000	—	112,000	—
1961	600,816	—	—	—
1974	1,324,053	—	—	50% are Taiwanese
1987	2,500,000	—	—	—
1992	2,600,000	—	—	—
2000 after PFP split	1,000,000 claimed	—	—	Re-registration 340,000 active
2004	970,000	—	—	Re-registration

SOURCE: Bergere, Marie-Claire. *Sun Yat-sen.* (Translated by Janet Lloyd from "La Chine au XX siecle: D'une revolution a l'autre 1895–1949". Paris: Librarie Artheme Fayard, 1994.) Stanford, CA: Stanford University Press, 1998; Dickson., Bruce D. *Democratization in China and Taiwan: The Adaptability of Leninist Parties.* Oxford: Clarendon Press, 1997; Wang Qi-sheng. *Zhan Shi Guomindang Dangyuan yu Jiceng Dang Zuzhi* (Guomingdang membership and base party organizations during the war period), ND. From website www.hoplite.cn.

Table 1

Totalitarian rule under martial law (which continued until 1987) repressed all voices of opposition. The GMD made clientelist alliances with existing Taiwanese factions to extend its control over local political life. This was intended to be a transitional measure, until Chiang Ching-kuo could train a new generation of Taiwanese cadres of his ideal Leninist party to replace them. After he became premier in 1972 Chiang accelerated organizational restructuring, replaced older cadres, and began the "Taiwanization" of the party. Among the new members of the GMD Central Committee that year was Li Denghui. In local elections Chiang replaced faction leaders with parachuted candidates from among his students. To defeat alienated local factions, the GMD made extensive use of electoral corruption.

When Chiang Kai-shek died in April 1975, Chiang Ching-kuo succeeded him as GMD chairman. In 1977 the GMD's attempt to eliminate local factions and replace them with a united party led to significant electoral losses. Much worse, blatant electoral corruption provoked the violent Zhongli Incident, a riot in Taoyuan involving mainly Hakka supporters of the losing GMD faction in that election. The incident revealed the strength of continuing ethnic tensions and popular hatred of the GMD in Taiwan.

Another significant development during this period was the accumulation of immense party assets as Taiwan's economy developed. The nominal distinction between party and state made state resources readily available to the party, and it gave the party privileged access to investments in Taiwan's economy. Party assets supported up to 6,000 full-time employees and ensured vast funds for elections and patronage.

THE ELECTION MACHINE, 1980–2008

In the late 1970s the GMD was challenged by a small and courageous Taiwanese opposition movement, the Dangwai (Tangwai), which grew with support from disaffected local factions. As a result, the GMD's goal of factional replacement was abandoned, and manipulation of factions, electoral corruption, and clientelism became permanent and standard GMD practice. When Chiang Ching-kuo became president in 1978, his vision of a revolutionary order led by an idealistic and disciplined GMD was already failing. After the failure of the Gao-xiong Incident (a rally on Human Rights Day, December 10, 1979, that was manipulated into a "police riot"), a final attempt to maintain control by arresting the entire Dangwai leadership backfired. New pressures on the GMD from foreign and domestic sources to improve human rights and democratize, along with the need to win elections, meant that small Dangwai victories took on huge significance even though they did not seriously threaten the GMD party-state.

The turning point came on September 28, 1986, when the Dangwai organized the Democratic Progressive Party (DPP, Minzhu Jinbu Dang) in defiance of martial law. On October 15 the GMD Central Committee announced that it would end martial law, legalize other political parties, and draft an election law: The DPP had forced the GMD to end sixty years of political tutelage. This pattern of the DPP proposing and the GMD disposing sums up the next decade of dizzying political changes that ended with Li Denghui becoming the first popularly elected president of a democratic Republic of China in 1996. Li had achieved the GMD dream lost when Sun Yat-sen surrendered the presidency to Yuan Shikai in 1912.

Chiang Ching-kuo died in January 1988 and was succeeded as president and party chairman by Li Denghui. Li survived challenges to his succession through clever factional alliances. At the Thirteenth GMD Congress in 1988 Taiwanese members for the first time became a majority of the Central Standing Committee. In the Fourteenth Congress (1993) local faction leaders and legislators entered the GMD Central Committee in large numbers. Under the new hegemony of public opinion, winning elections

President of Taiwan Li Denghui (Lee Teng-hui), Taipei, Taiwan, November 6, 1999. Founded by Sun Yat-sen in 1905, the Nationalist Party fled to the island of Taiwan in 1949 after losing control of China to the Communists. Also called the Guomindang, the Nationalist Party used military rule to govern the Republic of China, suppressing democratic elections until the end of the 1980s. © REUTERS/CORBIS

became the main source of GMD legitimacy. The GMD became a formidable election machine, but its reliance on local factions (often linked to criminal gangs) and massive vote buying created the political corruption known as black gold politics (Hei Jin Zhengzhi). As party primaries became the legitimate (though not only) method for choosing candidates for Taiwan's almost-annual elections, the ideal Leninist party dissolved into a kleptodemocracy. The Fourteenth Congress also elected the party chairman by secret ballot for the first time. Faction leaders and legislators, formerly clients of the party, now bargained for power and inserted their interests into party policies.

In 1993 a group of young Mainlanders, dissatisfied with Li's Taiwanese nationalism and black gold politics, defected to form the New Party (Xin Dang). As political reforms continued, tensions continually stressed the GMD along ethnic lines. These came to a head in the 2000 presidential election, when Li's covert support for the DPP candidate resulted in the unthinkable—the GMD lost the presidency. Li was forced to resign as GMD chair. Calls to return to its Chinese identity and the policies of Chiang Ching-kuo rallied the shaken party. Song Chuyu (James Soong, b. 1942), Li's former right-hand man, formed the People First Party (PFP, Qin Min Dang), taking huge numbers of GMD members and a significant corps of legislators with him. In 2001 Li himself rejected the GMD as a "foreign power" (*wailai zhengquan*) and organized the Taiwan Solidarity Union (Taiwan Tuanjie Lianmeng) taking more GMD legislators and many Taiwanese members. In that year's election the GMD lost control of the legislature. Active membership fell to under 350,000.

The surviving GMD went through another round of internal reforms, including direct election of the party chair by all members. The GMD still controlled vast wealth, and with the use of this lubricant, the promotion of the party as peacemaker with China, and election alliances with the New Party and the PFP, the GMD recovered. By 2004 membership had climbed to 970,000. In 2008 the PFP leader Song Chuyu agreed to reunite with the GMD, and the GMD regained control of both the legislature and the presidency. Back in power, the party took on a new role as the forum for negotiating policies and resolving conflicts between the GMD administration and GMD legislators. Of more interest to the people of Taiwan, and the world, was the role of the GMD in building a new relationship with the Chinese Communist Party. In May 2008 the GMD chairman Wu Boxiong (b. 1939)—a Taiwanese student of Chiang Ching-kuo—said he came to Beijing as chairman of the "Guomindang of China."

SEE ALSO *Chiang Ching-kuo (Jiang Jingguo); Chiang Kai-shek (Jiang Jieshi); Hakka; Li Denghui (Lee Teng-hui); Nanjing (Nanking); Northern Expedition; Political Parties, 1905–1949; Sun Yat-sen (Sun Yixian); Wang Jingwei; Warlord Era (1916–1928); Yuan Shikai.*

BIBLIOGRAPHY
Bedeski, Robert E. *State Building in Modern China: The Kuomintang in the Prewar Period*. Berkeley: University of California Center for Chinese Studies, 1981.

Bergère, Marie-Claude. *Sun Yat-sen*. Trans. Janet Lloyd. Stanford, CA: Stanford University Press, 1998.

Dickson, Bruce J. *Democratization in China and Taiwan: The Adaptability of Leninist Parties*. Oxford, U.K.: Clarendon Press, 1997.

Eastman, Lloyd, ed. *The Nationalist Era in China, 1927–1949*. Cambridge, U.K.: Cambridge University Press, 1991.

Fewsmith, Joseph. *Party, State, and Local Elites in Republican China: Merchant Organizations and Politics in Shanghai, 1980–1930*. Honolulu: University of Hawaii Press, 1985.

Fitzgerald, John. *Awakening China: Politics, Culture, and Class in the Nationalist Revolution*. Stanford, CA: Stanford Unversity Press, 1996.

Spence, Jonathan D. *The Search for Modern China*. New York: Norton, 1990.

Tien Hung-Mao. *Government and Politics in Kuomintang China, 1927–1937*. Stanford, CA: Stanford University Press, 1972.

Tien Hung-Mao. *The Great Transition: Political and Social Change in the Republic of China*. Stanford, CA: Hoover Institution Press, 1989.

Michael Stainton

NATURAL RESOURCES

With a territory of around 9,600,000 square kilometers, China has a vast pool of natural resources that are characterized by great diversity. This entry discusses various types of natural resources in China including water, forests, arable land, pastures, minerals, and wildlife. In addition to providing general information about China's natural resources, the entry will also treat the major dynamics and issues of exploitation that characterize the environment in China in the early years of the twenty-first century.

TOPOGRAPHIC AND CLIMATIC FEATURES

Modern China has a variety of topographic features and climatic zones that determines the diversity of its natural resources. The topography of China is marked by a gradual descent from the high west to the low east. The majority of the population resides in the plains in the east, including the Northeast Plain, the North China Plain, the Middle to Lower Yangzi Plain, and the Pearl River Delta Plain, which are China's important agricultural and industrial bases.

China is subject to a strong monsoon climate, leading to a distinctive weather difference between the wet southeast climatic zone and the dry northwest climatic zone. The average annual precipitation in China is 648 millimeters, which is 19 percent less than the world average of 800 millimeters on land. China's annual precipitation varies from more than 2,000 millimeters in the southeastern coastal areas to fewer than 200 millimeters in northwestern areas. Average annual evaporation from the surface varies from 700 to 800 millimeters in eastern areas to usually fewer than 300 millimeters in western areas.

The distribution of natural resources in China shows a regionally specific character. Forestry resources are concentrated in the northeastern and southwestern regions,

SURVEYS OF NATURAL RESOURCES

Modern surveying of natural resources in China dates back to the period of the Nationalist government; the geologist Weng Wenhao (1889–1971) was a pioneer. In 1912 Weng, the geologist Ding Wenjiang (1887–1936), and others founded an institute of geological survey under the Ministry of Agriculture and Commerce. Weng also is credited with finding and developing the Yumen Oil Field, China's first large oil field, in the Gobi Desert. In the early 1920s the geographer Zhu Kezhen (1890–1974) called for training Chinese geographers in surveying geomorphology, meteorology, ethnology, fauna and flora, and mineralogy.

Foreigners also were involved in early surveys of natural resources in China. Between 1927 and 1935, for example, a group of scientists from Germany, Denmark, and Sweden, led by Sven Hedin (1865–1952), joined their Chinese counterparts in a research expedition in the Gobi Desert.

After the founding of the People's Republic the Chinese government started to prioritize interdisciplinary, integrated, and comprehensive surveys of natural resources. These activities met the requirements of planned economic development, and they later sustained economic growth in the reform and opening period.

In the 1950s Zhu Kezhen, then vice president of the Chinese Academy of Sciences (CAS), organized multidisciplinary surveys in Tibet, Hainan Island, and southern Guangxi. In China's twelve-year plan for the development of science and technology (1956–1967), formulated by scientists and approved and issued by the State Council, there was an important component of surveying natural resources. Zhu Kezhen proposed establishing a commission within the academy to be in charge of surveying, which eventually evolved into a national organization to oversee nationwide surveys, the Commission for Integrated Survey of Natural Resources (CISNAR). Zhu not only chaired the commission, but also participated in its projects. The surveys covered almost the entire country, and in particular remote regions, thus laying a solid foundation for China's natural resources development and providing significant scientific evidence to be used in the formulation of national and regional economic development plans.

In 1999, when the CAS launched its Knowledge Innovation Program, the CISNAR joined the Institute of Geography to form the Institute of Geographic Sciences and Natural Resources. One of the institute's most important missions is to carry out surveys of natural resources that contribute to the reasonable and comprehensive use of natural resources, ecological and environmental protection, and sustainable development.

Cong Cao

water resources in the southeastern region, and mineral resources in the western region.

WATER RESOURCES

China has a large number of rivers with a total length of 420,000 kilometers. China ranks sixth among nations in total water resources, but the amount of water per capita and per unit of cultivated land is far below the world average. Most of China's rivers are situated in the wet eastern monsoon climatic zone, the major ones including the Yangzi, Yellow, Heilong, and Pearl. Northwestern China has a small number of rivers, with no connection to the sea and little runoff.

The Yangzi River and the Yellow River, the third- and sixth-longest rivers in the world, respectively, provide China with two prominent hydraulic systems. The Yellow River incubated the earliest Chinese civilization, but has also been identified as the "sorrow of China," due to its high seasonal volume and the high percentage of silt carried in its waters. The country's most disastrous flood, for example, which killed between 900,000 and 2,000,000 people back in 1887, occurred in the middle and lower reaches of the Yellow River. Nevertheless, the Yellow River provides great water resources for the North China Plain.

The Yangzi River, the biggest river in China, running across nine provinces and regions, provides abundant water resources to its river valley area, especially the Middle and Lower Yangzi Plain. Like the Yellow River, the huge water flow of the Yangzi is both blessing and woe: it provides enormous hydroelectric resources, but it also brings frequent floods during monsoon seasons. In 1931, 1954, and 1998, for example, large-scale flooding caused millions of deaths.

To deal with water calamities, Han Chinese civilization developed a system of water control—using dikes, dams, river diversions, and other measures. Inspired by confidence in human capacity to control nature, major waterworks were constructed to tame the rivers. Construction on the most recent example, the Three Gorges Dam, began in the mid-1990s. The project stirred great controversy regarding the issues of environmental protection, preservation of cultural heritage, mass relocation of upstream people, and the relationship between large-scale waterworks and an authoritarian government, among other issues. To solve the problem of uneven distribution of water resources, China is undertaking a major project to transfer more than 40 million cubic meters of water per year from the southern Yangzi Basin to the North China Plain by 2020. Another major water-control project—the Nu River Dam—is supposed to make the best use of the unspoiled Nu River resources in southwestern China and more efficiently distribute the potential water resources around the river basin. This project remained under debate among governments, experts, local people, and environmental groups as of 2009.

ARABLE LAND

Although China's territory is vast, the amount of arable land is relatively small with most of it concentrated on the river basins of eastern and southern China. Only 1.3 million square kilometers out of 9.6 million square kilometers are suitable for farming, about 14 percent of the total land area. Of the remainder, 28 percent is pasture, 24 percent forest, and the rest uncultivable and urban area.

The Chinese government has divided the country into seven regions for central conservation planning and in 2008 an extensive survey was done in these seven regions for better conservation planning (PRC National Survey for Soil and Water Conservation 2008 final report):

1. The Loess Plateau Region of North China

2. The Black Soil Region of Northeast China

3. The Red Soils Region of South China

4. The Northern Rocky Mountain Region

5. The Southwest Mountain Region

6. The Northwest Region

   The Agricultural Sub-region of Northwest China

   The Grassland Plains Sub-region of Northwest China

7. The Tibetan High Plateau and Mountain Region

The amount of arable land, in contrast with other natural resources, increased during the expansion of Han Chinese civilization. Large amounts of other types of land were converted to agricultural land to meet the needs of the growing population. As the population grew, and land reclamation progressed, urbanization reduced the areas available for cultivation. In addition, land degradation due to water and wind erosion, misuse of fertilizer, overgrazing, and other causes has contributed to the decrease in arable land.

Degraded grasslands in the PRC

Province	Grassland area (million ha)	Grassland area moderately to severely degraded	
		(million ha)	%
Tibet	82.4	21.4	26
Inner Mongolia	79.1	45.9	58
Xinjiang	56.4	26.0	46
Qinghai	36.0	10.8	30
Sichuan	21.1	6.1	29
Gansu	17.6	8.4	48
Yunnan	15.2	0.5	3
Other provinces	117.8	17.7	15
Total	**393.6**	**136.7**	**34**

SOURCE: Ministry of Agriculture. 1999. Cited in L. Berry, "Land Degradation in China: Its Extent and Impact," April 2003.

Table 1

FORESTS

China has a long history of deforestation. Over the course of Chinese civilization, the forest has been shrinking continuously, due to agricultural land reclamation and animal husbandry. Four thousand or five thousand years ago, about 60 percent of the land in China was covered with forests, declining to less than 50 percent around two thousand years ago, and to around 40 percent one thousand years ago. As a result of intensive land reclamation, wars, and demands for timber, China's forestland had decreased to 21 percent by the start of the last dynasty of China, more than 350 years ago. According to incomplete statistics compiled by the Forestry Society of China, the country's forest coverage had dropped sharply to 8.6 percent by 1948, before it was further devastated by the Great Leap Forward at the end of 1950s, during which a large number of trees were felled to fuel steel-industry development.

China also suffers from the poor quality of its remaining forest resources. Although China has the fifth-largest forest resources in the world after Russia, Brazil, Canada, and the United States, in terms of coverage rate, China is 1.83 times below the world average. The remaining forests in China are mainly located in the northeastern and southwestern regions, with some in the subtropical and tropical zone. These regions account for 29.9 percent, 19.6 percent, and 41 percent, respectively, of the national forest area. Few forests exist in the North China Plain and in northwestern China.

To address the problem of low forest quality and low productivity of forestland, the People's Republic of China (PRC) has implemented reforestation strategies, although the growth of forest resources is slow, with an average annual increment of 0.16 percent. According to the statistics of the sixth national forest survey between 1999 and 2003, the total forest coverage in China increased to 18.21 percent.

MINERALS

By 2002, 157 varieties of mineral resources with verified reserves had been discovered in China: 9 were energy-mineral resources, 54 were metallic mineral resources, 91 were nonmetallic mineral resources, and 3 were water-and-gas-mineral resources.

Energy-mineral resources include coal, petroleum and natural gas. Coal is the major mineral resource in China. In the 1980s, more than 80 percent of China's energy production was from coal; in the first decade of the 2000s, still more than 50 percent of China's energy production came from coal. China has high reserves of coal but only small reserves of high-quality coking coal and anthracite coal. The coal reserves are mostly found in the North China Plain, specifically in Shanxi Province.

China possesses rich metallic mineral resources, with reserves of almost every types of useful metallic mineral that has been discovered worldwide. Some of China's proven reserves, including wolfram, tin, stibium, tombarthite, tantalum, and titanium, are the largest in the world. The proven reserves of vanadium, molybdenum, niobium, beryllium and lithium are the second largest in the world. China's zinc resources are the fourth largest in the world, and China's reserves of iron, lead, gold, and silver are the fifth largest.

Although China's reserves of metallic mineral resources are large, their quality varies. Some, such as the reserves of wolfram, tin, molybdenum, and tombarthite, are high quality and are very competitive in world markets. However, some of China's mineral resources are poor quality and are less competitive in world markets. China's deposits of iron, aluminum, and copper ores, for example, are difficult to smelt.

China also has a relatively complete range of varieties of nonmetallic mineral resources. By 2009, there were more than five thousand nonmetallic mineral-ore production bases with proven reserves in China. The reserves of magnesite, graphite, fluorite, talc, asbestos, gypsum, barite, wollastonite, alunite, bentonite, and halite are among the largest in the world.

While the reserves of mineral resources are abundant and some of them are high quality, when they are subject to exploitation, these nonrenewable resources give rise to the dilemma of the "tragedy of the commons." At the present rate of exploitation, many of these reserves will be exhausted by the mid-twenty-first century.

PASTURES

China is the third-largest pasture resource country in the world. The total pasture area is 398,920,000 hectares. Most of the pastures are in the north (mainly Inner Mongolia), northwest, and Tibetan region. In ancient China, pastureland outside the Great Wall was occupied by nomadic people, including the proto-Turks, and other aboriginal tribes. In contemporary China, the pastures are an important source for the well-being of many ethnic peoples, including the Mongols, Tibetans, and Uygurs.

As many other types of natural resources, China's grasslands have suffered significant degradation both in history and present day. By 1999, 90 percent were degraded to some degree, with 34 percent moderately to severely degraded. In order to improve the deteriorating pasture eco-environment, the PRC has implemented several restoration plans—for example, allocating the grazing area more efficiently, and planting new pastures. Currently, the pastures are in the process of slow recovery.

WILDLIFE

China has a great diversity of wildlife. There are more than 4,400 species of vertebrates, more than 10 percent of the world's total. There are nearly 500 mammal species, 1,189 species of birds, more than 320 species of reptiles and 210 species of amphibians. China's topography contributes to this diversity. China lies in two of the world's major zoogeographic regions—the Palearctic and the Oriental. The Tibetan Plateau, Xinjiang and Inner Mongolia, northeastern China, and the North China Plain are in the Palearctic region. Central, southern, and southwestern China lie in the Oriental region. Such mammals as the river fox, horse, camel, tapir, mouse hare, hamster, and jerboa live in the Palearctic zone. The civet cat, Chinese pangolin, bamboo rat, tree shrew, and gibbon and various other species of monkeys and apes can be found in the Oriental region. The famous giant panda is found only in northern Sichuan along the Yangzi River.

With the intrusion of humans into their habitats, many of China's animal species are undergoing a severe drop in numbers. In order to prevent their extinction, the Chinese government surveyed the country's animals and categorized them into different levels based on their need for protection. For example, the giant panda is under level-one protection, the highest. In addition, many wildlife conservation areas were established to protect wildlife resources, for example, the Wolong Wildlife Conservation Area in Sichuan Province and Xishuangbanna Wildlife Conservation Area in Yunnan Province. In 2007 to 2008, two rare species—the white-flag dolphin and the South China tiger were pronounced extinct in China, which is a huge loss to China's wildlife pool. In general, however, the conservation policy set by the central government since the 1980s has saved many animal species.

ENVIRONMENTAL ISSUES AND RESOURCE MANAGEMENT

China is facing serious environmental challenges. During 2008, China had surpassed the United States to become the world's foremost emitter of greenhouse gases. Deforestation, desertification, water pollution, and other problems all besiege China currently. To tackle its environmental problems, the PRC decentralized the policy-making process for environmental issues, which means that provincial governments and even local governments are taking the lead in solving environmental problems. In addition, China has experienced a gradual increase in voices from the public space, especially nongovernmental organizations. Although in the context of Chinese society, nongovernmental organizations are closely tied to the government, they are becoming more and more proactive in addressing China's environmental issues.

SEE ALSO *Agricultural Production: Forestry and Timber Trade; Climate; Desertification; Endangered Species, Protection of; Energy: Overview; Environment; Land Use, History of; River Systems.*

BIBLIOGRAPHY

Berry, Leonard, Land Degradation in China: Its Extent and Impact. Food and Agriculture Organization of the United Nations. Land Degradation Assessment in Drylands. 2003.

China Mining Association. Characteristics and Distribution of China's Mineral Resources. 2006. http://www.chinamining.org/Investment/2006-07-25/1153812794d198.html.

Ministry of Water Resources of the P.R.C. 2007 Statistic Bulletin on China Water Activities.

Ministry of Water Resources of the P.R.C. Zhongguo shuitu liushi yu shengtai anquan zonghe kexue kaocha baogao [A report on People's Republic of China national survey for soil and water conservation], 2008.

Ministry of Water Resources of the P.R.C. Water Resources in China. 2004. http://www.mwr.gov.cn/english1/20040802/38161.asp.

Organization for Economic Cooperation and Development OECD. Working Party on Environmental Performance. Environmental Performance Review of China: Conclusions and Recommendations (Final). November 2006.

PRC Bureau of Forestry. Di liu ci quanguo senglin ziyuan qingcha zhuyao jieguo. [The statistics of the Sixth National Forestry Survey]. September 2006. http://www.forestry.gov.cn/distribution/2007/03/07/lygk-2007-03-07-2066.html.

Yan Gao

NEPOTISM AND *GUANXI*

Nepotism is the exercise of favoritism toward kin. This original meaning of nepotism is associated with monarchies or dynasties in which privileges and positions of power were reserved and assigned to relatives of incumbents. In modern China, nepotism is formally denounced in governmental and nongovernmental organizations, but its practice is widely observed in public and private domains as its meaning has extended to refer to an array of attitudes and behaviors of favoritism toward kin and nonkin of *guanxi* ties. Understanding what *guanxi* means and how *guanxi* is formed and carried out is thus a key to the legacy of nepotism in China today.

DEFINING FEATURES OF *GUANXI*

Guanxi refers to a dyadic (i.e., binary), particular, and sentimental tie that has the potential for facilitating the exchange of favors between the two parties connected by the tie. To Chinese people inside or outside mainland China, any blood or marital relationship qualifies for this definition; hence, kin ties are automatically *guanxi* ties. Persons with a nonkin tie, on the other hand, can develop *guanxi* between them if the parties repeatedly invest sentiment in the tie and at the same time build up obligations to each other, making the tie special to both parties. The word *special* here means *personal* and *personalized*, or what sociologists term *particular*. When *guanxi* goes beyond the dyadic basis to connect more than two persons, a *guanxi* network (or *guanxiwang*) emerges. In conventional social-network terms, a *guanxi* network is an egocentric network in which a focal actor (ego) is connected to two or more other actors (alters), who are connected to still others.

An adequate understanding of the cultural meaning of *guanxi* is a prerequisite to understanding patterns of nepotism and other behaviors of the Chinese. In Chinese culture, two parties that are connected by a mutually recognized *guanxi* tie tend to have at least three interrelated feelings toward each other: *ganqing* or feelings of affection; *renqing* or feelings of reciprocal obligation; and *mianzi* (face) or the feeling that one is gaining respect from the other party when affections are rewarded or expected obligations fulfilled. Inversely, *ganqing* is hurt when affection goes in only one direction, *renqing* is considered nonexistent when expected obligations are never recognized or favors never returned, and *mianzi* is lost when attitudes and actions of ignorance or rejection are signaled or implied by the other party. These negative relational processes ultimately lead to the dissolution of a *guanxi* tie. This means that *guanxi*, like any kind of social connection, is dynamic rather than static, and its effectiveness and duration depend on sentimental and behavioral exchanges between the parties involved.

GUANXI-BUILDING AND FAVORITISM

Guanxi-building is the process of developing mutual affection, strengthening reciprocal obligations, and increasing mutual respect between parties that are connected by a tie. Possible foundations for the cultivation of *guanxi* ties, apart from kinship, include a common hometown, residence, school, military experience, and organizational affiliation. During one's life course, new members may be added to and old members eliminated from one's *guanxi* network. For example, *guanxi* ties can be developed from among classmates (*tong xue*), roommates (*shi you*), army comrades (*zhan you*), and hometown folk (*tong xiang*). Very close friends are likely to become pseudo kin by addressing each other as brother or sister, especially among northerners. To be sure, *guanxi*-building is individualistic and is a behavioral art, requiring interpersonally justified strategies in such social interactions as conversations, banquets, and gift exchanges. The so-called "art of *guanxixue*" is about these strategies of relational cultivation, maintenance, and utilization at individual levels.

In everyday life, *guanxi*-building may not be a deliberate process, but the utilization of an existing *guanxi* tie is almost always intended to generate the benefit of favoritism. An applicant to a top music school receives an admissions offer not only because of her talent but also because of her teacher's strong connections with the school. A college graduate fails to get a job on his own but secures a good one through his uncle's influence over the hiring organization. In government bureaucracy, many people are appointed to positions of power and privilege because they have been loyal to the authorities who have promoted them. This last example points to the influences of cliques and factions that are formed around the *guanxi* networks of powerful politicians. A general proposition about the pervasiveness of *guanxi* influence suffices here: In competition over scarce resources or desirable positions, *guanxi*-facilitated favoritism is likely to rise.

SCHOLARLY ROOTS OF *GUANXI* STUDY

The term *guanxi* entered social science research through the works of Chinese scholars Liang Shuming ([1949] 1986) and Fei Xiaotong ([1949] 1992). Seeing the family and kinship as the cornerstones of Chinese culture and society, Liang considers *guanxi* as the extended familial ties defined by a set of ethical codes combining sentiment (*qing*) and obligation (*yi*). He argues that, under these codes, Chinese individuals are relationally oriented so that their normative behaviors toward others are confined to Confucian elaborations of the five cardinal dyadic ties (*wu lun*) connecting the ruler and the ministers, the father and the sons, the husband and the wife, the older brother and the

younger brothers, and friend and friends. While each of these dyadic ties has a corresponding set of sentimental and obligatory codes, these codes are thought to have extended to characterizing all interpersonal relations of social and personal significance, pushing every Chinese individual to develop his or her web of "pseudo families" with significant others. To Liang and Fei, a civilized Chinese individual makes a lifelong effort to build and rebuild his or her personal *guanxi* network.

Fei Xiaotong's work has had a wide and lasting impact on social science research in modern China and requires special attention. Fei makes a fundamental distinction between Chinese and Western social structures. He calls Western social structure an "organizational mode of association" (*tuan ti ge ju*) in which individuals make up groups and organizations as members based on their clearly defined interests. Under the organizational mode of association, members have basically the same relationships to groups or organizations and are consequently bound by rules that are universally applied to all members within the groups or organizations.

In contrast, Chinese social structure is a "differential mode of association" (*cha xu ge ju*) in which there are no fixed groups or organizations with defined memberships, but rather myriad overlapping networks of personalized *guanxi*. The pattern for this kind of network resembles "the circles that appear on the surface of a lake when a rock is thrown into it" (Fei Xiaotong [1949] 1992, p. 62); when many rocks (persons) are thrown into the lake (society), the aggregate structure is the interrelated and overlapped circles of strong and weak personalized *guanxi*. Under the differential mode of association, one's behavioral criteria are constantly shifting from one person to another, depending on one's sentiments and obligations to others as defined by and confined to the particularistic relationships one has with them. These relational sentiments and obligations, Fei claims, retain primacy over one's group or organizational affiliations.

The differential mode of association appears to be persistent in Mao Zedong's political culture of "principled particularism." For ordinary people, their *guanxi* ties to authorities are instrumental in obtaining a great array of life necessities, consumer items, and job opportunities that are allocated through the hierarchy of state-run organizations. While prior relationships and sentimental investments are still necessary for developing *guanxi*, instrumental reciprocity becomes the most important characteristic and the overarching goal of *guanxi*. This makes *guanxi*-building a deliberate and rational process under Communism, eroding the traditional-ethical basis of *guanxi* as a familial and pseudo-familial tie. This tendency reached its peak during the Cultural Revolution decade (1966–1976) and has continued to characterize the post-1980 reform era in which short-term rationality is the core of the new relational ethics shared by younger generations.

GUANXI PRACTICES AND NEPOTISM IN THE REFORM ERA

In reform-era China, empirical studies about *guanxi* and its significance in social, economic, and political spheres have generated diverse findings. In the social sphere, village case studies indicate that Chinese peasants normatively invest sentiment to maintain good kinship and neighborhood ties, and that the instrumental and emotional gains are the by-product or unintended consequence of *guanxi*-building as a way of life. Urban studies, on the other hand, show that *guanxi* development and maintenance are assisted through visitations, social eating, and gift exchanges during life events of personal and cultural significance. Those with advantageous social positions tend to have diverse *guanxi* ties across structural and institutional boundaries. These people in turn attend a greater number of social eating opportunities and identify higher social standing than people of otherwise equal social-demographic characteristics in China today. In light of these findings, researchers have conceptualized *guanxi* as a form of social capital.

In the economic sphere, studies of township and village enterprises (TVEs) show that labor-market information and economic resources flow consistently through *guanxi* networks that have been built up within the confines of kinship, home villages, and hometowns, making China a model of "network capitalism." Kinship networks also serve as governance structures and informal property-rights institutions of TVEs. In the urban labor markets, good *guanxi* ties are useful to both learn job information and obtain more substantial assistance from authorities for employment opportunities; studies show that a great majority of people obtained jobs through their *guanxi* ties. To entrepreneurs, personalized *guanxi* ties to local officials are the lifeblood of private businesses, interorganizational *guanxi* ties are important for the operation of business contracts, and *guanxi*-building is an integral part of enterprise management.

In the political sphere, *guanxi* networks are reportedly the informal mechanisms behind the wide spread of nepotism in office appointments, official corruption, and legal injustice. First, while promotions to positions of state power and authority are formally regulated by merit-based personnel rules, the system of political appointment opens up a huge area in which one wins favors from his or her superiors through *guanxi* ties. This form of nepotism can be as influential as in the private sector, in which entrepreneurs are less constrained in managerial and nonmanagerial appointments. Second, official corruption or abuse of public power for personal gain has increased because of rising opportunities for state officials to play direct and indirect roles in emerging market economies. Their power-money exchanges are facilitated by *guanxi* ties: prior ties or common go-betweens allow the flow of confidential information, maintain a desirable level of trust, and permit illicit transactions between officials and entrepreneurs. Finally, these illicit practices are widespread by and large because of a *guanxi*-eroded legal system. For example, successful Chinese lawyers tend to be well connected politically, and rural and urban residents who have political connections have an advantage in winning a civil dispute or a civil lawsuit.

While there is no systematic assessment of the roles of *guanxi* in the rise of nepotism in reform-era China, an important research task is to differentiate between good and bad influences of *guanxi* in social, economic, and political life. Economic sociology makes the distinction between information and favoritism that may have flowed through *guanxi* networks. In the labor markets, for example, *guanxi* networks may transform person-specific information, which in turn matches worker qualifications to the skill requirements of the jobs to which these workers are assigned. But *guanxi* networks may also allow people to gain favors from socially constrained employers, who would assign marginalized workers to jobs of superior earning opportunities. While both kinds of *guanxi* influences are visible in Chinese workplaces today, the practical question is how to reduce and minimize the bad *guanxi* influence while maintaining the good *guanxi* influence. Clues to answering this question may be gained by comparing Chinese *guanxi* networks to Western social networks.

SEE ALSO *Corruption; Identity, Chinese; Social Classes before 1949; Social Classes since 1978; Social Rituals.*

BIBLIOGRAPHY

Fei Xiaotong. *From the Soil: The Foundations of Chinese Society.* 1949. Eds. and trans. Gary G. Hamilton and Wang Zheng. Berkeley: University of California Press, 1992.

Liang Shuming. *Chongguo wenhua yaoyi* [The essential meanings of Chinese culture]. 1949. Hong Kong: Zheng Zhong Press, 1986.

Yanjie Bian

NEW DEMOCRACY, 1949–1953

New Democracy (*Xin Minzhu-zhuyi*), or the New Democratic Revolution (*Xin Minzhu-zhuyi Geming*), was the term for the stage of rule of the Chinese Communist Party (CCP) following its victory in 1949. The theoretical basis for it was outlined by Mao Zedong in his January

1940 speech "Xin minzhu zhuyi de zhengzhi yu Xin minzhu-zhuyi de wenhua" (The politics and culture of New Democracy), which was published in the Yan'an-based journal *Zhongguo Wenhua* (Chinese culture) in February of that year as "Xin Minzhu-zhuyi lun" (On New Democracy).

In the speech he argued that the Chinese revolution historically fell into two stages, democracy and socialism; the former was not democracy in general, but democracy of a special Chinese type to be called *New Democracy*. Mao took note of the special nature of Chinese society after the Opium War of 1840, which he defined as semicolonial and semifeudal in character. This preparatory period culminated in the Revolution of 1911, which Mao described as a bourgeois-democratic revolution and as the beginning of the wider Chinese revolution. The outbreak of World War I and the Russian October Revolution in 1917 brought the Chinese bourgeois-democratic revolution within the fold of the bourgeois-democratic world revolution, and the subsequent May Fourth movement in 1919, the founding of the CCP in 1921, and the Great Revolution from 1924 to 1927 brought the Chinese revolution into the fold of the proletarian-socialist world revolution. In his article Mao took great pains to cite Stalinist theory, quoting extensively from Stalin's 1918 article "The October Revolution and the National Question." In that article Stalin was attempting to erect a bridge between the proletariat of the socialist West and the toilers of the "enslaved" East, thereby making a strategic appeal to the Kemalist and other revolutions for support for the Russian Revolution. In Stalin's theory Mao found ideological justification for arguing that revolutions in colonies and semicolonies were able to break away from the old category and become part of the proletarian-socialist revolution. Mao's formulation of New Democracy also addressed the specifics of China's history and the relevance of the Chinese revolution for the world revolution and the Communist International (Comintern). In 1940 Mao remained troubled by the alliance of potential rival Chinese Communist leaders, such as Wang Ming (1904–1974), with the Comintern.

Within Marxist theory it was impossible to achieve socialism and communism in a society that had not reached the stage of capitalism. Mao's theory of New Democracy attempted to provide a theoretical basis for effecting the transition to socialism following a successful revolution led by a party representing the proletarian-socialist world revolution, namely the CCP, in a society whose modes of production could sustain only a bourgeois-democratic revolution. Mao argued that the CCP could initiate socialism by forging a relationship with a coalition of the four most progressive classes: proletarian workers, peasants, the petty bourgeoisie, and the nationally based capitalists. These four classes are represented on the flag of the PRC by the four stars surrounding the large yellow star, which represents the CCP.

The victory of the Chinese Communists in 1949 was hailed in China as marking the establishment of New Democracy, a preliminary stage prior to the establishment of the dictatorship of the proletariat. In Mao's analysis, there were only three basic types of state system in the world in terms of political power: republics under bourgeois dictatorship; republics under the dictatorship of the proletariat; and republics under the joint dictatorship of several revolutionary classes. His New Democracy fell into the latter category, and he held that this could only emerge as a form adopted by revolutions in colonial and semicolonial states. For him, the anti-Japanese united front was an alliance of several revolutionary classes, and this represented the kernel of the New Democratic power to be introduced after his revolution was successful. The united front that he mentions was also an effective mode of organization and co-option after 1949.

After 1949 the alliance of the CCP with local or "national" capitalists (the term *national* excluding counterrevolutionaries and traitors) was designed to ensure the continuation of economic growth, whereas the alliance with the petty bourgeoisie ensured that the CCP, which had remained entrenched in rural bases for much of the revolutionary period, could draw on urban support. The alliance with capitalists was theoretically troublesome for Mao. He took great pains to examine the dual character of China's capitalists and of the "big bourgeoisie," and argued that this social class was prone to seek conciliation with the Guomindang, who were the enemies of the revolution. Mao pointed out that between 1927 and 1937 China's "big bourgeoisie" had nestled in the arms of the imperialists, and in the anti-Japanese war the "big bourgeoisie" was represented by the puppet regime of Wang Jingwei. This betrayal meant that the unpatriotic Chinese bourgeoisie fell far short of the bourgeoisie in the French or American revolutionary periods. This highly developed tendency of the Chinese bourgeoisie to conciliation with the enemies of the revolution, as remarked upon by Mao, would have dire consequences for the Chinese bourgeoisie, and it betrayed Mao's belief in the existence of a social pathology in semicolonial China. Mao took great pains to distinguish the "big bourgeoisie" from the "petty bourgeoisie," and included the petty bourgeoisie among the four awakening classes that would necessarily become the basic components of the state and governmental structure in the democratic republic of China, the New Democracy, that would be established after victory over imperialism and the forces of feudalism. Mao also described this New Democracy as a republic of the genuinely revolutionary new Three People's Principles, reviving but totally redefining Sun Yat-sen's principles.

Mao argued firmly that this alliance was only a contingent arrangement, and his attempts to accelerate the pace of change in China in the late 1950s by establishing communes betrays his discomfort with his own model. But the model continued to have great appeal for Marxist parties operating in semicolonial nations: The Shining Path in Peru, the "Maoists" in Nepal, the New People's Army in the Philippines, and the Communist Party of India (Maoist), all cited Mao's concept of New Democracy as the goal of their revolutions, and invoked Mao's example of conducting a successful guerrilla war.

SEE ALSO *Chinese Marxism: Mao Zedong Thought.*

BIBLIOGRAPHY

MacFarquhar, Roderick, and John K. Fairbank, eds. *The Cambridge History of China,* Vol. 14, *The People's Republic,* Part 1. Cambridge, U.K.: Cambridge University Press, 1987.

Mao Tse-tung. On New Democracy. In *Selected Works of Mao Tse-tung,* Vol. 2, 339–384. Beijing: Foreign Languages Press, 1967.

Bruce G. Doar

NEW LEFT

Emerging in China in the 1990s, the New Left (Xin Zuopai) is a loose grouping of intellectuals often contrasted with the Liberals. Both groups include many intellectuals who were educated abroad, often in the United States. Neither group can be considered dissident, in the Cold War sense of the term, and members are perhaps best described as "critical intellectuals" or "public intellectuals."

Those intellectuals, typified by Wang Hui, who since the late 1990s were styled pejoratively, and then subsequently styled themselves, the New Left, generally adhere to a critique of the official "commodity market economy" model espoused by the Chinese Communist Party (CCP) after 1985. Although the initial wave of economic reforms initiated by the CCP under Deng Xiaoping in 1978 saw a freeing up of distribution networks, a development the Chinese New Leftists supported, the New Leftists became critical of economic and political developments in the 1990s.

Some date the emergence of the Chinese New Left from the December 24, 2004, Zhengzhou Incident, in which four protesters were sentenced to three-year prison terms for distributing leaflets praising Mao Zedong at a gathering honoring the anniversary of Mao's death. However, this incident belies the intellectual and academic nature of the New Left, and the group's general strategy of working with the Communist Party as a "leftist" think tank whose articles are read by many party members. The New Leftists generally oppose capitalist democracy, which

gives them something in common with the Euro-American New Left, but there are few other similarities. Most Chinese New Leftists evince an interest in and nostalgia for the "revolutionary Maoism" of the pre–Cultural Revolution period, even though most were educated in the United States, but they are not to be confused with the Ultra-Leftists of the Cultural Revolution period.

Born in Yangzhou in 1959, Wang Hui completed his undergraduate studies at Yangzhou University and his Ph.D. in the Graduate School of the Chinese Academy of Social Sciences in 1988. In 1989 he took part in the Tiananmen Square protests and was later punished for his involvement by being sent to rural Shaanxi for reeducation. Wang served as coeditor of the leading intellectual journal *Dushu* (Reading) from May 1996 to July 2007, and became a professor in the Department of Chinese Language and Literature at Tsinghua University in Beijing. As Pankaj Mishra wrote in the *New York Times* in 2006, "Wang has reflected eloquently and often on what outsiders see as the central paradox of contemporary China: an authoritarian state fostering a free-market economy while espousing socialism." Contrary to mainstream Western interpretations, Wang characterizes the 1989 protests as a revolt against such policies. As well as being a conduit for demands for democracy, Wang characterizes the protests as "a spontaneous resistance to the inequalities springing from the growth of markets" (Wang Hui 2003, p. 58).

Wang Hui is only one of many thinkers described as New Left. Cui Zhiyuan, educated at the Massachusetts Institute of Technology and a professor of politics and public management at Tsinghua University, is also referred to as a New Leftist thinker. Cui has called for a "second liberation of thought," an idea outlined in Wang Chaohua's *One China, Many Paths* (2003). Cui is critical of the privatization of state assets, and has praised the Cultural Revolution as an innovation in the field of politics. He referred specifically to the charter of the Anshan Steel Works for embodying a uniquely workable Chinese Communist management style. He is also the editor of the selected essays of the Brazilian legal scholar and political theorist Roberto Unger and has coauthored several books with him.

Another self-proclaimed New Left advocate is Chen Xin, a sociology professor at the Chinese Academy of Social Sciences. Chen argues that social justice is the major thrust of New Left philosophy, and this entails addressing the deep inequalities that emerged in Chinese society in the early 1990s.

Two other prominent members of the New Left are Gan Yang, a mentor of the mainland New Left who is based as a researcher in the Centre of Asian Studies of the University of Hong Kong, and Wang Shaoguang, who is a chair professor in the Department of Government and Public Administration at the Chinese University of Hong

Kong, as well as being a Changjiang Professor in the School of Public Policy and Management at Tsinghua University in Beijing. Gan Yang is best known for his research and commentary on the political economy of China's reform and his insights into intellectual politics in contemporary China, while Wang Shaoguang, a Ph.D. graduate in political science from Cornell University, is the editor of the influential journal in the greater China region, the *China Review.*

The New Left indirectly influences Communist Party policy, and the concerns of the New Left about the negative effects of privatization, marketization, and globalization have many followers in the CCP, not surprisingly because intellectuals of the New Left argue that the injustices arising from these social trends can be addressed by state power. Some political commentators have detected New Left influences in the attacks by Hu Jintao and Wen Jiabao on the Three Represents policy of Jiang Zemin, in the emphasis of the current leadership on harmonious society, and in calls to provide better material and social-security conditions for itinerant workers and farmers. The New Left's rhetoric meshes with that of the government of Hu Jintao, but officially the CCP neither acknowledges nor endorses influences from the New Left, New Left-Liberals, or Liberals. Sustained ideological diversity is not within the tradition of the CCP, but the party's use of think tanks and opinion polls is now a well-established practice. The New Left's issues are usually raised in the Chinese-language Internet, rather than in political meetings or in the heavily monitored publishing sector.

The emergence of the New Left—and of the Liberals—is evidence of the return of political debate to Chinese society since 1989, even though this debate takes place within narrow confines. The current prominence of the public intellectual in China is also an unprecedented phenomenon in the history of the People's Republic, but the phenomenon also points to the seriousness of social issues and the necessity to work for the establishment of social justice and welfare in a radically altered society that could rapidly destabilize if these issues are not effectively addressed.

SEE ALSO *Classical Scholarship and Intellectual Debates: Debates since 1949; Liberalism.*

BIBLIOGRAPHY

Mishra, Pankaj. China's New Leftist. *New York Times*, October 15, 2006.

Wang Chaohua, ed. *One China, Many Paths.* New York: Verso, 2003.

Wang Hui. *Sihuo chongwen* [Rekindling frozen fire: The paradox of modernity]. Beijing: People's Art and Literature Publishing House, 2000.

Wang Hui. *China's New Order: Society, Politics, and Economy in Transition.* Trans. Ted Huters. Cambridge, MA: Harvard University Press, 2003.

Wang Hui. *Xiandai Zhongguo sixiang de xingqi* [The rise of modern Chinese thought]. 4 vols. Beijing: SDX Joint Publishing Company, 2004.

Wang Shaoguang and Cui Zhiyuan, eds. *Political Economy of China's Reforms.* Hong Kong: Oxford University Press, 1997.

Zhang Xudong. *Whither China? Intellectual Politics in Contemporary China.* Durham, NC: Duke University Press, 2001.

Bruce G. Doar

NEW PRINT MOVEMENT

The twentieth century in China was an era of nearly constant social and political upheaval, often marked by fierce violence from both internal and external sources. Many Chinese students during the 1920s and 1930s, a period of cultural tumult, embraced the culture of the West as China's destiny. Born as China's imperial system was collapsing, they were educated at the moment of transition from the old to the new, a period of extraordinary hope and enthusiasm for China's modernization. Various literary movements, such as the May Fourth movement, sprang from the reformist cultural convictions of this era. The modern art that blossomed at approximately the same time, inspired by the same sources, can be considered part of the same cultural phenomenon. Many of that generation viewed modern art and Western art as synonymous and believed that by adopting Western forms China might create an art in keeping with its new domestic and international situation.

Chinese artists adapted modern trends, such as impressionism, postimpressionism, constructivism, cubism, surrealism, fauvism, and expressionism, for their own purposes. The woodcuts (woodblocks) of the new print movement, which by the late 1940s had become the de facto official art of the Communist Party, may be the most thoroughly published works of any type of twentieth-century Chinese art. This canonization, however, obscures the movement's avant-garde origins and has yielded somewhat oversimplified histories of its artists, the art form, and China itself in this extraordinarily complicated era. Woodcuts were a means by which young revolutionaries hoped to enlighten their countrymen, a call to arms. They were also a vehicle through which young artists sought to express themselves in ways that were often modernist and cosmopolitan. Although much of the Chinese art historical literature written after 1949 viewed the modern woodcut movement as the first chapter of the development of Communist art, in fact the art form's early history more closely parallels and intersects with developments in other Western media.

DEVELOPMENT OF THE CHINESE WOODCUT

Although the woodcut was invented in China, and reproduced and distributed throughout the Chinese empire in elegant imperial encyclopedias, state-sanctioned religious canons, poetry anthologies, the classics of history and philosophy, cheap popular books, medical manuals, dramas, stories, and elementary textbooks, most young practitioners of the new print movement in China considered the woodcut Western and modern. They initiated significant changes in the practice of making prints. Unlike the artists of the Ming and Qing periods, whose paintings were turned over to a highly skilled craftsman for carving on pear-wood blocks, the twentieth-century printmakers dispensed with the division of labor and learned to carve and print their own blocks. In addition, artists of the modern woodcut generally printed with European oil-based printing inks rather than traditional water-based inks.

The modern woodcut was thus a form of art that, from its inception, fully synthesized the cosmopolitan aspirations of its practitioners with the particularities of their Chinese situation. The most important inspiration for the development of the new movement, however, was Lu Xun (1881–1936). Lu Xun was not a visual artist but rather an educator and writer with a passion for books and an enthusiastic collector of antique rubbings, European and Japanese prints, and Chinese books and letter papers. During the last decade of his life, he strove to encourage visual artists who might realize the same cosmopolitan originality that he promoted in literature.

Lu Xun took as one of his missions during this period the promotion of European art, particularly art that seemed to deal with problems similar to those faced by China. He recognized the utility of the woodcut print as a medium as well as the effectiveness of the expressionist images in Germany produced under distressing social circumstances similar to those in China. Expressionist artists created work in several mediums, but the woodcut became a powerful means for conveying their message of social betterment via art. Aside from the obvious advantage of duplication to reach many people, prints from woodblocks produce bold lines and shapes that are conducive to suggesting emotional content. A woodblock print is gestural, usually symbolic or highly didactic. Lu Xun organized a number of events at which young artists had the opportunity to view his collection of European woodcuts and hear his views on the potential importance of this art form for improving China's art and society. Between 1928 and 1930 he published five volumes of foreign woodcuts, which ranged in style from

the art nouveau of the nineteenth-century British illustrator Aubrey Beardsley to Russian constructivism.

In the early 1930s, with the help of his friend Uchiyama Kanzō (1885–1959), a bookstore owner in Shanghai, Lu Xun held several foreign woodcut exhibitions in Shanghai. In the summer of 1931 Lu Xun organized a short course to teach printmaking and recruited a group of thirteen students from various art schools and clubs in the Shanghai area. He lectured on basic woodcut print art history, from ukiyo-e, which depicted ordinary people going about their daily lives, to the work of German expressionists in his collection; Uchiyama Kanzō's younger brother, Uchiyama Kakitsu (1900–1984), with the assistance of Lu Xun as translator, lectured and demonstrated the practical art of making woodcuts. The birth of the modern Chinese woodcut movement is often dated to this event. Lu Xun not only mentored young artists in the classroom setting but also corresponded with a great many others, providing advice, criticism, and occasionally even money to poor art students. A significant number of the group went on to careers as printmakers and teachers, forming the core around which later developments in printmaking developed in China.

Like German expressionist artists, Chinese woodblock printmakers held a utopian notion of that individual creativity could influence society. The artists of the movement rejected naturalistic representation in favor of a harsh antinaturalism that communicated their criticism of materialism in society while providing a guide toward a new, utopian future, justifying the primitive appearance of their work as signaling a break from tradition. Among them, Chen Tiegeng (1908–1969), Jiang Feng (1910–1982), Chen Yanqiao (1911–1970), Hu Yichuan (1910–2000), Wo Zha (1905–1974), and Li Hua (1907–1994) are most representative. In Shanghai, Hangzhou, Guangzhou, and other cities during the 1930s, these young artists organized many active art groups, such as the Yesui she (Wild Grain Society), Tiema banhuashe (Steel Horse Woodcut Society), Dazhong muke yanjiuhui (Mass Woodcut Research Society), MK muke yanjiuhui (MK Society), Xiandai banhuahui (Modern Prints Society), and Muling muke yanjiuhui (Dumb Bell Woodcut Research Society). They held print exhibitions and published catalogues and journals, such as *Mubanhua* (*Woodblock Prints*), *Huilan muke* (*Whirlpool Woodcut*), *Xiandai banhua* (*Modern Prints*), *Tiema banhua* (*Steel Horse Prints*), and *Weiming mukexuan* (*Unnamed Woodcuts*).

AFTER THE JAPANESE INVASION

The death of Lu Xun, followed within less than a year by the outbreak of the Second Sino-Japanese War (1937–1945), profoundly changed the dynamics of the modern woodcut movement. The Japanese invasion of 1937 is an important chronological break and a biographical marker for all Chinese artists. Although some prints produced before 1937 show leftist political inclinations, a more important trend is multifaceted modernism. Prints produced after the Japanese invasion—though still somewhat varied in style, particularly those made at the Communist Yan'an Base Area, which were often carved in realistic or easily readable styles—show a greater unity of purpose and a more urgently ideological tone. Woodcuts, seen in Shanghai as instruments of social change, now became weapons of national salvation. Woodcuts in this vein ranged from upbeat propaganda pictures to introspective domestic meditations to desolate images of war. The common connection among them was the link the artists made between the real conditions of life and their artwork. A similar shift may be seen in other media as well: with the very survival of the nation and its people in question, artists eschewed personal experiments in style and subject matter for works that contributed to saving the nation.

During the war many young artists went to the Yan'an Base Area, producing woodcut posters to encourage the local peasants to resist the Japanese and help the Communist army. Among them, including a number of the Shanghai veterans, were Jiang Feng, Hu Yichuan, Chen Tiegeng, Wo Zha, Luo Gongliu (1916–2004), Gu Yuan (1919–1996), Zhang Wang (1915–1992), Yan Han (b. 1916), and Liu Xian (1915–1990). In a striking stylistic shift, the woodcut artists largely abandoned shading and three-dimensional settings in their prints, striving for naive effects that more closely resembled folk prints to better satisfy the tastes of their audience, the peasants.

Work produced in the Nationalist areas, however, was slightly different in style and subject matter from that of the Yan'an artists. Themes common in prewar Shanghai, such as the persecution of patriots by the Nationalist government, remained lamentably relevant during the war years in works by Li Hua, Huang Xinbo (1916–1980), and Ding Cong (b. 1916), among others.

POSTWAR DEVELOPMENT

Following the victory over Japan in 1945, the civil war between the Communists and the Nationalists intensified. Artists in Yan'an tended to stay in the Communist-controlled areas, and their works were celebratory in nature, commemorating the heroism of a glorious military victory. Most other artists returned to Shanghai. Postwar work produced in Shanghai—quite naturalistic, readable, and far more technically refined than the work of the early 1930s—was more critical of the government than were prints of previous years. These artists expressed despair and anguish at the failings of their government in what should have been a time of peace. Among them, the

works of Li Hua, Yang Keyang (b. 1914), Zhao Yannian (b. 1924), and Shao Keping (b. 1916) were most representative. This art, with its desolate portrayals of the current situation, prepared urban people for the Communist victory.

The modern woodcut movement, in part because of the portability of its materials, underwent sustained and continuous development from its birth in the late 1920s through the Communist victory. The artists of this movement strove to create works comparable in quality to those of printmakers in the West. What made the modern woodcut movement a remarkable phenomenon was its ability to connect entire populations of people. Lu Xun recognized the potential for woodcuts to influence people's views and propagate social change. The work of the new print movement offers a concentrated sense of the struggles of the Chinese people during an era of radical change and great peril.

SEE ALSO *Art, History of; Art, Policy on, since 1949; Li Hua; Lu Xun; Luo Gongliu; Propaganda Art; Woodblock Printing (xylography).*

BIBLIOGRAPHY

Andrews, Julia F., and Kuiyi Shen, eds. *A Century in Crisis: Modernity and Tradition in the Art of Twentieth-Century China.* New York: Guggenheim Museum, 1998.

Burg, Christer von der, ed. *The Art of Contemporary Chinese Woodcuts.* London: Muban Foundation, 2003.

Danzker, Jo-Anne Birnie, Ken Lum, and Zheng Shengtian, eds. *Shanghai Modern 1919–1945.* Ostfildern-Ruit, Germany: Hatje Cantz, 2004.

Sullivan, Michael. *Art and Artists of Twentieth-Century China.* Berkeley: University of California Press, 1996.

Tang, Xiaobing. *Origins of the Chinese Avant-Garde: The Modern Woodcut Movement.* Berkeley: University of California Press, 2008.

Wachs, Iris, and Chang Tsong-zung. *Half a Century of Chinese Woodblock Prints: From the Communist Revolution to the Open-Door Policy and Beyond, 1945–1998.* Tel Aviv: Museum of Art Ein Harod, 1999.

Kuiyi Shen

NEW WAVE MOVEMENT, '85

The term *1985 movement* (*Bawu meishu yundong*), coined in 1986 by the art critic and curator Gao Minglu and later changed to *1985 Art New Wave* (*Bawu meishu xinchao*), originates from a flurry of exhibitions that took place throughout China in the mid-1980s. In practice, the term has been used to define an artistic and cultural current much wider in scope and historical perspective than the original group of events. The exceptional quality and historical significance of the New Wave movement is due to its dramatic break with the ideological atmosphere that had defined the art of the preceding three decades. For the first time since the founding of the People's Republic of China (PRC) in 1949, independent art groups and artistic practices were allowed to emerge and produce new expressive forms. This was a grassroots artistic movement begun in Chinese art academies in explicit opposition to the politicized art practices of the time. Eventually it transformed China's artistic development, allowing it to dialogue with international contemporary art practices.

A possible way to frame the phenomenon is to situate it within two landmarks exhibitions that can be considered the movement's prelude and conclusion. In September 1979 the Stars exhibition was hung on the railings of the park adjacent to the China Art Gallery in Beijing; in February 1989 the Avant-Garde exhibition was held inside the same building. The spatial and temporal transition between these events is framed by two crucial historical episodes: the creation of the Xidan Democracy Wall in fall 1978 and the crushing of the prodemocracy movement on June 4, 1989 at Tiananmen Square, only four months after the opening of the Avant-Garde exhibition. Although the Stars group is not normally considered part of the 1985 movement, it is widely accepted as having set the stage for many of the actions that defined the artistic wave of the following decade.

ARTISTIC PRECEDENTS

Two artistic trends that emerged at the end of the Cultural Revolution paved the way for the creative outburst of the mid-1980s. Scar painting (*shanghen huihua*), which emerged in the late 1970s, offered a profoundly emotional response to the tragic experience of the Cultural Revolution and the rustication movement (*xiaxiang*). Native soil painting (*xiangtu ziranzhuyi huihua*) in the early 1980s was defined by its representation of "antiheroes"—smaller characters who had been ignored by the celebratory style of socialist realism. The experience of rustication exposed the younger generation of artists to the harsh life of the countryside and facilitated their personal contact with the peasants and ethnic minorities that became their artistic subjects. Both scar painting and native soil painting were defined by a critical use of realism and a personal interpretation of experience that up to then had been represented according to an imposed political script.

Gao Minglu, a critic, curator, and art historian who was both a protagonist of the movement and its most thoughtful commentator, characterized the 1985 movement as more broadly cultural and conceptual than simply artistic, because it involved writers, poets, and philosophers as well as visual artists. The political and social conditions

that allowed the movement to emerge were favored by the more relaxed climate that followed Mao's death in 1976 and Deng Xiaoping's surge to power as head of the Communist Party in 1978. At that time Chinese intellectuals, driven by a widespread sense of mission and responsibility toward society, had begun to reclaim their centuries-old traditional role in creating a cultural and spiritual atmosphere.

By the early 1980s the class of students who had been readmitted to higher education in 1977 after the long interruption of the Cultural Revolution had graduated and entered the educational workforce. Almost all of the participants in the 1985 movement, though anti-institutional in their actions, were in fact either full- or part-time employees of official art educational institutions.

The decade preceding the tragic events at Tiananmen Square in June 1989 was a period of soaring excitement and widespread optimism closely linked with a regained faith in the potential for individual expression. The mood prompted a wave of heightened experimentalism that often was inspired by Western modernism, though it sprang from a very different range of social conditions than those associated with the emergence of modernism in Europe. In a sense, the 1985 movement can be seen as continuation of the modernist experiments initiated in China and abruptly aborted during the late 1930s: a period with which it shared an iconoclastic attitude toward preceding artistic practices and an acute experimentalism. In *The Wall: Reshaping Contemporary Chinese Art* (2005) Gao Minglu argues that the 1985 movement was avant-garde in its self-conscious participation in a project of both social and artistic modernization and its intrinsic iconoclasm toward past traditions (both socialist and Chinese).

UNOFFICIAL SPACES OF
INDEPENDENT EXHIBITIONS

In the mid-1980s artistic discussions and activities exploded nationwide. Conferences, debates, exhibitions, and manifestos were organized and publicized in art academies and in newly established art publications. According to Gao, more than eighty artists' collectives were founded nationwide in China between 1985 and 1987. The Advancing Young Artists exhibition (*Qianjin zhongde Zhongguo qingnian meishu zuopin zhanglan*) held in May 1985 at the China Art Gallery in Beijing is considered to be the official launch of the movement, and one of the paintings exhibited there, Zhang Qun (b. 1962) and Meng Luding's (b. 1962) *In the New Era: Revelation of Adam and Eve*, is considered to be a conscious representation of the spirit of movement. The painting depicts a modern, naked Adam and Eve in classic positions welcoming a young woman walking toward them. She carries a plate of red fruits and breaks through a series of empty painting frames, shattering a glass pane. A rising sun looms over the low horizon, signaling an era of renewed creativity symbolized by the breaking of a long series of forced limitations.

As implied by the choice of the location for the first Stars exhibition in 1979, many activities of the 1985 movement were defined by the inventive appropriation of unconventional venues. The use of garages, apartments, temporary exhibition halls, and often outdoor locations such as streets, parks, and squares came to signify both physically and metaphorically the occupation of a new space. Locations often were chosen for practical reasons, in order to circumvent the highly bureaucratized system of public exhibitions, but also with a sincere desire to create a more direct communication between artists and their audiences. Gao Minglu cites an eloquent slogan displayed on the occasion of the 1986 Zero exhibition organized in Shenzhen: "Art is the absolute possession of life, art is the absolute possession of space" (Gao Minglu 2005).

MAJOR GROUPS, EVENTS, AND FIGURES

Representative of this new form of artistic interaction were the activities organized by the Pond Society (*Chishe*) in Hangzhou, founded by Zhang Peili (b. 1957), Geng Jianyi (b. 1962), and Song Ling (b. 1961). In May 1986 the group mounted an outdoor exhibition of large cutout paper figures on the wall of a street close to the Zhejiang Art Academy. Subsequently, Zhang Peili organized a series of mailing projects to stimulate interaction between the society's activities and the public. These would involve sending absurd questionnaires or fragments of unusual material to a mailing list composed mostly of people working or active in the art world.

The changes in exhibition formats and the claiming of new spaces facilitated the emergence of performance art. The Southern Artists Salon First Experimental Art Exhibition (*Nanfang yishu jia shalun di yi hui shixian zhan*), organized in Guangzhou in September 1986, combined art, music, and performance. Another event of this type was the Concept 21 Action Art (*Guannian 21 xing-wei huodong*), at Peking University in December 1986.

In terms of its main themes and styles, in the genre of painting, which in the 1980s was still the most popular medium for formal experimentalism, a general distinction can be made between two types of works. On the one hand were paintings characterized by the disintegration of both form and composition; some of these were in an expressionist or surrealist vein. On the other hand were works created in a more rigorous formal style, typically with a hyperrealist approach. Works belonging to the first group had either an abstract style or a fragmented narrative, and paid close attention to the fabric of the painterly surface. The style has been interpreted as form of explo-

ration of the primordial unconscious. Artists active in this mode were Yu Youhan (b. 1943), Mao Xuhui (b. 1956), Pan Dehai (b. 1956), and Ding Fang (b. 1956).

Paintings of the second group, in the so-called rationalist style, were defined by a form of hyperrealistic representation—a cold and detached rendering of figures and situations, obsessively drained of any emotion or personal introspection. Works by Wang Guangyi (b. 1956), Zhang Peili, and Geng Jianyi (b. 1961) offer a punctilious representation of objects and an aseptic, nearly abstract idea of a dehumanized scene. Typical of this current were the works exhibited in the 1985 New Space Exhibition (*1985 xin kongjian*) in Hangzhou, and paintings produced by members of the Northern Art Group (*Beifang yishu qunti*), which was founded in Harbin in 1984 by, among others, Wang Guangyi, Shu Qun (b. 1958), Ren Jian (b. 1956), and Liu Yan (b. 1965). Both tendencies avoid any narrative reference, presenting instead a cryptic message. This practice ran against the didactic trend of Maoist art.

Another prominent group associated with this period was Xiamen Dada, founded in 1986 by Huang Yongping (b. 1954), Cai Lixiong (b.1960), Liu Yiling (b. 1964), Lin Chun (b. 1962), and Jiao Yaoming (b. 1957). Inspired by the French dadaist Marcel Duchamp (1887–1968), the group adopted a radically iconoclastic, nonsensical conception of artistic creation; in one of their most famous events the group burned their own paintings at the end of the exhibition.

Language art (*wenzi yishu*) shares the intrinsic iconoclasm of the 1985 movement. In the works of artists such as Xu Bing, Gu Wenda, and Wu Shanzhuan (b. 1960), the calculated misuse of language and written or printed characters repeatedly violates the sacred conceptual space associated with the Chinese script.

The final celebration of the 1985 movement took place in February 1989 with the opening of the historic China Avant-Garde exhibition at the China Art Gallery in Beijing. A few months later the repression of the student movement on Tiananmen Square brought to an abrupt end the idealistic spirit that had fueled the movement from the moment of its emergence.

A sober period followed, when experimentalism turned into the mature, even slick professionalism that is now is a staple of Chinese artistic production. The next period was defined by a cynical, nonparticipative attitude and a total lack of idealism that rests at the core of the rampant commercialism of the first decade of the 2000s. Yet, it can be argued that the antiestablishment spirit of the '85 movement was revived in February 2009 when a Beijing exhibition organized by Gao Minglu to celebrate the anniversary of the 1989 China Avant-Garde show was closed down by police before it had opened.

SEE ALSO *Art Exhibitions since 1949; Art, History of: Art since 1949; Art Market since 1949; Commercial Art; Gu Wenda; Scar (Wound) Art; Xu Bing.*

BIBLIOGRAPHY

Bai Yu. *Chuangzao lishi: zhongguo ershi shiji bashi niandai xiandai yishu jinian zhan* [Creating history: A commemorative exhibition of the art of the 1980s]. Guangzhou: Ling Nan Meishu Chubanshe, 2006.

Galikowski, Maria. *Art and Politics in China, 1949–1984.* Hong Kong: Chinese University Press, 1998.

Gao Minglu, ed. *Inside/Out New Chinese Art.* Berkeley: University of California Press, 1998.

Gao Minglu. *The Wall: Reshaping Contemporary Chinese Art.* Buffalo, NY: Buffalo Fine Arts Academy and the Millennium Art Museum, 2005.

Koeppel-Yang, Martina. *Semiotic Warfare: The Chinese Avant-Garde, 1979–1989, a Semiotic Analysis.* Hong Kong: Timezone, 2003.

Li Xianting. Major Trends in the Development of Contemporary Chinese Art. In *China's New Art, Post-1989,* ed. Valerie C. Doran, x–xxii. Hong Kong: Hanart T Z Gallery, 1993.

Lü Peng and Yi Dan. *Zhongguo xiandai yishu shi* [A history of China's modern art]. Changsha: Hunan Meishu Chubanshe, 1992.

Van Dijk, Hans. The Fine Arts after the Cultural Revolution: Stylistic Development and Theoretical Debate. In *China Avant-Garde Counter-currents in Art and Culture,* ed. Jochen Noth, Wolfger Pöhlmann, and Kai Reschke, 14–39. Oxford, U.K.: Oxford University Press, 1994.

Francesca Dal Lago

NEW YEAR'S MOVIES

New Year's movies (*hesuipian*) are released during the holiday season (Chinese New Year), when families get together and look for entertainment. To suit the occasion, they are, as a rule, lighthearted crowd-pleasers. Like Hollywood summer blockbusters, many of these productions have become milestones of popular culture.

New Year's movies were first produced in Hong Kong. Michael Hui Koon-Man (1942–), reviving Cantonese cinema and vying with the Shaw Brothers Studio, released *Security Unlimited* for New Year's 1982. The film's record-setting box-office success, followed by the similar achievement of *Aces Go Places* (1982), resulted in a slew of films timed for the holidays. Many New Year's movies feature New Year blessings in their Chinese titles and reunions in their plots. They are mostly romantic comedies and ribald spoofs, such as *All's Well That Ends Well* (1992) and *Eagle-Shooting Heroes* (1993), but over the years the trend has included every popular genre, such as the action flicks *Heroic Trio* (1993) and *Confessions of Pain* (2006), a number of Jackie Chan's kung-fu movies,

and swordplay pieces such as *A Battle of Wits* (2006). The comedian Stephen Chow has contributed to New Year's movies by starring in one almost every year in the 1990s, notably in the two-part *Chinese Odyssey* (1994).

When the mainland film industry shifted to a market economy in the mid-1990s, it emulated the model of New Year's movies. Paving the way for local productions were the successes of Jackie Chan's *Rumble in the Bronx* (1995) and Jeffrey Lau's *Chinese Odyssey* in the People's Republic—the latter became a cult hit on university campuses. The trend was initiated by Feng Xiaogang's *Dream Factory* (*Jiafang yifang*), made for New Year's 1998. The film originated in an attempt by Beijing Film Studio to address the issue of laid-off workers. The result was an updated version of state-owned studios' practice of putting a positive spin on current social problems. The plot describes the rise of laid-off workers to successful entrepreneurs. Their company gives common people the chance to play out their heroes for a day; their merrymaking is guided, however, by a genuine interest in doing good, and they eventually give up their profits to help people in need. The movie found a balance between social satire on people's unrealized desires and respect for social order.

Dream Factory, marketed as the first mainland-made New Year's movie, modified Hong Kong humor to suit the reality of the postsocialist mainland. In this and subsequent New Year's movies, Feng added linguistic wit and self-deprecating jokes, in the vein of the novels of Wang Shuo that inspired many of the scripts. New Year's movies were also influenced by the Spring Festival extravaganzas on China Central Television (CCTV), especially skits by comedians such as Feng Gong and Zhao Benshan, who have crossed over to the big screen.

While Feng Xiaogang has continued to churn out New Year's movies, the trend has expanded to include many genres, and the term now refers to all major productions released between the Christmas season and the first lunar month. These include staple comic pieces, such as *Happy Times* (*Xingfu shiguang,* 2000) and *Ordinary People's Life* (*Meili de jia,* 2000), martial arts films such as *Hero* (*Yingxiong,* 2002) and *The Promise* (*Wu ji,* 2005), art films such as *Still Life* (*Sanxia haoren,* 2006), and even foreign releases such as *Saving Private Ryan* (1998) and *Harry Potter and the Sorcerer's Stone* (2001).

New Year's movies signal the transition of the mainland film industry to a Hollywood-inspired production mode. Feng Xiaogang's films have supported the rise of Beijing Forbidden City Film Company, established to produce *Dream Factory.* With revenues exceeding RMB 500 million, Beijing Forbidden City is a model for many smaller production companies. *Crazy Stone* (*Fengkuang de shitou,* 2006), which made RMB 23 million at the box office, is further proof that the trend is helping to make filmmaking in mainland China commercially viable. New Year's movies have also ushered in greater integration among the film, television, and advertisement industries.

SEE ALSO *Feng Xiaogang; Film Industry: Overview; Wang Shuo.*

BIBLIOGRAPHY
Feng Xiaogang. *Wo ba qingchun xiangei ni* [I dedicate my youth to you]. Wuhan: Changjiang Chubanshe, 2003.
Tom.com Corporation. Zhongguo hesui dianying shi nian lu [A decade of Chinese New Year's films]. http://ent.tom.com/.

Yomi Braester

NEWSPAPERS

It is not only since Mao's 1959 dictum that "newspapers must be run by politicians" (Mao 1983, pp. 215–216) that newspapers in China have served politics. This has been the norm rather than the exception in the long history of Chinese newspaper history. The premodern Chinese "public sphere" was peopled mostly by officials and those with the educational qualifications to become officials, but the most powerful voice belonged to the court. This left little room for independent voices even though an easy flow of information—the openness of the *yanlu* (road of speech)—was a classical ideal that the court, the officials, and the educated elite upheld, at least in theory. Due to the secret-memorial system which was firmly in place by the nineteenth century, most officials were not privy to much important information, and the general public was quite unaware of politics at the highest levels.

EARLY NEWSPAPERS

Yet, the court published its own gazette as early as the Han dynasty (206 BCE–220 CE); this could be called the world's oldest newspaper. *Di* officials transmitted the news of the court to the provinces and vice versa. Their communications, the *dibao*, recorded summonses to office, promotions, and demotions, as well as edicts and memorials. In the early eighteenth century the *dibao* was officially renamed *jingbao* (capital/court announcements/gazette); other terms such as *dichao, tangbao, zhuangbao,* and *chaobao* were also used. The gazette took its information from the Grand Council documents received by official courier posts in Beijing. These documents were printed in *baofang* (publishing houses, many of which were private bookshops), then sent on to the provinces where they were expanded with news from the provincial administrations and sold or rented out by hawkers on the streets. The gazette was widely read by the literary elite,

as evidenced by letters, diary entries, *biji* (a literary style translated as "brush jottings"), and literary works that reference them. In the nineteenth century missionaries and merchants in China introduced the foreign-style press, and in an acknowledgment that the court gazette fulfilled an important function by spreading news, early foreign-style newspapers (both English- and Chinese-language papers) reprinted the gazette in their pages. Chinese-language papers even introduced telegraphed versions of the court news in order to speed up its delivery to readers in remoter parts of the country.

ESTABLISHING A "FREE PRESS"

Although the foreign-style newspapers reprinted the court news, they also criticized the gazette for reporting only official news. Indeed, China did not have a "free press" before the nineteenth century. Newspapers such as the Shanghai *Shenbao* (1872–1949) and the Hong Kong *Xunhuan Ribao* (1874–1947) were modeled on an idealized prototype of the foreign newspaper.

By the nineteenth century, the newspaper already had a history that dated back several centuries in Europe. Much of this history was dominated by official interventions: the imposition of stamp acts, and legal charges of libel, blasphemy, and sedition had been the rule rather than the exception. Mainstream newspaper production was dominated by publishing from official sources or under official supervision, and authorities often intervened to use the "dangerous instrument" for their own purposes by putting journalists and publishers on their payrolls, establishing censorship procedures, and publishing official papers. Although the historical record supports only a guarded evaluation of the independence of newspapers even as late as the nineteenth century, nevertheless it was the ideal of the free press that traveled abroad and became the model in China.

Extraterritoriality was the key to the establishment of a free press in China, evidenced by newspapers founded in Hong Kong (*Xunhuan Ribao*) and the international settlement in Shanghai (*Shenbao* and *Xinwenbao,* 1893–1941). No Chinese state entity had a real regulatory impact on the press in these areas, and consequently they were some of the world's most independent papers of the period.

This first group of influential and long-lasting daily newspapers (whose circulation numbers moved from the hundreds to the thousands in the first decades) was followed, after a brief upsurge of ephemeral papers and magazines, by a second group of important newspapers founded and supported by reformers around the turn of the century. *Shibao* (1904–1939) was certainly the most important of them. Following a Japanese model, it introduced many reforms in newspaper writing which also

Reflection of a man reading a newspaper, Shanghai, January 19, 2005. *In the early years of the People's Republic of China, the central government kept firm control over the content of China's few newspapers. As restrictions eased by the end of the twentieth century, the number of newspapers available in China swelled, with print media outlets competing for advertising revenue from businesses rather than relying on Communist Party subsidies.* © CLARO CORTES IV/REUTERS/CORBIS

affected older papers such as *Shenbao*, changing them significantly. One of these innovations was the introduction of short editorials (*shiping*) that replaced longer pieces in traditional Chinese discursive forms such as the *lun-* and *shuo*-essays, and the more subjective recordings of *ji*-jottings or *shu*-letters. The *shiping* became extremely popular during the Republican period in both the popular and elite press. In addition to serving as a political tool in the conflict-ridden last years of Qing rule, and not unlike the earlier treaty-port papers, the press in this period set out to perform an important cultural function as readership increased from the thousands into the hundred thousands. Those who wrote for the new newspapers and periodicals believed that the enlightening function of journalism was paramount, and that their medium would replace teachers and learned scholars in producing knowledge, cultural values, and shared beliefs. Whether or not the reformist press did indeed promote and bring

about social, cultural, and political change, it certainly was one of the preeminent institutions of the late Qing.

The early years of the Republic saw a growing market of newspaper readers from different classes and backgrounds, and a growing number of newspapers—over 900 by the 1930s (and a similar number of periodicals). Newspapers catered to a variety of interests; the spectacular rise of the *xiaobao* (little papers) tabloids, which first appeared in the 1920s and peaked in the 1940s, was a sign of the times. Beginning in the 1930s, censorship (often criminally enforced, as in the murder of *Shenbao*'s editor, Shi Liangcai) and paper shortages hindered the uninhibited growth of newspapers. Many newspapers, too, took an illiberal turn. Pluralism was still prevalent— the sheer number of papers made this possible—but political groups began to publish their own partisan papers: The Nationalist *Zhongyang Ribao* (1928–1949) and the Communist *Xinhua Ribao* (1938–1947) and *Jiefang Ribao*

38

(1941–1947) were the most important and influential. This development led directly to the political use of the press that has been seen as a hallmark of the People's Republic of China since 1949.

INFORMATION MEDIA UNDER CHINESE COMMUNIST PARTY RULE

After almost three decades during which the number and contents of Chinese newspapers was rigorously restricted and supervised by the Chinese Communist Party (except for a short phase of free, albeit single-minded, Red Guard papers produced in the mid-1960s), in the late 1970s local and even private newspapers (which were legalized with the structural reforms of the mid-1980s) began to grow exponentially. Though they were still required to print certain contents such as *Xinhua* (New China) news agency commentaries, these newspapers introduced some significant editorial changes, including a new orientation to their readers (and thus an increased amount of entertaining news), and an interest in authenticity and truth in reporting (and therefore more attention to the dark sides of life). These editorial changes put pressure on the established papers, which added features such as marriage (and commercial) ads and stories on interesting crime cases.

In 1979 the Communist Party publicly vowed that in its newspapers it would be "seeking truth from facts." Calls for truth and objectivity were persistently raised in the following years, but still, in 1989, party journalists, marching during the Tiananmen demonstrations, carried signs reading "Don't believe us, we tell lies!" It is said that Chinese readers are well practiced in reading between the lines of the official papers, and popular cynicism is high, especially toward the party's central newspaper *Renmin Ribao* (People's Daily)—one reason why it is delivered, not sold, to all work units. Although reporting has become more varied since the 1980s, journalists still have to be on guard not to breach boundaries if they do not want to be bullied out of their jobs, imprisoned, or even killed.

The introduction of the Internet, which took off in China in 1997, and the possibility of running and reading online newspapers opened the floodgates of information to China. But again, restrictions were enforced. The authorities installed a "golden shield" (*jindun gongcheng*) that delinks the Chinese Net from the Internet—only with proxy servers can one sail around blocked Web sites—and for easy control, international data traffic is limited to only three gateways (in Beijing, Shanghai, and Guangzhou). Commercial providers are not allowed to hire journalists; that is the prerogative of state-owned media. The provider Sina.com lists as its main cooperative partners mainstream media outlets such as *Xinhua* (New China),

Jiefang Ribao (Liberation Daily), *Nanfang Ribao* (Nanfang Daily), and *China Daily*.

Yet, there are national projects for online services and newspapers that receive massive state funding and support, and that are allowed to provide news: *Qianlongwang* (Dragon Net) is one of them. Thus the Chinese government has transferred the institutional structure of control of the news sector from the traditional media to the new domain of the Internet. Notwithstanding the frequent twists and turns since the Chinese Communist Party's assumption of power in 1949, the role and the functions of the news media have changed remarkably little over half a century. Even commercialization and globalization have not changed the fundamental tenets that have determined the Chinese Communist Party's media politics since Yan'an. The media have been a core instrument in the party's ambitious project of social engineering and they remain a crucial tool of governance today.

SEE ALSO *Internet; Journalism; Local Gazetteers; Publishing Industry.*

BIBLIOGRAPHY

Fitzgerald, John. The Origins of the Illiberal Party Newspaper: Print Journalism in China's Nationalist Revolution. *Republican China* 21, 2 (1996): 1–22.

Ge, Gongzhen. *Zhongguo baxueshi.* Reprint. Hong Kong: Taiping Shuju, 1964.

Janku, Andrea. *Nur leere Reden: Politischer Diskurs und die Shanghaier Presse im China des späten 19. Jahrhunderts* [Just empty speeches: Political discourse and the Shanghai news media in late 19th century China]. Wiesbaden, Germany: Harrassowitz, 2003.

Judge, Joan. *Print and Politics: "Shibao" and the Culture of Reform in Late Qing China.* Stanford, CA: Stanford University Press, 1996.

Klaschka, Siegfried. *Die Presse im China der Modernisierungen. Historische Entwicklung, theoretische Vorgaben und exemplarische Inhalte* [The press in modernizing China. Historical development, theoretical parameters and exemplary contents]. Hamburg, Germany: Kovac, 1991.

Lin Yuanqi. *Dibao zhi yanjiu* [Studies of the Dibao]. Taibei: Hanlin Chubanshe, 1977.

MacKinnon, Stephen R. Toward a History of the Chinese Press in the Republican Period. *Modern China* 23, 1 (1997): 3–32.

Mao Zedong. *Mao Zedong xinwen gongzuo wenxuan* [Writings by Mao on newspaper work]. Beijing: Xinhua Chubanshe, 1983.

Mittler, Barbara. *A Newspaper for China. Power, Identity and Change in the Shanghai News Media, 1872–1912,* Harvard East Asian Monographs 226, Cambridge, MA: Harvard University Press, 2004.

Mohr, Wolfgang. *Die moderne chinesische Tagespresse* [The modern Chinese daily press]. Wiesbaden, Germany: Steiner, 1976.

Narramore, Terry. *Making the News in Shanghai:* Shenbao *and the Politics of Newspaper Journalism, 1912–1937.* Ph.D. diss., Australian National University, 1989.

Stranahan, Patricia. *Molding the Medium: The Chinese Communist Party and the "Liberation Daily."* Armonk, NY: Sharpe, 1990.

Vittinghof, Natascha. *Die Anfänge des Journalisms in China (1890–1911)* [The beginnings of journalism in China (1890–1911)]. Wiesbaden, Germany: Harrassowitz, 2002.

Volland, Nicolai. *The Control of the Media in the People's Republic of China.* Ph.D. diss., Heidelberg University, 2003.

Ye, Xiaoqing. *The Dianshizhai Pictorial: Shanghai Urban Life, 1884–1898.* Ann Arbor: University of Michigan Press, 2003.

Zhu Junzhou. Shanghai xiaobao de lishi yange [The historical development of Shanghai tabloids]. *Xinwen yanjiu ziliao* 42 (1988): 163–179; 43 (1988): 137–153; 44 (1988): 211–220.

Barbara Mittler

NIAN UPRISING

The Nian Uprising (1851–1868), a peasant insurrection that engulfed North China, originated among proliferating criminal gangs (*nian*). By 1800 these gangs began using pillage, banditry, salt smuggling, gambling, and kidnapping to eke out a living in the impoverished, agriculturally unproductive flood- and drought-prone plain between the Huai and Yellow (Huang) Rivers, where Shandong, Jiangsu, Anhui, and Henan provinces meet. These mafia-style bands were based in villages that they fortified with earthen and brick walls and even moats. Within their so-called nests, the Nian organized militia forces to fight against imperial troops, who were seeking to eradicate them as well as to put down the civil unrest unleashed by the expeditionary forces of the Taiping Uprising (1851–1864), which in 1853 had established its heavenly capital in the lower Yangzi (Chang) River city of Nanjing.

Taking advantage of the region's abundant supply of horses, Nian raiding parties struck with lightning speed and effectively applied guerrilla tactics. Among these mounted "half-farmers, half-soldiers" were White Lotus sectarians and Triad secret society members. Mostly, though, they were a floating population of demobilized government mercenaries and displaced peasants. Their bandit chiefs allied with village elders, lineage heads, and gentry leaders in the common effort to control and thereby defend these territorial bases. As criminal elements merged with legitimate society, banditry and pillaging for food—often unchecked by incompetent and corrupt local officials—became the community's primary means of survival.

By 1852 the widely scattered, autonomous Nian groups had become increasingly coordinated. A number of bandit chiefs appointed Zhang Luoxing (1811–1863), a wealthy landlord and salt smuggler from Anhui, as their leader. He emulated the Taiping's top-down military organization by setting up five cohorts—under red, yellow, blue, white, and black banners—of 20,000 men each; at the same time Nian ranks swelled with refugees from devastating Yellow River floods.

The Nian projected insurrectionary fervor, martial discipline, and humanitarian concern as they incorporated teachings, rituals, and symbols from the Triad, White Lotus, and Taiping rebels. They employed such egalitarian slogans as "rob from the rich and succor the poor" while pillaging government food convoys, evenly distributing the spoils of their raids, and prohibiting unauthorized pillage and rape. They also turned increasingly anti-Manchu. In 1856 they hailed Zhang Luoxing as the "Great Han King with the Heavenly Mandate," a title reminiscent of Triad calls for the restoration of the Chinese emperors of the Ming dynasty (1368–1644) and White Lotus longings for an earthly utopia of peace and plenty under the Maitreya Buddha of the Future. Like the iconoclastic Taiping rebels, the Nian let their hair grow long in defiance of Manchu rule. For these "seditious" actions, the throne declared the Nian a rebel movement.

HIGH POINT AND COLLAPSE

By 1858 the Nian had established a large, well-stocked base area in northwestern Anhui. From there, full-time, professionalized Nian forces launched raids into eight northern provinces, inspiring local tax resistance and antigovernment insurrections along the way. They also captured and held cities, secured popular support by espousing philanthropy, economic justice, and humane treatment, and outmaneuvered the much larger Qing forces.

In 1860 the throne appointed the Mongol prince, Senggerinchin (1811–1865), to intensify suppression efforts. Relying on Mongol and Manchu horsemen, he succeeded in capturing and executing Zhang Luoxing in 1863. The following year, Zhang Zongyu (d. 1868), Zhang's nephew and successor, shifted from a base-area strategy to all-out, sustained cavalry assault. Nian forces, reinforced by but not allied to Taiping troops, now roamed the North China plain, threatening the imperial capital of Beijing. In May 1865 the Nian ambushed and killed Senggerinchin.

During the next three years, Zeng Guofan (1811–1872) and his protégés Li Hongzhang (1823–1901) and Zuo Zongtang (1812–1885), Qing officials who had crushed the Taiping Heavenly Kingdom in 1864, began a successful strategy of cleansing and isolating Nian enclaves, offering amnesty to defectors, registering loyalist peasants, and appointing progovernment village heads. Meanwhile,

40

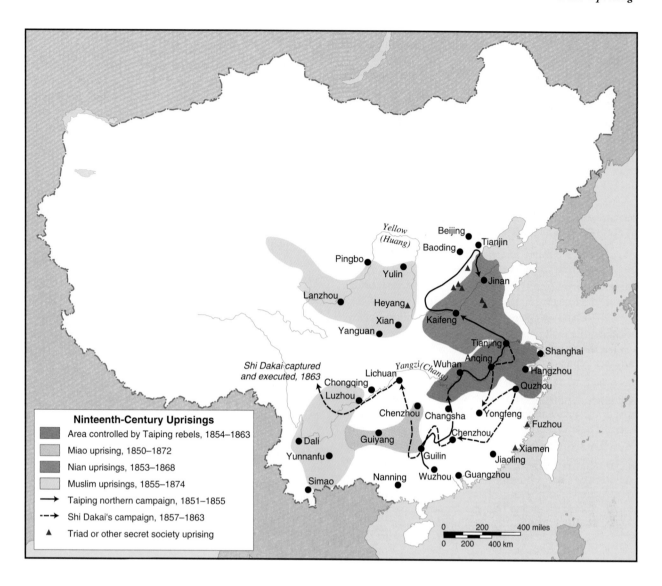

Ninteenth-Century Uprisings

- Area controlled by Taiping rebels, 1854–1863
- Miao uprising, 1850–1872
- Nian uprisings, 1853–1868
- Muslim uprisings, 1855–1874
- → Taiping northern campaign, 1851–1855
- ‑‑‑> Shi Dakai's campaign, 1857–1863
- ▲ Triad or other secret society uprising

Nian leaders blundered by dividing their forces into Eastern and Western divisions and campaigning far beyond their home turf. With better-fed troops and modern Western weapons, the Qing military encircled the Nian rebels, cutting off their food and recruits and then annihilating them. With Zhang Zongyu's suicide in August 1868, the Nian Uprising collapsed.

North China's socioeconomic ills continued to fester well after 1868. Unlike the more religiously inspired rebels of the day, the Nian insurgents never threatened China's dynastic system or its Confucian rationale. They lacked the millenarian aspirations and organizing principles of White Lotus Buddhist utopianism, the universal equality enforced by the Taipings' totalitarian land system, and the goal of an independent Chinese sultanate pursued by the Muslim separatists. But because they did pose a serious regional threat by rejecting imperial authority, the Nian are considered a model of traditional Chinese peasant rebellion. Ulti-

mately, their insurrection, with its insistence on base areas, mobile guerrilla tactics, and winning popular approval through humane actions, hampered imperial control throughout North China and significantly delayed the Qing campaign against the Muslim insurgents. In this sense, the Nian, along with other midcentury uprisings, contributed to the growth of an anti-Manchu nationalism that would precipitate the dynasty's downfall fifty years later.

BIBLIOGRAPHY

Chiang, Siang-tseh. *The Nien Rebellion.* Seattle: University of Washington Press, 1954.

Perry, Elizabeth J. *Rebels and Revolutionaries in North China, 1845–1945.* Stanford, CA: Stanford University Press, 1980.

Teng, S. Y. *The Nien Army and Their Guerrilla Warfare, 1851–1868.* Paris: Mouton, 1961.

P. Richard Bohr

NINGBO (NINGPO)

A subprovincial coastal port city in Zhejiang Province since 1994, Ningbo is a major shipping, fishing, and shipbuilding center. Ningbo city, with a population of 5.52 million (2000 census), covers 9,365 square kilometers on the edge of the Yangzi River Delta and at the confluence of the Feng, Yu, and Yong (Ningbo) rivers, and includes the deepwater port of Beilun. Ningbo sits on the southern shore of Hangzhou Bay, which contains the Zhoushan Archipelago, including Putuoshan Island. The location of a renowned ancient Buddhist monastery first established in the Song dynasty, this island is traditionally regarded as the home of the goddess Guanyin, known in Sanskrit as Avalokitesvara.

The city borders Shaoxing to its west and Taizhou to the south. The opening in May 2008 of the 35.67-kilometer Hangzhou Bay Bridge, a cable-stayed bridge that is the longest transoceanic bridge in the world, connected Ningbo municipality with Shanghai municipality, reducing the road journey between these two major urban centers from 400 to 80 kilometers. The bridge enabled Ningbo, with its port of Beilun, to compete with Shanghai's port of Pudong for international ocean trade. For economic purposes, Ningbo is one of five municipalities that come under the direct control of the central government. The municipality of Ningbo comprises Ningbo city, as well as six municipal districts (*shixiaqu*—Haishu, Jiangdong, Jiangbei, Beilun, Zhenhai, and Yinzhou), three county-level cities (Yuyao, Cixi, Fenghua), and two counties (Xiangshan, Ninghai). The names of these administrative divisions of greater Ningbo preserve many of the names by which Ningbo was historically known.

HISTORY

Ningbo became important as a maritime trading port during the Tang dynasty (618–907) and from the tenth century onward was known for producing merchants with commercial acumen and fierce loyalty to their home district. In the Qing dynasty (1644–1912) it was the capital of a large prefecture, including seven county-level jurisdictions. But its fame in modern times is due chiefly to the Ningbo *bang* (gang) of merchant bankers. In the nineteenth and twentieth centuries, many of China's most prominent merchants and traders came from Ningbo. As a result, the city was said to be the source of the capitalist elite of Shanghai. Already in the late seventeenth century Ningbo was a major source of migration to Shanghai. The relationship between the two places became even closer after the Opium War (1839–1842). Ningbo was the scene of fierce fighting in October 1841, when the British stormed the town of Zhenhai at the mouth of the Yong River. At the conclusion of the war it became one of five trading ports opened initially to the victorious British by the Treaty of Nanjing (1842).

Competition from Shanghai meant that until the end of the dynasty Ningbo retained a largely regional importance in trade, but the Ningbo merchants played an important role in Shanghai's economic development from the mid-nineteenth century onward. Ningbo merchants created an extensive network of associations that dominated finance in Shanghai and managed trade between Jiangnan and other regions. These Ningbo merchants preferred to deal with other members of the Ningbo network. Exemplifying this trend was Ye Chengzhong (1840–1899), who built up a business retail network and acquired from Standard Oil the distribution rights for kerosene throughout southern China.

Apart from producing famous merchants, the city's most famous son is the philosopher Wang Shouren (Wang Yangming) (1472–1529). Chiang Kai-shek (Jiang Jieshi) (1887–1975) also claimed Ningbo as his ancestral home, as do many prominent twentieth-century cultural figures, including Rou Shi (1902–1931), Zhou Xinfang (1895–1975), Pan Tianshou (1897–1971), Chen Yifei (1946–2005), Feng Jicai (b. 1942), and Yo-Yo Ma (b. 1955), to name only a few.

ECONOMY

Apart from trade, Ningbo was traditionally a center of silk weaving, fishing, and furniture production. After 1949 many modern light industries, including textile weaving, food processing, and electrical products, and some heavier industry, such as industrial tools, were introduced. The city is regarded as one of China's most prosperous, with per capita output competitive with that of Shanghai. Tourism has grown steadily since the late twentieth century and is focused mainly on Moon Lake (Yue Hu) and the nearby Tianyi Ge, the oldest surviving library building in China, said to have been built in 1516, and the Zhoushan Islands, most especially Putuoshan. The University of Nottingham has established a campus in Ningbo.

Set up in 1993, the Ningbo Economic and Technological Developmental Zone was one of the earliest state-level economic development zones to be established in China. Located 27 kilometers away from downtown Ningbo, the zone was strategically located with proximity to Shanghai and canal linkage to Hangzhou. The zone, administered by the ministry of commerce, was designed to attract finance, develop import-export high-tech industries, and facilitate technology transfer. It boasts a specialized port facility for handling liquidized chemical products. In November 2008 a Digital Park was established in the Ningbo Development Zone, which eventually aims to become the leading center of digital innovation in Zhejiang Province.

SEE ALSO *Banking; Commercial Elite, 1800–1949; Treaty Ports; Urban China; Zhejiang.*

BIBLIOGRAPHY

Cochran, Sherman. *Encountering Chinese Networks: Western, Japanese, and Chinese Corporations in China, 1880–1937.* Berkeley: University of California Press, 2000.

Yoshinobu, Shiba. Ningpo and Its Hinterland. In *The City in Late Imperial China*, ed. G. W. Skinner, 391–439. Stanford, CA: Stanford University Press, 1977.

Bruce G. Doar

NINGXIA

The Ningxia Hui Autonomous Region is among the smallest of China's province-level units, both in area (66,000 square kilometers) and population (6.04 million in 2006, 43% urban, 57% rural). Its capital, Yinchuan, formerly called Ningxia, had a population of 1.45 million in 2006.

PHYSICAL GEOGRAPHY

Ningxia is in northwestern China, bordering Inner Mongolia to the northwest, north, and northeast, Shaanxi to the east, and Gansu to the southwest, south, and southeast. Ningxia's north is plains, crossed by the northeast-flowing Yellow River. The south is more elevated and part of the great Loess Plateau. The north is the main farming area, but loess soil "contains many crop nutrients" with "natural fertility" (Ren Mei'e et al. 1985, pp. 195–196). Nearly half Ningxia's total land is pastoral.

Temperatures show a significant range. The annual average is 5 to 9 degrees Celsius, with an average temperature of negative 8 in January but over 30 in July and August. Most of Ningxia is dry, and Yinchuan has the lowest annual rainfall of any of China's province-level capitals (236 millimeters in 2006).

HISTORY

Xixia, a kingdom set up by the Tibetan-related Tanguts in 1038, centered on the Yinchuan area. In 1227 the Mongols conquered Xixia, establishing Ningxia Prefecture in 1288, the first time the present name was used. Under the Qing (1644–1912), Ningxia Prefecture occupied the northern part of present-day Ningxia Hui Autonomous Region, belonging to Gansu Province.

The 1911 revolution had little immediate impact on Ningxia administratively. However, in 1928 it became a province, with its area of about 275,000 square kilometers including some of present-day Inner Mongolia.

Haiyuan County, southwest of the geographical center of Tongxin, was the epicenter of an earthquake on December 16, 1920, measuring 8.5 on the Richter scale. Total deaths were approximately 230,000, almost all in Ningxia, Haiyuan itself being totally destroyed. Another

---

NINGXIA

■

Capital city: Yinchuan

Largest cities (population): Yinchuan (1,450,000 [2006]), Shizuishan, Guyuan

Area: 66,000 sq. km. (25,000 sq. mi.)

Population: 6,040,000 (2006)

Demographics: Han, 65%; Hui, 34%; Manchu, 0.4%

GDP: CNY 71 billion (2006)

Famous sites: Tombs of Xixia Kingdom National Park, Helan Shan, Baisikou Twin Pagodas, desert research outpost at Shapatou

---

earthquake occurred in Guyuan, southeast of Haiyuan, in April 1921, killing about 10,000 people.

The Republican period witnessed much local warfare, and also resistance to Japanese onslaughts. The main political and military power holder was the warlord Ma Hongkui (1892–1970), a Chiang Kai-shek (Jiang Jieshi) loyalist. Ma was chairman of the Ningxia provincial government from 1932 to 1949, and a member of the famous Ma clique of northwest China that included his father Ma Fuxiang (1876–1932) and cousin Ma Hongbin (1884–1960). The Chinese Communist Party's Shaanxi-Gansu-Ningxia border region, established in 1936, included two counties of Ningxia Province that witnessed land reform and experimentation in "mass line" politics and resistance against the Japanese. In October 1936, Mao Zedong formally set up the party's first county-level political power among the ethnic minorities, the Shaanxi-Gansu-Ningxia-Yuhai County Hui Autonomous Government at the Great Mosque of Tongxin. However, Ma Hongkui defeated this government in 1937, executing its leader Ma Hefu outside Tongxin in April.

Ningxia Province fell to the Communist Party in September 1949. Its provincial status was abolished in September 1954, and it was merged with Gansu. The Ningxia Hui Autonomous Region was established on October 25, 1958.

POPULATION AND ETHNICITY

The population expanded during the first half of the Qing period, reaching a high point late in the eighteenth century. Around 1850 the population was about 1.5 million, but a 1909 count shows only 523,516 people, the decline due to such factors as famine, poor economic conditions, and war, especially the Muslim rebellions. The early Republican period saw a slight increase to 668,362 in

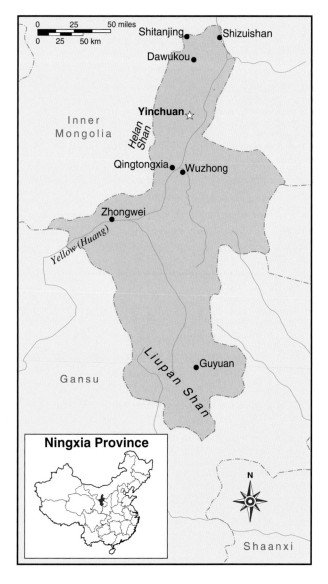

Ningxia Province

Populations of Ningxia Hui Autonomous Region in the four censuses since the region's establishment

Year	Total population	Hui population	Hui percentage	Han population	Han percentage
1964	2,107,490	646,961	30.69	1,457,116	69.14
1982	3,895,576	1,235,182	31.71	2,651,335	68.06
1990	4,655,451	1,524,448	32.75	3,107,370	66.75
2000	5,486,393	1,862,474	33.95	3,590,563	65.44

Table 1

In the 1940s, there were about 300,000 Hui in Ningxia, about 29 percent of the total population, with concentrations in the south over twice those of the north. In 1940 Tongxin County's population was about two-thirds Hui. Other than the dominant Han, Ningxia was home to small numbers of Manchus and Mongolians.

Table 1 shows the populations of Ningxia Hui Autonomous Region, plus the Hui and Han numbers, in the four censuses since the autonomous region's establishment.

Year-to-year figures show consistent rises, except for 1961 and 1962, when famine following the Great Leap Forward caused population falls almost everywhere in China. The census figures show a gradually rising Hui proportion. The total 2000 population was 51.28 percent male and 48.72 female, while among the Hui, 50.86 percent were male and 49.14 percent were female. The average life expectancy in the 2000 census was 70.17 years, against a national average of 71.40.

ECONOMY

Ningxia is a poor region, especially the south. However, it has good reserves of high-quality coal, gypsum, and other minerals. The Yellow (Huang) River and its tributaries enable the production of hydroelectricity. Irrigation has been practiced for many centuries. Agricultural products include wheat, rice, hemp, melons, and fruits, as well as furs, Tibetan lambskins featuring among Ningxia's "five treasures" (*wubao*).

Total agricultural and industrial value at current prices expanded twenty times between 1982 and 2006. In 2006 Ningxia's gross regional product per capita was 11,847 yuan (11.2% primary industry, 49.2% secondary, and 39.6% tertiary), against a national average of about 16,000. Total wealth, and in particular industry, is heavily concentrated in the north, especially in the Yinchuan region.

BIBLIOGRAPHY

Dillon, Michael. *China's Muslims*. Hong Kong: Oxford University Press, 1996.

1928, a rise that occurred despite the earthquakes of 1920 to 1921. Greater stability and economic improvement from 1930 led to a 1935 population of about 1.32 million. A fall to about 1.12 million by 1947 resulted from a catastrophic population decline in the north due to the Japanese occupation, although the continuing natural increase in the south partly compensated.

A prominent feature of Ningxia's population is the high number of Hui, an ethnic group characterized by adherence to Islam. Muslims first came to Ningxia during the Yuan period (1279–1368). However, it was only after the recapture of Muslim leader Ma Hualong's headquarters in Jinjipu (in present-day Ningxia) in 1871 that the resettlement of Muslim populations from there and Shaanxi to Guyuan and Jingyuan in southern Ningxia brought about Ningxia's still-existing Hui population distribution.

Dillon, Michael. *China's Muslim Hui Community: Migration, Settlement, and Sects.* Richmond, U.K.: Curzon, 1999.

Gladney, Dru C. *Muslim Chinese Ethnic Nationalism in the People's Republic.* Cambridge, MA: Harvard University Press, 1991.

Lipman, Jonathan N. *Familiar Strangers: A History of Muslims in Northwest China.* Seattle: University of Washington Press, 1997.

Ren Mei'e, Yang Renzhang, and Bao Haosheng. *An Outline of China's Physical Geography.* Trans. Zhang Tingquan and Hu Genkang. Beijing: Foreign Languages Press, 1985.

Colin Mackerras

NORTHERN EXPEDITION

The Northern Expedition (1926–1928) was a successful military campaign in central and northern China launched by the first United Front (1923–1927) of the Nationalist Party or Guomindang (GMD) and the Chinese Communist Party (CCP). The campaign's aim was to reunite militarily a warlord-dominated China under the leadership of Chiang Kai-shek (Jiang Jieshi), backed by the National Revolutionary Army, the military arm of the GMD. The 1,500-mile expedition defeated many northern warlords along the way, toppled the warlord regime in the ancient capital Beijing, and set up a new national government at Nanjing.

FIRST NORTHERN EXPEDITION

By striving for the military reunification of China, which had disintegrated into a patchwork of warlord satrapies after Yuan Shikai's death in 1916, the GMD was taking advantage of the tidal wave of militant left-wing nationalism sweeping the entire country as a result of the revolutionary May Thirtieth movement against Western imperialism and its Chinese warlord agents. Chiang Kai-shek also relied on the patriotic zeal, discipline, morale, and fighting spirit of the National Revolutionary Army's politically loyal officer corps, trained under his command at the Whampoa Military Academy.

When General Chiang began the long-delayed expedition to the north, the Nationalists controlled only Guangdong and Guangxi provinces in the south, but their military strength had been growing with substantial support from the Soviet Union. Though vastly outnumbered and outgunned by the private armies of the powerful northern warlords, the GMD military machine was better organized, better led, and much more disciplined. The Soviet-supplied National Revolutionary Army had eight army corps, consisting mainly of the Whampoa's First Army (also known as the "Party Army" of the GMD) and seven warlord armies which were aligned with the GMD and whose command structures were dominated by Whampoa graduates. Military planning was in the capable hands of legendary Soviet commander Vasily Blücher (1889–1938), who was Chiang Kai-shek's chief military adviser under the nom de guerre of "General Galen."

On July 9, 1926, the 100,000-strong National Revolutionary Army fanned out from its stronghold in Guangzhou, Guangdong Province, to challenge the power and separatist ambitions of the northern military overlords, who were seen as obstacles to China's national unity and were widely despised as the "running dogs" of Western and Japanese imperialism. Soviet military advisers were attached to every unit of Chiang's expeditionary force while Soviet aircraft and pilots flew reconnaissance missions over enemy positions and strafed warlord troops. Thousands of Communist agitators and propagandists spread out at the enemy's rear, persuading warlord subordinates to defect to the Nationalist side and fomenting industrial-worker strikes and peasant revolts against absentee landlords and other wealthy landowners.

Popular support for the United Front's progressive nationalist ideology was so strong and widespread, especially in the impoverished countryside, that the National Revolutionary Army—whose ranks had quickly swelled to more than 260,000 revolutionary soldiers reorganized into thirty army corps—was able to reach the Yangzi River before the end of 1926. Routing the mercenary armies of "philosopher general" Wu Peifu (1874–1939), "Nanjing warlord" Sun Chuanfang (1885–1935), and other northern militarists, the National Revolutionary Army had by March 1927 overrun Hunan, Hubei, Jiangxi, Guizhou, and Fujian provinces, as well as many important cities, including Shanghai, Nanjing, and Wuhan. Following these military successes, the GMD leadership moved the seat of the Nationalist government from Guangzhou to Wuhan, the capital of the recently captured Hubei Province in central China.

In the spring of 1927, a bitter feud erupted between Chiang Kai-shek and the left-wing GMD provisional government at Wuhan led by Wang Jingwei (Wang Zhaoming), a close associate of GMD founder Sun Yat-sen (Sun Yixian), who was demanding continued cooperation with the CCP and the Soviet Union, while accusing Chiang of having turned into a despotic and power-hungry warlord. Chiang, who by that time had severed most ties with Moscow and had unleashed a vicious and bloody purge of his former Communist allies known as the "White terror," was stripped of his military command and expelled from the GMD as a "traitor" and "counterrevolutionary" on April 17, 1927. Backed by wealthy right-wing bankers and criminal underworld bosses from Shanghai, he assumed full military power as a generalissimo and established a rival anti-Communist regime under his dictatorial leadership at

Nanjing, Jiangsu Province. Lacking sufficient military and financial resources to resist him, Wang Jingwei's Wuhan government was forced to break relations with the Communists in July 1927 and finally submitted to Chiang's authority in January 1928.

SECOND NORTHERN EXPEDITION

On April 7, 1928, Chiang resumed his northern offensive against the remaining warlord forces, primarily the Fengtian Army of Manchurian marshal Zhang Zuolin (1875–1928), also known as the "Mukden tiger." In what is often called the Second Northern Expedition, the million-strong National Revolutionary Army marched farther north to the Manchurian border, capturing Beijing on June 8, 1928. By the end of 1928, most of China had been brought under Chiang's control, thereby largely ending the chaotic era of warlordism, even though a few northern warlords continued to reject his authority until the Japanese launched full-scale war against China in 1937.

Although the Northern Expedition failed to fully reunify the country, as some old provincial overlords stayed in power and new regional overlords soon emerged, it managed to create a strong military-led central government at Nanjing, which would remain the Nationalist capital for the next decade (1928–1937). It also marked the ascendancy of Chiang Kai-shek as the GMD strongman and China's new authoritarian ruler. His right-wing military dictatorship was recognized internationally as the legitimate government of the Republic of China for many years to come, but by turning on his erstwhile CCP allies and overthrowing the GMD civilian leadership, Chiang ignited a prolonged civil war, which led to his ultimate military defeat and the expulsion of his Nationalist army from the Chinese mainland in 1949. For their part, the Soviet-backed Communists drew the lesson that they had to create their own army, the Red Army, if they wanted to achieve a military victory over Chiang Kai-shek's autocratic regime and accomplish on their own the daunting task of China's full reintegration and political centralization.

SEE ALSO *Chiang Kai-shek (Jiang Jieshi).*

BIBLIOGRAPHY

Chan, F. Gilbert, and Thomas H. Etzold, eds. *China in the 1920s: Nationalism and Revolution.* New York and London: New Viewpoints, 1976.

Fenby, Jonathon. *Chiang Kai-shek: China's Generalissimo and the Nation He Lost.* New York: Carroll & Graf, 2004.

Jordan, Donald A. *The Northern Expedition: China's National Revolution of 1926–1928.* Honolulu: University Press of Hawaii, 1976.

Van de Ven, Hans J. *War and Nationalism in China, 1925–1945.* London and New York: RoutledgeCurzon, 2003.

Wilbur, C. Martin. *The Nationalist Revolution in China, 1923–1928.* New York: Cambridge University Press, 1984.

Rossen Vassilev

O

OIL PAINTING (*YOUHUA*)

During the early twentieth century a significant development of Western art forms in China coincided with the efforts of Chinese intellectuals to revitalize Chinese art and culture. The adoption of Western art and its techniques were seen as a way of modernizing and revitalizing the Chinese tradition, and by the time of the 1902 educational reforms, Western drawing classes were incorporated into the general school curriculum that emphasized Western learning, sciences, and technology.

TRAINING IN WESTERN TECHNIQUES

Oil painting accompanied Western drawing techniques into China, and was made possible initially by the new schools that imported their art teachers from Japan. By 1912 most of these teachers had returned home because of increasing political instability in China and because their positions were replaced by the new Chinese art graduates and students returned from study abroad. Other sources for learning Western art were the workshops located in treaty ports such as Guangzhou and Shanghai. For example, the Tushan Wan Painting Workshop, an affiliate of the Tushan Wan Arts and Crafts Center in Shanghai, was founded by French Catholic missionaries in 1867 and remained active until the 1940s. The workshop was one of the first schools where students were given an extensive and systematic training in Western art and were taught to paint religious works and copy Western masterpieces by European instructors or the Chinese artists trained in the prior generation.

Workshop teachers taught many pioneers of the Western-style art movement in Shanghai (as well as commercial art for the new mass media) including Zhou Xiang (1871–1934), Ding Song (1891–1972), and Xu Yong-qing (1880–1953).

The early association of Western art with science and commerce had begun to change by 1912 with Cai Yuan-pei's (1868–1940) strong promotion of aesthetic education and his move to liberate Western art from its merely utilitarian functions. Cai's essays inspired many young people to look to the West at just the time that the first generation of graduates trained in Japan began to return home. Among them, Li Shutong (1880–1942) was one of the first Chinese students to receive a thorough Western art education at the Tokyo School of Art. Li enrolled at the school in 1906 and graduated in 1911, when Kuroda Seiki (1866–1924) was its head. As one of the few early twentieth-century Chinese artists to master the foreign medium, Li is a legendary figure in modern Chinese art history. He not only became an accomplished Western painter, but also was a well-known poet, Chinese ink painter, calligrapher, and seal engraver before embarking on his studies in Japan. Upon his return to China, Li taught briefly in Shanghai before joining the Zhejiang First Normal School in Hangzhou as a teacher of art and music in 1912. Although he later left the school, taking the tonsure as the Buddhist monk Hong Yi in 1918, his teaching methods had a lasting impact on the transmission of Western art in China. He had his students draw directly from plaster casts and still life arrangements rather than copy their teachers' paintings or reproductions in textbooks, which was the previous practice. Li also encouraged students to go outdoors to immerse themselves in the natural beauty of the West Lake, and he pioneered modern plein-air painting in China. In 1913 he introduced painting from nude models as the basic training method in Western painting, a historic event that was recorded in a photograph showing the first class of thirty students with the model. In addition to painting techniques, Li also taught graphic design, woodcuts, Western drawing, and music, and thus trained many students who later became influential figures in China's art and cultural worlds.

Other major oil painters of influence include Lin Fengmian, Xu Beihong, Liu Haisu, and Yan Wenliang (1893–1990), who headed important art schools in Hangzhou, Nanjing, Beijing, Shanghai, and Suzhou. In 1926, when Lin Fengmian returned to China from his studies in France, he was invited by Cai Yuanpei to head the National Beiping Art School (Guoli beiping meishu xuexiao) and later the National Hangzhou Art Academy in 1928. In Hangzhou Lin developed the academy into an important center of French modernist styles, with supportive teachers from France and other countries. As an artist conversant in both Western and Eastern styles of painting, Lin maintained a lively and freethinking academic atmosphere at the school and trained many important artists of the next generation. Xu Beihong, another artist trained in France, worked to promote an oil painting style that is both romantic and realist, while synthesizing Western and Chinese painting techniques into his Chinese ink paintings. As an educator, he was appointed principal of the National Beiping Art School in Beijing in 1928 and head of the art department in the National Central University in Nanjing in 1929, maintaining it as a center for the promotion of realist styles. During his tenure, Xu attracted many talented artists to teach at the school including Pan Yuliang, Fu Baoshi, Gao Jianfu (1879–1951), and Zhang Daqian. After 1949, Xu was appointed the first principal of the newly established Central Academy of Fine Arts in Beijing, where his realist style served him well under the new Communist government, preparing the ground for the growth of socialist realism after his death in 1953.

Xu Beihong also encouraged fellow artist Yan Wenliang to go to Paris for further training. Yan returned three years later, in 1931, to become the president of the Suzhou Academy (also known as Suzhou Art Training Institute, or Suzhou yishu xuexiao). As a teacher and painter, he took to heart Cai Yuanpei's reforms and strongly promoted Western art during his tenure as principal, while painting in his own romantic and impressionistic style. The art school flourished among the beautiful Suzhou gardens until the war, when it was sacked by the Japanese and Yan's precious plaster casts and copies of masterpieces brought from Paris were destroyed. Unfortunately, Yan was not able to revive the school. In Shanghai, Liu Haisu and his friends established the Shanghai Art Academy in 1913. The school developed into a thriving center of modernist trends in Western art, offering classes in Western painting, admitting women students as early as in 1920, and even offering controversial nude painting classes. The school also invited important political and literary figures such as Chen Duxiu, Hu Shi, and Xu Zhimo to give lectures on its premises. In its heyday, the academy was seen as a symbol of artistic freedom and garnered the support of many important figures on its board of directors, including Cai Yuanpei, Liang Qichao, and Wang Zhen.

In addition to the art schools, artists also banded together to form societies to promote their art. The Storm Society, for example, was established in 1931 by Ni Yide (1901–1970), Pang Xunqin, and friends to form a serious modernist art movement. Although Ni Yide was trained in Japan and worked in earlier styles inspired by Paul Cézanne (1839–1906) and the fauvists, he also advocated other more recent modes of modernist painting such as dadaism and cubism. Ni promoted an art that would express a Chinese mood yet retain a Western flavor and outlook—a goal similar to that of other artists of this same period who were working toward a synthesis of Chinese and Western art. Fellow founder Pang Xunqin was trained in Paris and also worked in modernist styles, though he chose to experiment in paintings of fragmented urban life with elements of social commentary. The society held annual exhibitions until its members parted ways in 1935, taking their art onto different paths.

WOMEN ARTISTS

During the 1920s women artists working in oils also rose to fame in the art world. They included Cai Weilian (1904–1940), Sun Duoci (1913–1975), Guan Zilan (Violet Kwan, 1903–1986), Fang Junbi (1898–1986), and Pan Yuliang. Cai Weilian, the daughter of Cai Yuanpei, studied oil painting in Belgium and Lyon, France, and was noted for her portraits in oils. In 1928 she was invited to teach at the National Art Academy in Hangzhou. Sun Duoci was a student of Xu Beihong and studied in the art department at the National Central University in Nanjing. In 1949 she moved to Taiwan with her husband and became active in the Taiwanese art circles, working in her teacher's realist and romantic mode.

Guan Zilan was an artist of Cantonese descent active in Shanghai during the late 1920s and early 1930s. She was a student of the Japanese-trained artist Chen Baoyi (1893–1945), and graduated in 1927 from the Shanghai Chinese Arts University (Shanghai zhonghua yishu daxue) before going to Japan to study at the Tokyo Institute of Culture. In 1930 she returned to China to hold a large solo exhibition of her postimpressionistic works. The show was highly publicized in the popular pictorial magazine *Liangyou* (Young companion), and she went on to teach at the Xiyang Academy of Fine Arts in the same year.

Fang Junbi was both an oil and Chinese ink painter; her style is noted for its romantic tendencies and often lauded for its melding of Western and Chinese painting techniques. Fang was trained in Bordeaux and later in Paris at the Académie Julian and École nationale supérieure des beaux-arts. Fang exhibited briefly at the Salon before her return to China in 1925, and she taught at Guangdong University from 1926 to 1930. After 1949 she moved to Paris and then settled in the United States. In 1984 Fang was honored with a large retrospective exhibition at the Musée Cernuschi in Paris. Pan Yuliang, another important female painter and sculptor, first studied under Liu Haisu at the Shanghai Art Academy, then traveled to Europe to study at Lyon, Paris, and Rome from 1921 to 1928. She returned to China in 1928 to teach at the art department of the Nanjing National Central University under Xu Beihong, before settling in Paris permanently in 1935. She worked in the postimpressionistic styles of Cézanne and Paul Gauguin (1848–1903), but incorporated distinctively expressionistic Chinese linear brushwork. She is particularly known for her nudes and self-portraits, and she was a frequent exhibitor and prize winner at the Salons, winning the prestigious Gold Medal of the City of Paris in 1959.

OIL PAINTING AFTER 1949

After 1949, developments in oil painting had a new focus in Communist China: to serve the needs of the masses. The style that emerged acquired strongly political connotations as the nation and the artists set about building a new China. Artist-revolutionaries, veterans of the Lu Xun Academy at Yan'an, took the lead in defining the path for China's new art, and aligned themselves with party policy favoring Soviet socialist realist models. Veteran Yan'an artists such as Luo Gongliu were sent for training at the Repin Academy of Arts in Leningrad; a Soviet portrait painter, Konstantin M. Maksimov (b. 1913), was sent to Beijing to teach oil painting to students at the Central Academy of Fine Arts in 1955. The establishment in 1951 of the Central Museum of Revolutionary History, located in the western part of Beijing's Forbidden City, and the erection of ten major architectural monuments in Beijing to celebrate the tenth anniversary of the People's Republic in 1959 ensured a steady demand for large-scale works, including monumental history paintings to fill the walls of these buildings. Prestigious painting campaigns were launched in 1959 and 1961 to select paintings from artists throughout the country. The oil works of the period are mainly historical in subject and often depict the new revolutionary iconography that was enshrined in the new galleries of the Museum of the Chinese Revolu-

tion. They include works depicting military valor and heroic battles such as Luo Gongliu's *Mao Zedong Reporting on the Rectification in Yan'an* (1951), Jin Shangyi's *Mao Zedong at the December Meeting* (1961), Zhang Jianjun's *Five Heroes of Mount Langya* (1959), Quan Shanshi's *Unyielding Heroism* (1961), and He Kongde's *Before the Attack* (1963).

Changes in style began to be evident after the Sino-Soviet rift in 1960, when there was a movement to nationalize oil painting by incorporating recognizably Chinese aesthetics. In one example, *Mao Zedong at Mount Jinggang* (1961), Luo Gongliu applied distinctively long brushstrokes and darker dots on the canvas to evoke the texture strokes and dots of traditional ink painting. If these experiments in oils presented a "national" feeling, with the onslaught of the Cultural Revolution a new Chinese aesthetic emerged in line with Jiang Qing's ideal of "red, smooth, and glowing" (*hong-guang-liang*) for figurative painting by 1971. This new ideal was widely practiced for the next five years, as evidenced in the popular propaganda posters promoting Mao and his policies. A positive view of the lives of sent-down youth was promoted also in propagandistic oil paintings of the time. Examples of this phenomenon include Chen Yanning's barefoot doctor in *Guangdong in His New Doctor in the Fishing Village* (1974), and Zhou Shuqiao's happy group of teenagers preparing to depart for their new rural homes in *Willows in Spring* (1974). Artists sent to the remote regions of China also began to depict in their private sketchbooks the people they encountered as they came to understand rural poverty and gained a genuine appreciation for the value of human labor and the people who worked in China's hinterlands.

It has been argued that the Maoist period "naturalized" oil painting in China, transforming it from a foreign art into an integral part of the Chinese social fabric. In this view, the widespread dissemination of socialist realist visual imagery throughout society as part of the Maoist propaganda effort not only indoctrinated an entire generation of Chinese politically, but also educated them to assume that it was natural for Chinese pictorial art to take a Western form.

When the Cultural Revolution came to an end in 1976, artists began to move away from its style and iconography to reflect a less Mao-centered view of history, depicting instead the real hardships of the era rather than only heroic images. New sets of history paintings were commissioned for the Beijing museums, including Chen Yifei and Wei Jingshan's *Taking of the Presidential Palace* (1977), which is a good example of the work from this transitional period. Its photographic realist style and grand depiction of the Communist victory over the Nationalist forces is a deliberate departure from the bright and artificial style of the prior period. In the late 1970s "scar" or "wound" literature lent its name to a group of paintings, now called scar painting, that depicted the terrible suffering and senseless killings of the Cultural Revolution. Cheng Conglin (b. 1954) recorded a particularly brutal episode between different factions of the young Red Guards in his *A Snowy Day in 1968* (1979). Similarly, rustic realism emerged from the art academies in the early 1980s as a reaction against the use of art for propaganda. The artists who had been sent down to the rural areas began to paint their unidealized experiences laboring on farms, at factories, and in military camps. These artists faithfully depicted the unvarnished reality of the lives of farmers and minority peoples in the countryside in an attempt to capture the humanity of their subjects. Key artists of the movement included Luo Zhongli (b. 1948), whose work *Father* (1980) caused a controversy at the Second Chinese Exhibition for Young Artists with its photorealistic bust portrait of a peasant rendered on the monumental scale previously reserved for important political figures such as Chairman Mao. With a more subjective and contemplative tone inspired by the works of Andrew Wyeth (1917–2009), He Duoling (b. 1948) and Ai Xuan (b. 1947) demonstrated great technical virtuosity in their sensitive depictions of people in the countryside and the Tibetans. Scar painting and rustic realism were two of the many groups and movements that came and went rapidly in the late 1970s and early 1980s; another was the Stars movement, whose exhibitions broke new ground in subject matter, style, and medium. These movements were attempts by Chinese artists to reject socialist realist conventions and to express their own experiences and understanding of China's history and its people by adopting Western art styles they discovered in books and magazines, from impressionism to dadaism and surrealism.

After the crushing of the Tiananmen demonstration in 1989, the idealism of the 1980s was replaced by a strong sense of disillusionment and cynicism. Among the paintings produced in this period, cynical realist works such as Fang Lijun's (b. 1963) satirical shaven-headed loiterers evince strong feelings of ambiguity and estrangement. Political pop paintings by Wang Guangyi (b. 1956), Li Shan (b. 1942), and Yu Youhan (b. 1943) drew their images from the propaganda art of the Maoist era, but robbed them of their political power. These familiar images are treated as part of Chinese folk culture, or repeated meaninglessly like the Campbell's soup cans of Andy Warhol (1928–1987). Wang Guangyi juxtaposes the images of Red Guards with corporate logos, thus reducing these potent images of China's revolutionary past to the level of commercial art, while paying tribute to China's rising consumerism. From this period onward, Chinese oil painters began to move beyond the Chinese art market to gain international acclaim and financial

success. Most contemporary stars were trained at prestigious art academies such as the Central Academy of Fine Arts (Beijing), Sichuan Academy of Fine Arts (Chongqing), Zhejiang Academy of Fine Arts (Hangzhou), and Lu Xun Academy of Fine Arts (Shenyang). They include such familiar names as Fang Lijun, Luo Zhongli, Zhou Chunya (b. 1955), Wang Guangyi, Zhang Xiaogang (b. 1958), and Wei Ershen (b. 1954).

SEE ALSO *Lin Fengmian; Liu Haisu; Luo Gongliu; Modernist Art of the 1920s and 1930s; Pang Xunqin; Political Pop and Cynical Realism; Propaganda Art; Rustic Realism in Art; Scar (Wound) Art; Socialist Realism in Art; Women in the Visual Arts; Woodblock Printing (xylography); Xu Beihong.*

BIBLIOGRAPHY

Andrews, Julia F., and Kuiyi Shen. *A Century in Crisis: Modernity and Tradition in the Art of Twentieth-Century China.* New York: Harry N. Abrams and Guggenheim Museum Publications, 1998.

Cohen, Joan Lebold. *The New Chinese Painting, 1949–1986.* New York: Harry N. Abrams, 1987.

Galikowski, Maria. *Art and Politics in China, 1949–1984.* Hong Kong: Chinese University Press, 1998.

Kao, Meiching. The Beginning of Western-Style Painting Movement in Relationship to Reforms in Education in Early Twentieth-Century China. *New Asia Academic Bulletin* (Hong Kong) 4 (1983): 373–400.

Sullivan, Michael. *Art and Artists of Twentieth-Century China.* Berkeley and Los Angeles: University of California Press, 1996.

Zhu Boxiong and Ruilin Chen, eds. *Zhongguo xihua wushi nian 1898–1949* [Fifty years of Chinese Western painting, 1898–1949]. Beijing: Renmin Meishu Chubanshe, 1989.

Ying Chua

OLYMPICS

The 2008 Olympic Games in Beijing marked the culmination of China's lengthy quest for athletic equality in the world. Equality in the Olympics stems as much from politics as it does from athletic competition, and international politics and nationalism have played a role in the modern Olympic Games since their initiation in 1896. China's participation in the Olympics has, through the years, evoked political controversy within China and internationally. Only recently have China's athletes themselves sparked much excitement.

EARLY COMPETITIONS

There is some disagreement concerning whether China was invited to send a team to the first modern Olympic

Games in Athens in 1896. There is evidence that the International Olympic Committee (IOC) sent a letter of invitation as early as 1894 but that the Qing government failed to respond. A more genial relationship had developed by 1920, when the IOC formally recognized the Far Eastern Athletic Federation and its championship games, in which China competed.

In 1922 Wang Zhengting (1882–1961), the chancellor of China University and a sponsor of the Far Eastern Championship Games, became the first Chinese official elected to a seat on the IOC. During the first decades of the twentieth century, China conducted its own annual National Games and participated in the Far Eastern Games. In addition, the Chinese government promoted *tiyu*, which combined Western sports and physical culture emphasizing hygiene with traditional Chinese activities such as martial arts, strategic chess, mountain climbing, boating, and military exercise. By the late 1920s, Chinese society had become engulfed in *tiyu*.

In 1928 the Chinese government sent a diplomatic representative, Song Ruhai (1897–1977), as an observer to the opening ceremony of the Ninth Olympic Games in Amsterdam. An overseas Chinese athlete, He Haohua, registered to compete in three cycling events in the name of China. Before he could actually compete, an injury sent him to the hospital, and ended his participation. In 1930 Song Ruhai published a history of the Olympics, *Wo neng bi ya* (I can compete), in which he exhorted his fellow Chinese to pursue their Olympic dreams.

CHINA AND THE 1930s OLYMPICS

China's participation in the 1932 Olympics in Los Angeles was controversial. By that time, the Olympics had become a powerful symbol of national accomplishment, strength, and participation. Initially, the Chinese National Amateur Athletic Federation (CNAAF) had no plans to send competitors to Los Angeles, but was forced to do so when Japan announced that two athletes from occupied Dalian, the runners Liu Changchun (1909–1983) and Yu Xiwei (1909–1980) would represent the puppet Manzhouguo (Manchukuo) government in the Olympics. In the resulting furor, Liu disassociated himself from the Japanese, stating, "I am Chinese and will not represent the bogus Manzhouguo." After that nationalist proclamation, Liu assured the Chinese public, "I still have a conscience, my hot blood still flows—how could I betray my nation and serve others like a horse or cow?" Liu and his coach Song Junfu agreed to travel to Los Angeles under the sponsorship of China's Guomindang (GMD) government. Yu, fearing for his family's safety after threats of reprisal from the Japanese, stayed in Dalian. The Chinese American community greeted Liu and his coach in Los Angeles, and they met with great sympathy from many other Americans as

well. Although Liu did not win any medals, he wrote home with pride about the "flag of the white sun on the blue sky fluttering over the Coliseum alongside the flags of other nations" (Liu changchun bei shou huanying, p. 2, quoted in Morris 2004, p. 171).

Civil war and attacks by the Japanese did not stop China's GMD government from establishing a training camp for athletes at Shandong University in 1934 in preparation for the 1936 Olympics in Berlin. Although the camp was designed to encourage camaraderie, cronyism and international politics plagued the selection of the Olympic squad. The sprinter Li Shiming was disqualified after the CNAAF learned that he had represented his hometown in the Manzhouguo National Games in 1933 and 1934. Despite his subsequent protestations of loyalty to China, the CNAAF barred him from the Olympic team, thereby depriving the nation of its best middle-distance runner.

After an exhausting voyage to Europe, the Chinese athletic delegation, made up of sixty-nine male and nine female athletes accompanied by dozens of officials, scholars, and journalists, arrived in Berlin on July 23, 1936, to take part in what has become known as the Nazi Olympics. The Chinese prepared to compete in track and field, basketball, soccer, weightlifting, boxing, swimming, and *guoshu* (martial arts). Aware of the political implications of their actions, the Chinese athletes did not salute Adolf Hitler (1889–1945), though they did stand in respect for the German national flag.

The Chinese competitors failed to win any medals, but the men and women *guoshu* teams thrilled the audience at the Berlin Olympic Stadium in a one-hour demonstration. The runner Cheng Jinguan (1912–2005) befriended the great American runner Jesse Owens (1913–1980). The two posed for a portrait, which has become an icon of Chinese Olympic history. Contemporary critics of the team's performance argued that China had failed to "produce men like Jesse Owens." The Chinese felt that their middleweight boxer Jin Guidi (1916–1937) was cheated out of victory when the British fighter Dick Shrimpton punched Jin while the referee was separating a clinch. The Chinese protest was disallowed, but Jin was selected to carry the Chinese flag during the closing ceremony.

China's athletes and supporters emerged from the 1936 Olympics with a powerful sense of failure, with a self-perception that the weak, sickly Chinese body was to blame. Humiliated, the Chinese authorities declared that the athletes had "brought back nothing more than a 'duck's egg.'" What the Chinese felt most gallingly was the success of the Japanese in the games. Chinese athletes and the public became determined to emphasize *tiyu* and to prepare a stronger delegation for the 1940 Tokyo Olympics, which was suspended because of World War II (1937–1945).

COLD WAR POLITICS
AND THE OLYMPICS

China fared no better in the first postwar Olympics in 1948 in London. One reason was lack of funding. The GMD government allotted only $25,000, which was augmented with private donations and proceeds from basketball tournaments around Asia. Yet, in the end, the Chinese delegation had to borrow money to return home after the games.

In 1949 the Chinese Communists established the People's Republic of China (PRC) while the GMD government fled to the island province of Taiwan. The IOC thus had to decide either to choose one as the legitimate Chinese state or to violate its own charter by admitting two delegations from one country. Initially, IOC president Avery Brundage (1887–1975), under pressure from the United States, insisted that the government in Taiwan represented China and had only changed its address. Brundage became irritated when PRC officials insisted that sports manifested political behavior, a position plain to the Chinese but antithetical to the IOC's declarations that the Olympics were apolitical.

There was little activity until just before the next Olympics, the 1952 games in Helsinki, Finland. Although the Korean War (1950–1953) was underway, the All-China Athletic Committee, based on the mainland, informed the IOC that it intended to send a delegation to Helsinki. The Taiwanese also signaled their wish to compete. IOC members voted twenty-nine to twenty-two to admit both teams. The Taiwanese withdrew in protest, while the PRC sent a forty-person delegation. Because of the political controversy, most Chinese athletes arrived too late to take part in their qualifying rounds, and only the swimmer Wu Chuanyu (1928–1954) managed to compete. Though Wu did not win a medal, he set a new national record for the 100-meter backstroke. The other athletes mingled with their peers from other nations. The primary impact of the games was ideological.

Mao Zedong had long recognized the importance of athletics. In "A Study of Physical Education" (1917), Mao argued for the importance of sports in national rejuvenation, a belief that later stipulated that sports should be a form of mass exercise. Impressed by the substantial progress shown by athletes from the Soviet Union and Eastern European socialist countries, the PRC determined to establish a State

Chinese speed skater Yang Yang (center), racing at the 2006 Winter Olympic Games, Turin, Italy, February 22, 2006. *Until the 1984 Olympics, the People's Republic of China (PRC) battled with the Republic of China (ROC) over which country should represent China at the international event. With the ROC eventually agreeing to compete as Chinese Taipei, the PRC has become an Olympic powerhouse, devoting many resources to developing medal-winning athletes.* **VLADIMIR RHYS/BONGARTS/GETTY IMAGES**

Commission for Physical Culture and Sports. He Long (1896–1969), a top People's Liberation Army marshal, became the commission's first chairman. Since then, sports have become a key part of the Chinese struggle for legitimacy and prestige on the world stage. Chinese athletes, like soldiers, were to strive in the international arena on behalf of socialism, the homeland, and national identity, a belief that remains in force today.

In the 1950s, politics took precedence over participation. In 1954 the IOC voted twenty-three to twenty-one to admit the PRC team to the 1956 games in Melbourne, Australia. The PRC expressed a desire to compete, but ultimately withdrew when the IOC refused to drop the "two Chinas" policy. The United States lobbied to keep the PRC out of regional athletic associations, which would disallow the mainlanders from Olympic qualification. In return, the Soviet Union dismissed Taiwan's team as "political leftovers." Even after the Sino-Soviet split beginning in the late 1950s, the Soviets continued to press for admission of the PRC to the Olympics. In a series of angry exchanges with Avery Brundage, the Chinese Communist members of the IOC referred to Brundage as a "faithful menial of the U.S. imperialists" who were intent on a "two Chinas" policy.

With that parting shot, the PRC severed ties with the IOC and did not participate in the 1960 Rome Olympics. The IOC did, however, remove the GMD government's right to represent China, and Taiwan's delegation was forced to march behind a sign that read "Formosa." One of Taiwan's athletes carried another sign that read "Under Protest." In the 1960 games, Yang Zhuanguang (Yang Chuan-Kwang or C. K. Yang, 1933–2007) won the first-ever medal for a Chinese Olympian, taking the silver in the men's decathlon.

During the remainder of the 1960s, the PRC remained outside of the Olympic movement and, increasingly alienated from the Soviet Union, turned to regional venues. In 1963 the PRC participated in the Games of the New Emerging Forces (GANEFO), which Indonesia organized in late 1962 to counter the Olympic Games. Established for the athletes of the so-called emerging nations (mainly newly independent socialist states), GANEFO stated in its constitution that politics and sports were intertwined. This view ran counter to the doctrine of the IOC, which strove to separate politics from sports.

The PRC enthusiastically took part in GANEFO, and China's athletes won the most medals, giving the Chinese their first major international victory. GANEFO posed problems for the Japanese organizers of the 1964 Tokyo Olympics when the IOC threatened to ban all nations taking part in the emerging nations' competition. Faced with a boycott from African and Asian nations, the IOC relented. The PRC supported GANEFO II, sched-uled to be held in Cairo with Beijing as a backup city. But when the president of Indonesia, Sukarno (1901–1970), was overthrown in 1965, the new Indonesian government moved toward alliance with the IOC. In the end, the Egyptian government could not handle the financial responsibilities of GANEFO II, and China, now in the throes of the Cultural Revolution, refused to allow an international sports festival to take place within its borders in the midst of chaos. GANEFO thus collapsed.

The IOC admitted Taiwan's team to the games in Tokyo in 1964 and Mexico City 1968. During the 1968 games, the Taiwanese regained the name "Olympic Committee of the Republic of China." Ji Zheng (Chi Cheng) won a bronze medal in the women's 80-meter hurdles, becoming the first Chinese woman to place in Olympic competition.

Shut out of international competition, the PRC engaged in what become known as ping-pong diplomacy, first with the Soviet Union, then famously with the United States. After Zhou Enlai's reception of the American ping-pong team in the Great Hall of the People in Beijing in April 1971, and the subsequent relaxation of tensions between the United States and China, the way was paved for the PRC's reentry to the Olympics. As Zhou put it, "a ping-pong ball fell over the net and the whole world was shocked."

The 1976 Montreal Olympics became a flash point. Canada had become a principal trading partner of the PRC and had established a one-China policy in 1970. The Canadian government announced that it would exclude athletes from the Republic of China unless they marched under a banner labeled "Taiwan." Furious negotiations with the IOC and the United States failed; the Canadians were unwilling to budge. Ultimately, the Republic of China's delegation refused to participate. Extensive negotiations over the next several years resulted in approval in 1981 of the name, flag, and emblem of the Chinese Taipei (Taibei) Olympic Committee, a solution that continued into the 2008 Olympic Games. Both Chinas boycotted the 1980 Moscow Games.

REJOINING THE OLYMPIC FAMILY

PRC athletes became powerful forces in the 1984 Los Angeles Olympics, winning fifteen gold, eight silver, and nine bronze medals; with a total of thirty-two medals, the PRC placed fourth among all nations. China lost some of its momentum in 1988 in Seoul, where its athletes took only twenty-eight medals, with a sharp drop to five golds. The team rebounded in 1992 in Barcelona by taking sixteen gold, twenty-two silver, and sixteen bronze medals, placing the PRC fourth among all nations. The Chinese also won three silver medals at the 1992 Winter Games in Albertville, France. The Chinese Taipei baseball team took the silver medal in baseball at the Barcelona Games.

The Chinese role behind the scenes was even more important. The Soviet Union announced a boycott of the 1984 games in Los Angeles and contended that more than one hundred nations would honor its call. As Peter Ueberroth, the chairman of the U.S. Olympic Committee later admitted, had the Chinese government heeded the Soviet boycott, the games may have been canceled. After intensive lobbying, the Chinese accepted the Olympic invitation, and the effect of the Soviet effort was muted.

In the 1996 Olympics in Atlanta, Chinese athletes took sixteen gold medals and fifty medals overall. Reminders of past controversies scarred China's participation in the Atlanta Games. Stung by the IOC's narrow rejection in 1993 of Beijing as host city for the 2000 Olympic Games, the Chinese threatened to boycott the Atlanta competition over the possible attendance of Taiwanese officials. The Chinese did appear in Atlanta, but new problems emerged. Westerners accused China's female swimmers of using performance-enhancing drugs. Chinese women had become dominant in world championships in the 1990s, but a number of them had been banned from the Asian Games in Hiroshima in 1994 for substance abuse. Some commentators suggested that Chinese athletes should be barred from the Atlanta Games. The Chinese angrily rejected such charges as ideological and denounced comments by NBC television host Bob Costas about human rights in China. Seventy-eight Chinese student associations from around the world purchased space in the *Washington Post* on August 14, 1996, to demand an apology from NBC and Costas. The network apologized, but Costas refused. China did gain one important victory when Deng Yaping beat Taiwan's representative, Chen Jing, for the women's table-tennis gold.

China increased its tally of gold medals to twenty-eight in the Sydney Olympics of 2000 and jumped to thirty-two in the Athens Games in 2004. China won one hundred medals at the 2008 Beijing Olympics, including fifty-one gold medals. During this productive period, China has won most of its Olympic gold medals in diving, table tennis, weightlifting, shooting, and gymnastics. China has also won numerous medals in badminton.

In addition, China has gradually improved its performance in the four Winter Olympics after Albertville. The speed skater Yang Yang won the women's 500- and 1,000-meter races in Salt Lake City, Utah, in 2002, giving China its first Winter Olympics gold medals. Han Xiaopeng won the freestyle skiing medal and Wang Meng won the 500-meter speed-skating competition in the 2006 games in Turin, Italy.

Chinese Taipei athletes won gold medals in men and women's flyweight taekwondo at the 2004 Athens Olympics. As of 2008, China Taipei had won twelve medals since the 1996 Atlanta Games. Taipei has never won a medal in winter competitions.

China's quest for medals points to a powerful ideological transformation in Chinese society since the Mao era, when participation was focused less on winning than on "Friendship First, Competition Second." Now, "championism" (*jinbiao zhuyi*), previously denounced by Mao and Zhou Enlai, motivates athletes in pursuit of individual glory and wealth, while the nation becomes a society of spectators. These patterns accelerated in the run-up to the 2008 Olympics.

SEE ALSO *Beijing; Leisure; Physical Education; Sports; Sports Figures.*

BIBLIOGRAPHY

Brownell, Susan. *Training the Body for China: Sports in the Moral Order of the People's Republic.* Chicago: University of Chicago, 1995.

Close, Paul, David Askew, and Xu Xin. *The Beijing Olympiad: The Political Economy of a Sporting Mega-event.* New York: Routledge, 2007.

Gao Yunxiang. Sports, Gender, and Nation-State during China's "National Crisis" from 1931 to 1945. Ph.D. diss., University of Iowa, 2005.

Kanin, David B. *A Political History of the Olympic Games.* Boulder, CO: Westview, 1981.

Large, David Clay. *Nazi Games: The Olympics of 1936.* New York: Norton, 2007.

Miller, David. *The Official History of the Olympic Games and the IOC: Athens to Beijing, 1894–2008.* Edinburgh, U.K.: Mainstream, 2008.

Mitchell, Andrea, and Helen Yeates. Who's Sorry Now? Drugs, Sports, and the Media toward 2000. In *The Olympics at the Millennium: Power, Politics, and the Games*, ed. Kay Schaffer and Sidonie Smith, 197–213. New Brunswick, NJ: Rutgers University Press, 2000.

Morris, Andrew. *Marrow of the Nation: A History of Sport and Physical Culture in Republican China.* Berkeley: University of California Press, 2004.

Segrave, Jeffrey O., and Donald Chu, eds. *The Olympic Games in Transition.* Champaign, IL: Human Kinetics, 1988.

Senn, Alfred E. *Power, Politics, and the Olympic Games.* Champaign, IL: Human Kinetics, 2000.

Xu Guoqi. *Olympic Dreams: China and Sports, 1895–2008.* Cambridge, MA: Harvard University Press, 2008.

Zinser, Lynn. Phone Call from China Transformed '84 Games. *New York Times*, July 14, 2008.

Gao Yunxiang

OLYMPICS, 2008 BEIJING OLYMPIC GAMES

China realized its Olympic goal on July 13, 2001, when the International Olympic Committee voted to make Beijing the host city for the 2008 Olympics. Nearly 400,000 people anxiously awaited the news in Tiananmen

Opening ceremony performers, 2008 Beijing Summer Olympics, August 8, 2008. *In an event viewed by millions around the globe, China used the opening ceremony of the 2008 Beijing Summer Olympics to promote its status as a world superpower. Featuring highly choreographed dance sequences, complemented by innovative uses of new technology, the event highlighted the capabilities of China in a new millennium.* **JEWEL SAMAD/AFP/GETTY IMAGES**

Square, and the Chinese nation exploded with pride and joy when news arrived that the International Olympic Committee elected the city by a sizable majority in the second round of voting. Jiang Zemin and other leaders appeared on the balcony of Tiananmen to join the celebration, the culmination of planning initiated in 1984. In the past, several issues were significant barriers: The suppression of the prodemocracy movement in Tiananmen Square in 1989, perceptions of China's poor record in human rights, the status of Tibet, and tensions leftover from the Cold War had damaged the country's appeal to the outside world. Beijing lost to Sydney by just two votes for the right to host the 2000 games. Bruised by this loss, which it blamed on "obstacles and interference that crudely trampled the Olympic spirit," China decided not to pursue the 2004 selection and concentrated on the choice for 2008. China's rise as a global power and rapprochement with the United States helped its 2008 bid. U.S. President George W. Bush openly supported Beijing's quest in 2001.

Having won the right to host the Olympics, the city of Beijing splurged on preparations for tens of thousands of visitors. Taxi drivers were taught English. The city constructed new subways and light rails, new highways, and a new airport terminal. Construction sites appeared all over the city. The Chinese government contracted with world-famous architects to build a new Olympic stadium, dubbed the Bird's Nest, for its intricate steel webbing, and a swimming site known as the Water Cube because of its unique exterior. Ai Weiwei, one of China's most notable contemporary artists, designed the Bird's Nest in collaboration with the Swiss architectural firm Herzog and de Meuron. The Water Cube was a collaborative product of PTW Architects (an Australian architecture firm), Arup International Engineering Group, China State Construction Engineering Corporation, and China Construction Design International of Shanghai. The city cleared hundreds of acres of old housing to make way for projects, thereby displacing nearly a million residents.

China geared up for the Olympics by creating a Beijing Organizing Committee for the Games of the XXIX Olympiad. The executive member was He Zhenliang, concurrently honorary president of the Chinese Olympic

Committee, member of the International Olympic Committee, and chairman of the Commission for Culture and Olympic Education of the International Olympic Committee. The president of the committee was Liu Qi, who announced the slogan for the games, "One World, One Dream," by sending it in a text message to China Mobile's 230 million phone subscribers. The slogan was advertised nationwide by the Olympic mascots, five good luck dolls designed by Han Meili, a noted Chinese artist. The names of the five dolls—Beibei, Jingjing, Huanhuan, Yingying, and Nini—together form the sentence "Beijing huanying ni," or "Beijing welcomes you."

In the lead-up to and even during the Olympics, political controversies over human rights simmered, with particular emphasis on religious freedom and China's involvement in Darfur, in western Sudan. Old conflicts with Taiwan resurfaced. The Olympic torch, a tradition started in Berlin in 1936, was rerouted because of conflicts between the People's Republic and Taiwan, and protests against Chinese control of Tibet. Worries about terrorist attacks and pollution did not materialize, but the Chinese

government received global criticism for its repression of dissent. Farcically, the Chinese government required would-be protestors to apply for permits, and then promptly arrested any who sought permission. Known dissidents were placed under house arrest amid reports of torture. One nonpolitical controversy was over the age of several young female gymnasts. Eventually the International Olympic Committee investigated their ages and cleared the Chinese Olympic authority of any wrongdoing.

The Beijing Olympics opened on August 8, 2008, with a total of 10,500 athletes from every one of the 204 member nations of the International Olympic Committee except Brunei. The opening ceremony started at 8:08 p.m. China Standard Time on August 8, reflecting the association in Chinese lore of the number 8 with prosperity and culture. Basketball player Yao Ming and Lin Hao, a nine-year-old survivor of the 2008 Sichuan earthquake, led the Chinese delegation of 1,099 people. Chinese filmmaker Zhang Yimou and choreographer Zhang Jigang codirected a spectacular show featuring 15,000 performers. Britain's Sarah Brightman and China's Liu Huan sang the official

Chinese gymnast Deng Linlin competing on the balance beam at the 2008 Summer Olympics, Beijing, August 13, 2008. In *the summer of 2008, the city of Beijing hosted the Summer Olympics, concluding several years of intense city-wide preparation for the event. Chinese Olympians performed exceptionally well before their home audience, earning fifty-one gold medals, the most of any competing nation.* AL BELLO/GETTY IMAGES

song, "You and Me," on a giant world globe. Fifty-six Chinese children in traditional garb, one from each of China's fifty-six officially recognized ethnic groups, carried a huge Chinese flag. One discordant note was retrospectively sounded when nine-year-old Lin Miaoke's performance of the song was revealed to have been lip-synched (the seven-year-old singer Yang Peiyi had been considered not cute enough for the stage). World audiences in the hundreds of millions watched daily events, shown in the United States on the National Broadcasting Company (NBC) television network. Time differences and the desire to present popular events during American prime-viewing time meant that most competitions were seen on tape delay. Audiences in China were enormous.

In the competitions, China led the world in gold medals with 51; the United States was second with 36, followed by Russia with 23 and Great Britain with 19. Chinese athletes accumulated 100 medals overall, second to the American total of 110. China's women table-tennis team had the distinction of winning the nation's 33rd gold medal, thereby eclipsing the nation's previous best of 32 set in Athens in 2004. China did best in gymnastics, earning 11 gold medals, while garnering 8 in weightlifting, 7 in diving, 4 in shooting, 4 in table tennis, and 3 in badminton. New heroes stepped forth. The female diver Guo Jingjing won 2 gold medals in Beijing to add to the pair she won in Athens in 2004. Her face adorns billboards across China. Lin Dan, who won the gold medal in badminton, is known as Super Dan and is loved in China for his ferocious serve and for the Chairman Mao button he sports on his shirt. Not all was glorious. The Chinese basketball and soccer teams did poorly. The Chinese nation suffered a major disappointment when the immensely popular hurdler Liu Xiang withdrew just before the race with a hamstring injury, apparently incurred during a false start initiated by another competitor.

Major accomplishments came from athletes of many nations. Michael Phelps of the United States won 8 gold medals in swimming, the most for an individual in a single Olympics. Jamaican sprinter Usain Bolt set world records in the 100- and 200-meter races. The U.S. men's and women's basketball teams easily won gold medals.

The Beijing Olympics closed on August 24, 2008. With its massive haul of medals, China forever dispelled the "sick man" image that plagued it during the early twentieth century. The Olympics surely succeeded in bolstering national pride and support for the ruling Communist Party. Longer-term social and economic impacts remain to be seen.

BIBLIOGRAPHY
Xu Guoqi. *Olympic Dreams: China and Sports, 1895–2008.* Cambridge, MA: Harvard University Press, 2008.

Gao Yunxiang

OPIUM, 1800–1950

Opium was used in China as a medicinal drug as early as the Tang dynasty (618–907). By the Ming (1368–1644), it was a regular part of the pharmacopeia. Opium was used to treat a number of ailments, and it remained a commonly used medicinal drug until 1949. Although it was traded as early as the Ming, it became a major import only after the habit of smoking opium began to spread in the mid-Qing. Opium smoking began to spread in China after 1750. By the early 1800s, opium imports were growing rapidly, as was opium smoking. The court was concerned with the spread of this new habit and above all with the silver that was supposedly flowing out of the country to pay for it.

THE FIRST ANTI-OPIUM CAMPAIGN

These concerns led to a court debate on opium policy in 1836 between those who favored strict prohibition of the importation and production of opium and those who favored legalization of opium smoking on the grounds that legalization would eliminate the problem of smuggling and might make it possible for domestic opium to supplant foreign opium and eliminate the silver drain. These, rather than the effects of opium use on the masses of Chinese, were the chief concerns of many in the bureaucracy. The prohibition side prevailed.

The anti-opium campaign that ensued was in some respects a model for later campaigns. There were attempts to eliminate opium production in southwest China, and there were at least some attempts (mostly focusing on elites) to encourage Chinese to stop smoking opium. Many of the problems these efforts faced were the same that would face later campaigns. Poppy cultivation was difficult to control, and it was difficult to distinguish illegal opium smoking from the medicinal use of opium. The state's ability to control behavior at the local level was limited, and most ordinary Chinese saw little point in abjuring opium. The main focus of the campaign however was on interdicting supplies of foreign opium, especially the British-controlled trade in Indian opium centered on Guangzhou (Canton). This led to Lin Zexu's (1785–1850) destruction of the foreign opium at Humen, which would later be regarded as the beginning of China's war against opium.

GROWTH IN PRODUCTION AND CONSUMPTION

China's defeat in the first Opium War (1839–1842) led to a complete change in China's opium policy and in its relationship with the West. Although opium importation, production, and sales remained illegal until 1860 (the Peking Convention), in practice the state paid little attention to

Chinese opium users, c. nineteenth century. *Despite efforts by the Qing government to curtail opium use, the drug flourished in China during the nineteenth century, fueled particularly by British traders importing Indian opium and the income local governments earned distributing the product. Efforts to control domestic consumption and production generally failed until the People's Republic of China effectively eliminated the opium industry in the 1950s.* **POPPERFOTO/GETTY IMAGES**

the opium trade and opium consumption after 1841. Still, many appreciated the benefit of opium *lijin* taxes, introduced in the 1860s, for the fiscal health of the state.

From 1841 to 1900, opium production and consumption grew steadily. Production came to be concentrated in western China, with Sichuan and Yunnan the largest producers. By 1906 Sichuan was producing 57,000 *piculs* (2,850 tons) of opium a year, slightly more than the total amount of foreign opium sold that year. Domestic opium production and marketing became increasingly important industries.

Opium smoking also seems to have spread steadily. Before 1840, it had largely been limited to elites and coastal areas, but by 1900 opium smokers could be found all over China. Opium smoking was becoming a common form of sociability, especially for men. Popular attitudes toward smoking were mixed during the Qing. The dangers of excessive opium use were widely publicized, and the first cures for opium smoking began to appear, often associated with foreign missionaries. At the same time, opium smoking was also regarded as a valuable tonic that could be used occasionally (or frequently) with no ill effects.

CHANGING ATTITUDES AND POLICIES

Chinese attitudes and state policies toward opium began to change in the late nineteenth century, in part because of greater state desire to control the trade and its revenue and in part because of the arrival of new ideas about addiction from the West. British and American doctors had been developing new ideas about drugs, which led to the view that there were certain substances that, once used, would force those who consumed them down a path of inevitable destruction. These ideas began to spread into China by 1900, as Chinese were trying to identify the causes of their national crisis. Opium became one of the standard evils bedeviling China in the rhetoric of all Chinese politicians, and all Chinese governments at least announced campaigns to end opium production and smoking. The first of the modern campaigns started under the Qing in 1906 and had some success. The Qing government was able to get the British to agree to gradually eliminate imports of Indian opium and both production and consumption of opium declined. However, although the state tried to teach the populace that opium use was bad for the nation, this lesson does not seem to have sunk in. The campaign ended as order disintegrated after 1916, and both production and use returned to their previous levels.

The late Qing campaigns had involved setting up state-run monopolies for the distribution and sale of opium. Originally these were intended to provide governments with a degree of control over the trade and assist in its eventual suppression, while also providing the revenue to fund that suppression. As China slipped into warlordism, control of the opium trade remained important for local governments, but the goal of raising revenue predominated over the (increasingly remote) elimination of the trade.

THE WARLORD PERIOD

The warlord period was the heyday of the opium trade and also the era that created many of the modern images of opium and China. Controlling the opium trade was a key goal of many regional militarists because it was the easiest way for them to generate revenue. It was particularly important for militarists in remote areas, such as Long Yun (1884–1962) of Yunnan, who was able to become a major figure in national politics in part because of his government's substantial revenues from opium.

The resurgence of the opium trade under the warlords was a source of embarrassment and concern for educated Chinese. China was signatory to a series of international opium control agreements, most notably the Geneva Conventions of 1925, and China's continued failure to live up to these agreements was the most obvious sign of its failure to create a modern nation. The opium trade and the warlordism it helped finance were the most obvious signs of the backwardness of Chinese people in the eyes of Chinese reformers and foreign governments.

NEW EFFORTS AT SUPPRESSION

After 1927, the new Nationalist government announced that opium suppression would be one of its chief goals. This would prove somewhat problematic, because during its Guangzhou period the Guomindang government had profited from the opium trade, as did the regional governments. Like other governments, Nanjing found itself bedeviled by the difficulties of controlling the drug trade and seduced by the lure of easy revenue from state involvement in the trade. For Nanjing, the drug trade was particularly important because opium profits financed many of the regional militarists (including the Communists) who were the government's chief domestic rivals and because the Japanese were closely connected with the trades in the new opium derivatives of morphine and heroin.

All of these problems were eventually dealt with by the announcement of the 1935 Six-Year Plan to Eliminate Opium and Drugs. The Nationalist set up a nationwide opium distribution and control system, partially based on existing systems established by regional warlords. As before, the system was intended to provide the central government with revenue, while also enabling it to control and supposedly eventually eliminate opium. Opium producers and smokers were licensed by the state, and, as before, both production and consumption were to be gradually eliminated. In this case, the plan actually did have considerable effect, in part because the government had developed a much better understanding of the trade and in part because, while opium control did provide revenue to the central government, the Guomindang was more interested in denying opium revenue to regional and local governments than in continuing the trade indefinitely.

Chiang Kai-shek (Jiang Jieshi), unlike some others in his government, was concerned with the effect of opium on the morality of the Chinese people. Although the campaign was interrupted by the beginning of the Sino-Japanese War in 1937, and opium and drug use expanded rapidly in Japanese occupied areas, the Nationalists continued the plan in "free China," and by 1940 could claim with considerable accuracy that they had broken the link between the Chinese state and the opium trade. At the same time, opium smoking was continuing its steady movement toward social unacceptability.

After 1949, the Communists effectively ended the production and consumption of opium, in large part borrowing the methods of the Nationalists' campaigns, but also taking advantage of their much greater control over local society and behavior. Although drug use has returned to China since the start of the reform period, it has done so as a deviant behavior rather than as a major part of China's political economy.

SEE ALSO *East India Company, 1800–1834; Opium Wars.*

BIBLIOGRAPHY

Baumler, Alan. *The Chinese and Opium under the Republic: Worse than Floods and Wild Beasts.* Albany: State University of New York Press, 2007.

Brook, Timothy, and Bob Tadashi Wakabayashi. *Opium Regimes: China, Britain, and Japan, 1839–1952.* Berkeley: University of California Press, 2000.

Madancy, Joyce A. *The Troublesome Legacy of Commissioner Lin: The Opium Trade and Opium Suppression in Fujian Province, 1820s to 1920s.* Cambridge, MA: Harvard University Asia Center, 2004.

McAllister, William B. *Drug Diplomacy in the Twentieth Century: An International History.* New York: Routledge, 1999.

Zhang Yangwen. *The Social Life of Opium in China.* Cambridge, U.K.: Cambridge University Press, 2005.

Alan Baumler

OPIUM WARS

The Opium Wars originated in trade disputes. The first war (1839–1842) was a confrontation between Britain and Qing China, precipitated in the 1830s by a rapid increase in the volume of opium shipped from British India to Guangzhou (Canton). China was defeated and signed the Treaty of Nanjing (1842), acceding to British demands for greater freedom to reside and do business in Chinese ports. In this manner, the aggressors forced China to accept what they called "free trade." In the second war (1856–1860) China was defeated by an Anglo-French allied force. Agreements signed in 1860 (the Conventions of Beijing) authorized the further extension of European and American privileges and granted Christian missionaries the right to proselytize throughout China.

SINO-WESTERN TRADE RELATIONS BEFORE 1839

From 1557, Portuguese-administered Macau was a trading base where Europeans purchased Chinese silk, tea, and other valuable goods. As the British colonization of India proceeded, agents of the East India Company (EIC) developed business opportunities in China. As the inhabitants of Britain became avid consumers of tea during the eighteenth century and the cultivation of tea in China expanded to meet the British demand, the EIC made large investments in the tea trade. In 1759 an EIC representative named James Flint traveled north to deliver protests to the emperor against the official restrictions and corruption that British merchants faced in China. The Qing government responded by imprisoning him for three years for sailing north without permission, presenting petitions to the court, and for having learned Chinese. In 1760 stricter restrictions were imposed; thereafter, foreigners could do business only at Guangzhou and only with a merchants' guild called the Co-hong (*gong-hang*). All communications with Chinese officials had to be conducted solely through them, and foreigners were not permitted to study the Chinese language. During the following decades, members of the Co-hong and agents of the EIC worked together effectively, entrusting one another with credit and large shipments of commodities. But the British traders came to view the Co-hong system as confining. They resentfully compared their profits with the large sums that were appropriated by Qing officials in the form of fees and gifts. The emperor benefited as well, through his appointment of an official of the Imperial Household Department to supervise the trade at Guangzhou. Referred to as the *hoppo* by foreigners, the trade superintendent remitted funds directly to the imperial palace. Meanwhile, the favorable balance of trade kept the empire well stocked with silver. One of the foundations of China's bimetallic monetary system, silver was

the means by which foreigners paid for the bulk of their purchases in China from the 1600s to about 1820. Despite these advantages, China rejected the arguments presented to the Qing court by emissaries of the British government in 1793 and 1816 that Sino-British relations should be placed on a more direct and equal footing.

COMMODITIES AND MONEY

The first Opium War followed a set of interrelated shifts in the pattern of Sino-British trade. Most remarkably, during the 1820s opium became the most important commodity in the two-way trade, greatly exceeding in value the foreign purchases of tea, silk, and other Chinese goods. The cultivation of opium in Bengal, established by an EIC monopoly in 1773, thus reversed the balance of trade, despite the fact that the importation and consumption of this narcotic substance had been prohibited by a series of Qing edicts beginning in 1729. Then, in 1833, an act of parliament terminated the EIC's monopoly on East Asian trade; private traders increased their shipments of opium to Guangzhou. At the same time, new policies encouraged the expansion of opium cultivation in India. The increased supplies and lower prices vastly expanded the volume of opium shipped to southern China, where it was quickly absorbed into the well-developed commercial networks of the Chinese Empire. "Opium is like gold; I can sell it anywhere," one trader declared (Wakeman 1978, p. 172). Imports rose from the level of about 4,000 chests a year during the period 1800 to 1818 to about 20,000 chests yearly by the mid-1830s. British merchants' impatience with the restrictions of the Co-hong system mounted as they eyed the profits to be made in direct dealings with Chinese buyers at various points beyond Guangzhou. They began to advocate a coercive approach to improving their access to China's vast hinterland. As their petition to Parliament argued in 1830, the failed missions of 1793 and 1816 proved "how little is to be gained in China by any refinements of diplomacy" (Wakeman 1978, p. 173).

The rising tide of opium imports was alarming. The most urgent concern was a monetary one. The rapid reversal of the Sino-Western trade balance severely disrupted China's financial system. Whereas 26 million Mexican dollars had flowed into China between 1800 and 1810, 38 million dollars flowed out during the eight-year period from 1828 to 1836. The outflow of silver bullion in payment for opium imports led to the appreciation of silver relative to copper, the other basis of China's monetary system. The problem was acute for China's farmers, who were compelled to pay taxes in silver exchanged for the copper coins they earned selling their produce. The officials also discussed the harmful effects of opium on the population of the empire. It was particularly

此物出在浙江處州府青田縣數十成群人獲之化為血水官兵持砲擊之刀箭不能傷現有不論軍民人才有能制除者從重獎賞此怪近聞官兵逐急旋即落水進人便食其奇怪哉

A Chinese cartoon describing European men encountered during the Opium Wars as hairy and fire-breathing, 1857. Upon learning that the Imperial government looked to halt the import of opium, the British government invaded the country to force the Chinese into more favorable trade conditions. After winning two separate wars, the British imposed heavy indemnities on the country and demanded increased access to Chinese ports, weakening the power of the Qing emperor and increasing resentment against Western nations. **HULTON ARCHIVE/ILLUSTRATED LONDON NEWS/GETTY IMAGES**

worrisome that opium addiction was said to have become common among imperial soldiers. Moreover, the open flouting of a long-established imperial ban on opium was insulting to the emperor. The proposals of officials who advocated legalization of the opium trade on the grounds that it would be easier to regulate a legitimate business than one driven underground were defeated when the Daoguang emperor (r. 1821–1850) accepted an opposing argument that the opium trade should be eliminated on moral grounds.

MILITARY ENGAGEMENT AND PEACE TERMS

Having decided on strict enforcement of the ban on opium trade and consumption, at the end of 1838 the emperor appointed a high-ranking official named Lin Zexu (1785–1850) as imperial commissioner for frontier defense, placing him in command of the naval forces of the southern coast. Within weeks of his arrival in Guangzhou, Lin took action to curb the importation of opium. After a standoff during which all trade at Guangzhou was suspended and foreigners were confined to their living quarters for

forty-seven days, Commissioner Lin confiscated the stocks of imported opium held by the British merchants. He then proceeded to destroy the contents of 20,283 chests, a year's supply of opium for the China market, dissolving the opium in water and lime and flushing it into the Pearl River.

In petitions to their government, the British traders demanded that military force be used against China, citing in justification their forty-seven days of detention and the destruction of their property by Lin Zexu. The matter was debated in Parliament in April 1840. In spite of a Tory resolution against a war aimed "to protect an infamous contraband traffic" (Wakeman 1978, p. 195), the motion to wage war on China passed by five votes. Opium was not an illicit substance in Britain then, and moreover, the foreign minister argued, the opium trade was not the central issue in the dispute with China.

An expeditionary force dispatched from India reached China in June 1840. Because Lin Zexu blockaded the Pearl River to defend Guangzhou, the British force continued northward, occupied Zhoushan Island close to the mouth of the Yangzi, and then landed on the northern coast, poised to advance toward Beijing. The Qing government opened negotiations, and an agreement was reached in January 1841. The war resumed after both London and Beijing refused to ratify the agreement. In spring 1842 British forces sailed northward again, demonstrating their superiority in military technology and tactics by overwhelming the Qing defenses at Xiamen and Ningbo on the coast and Zhenjiang on the Yangzi. At a cost of a few dozen casualties among the invading force, thousands of the defenders were killed and numerous Manchu commanders committed suicide in the face of defeat. The Qing government capitulated when the British threatened to attack the alternate imperial capital at Nanjing. The terms of peace were negotiated in meetings held on a British ship anchored in the river near Nanjing.

The Treaty of Nanjing of August 1842 set new terms for the conduct of trade and diplomacy between Britain and China. It provided for the opening to British trade of four ports in addition to Guangzhou (Xiamen, Fuzhou, Ningbo, and Shanghai), the payment of an indemnity in compensation for the confiscated opium and other costs, the permanent cession of Hong Kong to Britain, fixed limits on tariffs, and direct relations between Chinese and British officials on a basis of interstate equality. Detailed provisions for implementation of the Nanjing settlement, including extraterritorial privileges for British residents in the open ports, were specified in the supplementary Treaty of the Bogue (1843). On the basis of a most-favored-nation provision, according to which Britain was entitled to receive any privileges accorded by the Qing to another nation, the United States and France negotiated agreements similar to Britain's in 1843 and 1844, respectively.

THE SECOND OR THE *ARROW* WAR

Opium was not mentioned in the Treaty of Nanjing (except as compensation for the opium destroyed); nor was the imperial anti-opium prohibition rescinded until a second war had been waged. This conflict had its beginning in Guangzhou in October 1856 when Chinese officials boarded the *Arrow*, a Chinese-owned ship registered in Hong Kong, in search of a notorious pirate. The consul at Guangzhou protested that British rights had been violated by the search of the *Arrow*, and British naval forces bombarded the government offices in Guangzhou. Governor-general Ye Mingchen (1807–1859) did not yield to their demands, however. Instead, he ordered a halt to foreign trade at the port. When an expeditionary force arrived from India a year later and the authorities still refused to reopen the trade, Guangzhou was occupied. In response to the murder of a French missionary in Guangxi, France sent a task force to support the British campaign. After the allied forces occupied strategic points on the

northern coast, Qing authorities signed the Treaty of Tianjin (1858), providing for the opening of another ten ports to foreign trade all along the coast up to Manchuria, along the Yangzi, and on Taiwan, and the establishment of permanent French and British diplomatic missions in Beijing. The Tianjin agreement was not ratified, however, because when an Anglo-French delegation returned the following summer to implement the treaty, its leaders insisted on proceeding toward Beijing along a route that was officially closed to them. Qing forces attacked the party, inflicting heavy losses. An enlarged Anglo-French expeditionary force arrived in North China a year later, escorting a delegation of thirty-nine officials. In a skirmish near the capital, the entire delegation was captured by Qing troops. The foreign officials were imprisoned in Beijing, fighting continued, and the emperor fled to Manchuria. Twenty-six of the captives were killed as the allied force entered the city. In retaliation, the survivors imposed a destructive punishment, burning the emperor's summer palaces on the outskirts of Beijing. A peace settlement was then negotiated by the emperor's brother, Prince Gong (1833–1898), and the Conventions of Beijing were signed (1860). These agreements reiterated the provisions of the earlier Treaty of Tianjin, along with a few new terms, including the opening of Tianjin itself and the creation of a central government agency to handle China's foreign affairs.

SIGNIFICANCE OF
THE OPIUM WARS

Military defeats in the two Opium Wars did not result in the collapse of the Qing Empire or its colonization. The Qing system of government was well-organized and sophisticated enough for the foreign powers to work through it without taking over the country. Second, Britain, the leading foreign power by far, having taken over India in 1858, was not inclined to increase the burden of empire.

The Second Opium War also resulted in the continuation of the Inspectorate of Customs in Shanghai, expanding its operations to all the sixteen treaty ports, and additional treaty ports that were opened thereafter. This consolidation and centralized management of tariffs under a British inspector-general and a senior staff of foreign nationals was created under the pressure of foreign demands for fair and predictable commercial relations. Though it reported to the Chinese government, and generated revenue that contributed to China's modernization, it was nonetheless a foreign-dominated institution, opening a period of Sino-foreign authority in China's fiscal affairs.

Ultimately, the treaties that concluded the wars laid the foundation for a century of foreign domination. The most-favored-nation clause provided for shared and interlocking interests among the powers vis-à-vis China. Together with the military defeats, these treaty provisions undermined the credibility of Qing rule.

SEE ALSO *East India Company, 1800–1834; Foreign Trade, 1800–1950; Lin Zexu; Opium, 1800–1950; Treaty Ports; Wars and the Military, 1800–1912; Wars since 1800.*

BIBLIOGRAPHY

Fairbank, John K. The Creation of the Treaty System. In *The Cambridge History of China*, vol. 10, pt. 1, ed. Denis Twitchett and John K. Fairbank, 213–263. New York: Cambridge University Press, 1978.

Fay, Peter Ward. *The Opium War, 1840–1842.* Chapel Hill: University of North Carolina Press, 1975.

Fu Lo-shu. *A Documentary Chronicle of Sino-Western Relations, 1644–1820.* Tucson: University, Arizona Press, 1966.

Wakeman, Frederic, Jr. The Canton Trade and the Opium War. In *The Cambridge History of China*, vol. 10, pt. 1, ed. Denis Twitchett and John K. Fairbank, 167–212. New York: Cambridge University Press, 1978.

Waley, Arthur. *The Opium War through Chinese Eyes.* London: Allen and Unwin, 1958.

Wong, J. Y. *Deadly Dreams: Opium, Imperialism, and the Arrow War (1856–1860).* New York: Cambridge University Press, 1998.

Emily M. Hill

OVERSEAS CHINESE

SEE *Chinese Overseas.*

P

PAKISTAN, RELATIONS WITH

In the complex political, military, and diplomatic landscape that has shaped international relations in South Asia since 1947, one of the most salient factors has been the Sino-Pakistani entente. Its importance stems not only from its substance but also from its stability and continuity in this volatile region. The broad network of interactions between these two countries might seem a counterintuitive puzzle given the inherently different characteristics of China and Pakistan, especially the disparities in how they view the world and define their collective identities. Although these disparities initially fostered mostly indifference and some latent suspicion, they have not prevented both sides from reevaluating in time their initial approaches and developing mutual political trust and strategic bonding. Why? The short answer is the realpolitik perspective that informs the convergence and complementarity of their vital long-term, strategic interests. Time and the evolution of regional and global politics have strengthened the credibility of China's and Pakistan's perceptions of their mutual indispensability to each other's objectives.

MINIMAL ENGAGEMENT: 1947–1954

After its independence in 1947, Pakistan took a cautiously ambivalent position toward the struggle for control over China between the Chinese Communist Party and the Guomindang. When the Communist Party prevailed in 1949, Pakistan adopted a realistic view of its neighbor, and on January 4, 1950, became the first Muslim state to recognize the new regime, calling for the People's Repub-

lic of China (PRC) to take a seat in the United Nations General Assembly and in the Security Council. Pakistan was, however, concerned over the political implications of the ideological divide between itself and the PRC. The Pakistani leadership was also aware of the need to avoid the dual risks of antagonizing the United States, the PRC's main opponent, and of being isolated by the emergent close Sino-Indian relationship. China, for its part, kept a foot in Pakistan's door, having its own doubts about the sustainability of its relationship with India and being aware of the importance of Pakistan for its future interests in the Middle East, and more broadly its relations with the newly independent Muslim countries. These factors have led to symmetrical attitudes on China's and Pakistan's part, namely, cautious mutual deference tempered by suspicion.

As Sino-Indian relations blossomed in the early 1950s, China's attitude toward Pakistan became cooler but never hostile, even when Pakistan formally allied with the West and joined the Baghdad Pact and SEATO in 1954 and 1955, respectively, and CENTO in 1959. The mutual policy of low-level engagement and caution to leave future options open for a strategic relationship proved beneficial when circumstances changed (Vertzberger 1985, pp. 9–17).

THE TURNING POINT: THE BORDER AGREEMENT

Political instability in Pakistan led to a military coup in 1958. General Mohammad Ayub Khan, the head of state, and the new regime drifted further away from China, emphasizing Pakistan's special relationship with the United States. The failure of the Ayub-Nehru talks to settle the

Kashmir issue in 1959 and to establish a common defense policy along the northern border of India and Pakistan, on the one hand, and the rapidly deteriorating Sino-Indian relations since the late 1950s, on the other, encouraged the rising young minister in Ayub's government, Zulfikar Ali Bhutto, to try to convince Ayub Khan to change direction. He believed that the misguided, one-sided dependence on the United States had run its course and it was time to consider a closer relationship with China (Bhutto 1969, pp. 10–15). The military leadership was hesitant, doubting whether the PRC could be trusted. The litmus test that eventually convinced the Pakistani government to reexamine the China option was Chinese willingness to settle the border dispute with Pakistan, which in essence was an extension of the border problem with India, both left over from the colonial days of British India. Within a relatively short time, from October 1962 to March 1963, the two sides reached an agreement on the 523-kilometer disputed border between Pakistan's Azad Kashmir and China's Xinjiang, on terms that the Pakistani leadership considered favorable. Ayub Khan noted in his autobiography:

> This agreement on border demarcation was the first step in the evolution of relations between Pakistan and China. Its sole purpose was to eliminate a possible cause of conflict in the future, but as a result of this agreement, the Chinese began to have trust in us and we also felt that if one was frank and straightforward, one could do honest business with them. (1967, p. 164)

Underlying the Chinese goodwill and Pakistan's open-mindedness were shared strategic interests, which have proved highly resilient over time, and other issues that offered both parties important political and economic opportunities.

The main threat to Pakistan has been from India, which according to Pakistan had never accepted the "two-nations" concept, and the related pathology of the asymmetrical balance of power between India and Pakistan. In the context of the increasing disappointment with the weak role played by both the United States and the United Nations in containing India's ambitions for predominance in the subcontinent, a cooperative relationship with China that proved itself in October 1962 to be both willing and able to use its military power to defeat India and teach it a painful lesson, seemed a promising policy to enhance Pakistan's position vis-à-vis India through China's extended deterrence. This would serve Pakistan's principal goal of achieving strategic parity with India, would ensure that Pakistan could survive as an independent sovereign political entity, and would force India to negotiate with Pakistan on equal footing.

The concern over India's aggressive intention became even more acute with the strengthening of Indo-Soviet relations since the 1950s, and the Soviet Union's willingness to supply advanced weapons systems to India. The Soviet Union was perceived not only as a de facto ally of India but also as a threat in and of itself, taking into account West Pakistan's geostrategic location on the Soviet Union's path to the Indian Ocean and to the oil fields of the Middle East. Furthermore, Pakistan viewed building a close relationship with China as an important opportunity to reestablish its credentials among the more radical, anti-Western third world countries, which perceived Pakistan as completely under the spell of U.S. neocolonialism, an image the Pakistani leadership and intelligentsia were keen to dispel, especially given India's pivotal role among the nonaligned nations. Also of great importance were the traditional pan-Islamic aspirations of Pakistan and the hostility toward the United States and its allies in much of the Muslim world (Vertzberger 1985, pp. 24–29).

China's motivations were no less critical. China perceived India as a long-term dangerous protagonist, a strategic threat on its southern borders, and a source of support for a resurgent Tibet after it provided asylum to the Dalai Lama following his escape from Tibet in 1959. India was also viewed as the country where the interests of China's archenemies, the United States and the USSR, converged. Sino-Pakistani strategic cooperation would not only remedy the asymmetry in the balance of power in South Asia and force India to invest extensive resources in its conflict with Pakistan, but would also serve as a permanent warning to India of the cost of challenging China, whether by intervention in Tibet, by directly confronting China and applying a revanchist military policy toward it, or by serving the interests of the United States and/or the USSR in the region in return for economic, military, and political assistance. India could consequently face a three-front confrontation with Pakistan in the West and East and China in the North. Such coordinated efforts would have a number of additional advantages. They could pose a credible threat to cut off India's restive northeastern region by slicing through an Achilles' heel of Indian defense, the narrow Siliguri corridor. At the same time, China's improved relations with Pakistan would provide an important link to the policy of isolating India in South Asia by building close relations with Nepal, Sri Lanka, Burma (Myanmar), and potentially Bhutan.

China also viewed Pakistan as a gateway to improving relations with the Arab world, as well as with two important traditional Pakistani allies, Iran and Turkey, both bordering on the Soviet Union and both key members of the CENTO alliance. This would open new diplomatic options for China and undermine the American architecture of encirclement and isolation of China. Moreover, by gaining legitimacy through Pakistan in the Muslim world, China hoped to reduce criticism of its policies toward the restive Muslim region of Xinjiang, where the Communist regime encountered ongoing resistance that had been encouraged by subversive Soviet intervention since the 1960s. A Sino-Pakistani border agreement would eliminate the chance that Pakistan might get involved in offering support to Muslim separatists in Xinjiang (Syed 1974, pp. 81–93; Vertzberger 1985, pp. 29–33).

From 1963 to the present, most of these motifs have persisted in various permutations, keeping the Sino-Pakistani relationship one of enduring importance to both parties.

THE TESTS OF CRISES AND WARS: THE 1965 WAR

The emergent friendship faced its first test during the 1965 war between India and Pakistan. China's position was one of all-out support for Pakistan, describing its measures as "just actions" taken to repulse Indian aggression. As the war progressed, China's intervention escalated to the point of accusing India of multiple violations of China's sovereignty along the Sino-Indian border. It intensified its threats to India by building up the number of troops on the Tibetan border and eventually gave India a seventy-two-hour ultimatum to reverse its alleged violations of China's territory. At the same time, China also challenged the United Nations' fairness in the conflict and accused the United States and the Soviet Union of conspiring with India against Pakistan. China's role served to strengthen Pakistan's position in the post-cease-fire negotiations and made the point that the PRC could not be ignored in addressing major conflicts in Asia, thus asserting China's regional great-power status. Yet the war's real political winner was the USSR, which hosted the 1966 Tashkent Conference between India and Pakistan that resulted in a return to the status quo ante (Vertzberger 1985, pp. 37–45).

The launching of the Cultural Revolution placed China's foreign policy on the back burner. Still, Pakistan was one of the few countries where the Chinese Foreign Ministry made sure the Cultural Revolution would not disrupt the relationship. As the PRC started to remedy the disastrous consequences of the Cultural Revolution, and as U.S. policy in South Asia tilted toward Pakistan, the latter became in 1969 a pivotal facilitator in the process of normalizing U.S.-PRC relations (Kissinger 1979, pp. 180–182). The emergent Sino-American strategic axis eliminated a major source of tension that had been inherent in Pakistan's foreign policy: the necessity to reconcile its close relations with China and the United States.

The 1971 War Although the Sino-American strategic axis would soon prove its ability to cooperate and coordinate positions at the United Nations, it failed in its attempts to prevent the 1971 Indo-Pakistan war that resulted in Pakistan's military defeat in East Pakistan and the establishment of the new state of Bangladesh. Yet the Sino-American coalition had managed to make it patently clear to India

that any attempt to dismember West Pakistan would be intolerable. Through the crisis and war of 1971, China expressed its support for Pakistan, though the extent of its willingness to take risks was probably misunderstood by the Pakistani leadership. China backed its supportive statements with intense diplomatic activity at the United Nations and provided military supplies. At the same time, China advised Pakistan to resolve peacefully its domestic crisis that resulted from the 1970 election victory of the East Pakistan–based Awami League, and refused to be drawn into the confrontation with India for fear of a Soviet military reaction following the signing of the August 1971 Indo-Soviet Treaty of Peace, Friendship, and Cooperation. Article 9 of the treaty especially seemed to imply a Soviet military role in a confrontation between India and a third party. China's reluctance to risk even a remote chance of a military conflict with the Soviets was due to the dismal domestic situation in China, which had not yet recovered from the excesses of the Cultural Revolution, and the poor condition of the Chinese military as revealed in the 1969 clashes on the Ussuri River. Consequently, and unlike the 1965 war, the 1971 war involved almost no actual incidents along the Chinese-Indian border, though on December 15, 1971, China protested several alleged incursions of Indian troops into its territory along the Sikkim-Tibet border.

With the surrender of Pakistan's army in East Pakistan, and a military stalemate on the western Indo-Pakistan front, the war came to an end. With its ally defeated, China's immediate concern was to reestablish a balance of power on the subcontinent by encouraging India and Pakistan to resolve their outstanding issues peacefully, including support for the Simla Accords. China also set out to redress the military imbalance of power on the subcontinent through extensive resupply of weapons to Pakistan's army, aimed at avoiding an India-dominated South Asia (Sisson and Rose 1990, pp. 154–205, 221–265; Vertzberger 1985, pp. 47–61).

The Soviet Invasion of Afghanistan, 1979 The Saur Revolution of April 1978 brought to power the People's Democratic Party of Afghanistan. As the party faced increasing difficulties and intense opposition to its reforms, and a growing insurgency in the countryside by mujahideen groups, the Soviet Army invaded Afghanistan in December 1979. Pakistan became the frontline state in a deadly struggle in which the Soviet Union was believed to have long-term designs directed toward South and Southwest Asia, the Indian Ocean region, and the Persian Gulf. China and the United States viewed these designs as having critical implications for the global balance of power, with one of the Soviets' major goals being the strategic encirclement of China with the help of Soviet allies India and Vietnam.

From that perspective, Pakistan's ability to resist the Soviet push to extend all the way to the "warm waters" of the Indian Ocean became a critical concern for both the United States and China. Yet China had only limited ability to provide Pakistan with the large-scale military and economic aid needed to bolster its position. China's role mostly involved political support for Pakistan's position in international forums such as the United Nations, sustaining criticism of the Soviet Union, and supplying arms to Pakistan's military and the mujahideen. Although the United States bore most of the burden of military-economic assistance to Pakistan and the mujahideen through the years of Soviet intervention until the withdrawal of Soviet troops in 1988 and 1989 (Malik 1994, pp. 268–274; Vertzberger 1985, pp. 119–139), China remained an important ally because of latent suspicions within Pakistan's military regime under President General Zia ul-Haq of U.S. credibility as an ally due to deep-seated tensions with the United States that were temporarily dormant but bound to surface sooner or later (e.g., over issues such as democracy and the development of nuclear weapons).

China's Position on the Kashmir Conflict The end of the Cold War did not abate the intractable conflict over Kashmir, which posed for China the ongoing risk of being drawn into an Indo-Pakistani war over Kashmir (as might have happened in 1965, 1971, 1986–1987, 1990, 1999, and 2001–2002). That both countries had acquired nuclear weapons made such risks unacceptable.

The other main factor affecting China's position was its changing relations with India. Clearly, China's policy on Kashmir had been nothing but prudently pragmatic. During the 1950s, China's position on Kashmir was one of strict neutrality. This changed to a pro-Pakistani stance from the early 1960s and through the 1970s; but since the mid-1980s, China's policy in Kashmir tilted toward the position that the conflict there is a bilateral issue between India and Pakistan and should be solved through peaceful means that reflect the aspirations of the people of India and Pakistan. China, therefore, has declined to support internationalization of the Kashmir dispute, and therefore did not interfere in the 1999 Kargil War.

At the same time, China emphasizes that improved relations with India will not affect its support for the core national interests of its "all-weather" ally Pakistan. This position, while carefully framed not to alienate India, entails a promise of not abandoning Pakistan, and a subtle warning to India not to misrepresent the strength of the Sino-Pakistani long-term entente. China thus seeks to impress on Pakistan and India the urgent need to maintain the cease-fire along the line of control, and encourages both states to take active steps (Garver 2001, pp. 237–334; Garver 2004; Yuan 2005) toward a permanent peaceful solution.

Since 2001, this position has assumed an important additional dimension, namely, China's concern over the threat of the destabilization of the region by terrorist groups such as al-Qaeda, the Taliban, and their affiliates. Thus, China and Pakistan perceive the war on terror as a critical area of common interest, especially in light of the challenge of the Uygur separatist movement and its links to al-Qaeda and the Taliban, which are believed to supply training and weapons and then infiltrate the Uygur terrorists back into China (Niazi 2007). There was also acute concern over the security of the 2008 Beijing Olympic Games. China has been pressing Islamabad to take a proactive policy against militant groups. This has also led to joint exercises and military operations to control both Uygur separatists in western China and Baluch separatism in Pakistan. China and Pakistan have also been cooperating in fighting transborder crime, especially narcotics trafficking, which is bound to remain a problem for both countries for years to come (Kondapalli 2006, pp. 234–237; Niazi 2007). This policy places China on the same side as the United States and its NATO allies. China has probably been as concerned as the United States over the damaging consequences of reconciliation with the extremists that was attempted by the newly elected 2008 government of the Pakistan People's Party (PPP) and the Pakistan Muslim League (Nawaz Sharif; PML/N), and would prefer the military to continue to guide Pakistan's policy toward groups representing the "three evils": extremism, terrorism, and separatism.

China's Military and Civilian Assistance A key component of China's approach to managing relations with Pakistan has been to provide aid and to encourage investment, trade, and technological transfer in both the civilian and military domains. Most salient and controversial since the late 1970s was China's ill-advised assistance to Pakistan's nuclear and missile development programs. These included nuclear weapons design and development and the transfer of dual use nuclear technology and materials, including to unsafeguarded facilities. The nuclear assistance to Pakistan goes back to the late 1970s. Most likely in light of Pakistan's defeat in 1971 and India's progress in developing nuclear capabilities, China believed that a nuclear balance would be a quick fix for the asymmetric Indo-Pakistani power relationship, which would stabilize the region and reduce the chances that China might be required to intervene militarily in South Asia. Instead, it created new and dangerous risks and vulnerabilities (Braun 2008, pp. 313–331). China's aid covered a broad range of items and activities, including reactors (such as the heavy-water Khusab reactor, which plays a key role in Pakistan's production of weapons grade plutonium), custom-made ring magnets (used for uranium enrichment), nuclear warhead design, the Chasma reprocessing facility and electrical

Chinese and Pakistani troops conducting joint anti-terrorist training exercises, Xinjiang, China, August 6, 2004. *Despite being the first Islamic state to recognize the People's Republic of China (PRC) in 1950, Pakistan remained an indifferent neighbor of China for several years thereafter, generally siding with the United States against the PRC. In the mid-1960s, Sino-Pakistani relations improved greatly, with each country relying on the other to balance the growing powers of India and Russia in the region.*
AP IMAGES

generating reactor, heavy-water supply, and fuel-fabrication services. China insists that its cooperation with Pakistan has been strictly for peaceful purposes, denying any assistance for the nuclear devices that were used in the 1998 nuclear tests. Nuclear cooperation may have been mutually beneficial; for example, China's scientists gained access to Pakistan's more advanced uranium enrichment technologies (Medeiros 2007, pp. 51, 65–71). In May 1996 China, under heavy U.S. pressure, committed to stop assistance to unsafeguarded nuclear facilities. Since the 1990s, China has also supplied Pakistan with material, equipment, and technologies, and helped to construct a ballistic-missile production facility in Rawalpindi (Medeiros 2007, pp. 150–151, 203–204).

Despite and probably because of China's important role in developing Pakistan's nuclear capabilities, the Indian nuclear tests of 1998 prompted a sharp response from China. Pakistan's subsequent tests were viewed with concern by China but were construed as a reaction to India's tests. The blame for widely opening the door to further proliferation was placed on India, dismissing India's argument that it was merely responding to the "China threat" (Frazier 2000, pp. 11–31).

China also remains the chief supplier of weapons to Pakistan's military. This includes supply and coproduction of fighters, trainers, transport aircraft, helicopters, tanks, frigates, and fast attack boats, as well as radar systems, antitank and surface to air missiles. Pakistan's military manufacturing industries were largely built with China's assistance. The two countries plan to further expand cooperation in developing advanced military systems such as AWACS planes (Kondapalli 2006, pp. 228–265; Vertzberger 1985, pp. 87–99). On the civilian side, there is strong emphasis on trade expansion, including border trade. It got a major boost with the signing of the Free Trade Agreement (FTA) in 2006, which set a goal of $15 billion worth of trade by 2011. In transportation, assistance in railway and road construction has been a major priority, with the two countries cooperating effectively since the 1960s, including in the construction of the

Karakoram Highway (KKH). China and Pakistan agreed to significantly upgrade the KKH, which will also serve to link western China and the Central Asian Republics to Pakistan and the Middle East, Africa, and other countries in South Asia, especially after the completion of the new deep-water Gwadar port in southwestern Pakistan, which is planned to become a major transportation hub (Garver 2005, pp. 205–218). These developments are also part of a broader agenda for Baluchistan, including the development of its rich mineral resources of iron ore, copper, gold, and lead-zinc mining projects in which Chinese firms play a leading role. The construction of a network of road links, in addition to its commercial and economic development value, could also have important strategic implications for present and future cooperation between the two militaries against India, as well as the containment of terrorists and separatists in Baluchistan and Xinjiang. In addition, China's cooperation and assistance extends to health, family planning, meteorological research, fisheries, vocational training, criminal justice, pesticide management, dam building, and space sciences. Economic development and trade expansion programs are supported by soft loans and by an active drive to expand investments by Chinese companies that in 2008 reached $4 billion. China has also agreed to assist in Pakistan's financial crisis bailout diplomacy in 2008. All these activities take place within a context of regular and frequent consultations and exchange of visits at the highest levels of both governments and their military forces.

RETROSPECT AND PROSPECTS

Sino-Pakistani entente has survived the test of time and dramatic international changes and has become more robust. This is essentially because of the underlying shared strategic interests and the sustainability and expansion of beneficial cooperation opportunities. Pakistan and China mutually perceive each other as an important long-term asset and consider their relationship as realpolitik at its best. Their shared interests are institutionalized in the landmark 2005 Treaty of Friendship, Cooperation, and Good-Neighborly Relations. Pakistan's geostrategic significance for Chinese economic and political interests in the Persian Gulf, South and Central Asia, and Africa, as well as for China's naval capabilities projection in the Indian Ocean region, has not diminished and is likely to grow. China and Pakistan's shared suspicions of India despite Sino-Indian rapprochement since 1988 are there to stay. And while China must contain the spread of Islamic extremism along and across its borders, it has at the same time, for economic and political reasons, to build bridges to moderate, modernist Muslim states, to which Pakistan remains a useful conduit.

These imperatives are of the greatest relevance for regional and global stability and by implication for continued vibrant economic growth in China and a sustainable Pakistani economy that is considered essential for avoiding the failed-state syndrome there. These factors make the Sino-Pakistani entente essential for both parties.

SEE ALSO *India, Relations with.*

BIBLIOGRAPHY

Ayub Khan, Mohammad. *Friends Not Masters: A Political Autobiography.* London: Oxford University Press, 1967.

Bhutto, Zulfikar Ali. *The Myth of Independence.* London: Oxford University Press, 1969.

Braun, Chaim. Security Issues Related to Pakistan's Future Nuclear Power Program. In *Pakistan's Nuclear Future: Worries beyond War*, ed. Henry D. Sokolski, 277–346. Carlisle, PA: U.S. Army War College, 2008.

Frazier, Mark W. China-India Relations Since Pokhran II: Assessing Sources of Conflict and Cooperation. *AccessAsia Review* 3, 2 (2000): 5–36.

Garver, John W. *Protracted Contest: Sino-Indian Rivalry in the Twentieth Century.* Seattle: University of Washington Press, 2001.

Garver, John W. China's Kashmir Policies. *India Review* 3, 1 (2004): 1–24.

Garver, John W. China's Influence in Central and South Asia. In *Power Shift: China and Asia's New Dynamics*, ed. David Shambaugh, 205–227. Berkeley: University of California Press, 2005.

Kissinger, Henry. *White House Years.* Boston: Little, Brown, 1979.

Kondapalli, Srikanth. The Chinese Military Eyes South Asia. In *Shaping China's Security Environment: The Role of the People's Liberation Army*, eds. Andrew Scobell and Larry H. Wortzel, 197–282. Carlisle, PA: U.S. Army War College, 2006.

Malik, Hafeez. *Soviet-Pakistan Relations and Post-Soviet Dynamics, 1947–92.* Houndmills, U.K.: Macmillan, 1994.

Medeiros, Evan S. *Reluctant Restraint: The Evolution of China's Nonproliferation Policies and Practices, 1980–2004.* Stanford, CA: Stanford University Press, 2007.

Niazi, Tarique. China, Pakistan, and Terrorism. *Foreign Policy in Focus (FPIF) Commentary.* July 16, 2007. http://www.fpif.org/fpiftxt/4384

Sisson, Richard, and Leo E. Rose. *War and Secession: Pakistan, India, and the Creation of Bangladesh.* Berkeley: University of California Press, 1990.

Syed, Anwar Hussain. *China and Pakistan: Diplomacy of an Entente Cordiale.* Amherst: University of Massachusetts Press, 1974.

Vertzberger, Yaacov Y. I. *China's Southwestern Strategy: Encirclement and Counterencirclement.* New York: Praeger, 1985.

Yuan Jingdong. China's Kashmir Policy. *China Brief* 5, 19 (2005). http://www.jamestown.org/programs/chinabrief/

Yaacov Y. I. Vertzberger

PAN TIANSHOU

1897–1971

Courtesy name: Dayi. A major twentieth-century Chinese artist, Pan Tianshou experimented with color, composition, scale, and finger painting to create paintings that transcend traditional practice and sensibility through their modern expressive power. His art was inspired by the loose and spirited styles of Shitao (1642–1707), Badashanren (1626–1705), Gao Qipei (1660–1734), the Eight Eccentrics of Yangzhou (eighteenth century), and Wu Changshi (1844–1927). He was also an important theorist and art educator.

Pan Tianshou was born in Ninghai, Zhejiang Province, into a well-educated and cultured family. He began to learn painting by copying from the *Jieziyuan huapu* (Mustard Seed Garden manual of painting). In 1915 he entered the Zhejiang First Normal College in Hangzhou and studied art and music with Li Shutong (1881–1942), one of the first Chinese students to study art in Japan. After graduation Pan taught at schools in Ninghai and Xiaofeng in Zhejiang before moving in 1923 to Shanghai, where he taught at Shanghai Nationalist Women's Industrial Art School (Shanghai Minguo Nüzi Gongyi Xuexiao), Shanghai Art College (Shanghai Meishu Zhuanmen Xuexiao), and Xinhua Art College (Xinhua Yishu Zhuanke Xuexiao). In 1926 he met an urgent pedagogical need by compiling from Chinese and Japanese sources *Zhongguo huihuashi* (A history of Chinese painting), the first Chinese-language textbook of its kind. In 1928 he was appointed head of the Chinese Painting Department at the National Academy of Art (Guoli Yishu Yuan) in Hangzhou, and the following year he travelled to Japan as part of an art-education delegation. After the outbreak of the Sino-Japanese War, Pan accompanied staff and students inland to Zhejiang, Jiangxi, Hunan, Guizhou, Yunnan, and Sichuan. He occupied a number of different teaching posts before serving as director of the academy from 1944 to 1947.

In the late 1940s he developed a distinctive style in painting birds and rocks, notable for daring composition, bold expression, and use of wet ink. Many of these paintings were created using his finger and nail. From 1950 to 1952 he spent periods in the countryside in Zhejiang and Anhui and created a number of figure paintings using the outline technique (*baimiao*) in an attempt to accord with the Communist Party's expectations of artists. In the 1950s he developed a new genre of painting that combined ink and intense color, together with a close-up view traditionally found in bird-and-flower painting. This genre, inspired by the natural environment rather than convention, was in accord with Mao Zedong's directive to "weed through the old to bring forth the new" (*tui chen chu xin*).

In 1957 he published an art-historical monograph on the figure painter Gu Kaizhi (c. 344–c. 406), and he was instrumental in having the Chinese Painting Department reinstated at the National Academy of Art in 1959. He was appointed principal of the academy in that same year and president of the Zhejiang Artists Association in 1961. In the late 1950s and 1960s Pan Tianshou, like his contemporaries, painted many artworks for government officials and institutions. He also created works for publishing houses and the Hangzhou Municipal Parks and Cultural Heritage Management Bureau (Hangzhou yuanlin wenwu guanli ju) and a series of monumental ink paintings, including finger paintings, for hotels and public buildings.

In 1962 an exhibition of paintings by Pan Tianshou was held in Hangzhou and at the art gallery of the Central Academy of Fine Arts in Beijing, initiated by Kang Sheng, member of the Communist Party Central Committee. But this recognition was not sufficient to prevent Pan from being vilified during the Cultural Revolution (1966–1969). On June 3, 1966, Pan Tianshou was accused of being a "reactionary academic authority," and an exhibition of "black paintings" confiscated from the family home was held at the academy. Pan Tianshou was paraded through the streets of Hangzhou and Ninghai and publicly humiliated. He died in a hospital in Hangzhou on September 5, 1971, at the age of 75. Pan Tianshou was politically rehabilitated in 1977, and the following year a memorial service was held. A memorial museum, located in his former residence, was opened to the public in 1981, and in 1991 it was refurbished with funds provided by the Ministry of Culture. The Pan Tianshou Memorial Museum is administered by the China National Art Academy in Hangzhou.

SEE ALSO *Art Schools and Colleges; Chinese Painting (guohua); Epigraphic School of Art; Wu Changshi (Wu Junqing).*

BIBLIOGRAPHY

Lu Xin. *Pan Tianshou*. Beijing: Zhongguo Qingnian Chubanshe, 1997.

Lu Xin, ed. *Pan Tianshou yanjiu* [Pan Tianshou: Life and work]. 2 vols. Hangzhou: Zhejiang Meishu Xueyuan Chubanshe, 1989–1997.

Pan Gongkai, ed. *Pan Tianshou shuhua ji* [Collected calligraphy and paintings of Pan Tianshou]. 2 vols. Hangzhou: Zhejiang Renmin Meishu Chubanshe, 1996.

Pan Gongkai, ed. *Pan Tianshou tan yi lu* [Pan Tianshou on art]. Hangzhou: Zhejinga Renmin Meishu Chubanshe, 1997.

Pan Tianshou. *Zhongguo huihua shi* [A history of Chinese painting]. Shanghai: Shanghai Renmin Meishu Chubanshe, 1983.

Roberts, Claire. Tradition and Modernity: The Life and Art of Pan Tianshou (1897–1971). *East Asian History*, nos. 15/16 (June/December 1998): 67–96.

Claire Roberts

PAN YULIANG
1895–1977

Born in 1895 under the name of Chen Xiuqing, she later changed it to Zhang Yuliang. She is arguably as famous for her remarkable artistic achievements as for the dramatic events surrounding her life, portrayed in a 1994 movie starring Gong Li, *Hua hun* (*A Soul Haunted by Painting*).

Sold at age fourteen to a brothel after the early death of her parents, she was bought out to freedom by the wealthy official Pan Zanhua, whom she married as a secondary wife in 1913 and in gratitude to whom she changed her family name to Pan. In 1917 she began studying painting in Shanghai under the artist Hong Ye, and in 1918 she entered the Shanghai Tuhua Meishu Xueyuan (Shanghai Academy of Pictorial Art), where she studied under Wang Jiyuan and Zhu Qizhan. In 1921 she traveled to France, where she attended the Institut Franco-Chinois in Lyon and took courses at the local École des Beaux Arts. In 1924 she enrolled at the École Nationale Supérieure des Beaux Arts in Paris in the atelier of the painter Lucien Simon. In 1926 she entered the Accademia di Belle Arti in Rome, where she studied under the painter Umberto Coromaldi and began learning sculpture. In 1928 she returned to China for her first solo exhibition.

In 1929 she became the chair of the Oil Painting Department of the Shanghai Meishu Zhuanmen Xuexiao (Shanghai Art School) and took part in the First All-China National Exhibition. In 1930 she begun teaching at the Art Department of the Central University, Nanjing, where Xu Beihong was also teaching and where she would remain until 1935. Until 1937, the year she went back to France, she took part in various group and solo exhibitions in Nanjing and Shanghai. A catalog of her work was published in Shanghai in 1934. In 1936 one of her oil paintings was destroyed, and an insulting note referring to her past in the brothel was left next to it. In 1937 she returned to Paris, where she participated in the Exposition Universelle. She was never to return to her country, despite numerous attempts and her ongoing intention, as expressed in letters to her family. In 1945 she was elected president of the Association des Artistes Chinoises en France and participated in two exhibitions of Chinese painting in Paris, at the Musée Cernuschi and at the École des Beaux Arts. In 1953 a major solo exhibition of more than a hundred of her works—including paintings, sculptures, woodblock prints, and drawings—was organized at the Galerie d'Orsay in Paris. During the rest of her life and until the time of her death she participated in group and solo exhibitions, the Salons des Independents, and various artistic events held in the French capital and abroad. In 1963 she was invited to exhibit in San Francisco and New York. In the last exhibition in which she participated, Quatre Artistes Chinoises Contemporaines (Four Contemporary Chinese Women Painters), at the Musée Cernuschi in the spring of 1977, she was actively involved in the selection and curation. She died on July 22 of the same year.

Pan's oil paintings include still lifes, portraiture, self-portraiture, and nudes, the last genre being the most numerous. Her nudes are striking for their intimate atmosphere and the ease exhibited by her subjects, devoid of the eroticism normally associated with this genre. The effortlessness and the virtuosity of the lines executed with Chinese ink and brush technique, often employed in the last part of her career in her depiction of the female body, make Pan Yuliang one of the most successful and original painters of nudes in the history of Chinese painting.

SEE ALSO *Art, History of: 1911–1949; Women in the Visual Arts.*

BIBLIOGRAPHY
He Mengde [Christophe Comental], Jia Defang, et al. *Pan Yuliang.* Taibei: Yishujia Chubanshe, 2007.

Huan Xiuying, Li Zhiyi, Wang Dandan, et al., eds. *Huahun Pan Yuliang* [A soul haunted by painting, Pan Yuliang]. Taibei: Minsheng Bao, 2006.

Mao Yiwei, ed. *Pan Yuliang meishu zuopin xuan* [Selected artworks by Pan Yuliang]. Nanjing: Jiangsu Meishu Chubanshe, 1988.

Shi Nan. *Yidai huahun: Pan Yuliang* [A generation's soul haunted by painting: Pan Yuliang]. Beijing: Zuojia Chubanshe, 2006.

Wang Xutong, Shen Yizheng, et al., eds. *Zhongguo-Bali: Zaoqi lü Fa huajia huigu zhan.* [China-Paris: Seven Chinese painters who studied in France]. Taibei: Shili Meishu Guan, 1988.

Francesca Dal Lago

PAN-ASIANISM

Pan-Asianism originated as an ideology in Japan during the mid-nineteenth century in response to the encroaching Western imperial powers. The basic tenet of pan-Asianism is that Asian countries, especially those with shared Confucian and Sinic cultural heritages, should be united under Japanese leadership to resist Western imperial advancements. Many Japanese pan-Asianists regarded China as the key element to the success of pan-Asian enterprise, so early pan-Asian ideas centered very much on the idea of Sino-Japanese alliance.

This idea of cooperative Asian solidarity based on shared cultural heritage and common destiny initially appealed to many Chinese political and intellectual elites across the political spectrum. The most famous Chinese pan-Asianist was Sun Yat-sen, who formed enduring and intimate connections with Japanese pan-Asianists of various political persuasions including the liberal pan-Asianist Miyazaki

Torazō (1970–1922), the ultra-nationalist leader Toyama Mitsuru (1855–1944), and Japanese prime minister Inukai Tsuyoshi (1855–1932). Sun understood and interpreted pan-Asianism in the broader context of the threats of Western imperialism and revival of Asian civilization, and especially the renaissance of the Chinese civilization. Sun thought of Japan as a partner in the process of modernizing China and resisting Western imperialism. Essentially, he defined pan-Asianism in Sino centric terms and in line with China's national interest. Sun's ideas were cordially received by some Japanese pan-Asianists who shared the belief that the revival of China was the key to success of a new pan-Asian order, but this initial cordiality was gradually eclipsed by Japan's own growing stature and its belief in its manifest destiny to lead Asia.

Another influential Chinese pan-Asianist was Zhang Taiyan (1868–1936), a famous classical scholar and revolutionary. In an early article, "Lun yazhou yi zi wei chunchi" (Asian countries [Japan and China] should be as close to one another as the lips and teeth), he advocated for mutual dependence and assistance between China and Japan. He regarded tsarist Russia as the common enemy of both China and Japan, threatening the survival of both countries. In his other voluminous early writings he vividly described a deep racial and cultural bond between China and Japan and argued that in that time of Western imperialist expansion, only Japan shared the same destiny with China. The confrontations between China and Japan were brushed aside as benign fraternal disputes that posed no threat to a future relationship. However, this sense of Sino-Japanese fraternity gradually gave way to a deep sense of disappointment and outrage over Japan's adaptation of its own brand of imperialism toward its Asian brethren, in league with the white imperialists. Eventually, Zhang vehemently denounced Japanese imperialism and abandoned his early vision of Sino-Japanese alliance; instead, he came to believe that a Sino-Indian alliance would form the new nexus for Asian revival.

The early Chinese acceptance of pan-Asianism evaporated in the face of Japan's growing imperialist ambitions in continental Asia, especially after the infamous Twenty-one Demands in 1919, which sparked a nationwide student protest and outrage. Gradually, Japanese pan-Asianism was equated with imperialism. In a famous 1919 editorial, "Da yaxiya zhuyi yu xin yaxiya zhuyi" (On great Asianism and new Asianism), Li Dazhao (1888–1927) wrote that Japanese pan-Asianism was nothing but a crude imperialist design on China draped decorously in the cloth of "same letter and same race." Even the most sympathetic Chinese pan-Asianist, Sun Yat-sen, showed signs of deep frustration, urging the Japanese in 1924 to embrace the East's "kingly way" (Chinese: *wangdao*), or rule through benevolence and abandon the "despotic way" (*badao*) of the West.

Ironically, a decade after Sun's death, Japanese ideologues used pan-Asian rhetoric to justify its aggression into China and legitimize its "Asian Monroe Doctrine." Sun's kingly way concept was used to serve as the philosophical foundation for the new Japanese puppet state in Manchuria. The Chinese collaborationist government under the aegis of Wang Jinwei also attempted to assume Sun's pan-Asian mantle in an effort to legitimize its regime, and Wang actively promoted the Japanese-backed East Asian alliance movement through the 1940s. The taint of its association with Japanese imperialism in the 1930s and 1940s has largely overshadowed pan-Asianism's appeal to the Chinese before the 1930s.

BIBLIOGRAPHY

Duara, Prasenjit. Transnationalism and the Predicament of Sovereignty: Modern China, 1900–1945. *American Historical Review* 102, 4 (October 1997): 1030–1051.

Jansen, Marius B. *The Japanese and Sun Yat-sen*. Cambridge, MA: Harvard University Press, 1954.

Karl, Rebecca E. Creating Asia: China in the World at the Beginning of the Twentieth Century. *American Historical Review* 103, 4 (October 1998): 1096–1118.

Yuan Cai

PANG XUNQIN
1906–1985

Pang Xunqin (also known as Huinkin Pang) is revered as a modernist oil painter and designer. As an avid advocate of modernism in Chinese art, he is remembered for returning from Paris with a fervor to change China's art world. Despite cataclysmic political obstructions that hindered realization of many of his dreams, Pang Xunqin's efforts to establish China's first modernist painting society in 1931 and China's first academy of design in 1956 had lasting effects.

Pang was born in Changshu County in Jiangsu Province in 1906. As a child, he studied the classics and also began studying painting with private tutors. Pang later enrolled in Zhendan University (Université Aurore) in Shanghai to study medicine. While there, he enrolled in French classes and took painting lessons with a Russian oil painter. In 1925 Pang left school prior to graduation and traveled to Paris. While in Paris, he made the decision to become a painter and applied to the École des Beaux-Arts, but was not accepted. Instead, he entered the Académie Julian, where he began basic training in Western art. From 1927 to 1929, he studied at the Académie de la Grande Chaumière, where he recalled producing thousands of ink drawings.

After leaving the Académie Julian and exhibiting with friends in minor exhibits, he returned to China in 1930, where he taught at several art schools in Shanghai. In 1931 Pang and a Japanese-educated fellow artist, Ni Yide (1901–1970), established the first modernist art society in China, the Juelanshe, with the English name of "Storm Society." The word *juelan* refers to a crushing, forceful wave and implies a powerful impact and shock. This directly corresponded with the society's aim to develop a new atmosphere in the artistic community of twentieth-century China. The society held five very successful and well-publicized exhibitions from 1931 through 1935, but was not financially viable, and then found its artistic ideals overturned by the exigencies of war with Japan.

The only female member of the group was an artist known as Qiu Ti (1906–1958), who won the Storm Society Award in their second exhibition. Qiu Ti was a native of Fujian and had graduated from the Shanghai Art Academy in 1928. She traveled abroad to study art in Tokyo and came back to China in 1929, returning to the Shanghai Art Academy for graduate studies. She met Pang Xunqin at one of his exhibits in Shanghai and became more acquainted with the modernist art community in which he was active. The two were married in 1932.

As the war with Japan loomed, the Juelanshe dissolved and Pang joined the staff of the National Art School in Beijing in 1936. After the Japanese invasion of 1937, Pang Xunqin, Qiu Ti, and their young daughter and son fled to Shanghai, then to several other cities before finally settling in Kunming. In Kunming, Pang accepted a position with the National Museum working with the costume and decorative arts of the Miao people. This appointment took him to Guizhou to collect materials for the museum's collection and awakened a lifelong enthusiasm for China's indigenous design. He made countless careful illustrations of design motifs he found in his fieldwork, many of which are reflected in his own paintings of the 1940s.

Throughout the 1940s, Pang held various teaching positions in western China and then on the coast. His first appointment during this period was at the Provincial Art College in Chengdu. He then moved on to the National Sun Yat-sen University in Guangzhou, and finally to the National Academy of the Arts in Hangzhou, where he headed the department of applied arts. After the founding of the People's Republic of China, he worked to establish the Central Academy of Arts and Crafts in Beijing (now Qinghua University College of Arts) and became its founding director when it opened in 1956. Qiu Ti also contributed to the academy, working as a researcher for the school.

Shortly after the establishment of the academy, Pang Xunqin's career as an artist and teacher changed dramatically. In an attempt to suppress sentiment against the Chinese Communist Party, the Anti-Rightist campaign was launched, with many artists, including Pang Xunqin, as targets. Wrongly denounced as committing ideological crimes, his life and career suffered greatly until his case was overturned twenty-two years later. It was amid the pressure of this crisis, in 1958, that Qiu Ti died of a heart attack.

"Rightists" were particularly targeted during the Cultural Revolution (1966–1969), and in an effort to protect himself and his family from further accusations, Pang Xunqin destroyed many of his own early modernist paintings before they could be seized as evidence by the Red Guard. Nevertheless, the many reproductions of his paintings in magazines of the 1930s provide a record of his influential early work. Fortunately, a manuscript of design studies he sent to Europe for publication in 1944 was rescued by his British friend, the art historian Michael Sullivan, and returned to him in good condition after the Cultural Revolution.

Pang Xunqin exhibited work for the first time in many years at the New Spring Art Exhibition (Xinchun Huazhan) in February 1979. This exhibition of nonpolitical art, mainly by senior artists, marked the first open rejection of Cultural Revolution artistic standards by the mainstream Beijing arts community. Pang Xunqin died several years later, in 1985, after writing his autobiography. As China's modernist past is rediscovered by younger generations, his leading role in its history and his early career have been rediscovered, and his standing in the history of Chinese art has steadily risen.

SEE ALSO *Commercial Art: Graphic Design; Folk Art; Modernist Art of the 1920s and 1930s.*

BIBLIOGRAPHY

Croizier, Ralph. Post-Impressionists in Pre-War Shanghai: The Juelanshe (Storm Society) and the Fate of Modernism in Republican China. In *Modernity in Asian Art*, ed. John Clark, 135–154. Sydney: Wild Peony, 1993.

Danzker, Jo-Anne Birnie, Ken Lum, and Zheng Shengtian, eds. *Shanghai Modern, 1919–1945.* Ostfildern-Ruit, Germany: Hatje Cantz, 2004.

Sullivan, Michael. *Chinese Art in the Twentieth Century.* Berkeley: University of California Press, 1959.

Sullivan, Michael. *Art and Artists of Twentieth-century China.* Berkeley: University of California Press, 1996.

Sun Ping. *Pang Xunqin: Pang Jun, Pang Dao.* Shijiazhuang Shi, PRC: Hebei Jiaoyu Chubanshe, 2002.

Christina Wei-Szu Burke Mathison

PANTHAY REBELLION, 1855–1873

SEE *Muslim Uprisings.*

PARKS

SEE *Gardens and Parks; Urban China: Urban Planning since 1978.*

PARSIS

Parsis are the descendants of Persian Zoroastrians who moved from Gujarat, India, to the booming port of Bombay (Mumbai) throughout the eighteenth and nineteenth centuries. During this period, Parsis forged strong links with the British Empire and skillfully employed the commercial experience they had acquired in the Indian Ocean trade to become one of the leading commercial communities in Bombay.

Parsi merchants who acted as brokers for the East India Company as well as for British private traders enriched themselves through the so-called India-China trade. Quick fortunes were made by smuggling Indian opium to Guangzhou (Canton), the Chinese port where foreigners were allowed to carry out maritime trade under a tightly regulated monopolistic regime. By the early 1830s, Guangzhou had developed into an important node of the Parsi trade diaspora. According to one account, as many as seventy Parsi men sojourned in the city during the trading season; a priest took care of the spiritual needs of the community, and funds were collected for philanthropic endeavors. Parsis could also relax in Macau, where they had established recreational premises.

The obsolete Canton trade system was suppressed at the end of the Opium War (1839–1842) when the Treaty of Nanjing sanctioned the cession of Hong Kong to the British and the opening of five cities, the first treaty ports, to foreign commerce. Parsi traders based in Guangzhou immediately seized the opportunity to enlarge their commercial interests in other areas of China, and they extended their trading networks to nearby Hong Kong and as far north as Shanghai, thus establishing an interconnected commercial web that enabled them to keep their prominent position among foreign traders in China. At a later stage, Parsis also started to operate in Tianjin and Beijing.

After the opium trade became legal in 1858, Parsis continued to trade in the Indian variety of the drug, though Baghdadi Jews replaced them as the main suppliers of the drug to the Chinese market. Once the legality of the opium commerce started to be questioned toward the end of the nineteenth century, Parsis and Baghdadi Jews together defended this line of business and even founded a cartel in Shanghai that monopolized the local distribution of the drug before the ban on the trade at the end of 1917.

The Parsis' economic and financial interests in China were wide. They set up brokerage firms, pioneered the financial sector, especially in Hong Kong, and were involved in the import-export commerce of commodities, such as cotton yarn. Yet, as a whole, in the latter part of the nineteenth century, they failed to capitalize on their mercantile expertise and adopted an increasingly defensive commercial strategy. Their commercial decline might be partly attributed to their reluctance to choose China as their permanent abode. That said, women and children did take residence in Chinese cities in the twentieth century, and, according to a reliable statistic, sixty males, thirty-one females, and thirty-one children resided in Shanghai in 1934, making the city China's major Parsi center.

Though small, Parsi communities in China were well organized. Parsi institutions took care of the religious and social needs of their members and also collected funds for needy coreligionists in India and Iran, as well as for poor Chinese. The founding of the People's Republic of China in 1949 marked the end of the Parsi presence in China, except in the former British colony of Hong Kong, where a small community has continued to thrive until the present.

SEE ALSO *Opium, 1800–1950.*

BIBLIOGRAPHY

Betta, Chiara. The Trade Diaspora of Baghdadi Jews: From Ottoman Baghdad to China's Treaty Ports. In *Diaspora Entrepreneurial Networks: Five Centuries of History*, ed. Ina Baghdiantz McCabe, Gelina Harlaftis, and Ioanna Penepelou Minoglou, 269–285. Oxford and New York: Berg, 2005.

Hinnells, John R. *The Zoroastrian Diaspora: Religion and Migration.* New York: Oxford University Press, 2005.

Karaka, Dosabhai Framji. *History of the Parsis: Including Their Manners, Customs, Religion, and Present Position.* London: Macmillan, 1884.

Markovits, Claude. Indian Communities in China, c. 1842–1949. In *New Frontiers: Imperialism's New Communities in East Asia, 1842–1952*, ed. Robert Bickers and Christian Henriot, 55–74. Manchester, U.K.: Manchester University Press, 2000.

Chiara Betta

PEACE SETTLEMENT AFTER WORLD WAR II

The outbreak of war in Europe in 1939 brought China into alliance with the United States and Great Britain. Their alliance was further strengthened after the German attack on the Soviet Union in June 1941 and the start of the Pacific War in December 1941. China's status remained somewhat ambiguous, however, given the relative weakness of its military position and the fact that its fate was seen to lie largely in the hands of the British and the Americans. China took part in some of the major wartime conferences, including Cairo in 1943, but not others, notably Yalta in 1945.

The Cairo Declaration, later cited in the Potsdam Declaration (July 1945), stipulated that territories such as Manchuria, Taiwan, and the Pescadores would be returned to China upon Japan's defeat, and that Korea should gain its independence. However, at the Yalta Conference (February 4–11, 1945) Winston Churchill, Joseph Stalin, and Franklin D. Roosevelt agreed on a secret clause allowing for the Soviet Union's entry into the war against Japan within two or three months of a German surrender. The Soviet Union would also regain the rights it enjoyed before the Russo-Japanese War (1904–1905). In addition, the status quo in Outer Mongolia would be preserved, and the Soviet Union would be granted the Kurile Islands.

The Soviets invaded Manchuria on August 9, 1945. They arrested Emperor Kang De (Pu Yi, 1906–1967), which led to the disbanding of the puppet state of Manchukuo. They also handed stockpiles of weapons to the Communists who had moved their forces into the area in advance of Chiang Kai-shek (Jiang Jieshi). Soviet and Outer Mongolian troops also were active in Xinjiang and Inner Mongolia, where the Nationalists struggled to regain control. U.S. assistance in moving Nationalist troops to north and east China to accept the Japanese surrender after August 15 was only partially successful. Ultimately, the Nationalists were unable to reestablish authority across the country; some warlords retained power, and puppet troops were allowed to remain in place as a means of preventing Communist control. Hong Kong and Macau reverted to the control of the United Kingdom and Portugal, respectively.

Class A trials dealing with crimes against peace were held in Tokyo (the International Military Tribunal of the Far East) between 1946 and 1948, and military tribunals were held across Asia to try Class B and C criminals (those accused of war crimes and crimes against humanity). Trials were held in thirteen locations across China and Taiwan between 1946 and 1949 by the Nationalists, and later in Shenyang in 1956 by the Communists. The Tokyo trial has been criticized for marginalizing the Asian experience of the war and for failing to charge those responsible for military sexual slavery, forced labor, and chemical and biological warfare. The Nationalist trials also were overshadowed by the trials of Chinese collaborators and the burgeoning civil war.

Japan made partial reparations, in the form of machinery and equipment, to China between 1948 and 1949 under the plan put forward by U.S. president Harry Truman's adviser Edwin W. Pauley. However, the reparations program was cancelled in 1949 by the U.S. government, which came to view the reparations as detrimental to Japan's economic recovery.

Due to differences of opinion between the British and U.S. governments on the question of recognition of China, neither the People's Republic of China (PRC) nor the Republic of China (ROC) signed the San Francisco Peace Treaty in 1951, which signalled the end of the state of war. Amid growing Cold War tension, Japan was pressured by the United States to normalize relations with the ROC and subsequently, in April 1952, signed the Treaty of Peace in which Taiwan waived the right to demand reparations from Japan. The PRC and Japan normalized relations in 1972 with the signing of the Joint Statement, in which the former renounced its demand for war indemnities. The Treaty of Peace and Friendship was signed in 1978.

In settling with Japan, both the ROC and PRC governments focused more on dealing with strategic issues of the time than with reparations. However, starting in the 1990s PRC and Taiwanese (and indeed other Asian) citizens began to seek apologies and compensation through Japanese courts for their suffering at the hands of the Japanese imperial army. More than sixty cases have been brought against the Japanese government and companies by former forced laborers, so-called comfort women (military sex slaves), and victims of the Nanjing massacre (1937–1938), indiscriminate bombing, and Japan's biological and chemical warfare program. The majority have been rejected by the Japanese courts, although some Japanese companies involved in the use of forced labor have agreed to settle out of court. A number of cases continue to be fought in the Japanese courts.

The perceived failure to effect full reconciliation, legally, materially, and morally, continues to pose problems in the political relationship between the PRC and Japan.

BIBLIOGRAPHY

Dower, John. *Embracing Defeat: Japan in the Aftermath of World War II*. London and New York: Penguin, 1999.

Fairbank, John K., and Albert Feuerwerker, eds. *Republican China 1912–1949, Part 2*. Vol. 13 of *The Cambridge History of China*. London and New York: Cambridge University Press, 1986.

Pepper, Suzanne. *Civil War in China: The Political Struggle, 1945–1949*. Lanham, MD: Rowman and Littlefield, 1999.

Piccigallo, Philip R. *The Japanese on Trial: Allied War Crimes Operations in the East, 1945–1951*. Austin: University of Texas Press, 1979.

Caroline Rose

PEASANTRY, 1800–1900

China was largely a peasant society in the late imperial period. In 1800 the great majority of Chinese people were farmers living in villages, using traditional labor-intensive techniques on very small parcels of land. This is regarded as a fact of central importance to the processes of social change that China confronted in the nineteenth century and to the character of the Communist revolution that was to ensue in the twentieth century. What is a peasant?

And what relevance does this fact about Chinese society have for political and social behavior?

FACTS AND FIGURES

A peasant is a smallholding farmer, producing crops for family consumption and for market exchange, using family labor throughout the farming cycle (Netting 1993). Peasants live in villages; they engage in face-to-face relations with neighboring farmers; they possess a diverse range of cultural and religious beliefs and practices; and they fall within a diverse range of social networks and local organizations (kinship organizations, temples, labor-sharing networks). Zhao Gang (Chao Kang) estimates China's urban population in 1820, defined as people living in towns and cities with a population greater than two thousand, at 6.9 percent of China's population of 353 million (1986, p. 58). So the farm population exceeded 90 percent of the total population in the early nineteenth century. The basic unit of production in Chinese agriculture was the family, and family subsistence was dependent upon the labor efforts of all members of the family, including young children. In *Land and Labor in China* (1966), economic historian R. H. Tawney (1880–1962) describes this system of production in the early twentieth century, and his description is probably accurate for the previous several centuries as well.

The heart of China's peasant society in late imperial China in 1800 was in the Yangzi Delta, where an intensive rice economy supported the highest population density of any region in the early nineteenth century. Advanced rice cultivation and a dense network of waterways produced a combination that permitted the growth of a very large population based on farming. The dry farming of the North China Plain constituted a second large zone of Chinese peasant culture and population. The Lower and Middle Yangzi regions together possessed a population of about 150 million in 1843, and the North China region had about 112 million people at that time. The population density of the Lower Yangzi (348 persons per square kilometer) was more than double that of North China (150 persons per square kilometer) and the Middle Yangzi region (120 persons per square kilometer) (Naquin and Rawski 1987, p. 213). These population densities reflected the highly intensive agriculture that was characteristic of Chinese farming. Philip C. C. Huang (Huang Zongzhi 1985) and Ramon Myers (1980) provide extensive descriptions of the farm economy of North China, and Li Bozhong (1998) provides a definitive analysis of the farm economy of the Lower Yangzi region.

LOCAL AND REGIONAL DIVERSITY

"Peasant society" was not socially homogeneous. Small traders, martial arts instructors, bandits, minor officials, necromancers, priests, moneylenders, elites, scholars, and large landowners all played roles within peasant society, but they were not peasants. Their incomes derived ultimately from the farm economy, but their lifestyles, standards of living, values, and social status were all distinct from those of peasant farmers. In short, "peasant society" consists of many people who are not themselves "peasants."

Nor can peasants themselves be considered a homogeneous category. Farming in late imperial China was undertaken in a great range of social and natural environments, from the rice paddies and deltas of the Lower Yangzi, to the wheat farms of Hebei and Shandong in the north, to the mountainous plots of Yunnan in the southwest. These different environments fostered diverse local societies. Substantial cultural, social, political, and ecological variation pertained within the large population of farmers.

Chinese peasant farmers cultivated extremely small parcels of land, using techniques of cultivation that involved high land productivity and low labor productivity. Li Bozhong (1998) has provided careful estimates of the farm economy in the Lower Yangzi Delta in the eighteenth century. He describes a system of rice farming that made extensive use of human labor, fertilizer, and water control to yield a high level of grain output per hectare. He documents as well the extent of cultivation of cotton and silk in the region—important complements to the income stream for peasant families. The primary form of land tenure in the Lower Yangzi region was tenancy, and Li estimates that ground rents were about 50 percent of the chief crop (1998, p. 127).

The intensive use of human labor was the most important characteristic of the Chinese peasant economy. Li describes the many stages of labor involved in rice cultivation in the Lower Yangzi Delta: land preparation, transplanting, weeding, harvesting and threshing, and irrigating (1998, p. 73). Farming involved all members of the family, and the work was time-consuming and exhausting. Cultivation techniques were continually refined over centuries to produce the most efficient possible combination of irrigation, fertilizer application, pest and weed eradication, and cropping decisions. The marginal product of labor was extremely low, since the return of yet another catty of rice would justify a substantial additional investment of labor time on the part of an underutilized family member. Mark Elvin describes this system of agriculture as one that has approached a "high-level equilibrium trap," in which high-yield agriculture just barely suffices to satisfy the food needs of the population (1973, p. 285). Others describe the system as a highly efficient one, and one that permitted a standard of living for rural society that was comparable to that of English farmers in the early nineteenth century (Pomeranz 2000).

Conditions of farm life were different in North China, but the intensity of farm labor was comparable. Huang (1985) uses a variety of sources to estimate the features of the wheat peasant economy in North China. He finds that the average landholding was under 15 *mu* (one hectare). Twenty-five percent of households were made up of landless workers or tenants. But the majority of peasant families were smallholders, and the primary forms of surplus extraction they confronted were taxes and interest. Villages were more important than in eastern China, according to Huang, and the state had a more effective system of tax collection than in the rice-producing region of the Lower Yangzi.

SOCIETY AND POLITICS

Chinese rural society was primarily organized around farming villages and hamlets. As G. William Skinner (1971) has demonstrated, the landscape was structured by a network of cities, towns, villages, and hamlets, with periodic markets and urban products and services; but the great majority of the Chinese population in 1800 resided in places with a population of less than five hundred. Peasant society was organized around face-to-face relations in small villages, with social relationships among families that extended over multiple generations. Labor-sharing arrangements, burial societies, kinship organizations and temples, and heterodox religious societies were among the forms of social cooperation and interaction that characterized Chinese peasant society.

Because the effective reach of the state was limited to the county yamen for most purposes, village politics were subject to a variety of local influences. The informal realities of village elites, on the one hand, and bandits, salt smugglers, martial arts practitioners, and other interstitial social groups, on the other, defined a space of power relationships within which ordinary peasant families lived and worked. Rural society in China was a volatile social world, and local conflicts could spark rebellions in times of crisis.

The nineteenth-century rebellions (Taiping, Nian, Panthay, Dongan, among others) had different origins but were in general related to pressure on the land. There is little disagreement that the Chinese peasant economy had achieved an efficient combination of technologies, labor, and crops as of 1800. But there is also little disagreement that population increase had stretched this economy to its limits by midcentury. A steady erosion of the environment—soil, water, silting of rivers—narrowed the margin of subsistence in rural society. In the most densely populated regions of the country, population pressure on the land was an increasingly significant source of crisis at the local level. Internal migrations served to export the crisis from core to peripheral areas. Foreign wars, economic change associated with the altered international environment, and natural disasters were other contributing factors in the series of peasant rebellions that remain a defining feature of China's nineteenth-century history.

SEE ALSO *Education: Education in Rural Areas; Illiteracy; Land Tenure since 1800; Migrant Workers; Peasants; Poverty; Provincial and Subprovincial Government Structure since 1949: Villages; Standard of Living; Taxation and Fiscal Policies, 1800–1912.*

BIBLIOGRAPHY

Buck, John Lossing. *Chinese Farm Economy*. Chicago: University of Chicago Press, 1930.

Elvin, Mark. *The Pattern of the Chinese Past*. Stanford, CA: Stanford University Press, 1973.

Elvin, Mark. *The Retreat of the Elephants: An Environmental History of China*. New Haven, CT: Yale University Press, 2004.

Huang Zongzhi (Philip C. C. Huang). *The Peasant Economy and Social Change in North China*. Stanford, CA: Stanford University Press, 1985.

Li Bozhong. *Agricultural Development in Jiangnan, 1620–1850*. London: Palgrave Macmillan, 1998.

Myers, Ramon H. North China Villages during the Republican Period: Socio-economic Relationships. *Modern China* 6, 3 (1980): 243–266.

Naquin, Susan, and Evelyn S. Rawski. *Chinese Society in the Eighteenth Century*. New Haven, CT: Yale University Press, 1987.

Netting, Robert McC. *Smallholders, Householders: Farm Families and the Ecology of Intensive, Sustainable Agriculture*. Stanford, CA: Stanford University Press, 1993.

Perdue, Peter C. *Exhausting the Earth: State and Peasant in Hunan, 1500–1850*. Cambridge, MA: Council on East Asian Studies, Harvard University, 1987.

Pomeranz, Kenneth. *The Great Divergence: China, Europe, and the Making of the Modern World Economy*. Princeton, NJ: Princeton University Press, 2000.

Skinner, G. William. Chinese Peasants and the Closed Community: An Open and Shut Case. *Comparative Studies in Society and History* 13 (1971): 270–281.

Tawney, R. H. *Land and Labor in China*. Boston: Beacon, 1966.

Zhao Gang (Chao, Kang). *Man and Land in Chinese History: An Economic Analysis*. Stanford, CA: Stanford University Press, 1986.

Daniel Little

PEASANTRY SINCE 1900

The term *peasant* is controversial in Chinese studies because it implies a status closer to serf than to freehold or tenant farmer, whereas the word *farmer* suggests someone too much like a small businessman to be appropriate for the average cultivator in twentieth-century China. The fact that "peasant" is now generally used as the translation for *nongmin* has more to do with customary usage than with the unresolved controversy (see Han 2005). More broadly, the peasantry often serves as a byword for rural society, particularly since the demise of the landlord class in the wake of the Communist revolution. Rural society in fact encompasses many other occupational categories including teachers, health workers, mechanics, shopkeepers, and barbers. In a given peasant family, moreover, a grown son and daughter might be migrant workers in a distant city, having left their allocated land untilled.

Rural China is generally perceived as lagging well behind urban society in the pace of economic and social change over the last century. This urban-rural gap by no means signifies that peasants were nonparticipants in history. On the contrary, over the course of the twentieth century China's peasantry was massively exposed to the effects of political, military, and economic developments related to the struggle for state power. These effects are visible in patterns of peasant unrest, mortality, changes in land usage, migrations, and governmental policy affecting both urban and rural society. The trend of long-term change is evident in the changed balance of urban and rural sectors in the economy and in population distribution. In the early twentieth century the overwhelming majority of people in China were peasants. In the early twenty-first century about two-thirds of the population might still fit into this category, but they are not cultivators as the term suggests; agriculture accounts for only around 10 percent of the Chinese economy and well under half of the workforce.

PEASANTRY UNDER IMPERIAL AND REPUBLICAN RULE

Around 1900, rural society in China was reaching the limits of growth possible under the old labor-intensive mode of agriculture, and facing other pressures as well. The end of the Qing dynasty (1644–1912) was marked by numerous peasant riots involving attacks on county seats and the destruction of tax and land registers and other administrative documents. These revolts in rural areas were local, sporadic, chronic, desperate, and prompted by concrete grievances.

Three main factors explain the riots. The first was population growth. Following a massive population loss in the mid-century rebellions, the rural population recovered rapidly in the late nineteenth century. From 1873 it grew 8 percent in the twenty years to 1893, 17 percent by 1913, and 31 percent by 1933 (Bianco 1971). The second factor was the diminishing size of the family farm. At the end of the eighteenth century the (rural) per capita average of cultivable land was 3.75 *mu* (about 0.62 acre); in 1859 it was down to 1.78 *mu* (Fan 1984, p. 133). The third factor was that agricultural output was low and taxes high. The impact of high taxes and new levies often was exacerbated by official corruption. Although the commercialization of agriculture led to an increase in the numbers of wealthy farmers

in some regions, floods and drought leading to famines and general scarcity were common phenomena in rural China in the early years of the twentieth century. Rural immiseration encouraged the growth of secret societies such as the Triads, the Gelaohui, and the Dadaohui, which played a role in the fall of the dynasty by spreading antiforeign slogans and millenarian doctrines. For the peasantry, secret societies also played a protective role, providing their followers with food and with security from abuse by corrupt functionaries and bandits.

Sun Yat-sen's manifesto for the Tongmenghui (Chinese Revolutionary Alliance), promulgated in Tokyo in 1905, held out the promise of agrarian reform under a republic, but this promise was not fulfilled. Between the founding of the Republic of China in 1912 and the Nationalist Revolution of 1927, rural China carried the burden of increased taxation to support the 130 greater and lesser wars waged in that period. In North China a severe famine in 1920 and 1921 added to the misery of political chaos and ongoing warfare. As the situation worsened, peasants had a choice of joining either the bandits or the regular army. Society was militarized on a grand scale. In Sichuan, for example, 3 percent of the population had joined an army by 1932. It is estimated that the overall number of bandits in China was around 20 million in 1930. (Bianco 2001).

Nevertheless, a large area of rural China benefited from the relative political stability during the Nanjing decade (1927–1937), when there was significant growth in agricultural and industrial outputs, to levels not reached again until the mid-1950s. These successes were achieved despite ongoing hostilities against the Communists, which were suspended at the end of 1936 with the formation of the second United Front. Productivity and the scale of farming varied from place to place. John Lossing Buck found "a standard of living appreciably higher in East Central China than in North China" (Buck 1930, p. 454) despite that fact that more "farmers" (he did not talk of "peasants") owned their own land in the North, and he also found that larger farms were more efficient. The average size of the farms covered in his famous survey was very small, and even those of above average size were not dependably remunerative.

PEASANTRY IN THE COMMUNIST REVOLUTION

In the second and third quarters of the twentieth century the peasantry moved to the center of China's political stage. During the Nationalist Revolution in the 1920s, a Peasant Movement Training Institute (*Nongmin Yundong Jiangxi Suo*) in Guangzhou was one of the key centers for mass mobilization developed by the Guomindang (GMD). Mao Zedong, a founding member of the Chinese Communist Party, joined the GMD as part of the first United Front that combined the two parties between

1923 and 1927, and served as an instructor in the institute. His later study of peasant conditions in Hunan gave rise to the famous *Report on an Investigation of the Peasant Movement in Hunan* (*Hunan nongmin yundong kaocha baogao*, 1927), in which he identified the revolutionary potential of the peasantry and gave notice of the role they were to perform in the subsequent Maoist revolution.

After the Communists established their base in Jiangxi in 1929, Mao undertook experiments in gaining peasant support by land reform, ideological work, and military training. This would be systematized later in Yan'an, where Mao and a few thousand survivors of the Long March reestablished themselves in 1935. From these early experiences of peasant society, he gained valuable knowledge that would be put to use in implementing nationwide agrarian reform during the first decade of the People's Republic of China (PRC). Mao drew on the peasantry to rebuild the CCP, and the mobilization of peasants during and after the Anti-Japanese War (1937–1945) was crucial to the Communist victory. Yet it was not easy to transform peasants with highly localized and concrete concerns into revolutionaries with national and ideological aims, and eventually only a minority actually joined the Party.

Land reform was started in the areas "liberated" by the Communists and it continued after the Communists won power. The agrarian law of 1950 was one of the first laws promulgated in the PRC. By autumn 1952 land reform has been carried out throughout China. Around 50 percent of the cultivated land changed ownership and about one million landlords were executed. "Landlord" was one of the five black categories used to identify class enemies during the class struggles by which the revolution was waged in local society during the Maoist era; the other black categories were rich peasants, counter-revolutionaries, bad elements, and rightists. People carried these labels for years, in most cases until the late 1970s and the beginning of the Reform Era. In rural areas of China during the Mao years, the label "poor peasant" was keenly sought after. Categorization as a poor peasant ensured a good land allocation and likely exemption from persecution during political campaigns.

In addition to gaining land during the revolution, peasants received education. It is estimated that 80 percent of the Chinese population was illiterate before 1949, and the vast majority of the illiterate people lived in rural areas. Except during the Cultural Revolution period, the government has prioritized literacy campaigns, with remarkable success. In the 1982 census illiteracy stood at nearly 32 percent (45 percent for women), and by 2000 it had fallen to around 6 percent (National Bureau of Statistics of the PRC 2003). Health care in rural areas also improved greatly during the early decades of the revolution, especially through the system of "barefoot doctors" (*chijiao yisheng*) developed during the Cultural Revolution. With their albeit very basic training, barefoot doctors made elementary health care widely available in rural China. The system was abandoned during the Reform era, and by the early twenty-first century the lack of health services in rural areas had become a major problem.

1958, A TURNING POINT

In 1949 nearly 90 percent of China's population was rural (Mackerras and Yorke 1991, p. 171), a proportion that quite quickly changed over the next half century. At the time of the revolution, landlords owned more than 50 percent of cultivated fields, and received around half of the grain produced in rent payments. Between 1949 and 1958 land redistribution was effected, with poor and lower-middle peasants receiving fields taken from former landlords. At *chiku* ("speak bitterness") meetings the former landlords were publicly criticized by their sometime tenants, who typically would use the occasion to talk of the bitterness of their past lives. This was also a time when heavy industry was being developed in the cities. Between 1950 and 1958 about forty million peasants were recruited to boost the urban industrial sector, following the Soviet model.

Collectivization of farmlands commenced in 1952 with the formation of cooperatives. In 1958, at the beginning of the Great Leap Forward, a more intensive process of collectivization led to the formation of communes. From 1958 until 1982 the hierarchy of rural administrative organization was, from top down, the county, the commune, the brigade, and the production team. A county included eight to fifteen communes and a commune between 2,000 and 7,000 households. The communes provided in the countryside what the work units provided in the cities—education, health care, and social services—and they guided and carried out the central government planning. The establishment of communes marked the apogee of the centralized and planned rural economy. After 1982 the system was dismantled and the original administration system restored.

The Great Leap Forward, which emphasized the supremacy of industry even at grassroots level, encouraged a wave of rural migrants to the cities to participate in an accelerated industrialization process. The goals of the Great Leap Forward were soon revealed as unreachable. Between twenty-five and thirty million rural laborers were sent back to the countryside, which by 1959 was in the grip of famine that lasted for three to four years. The official figure for the deaths caused by this famine long stood at fifteen million, but in 2009, researchers in recently opened archives were reporting a figure of thirty-seven million deaths.

In 1958 the Regulation on Household Registration—known as the *hukou*—was promulgated. This marked the end of the migration from rural areas to the cities. A few attempts have been made since then to reform the *hukou*, which requires every Chinese person to register at his or her birthplace and determines rights to some social benefits based on residency, but so far it is still a necessary document of identification.

PEASANTS AFTER REFORMS

In 1978 the household responsibility system was implemented. Land use rights were returned to individual farmers, though the property remained collective. This was initially successful, leading to a rapid increase in agricultural output, but a problem of surplus labor quickly became evident. In the late 1970s the rural population was 790 million, or 82 percent of the total population (Mackerras and Yorke 1991, p. 172). In the first phase of the economic reforms a number of township and village enterprises (TVEs) were established for local industrialization. A decade later, it was clear that this type of development was not enough to absorb the rural surplus of manpower. Leaving the land to work in other economic sectors was a growing trend. In 2002 nonagricultural income accounted for 54 percent of all rural income (National Bureau of Statistics of the PRC 2003).

In the 1990s the central government attempted first to restrict migration and then to regulate it. In the following decade, attempts were made to alleviate the difficulties faced by rural migrants employed in the cities. When Wen Jiabao became prime minister in 2003 he made agricultural problems his priority. Together with President Hu Jingtao, he acknowledged the imbalance between rural and urban development, and identified the "three rural issues" needing attention: agriculture, rural areas, and farmers. Agricultural taxes were abolished in 2005 and a number of administrative measures were implemented to stimulate rural development. These included providing new infrastructure, lifting agricultural output, improving health care and education, and ensuring fair pay for rural migrants.

In 2008, for the thirtieth anniversary of the rural reforms, the reorganization of land property rights was announced. In 1978 peasants had gained individual rights to land use: They could transmit land to their heirs but could not sell to other people, and in accordance with the constitution, the land was still collectively owned by the village authorities. The 2008 reform allowed peasants to trade their rights to use of the land, so that some peasants will cultivate more land and others will seek alternative employment. The aim of the reform is to boost rural income: The urban-rural income gap was three to one in 2003.

SEE ALSO *Land Use, History of; Rural Development; Rural Development since 1978.*

BIBLIOGRAPHY

Buck, John Lossing. Chinese Rural Economy. *Journal of Farm Economics* 12, 3 (July 1930): 440–456.

Bianco, Lucien. *Origins of the Chinese Revolution 1915–1949.* Stanford, CA: Stanford University Press, 1971.

Bianco, Lucien. *Peasants without the Party, Grass-roots Movements in Twentieth-century China.* Armonk, NY: Sharpe, 2001.

Cao Jinqing, *China Along the Yellow River—Reflections on Rural Society.* London: Routledge, 2005.

Chen Guidi, and Wu Chuntao. *Will the Boat Sink the Water? The Life of China's Peasants.* New York: Public Affairs, 2006.

Fan Shuzhi. Nongdian yazu guili di lishi kaocha [Investigation of the history of agricultural tenants deposit practices] *Jingji shi* [Economic history] 5 (1984): 129–135.

Han, Xiaorong. *Chinese Discourses on the Peasant, 1900–1949.* Albany: State University of New York Press, 2005.

Mackerras, Colin, and Amanda Yorke. *Cambridge Handbook of Contemporary China.* Cambridge, U.K.: Cambridge University Press, 1991.

Mao Zedong. *Report from Xunwu.* Trans. Roger R. Thompson. Stanford, CA: Stanford University Press, 1990.

National Bureau of Statistic of the PRC. *China Economic Yearbook 2003.* Beijing: China Statistics Press.

Florence Padovani
Antonia Finnane

PEASANTS

Sociologists define a *peasant* as a smallholding farmer, producing crops for family consumption and for market exchange, using family labor throughout the farming cycle. Peasants have continuing access to land, either through ownership or tenancy; their plots are usually small; and the margin between product and the subsistence needs of the family is usually small as well. The most important economic necessities defining the situation of the peasant are the subsistence needs of the family, taxes, interest, and rent (if the peasant is a tenant). In some historical settings, peasants were also subject to corvée labor on public-works projects. If crop production is reduced in a given year, the peasant family is likely to fall short in its obligations to rent, interest, taxes, and subsistence, and subsistence is often imperiled.

By this definition, China has been a peasant society for millennia. At the time of the collapse of the Qing dynasty (1644–1912), China's population consisted of a majority of poor farmers, under a variety of forms of land tenure. They were poor, had little land, and were subject to exploitation by landlords, lenders, and the state. Social and economic conditions in the countryside were documented by survey teams under the direction of agricultural economist John Lossing Buck (1890–1975) in the 1920s (Buck 1930). This is the social reality that economic historian R. H. Tawney (1880–1962) described so vividly as "a man standing permanently up to the neck in water"

(1966, p. 77). Subsistence crises were common during times of drought, flood, or war, and life was precarious.

These facts are highly relevant to China's political history in the twentieth century. Peasants were poor, they were a large majority throughout China, and they were potentially revolutionary as a result of their poverty and exploitation. And, of course, imperial China had a long history of peasant rebellions and uprisings with indigenous leadership. All that was needed was a party that could mobilize and activate them.

However, the transformation from peasant hardship and exploitation to committed political mobilization is a complex process. Political scientists have identified some of the factors that are needed before a group is likely to come together in successful collective action in pursuit of common interests. The group needs to come to possess a common group identity; there need to be organizations and leaders who can help to mobilize political action; and there need to be processes that escalate protests from local to regional and national arenas. A "farmer" (*nongmin*) is an agricultural producer; but this fact about production status tells little about how rural people defined their own social realities or the way that others defined them. Before the peasantry could become a politically important force in China, it was necessary for peasants to come to possess a collective identity as a peasant class. The mobilization of peasants along class lines requires an organized political effort by a party that promotes the salience of class over other affinities. In order for a population to become a self-conscious identity group, a deliberate process of identity-formation must take place.

The issue of the social reality of the peasant was a central focus of Chinese intellectuals' discourse in the first two decades of the twentieth century. These years witnessed the "creation" of the Chinese peasant in the discourses of intellectuals. And these constructions were intimately connected to the political goals of the intellectuals for the transformation of China.

PEASANTS UNDER CHINESE COMMUNISM

The Chinese Communist Party (CCP) worked single-mindedly to create the affinity with class identity throughout the 1920s and 1930s in rural China. One way of doing this was to promote organizations to represent and advocate for the interests and identity of peasants. One of the most important among these organizations was the Guangdong Provincial Peasant Association, founded by activist and revolutionary Peng Pai (1896–1929) in 1926. This organization, which claimed 200,000 members, came to play a crucial role in the development of CCP doctrines as a peasant revolutionary party.

Mao Zedong's political strategies were shaped by several main influences, including the doctrines of Marxist-Leninist thought and the concrete experience of political struggle in the 1920s and 1930s. The doctrines of Marxist-Leninist thought brought revolutionary thinkers, including Mao, to focus on the urban proletariat as the likeliest revolutionary class. In the mid-1920s, Mao turned his focus to the exploited rural classes—peasants. He offered his analysis of the class structure of China in a report written in 1926 (Mao Zedong [1926] 1956). A few months later, he conducted an investigation of the conditions of peasants in Hunan in 1927, which resulted in the *Report of an Investigation into the Peasant Movement in Hunan* (Mao Zedong [1927] 1953). Here is an important statement of his view of the role of peasants in the Chinese revolution:

> Without the poor peasants it would never have been possible to bring about in the countryside the present state of revolution, to overthrow the local bullies and bad gentry, or to complete the democratic revolution. Being the most revolutionary, the poor peasants have won the leadership in the peasant association.…This leadership of the poor peasants is absolutely necessary. Without the poor peasants there can be no revolution. To reject them is to reject the revolution. To attack them is to attack the revolution. Their general direction of the revolution has never been wrong. (Mao Zedong 1971, pp. 34–35)

The mobilization strategies of the CCP of the 1930s were aimed at creating a large and energized supporting population of poor and middle peasants. The party pursued this goal by recruiting local cadres who could communicate the party message to their intended supporters and by offering a program of land reform and social reversal that would strongly appeal to this group. Their efforts were successful in several important base areas, and the CCP was in fact able to cultivate a loyal base among poor and middle peasants. Moreover, this group increasingly provided recruits for middle and higher positions of leadership in the military and political organizations of the party. So we might say that the modern Chinese peasant movement was in fact created and shaped by CCP doctrines in the 1930s, and the Chinese revolution of 1949 was a peasant revolution.

Conditions for Chinese rural people since 1949 have changed abruptly and sometimes catastrophically. The land-reform policies of the early 1950s (redistributing land from large landowners to small landowners, tenants, and landless workers) quickly evolved into the Great Leap Forward and the collectivization of agriculture in 1956. Large collective farms were created, and peasants became agricultural workers within communes, living collectively and taking meals in collective dining halls. Communes were very large, with an average size of about 25,000 people. The Great Leap Forward famine (1958–1961) resulted from a massive dislocation of farm production associated with rapid collectivization; estimates of excess deaths during the famine years go as high as thirty to forty million people. Rural society was also affected by the social disturbances of the Cultural Revolution (1966–1969), and some of the worst examples of mass killings of that period took place in rural and commune areas. This was a period of wide suffering and hardship in the Chinese countryside.

THE IMPACT OF THE REFORM ERA

The fundamental reforms of agriculture that began in 1978—creation of the *household responsibility system*—brought a new period of change for Chinese peasants. The household responsibility system marked the end of collective farming. Farm families were given relatively secure claims to plots of land and were encouraged to be productive, and they were permitted to sell their products on the market once mandatory production quotas were achieved. These reforms were successful and agricultural output rose rapidly throughout the 1980s. At the same time, some of the forms of the social safety net that had protected the welfare of the poor and elderly in China began to dissolve, and inequalities between regions in China began to accelerate. These changes often led to greater insecurity in the lives of rural families even as the standard of living rose.

A second major effect on rural society since 1990 has been the rise of export manufacturing in China. Peasant men and women make up the majority of China's migrant workforce in export factories and construction—a population of upward of one hundred million people. These rural migrant workers often continue to maintain an affiliation with their home villages but travel to major industrial cities to find work. They are often subject to bad working conditions in the factories where they find work. Protests around issues of health, safety, and payment of wages are increasingly common among these migrant rural worker communities.

Since 1978, then, China's rural population has improved its standard of living significantly; farmers have gained direct access to land and their crops; and inequalities have increased between rural and urban populations. However, as is so often the case, peasant society in China has benefited less than the urban sector from the rapid economic growth that China has witnessed since 1990.

SEE ALSO *Social Classes before 1949.*

BIBLIOGRAPHY

Buck, John Lossing. *Chinese Farm Economy.* Chicago: University of Chicago Press, 1930.

Mao Zedong. *Report of an Investigation into the Peasant Movement in Hunan.* 1927. Beijing: Foreign Languages Press, 1953.

Mao Zedong. *Analysis of the Classes in Chinese Society.* 1926. Beijing: Foreign Languages Press, 1956.

Mao, Zedong. *Selected Readings from the Works of Mao Tsetung.* Beijing: Foreign Languages Press, 1971.

Peng Pai. *Seeds of Peasant Revolution: Report on the Haifeng Peasant Movement.* Trans. Donald Holoch. Ithaca, NY: China-Japan Program, Cornell University, 1973.

Tawney, R. H. *Land and Labor in China.* Boston: Beacon, 1966.

Daniel Little

PEI, I. M.
1917–

Pritzker Prize–winning U.S. architect Ieoh Ming Pei (Putonghua: Bei Yuming), usually known by his initials I. M. Pei, was born in Guangzhou in 1917 to a prominent old family from Suzhou. Internationally renowned, and feted in China and Hong Kong, I. M. Pei was educated in Hong Kong, Shanghai, and the United States. His father, Pei Tsuyee (Bei Zuyi), a director of the Bank of China and later governor of the Central Bank of China, moved the family to Hong Kong and later back to Shanghai. I. M. Pei attended primary school in Hong Kong and high school in Shanghai, then moved in 1935 to the United States at the age of eighteen to study architecture at the University of Pennsylvania. He received a bachelor of architecture degree from Massachusetts Institute of Technology in 1940. Pei won many awards before enrolling at the Harvard Graduate School of Design. He later worked for the National Defense Research Committee in New Jersey. In 1944 he returned to Harvard, where he studied under the renowned German-born architect Walter Gropius (1883–1969), receiving his master's degree in architecture in 1946 and becoming a faculty member. In 1954 Pei became a naturalized citizen of the United States.

Pei's early influences were Gropius, Le Corbusier (1887–1965), Marcel Breuer (1902–1981), and Ludwig Mies van der Rohe (1886–1969). His first professional recognition came when he was hired in 1948 by William Zeckendorf (1905–1976) to work as director of architecture for the real-estate development company Webb and Knapp. Pei's innovation created a new benchmark in American commercial and residential architecture. In 1955 he founded I. M. Pei and Associates, which became I. M. Pei & Partners in 1966 and continued under this name until 1989, when the firm was renamed Pei Cobb Freed and Partners.

Bank of China Tower, Hong Kong, June 25, 1997. *Growing up in Shanghai, award-winning architect I. M. Pei received early exposure to Western-style buildings, later increasing this knowledge through university studies in the United States. By blending elements from both East and West, Pei has earned a reputation for unique treatments of glass, concrete, and steel in structures throughout the world, including this Hong Kong skyscraper housing offices for the Bank of China.* AP IMAGES

MAJOR PROJECTS

There is no greater testimony to Pei's architectural inventiveness than his continual move toward more innovative sculptural forms, using cement and glass to full advantage while ensuring that shapes blend with landscapes and context. Pei is little given to theorizing about architectural principles or producing postmodern manifestoes, but the following incomplete list of acclaimed buildings documents a continually widening architectural vision. Among his early architectural triumphs are: Luce Memorial Chapel, Tunghai University, Taiwan, 1954–1963; National Center for Atmospheric Research, Boulder, Colorado, 1961–1967; East Building of the National Gallery of Art, Washington, D.C., 1968–1978; and John F. Kennedy Library, Boston, 1965–1969. In the course of his career, he has designed more than thirty institutional projects, including more than a dozen museums.

From the 1970s onward, more international commissions came his way. Among his most prominent later works are: Raffles City, Singapore, 1973–1986; Bank of China Tower, Hong Kong, 1982–1989; Grand Louvre, Paris, 1983–1989; Rock and Roll Hall of Fame and Museum, Cleveland, Ohio, 1987–1995; and Miho Museum, Shiga, Japan, 1991–1997. The Louvre extension with a glass pyramid was a controversial project that reconciled the need to expand the Louvre and to provide a new entrance and the lighting required by a modern museum. The unlikely choice of a pyramidal structure fortunately enhanced, rather than detracted from, the character of the original museum. The iconic Bank of China Tower in Hong Kong provided reassurance to Hong Kong's citizens that the mainland would respect the entrepreneurship, innovation, and openness of Hong Kong after the colony reverted to the sovereignty of the People's Republic of China. At the same time, the extensive use of glass elevators and the placement of cameras created a sense that the bank was a secure and dependable institution.

PROJECTS IN MAINLAND CHINA

Although I. M. Pei's family has a historical association with the renowned Shizilin (Lion Grove) Garden in Suzhou, a masterpiece of Ming-Qing dynasty urban landscape design, Pei himself has designed few buildings in mainland China. The first project he undertook there was the Xiangshan Hotel, located in the Fragrant Hills in northwest Beijing. Built in 1982, the low-key hotel complex blends exquisitely with its surroundings and attempts to integrate Chinese architecture of a southern style, evocative of his "hometown" of Suzhou, with elements suggestive of more monumental fortress architecture. The subtlety of the building, and the hotel's poor management and maintenance at different times, have detracted from its reputation among locals. In 1995 Pei's company also designed the Bank of China Building at Xidan in Beijing, the credit for which must go to his two sons, who are also

architects (Pei has four children). The main feature of this building is the vast skylit atrium, which contains a massive rock garden with boulders shipped from Yunnan's Stone Forest. This building also features a beam-free auditorium that can accommodate two thousand people. The new Suzhou Museum complex, completed in 2002, in time for a UNESCO conference, is the other project I. M. Pei himself designed on the mainland. The composite style of this complex, integrating functional Western and Chinese traditional elements, is now widely emulated by many Chinese architects.

The Suzhou Museum was part of a larger project for urban renewal in the Pingjiang area of Suzhou, initiated originally by the city's mayor during a visit to New York to discuss with Pei the design of a new museum and environs. In 1996 a workshop organized by Pei's company and EDAW, a landscape architecture firm based in San Francisco, brought together experts from EDAW and Chinese architectural students and professionals from the Suzhou Planning Bureau. The completion of the museum served to transform the site into an open area for pedestrians using old houses in a mix of retail and commercial development, accessible from the adjacent canal from a renovated landing with granite steps leading to the new museum's entrance. Although more conservative Chinese architects wanted Pei to preserve the familiar whitewashed walls from the traditional architecture of Suzhou, Pei's placing of traditional diamond shapes brought new elements to the structure.

I. M. Pei has received many awards and accolades. As a student, he was awarded the MIT Traveling Fellowship and the Wheelwright Traveling Fellowship at Harvard. Among his most prominent awards are the Gold Medal of the American Institute of Architects (1979), the Gold Medal of the French Académie d'Architecture (1981), and the prestigious Pritzker Architecture Prize (1983), described by some as the Nobel Prize of architecture.

In China, I. M. Pei is regarded as one of the most successful overseas Chinese, and his family has been involved in a number of projects in China, but his major works are all to be found outside the mainland.

SEE ALSO *Architecture, History of.*

BIBLIOGRAPHY

Deitz, Paula. Stones, Scrolls, and Scholars: I. M. Pei Makes a Poignant Return to His Native Suzhou. *Architectural Review* 222, 1328 (October 2007): 64–73.

Boehm, Gero von. *Conversations with I. M. Pei: "Light Is the Key."* New York and London: Prestel, 2006.

Jodidio, Philip, and Janet Adams Strong. *I. M. Pei: Complete Works.* New York, Rizzoli, 2008.

Suzhou Museum. http://www.szmuseum.com/szbwgcn/html/xw/2006/0930/165.html.

Bruce G. Doar

PEKING OPERA AND REGIONAL OPERAS

Traditional Chinese opera in its mature form first appeared a millennium ago during the Northern Song dynasty (960–1127). In the subsequent centuries it evolved into many regional forms, incorporating local language and musical characteristics, and influencing one another in a complex web of relationships. Shortly before 1800, several regional styles of singing from various provinces amalgamated into one style in Beijing and quickly spread and gained prominence throughout the land. This style later became known as Jingxi or Jingju (capital opera). Since the twentieth century, it also became internationally renowned, attracted scholarly attention from the West, and was named Peking Opera (also Beijing Opera in recent years by some scholars and some in the media). The history of Chinese opera in the modern period has been dominated by the development of Peking Opera.

Chinese opera, particularly Peking Opera, a repository through the centuries of creative literary, musical, and other artistic expression, is recognized as among the most sophisticated theatrical genres in the world. Until the middle of the twentieth century, Chinese opera also served several social functions. First, it was probably the most widespread form of entertainment, for both the elite and the masses, in both urban and rural areas. Second, most regional operas were intimately connected to many kinds of ritual, serving either as the core of the ritual or as a supplement to other ritual activities. Third, operas functioned as an important medium of communication and education, since before the twentieth century the vast majority of Chinese people were illiterate or semiliterate. Opera offered them a view of the wider world and played a major role in giving them a shared sense of history and mores. It thus helped to forge a cultural identity. These social functions have diminished in significance in since the 1980s in the face of newer forms of mass-media entertainment, reduced practice of formal religious rituals, and greatly improved levels of literacy.

The development of Peking Opera and other regional operas in the modern period was founded to a large extent on their most eminent predecessor, Kun Opera (Kunqu), which emerged early in the Ming dynasty (1368–1644). Evolved from Kunshan melodies of the Wu region (around modern Suzhou), Kun Opera for centuries had attracted the interest and resources of the literati, who produced a large number of opera scripts, created refined verse for its lyrics, developed complex melodies for its singing, devised intricate and delicate gesture and dance movements, and established theatrical practices ranging from costumes and makeup to staging. By 1800, however, Kun Opera had declined in popularity and soon largely disappeared on the stage, although new scripts continued to be written for reading enjoyment. Though Kun Opera was no longer a major theatrical presence in the modern period, its performative elements exerted great influence on Peking Opera and regional operas. Prominent Peking Opera actors either were first trained in Kun Opera or later studied its singing and acting techniques, and they incorporated its repertoire into Peking Opera. In recent years Kun Opera has shown signs of revival, particularly after being declared a "masterpiece of the oral and intangible heritage of humanity" by the United Nations Educational, Scientific, and Cultural Organization (UNESCO) in 2001.

PEKING OPERA

The origin of Peking Opera traces back to the late 1700s. After a century of stability, the Qing dynasty reached its peak of prosperity during the reign of the Qianlong emperor (r. 1736–1796). Government officials indulged in artistic pursuits and extravagant entertainment, including opera, as did the ordinary citizenry, particularly in the capital city. As the center of political, economic, and cultural activities, Beijing naturally attracted talented performers from other parts of the country, who congregated in the capital to vie for fame and fortune. Among the best-known actors of this period was Wei Changsheng (c. 1744–1802), who specialized in female roles in the regional opera of Sichuan, where he came from. Wei was the first of many stars who raised the popularity of opera in the capital, and he exerted tremendous influence on later generations through his many disciples.

Significantly, the Qianlong emperor himself was an opera aficionado, and in one of his famous six tours of the southern provinces, he was so impressed by the local operas that he personally brought performers back to Beijing. A seminal event was his eightieth birthday in 1790, when wealthy merchants in Yangzhou in the South sent opera companies, known as Anhui troupes, to celebrate the occasion. After performing in the Imperial Palace to great acclaim, these troupes stayed to entertain the masses. Their success induced more troupes from Anhui and other southern provinces to come. Two particular styles of singing, one called *xipi*, the other *erhuang*, combined to result in a new style called *pihuang*, a blend of the other two terms. *Pihuang* became enormously popular in Beijing and spread to many provinces during the first half of 1800s; it later became known as Jingxi, or Peking Opera.

Some of the most renowned actors during that period were Cheng Changgeng (1811–1879), from Anhui Province; Yu Sansheng (1796–1868), from Hubei Province; and Zhang Erkui (1814–c. 1865), who was from southern Hebei but grew up in Beijing. Cheng, who was trained in Kun Opera and Anhui regional opera, introduced the *erhuang* style of singing. Yu brought in the *xipi* style. Zhang used Beijing pronunciation and local singing styles. All three were credited with critical contributions to the development of *pihuang*. Notably, all three specialized in the *laosheng* (mature male) role type, since considered an important singing part.

The social instability caused by the Taiping Uprising from 1851 to 1864 temporarily halted the artistic development of opera. But performances resumed soon thereafter, and in the second half of the century Peking Opera continued to flourish and established its identity. The imperial family, notably Empress Dowager Cixi (1835–1908), became avid patrons, and this support further raised its stature and attracted talented performers to join its ranks. The city of Shanghai, as it grew in prosperity from the mid-1800s, soon became a second center for Peking Opera, attracting performers from provinces along the Yangzi River basin.

In the second half of the century a new generation of actors creatively moved the art forward. While Cheng Changgeng continued for a few years as the dominant figure, a few outstanding younger actors asserted their presence and became the direct link to the great stars of the twentieth century. Tan Xinpei (1847–1917), from a Hubei acting family, began performing at age eleven, first in the *wusheng* (martial male) role type, later switching to the *laosheng* role type. Having performed in over 300 different plays—among which the most famous, such favorites as *Kongcheng ji* (Ruse of the empty city), *Jigu ma Cao* (Scolding Cao Cao while beating the drum), and *Wulong Yuan* (Black dragon compound), are still in today's repertoire—he established his own style of performance, known as the Tan school (*Tan pai*). A generation younger, Wang Yaoqing (1882–1954), from Jiangsu Province but born in Beijing, was also from an acting family, his father being a famous Kun Opera performer specializing in *dan* (female) role types. Trained from the age of twelve in the *qingyi* (virtuous female) role type, Wang Yaoqing performed on stage shortly thereafter. He often partnered with Tan Xinpei, most notably in 1905–1906, when the two paired up to perform in the imperial palace. From 1926 Wang began teaching a younger generation of singers, and thereby influenced the next generation of *qingyi* performers, including Mei Lanfang.

The first half of the twentieth century witnessed political and military traumas, with resulting social instability and chaos, yet Peking Opera continued to thrive. Some of the most notable actors of the time were Yu Shuyan (1890–1943) and Ma Lianliang (1901–1966), both actors of the *laosheng* role type. However, the period was renowned for the popularity of singers of *dan* role type, headed by Mei Lanfang (1894–1961). He and his fellow actors Cheng Yanqiu (1904–1958), Shang Xiaoyun (1900–1976), and Xun Huisheng (1899–1968) were crowned by the public as "the four great female-role actors." In collaboration with the scholar Qi Rushan (1877–1962), Mei spearheaded

many new plays and innovations in artistic expression, borrowing liberally from Kun Opera and Western-style theater. Some of the more prominent plays that gained a foothold in the repertoire were *Bawang bie ji* (Farewell my concubine) and *Guifei zui jiu* (Guifei is intoxicated).

For centuries, troupes were either all male or all female, the mixing of sexes on stage being considered immoral. Ironically, the age of the great female impersonators in the early decades of the twentieth century saw the first appearance of female roles being played by women opposite male roles played by men. These women thus broke the longstanding tradition of single-sex performance. After the founding of the People's Republic in 1949, female impersonation disappeared almost completely from the stage. The new century also saw the establishment of operatic training schools with a systematic and comprehensive curriculum, including language and culture courses, as opposed to the traditional apprentice system.

As Shanghai prospered and operatic activities thrived, there soon emerged two styles of performance, one identified with Beijing, noted for rigidly upholding high standards for acting and singing styles, and the other with Shanghai, known to be progressive in creating new plays and performance practices. Many prominent artists performed in both cities, and the rivalry cross-fertilized further artistic development.

The establishment of the People's Republic in 1949 led to a major reorganization of opera troupes and performance practices, such as the establishment of modern Peking Opera companies in Beijing, Shanghai, Tianjin, Wuhan, and other cities and the creation of operatic schools to train professional actors. Old plays considered "superstitious" and "feudal" were banned, and new plays with "healthy" content were created. Some new plays were based upon preexisting stories but were given new treatments to convey "correct" messages, for example, *Baishe zhuan* (The story of the white snake) and *Yangmen nüjiang* (Women warriors of the Yang family), while others had contemporary settings, such as *Baimao nü* (The white-haired girl).

During the Cultural Revolution all traditional plays were banned, and only a handful of newly created modern revolutionary Peking Operas (*geming xiandai jingju*), also known as model operas (*yangban xi*), were staged. Being associated with Mao's wife Jiang Qing, these plays disappeared from the stage after Jiang was purged in 1976. But their artistic merits were subsequently recognized, and several of them, such as *Zhiqu Weihushan* (Taking Tiger Mountain by strategy), have reappeared to great acclaim.

On Taiwan, Peking Opera experienced a unique trajectory following the retreat of the Nationalist regime to the island in the late 1940s. Supported by mainland immigrants and financed largely by the government, which declared it national opera, Peking Opera thrived from the 1950s

A visiting production of **The Legend of the White Snake** *by the National Beijing Opera Company of China, London, England. In the late 1700s, a variety of singing traditions merged to become Peking Opera, a form of entertainment that also served a dual purpose of educating a largely illiterate population. Despite political instability in China throughout the nineteenth and twentieth centuries, Peking Opera has continued into a new millennium as a vibrant reflection of Chinese culture.* © **ROBBIE JACK/CORBIS**

through the mid-1990s. During the Cultural Revolution, when all traditional fare was banned on the mainland, Taiwan troupes prided themselves for preserving the traditional art. However, with the opening of the mainland in the late 1980s, with greater cross-strait flows of people and ideas in the 1990s, and with growing pressure from native Taiwanese to promote Taiwan's own arts, Peking Opera lost its privileged status and came under heavy influence from the mainland.

China's official policy of reform and opening up, launched in the late 1970s and developed in subsequent decades, has transformed China's business, finance, media, and technology. As troupes and schools were privatized and popular entertainment in the mass media diversified and grew to compete for audience attention, Peking Opera suffered. Many talented performers moved abroad, while others were attracted to better paying jobs in film, television, and other forms of entertainment. To overcome the crisis and meet these challenges, producers and actors have struggled to preserve the art by drastically rethinking and redefining

Peking Opera and plotting its future through bold innovation. One innovation is a breakdown of rigid performance practices, such as the singing and acting styles of role types. Another is adaptation of well-known Western plays and incorporation of performance concepts and techniques of contemporary avant-garde theater and other performance media, such as films and spoken plays. Examples include the staging of the Greek tragedy *Bacchae* by Zhou Long of Beijing in 1998, and of several Shakespearean tragedies (*King Lear, Macbeth*) by Wu Xingguo of Taibei beginning in the mid-1980s.

REGIONAL OPERAS

A survey conducted in the 1950s reported that there were over three hundred regional operas, each with its distinctive linguistic and musical features. The majority had small troupe sizes, limited repertoires, and relatively simple artistic expression. For example, the performance might consist of only two actors, one or two percussion instruments, and a single tune repeated over and over again. These theatrical

88

forms were localized, often known only within a county or a small part of a province, and referred to in the literature as folk and minor operas.

In contrast, a few regional operas were known as major operas, with extensive repertoires, rich musical vocabulary, complex artistic expression, and large-scale productions involving many actors and instrumentalists, and elaborate makeup and costumes. They often have extensive audiences spread out to many parts of the country or even abroad among immigrants. For example, Chaozhou Opera and Fujian Opera are known in many parts of Southeast Asia, while Cantonese Opera is known in the Chinatowns of some North American and European cities.

Many major operas established their identities during the stable and prosperous reigns of Qianlong (r.1736–1796) and Jiaqing (r.1796–1820). For example, Sichuan Opera became renowned for its dance, acrobatics, and narrative songs, and during the 1800s spread beyond Sichuan to Guizhou, Yunnan, Hubei, and other provinces. Since Sichuan Opera faced the same challenges as Peking Opera in the late twentieth century, actors began seeking new directions. In 1999 the young actress Tian Mansha created a new opera based on the character Lady Macbeth, and in 2002 she collaborated with Zuni Icosahedron, an avant-garde theater group of Hong Kong, to develop new concepts of performance style based on traditional techniques.

Cantonese Opera developed in the 1800s after Canton (today known as Guangzhou) was declared in 1759 to be the only port allowed to handle China's trade with foreign countries. This privileged status attracted from the northern provinces large numbers of businessmen, who brought great wealth as well as operatic troupes from their native areas. Popular throughout the Pearl River Delta, Cantonese Opera was known for its bold experimental spirit, and in the 1920s through the 1940s, it adopted many Western elements, which were easily accessible in Hong Kong. Hundreds of new plays were created and staged in the first half of the twentieth century, among which probably the best known was *Dinü Hua* (The flower princess), by the scriptwriter Tang Disheng (1917–1959), which still regularly draws large audiences.

While most major operas trace their origins to the Ming or Qing dynasties, there were exceptions, among which an outstanding example is Huangmei Opera of Anhui Province. It began as a minor opera, with two performers singing folk tunes and enacting simple stores, but through the creative energy of a few actors, particularly Yan Fengying (1930–1968), Huangmei Opera—with its gentle and melodious tunes, romantic stories, and simple performance style rooted in folk culture—became one of the most popular regional operas since the 1950s.

For centuries, the regional operas influenced one another as people migrated. Such cross-fertilization not only resulted in Peking Opera, but also further developed the artistic expression of these regional operas. Throughout its history, Chinese operas have depended critically on their social and economic environments. In the early twenty-first century, they face enormous obstacles as China undergoes unprecedented social change and economic growth in a global environment that provides both opportunities and challenges. This century will inevitably see major changes to Peking Opera and other forms of Chinese opera.

SEE ALSO *Mei Lanfang.*

BIBLIOGRAPHY
Guy, Nancy. *Peking Opera and Politics in Taiwan.* Urbana: University of Illinois Press, 2005.
Li, Siu Leung. *Cross-Dressing in Chinese Opera.* Hong Kong: Hong Kong University Press, 2003.
Mackerras, Colin. *The Chinese Theatre in Modern Times, from 1840 to the Present Day.* Amherst: University of Massachusetts Press, 1975.
Mackerras, Colin. *Peking Opera.* New York: Oxford University Press, 1997.
Provine, Robert, Yosihiko Tokumaru, and J. Lawrence Witzleben, eds. *The Garland Encyclopedia of World Music.* Vol. 7, *East Asia.* New York: Routledge, 2002. The entries "Chinese Opera: An Overview," "Peking Opera," "Kunqu," "Huju," "Cantonese Opera."
Stock, Jonathan P. J. *Huju: Traditional Opera in Modern Shanghai.* Oxford: Oxford University Press, 2003.
Wichmann, Elizabeth. *Listening to Theatre: The Aural Dimension of Beijing Opera.* Honolulu: University of Hawaii' Press, 1991.
Yung, Bell. *The Music of Cantonese Opera: Performance as Creative Process.* New York: Cambridge University Press, 1989.

Bell Yung

PENAL SYSTEMS, 1800–1949

The penal system in late imperial China was based on legal regulations in the Qing Code (*Da Qing lüli*) of 1740. The Qing code was modeled on earlier codes issued by each dynasty on its inception. The code was a body of core criminal laws containing rules that prescribed punishments for every infraction. Each offense was allocated an exact degree of punishment. The task of the judge (magistrate) was to identify the proper name of the offense disclosed by the facts. Determination of the correct punishment then had to follow the text of the law, with theoretically little discretion on the part of the judge. Imperial Chinese criminal justice operated on the basis of precise and complex regulations that provided guidelines to determine how officials

Painting of an accused criminal before a magistrate, c. 1840–1860. *Based upon the penal codes of previous dynasties, the Qing code outlined the consequences for criminal behavior. Accused citizens faced a magistrate, who then examined the situation, judged if a crime was committed, and then announced a punishment based on laws established by Qing officials.* © **BRITISH LIBRARY BOARD.**

responded to crime and to ensure that they produced consistent judgments and handed down predictable sentences. In practice, however, the judge enjoyed discretion when deciding on intent, culpability, and the rubric of the code under which he would enter the criminal offense.

The Qing code, like its predecessors, listed five punishments (*wu xing*), which were all executed in public: death (*si*), exile (*liu*), penal servitude (*tu*), beating with a heavy stick (*zhang*), and beating with a light stick (*chi*). Each punishment was available in different grades. For instance, beating was available in five degrees ranging from ten to fifty blows. Penal servitude and exile were graded according to the length of the banishment and the distance of deportation from the native place of the convict. The code recognized two degrees of death penalty. The lighter degree was strangulation, and the heavier, decapitation. The gradations

in penalties provided the judge with fine, scaled sentencing distinctions.

Chinese theories of punishment and criminal justice were based on the principle that the penalty should correspond precisely to the severity of the crime it punished. Therefore, legal punishment had to be graded in relation to the harm done by the crime and in anticipation of the moral consequences it might produce in society. Chinese penal philosophy resulted from a syncretistic merger of legalist and Confucian arguments. The penal system accommodated a Confucian view that was reluctant to concede legal punishments an important position in the state, as well as the legalist view that the harsh penal apparatus that had been inherited was useful for dealing with unruly elements and enforcing morality. Imperial penal philosophy came to accept the necessity for punishments when dealing with members of society who could not be changed through education, but it infused the penal practice with Confucian norms and ideas. In this system, punishments should be painful lessons designed to transmit moral values and inform people who have morally failed. Public shame should lead to moral improvement. This process was also called "self-renewal" (*zixin*), a term that can be frequently found in Chinese legal documents.

From the late Qing onward and throughout the Republican period, a series of reforms was implemented to establish a new Western-inspired system of criminal justice that was modeled on German and Japanese prototypes. These reforms were driven by two goals. First, by adopting international standards, the government hoped to respond to Western criticism and hence rid China of extraterritoriality. Second, the reforms were a central part of a more internal and large-scale attempt to strengthen the Chinese state. Both motives imputed a high priority to the creation of a new criminal system.

Starting in the 1900s, a wave of legislation gradually introduced a new criminal justice system. A new court system was established that was governed by newly drafted procedural laws (1928, 1936) and criminal laws (1928, 1935). The penal system was reshaped as well. Already in 1905, the five physical punishments were all abolished and replaced by fines and imprisonment. The death penalty was retained, but was no longer executed in public. A prison law went in effect (1913, revised in 1928) that included regulations for the administration of prisons and the treatment of sentenced offenders.

The development of the penal system in Republican China can best be characterized by the general tendency to redirect the focus of criminal justice away from the crime toward the criminal. The criminal process, as well as the execution of punishments, both focused on the individual by taking into account his or her specific past, criminal record, deficiencies, problems, needs, and possible responses. The proper management of crime and the criminal required individualized, corrective measures adapted to the specific case or the particular individual. This principle was called "individualization" (*ge ren hua*). The judge was directed, before passing sentence, to consider the state of the offender's mind, motives, general intelligence, and conduct subsequent to the offense. In the imposition of fines, too, the judge was instructed to take into account individual circumstances, that is, the economic condition of the offender.

In a similar way, imprisonment was supposed to offer individualized treatment of an offender after he or she was sentenced. The policy of reform (*ganhua*) shaped the Chinese prison. The maladjusted delinquent was the problem, and reformative correctional treatment was the solution. Accordingly, correctional intervention by the authorities should take on the form of advice, lectures, and therapeutic treatment, thereby combining punitive measures with education and instruction.

The full implementation of the criminal justice reforms was made difficult by the political turbulence of the 1930s and 1940s. While some hundred new prisons were built and new courts operated in urban China, wide stretches of rural China still saw the imposition of punishments stemming from the imperial penal system.

SEE ALSO *Death Penalty since 1800; Law Courts, 1800–1949.*

BIBLIOGRAPHY

Bodde, Derk, and Clarence Morris. *Law in Imperial China.* Cambridge, MA: Harvard University Press, 1967.

Brook, Timothy, Jérôme Bourgon, and Gregory Blue. *Death by a Thousand Cuts.* Cambridge, MA: Harvard University Press, 2008.

Dikötter, Frank. *Crime, Punishment, and the Prison in Modern China, 1895–1949.* New York: Columbia University Press, 2002.

MacCormack, Geoffrey. *Traditional Chinese Penal Law.* Edinburgh, U.K.: Edinburgh University Press, 1990.

MacCormack, Geoffrey. *The Spirit of Traditional Chinese Law.* Athens: University of Georgia Press, 1996.

Meijer, Marinus J. *The Introduction of Modern Criminal Law in China.* Batavia, Indonesia: De Unie, 1950.

Mühlhahn, Klaus. *Criminal Justice in China: A History.* Cambridge, MA: Harvard University Press, 2009.

Xu, Xiaoqun. *Trial of Modernity: Judicial Reform in Early Twentieth-Century China 1901–1937.* Stanford, CA: Stanford University Press, 2008.

Klaus Mühlhahn

PENAL SYSTEMS SINCE 1949

After the founding of the People's Republic of China in 1949, the new government did away with the Republican laws root and branch, including the criminal justice system. But the new state delayed supplying substitutes. While discussions soon started about the drafting of various criminal laws, such as a penal code or regulations of judicial procedure, no laws were made public until 1978. Instead of producing comprehensive legal codes, the socialist state issued numerous single decrees, orders, resolutions, and regulations, many of them carrying the threat of punishment. Among the earliest and most significant legislative measures were the Statutes for the Punishment of Counterrevolutionary Activity (1951). The statutes were promulgated in conjunction with several nationwide political campaigns. Between 1950 and 1953 several social groups were singled out and purged in the course of these campaigns: landlords (the Land Reform campaign), counterrevolutionaries (the campaign to suppress counterrevolutionaries), corrupt bureaucrats (the Three-Anti's campaign: anti-corruption, anti-waste, anti-bureaucratism), capitalists and private entrepreneurs (the Five-Anti's campaign: anti-bribery, anti-tax evasion, anti-fraud, anti-theft of state property, anti-leakage of state economic secrets), and the educational sector and intellectuals more generally (the Thought Reform campaign). The statutes thus provided the regime with a powerful leverage to enforce compliance with the campaigns, setting the perimeters of the penal system early in the regime. The quick promulgation of those statutes demonstrated that the new state was above all concerned with domestic security and hence with the suppression of forces and groups deemed unreliable or dangerous for the new order. Other regulations dealt with corruption, land reform, and the maintenance of public order. The protection of the socialist order and socialist transformation was regarded as a major function of the criminal justice system.

THEORIES OF CRIME AND PUNISHMENT IN SOCIALIST CHINA

Theories of crime and punishment accordingly suggested that crime principally resulted from thoughts and habits acquired in the old society and therefore stemmed from a deeply rooted, wrong ideological consciousness. The occurrence of crime and the need for punishment in socialist China were explained as historical remnants of class society and therefore considered to be transitional. This conception of crime as a conscious or unconscious harmful act against the existing social order had far-reaching consequences: All crime was thus politicized; every criminal act became a genuine political matter.

Punishments in this approach had a distinct function. They should reform and reeducate the criminal into a new man (*xinren*) who could be allowed to return to socialist society. Emphasis was placed on the leniency of the penal policy adopted in socialist China. The official policy was that death sentences should be only rarely meted out. As a general rule, offenders would rather be given the opportunity to renew themselves. Official theory accentuated that the spirit of reeducation and reform would permeate and inform the whole criminal justice system in socialist China. Physical labor and political instruction were the main tools to achieve reform of the offenders.

TYPES OF PUNISHMENT

Five types of main punishments and three types of supplementary punishments were used. Main punishments included: (1) work under surveillance; (2) detention (for one month to six months); (3) fixed-term imprisonment (six months to twenty years), carried out as reform

through labor (*laogai*); (4) life imprisonment, carried out as labor reform; and (5) the death penalty (*sixing*), with or without a two-year period of delay (during which the sentence could be commuted to imprisonment due to a successful reeducation). Supplementary punishments, regardless of the opposite meaning conveyed by their name, could be imposed independently. These included: (1) fines (the amount imposed depended on the circumstances of the crime); (2) the deprivation of political rights; and (3) the confiscation of property.

In this approach to criminal justice, the class-struggle ideology also justified the implementation of differential treatment based on a friend/foe distinction. The Communist Party held that enemies of the "people" had no rights, which were only available to the people (friends). Crime and punishments served as potent tools to protect socialism and to implement social and political transformation. The broad state powers, which were invoked by the people's government to punish enemies and counterrevolutionaries, were time and again challenged by courts and legal scholars. In the 1950s, there often was a courageous readiness of the courts to challenge the administration's procedures, but all attempts were ultimately crushed by mass movements such as the anti-rightist movement, the Great Leap Forward, and the Cultural Revolution (1966–1969), which aimed, among other things, to eliminate judicial independence.

THE REFORM PERIOD SINCE 1978

After 1978, there was a general agreement that the criminal justice sector was an area in need of rebuilding and reform. Many party members and cadres had become victims of the campaigns and purges. In 1979 the People's Congress passed China's first-ever Law of Criminal Procedure, which defined the roles of procurators in criminal prosecution, investigation, and the powers of "supervision" in the criminal process. Another law adopted in the same legislative package included China's first Criminal Law. This law retained the main punishments that were in use since the 1950s. The Chinese government thus (re)established a formal legal and criminal justice system.

Beginning in the 1990s, the pace of criminal justice reforms accelerated. China succeeded in making a series of important changes to its criminal law (1997), the law of criminal procedure (1996), the laws governing administrative punishments (1996), and the law regulating the system of administrative punishments (1997), including administrative detention. These changes included the abolishment of the crime of counterrevolution, an enhanced concept of judicial independence, redefined roles of the prosecutors, limits on police power in law, a right to legal aid, growing independence of the legal profession, enhanced professional qualifications of judges and prosecutors, recognition of the

Inmates of Shaanxi Women's Jail visiting the city of Xi'an as a reward for good behavior, March 7, 2006. *The early criminal justice system of the People's Republic of China lacked a formal structure, being instead a collection of laws, decrees, and pronouncements made by government officials. By the late 1970s, however, Communist Party leaders constructed a more unified penal code, shifting power to a criminal court system designed to depoliticize the legal process.* **AP IMAGES**

right to defense in pretrial detention, provision of legality in substantive criminal law, and the abolition of retroactive application of the criminal law.

A new Prison Law was made public in December 1994. The purpose of imprisonment was defined as protecting the safety of society and assisting the rehabilitation of offenders.

The law recognized and implemented common principles, such as fairness, justice, and the rule of law. It also strove to recognize and respect the basic rights of offenders. There was a clear effort to maintain a balance between the rights and interests of the offenders and those of the victims and public safety.

Overall, the party has gradually ceded a good deal of authority in the ordinary course of criminal justice matters to the courts and other institutions. It tried to depoliticize crime and punishment. This partial withdrawal by the party provides a degree of political space for the development of "rule of law with Chinese characteristics," as it were.

Yet despite the growth of an increasingly robust criminal justice system and legal consciousness, the Communist Party retains ultimate control, especially over handling sensitive issues, through the committees on political and judicial matters (*sifa weiyuanhui*). The maintenance of social order has become increasingly important in legitimizing the Chinese government. Rising crime rates long have accompanied China's march to market liberalization and prosperity, leading the government to consider law and order as central a priority as economic growth and the promise of prosperity. Several "strike hard" (*yanda*) campaigns were carried out in the 1990s and first decade of the 2000s that by way of public rallies and abridged procedures sought to reduce crime rates and increase the number of criminal convictions.

SEE ALSO *Death Penalty since 1800; Education through Labor, Reform through Labor; Penal Systems, 1800–1949.*

BIBLIOGRAPHY

Bakken, Børge, ed. *Crime, Punishment, and Policing in China.* Lanham, MD: Rowman and Littlefield, 2005.

Cohen, Jerome Alan. *The Criminal Process in the People's Republic of China, 1949–1963.* Cambridge, MA: Harvard University Press, 1968.

Dutton, Michael. *Policing Chinese Politics: A History.* Durham, NC: Duke University Press, 2005.

Leng Shaochuan and Qiu Hongda (Chiu Hungdah). *Criminal Justice in Post-Mao China: Analysis and Documents.* Albany: State University of New York Press, 1985.

Mühlhahn, Klaus. *Criminal Justice in China: A History.* Cambridge, MA: Harvard University Press, 2009.

Tanner, Harold. *Strike Hard! Anti-Crime Campaigns and Chinese Criminal Justice, 1979–1985.* Ithaca, NY: East Asia Program, Cornell University, 1999.

Klaus Mühlhahn

PENG DEHUAI

1898–1974

Marshal Peng Dehuai is today honored in China primarily for commanding Chinese forces during the Korean War (1950–1953), but he played a major role in helping Chairman Mao Zedong rise to power. Five years Mao's junior, Peng rose to become his top military commander before being purged in 1959. Like Mao, he was born in Xiangtan County in Hunan Province in 1898, just a few miles from Mao's birthplace. Many other top Chinese leaders came from Hunan, but Peng was one of the few from an impoverished peasant family. Two of his brothers starved to death in one of China's frequent famines, and by the age of nine, Peng had finished school and started work. At thirteen he was a coal miner, and by fifteen he was a day laborer maintaining the dikes on Dongting Lake.

During another famine, Peng joined an effort to seize grain from a wealthy landlord and had to flee. At sixteen, he joined the army of a local warlord. Later, he was selected to attend the newly established Hunan Military Academy as an officer cadet. By 1926, when Chiang Kai-shek (Jiang Jieshi) had established himself in power after the Northern Expedition, Peng was a twenty-eight-year-old brigadier in the Guomindang (GMD) army.

When the Chinese Communist Party (CCP) and GMD split, Peng was expelled from the GMD. In 1928 he officially joined the CCP, and with 1,500 troops he led a rebel uprising in Pingjiang County. After the uprising was severely crushed, Peng and his remaining 600 soldiers joined Mao in the "soviet" established in the Jinggan Mountains on the border of Hunan and Jiangxi provinces. In 1930 Peng led an attack on Changsha, the provincial capital, which he abandoned after eleven days, suffering heavy losses.

When the GMD besieged the Communist bases, forcing the CCP to embark on the Long March, Peng emerged as a trusted commander. Several attempts were made to have Peng replace Mao as front commander. Among a leadership dominated by intellectuals, often acting on orders from Moscow advisers, Peng was exceptional because he had both military training and a personality that enabled him to gain the trust and loyalty of the peasants enlisted into the Red Army. However, for the next twenty-five years, Peng stayed loyal to Mao and never seemed to have harbored an ambition to become a political leader in his own right. Along with Lin Biao and Zhu De, Peng became one Mao's most trusted generals.

In 1940, as acting commander of the Eighth Route Army, Peng led the only significant Communist offensive, the monthlong Hundred Regiments campaign, against the Japanese during the United Front period with the GMD. In 1943 Mao brought Peng back to Yan'an, where Peng voiced opposition to the growing Mao cult. In 1945 Mao set out to tarnish Peng's reputation by attacking him and subjecting him to weeks of interrogations.

During the civil war, Peng led armies in Northwest China. In 1949 he became the first secretary of the Northwest Bureau of the Party, chairman of the Political Committee of the Northwest Army, commander of the Northwest military area, and vice president of the Military Commission of the Central Committee and the National Defense Committee.

KOREAN WAR

In 1950 Peng backed Mao's decision to invade Korea, while other military leaders urged the conquest of Taiwan. Consequently, in September 1950 Peng arrived in Shenyang, tasked with the enormous problem of assembling an army of a quarter of a million with field officers who had no experience fighting a conventional war. By mid-October, the first troops crossed the Yalu River, and soon Peng was commanding 380,000 troops. His forces eventually suffered a million casualties in a three-year war, which ended in stalemate and an armistice. Peng had difficulties dealing not only with Mao but also with Joseph Stalin (1879–1953) and Kim Il Sung (1912–1994), and on several occasions Peng offered to resign.

In 1954, in recognition of his success in fighting the United Nations forces to a standstill in Korea, Peng was made minister of defense, a largely honorary position. The following year, he was declared a field marshal and joined the Politburo. The outspoken soldier continued to complain about Mao's personality cult and raised objections to his policies, especially after Nikita Khrushchev's (1894–1971) denunciations of Stalin. Matters came to a head after the launch of the Great Leap Forward. In 1958 Peng toured parts of the country and discovered things were far different from what was being reported. In Gansu, he found orchards cut down to fuel furnaces, while harvests were left to rot in fields. After visiting Jiangxi and Anhui and his home village in Hunan, Peng sent telegrams to Beijing warning that the "masses are in danger of starving." In early 1959 he visited Mao's home village and found untilled fields, falsified production figures, and peasants dying of starvation.

LUSHAN PLENUM

At the Lushan Plenum, which Mao called in 1959 and which lasted six weeks, Peng was encouraged by more sophisticated leaders such as Zhang Wentian (1900–1976) to write Mao a petition, a handwritten letter that ran to ten thousand characters. The mildly worded petition did not even refer to a famine and instead praised the accomplishments of the Great Leap Forward, observing there were more gains than losses. In a meeting with Mao at the plenum, however, Peng's temper exploded, and he accused Mao of acting despotically, like Stalin in his later years, and of sacrificing human beings on the altar of unreachable production targets. Peng warned of a rebellion and said the Soviet army might be called in to restore order. Mao interpreted this as a plot to overthrow him and believed that Peng, during his recent trip to Eastern Europe, had sought Soviet backing for a coup. At a showdown in Lushan, Mao summoned his military leaders to ask if they backed him or Peng. Afterward, Peng was dismissed as a rightist and put under house arrest in Sichuan. In the ensuing purge of the "rightist opportunists," large numbers of Peng's real or suspected followers and sympathizers were arrested and sent to labor camps. Many of them died of starvation.

When the Cultural Revolution started in 1966, Peng was arrested and taken to Beijing. In one of numerous struggle sessions, he was forced to kneel before forty thousand people and was savagely kicked and beaten. Peng was kept in a prison cell, where he was not permitted to sit or use the toilet. He was interrogated more than two hundred times, and finally died in prison in 1974 after an eight-year ordeal. He was cremated in secrecy. Peng was rehabilitated in 1979, three years after Mao's death.

SEE ALSO *Communist Party; Cultural Revolution, 1966–1969; Korean War, 1950–1953; Mao Zedong; People's Liberation Army; Rural Development, 1949–1978: Great Leap Forward.*

BIBLIOGRAPHY

Becker, Jasper. *Hungry Ghosts: Mao's Secret Famine.* London: Murray, 1996.

Domes, Jürgen. *Peng Te-huai: The Man and the Image.* Stanford, CA: Stanford University Press, 1985.

Hu Sheng. *A Concise History of the Communist Party of China.* Beijing: Foreign Languages Press, 1994.

Li Zhisui. *The Private Life of Chairman Mao: The Memoirs of Mao's Personal Physician.* London: Chatto Windus, 1994.

Zhang Rong (Jung Chang) and Jon Halliday. *Mao: The Unknown Story.* London: Cape, 2005.

Jasper Becker

PEOPLE'S LIBERATION ARMY

This entry contains the following:

OVERVIEW

The People's Liberation Army (PLA) is one element of the Chinese armed forces. The Chinese armed forces are composed of the active and reserve units of the PLA, the People's Armed Police (PAP), and the People's Militia. The Central Military Commission is the highest command and policy-making authority for the Chinese armed forces (sharing command of the PAP with the State Council through the Ministry of Public Security). In 2008, the PLA had about 2.3 million active-duty troops and an estimated 800,000 personnel in

Joint Chinese and Russian military exercises, Shandong Peninsula, August 24, 2005. *The People's Liberation Army (PLA), together with the people's militia and the People's Armed Police, form the basis of the armed forces in China. At the turn of the twenty-first century, the PLA has embarked on an aggressive modernization campaign, investing in new weapons systems and conducting military training exercises with neighboring countries.* **AFP/GETTY IMAGES**

reserve units. The 1997 National Defense Law states that the PLA has a "defensive fighting mission, [but] when necessary, may assist in maintaining public order in accordance with the law." The PAP, which is primarily responsible for domestic security, officially numbers about 660,000 personnel, though another 230,000 PAP personnel may be under the daily command of the Ministry of Public Security. The primary militia consists of about 10 million personnel and is tasked to provide support to both the PLA and PAP. The PLA is divided into the ground forces, the People's Liberation Army Navy (PLAN), the People's Liberation Army Air Force (PLAAF), and the strategic-missile forces (Second Artillery). At least 200,000 PLA coastal and border-defense units and roughly 100,000 PAP troops are responsible for border defense. All elements of the Chinese armed forces engage in societal activities (e.g., disaster relief and some infrastructure development). An unknown number of civilians (technical specialists, administrative and custodial staff, administrative contractors, and local government-paid staff) also support PLA operations.

Following the decade of the Cultural Revolution (1966–1976), the PLA has become increasingly professional. Training has become increasingly sophisticated and realistic since the 1980s. Officers are being educated at a smaller number of more-advanced institutions, including civilian universities. Measures such as a National Defense Scholarship Program, initiated in 2000, have attempted to attract high school graduates to study in civilian institutions with the obligation to serve in the PLA upon graduation. This program, also known as the National Defense Student program, seeks to produce junior officers with the technical qualifications necessary for PLA modernization. Some military academies have been converted to training bases for the technical training of officers, noncommissioned officers, conscripts, and civilian college graduates, as well as small units.

The 1999 Service Law reduced the conscript service period to two years for all conscripts, but the overall quality of recruits remains low and the system is subject to corruption. The PLA has gradually increased its military exchanges, attaché offices abroad (though few have PLAAF and PLAN attachés), and educational exchanges, and has conducted a variety of joint exercises with Russia and Western nations. A limited number of port calls and the PLAN's first global circumnavigation in 2002 by the destroyer *Qingdao* and the support ship *Taicang* have furthered diplomacy. Since 1990, when it first deployed military observers, the PLA has greatly increased its role in United Nations peace-keeping. China has contributed roughly 6,800 personnel to twenty-one United Nations peacekeeping missions since first sending military observers in 1990. In February 2008, 1,962 Chinese personnel were deployed on peace-keeping missions. These activities are supported by training facilities at the PLA International Relations Academy in Nanjing and the China Peacekeeping Police Training Center in Langfang, Hebei Province.

PLA GROUND FORCE

The approximately 1.6-million-person (and gradually decreasing) ground force has historically dominated the PLA, both numerically and politically. Long equipped with obsolete Soviet equipment, since the 1980s it has been periodically downsized and restructured, and its equipment modernized. Its eighteen Group Armies, divided among seven military regions, each now generally have two or three infantry divisions or brigades and one armored division or brigade, plus other units.

A variety of paramilitary forces support the PLA. In the mid-1980s, as part of a major restructuring and personnel reduction, several organizations with largely nonmilitary functions were at least partially removed from PLA ground-force command. The PAP was formed in April 1983 from PLA units tasked with internal security missions and from the Ministry of Public Security's armed police, border-defense police, and firefighting police units. In wartime, the PAP will assist the PLA ground forces in defensive operations; in peacetime, the PAP performs such missions as internal security (in support of the Ministry of Public Security) and protection of China's forests, gold mines, and hydroelectric facilities, as well as firefighting, personal security, and border-defense tasks.

The People's Militia, which supports security operations during war or national emergency, has been augmented by the PLA reserve force (established in 1984). PLA reserve units are commanded by PLA provincial military district headquarters. The Xinjiang Production Construction Corps (XPCC), which operates state farms structured along military lines in remote regions, was formed in October 1954. While the XPCC (like the Railway Corps and the Capital Construction Corps) was removed from PLA control in the early 1980s, it still performs economic and social functions. Several militia units have been formed from personnel assigned to its work units. The XPCC also cooperates closely with PAP forces in the area.

PLA NAVY (PLAN)

In 1949 Mao Zedong declared, "to oppose imperialist aggression, we must build a powerful navy." Founded on April 23, 1949, the PLAN established its headquarters in Beijing in April 1950 and its first base in Qingdao in September 1950. Assisted by 2,500 Soviet advisers, the PLAN was initially led by PLA ground-force commanders, whose forces were primarily former Nationalist sailors, many of whom had defected voluntarily, and their vessels. During the Cold War, the PLAN was repeatedly reorganized, largely in attempt to improve equipment and maintenance. Until 1985, the PLAN was charged with coastal defense. As a subordinate organization, the PLAN would support the PLA in what Mao envisioned to be a major ground war against the superpowers. Following rapprochement with the United States in 1972, this concern was directed solely at the Soviet Union.

During the late 1970s, however, evidence emerged that China might be moving beyond a policy of coastal defense. The PLAN sent submarines into the South China Sea and beyond the first island chain into the Pacific Ocean for the first time. An "offshore defense strategy" was officially approved by the Central Military Commission in 1985 (Chiang Shang-chou 1998). This major paradigm shift was driven by Deng Xiaoping's assessment that a great-power war would not occur for some time and that coastal economic development should take precedence, and it was accelerated by increasing People's Republic of China (PRC) concerns with maritime resources and sovereignty (particularly over Taiwan as it began to democratize in the late 1980s, a process that would raise popular questions about its status vis-à-vis the mainland). This shift was further articulated and implemented by PLAN commander Admiral Liu Huaqing, who served as deputy director of the Defense Science and Technology Commission in the 1960s, chief of the PLAN (1982–1988), and vice chairman of the Central Military Commission (1989–1997), and who helped transform the PLAN into a more modern and professional force.

China's evolving platforms and weaponry suggest an "access denial" strategy consistent with Beijing's focus on Taiwan. Apparent inability to challenge U.S. Navy intervention in the 1995–1996 Taiwan Strait crisis may have motivated Beijing to accelerate PLAN development, with submarines as a major focus. China is simultaneously constructing two classes of indigenously designed diesel vessels (Song/Type 039 and Yuan/Type 041) and two classes of nuclear vessels (Shang-class/Type 093 submarines and Jin-class/Type 094 ballistic missile submarines), while importing Kilo-class diesel submarines from Russia. Rapidly upgrading its previously backward destroyer fleet, China has built five new classes of destroyers since the early 1990s. China's inventory of frigates has likewise substantially improved since the early 1990s, with major upgrades taking place both within and between four successive indigenously built classes—some of which have entered series production.

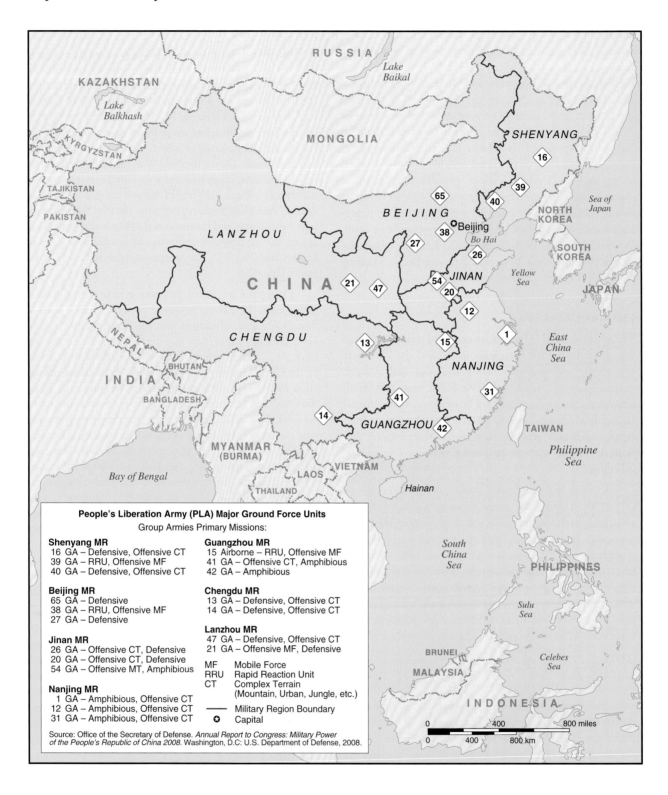

People's Liberation Army (PLA) Major Ground Force Units
Group Armies Primary Missions:

Shenyang MR
16 GA – Defensive, Offensive CT
39 GA – RRU, Offensive MF
40 GA – Defensive, Offensive CT

Beijing MR
65 GA – Defensive
38 GA – RRU, Offensive MF
27 GA – Defensive

Jinan MR
26 GA – Offensive CT, Defensive
20 GA – Offensive CT, Defensive
54 GA – Offensive MT, Amphibious

Nanjing MR
 1 GA – Amphibious, Offensive CT
12 GA – Amphibious, Offensive CT
31 GA – Amphibious, Offensive CT

Guangzhou MR
15 Airborne – RRU, Offensive MF
41 GA – Offensive CT, Amphibious
42 GA – Amphibious

Chengdu MR
13 GA – Defensive, Offensive CT
14 GA – Defensive, Offensive CT

Lanzhou MR
47 GA – Defensive, Offensive CT
21 GA – Offensive MF, Defensive

MF   Mobile Force
RRU Rapid Reaction Unit
CT   Complex Terrain
       (Mountain, Urban, Jungle, etc.)

——— Military Region Boundary
⊙ Capital

Source: Office of the Secretary of Defense. *Annual Report to Congress: Military Power of the People's Republic of China 2008*. Washington, D.C: U.S. Department of Defense, 2008.

In 2008 the PLAN commander, Admiral Wu Shengli, together with coequal political commissar, Admiral Hu Yanlin, led approximately 290,000 personnel in submarine, surface, naval aviation, coastal defense, and marine corps units, as well as ten institutions of professional military education. Personnel include 25,000 naval aviation personnel in seven divisions with twenty-seven regiments, 8,000 to 10,000 marines, and a coastal defense force of 28,000, reportedly including members of civilian militias. The PLAN has approximately 97,000 each of officers, noncommissioned officers, and conscripts, with the former being further divided into command, political, logistics, equipment, and technical career tracks.

MILITARY REGIONS

China's vast territory, diverse populations, and complex geography, with attendant transportation and logistics challenges, initially necessitated a regional approach to national defense, with centralized control imposed on decentralized operations. The area control of the People's Liberation Army was originally divided into six levels (see Table 1), though terms have varied over time, restructuring has occurred, and mission overlap persists.

Since February 1949 the People's Liberation Army has employed a geographically delineated system of military regions (*junqu*), which comprise military units permanently allocated to them. During wartime, a theater of war (*zhanqu*) encompasses both these geographically based units and any additional units deployed or otherwise operationally assigned there.

In the late 1940s Red Army forces were organized into five field armies (*yezhan jun*) (see Table 2). As part of a larger consolidation of forces at multiple levels, in 1948 the Central Military Commission combined the field armies into five military regions, and four military-region levels were established. The Central Plain (Zhongyuan) Military Region, later renamed the Central South (Zhongnan) Military Region, comprised Henan, Hubei, Hunan, Guangdong, and Guangxi; the East China (Huadong) Military Region comprised Shandong, Jiangxi, Jiangsu, Anhui, Zhejiang, and Fujian; the Northeast (Dongbei) Military Region comprised Heilongjiang, Jilin, and Liaoning; the North China (Huabei) Military Region comprised Shanxi and Hebei; and the Northwest (Xibei) Military Region comprised Xinjiang, Qinghai, Gansu, Ningxia, and Shaanxi. In February 1950 it established a sixth military region, the Southwest (Xinan) Military Region, comprising Sichuan, Yunnan, Guizhou, and Xizang.

In 1955, under Soviet influence, China's six military regions were reconfigured into twelve ground-operations military regions: Shenyang, Beijing, Jinan, Nanjing, Guangzhou, Wuhan, Chengdu, Kunming, Lanzhou, Xinjiang, Inner Mongolia, and Xizang. Each was under a single commander, with some of the thirty-five infantry corps of the People's Liberation Army directly subordinate. The People's Liberation Army Navy was divided into the current North, East, and South Sea Fleets. The operations of the People's Liberation Army Air Force were divided into six air-defense regions. The following year, a thirteenth military region, Fuzhou, was added.

By 1969 the military regions of the People's Liberation Army were reduced to eleven: Shenyang, Beijing, Jinan, Nanjing, Guangzhou, Wuhan, Chengdu, Kunming, Lanzhou, Fuzhou, and Xinjiang (renamed Wulumuqi Military Region in May 1979). (In May 1967 the Inner Mongolia Military Region was reduced to a provincial military district (*sheng junqu*) subordinate to the Beijing Military Region, and in December 1969 the Xizang Military Region was reduced to a provincial military district subordinate to the Chengdu Military Region.)

In 1985 the eleven military regions were reduced to the current seven (with over twenty provincial military districts) as part of a major demobilization. The Shenyang Military Region contains Liaoning, Jilin, and Heilongjiang; the Beijing Military Region contains Hebei, Shanxi, and Inner Mongolia; the Lanzhou Military Region contains Gansu, Shaanxi, Xinjiang, Ningxia, and Qinghai; the Jinan Military Region contains Shandong and Henan; the Nanjing Military Region contains Jiangsu, Zhejiang, Anhui, Fujian, and Jiangxi; the Guangzhou Military Region contains Guangdong, Guangxi, Hunan, Hubei, and Hainan; and the Chengdu Military Region contains Yunnan, Xizang, Guizhou, and Sichuan—as well as the Hong Kong and Macau garrisons.

Below the military-region level, military units answer to the local government/party. The headquarters of provincial military districts command local border, coastal defense, and logistics units of the People's Liberation Army, for example.

BIBLIOGRAPHY

Allen, Kenneth W. Introduction to the PLA's Administrative and Operational Structure. In *The People's Liberation Army as Organization*, ed. James Mulvenon and Andrew Yang, 1–44. Santa Monica, CA: RAND, 2002.

Allen, Kenneth W. History of the PLA's Ground Force Organizational Structure and Military Regions. *Chinese Military Update* (Royal United Services Institute for Defence and Security Studies), May 2004.

Yuan Wei, ed. Zhongguo Renmin Jiefan Jun wu da yezhan budui fazhan shilüe [A brief history of the five field armies of the People's Liberation Army]. Beijing: Jiefangjun Chubanshe, 1987.

Andrew S. Erickson

Functional groups and missions of the People's Liberation Army*

Functional groups	Organizational entity	Missions
General departments	General departments (*zongbu*)	National military strategy (*zhanlüe*)
Theaters of war (*zhanqu*)	Military regions (*dajunqu*)	Theater strategy
Front army (*fangmian jun*), Field army (*yezhan jun*)	N/A	Eliminated in the 1950s
Army group (*bingtuan*)	N/A	Eliminated in the 1950s
Units (*budui*)	Corps (*jun*) / combined Arms group army (*hecheng jituan jun*)	Operational and tactical (*zhanyi zhanshu*)
	Division (*shi*)	Operational and tactical
	Brigade (*lü*)	Operational and tactical
	Regiment (*tuan*)	Tactical (*zhanshu*)
Elements (*fendui*)	Battalion (*ying*)	Tactical
	Company (*lian*)	Tactical
	Platoon (*pai*)	Tactical
	Squad (*ban*)	Tactical

*Major reorganization is in progress to reduce bureaucracy and thereby further mechanization and informatization. For example, some combined arms group armies (particularly ones of secondary importance) have transitioned from division-regiment-battalion format (with its numerous bureaucracies) to brigade-battalion format (with its substantially reduced bureaucracy), thereby eliminating one layer of bureaucracy.

Table 1

The five field armies

Long March	Anti-Japanese War	Civil War
First Front Army	115th Division of the Eighth Route Army	Fourth Field Army, North China Field Army
Second Front Army	120th Division of the Eighth Route Army	First Field Army
Fourth Front Army	129th Division of the Eighth Route Army	Second Field Army
Red Army remnants in Southern China evacuating for the Long March	New Fourth Army	Third Field Army

Table 2

NAVAL AVIATION FORCE

Under Soviet guidance, the PLA established a Naval Aviation Force in 1951. Initially subordinated to the PLAAF, it subsequently was divided into three fleet air divisions. In 1950 a naval air academy was established in Qingdao to provide fifteen months of primarily technical instruction. By January 1953, the PLA Naval Aviation Force had a fighter division and a light bomber division. By 1958, the force had grown to a shore-based force of 470 aircraft charged with coastal air defense.

MARINE CORPS

Taiwan long expected that China would develop a marine corps to defend its offshore islands. Despite persistent rumors, however, the PLA lacked air-cover capabilities and did not deploy such a force in a meaningful way. Since the 1990s, China has made significant progress concerning amphibious warfare, probably because of its perceived relevance to a Taiwan contingency. In 2008 the PLAN possessed at least fifty medium and heavy amphibious lift vessels.

PLA AIR FORCE (PLAAF)

Founded on November 11, 1949, the PLAAF began operations with captured Nationalist and Japanese aircraft. Like the PLAN, its early leaders had only ground experience. The PLA Air Defense Force was merged into the PLAAF in 1957. Lin Biao's doctrine of imminent war during the Cultural Revolution was particularly damaging to the PLAAF, which suffered from a low level of training and high accident rates on aircraft that were poorly constructed and maintained.

Since 1949, the PLAAF has implemented six reductions in force (1960, 1970, 1975, 1985, 1992, 2003), all of which were part of larger PLA force-reduction programs designed to create a more capable, professional force. Early programs were aimed primarily at cutting the size of headquarters staffs from 15 to 20 percent. In December 1975, the PLAAF reduced its entire force by 100,000 people, and in August 1985, it further downsized 20 percent by eliminating some organizations, reforming the unit-organization structure, and eliminating old equipment. In October 1992, it carried out yet another 20 percent reduction. In September 2003, the PLA initiated its tenth downsizing since 1951 (Zhu Rongchang 1996, pp. 973, 977, 980, 982). The

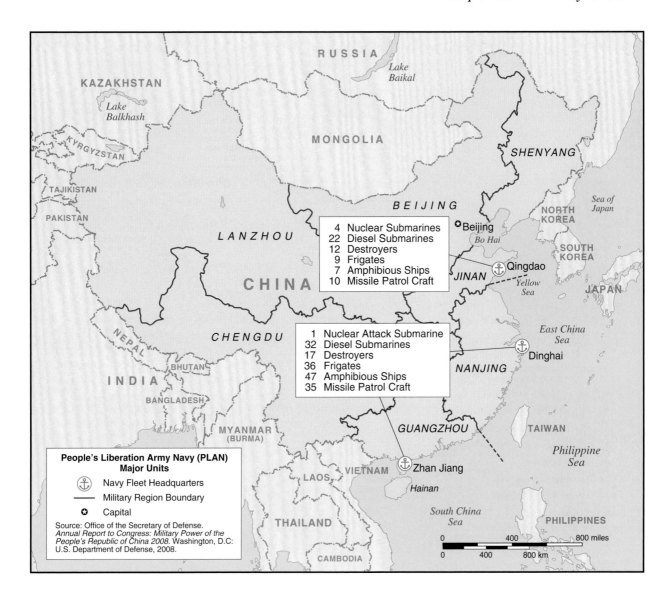

People's Liberation Army Navy (PLAN)
Major Units

⚓ Navy Fleet Headquarters

— Military Region Boundary

⊙ Capital

Source: Office of the Secretary of Defense.
*Annual Report to Congress: Military Power of the
People's Republic of China 2008.* Washington, D.C:
U.S. Department of Defense, 2008.

4	Nuclear Submarines
22	Diesel Submarines
12	Destroyers
9	Frigates
7	Amphibious Ships
10	Missile Patrol Craft

1	Nuclear Attack Submarine
32	Diesel Submarines
17	Destroyers
36	Frigates
47	Amphibious Ships
35	Missile Patrol Craft

2003–2004 downsizing included 200,000 troops, of which 170,000 (85%) were officers (*People's Daily* 2006).

The PLAAF also has a surface-to-air missile and antiaircraft artillery corps and three airborne divisions assigned to the Fifteenth Airborne Army. It has multiple academies and research institutes. Together with the PLA Naval Aviation Force, the PLAAF possessed 2,300 operational combat aircraft of varying degrees of capability in 2008. Their range is severely limited by lack of deck-aviation platforms, substandard aerial-refueling capabilities, and overseas bases. Long hampered by the inadequacy of China's domestic aviation industry, the PLAAF still relies on massive imports of Russian planes and their components, particularly aerial-refueling tankers and jet engines. Helicopters have been an area of particular weakness for the PLA. Most platforms in its disproportionately small fleet (roughly three hundred in the PLA and forty in the PLAN) are either imports or copies of foreign models.

SECOND ARTILLERY FORCE

The PLA's surface-to-surface missile troops were established under the Central Military Commission's artillery troops in December 1957. Following China's successful detonation of a nuclear weapon in 1964, the PLA Second Artillery headquarters was established in 1966. The following year, it received China's artillery corps' missile troops and schools. Guided and directed by the Central Military Commission (which has had wartime release authority for all nuclear and strategic weapons since at least 1982), Second Artillery has operational control for all nuclear missiles and is responsible for most of China's conventional and nuclear ballistic missiles (although the PLAN may have operational control of ballistic missile submarines).

In 2008 Second Artillery had approximately 90,000 personnel and 100 to 400 nuclear weapons, divided among a headquarters, two command academies, one engineering

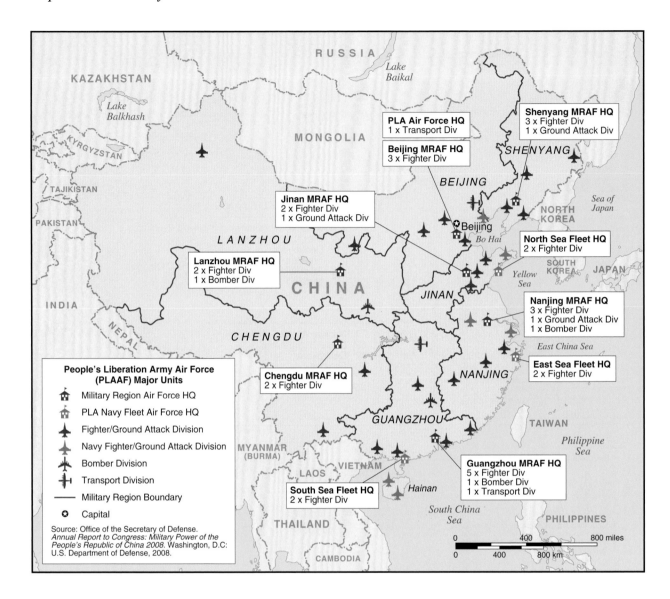

design academy, four research institutes, and six corps-level launch bases that have multiple missile-launch brigades: Shenyang, Huangshan, Kunming, Luoyang, Huaihua, and Xining. China has positioned 675 to 715 mobile DF-11 (300-kilometer range) and 315 to 355 DF-15/CSS-6 (600-kilometer range) SRBMs (short-range ballistic missiles) in coastal areas opposite Taiwan. At least five brigades are presumably commanded by the Huangshan base, two by PLA ground forces. China is also fielding a number of new strategic nuclear systems. An upgraded version of China's twenty DF-5/CSS-4 liquid-fueled ICBMs (intercontinental ballistic missiles) have a range of more than 13,000 kilometers and may be equipped with multiple independently targetable reentry vehicles. Based on the JL-1 SLBM (submarine-launched ballistic missile), China's sixty to eighty 2,500-kilometer-range DF-21s are solid-propellant and road mobile. China's 7,250-kilometer-range DF-31/CSS9 ICBM and its 11,200-kilometer-range-31A variant are also solid-

propellant and road mobile (initially deployed c. 2007), making them extremely difficult to target, as would be any 8,000-kilometer-range JL-2 SLBMs (said to be a derivative of the DF-31) eventually based on Type 094 ballistic missile submarines at sea (Office of the Secretary of Defense 2008).

HISTORY

Founded during the Nanchang Uprising on August 1, 1927, and throughout the Long March, the War of Resistance against Japan (1937–1945), and the War of Liberation (1945–1949), the Red Army gradually incorporated subordinate units until the PRC's establishment on October 1, 1949. While the term *People's Liberation Army* was used to describe individual units as early as 1945, only a Central Military Commission order on November 1, 1948, made the term *PLA* broadly applicable to the Chinese Communist Party (CCP) armed forces. In 1949 the PLAN and PLAAF were

NEW FOURTH ARMY

The New Fourth Army was the smaller of two Communist armies that fought against Japan's aggression during the Anti-Japanese War (1937–1945) as part of the National Revolutionary Army led by Chiang Kai-shek (Jiang Jieshi), head of the Guomindang, or Nationalist Party, and military ruler of the Republic of China.

The New Fourth Army, twelve-thousand men strong, was organized at the time of the anti-Japanese second United Front of the Guomindang and the Chinese Communist Party. First established under nominal Nationalist command on December 25, 1937, in Hankou, the army was in fact controlled by the Communist Party leadership. Its original four divisions and one special-operations battalion, which assembled for action in Anhui Province in April 1938, were composed of survivors from the Communist guerrilla units that stayed behind in Jiangxi and Fujian provinces under the command of Xiang Ying (1895–1941) after the main Red Army forces had embarked on their historic Long March to the northwest in 1934–1935.

The New Fourth Army was led by Communist commander Ye Ting (1897–1946), with Xiang Ying as his deputy. The Guomindang War Ministry assigned it to conduct military operations in an area south of the Yangzi River near Shanghai. Much like the Eighth Route Army, the New Fourth Army operated in Japanese-occupied territory, employing the same tactics of large-scale guerrilla warfare that had proved so effective in southern China during the civil war with the Nationalists following the collapse of the first United Front in 1927.

Sporadic skirmishes between Nationalists and Communists erupted into full-scale fighting during the New Fourth Army incident, when Nationalist troops ambushed and destroyed the New Fourth Army on January 6–7, 1941. Thousands of Communist soldiers, including the deputy commander Xiang Ying, were killed. About 4,000 survivors were captured and imprisoned, including the wounded army commander Ye Ting, while only about a thousand men escaped and joined the Eighth Route Army. Even though President Chiang had officially disbanded it, the New Fourth Army was reorganized by the Communists on January 20, 1941. Based at Jiangsu, the army remained operationally active until the end of the Anti-Japanese War under the leadership of the commander Chen Yi (1901–1976) and his deputy Liu Shaoqi (1898–1969). Amid bitter recriminations from both sides, the New Fourth Army incident ended all substantive cooperation between Communists and Nationalists, thus confirming the virtual collapse of their second United Front.

During the renewed civil war (1946–1949) between Nationalists and Communists, the New Fourth Army was incorporated into the new People's Liberation Army. Its heroic military exploits and temporary defeat at the hands of Guomindang troops have now acquired an iconic, almost mythical role in Chinese Communist historiography, especially as a symbol of Chiang Kai-shek's treachery.

BIBLIOGRAPHY

Benton, Gregor. *New Fourth Army: Communist Resistence along the Yangtze and the Huai, 1938–1941.* Berkeley: University of California Press, 1999.

Xiang, Lanxin. *Mao's Generals: Chen Yi and the New Fourth Army.* Lanham, MD: University Press of America, 1998.

Rossen Vassilev

established. In practice, however, these services would be subordinated to the army through the end of the Cold War. A survey of PLA uses of force during the latter half of the twentieth century reveals primarily ground-force actions on China's land borders with some degree of air support, but also several naval efforts to assert sovereignty over disputed islands.

The War to Resist U.S. Aggression and Aid Korea (Korean War, 1950–1953) came at a terrible human cost and convinced Mao's generals that modernization and professionalization were essential. By 1958, however, Mao determined that "people's war" of attrition was the correct choice for China, and by 1965 officers seeking to emphasize professional training were actively persecuted.

In the first decades after Chiang Kai-shek (Jiang Jieshi) and the Nationalists retreated to Taiwan, many low-level skirmishes took place between Communist and Nationalist forces near the mainland's coastal islands. The most dramatic of these was part of the 1954 Yijiangshan campaign, the PLA's one truly "joint" campaign as of 2008. On October 25, 1949, thirty-thousand Third Field Army soldiers had attempted to take Jinmen via small boats across the 10-kilometer strait, but suffered heavy casualties and only seized a small beachhead, which they failed to reinforce, and withdrew. In spring 1954, the PLAN began to shell Jinmen and Mazu, prompting U.S. naval and air force deployment to the region and support for the Nationalist garrisons. In September, the PLA amassed

RED ARMY

The Nanchang Uprising of August 1, 1927, was the Chinese Communist Party's (CCP) first independent military action and—even though a dismal failure—August 1 (*ba-yi*) is still celebrated annually as the birth of the People's Liberation Army (PLA). Survivors of the Nanchang Uprising, including Zhu De, He Long, Zhou Enlai, and Ye Jianying, eventually joined with Mao Zedong to form the Red Army and organize a peasant-based revolutionary movement.

By 1930, the rural Jiangxi Soviet was composed of about a dozen liberated areas, while the Red Army had grown to approximately 60,000 to 65,000 soldiers. Beginning in December 1930, Chiang Kai-shek (Jiang Jieshi) launched a series of five encirclement campaigns. In October 1933, the Fifth Encirclement campaign, with a combined force of 700,000 soldiers, successfully used a blockhouse strategy devised by Chiang's German military advisers (who had replaced the Soviet advisers expelled in 1927) to surround and blockade the Jiangxi Soviet.

The Communists retreated from South China on the Long March to Yan'an in China's northwest. Although the CCP later treated this as a heroic era, in reality, the Long March was a strategic disaster. For example, after the yearlong 6,000-mile Long March, only about 10,000 Red Army soldiers reached Yan'an in October 1935.

Subsequently, following Mao's adoption of guerrilla tactics, the Red Army played a key role in the Communists' rise to power. During the War of Resistance (1937–1945), the Communists cooperated with the Nationalists, and the Red Army was divided into the Eighth Route Army and the New Fourth Army. On August 9, 1945, the two armies were merged to form the PLA as Mao declared the anti-Japanese offensive.

Bruce Elleman

forces near the Dachen Archipelago's Yijiangshan Islands, engaged in drills, and conducted aerial reconnaissance. On November 1, the PLAAF and PLAN staged a seventy-eight-day blockade of the islands. On January 18, 1955, with an amphibious landing supported by air and naval forces, the PLA captured the island. From February 2 to February 9, the PLA seized four other islands.

In the 1958 Taiwan Strait crisis, mainland China fought seven air battles with Taiwan, while U.S. ships escorted Nationalist ships to resupply Nationalist-held offshore islands and the Soviet Union supplied SA-2 missiles to China. Following Sino-Soviet disagreement, the crisis ended inconclusively (although intermittent shelling would continue until Beijing and Washington normalized relations on January 1, 1979). The crisis highlighted the fact that PLA and PLAN limitations and U.S. support precluded Beijing from taking Taiwan and that Moscow would not provide Beijing with a nuclear umbrella. Before the crisis, Nationalist aircraft were able to overfly the mainland as far north as Tianjin; subsequent deployment of PLAAF aircraft opposite Taiwan limited Nationalist overflights to U.S.-sponsored U-2 reconnaissance flights. Five were shot down before the program ceased in 1967.

The McMahon Line is a product of the 1914 Simla Convention between Britain and Tibet. Though as late as 2008 it represented the effective boundary between India and China (and is accepted by the former), the PRC has always maintained that Tibet lacked the sovereignty to conclude treaties and has claimed 150,000 square kilometers of territory south of the line. Following a series of border disputes beginning in 1959, in a series of attacks in 1962 the PLA routed Indian forces before unilaterally declaring a cease-fire and withdrawing 20 kilometers behind the "line of actual control." Three years later, China conducted a noninvasive mobilization to assist ally Pakistan.

During the Vietnam War (1957–1975), China provided military assistance to Communist allies in Southeast Asia. The PLA made incursions into Burma (Myanmar) in 1960 and 1961. In the 1960s, the PLA assisted Laos by constructing roads and providing air defense. China supplied North Vietnam with large amounts of weaponry throughout the Vietnam War.

Despite major Chinese preparations for a conflict with the Soviet Union, which absorbed considerable resources and planning from the mid-1960s through the early 1980s (and impeded development of a rationally configured defense industrial base or significant efforts to assert sovereignty over territorial claims on China's maritime periphery), actual hostilities erupted only once, and on a minor scale, in the Zhenbao Island conflict of March 2, 1969, when fire was exchanged as Chinese troops approached the island in the middle of the Ussuri River (Beijing claimed it represented the boundary demarcation line based on the "thalweg principle"). Subsequent Russian attempts to retake the island failed, both sides desisted, and tensions eased several years later. The question of which side initiated the conflict remains disputed. Some scholars believe Mao ordered the conflict to demonstrate resolve and thereby deter Soviet invasion.

While supporting North Vietnamese forces during the Vietnam War, Beijing opposed Saigon (Ho Chi Minh City) during the 1974 Xisha Islands defensive campaign. On January 11, the PRC Ministry of Foreign Affairs declared that China had incontestable sovereignty over the Xisha and their

EIGHTH ROUTE ARMY

The Eighth Route Army was the larger of two Communist armies that fought against Japan's aggression and occupation during the Second Sino-Japanese War (1937–1945). It formed part of the National Revolutionary Army led by Generalissimo Chiang Kai-shek (Jiang Jieshi, 1887–1975), head of the ruling Nationalist Party (Guomindang) and the Republic of China.

On September 6, 1937, during the anti-Japanese second United Front alliance between the Guomindang and the Chinese Communist Party, the Eighth Route Army was created by combining three divisions of the Red Army, the Communist military arm, and placing them formally under Nationalist command. Comprising the 115th, 120th, and the 129th Divisions, the newly created army, 45,000-men strong, was led by legendary Red Army commander Zhu De (1886–1976) and his deputy Peng Dehuai (1898–1974). On September 25–26, 1937, the 115th Division, under the command of Lin Biao (1907–1971), ambushed units of the Japanese Imperial Army at the Great Wall pass of Pingxingguan and won China's first major military victory in the Second Sino-Japanese War.

In 1938 the Eighth Route Army was reorganized into the Eighteenth Army Group, nominally under the command of Nationalist-aligned warlord Yan Xishan (1883–1960), the "model governor" of Shanxi Province. But the army group, which grew to some 600,000 troops by 1945, remained under Zhu De's direct control throughout the war and operated behind Japanese lines independently of the Nationalists, especially after the collapse of the second United Front in December 1940. As early as December 1939, Guomindang armies in southern Shanxi joined the Japanese in attacking the troops of the former Eighth Route Army that were waging large-scale guerrilla warfare in northern China. From August to December 1940, Zhu De and Peng Dehuai directed the successful Hundred Regiments campaign (which involved 115 regiments from the 115th, 120th, and the 129th Divisions), launching a series of conventional military attacks against Japanese-held cities and railway links in central China.

American observers visiting Communist-held Yan'an during the Second Sino-Japanese War reported that the highly mobile and self-sustaining Eighth Route Army was the best-organized and best-led fighting force in the world for its size and purpose, skillfully using rural guerrilla operations to defeat an enemy that was many times superior in numbers and heavy weaponry. During the renewed civil war between the Nationalists and Communists (1946–1949), all units of the former Eighth Route Army were incorporated into the new People's Liberation Army. The famous military exploits of the Eighth Route Army later acquired an iconic, almost mythical role in Chinese Communist historiography.

BIBLIOGRAPHY

Carlson, Evans F. *The Chinese Army: Its Organization, and Its Military Efficiency*. New York: Institute of Pacific Relations, 1940.

Carlson, Evans F. *Twin Stars of China: A Behind-the-Scenes Story of China's Valiant Struggle for Existence by a U.S. Marine Who Lived and Moved with the People*. Westport, CT: Hyperion Press, 1975.

Carlson, Evans F. *China at War, 1937–1941*. Ed. Hugh Deane. New York: China and U.S. Publications, 1993.

Smedley, Agnes. *China Fights Back: An American Woman with the Eighth Route Army*. Westport, CT: Hyperion Press, 1977.

Rossen Vassilev

---

surrounding waters. Over several days, a PLAN force of eleven vessels and 600 assault troops attacked South Vietnamese ships after they reportedly resisted PRC patrol boats and fishermen. Within two days, this largest PLA amphibious operation to date gained Chinese control of the islands, reportedly at the cost of 300 South Vietnamese casualties. In 1978 the PLAN confronted Japanese forces in the area surrounding the disputed Senkaku/Diaoyu Islands.

China launched a "self-defensive counterattack against Vietnam" from February 17 to March 17, 1979. While moving thirty to forty divisions to the Vietnamese border, China simultaneously prepared to deter an attack by the Soviet Union. Encountering heavy resistance when its forces crossed the border, Beijing stated that the PLA would not proceed farther than 50 kilometers into Vietnam. The PLAAF did not engage in air combat. After sustaining what it claimed were 20,000 casualties, which Vietnam claimed were 42,000, the PLA withdrew systematically. Severe problems with coordination, command, control, and logistics demonstrated how unprepared for combat the PLA had become.

In March 1988, the PLAN sank three Vietnamese supply vessels and seized several reefs in the disputed Nansha

Chinese soldiers watching an outdoor military movie, July 26, 1997. *Protecting the border of China for over seventy years, the People's Liberation Army continues to be influenced by traditional Confucian values of self reliance that have been practiced by military leaders throughout the history of China.* **AP IMAGES**

Islands. In 1995 the PLAN seized Mischief Reef in the Nansha Islands, also claimed by the Philippines.

The PLA was directly involved in politics through the PRC's founding in 1949, and became reinvolved during the Cultural Revolution, but since then has minimized its political activity. A challenge for civil-military relations

emerged when, despite protests from retired senior generals, Deng Xiaoping ordered the PLA to crack down on popular demonstrations in Beijing on June 4, 1989, after police and PAP units failed to disperse protesters, many of whom were killed. Reportedly, some commanders and units refused to participate in the crackdown. The PLA had also suppressed an uprising in Xizang earlier that year. For the next few years after Tiananmen, many PLA units were subject to intensive political indoctrination.

During the 1995–1996 Taiwan Strait crisis, the PLA fired ten DF-15 SRBMs to the north and south of (not over) Taiwan (or in the strait) as part of large-scale military exercises and accompanying political rhetoric to discourage independence moves by Taiwan president Lee Teng-hui (Li Denghui) before and during his election.

MAJOR LEADERS

In its initial decades, the Red Army had considerable leadership continuity, as commanders of the campaigns from the 1930s to the 1950s largely rose through the ranks together in the same military regions and forged a variety of reciprocal bonds. Schooled on the battleground of "people's war," these first-generation commanders had little naval or air experience. They also played a major role in affairs of state: Mao and Deng became national leaders; Zhou Enlai became premier; and Chen Yi became foreign minister.

Paramount leaders have always had disproportionate influence on the PLA because it is a party army. Mao Zedong is the most prominent example of the interrelation between PRC political and military leadership. He led the Chinese Communist Party (CCP) to victory in the anti-Japanese and civil wars, and was China's paramount leader from 1949 to 1976. During that time, he commanded the PLA as head of the Central Military Commission and served as China's foremost military strategist. In developing PLA tactics, Mao drew on both traditions of peasant insurgency and guerrilla warfare experience. Deng Xiaoping served in a variety of military leadership roles during the civil war. In 1975 he was named CCP vice chairman, Central Military Commission vice chairman, and PLA General Staff Department head. From 1978 until his last public appearance in 1994, he was China's preeminent leader. In 1979 he ordered China's self-defensive counterattack against Vietnam, and in 1989 he ordered the PLA Tiananmen crackdown. Deng stepped down as CCP Central Military Commission chairman in 1989 and as State Central Military Commission chairman in 1990. Jiang Zemin increased PLA budgets and directed significant PLA modernization. Hu Jintao, like his predecessors, chairs the Central Military Commission, in addition to serving as general secretary of the CCP and president of the PRC.

In 1955 the PLA's postwar military leadership was established. Ten leading officers were named marshals: Zhu De, Peng Dehuai, Lin Biao, Liu Bocheng, He Long, Chen Yi, Luo Ronghuan, Xu Xiangqian, Nie Rongzhen, and Ye Jianying. Ten were named senior generals: Su Yu, Xu Haidong, Huang Kecheng, Chen Geng, Tan Zheng, Xiao Jingguang, Zhang Yunyi, Luo Ruiqing, Wang Shusheng, and Xu Guangda. Fifty-seven were named generals, including Chen Zaidao, Han Xianchu, Hong Xuezhi, Li Kenong,

Song Renqiong, Ulanhu, Wang Zhen, Xie Fuzhi, Yang Dezhi, and Zhang Aiping. One hundred and seventy-seven were named lieutenant generals.

Like other governmental systems, the PLA has vertical and horizontal lines of authority. The PLA has long had a specific institutional culture (focused on taking orders based on hierarchy) and a significant degree of autonomy. At various times, such horizontal factors as localism, provincialism, and factionalism have undermined the vertical system. As the PLA becomes more like other large Chinese government bureaucracies, policy processes are becoming more complex and negotiated.

SEE ALSO *Army and Politics; Central State Organs since 1949: Central Military Commission; Lin Biao; Military Culture and Tradition; Peng Dehuai; Zhu De.*

BIBLIOGRAPHY

Allen, Kenneth W. Introduction to the PLA's Administrative and Operational Structure. In *The People's Liberation Army as Organization*, ed. James Mulvenon and Andrew Yang, 1–44. Santa Monica, CA: RAND, 2002.

Blasko, Dennis J. *The Chinese Army Today: Tradition and Transformation for the 21st Century.* New York: Routledge, 2006.

Chen Jian. *Mao's China and the Cold War.* Chapel Hill: University of North Carolina Press, 2001.

Chiang Shang-chou. China's Naval Development Strategy: Building an Offshore Defensive Naval Armed Force. *Wide Angle* (FBIS). December 16, 1998.

Christensen, Thomas J. *Useful Adversaries: Grand Strategy, Domestic Mobilization, and Sino-American Conflict, 1947–1958.* Princeton, NJ: Princeton University Press, 1996.

Cole, Bernard D. *The Great Wall at Sea: China's Navy Enters the Twenty-First Century.* Annapolis, MD: Naval Institute Press, 2001.

Dangdai Zhongguo haijun [China today: Navy]. Beijing: China Social Sciences Press, 1987.

Jiang Siyi, ed. *Zhongguo renmin jiefangjun dashi dian* [The dictionary of the PLA's major events]. Tianjin, PRC: Tianjin People's Press, 1992.

Kamphausen, Roy, and Andrew Scobell, eds. *Right-Sizing the People's Liberation Army: Exploring the Contours of China's Military.* Carlisle, PA: Army War College, 2007.

Liu Huaqing. *Liu Huaqing hui yi lu* [The memoirs of Liu Huaqing]. Beijing: People's Liberation Army Press, 2004.

Liu Xunyao, ed. *Kongjun da cidian* [Air force dictionary]. Shanghai: Shanghai Dictionary Press, 1996.

Mao Zedong. *Selected Military Writings of Mao Tse-tung.* Beijing: Foreign Languages Press, 1967.

People's Daily Online. China Cuts Army by 200,000 with Ground Army Ratio to Record Low. January 9, 2006.

Office of the Secretary of Defense. *Annual Report to Congress: Military Power of the People's Republic of China, 2008.* http://www .defenselink.mil/pubs/pdfs/China_Military_Report_08.pdf.

Ryan, Mark A., David M. Finkelstein, and Michael A. McDevitt, eds. *Chinese Warfighting: The PLA Experience since 1949.* Armonk, NY: Sharpe, 2002.

Swanson, Bruce. *Eighth Voyage of the Dragon: A History of China's Quest for Seapower.* Annapolis, MD: Naval Institute Press, 1982.

Whiting, Allen S. *The Chinese Calculus of Deterrence: India and Indochina.* Ann Arbor: University of Michigan Press, 1975.

Xin Ming, ed. *Zhongguo renmin jiefangjun kongjun shouce* [People's Liberation Army Air Force handbook]. Qingdao, PRC: Qingdao Press, 1991.

Yang Zhiben, ed. *Zhongguo haijun baike quanshu* [China navy encyclopedia], Vols. 1 and 2. Beijing: Sea Tide Press, 1998.

Zhang Xusan, ed. *Haijun da cidian* [Naval dictionary]. Shanghai: Shanghai Dictionary Press, 1991.

Zhongguo junshi baike quanshu [Chinese military encyclopedia]. Beijing: Academy of Military Science Publishers, 1997.

Zhongguo renmin jiefangjun da shiji 1927–1982 [People's Liberation Army chronicle, 1927–1982]. Beijing: PLA Academy of Military Science, 1983.

Zhongguo renmin jiefangjun shi de 70 nian [Seventy years of the PLA]. Beijing: Military Science Press, 1997.

Zhu Rongchang, ed. *Kongjun da cidian* [Air force dictionary]. Shanghai: Shanghai Dictionary Publishing House, 1996.

Andrew S. Erickson

The views expressed in this entry are those of the author alone and do not represent the official policies or estimates of the U.S. Navy or any other element of the U.S. government.

COMMAND STRUCTURE OF THE ARMED SERVICES

Like all other major parts of government, the People's Liberation Army (PLA) has parallel Communist Party– and state-bureaucratic structures. Every headquarters of the PLA has a party committee (*dangwei*) and a party standing committee (*dangwei changwei*). Political commissars (usually the committee secretary) and military commanders (usually the deputy secretary) make decisions using a party-committee system that brings them and their deputies into a collective decision-making process. Staff departments (e.g., command, political, logistics, armaments) support their decisions by providing information and analysis to relevant party committees and then monitor and guide implementation at lower levels.

On the party side, the Central Military Commission (Zhongyang Junshi Weiyuanhui), established in February 1930 as part of a gradual, negotiated process, makes decisions on operational policy (*zuozhan fang'an*) for the PLA as its party committee and determines national military strategy, as China's national command authority. It currently has eleven members: Chairman Hu Jintao, China's president; two vice chairs; a defense minister; four general department heads, and the commanders of the PLA Navy, Air Force, and Second Artillery. The general office (*bangongting*) of the Central Military Commission (CMC) coordinates the general departments, services, and premier professional-military-education institutions (the National Defense University and the Academy of Military Science) to realize national military strategy. Four general departments, led by commission members, are responsible for operational command (*zuozhan zhihui*), and assist in the promulgation and implementation of CMC policy (e.g., by

A comparison of administrative levels

Organization	First level	Second level*	Third level**
General departments (*zongbu*)	4 departments (*bu*)	Department (*bu*), general office (*bangongting*), bureau (*ju*)	Bureau (*ju*)
Service headquarters (*junzhong*)	4 departments (*bu*)	Department (*bu*), office (*bangongshi*), bureau (*ju*)	Division (*chu*)
Military-region headquarters (*junqu*)	4 departments (*bu*)	Department (*bu*), office (*bangongshi*)	Division (*chu*)
Military region of the Air Force/fleet headquarters (*junqu* Kongjun/ Jiandui)	4 departments (*bu*)	Office (*bangongshi*), division (*chu*)	Office (*ke*)
Army/corps (*jun*)	4 departments (*bu*)	Division (*chu*)	Office (*ke*)
Base (*jidi*)	4 departments (*bu*)	Division (*chu*)	Office (*ke*)
Division (*shi*)	4 departments (*bu*)	Office (*ke*)	
Brigade (*lü*)	4 departments (*bu*)	Office (*ke*)	
Regiment (*tuan*)	Headquarters department (*bu*); political, logistics, and armament/ maintenance divisions (*chu*)	Branch (*gu*)	
Battalion (*ying*), group (*dadui*)	N/A		
Company (*lian*), squadron (*zhongdui*)	N/A		

*Some second level departments are in the process of being consolidated.

**Third level organizations are in the process of being consolidated and reduced, particularly below the division level.

Table 1

Officer grades and ranks of the People's Liberation Army

Grade (*zhiwu dengji*)	Military rank (*junxian*)	Service limit age	Army	Navy	Air Force	2nd Artillery
1. Central Military Commission chairman (Junwei *zhuxi*), vice chairman (*fuzhuxi*)	Chairman: none; vice chairman: general					
2. Central Military Commission member (Junwei *weiyuan*)	General		General departments			
3. Military-region leader (*daqu zhengzhi*)	General, lieutenant general	65	Military region/general department deputy leader	Headquarters	Headquarters	Headquarters
4. Military region deputy leader (*daqu fuzhi*)	Lieutenant general, major general	63		Fleet/naval aviation	Military region of the Air Force	
5. Army leader (*zhengjun*)	Major general, lieutenant general	55	Army (*jituan jun*), military district	Base, fleet aviation	Airborne army	Base
6. Army deputy leader (*fujun*)	Major general, senior colonel	55				
7. Division leader (*zhengshi*)	Senior colonel, major general	50	Division	Garrison (*zhidui*), flotilla (*jiandui*)	Division command post	
8. Division deputy leader (*fushi*), brigade leader (*zhenglü*)	Colonel, senior colonel	50	Brigade		Brigade	Brigade
9. Regiment leader (*zhengtuan*), brigade deputy leader (*fulü*)	Colonel, lieutenant colonel	45	Regiment	Group (*jianting dadui*)	Regiment, brigade deputy leader	Brigade deputy leader
10. Regiment deputy leader (*futuan*)	Lieutenant colonel, colonel	45				
11. Battalion leader (*zhengying*)	Major, lieutenant colonel	40	Battalion	Squadron (*jianting zhongdui*)	Battalion, group (*dadui*)	Battalion
12. Battalion deputy leader (*fuying*)	Captain, major	40				
13. Company leader *zhenglian*)	Captain, 1st lieutenant	35	Company		Company, squadron (*zhongdui*)	Company
14. Company deputy leader (*fulian*)	1st lieutenant, captain	35				
15. Platoon leader (*zhengpai*)	2nd or 1st lieutenant	30	Platoon		Platoon, flight (*fendui*)	Platoon

Table 2

helping line officers make decisions): the General Staff Department (strategy and operations); the General Political Department (in charge of personnel, party indoctrination, internal security, and psychological operations since 1931, save for 1937–1946); the General Logistics Department (finance, supply, military-matériel industries, construction, and medical); and the General Armaments Department (in charge of weapons development, production, and acquisition since 1998). The General Staff Department's Second and Third Departments, as well as the General Political Department's Liaison Department, are responsible for intelligence. This bureaucratic pattern is replicated in the military regions, where communications-intercept stations are based (see Table 1).

The fact that the PLA remains a party army is revealed by its small, relatively noninfluential state-side organizations that are counterparts to party organizations. The State Council oversees the Ministry of National Defense (whose minister is a senior member of the CMC, as provided for by China's 1982 constitution) and the state CMC (which merely approves decisions by the party CMC). The Ministry of National Defense was created specifically to interface with foreign counterparts and lacks independent authority. Party pronouncements stipulate that the PLA will remain a party army for the foreseeable future.

This system has the benefit of maintaining political consensus and avoiding rash decisions, but in comparison with Western military systems with complete civilian leadership and a single chain of command, it suffers from two major challenges aggravated by the requirements of modern warfare. First, it is sometimes difficult to divide responsibilities clearly under the unified party-committee leadership. Second, it may be difficult to decide which decisions are sufficiently important to forward to the party committee. This might slow the deployment of troops into combat situations or limit their ability to react quickly to changing conditions once there.

GRADES AND RANKS

The Officer Grade and Rank System (Ganbu Dengji Zhidu) of the PLA has evolved fitfully. In the early years of the PLA,

Enlisted grades and ranks of the People's Liberation Army			
Time in service	**Service period**	**Grade (*sandeng liuji*)**	**Rank (*junxian*)**
1st year	Conscript (2 years)	Conscript (*shibing*)	Private 2nd class (*liebing*)
2nd year			Private 1st class (*shangdengbing*)
2–4 years	1st period (3 years)	1st grade, basic noncommissioned officer (*chuji shiguan*)	Sergeant 1st grade (*yiji shiguan*)
5–7 years	2nd period (3 years)	2nd grade, basic noncommissioned officer (*erji shiguan*)	Sergeant 2nd grade (*erji shiguan*)
8–11 years	3rd period (4 years)	3rd grade, intermediate noncommissioned officer (*zhongji shiguan*)	Sergeant 3rd grade (*sanji shiguan*)
12–15 years	4th period (4 years)	4th grade, intermediate noncommissioned officer (*zhongji shiguan*)	Sergeant 4th grade (*siji shiguan*)
16–20 years	5th period (5 years)	5th grade, advanced noncommissioned officer (*gaoji shiguan*)	Sergeant 5th grade (*wuji shiguan*)
21–30 years	6th period (9 years)	6th grade, advanced noncommissioned officer (*gaoji shiguan*)	Sergeant 6th grade (*liuji shiguan*)

Table 3

there was tension between Mao Zedong, who championed an egalitarian "red" peasant army, and Marshals Zhu De and Peng Dehuai, who advocated a more professional "expert" Western-style military hierarchy. Soviet-style ranks were established in 1955, when ten officers were promoted to marshal and ten to senior general. The call to be red was taken to extremes during the decade of the Cultural Revolution (1966–1976), when many professional-military-education schools were closed, instructors were harassed and in many cases killed, and political study supplanted operationally useful training. Ranks were abolished in 1965 and not reinstated until October 1, 1988, following poor performance during the 1979 "self-defensive counterattack" against Vietnam. The rank of marshal was eliminated. Seventeen officers were promoted to full general, and many officers persecuted during the Cultural Revolution were rehabilitated. By 1993 most of these generals had retired, and Jiang Zemin promoted twenty-five officers to full general both to further standardize and professionalize the officer corps and to consolidate his civilian authority. Tables 2 and 3 outline the PLA's grades (which are more important) and ranks for officers and the enlisted.

BIBLIOGRAPHY

Allen, Kenneth W. Understanding the PLA's Organizational Structure. Strategic Comments (Institute for International Strategic Studies, London), August 2005.

Swaine, Michael. *The Military and Political Succession in China.* Santa Monica, CA: RAND, 1992.

Whitson, William W., with Chen-hsia Huang. *The Chinese High Command: A History of Communist Military Politics, 1927–71.* New York: Praeger, 1973.

Xun Zhenying, ed. *Jundui ganbu guanlixue* [Military cadre management studies]. Beijing: Zhongguo Remin Jiefangjun Guofang Daxue Chubanshe, 1989.

Yao Yanjing, Lai Mingchuan, and Wang Yamin. *Junshi zuzhi tizhi yanjiu* [Military organization system research]. Beijing: Zhongguo Remin Jiefangjun Guofang Daxue Chubanshe, 1997.

Andrew S. Erickson

MILITARY DOCTRINE

Since the Chinese Communist Party (CCP) developed its own military forces in the late 1920s, top Communist leaders have, at least until the 1990s, seen the definition of basic military doctrine as a core role, primarily in their capacity as chair of the Military Affairs Commission of the CCP. Certainly Mao Zedong and, to a lesser extent, Deng Xiaoping, played the leading role in the codification of People's Liberation Army (PLA) military doctrine. Since the 1990s, military professionals have increasingly defined doctrine, with the concurrence of the chairman of the Military Affairs Commission (often also the general secretary of the CCP). The core national interests of China (as defined by the CCP) are to maintain the CCP's leadership position in Chinese society, to defend China's territorial integrity (including creating the ability to bring Taiwan under Chinese control), and increasingly to defend and protect Chinese interests internationally. China's defense doctrine takes these core interests as the starting point to develop systematic ideas governing the role of the use of force and the conditions under which force is used, and to guide the acquisition of capabilities (weapon systems) that make it possible for the successful implementation of doctrine.

The U.S. Department of Defense (DOD) defines *doctrine* as "fundamental principles by which the military forces or elements thereof guide their actions in support of national objectives. It is authoritative but requires judgment in application" (DOD 2001, p. 169). Whatever the U.S. definition, China's definition of doctrine is sufficiently unclear that leading Western experts disagree on what it is. Moreover, while China appears to have a formal written military doctrine, it is not publicly revealed. While there has been some movement toward improved transparency, available public statements are at a high level of generality. These vague statements are often combined with sanitized intelligence reports released by national governments, particularly the U.S. government, to make reasonable assessments about what Chinese military doctrine is. Over time, instead of a formal definition, it is more useful to distinguish among the

110

following: nuclear weapons doctrine; "rhetorical" doctrine (a "doctrine" that served as a deterrent, even if was not one that actually guided military planning); actual uses of force and actual (to the extent they can be determined) plans to use force (from the actual uses of force and what is known about plans to use force, it is possible to work backward and try to infer the military doctrine that explains the apparent pattern of China's use of force). In general, China has been quite circumspect in revealing its military doctrine.

NUCLEAR WEAPONS DOCTRINE

China tested its first nuclear weapon in 1964. At that time, China promised "no first use"—meaning that in a conflict, it would not be the first power to use nuclear weapons. But for the remainder of the Mao period and shortly thereafter, China had no formal nuclear weapons doctrine. Mao simply did not state one, and no other political or military leader discussed the issue as long as the chairman was alive. From the 1970s until the present, China's nuclear weapons doctrine seems consistent with a strategy of minimal deterrence. This means no first use of nuclear weapons, and deploying only a small nuclear force to be used in reprisal after a nuclear attack on China. This threat of retaliation after a nuclear attack was seen as sufficient to deter an attack by a stronger nuclear power in the first place. However, the situation may be changing, as China appears to be in the process of deploying new generations of strategic missiles and nuclear submarines. Currently, however, China's nuclear forces and their training seem consistent with minimal deterrence.

RHETORICAL DOCTRINE

In terms of rhetorical (and sometimes real) doctrine, China has often articulated a doctrine of people's war. Again, this was particularly true of the Mao period in general, and especially from the mid-1960s until the late 1970s. This doctrine argued that should either (or both) superpowers (the United States and Soviet Union) attack China, they would be confronted by the mobilized might of the Chinese people and army. The problem with this as a military "doctrine" was that, were the United States to fight a war with China, it was extremely unlikely to invade the whole of China. Soviet plans were less clear, but the doctrine of people's war played to China's relative strengths, and military planning emphasizes either playing to one's enemies' weaknesses or to one's own strengths. Thus, U.S. and Soviet plans against China would emphasize airpower and missile strikes, rather than a repeat of the Japanese war with China from 1937 to 1945.

While people's war is often associated with guerrilla warfare, in fact, there was more to it. China's leaders understood that the United States and Soviet Union had more technologically sophisticated weapons than China did, and that in the event of an attack on China, Chinese forces would have to be on the defensive. As in the war against Japan, the idea of people's war was that the main force units of the PLA would be preserved (as well as possible) while the population and militia units carried out sabotage, small-scale attacks, and generally wore down the invader. At some point, the tide of battle would turn, and then the main force units of the PLA would attack and destroy the invader. As a rhetorical device, Mao promised that any nation that invaded China would face a situation from which it could not extricate itself. Put forward at a time when the United States was engaged in a smaller-scale people's war in Vietnam, the doctrine of people's war was a rhetorical device used to deter a conventional attack on China. To the extent that China was not attacked by either superpower, it worked.

There is an element of rhetorical doctrine with China's war of words concerning Taiwan as well. Central to China's efforts to prevent Taiwan's de jure independence has been explicit threats to use force (and even to appear to threaten nuclear war with the United States should the United States aid Taiwan's defense). These threats seem to have discouraged a plurality of Taiwan's population from advocating a change in the existing status of de facto independence. Increasingly, however, China's military acquisitions and deployments are focused on Taiwan scenarios. While there is a great deal of rhetoric about China's willingness to use force against Taiwan as a last resort, increasingly China is developing robust capabilities to be able to impose its will and control over Taiwan.

ACTUAL USE OF FORCE

In terms of China's actual use of force, a doctrine of active defense is perhaps a more accurate characterization of China's military doctrine. A major study of China's use of force determined that, after the United States, China was the major power most likely to use force in the 1950–1990 period. Many times when China employed force, it occurred on the Chinese border and over the border. The enemy was not, in classical Maoist guerrilla doctrine, "lured in deep." Rather, the PLA fought the enemy before it could invade China, as in Korea in the 1950s and Vietnam in the 1960s, probably with the idea of preempting a larger attack against China later. In most of these cases, China initiated the actual use of force, and therefore acted offensively, not defensively.

China, like most other countries, portrays its use of force as defensively motivated. This means that, in practice, China's effective or real military doctrine has been concerned with using force offensively to secure China's borders, although hard-and-fast statements are impossible. In the 1960s, China deployed military units in North Vietnam and had many regular force units near the border with North Vietnam, prepared to intervene had the United States invaded North Vietnam (repeating the development of the Korean War). At the same time, China's main force units were deployed far away from the border with the Soviet Union, even as the danger of war became acute in 1969.

Since 2000, the PLA has been preparing to fight "local wars under conditions of informationization." Increasingly, China's capabilities and presumed or inferred doctrine are primarily oriented toward preventing Taiwan from declaring independence, and should that fail, using force to bring about the submission of Taiwan to Beijing's control. This means that China is preparing capabilities and doctrines to challenge U.S. power, should the United States come to the assistance of Taiwan. But Taiwan scenarios are just the beginning of the PLA's rethinking of doctrine and its building of new capabilities in coming years. China's rapid economic growth has made it increasingly dependent on resource flows from around the world, especially oil from the Persian Gulf. The United States (and, to an extent, India) have the capability to interdict oil bound for China, which would fundamentally threaten the Chinese economy, China's power, and the position of the CCP. Currently, China has limited ability to project power much farther than about 150 miles beyond its land borders. But concerns about economic security will increasingly drive it to develop more robust capabilities (if only to protect its vital supply lines), and this in turn will necessitate the creation of new doctrine for the PLA.

BIBLIOGRAPHY

CHINESE VIEWS

Hu Zhefeng. Jianguo yilai ruogan junshi zhanlue fangzhen tanxi [An exploratory analysis of several guiding principles of military strategy since the founding of the PRC]. *Dangdai zhongguo shi yanjiu* [Contemporary China historical studies] 7, 4 (2000): 21–32.

Mao Zedong. *Six Essays on Military Affairs*. Beijing: Foreign Languages Press, 1972.

Peng Guangqian and Yao Youzhi, eds. *The Science of Military Strategy*. Beijing: Military Science Publishing House, 2005.

Pillsbury, Michael, comp. and ed. *China Debates the Future Security Environment*. Washington, DC: National Defense University Press, 2000.

State Council Information Office. *White Paper on National Defense in 2006*. Biennial. http://www.china.org.cn/english/China/194332.htm.

U.S. GOVERNMENT VIEWS

U.S. Department of Defense (DOD). Joint Chiefs of Staff. Joint PUB 1-02: *DOD Dictionary of Military and Associated Terms*. Washington, DC: Author, 2001 (as amended through May 2008).

U.S. Department of Defense (DOD). Office of the U.S. Secretary of Defense. *Annual Report to Congress: Military Power of the People's Republic of China*. 2008. http://www.defenselink.mil/pubs/china.html/.

SCHOLARLY SOURCES

Lewis, John Wilson, and Xue Litai. *China's Strategic Seapower: The Politics of Force Modernization in the Nuclear Age*. Stanford, CA: Stanford University Press, 1994.

Lewis, John Wilson, and Xue Litai. *Imagined Enemies: China Prepares for Uncertain War*. Stanford, CA: Stanford University Press, 2006.

Ryan, Mark A., David M. Finkelstein, and Michael A. McDevitt, eds. *Chinese Warfighting: The PLA Experience since 1949*. Armonk, NY: Sharpe, 2003.

Shambaugh, David. *Modernizing China's Military: Progress, Problems, and Prospects*. Berkeley: University of California Press, 2002.

David Bachman

MILITARY ENTERPRISES AND INDUSTRY SINCE 1949

The economic activity of the People's Liberation Army (PLA) can be divided into four eras, as Thomas Bickford (1994) notes. From 1927 to 1949, the PLA's economic activity supported the Chinese Communist Party (CCP) politically, sustained base areas, and provided military logistical support. From 1949 to 1978, it supported Mao Zedong's goals of rendering China self-sufficient through labor-intensive light industrialization, agricultural collectivization, and military production. From 1978 to 1998, the PLA's economic activity helped fund the PLA itself amid declining defense budgets—at the expense of corruption and diversion. Since 1998, PLA commercialism has been severely restricted, professionalism has increased, and the PLA's overall role in China's economy has declined to its lowest level ever.

CIVIL WAR

The CCP established its first "bases," the Jiangxi Soviet, in a weakly controlled interprovincial border region. A rapidly expanding and diversifying system of farming and production of munitions as well as other necessities supplied the PLA and minimized its material dependence on local peasants, whose loyalty the CCP was trying to court (e.g., by helping peasants harvest crops). After the CCP established the Yan'an Base Area in 1937, small PLA factories (many captured, some of the equipment hauled on the Long March) provided a range of goods, while soldiers (e.g., Wang Zhen's 359th Brigade) cultivated wasteland. By the time of the founding of the People's Republic of China (PRC) in 1949, military enterprises had become firmly entrenched as the CCP's "economic vanguard."

MAO ERA

While Mao approved the establishment of a civilian-controlled armaments industry, he preserved and nurtured PLA production as an essential component of his ideology, and on December 5, 1949, he directed the PLA to engage in major production starting in spring 1950. The PLA played a major role in China's economy and infrastructure development, with an initial 340,000 troops dedicated full-time to agricultural construction divisions, forestry construction divisions, aquaculture, animal husbandry, and mines. In addition, three principal organizations were formed to conduct economic construction activities.

The Railway Construction Corps can be traced to the CCP's Fourth Field Army in the Chinese civil war. First commanded by Lü Zhengcao, it was responsible for building and maintaining strategic rail links. In this capacity, it played a major logistical support role in the Korean War (1950–1953), the 1958 Taiwan crisis, the Vietnam War (1957–1975), and Mao's effort to disperse roughly half of all armaments production among a "third line" network in China's vast interior in the 1960s and 1970s.

The Xinjiang Production Construction Corps (XPCC) was founded by former PLA corps commander, commissar, and first party secretary Wang Zhen under Mao's orders on October 9, 1954. This was part of a larger process of emulating China's Han-era "agricultural garrisons" and Qing-era "military colonies" in establishing "construction corps" to settle, render agriculturally self-sufficient, and develop economically remote regions (e.g., Heilongjiang, Inner Mongolia, and Xinjiang) while engaging in border defense and preparing to resist potential invaders. The XPCC's initial force of 175,000 military personnel, commanded by Tao Zhiyue, was drawn from the First Field Army's Second and Sixth Corps, former Guomindang soldiers, and former military forces of the interwar East Turkestan Republic (Ili National Army), and was subsequently augmented with young civilians. By 1956, the XPCC's 300,000 troops were under the control of the new State Farms and Land Reclamation Ministry. In the 1962 Sino-Indian War, the XPCC supported frontline forces and furnished reserves. Following the 1962 Yining riots, in which thousands of Kazakhs and Uygurs fled to the Soviet Union, XPCC's force rose to 1.48 million. Following Xinjiang leader Wang Enmao's dismissal in 1968 on charges for having used the XPCC as his own regional army, the corps assumed a greater economic role and was stripped of its military designation and absorbed by Xinjiang's provincial government in 1975. Deng Xiaoping restored the XPCC's military role in 1981 amid fears of economic stagnation, Soviet aggression, Islamic fundamentalism, and ethnic separatism.

The Capital Construction Corps was established under the State Council in 1965 by consolidating construction units from various civilian ministries (e.g., transportation). It was responsible for constructing roads (e.g., into Tibet) and hydroelectric facilities, managing forests and gold mines, and engaging in disaster relief. It retained some preexisting responsibilities of subordinate units, such as construction of the Beijing subway (and probably the associated tunnels for use by the military and civilian leadership). The Capital Construction Corps even had a subordinate unit, jointly managed by the Second Ministry of Machine Building, responsible for uranium extraction.

In addition to these major organizations, the PLA also ran a variety of small-scale enterprises. The General Logistics Department controlled most of the largest PLA enterprises, but the General Staff and General Political departments each had their share, as did nearly every PLA organization down to the regiment level. The PLA, the People's Liberation Army Navy (PLAN), and the People's Liberation Army Air Force (PLAAF) ran their own vehicle, ship, and airplane repair factories. The General Logistics Department ran factories to produce military uniforms (e.g., Beijing's 3501 Factory); warehouses to store weapons, food, and uniforms; and one "all-Army" farm (in Heilongjiang). Smaller farms were run by various organizational levels.

What the PLA has never run are the large state-owned military industrial enterprises responsible for armaments production. These have always been civilian-controlled, subordinate to China's State Council. PLA representatives, who report to either the General Armaments Department or service headquarters, are seconded to these enterprises in Military Representative Offices (factories) and Military Representative Bureaus (industrial cities) to serve as liaisons and ensure quality control.

Beyond these core organizational responsibilities, PLA involvement in agriculture, hydrological construction, and other production rose sharply during Mao's political campaigns (e.g., the Great Leap Forward and the Cultural Revolution [1966–1969]), and fell at other times. Even before Mao's death in 1976, the PLA had already begun to reduce its sideline production because of pressing concerns regarding the Soviet Union.

DENG ERA

Deng Xiaoping's post-1978 reforms brought needed technology transfer, foreign direct investment, and export markets. During the Sixth Five-Year Plan (1980–1985), defense was prioritized as the "fourth modernization," but personnel were reduced and armaments spending declined in relative terms (from 17.5% to 10.4% of the national budget) so that resources could be focused on developing the civilian economy. As part of a major restructuring and personnel reduction, first formally discussed by the Central Military Commission in 1981 and organized by a General Logistics Department Leading Small Group established in 1982, several large organizations with largely nonmilitary, commercial functions were at least partially removed from PLA ground-force command. This move was supported by the PLA itself, whose leadership viewed the sprawling nonmartial responsibilities as impediments to professionalization.

From 1982 to 1983, the three principal economic construction organizations were transferred to civilian authority. In September 1982, the Railway Construction Corps was directly transferred to the Railway Ministry. The Capital Construction Corps, and many of its previous responsibilities, were transferred to ministries and local governments in 1983. Some of its forces (e.g., those involved in gold-mine, forestry, transportation, and hydrological work) were transferred to the People's Armed Police, which was established in April 1983. The XPCC was moved to the joint jurisdiction of the PRC central government and the Xinjiang Uygur Autonomous Region; the Wulumuqi (Ürümqi) Military Region assumed the military aspects of its duties in 1982 (after 1985, this became the Xinjiang [provincial] Military District of the Lanzhou Military Region). As a paramilitary organization, the XPCC currently employs reservists and roughly 100,000 militia and cooperates closely with People's Armed Police forces (e.g., in border defense) in addition to playing a policing function and running prisons and labor camps.

By 1983, Deng decided to eliminate one million military billets. After this "strategic transition," the PLA became involved in commercial activities. To compensate the PLA for budgetary reductions, Deng gradually opened the door for PLA development of a wide range of commercial enterprises and civilian light-industrial production. This unprecedented allowance for utilitarian profit-oriented commerce was first raised at a Central Military Commission meeting on October 25, 1984, following arguments in favor by Deng and Yang Shangkun. On January 23, 1985, China's State Council, Central Military Commission, and General Logistics Department established China Xinxing Corporation to oversee the military-commercial complex. In February 1985, the State Council and Central Military Commission ratified related regulations that envisioned long-term, uneven development of PLA commercial activities but prohibited the use of active-duty troops or their funds and equipment for commerce. After becoming first vice chair of the Central Military Commission in 1987, Zhao Ziyang furthered the commercialization process.

At the peak, as many as several million (mostly demobilized soldiers, PLA dependents, and unrelated civilians) worked for a multibillion dollar "PLA Inc." of nearly 20,000 enterprises. Weapons exports were also encouraged, the most prominent purveyor being China Polytechnologies (Baoli), established by the General Staff Department in 1984 to export surplus military equipment (e.g., rifles) from warehouses controlled by the department—often in competition with such (non-PLA) armaments industry import-export companies as China North Industries Corporation (NORINCO). Personal living standards (particularly for senior PLA officials in coastal regions) and profits rose rapidly, but only about 1 percent of revenue was devoted to weapons acquisition.

Significant corruption, ideological decay, and diversion from military preparation, as well as illegal activities (e.g., inaccurate accounting, prostitution, counterfeiting and illicit use of PLA license plates, and smuggling), ensued. Despite repeated inspections, this high volume of PLA business activity (some by princelings, much using subsidized inputs and

prioritized transportation access, preferentially taxed, exempt from many fees and forms of oversight, and often enjoying monopolies) presented unfair competition, thwarted local revenue collection, often enjoyed immunity from prosecution, and hampered Premier Zhu Rongji's efforts to control prices and inflation in the mid-1990s. New regulations (particularly during 1993–1995 and 1996 rectifications) transferred key PLA assets into holding companies.

JIANG ERA AND BEYOND

At an enlarged Central Military Commission session on July 22, 1998, Jiang Zemin ordered the PLA to divest itself from a majority of its civilian businesses (over 6,000) in conjunction with the downsizing of 500,000 personnel. The sensitive decision had already been made in May 1997, buttressed by a PLA leadership that favored professionalism, was tired of corruption investigations, and had been promised substantial compensation. The PLA managed to retain control of its guesthouses, some military hospitals (which earn revenue by serving civilian patients), some strategic telecommunications companies, and considerable real estate—the last under the operation of management companies, which return revenue to PLA units. Some agricultural sideline production and factories employing military dependents were retained, particularly in remote areas.

To facilitate foreign commercial relations, even XPCC units have been restructured along corporate lines, adopted a variety of civilian names (e.g., Xinjiang State Farm Organization), and reduced the use of military grades and terminology. Now tasked with both economic development and the prevention of separatism, the XPCC remains Xinjiang's largest single employer and landowner, with 175 farms, 4,390 large and small enterprises, and one-third each of the province's Han and arable land under its jurisdiction. In this sense, it is China's last "Maoist" organization, combining paramilitary and diverse civil economic roles.

In a two-phase process, most other PLA enterprises, some burdened with major welfare costs and debts, were transferred to local and provincial governments. Rather than retaining their pre-1985 responsibilities, PLA organizations have since outsourced the vast majority of nonessential logistics. This ameliorates reduced manpower, increases efficiency and cost control (particularly given inflation), and may even stimulate development of a service economy. Procurement (for example, food services) has been centralized and automated for some PLA units. General Logistics Department warehouses that were not already downsized may have outsourced nonessentials (e.g., food, uniforms) to civilians, while retaining munitions and weaponry still used by the PLA.

Reforms have been largely successful, thanks in part to rapid economic growth. This has allowed for substantial annual official defense budget increases (averaging 15% between 1990 and 2005). Corresponding improvements in salaries and living conditions have left the PLA increasingly satisfied to "eat imperial grain."

BIBLIOGRAPHY

Bickford, Thomas J. The Chinese Military and Its Business Operations: The PLA as Entrepreneur. *Asian Survey* 34, 5 (1994): 460–474.

Blasko, Dennis J. *The Chinese Army Today: Tradition and Transformation for the 21st Century.* New York: Routledge, 2006.

Cheung Tai Ming. *China's Entrepreneurial Army.* New York: Oxford University Press, 2001.

Ku Guisheng and Jiang Luming. *Zhongguo guo fang jingji shi* [History of the Chinese national defense economy]. Beijing: Military Science Press, 1991.

Li Nan, ed. *Chinese Civil-Military Relations: The Transformation of the People's Liberation Army.* New York: Routledge, 2006.

Mulvenon, James. *Soldiers of Fortune: The Rise and Fall of the Chinese Military-Business Complex, 1978–1998.* Armonk, NY: Sharpe, 2001.

Zhongguo junshi jingji shi [Chinese military economic history]. Beijing: People's Liberation Army Press, 1991.

Andrew S. Erickson

The views expressed in this entry are those of the author alone and do not represent the official policies or estimates of the U.S. Navy or any other element of the U.S. government.

PERSONALITY CULTS

During the decade of the Great Proletarian Cultural Revolution (1966–1976), Mao Zedong, his writings, and the quotations that were based on them became the object of the ultimate form of leader worship. As the embodiment of the Chinese Communist Party (CCP), Mao's countenance beamed down from huge billboards along the streets and avenues in China's urban areas. Photographs showing his face were placed in the fields. The people wore Mao badges in varying sizes pinned to their chests. His quotations were often compared to a magical or supernatural weapon, a "spiritual atom bomb," or even a "beacon light." His words graced every imaginable surface. Seen as the embodiment of change, Mao became a source of inspiration for restive youths in the West and a beacon for revolutionary movements in Africa, Latin America, and Asia.

ROOTS OF THE MAO CULT

The personality cult around Mao did not begin with the Cultural Revolution. The use of his writings as a repository of ideological truth began to evolve after he attained power over the party in Zunyi in 1935. In the Yan'an period (1936–1947), Mao had the time and opportunity to study and adapt the writings of Marxism-Leninism and to develop his own brand of sinicized Marxism. At the Seventh Party Congress in April 1945, the correctness of Mao's "Thought," principles, and political line were

affirmed and his position became unassailable: Mao and the party became one. From then on, the propagation of the cult of the leader, against which he himself raised ambiguous warnings at the time, started in earnest.

THE MAO CULT DURING THE FIRST DECADES OF THE PRC

In the first decade of the People's Republic of China (PRC), Mao became omnipresent in writings and portraits, but by the early 1960s, he was forced into the background as a result of the policy failures of the Great Leap Forward campaign. He plotted his return to prevent the nation from sliding in a direction he felt was a betrayal of his revolution, and turned to the People's Liberation Army to support his bid for power. The army was turned into "a great school of Mao Tse-tung Thought" after it published the *Quotations from Chairman Mao* (the "Little Red Book") in 1961 for study purposes. The goal was to make politics (i.e., Mao Zedong Thought) "take command" again. The intensity with which Mao's image and ideas were pushed in the mid-1960s, first by the army and later by secondary-school pupils and students supporting his comeback, was unparalleled. This time around, it all took place with Mao's explicit consent.

Mao's official portrait, bust, or other type of statue became regular presences in every home during the Cultural Revolution. Not having Mao on display indicated an unwillingness to take part in the revolution, or even a counterrevolutionary outlook, and refuted the central role Mao played in politics and in the lives of the people. The portrait often occupied the central place on the family altar, or the spot where that altar had been located before it had been demolished by Red Guards. A number of rituals were centered around the image, such as the daily practice of "asking for instructions in the morning, thanking Mao for his kindness at noon, and reporting back at night." This involved bowing three times, the singing of the national anthem, and reading passages from the Little Red Book, and would end with wishing Mao "ten thousand years" (i.e., eternal life).

Mao also invaded the private space of the people. His portrait was carried close to everyone's heart, either in the form of the photograph of Mao that was included in the Little Red Book that everybody carried in his or her left breast-pocket, or in the form of the Mao badges that many wore and collected. In the early 1970s, the extreme and more religious aspects of the cult were dismantled, but the adulation of Mao remained, and a new crime arose—"vicious attacks on the Great Leader" (*e du gongji weida lingxiu*).

In the late 1960s, even young people in the West who rebelled against the existing political and social order projected their hopes onto Mao. Waving images of Mao and translated copies of the Little Red Book, they copied events

Chinese school children marching with a red communist flag and picture of Mao Zedong, 1971. *During his tenure over China, Mao Zedong created a society devoted to his image, teachings, and leadership. Chairman Mao ensured objectors received swift punishment, resulting in many citizens following Mao's edicts out of fear they might be considered dissenters, a crime punishable by death.* **FRANK FISCHBECK/TIME & LIFE PICTURES/GETTY IMAGES**

that were taking place in China, even though they often only dimly understood what was actually happening there. The utopian and millenarian aspects of the Cultural Revo-

lution also inspired and influenced a number of liberation movements and revolutionary groups in newly independent, less-developed nations in Asia, Africa, and Latin

116

America. Following China's claims for the validity of its example, these groups subscribed to the idea that their own revolutionary experiences corresponded with those of Mao and the CCP, in particular the notion that they, as the world's "countryside," could successfully rise against the "cities," personified by the superpowers and the developed nations.

HUA GUOFENG

When Mao died in September 1976, his handpicked successor, Hua Guofeng (1921–2008), took over. Hua's legitimacy was pictured in a popular poster showing Mao, with a hand on Hua's knee, saying: "With you in charge, I feel at ease" (*ni banshi, wo fangxin*).

Once Hua was ensconced firmly in power, the mechanisms that had been instrumental in propagating Mao and his ideas continued to dominate. Whereas Mao had been referred to as the "Great Leader" (*weida lingxiu*), Hua had himself called the "Clairvoyant Leader" (*yingming lingxiu*). But it was more like a farce. Hua tried to take over Mao's political legacy by adopting most of his policies, stating that "We firmly uphold whatever policy decisions Chairman Mao made and we unswervingly adhere to whatever instructions Chairman Mao gave." Additionally, he restyled his image in such a way that he became somewhat of a Mao look-alike, even adopting his predecessor's hairstyle. In a number of cases, Hua stole the limelight formerly reserved for his predecessor. Posters were made that showed him in settings similar or identical to those associated with Mao. For example, where Mao had put in hard labor at the Ming Tombs in the late 1950s, Hua was shown to do likewise at the Miyun Reservoir in the late 1970s. Where Mao was depicted with Chen Yonggui (c. 1913–1986) on visits to Dazhai that never took place, Hua—who actually did visit the model commune—was shown in similar circumstances. Hua also claimed Mao's position as an object of reverence: Formal portraits of Mao and Hua hung side by side in rooms and offices in the late 1970s.

THE DENG XIAOPING ERA

Once Deng Xiaoping took over from Hua Guofeng in 1977, leadership worship ceased. Deng abhorred the personality cult in all its forms and was convinced that leaders should remain in the background. Under Deng, a process of de-Maoification was started in the early 1980s, leading to a reassessment of Mao's contributions. In the *Resolution on Certain Questions in the History of Our Party since the Founding of the People's Republic of China*, adopted by the Sixth Plenum of the Eleventh Central Committee of the CCP in 1981, Mao Zedong Thought was now interpreted as the crystallization of the collective wisdom of all of China's veteran revolutionary leaders. But Mao did not disappear from the scene altogether.

Embracing Mao in the 1980s and 1990s effectively meant delegitimating the regime and giving expression to a yearning for a less-complicated and more-caring past. Many Chinese continued to see Mao as the leader who always took the well-being of the people to heart. The privations and persecutions of the past seemed to have been forgotten. Many believed that Mao himself had not been responsible for these aberrations, but that they should be attributed to the evil forces and bad officials and leaders surrounding him. They contrasted this reinvented view of history with the harsh and uncaring policies, the social and income inequalities, that resulted from the reform and modernization process.

The leadership clearly employed—and continues to employ—icons such as Mao as legitimating symbols and, at the same time, as magic wands to protect against disunity and chaos. This was clearly visible in 1993, when the centenary of Mao's birth was celebrated. The event was marked by the publication and production of a flood of posters, memorabilia, and other Mao-related kitsch. Once the Mao fever cooled down after 1993, a wide selection of Mao memorabilia remained available, although mainly in the larger urban centers. By that time, Chinese customer interest seemed to have waned or shifted to other objects. Still, Mao continues to be considered the most admired Chinese personality. In some rural areas, Buddhist-style temples dedicated to Mao have sprung up.

Mao, as the Great Teacher, the Great Leader, the Great Helmsman, the Great Commander, has come full circle in a remarkable way. More important even than the fact that his portrait continues to dominate Tiananmen Square, his face graces the new currency that went into circulation in 1999 to mark the fiftieth anniversary of the founding of the PRC. Mao may no longer reside in the hearts of the people, but they all want him in their pockets.

SEE ALSO *Chinese Marxism: Mao Zedong Thought; Cultural Revolution, 1966–1969; Mao Dun.*

BIBLIOGRAPHY

Apter, David, and Tony Saich. *Revolutionary Discourse in Mao's Republic.* Cambridge, MA: Harvard University Press, 1994.

Barmé, Geremie. *Shades of Mao: The Posthumous Cult of the Great Leader.* Armonk, NY: Sharpe, 1996.

Cong Dachang. *When Heroes Pass Away: The Invention of a Chinese Communist Pantheon.* Lanham, MD: University Press of America, 1997.

Landsberger, Stefan R. The Deification of Mao: Religious Imagery and Practices during the Cultural Revolution and Beyond. In *China's Great Proletarian Cultural Revolution: Master Narratives and Post-Mao Counternarratives,* ed. Woei Lien Chong (Zhuang Ailian, 139–184). Lanham, MD: Rowman & Littlefield, 2002.

Martin, Helmut. *Cult & Canon: The Origins and Development of State Maoism.* Armonk, NY: Sharpe, 1982.

Schrift, Melissa. *Biography of a Chairman Mao Badge: The Creation and Mass Consumption of a Personality Cult.* New Brunswick, NJ: Rutgers University Press, 2001.

Teiwes, Frederick C. *Politics and Purges in China: Rectification and the Decline of Party Norms, 1950–1965.* 2nd ed. Armonk, NY: Sharpe, 1993.

Yan Jiaqi and Gao Gao. *Turbulent Decade: A History of the Cultural Revolution.* Trans. and ed. D. W. Y. Kwok. Honolulu: University of Hawai'i Press, 1996.

Stefan R. Landsberger

PHOTOGRAPHY, HISTORY OF

This entry contains the following:

ART PHOTOGRAPHY
Yi Gu

DOCUMENTARY PHOTOGRAPHY
Eliza Ho

PROPAGANDA PHOTOGRAPHY
Eliza Ho

ART PHOTOGRAPHY

The twentieth century witnessed many changes in how art was understood, perceived, created, and criticized in China. These changes are reflected in the history of art photography. Photography acquired the stature of an art form in China in the early 1920s. Unlike in the West, where photography secured this status through decades of heated debate, art photography in China gained legitimacy with little resistance. This willingness to accept photography as a fine art reflected a contemporaneous redefinition of art in general. Three influences combined to add new elasticity to what counted as art. First, the New Culture movement triggered the iconoclastic rethinking of tradition. Second, reformers such as Cai Yuanpei (1876–1940) promoted aesthetic education. And third, images made in a pictorial language that was vastly different from that of traditional brush painting flooded into China. Under these circumstances, phrases like *yishu sheying* (art photography) and *meishu sheying* (fine art photography) first appeared in pictorials such as *Shishi huabao* (Pictorial of current affairs), *Liangyou huabao* (Young companion) and *Beiyang huabao* (North China pictorial). Photographs of various subjects—female social celebrities, architecture, and scenic spots—were now juxtaposed with paintings, and were dubbed *art photography*. In addition, manuals aimed at amateur photographers, whose numbers dramatically increased due to such technical breakthroughs as dry film and hand cameras, contributed to the dissemination of the idea of art photography.

EARLY PHOTOGRAPHIC SOCIETIES

The artistic aspirations of photographers eventually crystallized in societies devoted to the study and promotion of art photography. In 1923 the first such society, Yishu Xiezhen Yanjiushe (Art Photography Research Society), which was soon renamed Guangshe (Light Society), was established by a group of amateur photographers anchored in Beijing University. Guangshe launched four well-received annual exhibitions from 1924 to 1928 and published two annals featuring members' photographic works, along with writings that preached artistic expression in photography. In 1924 Chen Wanli (1892–1969), one of the founding members, published *Dafengji* (The book of great wind), the first photography catalog showcasing the work of an individual photographer. In 1927 another member, Liu Bannong (1891–1934), published *Bannong tanying* (Bannong on photography), the first example of theoretical writing on the aesthetics of photography in China.

Guangshe predated other photographic societies that pervaded China during the late 1920s and 1930s. Among them, Zhonghua Sheying Xueshe (Society of Chinese Photography)—often known by its abbreviation, Huashe—launched in Shanghai in 1928, was the most influential. Although it lasted only two years, Huashe became well-known because members such as Lang Jingshan (1892–1995) and Hu Boxiang (1896–1989) were famous figures in the Shanghai art world. Moreover, the four exhibitions organized by Huashe between 1928 and 1930 were huge successes. Members of this society published two journals on art photography, *Tianpeng* (China focus) and *Zhonghua sheying zazhi* (Chinese photographic journal). Similar organizations included Heibai Yingshe (Black and White Society), Zhongguo Sheying Xuehui (Chinese Association for Photography), and Shanghai Sheying Xuehui (Shanghai Association for Photography) in Shanghai; Jingshe (Aperture Society), Bailü Sheying Xuehui (White and Green Association for Photography), and Hongchuan Sheying Yanjiushe (Red Window Association for Photography) in Guangzhou; and Meishe (Art Society) and Nanjing Yingshe (Nanjing Photographic Society) in Nanjing; along with many others in smaller cities such as Suzhou, Fuzhou, Ningbo, and Wuxi. These societies launched exhibitions and published journals or annals to promote photography as art. The period's new recognition of art photography was evidenced by the fact that two national exhibitions of fine art, launched by the Nanjing government in 1929 and 1937, included a section for photography.

PICTORIALISM, MODERNISM, AND OTHER TRENDS

The development of art photography in China in the 1920s and 1930s was linked with the international photographic movement known as *pictorialism*, which was based on the belief that photography was a means of personal artistic expression. In an effort to lift photography to the status of fine art, pictorialists differentiated themselves from both commercial photographers and snapshooters—disdaining the former for diminishing photography as industry and the latter for technical inadequacy. Through societies that launched exhibitions and publications, the lofty pictorialists canonized a painterly style that was often achieved through careful framing, soft focus, and various manual manipulations. In vogue since the mid-1880s, pictorialism began to decline rapidly around the time of World War I (1914–1918) due to the prevalence of modernism, which encouraged innovative angles and sharp focus in photography. Nonetheless, pictorialism continued to attract followers among amateurs and promotion from the corporate photographic industry, especially Kodak.

Although the first three decades of the twentieth century witnessed a major transition from pictorialism to modernism in art photography in the West, neither this stylistic shift nor its ideological implications received recognition in China. Instead, what poignantly registered in the minds of Chinese photographers was China's absence in the world of art photography, a situation lamented in almost every piece of writing on photography as one more sign that China had fallen behind in the march toward modernity. The urgency of catching up thus became the prominent issue underlying the pursuits of ambitious art photographers, which led to three interrelated phenomena.

The first was stylistic pluralism. Photographers eagerly sought inspiration from photographic journals and exhibition catalogs of the West and Japan, freely experimenting with what they learned from these publications. Although certain societies exhibited preferences—for example, most Huashe members adopted the romantic style of pictorialism, while the members of the Heibai Yingshe subscribed to modernist photography—there was no artistic school or clearly defined style aside from a common yearning to learn it all.

The effect of the first phenomenon was countered by the second: the explicit desire to find a style that was quintessentially Chinese. Thus, many photographers appealed to traditional styles of painting for inspiration. Lang Jingshan's composite photography, each print made of segments of several negatives that were superimposed to resemble traditional painting, was acclaimed as a huge success in this regard.

The third phenomenon was the effort of early Republican photographers to participate and excel in international salons. Chinese art photographers openly claimed that acceptance by international salons was the ultimate achievement. In parallel with increased aggression from Japan, Chinese photographers treated the salon as a battlefield, celebrating the number of acceptances and awards given to Chinese photographers as a victory over Japan. The focus on a national style and national pride in art photography echoed the widespread nationalism of the early Republican era.

Starting in the second half of the 1930s, the Chinese photography world bifurcated. In essence, this difference was about the relationship between art and society, echoing debates in the art and literary world as to whether the practice of art as an intuitive and subjective expression was legitimate amid a national crisis. The gap between those who believed in the legitimacy of art photography itself and those who emphasized photography's social function became increasingly wide. Left-leaning photographers accused art photography of being irrelevant to society. The Anti-Japanese War (1937–1945) further confirmed their dismissal of photography that was preoccupied with formal qualities and personal expression. Instead, photojournalism was given full attention. Photographers such as He Tiehua (b. 1909) provided antiwar propaganda by shifting from visually pleasant subjects to scenes that illustrated the brutality of war. Meanwhile, art photographers such as Lang Jingshan continued pursuing international recognition as a means of national salvation. The activities of Lang and like-minded photographers remained the same as in the prewar period: organizing societies, publishing catalogs, launching exhibitions, and submitting works to international salons.

PHOTOGRAPHY IN THE PEOPLE'S REPUBLIC

Photography, like other means of representation, was under firm control after the Communist Party won the war against the Guomindang and established the People's Republic of China (PRC) in 1949. The word *yishu sheying* (art photography) was replaced by *sheying yishu* (the art of photography). The nominal difference revealed the awkward position of art photography in the new state. Photography was still considered a form of art, but as with all the other art forms, its artistic quality was only considered meaningful in the service of the party. Indeed, the Communist Party used photography to produce some of the most powerful works of propaganda, among which were the illustrations in *Renmin huabao* (People's pictorial), an official pictorial devoted to portraying a lively prospering new state. This type of photography was categorized as photojournalism, which dominated in Maoist China and swept aside all other types of photographic representation. In 1956, when the Association of Chinese Photographers was established, the majority of its members were photojournalists, accompanied by a small number of famous early Republican art photographers, who apologized for their earlier passion for art photography and expressed eagerness to serve the PRC with their art.

The idea of art photography as personal expression did not thrive again in China until the end of the 1970s, after the Cultural Revolution came to an end. Private photography clubs and exhibitions started to emerge in Beijing in 1976, eventually leading to the establishment

Rhapsody *by Chen Fuli, 1952.* *In 1979, Hong Kong artist Chen Fuli earned attention for his photo exhibition in mainland China. As most photography in the People's Republic of China served as a propaganda tool, Chen's work introduced audiences to a different use of the artistic medium, the chance to express oneself, rather than Communist Party ideals, through photographs.* TCHAN FOU-LI/FOTOE

in 1979 of the famous Siyue Yinghui (April Photo Society), which pronounced that photojournalism did not equal the art of photography. Siyue Yinghui organized three exhibitions all under the title *Nature, Society, and Man*, aiming to foster an aesthetic variety that had been long forbidden in China. Although eager to break away from the photo propaganda that had dominated China for decades, photographers struggled due to the limited availability of resources from which to draw inspiration. Thus, photographs by Hong Kong photographer Chen Fuli (b. 1916) imitating the aesthetics of traditional Chinese painting caused a huge sensation when he exhibited them in 1979 on the mainland. The style featured in Chen's works was actually very similar to Huashe members' painterly photography of the late 1920s and 1930s. Chen's style, along with other works preoccupied with formal qualities and technical sophistication, became known in China as the "salon style" and regained currency.

China of the 1980s had a thirst for knowledge, ideas, and thoughts from the outside world that had been absent since the Cultural Revolution. Works of various contemporary Western and Japanese photographers were introduced into China through photo journals, especially *Xiandai sheying* (In photography), which was launched in 1984. This renewed cultural contact initiated a new period in photography, later described by critics as *sheying xinchao* (photographic new wave). Documentary photographs in the West, as well as photographs in documentary style, particularly interested Chinese photographers, who were eagerly searching for alternatives to the two dominant styles in mainstream photography: the romanticized portrayal of social reality that was a residue of the photo propaganda dominating the first three decades of the PRC, and the salon style that also romanticized the world through aestheticization. The significant photographic societies of the mid-1980s included Beihemeng (North River League) in Shanghai and Liebian Qunti (Rupture Group) in Beijing, among many others. Unlike Siyue Yinghui, these societies no longer praised or promoted the idea of art photography.

The *guannian sheying* (conceptual photography) and *shiyan sheying* (experimental photography) that has been booming in China since the early 1990s can hardly be categorized as art photography. Not only do artists who engage with photography rarely identify themselves as photographers, some also deny being photographers and deliberately distance themselves from official photographic institutions, such as the Association of Chinese Photographers. Avant-garde artists have adopted photography to create two-dimensional works, and they have integrated photography into their installation and performance projects. This trend parallels postmodernist photography in the West, in which artists have taken on photography as a special criticism of a culture replete with mass-media images. The rapid urbanization, commercialization, and globalization of China since the 1990s have allowed artists to engage much more profoundly with Western postmodernist photography, as opposed to mere stylistic borrowing. Owing little to the tradition of art photography, this new trend has agitated photographic circles and engendered animated discussions about the future of photography.

SEE ALSO *Pictorial Magazines since 1880.*

BIBLIOGRAPHY

Hu Zhichuan, Ma Yunzeng, Chen Shen, et al. *Zhongguo sheying shi: 1840–1937* [History of Chinese photography: 1840–1937]. Beijing: Zhongguo Sheying Chubanshe, 1987.

Jiang Qisheng. *Xinwen sheying yibai sishinian* [A hundred and forty years of photojournalism]. Beijing: Xinhua Chubanshe, 1989.

Jiang Qisheng, ed. *Zhongguo sheying shi: 1937–1949* (History of Chinese photography: 1937–1949). Beijing: Zhongguo Sheying Chubanshe, 1998.

Long Xizu. Zhongguo jindai sheying yishu meixue wenxuan [Collected essays on the photography aesthetics in early Republican China]. Tianjin: Tianjin Renmin Meishu Chubanshe, 1988.

Phillips, Christopher. The Great Transition: Artists' Photography and Video in China. In *Between Past and Future: New Photography and Video from China*, eds. Wu Hung (Wu Hong) and Christopher Phillips, 37–50. Chicago: Smart Museum of Art, University of Chicago, 2004.

Shanghai sheyingjia xiehui and Shanghai daxue wenxueyuan. *Shanghai shying shi* [History of photography in Shanghai]. Shanghai: Shanghai Renmin Meishu Chubanshe, 1992.

Shanxi laonian sheying xue hui. Shanxi sheying shihua [History of photography in Shanxi]. Xi'an: Shanxi Sheying Chubanshe, 1994.

Tong, Elizabeth. Chinese Photographic Societies Reminiscences. *Echo of Things Chinese* 6, 8 (1978): 20–24, 58–59.

Wu Hung (Wu Hong). Between Past and Future: A Brief History of Contemporary Chinese Photography. In *Between Past and Future: New Photography and Video from China*, eds. Wu Hung (Wu Hong) and Christopher Phillips, 11–36. Chicago: Smart Museum of Art, University of Chicago, 2004.

You Di, ed. Dangdai Zhongguo sheying yishu sichao [Trends of art photography in contemporary China]. Beijing: Guoji Wenhua Chuban Bongsi, 1989.

Zhongguo sheyingjia xiehui, ed. *1989–1994 sheying yishu lunwenji* [Collected essays on photographic art, 1989–1994]. Beijing: Zhongguo Sheying Chubanshe, 1994.

Zhu Qi, ed. *1990 nian yilai de Zhongguo xianfeng sheying* [Chinese avant-garde photography since 1990]. Changsha, PRC: Human Meishu Chubanshe, 2004.

Yi Gu

DOCUMENTARY PHOTOGRAPHY

Except for those created solely for aesthetic experimentation, all photographs are, to some degree, documentary because of their inherent capacity to capture and reflect reality objectively. Documentary photographs are also historical photographs because they convey information of the past, specific moments in time. Documentary photography, more specifically, refers to photographs that record a real world situation on which the photographer intends to comment on and demonstrate the need for change. It is different from, although closely related to, news photography or photojournalism, whose main role lies in recording reality and reporting that reality in an objective and timely manner.

FOREIGN ORIGIN AND PRECEDENTS

The term *documentary photography* was first used in the mid-1930s to describe the U.S. Farm Security Administration's photographs, taken by Dorothea Lange (1895–1965), Walker Evans (1903–1975), Russell Lee (1903–1986), and Arthur Rothstein (1915–1985), among others, which depict the plight facing farm tenants and sharecroppers in rural America during the Great Depression. The concept of documentary photography was presaged much earlier however, when nineteenth-century Scottish photographer John Thomson's (1837–1921) photographs of the grim reality of the London poor were published in *Street Life in London* (1877–1878). This work is considered to be the first project of socially concerned, documentary photography. Following Thomson's footsteps, the Swiss-born American journalist Jacob Riis (1849–1914), at the end of the nineteenth century, took photographs that disclosed the distressing living conditions in the slums of New York City, which later helped lead to legislation improving housing in the city. Photography's potential in educating the public and triggering social reforms, therefore, became the defining characteristic for social documentary photography as it is understood today.

EARLY DEVELOPMENT OF CHINESE DOCUMENTARY PHOTOGRAPHY

In China, such socially oriented documentary photography did not appear until the 1920s, when a scholar at Beijing University, Chen Wanli (1892–1969), photographed the Forbidden City immediately after the expulsion of China's last imperial emperor, Puyi (1906–1967), from the palace on November 5, 1924. Chen captured the moments of the authorities taking over the palace, removing the furniture and treasures of the former regime, and escorting the maids and servants from the palace. These photographs, eighty-four of them in total, were published four years later in a book titled *Min shisan zhi gugong* (The palace in the thirteenth year of the Republican period). In the preface, Chen expresses his contempt for his countrymen's obsolete reverence for the imperial family even after the overthrow of the Qing dynasty thirteen years earlier. The book was a rarity in the 1920s in the

sense that the author-photographer made his social commentary through a combination of words and photographs.

Toward the end of the 1920s, photographs depicting the lives of working people in cities appeared in Chinese newspapers and illustrated magazines. For example, the Beijing-based newspaper *Jingbao* (Beijng daily), published a column called *Jiuduhui xiezhen* (Social images of the Old Capital) beginning in 1929. Composed of an uncredited photograph and a short text, the column investigated the engagement of Beijing's urban dwellers in their lowly jobs, such as collecting feces, mending shoes, or selling foods. While the photographs are ethnographic in flavor, the descriptions are satirical in tone, voicing complaints about the social injustice the laboring population faced. A rarity of its time, these photographs can be seen as prototypes of the genre of social documentary in the history of Chinese photography.

With the growing population of amateur photographers and the popularization of the small, portable Leica in the 1930s, some practitioners, such as Chen Chuanlin (1897–1945), Lu Sifu (1898–1983), and Sha Fei (1912–1950), to name only a few, took their cameras to the streets to capture the mundane lives of ordinary Chinese. By depicting the less-than-grandiose aspects of city life, they aimed to create images that would evoke public sympathy for the poor. Other photographers, such as Chen Jinshi, who made farmers and fishermen his subject, created picturesque photographs, showing his own nostalgia for the vanishing idyllic life of rural China. Despite their social content, these photographs were mostly published as *meishu sheying* (fine art photography) in mass-circulated pictorial magazines.

With the acceleration of Japanese aggression in 1931, both professional and amateur photographers began to devote their photographic practice to documenting the increasing violence. Although other strands of photography, namely pictorialist and modernist photography, existed in the 1930s, it was clear that photographs with strong social content were becoming the dominant mode before and after the outbreak of the War of Resistance against Japan in 1937. During the war years, from 1937 to 1949, photographs of military preparations and aggression, damaged cities and villages, fleeing refugees, and wartime atrocities filled the pages of a handful of illustrated magazines and newspapers.

THE MAOIST PERIOD (1949–1976)

Upon the founding of the People's Republic of China (PRC), the Communist Party began to centralize every aspect of photographic practice, from its production to its dissemination and distribution, to ensure that the medium fulfilled a prescribed function—to educate the public and to promote socialist ideals. Because of the radical changes in China's political system, individual freedom to create was

Crying for Life, *1937, photograph by Sha Fei. With the advent of smaller cameras in the 1930s, photographers took advantage of this new portability to record the experiences of average Chinese citizens. Sha Fei, creator of the above image, became well known for documenting the impact of the Japanese invasion on the people of China, publishing his photos in a variety of magazines and newspapers.* **SHA FEI / FOTOE**

further restricted, and individually initiated documentary photography vanished. Photographers, regardless of their previous status as professional or amateur, were now "employed" by the government to work at their assigned work units. All photographic projects were state-sponsored, and they were screened, selected, and published in official publications. To get a sense of the typical photographs of the period, one only needs to look at *Zhongguo* (China), a large-scale photographic album published in 1959 to celebrate the tenth anniversary of the establishment of the PRC. The photographs included are limited to the successes of

Communist rule: modernization and industrialization, the betterment of Chinese lives, harmony between soldiers and civilians, and the healthy and optimistic younger generation. These photographs were used to convey the preferred political ideology and messages. The critical edge of the socially concerned documentary photographs in the 1930s had disappeared.

The situation only worsened during the decade of the Proletarian Cultural Revolution from 1966 to 1976. While normal lives and all government operations were entirely disrupted, photographic output dramatically decreased.

Photographs, if taken at all, were highly restricted in content and contrived in appearance, and served purely to glorify Mao Zedong's continued revolutions. Amateur photographers were extremely rare because cameras were not easily accessible to ordinary Chinese. One surprising body of work that recently came to light was published as *Red-Color News Soldier* (2003). It includes documentary photographs taken in Heilongjiang by photojournalist Li Zhensheng during the Cultural Revolution. The images portray the fanatical activities of the Red Guards and the cruelty inflicted upon many ordinary Chinese, documenting a sad story in the history of modern China.

THE POST-MAO PERIOD

Documentary photography witnessed a revival at the end of the Cultural Revolution, and more specifically during the April Fifth movement, the apex of the four-month public mourning of the death of the country's premier, Zhou Enlai, on January 8, 1976. Amateur photographers such as Li Xiaobin and Wang Ziping took pictures of the mass gatherings and the public demonstrations at Tiananmen Square, and the photographs, around five hundred, were published three years later in the catalogue *Renmin de daonian* (People's mourning, 1979). Originally funded by private sources, the catalogue, published after the rehabilitation of the April Fifth movement, later received the Chinese government's support and became an official project, endorsed by China's top leaders at the time.

The years immediately after Mao's death in 1976 also saw the rise of unofficial or underground photo clubs in Beijing and Guangzhou; even the more remote cities, such as Xi'an in Shaanxi Province, had their photographers. Art historian Wu Hung (Wu Hong) has described the activity of the period between 1980 and 1990 as *sheying xinchao* (the photographic new wave), in which documentary photographs can be divided into two types: *shanghen sheying* (scar photography) and *xiangtu sheying* (native-soil photography). These types corresponded to or were named after contemporary art and literary movements, and provide a parallel to root-seeking literature and rustic realist painting. While *shanghen sheying* is characterized by its critical attitude toward the pain and damage left behind by the Cultural Revolution's chaos, *xiangtu sheying* is defined by its nostalgic sentiments for an idealized unspoiled land where innocence was preserved.

The 1980s also saw the publication of specialized photography journals such as *Renmin sheying bao* (People's photography daily) in Shanxi (1983) and *Xiandai sheying* (In photography) in Shenzhen (1984), which featured photographs and articles that were less ideologically driven and more academically oriented. A summary of the development of Chinese photography during the 1980s may be found in two exhibition catalogues: *Shinian yixunjian* (Flashback: A decade of changes, 1976–1986, 1986) and *Zhongguo sheying*

sishi nian (Forty years of Chinese photography, 1988). Both catalogues contain photographs concerning lives of ordinary Chinese under socialist rule. *Zhongguo renben* (Humanism in China), an exhibition organized by the Guangdong Museum of Art in 2003, surveyed the development of Chinese documentary photography from 1951 to 2003. By bringing together 600 works produced by 248 Chinese photographers for the exhibition, and having them added to the museum's permanent collection, the Guangdong Museum of Art has aimed to promote and encourage scholarly research on Chinese documentary photography.

THE 1990s TO PRESENT

Since the beginning of the 1990s, documentary photography has entered a pluralistic stage in which the photographers' subject matter has expanded, their styles have diversified, and their intentions have varied. While some photographers continue to explore China's contemporary social landscape in a realistic style, others have adopted a more experimental approach by incorporating photography with other mediums. These works draw upon the artists' own experience, and tend to be individualistic. In some cases, digital manipulation is involved. The traditional definition of documentary photography is thus challenged, and in need of revision.

SEE ALSO *Pictorial Magazines since 1880; Scar (Wound) Art.*

BIBLIOGRAPHY

Capa, Cornell, ed. *Behind the Great Wall of China: Photographs from 1870 to the Present.* Greenwich, CT: New York Graphic Society, 1972.

Chen Changlian et al. *Dandai zhongguo sheying yishu shi (1949–1989)* [The art history of Chinese contemporary photography (1949–1979)]. Beijing: Zhongguo Sheying Chubanshe, 1996.

Chen Wanli. *Min shisan zhi gugong* [The Forbidden City in the thirteenth year of the Republic]. Shanghai: Kaiming Shudian, 1928.

Hu Wugong. *Zhongguo yingxiang geming* [Image revolution in China]. Beijing: Zhongguo Wenliang Chubanshe, 2005.

Li Zhensheng. *Red-Color News Soldier.* London and New York: Phaidon, 2003.

Ma Yunzeng et al. *Zhongguo sheying shi: 1840–1937* [History of Chinese photography: 1840–1937]. Beijing: Zhongguo Sheying Chubanshe, 1987.

Moore, Oliver. *IIAS Newsletter* 44 (Summer 2007): 6-7.

Wu Hung (Wu Hong) and Christopher Phillips. *Between Past and Future: New Photography and Video from China.* Chicago: Smart Museum of Art, University of Chicago, 2004.

Wue, Roberta, et al. *Picturing Hong Kong: Photography, 1855–1910.* Hong Kong: South China Printing, 1997.

Eliza Ho

PROPAGANDA PHOTOGRAPHY

Propaganda photography or *xuanchuan sheying* refers to photographs that were taken or used primarily to influence people's opinions of certain social, ideological, and religious issues and to modify their behavior by appealing to their emotions. Beyond simple advocacy, propaganda is also characterized by deliberate planning and, particularly when unchecked by free public discourse, may also exhibit a disregard for factual accuracy. In modern times, during war or peace, propaganda photographs appeared in both democratic and totalitarian societies; their governments and private sectors sponsored the production of propaganda photographs or adapted photographs to propagate their interests and ideologies. In the 1930s, Soviet photographic theoretician Lazar Mezhericher observed that American advertising photography, with its immense power to persuade, was so successful that it could be "put in direct and concrete service of [the Soviet] party line" (Bendavid-Val 1999, p. 59).

FOREIGN PRECEDENTS

Although China has a venerable tradition of imperial art, photographs deployed for propaganda purposes have a longer history in the West than in China. For example, as early as the middle of the nineteenth century, Napoléon III (1808–1873) and his government were known for their attempts to use photographs to promote and publicize the Second Empire's (1852–1870) achievements. At around the same time, leadership imagery was born; it grew into a genre of its own and became essential to any leader's self-aggrandizement, as well as to political campaigns. This genre evolved from simple, straightforward portraiture to photographs embedded with a narrative. The main objective of such photography is to cast a positive and believable light onto the leader by using realistic imagery, and therefore to solicit public support for the leader and his or her policies and administration.

Photography's claim for truthfulness, and its reproducibility and manipulability have made it a prime visual medium for propaganda in modern times. In the 1920s in Soviet Russia, the government began to mobilize such progressive photographers, artists, and designers as El Lissitzky (1890–1941) and Alexander Rodchenko (1891–1956) to create dramatic, and sometimes abstract, images to promote Soviet successes under socialism. With Joseph Stalin's gradual consolidation of power and the official sanction of socialist realism in 1934, Soviet photographers were obligated to take realistic pictures, which were easily accessible to the largely illiterate population, in order to propagate Socialist ideals.

While propagation of falsehoods, particularly by totalitarian governments or nations at war, has tainted the English term *propaganda* with a negative connotation, viewers of photographs should be aware that the line between documentary and propaganda photography is sometimes blurred. A case in which the functions of documentation and advocacy overlapped may be seen in 1930s America. Aiming to provide evidence of the difficult situation of the country's agricultural population, the now-famous Historical Section of the Farm Security Administration employed both established and novice photographers to document the nationwide plight facing tenant farmers and sharecroppers in the rural United States. The resulting photographs were centrally archived and distributed for publication in government reports and popular illustrated magazines to rally public support for the government's depression-era federal aid policy.

Under contemporary scrutiny, we are now more aware of the ideological messages embedded in these presumably documentary photographs and how they were used as tools of political advocacy. These cases highlight the fact that photographic meanings are, by nature, fluid and multiple. Texts and captions are essential to anchor the intended meanings, and to make propaganda photographs effective.

EARLY DEVELOPMENT OF CHINESE PROPAGANDA PHOTOGRAPHY

Relatively speaking, the Chinese came late to the utilization of photographs for propaganda purposes. Since the introduction of the technology to China in the 1840s, photography, to a large extent, remained part of the trade of portrait-making. The Qing rulers did not recognize the technology's potential usefulness to promote their regime; they used it, from the time of the empress dowager in the late nineteenth century, to record their own lives in the Forbidden City and as entertainment. *Zhenxiang huabao* (True record, 1911–1913), an art magazine financially sponsored by the fledgling Nationalist Party, published some photographs in praise of the revolutionary efforts that had led to the establishment of the Republic, but it was short-lived and its editors soon returned to painting. In the early Republican period, while warlord conflicts plagued China, no warlord is known to have used photographs consciously and systematically to promote his political causes. However, with the growth of celebrity culture, and the successful manipulation of mass-media imagery by some cultural figures, the ground was prepared for more widespread political propaganda photography.

Upon its consolidation of power in 1927, the Nationalist Party established the Central News Agency to centralize and monopolize the entire country's news supply. In Nationalist-supported newspapers and magazines, photographs were used selectively to promote the party and its leader Chiang Kai-shek (Jiang Jishi). No effectively organized attempts to produce photographs for political propaganda had yet emerged. It was during the War of Resistance

Chinese soldiers fighting along the Great Wall in Hebei province, spring 1938. *Not until the War of Resistance with Japan did propaganda photographs become widely used in China. The Chinese Communist Party, in particular, promoted their message through photos in a variety of publications, using pictures to influence the opinions of both literate and illiterate citizens.* SHA FEI / FOTOE

against Japan from 1937 to 1945 that a more systematic application of photography for propaganda emerged. One example is a Chinese Communist Party (CCP) publication of 1942, *Kangzhan zhong de balujun* (Eighth Route Army in the War of Resistance). Published at Yan'an, the wartime headquarters of the CCP, the book is composed of photographs accompanied by brief texts that document (and glorify) the heroic deeds and survival of the Eighth Route Army and its resistance efforts against the Japanese over the preceding five years.

During the war years in various CCP-controlled areas such as the Jin-Cha-Ji (Shanxi-Chahaer-Hebei) border region, illustrated pictorials mushroomed. The earliest such pictorial was the *Jin-Cha-Ji huabao* (Jin-Cha-Ji pictorial), whose inaugural issue appeared on July 7, 1942, soon after Mao Zedong's Yan'an Talks on Literature and Art, to commemorate the fifth anniversary of the war. The *Jin-Cha-Ji huabao* is known as the model for other resistance areas' pictorials because of its sophisticated use of photographs to convey the wartime situation and promote the CCP by emphasizing the party's effective reforms in improving peasants' lives and its military success in defeating the Japanese.

This publication was also unique in its sole reliance on photographs taken by homegrown photographers such as Sha Fei (1912–1950), Shi Shaohua (1918–1998), and Luo Guangda (b. 1919), among many others. Their photographs were straightforward and easily accessible to a broad range of audiences, including illiterate peasants. The Nationalist Party also published its own pictorials in the wartime capital in Chongqing, the most prominent of which was *Lianhe huabao* (United pictorial). Unlike the *Jin-Cha-Ji huabao* and other CCP-sponsored pictorials, *Lianhe huabao* relied heavily on photos supplied by freelance photographers, foreign news agencies, and the American News Agency.

THE PEOPLE'S REPUBLIC ERA

The development of Chinese photography in the People's Republic was, as noted by Regine Thiriez, overshadowed by the CCP's command of the medium to promulgate socialist ideology and educate the masses about the new Communist China, and it was achieved at the cost of sacrificing the diversity of viewpoints that had existed in the bygone Republican period. There is some truth in contrasting the pluralistic Republican and the monolithic Maoist periods,

---

even if both, to different degrees, experienced information control and censorship. At any rate, it is safe to say that the category of *meishu sheying,* or fine art photography, which had flourished during the 1920s and 1930s, was drastically reduced as soon as the CCP took power in 1949. *Xinwen sheying,* or journalistic photography, with approved subject matters rendered in acceptable style, took primacy.

In 1950 the CCP centralized the production and dissemination of news photographs when Xinwen Sheying Chu (Photographic Department of the News Bureau) was formed. Two years later, the bureau was transformed into the present Xinhuashe Sheying Bu (Photographic Department of the New China News Agency). This organization selected, approved, and distributed news photographs to central, regional, and local newspapers, journals, and magazines for publication. *Renmin huabao* (China pictorial) and *Zhongguo jianshe* (China reconstructs; now *Xiandai Zhongguo* or China today) have been the two major propaganda magazines in which photographs were published. All Chinese photographers' job placements were centrally coordinated. Zhongguo Sheying Xuehui (Chinese Photography Society), a state-administrated organization under the Federation of Literary and Art Circles, was established in December 1956. The society, aiming at professionalizing photographers in its select membership, launched two specialized magazines: *Zhongguo sheying* (Chinese photography) and *Dazhong sheying* (Mass photography) in order to provide publishing channels to its members. Without any kind of support from the government, amateur photographers and their activities were virtually suppressed. Generally speaking, officially sanctioned news photography dominated the development of Chinese photography from 1949 to 1976. Photographs produced in this period can be seen as propagandistic because of their predetermined function to promote the regime.

These propaganda photographs are characterized by the following: creation of heroic models; a focus on workers, peasants, and soldiers; successes in mechanization and industrialization; and achievements in collectivization. Along with their limited subject matter, these photographs were rendered in the uniform style of socialist realism. Frequently seen images, for example, were low-angled shots of soldiers, close-ups of exemplary characters, action shots of workers laboring with machines, high-angle shots of applauding crowds, and monumental views of industrial complexes and dams.

The genre of leadership imagery continued to be popular. Hou Bo (b. 1924), Mao Zedong's personal photographer, was given rare access to photograph both Mao's private and official life. Her photographs, some collaboratively produced with her husband, Xu Xiaobing (b. 1916), represent Mao as an approachable and benevolent leader, and were used in many contexts to promote the cult of Mao. Portraits of Mao Zedong were widely circulated, collected,

and hung in ordinary people's homes for adulation during the Cultural Revolution. The ultimate propagandistic touch was the high degree of retouching suffered by many such photographs before they were released to the public.

The term *xuanchuan* in contemporary Chinese may be translated as both propaganda and publicity, thus acknowledging both the informational and the manipulative meanings attached to the word. The advent of the digital camera and the Internet has launched a new era, with the potential to further blur the borders between news, documentary, historical, and propaganda photography. At the same time, the possibility that fraud will be publicly exposed has become greater.

SEE ALSO *Pictorial Magazines since 1880; Propaganda; Propaganda Art.*

BIBLIOGRAPHY

Bendavid-Val, Leah. *Propaganda & Dreams: Photographing the 1930s in the USSR and the U.S.* Zurich and New York: Edition Stemmle, 1999.

Chen Changlian et al. *Dandai Zhongguo sheying yishu shi (1949–1989)* [The art history of Chinese contemporary photography (1949–1979)]. Beijing: Zhongguo Sheying Chubanshe, 1996.

Ma Yunzeng et al. *Zhongguo sheying shi: 1840–1937* [History of Chinese photography: 1840–1937]. Beijing: Zhongguo Sheying Chubanshe, 1987.

Thiriez, Regine. *Barbarian Lens: Western Photographers of the Qianlong Emperor's European Palaces.* Amsterdam: Gordon and Breach, 1998.

Thiriez, Regine. China. *The Oxford Companion to the Photograph.* Ed. Robin Leman. New York: Oxford University Press, 2005.

Wue, Roberta, et al. *Picturing Hong Kong: Photography, 1855–1910.* Hong Kong: South China Printing, 1997.

Wu Hung (Wu Hong) and Christopher Phillips. *Between Past and Future: New Photography and Video from China.* Chicago: Smart Museum of Art, University of Chicago, 2004.

Eliza Ho

PHYSICAL EDUCATION

Physical education (PE) as an integral part of the modern Chinese educational system was developed during the last decades of the Qing dynasty (1644–1912). PE has been closely associated with Chinese nationalism and modern state-building ever since.

When modern sports were introduced to China by foreign missionaries and educators, they were readily embraced by reformist Chinese who sought means to empower the nation in the face of imperialist encroachment. PE in the form of *ticao,* a combination of gymnastics and militaristic calisthenics, was first incorporated into new schools established by self-strengtheners, late Qing reformers, and foreign missions, such as the YMCA. Sports were also introduced to schools

A Chinese boy training in gymnastics, Bozhou, Anhui province, August 3, 2005. *In the late 1800s, many Chinese reformers added physical education requirements to modernize school curriculums. Physical education continues to play an important role in Chinese schools, as authorities consider a physically fit populace an important image to project to the world at large.* © **CHINA NEWSPHOTO/ REUTERS/CORBIS**

as extracurricular activities and interscholastic competitions in the late Qing. In 1902 the government made *ticao* mandatory in the country's new educational program; reformers and early revolutionaries had linked PE with physical and military fitness and thus regarded it as crucial for making China strong.

Physical education remained prominent in the early Republic. In its first educational law issued in 1912, the new government again declared *ticao* mandatory. Professional Chinese *ticao* schools, including women's *ticao* schools, emerged as a result, and a generation of young Chinese students embraced physical fitness as part of the new republican nationalism. In 1917 the young Mao Zedong's essay "On Physical Education" articulated such sentiment.

In the 1920s, PE underwent changes in theory and practice due to the May Fourth movement and the introduction of Western liberal-education philosophy. PE was now seen as promoting democracy, freedom, and a new breed of youth. More lively sports, such as track and field, were favored over rigid calisthenics. PE pedagogy also received more atten-

tion. Reacting to this intellectual trend, the Chinese government in 1922 issued a new law to replace *ticao* with *tiyu,* a broader concept of "physical culture, physical education or more literally, body-cultivation" (Morris 2000, p. 877).

The Nanjing government made efforts to systematize PE. The Ministry of Education issued the Citizen's Physical Education Law in 1929, established the PE Bureau, held the first national PE conference in 1932, and standardized PE instruction in 1936. In Jiangxi Soviet, the Chinese Communists regularly held sports meets and established their own PE association in 1933. After the outbreak of the Second Sino-Japanese War in 1937, both the Nationalists and Communists linked physical fitness with China's victory over Japanese aggression. In 1940 the Nationalist government held a national PE conference in Chongqing, while the Communists established a PE association in Yan'an. In 1941, while the Nationalists published guiding principles for implementing a national PE program, the Communists also established a PE department at Yan'an University.

After the establishment of the People's Republic of China, its school system was designed to provide moral, intellectual, and physical education to Chinese youth. PE was a mandatory twice-a-week subject in all levels of school, and students were required to spend at least one-and-a-half hours on extracurricular physical activity each day. By 1955 students were required to do daily freestanding exercises to radio music once in the morning and once between classes. PE was seen as crucial in training students to become fit workers for socialist construction and defenders of the country. A *lao wei zhi* (labor and defense) program was established and later standardized to measure the fitness of students and the success of the PE program. In 1957 health education was added to PE, and by 1958 students from the elementary to university level were required to attain their respective physical-fitness standard set up by the *lao wei zhi* before graduation. In the early 1960s, students were encouraged to participate in interscholastic sports competitions, and an annual university-level national sports meet was launched.

With China's rise in global status, Chinese people's physical fitness has become an important symbol of China's strength and world image. After its disruption during the Cultural Revolution (1966–1969), PE has again been made mandatory at all levels of schooling since the 1980s. At the first- through twelfth-grade level, students are required to have at least one hour of daily physical activity, three after-school physical activity sessions, and two PE classes each week. Students must pass PE classes and meet fitness standards to move to a higher grade. In 1995 the National People's Congress passed the Physical Education and Sports Law to legalize PE as an integral academic subject and to require schools to provide facilities and equipment for physical activities, organize after-school athletic events, competitions, and annual meets, and ensure that students meet fitness standards. In 2001 the Ministry of Education issued the first national standards for PE and health for students of all levels, including postsecondary. However, given China's uneven social and economic development, disparities in the implementation of the 1995 law and the 2001 standards still exist between rural and urban, coastal and interior regions. Hosting the 2008 Beijing Olympics has stimulated new debate and discussion on how to improve China's physical education.

SEE ALSO *Education; Olympics; Sports; Sports Figures.*

BIBLIOGRAPHY

Brownell, Susan. *Training the Body for China: Sports in the Moral Order of the People's Republic.* Chicago: University of Chicago Press, 1995.

Cui Lequan. *Zhongguo jindai tiyu shihua* [History of modern Chinese physical education]. Beijing: Zhonghua Shuju, 1998.

Department of Secondary Education, State Education Commission, the People's Republic of China. *Secondary Education in China.* Beijing, 1986.

Graham, Gael. Exercising Control: Sports and Physical Education in American Protestant Mission Schools in China, 1880–1930. *Signs* 20, 1 (1994): 23–48.

Ma Mingbing and Wang Qingbo. Cong 2008 nian Beijing auyunhui kan zhongguo xuexiao tiyu de fazhang [View the development of Chinese physical education from 2008 Beijing Olympic Games]. *Hubei tiyu keji* (Journal of Hubei sports science) 2 (2006): 149–150.

Morris, Andrew. "To Make the Four Hundred Million Move": The Late Qing Dynasty Origins of Modern Chinese Sport and Physical Culture. *Comparative Studies in Society and History* 42, 4 (2000): 876–906.

Zhongguo jiaoyu nianjian bianji bu, ed. *Zhongguo jiaoyu nianjian, 2005* [China education yearbook, 2005]. Beijing: Renmin Jiaoyu Chubanshe, 2006.

Zhongyang jiaoyu kexue yanjiusuo, ed. *Zhonghua renmin gongheguo jiaoyu dashi ji, 1949–1982* [Chronicle of events of education in the People's Republic of China, 1949–1982]. Beijing: Jiaoyu Kexue Chubanshe, 1983.

Zhou Chengyong and Li Lin. 2008 nian Beijing auyunhui yu zhongguo xuexiao tiyu fazhang [2008 Beijing Olympics and the development of Chinese physical education]. *Beijing Tiyu daxue xuebao* [Journal of Beijing University of Sports] 12 (2007): 1679–1683.

Li Danke

PICTORIAL MAGAZINES SINCE 1880

In the 1920s, China, like its Western counterparts, experienced a boom in the publication of pictorial magazines. The boom was precipitated by a combination of factors that had begun to take effect as early as the last decades of the nineteenth century: the importation of Western printing technologies, a multiplication of markets, and an expansion of readership owing to the affordability of printed matter and people's growing thirst for knowledge and information about the contemporary world.

What distinguishes print culture of the modern period from that of previous times are matters regarding patronage and the production, distribution, and consumption of printed works, including books and the new genre of illustrated magazines. The beginning of Chinese print history can be traced back to the ninth century, during the Tang dynasty (618–907), when printing occurred largely to fulfill demands for the reproduction of Buddhist scriptures. In addition, the imperial court, the dominant cultural trendsetter of all dynasties, commissioned the printing of the canonical texts and the Confucian classics. The system of civil service examinations also created a market for the publication of examination guides. Toward the end of the Ming period (1368–1644), illustrated novels became popular among ordinary citizens who sought entertainment from reading.

PREDECESSORS OF MODERN PICTORIAL MAGAZINES

The emergence of pictorial magazines in the Republican period was prefigured by late-Qing predecessors, notably *Dianshizhai huabao* (Dianshizhai pictorial). This publication originated as a supplement for *Shenbao*, the longest-running and one of the most-read dailies in pre-1949 China, established by the British merchant Ernest Major (1842–1908) in 1872. *Dianshizhai huabao* showed many traits that defined modern picture magazines, such as the use of images to illustrate current events and to visualize curiosities and oddities (*qi*) of the world. With hand-drawn illustrations by such skilled artists as Wu Youru (Wu Jiayou, d. 1894), this popular pictorial retained the otherwise traditional appearance of an illustrated publication. It was printed by lithography, a Western-inspired technique that could preserve the aesthetic of the Chinese characters and the line-work of the hand-drawn illustrations.

PICTORIAL MAGAZINES IN THE REPUBLICAN PERIOD

The renowned Chinese journalist Ge Gongzhen (1890–1935) maintained that "the readers nowadays demand visual evidence along with the news" (Ma 1987, p. 114). Inspired by Western-illustrated magazines, Ge saw the need and market for photographic illustrations for Chinese newspapers. In 1920 he created a supplement, *Tuhua zhoukan* (Pictures weekly), for *Shibao* (China times), that was illustrated by news photographs. Many newspapers followed suit, and the trend gave rise to the subsequent burgeoning of picture magazines in the late 1920s and early 1930s.

A tabloid-format entertainment newspaper, *Shanghai huabao* (Pictorial Shanghai), founded by the literary figure Bi Yihong (Bi Zhenda, 1892–1926) in 1925, was one of the most prolifically illustrated of the Republican era. Characterized by the primacy of its photographic illustrations, and its emphasis on current events, it laid the groundwork for subsequent developments. *Liangyou huabao* (Young Companion), inaugurated in 1926, a general interest magazine that showcases urban, modern lifestyle, is one of the earliest popular pictorials and is representative of those that circulated far and wide throughout China and abroad. In addition to its featuring of fashionable women for its front covers, *Liangyou* was also known for its use of collotype and photogravure, which contributed to its high production quality.

Besides the newly available technologies for photographic reproduction, the popularization of portable cameras also contributed to the mushrooming of pictorial magazines. The availability of Leica and Contax cameras to both amateur and professional photographers beginning in 1930 opened up opportunities for otherwise unforeseeable subjects, especially candid and spontaneous pictures of people. Improvements in camera technology, such as faster shutter speed and more light-sensitive film, also enabled photographers to capture the fleeting realities of commoners' lives on the street. The increasing number and variety of reproducible photographs made pictorial magazines appealing to a broader spectrum of readers. Toward the 1930s, Chinese pictorial magazines began to adopt the format of the photo-story, in which a topic was explored by a series of related photographs accompanied with text. Topics of interest were no longer confined to news events but included a wide variety of human-interest subjects to fulfill people's continuing fascination with the world's curiosities.

Besides the commercially oriented picture magazines, there were socially and politically concerned pictorials that had backing from political parties and warlords. An early example was the art periodical *Zhenxiang huabao* (True record), which was founded in 1912 by two Guangdong painters, Gao Jianfu (1879–1951) and Gao Qifeng (1889–1933), and was reportedly financed by the newly formed Nationalist Party. Besides its intent to disseminate new learning and ideas of revolution, *Zhenxiang huabao*'s historical significance also lies in its early adoption of the technology of photolithography for colored reproductions. People's demand for new knowledge intensified during and after the May Fourth and New Culture movements, and contributed to the multiplication of markets and the expansion of readership. Specialized pictorials targeting specific audiences, such as workers, women, and students, appeared. Besides covering new knowledge and technologies of the day, these pictorials also regularly contained self-help articles to accommodate the special interests and individualized needs of their readers.

When armed conflict between China and Japan became imminent toward the middle of the 1930s, some pictorial magazines turned to politics. For example, *Dazhong shenghuo* (Mass life), a progressive pictorial published by Zou Taofen (1895–1944), was particularly successful in using news photographs for its cover images. *Dazhong shenghuo* was also known for its boldness in criticizing the Nationalist government's appeasement policies toward the Japanese.

THE WAR PERIOD, 1937–1949

Although they had established their own news agencies during their formative years, the Communists and the Nationalists did not fully utilize the medium of pictorial magazine for propaganda until the war years from 1937 to 1949. The Chinese Communist Party-sponsored *Jin-Cha-Ji huabao* (Jin-Cha-Ji pictorial) and the Nationalist government-sponsored *Lianhe huabao* (United pictorial) were early "official" pictorials that came into being in 1942, in the midst of the Anti-Japanese War. These pictorials promoted the parties' agendas and ideologies by printing numerous war-related photographs, which reached high-level officials and cadres, as well as international audiences. Other Chinese pictorial magazines diverted all their pages to the war.

The protracted war eventually led to the displacement and relocation of many publishers and their printing facilities, resulting in a drastic shrinkage of the pictorial-magazine industry.

AFTER 1949

The establishment of the People's Republic of China in 1949 meant the beginning of state centralization of news production and distribution. As a popular medium, pictorial magazines became a tool to propagate Communist policies and ideologies. Complying with the prescribed functions of journalism to serve the needs of the party, pictorial magazines such as *Renmin huabao* (China Pictorial) and *Zhongguo jianshe* (China reconstructs) assumed the role of the party's mouthpiece. Along with domestic distribution, these official pictorials are published in many different languages for international circulation. After a drought during the decade of the Cultural Revolution (1966–1976), pictorial magazines reemerged, and their contents reflected the partial and selective loosening up of information control as well as the new demands of a market economy that Deng Xiaoping's reform inaugurated. The function of the pictorial magazine was thus redirected toward entertainment and consumption. Among the popular titles are *Waitan huabao* (The Bund pictorial) and *Sanlian shenghuo zhoukan* (Sanlian life weekly). Both are general-interest picture magazines, covering a variety of subjects ranging from politics to business to technology to art and culture. As contemporary media, both have electronic versions that are also loaded with still images.

SEE ALSO *Commercial Art; Photography, History of.*

BIBLIOGRAPHY

Lin Yu-tang. *History of the Press and Public Opinion in China.* 1936. New York: Greenwood Press, 1968.

Ma Yunzeng et al. *Zhongguo sheying shi: 1840–1937* [History of Chinese photography: 1840–1937]. Beijing: Zhongguo Sheying Chubanshe, 1987.

Reed, Christopher A. *Gutenberg in Shanghai: Chinese Print Capitalism, 1876–1937.* Vancouver: University of British Columbia Press, 2004.

Waara, Carol Lynne. Arts and Life: Public and Private Culture in Chinese Art Periodicals, 1912–1937. Ph.D. diss., University of Michigan, 1994.

Zhao Yuezhi. *Media, Market, and Democracy in China: Between the Party Line and the Bottom Line.* Urbana: University of Illinois, 1998.

Eliza Ho

PIRACY, MARITIME

Piracy has existed in China in all ages. In modern times, there were three major episodes: during the late eighteenth and early nineteenth centuries, during the Opium War and Taiping Uprising in the mid-nineteenth century, and between the Revolution of 1911 and World War II (1937–1945). Pirates continue to operate in the geographically and politically complex waters between Japan and Australia, but the days of the great pirate fleets have long passed.

After a lull of about a century, Chinese piracy rose again and reached unprecedented heights between 1780 and 1810. During those years South China was plagued by several competing pirate leagues, composed of self-contained fleets that functioned independently of one another. While petty gangs of pirates continued to operate, they were overshadowed by the larger, better-organized pirate leagues. Large-scale piracy reappeared in the South China Sea in the 1780s, when Tay Son rebels in Vietnam sanctioned raids into Chinese waters to bolster their revenues and increase their manpower with the addition of Chinese pirates. Before their defeat in 1802, pirate fleets set out each spring and summer from bases along the Sino-Vietnamese border to plunder vessels and villages along the China coast.

By far the most impressive group of pirates in Chinese history was the Guangdong confederation between 1802 and 1810. Composed of the remnants of Tay Son privateers and Chinese pirates, at its height in 1809 the confederation consisted of hundreds of vessels and anywhere from 40,000 to 60,000 followers, including men, women, and children. Until his death in 1807, Zheng Yi, who hailed from a family of professional pirates, led the confederation, which was divided into seven, later six, well-armed and highly organized fleets. After Zheng Yi's death, leadership passed into the hands of his capable widow, Zheng Yi Sao, and the charismatic young Zhang Bao.

Although at the height of its power in 1809, the confederation collapsed within a year. Unable to stop the pirates, the Jiaqing emperor (r. 1796–1820) offered the pirates pardons and rewards for their surrender. The confederation began to fall apart as rogue gangs entered into allegiance to the state. Finally in April 1810, Zheng Yi Sao and Zhang Bao surrendered. The government quickly rewarded Zhang Bao with money and a naval commission, and then sent him and his fleet to fight the remaining pirates in western Guangdong.

Huge pirate leagues never re-formed, but piracy persisted, with a marked upsurge between 1840 and 1870 brought on by the chaos of the Opium War (1839–1842) and the Taiping Uprising (1851–1864). Piracy increased during the first years of the British colony, partly owing to the inefficiency of the new Hong Kong government and partly owing to the growth in trade. The two most notorious Chinese pirates at that time were Shi Wu Zai (Shapng-tsai) and Xu Yabao (Chu-apoo). At the same time, European and American renegades, runaway slaves, and the so-called "Manilla-men" from the Philippines occasionally joined with native pirates or formed gangs of their own.

CHINESE PIRATES ATTACKING A TRADER.—Drawn by J. O. Davidson.—[See Page 226.]

Chinese Pirates Attacking a Trader, *by American marine artist Julian Oliver Davidson, 1876. Piracy on China's coast increased during the mid-nineteenth century as the Opium Wars and Taiping Rebellion weakened the power of the Imperial government to police the seas. Despite fewer incidents, pirates remain active in the twenty-first century.* © **CORBIS**

After Hong Kong became the headquarters of its China station, the Royal Navy increased its presence, and piracy began to recede in the area. In 1847 the Hong Kong government also enacted its first antipiracy legislation, and in 1860 the Treaty of Tianjin allowed British warships to pursue pirates into Chinese harbors. British steam warships drove the pirates' sailing junks into China's inland rivers and into the waters of Southeast Asia.

The calm lasted forty years until the Revolution of 1911, subsequent warlordism, and the civil war between the Nationalists and Communists provided opportunities for a resurgence in piracy along the southern coast. Successive Chinese governments were too weak or too corrupt to curb piracy, and foreign governments were often reluctant to get involved because of the sensitive issue of Chinese sovereignty. One of the most unforgettable pirates of this era was a woman named Lai Caishan (Lai Choi San), who was dubbed the queen of Macau pirates. Like Zheng Yi, she too came from a family of pirates.

Between the two world wars there were fifty-one reported cases of piracy against modern coastal steamers, most of which

were British ships. What was important about these piracies was that they all involved a relatively new modus operandi: hijacking. The most notorious heists were the so-called Bias Bay piracies, named after the area out of which the pirates operated (modern-day Daya Bay, east of Hong Kong). Pirates had adapted to the modern world of steamships and modern shipping practices. In the Pearl River Delta, pirates worked in business-like syndicates and spent weeks in preparations for their operations. Hijacking remained the dominant pirate tactic even as late as 2008.

With the outbreak of the Second Sino-Japanese War in 1937, piracy began to decline, or at least there were fewer reported cases. It picked up for a time during the Chinese civil war (1945–1949) and during the first few years of Communist rule, but by the late 1950s piracy seemed a thing of the past along the South China coast. Although there still are many petty piracies that go unreported, the number of professional piracies has certainly decreased. In the first decade of the twenty-first century, most of these latter forms of piracy take place in Southeast Asian waters, though bosses may still hail from China.

BIBLIOGRAPHY

Antony, Robert J. *Like Froth Floating on the Sea: The World of Pirates and Seafarers in Late Imperial South China.* Berkeley: Institute of East Asian Studies, University of California, 2003.

Fox, Grace. *British Admirals and Chinese Pirates, 1832–1869.* London: K. Paul, Trench, Trubner, 1940.

Lilius, Aleko. *I Sailed with Chinese Pirates.* London: Arrowsmith, 1930.

Murray, Dian. *Pirates of the South China Coast, 1790–1810.* Stanford, CA: Stanford University Press, 1987.

Robert J. Antony

PLAYS (*HUAJU*)

Hong Shen, a Harvard-educated writer and director of stage and film productions, is credited with introducing the term *huaju* (spoken drama) in 1928 to define and discipline a modern form of drama inspired by Western theater and distinct from operatic traditions within China. Since the nineteenth century, Chinese students in missionary schools or studying overseas had been introduced to Western drama in dialogues without musical arias. By 1906 to 1907, the political ferment among Chinese students in Japan prompted them to form a drama club, Chunliu She (Spring Willow Society), to stage adaptations of Harriet Beecher Stowe's *Uncle Tom's Cabin* (1851–1852) and Alexandre Dumas's (fils) *La Dame aux camélias* (1848) as suggestive commentary on conditions within Chinese society. These productions inspired numerous performances within China that became known as *wenming xi* (civilized or enlightened drama). However, scripts for these productions were not published as a literary form in themselves, and, following the Republican revolution of 1912, as a performance art they were censored and transformed into vaudeville, with some scripts later revised for early Chinese films in the 1920s and 1930s.

A NEW WAVE OF INTEREST IN MODERN THEATER

In the United States, a Chinese graduate student, Hu Shi, wrote and staged a realistic one-act comedy for Chinese students at Columbia University in New York titled *Zhongshen dashi* (The greatest event in life, 1919). The play depicted a young woman eloping with her admirer after her parents object to her choice of a spouse on the grounds of violating one or another form of traditional belief, custom, or propriety. Hu Shi's daringly rebellious script, its contemporary Chinese setting, and its realist prescriptions requiring both male and female performers to share the stage, together with translations of provocative plays by Henrik Ibsen and others, all provoked a new wave of interest in modern theater among the youthful educated elite in Beijing and Shanghai.

By the early 1920s, this movement resulted in a variety of dramatic associations and scripts, among them one-act comedies by Ding Xilin inspired by Oscar Wilde and George Bernard Shaw, Guo Moruo's innovative historical dramas on "three rebellious women" (*Wang Zhaojun*, 1923; *Zhuo Wenjun*, 1923; *Nie Ying*, 1925), and romantic plays by Tian Han in which despair over disappointed love drives characters to drink or suicide, as in *Kafei dian zhi yiye* (A night in a café, 1922) and *Huo hu zhi ye* (The night the tiger was caught, 1924). As China's first professionally trained dramatist, Hong Shen introduced a more powerfully ambitious form of modernist drama by adapting Eugene O'Neill's 1920 play *The Emperor Jones* as *Zhao Yanwang* (Yama Zhao, king of hell, 1923), on the fate of a rebellious peasant joining the Boxer insurrection of 1900. Hong also introduced unified production under a director and acting methods that further distinguished the practice of spoken drama.

From the 1920s on, a wide range of writers in all genres tried their hand at spoken drama, from the poet Xu Zhimo and the novelist Mao Dun to the cultural critics Lu Xun and Lin Yutang, as well as young women writers like Bai Wei, Yuan Changying, and Yang Jiang. Together with the pioneering writers, their plays created controversy, introducing men and women together on the stage, acting out provocative themes of cultural or political criticism for which authorities banned numerous productions, generating more attention to spoken drama. In 1936 the sole professional drama troupe, the China Traveling Dramatic Company (Zhongguo Luxing Jutuan), discovered a domestic tragedy by a recently graduated university student, Cao Yu, titled *Leiyu* (Thunderstorm) and gave the play a performance that startled audiences in Shanghai and thereby established an audience for spoken drama that would support theater as a professional, commercial enterprise.

WAR AND POLITICS IN THE 1930s AND 1940s

At the same time, a surge of writers joining leftist organizations included a number of dramatists, and among the new playwrights working with the Communist Party, Xia Yan, Yang Hansheng, and Chen Baichen made distinctive contributions. Xia Yan's *Shanghai wuyan xia* (Under Shanghai eaves, 1937) has been recognized as a classic piece of "slice of life" social realism in the tradition of Maxim Gorky's *The Lower Depths* (1902) and Elmer Rice's *Street Scene* (1929). The Communist-organized movement for a "literature of national defense" against Japanese aggression increased audiences with street theater, the most famous of which was *Fangxia nide bianzi* (Put down your whip, 1931), its earliest script credited to Chen Liting, an adaptation of an episode in Goethe's novel *Wilhelm Meister's Apprenticeship* (1795). The play presents a street performance of folk tunes by a father and his daughter. When the father begins to beat his daughter

A People's Liberation Army Dramatic Troupe performance of The Sound of Galloping Horses, *Beijing, October 22, 1996.* Plays written in the style of socialist realism provided the People's Republic of China a way of communicating Communist Party beliefs to a wider public. Work created by artists at the end of the twentieth century, however, reflected less on politics and more on the societal effects of China's transition to a market-based economy. AP IMAGES

after she collapses from hunger, a performer in the street audience intervenes, and the daughter reveals the oppression of life under Japanese occupation that has ruined both her life and her father's, leading the performers into arousing the audience to join in singing songs of patriotic resistance.

Leftist criticism of Nationalist Party policy evading resolute action against Japanese aggression also took the form of historical dramas, such as Xia Yan's *Sai Jinhua* (1936) on the Boxer insurrection of 1900 and Chen Baichen's *Shi Dakai de molu* (The last days of Shi Dakai, 1936) on a general of the nineteenth-century Taiping Uprising (1851–1864). Historical drama would become even more prevalent after the outbreak of war. The plays recalled Chinese resistance to Mongol or Manchu-led invasions, as in *Mingmo yihen* (Sorrow for the fall of the Ming, 1940) by A Ying, or continued the criticism of Nationalists, as in Guo Moruo's *Qu Yuan* (1942), on the famous ancient official whose sage advice to the king of Chu only led to his rivals' calumny of him and to his punishment.

As much as spoken drama contributed to patriotic propaganda at the outset of the War of Resistance against Japan (1937–1945), by 1940 spoken drama was turning to other material. The dominant theme in contemporary realist drama was the corruption of Nationalist officials who frustrated the work of the educated elite and squandered dedicated human resources, as in Xia Yan's *Faxisi xijun* (Fascist bacillus, 1942) and similar plays by Lao She, Cao Yu, Mao Dun, and others. However, Nationalist-supported playwrights offered responses, whether through spy dramas like *Ye meigui* (Wild rose, 1941) by Chen Quan or historical plays like *Qing gong yuan* (1941, translated as *Malice of Empire*) by Yao Ke. More and more, spoken drama survived in well-written plays and accomplished productions that incorporated elements of Chinese musical theater, the most successful being *Qiu Haitang* (1942) by Qin Shouou, depicting the fate of a Peking opera *huadan* female impersonator's romance with the concubine of a warlord, providing the occasion for opera scenes. The success of such hybrid forms was not lost on Communist dramatic producers, who inaugurated a "new music theater" (*xin geju*) that proved popular for several decades.

DRAMA IN THE PEOPLE'S REPUBLIC

Following the founding of the People's Republic of China (PRC), the state supported spoken-drama troupes nationwide, as well as a Central Drama Academy in Beijing, and tasked them to provide works of socialist realism following Mao Zedong's prescriptions. Comedies like *Buguniao you jiaole* (Cuckoo sings again, 1957) by Yang Lüfang celebrated a peasant girl's struggle to become a production cooperative's tractor driver, incorporating folk songs into the action. Experimental dramas like *Jiliu yongjin* (Braving the current, 1963) by Hu Wanchun, Huang Zuolin, and Tong Luo presented the rehabilitation of an industrial manager dedicated to socialism. Devotional works like *Lei Feng* (1964) by Jia Liu and others memorialized such figures as model soldiers.

In addition to such celebrations of workers, peasants, and soldiers, many veteran writers turned to historical dramas, among them Tian Han, whose most noted script, *Guan Hanqing* (1958), commemorated the social criticism of a thirteenth-century playwright. Yet, by 1966 a new group of cultural leaders led by Mao Zedong's wife, Jiang Qing, deemed all such dramas inadequate or resistant to Maoist prescriptions for literature and art and purged spoken drama from the stage, consigning its writers and artists to reform through labor or reeducation, and replacing their work with "revolutionary model performances" (*geming yangban xi*) in operatic and ballet forms.

Following the collapse of Jiang Qing's authority in 1976, writers were rehabilitated and theater groups were reformed. Historical dramas, such as *Qin wang Li Shimin* (Li Shimin, Prince of Qin, 1981) by Yan Haiping, opened reconsideration of the nation's imperial past. Satirical plays, such as *Jiaru wo shi zhende* (Sha Yexin, If I really were, 1979), probed the ethics of the present. Modernist scripts, such as *Che zhan* (Bus stop, 1983) by Gao Xingjian, brought themes of absurdity to questions about contemporary Chinese culture. While the state sanctioned plays offering a new appreciation of the traditions of entrepreneurship, as in the popular realist drama *Tianxia diyi lou* (World's finest restaurant, 1988) by He Jiping on the history of a Peking-duck restaurant, avant-garde playwrights like Zhang Guangtian sought to stir audiences with the memory of socialist ideals in such plays as *Qie Gewala* (Che Guevara, 2001), or questioned foreign and local cultures and the place of the common person in modern revolutions and market reforms, as in Guo Shixing's *Niaoren* (Birdmen, 1993) and *Cesuo* (Toilet, 2004).

The more the theater of spoken drama was challenged by television and the Internet, the more it moved into the experimental and avant-garde, notably in the brief successes of Meng Jinghui and the more sustained work of Lai Shengchuan with the Performance Workshop (Biaoyan gongzuo fang), based in Taiwan. The Performance Workshop's productions since the 1980s have repeatedly returned to the theme of the fragmentation of experience in modern life and its relation to disappearing features of a premodern culture in such plays as Lai's *Anlian taohuayuan* (Secret love for peach blossom spring, 1986) and *Ru meng zhi meng* (A dream like a dream, 2005).

SEE ALSO *Cao Yu; Gao Xingjian; Guo Moruo; Lao She; Mao Dun; Model Operas and Ballets; Translation of Foreign Literature.*

BIBLIOGRAPHY

Chen Xiaomei. *Acting the Right Part: Political Theater and Popular Drama in Contemporary China.* Honolulu: University of Hawai'i Press, 2002.

Chen Xiaomei, ed. *Reading the Right Text: An Anthology of Contemporary Chinese Drama.* Honolulu: University of Hawaii Press, 2003.

Cheung, Martha P. Y., and Jane C. C. Lai, eds. *An Oxford Anthology of Contemporary Chinese Drama.* Hong Kong and New York: Oxford University Press, 1997.

Eberstein, Bernd, ed. *A Selective Guide to Chinese Literature, 1900–1949.* Vol. 4: *The Drama.* New York and Leiden, Netherlands: Brill, 1990.

Gunn, Edward, ed. *Twentieth-century Chinese Drama: An Anthology.* Bloomington: Indiana University Press, 1983.

Yan Haiping, ed. *Theater and Society: An Anthology of Contemporary Chinese Drama.* Armonk, NY: Sharpe, 1998.

Edward Mansfield Gunn Jr.

POETRY

This entry contains the following:

CLASSICAL POETRY
Michelle Yeh

MODERN POETRY
Michelle Yeh

MISTY POETRY
Michelle Yeh

CLASSICAL POETRY

Classical poetry began with the *Shijing*, commonly translated as *Book of Songs, Book of Odes*, or *Classic of Poetry*, a collection of folk songs, courtly compositions, and ritual hymns compiled in the sixth century BCE. This genre, known as *shi* ("poetry"), evolved into several major forms in the next two millennia and continues to be written to this day. The forms are: (1) quatrain (*jueju*), in which all four lines contain either five or seven characters per line; (2) regulated verse (*lüshi*), in which all eight lines contain either five or seven characters per line; (3) song lyric (*ci*), which contains a varying number of lines of irregular lengths and is set to a preexisting tune; and (4) aria (*qu*), which contains irregular lines set to a preexisting tune for drama. Unlike poetry in European civilization, classical poetry is highly regarded in Confucian China not only for its artistry but also for its educational, moral, and political import. It is no exaggeration to say that classical poetry is a defining feature of Chinese culture and an integral part of Chinese civilization.

In view of the remarkable longevity and superb talents that characterize classical poetry, latecomers are inevitably met with the daunting challenge to "make it new." Poets in the late Qing dynasty (1644–1912), for example, tended to follow one of two paths: first, by reviving a poetic style from earlier times against the prevailing style, and, second, by injecting new elements into the ancient form. The first path is represented by several schools of poets, including the Tong-Guang style, which exalted and emulated Du Fu (712–770), Han Yu (768–824), and, above all, Huang Tingjian (1045–1105); the Han-Wei–Six Dynasties school; the Mid- and Late Tang school (or Xikun style); and the Changzhou school of the song lyric, which exalted and emulated Wu Wenying (c. 1200–1260), famous for his dense, allusive style.

Partly in reaction to the revivalist paradigm described above, Liang Qichao (1873–1929) and several young intellectuals ushered in the "poetry revolution" in December 1899. Inspired by poets both earlier and contemporary, such as Gong Zizhen (1792–1841), Jin He (1818–1885), Kang Youwei (1858–1927), and, above all, Huang Zunxian (1848–1905), Liang advocated a "new-style poetry" that boasted "new meanings and atmospheres," "new words and expressions," and restored the "styles of the ancients." For the first time, images and vocabularies of modern science and technology and, of the discovery and colonization of the New World, found their way into classical poetry. Along with the "fiction revolution" and "literature revolution," also led by Liang, the poetry reform underscored China's effort to modernize itself on the global stage.

Although the late Qing poetry revolution was short-lived, it inspired Hu Shi (1891–1962) to call for a more radical and ambitious reform—from classical Chinese to the modern vernacular, from traditional forms to complete freedom in form. But even here, the influence of classical poetry was inescapable. His idea, Hu argued, was not as radical as it sounded; there had been six previous "revolutions" as classical poetry evolved from the earliest *Shijing* to the *qu*, the last major form to emerge in the Yuan dynasty (1279–1368). While highly critical of the regulated verse for its rigidity, Hu was favorably disposed toward the more vernacular *ci* and *qu*.

Hu Shi's own "modern poetry" also displayed unmistakable traces of classical poetry. In fact, he wrote classical poetry his entire life, as did most pioneers of modern poetry and modern fiction. Some of them, such as Zhou Zuoren (1885–1967) and Yu Pingbo (1900–1990), stopped writing modern poetry and wrote classical poetry exclusively; others

like Lu Xun (1881–1936) and Yu Dafu (1896–1945) left behind memorable classical-style poems. After millennia, classical poetry has become so deeply embedded in the Chinese language and the collective memory of the Chinese people that it is a natural vehicle for expressing emotions and aspirations, not only for intellectuals and political figures (most notably, Mao Zedong), but for common folks as well. This was evident during and after the Cultural Revolution (1966–1969), when grievances and protests often took the form of classical poetry.

In the more liberal atmosphere of the 1980s, classical poetry underwent a robust revival, as new poetry clubs devoted to the writing of the genre mushroomed. Typically, these clubs were registered with the local government, received subsidies from it, held poetry gatherings, and published original poetry in journals. Since the 1990s, with the spread of the Internet, classical poetry has found another fertile ground. The renewed interest in traditional culture as China seeks to redefine itself in the world also helps to promulgate classical poetry in formal education and popular culture. Paradoxically, although modern poetry is written in the vernacular while classical poetry is written in classical Chinese, readers usually find the latter more accessible; while modern poetry has replaced classical poetry as the representative poetic form in modern literature, the latter seems to be closer to everyday life. It is beyond doubt that so long as the Chinese language exists, classical poetry will be read and written.

SEE ALSO *Hu Shi; Kang Youwei; Liang Qichao; Yu Dafu.*

BIBLIOGRAPHY

Cai, Zongqi, ed. *How to Read Chinese Poetry: A Guided Anthology.* New York: Columbia University Press, 2008.

Kowallis, Jon Eugene von. *The Subtle Revolution: Poets of the "Old Schools" during Late Qing and Early Republican China.* Berkeley: University of California Institute of East Asian Studies, 2006.

Owen, Stephen. *An Anthology of Chinese Literature: Beginnings to 1911.* New York: Norton, 1997.

Watson, Burton. *The Columbia Book of Chinese Poetry: From Earliest Times to the Thirteenth Century.* New York: Columbia University Press, 1984.

Wu, Shengqing. Contested *Fengya*: Classical-style Poetry Clubs in Early Republican China. In *Literary Societies of Republican China*, ed. K. A. Denton and M. Hockx, 15–46. Lanham, MD: Lexington Books, 2008.

Michelle Yeh

MODERN POETRY

In the Chinese context, *modern poetry* refers to poetry that is written in the modern vernacular in nontraditional forms, from the early twentieth century to the present. As such, it is distinguished from *traditional poetry* (or *classical*

136

poetry) linguistically and formally. Although the use of the vernacular is not uncommon in classical poetry (e.g., traditional ballads, folk songs, and song lyrics), modern poetry employs everyday language used in present-day China. Although modern poetry adapts certain forms from other literatures (e.g., the sonnet from European poetry), it shuns traditional Chinese forms with their prescribed tonal patterns and rhyme schemes.

Classical poetry has a long, glorious tradition going all the way back to the *Classic of Poetry* (also translated as *Book of Songs*, or *Shijing*), compiled around the sixth century BCE. Through the ensuing centuries, classical poetry has developed into a supreme art, as exemplified by a variety of genres and a pantheon of talented poets. Moreover, poetry occupies a canonical place in Confucianism, serving moral, educational, social, and political functions. It is no exaggeration to say that classical poetry is a defining feature of Chinese culture and an integral part of the Chinese language (which remains true in the twenty-first century). Chinese people are proud of this heritage and often refer to themselves as a "nation of poetry."

We may ask then, why modern poetry? Why not continue to write classical poetry? Indeed, classical poetry has never ceased to be written. Not only did many literary and political figures in the twentieth century write in the genre, but poetry clubs devoted to classical poetry have been formed in the sinophone world and have in fact mushroomed in mainland China in recent decades. Classical poetry has existed alongside modern poetry since the early twentieth century, and no doubt the situation will continue in the foreseeable future.

THE POETRY REVOLUTION

However, by the late Qing, the call for poetry reform arose from young intellectuals. The so-called poetry revolution at the end of the nineteenth century was inspired by the swiftly changing world and the notion of literature as an agent of social change and political reform. The poetry revolution sought to modernize the diction and (to some extent) content, but not the form, of poetry. Radical reform would have to wait till 1917, when a Chinese student studying in the United States named Hu Shi (1891–1962) formulated a theory of *new poetry* and penned some samples in the new genre. In "A Modest Proposal for Literary Reform" ("Wenxue gailiang chuyi") published in the *New Youth* (*Xin qingnian*) in January 1917, Hu lists the "eight don'ts" as follows: (1) Make sure there is substance; (2) Do not imitate poets of the past; (3) Observe grammar; (4) Do not groan if you are not sick; (5) Get rid of clichés and formulaic expressions; (6) Do not use allusions; (7) Do not observe parallelism; and (8) Do not avoid colloquial words and expressions.

The list of "eight don'ts" serves as a succinct manifesto of an unprecedented revolution. It rejects stylistic and aesthetic conventions of classical poetry, such as imitation, as a legitimate, even requisite, practice; use of stock motifs and imagery; and formal parallelism. Instead, Hu envisioned a new poetry based on formal "emancipation," personal experience, and original expression, as suggested in "Dream and Poetry" ("Meng yu shi"), written in 1920: "You cannot write my poem / Just as I cannot dream your dream." Going further than the late-Qing poetry revolution, Hu drew on English poetry—from Robert Browning (1812–1889) to Sarah Teasdale (1884–1933)—for inspiration. Although Hu's own poems bear heavy marks of classical poetry, especially the song lyric or *ci*, his call for new poetry (*xinshi*) or vernacular poetry (*baihua shi*), made him a pioneer of literary experimentation. The literary revolution in which modern poetry was born harbingered the wholesale iconoclastic cultural reform of the May Fourth movement, which began in 1919.

Hu Shi also authored China's first individual collection of modern poetry, appropriately titled *Experiments* (*Changshi ji*), which was published in August 1919. Other pioneers in the late 1910s and early 1920s include: Liu Dabai (1880–1932), Zhou Zuoren (1885–1967), Kang Baiqing (1885–1959), Liu Bannong (1891–1934), Guo Moruo (1892–1978), Lu Zhiwei (1894–1970), Xu Zhimo (1897–1931), Wen Yiduo (1899–1946), and Yu Pingbo (1900–1990), among others. Whereas romanticism dominated the formative period, symbolism and modernism exerted significant influences in the 1930s and 1940s. A younger generation of poets, such as Feng Zhi (1905–1993), Dai Wangshu (1905–1955), Bian Zhilin (1910–2000), He Qifang (1912–1977), and Mu Dan (1918–1977), took modern poetry to a new height of sophistication and maturity.

CHALLENGES TO MODERN POETRY

Since its inception, modern poetry has been much maligned for its alleged obscurity, lack of musicality, and Westernization. Compared with classical poetry, it sounds strange, un-Chinese, and "unpoetic." But the root cause is twofold: the marginalization of poetry in modern society, and the difficulty of introducing a new aesthetic paradigm to a poetic tradition of glorious longevity. Although poetry still retains some of its old prestige, it no longer plays a functional role in more "important" or "practical" spheres of modern society, such as education and politics. Insofar as it is unimaginable today that, before the twentieth century, to become a government official one had to be not only well versed in, but also a competent practitioner of, poetry, modern poetry is only one of many genres of modern literature and art.

The other challenge modern poetry faces stems from its radical differences from classical poetry. Chinese readers have long internalized classical poetry not only as cultural heritage but also as part of the spoken and written language.

Understandably, many tend to judge modern poetry by the standards of classical poetry and find it lacking. But this is not unlike comparing apples and oranges. Central to the self-validation of modern poetry is the cultivation of a new community of competent readers. Over the decades, this has been accomplished gradually with its presence in the print media and integration into the education system.

Like other genres, modern poetry may be mobilized for political purposes. During the Second Sino-Japanese War (1937–1945), it served as a powerful tool of resistance as it was recited in public spaces—from school auditoriums to street corners—to raise morale and promote patriotism. In the Mao era, modern poetry, based on the formula of "classical+folk song," was mass produced. In postwar Taiwan, the Nationalist regime under Chiang Kai-shek (Jiang Jieshi) offered handsome rewards for anticommunist poetry. It comes as no surprise that most of the poetry written under these circumstances has long been forgotten.

More often than not, poetry of the first order reacts against adverse conditions and external demands. In the midst of wartime harshness, Feng Zhi wrote the masterpiece *Sonnets* (*Shisihang ji*), and Mu Dan his "Eight Poems" ("Shi ba shou"). The 1950s and 1960s witnessed the golden age of modernist poetry in Taiwan, spearheaded by Ji Xian (b. 1913), Qin Zihao (1912–1963), Luo Fu (b. 1928), Shang Qin (b. 1930), Ya Xian (b. 1932), and Zheng Chouyu (b. 1933). In post-Mao China, "misty poetry" (*menglong shi*) ushered in a renaissance in literature and art. Going beyond the critical "scar literature" (*shanghen wenxue*), experimental poetry in the 1980s and 1990s reasserted the independence of art and expanded the aesthetic horizon. At the same time, a new generation of poets in Taiwan rebelled against the commercialization of culture with bold experiments in language and form.

Despite all the challenges, modern poetry has firmly established itself as a major genre of Chinese literature, having produced an impressive array of individual talents and landmark works. Since the 1990s, it has been thriving on the Internet. While it may always be a "minority" genre compared with fiction or film, modern poetry has been a vanguard in literary experimentation and a harbinger of cultural trends.

SEE ALSO *Guo Moruo; Xu Zhimo.*

BIBLIOGRAPHY

Hockx, Michel. *A Snowy Morning: Eight Chinese Poets on the Road to Modernity.* Leiden, Netherlands: CNWS, 1994.

Lin, Julia. *Modern Chinese Poetry: An Introduction.* Seattle: University of Washington Press, 1972.

van Crevel, Maghiel. *Language Shattered: Contemporary Chinese Poetry and Duoduo.* Leiden, Netherlands: Research School of Asian, African, and Amerindian Studies, 1996.

van Crevel, Maghiel. *Chinese Poetry in Times of Mind, Mayhem, and Money.* Leiden, Netherlands: Brill, 2008.

Yeh, Michelle. *Modern Chinese Poetry: Theory and Practice since 1917.* New Haven, CT: Yale University Press, 1991.

Michelle Yeh

MISTY POETRY

The term *misty poetry* (*menglong shi*) was originally a derogatory one, referring to the allegedly obscure and obfuscating poetry that emerged in China in the late 1970s and early 1980s. Following the end of the Cultural Revolution, Mao Zedong's death, and the arrest of the Gang of Four in 1976, Deng Xiaoping introduced an era of reform ("the Four Modernizations") and an open-door policy in the international arena in 1978. After almost three decades of near isolation, China was reconnected with the outside world. Writers and artists took advantage of the liberalizing trend and started publishing works that would have incurred political persecution in an earlier time. The long-awaited "thaw" led to a renaissance in literature and art.

The renaissance in post-Mao China was powerfully represented in misty poetry. The immediate forerunner of misty poetry was underground poetry, which can be traced back to the 1960s. Individually or as a group, in Beijing as well as other cities around China, young poets were secretly writing poetry that departed from the officially sanctified norm and expressed personal sentiments. During the Cultural Revolution some of the poetry was circulated underground and gained popularity among the youth. Guo Lusheng (penname Index Finger or Shizhi, b. 1948) from Beijing was famous for his lyrics of hope and love; Huang Xiang (b. 1941) from Guiyang, Guizhou province, wrote rhapsodic free verse of defiant individualism. Both had been writing since the 1960s and both suffered greatly for their art: Guo was institutionalized in the early 1970s for schizophrenia, and Huang was repeatedly imprisoned by the authorities.

A breakthrough came in 1978 when Huang Xiang founded the journal *Enlightenment* (*Qimeng*) in October, and Bei Dao (b. 1949) and Mang Ke (b. 1950) founded *Today* (*Jintian*) in December. Like many underground journals appearing at the time, the first issues of *Enlightenment* and *Today* were posted in Beijing, on what came to be known as the Democracy Wall (*mingzhu qiang*) in the commercial district Xidan. Many of these underground journals not only voiced grievances against the Cultural Revolution but also called for human rights and democratic elections, and were increasingly critical of the Communist regime. Such expressions incurred the wrath of Deng Xiaoping and led to the arrest of some of the editors and writers in March–April 1979, including Wei Jingsheng (b. 1950)—founder of *Exploration* (*Tansuo*)—and Ren Wanding (b. 1944)—founder of *Beijing Spring* (*Beijing zhi chun*), thus ending the brief period of political liberalization known as "Beijing Spring."

Unlike most journals during the Beijing Spring, *Today* was devoted exclusively to literature, publishing poetry, fiction, translations, and literary and art criticism. Although it was forced to fold in 1980, by then it had reached millions of readers. Some of the young poets who contributed to *Today* were catapulted to national fame and began to appear in official journals. Gu Cheng's (1956–1993) "A Generation" (*Yidairen*), which contains only two lines—"Dark night gave me dark eyes, / With which I look for light"—became the manifesto of the youth of the Cultural Revolution, speaking of hope in the midst of dark despair. Also representative is Bei Dao's line "I—Do—Not—believe!" which expresses skepticism of the official ideology. Responses to historical trauma also came from Jiang He (b. 1949), Yang Lian (b. 1955), and Duoduo (b. 1951). Whereas Jiang He and Yang Lian wrote about national history in an elegiac mode, Duoduo leaned toward the surrealist and absurdist. In a different vein, Shu Ting's (b. 1952) longing for, and faith in, romantic love was a refreshing return to lyricism, and Wang Xiaoni's (b. 1955) celebration of female independence was a precursor of women's poetry in the 1980s. Liang Xiaobin (b. 1954), Yan Li (b. 1954), Tian Xiaoqing (b. 1953) and others also were considered misty poets.

The cultural establishment and some senior poets were quick with criticism for several reasons. First, in both style and content, the poetry was so different from what Chinese readers had been used to that it was puzzling, even incomprehensible—hence the epithet *misty* (*menglong*). Features such as extensive parataxis, densely metaphorical language, obscure symbols, and stream of consciousness were a radical departure from the formulaic language and oratorical style typical of poetry in the Communist literary tradition. Senior poets such as Ai Qing (1910–1996) and Gong Liu (1927–2003) expressed their shock. Even Gu Gong, Gu Cheng's father and a veteran writer, admitted that he could not understand his son's work. In a socialist system in which literature was supposed to serve the masses, obscurity was seen as elitist and reactionary. The establishment attributed the strangeness of the new poetry to Western influence, especially the influence of modernism, and accused the poets of imitating the West in their display of individualism, escapism, nihilism, and decadence. Some of the themes, such as alienation and skepticism, were deemed undesirable because these "spiritual maladies" could only exist in a capitalist society, but not in China.

Misty poetry was the target of several campaigns launched by the government against "bourgeois liberalism" and "spiritual pollution" throughout the 1980s. These attacks did nothing to stem the tide, however. Misty poetry had been especially popular among students, and it quickly achieved canonization as readers thirsted for new voices in the wake of the Cultural Revolution. The most persuasive defenses came from Professor Xie Mian (b. 1932) at Peking University, the literary critic Sun Shaozhen (b. 1936), and the poet Xu Jingya (b. 1953). They referred to the rise of misty poetry as an awakening of aesthetic consciousness and a harbinger of a new epochal spirit. These defenses were collectively known as "the three rises" (*san ge jueqi*).

The significance of misty poetry has been profound and lasting. In its somber reflections on historical trauma, it was a poetic expression of "scar literature" and the overall critical spirit manifest in post-Mao literature. In its introspection, it portended the rebirth of humanism and individualism in the 1980s. In its explorations of form and stylistics, it represented the first wave of experimental literature in the People's Republic of China, a true avant-garde movement that inspired not only a new generation of poets but also fiction writers and visual artists.

The popularity of misty poetry also invited rebellion, which appeared as early as 1986, when younger poets all over the country rose to challenge it. The self-proclaimed "Newborn Generation" (*xinshengdai*) veered away from the intense, contemplative voice, the metaphoric and symbolic language, and the heroic humanism of misty poetry, and employed instead a language that was colloquial and low-key to depict quotidian experiences of ordinary people trying to make it in the world. The vitality of the post-misty (*hou menglong*) movement owed to misty poetry itself but also underscored the anxiety of influence that the late-comers felt toward their groundbreaking predecessors. In practice, the distinction between misty and post-misty poetry is not always clear; there is such diversity that it is not hard to find affinity and continuity. What is beyond doubt is that misty poetry is a shining landmark in Chinese literature and a moving witness to Chinese history.

SEE ALSO *Scar (Wound) Art; Scar (Wound) Literature.*

BIBLIOGRAPHY

Emerson, Andrew G. The Guizhou Undercurrent. *Modern Chinese Literature and Culture* 13, no. 2 (2001): 111–133.

Tay, William. How Obscure Is "Obscure Poetry"?—On a Recent Controversy in the P.R.C. In *After Mao: Chinese Literature and Society, 1978–1981*, ed. Jeffrey Kinkley, 133–158. Cambridge, MA: Harvard University Press, 1985.

van Crevel, Maghiel. *Language Shattered: Contemporary Chinese Poetry and Duoduo.* Leiden, Netherlands: Research School of Asian, African, and Amerindian Studies, 1996.

Yeh, Michelle. Light a Lamp in a Rock: Experimental Poetry in Contemporary China. *Modern China* 18, 4 (October 1992): 379–409.

Michelle Yeh

POLICE, 1800–1949

The roots of China's city police are among the oldest in the world. Several early capitals were populous enough to include ethnic, occupational, and other subcultures. Such mixtures in crowded conditions can lead to spatial differentiation and bureaucratic police activity. Moreover, Chinese cities usually were secured by boundary walls, watchmen, census registration, and groupings of households in relationships of mutual responsibility. In capital cities, these social characteristics and traditional practices, along with the rulers' wish for control, fostered systematic police operations.

BEIJING BEFORE 1912

In Beijing during the Yuan, Ming, and Qing eras (1279–1912), both the disposition of space and large-scale human institutions were fundamental to urban order. Walls and gates were physical barriers that were reinforced by police patrols. Especially important among several Beijing forces under the Qing dynasty (1644–1912) was the joint Eight Banner–Green Standard gendarmerie. The head of the gendarmerie was the *bujun tongling* (commander of the gendarmerie, also known as the *tidu jiumen,* commander of the nine gates), always a powerful Manchu or Mongol.

The gendarmerie of Beijing took a broad view of its responsibilities. In addition to regular day-and-night patrols, these responsibilities included a biannual census, street maintenance, firefighting, food security, commercial regulation, mediation of street disputes, observation of large gatherings, control of traffic, and welfare operations. At its height in the later eighteenth century, the Beijing gendarmerie numbered about 23,000 soldiers and 10,000 officers, though at least some of these were only part-time policemen. The gendarmerie operated in a context of multiple, often competitive, police institutions representing different government offices (such as the censorate) and territorial jurisdictions (such as two local districts or the prefecture). Reform at the end of the Qing era added a new, modernizing Beijing police organization to the older ones.

The gendarmerie of Qing Beijing resembled modern city police in some ways but also differed from them. It was a military organization rather than a civilian and community one; its personnel, especially at lower levels, worked in a relatively unspecialized and nonprofessional institutional context; and its interests focused on political security and public order rather than on the safety of individuals or on crimes with mainly private implications. Similar patterns of police activity existed in other large Qing cities, but Beijing as the capital appears to have received by far the most attention.

MODELS FOR POLICE MODERNIZATION

Between the end of the Opium War (1839–1842) and about 1900, important examples of modern urban police developed in foreign concessions in treaty ports such as

Shanghai and Tianjin, in the British colony of Hong Kong, and in Tokyo under Meiji imperial rule (1868–1912). The Japanese-coined term *bunmei* (civilization, Chinese *wenming*) referred especially to a modern urban environment that would be clean, healthy, hygienic, spacious, and orderly. Toward the end of the nineteenth century, East Asian and European police models deeply influenced Chinese reformers in an era of growing nationalism. They increasingly saw city policing as an effective way to achieve "civilization" and thereby enhance national productivity, wealth, and power. The modern Chinese term for police, *jingcha,* originated in another Japanese coinage, *keisatsu.*

NEW POLICIES

During the first decade of the twentieth century, corresponding to the New Policies (Xinzheng) reform in the last decade of the Qing dynasty, a historic transition began in Chinese local administration and police. In North China, Yuan Shikai, as governor-general of Zhili, experimented with modern forces in Baoding and Tianjin (1902). After the Boxer Uprising, Japanese occupiers introduced trained police in the northern part of Beijing's Inner City, and the Qing government was inspired by this example. With the end of the state examination system in 1905, a stream of Chinese students studied police work in Japan; they became familiar with both Japanese and European—especially French and Prussian—models.

Because it was easier to create a fresh organization than to change the gendarmerie and other Beijing forces, reformers founded the new Beijing police in 1901 to 1902. Two of its early heads (the Manchu nobleman Shanqi, better known as Prince Su [1863–1921], and Natong [1856–1925]) served simultaneously as commanders of the gendarmerie. The new police were known by a series of names, of which the most enduring was Capital Police Board (Jingshi Jingcha Ting) in 1914 and after. They maintained their own academy (Jingwu Xuetang), where gendarmerie experts participated by lecturing on Qing law. The prestige of foreign models caused the status of police work to rise, and to suffer less than before from association with abusive, low-level *yamen* runners. The scope of police interests began to extend into the workplace and the home. Their public-health-oriented operations, for example, grew rapidly.

As early as 1898, modern police institutions under Chinese rather than foreign auspices started to emerge in the Chinese City in Shanghai. Acceptance of police by the populace there and in several eastern Chinese cities was notably rapid. In smaller inland cities such as Chengdu in the southwest, the numbers of traditional police were lower in proportion to the population and less active than in larger cities; moreover, foreign-style police were less well known. Chengdu residents reacted sharply against "civilizing" regulation, and police modernization was delayed until 1934 and after.

Thus, developments that occurred from around 1901 to 1912 initiated a synthesis between age-old Chinese city

Police force in Beijing, 1919. *Prior to the 1900s, China did not employ professional modern police forces in its cities. Only near the end of the Qing dynasty were local police departments formed, with the development of trained law enforcement continuing into mid-century.* © **CORBIS**

police organizational patterns and foreign models. Other traditional influences—gentry assemblies, gentry-run charities, and trade or merchant guilds—also were important in cities where policing developed partly or mainly under community rather than governmental auspices (as occurred in Shanghai and Hankou).

CITY POLICE UNDER THE REPUBLIC

The new police of Beijing and of the Chinese City of Shanghai became national exemplars. In Shanghai, separate foreign forces continued to operate in the International Settlement and the French Concession. At Beijing, the Capital Police Board managed to maintain institutional continuity throughout a period (1912–1928) when

political authority over the city was in flux. From 1912 until his death in 1916, President Yuan Shikai allowed the gendarmerie to continue in existence, perhaps to enhance his control of all police by means of a multiple structure. Like the gendarmerie, which was finally extinguished by a warlord government in 1924, the new police were unusually numerous in proportion to the population and defined their mission in expansive terms.

Soon after national unification under the Guomindang in 1928, China's eastern cities faced pressures generated by the intensifying conflict with Japan, as well as by the ideological struggle between the Nationalist and Chinese Communist parties. In this atmosphere, the Nationalist government revealed a distinctly authoritarian view of police both in the New Life movement, which harked back to the earlier theme of "civilization," and the development of secret police (Blueshirts) inspired by then-contemporary fascism. During the 1928–1937 period at Nanjing, Chiang Kai-shek tried to centralize China's national police and to modernize local policing. These goals competed with each other for resources and also conflicted with a growing flow of revenue to government from criminal activities such as the drug trade. Chiang's police efforts were still at an early stage when the outbreak of war cut them short. After eight years of war (1937 to 1945) and the ensuing civil war ended in 1949, the confluence of traditional, European, Japanese, and early twentieth-century Chinese police models facilitated unprecedented levels of urban control under Communist rule.

SEE ALSO *Penal Systems, 1800–1949.*

BIBLIOGRAPHY

Dray-Novey, Alison J. Spatial Order and Police in Imperial Beijing. *Journal of Asian Studies* 52, 4 (1993): 885–922.

Dray-Novey, Alison J. The Twilight of the Beijing Gendarmerie, 1900–1924. *Modern China: An International Quarterly of History and Social Science* 33, 3 (2007): 349–376.

Goodman, Bryna. *Native Place, City, and Nation: Regional Networks and Identities in Shanghai, 1853–1937.* Berkeley: University of California Press, 1995.

Han Yanlong and Su Yigong, comps. *Zhongguo jindai jingcha zhidu* [China's modern police system]. Beijing: Zhongguo Renmin Gongan Daxue Chubanshe, 1993.

Rowe, William T. *Hankow: Commerce and Society in a Chinese City, 1796–1889.* Stanford, CA: Stanford University Press, 1984.

Rowe, William T. *Hankow: Conflict and Community in a Chinese City, 1796–1895.* Stanford, CA: Stanford University Press, 1989.

Stapleton, Kristin. *Civilizing Chengdu: Chinese Urban Reform, 1895–1937.* Cambridge, MA: Harvard University Press, 2000.

Strand, David. *Rickshaw Beijing: City People and Politics in the 1920s.* Berkeley: University of California Press, 1989.

Wakeman, Frederic, Jr. *Policing Shanghai, 1927–1937.* Berkeley: University of California Press, 1995.

Zarrow, Peter Gue. *China in War and Revolution, 1895–1949.* Oxford and New York: Routledge, 2005.

Alison J. Dray-Novey

POLICE, SECRET

The secret police of the People's Republic of China has always been a powerful, centralized, and autonomous body. Since the beginning of the reform era in the late 1970s, some of its privileges and discretionary powers have been curbed. It has also appeared more openly, after the establishment in 1983 of the Ministry of State Security (*guojia anquan bu*), a structure distinct from the Ministry of Public Security (*gong'an bu*), which has come to be in charge of the

country's internal security, public order, and the armed police forces (*wuzhuang jingcha*). However, China's opening to the outside world, its development and empowerment strategy, and its security challenges have intensified rather than diminished the role of the secret police, both inside and outside the country.

The secret police is the direct heir of the Central Social Affairs Department (*zhongyang shehui bu*) established by the Chinese Communist Party in Yan'an at the beginning of the Second Sino-Japanese War (1937–1945). This department was headed by Mao Zedong's right-hand man, Kang Sheng (1898–1975), a sinister individual trained by the Soviet secret police, the NKVD, in the 1930s. Its purpose was to protect the party against both pro-Soviet and pro-Guomingdang (Nationalist Party) agents. The department and its director played a key role in the Yan'an rectification campaign (1942–1944), ferreting out many real or supposed Guomindang spies (perpetrating at least 40,000 executions).

After the establishment of the People's Republic, the Central Social Affairs Department remained active for some time but gradually transferred its domain to the Central Investigation Department (CID, *zhongyang diaocha ju*), an arm of the party and the state, and the Ministry of Public Security. In the 1950s Kang Sheng's influence waned, mainly because of de-Stalinization. He was replaced by his deputy, Li Kenong (1899–1962), who as CID director controlled both the party and the state secret services until his death. Li was also vice minister of foreign affairs, director of the General Intelligence Department of the Central Military Commission, and deputy chief of the General Staff of the People's Liberation Army, underlining the close connection at that time between the civilian and military intelligence services. In 1962 Mao promoted Kang Sheng to the party's Central Secretariat and relied heavily on him to spy on his rivals in the party leadership and apparatus, in particular after the beginning of the Cultural Revolution decade (1966–1976).

After Kang Sheng's death in 1975, the secret police was taken over by Hua Guofeng (1921–2008), the minister of public security who was Mao's designated successor, and Wang Dongxing (b. 1916), Mao's former bodyguard and head of the Central Committee's guard unit 8341. Both played a key role in the arrest of the Gang of Four in October 1976, a month after Mao's death. From 1976 to 1982, the CID was headed by Zhou Shaozheng, a close associate of Wang and a veteran of the Central Investigation system.

After Deng Xiaoping's rehabilitation in 1977, the secret police went through a transition period and was gradually overhauled. After 1978 the release of many political prisoners or people unduly arrested weakened Hua and Wang and put the secret police back under the command of the Central Committee, and more specifically of Deng Xiaoping's people. After 1980, once he was in control of the People's Liberation

Army, Deng separated the civilian and the military intelligence services.

This reform process led in 1983 to the establishment of the Ministry of State Security (MSS), along the lines of the Soviet KGB (although its model is the U.S. Central Intelligence Agency). This new ministry merged the activities of the CID and the counterintelligence department of the Ministry of Public Security. As Liu Fuzhi, public security minister and a key architect of the new secret police, indicated, the mission of the MSS is to ensure "the security of the state through effective measures against enemy agents, spies, and counterrevolutionary activities designed to sabotage or overthrow China's socialist system."

Since its establishment, the MSS has been headed by four successive ministers: Ling Yun (1983–1985), Jia Chunwang (1985–1998), Xu Yongyue (1998–2007) and Geng Huichang (since 2007). Jia played a key role in building a more modern, sophisticated and efficient secret police. Geng, an expert in commercial intelligence, was the director of China's Institute of Contemporary International Relations (CICIR) from 1990 to 1995 and spent most of his career in the MSS. Every minister of the MSS sits in the Chinese Communist Party's powerful Central Political and Legal Commission, headed by Zhou Yongkang (b. 1942) since 2007.

GOALS OF THE ESPIONAGE SYSTEM

Although presented by Chinese leaders as defensive, the mission of the MSS is of course also offensive. Among its ten bureaus, only the sixth is in charge of counterintelligence. The other bureaus deal with domestic and foreign intelligence; Hong Kong, Macau, and Taiwan; scientific and technological information; and antidefection and countersurveillance. A research bureau supervises the activities of the CICIR, a well-known think tank that maintains continuous interactions with foreign and in particular Western international affairs experts.

Among these activities, two areas have become particularly important for China: (1) acquisition of modern technologies, and (2) surveillance of political opponents. Toward the first goal, gathering advanced and well-protected scientific and technological information in developed countries—the United States, Western European nations, and Japan—the MSS has mobilized thousands of agents. Working with local intermediaries, often of Chinese descent, or students and businesspeople from the People's Republic, these agents endeavor to secretly acquire as many military and dual-use (military and civilian) technologies as possible, not only to help China catch up in terms of its technology and industry but also to speed up the modernization of its weaponry. Since the military suppression of the Tiananmen Square protests of 1989, the West and Japan have imposed an arms embargo that forces China to rely almost exclusively on Russia. In their professionalism and

aggressiveness, the MSS agents have no reason to envy their former Soviet colleagues. Some of these Chinese spies and their local collaborators have been caught and prosecuted, mostly in the United States. For diplomatic reasons, in the European Union or in Japan such arrests have remained less frequent and more discreet.

The secret police conducts close surveillance of dissidents to fulfill its ultimate priority, protection of the regime, and the party-led political system, against its enemies. A large number of agents have been mobilized both inside and outside the country, with the assistance of the Chinese embassies, to eavesdrop on and sabotage activities deemed oppositional, prodemocracy, or merely independent-minded. Such activities are targeted whether conducted by Chinese dissidents; Tibetan, Uygur, or Mongol "separatists"; or Chinese or foreign nongovernmental organizations, including religious organizations that are or are trying to become active in China.

The division of labor between the secret police and Ministry of Public Security in controlling and repressing activities regarded by the party as threatening the regime or social stability is far from consistently clear. The latter usually intervenes first and handles most if not all criminal cases related to organized crime, corruption, or even petty dissident activities. However, as soon as a case is considered politically serious or has an international dimension, the secret police is alerted and takes over investigation and surveillance. For instance, after Jiang Zemin decided to dismantle the nationwide Falun Gong network, a Buddhist sect practicing *qigong* (a Chinese healing and exercise system) and headed by Li Hongzhi (b. 1952), the secret service stepped in and conducted the arrest of its main followers while looking into Falun Gong activities abroad. The same pattern applies to foreign (in particular American) Protestant churches whose proselytism is viewed as too aggressive; underground activities conducted by Catholics who maintain their allegiance to the Vatican; and well-known political dissidents. For instance, for a long period the secret police tightly controlled the activities and movements of Hu Jia (b. 1973), an activist famous for helping HIV/AIDS sufferers. After addressing the European Parliament by webcam, Hu was arrested in December 2007 for "inciting subversion of state authority." The secret police also prepared his judicial prosecution. Because his case file involved state secrets, his lawyers were not given access to it nor were they authorized to see him. In April 2008 Hu was sentenced on the same charge to three-and-a-half years in jail.

SEE ALSO *Communist Party.*

BIBLIOGRAPHY

Byron, John, and Robert Pack. *The Claws of the Dragon: Kang Sheng, the Evil Genius behind Mao and His Legacy of Terror in People's China.* New York: Simon and Schuster, 1992.

Faligot, Roger. *Les services secrets chinois: De Mao aux JO.* Paris: Nouveau Monde, 2008.

Faligot, Roger, and Rémi Kauffer. *The Chinese Secret Service.* Trans. Christine Donougher. New York: Morrow, 1989.

Select Committee on U.S. National Security and Military. *Commercial Concerns with the People's Republic of China.* Washington, DC: U.S. Government Printing Office, 1999. http://www.fas.org/spp/starwars/congress/1999_r/cox/

Tanner, Murray Scot. "The Institutional Lessons of Disaster: Reorganizing the People's Armed Police after Tiananmen." In *The People's Liberation Army as Organization.* Santa Monica, CA: RAND, 2002.

Jean-Pierre Cabestan

POLITICAL CONTROL SINCE 1949

The Chinese Communist Party exercises political control as a means to maintain its authority and legitimacy. During the Maoist era, the party exerted this influence in virtually all areas of citizens' lives, including marriage, childbearing, religious practices, employment, and place of residence. Instruments used to monitor, track, or shape citizens' behaviors and actions include the household registration record, the *danwei* (work unit), the personal dossier, reeducation camps, and the *nomenklatura* system. Since the reform era of the late 1970s, with the important exceptions of family planning and challenges to the party, political control over people's lives has generally relaxed, becoming more institutionalized and rational in approach, thus largely replacing the chaotic and draconian measures of the past.

THE MAOIST ERA

Political control in the Maoist era (1949–1976) was personal, total, unpredictable, and violent in large part because of Mao Zedong himself. At the elite level, Mao took criticisms personally and lashed back in ways that muted dissent, setting a pattern that allowed his whims to dictate policies. At the popular level, citizens experienced this style of political control through campaigns. Life became unpredictable because one's actions, lauded by Mao in one campaign, might be punished in the next, as demonstrated by the intellectuals who criticized the government in the Hundred Flowers Campaign (1956–1957) but were then persecuted in the anti-rightist campaign (1957). Mao also sanctioned violence in these campaigns. In the Cultural Revolution (1966–1969) the Red Guard youth believed that they were implementing his will by beating up "bad" teachers. They destroyed places of worship because Mao regarded religious belief and practice as superstitious and backward.

Mao employed several instruments of political control over the population. In 1959 the government instituted the household registration record (*hukou*), which froze urban and rural dwellers in their respective regions, thus limiting geographical mobility and ensuring that the countryside supported the cities. In 1962 it instituted the work unit (*danwei*) to restrict urban workers' job mobility. In addition to creating a self-contained community where one had a secure job, affordable health care, and inexpensive housing, the *danwei* also regulated minute aspects of its employees' private lives by controlling their personal dossiers (*dang'an*). If an individual received a "black mark" in his or her *dang'an*, this resulted in far-reaching consequences, including denials of promotion, permission to marry or have children, or even to travel. Other instruments of Mao's political control to ensure order and "proper" ideological orientation included reeducation through labor (*laojiao*), the more punitive reform through labor (*laogai*), and "sending down" youths to the countryside to learn from the peasants (*xiafang*). Ultimately, the totalitarian control that characterized this era failed to achieve or sustain any tangible long-term goals.

THE REFORM ERA

In the reform era (since 1978), political control relaxed in certain spheres. During his leadership (1978–1992) Deng Xiaoping applied a pragmatic approach to economic development. By partially lifting control over agricultural production through the Household Responsibility System of 1980, he enabled farmers to keep surplus crops once they met government quotas. He also eased control over development by creating special economic zones, which welcomed foreign direct investment and allowed enterprises to operate on market principles.

His successor, Jiang Zemin (1992–2002), continued loosening control by cutting the staff of the economic apparatus in the central and provincial administration by one-half and at the township level by one-fifth between 1998 and 2002. Jiang also introduced his Three Represents to the Sixteenth Party Congress in 2002; this policy signaled that the party would welcome members from the bourgeoisie, thereby eliminating political controls based on one's class background.

The economic reforms in effect weakened the *hukou* and the *danwei*. As market forces began replacing the need for rural subsidization of urban areas, the rationale behind the *hukou* system began to break down. In addition, the need for labor to fuel economic development in China's southeastern coastal region encouraged millions of peasants to seek work in the cities. Instead of clamping down on this mobility, the party adjusted by introducing the temporary urban resident permit in 1985 and the blue-seal *hukou* in 1993 (revised in 1998), the latter allowing educated or wealthy citizens to move permanently to an urban area. The *danwei* also weakened because state-owned enterprises had to compete with market enterprises, which often had no need to inspect one's *dang'an* for a job. By the mid-1990s, workers could finally choose their employment in many regions, and by 2003 one no longer needed permission to marry.

Student protestor surrounded by People's Liberation Army soldiers in Tiananmen Square, Beijing, June 4, 1989. *After the start of economic reforms in the mid-1970s, some Chinese pressed for similar political reforms in the late 1980s, giving rise to large pro-democracy demonstrations in Beijing's Tiananmen Square in early 1989. Nearly seven weeks of protesting came to a bloody conclusion on June 4, as government troops ended the gatherings, killing hundreds of protestors in the process.* © **JACQUES LANGEVIN/CORBIS SYGMA**

In addition to the economy, the party also relaxed control over religion. In 1982 the party issued a directive ("Document 19") granting protection of freedom of religious belief. The reasoning behind the directive held that, though belief in religion would eventually disappear when a genuine socialist state was achieved, stamping it out before that was achieved, as attempted during the Cultural Revolution, was unfeasible.

Despite these relaxations in control, both Deng and Jiang remained unyielding in exercising political control to preserve party authority and legitimacy. Based on Deng's Four Basic Principles (*sixiang jiben yuanze*), which upheld the party's absolute political dominance, the protection of a citizen's right to practice religion, for instance, was conditioned on his or her submission to the directives of the party. In addition, the *dang'an* and the classified designation of targeted persons (*zhongdian renkou*) on a particular *hukou* still allowed the government to track and monitor citizens as well as deny them travel permission. Finally, Jiang reasserted and further strengthened the party's *nomenklatura* prerogative. The Soviet-style *nomenklatura* is a list of people deemed eligible to hold elite positions of power in all spheres, over which the party exercises absolute power of appointment and dismissal. Ambitious Chinese who aspire to leadership positions must conform to the norms and standards of the Communist Party in hope of getting their names on the list.

Other examples of actions taken to maintain party authority and legitimacy are Jiang's suppression of the China Democracy Party (Zhongguo Minzhu Dang) and the spiritual practice group Falun Gong in 1999. Jiang's administration sent members of both groups, the latter numbering in the thousands, to labor reeducation camps.

The party leadership has also exercised tight control in the sphere of childbearing. Based on a missile scientist's dire overpopulation projections, the party implemented the one-child policy (allowing most couples to have only one child) in 1980 and made a big push in 1983 to achieve its goal. The magnitude of the resulting social suffering—twenty-one million sterilizations and fourteen million abortions that year—made the leadership step back from such a strict policy; though still advocating for the one-child rule, the party instituted more conditions that would permit having second children. Although the policy has produced an aging population and a skewed sex ratio (120 boys per 100 girls born in 1999), under Hu Jintao, who came to power in 2003, the party has decided to extend the one-child policy until 2018.

THE TWENTY-FIRST CENTURY

Compared to the Maoist era, in the 2000s the party's application of political control is less oppressive in people's everyday lives. Aside from family planning, citizens exercise greater economic, social, religious, and some limited political freedoms. Their ability to dissent is an important indication of these new freedoms. Between 1978 and 1999, lawsuits increased by 12,000 percent. From 1994 to 2003, the number of farmer and worker protests increased from 10,000 to 60,000. One must note, however, that although the party has allowed farmers and workers to protest—viewing this as a safety valve for releasing frustration—these protests usually occur at the local, and sometimes at the regional, level but never rise to a national level where they could threaten party legitimacy.

In areas of potential challenge to party authority and legitimacy, political control continues to be arbitrary and nontransparent to the Chinese people, especially in the party's censoring of the media and Internet and sending people to labor reeducation camps. As long as the party sustains China's impressive economic growth and development, such arbitrary political control will quite likely continue.

SEE ALSO *Censorship; Dissidents; Education through Labor, Reform through Labor; Human Rights since 1949; Police, Secret; Sent-down Educated Youth; Unit (danwei); Xiafang.*

BIBLIOGRAPHY

Dittmer, Lowell. Leadership Change and Chinese Political Development. *China Quarterly* 176 (2003): 903–925.

Goldman, Merle. *From Comrade to Citizen: The Struggle for Political Rights in China.* Boston: Harvard University Press, 2005.

Greenhalgh, Susan. Missile Science, Population Science: The Origins of China's One-Child Policy. *China Quarterly* 182 (2005): 253–276.

Lam, Willy Wo-Lap. *Chinese Politics in the Hu Jintao Era: New Leaders, New Challenges.* Armonk, NY: M.E. Sharpe, 2006.

Lieberthal, Kenneth. *Governing China: From Revolution through Reform.* 2nd ed. New York: W.W. Norton, 2004.

Lu, Xiaobo, and Elizabeth J. Perry. *Danwei: The Changing Chinese Workplace in Historical and Comparative Perspective.* New York: M.E. Sharpe, 1997.

Wang, Fei-Ling. *Organizing through Division and Exclusion: China's Hukou System.* Stanford, CA: Stanford University Press, 2005.

Grace C. Huang

POLITICAL CULTURE 1800–1900

Political culture not only serves as a motivational tool for central control and local mobilization, it provides a system of meaning to make sense of specific political events and individual attitudes or behaviors toward them. In the case of Qing China (1644–1912), its political culture envisioned an ideal state ruled by an exemplary emperor loyally assisted by virtuous and competent scholar-officials. This centralized bureaucratic monarchy, sanctioned by the "mandate of heaven," aimed to implement a Confucian agenda for benevolent rule as part of its effort to promote the continued reproduction of the agrarian empire.

Research on Qing political culture has produced four intersecting bodies of literature. The first focuses on the long-term evolution of key government institutions and how they structured power relationships and political maneuvering. The second body of work studies key events like "political campaigns" through which the emperor asserted his monarchical arbitrary power and restrained routine bureaucratic authority. The third approach places agency at the high layers of intellectual and official elites by explaining how factional literati politics fostered the shift of intellectual tides and provided new politico-cultural initiatives during periods of crisis. To break away from the conventional mode of top-down analysis, the last and a growing body of literature incorporates key dimensions of popular culture and local patterns of power into an examination of how popular protest and grassroots conceptions of political legitimacy influenced government policies and state-society relations.

HIGH QING

A structural feature of Qing political culture was that the overburdened state was far too small to handle all the business of governing an increasingly expansive, complex, and densely populated society. A persistent overproduction of educated degree-holders and the increasing competition for employment, in particular, had inflamed a wide range of sociopolitical crises that undermined the High Qing order. Bureaucrats at all levels were locked in a sort of survival politics driven by increasing rivalry, patronage, and corruption. Some politically frustrated literate men, under the pressure of literary inquisition, absorbed themselves in pedantic "evidential research" (*kaozheng*) of deciphering the ancient classics through philology and language. Others became troublemakers in nonstate or antistate activities, leading most of the incidents of social unrest during the late Qing.

THE TURN OF THE NINETEENTH CENTURY

Cast in the shadow of runaway imperial corruption and soaring turmoil, the turn of the nineteenth century marked a watershed in the shaping of Qing political culture. The acute crises acted as a sort of cultural catalyst that turned China outward by redirecting intellectual commitments from "perfecting the past" to "improving the present." The socio-moral indifference of High Qing evidential research was replaced by bottom-up social mobilization of practical statecraft studies (*jingshi*), as well as top-down political idealism of pure moral leadership (*qingyi*) and political remonstrance.

This period also saw the revival of the kind of literati networks that had promoted late Ming reform. The clas-

sical legitimization for autocratic government was challenged by increasing literati dissent and broader political participation. Provincial academies like the Yuelu Academy (Yuelu Shuyuan) became key arenas for political discussion and elite activism under direct government support. The resulting institutionalization of statecraft studies led to the recruitment of a new generation of reform-minded scholar-officials committed to pragmatic local administration.

MID-NINETEENTH CENTURY

Heading toward midcentury, the dynasty had to contend with an increasingly aggressive West while dealing with a series of large-scale peasant rebellions. This combined threat reshaped state commitments and exacerbated regional differences. The government reduced traditional "reproductive" responsibilities like preventing floods and providing emergency relief through a granary system in inland North China, shifting its priorities to meeting more urgent challenges in newly strategic coastal regions, as well as mobilizing new commercial revenue and encouraging "modern" development there in order to compete with other states. This pragmatic adjustment compelled more gentry to take greater initiative in managing local affairs, but the dilemma was that there were few resourceful local elites in the poor "marginalized" areas. The result was a more fundamental socioeconomic decay, with environmental degradation, diminishing government effectiveness, and mounting social disturbance feeding on each other catastrophically. The state retreat from paternalistic responsibilities toward those regions and the resulting polarization of society sapped popular support and spurred the development of heterodox organizations.

Thus, late Qing society was marked by the extraordinary degree to which unorthodox values and rebellious beliefs permeated popular consciousness and challenged Confucian orthodoxy. Moreover, the repeated failure of the Manchu court in resisting foreign assaults and the great nineteenth-century shift in China's global position reinforced simmering ethnic nationalism among Han Chinese. All these tendencies eroded the government's legitimacy and capacity to mobilize local communities for national purposes like dynastic restoration and preservation. They also undermined the shared commitments to the time-honored Confucian agenda of rule, which had held the state and society together.

THE TURN OF THE TWENTIETH CENTURY

In the late nineteenth century, furthermore, progressive political actors and scholar-activists bifurcated into three general camps at different levels. While a set of top-down reformers designed to shift China toward a constitutional monarchy (*junzhu lixian*), more provincial elites promoted

Western-style local self-government (*zizhi*). Some small groups of radical revolutionaries, by contrast, strived to overthrow the Manchu regime and establish a model of a republican polity (*gonghe*). They contended over the issue of how to provide a workable formula for creating a stronger Chinese state that could survive in an "eat or be eaten" competitive world of predatory powers. The social Darwinist struggle underpinned the ideology of state nationalism, both of which further fueled the deep-seated sense of ethnic nationalism. These interlocking ideologies replaced Confucianism as the dominant political culture and facilitated the transition from imperial to republican China.

In this momentous process of transformation, Chinese political culture proceeded through three levels of change from *material* borrowing (the Opium War of 1839 to the 1890s) to *institutional* reform and anti-Manchu revolution (the Hundred Days' Reform of 1898 to the 1911 revolution) to new *cultural* movement (the 1910s and after). Its development in the nineteenth century was neither stagnant nor simply a defensive response to Western challenges. Instead, it was reshaped by a series of internal dialogues that began as officials, literati, and elites groped toward more realistic state-making strategies in light of a combination of domestic and foreign crises.

SEE ALSO *Qing Dynasty in 1800.*

BIBLIOGRAPHY

Elman, Benjamin A. *From Philosophy to Philology: Intellectual and Social Aspects of Change in Late Imperial China.* Cambridge, MA: Harvard University Press, 1984.

Huters, Theodore, R. Bin Wong, and Pauline Yu, eds. *Culture and State in Chinese History: Conventions, Accommodations, Critiques.* Stanford, CA: Stanford University Press, 1997.

Kuhn, Philip A. *Origins of the Modern Chinese State.* Stanford, CA: Stanford University Press, 2002.

Polachek, James M. *The Inner Opium War.* Cambridge, MA: Harvard University Press, 1992.

Pomeranz, Kenneth L. *The Making of a Hinterland: State, Society, and Economy in Inland North China, 1853–1937.* Berkeley: University of California Press, 1993.

Wensheng Wang

POLITICAL CULTURE SINCE 1900

Political culture, broadly defined as the symbolic dimension of politics, bespeaking the values, beliefs, and feelings people have about political institutions and activities, has consistently played a major role in contemporary China, helping to stimulate intellectual engagement and mass participation. Political culture is embedded in the institutional structure of society, which before the revolution consisted of three relatively stable

and congruent elements: Confucianism as a belief system, a bureaucratic government with an emperor at the apex, and a social system with the extended family as the primary organizational unit and the scholar-official as the modal personality.

THE CONFUCIAN ORDER

Confucianism was a belief system that on the one hand legitimated the rule of the emperor and on the other placed normative constraints on that rule; it is mistaken to characterize it as either democratic (though it called for elite responsiveness to the people, it provided no institutional mechanism for this) or as a mere ideological tool for imperial despotism (it imposed normative limits on authority, which Confucian officials were sometimes willing to give their lives to defend). According to William De Bary (1964), Confucianism was typified by five characteristics:

1. humanism—that is, it focused on mundane human existence rather than an afterlife;

2. rationalism or reasonableness, rather than divine inspiration or charismatic spontaneity;

3. historic-mindedness ("using the past to serve the present");

4. fundamentalism—that is, belief in a foundation myth of superior normative order; and

5. restorationism—that is, revival of fundamental truths.

Max Weber (1864–1920) termed Confucianism a form of inner-worldly asceticism: It obliges the people to obey and defer to the emperor but also obliges the latter to care for the welfare of the people or risk loss of the "mandate of heaven."

China had the world's first bureaucracy to hold regular civil service exams based on universalistic value criteria (namely, the Confucian Four Books and Five Classics), earning popular respect for the intelligence and learning of the officials while ensuring a periodic turnover of elites (though vertical mobility tended to decline over time, particularly during dynastic decline). The bureaucracy (headed by a prime minister) deemed it proper to admonish the emperor to adhere to the norms of Confucianism, whereas the emperor preferred to exercise power without constraint. The emperor, though remote and mysterious, was worshipped as an exemplary leader (rule of man, not rule of law) and mediator between the welfare of the common people and the incalculable forces of "heaven." Though from the Han (206 BCE–220 CE) to the Song (960–1279) the bureaucracy strengthened its rule at the expense of the emperor, in the late eighteenth and early nineteenth centuries this gave way to a more autocratic trend in response to the series of internal rebellions and imperialist wars that occurred at that time.

The Chinese extended family, an endogamous unit defined by patriarchal lineage and intense filial loyalty, sustained the political system in three ways. First, the political system was the family system writ large, with the emperor occupying a position analogous to that of the patriarch. The five fundamental relationships in Confucianism—parent to child, older sibling to younger sibling, husband to wife, emperor to subject, and friend to friend—were focused almost entirely on parental authority as the model, and the emperor was referred to as the father of his people. Filial piety engendered a cult of obedience to authority figures and created the basis for political authoritarianism. Harry Eckstein (1980) has pointed to the importance of congruent authority patterns in enhancing political stability, and in Confucian China family (and clan) authority dovetailed very closely with the authority of the imperial government (though there were exceptions in which the interests of the family and those of the state clashed). Second, Confucianism rested on the assumption of a collective ethic, rather than individualism, which was first engendered within the family. Third, the Chinese family produced a type of morality that was situation-oriented and psychosocially dependent upon others, thus authority was ubiquitous but in effect coincident with social control: The emperor was "high and far away."

This "traditional" political culture left the Republican era that was inaugurated upon the overthrow of the Qing dynasty in 1912 with a legacy of benign authoritarianism, bureaucratic rationality, and respect for learning and the established order. It was to be subjected to three great forces of change in the course of the twentieth century, which might be termed *modernization*, *revolution*, and *nationalism*. The first refers to the processes of economic industrialization, rationalization, and mechanization; the second to the political assault on traditional culture by a series of mass movements or campaigns in an attempt to refashion it in some ideological, preconceived way; the third to the cultivation of loyalty to the Chinese nation-state. These three challenges were unleashed by the 1911 Revolution and have alternated in their relative intensity throughout the following decades.

MODERNIZATION, REVOLUTION, NATIONALISM

The force of economic modernization, borne by cinema, tourism, and commodity consumerism all along China's eastern seaboard throughout this period, had a subtle undermining and fragmenting effect on the old cultural order by making certain culturally sanctioned institutions impractical and rewarding the introduction of culturally heterodox alternatives: Rapid urbanization and accelerated horizontal and vertical mobility split up the family. The younger generation grew up in a different world than their parents, with whom they found it increasingly difficult to communicate, sometimes resulting in generational ruptures that unleashed the younger generation from many of the bonds of the older generation (such as arranged child marriage), and contributed to political radicalization. These disruptions were exacerbated by the collapse of the old order, beginning with elimination of the meritocratic Confucian examination system in 1905 and culminating in the fall of the dynasty itself in 1911. The forces of modernization coexisted uneasily with the force of revolution during the Maoist era, but truly came into their own during the "reform and opening" policy introduced by Deng Xiaoping at the Third Plenum of the Eleventh Party Congress in December 1978.

The revolutionary assault on traditional culture was launched in a series of mass movements erupting spasmodically throughout the twentieth century, beginning most famously with the May Fourth movement, a youth movement triggered in May 1919 by popular indignation against Japanese "21 demands" (1916) which introduced vernacular writing and a literary revolution, a boycott of Japanese consumer goods, an assault on arranged marriage and other Confucian traditions, and an intense search for political solutions in Western political thought (e.g., "Mr. Democracy and Mr. Science"). The two political parties that vied for power for the next three decades, the Nationalist Party (Guomindang, or GMD) and the Chinese Communist Party (CCP), were both deeply influenced by this movement: The former was reorganized under Comintern auspices from 1924 to 1925, whereas the latter was founded in Shanghai in 1921 with Comintern advice. Under the slogan "continuing the revolution under the dictatorship of the proletariat," the CCP continued these movements even after seizing power in October 1949, resulting in the Hundred Flowers movement (1956–1957), the decade of the Cultural Revolution (1966–1976), the April 5, 1976, movement upon the death of Zhou Enlai, and the Tiananmen uprising of April to May 1989. Although all of these movements were chaotic and filled with mutually contradictory trends, common to all were an initially emancipatory thrust and a spontaneous impulse for an ill-defined populist democracy. Psychologically, they relied on a counterphobic iconoclasm in which participants were encouraged to shatter the inhibitions cultivated by the old order and thereby create the psychological space for adoption of more altruistic, national salvation–oriented cultural patterns. But the chaotic, anarchic thrust of these movements made it impossible to organize them to constructive account, and all were violently suppressed.

Since the death of Mao Zedong in September 1976, the Chinese political community has attempted with some trepidation to come to grips with the Cultural Revolution, at first containing the turmoil while rhetorically reaffirming

The Tenth Panchen Lama of Tibet during a struggle session, Lhasa, Tibet, 1964. *Throughout the twentieth century, China experienced periods of extreme political unrest as citizens rejected traditional teachings, leadership, and social order. In the early years of the People's Republic of China, party leaders joined in the purging of old ways, as demonstrated by this photo recording the treatment of the Tenth Panchen Lama of Tibet during a struggle session.* **AP IMAGES**

it under Hua Guofeng, then criticizing it as "feudal despotism" while encouraging "emancipation of thought" during Deng Xiaoping's early years (1978–1980), and finally officially repudiating it at the Sixth Plenum of the Eleventh Central Committee in June 1981. A new wave of literature was launched to reevaluate the emotional impact of the Cultural Revolution, followed by hundreds of memoirs by former victims and detailed historical analyses. After suppression of the Tiananmen movement in June 1989, which the elite had identified with its anarchist spirit, a movement was launched in the 1990s to "totally negate" the Cultural Revolution. In the vacuum left by the increasingly explicit repudiation of revolutionary ideals, traditional Chinese political culture has been largely rehabilitated, including respect for older generations and an appreciation of the values of harmony and stability.

Nationalism was the first of Sun Yat-sen's Three Principles of the People, because he thought the Chinese people were a "sheet of loose sand" lacking loyalty to the nation-state (indeed, the word *nationalism* itself was newly translated from

the Japanese). Nationalism involved turning the group loyalty implanted by Chinese socialization mechanisms from the small filial group to the larger collectivity. According to the scholar Chalmers Johnson (1962), during the turmoil that swept the country in the first half of the twentieth century, the Chinese Communists were more successful than the rival Guomindang in cultivating peasant nationalism because they remained in enemy-occupied areas and helped to mobilize peasant resistance against the Japanese invaders, accounting for the surprisingly swift postwar "liberation" of China by the Chinese Communist Party. During CCP rule nationalism was initially subsumed by the "world revolution," but when revolutionary loyalties were undermined first by the Cultural Revolution and then by the collapse of the Communist bloc (1989–1991), the leadership shifted to a more pragmatic and less ideological approach to economic construction, quietly abandoning revolutionary rhetoric. In the subsequent era of "reform and opening," the appeal to nationalism has become more culturally focused, adopting some traditional Chinese values (e.g., respect for experience, learning, and meritocratic hierarchy) and adhering to a "realist" conception of the national interest.

SOCIALIST HARMONY

Meanwhile, the forces of modernization and globalization, enhanced by the "reform and opening" policy launched by Deng Xiaoping, have continued to exert a less direct but perhaps even more profound impact on Chinese political culture. The thrust of this impact is similar to that already experienced in the industrialized Western countries, including sexual emancipation, ideological pluralization, enhanced mobility and communications, and rampant consumerism. These trends coexist uneasily with the force of a distinctive Chinese nationalism that has gathered momentum with growing elite and intellectual support since the end of the Cold War, under a political regime that appears determined to maintain political stability above all and avoid major disturbances of its own structural integrity. The growing strain between these conflicting forces has manifested itself in a growing number of spontaneous local protests—nearly 90,000 violent incidents were reported by the Department of Civil Affairs in 2005, though to be sure, these protests were directed not at the regime per se but at its local representatives. This growing strain helps explain the leadership's resolve at its Seventeenth Party Congress in October 2007 to adhere to a "scientific outlook on development" and construct a "socialist harmonious civilization," hoping to counteract social turmoil by emphasizing a synthesis of Western ("scientific") and traditional ("harmonious") values.

SEE ALSO *Constitutionalism; Dissidents; Personality Cults; Political Parties, 1905–1949.*

BIBLIOGRAPHY

Barme, Geremie. *In the Red: On Contemporary Chinese Culture.* New York: Columbia University Press, 1999.

Chen Fangzheng, and Jin Guantao. *From Youthful Manuscripts to River Elegy: The Chinese Popular Cultural Movement and Political Transformation.* Hong Kong: Chinese University Press, 1997.

De Bary, William Theodore. *Sources of Chinese Tradition.* New York: Columbia University Press, 1964.

Eckstein, Harry. *The Natural History of Congruence Theory.* Denver, CO: Graduate School of International Studies, University of Denver, 1980.

Hua Shiping, ed. *Chinese Political Culture, 1989–2000.* Armonk, NY: M. E. Sharpe, 2001.

Johnson, Chalmers. *Peasant Nationalism and Communist Power: The Emergence of Revolutionary China, 1937-1945.* Stanford, CA: Stanford University Press, 1962.

Liu, Alan P. L. *Political Culture and Group Conflict in Communist China.* Santa Barbara, CA: ABC-Clio, 1976.

Pye, Lucian W. *The Spirit of Chinese Politics: A Psychocultural Study of the Authority Crisis in Political Development.* Cambridge, MA: M.I.T. Press, 1968.

Pye, Lucian W. *The Dynamics of Chinese Politics.* Cambridge, MA: Oelgeschlager, Gunn, and Hain, 1981.

Pye, Lucian W. *The Mandarin and the Cadre: China's Political Cultures.* Ann Arbor: Center for Chinese Studies, University of Michigan, 1988.

Solomon, Richard H. *Mao's Revolution and the Chinese Political Culture.* Berkeley: University of California Press, 1971.

Weber, Max. *The Religion of China: Confucianism and Taoism.* Translated and edited by Hans H. Gerth. Glencoe, Ill.: The Free Press, 1952.

Zarrow, Peter. *Anarchism and Chinese Political Culture.* New York: New York University Press, 1990.

Lowell Dittmer

POLITICAL PARTIES, 1905–1949

Modern Chinese political parties did not come into being until after 1911. Before then, in the last years of the Qing dynasty, there were political groupings that either advocated a constitutional monarchy or sought to overthrow Manchu rule. Most notable of these were the Constitutionalists, led by Liang Qichao (1873–1929), which grew out of the Save the Emperor Society (Baohuang Hui), and their opponents, the Revolutionary Alliance (Tongmeng Hui), formed in Tokyo in 1905 under the leadership of Sun Yat-sen (1866–1925). The Revolutionary Alliance was factionalized along provincial lines, with internal disputes over leadership, revolutionary strategies, finance, and other issues. Back in China, it set up regional bureaus in many parts of the country. Its Central China Bureau was involved in subverting the Hubei New Army, whose officers launched the October 10, 1911, uprising that led to the overthrow of the dynasty.

THE EARLY REPUBLICAN PERIOD

Following the establishment of the Republic in 1912, the Constitutionalists were transformed into the Democratic Party (Minzhu Dang), which later merged with the newly formed Unification Party (Tongyi Dang) to become the Progressive Party (Jinbu Dang). It supported President Yuan Shikai in the new Parliament until 1915, when he attempted to restore the monarchy. Opposed to Yuan was the Nationalist Party, which succeeded the Revolutionary Alliance. Its leader Song Jiaoren (1882–1913) was assassinated in 1913, allegedly on Yuan's order, an event that triggered the so-called Second Revolution. After Yuan's death in 1916, China descended into chaos and was ruled by a succession of militarists. The Nationalist leader Sun Yat-sen established a revolutionary military government in Guangzhou in 1917, and in 1923 he formed a United Front with the infant Chinese Communist Party to fight warlordism and imperialism. The United Front collapsed in late

1926 as the Northern Expedition swept across Central and East China and Chiang Kai-shek (1887–1975) began a purge of the Communists in Shanghai the next April.

After the National Government was established in Nanjing in 1928, all political parties other than the ruling Nationalist Party were outlawed. The ruling party itself was far from united, with a left-wing faction led by Wang Jingwei (1883–1944) and a right-wing faction rallying behind Hu Hanmin (1879–1936). Soon power was concentrated in the hands of Chiang Kai-shek, whose control of the army enabled him to turn the regime virtually into a personal dictatorship. A dissident group led by Deng Yanda (1895–1931) formed the Provisional Action Committee of the Nationalist Party (Guomindang Linshi Xingdong Weiyuanhui), which pledged to fight imperialism, feudalism, and capitalism and to establish a people's regime, with workers and peasants at its core. Deng was arrested and executed in November 1931. In 1935 the Provisional Action Committee was renamed the China Liberation Action Committee (Zhongguo Minzu Jiefang Xingdong Weiyuanhui), better known as the Third Party (Disan Dang), led by Zhang Bojun (1895–1969). In 1947 it became known as the Chinese Peasants and Workers Democratic Party (Zhongguo Nonggong Minzhu Dang).

Another minor party was the Chinese Youth Party (Zhongguo Qingnian Dang), formed in Paris in 1923 by a group of patriotic students who returned to China the next year to set up headquarters in Shanghai. Led by Zeng Qi (1892–1951), Li Huang (1895–?), and Zuo Shunsheng (1893–1969), the Youth Party was conservative, nationalistic, and anticommunist, bearing a resemblance to the Nationalist Party but differing from it in that it advocated parliamentary democracy, less economic planning and more private enterprise, and provincial autonomy under a federal system.

A third minor party emerged early in the 1930s—the State Socialist Party (Guojia Shehui Dang), formed by Zhang Junmai (1887–1969) and associates. It advocated a form of state socialism marked by planning, a mixed economy, and a social democratic platform. Influenced by the social democracy of Weimar Germany, Fabianism, and the British Labour movement, it basically advocated democratic socialism. It had nothing to do with Nazism or fascism.

There were also several political groups (*pai*), namely, the Rural Reconstructionists (Xiangjian Pai), the Vocational Education Society (Zhijiao Pai), and the National Salvation Association (Jiuguo Hui). Collectively, the minor parties and groups stood for those educated Chinese who were disaffected with both the Nationalists and the Communists. Despite their small memberships and lack of political muscle, they had a collective importance far beyond their actual numbers. Diverse yet united by common concerns about the national crisis, they were critical of the government over its Japan policy, one-party rule, political tutelage, and Chiang Kai-shek's personal dictatorship. Each sought a

way of saving the nation, and all professed to be democratic and socialistic.

THE LATE REPUBLICAN PERIOD

In 1936 Chiang Kai-shek resolved to fight the Japanese, formed a second United Front with the Communists, lifted the ban on minor political parties, and invited representatives of all the political parties and groups to participate in the wartime People's Political Council (Renmin Zhengzhi Huiyi), which opened in Hankou in 1938. While supporting the government's war efforts, the minor political parties maintained the momentum of a constitutional movement and did not falter in their demand for an early end to one-party rule. In 1941 they coalesced to form the China Democratic League (Zhongguo Minzhu Tongmeng), whose forerunner was the United National Reconstruction Comrades Association (Tongyi Jianguo Tongzhi Hui).

The league came into being at a point when the conflict between the government and the Communists reemerged following the New Fourth Army incident of January 1941, which virtually put an end to the second United Front. The league was a collection of diverse elements, mainly intellectuals, with members maintaining a dual identity and divided loyalty. Its immediate aim was to maintain national unity by seeking a political settlement of the differences between the Communists and Nationalists. The league's headquarters were in Chongqing, but its stronghold was Kunming, the site of the wartime Associated Southwest University, many of whose faculty were its members, including some of China's best known and most highly respected scholars. The league conceived of democracy in terms of multiparty rule, representative government, free elections, competitive politics, respect for civil liberties, and regard for political and human rights. In the specific Chinese context, it demanded an end to one-party rule, a coalition government, nationalization of all armies, and a cessation of civil war. The league represented a third-force movement, attempting to steer a path between the government and the Communists. In economics, it advocated planning and a mixed economy. And it claimed socialism to be its ultimate goal.

No sooner had the war against Japan ended than civil war threatened to resume. This prompted the minor parties and groups to renew their efforts to search for a peaceful settlement. But disputes arose over the November 1946 opening of the National Assembly, which was boycotted by the Communists and leftist members of the Democratic League. The Youth Party and the State Socialist Party, which was renamed the Democratic Socialist Party after merging with an American-based constitutionalist group, decided to attend the National Assembly, and so withdrew from the league. A disaffected group who resented Zhang Junmai's unilateral decision to attend the National Assembly formed the breakaway Democratic Socialist Party (Reformist). What remained of the Democratic League lurched to the Communists, while representatives from the Youth Party and the Democratic Socialist Party joined the National Government when it was reorganized under the new 1947 constitution adopted the previous December. Half a dozen small pro-Communist groups also came into existence. Known in Communist parlance as democratic parties and groups (*minzhu dangpai*), they were all co-opted into the Communist Party and state after 1949, along with the Democratic League.

SEE ALSO *Classical Scholarship and Intellectual Debates: Intellectuals, 1900–1949; Communist Thought in China, Origins of; Nationalist Party; Zhang Junmai (Carsun Chang).*

BIBLIOGRAPHY
Ch'ien Tuan-shêng. *The Government and Politics of China, 1912–1945.* Cambridge, MA: Harvard University Press, 1950.

Fung, Edmund S. K (Feng Zhaoji). *In Search of Chinese Democracy: Civil Opposition in Nationalist China, 1929–1949.* New York: Cambridge University Press, 2000.

Jeans, Roger B., ed. *Roads Not Taken: The Struggle of Opposition Parties in Twentieth-Century China.* Boulder, CO: Westview Press, 1992.

Liew, Kit Siong. *Struggle for Democracy: Sung Chiao-jen and the 1911 Chinese Revolution.* Berkeley: University of California Press, 1971.

Van Slyke, Lyman P. *Enemies and Friends: The United Front in Chinese Communist History.* Stanford, CA: Stanford University Press, 1967.

Edmund S. K. Fung (Feng Zhaoji)

POLITICAL POP AND CYNICAL REALISM

Political pop (*zhengzhi popu*) and cynical realism (*popi*) are two artistic currents that emerged on the Chinese scene in the early 1990s. Considered to be the result of the drastically transformed intellectual and spiritual atmosphere that followed the crushing of the idealistic aspirations advocated by the 1989 Tiananmen democratic movement, political pop and cynical realism follow the heightened atmosphere of experimentation that characterized the decade of the 1980s, which in turn had emerged as a reaction to the stifling conditions of the Maoist years. The early 1990s, in contrast, were defined by a process of sobering up, of coming to terms with a much less idealistic reality. Disillusionment and cynicism were widespread spiritual conditions among the younger generations, an attitude accompanied by a lack of attachment to any form of lofty ideal, since such ideals had so often proved misleading.

POLITICAL POP

The artists grouped under the name of political pop chose to no longer celebrate socialist victories through an idealistic description of reality, but to denounce its contradictions and fallacies by employing the same language that in the previous period had been used to reinforce such reality. Their works suggested a critical reflection on the contemporary political situation, making use of formulas that were familiar to the Chinese public at the time. Through common and ubiquitous signifiers, these works denounced a moral and spiritual impoverishment and the absurdity of all political symbolism. Their didacticism and choice of images and colors were both directly and indirectly related to the iconography and language of political propaganda. These artists, most of whom were born in the 1940s or 1950s, had shared unique experiences that equipped them with both a personal sense of mission and a desire to deconstruct the traditional forms of political culture that had frustrated individual expression. Artists associated with political pop include Li Shan (b. 1942), Yu Youhan (b. 1943), Zhang Hongtu (b. 1943), Wang Guangyi (b. 1957), Wang Ziwei (b. 1963), Geng Jianyi (b. 1962), Feng Mengbo (b. 1966), and, to a limited extent, Zhang Peili (b. 1957), but many other artists have used references to the political past in their art.

Wang Guangyi adopts the most stereotypically figurative language of socialist propaganda borrowed from the iconography of the posters of the Cultural Revolution and pairs it with explicit symbols of Western consumerism to denounce the untenable contradictions of a political system that accepts the practice of capitalism while condemning it on an ideological level. Yu Youhan has ridiculed the familiar imagery of the Cultural Revolution to the point where its "popular" characteristics become comical, if not grotesque. In the 1992 series *Rays*, Geng Jianyi metonymically suggested the figure of Mao Zedong by quoting a formal attribute immediately associated with his official representations, but replacing the central icon of the halo with nonsensical figures, like pandas or workers, peasants, and national minorities such as those featured on Chinese banknotes. The image of Xin Zhibin (China's most famous newscaster for China Central Television and one of the official voices of authority during the summer of 1989) was used by Zhang Peili in the triptych *1989 Standard Pronunciation* as a recognizable symbol of unimpeachable officialdom. Her image scrolls relentlessly on the painted screen, alluding to the chronic impossibility of fixing into a precise definition the real meaning of authority and political power.

CYNICAL REALISM

As discussed by critic and curator Li Xianting—to whom we owe the first definition in print of political pop and cynical

A viewer before **A Big Family** *by Zhang Xiaogang, 1995. Coming of age during the Cultural Revolution, Zhang Xiaogang is considered by critics an important contributor to the Political Pop art movement, a collection of artists examining the contradictions of the socialist teaching of their youth with the political messages of contemporary society.* © **NETWORK PHOTOGRAPHERS / ALAMY**

realism—the term *popi* "is a colloquial expression whose original meaning is close to 'bored,' 'senseless,' 'rogue,' 'small ruffian.' The term also bears the reference to 'dissipated,' 'cynical,' 'indifferent to everything' and 'jaded'" (Li Xianting 1992). Artists representative of this trend are Fang Lijun (b. 1963), Liu Wei (b. 1965), Yue Minjun (b. 1962), Yang Shaobin (b. 1963), Liu Xiaodong (b. 1963), Yu Hong (b. 1966), Song Yonghong (b. 1966), Wang Jinsong (b. 1963), and Zhao Bandi (b. 1966). For these artists, who were children during the first years of the Cultural Revolution, painting by the early 1990s had become their only serious endeavor, yet they nevertheless display fun and mockery in their art. Realism, which for nearly four decades was the official visual idiom of the People's Republic, becomes a weapon directed against the false formality and conformity with which the artists were confronted everyday. Because reality is often contradictory, absurd, and hypocritical, their works frequently show a surrealist vein and a nihilistic, disenchanted view. After decades of artistic production geared toward the representation of models of political and spiritual practice, these artists wholeheart-

edly rejected all heroic connotations, focusing instead on the description of people and situations who are hyperordinary, antiheroes who could not fit into any grand narrative. Most of the characters featured in their works are in fact portraits of actual people: friends, schoolmates, relatives, and even themselves.

Fang Lijun's *Series 2 No. 2* (1991–1992) is one of the icons of this particular ethical stance. A bald young man appears in the foreground, yawning in apathy against a blue background, while a series of older, clonelike men look on. The rogue with the bald head is the epitome of the antihero: he is young, somehow cool with his spotless white polo shirt, and bored. The faces and the expressions of the characters in Fang Lijun's early paintings are always more or less identical. There might be several people in a composition, but also a feeling of a chronic distance among them. The characters, repeated obsessively, become surreal and take on new meanings, producing an effect of a great loneliness and alienation. In *New Generation* (1990), Liu Wei produces a portrait of himself and his brother as babies posing for a photographic session in front of an official poster of Mao Zedong. The chairman is confined to the position of backdrop for the ritual photographic portrait; the tension produced by juxtaposing the expressionless look on Mao's face with the liveliness of the children illustrates the huge generational gap. Mao is just a reminiscence of the past, a flat poster on the wall, while a new generation strives in the foreground, taking up the center of the stage.

POPULARITY IN THE WEST

The artworks of political pop and cynical realism, in their later manifestations and endless replication, have been most successful with Western buyers. Most of the record-breaking auction prices reached by Chinese contemporary art in the early 2000s were scored by works produced in the style of these two currents. Yet in many later works, the original tension and brash ingenuity have been replaced by mannerist repetitiveness and stylistic bravura that undermine the critical significance of this art.

SEE ALSO *Art in New Media; New Wave Movement, '85.*

BIBLIOGRAPHY

Dal Lago, Francesca. Personal Mao: Reshaping an Icon in Contemporary Chinese Art. *Art Journal* 58, 2 (1999): 46–59.

Dal Lago, Francesca. Images, Words, and Violence: Cultural Revolutionary Influences on Chinese Avant-garde Art. *Chinese Art at the Crossroads: Between Past and Future, Between East and West*, ed. Wu Hong, 32–39. Hong Kong: New Art Media, 2001.

Dal Lago, Francesca. The Voice of "Superfluous People": Painting in China in the late 1980s and early 1990s. *Writing on the Wall: Chinese New Realism and Avant-garde in the Eighties and Nineties*, ed. Barbera van Kooij, 21–32. Groningen, Netherlands: Groninger Museum; Rotterdam: NAI, 2008.

Li Xianting. Hou '89 yishu zhong de wuliaogang he jiegou yishi [Apathy and deconstruction consciousness in post-1989 art]. *Yishu chaoliu* [Art currents], Taiwan inaugural issue (1992).

Li Xianting. Major Trends in the Development of Contemporary Chinese Art. In *China's New Art, Post-1989*, ed. Valerie C. Doran, x–xxii. Hong Kong: Hanart Gallery, 1993.

Li Xianting. The Imprisoned Heart: Ideology in an Age of Consumption. *Art and Asia Pacific* 1, 2, (1994): 25–30.

Smith, Karen. *Nine Lives: The Birth of Avant-garde Art in New China*. Zurich: Scalo, 2004.

Francesca Dal Lago

POLITICAL REPRESENTATION

In China the theory of representation derives more from the tradition of direct democracy, familiar to Communists from the model of the 1871 Paris Commune, than from representative democracy. Therefore, Chinese elections confirm the authenticity of political consultation during the leadership selection rather than allowing voters to delegate power to their representatives. In China voting does not transfer sovereignty but appoints someone to inform those engaged in decision-making processes about group needs, interests, and viewpoints. Representatives are not elected because they share political visions with voters, but for their ability to represent the group well. Commonly, the government and voters alike evaluate candidates according to their demonstrated talent in work and other pursuits. This approach leaves representation relatively apolitical. Yet, as An Chen finds in his 1999 study, Chinese voters are largely satisfied with representatives who tackle concrete issues affecting daily life.

The Chinese Communists see that consultation of all relevant interests, geographic areas, and social groups to know various needs and interests must precede policy making that aims to find a balance among these interests. The Chinese Communist idea of representation thus belongs to the type of representation that Anthony Birch (2001) calls "microcosmic representation" and Jane Mansbridge (1998) calls "surrogate representation." In this kind of representation, people are represented as members of a certain social group, such as workers, soldiers, women, or entrepreneurs, or as members of an ethnic group, not as proponents of particular political beliefs. Apart from elections, this kind of representation is apparent in the pattern of political organization in China. The state and the party have established various official organizations to represent one social group or stratum, such as labor, women, youth, overseas Chinese, or a certain profession, in order to consult these organizations during policy-making processes.

REPRESENTATIVE ELECTORAL RESULTS AND INSTITUTIONS OF REPRESENTATION

The need to guarantee the balance of various interests has an impact on the electoral system. Electoral districts follow not geographic but functional divisions. For example, universities, schools, factories, hotels, even temples, form a separate electoral district alone or with other similar units. Each electoral district is assigned certain criteria for appointing candidates—for example, soliciting one female, one entrepreneur, one lawyer, or one member of a democratic party. Balanced representation of all interests means that all interests, especially the groups central for modernization, should be heard. Consequently, peasants are numerically underrepresented to prevent them from overwhelming other interests through weight of numbers, while intellectuals and workers, and nowadays entrepreneurs, are overrepresented.

From the perspective of Chinese Communists, the best policies emerge from extensive consultation of all social groups. Thus it makes sense to have several overlapping systems of consultation and representation. The main institutions for representation are people's congresses and people's political consultative conferences, both of which have organs at the national, regional, and local levels. In addition, political parties, professional or religious associations, mass organizations, and even trade associations and nongovernmental organizations have representative functions. All political parties explicitly represent certain social classes or strata, the Communist Party being the party for the workers and peasants, while small democratic parties represent intellectuals, overseas Chinese, and entrepreneurs. Only since the turn of the century has the Communist Party invited entrepreneurs under its own representative umbrella.

FROM THE MAOIST ERA THROUGH THE REFORM ERA

The Chinese People's Political Consultative Conference (CPPCC) convened for the first time in September 1949 to prepare for the Communist takeover of national political power and served as the legislature until 1954. It was, and still is, a united front organization. Along with political parties and mass organizations, it brings together nonparty notables, such as religious leaders, political persons who aligned with the Communists during the republican era, representatives of minority nationalities, and overseas Chinese dignitaries. People's political consultative congresses make and evaluate policy proposals, investigate administrative misconduct and other unlawful affairs, and relay public concerns to decision makers.

In 1954 a new organ, the National People's Congress (NPC), took over the legislative function from the CPPCC. The NPC nominates the government and the president, supervises the work of the government and the judiciary, approves budgets, and ratifies treaties. It deliberates and votes on bills, and its members can make legislative proposals. According to Kevin O'Brien in his 1994 article, many representatives take seriously their right to investigate malpractice in administration and society and convey the voice of their constituency to decision makers. Provincial and local-level congresses have comparable tasks on their own administrative level. The role of people's congresses has strengthened since 1979 with the attempt to build the rule of law in China. The emphasis on the law and the division of power between the Communist Party and various state organs has provided people's congresses a role in consensus building among the legislature, the administration, and the Communist Party.

Although Western observers often dismiss people's congresses as rubber stamps, the congresses do participate in lengthy consensus building during the policy formulation process and have a supervisory role over government officials, exercised in yearly hearings. In individual cases the NPC has forced ministers to resign. The fact that it has only ever rejected one law proposal is explained as an outcome of the above-mentioned lengthy process of consensus building. It is common to take years to pass a law that often goes through consultation of relevant state organs and social

groups, local experimentation, public press discussion, and citizen input during its drafting process. At the provincial and local levels, people's congresses have impeached officials, rejected government-initiated policies, and elected their own gubernatorial candidates instead of the ones nominated by the party. Although the Communist Party can force its will on the process through its prestige, its role in candidate setting, and its representatives with party affiliation, it usually prefers more a deliberative approach of persuasion and technical expertise. People's congresses, for their part, seek a cooperative, not oppositional, relationship with the Communist Party and seek to avoid deadlock when pursuing their own position.

During the decade of the Cultural Revolution (1966–1976), the whole representative system, including the people's congresses, the CPPCC, mass organizations, and democratic parties, collapsed as symbols of established and bureaucratized power. Between 1966 and 1977, the NPC convened only once; the CPPCC and democratic parties were dismantled; and purges inactivated mass organizations or rivaling organizations challenged their position. Revolutionary committees replaced people's congresses. Their composition was based on class representation benefiting political activists, the Communist Party members, workers, and soldiers. The proletarian emphasis of the movement made other social interests less legitimate. The Communist Party as the organization representing the proletariat and peasantry was consequently strengthened vis-à-vis state organs and organizations representing other social groups.

LIMITATIONS

On the stated grounds that people's representatives' need strong social integration with their constituencies, people's congresses convene only briefly. For example, the yearly NPC sessions take less than two weeks. Consequently, most people's representatives develop little legislative expertise and supportive networks within the legislature. This has negatively affected the powers people's congresses have vis-à-vis government and party organs. Since the later decades of the twentieth century, their standing committees have been gaining strength, thus enhancing their legislative and supervisory capacities.

In China the state, not social groups themselves, decides whether a certain interest is represented. Consequently, the inclusion of new social interests, such as the migrant population, has been slow, with the outright exclusion of some social groups, such as those deemed class enemies (until 1979). Moreover, the state can evaluate different interests autonomously. For example, the peasants, underrepresented in the legislature and lacking a national peasant organization, have been unable to challenge the developmental model directing resources coming from agriculture to urban development and industrialization. Nevertheless, they have managed to draw the government's attention to rural problems, of which the launching of the economic reforms from the countryside is one example. The Chinese representational system thus makes the government consult and consider various social interests, but on its own terms.

SEE ALSO *Communist Party; Migrant Workers; United Front Work.*

BIBLIOGRAPHY

Birch, Anthony. *The Concepts and Theories of Modern Democracy.* London: Routledge, 2001.

Chen, An. *Restructuring Political Power in China: Alliances and Opposition, 1978–1998.* Boulder, CO: Lynne Rienner Publishers, 1999.

Jacobs, Bruce. Elections in China. *Australian Journal of Chinese Affairs* 25 (1991): 171–199.

Kelliher, Daniel. The Chinese Debate over Village Self-Government. *China Journal* 37 (1997): 63–91.

Mansbridge, Jane. *Many Faces of Representation.* Kennedy School of Government Politics Research Group Working Paper 17 (1998).

Mao Zedong. "On Ten Major Relationships" (1957). In *Selected Works of Mao Tse-tung*, vol. 5, 284–307. Peking: Foreign Languages Press, 1977.

O'Brien, Kevin J. *Reform without Liberalization: China's National People's Congress and the Politics of Institutional Change.* New York: Cambridge University Press, 1990.

O'Brien, Kevin. Chinese People's Congresses and Legislative Embeddedness. *Comparative Political Studies* 27, 1 (1994): 80–107.

Salmenkari, Taru. *Democracy, Participation and Deliberation in China: The Discussion in Official Chinese Press, 1978–1981.* Helsinki: Finnish Oriental Society, 2006.

Shih, Chih-yu. *Collective Democracy: Political and Legal Reform in China.* Hong Kong: Chinese University Press, 1999.

Tanner, Murray Scot. *The Politics of Lawmaking in Post-Mao China: Institutions, Processes, and Democratic Prospects.* Oxford: Clarendon Press, and New York: Oxford University Press, 1999.

Townsend, James. *Political Participation in Communist China.* Berkeley: University of California Press, 1967.

Xia, Ming. "Political Contestation and the Emergence of the Provincial People's Congresses as Power Players in Chinese Politics." *Journal of Contemporary China* 9, 24 (2000): 185–214.

Taru Salmenkari

POLITICAL SUCCESSION

Political succession is both important and problematic in all communist party-states. It is important because power tends to be monocratically concentrated and political policy is highly variable depending on the person who holds the leadership position. It is problematic because no reliable mechanism has been found for the transfer of power in a regime in which authority flows from the top down. The two main types of succession arrangement are *premortem* succession, in which the departing incumbent attempts to install an heir apparent and invest him or her with power before succession occurs, and *postmortem* succession, in which the incumbent may leave a last will and testament or not even that and the successor is selected via open-ended competition among those strong enough to compete. Because of the difficulties in arriving at elite consensus in premortem succession, most such systems have opted for postmortem succession, which is, however, uncertain because the death of the incumbent changes the elite balance of power unpredictably.

Thus, although Zhou Enlai attempted to arrange for Deng Xiaoping's succession to the premiership before Zhou's death in January 1976, Mao Zedong outlived Zhou, allowing Mao to derail these arrangements. Premortem succession offers a way of reducing the uncertainty of the transition because it allows the successor to consolidate his or her power with the assistance of the retiring incumbent. There are, however, two inherent difficulties. The first is that the incumbent may be ambivalent about arranging for his or her own succession, either due to unforeseen inadequacies in the heir apparent's performance or simply because the incumbent is reluctant to relinquish power, and this ambivalence may derail a smooth succession. This seems to have been the case, for example, with Mao Zedong's successions first to Liu Shaoqi and then to Lin Biao. Part of the reason for the incumbent's ambivalence has to do with the second problem with premortem succession: The heir apparent, anticipating an incumbent's change of heart and other uncertainties, may usurp power prematurely and purge the incumbent, or simply usurp sufficient power plausibly to threaten the incumbent. The first possibility is illustrated by Leonid Brezhnev's succession in 1964 to Nikita Khrushchev, the second by Liu Shaoqi's growing power base during the early 1960s when he and Deng Xiaoping took charge of recovery efforts from the economically disastrous Great Leap Forward.

Despite these liabilities, the greater possibility of stabilizing a premortem than a postmortem succession has made premortem succession the preferred model in the People's Republic of China—only the succession to Mao himself was clearly postmortem, after premortem arrangements broke down. Political succession in China may be divided into three periods: the preliberation period, the Maoist period, and finally the post-Mao succession experience.

PRELIBERATION PERIOD

During the preliberation period (1921–1949), succession was invariably premortem but also secretive and nonconsensual, taking the form of frequent involuntary removal of incumbents by senior colleagues (i.e., purges). Inasmuch as power and policy were highly centralized and personalized, ending a particular set of policies or "line" (e.g., the "Li Lisan line" or the "Qu Qiubai line") could be most efficiently achieved by blaming the top leader for all previous policy errors and deposing him or her. Thus the founding chair of the Chinese Communist Party (CCP), Chen Duxiu, was purged in 1927 (and evicted from the Party in 1929) for the failure of the first United Front with the Guomindang. Though this form of policy change via elite purge resulted in great leadership instability, it permitted the leadership to adjust flexibly to environmental exigencies without inheriting responsibility for failed policies.

MAOIST PERIOD

During Mao's tenure, leadership instability at the top was largely avoided; indeed, Mao and a few of his close colleagues retained lifetime tenure. There were, however, frequent shifts of policy "line," which could be negotiated without admitting error or inconsistency by positing a leadership disagreement in which the dissident leader would be blamed for the wrong policies, criticized, and dismissed. Often such leadership disputes would be conflated with premature succession crises. Mao, recognizing the need to anchor the revolutionary values he wished to endure beyond his own person, would anoint an official heir apparent, only to later repent of his choice and reverse his own decision. This created a crisis around the succession issue that mounted over time as Mao grew older and more infirm and his personal power increased. And the crisis transcended the personnel issues, as Mao tended to use premortem succession as a political device to boost a specific (if shifting) policy agenda.

In the case of Liu Shaoqi, heir apparency was awarded in the late 1950s, probably to ensure his support for the Great Leap Forward in 1958 to 1959 (which Liu indeed supported). But when Liu then retracted that support in the early 1960s in the light of the economically disastrous consequences of the Leap and took the lead in implementing more economically flexible policies in order to facilitate economic recovery, the result was an elite split between what became known as the "proletarian revolutionary line" and the "bourgeois reactionary line," leading Mao to rescind his succession arrangements and helping to precipitate the mass upheaval known as the Great Proletarian Cultural Revolution (1966–1969).

Mao then replaced Liu with Lin Biao because of Lin's more enthusiastic embrace of the Cultural Revolution and to ensure the support of the People's Liberation Army (PLA) that he commanded, even writing Lin's succession into the Party Statute (i.e., constitution) at the Ninth Party Congress in 1969. But when Mao then decided that the army had assumed too much power in the course of restoring order and that Lin himself was threatening Mao's primacy, Mao's attempt to reverse succession arrangements resulted in the death of Lin Biao and several of this family members and in the subsequent purge of the PLA. It also undermined the credibility of the Cultural Revolution itself,

as did Mao's subsequent short-lived infatuation with would-be successor Wang Hongwen (who was appointed CCP vice chair at the Tenth Party Congress in 1973) as representative of the Red Guard generation. Mao's inability to resolve the succession conundrum thus helped to undermine the revolutionary revitalization he had hoped to bequeath as his legacy to postrevolutionary China.

POST-MAO PERIOD

Deng Xiaoping eventually succeeded Mao by outmaneuvering Mao's chosen successor, Hua Guofeng (1921–2008), and championing a much more pragmatic and flexible policy orientation, but like Mao he recognized the importance of premortem succession arrangements as a way of ensuring the posthumous continuity of his policy line. While Mao sought to tie his own succession to the question of revolutionary generational succession, Deng attempted to demobilize the masses and to limit the issue to one of leadership succession—defined now, however, as a cadre stratum rather than as an individual. Thus, under Deng Xiaoping for the first time, all central government leaders were appointed for a limit of two five-year terms, and the Central Advisory Commission was introduced at the Twelfth Party Congress in 1982 (and terminated at the 14th Congress in 1992) to provide a provisory forum to which superannuated cadres could retire gracefully. Compulsory retirement at age 65 was also introduced in 1982 for all central and provincial government officials; though the CCP adopted no formal age limits, an informal norm was introduced at the 15th Party Congress for all Politburo members to retire by the age of 70 (later lowered to 68).

Meanwhile, however, Deng's personal succession arrangements proved more complicated, as he changed his mind about the succession of first Hu Yaobang in 1986, replacing him with Zhao Ziyang (at no cost to the reform policies both supported); but when he then again changed his mind about Zhao Ziyang in 1989, this reversal had a divisive impact on elite solidarity in response to the Tiananmen protests that were crushed on June 4, a split that at least temporarily slowed the momentum of the reform agenda.

Ultimately the leadership did achieve consensus on the choice of Jiang Zemin after suppressing the "turmoil" at Tiananmen, and Jiang proceeded to consolidate his leadership in China's first successful premortem succession. This he managed to do despite the survival of Deng Xiaoping as an internationally visible alternative (informal) power locus from 1992 until his death in early 1997. And five years later at the Sixteenth Party Congress, Deng Xiaoping's candidate, Hu Jintao, succeeded Jiang Zemin even more smoothly and with less display of incumbent ambivalence. At the Seventeenth Party Congress in 2007, the first steps were taken toward a fourth smooth succession of leadership generations with the promotion of relatively young cadres, Xi Jinping and Li Keqiang, to positions in the Politburo Standing Committee from which they were expected to assume leading positions in the party and state in 2012.

Thus, over time, considerable progress has been made in institutionalizing a political-succession process previously prone to crises that split the country's leadership and had disruptive political repercussions throughout the system. Deng Xiaoping began by placing much greater emphasis on fostering greater civility within the elite, as symbolized by the wholesale rehabilitation of cadres who had been purged during the Cultural Revolution, as well as by the relatively lenient treatment of those he clashed with in the process of consolidating his own power (e.g., Hua Guofeng). The introduction of cadre term limits and age limits and the institutionalization of compulsory retirement reduced the stakes of elite power struggles. Since the split over Tiananmen, factional divisiveness within the leadership has also been more successfully controlled. Policy continuity during the second and third generational leadership successions was further enhanced by (1) detaching the choice of successor from the incumbent's personal discretion (i.e., Jiang Zemin was reportedly selected by a moderate grouping led by Chen Yun and Li Xiannian, and Hu Jintao was selected not by Jiang Zemin but by Deng Xiaoping, as early as 1992), and (2) permitting the incumbent to remain in a powerful position (a "regency") to monitor the new leader for an indefinite period after succession.

While this institutionalization of succession is impressive, it is not without drawbacks. First, the emphasis on elite continuity has perhaps deprived the leadership of a mechanism for dramatic policy innovations of the sort that launched the "reform and opening policy" in 1978. Second, the demobilization of the masses in succession crises has deprived the system of not only opposition but mass support, contributing to a progressive weakening of the leadership's policy implementation capabilities.

SEE ALSO *Deng Xiaoping; Hu Jintao; Jiang Zemin; Liu Shaoqi; Mao Zedong.*

BIBLIOGRAPHY

Dittmer, Lowell, Haruhiro Fukui, and Peter N. S. Lee, eds. *Informal Politics in East Asia.* Cambridge, U.K., and New York: Cambridge University Press, 2000.

Gardner, John. *Chinese Politics and the Succession to Mao.* London: Macmillan, 1982.

Lieberthal, Kenneth. *Governing China: From Revolution through Reform.* 2nd ed. New York: Norton, 2004.

MacFarquhar, Roderick, ed. *The Politics of China: The Eras of Mao and Deng.* 2nd ed. Cambridge, U.K., and New York: Cambridge University Press, 1997.

Teiwes, Frederick C. *Leadership, Legitimacy, and Conflict in China: From a Charismatic Mao to the Politics of Succession.* Armonk, NY: Sharpe, 1984.

Wong, John, and Zheng Yongnian, eds. *China's Post-Jiang Leadership Succession: Problems and Perspectives.* Singapore: Singapore University Press; Rivers Edge, NJ: World Scientific, 2002.

Lowell Dittmer

POPULAR RELIGION

Any effort to understand Chinese popular religion must begin by conceding the problematic nature of this term. The term for *religion* in Chinese (*zongjiao*) is in fact a Japanese neologism derived from Western culture, and has but tenuous links to traditional Chinese concepts and organizations. The term *popular* is equally problematic, with some scholars (and officials) using it to describe beliefs and practices not considered to be a part of institutionalized religions such as Buddhism and Daoism. Others apply the term *popular religion* to commonly held facets of religious life, and still others use it to refer to religions considered distinct from so-called elite religion. For these reasons, some scholars prefer a newer term, *communal religious traditions*, defined as an integrated Chinese system of religious life that incorporates practices for individual well-being and salvation, family-based mortuary ceremonies, and rites to ensure communal harmony, all of which involve the participation of ritual specialists ranging from Buddhist, Daoist, and Confucian clerics to a wide variety of local religious experts such as ritual masters, spirit-mediums, diviners, geomancers, and so on.

Organizationally speaking, Chinese communal religious traditions can be divided roughly into ascriptive groups and voluntary associations. The former include territorial communities (temple cults and tutelary deities), lineages (ancestor worship and mortuary ceremonies, but also the worship of guardian deities), and corporations (especially native-place associations and guilds that worship patron deities). Voluntary associations include lay Buddhist and Daoist groups, pilgrimage associations, redemptive societies, and so on. Members of such organizations tend to focus on individual self-cultivation and salvation, while engaging in practices such as lectures, meditation, and spirit-writing.

Not all of the above-mentioned groups built temples, because the presence of an incense burner, statue or spirit tablet, and ritual specialists were sufficient to maintain a community's ritual existence. Some groups used household altars or small private shrines, but those that had the material resources and had not been subjected to official persecution made every effort to construct temples. The resulting temple cults featured reciprocal interaction between the community and its deities, with worshippers providing sacrifices and financial support in exchange for the performance of miracles. If miracles failed to materialize, a cult could easily die out, but new ones often arose to take its place or even surpass it in terms of influence. In addition to rites celebrating deities' birthdays and other important occasions in the local ritual calendar, the better endowed temples also organized festivals featuring processions that defined the cult's territory and the jurisdiction of its deities.

Prior to the modern era, the Chinese imperial state's religious policies toward communal religious traditions were based on a utopian vision of imposing an ethical order on society from the top down. In practical terms, this meant protection and occasional financial or literary patronage of state cult sacred sites, monasteries belonging to institutionalized religions such as Buddhism and Daoism, and temples or shrines to ancestors and local deities deemed to be "orthodox" (*zheng*). Other sacred sites were allowed to exist or simply ignored, but those labeled "illicit/lascivious" (*yin*) or "heterodox" (*xie*) could be subject to suppression. In addition, the imperial state tended to be more tolerant of ascriptive communities, especially those that adhered to traditional patriarchal structures, and was distrustful of or even hostile to voluntary associations with traces of millenarian ideology.

CHALLENGES AND ADAPTATIONS

By the end of the nineteenth century state and elite attitudes toward religion were dramatically transformed as part of China's effort to join the community of modern nation-states. To many intellectuals, the formation of Chinese modernity necessitated a total reconstruction of culture and society, including religious traditions, whereas reformers viewed temple cults as hindrances to nation-building that merited destruction and/or expropriation of their assets. Moreover, the influence of Western concepts of religion (*zongjiao*) and superstition (*mixin*) prompted Chinese officials and intellectuals to reclassify the criteria for determining the legitimacy of religious traditions, which meant that by the Republican and PRC eras groups with coherent doctrinal and canonical traditions (Buddhism, Daoism, Catholicism, Protestantism, and Islam) gained acceptance as religions, whereas temple cults and their practices ended up labeled "superstitions" and targeted for repression. The category of superstition also encompassed practices such as geomancy and divination, and even state cult deities such as Wenchang and Guandi, thereby challenging the role of Confucianism as the religion of China's elites (Confucianism continued to occupy a prominent place in spirit-writing groups and redemptive societies, however).

The new classification systems spelled doom for Chinese communal religious traditions. Political leaders and intellectual elites implemented new policies, with religious organizations and specialists being forced to adapt, resist, or even reinvent themselves. It began with Kang Youwei's (1858–1927) memorial of July 10, 1898, which recom-

mended establishing Confucianism as China's national religion (*guojiao*), outlawing other religious institutions, and destroying all temples except those linked to the state cult. Kang's calls went largely unheeded, but beginning with the New Policies in 1901, increasing numbers of temples were turned into schools, police stations, post offices, and other government buildings, despite efforts by local elites to effect compromises whereby these edifices could be shared for dual usage. In addition, the termination of the state practice of granting titles to prominent local deities, as well as the abolition of state rituals in favor of Western-style ceremonies featuring flags and a national anthem, further served to decrease religion's power and prestige in Chinese public life.

Things turned even worse during the Nationalist anti-superstition campaigns of the late 1920s and 1930s, when the central government began to play an active role in the seizure and destruction of prominent sacred sites at the center of local political systems (such as City God temples). One significant piece of legislation was the Standards for Determining Temples and Shrines to be Destroyed or Maintained (*Shenci cunfei biaozhun*), according to which sacred sites belonging to authentic "religions" (particularly Buddhism and Daoism) and those dedicated to historical worthies (such as Confucius) were to be preserved, with the rest slated for elimination. The Nationalist government also levied taxes on temples, ritual items, and festivals, thereby bankrupting communal religious traditions already facing the devastating effects of that era's poverty, natural disasters, and warfare.

These policies marked a new level of state intrusion into local society, with officials attempting to gain control over the management of communal religious assets such as temples, not to mention related socioeconomic systems (irrigation, marketing, philanthropy). In areas where temple cults had been thoroughly blended into networks of power (notably southeastern China), elites and worshippers employed a wide range of tactics to resist the authorities, including rhetorical and symbolic challenges, legal action, and even acts of violence. However, throughout much of northern China, where religious life tended to be more loosely structured, the state proved far more effective at achieving its aims. Urban temples with conservative elites fared better than those that served as hotbeds of revolutionary activity.

At the same time, however, the destruction of temples hardly spelled the end of communal religious activities, because other movements that proved more adaptable to the vicissitudes of China's modernization efforts arose to take their place. This was especially true for redemptive societies that practiced spirit-writing and actively proselytized their teachings, including the Tongshanshe, Daoyuan, and Yiguandao. Like temple cults, these religious associations offered healing and ritual services, yet also professed aversion to superstition while emphasizing morality and body discipline in ways that conformed to state discourse. Interestingly, prior to its rise to power, the Chinese Communist Party (CCP) was willing to interact with rural religious groups based on a common agenda of resisting the intrusions of pro-Guomindang urban elites.

Under CCP rule, the state devoted unstinting efforts to reorganizing China's institutional religions along corporatist lines under the Religious Affairs Bureau of the United Front Department (Tongyi zhanxian gongzuobu zongjiao shi-wuju), vigorously cracking down on redemptive societies, reforming marital and mortuary customs, and extirpating temple cults by seizing their lands and wiping out elite patrons. During the Great Leap Forward and the Cultural Revolution (1966–1969) in particular, countless sacred sites were destroyed or desecrated, but some religious traditions persisted in the form of rumors claiming that the chaotic times people were experiencing were the result of divine retribution for abandoning worship of their gods. By the 1970s China's communal religious traditions had been systematically destroyed or forced underground, whereas those beliefs and practices that survived in Taiwan, Hong Kong, and overseas Chinese communities were viewed as little more than quaint remnants of a traditional culture that would soon wither in the face of rapid modernization. This was not to be.

RELIGIOUS REVIVAL

Beginning in the late 1970s, reform efforts in China contributed to a remarkable renewal of communal religious traditions on a scale that few had anticipated. Recent research has identified a number of factors underlying this renewal, including:

1. the importance of temple cults and their rituals in supporting traditional values, as well as their links to deeply rooted peasant organizations;

2. the importance of local elites who utilize temples and temple associations as a valuable political, economic, and symbolic resource, and who negotiate with the state to legitimize their local traditions;

3. the shift of some central government power to local governments; and

4. the impact of economic prosperity, which allowed temples to thrive on donations, including those deriving from the provision of ritual services, even if their lands had been confiscated.

Although nationwide statistics have yet to be compiled, fieldwork throughout China suggests that many areas average around one temple per every 400 persons, nearly identical to figures reported in 1900 (Goossaert and Palmer 2008, p. 141).

One of the most important changes to shape China's intellectual and official realms came in the early 1980s, when scholars were given the freedom to reconsider Karl Marx's comments on religion as the opium of the masses. In addition, a new set of regulations on religious affairs promulgated in 2005 raised the option of unaffiliated temples being allowed to register with the state, but the details of how such a policy might actually be implemented remain unclear. Another new development, the formation of an office for "popular beliefs" (*minjian xinyang*) under the policy development section of the State Administration of Religious Affairs, clearly suggests that the state is considering communal religious traditions as a distinct phenomenon meriting some degree of legitimation. The state also has begun to patronize temples that conform to its nationalist agenda, such as those that honor the Yellow Emperor (the mythical founder of the Chinese nation).

Globalization also has contributed to the renewal of China's religious life. On example of this is the state's decision to adopt UNESCO's guidelines and subsequently establish an administrative system for preserving Chinese forms of "intangible cultural heritage" (*fei wuzhi wenhua yichan*). This decision was enthusiastically welcomed by local officials and elites, who worked hard to legitimize communal religious traditions by applying for state recognition under this framework. There is also the fascinating case of the goddess Mazu, whose cult has become linked to a wide range of political agendas and identities on both sides of the Taiwan Straits.

China's religious revival is especially striking in light of the rapid urbanization that has swept the land, because state and private developers have ended up demolishing numerous sacred sites and erasing urban communal memories. As a result, many Chinese urbanites tend to encounter religion in state-sponsored sacred sites that double as tourist destinations, and in museums. Nonetheless, people remain interested in religious activities, especially vegetarianism, self-cultivation (including *qigong*), and rites performed at private shrines, and are able to learn about these subjects through visiting bookstores and surfing the Web.

Another, different form of religious revival has swept through Taiwan, Hong Kong, and the overseas Chinese populations. Surprisingly, economic growth and technological development have not resulted in the decline of religious practice; on the contrary, many educated men and women who use the Internet on a daily basis feel no qualms about practicing religion (in fact, most large religious organizations and temples now have their own Web sites). Religion continues to play an integral role in individual, family, and communal life, and temple cults have retained their importance as sites for daily worship, community service, and massive festivals, while also addressing more modern concerns by, for example, promoting the worship of aborted or miscarried fetuses.

SEE ALSO *Falun Gong; Family; Fengshui; Qigong; Religious Policy.*

BIBLIOGRAPHY

Chau, Adam Yuet. *Miraculous Response: Doing Popular Religion in Contemporary China.* Stanford, CA: Stanford University Press, 2006.

Clart, Philip A., and Charles B. Jones, eds. *Religion in Modern Taiwan: Tradition and Innovation in a Changing Society.* Honolulu: University of Hawaii Press, 2003.

DeBernardi, Jean. *Rites of Belonging: Memory, Modernity, and Identity in a Malaysian Chinese Community.* Stanford, CA: Stanford University Press, 2004.

Duara, Prasenjit. Knowledge and Power in the Discourse of Modernity: The Campaigns against Popular Religion in Early Twentieth-Century China. *Journal of Asian Studies* 50 (1991): 67–83.

DuBois, Thomas David. *The Sacred Village: Social Change and Religious Life in Rural North China.* Honolulu: University of Hawaii Press, 2004.

Fan Lizhu, James D. Whitehead, and Evelyn Eaton Whitehead. Fate and Fortune: Popular Religion and Moral Capital in Shenzhen. *Journal of Chinese Religions* 32 (2004): 83–100.

Goossaert, Vincent. 1898: The Beginning of the End for Chinese Religion? *Journal of Asian Studies* 65, 2 (2006): 307–336.

Goossaert, Vincent, and David Palmer. *The Religious Question in Modern China. A History, 1898–2008.* Unpublished book manuscript, 2008.

Katz, Paul R., and Murray A. Rubinstein, eds. *Religion and the Formation of Taiwanese Identities.* New York: Palgrave Macmillan, 2003.

Lang, Graeme, and Lars Ragvald. *The Rise of a Refugee God. Hong Kong's Wong Tai Sin.* Hong Kong: Oxford University Press, 1993.

Madsen, Richard. *Democracy's Dharma: Religious Renaissance and Political Development in Taiwan.* Berkeley: University of California Press, 2007.

Moskowitz, Marc L. *The Haunting Fetus: Abortion, Sexuality, and the Spirit World in Taiwan.* Honolulu: University of Hawaii Press, 2001.

Nedostup, Rebecca. Ritual Competition and the Modernizing Nation-State. In *Chinese Religiosities: Afflictions of Modernity and State-Formation*, ed. Mayfair Mei-hui Yang, 87–112. Berkeley: University of California Press, 2008.

Overmyer, Daniel L., ed. Religion in China Today. *The China Quarterly Special Issues*, New Series, No. 3. Cambridge: Cambridge University Press, 2003.

Smith, Steven A. Talking Toads and Chinless Ghosts: The Politics of "Superstitious" Rumors in the People's Republic of China. *American Historical Review* 111, 2 (April 2006): 405–427.

Watson, James L., and Evelyn S. Rawski, eds. *Death Ritual in Late Imperial and Modern China.* Berkeley: University of California Press, 1988.

Yang Fenggang. Between Secularist Ideology and Desecularizing Reality: The Birth and Growth of Religious Research in China. *Sociology of Religion* 65, 2 (2004): 101–119.

Paul R. Katz

POPULATION POLICY

This entry contains the following:

OVERVIEW

After the founding of the People's Republic of China in 1949, Chinese population policy started from the premise of severe population losses during the preceding era and the need for high population numbers in order to defend and build up the country. Polemics against the concept of birth control were further buttressed by the traditional Marxist critique of Malthusianism. With a strong statement in 1949, Mao Zedong acted as the herald of the pronatalist position.

Doubts began to surface in 1954, when China's first population census yielded larger population numbers than were expected. This triggered concerns about the sufficiency of the country's resources for feeding, clothing, employing, and schooling the growing population. The ban on contraceptives, abortions, and sterilizations was relaxed progressively during the following years. The policy change culminated in the first birth planning campaign of 1954 to 1958, which was largely limited to the large coastal cities. This campaign relied strictly on educational approaches, avoided any coercive measures, and propagated measures such as late marriage, contraception, and birth spacing. It was accompanied by efforts to restrict rural-urban migration to the big cities, to replace the free urban labor market with work allocation, and to limit the expansion of urban schools. Another campaign tried to redirect the migration streams to land reclamation areas and scarcely populated borderlands. Most of these policies were terminated in 1958 by the Great Leap Forward. Prominent proponents of birth planning were dismissed and silenced; urban areas registered a huge wave of new in-migrants.

Another by-product of the first population census was the official recognition and designation of national minorities, which were counted as distinct entities for the first time in Chinese history. This altered the ethnodemographic map of the country and served as the basis for establishing autonomous nationality areas. But once again, the Great

Passengers lining up for train tickets, Guiyang, Guizhou province, February 3, 2006. Concerns about the impact of unchecked population growth began in the late 1950s, as the Chinese government began estimating optimal population levels for the country. Fears about exceeding these targets have led to laws designed to limit population growth, such as one child per family policies designed to lower national birthrates. **AP IMAGES**

Leap produced a policy reversal, as prominority policies were followed by assimilationist pressures and drives against local nationalism. Many minority nationals found it prudent to claim Han Chinese nationality instead of clinging to minority status, a stance that was only reversed with the return to prominority policies in 1980.

The second birth planning campaign was waged from 1962 to 1966 in reaction to the economic crisis produced by the Great Leap. It coincided with a major drive of deurbanization that tried to rid the cities of recent in-migrants, to promote the construction of small towns, and to resettle unemployed urban youth in the countryside. Starting in 1962, peasants received permits for permanent migration to the cities only in exceptional cases. Birth planning gradually spread from the cities to the densely populated rural areas and started to include some punitive elements. Propaganda focused on the need to limit child-bearing to two or at most three children per woman. Abortions were completely liberalized in 1963, and sterilizations were performed free of charge. But once again the campaigns were interrupted by political turmoil. During the heyday

of the Cultural Revolution from 1967 to 1970, birth planning ceased in most parts of the country.

The rustication program for urban youth had been resurrected in late 1968, when its economic motives coalesced with the wish to discipline unruly Red Guards, to reeducate them in the villages, or to send them off for land reclamation, construction, and settlement projects in faraway border areas. With few exceptions, years of rustication became mandatory for everybody. Although the campaign at first could still muster some of the ideological fervor of the Cultural Revolution, later there were huge implementation problems and disillusionment. Large oscillations in the rustication numbers testified to wavering attitudes of the leadership and to a rising tide of return to the cities. In 1980 the program was terminated altogether. Ever since, migration controls for the urban areas have been further relaxed, though not abolished. Various new regulations in the mid-1980s permitted peasant migration to the small towns and cities under renewable provisional registration status.

The fortunes of birth planning were different, as the tightening of goals and instruments persisted after the

MA YINCHU

Ma Yinchu, one of the most influential Chinese economists of the twentieth century, is regarded as the father of China's post-1978 population policy. He also anticipated essential aspects of Deng Xiaoping's new development policy as early as the mid-1940s. During Ma's career as a scholar and adviser to the Guomindang (GMD) and the Chinese Communist Party (CCP) governments, he was an example of the best Chinese tradition of uniting intellectual brilliance and moral uprightness. Born on June 24, 1882, his life spanned a full century—he died in 1982—enjoying great and universal respect as the honorary president of Peking University.

Ma was born in Shaoxing, Zhejiang Province. After a personal conflict with his father about his future career, Ma pursued the way of learning independently. Without any financial support, he studied mining and metallurgy at Beiyang University and won a government scholarship for study in the United States. He left China in 1906 and returned in 1915 after studying economics at Yale University and earning a Ph.D. from Columbia University. In the 1920s, he was active as a founder of the Shanghai College of Commerce and the China Society of Economics. In 1927 he started his political career as a member of the Zhejiang Provincial government and of the Nanjing Legislative Council. During the Anti-Japanese War (1937–1945), he moved to Chongqing and became president of the College of Economics.

During this period, Ma began to sharply criticize the Nationalist economic policy, exposing the rampant corruption, the inflationary financing of the state, and the monopolization of the economy under four families—those of Chiang Kai-shek (Jiang Jieshi), T. V. Soong (Song Ziwen), H. H. Kung (Kong Xiangxi), and the Chen brothers (Chen Li-fu [Chen Lifu] and Chen Kuo-fu [Chen Guofu]). Between 1940 and 1942, Ma was held under house arrest. From that time onward, he enjoyed the protection of the CCP and especially Zhou Enlai. After challenging GMD leaders again in Nanjing and facing even the threat of murder, Ma was secretly transported to Beijing via Hong Kong in 1948. After the founding of the People's Republic in 1949, he became an independent member of the People's Consultative Conference.

In the 1950s, Ma served in many influential positions in academia and politics. He became president of both Zhejiang and Peking universities and vice chairman of the Central Committee of Finance and Economics. As a delegate, he was invited to give a speech at the Meeting of the National People's Congress in June 1957, in which he famously explicated his theories about population and growth. With the subsequent radicalization of Maoist economic policies, he faced Mao Zedong's personal wrath. The main bone of contention was his vigorous defense of birth planning, which he presented as the "new population theory" (*xin renkou lun*). This opinion clashed with Mao's emerging view that strong population growth would support China's rise, even though the Third Plenum of the Eighth Central Committee had adopted birth planning as a part of the Twelve-Year Agricultural Development Plan. After two years of struggle, Ma was finally removed from all positions; only Zhou Enlai's continuing protection sheltered him from the worst. On July 26, 1979, the CCP Central Committee expressed formal apologies to him, explicitly stating that historical developments had proven his view to be correct.

As a trained economist, Ma advocated an economic policy that would foster growth by boosting the investment rate and by controlling the birth rate of the population. In this sense, his approach was a neoclassical one, and he explicitly denied the relevance of Keynesian theory for China. Ma highlighted the crucial role of the rural sector for Chinese economic development. Based on principled philosophical views on the circularity of all relations in the economy, Ma proposed that the development of light industry would be the most appropriate strategy for China, because light industry relies on agricultural inputs and allows for high profit rates. The positive returns on rural incomes would increase rural demand, which in turn would support a further growth of production. Thus, Ma welcomed the economic conception of the "new democracy," in which free competitive markets would reign and private entrepreneurship would enjoy protection. In 1945 he described the "Chinese way" to prosperity as being midway between Soviet planning and American capitalism. Only certain core sectors of the economy, such as parts of the railway system, military technology, and large-scale hydropower stations, should be controlled by the government. Equal opportunities for Chinese farmers would be key to the economic development of China. After 1978, many of these ideas became an integral part of Chinese economic reforms.

Carsten Herrmann-Pillath

death of Mao Zedong. Birth planning was revived in 1971 and 1972 with the third birth planning campaign. It integrated population targets into the economic plans, and introduced strict late-marriage requirements, free distribution of contraceptives, and a general two-child limit, which was enforced with increasing sanctions. This time, the campaign engulfed all rural areas, and only the national minorities remained exempt. After 1979 and 1980 the campaign developed into the one-child policy, which is viewed as an escape from the population predicament but controversial both inside and outside China. Six failed attempts to replace it with the earlier two-child rule can be documented. Even though an increasing number of second-child exemptions have been granted since the mid-1980s, the policy remains in force. United Nations population programs aim at turning it into a less intrusive version of reproductive health care. This is aided by recent socioeconomic developments, which lower the demand for children and ease some of the tensions caused by the policy.

SEE ALSO *Family; Social Policy Programs.*

BIBLIOGRAPHY

Banister, Judith. *China's Changing Population.* Stanford, CA: Stanford University Press, 1987.

Greenhalgh, Susan, and Edwin A. Winckler. *Governing China's Population: From Leninist to Neoliberal Biopolitics.* Stanford, CA: Stanford University Press, 2005.

Scharping, Thomas. *Birth Control in China 1949–2000: Population Policy and Demographic Development.* London and New York: Routledge, 2003.

Zhao Zhongwei and Guo Fei, eds. *Transition and Challenge: China's Population at the Beginning of the 21st Century.* Oxford: Oxford University Press, 2007.

Thomas Scharping

DEMOGRAPHIC TRENDS
SINCE 1800

China experienced rapid population growth during the second half of the eighteenth century and reached a peak population of 430 million around 1850 (see Figure 1). This was also a period when China conducted nationwide population numerations. After 1850, a century of civil wars, dynastic change, and armed invasion slowed population growth in China. The first national census took place in 1953 and showed that China had a population of 582.6 million. With nearly universal marriage, fertility of five to six births per woman, and a dramatic decline in infant mortality during the 1950s and 1960s, the population grew rapidly. From 1964 to 1974, the population increased 200 million in a decade. Although the total fertility rate declined rapidly during the 1970s, the population in China has

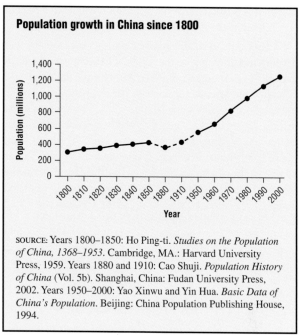

Population growth in China since 1800

SOURCE: Years 1800–1850: Ho Ping-ti. *Studies on the Population of China, 1368–1953.* Cambridge, MA.: Harvard University Press, 1959. Years 1880 and 1910: Cao Shuji. *Population History of China* (Vol. 5b). Shanghai, China: Fudan University Press, 2002. Years 1950–2000: Yao Xinwu and Yin Hua. *Basic Data of China's Population.* Beijing: China Population Publishing House, 1994.

Figure 1

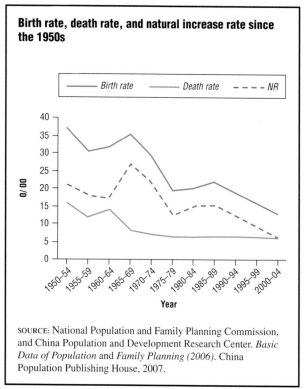

Birth rate, death rate, and natural increase rate since the 1950s

SOURCE: National Population and Family Planning Commission, and China Population and Development Research Center. *Basic Data of Population* and *Family Planning (2006).* China Population Publishing House, 2007.

Figure 2

continued to grow with great momentum. The population surpassed 1 billion in 1982 and had hit 1.3 billion by early 2005. Even though the rate of growth has been slowing down, it is predicted that the population will reach a peak of 1.5 billion in the mid-2030s.

There are no reliable national statistics on mortality and fertility in China before the 1950s. One estimate is a birth rate of 41 per thousand, a death rate of 33 per thousand, and a natural increase rate of about 8 per thousand in relatively peaceful rural China from 1929 to 1931. From China's first fertility survey in 1982, infant mortality rate was estimated at about 200 per thousand from 1945 to 1949. The birth rates, death rates, and natural increase rates since 1950 show a clear demographic transition in China in the last half of the twentieth century (see Figure 2). Life expectancy is estimated to have been below 40 years of age in the 1940s; it was 75.25 for women and 70.83 for men in 2005.

Zheng Zhenzhen

POPULATION CENSUSES

Censuses provide the most reliable population figures for China. Their history clearly reflects the changing agenda of the state, the problems met in extending their reach, and the changing social setting in which they operate. After two failed attempts, in 1910 to 1911 and 1928 to 1929, the census of July 1, 1953 was the first successful modern population census in Chinese history. Actual census work continued into 1954, and the official results were published in November that year. They were limited to a brief bulletin with highly aggregated data at national and provincial levels. Further figures leaked through during the 1950s, but the detailed population structure by age and sex was released twenty-eight years later. The census covered age, sex, nationality, place of residence, and relationship to the head of household, and yielded a population total of 583 million. Its quality is considered to be good, with deficiencies in regard to patchy implementation in Tibet and certain other minority areas.

The second census, of July 1, 1964, was conducted in secrecy. Due to the sensitive implications of scanty births and surplus deaths during the Great Leap Forward, the results were published only in 1982. In addition to the items included in 1953, the questionnaire covered also educational level, occupation, and class status. Because standardized categories for the last two items were lacking, they were never tabulated. As in all later censuses, definitional change affected some other items. The population total for the Chinese mainland was 695 million, about 50 million less than would have been plausible under normal circumstances.

There were large improvements in the third census, of July 1, 1982. It involved foreign experts, introduced computer technology, and received unprecedented publicity. Detailed results in book form became available in 1985. They contained information from the much enlarged ques-

tionnaire that now included items on registration status, sector of employment, type of nonemployment, marital status, type and size of household, children ever born, and births and deaths during the last year. This reflected the increasing importance of employment policy and birth control since the start of the reform period. Among all Chinese censuses, the quality of the 1982 count (1.008 billion) is considered best. Still, retrospective analyses demonstrate underregistration of births due to birth control evasion.

Quality deteriorated in the fourth census, of July 1, 1990, which registered 1.134 billion people but struggled with the difficulties of defining and counting China's growing flood of migrants. Moreover, there are signs of underregistration of children younger than nine, by an average 6 percent. The census questionnaire was expanded again, particularly in regard to registration status, former place of residence, and migration reasons. With the issuing of a three-volume compendium of national census results and a series of provincial materials in eighty-five volumes, access to information improved dramatically.

The most recent and most problematic population count was the fifth census, of November 1, 2000. It gave a total population of 1.266 billion, but suffered from serious defects in the registration of child cohorts, the full extent of which has not been ascertained. Numbers for migrant age groups are defective, too. The census questionnaire was again enhanced by refining the migration items and adding a battery of fifteen questions on private housing. It was divided into a short form for all persons and a long form administered to a 10 percent sample. The census implementation suffered from inadequate funding and personnel, as well as from bureaucratic conflicts and popular resistance to breaches of privacy.

BIBLIOGRAPHY

Banister, Judith. *China's Changing Population*. Stanford, CA: Stanford University Press, 1987.

Scharping, Thomas. *Birth Control in China 1949–2000: Population Policy and Demographic Development*. London and New York: Routledge, 2003.

Zhao Zhongwei and Guo Fei, eds. *Transition and Challenge: China's Population at the Beginning of the 21st Century*. Oxford: Oxford University Press, 2007.

Thomas Scharping

POPULATION GROWTH PROJECTIONS

Population projections serve to calculate either likely or desirable population numbers. They can provide figures for future population structure and be split up into a number of variants to demonstrate the effects of different political, socioeconomic, and demographic scenarios.

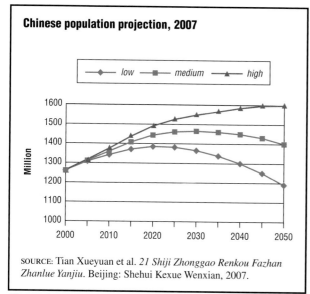

Chinese population projection, 2007

SOURCE: Tian Xueyuan et al. *21 Shiji Zhonggao Renkou Fazhan Zhanlue Yanjiu.* Beijing: Shehui Kexue Wenxian, 2007.

Figure 1

Chinese population projections began in 1957, when debates about the sufficiency of the country's resources began, and social scientists calculated an optimum population of 700 to 800 million, a figure that is still cited. If instead the supportable maximum number is used as a yardstick, the figure swells to more than double that size. Growing sophistication has led to the awareness that ceilings depend on factors such as ethical criteria and welfare standards, economic patterns, and technological progress. Nevertheless, the projections testify to the continuing anxiety over the detrimental effects of high population numbers. The decline in births since the mid-1990s has shifted attention to the future growth of the elderly population.

Although problems with implementing birth planning policy during the 1980s led to upward revisions of the projected population total for 2050, that number has shrunk again since the late 1990s. The precise figure depends not only on future birth policies but also on the social effects of China's rapid economic growth. The most important variables are the fate of the birth planning policy (*jihua shengyu*, often referred to as the "one-child policy"), the pace of urbanization, the rising life expectancy, changes in lifestyles, and the evolution of the social security regime. Most medium variants of current projections reckon with a likely population of 1.4 billion in midcentury, with a life expectancy of seventy-eight and a 75 percent urban population. Whereas the share of the young population will decline to 16 percent, the share of people aged sixty-five and older will reach 23 percent, with some 35 percent in the urban areas. The working-age population will start to shrink after 2025. Calculations are hampered by some uncertainty about current and expected fertility levels.

BIBLIOGRAPHY

Scharping, Thomas. *Birth Control in China 1949–2000: Population Policy and Demographic Development.* London and New York: Routledge, 2003.

Tian Xueyuan et al. *21 Shiji Zhongguo Renkou Fazhan Zhanlue Yanjiu.* Beijing, Shehui Kexue Wenxian, 2007.

Thomas Scharping

BIRTH-PLANNING POLICY

The Chinese government has called on Chinese couples to limit their families to a single child since the beginning of the 1980s. The policy has been modified in various ways, and it is claimed that exemptions now mean that over half of all couples are allowed to have a second child. However, the government remains strongly committed to birth planning. China has a population of about 1.3 billion people, 20 percent of the global total, and has pledged to keep it under 1.36 billion by 2010 and under 1.45 billion by 2020.

Chinese policy documents tend to use the expression "birth planning" (*jihua shengyu*) rather than "family planning" (*jiating jihua*), reflecting a view of birth limitation as a national project rather than a private matter. Other governments have, of course, introduced family planning in the interests of reducing population growth, but none has adopted a policy as strict as China's.

THE DEVELOPMENT OF THE POLICY

China experienced a steep decline in the death rate in the 1950s due to the establishment of civil order and of a comparatively effective health system focusing on preventive measures. The birth rate remained high, and according to census data the population grew from 583 million in 1953 to just over one billion by 1982.

The need for birth control was a contested issue in the 1950s. Arguing that China's population could be an asset if everyone was productive, Mao Zedong rebuked the experts for seeing people as "mouths not hands." Leading Communist women, however, wanted contraception to be available, and planners were concerned about the difficulty of feeding China's huge population, especially after the results of the 1953 census became available. By 1957 Mao himself had begun to speak of the need for birth planning. In the early 1960s, the government introduced a "planned births" campaign backed up by exhibitions and meetings. The campaign was disrupted by the Cultural Revolution from 1966, but reintroduced with the promotion of the "two-child family" as an ideal in the 1970s. The slogan "late, spaced, few" was used to sum up the new demands: couples should delay the birth of their first child, they should leave a long gap before the second, and they should stop at two.

After Mao's death in 1976, there was concern that hard-won gains in agricultural growth had been cancelled out by population growth, with the result that by the late 1970s per capita output of grain was hardly greater than it had been in 1957. China had to feed almost a quarter of the world's population on only 7 percent of the world's cultivated land. The shortage of cultivable land severely limited the potential for agricultural growth. The age structure of China's population was also identified as a threat. According to the 1982 census, 45 percent of the population was under twenty, and nearly two-thirds were under thirty. Demographers working with computer-modeled projections warned that China's population of one billion would double within less than half a century if each woman averaged three children. The policy response was the one-child family rule, first discussed in 1978 and implemented with increasing severity from 1980.

ONE-CHILD REGULATIONS

Although the general principle of one child per family is national policy, the national birth-planning law that now underpins it was not agreed upon until December 2001. In the 1980s and 1990s, the provinces and many of the big cities produced their own regulations, so that local implementation could be modified for local circumstances. However, though they varied in the details, these regulations were broadly similar. All couples were asked to have only one child unless they fell into certain exempt categories. These usually include ethnic minorities, people living in the border areas, returned overseas Chinese, those whose first child was handicapped and would not be able to work, and parents who themselves were both an only child. The most important exception, which became general in regulations for rural areas after 1986, was that peasant couples whose first child was a girl could have a second child.

The regulations encompass a range of incentives and penalties through which the policy is enforced. Parents who apply for a birth-permission certificate and promise to have only one child receive a small monthly allowance and have privileged access to housing, health care, and schooling. There are penalties for "out-of-plan births," including births to parents under the age for legal marriage (set at twenty for women and twenty-two for men) and second or subsequent births for which there has been no permission. The severity of the penalty increases with the parity of the child. State employees who defy the policy may have 10 percent or more of their salaries withheld for fourteen to sixteen years to represent the supposed costs to the state of the additional child. Others pay large fines. Medical fees for the birth and subsequent health and educational costs fall wholly upon the parents. The state produced extensive publicity materials to explain and justify the policy, arguing that rapid population growth threatened living standards and compromised economic growth.

IMPLEMENTATION AND ACCEPTANCE OF THE POLICY

The one-child policy encountered resistance, especially in the countryside, where children are still seen as a source of prosperity and security. Sons are traditionally preferred to daughters because they remain members of their natal families on marriage, support their parents in old age, and their sons carry on the family name. By contrast, a daughter marries out of her natal family, cares for her parents-in-law, and cannot supply heirs to her natal family. A daughter may be loved and welcomed if a couple can also have a son, but where the one-child rule is strictly enforced, the birth of a girl is perceived as a disaster if it means her parents lose the chance to produce a boy.

According to Chinese statistics, boys increasingly outnumber girls among registered newborns in both rural and urban areas. Several factors are responsible for the imbalance. Some parents may simply not register female births in order not to be barred from having further children. The practice of female infanticide is difficult to quantify but certainly reappeared after the introduction of the one-child rule. However, it is widely acknowledged that sex-selective abortion is increasingly implicated in producing the deficit of girls. Although illegal, the practice is clearly widespread. The increasing availability of technology to determine the sex of the fetus has coincided with the worsening sex ratio. The international norm is 105 to 106 male births to 100 female ones. Chinese census figures for children under one year old indicate that there were 107.6 boys for every 100 girls in 1982, 112 in 1990, and 118 by 2000. The ratio is much worse for second and subsequent parity births than for first births, reflecting the fact that many parents will bring up a firstborn girl but are determined that subsequent children should be male. Infanticide and the abandonment of girl babies forced the government to concede as early as 1986 that rural parents whose firstborn was female could have a second child. However, the distorted sex ratio among children continues to give rise to government concern.

The one-child policy is better accepted in urban areas, although even here the sex ratio is unbalanced. However, as accommodation, child care, and education have become increasingly expensive, and with dual-career families the norm and consumerism transforming people's aspirations, many urban couples now only want one child and may be satisfied with a daughter. They lavish time, attention, and money on their single children, investing in the future through them. This consequence of reduced family size fits in well with the state advocacy of "reducing the quantity and enhancing the quality" of the population. On the other hand, there has been concern about the likely character of a generation without brothers and sisters. It is often claimed that these singletons are spoilt, selfish, and lacking in social skills. Another worry is that

A young child waits as her mother meets with a family-planning specialist, Hebei province, January 29, 1997. In 1980, the Communist government began instituting population controls on a large segment of the country, limiting the number of children a married couple could produce. Government planners allow for one child in most urban families, with rural residents often permitted a second child if a daughter is born first. **AP IMAGES**

the enormous pressure on children to succeed academically may have some negative consequences.

Acceptance is more difficult in the countryside where the economic need for sons is greatest, social-welfare provision is limited, and the system of patrilocal marriage leads peasants to see sons as a guarantee of prosperity and old-age security. Conflict has been reduced by the concession that allows rural couples a second child if their first is a girl. However, many other aspects of birth-planning policy still clash with rural traditions and aspirations. The minimum ages for marriage of twenty-two for a man and twenty for a woman are high by rural standards. Couples whose circumstances qualify them to have a second child are still required to seek permission to do so and must leave a four-year gap between births. Those who have had a second child are supposed to undergo sterilization or employ an approved method of contraception.

Local officials, who may themselves be fined or demoted if they fail to meet targets set for their area concerning the number of single-child families, births, and contraceptive use,

are often tempted to use coercion. There have been many reports of women who have an "out-of-plan" pregnancy being forced to abort. On the other hand, village officials may sympathize with the people they are supposed to police, and ignore infringements of the regulations. Since the death of Mao in 1976, the state has relaxed its control over many areas of the economy, cultural life, and even politics. Yet through the single-child family policy, it has intruded into what is normally the most private area of life.

Birth planning has not brought Chinese women reproductive freedom. Rather they are subject to conflicting pressures from the state and their families over the control of their reproduction. A woman who gives birth to a girl when a boy is desired may be blamed. Women bear the main burden of contraception and sterilization. Their menstrual cycles may even be officially monitored at their place of work. On the other hand, birth-planning policy has brought them some benefits. Even in the poorest and most remote parts of the Chinese countryside they have access to the contraceptive knowledge and supplies that are still denied to women in much of the developing and even the developed world.

CHINA'S CHANGING FERTILITY

The total fertility rate in China, an indicator of the number of children each woman may be expected to give birth to, declined from around 6.0 in the 1950s and 1960s to 4.51 in 1973, 2.19 in 1984, and 1.7 to 1.8 since the mid-1990s, an extraordinary achievement in what is still overwhelmingly a low-income country with a large rural population. There is, of course, considerable variation. Fertility in the urban areas and in the coastal provinces is much lower than in less-developed central and western provinces. National birth rates increasingly resemble those of a developed country.

The factors that contributed to this decline no doubt include those associated with demographic transition all over the world: increased urbanization, rising living standards, improved literacy rates especially among women, and higher female labor participation rates. It is impossible to be certain how much of the fertility decline can be attributed to the one-child policy. Birth rates had begun to fall in the 1970s when the state was already advocating birth planning but before the introduction of the draconian one-child limit. It is clear, however, that the state's promotion of small-family goals, its constant pressure on the population to accept these goals, and its huge investment in making contraception generally available, have contributed to China's extraordinarily rapid fertility reduction. Most urban families now have one child while the majority of rural families have two, but the vast majority of couples use contraception for a large part of their reproductive lives, and even in the countryside, families with more than three children are rare.

The rapid fertility decline has affected the age structure of the population. It is a mark of the success of China's birth-planning policy that the state must now be concerned with the problems that will arise with the graying of the population as the proportion of the elderly rises.

The Chinese government claims that birth planning has helped prevent 400 million births and has aided the nation's rapid economic development. Internationally, there has been widespread controversy over China's birth-planning policy. It has been condemned, especially in the United States, by campaigners against abortion and also by those who regard reproductive freedom as a basic human right. Others argue that there can be no absolute right to reproductive freedom where it threatens the nation's development goals and the environment, especially in an age when global warming has become a major concern. They applaud the Chinese success in lowering fertility and raising living standards.

SEE ALSO *Family: Infanticide; Family: One-Child Policy; Sex Ratio.*

BIBLIOGRAPHY

Croll, Elisabeth, Delia Davin, and Penny Kane, eds. *China's One-child Family Policy.* London: Macmillan, 1985.

Greenhalgh, Susan, and Edwin A. Winckler. *Governing China's Population: From Leninist to Neoliberal Biopolitics.* Stanford, CA: Stanford University Press, 2005.

Milwertz, Cecilia. *Accepting Population Control: Urban Chinese Women and the One-child Family Policy.* Richmond, U.K.: Curzon, 1997.

Scharping, Thomas. *Birth Control in China, 1949–2000: Population Policy and Demographic Development.* London and New York: RoutledgeCurzon, 2003.

White, Tyrene. *China's Longest Campaign: Birth Planning in the People's Republic of China, 1949–2005.* Ithaca, NY: Cornell University Press, 1994.

Delia Davin

POVERTY

Throughout most of Chinese history, the majority of Chinese have lived in poverty. As the hundreds of famines that have killed millions of Chinese attest, Chinese poverty has often been absolute, that is, characterized by a lack of the very material resources needed to sustain life and maintain health. However, poverty is most often defined relatively: being materially disadvantaged vis-à-vis the standards of one's society—for example, official poverty lines. Poverty was first defined by the government of the People's Republic of China (PRC) when it set criteria to define "poor peasants." In this entry, *poverty* will generally refer simply to severe levels of material deprivation.

POVERTY IN IMPERIAL CHINA

Preindustrial, agriculture-based regimes such as China typically extracted surplus from the agricultural producers, leaving them just enough to reproduce the labor force while the elite lived in relative luxury. Another characteristic of such regimes was that the major means by which peasant families could get ahead was to increase labor power, in the form of sons, with land resources. A 1930s study of three Hebei villages, where conditions would not have differed significantly from those in the nineteenth century and earlier, shows a direct correlation between family size and family income, higher-income families having ten or more members (Brandt and Sands 1992, p. 196). Together with natural fertility, this maintained high levels of population.

This situation created a Chinese population that historically was usually at, just under, or sometimes slightly over carrying capacity. The first Chinese census in 2 CE set the population at 60 million, where it remained for many centuries, falling in the wake of war or severe natural disaster, then increasing back to carrying capacity within a generation or two. A Nanjing University study found that

Poor residents of Hong Kong, renting sleeping space in a communal room, August 9, 2007. To escape widespread poverty in rural areas, many Chinese migrated to larger cities, hoping to take advantage of China's economic progress at the turn of the twenty-first century. However, many individuals remain poor, despite efforts by the Communist government to elevate the standard of living for all citizens.
© ALEX HOFFORD/EPA/CORBIS

between 108 BCE and 1911 CE there were 1,828 famines in China, almost one per year (Mallory 1926, p. 1). Carrying capacity increased twice during this period, first to 100 million in the twelfth century when wheat, sorghum, and Champa rice were introduced, and again in the sixteenth century when China received potatoes, sweet potatoes, and maize from the New World, which could be sown in previously uncultivable areas. Following the latter development, person-cultivated land ratios fell from 7.92 *shimu* per person (1 *shimu* equals 693.6 square meters) in 1657 to 3.3 in 1776, 3.19 in 1800, and 2.7 in 1848 (Zhao Gang 1986, p. 89).

By 1850, the population was estimated at an unsustainable 430 million, which brought on Malthusian checks, such as war, starvation, and disease. Already in 1796, the White Lotus Rebellion occurred in an economically marginal area of Sichuan, Hubei, and Shaanxi. The nineteenth century saw much more serious unrest, including the Taiping, Nian, and Miao uprisings, plus many smaller bandit uprisings and rice riots (Xiao Gongquan 1960). A major factor in all of these was hunger caused by too many people on too little land.

According to Edwin Moise, by 1850 the land-person ratio in China had reached such a level that,

> Mobility for individual men and for families was predominantly downward...the families at the bottom of the economic scale tended to die out. The poorest men often were unable to have children [and] any children they did have were rather likely to die young. [Thus] the poorest 15 percent of the men in one generation could not be the children of the poorest 15 percent in the preceding generation....They had to be the children of parents farther up the economic scale....The average Chinese man was significantly poorer than his father. (Moise 1977, p. 4)

There were no systematic poverty-alleviation measures in dynastic China. However, well aware that hungry people could threaten stability, governments had for centuries instituted "ever-normal" granaries to supply relief grain, and utilized price controls and other measures to prevent speculation, particularly in the wake of disasters.

Moreover, the Qing code required that magistrates provide "'sufficient maintenance and protection' to all 'poor destitute widowers and widows, fatherless children, and the helpless and infirm.'" The code also established "a penalty of 60 strokes of the bamboo for any magistrate found derelict in this responsibility" (Rowe 1989, p. 100).

During emergencies such as the North China famine (1876–1879), charitable donations from merchants and gentry were common. There were also poorhouses (*puji-tang*) and orphanages, originally private ventures but gradually mandated by the emperor (Rowe 1989, pp. 100–103). Buddhists established soup kitchens (*zhouchang*) and provided lodgings to the poor, and foreign missionaries were a third source of relief, their generosity and sacrifice earning even the respect of initially hostile officials (Bohr 1972). These measures, taken together, were piecemeal compared to the number of needy. However, the Qing government had become corrupt and inept by the nineteenth century. Officials neglected infrastructure, such as flood control, and let the emergency granaries become empty. Such actions or inactions resulted in more frequent natural disasters and exacerbated the level of suffering when disasters happened.

Other factors also contributed to nineteenth-century Chinese poverty. Wars with Western powers reduced the government's financial capacity to prevent or alleviate disasters, and internal rebellions caused great damage to crops. The drain of silver to pay for imported opium inflated the value of silver, resulting in a de facto devaluation of the copper coinage ordinary people used. This, in effect, raised people's taxes, which they had to pay in silver, causing further emiseration. And, from 1853, the *likin* (*lijin*) tax increased the cost of transport, which depressed the entire rural economy.

POVERTY IN REPUBLICAN CHINA

The fall of the Qing dynasty and the dynastic system in 1911 changed China significantly, but the major change to the condition of the peasantry was due to armed conflict. Between 1911 and the Communist takeover in 1949, China suffered thirty years of warfare that included battles between warlord armies over territory, the Northern Expedition leading to the establishment of the Nationalist government in Nanjing, the extermination campaigns against the Communists, the deadly war against the Japanese (1937–1945), and the resumption of the civil war from 1946 to 1949. Aside from the destruction caused by the battles themselves, marauding armies often confiscated crops and forcibly conscripted men, leaving the peasants with no resources. Moreover, competing warlords taxed the peasants, sometimes many years in advance.

In the first half of the twentieth century, Western, often Christian, organizations and local researchers carried out numerous studies of China's agricultural conditions and the lives of its peasants, providing greater understanding of

Farm sizes based on survey of fifty million farms, 1920

Size of farm	Percentage
under 10 mu	36%
10–29 mu	26%
30–49 mu	25%
50–99 mu	10%
100 mu or more	6%

1 mu = 0.0667 hectares

SOURCE: Tawney, Richard H. *Land and Labour in China.* New York: Harcourt Brace, 1932, pp. 38-40.

Table 1

the causes of Chinese poverty and quantitative indications of its depth. As Table 1 demonstrates, the major problem was tiny farm size.

Families with 20 *mu* (1 *mu* equals 0.0667 hectares) were middle peasants, and those with 100 *mu* were rich peasants (Huang Zongzhi 1985, p. 109). In Ding County (Hebei), 55 percent of farms were under 4 *mu* (0.267 hectares) and just over 7 percent were above 10 *mu* (0.667 hectares). In the north, where wheat is the staple, a family of five needed 1.88 hectares (28 *mu*) to meet basic food needs, but 55 percent of families had no more than 0.6 hectares (9 *mu*) (Mallory 1926, p. 13). A Department of Agriculture survey found that close to half of China's peasant families lacked sufficient land even to provide sufficient food, let alone other needs. John Buck noted in 1926 that "the small incomes reduce most farmers and their families to a mere subsistence basis. In fact the people feed themselves in the winter...by consuming as little and as poor food as possible" (Tawney, p. 73). And Elsworth Huntington reported that villagers in areas where harvests were too poor to provide sufficient food for the entire year boarded up their homes in winter and begged until springtime, when they could return to plant the next crop (1945, pp. 188–189).

Graphic descriptions of poverty are many. Richard Tawney observed that "if the meaning of [famine] is a shortage of food on a scale sufficient to cause widespread starvation, then there are parts of the country from which famine is rarely absent" (1932, p. 76). Those who did not starve ate very simply. Poor villagers in Taitou in Shandong Province ate sweet potatoes at every meal, year round; the better-off ate millet, wheat, and some meat and rice (Yang Maochun 1945, pp. 32–33). According to Philip C. C. Huang (Huang Zongzhi), half the rural population was poor: "[They] lived in shabby dwellings, struggled to keep from starving; seldom, if ever, tasted meat; dressed in rags, and lived a life of constant toil. [They] struggled between the margins of hunger and starvation...[from] widespread indebtedness, endemic malnutrition, sale of daughters [and] periodic massive starvation" (1975, pp. 132–133).

Describing the 1921 North China famine, Walter Mallory claimed it killed half a million and reduced 20 million to destitution. Families sold their roof timbers, women, and children. Many were reduced to eating chaff, bark, roots, flour made from leaves, corncobs, sawdust, and thistles. "Some of the food was so unpalatable that the children starved, refusing to eat it" (Mallory 1926, p. 2).

Farm size varied from region to region; those in the northeast (Manchuria) were double those in Hebei and Shanxi, which were almost double those in Jiangsu and Zhejiang (Tawney 1932, p. 30). However, size often reflected differences in soil quality, the reliability of rainfall, and the length of the growing season, which tended to equalize productivity. Also important were proximity to urban population centers, where crops could be sold and off-farm work was available, and tenancy, which was much more common near cities, imposing an additional burden on the farmer.

With China's population over 70 percent rural, urban poverty was less of a problem; however, conditions for ordinary city people were little better than for those in the countryside (Lamson 1935, pp. 1–32). The central problem was similar to that in the rural areas: too many people chasing too few resources. Jean Chesneaux (1968) describes factories hiring day laborers by throwing the number of tallies for the number of workers they wanted into a crowd of jobseekers and letting the workers fight over them. Tawney states that factory employees worked a daily twelve-hour night or day shift, child workers included. Their wages were very low, and there were high rates of industrial accidents and disease (1932, pp. 142–149). Ida Pruitt (1945) and Lao She (1979) offer detailed descriptions of the lives of the urban poor.

POVERTY IN THE PEOPLE'S REPUBLIC OF CHINA

The PRC was the first Chinese government to attempt systematically to reduce both inequality and poverty. In urban areas, the state appropriated all income-producing property and made all employing units state enterprises. The wages and wage goods these provided gave employees a meager but adequate level of living. From the 1950s to the 1970s, the urban Gini coefficient was around 0.25, slightly more than half that of contemporary developing countries (Parish 1984, pp. 88–89), and it decreased to only 0.21 in 1981 (Yao Shujie 2005, p. 172). In rural areas, land reform greatly reduced inequality. According to a 1954 survey of 192,760 households in twenty-two provinces, the PRC reduced landlords to the material level of poor peasants and lifted considerable numbers of poor peasants to middle-peasant status (Wong 1973, pp. 181–187). For example, in the mid-1960s villagers suffered from poor housing,

clothing, and food, their routine diets consisting of rice or rice congee flavored with "bits of tiny salt-dried fish, pickles, fermented bean curd, and fermented black beans." A decade later they consumed vegetables daily and usually had meat (Chan, Madsen and Unger 1992). However, while such efforts alleviated poverty for many, poverty was not eliminated. The survey shows that per household average acreage, converted to metric, was only 1.1 hectares of land, well below the needed 1.88 hectares noted above.

Thus, while the unfavorable population-arable land ratio is still a major cause of rural poverty in China, it has also been exacerbated by government policy. The Great Leap famine (1958–1962), which killed somewhere between 9 million and 43 million and during which there were reports of cannibalism, was caused by communization, the diversion of grain land to the production of industrial crops, mandated deep plowing, close planting, and the elimination of sparrows, in addition to the often-blamed unfavorable weather. From 1966 to 1976, the Cultural Revolution "grain first" policy, which ignored comparative advantage and required each area to be self-sufficient in grain, produced privation in large parts of rural China (Lardy 1983, pp. 47–53; Becker 1996). A 1981 Agricultural Ministry report stated that almost 88 million people lived in counties that had suffered three consecutive years (1977–1979) of dire poverty, during which people were unable even to afford sufficient food. This does not include chronically poor work teams elsewhere. The report also linked poverty and life expectancy. People in the poorest province, Guizhou, lived an average of fifty-nine years, while the national average was sixty-five (Lardy 1983, pp. 171–172).

The response of the post–Cultural Revolution government included the household-responsibility system, which restored the price mechanism, and state allocation of resources to agriculture. Between 1978 and 1984, these changes brought an average annual 14 percent rise in farm incomes and reduced rural poverty from a reported 600 million to fewer than 58 million. Since 1985 economic policy has tilted toward industrialization, which, together with imposts to build local infrastructure, halted rural poverty reduction (Khan and Riskin 2001, pp. 53–55, 103–105; Yao Shujie 2005, p. 7) until the mid-1990s when the government implemented the Eight-Seven Poverty Reduction Plan to lift the remaining 80 million out of poverty in seven years (1994–2000). Since then, poverty reduction has targeted the chronically poor areas in the northwest, southwest, and central mountain areas.

China began to define rural poverty in 1984 based on an extensive survey of the consumption habits of rural dwellers. Its 2007 poverty indicators are explained in Table 2.

The government ignored urban poverty until the mid-1990s, claiming it was only 0.3 percent in 1981 and was insignificant compared with poverty in the countryside.

Rural poverty lines used in the PRC			
	"Food line"	"Low" poverty line	"High" poverty line
Established	1984, revised 1998, indexed	2004	2004
Definition	Income needed to buy 2100 calories, ≤75% from grain, and 62 grams of protein	US$1.00/person/day; extra amount of food needed for good health	US$2.00/person/day; food and non-food needed for a healthy life
2007 cash value	686 yuan	889 yuan	1454 yuan
Number (percentage of population)	26.52 million (2.8%)	67.94 million (7.2%)	160.00 million (17%)

SOURCE: Guo Hongquan (Guo Hungchuan). Woguo nongcun zuidi shenghuo baozhang de zhengcixuanze [The Policy Choices to Safeguard China's Poorest Rural Villagers]. June 2006. *China Social Sciences Academy Bulletin*. http://myy.cass.cn/file/2007060727868.html.

Table 2

Urban workers were protected against privation through their employment in state enterprises. However, millions lost their jobs and some even their homes in the 1990s following the restructuring of state enterprises. Moreover, economic development seriously eroded the relative equality that had existed in cities, the Gini coefficient reaching 0.45 in 2004 (Li Cheng 2006, p. 2). Despite these developments, China has implemented no national urban poverty line or reduction programs, although there are projects to develop them (Asian Development Bank 2007). Local Ministry of Civil Affairs offices examined cases based on such indicators as employment, housing, ability to work, and health to determine a monthly subsidy, capped in 2003 at fifty-six yuan (Wang Sangui 2004). Moreover, migrant workers are excluded from consideration.

Between 1986 and 2004 the central government spent 212 billion yuan on poverty-reduction programs. Moreover, China had strong average growth rates: Real 2002 gross domestic product was 6.2 times that of 1978, the agricultural sector expanded 4.6 times, and per capita net rural household incomes averaged 6.3 percent annual growth to 586 yuan (Wang Sangui 2004). However, the 2002 food poverty line, which denotes absolute poverty, was 627 yuan per capita, so rural productivity still fell short by 9.3 percent—thirty-one yuan per person—in providing all with minimal nutrition. These are aggregated figures that ignore variations in farm household earnings. Jonathan Unger states that the rural Gini index increased from 0.2 to 0.4 between 1978 and 1995 (2004). But the fact that farmers in fertile areas near cities have comfortable incomes only emphasizes how badly off farmers in marginal areas are.

In 2005 there were still 100 million villagers and 20 million urban residents living in absolute poverty (Yao Shujie 2005, p. 50); the 2007 World Bank reevaluation of Chinese poverty puts the number at 300 million. Rural poverty is alleviated mainly by villagers working in cities and coastal regions and remitting money back home. A World Bank group estimates that some 95 million migrant workers sent over $30 billion in remittances in 2005 (Torre 2005). China's only hope in alleviating poverty is continued economic growth and ensuring that those living in marginal areas are able to benefit.

SEE ALSO *Labor: Unemployment; Migrant Workers; Peasantry since 1900; Peasantry, 1800–1900; Standard of Living.*

BIBLIOGRAPHY

Asian Development Bank. 37600: PRC Urban Poverty Strategy Study. 2007. http://www.adb.org/projects/project.asp?id=37600.

Becker, Jasper. *Hungry Ghosts: China's Secret Famine*. London: John Murray, 1996.

Bohr, P. Richard. *Famine in China and the Missionary: Timothy Richard as Relief Administrator and Advocate of National Reform, 1876–1884*. Cambridge, MA: East Asian Research Center, Harvard University, 1972.

Brandt, Loren, and Barbara Sands. Land Concentration and Income Distribution in Republican China. In *Chinese History in Economic Perspective*, ed. Thomas Rawski and Lillian M. Li, 179–206. Berkeley: University of California Press, 1992.

Buck, John Lossing. *An Economic and Social Survey of 105 Farms Yenshan County, Chihli Province, China*. Nanjing: University of Nanking, 1926.

Chan, Anita, Richard Madsen, and Jonathan Unger. *Chen Village: The Recent History of a Peasant Community in Mao's China*. Berkeley: University of California Press, 1992.

Chesneaux, Jean. *The Chinese Labor Movement, 1919–1927*. Trans. H. M. Wright. Stanford, CA: Stanford University Press, 1968.

Guo Hongquan (Guo Hungchuan). Woguo nongcun zuidi shenghuo baozhang de zhengcixuanze [The policy choices to safeguard China's poorest rural villagers]. June 2006. *China Social Sciences Academy Bulletin*. http://myy.cass.cn/file/2007060727868.html.

Huang Zongzhi (Philip C. C. Huang). Analyzing the Twentieth-century Chinese Countryside: Revolutionaries versus Western Scholarship. *Modern China* 1, 2 (1975): 132–160.

Huang Zongzhi (Philip C. C. Huang). *The Peasant Economy and Social Change in North China*. Stanford, CA: Stanford University Press, 1985.

Huntington, Elsworth. *Mainsprings of Civilization*. New York: Mentor, 1945.

Khan, Azizur Rahman, and Carl Riskin. *Inequality and Poverty in China in the Age of Globalization*. Oxford: Oxford University Press, 2001.

Lamson, Herbert Day. *Social Pathology in China: A Source Book for the Study of Problems of Livelihood, Health, and the Family*. Shanghai: Commercial Press, 1935.

Lao She. *Rickshaw: The Novel Lo-t'o Hsiang-tzu*. Trans. Jean M. James. Honolulu: University of Hawai'i Press, 1979.

Lardy, Nicholas R. *Agriculture in China's Modern Economic Development*. Cambridge, U.K.: Cambridge University Press, 1983.

Li Cheng. China's Inner-party Democracy: Toward a System of "One Party, Two Factions?" *China Brief* 6, 24 (2006). http://www.jamestown.org/china_brief/article.php?articleid= 2373247.

Mallory, Walter H. *China: Land of Famine*. New York: American Geographical Society, 1926.

Moise, Edwin E. Downward Social Mobility in Pre-revolutionary China. *Modern China* 3, 1 (1977): 3–31.

Parish, William L. Destratification in China. In *Class and Social Stratification in Post-revolution China*, ed. James L. Watson, 84–120. Cambridge, U.K.: Cambridge University Press, 1984.

Pruitt, Ida. *A Daughter of Han: The Autobiography of a Chinese Working Woman*. New Haven, CT: Yale University Press, 1945.

Rowe, William T. *Hankow: Conflict and Community in a Chinese City, 1796–1895*. Stanford, CA: Stanford University Press, 1989.

Smith, Arthur H. *Village Life in China: A Study in Sociology*. Edinburgh: Oliphant, Anderson and Ferrier, 1900.

Tawney, Richard H. *Land and Labour in China*. New York: Harcourt Brace, 1932.

Torre, Ulysses de la. China-labor: Urban Workers Sent $30 Billion to Rural Homes—Study. Inter Press Service English Newswire. December 13, 2005.

Unger, Jonathan. *The Transformation of Rural China*. Armonk, NY: Sharpe, 2004.

Wang Sangui. Poverty Targeting in the People's Republic of China. Asian Development Bank Institute: Discussion Paper No. 4. 2004. http://www.adbi.org/discussion-paper/2004/01/04/83.poverty.targeting/.

Wong, John. *Land Reform in the People's Republic of China: Institutional Transformation in Agriculture*. New York and London: Praeger, 1973.

Xiao Gongquan (Hsiao Kung-chuan). *Rural China: Imperial Control in the Nineteenth Century*. Seattle: University of Washington Press, 1960.

Yang Maochun (Martin C. Yang). *A Chinese Village: Taitou, Shantung Province*. New York: Columbia University Press, 1945.

Yao Shujie. *Economic Growth, Income Distribution, and Poverty Reduction in Contemporary China*. New York: RoutledgeCurzon, 2005.

Zhao Gang (Chao Kang). *Man and Land in Chinese History: An Economic Analysis*. Stanford, CA: Stanford University Press, 1986.

David C. Schak

POVERTY ALLEVIATION PROGRAMS

SEE *Social Policy Programs*.

PRICE SYSTEM

A *price system* is a defining feature distinguishing a planned economy from a market economy. Correspondingly, reforms to the price system were a central issue in the Chinese transition to a market economy after 1978. In a market economy, prices have the function of equilibrating supply and demand, whereas in a planned economy, they serve the purpose of guiding resources into politically determined priority sectors and of controlling plan implementation via budgeting.

Under the Maoist command economy, the price system was a major instrument for reallocating resources from agriculture to industry. Urban real wages were repressed for two decades by keeping agricultural output prices low, so that accumulation of capital via retained industrial profits could be maximized. This "price scissor" was a stable feature of the Chinese economic system into the 1980s, because the full-scale marketization of major agricultural staples proceeded only gradually. Because centrally planned prices are not changed frequently, the pre-reform price system did not reflect changing national and regional conditions of supply and demand, so that periodic shortages and hoarding were typical phenomena, along with weak incentives for raising productivity in sectors with artificially suppressed prices.

After 1949, the price system underwent a gradual change from market pricing to complete administrative pricing by the end of the 1950s. However, this change did not imply that all prices were set by the central government. Goods were classified into groups according to national priorities (*yilei*, *erlei*, and *sanlei shangpin*, or category one, category two, and category three goods), with prices of grains, cotton, or oil determined centrally. Other goods of less-strategic significance were administrated by lower-level planning units. Furthermore, pricing policies differed for the different systems of state purchasing, reaching from the state monopoly (*tonggou*) to the quota system (*paigou*) to different forms of negotiated prices (*yigou*). The task of fixing prices was given to special price commissions. With the transition to administrative prices, the issue of the appropriate pricing method emerged. Already in the 1950s a discussion was taking place between protagonists of a labor theory of value and those who favored the capital-based method that actually reproduced the Marxian price formula for capitalism. After 1978, this formula was determined to be the appropriate method for the so-called planned commodity economy, which was the initial stage of economic reforms. This stage prepared the country for the transition to market pricing in the 1980s.

Until the early 1990s, the Chinese price system exhibited dual-track pricing, which refers to the coexistence of administrative prices and market prices for the same goods and industries. The category of "negotiated purchases" (*yigou* in agriculture, *dinggou* or *xuangou* in industry) allowed for many hybrid forms of pricing. Under this regime, enterprises were permitted to sell beyond-quota-production with market-pricing, so that they could earn additional profit, given the sellers' market in the early years of reforms. Coexisting with distorted administrative prices, the dual-track system caused such phenomena as parallel investment in downstream industries across the provinces and interprovincial trade conflicts. With the expansion of production, market prices tended to fall even below administrative prices, so that administrative prices were finally crowded out of the system. However, for some strategic goods this process did not operate smoothly—in particular in the agricultural sector, which manifested stronger fluctuations of production. In such sectors, price guarantees remain a discretionary policy instrument today. Administrative prices continue to be used in the natural resources sector—in prices for water and energy resources, for example. The vast majority of prices in China are determined by market forces. The Price Law of 1998 allows for discretionary government intervention in cases of serious market disorder, but generally prohibits anticompetitive pricing by market participants. The administrative practice of price registration and price surveillance also remains in place.

One major effect of administrative pricing is the rupture between world prices and domestic price relations. After China's entry into the World Trade Organization (WTO) in 2001, the alignment of Chinese prices with world prices proceeded, a process also resulting from the tarification of trade barriers and their subsequent stepwise lowering of rates. However, the extent of the gap between world prices and domestic prices is also determined by the relation between traded and nontraded goods. Because most services, as well as construction business and land, are nontraded, market prices differ systematically from price structures in other countries. This leads to divergent purchasing power across different currencies, with currencies of less-developed countries being systematically undervalued. This is the main reason why China's gross domestic product per capita is much higher in terms of purchasing power than when evaluated by exchange rates.

SEE ALSO *Economic Reform since 1978.*

BIBLIOGRAPHY

Ishihara Kyōichi. *China's Conversion to a Market Economy.* Tokyo: Institute of Developing Economies, 1993

Kennedy, Scott. The Price of Competition: Pricing Policies and the Struggle to Define China's Economic System. *China Journal* 49 (2003): 1–30.

Carsten Herrmann-Pillath

PRINCELINGS

SEE *Social Classes since 1978.*

PRIVACY

In discussing privacy in China, it is pertinent to note that privacy, as a legal concept, is of relatively recent origin in Western countries. Although Samuel Warren and Louis Brandeis first formulated the concept in an 1890 *Harvard Law Review* article, privacy has still not been recognized as a constitutional right per se in most Western countries, including the United States. In its 2007 ranking of twenty-seven European Union and nineteen other countries, including China, as well as Taiwan on privacy, Privacy International, a non-governmental organization, ranked China second last on the list, with a score of 1.3 out of 5.0 (tied with Malaysia and Russia) denoting an "endemic surveillance society." Both the United Kingdom, which scored 1.4, and the United States, which scored 1.5, fell under the same category (National Privacy Ranking 2007). Privacy is strongly correlated with how a society is governed. As Raymond Wacks discerns, "at the heart of the concern to protect 'privacy' lies a conception of the individual and his or her relationship with society" (Wacks 1989, p. 7).

In Chinese language, the word *si* (private/privacy) has generally negative connotations (except in the context of family) such as secrecy and selfishness, whereas *gong* (public) and *guan* (official) are used in relation to fairness and justice (McDougall 2004). Bonnie McDougall argues that "[t]he emphasis on public service as a personal goal and on the public good as a national objective by Chinese political figures throughout the greater part of the twentieth century is partly responsible for the perception that privacy as a value is foreign to China" (2004, p. 2). Nevertheless, in traditional Confucian culture, family is considered a realm separate from the state, within which individuals may enjoy freedom from public scrutiny—albeit as a family unit and not as individuals (McDougall 2004).

While McDougall's observation on the negative connotations of privacy in Chinese society remains valid, the excesses of the Red Guards during the Cultural Revolution and China's subsequent economic reforms and progress have resulted in increasing acceptance in society, by the state and among individuals, of the notion that certain activities and values should be regarded as entirely personal and free from scrutiny outside the confines of one's home. In particular, privacy is now recognized and protected in China as a legal and constitutional right to reputation. Under Article 38 of the 1982 Constitution of the People's Republic of China, "[t]he personal dignity of citizens of the People's Republic of China is inviolable. Insult, libel, false charge or frame-up directed against citizens by any means is prohibited." Article 39 guarantees the inviolability of the home and prohibits unlawful search or intrusion. Article 40 provides that "[n]o organization or individual may, on any ground, infringe upon the freedom and privacy of citizens' correspondence except in cases where, to meet the needs of state security or of investigation into criminal offences, public security or procuratorial organs are permitted to censor correspondence in accordance with procedures prescribed by law." Article 252 of the General Principles of Criminal Law prohibits infringement of a person's "right of communication freedom by hiding, destroying, or illegally opening" of letters belonging to another, and illegal search or intrusion into another person or his or her home. Article 101 of the General Principles of Civil Law protects a "right of reputation," stating that "[t] he personality of citizens shall be protected by law, and the use of insults, libel or other means to damage the reputation of citizens or legal persons shall be prohibited." However, privacy of information relating to public affairs or immoral conduct will not be protected (Cao 2005). As the Party-state controls the media and alternative sources of information, the advent, accessibility and supposed anonymity of the Internet, which in 2006 was used by 123 million Chinese people (Kong 2007, p. 158), has raised significant issues relating to privacy protection. According to a government survey, 23.2 percent of Internet users and 18.6 percent of nonusers regarded Internet use as very likely to lead to unauthorized disclosure of personal information (Kong 2007, p. 159). As a member of the World Trade Organization since 2001, China is obliged to meet relevant privacy protection requirements.

Within the confines of the home, Shengming Tang and Xiaoping Dong (2006) in their survey of 338 students attending three high schools in Shanghai and 256 parents of students attending those schools found that despite the pervasive role of family in Chinese culture, many students asserted strong desires for individual privacy within their families, and parents endeavored to respect their children's privacy. Yao-Huai Lü (2005, p. 8) observed generally that whereas Chinese parents previously would have taken it for granted that they might freely open or read letters belonging to their children and enter their rooms without knocking, nowadays more and more Chinese children in the cities expect that their consent will first be sought. Lü also refutes the idea that space in an increasingly overcrowded society has any bearing on perceptions about privacy in China,

finding that Chinese people living in rural areas, as "acquaintance societies," tend to be more interested in the private matters of acquaintances than are those in the cities, who live in greater and reciprocated anonymity (2005, p. 12). It should be noted that a right to privacy is increasingly asserted by perpetrators of domestic abuse as a pretext to circumvent sanctions for their conduct. In this context, the notion of privacy has helped construct a realm to which women's lives and voices are relegated and dismissed as unimportant or irrelevant to (male) society (McDougall 2004; Milwertz and Bu 2007).

SEE ALSO *Internet.*

BIBLIOGRAPHY

Cao, Jingchun. Protecting the Right to Privacy in China. *Victoria University of Wellington Law Review* 36 (2005): 645–664.

Deibert, Ronald J. Dark Guests and Great Firewalls: The Internet and Chinese Security Policy. *Journal of Social Issues* 58 (2002): 143–159.

Kong, Lingjie. Online Privacy in China: A Survey on Information Practices of Chinese Websites. *Chinese Journal of International Law* 6 (2007): 157–183.

Lü, Yao-Huai. Privacy and Data Privacy Issues in Contemporary China. *Ethics and Information Technology* 7 (2005): 7–15.

McDougall, Bonnie S. Privacy in Modern China. *History Compass* 2 (2004): 1–8.

Milwertz, Cecilia, and Wei Bu. Non-Governmental Organising for Gender Equality in China—Joining a Global Emancipatory Epistemic Community. *International Journal of Human Rights* 11 (2007): 131–149.

Privacy International. National Privacy Ranking 2007—Leading Surveillance Societies around the World. http://www. privacyinternational.org/survey/rankings2007/phrcomp_sort.pdf

Tang, Shengming, and Xiaoping Dong. Parents and Children's Perceptions of Privacy Rights in China: A Cohort Comparison. *Journal of Family Issues* 27 (2006): 285–300.

Taubman, Geoffry. A Not-So World Wide Web: The Internet, China, and the Challenges to Nondemocratic Rule. *Political Communication* 15 (1998): 255–272.

Wacks, Raymond. *Personal Information: Privacy and the Law.* Oxford: Clarendon Press, 1989.

Warren, Samuel D., and Louis D. Brandeis. The Right to Privacy. *Harvard Law Review* 4 (1890): 193–220.

Yang, Guobin. The Co-Evolution of the Internet and Civil Society in China. *Asian Survey* 43 (2003): 405–422.

Yang, Guobin. The Internet and Civil Society in China: A Preliminary Assessment. *Journal of Contemporary China* 12 (2003): 453–475.

Phil C. W. Chan

PRIVATE ENTERPRISES

In the 1950s, almost all of China's private companies were transformed into state or collective organizations. Such privately owned companies were considered to be part of a capitalist sector with an antagonistic character.

Beginning in the mid-1960s, every form of self-employment was also forbidden. In 1978 only about 330,000 people were officially working in the private sector. It was not until March 1979 that the political leadership permitted the reemergence of individual economic structures (self-employment), although such entrepreneurs could not employ wage earners. In July 1981 a directive from the political leadership characterized individual companies as a necessary complement of state-owned and collective forms of ownership.

EARLY DEVELOPMENTS

In March 1979 the Chinese State Council explicitly endorsed the readmittance of self-employment (individual economy). From 1981 onward a package of regulations legalized this sector. Self-employed people were declared to be "socialist laborers" and thus formally equated to workers and peasants.

The starting point for the development of the private sector in the 1980s was poverty in the countryside. Already in the mid-1970s—that is, before the beginning of reform policies—a spontaneous shadow economy had developed, primarily in poverty stricken areas. As a consequence, markets developed that were considered at that time to be illegal. During the economic crisis in the second half of the 1970s, pressure from the countryside became ever greater, and some provinces with a high level of poverty (Anhui, Sichuan) tolerated this development. The success of private industry and commerce led in 1979 to the emergence of a small-scale private sector (individual businesses).

According to Chinese scholars, the return of family management in agriculture led to the redundancy of 150 million to 200 million members of the rural workforce. These workers had no access to the urban labor market or the state sector. The only way to absorb them was self-employment in commerce and craft-based work. Such employment was at first prohibited. Yet increasingly, with businesses based on employed "family members" or "relatives," paid work became a reality. Hesitantly, the state in the first half of the 1980s permitted private employers to maintain two, then five, then seven staff members.

NEW REGULATIONS AND CHANGING ATTITUDES

Beginning in February 1984, regulations for individual rural industrial and trade companies became legally binding. According to official statistics, however, by 1983 there were already around 5.8 million such companies with 7.5 million employees. These companies were retrospectively legalized by the "Regulations for Individual, Rural Industrial and Trade Companies" of 1984. The same phenomenon occurred in 1988 with the regulation of private firms stemming from administrative channels, which permitted expansion into various commercial fields, excluding the

defense and finance sectors. If such a firm had more than seven employees, it constituted a private company (*siying qiye*); with fewer than eight employees, it constituted an individual or household enterprise (*getihu*).

Concurrently new laws governing foreign capital, joint ventures, shareholding enterprises, and limited liability companies were enacted, for example, the Sino-Foreign Equity Joint Ventures Law (1979, amended 1990 and 2001); the wholly foreign-owned enterprise law (1986, revised 2000); the Sino-Foreign Cooperative Joint Venture Law (1988, revised 2000), and the Company Law (1994, amended 2006). The latter regulates shareholders' rights and limited liability companies and determines how foreign shareholders establish and manage their operations in China.

The actual developments were always one step ahead of the political process. Eventually, the development of the private sector was no longer controllable, not least because the advantages for employment, supply of goods, and income for the local authorities had become very apparent. In June 1988 the People's Republic of China (PRC) State Council issued provisional regulations for private companies. Limits on employment were abolished and, with that, the main block against the development of the private sector. However, by the end of 1987, some 225,000 private companies had already come into being. These were registered as individual, collective, or cooperative organizations that employed more than seven staff members dependent on wages.

The private sector quickly proved to be the most dynamic sector and so became a major pillar of economic development. As a result, in 1995 the Chinese Communist Party (CCP) leadership saw that it was necessary to make a statement to the effect that all forms of ownership should develop along parallel tracks and with equal rights. The prospering provinces in the eastern part of the country soon termed the private sector the "motor" of the "socialist market economy." The Fifteenth Party Congress of the CCP in September 1997 even declared this sector to be part of the "socialist" sector. The new Article 16 of the March 1999 constitutional change finally established that these individual and private companies were "important constituents of the socialist market economy" that were protected by the state.

At the 2002 Sixteenth Party Congress, CCP General Secretary Jiang Zemin argued that private entrepreneurs, like workers, peasants, intellectuals, cadres, and soldiers, were "builders of socialism with Chinese characteristics." The Congress agreed to that position, and thereafter private businesspeople were permitted to join the CCP.

In contrast to the Soviet Union and the former socialist countries of Eastern Europe, China was facing less of a top-down privatization—that is, a complete transfer of state-owned enterprises to private owners by the state—than a bottom-up privatization by virtue of an enhancement of private ownership as individuals set up private firms.

A Chinese investor in a private securities firm in Shanghai, August 16, 2007. *In the 1980s, the Communist government began to allow individuals to privately own companies, in part to gain control of the illegal businesses started out of necessity in impoverished rural areas. Investors, too, welcomed the changes, leading to the development of stock markets in China and greater amounts of foreign capital entering the Chinese economy.* **MARK RALSTON/AFP/GETTY IMAGES**

EXTENT OF PRIVATIZATION

Undoubtedly, the quantitative development of the private sector is underestimated. According to official Chinese data from mid-2007, 153.8 million people held jobs in both the "private" and the "individual" sector. The *Blue Book of Chinese Society*, published by the Academy of

Social Sciences in 2007, revealed that at the end of 2005, 208 million urban people were working in both sectors, 76.3 percent of China's entire urban labor force. In rural areas, almost all businesses are private, and no reliable data on this sector are available.

The private sector in this sense encompasses registered small, middle-sized, and larger enterprises, enterprises with foreign investment, private traders and craftspeople, and enterprises that are falsely registered as state- or collective-owned enterprises but are in fact private, as well as non-registered and underground enterprises (i.e., the shadow economy).

In 2005 the private sector was said to have generated more than 70 percent of the gross national product and three-quarters of the economic growth for that year. Furthermore, it created more than three-quarters of the new jobs. The latter figure suggests that China's party state is highly dependent on the private sector.

Interestingly, by the end of the 1990s, according to official statements, the following kinds of companies were already registered as private industries:

- 31,202,000 individual companies (*getihu* with fewer than eight employees) with 61,144,000 employees overall

- 1,201,000 private companies (*siying qiye* with more than seven employees) with 2,638,000 owners and 17,091,000 employees overall

In addition, the number of employees to be found in other private industrial sectors was:

- joint stock companies: 5,460,000

- limited liability companies: 4,840,000

- companies with investments from Hong Kong, Macau, and Taiwan: 2,940,000

- companies with investments from foreign countries: 2,930,000

These figures add up to a total of around 97 million people engaged in the private sector during that period. Additionally, there were about 25.83 million private companies operating in rural areas and employing about 72.8 million people; 120,000 private "scientific-technical" firms (mostly in the sphere of consulting) with around 2.1 million employees; and 220,000 companies with foreign capital employing about 25.1 million people. These must also be classified as private companies. Assuming that these numbers remained constant until the end of 1990s (although it is likely that they, in fact, increased), then at the end of the 1990s China's private sector may have involved more than 200 million people.

The statistical data says little about the actual extent of privatization, however. Some research indicates, for example, that the number of nonregistered companies in large and middle-sized cities in the second half of the 1990s was double or at least as high as the number of registered companies. In smaller towns, this ratio may be as high as four to one, and in rural areas the number of nonregistered companies is supposed to be even higher. In addition, some private companies may misleadingly register as state or collective companies.

The reasons that a private company may falsely register as a state or collective company may be *political*, including the need for political correctness and safeguards (in the hierarchy of the companies, state and collective firms are still ranked higher than private ones). Company leaders may also wish to obtain membership in the CCP (officially, private entrepreneurs were refused CCP membership until 2002) to gain access to political networks. The reasons may also be *economic*, such as better access to credit, tax advantages, more extensive information about markets or support from the local authorities, or they may be *social*, since a registered company can bring greater prestige.

In general, nonregistered enterprises comprise the following groups: illegal individual and private companies; family members helping out; persons with a second job; moonlighters who follow a second job in their free time; sections of the rural collective industries that in reality are actually in private hands (approximately 90 percent); and a great number of companies that are nominally state-owned or collective but are actually privately run. All together, the figures add up to between 250 million and 300 million people who may have been working in the private sector of the Chinese economy in 2002, approximately 35 to 40 percent of the total workforce.

Meanwhile, even the term *state ownership* has to be put into question. The following phenomena have made it difficult to estimate the actual amount of privatization in the Chinese economy: (1) the multiplicity of forms of ownership (ranging from large, state-sector firms centrally directed and organized according to the planned economy to firms directed by a province, city, or county, down to the small companies leased to private persons); (2) the different mixed-ownership constructions; and (3) misleading classifications and misclassifications.

GENESIS OF THE PRIVATE SECTOR

The private sector had its genesis in the countryside, even if the proportion of private enterprises in urban areas has risen relative to rural areas. In 1997 the proportion of private urban companies had passed the 60 percent barrier for the first time (62.1%), while that of rural areas stood at 37.9 percent. The increase in private economic activity in urban areas may result from more and more rural entrepreneurs basing themselves in urban areas with a view to expanding their entrepreneurial activities. They do so for a number of reasons, including the proximity of markets to raw materials, better marketing prospects, and less-heavy bureaucratic controls.

Chinese development confirms certain theories concerning rural entrepreneurs in East Asia, according to which a productive upswing in agriculture (as it developed, for example, in the course of the rural reforms and restructurings) led to the emergence of entrepreneurs who make use industrially of new potentials in agriculture (e.g., in the form of firms specializing in processing agricultural produce). The agricultural sector is thus connected with modern industry and urban markets. The genesis of industrial production potential in the countryside is also based on traditional clan and village bonds that help entrepreneurs minimize costs.

Rural industrialization has also had the effect that increases in income are not only concentrated in the urban areas, but also include the countryside; consequently, the flight from the countryside to urban zones and the urban poverty that results from that process can be managed. At the same time, rural entrepreneurs build interconnections with urban areas. What is specific about developments in China is that the transition from a planned economy to market structures enables new opportunities for entrepreneurs not only in the domain of the market but also in the links that develop in the mixing of elements from both market and planned economies. The latter has resulted in a connection between the market and the bureaucracy, as well as between private and state sectors.

Most of China's private companies are small firms in such sectors as small industry and crafts, transport, construction, retailing, catering, trade, and other service industries. The private rural industries, in particular, have become motors of industry, such that most of them, at the end of the 1990s, were still registered as "collective firms" because by doing so they hoped to obtain greater political security, protection by local authorities, and lower taxes and social contributions. Larger companies are only gradually emerging, even if their numbers are continually rising.

RELATIONSHIP TO THE STATE SECTOR

Private firms constituting the second economy at first stood in the shadow of a mighty state sector; they were concentrated in economic niches, and were founded through the initiatives of individuals, in contrast to the state sector, which remains protected and subsidized. But such private companies by no means constitute a separate second economy alongside the state and collective sector; instead, there are numerous interconnections. These are evidenced in the informal zone (individual relationships or networks between persons in public and private sectors

with the goal of reciprocal enrichment), as well as in the form of delivery firms, or relationships linked by providers of supplies and purchasers or providers of capital.

At the same time, the private sector also functions as a competitor that in certain spheres of the economy has ousted state and collective companies. There is rivalry too in the labor market between organizations operating under different forms of ownership, whereby private companies, insofar as they pay higher wages and salaries, attract qualified blue- and white-collar workers from the public sector. Due to the greater earning potential and mounting insecurity concerning future developments in the public sector, an increasing number of trained employees from the state sector are becoming self-employed. To describe the change to the private sector, the familiar word *xiahai* (diving into the sea) enjoys widespread circulation.

In the 1990s, numerous state and collective firms took on new forms of ownership, such as shareholding or limited liability (i.e., limited companies), or they were sold to private firms. The emergence of pluralism in company forms led to a further decentralization of decision making in the economy, and to a change in the structure of company ownership. The state companies began in this way to lose their dominant position in the Chinese economy. In 1978 state companies produced 77.6 percent (collective firms produced 22.4 percent) of the gross output. The percentage of private companies at that point was zero. By the end of the 1990s, the figure for state companies had fallen to 26.5 percent (36 percent for collective firms). The number of private companies (including shareholding companies and firms with foreign capital) was then 37.5 percent and already the largest sector. At the same time, the private sector has for years had the highest growth rate.

PROBLEMS FACING THE PRIVATE SECTOR

A range of problems continues to stand in the way of further rapid growth in the private sector. Among these are: (1) discrimination and handicaps in competition experienced by private companies against state companies (e.g., in the provision of commodities and raw materials, or when trying to obtain credit allocation or real estate); (2) an absence of legal safeguards; (3) interventions by the bureaucracy (e.g., the imposition of higher taxes or contributions), as well as corruption among officials; (4) a lack of confidence among entrepreneurs in government policies, with the consequence that profits are consumed and not reinvested; and (5) the continuing existence of a negative social view of the private entrepreneurial strata.

These problems contribute to another serious problem—the short life span of companies. The average life of a private company is estimated to be 2.9 years. As a result, an entrepreneur from Shandong demanded, in his role as a member of the National People's Congress, a "turtle philosophy" for private companies—that is, political measures for guaranteeing longer life spans.

Chinese surveys of private entrepreneurs suggest that confidence in the continuity of policies, social pressure, lack of state support, the limitations of the market, and distortions of competition in favor of state-sector firms are core problems. The leadership has responded to such expressions of dissatisfaction by recognizing that the interests of private entrepreneurs must be legally safeguarded, with authorities given fixed and unambiguous regulations and guidelines about frameworks, along with the strengthening of organizations representing the interests of entrepreneurs, the establishing of special banks for private entrepreneurs, and the granting to private companies of equal status for tax payments and provision of credit.

SEE ALSO *Companies; Entrepreneurs since 1949; Shops; Sincere Department Stores; Wing On Department Stores.*

BIBLIOGRAPHY

Dickson, Bruce J. *Red Capitalists in China: The Party, Private Entrepreneurs, and Prospects for Political Change.* Cambridge, U.K.: Cambridge University Press, 2003.

Garnaut, Ross, and Song Ligang, eds. *China's Third Economic Transformation: The Rise of the Private Economy.* London: RoutledgeCurzon, 2003.

Heberer, Thomas. *Private Entrepreneurs in China and Vietnam: Social and Political Functioning of Strategic Groups.* Trans. Timothy J. Gluckman. Leiden, Netherlands, and Boston: Brill, 2003.

Heberer, Thomas. *Doing Business in Rural China: Liangshan's New Ethnic Entrepreneurs.* Seattle: University of Washington Press, 2007.

Liu Shuanglin and Zhu Xiaodong, eds. *Private Enterprises and China's Economic Development.* London: Routledge, 2007.

Tsai, Kellee S. *Back-Alley Banking: Private Entrepreneurs in China.* Ithaca, NY: Cornell University Press, 2002.

Tsui, Anne S., Bian Yanjie, and Leonard Cheng, eds. *China's Domestic Private Firms: Multidisciplinary Perspectives on Management and Performance.* Armonk, NY: Sharpe, 2006.

Thomas Heberer

PRODEMOCRACY MOVEMENT (1989)

The prodemocracy movement in the People's Republic of China (PRC) is not a movement in the usual sense of the term. Given the effective hegemony of the Communist Party, since 1949, no opposition party has been able to exist. Therefore, rather than a political organization, the prodemocracy movement is a set of ideas that periodically are made public in demonstrations.

This set of ideas can be summed up as follows: The goal of the democrats is to allow the citizens of the PRC to enjoy the basic freedoms of association, expression, publication, and demonstration; they must be able to criticize the Communist Party without being sent to jail.

Tactics have varied, actors have changed, but these ideas have remained. From late 1954, when the literary critic Hu Feng (1902–1985) sent a 30,000-character letter to the Central Committee asking Mao to put an end to party control over the literary field, to December 2008, when the Charter 08 manifesto demanding constitutional democracy was made public, actors in the prodemocracy movement have fought for the same basic principles and have met with the same retribution: imprisonment. The party's ideology has been through many changes, from Mao Zedong's "new democracy" to the extreme radicalism he imposed during the Cultural Revolution (1966–1969), from Deng Xiaoping's policy of reform and opening up to Hu Jintao's attempt at creating a "harmonious society"; but the attitude of the successive leaders toward the prodemocracy movement has not changed: With few exceptions, democracy activists have been banned from expressing their ideas in public and, of course, from creating political organizations. They have been branded counter-revolutionaries or rightists, and have been accused of attempting to subvert the state, or of divulging state secrets.

Despite this, as shade accompanies the sun, the call for democracy has always been present at the side of the Communist Party in Chinese society, and it has been expressed in public under special circumstances.

STRUGGLE AT THE TOP

The first circumstance is disunity as the top of the central leadership. Even though it has never admitted it publicly, the party has always been divided into factions. Sometimes struggles erupt between them and they coalesce into two groups that support different political positions. Given the absence of transparency in the political system and the impossibility of bringing divergences into the open, the various factions resort to political maneuvers to settle their differences. When one of the leaders is charismatic, he does not hesitate to ask the masses to express their discontent in order to topple his adversaries. This provides the prodemocracy movement with an opportunity to appear in public.

It happened in 1956: In the wake of the de-Stalinization that was developing in the USSR, the Sixth Party Congress removed references to "Mao Zedong thought" from the Communist Party charter. Seeing this as an attempt to sidestep him, and hoping to weaken his rivals in the apparatus, Mao called on the citizens to criticize the new regime, thereby launching the Hundred Flowers campaign.

In another example, after the disaster of the Great Leap Forward of 1958 Mao was forced by Liu Shaoqi and

Student protestor, Tiananmen Square, Beijing, June 3, 1989. *In response to a wave of prodemocracy demonstrations in Tiananmen Square, Chinese government authorities mobilized military troops against the protestors, killing several hundred individuals during the June 3, 1989, crackdown.* **CATHERINE HENRIETTE/AFP/GETTY IMAGES**

his allies to "retire to the second line." Once again seizing the initiative, he made it possible for young students to organize and to denounce power holders. The Cultural Revolution also provided an opportunity for some proponents of democracy to express their opinions.

In 1976 the struggle between Deng Xiaoping and the radicals who supported Mao again opened a space for the people to express their demands. Deng Xiaoping was not opposed to using Chairman Mao's tactics: When in 1978 he decided to get rid of his neo-Maoist rivals, he endorsed the posting of *dazibaos* (big character posters) on the Democracy Wall.

Another circumstance that can allow an appearance by the prodemocracy movement occurs when a respected leader dies in disgrace. After Zhou Enlai died in 1976, at the Qingming festival, under the pretext of paying tribute to the deceased leader, a big demonstration took place on Tiananmen Square. In 1989 Hu Yaobang's death trig-

gered the Tiananmen prodemocracy movement. In fact, the death of a leader is an excellent opportunity for ordinary citizens to express their demands, which they present as having been supported by the deceased leader.

HELPING THE PARTY TO CORRECT ITS MISTAKES

One of the characteristics of the prodemocracy movement since 1949 is that its actors have almost never denounced the Communist regime itself. On the contrary, they always state that they want to enforce the principles defended by the party. Because the constitution recognizes the fundamental freedoms that are at the core of the demands of the prodemocracy movement, the movement does not position itself outside the system. The critics of 1957—such as Lin Xiling, who demanded the establishment of the rule of law—presented their demands as a way to help the party realize socialism. The same was true of Chu Anping, who

---

WANG DAN

■

Wang Dan was a key student leader during the national protest movement in 1989. Born in 1969 into a family of intelligentsia, Wang grew up in Beijing and studied politics and history at Peking University beginning in 1987. Inspired by the relatively relaxed political atmosphere of the 1980s, Wang became part of the movement for political reform, organizing "democracy salons" and editing dissident publications such as *Xin Wusi* (New May Fourth) and *Yanyuan Feng* (Yanyuan style). His activities were catalysts for student radicalization, and he played an important role in organizations such as the Beijing Students' Autonomous Federation. Wang was one of the first to launch a hunger strike to pressure the government into engaging in dialogue, and his televised confrontations with Chinese leaders such as Li Peng turned Wang into a celebrity.

After the June 4 crackdown, Wang topped the list of most-wanted student leaders and was soon arrested. In 1990 he received a four-year sentence for "counterrevolutionary activities," but was released on parole in 1993. Rearrested in 1995 for appealing for the release of others implicated in the 1989 movement, he received another eleven-year sentence. Immediately prior to President Bill Clinton's visit to China in 1998, Wang was granted medical parole to go to the United States.

In the United States, Wang earned a master's degree in East Asian history from Harvard University in 2001 and a doctorate in 2008. While most former student leaders moved on to other careers, Wang soldiers on as a democracy activist through affiliation with the Chinese Constitutional Reform Association and other dissident organizations, and through writing and lecturing. Among his many publications are memoirs, poetry, and political essays.

Although by 2007 Wang's prison sentence had expired, the Chinese government refused to renew his passport, depriving him of the right to return. His latest cause has been to champion citizenship rights for himself and other exiled dissidents similarly affected.

BIBLIOGRAPHY

Calhoun, Craig. *Neither Gods nor Emperors: Students and the Struggle for Democracy in China*. Berkeley: University of California Press, 1994.

Shen Tong, with Marianne Yen. *Almost a Revolution*. Boston: Houghton Mifflin, 1990.

Alfred L. Chan

---

denounced the wholesale domination of the party over society (*dang tianxia*). The demonstrators of 1976 wanted to put an end to the "dictatorship of Qin Shihuang" and demanded that "real Marxism-Leninism" be enforced. In 1978 to 1979 most of the activists of the Democracy Wall demanded their basic liberties—freedom of association, demonstration, and opinion—but did not question the legitimacy of socialism, with the notable exception of Wei Jingsheng. And in 1989, the students at Tiananmen Square insisted that their movement for democracy was "patriotic," and never directly questioned the legitimacy of the regime. More recently, the authors of the Charter 08 manifesto were the first since Wei Jingsheng to directly ask for an end to the dictatorship of the party, although they called not for the party's destruction, but for an end to the domination of one party over all others.

Except in 1957, when they represented the core of the Communist intelligentsia, most of the actors in the prodemocracy movement have been marginal intellectuals, such as the former Red Guards of 1976 and 1978, the freelance intellectuals of 2008, and the students of 1957 and 1989. The prodemocracy movement has never been very successful among the working people.

INABILITY TO ACCUMULATE EXPERIENCE

Ultimately, the main characteristic of this movement is that it has no continuity. After every episode, the actors are either jailed or exiled abroad or to the countryside. The effective monopoly of the Communist Party on the writing of history, and the pressure put on the families of activists to keep them from transmitting their experience to their children, make it difficult for later generations to draw lessons from earlier activists' experiences. For example, the former Red Guards who denounced the regime in 1978 had not read the writings of the 1957 rightists; they had to start from scratch, and it took them a long time to rediscover the demand for equality of all citizens before the law. The student activists of 1989 had not read the works of the rightists or the Democracy Wall activists, and during the two months that their movement lasted, they were unable to produce analyses of the regime that went deeper than those of their predecessors.

The Chinese prodemocracy movement cannot sum up and build on past experiences; it lacks a structured and structuring memory.

SEE ALSO *Classical Scholarship and Intellectual Debates: Debates since 1949; Cultural Revolution, 1966–1969; Democracy Wall; Deng Xiaoping; Hu Yaobang; Hundred Days' Reform; Hundred Flowers Campaign; Tiananmen Incident (1976); Zhao Ziyang.*

BIBLIOGRAPHY

Béja, Jean-Philippe. *A la recherche d'une ombre chinoise: Le mouvement pour la démocratie en Chine, 1919–2004* [In search of a shadow: The movement for democracy in China, 1919–2004]. Paris: Seuil, 2004.

Béja, Jean-Philippe. Forbidden Memory, Unwritten History: The Difficulty to Structure an Opposition Movement in the PRC. *China Perspectives* 4 (2007): 88–98.

Ding Yijiang. *Chinese Democracy after Tiananmen.* Vancouver: University of British Columbia Press, 2001.

Goldman, Merle. *From Comrade to Citizen: The Struggle for Political Rights in China.* Cambridge, MA: Harvard University Press, 2007.

Zhang Gang. *The Tiananmen Papers.* New York: Public Affairs, 2001.

Jean-Philippe Béja

PROPAGANDA

Propaganda and thought work (*xuanchuan yu sixiang gongzuo*) has always been an essential element of the Chinese Communist Party's hold on power. From 1949 to 1978, the era under Mao Zedong, propaganda and thought work played a key role in the socialist transformation of Chinese society. In the 1980s the party leadership was divided on the issue of what role propaganda and thought work had in China's modernizing economy and polity. This debate was brought to an effective end after the June 4, 1989, crackdown on the student protest movement. The post–June Fourth leadership established a new line, which has been followed since then: that the party would focus on both economic growth and a renewed emphasis on propaganda and political thought work. Since the 1990s, propaganda and thought work has frequently been described as the life blood (*shengmingxian*) of the party-state. It is regarded as one of the key means for guaranteeing the Communist Party's hold on power.

The Communist Party–led propaganda sector (*xuanchuan kou*) consists of four connected parts:

- the network of propaganda cadres and offices installed in party committees and branches at all levels of organizations in the state bureaucracy, as well as Chinese- and foreign-run private enterprises with party cells;

- the culture, education, sport, science, social-science, health, technology, and media sectors;

- the political-department system of the People's Liberation Army;

- all mass organizations, from the more traditional, such as the All-China Women's Federation, to nongovernmental organizations and government-operated nongovernmental organizations.

Despite moves toward privatization since the 1990s, even propaganda-related enterprises that receive little or no state funding are still controlled within this system. A handful of leaders at every level of government coordinate these various channels by holding concurrent key positions within the four parts of the propaganda sector.

Propaganda and thought work is controlled by the party propaganda system (*xuanjiao xitong*). At the pinnacle of this system is a senior leader responsible for overseeing all propaganda and thought work. This figure is always a member of the Politburo. Since 2002 the leader in this role, Li Changchun, has actually been a member of the Standing Committee of the Politburo. This is an indication of the increased importance of propaganda and thought work in recent years.

Bureaucratic arrangements have changed considerably between 1949 and now. Mao Zedong was the equivalent of the leader in this role from the mid-1940s and up to his death. This role is not the same as being head of the Central Propaganda Department, but is held by someone else (from 1949 to 1966, for example, this role was held by Lu Dingyi). In 1978 Hu Yaobang took on the propaganda leadership, until his downfall in 1987. Hu Qili then took over until the crisis of 1989. Li Ruihuan was in charge from 1989 to 1992. There was then a ten-year period when Ding Guan'gen controlled all the most important positions in the Party propaganda system, but was not on the Standing Committee of the Politburo. This may have been because he was rumored to have betrayed the Party in the late 1940s.

The next level of the propaganda system consists of the party's Propaganda and Thought Work Leading Group and the Foreign Propaganda Leading Group. These bodies consist of leading figures within the party-state propaganda system, such as the head of the Xinhua News Service, the head of China Central Television, and the head of the Ministry of Culture. There are Propaganda and Thought Work Leading Groups at the central, provincial, city, and district levels of government. The leading groups guide and coordinate party propaganda and thought work across a wide range of organizations. The next level of administrative control within the propaganda system is the Communist Party Central Secretariat. This body also has a coordinating role, facilitating the linkages between the various central and

***Propaganda poster titled* Survey the Enemy, *c. 1970.** Since the beginning of the People's Republic of China, the government has coordinated a multilayered approach to disseminating pro-Communist Party propaganda throughout Chinese society. Despite Deng Xiaoping's decision in the 1970s to adopt a market-based economy, the government has redoubled efforts to control the content of information in all other spheres of Chinese society.* © SWIM INK/CORBIS

provincial party organizations involved in propaganda and thought work.

The most important of all organizations in the propaganda system is the Communist Party Central Committee's Propaganda Department, or Central Propaganda Department (Zhonggong Zhongyang Xuanchuan Bu). The Central Propaganda Department has a guiding role over the entire propaganda sector. In 1998 the department's English title was formally changed to the Central *Publicity* Department—a reflection of an awareness of the negative connotations *propaganda* holds in English and an indication of changes in China's foreign propaganda strategies. The Chinese name has not changed, however, and in English the new name has not caught on, other than in official Chinese propaganda materials.

The Central Propaganda Department is in charge of planning China's overall ideological development. It has a

direct leadership role over some parts of the propaganda sector, while over other parts it has only a guiding role. The department has a leadership role over the entire media and culture sector in China, as well as over the offices in charge of state management of those sectors: the General Administration of Press and Publishing; the State Administration of Radio, Film, and Television; the Ministry of Culture; and the State Administration for Industry and Commerce. The Central Propaganda Department formally holds a leadership role in partnership with the State Council; it is in charge of ideological matters, while the State Council—through its subsidiary bodies the General Administration of Press and Publishing; the State Administration of Radio, Film, and Television; the Ministry of Culture; and the State Administration for Industry and Commerce—is in charge of ideology-related administrative matters. The Central Propaganda

Department also has a leadership role over the Central Party School and its local-level equivalents, as well as over the Institutes of Socialism (Zhongyang Shehuizhuyi Xueyuan), which provide ideological training to nonparty government cadres, and the Institutes of Administration (Guojia Xingzheng Xueyuan), which are in charge of educating government officials in modern management techniques.

The State Administration of Radio, Film, and Television supervises radio, film, and television in China and directly controls China Central Television, China National Radio, and China Radio International. The Central Propaganda Department is empowered to approve or disapprove any programming changes in these three media outlets and monitors overall developments relating to the media. The General Administration of Press and Publishing supervises all printing and publishing activities in China, including various forms of electronic publishing and reproduction of information.

The Ministry of Culture supervises everything from fashion contests, ten-pin bowling, karaoke bars, and tea shops to magazine and book selling, art exhibitions, and other culture-related enterprises. It also has authority over advertising (a role that it shares with the State Administration for Industry and Commerce). Since the mid-1980s the Central Propaganda Department has gradually relaxed its controls over cultural activities in China, and in comparison with the Chinese media, there is a relatively free atmosphere in this sector. However, some subjects are still taboo, mainly political themes.

The Central Propaganda Department also has a leadership role (with no state intervention) over the nationwide system of Spiritual Civilization Offices and over provincial, local, and party-branch-level propaganda departments. Spiritual Civilization Offices are in charge of propaganda-and-thought-work activities targeted at the masses. *Spiritual civilization* is a euphemism for the new era's soft propaganda and soft social control, such as public education on ethics and polite behavior. The Central Propaganda Department has a leadership role over the various professional associations that help manage the activities of personnel within the various parts of the propaganda sector, such as the Publishers Association, the Journalist Association, and the Internet Association.

The Central Propaganda Department has a guiding role over much of China's bureaucracy, including the General Political Office Propaganda Department of the People's Liberation Army; the Ministry of Health; the Ministry of Tourism; the Central Sport Commission; the Ministry of Education; the Chinese Academy of Social Sciences (China's provincial Academies of Social Science are under the direct leadership of provincial propaganda departments); all of China's mass organizations; and the network of press spokespersons and information departments that every government department has set up since 2002.

The leadership/guidance role of the Central Propaganda Department over large sections of the Chinese bureaucracy greatly assists its powers to manage the flow of information within China. Thus, every means of communication and form of organized social interaction in China is ultimately under the formal supervision of the Central Propaganda Department and its subsidiaries. Since the 1990s, however, the Central Propaganda Department has taken a macro view of control and is very selective in its interventions, in contrast to the microcontrol approach of the Mao era.

The Communist Party has historically divided propaganda work into two categories, domestic and foreign; and into four types: political, economic, social, and cultural propaganda. The Central Propaganda Department is in charge of domestic propaganda, while its brother organization, the Office of Foreign Propaganda, is in charge of foreign propaganda. To deal with the issue of the technical separation between party and state in China, the Office of Foreign Propaganda has another more commonly known nameplate: the State Council Information Office. Since the turn of the twenty-first century, as a result of the impact of information-communication technology, which knows no borders, the distinctions between domestic and foreign propaganda have become somewhat blurred, and there is some overlap between the duties of the Office of Foreign Propaganda and the Central Propaganda Department.

The content of propaganda and thought work has changed dramatically since 1989. Instead of political thought reform and social transformation, as in the Mao era, the focus since 1989 is on economic thought reform and social stability. Propaganda and thought work is considerably depoliticized in comparison to that of the Mao years. The main targets of party-political indoctrination are now youth and party members, while the masses are educated with the soft propaganda of spiritual civilization.

The Central Propaganda Department and the propaganda system it leads are commonly thought of as the most conservative of all the party-state organs in the Chinese system. Yet in the post-1989 period the Central Propaganda Department has overseen and encouraged a radical restructure of China's public sphere at the same time as adopting modern methods of mass persuasion and information control. In doing so, it has made a major contribution toward creating the conditions for ongoing Communist Party rule in China. The propaganda state is alive and well in China today and looks set to continue that way for the near future.

SEE ALSO *Communist Party; Influences Abroad: Maoism and Art; Music, Propaganda, and Mass Mobilization; Photography, History of: Propaganda Photography; Propaganda Art.*

BIBLIOGRAPHY

Brady, Anne-Marie. *Marketing Dictatorship: Propaganda and Thought Work in Contemporary China*. Lanham, MD: Rowman & Littlefield, 2007.

King, Vincent V. S. *Propaganda Campaigns in Communist China*. Cambridge, MA: Center for International Studies, Massachusetts Institute of Technology, 1966.

Liu, Alan P. L. *Communications and National Integration in Communist China*. Berkeley: University of California Press, 1971.

Lynch, Daniel C. *After the Propaganda State: Media, Politics, and "Thought Work" in Reformed China*. Stanford, CA: Stanford University Press, 1999.

Yu, Frederick T. C. *Mass Persuasion in Communist China*. London: Pall Mall Press, 1964.

Zhao, Yuezhi. *Media, Market, and Democracy in China: Between the Party Line and the Bottom Line*. Urbana: University of Illinois Press, 1998.

Anne-Marie Brady

PROPAGANDA ART

This entry contains the following:

OVERVIEW
Maria Galikowski

NEW NIANHUA
James Flath

POSTERS
Maria Galikowski

PEASANT PAINTING
Vivian Y. Li

ART PRODUCTS OF THE CULTURAL REVOLUTION
Maria Galikowski

OVERVIEW

Propaganda is information disseminated by various means, often by elite groups within a society, especially the politically powerful, to influence people's thinking and behavior. Although propaganda, in one guise or another, has been in existence since the development of complex societies, the modern connotations of the word stem from the explicit advocacy of propaganda as an ideological tool during the early years of the Soviet Union. Communist theorists like Nikolai Bukharin (1888–1938) asserted that propaganda had an important role to play in eradicating the bourgeois ideology of the old society and in firmly establishing the new ideology of socialism.

Under the direct influence of the Soviet Union and the almost constant threat of extinction at the hands of the ruling Nationalist Party, the early Chinese Communist Party (CCP) focused on propaganda as a means to win over sections of the population to the Communist cause and convey party principles to a wider audience. A Soviet-style Department of Propaganda was established in 1924 as a conduit for conveying policy formulations to the various left-wing cultural branches that were in the process of being set up. The central function of the new department was to direct all cultural workers toward propaganda work. In the intense struggle to win popular support for the CCP agenda against the Nationalists and subsequently the Japanese, propaganda, including visual images as a major component, became a key weapon in the CCP arsenal.

As party thinking on art-related matters evolved, particularly following Mao's Yan'an Forum in 1942, artists were increasingly obliged to adhere to the propaganda imperative. Free thinking and unfettered creativity were no longer to be tolerated. Gradually, however, the CCP was forced to acknowledge that to make art effective as propaganda—conveying a political message in ways readily accessible to the populace—required some accommodation of established aesthetic conventions.

THE WOODCUT MOVEMENT

The need to apply an aesthetic dimension to propaganda surfaced early on in the woodcut movement of the 1930s and 1940s. The history of woodcuts and woodcutting techniques in China reaches back at least as far as the Tang dynasty; but it was the writer Lu Xun (1881–1936) who in 1931 brought German expressionist woodcuts, particularly those of Käthe Kollwitz, and the stark work of the Russian constructivists to the attention of left-wing artists in Shanghai. As a relatively inexpensive art form that could be easily reproduced in the many urban underground publications, the woodcut was avidly embraced by left-wing artists such as Jiang Feng (1910–1982) and Hu Yichuan (1910–2000), two prominent figures in the post-1949 art establishment who modeled their work on the bold, grim styles of their European and Soviet counterparts.

The establishment of the Lu Xun Academy of Arts in 1937—the year of the Japanese invasion, igniting the Anti-Japanese War—at the Communist base in Yan'an formalized the training of left-wing artists in the theories and techniques of art as propaganda (at this stage, principally woodcuts). However, it soon became apparent that the somber, heavily shaded, black-and-white prints favored by the urban artists were proving unpopular with peasants, their primary audience. It was not until artists adapted folk-art print styles, incorporating the use of vivid primary colors and repetitive motifs, to promote the political themes of the day—opposing the Japanese invaders and exposing the corruption and incompetence of the Nationalist government—that the peasants became more receptive to the political message conveyed by these new-style prints.

SOCIALIST REALISM

How to achieve what was later termed a "unification of revolutionary political content and the most perfect artistic form possible" remained an issue after 1949. The orthodox Marxist political line, as propounded by prominent Marxists like Georgy Plekhanov (1857–1918) in Russia and Qu Qiubai (1899–1935) in China and adopted by Mao during his Yan'an Forum, became the prescribed content for all creative endeavors. There was to be no "art for art's sake"; the sole purpose of art was to guide "the people"—workers, peasants, soldiers—in the principles of socialism. China's adoption in the 1950s of Soviet socialist realism, whose stated purpose was the general dissemination of Communist ideology, ensured art's role as essentially a propaganda tool. Soviet artists and art theorists were hugely influential in promoting art as a vehicle for propaganda, and Soviet painting and sculpture were taken as models for the new socialist art. The range of permissible themes became increasingly circumscribed, including such officially sanctioned topics as party leaders and party history, the promotion of specific policies, and depictions of socialist heroes. In line with socialist realist precepts, the mode of representation also tended to be severely limited: artists had to adopt the correct ideological stance toward their subject, portraying revolutionary figures and events in a positive light and enemies of the people in a negative light. Workers, peasants, and soldiers were thus represented as contentedly enjoying the fruits of socialism, enthusiastically participating in ideological movements, or determinedly smashing enemies of the people. Party leaders, as long as they were still in political favor, were invariably depicted as strong, sympathetic supporters of the people; once out of favor, they were depicted in cartoons as weasel-like and devious or arrogant and bombastic.

To achieve "the most perfect artistic form possible," some individuals, including several high-ranking establishment figures like Jiang Feng, favored Western-style scientific drawing and oil painting as the most appropriate artistic means for conveying the new socialist society. Such artists considered most Chinese ink painting genres, with the exception of portraiture, as being particularly unsuitable for propaganda. Others argued that because traditional art forms were more readily recognizable to ordinary folk, utilizing them would enhance the effectiveness of a work of art as propaganda. Mao himself was a strong supporter of "national forms," which referred not so much to traditional Chinese ink painting as to those that grew from the lives and experiences of the masses, such as New Year pictures (*nianhua*), murals, and local sculpture styles. But even Chinese ink painting could serve a useful propaganda purpose under certain circumstances, such as during the initial phase of the Great Leap Forward (1958–1960), when deteriorating relations with the Soviet Union led China to forge its own route to socialism. To encourage a strong sense of national identity, which was required to unify the populace behind China's ambitious socialist construction program, party officials criticized those seen as having denigrated China's "national heritage," and Chinese ink painters were temporarily allowed to pursue more traditional motifs.

With such limited creative scope, and the danger of serious sanctions against those who contravened the restrictive guidelines laid down by the party, artists often had to fall back on convention, producing formulaic work. Ironically, both the cultural establishment and professional artists themselves complained that much of the art produced was dull and lifeless, more propaganda than art.

THE PEOPLE AS PROPAGANDISTS

Art was used to galvanize the entire population to participate in Mao's grandiose schemes to surpass the West in industrial production and achieve a Communist utopia. During the Great Leap Forward and the decade of the Cultural Revolution (1966–1976), a visual saturation of unambiguous propaganda conveyed the official goals of the two movements. The party exhorted factory workers, peasants, and soldiers to take up the brush and become artists themselves so as to feel like co-creators of the envisioned utopia. Many did so enthusiastically. Peasants produced simple depictions of the successes of the Great Leap in "new murals" (*xin bihua*), while workers created monochrome cartoons attacking the key political targets of the Cultural Revolution. In 1975 the Hu county peasant paintings, the best-known example of worker-peasant-soldier art, became the first paintings from Communist China to be exhibited abroad. The peasants' use (with some "guidance" by professional artists) of Western-style perspective and three-dimensional modeling raised the quality of their work from something purely amateur to a standard worthy of presentation on the international stage. Domestically, these paintings were touted as models to be emulated. By presenting visions of a rural idyll, with enthusiastic, ruddy-faced peasants busily engaged in hoeing the fields, building irrigation works, or attending political meetings, the paintings perfectly served the propaganda purposes of the authorities. As the decade of the Cultural Revolution began, art as propaganda was no longer something externally imposed by an authoritarian regime; instead people were co-opted to participate in the propaganda drive themselves. Anyone and everyone, in theory, was now a propagandist.

THE MAO CULT

Central to the successful implementation of the CCP political agenda was an enhancement of the status of the Communist leadership, in particular Mao Zedong. Mao had appeared in propaganda posters from the early 1940s, but the establishment of the Communist government in Beijing in 1949 was accompanied by a steady increase in the number and scale of works with Mao as the central focus, epitomized in the series of Mao portraits that have since hung in Tiananmen Square. A major upsurge in Maoist iconography occurred during the Cultural Revolution as a key means of bolstering the prestige of the chairman; further, it helped to ensure the success of this unprecedented movement, which would topple Mao's main political rivals and shake to the core the party he had been instrumental in building up. Mao's image was reproduced countless times, in paintings, posters, statues, and badges. It was ubiquitous in all public places—large-scale statues stood on university campuses and in public squares and portraits hung in factories, shops, offices, and homes. Together with Mao's *Little Red Book*, of which up to 800 million copies may have been sold during the Cultural Revolution, the visual image of the Great Helmsman reinforced Mao's power and prestige, raising him to almost godlike status. The cult surrounding him had its antecedents in the Soviet Union in the cult of Stalin and, to a lesser degree, of Lenin, but it also had resonances with traditional ideas of the emperor as mediator between Heaven and Earth. Thus the Mao cult took hold not simply through a process of coercive action on an unwilling populace, but also by being linked to traditional patterns of cultural receptivity and the quasi-religious acceptance of a powerful, paternalistic, authoritarian figure. Many portraits of Mao, including one of the most famous images to emerge from the Cultural Revolution, Liu Chunhua's (b. 1944) *Mao Goes to Anyuan* (*Mao zhuxi qu Anyuan*), portray him as a colossus striding the earth; the masses, if they figure at all, are secondary, often diminutive elements, whose only purpose seems to be to contrast with Mao's impressive stature.

REINVENTING HISTORY THROUGH ART

One of the primary uses of art as propaganda was to distort or reinvent history so as to accommodate political imperatives. Though arguably most, if not all, propagandist art distorts complex reality to serve an ideological agenda, a more blatant practice involved altering already existing paintings to conform to the prevailing political orthodoxy: Individuals who had fallen out of political favor were painted out, and individuals who served a minimal role in or were completely absent from a historical event were painted in. The rewriting, repainting, and resculpting of history occurred on a regular basis during the Cultural Revolution, when the party machine came under Mao's severe attack and many leading officials lost their positions or their lives. Mao was thus linked inaccurately in art to particular moments in party history, becoming, for example, the central figure in works commemorating the First Communist Party Congress in 1921 when in reality his contribution at that event was decidedly peripheral. The often-reproduced oil painting *Mao Goes to Anyuan* was raised to iconic status essentially because it implied a leading role for Mao in the successful Anyuan miners' strike of 1922, a landmark event in Communist Party history, in which Mao had in fact played only a minor role.

One of the most extreme, and perhaps also most famous, examples of art being used to reinvent history is Dong Xiwen's (1914–1973) monumental oil painting *Founding Ceremony* (*Kaiguo dadian*), which hung for many years in the Museum of Chinese Revolutionary History. Originally completed in 1952, it portrays the momentous point in China's modern history when Mao, joined by his close political comrades, stood atop Tiananmen Square and proclaimed the establishment of the People's Republic. Over the years a number of the figures that accompanied Mao on that day were purged, and Dong was forced to revise his painting by expunging first the figure of Gao Gang (purged in 1954) and then Liu Shaoqi (purged in 1966). In 1972 Dong was ordered to remove a third figure, Lin Boqu, from the leadership lineup, but he bravely refused to desecrate his painting a third time. A close (though inferior) copy was eventually made by two other artists, this time without the Lin Boqu figure. After the death of Mao, the official rehabilitation of many of his political opponents required a similar "rehabilitation" of numerous art works, and the copy version of *Founding Ceremony* was altered to incorporate, once again, all the individuals in Dong Xiwen's original.

Since the late twentieth century, propaganda art has been limited mainly to posters and street billboards. It has become less commonly used for overtly political purposes and more often to raise public awareness about relatively neutral issues, such as HIV/AIDS, severe acute respiratory syndrome (SARS), and the introduction of new laws. However, politically motivated visual images continue to appear, in propaganda posters that attempt to demonize the Falun Gong or cultivate nationalist sentiment by, for example, lauding the achievements of China as a developing power or emphasizing congenial relations between China's Han majority and its 55 minorities. Posters have been used periodically, and often extensively, to promote the government's capitalist-style economic reforms and social agendas, notably Deng Xiaoping's Four Modernizations, Jiang Zemin's Three Represents, and Hu Jintao's Eight Honors and Eight Disgraces.

SEE ALSO *Influences Abroad; Lu Xun; Mao Zedong; Music, Propaganda, and Mass Mobilization; Yan'an Forum.*

BIBLIOGRAPHY

Andrews, Julia F. *Painters and Politics in the People's Republic of China, 1949–1979.* Berkeley: University of California Press, 1994.

Fine Arts Collection Section of the Cultural Group under the State Council of the People's Republic of China. *Peasant Paintings from Huhsien County.* Peking: People's Fine Arts Publishing House, 1976.

Galikowski, Maria. *Art and Politics in China, 1949–1984.* Hong Kong: Chinese University Press, 1998.

Jiang, Joshua J. H. The Extermination or the Prosperity of Artists? Mass Art in Mid-Twentieth-Century China. *Third Text* 18, 2 (2004):169–182.

Laing, Ellen Johnston. Chinese Peasant Painting, 1958–1976, Amateur and Professional. *Art International* 27, 1 (1984): 1–12.

Laing, Ellen Johnston. *The Winking Owl: Art in the People's Republic of China.* Berkeley: University of California Press, 1988.

Maria Galikowski

NEW *NIANHUA*

In 1942 Mao Zedong and the Chinese Communist Party (CCP) called on affiliated artists to reconsider their "bourgeois" sensibilities and learn to appreciate the art of the common people of China. The party's cultural elite believed that by infusing folk art with modern messages the CCP could produce more effective propaganda for China's peasant and working classes. For artists then living in the rural Yan'an Base Area, the one variety of graphic art that appeared to have the greatest potential for such reform was the popular print known as *nianhua* (New Year pictures). These diverse, brightly colored woodblock prints were manufactured predominantly in rural areas and marketed across China in advance of the Lunar New Year. The reformed genre would come to be known as the new *nianhua* [*xin nianhua*].

Although *nianhua* prints often depicted themes that were considered "feudal" or "superstitious" by Communist ideologues, the medium itself was interpreted as inherently wholesome thanks to its peasant origins. By contrast, the artistic style favored by many CCP affiliated artists was derived from the socially conscious but overwhelmingly dark modern woodcut movement centered in Shanghai. When those artists moved to Yan'an in the mid-1930s they continued to create politically appropriate woodcuts but found that much of their work was visually incomprehensible to their target audience. To resolve this conflict artists

Revolutionary Wedding, c. 1950s. *In the late 1940s, Chinese Communist Party artists began disseminating propaganda in rural areas using traditional wood-block prints typically distributed before the Lunar New Year. Called* nianhua, *these posters featured bright, contrasting colors and revolutionary themes designed to be comprehended easily by uneducated citizens.* **COURTESY OF JAMES FLATH**

such as Li Qi (b.1928) and Gu Yuan (1919–1996) applied their woodcut skills to *nianhua*, replaced problematic subject matter with revolutionary themes, and adopted the bold colors and strong contrasts of the single outline and flat color (*danxian pingtu*) technique. In this way the CCP began to mass-produce simple but vivid propaganda posters that called on the people to support their initiatives of military resistance and agrarian reform. Even though these new *nianhua* grew increasingly dissimilar to the folk art that inspired them, they nonetheless represented an aesthetic link to the rural population from which the CCP drew much of its strength.

By 1949 new *nianhua* had gained favor at high levels within the party, and almost immediately after coming to power the CCP issued a "Ministry of Culture Directive Concerning the Development of New-*Nianhua* Work." To further encourage the production of new *nianhua*, the national Art Workers Association (AWA; the forerunner of the Chinese Artists Association) sponsored the National *Nianhua* Awards, inviting submissions from across the country. The purpose of these annual competitions was to select appropriate graphic models that demonstrated how people could achieve realistic socialist objectives. Although artists and art critics frequently cited the authority of the "masses" when making and critiquing new *nianhua*, they faced considerable difficulties in persuading these same masses to join in their production and appreciation.

During the 1950s arts cadres began to seek out the roots of the original *nianhua* genre in rural China, where the traditional industry still employed the woodblock printing technique. The goal was both to suppress the circulation of thematically "poisonous" prints that continued to reflect "reactionary" and "superstitious" themes and to promote political and social awareness in the local industry. Under the cadres' direction, peasant artists in villages like Yangjiabu in Shandong and Wuqiang in Hebei did produce a number of striking images illustrating the peace and prosperity that would ideally develop under the guidance of the CCP (see figure 1). However, many of these images were also criticized for ignoring the didactic principle of propaganda art and for simply replacing prerevolutionary symbols with revolutionary icons. Meanwhile, consumers showed little interest in the new images, preferring the brighter and more festive "old" *nianhua* that still appeared in New Year markets. Although new *nianhua* were continually produced in rural printing centers throughout the 1950s, these experiments never achieved satisfactory results, either in terms of political themes or production levels.

Instead, new *nianhua* would remain under the control of arts professionals and industrialized printers in urban China. In making new *nianhua* the standard art form it was implicit that other popular graphic arts, especially the sexually charged calendar posters (*yuefenpai*) made famous by the Shanghai cigarette industry, would have to meet new *nianhua* standards. In merging *yuefenpai* techniques and new *nianhua* principles, *yuefenpai* artists such as Zhang Biwu were able give new *nianhua* a vivaciousness and dramatic appeal that had so far been absent in Chinese propaganda art. The reconciliation of the *nianhua* tradition and the modernity of *yuefenpai* within the boundaries defined by China's art establishment helped to move Chinese propaganda art beyond the limitations of the Yan'an style. Although the genre was eventually marginalized by the development of Soviet-style socialist realism, the new *nianhua* movement was nonetheless a critical step in the development of Chinese socialist modernism.

SEE ALSO *Calendar; Folk Art; Luo Gongliu; New Print Movement; Rustic Realism in Art; Woodblock Printing (xylography); Yan'an Forum.*

BIBLIOGRAPHY

Andrews, Julia. *Painters and Politics in the People's Republic of China, 1949–1979.* Berkeley: University of California Press, 1994.

Flath, James. It's a Wonderful Life: *Nianhua* and *Yuefenpai* at the Dawn of the People's Republic. *Modern Chinese Literature and Culture* 16, 2 (2004): 123–159.

Hung, Chang-tai. Repainting China: New Year Prints (Nianhua) and Peasant Resistance in the Early Years of the People's Republic. *Comparative Studies in Society and History* 42, 4 (2000): 770–810.

Shen, Kuiyi. Publishing Posters Before the Cultural Revolution. *Modern Chinese Literature and Culture* 12, 2 (2000): 177–202.

James Flath

POSTERS

The propaganda poster is a modern visual art form that lends itself readily to mass production. Historically, governments have used the propaganda poster to convey a message, often of a highly emotive and ideological nature, to the general public. Nations used it extensively during both world wars as a way to legitimize involvement in these conflicts and as a means to mobilize human resources to engage in the war effort. Totalitarian regimes, most notably the Nazis in Germany and the Bolsheviks in the Soviet Union, have commonly made use of the poster to inculcate in the populace a particular worldview and to encourage mass participation in political campaigns.

In its efforts to implement socialism, the Chinese Communist Party (CCP), under the influence of its Russian counterpart, recognized the value of the propaganda poster as an important political tool for raising the ideological consciousness of the laboring classes. Unencumbered by the established conventions governing more traditional art forms,

Propaganda poster featuring Mao Zedong teaching children, created by Na Siu-ming and Che Ing-Jin, 1975. *Inexpensive to produce in mass quantities, propaganda posters became an important method of communicating Communist ideas to the general population. Many posters featured Mao Zedong in a variety of settings, contributing to a cult of personality aimed at elevating the leader to superhuman status.* **PVDE/RDA/GETTY IMAGES**

such as Chinese ink painting, original propaganda poster designs could more easily accommodate the principles of Soviet-inspired socialist realism, the cultural orthodoxy adopted by the CCP after 1949 to guide all creative work. Paintings, woodcuts, and New Year pictures (*nianhua*) that were considered to have particular didactic value could also be readily converted to the poster format (*huapian*).

The takeover of China's urban centers in 1949 secured for the CCP the printing facilities and other resources required for the mass production and distribution of posters. Millions of copies a year were subsequently produced, especially during periods of radical Maoism, as happened during the Great Leap Forward (1958–1960) and the decade of the Cultural Revolution (1966–1976). With their bright, eye-catching colors and dramatic designs, posters were displayed in homes, factories, shops, railway stations, and indeed every suitable public space. They could be produced cheaply and speedily; from conception and design to final lithographic printing, an individual poster might be

completed in ten hours or less, ready for sale to the general public through commercial outlets nationwide or for free distribution to urban *danwei* (units). The propaganda poster thus became the most flexible mass visual tool in what was often a rapidly changing political environment. It was used to reflect a wide range of social and political themes, extolling the virtues of Communism and railing against the evils of capitalism and imperialism, and was a chief visual component in all large-scale political campaigns.

Most Chinese propaganda posters inherited certain general characteristics from the Soviet Union, including the compositional centrality of human figures, bold images, and simple, direct slogans. These features gave the poster form a high level of immediacy and clarity, ideal for conveying a political message to a mass audience. However, different styles of propaganda posters did evolve over time, depending on the era in which it was produced and its core themes. One type, for example, closely aligned with Soviet posters, comprised images of androgynous workers or peasants, flexing bulging muscles and extending clenched fists, rendered using a minimalist palette of red, white, and black for maximum dramatic impact (as well as to keep down the costs of production). This type of poster was often used to attack "class enemies" or "foreign imperialists." A second, common type, particularly popular with the peasants, drew heavily on the traditional New Year picture and featured bright, unmodulated color schemes, less emphasis on shading and perspective, and the inclusion of images and symbols with lucky connotations, such as plump babies, smiling, obedient children, and overflowing food baskets. A third type, a product generally of the more moderate stages of Communist politics, reveals the influence of traditional Chinese ink painting: for example, Jinggangshan, the Communist stronghold of the 1920s and 1930s, might be rendered as a Song-style mountain scene, or the Communist base at Yan'an might be transformed into a soft, misty landscape.

Since the beginning of the reform era of the 1980s, the propaganda poster has gradually lost much of its function as an ideological "whip" for the masses. Instead, it has taken on a largely educational role, providing simple information about important health issues, such as HIV/AIDS and severe acute respiratory syndrome (SARS). It has not, however, entirely lost its more controversial propaganda function, as evidenced by posters warning of the dangers of the Falun Gong "cult"—though how effective such political messages have become is unclear.

BIBLIOGRAPHY

Cushing, Lincoln, and Ann Tompkins. *Chinese Posters: Art from the Great Proletarian Cultural Revolution*. San Francisco: Chronicle Books, 2007.

Evans, Harriet, and Stephanie Donald, eds. *Picturing Power in the People's Republic of China: Posters of the Cultural Revolution*. Lanham, MD: Rowman & Littlefield, 1999.

Galikowski, Maria. *Art and Politics in China, 1949–1984*. Hong Kong: Chinese University Press, 1998.

Landsberger, Stefan. *Chinese Propaganda Posters: From Revolution to Modernization*. Armonk, NY: Sharpe, 1995.

Maria Galikowski

PEASANT PAINTING

Peasant painting (*nongmin hua*) was nonexistent until the Great Leap Forward of 1958 to 1960, when peasants were encouraged to visually record the modernization projects and reforms then under way. Traditionally, peasant art consisted of decorative papercuts for windows, stenciled fabric patterns, printed religious images and charms, and New Year pictures (*nianhua*). The boldly rendered shapes and stylized figures and motifs of peasant painting recall the heritage of peasant art in these earlier mediums.

During the Great Leap Forward peasant paintings enjoyed some popularity as the mainstream form of art. Peasant painters from Pixian county in Jiangsu province and Zhejiang province received the most attention. Drawings, paintings, and photographs of peasant wall paintings from Pixian county were exhibited in Beijing in September 1958. In the years following the failed Great Leap Forward, however, peasant painting lost its prominence in publications, such as the official art journal *Meishu*, and media coverage turned elsewhere, though the paintings continued to be included in national exhibitions and local displays.

REVIVAL DURING THE CULTURAL REVOLUTION

It was not until the Cultural Revolution began in 1966 that peasant painting was recognized as an officially sanctioned art form. Earlier, painting was seen as a pastime for peasants. During the decade of the Cultural Revolution (1966–1976), by contrast, party officials regarded painting as an important activity to cultivate among the peasants for the development of art and culture for the masses. Mao's wife, Jiang Qing, who tightly controlled the art and cultural spheres of Chinese society during this period, officially endorsed peasant paintings. At the height of Jiang's power, from 1972 to 1976, articles about peasant paintings and painters began noticeably to reappear. Jiang ardently supported peasant painting as a means to emphasize the essential role of the worker and peasants in the fulfillment of Mao's revolutionary vision through cultural activities. As amateur artists, peasant painters were publicly esteemed as model citizens for their ability to excel at manual as well as mental labor.

Peasant paintings, usually gouache on paper but also sometimes appearing as murals on public structures and houses, used bright colors, black outlines, blocks of flat color, and repeated motifs for decorative effect. Their simple and structured compositions completely covered the picture plane, with no horizon line. In these paintings, figures were drawn in a cartoonlike fashion, and overall the paintings had a naïve pictorial quality. The art historian Ellen Johnston Laing argues convincingly in her 1984 article that the peasant painters of the Cultural Revolution were more skilled than those working during the Great Leap Forward because they benefited from training by professional artists. Beginning in 1963, in the years leading up to the Cultural Revolution, there were reports of teams of cultural workers composed of theatrical professionals, writers, and artists being sent to the countryside to learn from the peasants as well as to educate the peasants in socialism. There is also evidence of do-it-yourself copybooks prepared by professional artists to teach peasants how to paint; the use of such copybooks explains the formulaic treatment of figures and compositions found in several peasant paintings made during the Cultural Revolution.

For the most part the subject matter of peasant paintings falls into two categories: the heroic peasant enjoying the opportunities and prosperity of life under Mao, and the diligent peasant contributing to the reconstruction of China. Drawing from their everyday lives, peasant painters depicted such scenes as a peasant consumed in his reading of Mao's teachings, and peasants working together to dig a well. Peasant paintings were also used to promote campaigns, such as the attack against the military leader Lin Biao (1907–1971?), who was purported to have believed that the masses lacked creativity. Peasant paintings thus served as propaganda art in two ways: in their subject matter, and as evidence of the common peasant's ability to wield the brush.

HU COUNTY PEASANT PAINTINGS

The increased attention to peasant painting during the Cultural Revolution culminated in October 1973 in the Beijing exhibition of Hu county peasant paintings, which was attended by over two million visitors. Hu county in Shaanxi province, thirty-five miles outside Xi'an, was the designated "home of peasant painting." In 1972 Jiang named Hu county the model

art commune. Hu county's star distinction was matched only by the Dazhai brigade, which was considered the national model for agriculture, and Daqing, which was viewed as the best in the oilfield industry. By 1972 there were reportedly 550 peasant painters in Hu county, in twenty of the twenty-two communes in the area.

During his visit to the 1973 exhibition of Hu county peasant paintings, Zhao Wuji (Zou Wu-ki; b. 1921), a prominent Chinese artist who had immigrated to Paris, was impressed by the artworks and endeavored to have the show travel abroad. As a result, in the fall of 1975 eighty paintings from the exhibition went on view at the Ninth Paris Biennial Exhibition. Because this was the first time the People's Republic of China had participated in an international exhibition of contemporary art since the Cultural Revolution began, the show attracted wide attention as representing the official art of China. The selection of Hu county peasant paintings then continued to tour other major European cities, including London in 1976.

The Library of the Production Brigade, *by peasants from Huxian, 1958.* *In the late 1950s, Communist leaders encouraged peasants to express through painting the positive effects the People's Republic of China had on their lives. Generally abandoned after the failure of the Great Leap Forward, peasant art was again promoted by the government during the Cultural Revolution, often featuring images of workers benefiting from life under Mao Zedong or contributing to the building of a stronger China.* SNARK/ART RESOURCE, NY

FROM PROPAGANDA TO COMMERCIAL ART

Peasant painting continued to be endorsed at the official level in the 1980s and early 1990s, most evidently through the national exhibitions. In 1980 a well-received exhibition of peasant paintings from Jinshan, a suburb of Shanghai, was held at the National Art Gallery in Beijing and museums abroad. In subsequent years peasant art groups from Ansaixian and Yijunxian in Shaanxi province also showed works at the National Art Gallery.

Even with the opening of China after Mao's death in 1976, the Hu county peasant painters were kept guarded from foreigners. Commercialization changed this situation in 1983, when Deng Xiaoping undertook pragmatic economic policies. In her 1987 study, Joan Lebold Cohen hypothesizes that this caution surrounding the Hu county peasant painters may have signaled the government's wish to protect the peasants' naïveté from the corruption of foreign influence, or its fear that the close relationship between the amateur painters and professional artists would be exposed.

In contemporary entrepreneurial China, peasant art has since become commercial rather than propaganda art. Although art groups continue to meet and produce work, they have increasingly become concerned with selling their works. Pictures are usually exhibited with a price tag, and teams of art-sales representatives are sent to Beijing and other large tourist cities to find customers among foreign visitors and residents. The peasants' subject matter has also changed to reflect the present realities of China, with paintings depicting chic hairdressers, high-rise apartment buildings, and children playing in snowy Christmas scenes.

SEE ALSO *Federation of Literary and Art Circles; Folk Art; New Print Movement.*

BIBLIOGRAPHY

Cohen, Joan Lebold. *The New Chinese Painting, 1949–1986.* New York: H. N. Abrams, 1987.

Fine Arts Collection Section of the Cultural Group under the State Council of the People's Republic of China. *Peasant Paintings from Huhsien County.* Peking: People's Fine Arts Publishing House, 1976.

Galikowski, Maria. *Art and Politics in China, 1949-1984.* Hong Kong: Chinese University Press, 1998.

Laing, Ellen Johnston. Chinese Peasant Painting, 1958–1976: Amateur and Professional. *Art International* 27, 1 (January–March 1984): 2–12, 40, 48, 64.

Laing, Ellen Johnston. *The Winking Owl: Art in the People's Republic of China.* Berkeley: University of California Press, 1988.

Vivian Y. Li

ART PRODUCTS OF THE CULTURAL REVOLUTION

The decade of the Cultural Revolution (1966–1976) was the culmination of Mao Zedong's ambitious plan to effect a thorough transformation of Chinese society. As the name implies, the key focus of the movement was to be the cultural sphere, which had, according to Mao, lapsed into bourgeois thinking and needed radical restructuring. The position of professional artists, like all intellectuals, thus became precarious; leading figures in the art establishment were purged, and members of the official Artists Association were ultimately sent, in 1969, to "May 7th" cadre schools and military farms to reform themselves through agricultural labor. Much of the professional artwork produced before 1966, now regarded as bourgeois, feudalist, or revisionist, was destroyed by zealous Red Guards. All art now became in theory "mass art," as professional artists were sidelined, acting only as "advisers" to the new "mass artists," that is, the workers, peasants, and soldiers.

The visual image constituted a major element of the movement, and it overwhelmingly took on a propagandist role—propaganda posters, often cheaply produced woodcut prints using inks and gouache, served to highlight the successes of the Cultural Revolution, while cartoons became the most effective means to criticize and satirize the movement's main political targets. Images of Mao were ubiquitous, with other major themes including popular heroes such as Lei Feng, the People's Liberation Army, glowing relations between the Han Chinese majority and the national minorities, and the positive changes brought about in people's daily lives since the Cultural Revolution's inauguration.

Public and private spaces, both urban and rural, became saturated with propaganda images, usually accompanied by exhortatory text, directing human thought and behavior. Every house, every factory, every street wall was festooned with these political promptings. Cultural Revolution propaganda art thus became a key means for reinterpreting the more abstract political messages of the authorities in terms of simple, striking images that were accessible to ordinary people, across all walks of life, even illiterate peasants. Such art was, of necessity, relatively temporary in nature; it could be speedily and cheaply replaced with more contemporary examples, to ensure it remained in alignment with current policies—illustrations for blackboard and wall newspapers were, for example, changed regularly to contribute to the propaganda drive, and to ensure individuals were kept aware of the latest developments in official policy.

Most Cultural Revolution art had the purpose of conveying a clear and simple political message; it was designed to be as unambiguous as possible, with virtually no scope for personal interpretation. In the initial stages of the movement, when enthusiastic Red Guard groups began pasting posters or daubing images on every available flat surface, there was a definite spontaneity about the endeavor that informed the lively, if naive, artwork produced. By the end of the 1960s, however, with the exuberant young Red Guards having been reined in and sent down to the countryside to learn from the peasants, art was now firmly in the hands of amateur workers and peasants, whose relative lack of professional training and innate conservative tastes tended to militate against even minimal stylistic innovation. Art, with some rare exceptions, thus became largely repetitious and formulaic. This was especially so after the principle of "the three prominences" (*san tuchu*) was formalized as an essential component of aesthetic discourse—in a painting or sculpture, prominence was to be given to positive figures; greater prominence to heroes and heroines; and greatest prominence to the principal hero or heroine. The aim was to create healthy and youthful models or stereotypical worker-peasant-soldier figures, who dominate the picture area, with their robust physical appearance and their strong and determined facial features, revealing great strength of character. Ideas akin to "the three prominences" had, of course, been in existence prior to the Cultural Revolution, but in the late 1960s they reappeared in a particularly rigid and formulaic guise. The conventional images that resulted from the official adoption of this new doctrine caused later commentators to sardonically define the paintings of the era in terms of their main characteristics—"red, bright, vivid" (*hong, guang, liang*), a reference to the blanket banality of unmitigated optimism that pervaded much Cultural Revolution art.

It is probably fair to say that, ultimately, the extreme simplification, homogenization, and politicization of art during the ten years of the Cultural Revolution, as well as the overexposure individuals had, year after year, to such art, reduced its effectiveness as a propaganda tool, as well as its aesthetic appeal.

Somewhat ironically, the early 1990s saw a resurgence of popular interest in Cultural Revolution propaganda paraphernalia, from posters and political cartoons to Mao badges and copies of Mao's *Little Red Book*. For some, the craze was no doubt a nostalgic yearning during a time of social and economic transition for the certainties of a bygone era provided by an absolutist political authority; for others, it harked back to a period of heady youthful idealism, and liberation from the control of parents, teachers, and other authority figures; for yet others, the Cultural Revolution kitsch craze was a way of helping to lessen or neutralize the immense psychological power the images and symbols of the movement once wielded. It thus served as part of the ongoing process of catharsis, of coming to terms with the nature of this unprecedented mass political experiment.

SEE ALSO *Art, Policy on, since 1949; Cultural Revolution, 1966–1969.*

BIBLIOGRAPHY

Andrews, Julia F. *Painters and Politics in the People's Republic of China, 1949–1979.* Berkeley: University of California Press, 1994.

Andrews, Julia F., and Shen Kuiyi, ed. *A Century in Crisis: Modernity and Tradition in the Art of Twentieth-century China.* New York: Guggenheim Museum, 1998.

Chiu, Melissa, and Zheng Shengtian, ed. *Art and China's Revolution.* New York: Asia Society; Hartford, CT: Yale University Press, 2008.

Croizier, Ralph. Chinese Art in the Chiang Ch'ing Era. *Journal of Asian Studies* 38, 2 (1979): 303–311.

Galikowski, Maria. *Art and Politics in China, 1949–1984.* Hong Kong: Chinese University Press, 1998.

Laing, Ellen Johnston. Chinese Peasant Painting, 1958–1976: Amateur and Professional. *Art International* 27, 1 (1984): 1–12.

Laing, Ellen Johnston. *The Winking Owl: Art in the People's Republic of China.* Berkeley: University of California Press, 1988.

Landsberger, Stefan R., and International Institute of Social History, Amsterdam, comps. Chinese Posters, 1937–Present: Propaganda, Politics, History. http://chineseposters.net/

Maria Galikowski

PROSTITUTION, HISTORY OF

Prostitution in China from 1800 to 2000 is an unevenly documented social phenomenon subject to great regional differences and major, often radical, change. In traditional China, attitudes to prostitution were subject to class distinctions: Members of the upper-class literati had a romanticized notion of the prostitute as an entertainer and courtesan, but most prostitutes were in fact members of a socially invisible class of oppressed women who were regarded as little different from slaves.

The patronage of prostitutes was largely free from religious or ethical condemnation in nineteenth-century urban China, and major Chinese cities had conspicuous pleasure districts where brothels, opium dens, restaurants, theaters, and bathhouses were concentrated. Districts such as Qinhuaihe in Nanjing and the West Lake in Hangzhou are well documented, even by effective guidebooks of these areas such as Li Dou's *Yangzhou huafang lu* (Record of the Painted Boats of Yangzhou, c. 1795). In his pioneering history of prostitution, Wang Shunu discussed in detail traditional regional differences in prostitution and the local terminologies describing brothels, prostitutes, and patrons. Wang, who used Beijing to exemplify trends in North China, pointed out that after the Opium War (1839–1842) prostitution in Guangzhou, Shanghai, and other treaty ports developed along different lines from traditional prostitution. The International Concession Area of Shanghai attracted many prostitutes, as well as many Chinese merchants, who were fleeing the depredations of the Taiping Rebellion in the Yangzi River

Valley. Sun Guoqun (1988, p. 7) cited an 1865 issue of the newspaper *Zilin Xibao* (North China Daily News), produced by the Labor Department of the International Concession Area, that reported that of the 10,063 Chinese establishments and households in the concession, 668 establishments (roughly 6.6%) were brothels.

Prostitution at higher social levels, functioning as an adjunct to the entertainment and theatrical fields, was romanticized and formed the basis for a genre of "semidocumentary" fiction called *yanqing xiaoshuo*, which provides historians of prostitution and sexuality with details of the organization of urban prostitution in the late Qing period. It is also clear from these fictional works that there were hazy boundaries between prostitutes and admired male performers of female theatrical roles. Lu Xun, who pioneered studies of *yanhua xiaoshuo*, noted that it was not until 1892, with the publication of *Haishang hua liezhuan* (Lives of Shanghai Singsong Girls), that the genre began to document the iniquities of brothels and to expose the evils of prostitution. In contrast to this wealth of evidence of prostitution among the upper classes, knowledge of nineteenth-century prostitution in the Chinese countryside and among the lower classes is extremely scant, despite the fact that the great majority of prostitutes were impoverished.

THE EARLY TWENTIETH CENTURY

The plight of prostitutes was addressed by some reformers in the first decade of the twentieth century, and much of the condemnation of prostitution in the late Qing years was inspired by Christian missionaries and their followers. The nascent feminist movement, which was very much in its infancy and championed largely by enlightened male reformers, sometimes highlighted the injustices brought about by prostitution, but social attitudes toward prostitution were little changed, and a romantic, albeit historical, view of prostitution remained part and parcel of male scholarly attitudes. The New Culture movement and the subsequent May Fourth movement of 1919 saw an upsurge in calls for the abolition of prostitution, and many of the leading reformers of the period, including Hu Shi and Li Dazhao (1888–1927), wrote articles advocating its prohibition. Apart from Li Dazhao, some of the other early Communists who called for the abolition of prostitution included Qu Qiubai (1899–1935) and the feminist Xiang Jingyu (1895–1928). However, among the plethora of concerns raised by early feminists, who also targeted footbinding, arranged marriage, enforced widowhood and concubinage, and the need for women's education and greater literacy, prostitution had low priority.

Prostitution continued to flourish in Beijing during the period after the 1911 Revolution and in the Warlord era (1916–1928). According to Wang Shunu, in 1913 there were 353 brothels and 2,996 prostitutes in Beijing; in 1918 there were 406 brothels and 3,880 prostitutes (Wang Shunu [1933]

1988, p. 330). In November 1915 the Beijing government proclaimed a new set of laws covering criminal offenses (*weijing fafa*) that included engaging in prostitution, pimping, and running a house of prostitution; conviction of one of these crimes would incur detention for not more than fifteen days or a fine of not more than 15 yuan. Provisional supplementary new laws and regulations (*zanxing xin xinglü buchong tiaoli*) made it a criminal offense for relatives to force into prostitution their granddaughters (or granddaughters-in-law), daughters (or daughters-in-law), and wives. Not far from Beijing's main brothel district in the Bada Hutong district, the government established a shelter for prostitutes, though this was in fact a harshly supervised workhouse.

In early Republican Shanghai, benevolent societies set up shelters for prostitutes that often were run by regional guilds. In December 1912 the Shaoxing Compatriots Society in Shanghai (Shaoxing Lü Hu Tongxiang Hui), together with ten other organizations representing merchants from Huzhou, Ningbo, and other cities, established the National Women's and Children's Salvation Society (Quanguo Furu Jiuji Hui), which included the rescue of prostitutes in its social charity work. By 1914 the society had 2,000 members, and by 1915 a budget of 24,000 yuan. In the Republican period the laws and regulations governing prostitution, as well as its situation and cultural profile, varied greatly from region to region and city to city. For example, in contrast with Shanghai and Beijing, in Fengtian (contemporary Liaoning) the warlord Zhang Zuolin in 1917 introduced laws regulating prostitution (*Guanli jiguan yingye guize*) that were intended to lessen the influence of criminal elements in the business of prostitution and to ensure that prostitutes had regular medical examinations to prevent the spread of venereal diseases.

COMFORT WOMEN

The Japanese invasion of China and other East Asian countries of East Asia ushered in a particularly tragic period in the history of prostitution with the introduction of military brothels staffed by "comfort women" (*weianfu*). Previously, the Japanese army's "comfort women" had been Japanese prostitutes who had volunteered for such service, but with military expansion, the Japanese army forced women from the local populations into sexual slavery. The first "comfort station" (*weiansuo*), the Daiichi Salon, was established in the Japanese concession of Shanghai in 1932. This system of military brothels, which eventually included women from all countries invaded by the Japanese army, was exposed in the international media only in the 1990s. Perhaps because the issue did not come before Allied war crimes tribunals at the end of World War II, the numbers of women forced into service are not officially documented, but the Japanese government acknowledged in 1993 that the Japanese military was directly and indirectly involved in the

SELLING AND BUYING SEX IN CONTEMPORARY CHINA

Prostitution, which the Communist Party allegedly eradicated from Maoist-era China as a feudal-capitalist phenomenon that oppressed women, resurfaced and spread throughout the mainland coincident with the post-1978 shift in the People's Republic of China (PRC) from a planned to a market-based economy. In terms of the number of Chinese women in prostitution, figures range from PRC government estimates of three million women nationwide, to U.S. State Department reports of ten million, to claims by a Chinese economist, Yang Fan, that there are twenty million sex workers, accounting for 6 percent of China's gross domestic product (French 2006; Jeffreys 2009, p. 27). Official reports suggest that sellers and buyers of sex come from all sectors of Chinese society, including government officials, intellectuals, urban workers, and rural migrant workers. Recent reports also indicate that the demand for male-male prostitution and male-female (i.e., male prostitute and female buyer) prostitution is increasing (Jeffreys 2007, pp. 151–175; Miller 2006). The spread of prostitution is a politically sensitive issue because it challenges the Communist Party's claim in the late 1950s and early 1960s to have eradicated prostitution in China, and, in the process, to have eradicated venereal disease and created more equitable sociosexual relations.

China adopted and retained an abolitionist approach to prostitution. Organizing, introducing, facilitating, or forcing another person to engage in prostitution is a criminal offense punishable by up to ten years' imprisonment with the possible addition of a fine, according to the PRC's first criminal code of January 1980 and the revised 1997 code. First-party participation in the prostitution transaction is not criminalized, but rather banned as a social harm punishable by a maximum of five days of administrative detention or a fine of 500 yuan, and in more serious cases, by ten to fifteen days of detention with the possible addition of a fine up to 5,000 yuan, according to the PRC's Public Security Administrative Punishments Law of March 2006. The 2006 law significantly changed penalties for first-party engagement in the prostitution transaction, reducing the possible term of administrative detainment from a maximum of two years to fifteen days, and the average fine from 5,000 yuan to 500.

These penalties were reduced to meet the challenges posed by the spread of the prostitution industry and associated social problems such as organized crime, corruption, and sexually transmitted infections (STIs). Forced prostitution and violence against women in prostitution is a major problem (Jeffreys 2006b, pp. 1–27; Jeffreys 2009, pp. 24–42). Sex-related bribery and corruption in the form of officials using public funds to obtain commercial sexual services is widespread (Jeffreys 2006a, pp. 159–178). STIs are rampant, including HIV, which once was viewed as a "foreign import" (UNAIDS 2002). The 2006 and 2007 rollout of the 100 Percent Condom Use Program for all providers of commercial sex in all recreational venues demonstrates China's commitment to involvement in global HIV-AIDS governance regimes. Such programs aim to prevent the spread of STIs/HIV-AIDS by encouraging a commitment to 100 percent condom use in all commercial sex encounters on the part of women who sell sex, and by the owners, managers, and employees of venues that facilitate the provision of commercial sex. They offer participatory workshops on the nature of STIs/HIV-AIDS transmission and how to use condoms, and encourage the managers of public entertainment venues to provide visible supplies of condoms and put up 100 percent condom use posters in their establishments. It is unclear whether that commitment signifies a shift toward decriminalizing the prostitution transaction; many academic and media commentators contend that the PRC government should abandon its historical ban on prostitution in order to protect the lives of women in prostitution, help in the task of disease prevention, and fight corruption.

BIBLIOGRAPHY

French, Harold. Shenzhen's Public Humiliation of Sex Workers Provokes a Backlash. *International Herald Tribune*, December 8, 2006.

Jeffreys, Elaine. *China, Sex, and Prostitution*. London: Routledge, 2004.

Jeffreys, Elaine. Debating the Legal Regulation of Sex-related Bribery and Corruption in the People's Republic of China. In *Sex and Sexuality in China*, ed. Elaine Jeffreys, 159–178. London and New York: Routledge, 2006a.

Jeffreys, Elaine. "Over My Dead Body!" Media Constructions of Forced Prostitution in the People's Republic of China. *PORTAL Journal of Multidisciplinary International Studies*, Women in Asia Special Issue, 3, 2 (2006b): 1–27.

Jeffreys, Elaine. Querying Queer Theory–Debating Male-Male Prostitution in the Chinese Media. *Critical Asian Studies* 39, 1 (2007): 151–175.

Jeffreys, Elaine. Serial Prostitute Homicide in the Chinese Media. In *Local Violence, Global Media: Feminist Analyses of Gendered Representations*, ed. Lisa Cuklanz and Sujata Moorti, 24–42. Bern: Peter Lang, 2009.

Miller, Tom. Boys Flocking to Be "Ducks" for China's Bored Housewives. *Observer*, May 7, 2006.

UNAIDS. HIV/AIDS: China's Titanic Peril–2001 Update of the AIDS Situation and Needs Assessment Report. 2002 http://www.gateway2china.com/report/AIDSchina2001 update.pdf

Elaine Jeffreys

establishment and management of comfort stations. According to the researcher Su Zhiliang (1999), there were eventually as many as 160 comfort stations set up by the Japanese military in Shanghai alone, and approximately 410,000 comfort women—one for every thirty Japanese soldiers. In 2009, several criminal cases brought by Chinese comfort women remained before the courts in Japan. The establishment of the world's first comfort station museum, an archive located in Shanghai Normal University that opened to the public in July 2007, and the preservation of the first comfort station in Shanghai as a cultural relic have been controversial in China. After World War II many prostitutes in China were charged with collaboration with the enemy; this occurred also in many of the European countries that had been occupied by the Germans.

After World War II it seems that there was a contraction in the number of brothels and prostitutes in China. According to Shao Yong (p. 390), many brothels might have gone underground to avoid new local taxes and regulations, though he notes that the available figures for the number of brothels in Changsha and other major cities do not indicate any reduction in the incidence of prostitution.

PROSTITUTION SINCE 1949

The Soviet defeat of the Japanese in Manchuria saw the establishment of Chinese Communist rule in parts of the northeast, and the new government made moves to eliminate prostitution. The new Communist administrations in Harbin, Jiamusi, Mudanjiang, and Qiqihar closed brothels and enacted legislation to outlaw prostitution and engagement in the business of prostitution. When Shenyang was liberated in November 1948, the city had 144 known brothels with 660 prostitutes and many more underground brothels, called *zudakang*. The new government ordered in May 1949 that brothels and prostitutes in Shenyang were required to register with the government, after which time no new premises could be opened. By February 1951 Shenyang had only thirty-six brothels with 150 prostitutes, as well as another 780 streetwalkers. In October 1951 a task force of nearly 150 government workers from the Public Security Bureau (Gong'an Ju), the Women's Association (Funü Lianhehui), and the Civil Affairs Bureau (Minzheng Ju) conducted an all-night roundup, arresting prostitutes and putting them into detention centers and clinics for the treatment of venereal diseases. The women were subjected to re-education in sessions in which they were encouraged to publicly recount their suffering (*suku*), and to rehabilitation in reform through labor, with jobs provided upon graduation from training. The government's gradualist approach to eradicating prostitution as part of the overall process of liberation in the northeast of China became a model later emulated throughout much of the rest of the country, including Shanghai. In Beijing, however, the process of eradication and rehabilitation

was accelerated: Regulations designed to lead to the closure of brothels were introduced in March 1949, and by November the government reported success in ending prostitution in the city. Because prostitution was tackled as an institution that exposed the exploitative nature of China's semifeudal and semicapitalist society, the new measures were politically successful in removing visible signs of prostitution from Chinese society, and by the early 1960s prostitution had been largely eliminated. In acknowledgement of this, in 1964 the government closed down all research institutes dedicated to studying sexually transmitted diseases. Throughout the 1960s and 1970s China enjoyed a reputation as a center of sexual puritanism.

Outside the People's Republic of China, in Hong Kong prostitution remained a vibrant industry even though it was criminalized in 1932 and the system of licensing brothels was terminated in 1935. Brothels continued to operate within strict limits, and the industry was effectively controlled by criminal gangs. With the influx of Mainlanders and women from East and Southeast Asia in the 1990s, there was a resurgence of the sex industry in Hong Kong, and criminal control of prostitution weakened. In Taiwan, prostitution had flourished from 1895 to 1945, when the island was a colony of Japan. Following the flight of the GMD government to Taiwan, there was tight government regulation, though prostitution operated out of massage parlors, hairdressing salons, and dance halls. In 1997 the Taibei City Council declared prostitution illegal, but this move was opposed by licensed sex workers.

Prostitution reemerged in China in the 1980s in the wake of economic reform and opening and the social migration that ensued. The government's abolitionist response was harsh at first, but it was somewhat tempered in the late 1990s and early in the 2000s when health authorities recognized that problems of sexually transmitted diseases can be better tackled by government regulation and public awareness campaigns than by draconian punishment of sexual offenders.

SEE ALSO *Law on the Protection of Women and Children; Sexuality; Women, Employment of; Women, Status of.*

BIBLIOGRAPHY

Henriot, Christian. *Prostitution and Sexuality in Shanghai: A Social History, 1849–1949.* Trans. Noel Castelino. Cambridge, U.K.: Cambridge University Press, 2001.

Hershatter, Gail. *Dangerous Pleasures: Prostitution and Modernity in Twentieth-century Shanghai.* Berkeley: University of California Press, 1999.

Lu Xun. *A Brief History of Chinese Fiction.* [1925]. Trans. Yang Hsienyi and Gladys Yang. Beijing: Foreign Languages Press, 1959.

Shao Yong. *Zhongguo Jindai Jinü Shi* [A history of Chinese prostitution in the modern period]. Shanghai: Shanghai Renmin Chubanshe, 2005.

Su Zhiliang. *Wei'anfu yanjiu* [Research on comfort women]. Shanghai: Shanghai Shudian, 1999.

Sun Guoqun. *Jiu Shanghai changji mishi* [The secret history of prostitution in old Shanghai]. Zhengzhou, China: Henan Renmin Chubanshe, 1988.

Wang Shunu. *Zhongguo Changji Shi* [History of Chinese prostititution]. 1933. Reprint Shanghai: Shanghai Sanlian Shudian, 1988.

Yang, Yeeshan. *Whispers and Moans: Interviews with the Men and Women of Hong Kong's Sex Industry.* Hong Kong: Blacksmith Books, 2006.

Bruce G. Doar

PROTESTANTISM

The history of Protestantism in China can be divided into four periods. In the nineteenth century Protestantism was characterized by a dearth of conversions, denominational rivalries between foreign missions, and the growth of anti-Christian violence. In the face of rising nationalism in the early twentieth century, the Chinese staff within the Western missions and among the independent Christian churches began to develop an indigenous Protestantism. After the Communist Revolution of 1949, a three-decade-long period of oppression and persecution finally gave way to an era of rapid growth of believers.

THE NINETEENTH CENTURY

Evangelization by foreign missionaries was banned in the eighteenth century. The first Protestant missionary, Robert Morrison, came to China in 1807, but the appearance of European and American Protestant missionaries in any significant numbers occurred only in the wake of the Opium Wars (1839–1842 and 1856–1860). The ensuing treaties of Tianjin (1858) and Beijing (1860) provided for toleration of Christianity; permitted Catholic and Protestant missionaries to travel freely, preach, acquire properties, and build churches across China; and required the imperial government to protect Chinese Christians from persecution. On account of doctrinal differences, the Catholic and Protestant missions ridiculed and competed with each other. They used different Chinese terms to refer to Christianity, namely Jidujiao (Protestantism, literally "the religion of Christ") versus Tianzhujiao (Catholicism, literally "the religion of the Lord of Heaven"), and created the impression that Protestantism and Catholicism were two different religions.

Throughout the nineteenth century, a variety of Protestant missions came to China from Europe and America, including the Basel Mission Society, the Church Missionary Society, the Foreign Mission Committee of the Presbyterian Church of England, the London Missionary Society, the Methodist Missionary Society, the American Board of Commissioners for Foreign Missions, the American Baptist Foreign Mission Society, and the American Presbyterian

Mission. These foreign missions appealed to their denominational churches in Europe and America for funds and largely operated in China's coastal regions. In 1865 Hudson Taylor founded the China Inland Mission, an interdenominational body that relied on unsolicited contributions and concentrated on the evangelization of China's inland provinces. At the time, popular feeling toward the Protestant missions was mixed. Rural areas witnessed a tendency to affiliate with the church and seek the protection offered by missionaries, whereas provincial, prefectural, and district cities experienced the rise of anti-Christian sentiment among some Confucian scholar-officials and lineage and temple leaders. Overall, Protestantism grew as a grassroots movement in some areas where believers succeeded in recruiting converts, building churches, and integrating Christianity with traditional customs and social structures. Christians identified themselves with particular denominations and their lineages and villages. This overlap of religious, kinship, and territorial identities characterized most Protestant communities in China. This pattern of church growth fitted well with the missionary expectation of self-propagation through native Chinese and marked the beginning of mass conversions.

An idea of the complexity involved in Sino-Christian interaction can be gained from the Taiping movement in South China, where Hong Xiuquan, inspired by a Christian tract, proclaimed himself the Chinese son of God and the younger brother of Jesus. He founded the Society of God Worshippers (Bai Shangdi Hui), a movement that developed into an uprising against the Qing dynasty. Hong and his followers defeated the imperial armies, founded the Heavenly Kingdom of Great Peace (Taiping Tianguo) in Nanjing, and controlled China's economic heartland from 1851 to 1864. They propagated a doctrine of universal brotherhood and sisterhood under God. They banned opium smoking, footbinding, prostitution, and drinking of alcohol. They treated women as equals of men, and divided all land among the Taipings and their supporters according to family size, with men and women receiving equal shares. Yet factional struggles among the leaders and hostility from the West undermined the Taiping movement. Even though Taiping ideology drew on many Christian principles, few of its policies were successfully implemented. After the Heavenly Kingdom fell in 1864, the Qing imperial government effaced all evidence of the Taipings. The Taiping movement, far from giving rise to a native tradition of Christianity, merely caused Protestant influence to wane and led to greater suspicion and hostility among Chinese toward any form of Christianity in the late nineteenth century.

ANTI-CHRISTIAN MOVEMENTS

Despite the collapse of the Taiping movement, Protestant Christianity took root in rural communities where proselytizing met with success. Yet political issues involving Western missionaries and Chinese converts were complex. Initially, cases of antiforeign disputes broke out in treaty ports, provincial capitals, prefectural cities, and district cities where missionaries were concentrated. The disputes spread into rural areas and were woven into existing kinship, lineage, and village conflicts. Missionaries were often at a loss because local conflicts over resources and anti-Christian violence frequently overlapped. Missionaries' ability to intervene successfully in local conflicts depended on powerful backing from Western powers in treaty ports and beyond. When they did intervene effectively, it was often at the cost of hostility from local Chinese officials and village leaders.

The turn of the twentieth century was marked by the outbreak of the Boxer Uprising, a movement directed against all forms of foreign presence, especially the missionaries and their converts. Such anti-Christian sentiments came to the surface in North China amid widespread drought and famine in 1899–1900, for which the Christians were blamed. Violence against missionaries and native converts broke out not only in areas far from the capital but also within the foreign concession in Tianjin and the legation quarter in Beijing. The foreign powers sent an expeditionary force to suppress the uprising, and the failure of the Boxers increased the prestige of Western missionaries.

CHRISTIANITY AND NATIONALISM

Meanwhile, the Chinese identified modernization as a critical component of national salvation, and this realization resulted in a nationwide conversion to science and technology. By comparison, conversion to Christianity proceeded slowly. Nationalism and modernization became the dominant discourse in politics, and this rising tide of nationalism, exemplified by the May Fourth and May Thirtieth movements, brought new challenges to the church. Early-twentieth-century nationalism differed from late-nineteenth-century anti-Christian movements in that many modern Chinese intellectuals were involved, and they accused the missionaries of using religious conversion and education to facilitate Western imperialists' agenda of political, economic, and military dominance over China. Faced with the charge of "cultural imperialism," more educated Chinese Christians and enlightened foreign church leaders called for a Three-Self movement, which sought to create self-governing, self-supporting, and self-propagating churches. They advocated that foreign missionaries learn to be advisers rather than commanders, and that Chinese Christians work independently, without missionary protection and support. The actual practices of implementing this principle varied from place to place and from denomination to denomination. Debate about the structure of a Three-Self church became an important topic in China throughout the 1920s and 1930s.

Coinciding with the call for an indigenous Chinese church, different strands of Protestantism emerged. The Young Men's Christian Association and Young Women's Christian Association initiated many programs for social change in urban areas, and fundamentalist movements upheld the supreme authority of the Bible, supernatural Christology, and the importance of repentance and rebirth. Even though popular Chinese itinerant preachers such as Wang Mingdao (1900–1991), John Sung (1901–1944), and Marcus Cheng (Chen Chonggui, 1884–1964) operated outside the Protestant missionary establishment, they adhered to conservative doctrines about the Bible, Christology, and conversion, and stressed the importance of training evangelists and building churches. In addition, Watchman Nee (Ni Tuosheng, 1903–1972) founded the Christian Local Assembly, widely known as the Little Flock, and called for return to congregational egalitarianism, as shown in the New Testament. The True Jesus Church, founded in 1917, appropriated Pentecostalism and emphasized the use of supernatural gifts such as healing, prophecy, and speaking in tongues. The Jesus Family, another Pentecostal communitarian church, was founded in rural Shandong Province around 1927. It believed in the imminent return of Jesus Christ and required members to live together and hold property in common. These independent Christian groups advocated an autonomous Chinese church independent of any external control.

PROTESTANT CHRISTIANITY IN THE PEOPLE'S REPUBLIC

After 1949, Y. T. Wu (Wu Yuzong, 1893–1979), general secretary for publications of the national committee of the Young Men's Christian Association, revived the call for a Three-Self movement, which gained wider support in Protestant circles. The Communist state appropriated this principle and launched the Three-Self Patriotic Movement to control Protestant congregations. With the outbreak of the Korean War (1950–1953), the state ended the missionary era by expelling all foreign missionaries and taking over all mission properties and church institutions. This policy further integrated all the churches into the state-controlled Three-Self Patriotic Movement. In the 1950s, the state organized countless campaigns to purge Christians. Tens of thousands of church leaders, such as Wang Mingdao and Watchman Nee, were sent to labor camps for reeducation from the late 1950s through the Cultural Revolution (1966–1969), the death of Mao, and the demise of the Gang of Four.

As the political campaigns of the Maoist era faded, most church leaders tried to articulate the experience of religious persecution. Many elderly church leaders used the word *chiku*, literally, to experience bitterness, to refer to the persecution. They drew on the memory of suffering to create a common bond among themselves and fight against the state's antireligious propaganda. They refrained from attacking the

Shanghai Community Church Choir on Easter Sunday, March 30, 1997. *Protestant missionaries first arrived in China in the early nineteenth century. Despite much anti-Christian sentiment, many Protestant churches attracted significant members, particularly in rural areas, blending Western theology with traditional Chinese customs.* **AP IMAGES**

Three-Self Patriotic Movement, but they opposed state intervention into the spiritual affairs of the church. In the early 1980s, Deng Xiaoping's economic-reform and open-door policies departed from the antireligious ideology of Mao's rule. The central government released many Protestant church leaders from labor camps and prisons, and permitted them to organize religious activities and join the Three-Self Patriotic Movement. Since then these church leaders have used the Three-Self Patriotic Movement to support the autonomous Christian groups known as "house churches" (*jiating jiaohui*).

The social landscape of Chinese Protestantism is characterized by rapid growth of membership in the state-controlled Three-Self Patriotic churches and the autonomous Christian groups. Most Protestants are from the countryside. Seeking salvation in miracles, healing, and exorcism, they harbor syncretic attitudes toward Christianity. These linkages between Protestantism and folk-religious practices are manifested in dozens of Christian-inspired sectarian movements. For example, Wu Yangming, a peasant, founded a movement called the Established King (Beili Wang) in Anhui Province in 1988. Wu proclaimed himself to be the Messiah and declared that the end of the world was imminent. He bitterly opposed the Three-Self Patriotic Movement and strongly criticized the Communist state as anti-Christ. In

1995 Wu was arrested and executed. But his loyal followers continued to expand the Established King into the interior.

Another well-organized movement, Eastern Lightning (Dongfang Shandian), was founded in North China during the early 1990s and has spread across the country and abroad. The term *Eastern Lightning* implies that the salvation of mankind will come from China. This group rejected the doctrine of the Trinity, renamed the God of Christianity as Lightning, and claimed that a female Christ had come to Henan Province in central China. Stressing the second coming of Jesus Christ in a manner similar to the advent of Buddhist saviors, these sectarian groups had in common a strong belief in millenarianism. In areas far from metropolitan cities, people could appropriate certain Christian doctrines to establish new teachings. But after the assault on Falun Gong in 1999, the state labeled these Christian-inspired sectarian movements as "evil cults" (*xiejiao*) and banned their activities.

As China's economy progressed, people sought prosperity and security in a fast-changing world. A group of "boss Christians" (*laoban jidutu*) emerged in the cities. Boss Christians attribute business success to their faith in Jesus Christ and proclaim to work for God in the commercial sector. In addition, since the 1990s there has been a group of scholars known as "cultural Christians" (*wenhua jidutu*).

They reject socialism and traditional Confucianism, and consider Christianity to be a new ethical system for China. Ryan Dunch best summarizes these diverse features of Chinese Protestantism as "a warm, experiential piety, centered on a concern for salvation and for tangible blessings in this life; literal faith in the Bible." The rapid growth of Christianity is "accompanied by institutional diversity and fragmentation, expanding with China's market economy" (2001b, p. 215).

Over the more than two centuries since the arrival of the first missionary, Robert Morrison, in 1807, Protestantism has transformed itself from an alien faith into a Chinese religion. This transformation has been characterized by state-controlled Three-Self Patriotic churches coexisting with autonomous Christian groups, the growth of Christian-inspired sectarian movements, and the appeal of Christianity as a new moral-ethical system.

SEE ALSO *Boxer Uprising; Missionaries; Three-Self Patriotic Movement.*

BIBLIOGRAPHY

Bays, Daniel H., ed. *Christianity in China: From the Eighteenth Century to the Present.* Stanford, CA: Stanford University Press, 1996.

Cheng, May M. C. House Church Movements and Religious Freedom in China. *China: An International Journal* 1, 1 (March 2003): 16–45.

Cohen, Paul A. *China and Christianity: The Missionary Movement and the Growth of Chinese Antiforeignism, 1860–1870.* Cambridge, MA: Harvard University Press, 1963.

Cohen, Paul A. Christian Missions and Their Impact to 1900. In *The Cambridge History of China*, vol. 10, *Late Ch'ing, 1800–1911*, ed. John King Fairbank, 543–590. Cambridge, U.K.: Cambridge University Press, 1978.

Dunch, Ryan. *Fuzhou Protestants and the Making of a Modern China, 1857–1927.* New Haven, CT: Yale University Press, 2001a.

Dunch, Ryan. Protestant Christianity in China Today: Fragile, Fragmented, Flourishing. In *China and Christianity*, ed. Stephen Uhalley Jr. and Xiaoxin Wu, 195–216. Armonk, NY: M. E. Sharpe, 2001b.

Hunter, Alan, and Kim-Kwong Chan. *Protestantism in Contemporary China.* Cambridge, U.K.: Cambridge University Press, 1993.

Lee, Joseph Tse-Hei. *The Bible and the Gun: Christianity in South China, 1860–1900.* New York: Routledge, 2003.

Lee, Joseph Tse-Hei. Christianity in Contemporary China: An Update. *Journal of Church and State* 49, 2 (Spring 2007): 277–304.

Lian, Xi. The Search for Chinese Christianity in the Republican Period (1912–1949). *Modern Asian Studies* 38, 4 (2004): 851–898.

Uhalley, Stephen, Jr., and Xiaoxin Wu, eds. *China and Christianity: Burdened Past, Hopeful Future.* Armonk, NY: M. E. Sharpe, 2001.

Yang, Fenggang. Lost in the Market, Saved at McDonald's: Conversion to Christianity in Urban China. *Journal for the Scientific Study of Religion* 44, 4 (2005): 423–441.

Yang, Fenggang. The Red, Black, and Gray Markets of Religion in China. *The Sociological Quarterly* 47 (2006): 93–122.

Joseph Tse-Hei Lee

PROVINCIAL AND SUBPROVINCIAL GOVERNMENT STRUCTURE SINCE 1949

This entry contains the following:

OVERVIEW

For most of the period since 1949, the People's Republic of China (PRC) has had four levels of local government: the province (*sheng*), the prefecture (*diqu*), the county (*xian*), and the township (*xiang*). According to the 1982 constitution, villages are considered "grassroots mass autonomous organizations," and have never been part of the government system. The province and the county are the two most prevalent levels of local government in China's history, but the prefecture is the heir of the imperial circuit (*dao*) or prefecture (*zhou*), and the township is an indirect perpetuation of the old rural region or district.

After the launching of the Great Leap Forward in 1958, township governments were replaced by "people's communes" (*renmin gongshe*), and villages were replaced by "production brigades" (*shengchan dadui*) or sometimes "production teams" (*shengchan dui*). The previous structure was restored in the early 1980s. While this administrative pattern refers to the state organization enshrined in the 1982 PRC constitution, it also applies to the Chinese Communist Party (CCP) territorial apparatus, whose committees exert a leading role in the local governments and state organs at each level.

The PRC is a multinational unitary state. This means that although nonfederal, it has established autonomous administrative units at the four levels of local government in areas mainly inhabited by ethnic, or non-Han, minorities (9 percent of the 2008 population). In 1949 there was only one "autonomous region" (*zizhiqu*) at the provincial level: Inner Mongolia. Four other provinces were later renamed "autonomous regions": Xinjiang (1955), Guangxi (1958), Ningxia (1958), and Xizang (Tibet, 1965). At the lower levels of government, a growing number of "autonomous prefectures" (*zizhizhou*) or "leagues" (*meng*) (fourteen in 1952, and thirty-three in 2007), as well as "autonomous counties" (*zizhixian*) or "(autonomous) banners" (*qi* or *zizhiqi*) (forty-three in 1955, and 169 in 2007), have been established. Only the number of nationality townships (*minzu xiang*) has decreased, due to both administrative simplification and urbanization (around 1,500 in 2007 against 2,794 in 1985).

China has traditionally been a rural society in which cities and marketplaces were subordinated to the territorial constituencies mentioned above and tightly controlled by the imperial bureaucracy. Nevertheless, after the 1911 revolution, urbanization forced the Republic of China government (the Guomindang) to modify the administrative map. In the late 1920s, twelve provincial-level municipalities, directly under the jurisdiction of the central government (*zhixiashi*), were established. The PRC authorities provisionally kept most of these municipalities until 1954, when they downgraded all but three of them (Beijing, Shanghai, and Tianjin) to the prefecture level. This situation remained unchanged until 1997, when a fourth "large municipality," Chongqing, was created and therefore separated from Sichuan Province.

Municipalities have always existed at the prefecture and county levels, but their numbers increased only after the beginning of reforms in 1978. Administered separately from the rural areas (prefectures and counties), the subprovincial municipalities nevertheless controlled a substantial rural zone outside of the city limits—a few counties or townships—whose main role was to feed the urban population with fresh agricultural products. This system was reformed in the 1980s in order to better integrate urban and rural administrations and economic development: The prefecture-level municipalities (283 in 2007 against 170 in 1987) have gradually replaced the prefectures (17 against 117) and directly govern most of the counties (1,463 against 1,817) and county-level municipalities (369 against 208).

In addition, more and more provincial and prefecture-level municipalities include urban districts (*shiqu*), which set up their own local government (856 in 2007 against 632 in 1987). Many of these latter governments have also set up several delegated organs called "neighborhood committees" or "street offices" (*jiedao banshichu*) in the various sections of the district (6,152 in 2006). Finally, urbanization has contributed both to the transfer of more townships to county-level municipalities and to an increase in the number of towns (*zhen*) (19,391 in 2007 against 12,500 in 1985), to the detriment of rural townships (15,365 in 2007 against 91,590 in 1986).

The provincial map of China has been relatively stable since 1949, after noticeable changes affected northern China, Manchuria, and Tibet. An additional (twenty-second) province was founded in 1988 when Hainan Island was separated from Guangdong Province. Provincial boundaries have otherwise not much changed. The major alteration concerned Inner Mongolia, which was gradually expanded until 1956; then, from 1969 to 1979, mainly because of the Sino-Soviet conflict, Inner Mongolia was deprived of half of its territory, to the benefit of Gansu, Ningxia, Liaoning, Jilin, and Heilongjiang, before being restored to its original limits.

In 2008 the PRC comprised thirty-three provincial-level administrative units (Taiwan excluded): twenty-two provinces, five autonomous regions, four large municipalities, and, since 1997 and 1999 respectively, two "special administrative regions," Hong Kong and Macau.

According to the constitution (apart from the two special administrative regions, which enjoy a special status), local provincial and subprovincial "people's governments" are elected by a "people's congress," itself elected directly by the voters up to the county level, and by the lower-level people's congress above that level. Prefectures are provincial governments' delegated organs (*paichu jigou*) and therefore do not have a people's congress (although prefecture-level municipalities have one). The same rule applies to the urban neighborhood committees. In reality, at these four levels of local administration, all state governmental organs, including the people's congresses and the judicial institutions, are led by the CCP committee at the corresponding level. And although autonomous areas benefit from special rules, such as the obligation to appoint a representative of the main ethnic group as chairperson of the local government, they are also led by the CCP and very often a Han party secretary, in particular in sensitive areas, such as Tibet or Xinjiang.

SEE ALSO *Central-Local Relationships; Provincial and Subprovincial Government Structure since 1949: Provinces; Provincial and Subprovincial Government Structure since 1949: Autonomous Regions.*

BIBLIOGRAPHY

Xie Jiaomin (Chiao-min Hsieh) and Max Lu, eds. *Changing China: A Geographic Appraisal.* Boulder, CO: Westview, 2004.

Zhong Yang. *Local Government and Politics in China: Challenges from Below.* Armonk, NY: Sharpe, 2003.

Zhonghua renmin gongheguo xingzheng quhua jiance [Overview of the administrative division of the People's Republic of China]. Beijing: Cehui Chubanshe, various years.

Jean-Pierre Cabestan

PROVINCES

The province (*sheng*) is the highest and most important level of local government in China. Most Chinese provinces are about the size of a middle-sized U.S. state or European country, such as Britain, but they are sometimes more populated—Henan, for example, counts over one hundred million people. Thus, Chinese provinces cannot be ruled in a centralized manner. The number of provinces remained stable at twenty-one after 1949, until, in 1988, Hainan Island was separated from Guangdong to form China's twenty-second province. Provincial boundaries have not otherwise changed, apart from those of Inner Mongolia, which were altered from 1969 to 1979, and Sichuan, which lost the Chongqing Municipality in 1997.

POLITICAL AUTONOMY

Although the People's Republic of China (PRC) has always been a unitary state, since 1958 and particularly after the launching of reforms in 1978, the provinces have been granted increasing, quasi-federal, and sometimes problematic economic and financial autonomy. Of course, like other levels of local government led by the provincial committee and secretary of the Chinese Communist Party (CCP), the provincial state institutions by no means enjoy genuine political autonomy. The provincial people's congresses are only formally elected by the people's congress of the lower level (prefecture-level municipalities or counties where prefectures have been kept), and, similarly, the leaders of provincial governments and judicial institutions are only officially designated by the provincial people's congresses. Such officials are actually selected by the CCP, and because of their high position in the hierarchy, most of them are selected by central party authorities, under the recommendation of the Central Committee Organization Department. However, this selection process does not guarantee centralization or even less obedience to the center in every respect.

In each province, the provincial party secretary and the governor (the governor is always the number-two official of the provincial party committee and often the party secretary's potential successor) are powerful "bureaucratic politicians." Following an unwritten rule, nearly all of them sit in the CCP Central Committee (the former as members and the latter often as alternate members). These leaders also try to use their provincial position as a career springboard, hoping to be promoted to the center, as minister, vice-premier, or eventually a CCP Politburo member. For central government ministers and a growing number of high cadres (including diplomats), provincial experience usually speeds up their career advancement, as long as nothing unexpected happens during their time in the provinces, such as social unrest, a human-caused catastrophe, or a corruption scandal.

As at the center or at other levels of government, the provincial party committee mainly deals with political, security, personnel, and propaganda issues. This committee, apart from the secretary and the governor, usually includes the secretary of the CCP commission in charge of politics and law (*zhengfa weiyuanhui*), which supervises all public security and judicial organs, as well as the heads of the provincial organization and propaganda departments. Economic and social matters are administered by the people's government, which operates under the leadership of the party committee. At the provincial level, every central government (or State Council) commission or ministry is represented by a corresponding functional department (*ting*) or bureau (*ju*). Since 1997, these departments have gradually stopped directly managing the enterprises controlled by the provinces and have focused on regulatory work and social policies (e.g., education, health care, and pension systems). However, provincial governments keep a close interest in these enterprises because of the revenue they bring to provincial coffers.

INEQUALITIES AMONG THE PROVINCES

Reforms and opening since 1978 have largely benefited the provincial authorities. In 1980 Beijing introduced a contractual fiscal relationship with the provinces that rapidly increased the latter's budgetary and extrabudgetary income. This reform also triggered widening inequalities between rich and poor provinces. The former are mostly located in the coastal areas (Guangdong, Jiangsu, Shandong, and Zhejiang), while the latter are concentrated in the hinterland (Gansu, Guizhou, Henan, Shaanxi, and Sichuan). The 1980 decentralization also impoverished the central government and weakened its redistribution powers.

In 1995 Premier Zhu Rongji decided to modify the fiscal system and the manner in which fiscal revenues were shared between the center and the provinces. As a result, Beijing's directly levied taxes increased from 45 percent to 55 percent of China's total fiscal revenues. Though this reform did not meet the premier's ambitious target of 66 percent, it strengthened the central government's grip over the consolidated state budget, as well as its capacity to assist the poorer provinces.

In 2000, in order to slow if not reduce the widening gap among provinces, Jiang Zemin decided to launch a new policy aimed at accelerating "the development of the west" (*xibu kaifa*). This policy contributed to the transfer of more foreign and domestic investments to provinces such as Gansu, Guizhou, Shaanxi, Sichuan, Yunnan, and even Xinjiang, as well as Qinghai and Tibet to a lesser extent. However, central provinces (Henan, Hunan, Shanxi, and to some degree Hubei) and northeastern provinces (Heilongjiang, Jilin, and Liaoning) felt neglected, and numerous economic and social problems (unemployment, AIDS, social unrest, and public insecurity) arose. These provinces have thus become more difficult to administer.

These inequalities have also had clear political consequences. Rich provinces, which could afford to say no to Beijing, enjoyed much larger de facto autonomy than poor provinces, which have continued, in spite of the efforts deployed since the mid-1990s, to depend upon the center's generosity.

While the provincial governments have remained Beijing's main local interlocutors, China's urbanization and the increasing number of prefecture-level municipalities (283 in 2007 against 170 in 1987) have contributed to empowering the latter to the detriment of the former. But here again, inequalities tend to persist: Municipalities that are also the seat of the provincial government (such as Wuhan in Hubei or Guangzhou in Guangdong) do not enjoy as much economic autonomy from the provincial authorities as do Dalian in Liaoning or Qingdao in Shandong. Today, the leaders of these cities are also more often elected to the CCP Central Committee.

PROVINCIAL REPRESENTATION IN THE PARTY'S TOP LEADERSHIP

Finally, a small minority of provincial leaders sits in the Politburo, the party's top leadership. Apart the Beijing, Shanghai, and Tianjin secretaries, only two provinces and one autonomous region were represented in the Politburo from 2002 to 2007 (Hubei's Yu Zhengsheng, Guangdong's Zhang Dejiang, and Xinjiang's Wang Lequan). And since 2007 only Wang Lequan and Guangdong's Wang Yang have been Politburo members. However, since the 1980s, a larger but carefully selected group of former provincial leaders has been promoted to the Politburo and its standing committee. Actually, by 2008, all Politburo members in China had acquired provincial experience, and most of them had served as provincial party secretaries (Hu Jintao in Tibet, Xi Jinping in Zhejiang, Jia Qinglin in Fujian [and Beijing], Li Changchun in Liaoning and Guangdong, and Li Keqiang in Henan and Liaoning) before being promoted to the center. But not every provincial leader moves to the top.

SEE ALSO *Central-Local Relationships.*

BIBLIOGRAPHY

Bo Zhiyue. *Chinese Provincial Leaders: Economic Performance and Political Mobility since 1949.* Armonk, NY: Sharpe, 2002.

Breslin, Shaun Gerard. *China in the 1980s: Centre-Province Relations in a Reforming Socialist State.* London: Macmillan, 1995.

Goodman, David S. G. *Centre and Province in the People's Republic of China: Sichuan and Guizhou, 1955–1965.* Cambridge, U.K.: Cambridge University Press, 1986.

Goodman, David S. G. *China's Provinces in Reform: Class, Community, and Political Culture.* New York and London: Routledge, 1997.

Li, Linda Chelan. *Centre and Provinces—China 1978–1993: Power as Non-zero-sum.* Oxford: Clarendon Press, 1998.

Jean-Pierre Cabestan

AUTONOMOUS REGIONS

Autonomous regions (*zizhi qu*) are province-level units in the People's Republic of China in which ethnic minorities exercise a form of autonomy governed by the state constitutions

China's autonomous regions

Autonomous region	Capital city	Date of establishment
Inner Mongolia	Hohhot	May 1, 1947
Xinjiang Uygur	Ürümqi	October 1, 1955
Guangxi Zhuang	Nanning	March 15, 1958
Ningxia Hui	Yinchuan	October 25, 1958
Tibet	Lhasa	September 9, 1965

Table 1

and the Law on Regional National Autonomy (*Minzu quyu zizhi fa*).

There are five autonomous regions in China, listed in Table 1 with capital cities and dates of establishment. There are also thirty autonomous prefectures, eight in Yunnan, six in Qinghai, five in Xinjiang, three in Guizhou, two in Gansu, three in Sichuan, and one in each of Jilin, Hubei, and Hunan, as well as about 120 autonomous counties.

HISTORICAL BACKGROUND

The *tusi* system in southwest China involved allowing local minority chiefs to exercise some autonomy among their own people. By the eighteenth century, the system was largely replaced by a power structure in which centrally appointed officials exercised control in the minority areas. In 1924 Sun Yat-sen signaled his belief in self-determination (*zijue*) and autonomy (*zizhi*) for smaller ethnic minorities. However, Chiang Kai-shek retreated from this idea in favor of tighter unity among the nationalities on the basis of nationalism. The Chinese Communist Party's (CCP) Chinese Soviet Republic Constitution (adopted November 7, 1931) explicitly allowed ethnic minorities either to secede or to set up their own autonomous region within China. The CCP had withdrawn permission for secession by 1949, but persisted in the idea of autonomy. The CCP's first autonomous government was established in October 1936 for the Hui area centered in Tongxin in central Ningxia. Inner Mongolia became an autonomous region before the PRC's establishment.

The CCP accepted the notion of autonomy in its Common Program of September 29, 1949, and in its four constitutions of 1954, 1975, 1978, and 1982. However, the 1975 constitution was written under the influence of the Cultural Revolution, when CCP Chairman Mao Zedong's obsession with class struggle had resulted in assimilationist ethnic policies, and it had much less about autonomy than the other three constitutions. The 1982 constitution has considerable detail on autonomy, while the Law on Regional National Autonomy of May 31, 1984, embellishes still further. Katherine Palmer Kaup states that of the 133 laws that the National People's Congress passed between 1979 and April 1992, "33 contained specific regulations on minority issues" (2000, p. 116). The 1984 law on autonomy was amended in February 2001, the new version strengthening several aspects of autonomy.

THE NATURE OF AUTONOMY

The essence of autonomy is that ethnic minorities establish self-government organs for the practice of regional autonomy in areas where they live in concentrated communities. Autonomy is not the same as independence, policy at all times emphasizing that all autonomous places are integral parts of the People's Republic of China and strongly advocating "the unity of the nationalities."

The main points of autonomy include: (1) all ethnic groups are equal and should be treated equally; (2) the organs of self-government may adopt laws and policies special to their area; and (3) the government head of autonomous places must belong to the ethnic group exercising autonomy in the area concerned. Encouragement should be given to training and promoting cadres belonging to ethnic minorities. Article 22 of the Law on Regional National Autonomy as amended in 2001 states that in recruiting working staff, self-government organs "shall give appropriate considerations" to members of minorities, especially the one exercising autonomy in the relevant area. The self-government organs have the right to frame budgets, administer finances, and allocate resources within the area they govern.

Ethnic minorities enjoy freedom of religion, but may not use it to threaten the state or social stability, and religious bodies may not be subject to foreign domination. Ethnic minorities have the right to follow and protect their own culture and use their own language not only in the private sphere but also in government, the law system, and the education system. Schools where most of the students belong to minorities are by law entitled to use the local minority language, both for textbooks and as the medium of instruction. In general, however, the higher in the educational system, the more likely are the textbooks and instruction to be in Chinese.

Self-government organs must help develop cultural phenomena such as literature, art, films, broadcasting, and publishing in forms and with characteristics unique to the ethnic minorities. State organs at higher levels must help autonomous areas train cadres from among the local ethnic minorities, as well as providing support for eliminating poverty.

Since the mid-1980s, autonomy has given rise to and facilitated a range of "preferential policies" (*youhui zhengce*) for ethnic minorities. The most important is a policy of greater flexibility in family planning, especially as it involves the one-child-per-couple policy, with autonomous governments adopting their own policies to suit local needs. Other preferential policies relate to school and university admissions, hiring and promoting, and financing and taxation in

Minority membership in the Chinese Communist Party (CCP)			
Year	Minority CCP membership	Total CCP membership	Minority proportion
1990	2.8 million	49 million	5.7%
1995	3.19 million	55 million	5.8%
2001	4 million	64.5 million	6.2%

Table 2

business, with government asked to give minorities preference in these areas.

LIMITATIONS ON AUTONOMY

Despite the preferential policies, some observers claim that ethnic minorities suffer discrimination, notably Tibetans and Uygurs. Representatives of the Tibetan and Uygur diasporas have made frequent accusations concerning such matters as forced abortions and discrimination in employment. There is doubt over the accuracy of some such claims, but what is clear is that whatever actions took place were illegal and represent failures of policy (see Mackerras 2003, pp. 136–138).

A major limitation on autonomy is that in crucial areas it does not apply to the CCP. While the government head of an autonomous place must by law belong to the ethnic minority exercising autonomy, the CCP secretary need not. A major qualification for membership in the CCP is belief in Marxism-Leninism, implying that members should be atheists. Mutual suspicion is thus common between the CCP and Islamic and other religiously committed ethnic groups. A common pattern is to appoint minorities to senior government positions, but Han to vital CCP positions. Bo Zhiyue (2002, pp. 61–63) shows that there were fewer minority party leaders than government leaders in all years from 1949 to 1998, except during the 1969–1977 period and six years from 1985 to 1992.

Bo suggests (2002, p. 64) that minorities were overrepresented in provincial leadership from 1949 to 1998. In total CCP membership, however, the contrary was the case, at least between 1990 and 2001, even though both the absolute figures and the proportions of total minority CCP membership rose during those years. The 2000 census had ethnic minorities with 8.41 percent of China's total population. Table 2 shows relevant data on CCP membership (see Mackerras 2003, pp. 41–42).

EVALUATION

Despite limitations, autonomy policies have produced significant benefits. Several studies have shown the growth of identity among the ethnic minorities. In particular, Kaup suggests that autonomy was originally a device to integrate China's most populous ethnic minority, the Zhuang, but autonomy has also had the effect of awakening feelings of ethnic identity among this people, with the result that since the 1980s Zhuang leaders have demanded ever more preferential treatment. "The CCP took a risk in promoting the development of a largely state-created nationality [the Zhuang]. It appears to be a risk that has paid off" (Kaup 2000, p. 180).

SEE ALSO *Central-Local Relationships; Minority Nationalities.*

BIBLIOGRAPHY

Bo Zhiyue. *Chinese Provincial Leaders, Economic Performance, and Political Mobility since 1949.* Armonk, NY: Sharpe, 2002.

Dreyer, June Teufel. *China's Forty Millions: Minority Nationalities and National Integration in the People's Republic of China.* Cambridge, MA: Harvard University Press, 1976.

Heberer, Thomas. *China and Its National Minorities: Autonomy or Assimilation?* Armonk, NY: Sharpe, 1989.

Kaup, Katherine Palmer. *Creating the Zhuang: Ethnic Politics in China.* Boulder, CO: Lynne Rienner, 2000.

Mackerras, Colin. *China's Minorities: Integration and Modernization in the Twentieth Century.* Hong Kong: Oxford University Press, 1994.

Mackerras, Colin. *China's Ethnic Minorities and Globalisation.* London and New York: RoutledgeCurzon, 2003.

Colin Mackerras

COUNTIES

The county (*xian*) was the lowest level of government in China for more than two thousand years. Developed during the Warring States period (475–221 BCE), the county stabilized after China's unification by Qin Shihuang (259–210 BCE) in 221 BCE and the establishment of the Han dynasty (206 BCE–220 CE). The county's *yamen* remained the seat of the emperor's lowest direct magistrate (*guan*) until the end of the Manchu dynasty in 1912. The number of counties increased from about 1,000 to 1,400 under the Sui (581–618) and to 2,000 by the end of the Qing dynasty (1644–1912), but thereafter remained more or less the same until the beginning of China's belated urbanization in the 1990s.

NEW COUNTY LAW DURING REPUBLICAN PERIOD

After the establishment of the Republic of China (1912–1949), the Guomindang authorities in the late 1920s tried to simplify local administration and to strengthen both the provincial and county governments. They abolished the circuit (*dao*), an intermediate level between these two levels, and they promulgated a new county law. But rapidly this revealed itself to be unfeasible: On the one hand, they had to establish the ward (*qu*), an important subdivision of the county that took care of most administrative affairs at the town (*zhen*) or township (*xiang*) level, and, on the other hand, they effectively restored the circuit in some areas for public security purposes.

COUNTY STATUS IN THE PRC

After the foundation of the People's Republic of China (PRC) in 1949, this four-level style of administration was strengthened, reducing the role of the county government. Below the county, a town or township government was established, which then became the lowest level of bureaucracy. After the launching of the Great Leap Forward in 1958, the townships were replaced by the people's communes until their dismantlement in the early 1980s, weakening the role of the county governments even more. Above the county and under the province, the circuit was replaced by the prefecture (*diqu*), a delegated and decentralized administrative organ (*paichu jigou*) of the provincial government.

However, in rural China, the county's power and autonomy has remained strong and sometimes problematic. The *xian* government administers a territory about the size of a French *département* or an American county and a population that can be ten times larger (up to 500,000 and sometimes a million). The prefecture is far away and the provincial government even farther, allowing county bureaucrats, in particular the Communist Party secretary and the county magistrate—who is also, as a rule, the number-two official of the county party committee—to enjoy much freedom to run the county's affairs. The county government controls the local finances and most of the local enterprises, to the detriment of the townships. The establishment in the early 1980s of contractual financial relations between the county and the prefecture has enhanced this autonomy. Of course, the economic and financial situation of each county can vary greatly, and poor counties have been unable to take advantage of this new autonomy, contributing to the deterioration of public services, including education and health care. However, the leading role taken by the Chinese Communist Party and the coordinating powers of the county party committee in every area of government, including the judiciary and the inspection or audit organs, tend to enhance rather than limit the counties' autonomy, as well as county leaders' temptation toward corruption or autocracy.

IMPACT OF URBANIZATION

Urbanization has been the main challenge to the county's autonomy and *raison d'être.* In the 1980s, in some developed rural areas, counties were placed under the leadership of prefecture-level municipalities (as occurred in Jiangsu, Guangdong, Shandong, and Zhejiang). This reform slowed in the early 1990s, but has been extended to most provinces since then. In 2007 the only remaining prefecture-led counties were located in poor provinces (such as Guizhou) or in areas of national minorities (such as Gansu, Qinghai, Sichuan, Tibet, Yunnan, and Xinjiang). Although municipality-led counties benefited from this new organizational pattern in terms of industrialization and communications, they have also lost some of their autonomy. This reform directly facilitated the urbanization of a growing number of counties: Since the early 1990s, many of them have become county-level municipalities (*xianjishi*). As a result, the number of these municipalities increased from 208 in 1987 to 442 in 1997. In 2007 this number fell to 369 because some county-level municipalities were upgraded to prefecture-level municipalities (*dijishi*, 283 against 222 in 1997) or merged. Conversely, the number of counties fell from 1,817 (1,986 county-level rural administrative units) to 1,520 (1,693) in 1997 and 1,463 (1,635) in 2007.

Below the county level, urbanization has also favored the multiplication of towns (*zhen*), not only as traditional marketplaces but also as new loci of industrialization. Since the 1980s, a growing number of towns have themselves become municipalities, contributing to the further weakening of county governments.

Nevertheless, as the numbers mentioned above indicate, the county is bound to remain a key administrative unit in rural and suburban China. For one thing, prefecture-level municipalities continue to rely on them for a large array of governmental tasks, from land management to birth planning and from agricultural production targets to basic education and health care. Since the early 2000s, Beijing has funneled more resources to the counties to help them fulfill these tasks. Moreover, there have been discussions about the abolition of township governments in order to strengthen the role and competence of counties both as administrative actors and agents of economic development. This reform has been put on hold because of the need to keep some government organs close to the villages or in the new towns. But it underscores the central authorities' priorities, according to which the county will remain, with the municipality, one of the two pillars of local and territorial administration at the subprovincial level.

ETHNIC MINORITY AREAS

Finally, the county remains a crucial level of government in the areas inhabited by ethnic minorities. In 2007 there were 169 county-level autonomous administrative units, including 117 "autonomous counties" (*zizhixian*), forty-nine "banners" (*qi*), and three "autonomous banners" (*zizhiqi*), mostly in "autonomous regions" or provinces mentioned above, but also in Inner Mongolia, Guizhou, Hubei, Hunan, and Jilin. According to the law on national minority areas, in these constituencies, the government and the people's congress should be chaired by a representative of the county's (or banner's) main nationality. However, this rule does not apply

to the party, whose secretary can also be (and is often) a Han, particularly in sensitive areas.

SEE ALSO *Central-Local Relationships.*

BIBLIOGRAPHY

Blecher, Marc, and Vivienne Shue. *Tethered Deer: Government and Economy in a Chinese County*. Stanford, CA: Stanford University Press, 1996.

Fitzgerald, John. Autonomy and Growth in China: County Experience in Guangdong Province. *Journal of Contemporary China* 5, 11 (1996): 7–22.

Zhonghua renmin gongheguo xingzheng quhua jiance [Overview of the administrative division of the People's Republic of China]. Beijing: Cehui Chubanshe, various years.

Jean-Pierre Cabestan

MUNICIPALITIES UNDER CENTRAL CONTROL

There were four municipalities directly under the jurisdiction of the central government (*zhixiashi*) of the People's Republic of China (PRC) in 2008: Beijing, Shanghai, Tianjin, and Chongqing. This type of organization dates back to the Republic of China era, when the Guomindang-led government established twelve "special municipalities" (*tebieshi*), rapidly relabeled *zhixiashi*. In 1949 the PRC authorities provisionally kept most of these municipalities, and added several more. However, in 1954, when the first state constitution was enacted, only three municipalities—Beijing, Shanghai, and Tianjin—were retained. The others were downgraded to subprovincial municipalities and subordinated to the government of the province in which they were located; most of them became provincial capitals (Guangzhou, Nanjing, and Wuhan), but some did not (Dalian, Qingdao, and Chongqing). For more than four decades, this administrative map remained unchanged, largely due to the Maoist policy of preventing the development of large cities and postponing urbanization.

THE CHONGQING MUNICIPALITY

China's urbanization in the 1980s and the 1990s increased the pressure for change. However, most provinces fiercely resisted alteration of their boundaries, since a growing part of their revenues originated from the large and booming cities under their jurisdiction. The only exception has been Chongqing, which in 1997 became the fourth municipality under central control. But this decision was not motivated by this city's exceptional dynamism, nor by its competition with Sichuan's capital city Chengdu, or its former status as the wartime national capital (under the name of Chungking). It was the construction of the gigantic Three Gorges Dam downstream in Hubei Province that triggered this reform.

In the late 1980s, the central authorities considered creating a "Three Gorges Province" (*sanxia sheng*), an idea that was rapidly abandoned due to opposition from both Sichuan and Hubei, which would have been deprived of large chunks of their territory. The change in the ecosystem that the dam would provoke and the need to relocate 1.4 million inhabitants because of the elevation of the Yangzi River water level were the main factors precipitating the separation, not only of Chongqing municipality but also the counties between this city and the Hubei border with Sichuan Province (two-thirds of Chongqing municipality's thirty-one million inhabitants are farmers). And it was easier for Beijing to negotiate only with Sichuan, which was given generous financial compensation, rather than both provinces.

ADVANTAGES AND DISADVANTAGES OF MUNICIPALITY STATUS

These municipalities enjoy a number of privileges, although they have become less valuable than they were under Mao Zedong or at the beginning of the reform period. Having been granted provincial status, they report directly to the central government and are listed on the plan separately from the twenty-two provinces and five autonomous regions of the PRC. Before 1979, they also had better access to food supplies and a much higher standard of living. In addition, these large municipalities administer not only the urban areas under their jurisdiction but also a number of rural counties from which most of their fresh produce used to come, especially during the time of Mao, and where today they are allowed to expand as part of their urbanization plan. Politically, the four large municipalities are headed by Chinese Communist Party (CCP) heavyweights and benefit from a high degree of autonomy, partly based on their capacity to attract investment and create wealth.

Since 1987, the party secretaries of Beijing, Shanghai, and Tianjin have sat in the Politburo, the inner circle of the country's leadership. This unwritten privilege was extended to Chongqing in December 2007 when former minister of commerce and Politburo member Bo Xilai was appointed Chongqing party secretary. These promotions reflect a new and more favorable policy toward large cities. Although Beijing has always benefited from its position as the seat of the national capital, it also suffered the consequences of this status, being more tightly scrutinized by the central government. Shanghai and Tianjin, however, have taken great advantage, since the end of the 1980s, of the new leadership policy. They have been allowed to keep a larger portion of their fiscal revenues (around 50%) and have been granted greater autonomy to implement their own economic development strategy, attract foreign investment, expand their harbors, and become regional hubs. As a consequence, these municipalities have often become a springboard for the careers of leading cadres. For example, Li Ruihuan (Tianjin) was promoted in 1997 to the post of national propaganda czar. And Jiang Zemin, Zhu Rongji, Wu Bangguo, and Huang Ju (Shanghai) have been among the most famous leaders called to the center of government: Jiang succeeded Zhao Ziyang as CCP general secretary in 1989, Zhu became premier in 1993, Wu was promoted to vice premier in 1998 and National People's Congress chairman in 2003, and Huang was given a vice premiership in 2003.

Shanghai's success, however, has also been its Achilles heel. Jiang's elevation to the country's top political position contributed to the formation of what some observers called the "Shanghai gang" (*Shanghai bang*). This favoritism provoked resentment among the political elite, as well as a good deal of corruption in Shanghai. While Huang Ju's early death in 2007 saved him from shame and prosecution, in September 2006 his successor, Politburo member Chen Liangyu, was dismissed, detained, and later expelled from the party and sentenced to eighteen years' imprisonment for bribery, abuse of power, and living a decadent life, and more specifically for his involvement in a major scandal regarding the diversion of pension funds that also led some well-known property developers to jail. Chen Liangyu's fate repeated Beijing's party secretary and Politburo member Chen Xitong's purge a decade earlier, also for corruption.

These examples underscore the CCP leadership's willingness to keep the large municipalities under check and rebalance the country's economic strategy. To some extent, Chongqing's elevation was part of a plan to speed up the "development of the west" (*xibu kaifa*) initiated by Jiang but deepened by Hu Jintao, which also benefited less-urbanized Sichuan, Gansu, and Yunnan.

Yet, China's four large municipalities will continue to take advantage of their special status to set more ambitious development plans, increase their international relations, intensify their globalization, and mobilize more resources to fulfill their ambitions. While Beijing organized the Olympic Games of 2008, Shanghai will host the 2010 World Expo and hopes to become not only China's financial center but also a counterweight to the international influence of New York and Hong Kong. Similarly, Tianjin wishes to use its proximity to Beijing to become a key technological and maritime transportation hub. And Chongqing's leaders dream about becoming a logistical center and industrial base for the entire hinterland, and later the entire country. Other cities, such as Shenzhen, aspire to join this group of large municipalities. However, facing strong decentralizing trends, the central government's intention is to keep this club as exclusive and small as possible.

SEE ALSO *Beijing; Central Planning; Central-Local Relationships; Chongqing; Shanghai; Tianjin*

(Tientsin); Urban China: Real Estate Management; Urban China: Urban Planning since 1978.

BIBLIOGRAPHY

Chung Jae Ho, ed. *Cities in China: Recipes for Economic Development in the Reform Era.* London and New York: Routledge, 1999.

He Shenjing. State-Sponsored Gentrification under Market Transition: The Case of Shanghai. *Urban Affairs Review* 43, 2 (2007): 171–198.

He Shenjing, Li Zhigang, and Wu Fulong. Transformation of the Chinese City, 1995–2005: Geographical Perspectives and Geographers' Contributions. *China Information* 20, 3 (2006): 429–456.

Wu Fulong and Zhang Jingxing. Planning the Competitive City-Region: The Emergence of Strategic Development Plan in China. *Urban Affairs Review* 42, 5 (2007): 714–740.

Yeung Yueman and Song Yunwing, eds. *Shanghai: Transformation and Modernization under China's Open Policy.* Hong Kong: Chinese University Press, 1996.

Jean-Pierre Cabestan

TOWNSHIPS

Townships occupy the lowest state administrative level below the county. There are two types of townships in China: urban (*zhen*) and rural (*xiang*). Townships have a long history in China. In the 1930s the Nationalist government fostered local self-government and experimented with village and township assemblies directly elected by inhabitants. After the founding of the People's Republic of China (PRC) in 1949, the new government retained the township designation. According to the constitution of 1954, townships were governed by a mayor and a people's congress. In 1958 the *xiang* level was replaced by *people's communes.* Townships were restored in 1982, and rewritten into the 1982 constitution. In 2006 China encompassed 41,040 units at the *xiang* and *zhen* level, of which 14,119 were rural townships.

In the PRC, *xiang* and *zhen* are distinguished according to their administrative-political status. The conditions for the assignment of town status have been changed three times. In 1955 the State Council laid down a number of criteria for the designation of towns. According to these norms, settlements could be granted *zhen* status if they had at least 2,000 inhabitants and 50 percent of the population was nonagrarian, or if they had between 1,000 and 2,000 inhabitants and had a 75 percent nonagrarian population. The latter regulation applied in particular to industrial and mining centers, railway and other traffic junctions, and trade centers.

In December 1963 the State Council tightened the preconditions for *zhen* status. The new norms were valid until 1984, and provided the following criteria for the designation of towns. There had to be more than 3,000 inhabitants, and the nonagrarian population had to make up more than 70 percent of the population. If there were between 2,500 and 3,000 inhabitants, the nonagrarian population had to be over 85 percent.

After the people's communes were dissolved, the preconditions for the status of *zhen* were modified again. In a report from October 1984, the Ministry of Civil Affairs complained that the development of towns did not follow a straight line, and the main problem was the absence of uniform norms to install *zhen* status. This situation had a negative effect on the development of industry, services, and leisure activities. To remove these obstacles, the following norms were proposed. Now all *xiang*—more or less comparable to former people's communes—could become a *zhen* if they were the seat of state authority at the county level, had fewer than 20,000 inhabitants but at least 2,000 nonagrarian inhabitants, or had more than 20,000 inhabitants with at least 10 percent belonging to the nonagrarian population in the seat of the township administration.

The rapid development of *zhen* was mainly due to economic reforms in rural areas. Among the main changes that revived *zhen* were the introduction of the production-responsibility system for peasant households, a diversification and specialization in agriculture, an increase of part-time jobs among peasants, the reopening of private markets, and industrialization.

The position and especially the functions of *zhen* in the urban hierarchy are not only conditioned by their administrative status and the number of agrarian and nonagrarian inhabitants; in many cases, their role and position are also determined by their proximity to large urban agglomerations or by special functions, such as mining or tourism. These special functions are limited to a small number of *zhen*; the main function of most *zhen* is to supply rural areas with market goods and services. By 2008, the economic functions of *zhen* in well-developed regions in China went far beyond their traditional role as markets—that is, they are not only centers for the collection and distribution of goods; they have also become pivots of rural industrialization.

The significance of *zhen* consists not only in their role as mediators between countryside and city; their significance is mainly due to their function as a focal point for the workforce that left agriculture and found employment in the nearby rural factories, or for peasant workers who combine agricultural and nonagrarian activities.

SEE ALSO *Education: Education in Rural Areas; Rural Development since 1978: Rural Industrialization; Township and Village Enterprises.*

BIBLIOGRAPHY

Fan Jie, Thomas Heberer, and Wolfgang Taubmann. *Rural China: Economic and Social Change in the Late Twentieth Century.* Armonk, NY: Sharpe, 2006.

Guldin, Gregory E., ed. *Farewell to Peasant China: Rural Urbanization and Social Change in the Late Twentieth Century.* Armonk, NY: Sharpe, 1997.

Yang Zhong. *Local Government and Politics in China: Challenges from Below.* Armonk, NY: Sharpe, 2003.

Thomas Heberer

VILLAGES

The word *village* (*cun*) has two meanings in Chinese: (1) a natural village or hamlet composed of residents who live together (*ziran cun*), or (2) an administrative rural area (*xingzheng cun*). According to the second definition, there were 652,718 villages in China in 2004, and approximately three million "village officials." Village size varies: Some villages have no more than thirty households, while others have between two hundred and five hundred households. An average village comprises roughly 380 households.

In each village, there is a branch of the Chinese Communist Party, as well as a village committee and a village representatives' assembly. These three organizations generally constitute the village political power structure. By law, the party branch constitutes the heart of the village power structure, and it is widely accepted in most villages that the village leader is the party secretary rather than the elected village head.

Before 1949, the village lay outside of the formal administrative system in China, and this continues to be the case insofar as the township is the lowest level of formal government in the People's Republic of China. In the Maoist era, under collectivization, introduced between 1955 and 1958, villages and townships were reconstituted as production brigades (*shengchan dadui*) and communes. Decollectivization in the early 1980s meant a reversal of this process, and production brigades were replaced by village committees (*cunmin weiyuanhui*) responsible for self-government (Zhong Yang 2003, p. 159). Since then, rural politics has undergone great changes, including the introduction of village committee elections, the redrawing of village boundaries, and a changing relationship between village and township.

VILLAGE ELECTIONS

The development of self-governance and village elections occurred in three stages. In the first stage (1978–1987), both were adopted in rural areas. In the second stage (1988–1998), trial elections were initiated. In 1990 up to a dozen villages in each county were selected for trial elections, and a basic institutional framework was established. The third stage began with the promulgation of the New Organic Law of Village Committees in 1998, followed by fairer and more open elections (from 1998 to the present).

The processes of rural democratization are full of contradictions, conflicts, and confusions, with a great number of variations. Four models can be used to describe the current state of affairs in Chinese village elections. They are (1) the absence of democracy, (2) formalistic democracy, (3) semidemocracy, and (4) established democracy.

The absence of village democracy has the following features: the denial of rights to women, the absence of formal democratic procedures, the nonexistence of elections, and the absence of a village representatives' assembly. In this category, authoritarian village leaders control village affairs without being subject to elections or to the village representatives' assembly; a few township leaders refused to hold village elections, and they themselves appointed village committee members. These townships even defied the order of the Ministry of Civic Affairs and continued their illegal practices, such as appointing village heads, as revealed by an analysis of 850 letters and visitors received by the office of the Ministry of Civic Affairs in 2001.

Formalistic democracy makes some progress in terms of the recognition of, and partial compliance with, formal democratic procedures, but there is an absence of any meaningful democracy. Village elections might be held and most electoral procedures are probably followed, but there is an absence of competition and therefore choice for the voters. Village representatives' assemblies exist, but are held only once a year merely as a ritual or formality. In addition, village representatives are appointed by village party secretaries rather than being elected by villagers. In some cases, village party secretaries control the entire election process, including mobilization of mass participation and the buying of votes through the resources they control.

Three types of noncompetitive elections occur where formalistic democracy prevails. The first is the muddled election in which electors lack information about electoral procedures, and township and villager leaders conduct elections without providing detailed information about candidates and procedures. These elections are nothing more than a formality. The second type is the manipulated election in which village party secretaries manipulate electoral procedures, select their own favored candidates, and predetermine the result. Prior to these elections, electors already know who will win, and elections lack uncertainty and excitement. These manipulated elections take place in authoritarian villages where competitiveness is absent and popular participation is low. The third type of noncompetitive election is the hoodlum election, in which a village ruffian stands for a leadership position and wins the election by means of threats and intimidation. For example, an addicted gambler was elected head of Nanyang village, Reian County, Zhejiang Province, and in 1996 the elected head of Hongguang village was a former convict.

These muddled, manipulated, and hoodlum elections tend to invite villagers' criticism, skepticism, and resistance, and contribute little to good village governance. Villagers adopt various measures against these forms of elections, such as nonparticipation, appeal to upper levels, or nomination of their own candidates. Through villagers' constant struggles, semicompetitive elections have gradually developed.

Semidemocracy takes a few steps toward partially meaningful democracy in terms of semicompetition and the increasing uncertainty of elections, and active participation by some villagers who fight for their village citizenship. Village representatives' assemblies are held several times each year, and they occasionally make village policy. Nevertheless, the competitive nature of village elections is constrained, with political liberty being very limited, political competition severely restricted, and the fairness of elections compromised. In addition, the effective power of elected village chiefs is limited, and village party secretaries still dominate village life.

Established village democracy involves a great advance in terms of fair and free village elections. Elected village chiefs are able to control village affairs, and village party secretaries are elected either by all villagers or by party members. Village leaders follow democratic rules and learn to use democratic means to solve social problems more and more often. Village representatives' assemblies are held more than ten times a year, and they make decisions about important issues, such as distribution of village income, land use, and village enterprises. There is an active citizenship and wide participation in the political process. This established village democracy, however, cannot be regarded as fully democratic, because it is still embedded in authoritarian structures.

ASSESSING VILLAGE DEMOCRACY

Among these four types, absence of democracy and well-established village democracy are both very rare. Few villages, probably less than 2 percent, refuse entirely to hold elections, putting them in the "absence of democracy" category. Most villages fall between formalistic democracy and semidemocracy; while the number of villages practicing formalistic democracy remains a majority, the number of semidemocratic villages is increasing.

Despite the vagaries of the process, the trend is a move from the absence of democracy to formalistic democracy, from formalistic democracy to semidemocracy, from semidemocracy to established village democracy, and from a phony to a partially true village democracy with democratic elements increasing to an impressive level.

The national surveys conducted by the Ministry of Civic Affairs found that 65.8 percent of respondents reported that the procedures of village elections were fair and being properly followed in 1998; this figure increased to 71.7 percent in 1999, dropped to 69.5 percent in 2000, and increased to 79.4 percent in 2001, reaching 95.3 percent in 2003. More and more villages are adopting formalistic democracy in terms of following electoral procedures, but,

of course, such procedural democracy does not guarantee substantive democracy. Chinese villages are still a long way from developing substantive democracy in terms of democratic and deliberative decision-making processes.

SEE ALSO *Population Policy: Birth-Planning Policy; Rural Development, 1949–1978: Collectivization; Rural Development since 1978.*

BIBLIOGRAPHY

He Baogang. *Rural Democracy in China: The Role of Village Elections.* New York: Palgrave Macmillan, 2007.

Li Lianjiang. The Empowering Effect of Village Elections in China. *Asian Survey* 43, 4 (2003): 648–662.

O'Brien, Kevin. Village Committees: Implementing Political Reform in China's Villages. *Australian Journal of Chinese Affairs* 32 (1994): 33–59.

Shi Tianjian. Village Committee Elections in China: Institutionalist Tactics for Democracy. *World Politics* 51, 3 (1999): 384–412.

Zhong Yang. *Local Government and Politics in China: Challenges from Below.* Armonk, NY: Sharpe, 2003.

Baogang He

STREET COMMITTEES, COMMUNITIES

Since 1949, China's urban organizational policy has been characterized by a threefold approach: (1) the creation of a network of political control (through street offices and residents committees); (2) the development of the urban population's economic potential (e.g., by setting up street and neighborhood businesses); and (3) the establishment of stable communities with community ties and awareness similar to villages or *danwei* (work units).

Street offices and resident committees had the task of implementing centrally determined policies (e.g., mass campaigns) in the neighborhoods. They also attended to social problems and "problem groups" (the unemployed, retirees, disabled persons, local people with criminal backgrounds, etc.). They founded kindergartens, health-care institutions, and small businesses; exercised political-aid functions; and acted as bureaus of registration and social services. In times of political radicalization, they became agents of political and ideological surveillance and control.

Street offices and resident committees were primarily established in neighborhoods that were not under the control of *danwei.* Their main purpose was the social organization of persons not belonging to *danwei.* These persons were principally family members of people who worked in larger *danwei,* employees in small enterprises, retirees, housewives, or the unemployed. Members of *danwei* did not usually participate in the activities of resident committees. In this way, city residents were integrated into a two-tier organizational network: They were either members of a work unit or a community unit.

With the Great Leap Forward in 1958, the economic function of the neighborhoods, together with political and ideological objectives, became the center of focus. Housewives, in particular, were integrated into the production process through "street factories." The idea of joining social control with economic production led to the formation of urban people's communes, modeled after their rural counterparts. In contrast to resident committees, urban communes were conceived as quasi-self-sufficient units that were supposed to link residential, production, education, and military functions, and assume the tasks of political and social mobilization. The experiment failed due to the reality of living conditions. Unlike rural areas, it proved impossible to unite the spheres of living, production, and administration because many residents pursued work in other neighborhoods, among other reasons. Furthermore, a latent resistance existed among the people, as well as among officials, against the continued forced collectivization of daily and private life. During the Cultural Revolution, however, street offices and the resident committees developed into breeding grounds for a totalitarian regime.

Economic reforms beginning in the late 1970s and the accompanying socioeconomic transformation and rise in social mobility have had a major impact on the structure of China's residential areas. Traditional community structures, such as *danwei*, eroded due to factory shutdowns or the collapse of enterprises. After reforms in residential policy, apartments were sold to their lodgers and new residential areas emerged, with condominiums owned by residents from a combination of different social groups. Homogenous residential structures based on the collective residence of enterprise employees were thus dissolved. The traditional resident committees, with their negative reputation and employees who were mainly older persons with low educational levels (predominantly female retirees), appeared incapable of meeting the communities' new requirements. The erosion of *danwei*, the increase in temporary residents, the growth of unemployment and urban poverty, as well as the lack of organizational structures for the private economy, were the most important factors. The dissolution of families (through rising divorce rates) and traditional values, as well as the decay of social and public security, were also factors.

Moreover, economic privatization and social individualization are no longer directed and regulated by the street offices. Conflicts are now resolved directly at the neighborhood level so as to disencumber the state and make rulings from higher organs more acceptable to local residents. Other functions, such as the responsibility for improving living spaces and infrastructure, the organization of leisure activities, and social care were also shifted to the neighborhood

level. Decentralized and communal solutions to problems are thus understood as contributing to good governance, to the extent that the population is more strongly integrated in participation, and resources and services are provided to citizens and available when needed.

Nonetheless, the restructuring of urban residential areas was not undertaken until the end of the 1990s. The administrative areas of the existing resident committees were merged into larger "neighborhood communities," with resident committees constituting the administrative and executive organs of control in the neighborhoods. This reorganization broke with the widespread residential organization according to *danwei*.

The term *shequ*—most closely translated into English as "community"—refers to a geographically defined living area. *Shequ* incorporate three dimensions: (1) a spatial aspect in terms of an administrative subunit (classified in China as a self-administration level below the street offices) with a population between 3,000 and 16,000; (2) a social dimension in regard to human actors and social relationships within a defined space; and (3) a normative or functional aspect, that is, a determined objective for a population segment, characterized by spatial proximity, mutual interests, and social control.

The 1989 law governing the organization of resident committees delegated two main areas of responsibilities to the committees: (1) supporting the government by safeguarding social stability; and (2) providing community and social services for residents. On the local level, however, a wide variety of perspectives exist as to what the main tasks and responsibilities of the *shequ* should be. They range from strictly administrative and control functions to income support, social care, family planning, employment procurement, hygiene, leisure organizing, and the political participation and self-administration of residents.

Formally, the resident committee answers to the delegate assembly of the *shequ* residents. In the neighborhoods, this assembly elects the members of the resident committee, accepts the committee's annual report, and is regarded as the primary decision-making authority. The size of a resident committee depends on the number of residents in a neighborhood. Most committees are comprised of six to eight persons. Funds for salaries and office expenses are provided by the city districts through the street offices.

SEE ALSO *Unit (danwei); Urban China: Urban Housing; Urban China: Urban Planning since 1978.*

BIBLIOGRAPHY

Chen Jie. *Popular Political Support in Urban China.* Washington, DC: Woodrow Wilson Center; Stanford, CA: Stanford University Press, 2004.

Chen, Nancy N., Constance D. Clark, Suzanne Z. Gottschang, and Lyn Jeffery, eds. *China Urban: Ethnographies of Contemporary Culture.* Durham, NC: Duke University Press, 2001.

Forrest, Ray, and Yip Ngai-Ming. Neighbourhood and Neighbouring in Contemporary Guangzhou. *Journal of Contemporary China* 50 (2007): 47–64.

Heberer, Thomas. Institutional Change and Legitimacy via Urban Elections? People's Awareness of Elections and Participation in Urban Neighbourhoods (*Shequ*). Duisburg Working Papers on East Asian Studies, no. 68. Duisburg, Germany: University Duisburg-Essen, Institute of East Asian Studies, 2006.

Heberer, Thomas, and Gunter Schubert. *Politische Partizipation und Regimelegitimität in der VR China* [Political participation and regime legitimacy in the PR China]. Vol. 1: *Der urbane Raum* [The urban space]. Wiesbaden, Germany: Verlag Sozialwissenschaften, 2008.

Read, Benjamin L. Democratizing the Neighbourhood? New Private Housing and Home-Owner Self-Organization in Urban China. *China Journal* 49 (2003): 31–59.

Thomas Heberer

PUBLIC FINANCE SINCE 1900

At the beginning of the twentieth century, China's public finances were challenged by an international debt crisis unleashed but not restricted to war indemnities, a balance-of-payment crisis that caused a massive outflow of silver, and deficit spending by successive governments leading to inflation and eventually hyperinflation after World War II (1937–1945). Although the Communist Party put an end to the debt crisis and inflation in the early 1950s, sound public finances and a rational public finance system only took shape after the reforms of 1978.

China's public finance system was launched on November 6, 1906, with an imperial edict. The court attempted to stem the financial anarchy into which China had fallen since the Opium Wars. It acknowledged that the traditional methods of public accounting could cope with neither the war expenditures (and accompanying war indemnities) nor the rapidly increasing imports. Although the financial crisis was seen as part of the general political crisis, the edict concentrated on reforms in tax administration rather than searching for new revenue sources. The reforms, which were never implemented, introduced ministerial responsibilities for a Board of Finance (Hubu). This board was to be organized in functional instead of territorial divisions, which reflected the Qing version of decentralization. The edict also, and for the first time, stipulated bank control in loan management.

REPUBLICAN CHINA (1911–1949)

Before the imperial reforms could be tested, China became decentralized, with different political and military alliances claiming to represent a "national" government. In actuality, these alliances seldom controlled more than the immediate vicinity surrounding the city they made their capital: Beijing, Nanjing, and Chongqing. The propagation of different constitutions or programs that attempted to reform public finance remained an exercise in either the written word or good intentions.

Four factors characterized public finances in Republican China: (1) size of jurisdiction; (2) lack of financial control; (3) intergovernmental transfers; and (4) a short-lived emergence of private banking. Those territories controlled by "independent" warlords, the Red Army, or the Japanese limited the geographical reach of public finances. Furthermore, no national government had control over revenue collection from local semiautonomous villages. Thus no national administration was able to tax agriculture, leaving only the narrow base of the nascent urban sector as a revenue source, since tariffs were linked to (foreign) debt service. What posed as intergovernmental transfers were in fact money flows in return for political support or war expenditures.

The two antecedents of private banking (*piaohao* and *qianzhuang*) were unable to reform into modern retail banks and disappeared with the end of the Qing dynasty (1644–1912). Instead, modern private banking emerged in 1912, but could not develop into a capital market large enough to accommodate private and state needs. This occurred for several reasons: the banks were concentrated in Shanghai, the capital market remained small with at maximum 106 banks, and the nascent capital market became strangled by the banking coup of 1935, after which banks were forced to concentrate on the issuance of state bonds instead of corporate stocks and bonds.

SOCIALIST CHINA (1949–1978)

In 1949 China united as one jurisdiction, becoming a single currency area under a unitary regulatory regime. China also introduced a socialist system characterized by the demonetization of the economy and contraction of the private sector, which inevitably led to a shrinking tax base. Between 1949 and 1983, taxation was limited to: (1) a tax on industrial production and commerce; (2) the agriculture tax; and (3) tariffs. These policies led to a taming of inflation, which was sidestepped by the rationing of goods. Instead of rising prices, queues and waiting lists indicated that demand could not find an appropriate (real) supply.

In budgetary terms, public finance in socialist China refers to small government. For example, the huge outlays for social security that characterize market economies were missing. However, in real terms, the scope of government activities became maximized, in that there was no longer a difference between the private sector and the public finance system.

REFORM CHINA (AFTER 1978)

In the early 1980s, the People's Bank of China began exercising control over the money supply and exchange

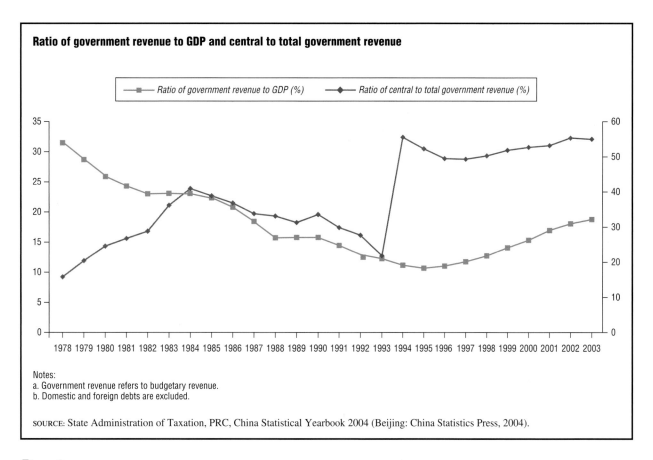

Ratio of government revenue to GDP and central to total government revenue

— ■ — *Ratio of government revenue to GDP (%)*   — ◆ — *Ratio of central to total government revenue (%)*

Notes:
a. Government revenue refers to budgetary revenue.
b. Domestic and foreign debts are excluded.

SOURCE: State Administration of Taxation, PRC, China Statistical Yearbook 2004 (Beijing: China Statistics Press, 2004).

Figure 1

rates, thereby functioning as a central bank. Yet a new, "rational" fiscal system was still missing. Traumatized by waves of inflation and debt crises in the twentieth century, the political leadership committed itself to a strict anti-inflationary and foreign-trade policy that facilitates foreign-exchange hoarding. The challenge for reform-era China has been to design a new public finance system that responds to revenue sources while ensuring that taxation does not hinder the emergence of new market-conforming organizations and innovations. Toward this goal, domestic reforms turned state-owned companies and collective enterprises into taxpayers, and since the 1990s all incorporated firms as well. A value-added tax (VAT) with a unified rate was introduced in 1994 in order to streamline the numerous taxes on specific goods, most of which were levied by local government agencies. In 2005 the income tax, first reintroduced for foreign joint ventures, was applied to all companies irrespective of ownership.

The most striking feature of China's public finance system is its "fiscal federalism." China has two tax systems: the national tax administration in charge of standardized national taxes, and local tax-sharing contracts. The latter means that government agencies levy local taxes and either keep the revenue for themselves or share a certain percentage with superior tax bureaus. Thus, public finance has become an aspect of central-local politics, where the center (Beijing) transfers regulatory power to the local state, in return for support of the overall reform course. Since the 1980s, after it became clear that localities profited much more from economic development than the center, the central government has tried to redress the financial imbalance. It forbade surtaxes and local levies, changed the sharing formulas of (joint) tax revenues, strengthened the national tax bureaucracy, and sought a better coordination of the intergovernmental transfer of revenue. Though the reforms streamlined the process of revenue appropriation for the central government, the overall effect has been limited, as shown in Figure 1.

While the 1950s saw the emergence of efficient monetary institutions, fiscal institutions emerged between 1980 and 2004. Although these institutions remain in flux, the new institutional framework and monetary and fiscal policy have rendered impressive results. By 2008, China had the largest foreign-exchange reserves in the world, and had become a major lender in international financial markets. In addition, China offered limited convertibility of its currency; controlled the money supply via a central bank aiming at price stability through unilaterally pegging the renminbi to the U.S. dollar; became an open economy whose integration into international value chains is facilitated by low tariffs and membership in international organizations; pursued a conservative budget policy, avoiding deficit spending; redesigned its tax base and tax rates in line with general economic growth and the expansion of the private business sector; and used taxes not only for revenue generation but also for encouraging or discouraging economic activities. China launched reforms of the banking sector much later than in other sectors, which left the economy with an underdeveloped stock and bond market, so that tradable (i.e., not government owned) shares account for only one-third of stock-market capitalization.

To conclude from this record that China "pragmatically" copied the best practices in monetary and fiscal policies from other (developed) countries is, however, inaccurate. Instead, China is a reminder that different institutions and policies can produce similarly positive results. The following section describes how some degree of continuity can be observed in China's public finance institutions, and points to features that appear to have been shaped more by China's own past practices than by international practices.

PATH DEPENDENCY IN INSTITUTION BUILDING

Three features can be identified as "Chinese," in that they are independent and unique to China: (1) ambivalence in central-local relations; (2) a missing link at the grassroots level; and (3) financial aloofness toward local funding.

Ambivalence in Central-Local Relations The question of how to govern an empire from the political center accompanies all political regimes. History shows that experiments with different degrees of decentralization follow functionality and power, that is, the need to compromise with local power holders. Usually, a political center transfers regulatory power to territorial jurisdictions (kingdom, province, state) in return for political support (and peace) and stable revenues.

In China, however, two modes of governance—namely, centralized tax administration and decentralized tax farming—were employed simultaneously. The only interruption of this trend occurred during the socialist era. In 1980 China started experimenting with tax farming, which was followed (in the 1990s) by a widespread (tax) sharing system (*fenshuizhi*). National taxes (*guojia shui*) are managed by a state bureaucracy, which operates under a unified tax code. Local taxes (*difang shui*) are managed by local bureaus and connected to the national tax bureau via tax contracts. Tax contracts are also used between local tax administrators and individual firms. A standard three-year

Tax sharing system (2006)	
Collecting agency	**Tax**
National tax bureau	Consumption tax, value-added tax (VAT), income tax on enterprises, income tax on foreign companies, stamp tax on security transaction, vehicle acquisition tax
Local tax bureaus	Business tax, individual income tax, resource tax, urban and township land usage tax, urban maintenance and construction tax, real estate tax, urban real estate tax, land appreciation tax, vehicle and vessel usage tax, slaughter tax, banquet tax, other stamp taxes
Customs	Tariffs, vessel tonnage tax

Table 1

Distribution of shared taxes		
Shared taxes	**Central**	**Local**
VAT	75% (2003)	25% (2003)
Enterprises income tax	50% (2002)	50% (2002)
	60% (2003)	40% (2003)
Individual income tax	50% (2002)	50% (2002)
	60% (2003)	40% (2003)

Table 2

contract defines the total tax obligation, which is then allocated to different tax obligations. Table 1 provides a short description of the 2006 tax-sharing system.

As in the Ming (1368–1644) and Qing dynasties, *decentralization* refers to delegating regulatory power and revenue sharing within an authoritarian regime, rather than a constitution-based separation of powers, as the term *fiscal federalism* suggests. Devolution relies on different tax administrations and revenue sharing, the largest of which are distributed as shown in Table 2.

The Missing Link at the Grassroots Level Closely linked to the problem of competing tax administrations and revenue sharing is the "failure" to build up a (tax) bureaucracy at the county level and below. The question is whether the different regimes did or did not want to penetrate the Chinese economy further. For example, the Qing dynasty as an occupying force expected the domestic (Han) magistrates to transfer revenues to the central (Manchu) coffer. In this case, the boundary between tax farming and tributes becomes blurred. Another example occurred in Nationalist China, where shaky alliances with local warlords left local tax authority, in particular the land tax, in the hands of those who actually controlled the land.

Bank worker counting money, Shanghai, November 24, 2000. *Beginning in the 1980s, China began enacting reforms on public finance, reflective of changes in the economy. Taxation of all companies, Chinese and foreign, became the rule, as did value added taxes on many business transactions.* **LIU JIN/AFP/GETTY IMAGES**

The most serious attempt to establish a unified, centrally controlled administration occurred during the Great Leap Forward with the attempt to make people's communes the basic economic unit. This effort was discontinued in the early 1960s, after which production brigades, or production teams, became once again the basic units of organization.

More recently, central-local aloofness is apparent in China's financial constitution, which differentiates only between national and local taxes, without specifying which subprovincial level executes which kind of tax authority. It is, rather, left to the province how to further decentralize regulatory power.

Financial Aloofness toward Local Funding Fiscal aloofness with respect to local funding is a consequence of the missing grassroots-level administrative link. Local government agencies, whether magistrates or townships, have always relied on alternative revenue sources, many of which continue to be used. These sources include surtaxes and customary fees, such as the so-called extrabudgetary reve-

nues (*yusuanwaishouru*) and off-budgetary revenues (*zhiduwaishouru*). Historically, these fees can be traced back to the socialist and Nationalist eras, as well as to the "meltage fee" (*haoxian*) of the Ming and Qing periods.

As in the past, by far the most crucial source of funding is land in rural China that is controlled, if not owned, by local government agencies. In the richer areas in southeast China, profit from land deals adds up to approximately 60 percent of total revenue, to the effect that the local government agencies become independent from the provincial or central money purse. Land ownership and lease contracts have reemerged in China, with the difference that peasants now face a "corporate" landlord in the form of a local government agency, often working in cooperation with development firms.

Surtaxes (*fei*) and land deals are not the only means by which local government agencies supplement revenues; informal networks are also a decisive factor. As poor counties and villages in Qing, Republican, and Nationalist China knew, the financing of even routine tasks depends on cooperation with or cooptation of nonbureaucrats. Even revenue-rich villages profit from cooperation with landowners, merchants, or private owners of companies or foreign firms, because this means more revenue outside of administrative budget control. In other words, what further characterizes China's public finance system at the local level is its reliance on informal networks for securing a sufficient resource, if not a prospering tax base. One such source is local banks that are neither sub-branches of state banks nor "private" companies. As in the past, these banks do not need to follow "sound" business practices, since the scope of business depends less on private savings than on financial transfers from superior bureaucracies and the cash flow that companies are forced to keep in these banks. In most cases, the banks represent a kind of joint venture between the successors of the old merchants (i.e., the new local business community) and local government agencies. This would point to another historical path dependency—namely, the missing or underdeveloped capital market—were it not for the fact that China, with its 2001 accession to the World Trade Organization, had committed itself to liberalizing the financial sector.

Another network-generated revenue source is the minority shares that local government agencies keep in commercial companies. These shares indicate more than an unfinished privatization of the local industrial sector. Local government agencies, if not individual government officials, are often invited to become co-owners, participating in daily management in return for patronage. In other words, while government officials become (at least part-time) entrepreneurs by controlling banks and incorporated companies, the local business community becomes a (part-time) administrator in charge of the smooth running of the local economy—just as in the past.

SEE ALSO *Banking: Overview; Banking: People's Bank of China; Taxation and Fiscal Policies, 1800–1912; Taxation since 1978.*

BIBLIOGRAPHY

Bastid, Marianne. The Structure of the Financial Institutions of the State in the Late Qing. In *The Scope of State Power in China*, ed. Stuart R. Schram. Hong Kong: Chinese University Press; London: School of Oriental and African Studies, University of London, 1985.

Brean, Donald J. S., ed. *Taxation in Modern China*. New York: Routledge, 1998.

Cheng Linsun. *Banking in Modern China: Entrepreneurs, Professional Managers, and the Development of Chinese Banks, 1897–1937.* Cambridge, U.K.: Cambridge University Press, 2003.

Faure, David. *China and Capitalism: A History of Business Enterprise in Modern China*. Hong Kong: Hong Kong University Press, 2006.

Feuerwerker, Albert. Economic Trends in the Late Ch'ing Empire, 1870–1911. In *Cambridge History of China*, Vol. 2: *Late Ch'ing, 1800–1911*, Pt. 2, eds. Denis Twitchett and John K. Fairbank, 1–69. Cambridge, U.K.: Cambridge University Press, 1980.

Kellee, S. Tsai. *Back-Alley Banking: Private Entrepreneurs in China*. Ithaca, NY: Cornell University, 2004.

Krug, Barbara, and Hans Hendrischke, eds. *The Chinese Economy in the 21st Century: Enterprise and Business Behaviour.* Cheltenham, U.K.: Elgar, 2007.

Musgrave, Richard A. *Fiscal Systems*. New Haven, CT: Yale University Press, 1969.

Nee, Victor. The Role of the State in Making a Market Economy. *Journal of Institutional and Theoretical Economics* 156 (2000): 66–88.

Qian Yingyi and Barry R. Weingast. China's Transition to Markets: Market-Preserving Federalism, Chinese Style. *Journal of Policy Reform* 1 (1996): 149–85.

State Administration of Taxation of the People's Republic of China. *China Statistical Yearbook 2004*. Beijing: China Statistics Press, 2004.

Teiwes, Fred. The Establishment and Consolidation of the New Regime, 1949–57. In *The Politics of China*, ed. Roderick MacFarquhar, 5–86. Cambridge, U.K.: Cambridge University Press, 1997.

Twitchett, Denis, and John K. Fairbank, eds. *Cambridge History of China*, Vol. 12, *Republican China, 1912–1949*, Pt 1. Cambridge, U.K.: Cambridge University Press, 1983.

Wong, Christine P. W., Christopher Heady, and Wing T. Woo. *Fiscal Management and Economic Reform in the People's Republic of China*. Manila: Asian Development Bank, 1995.

Zelin, Madeleine. *The Magistrate's Tael: Rationalizing Fiscal Reform in Eighteenth-century Ch'ing China*. Berkeley: University of California Press, 1984.

Barbara Krug

PUBLISHING INDUSTRY

Print culture in late imperial China was dominated by literati culture, the examination system that provided entry into the scholar-official elite, and by the widespread use of xylography, or woodblock printing. Woodblock printing was invented and in public use by the early eighth century; the oldest surviving printed book appeared in 868. Some works were carved in stone. By the eleventh century Chinese publishers practiced a newly invented method of printing by movable type.

HISTORICAL OVERVIEW

China's first emperor Qin Shi Huangdi (r. 221–210 BCE) understood the power of the written word and its importance as a political tool. Ever since he burned books and buried scholars alive, Chinese writers have lived with the fear or fact of censorship. The court supervised official publishing, mainly the production of imperially ordained works of history and anthologies for imperial libraries. In late imperial times both the court and local officials banned books, yet commercial publishing rendered prohibition ineffective.

The Beginnings of Mass Print Culture Mass communication society and mass print culture began in the late Ming era with the rise of commercial woodblock publishing. The worldwide economic boom of the seventeenth century and the growth of prosperous market towns and cities increased the market for books. The publishing industry gradually shifted its center from Fujian to Nanjing, Suzhou, and Hangzhou. Individual enterprises and commercial bookstores began to dominate the market. Technological advances and changes in production such as the simplification of fonts and the division of labor in woodblock cutting facilitated the production and distribution of books. The Jesuit missionary Matteo Ricci (1552–1610) noted "the exceedingly large number of books in circulation here and the ridiculously low prices at which they are sold" (Gallagher 1953, p. 21).

Private and commercial publishing enterprises catered to the tastes of urban readers and the needs of the rising merchant class. Commercial publishers supplied what the market demanded, producing anything from handbooks on literati taste to textbooks for civil service examinations, travel guides for merchants, novels, and erotic literature. Early Qing commercial publishers confessed to having become "filthy rich" (Widmer 1996, p. 91). Elite women emerged on an unprecedented scale as the authors and readers of poetry. In the eighteenth century Beijing became the new capital of commercial publishing. Reading habits changed before the Opium War (1839–1842) as women began to read and write fiction, too.

The imperial court published daily official gazettes and distributed the manuscripts through an official delivery system. Commercial news production began in 1582 as small-scale entrepreneurs published and sold hand-copied newssheets containing summaries from the *Beijing Gazette* (*Jingbao*). In 1638 the *Beijing Gazette* for the first time appeared in movable type replacing handwriting as the copying technology in response to an increased demand for information because movable type made it possible to produce more copies while keeping production at a lower price than woodblock cutting.

Print Capitalism and Print Communism In the late nineteenth century the introduction of Western mechanized movable lead-type printing and photogravure printing plates began China's "Gutenberg revolution," allowing rapid and large-scale reproduction of texts and catering to a new mass readership. The Commercial Press (Shangwu yinshuguan, established 1897) and the China Publishing House (Zhonghua shuju, established 1912) were among the first modern and largest publishing houses. *Shenbao* (*Shanghai News*) emerged in 1872 as the first mass-market newspaper. *Haishang qishu* (*Marvelous Writings from Shanghai*) became the first Chinese literary journal in 1892.

The new publishing methods and new commercial business forms made Shanghai the new publishing center and contributed to the establishment of "print capitalism"

in the Republican era (1912–1949). Nationalist-dependent publishers controlled the press until 1937. Shanghai's modern publishers issued lithographic (*shiyin*) or lead-type (*qianyin*) texts, building on traditional channels and distribution patterns. Woodblock printing and modern-style publishing coexisted until the 1940s.

The structures of "print communism" emerged with the founding of the Chinese Communist Party (CCP) in 1921 and the establishment of the People's Publishing House (Renmin chubanshe) the same year. Recognizing the importance of the print media, Mao Zedong (1893–1976) organized a print workers union in the early 1920s. Underground and commercial CCP publishers operated in secrecy, surviving against the odds until the outbreak of the Anti-Japanese War in 1937. As the war destroyed Shanghai's print capitalism, the CCP moved its print center first to Yan'an and then to Beijing.

The Party Central Committee's Publishing and Distribution Department established the party's major publication organ and official distribution service, New China Publishing House (Xinhua shudian), in Communist-controlled areas during the Anti-Japanese War (1937–1945). Xinhua officially opened in 1939 and gradually expanded across China. *Liberation Daily* (*Jiefang ribao*, 1941–) became the first standard-sized party newspaper using lead-type print.

When Mao Zedong founded the People's Republic of China (PRC) on October 1, 1949, the previously underground CCP publishers secured a state monopoly over the print media. Only two days later, the First National Publishing Work Conference opened, highlighting themes of unification and centralization of the press. The Communist propaganda culture regarded texts as basic to the CCP and the revolution. Heralding the era of print communism, the General Publishing Office (GPO, Chuban Zongshu, established 1949) declared the purpose of the new publishing industry to be for the benefit and service of the masses (Reed 2004b).

Publishing became party-dominated, heavily subsidized, and noncommercial. The government nationalized all Xinhua branches, entrusting them with publishing, printing, and distribution. In 1951 only 12 out of 304 book-printing plants in China were state-run, but in the next few years the privately owned plants were converted into public/private joint-run enterprises concentrated in Beijing. The state achieved full-scale nationalization of publishing units by 1956, and reduced their number to 103 (Reed 2004b).

Political objectives determined distribution, printing supplies, and publishing goals. Demand for books outstripped supply. Permitted publishing categories between 1949 and 1966 included works by Marx, Engels, Lenin, Stalin, and Mao; textbooks (57 million in 1950); popular literature for workers, peasants, and the masses; children's books; science and technology; and "books for cadres only" (*neibu*). Diverse works including reprints of classics and traditional literature appeared during the Hundred Flowers movement (1956–1957) but the industry suffered setbacks after the anti-rightist campaign (1957). The Cultural Revolution limited publications to political tracts and Mao's works in millions of copies.

PRINT CULTURE IN REFORM-ERA CHINA

The publishing industry enjoyed a renaissance in the era of reforms (1979–) characterized by decentralization, deregulation, and diversity. The General Administration of Press and Publication (GAPP, Xinwen chuban zongshu), a government body under the control of the State Council but overseen by the Party Central Committee's Propaganda Department, monitors and regulates all print media.

China National Publishing Administration (Zhongguo Guojia Chubanju,), the umbrella organization for the publishing industry, controlled the Xinhua distribution network and the Publishers Association of China until 1987 when it was replaced by GAPP. Chinese official sources counted 418 state publishing establishments in 1984 (the majority located in Beijing); 568 (plus 292 audio-video publishers) in 2006; and 572 in 2007 (Gov.cn; Barry 2007, p. 65). Publications of periodicals increased from 257 in 1949 to 1,470 in 1979 and 8,000 in 2004 (Gov.cn). The annual output of new and reprinted books increased from 15,000 titles in 1978 to 45,600 in 1985, and 222,473 individual titles in 2005 (Feldman 1986, p. 521; Barry 2007, p. 29).

In 1987 two news agencies, the Xinhua News Agency and the China News Service (Zhongguo xinwenshe), supplied information to the official national newspapers—notably *Renmin ribao* (*People's Daily*), *Guangming ribao* (*Enlightenment Daily*), and *Jiefangjun bao* (*Liberation Army Daily*)—and to the English-language *China Daily* and other specialized, local newspapers in China. In the 1980s translated foreign news was restricted to special newspapers for cadres only. Chinese government sources estimate the publishing output in 2004 as 25.77 billion copies of newspapers, 2.69 billion magazines, and 6.44 billion books (Gov.cn).

The Commercial Publishing Industry In the 1980s the commercial publishing industry began to expand rapidly, catering to investors' interests and consumer demands. The privatization of China's economy ended the state monopoly on publishing held by the Party Central Committee's Propaganda Department. A nongovernmental publishing industry, or "second channel," emerged as an alternative to the "red channel," the state-run Xinhua publishing network.

Wealthy private entrepreneurs known as "book kings" (*shuwang*) set up the second channel, which includes the "white channel" (previously licensed, limited local distribution networks that moved into unlicensed commissioning and publishing; these were semilegal operations that shied away from publications with controversial contents) and the "black channel" (illegal underground publishing operations that never received any license, were driven by profit, and therefore willing to publish sensitive, censored, or restricted works). Authors find second-channel operators attractive because they pay more and more quickly than state publishers. The private publishing industry has been holding its own trade conventions since 1987. Since second-channel operations lack legal status and are still officially prohibited, they do not appear in the official statistics and estimates about their outputs differ considerably. Recent estimates attribute around 25 percent of all titles, but most literary works, and 80 percent of all best sellers to second-channel publications (Kong 2004, p. 75; Barry 2007, p. 87). Estimates of the number of second-channel publishers in 2007 vary from at least 5,000 to 30,000 (Barry 2007, p. 87; Soong 2005a).

The development of new types of publishers has aided the commercialization of fiction writing. These new publishers help authors promote their books. Entrepreneurs have turned publishing houses into best-seller machines, and book traders (*shushang*) use semiofficial or unofficial channels of publishing to satisfy readers' demands for literary entertainment while maximizing their profits. Acting as publishers, agents, and editors, the book traders emerged as major players in the publishing industry in the 1990s.

Technological Change In the 1980s computers and laser typesetting technology replaced manual movable typesetting. In the 1990s software helped manage editing, printing, and issuance. China was first connected to the Internet in 1994; its use had been popularized by 1998 with one million users (CNNIC). In the early 2000s advanced digital technology facilitated electronic publications, online sales, and printing on demand.

The digital revolution has transformed the dynamics of publishing in China. In 2008 China's Web population became the world's largest with 253 million users (CNNIC). Digital publishing has replaced both paper and compact disc publications as the most profitable and stable source of income. The total digital publishing scale in China increased from 1.59 billion yuan in 2000 to 30 billion yuan in 2007 (Zhuang Guangping 2008). Government statistics count more than 2,000 new electronic publications annually (Gov.cn).

STATE REGULATION AND CONTROL

The Chinese government controls the print media through licensing policies and censorship. The constitution grants all citizens the right to publish, but administrative policies strictly regulate publishing. Manuscripts undergo editorial

Display at a book fair, Beijing, December 26, 2004. *Relaxing of regulations in the 1980s began an explosion in the amount of books published in China, with private companies becoming allowed to produce books not officially approved by the Communist government. These publishers offer an alternative to government-approved books, though the material they produce may be censored after publication if deemed subversive.* **CANCAN CHU/GETTY IMAGES**

review at publishing houses. GAPP administers copyright, issues the registration numbers (*shuhao*) legally required for books and periodicals, and has the power to censor or ban any publication. Until the 1980s all writers were screened and salaried members of China's Writers' Association. Wang Shuo (b. 1958) set a new trend in the 1980s as an independent freelance writer making a living from commercial publishing.

Neibu **Circulation** From 1949 to 1979 the official guidelines allowed publication of a limited number of works fulfilling all the criteria of political correctness, but internal circulation (*neibu*) provided an alternative channel for works that fell beneath the mark, including foreign translations. These works "for insiders' eyes only" were reserved for high-ranking cadres; their perusal or possession was illegal for ordinary citizens. The government lost control over their dissemination during the Cultural Revolution. Internal publications declined in the 1980s due to the proliferation of commercial and underground publishing. According to

PRC official sources, 18,301 internal publications appeared between 1949 and 1979 (Kong 2004, p. 122); in the 1990s the number of internal publications diminished (to about 15 in 1994), and publishers foresaw their demise (Gumbrecht 1995).

Censorship Ideological pressures encourage self-censorship, but the Chinese government also has a postpublication censorship system. If a book does not meet approval after publication it can incur a ban, and the author, editor, or publisher can be fined, blacklisted, or punished. This occurs with some regularity: Yunnan Province, for example, listed forty-one closed state publishing houses and 1,300 banned books in 1990 (Schell 1995, p. 301). According to government figures, government agencies confiscated over 55 million copies of illegal publications, closed 743 illegal printing enterprises and 15,000 publication stores, and fined another 22,000 publication stores in early 2006 (Barry 2007, p. 132). Book bans can create publicity, and some authors remain defiant. *Shanghai Baby* (*Shanghai baobei*, 1999) author Wei

Hui (b. 1973), for example, claims on her personal Web site that she is proud to be banned. Provoking the establishment can become a marketing strategy but the perils of publishing are well known, and the International PEN writers' association warned in 2002 that Chinese authors increasingly faced censorship, persecution, and imprisonment (*Mail & Guardian Online* 2002).

Despite periodic crackdowns, the government has been losing control over the press. Official and academic presses have been punished for selling ISBNs (book registration numbers) to book traders, who in turn received heavy fines for trafficking in the numbers. Books banned in print appear on the Internet, and vice versa. Censored Internet sites move to alternative or international electronic platforms.

MONIES, ROYALTIES, AND PROBLEMS OF MARKETIZATION

All media were state subsidized under Mao. Publishing units belonged under administrative units, business entities, or academic institutions. The reform era introduced competitive market conditions, turning publishing units into business units under pressure to become profitable. The first state-run shareholding publishing company, Shanghai Century Publishing, appeared in 2005, drawing on diversified fund sources. In 2008 government officials called for an internationally competitive publishing industry.

Wang Shuo was the first Chinese author to issue his collected works (1996) in four volumes, an honor previously reserved for paramount leaders or deceased literary icons. He pioneered the use of advertisements to promote his books in the 1980s, and in the first decade of the 2000s his books contained advertisements to boost profits. In 1993 Jia Pingwa (b. 1952) was the first author to receive a one million–yuan advance, from an independent publisher for his novel *Feidu* [Ruined capital]. In the early 2000s publishers spent millions of yuan in marketing print and Internet authors as brands. Twenty-first century bestselling authors including Han Han (b. 1982), Anni Baobei (b. 1975), and Guo Jingming (b. 1983) earn three million to four million yuan in advances and royalties per book, according to their publisher (Martinsen 2007).

The proliferation of pirate editions deprives authors of royalties (usually 8–10%) but brings more publicity and greater circulation. The estimated ratio of official to pirated books is 40 percent to 60 percent. Pirate editions are cheap to produce because they dispense with royalties, advances, or fixed costs: The cover price includes 78 percent for printing costs, distribution, and retailing, and 22 percent for profit. In 2005 an estimated 100 underground publishers thrived on an organized system of 4,000 underground publishing factories able to deliver print runs of 100,000 copies within days to 2,600 sales venues nationwide (Soong 2005b).

Second-channel publishing plays a key role in China's new print culture and forecasts assume that the second channel may be legitimized in the near future (Barry 2007, p. 88). While this may be true for some white-channel operations, however, it seems unlikely for the time being that such predictions will apply to all parts of the second channel (in particular the black channel).

SEE ALSO *Avant-garde Fiction; Censorship; Jia Pingwa; Journalism; Literature since 1800; Wang Shuo; Woodblock Printing (xylography).*

BIBLIOGRAPHY

Barry, Virginia. Red—The New Black: China-UK Publishing. London: Arts Council England, 2007. http://www.artscouncil.org.uk/publications/publication_detail.php?sid&=24&id&=593.

Berg, Daria. Portraying China's New Women Entrepreneurs: A Reading of Zhang Xin's Fiction. Durham East Asian Papers 12. Durham, U.K.: Department of East Asian Studies, 2000.

Berg, Daria. Carnival in China: A Reading of the Xingshi yinyuan zhuan. Leiden, Netherlands: E. J. Brill, 2002.

Berg, Daria. Miss Emotion: Women, Books, and Culture in Seventeenth-Century Jiangnan. In *Love, Hatred, and Other Passions: Questions and Themes on Emotions in Chinese Civilization*, ed. Paolo Santangelo and Donatella Guida, 314–330. Leiden, Netherlands: E. J. Brill, 2006.

Berg, Daria. Female Self-Fashioning in Late Imperial China: How the Gentlewoman and the Courtesan Edited Her Story and Rewrote Hi/story. In *Reading China: Fiction, History and the Dynamics of Discourse: Essays in Honour of Professor Glen Dudbridge*, ed. Daria Berg, 238–289. Leiden, Netherlands: E. J. Brill, 2007.

Brokaw, Cynthia. Commercial Woodblock Publishing in the Qing: The Dissemination of Book Culture and Its Social Impact. Paper presented at the conference "From Woodblocks to the Internet: Chinese Publishing and Print Culture in Transition." Ohio State University, Columbus, November 3–6, 2004.

Brokaw, Cynthia. *Commerce in Culture: The Sibao Book Trade in the Qing and Republican Periods.* Cambridge, MA: Harvard University Press, 2007.

Brook, Timothy. *The Confusions of Pleasure: Commerce and Culture in Ming China.* Berkeley: University of California Press, 1998.

China Internet Network Information Center (CNNIC). *Survey Report* 22 (July 2008). http://www.cnnic.cn/index/0e/00/11/index.htm.

Feldman, Gayle. The Organization of Publishing in China. *China Quarterly* 107 (1986): 519–529.

Gallagher, Louis, trans. *China in the Sixteenth Century: The Journals of Matteo Ricci, 1583–1610.* New York: Random House, 1953.

Gov.cn. Publishing. Chinese Government's Official Web Portal. http://english.gov.cn/2006-02/08/content_182635.htm.

Gumbrecht, Cordula. Report on an Information and Acquisition Tour to Japan, Hong Kong, Macao, Taiwan, and Singapore. *Bulletin of the European Association of Sinological Librarians* 8 (1995). http://www.easl.org/beasl/be9tour.html.

Kong, Shuyu. *Consuming Literature: Best Sellers and the Commercialization of Literary Production in Contemporary China.* Stanford, CA: Stanford University Press, 2004.

Mail and Guardian Online. The Pen Is Still Mightier than the Sword. January 1, 2002. http://www.mg.co.za/article/2002-01-01-the-pen-is-still-mightier-than-sword.

Martinsen, Joel. Lu Jinbo: Marketing the Wang Shuo Brand. June 21, 2007. http://www.danwei.org/books/lu_jinbo_marking_the_wang_shuo.php.

McDermott, Joseph P. *A Social History of the Chinese Book: Books and Literati Culture in Late Imperial China.* Hong Kong: Hong Kong University Press, 2006.

Mittler, Barbara. *A Newspaper for China? Power, Identity, and Change in Shanghai's News Media, 1872–1912.* Cambridge, MA: Harvard University Press, 2004.

Ōki Yasushi. Minmatsu Kōnan ni okeru shuppan bunka no kenkyū [Research on print culture in late Ming Jiangnan]. *Hiroshima daigaku bungakubu kiyō* [Research bulletin of the faculty of literature at Hiroshima University] 50, 1 (1991): 74–102.

Reed, Christopher A. *Gutenberg in Shanghai: Chinese Print Capitalism, 1876–1937.* Vancouver: University of British Columbia Press, 2004a.

Reed, Christopher A. Oppositionists to Establishmentarians: Print Communism from Renmin to Xinhua, 1921–1966. Paper presented at the conference "From Woodblocks to the Internet: Chinese Publishing and Print Culture in Transition." Ohio State University, Columbus, November 3–6, 2004b.

Schell, Orville. *Mandate of Heaven: A New Generation of Entrepreneurs, Dissidents, Bohemians, and Technocrats Lays Claim to China's Future.* London: Little, Brown, 1995.

Soong, Roland. The "Malignant Tumor" in Chinese Book Publishing. EastSouthWestNorth Web site. January 27, 2005a. http://zonaeuropa.com/20050130_1.htm.

Soong, Roland. The Underground Publishing Industry in China. EastSouthWestNorth Web site. June 14, 2005b. http://zonaeuropa.com/20050614_1.htm.

Wei Hui. Personal Web site. http://goldnets.myrice.com/wh/.

Widmer, Ellen. The Huanduzhai of Hangzhou and Suzhou: A Study in Seventeenth-Century Publishing. *Harvard Journal of Asiatic Studies* 56, 1 (1996): 77–122.

Widmer, Ellen. *The Beauty and the Book: Women and Fiction in Nineteenth-Century China.* Cambridge, MA: Harvard University Asia Center, 2006.

Zhuang Guangping. Domestic Publishing Industry on Information Highway. China Economic Net Web site. July 10, 2008. http://en.ce.cn/Insight/200807/10/t20080710_16110098.shtml.

Daria Berg

Q

QIAN ZHONGSHU
1910–1998

One of the most prominent scholars in the literature of modern China, Qian Zhongshu was also a novelist, short-story writer, and essayist known for his unique narrative style.

EARLY YEARS AND EARLY WRITINGS

Qian was born in 1910 in Wuxi, Jiangsu Province, and received rigorous training in classical Chinese at an early age. In his teens, he learned English in a missionary school and was extensively exposed to Western literature. From 1929 to 1933, Qian studied in the Department of Foreign Languages at Qinghua University. At the university, he began publishing traditional-style Chinese poetry and critical essays. In 1935 Qian, together with his wife, Yang Jiang, went to Oxford University on a government scholarship to study English literature. After receiving a bachelor of literature degree at Exeter College in 1937, Qian moved to the University of Paris, where he studied for one more year before returning to China in 1938 due to the outbreak of the Sino-Japanese War (1937–1945). Back in China, Qian taught at several universities and wrote extensively.

In 1941 Qian published *Marginalia of Life*, a collection of ten short essays. As the title indicates, these essays deal with various topics from unconventional and dialectical perspectives. For instance, Qian writes that a prejudice usually speaks of truth ("A Prejudice"), and that a demon can see through human hypocrisy ("A Demon Visits Mr. Qian Zhongshu at Night"). He also takes the opportunity to satirize contemporary literary practice and criticism, which he believes vulgarize literature ("On Laughter," "On Illiteracy," "On Writers").

In 1946 he published *Humans, Beasts, and Ghosts*. This was a collection of four short stories that Qian wrote in the mid-1940s. "God's Dream" reimagines the story of Genesis in an allegorical and playful manner. "The Cat" satirizes the shallowness of the aristocratic lifestyle. "The Inspiration" is a sarcastic caricature of a vain and shabby writer. "The Souvenir" is a family drama with deep psychological insight. Qian's distinctive narrative style in fiction writing was beginning to emerge in these stories.

FORTRESS BESIEGED (WEICHENG)

In 1944 Qian began writing his only novel, *Fortress Besieged*, which would take him two years to complete. *Fortress Besieged* was serialized in the journal *Literary Renaissance* in 1946 before it was published as a book in 1947. The novel gives a poignant portrayal of the shallow and inept lifestyle of modern "intellectuals."

In the novel, Fang Hongjian returns to China with a spurious Ph.D. certificate after loitering at several universities in Europe for four years. Back in Shanghai, Fang is given a petty job in the bank run by his former in-laws. Bored and frustrated, he goes to visit Miss Su Wenwan, a former classmate he met in France; during this visit he meets her cousin, Miss Tang Xiaofu. Fang falls in love with Tang but is too weak to tell Su, who is pretentious about Fang's love for her. The love triangle ends in Fang's breakup with Tang because of malicious things that Su says about him. Heartbroken, Fang takes a job in the newly established Sanlü University in interior Hunan Province. The tenuous and arduous journey from the

Japanese-occupied east coast to the interior turns out to be another frustrating experience for Fang, because of a series of cruel tricks played by his future colleagues who accompany him. At school, Fang is offered only a minor position and is inadvertently drawn into factional conflicts involving a group of vulgar charlatans and hypocrites. He is also entrapped into engagement by his seemingly guileless colleague, Miss Sun Roujia. A victim of the college politics, Fang gets fired. The young couple returns to Shanghai via Hong Kong, where they get married hastily. In Shanghai, their relationship deteriorates as both families inevitably get involved. The story ends with the separation of the couple after an ill-fated quarrel.

Fortress Besieged has been praised as one of the greatest novels in modern Chinese literature. It portrays an array of intellectual figures, whose folly, pretension, vanity, moral cowardice, and psychological weakness make them at once laughable and pitiable—and very identifiable. The central symbol of the *"forteresse assiégée"* comes from a French saying about marriage: people outside the fortress want to rush in and people inside want to get out. But the novel suggests that this paradox is applicable to other aspects of life. Qian's narrative style is marked by poignant satire, figurative language, witty expressions, and playful displays of erudition that are unrivaled by any other Chinese writer.

Fortress Besieged became popular with the broadcast on television of a serialized adaptation of the work in the 1990s in China. The novel has been translated into English, French, German, Spanish, Russian, and Japanese.

SCHOLARLY WORKS AND LATE YEARS

In 1948 Qian published *On the Art of Poetics*, a work of literary criticism written in classical language and taking the format of the short essay and reading note, similar to the traditional form of *shihua* (poetry critique). The work addresses issues in poetics such as aesthetics, rhetoric, and the appreciation and criticism of poetry. In this book, Qian exhibits his astounding range of knowledge of both Chinese and Western literary traditions by quoting extensively from over one thousand works.

On the Art of Poetics was surpassed only by his five-volume study of Chinese classics, *Pipe and Awl Collection* (also known as *Limited Views: Essays on Ideas and Letters*, 1979–1982). The work was written during the Cultural Revolution when the Qians were sent to the countryside of Henan Province to be "reeducated" and "remodeled." *Pipe and Awl Collection* is an ambitious study that traverses disciplinary boundaries. Qian quotes freely from a tremendous number of resources, both Chinese and Western. He awed his contemporaries with this cornucopia of sharp insights, intelligent thoughts, and extensive learning.

For many people, Qian's scholarly works mark a peak in the traditional scholarship of Chinese literature. However, his studies are difficult to classify due to his immersion in both Chinese and Western literature and his comparatist vision. For modern scholarship, which mostly relies on rational methodologies, Qian's critical approach defies the usual categories.

In the 1950s, Qian became a senior fellow at the Chinese Academy of Social Sciences, and he held this position for the rest of his life. In the 1950s and 1960s, he was appointed to be in charge of the English translation of Mao Zedong's works. Qian died in 1998 in Beijing.

Other works by Qian include *An Annotated Selection of Song Dynasty Poetry* (1958), *Four Old Essays* (1983), *Also So Collection* (1984), *Collection of Seven Patchings* (1985), *Words of Stone* (1986), and *Extant Poems of Huaiju* (1995).

Qian xue (Qian studies) has now become an academic subfield and has its own journal, *Studies on Qian Zhongshu*, to which scholars in and outside China contribute extensively. In the West, Qian is attracting more and more attention. C. T. Hsia and Theodore Huters are among the first scholars to introduce Qian to academics in the United States. Other scholars approach Qian's works from various perspectives, such as modernism, postmodernism, and linguistic studies.

BIBLIOGRAPHY

Chang Sheng-Tai. Reading Qian Zhongshu's "God's Dream" as a Postmodern Text. *Chinese Literature: Essays, Articles, Reviews (CLEAR)* 16 (1994): 93–110.

Egan, Ronald. Introduction. In *Limited Views: Essays on Ideas and Letters*, by Qian Zhongshu, ed. and trans. Ronald Egan, 1–26. Cambridge, MA: Council on East Asian Studies, Harvard University, 1998.

Gong Gang. *Qian Zhongshu: Ai zhi zhe de xiaoyao* [Qian Zhongshu: Spiritual freedom of a scholar]. Beijing: Wenjin Chubanshe, 2005.

Hu, Dennis T. A Linguistic-Literary Approach to Ch'ien Chung-shu's Novel *Wei-ch'eng. Journal of Asian Studies* 37 (1978): 427–443.

Huters, Theodore. *Qian Zhongshu*. Boston: Twayne, 1982.

Linsley, Robert. Qian Zhongshu and the Late, Late Modern. *Yishu: Journal of Contemporary Chinese Art* 1, 1 (2002): 60–67.

Tian Huilan, Ma Guangyu, and Chen Keyu, eds. *Qian Zhongshu, Yang Jiang yanjiu ziliao ji* [Collection of research materials on Qian Zhongshu and Yang Jiang]. Wuhan, PRC: Huazhong Shifan Daxue Chubanshe, 1990.

Wong Yoon Wah. Symbolism in Qian Zhongshu's Novel *Fortress Besieged*. In *Essays on Chinese Literature: A Comparative Approach*, 82–95. Singapore: Singapore University Press, 1988.

Xia Zhiqing (C. T. Hsia). Ch'ien Chung-shu. In *A History of Modern Chinese Fiction*, 432–460. 3rd ed. Bloomington: Indiana University Press, 1999.

Yang Xiaobing. Qian Zhongshu. In *Dictionary of Literary Biography: Chinese Fiction Writers, 1900–1949*, ed. Thomas Moran, 183–191. Detroit, MI: Thomson Gale, 2007.

Yang Yize, ed. *Qian Zhongshu* Weicheng *pipan* [Critiques on Qian Zhongshu's *Fortress Besieged*]. Changsha, PRC: Hunan Daxue Chubanshe, 2000.

Yu Hong. Qian Zhongshu's Essays. In *The Modern Chinese Literary Essay: Defining the Chinese Self in the 20th Century*, ed. Martin Woesler, 147–169. Bochum, Germany: Bochum University Press, 2000.

Haomin Gong

QIGONG

Qigong ("the discipline of the vital force") is the contemporary term, popularized in China in the 1950s, for a body of physical and mental disciplines loosely based on traditional Chinese medical and spiritual practices. The primary goal of *qigong* cultivation is physical health and well-being, but this "wellness" can readily expand to include the search for supernormal powers, moral transformation, or even immortality. In the 1980s, urban China experienced a "*qigong* boom" as hundreds of millions of Chinese joined one school or another in a pan-Chinese craze. The movement came to an end in the summer of 2000 as part of the Chinese government's campaign against Falun Gong.

THE RISE OF *QIGONG*

Like "traditional Chinese medicine," *qigong* is a "reinvented tradition" conceived in the 1950s as part of a nationalistic reaction to the perceived preeminence of biomedicine. *Qigong* enthusiasts within the Chinese medical establishment reappropriated traditional regimes of meditation, visualization, and *taiji*-like exercises, replacing the superstitious language that surrounded such practices with new scientific terminology, and training technicians to administer *qigong* on ailing patients in clinical settings. Although *qigong* therapeutics received modest state support through the mid-1960s, during the Cultural Revolution *qigong* was criticized as "feudal superstition," and institutional support for *qigong* was discontinued.

In the mid-1970s, small numbers of *qigong* masters began to appear in public parks in Beijing. Unlike the *qigong* clinicians of the pre–Cultural Revolution period, these masters were not part of the medical establishment; the best known figure, Guo Lin (1906–1984), claimed to have cured her own uterine cancer through special breathing practices, developed on the basis of Daoist techniques learned from her grandfather. She and others used the term *qigong* without official sanction and for want of a better alternative, and offered *qigong* training on an informal—and largely illegal—basis to those in search of a cure for pain and suffering.

Qigong returned to official favor after scientific experiments by respected Chinese scientists in the late 1970s claimed to prove the material existence of *qi*, often translated as "vital force" or "cosmic breath." This discovery meant that *qi*, and hence *qigong*, possessed a supposedly scientific basis, and could be incorporated into China's quest for modernization and the Communist Party's new quest for legitimacy. A "*qigong* world" (*qigong jie*) rapidly sprang into being on the basis of these claims. This *qigong* world was made up of scientists who continued to conduct experiments on *qi* and *qigong*, journalists who embraced *qigong* and spread the word of *qigong*'s power and benefits to the Chinese public, *qigong* masters, whose numbers increased exponentially in step with the burgeoning general enthusiasm for *qigong*, and—most importantly—party and government officials who saw in *qigong* a uniquely powerful "Chinese science," as well as a practical, economical means to achieve a healthier population (and thus a less expensive healthcare system). The China Qigong Scientific Research Association was established in April 1986 as a state organization mandated to oversee *qigong* activities.

THE *QIGONG* BOOM

The result was a *qigong* "boom" (*qigong* re) in the 1980s, a mass movement in which as many as 200 million people participated as active *qigong* practitioners. Many of these practitioners followed one of many charismatic *qigong* masters, who often became the equivalent of rock stars. The first master to achieve this status was Yan Xin, a previously unknown Chinese medical practitioner, but he was followed by hundreds of others, including Zhang Hongbao, Zhang Xiangyu, and Li Hongzhi. Many masters built nationwide organizations and carried out national (and even international) lecture tours; thousands of *qigong* enthusiasts bought tickets for such events, often held in a local arena or stadium, and lasting for several hours at a time.

Many schools of *qigong* preached traditional morality and spirituality in addition to *qigong* techniques, giving the *qigong* boom the overtones of a new religious movement or a cultural revitalization movement. Some masters claimed to "emit *qi*" in the course of their "lectures," a telling indication of the difference between the *qigong* of the 1950s and that of the 1980s: *Qigong* in the 1950s had been a therapeutic regime administered on an ailing patient by a trained professional; *qigong* of the *qigong* boom was a magical power possessed by a charismatic hero whose therapy consisted of diffusing his personal *qi* toward a mass of followers. Miracle cures were the most spectacular manifestation of *qigong*'s efficacy, but *qi* also manifested itself in the development of supernormal powers—a possibility of great interest to China's military-

Participants of a Qigong session, Guiyang, Guizhou province, August 8, 2007. *Practitioners of Qigong look to traditional elements of Chinese medicine to cure the human body of disease or maintain well being. Special breathing exercises form a large component of Qigong, along with meditation and attention to spiritual issues.* © QIAO QIMING/XINHUA PRESS/CORBIS

industrial complex, which hoped to use *qigong* to speed China's acquisition of great power status.

On a more mundane level, many *qigong* masters took advantage of the newly liberated Chinese economy to produce *qigong* books, audio- and videocassettes, and a wide variety of paraphernalia, all of which was sold to an eager and undiscriminating public. Journalists penned adoring biographies of *qigong* masters, which became best sellers.

Official support for *qigong* waxed and waned over the course of the 1980s. Many top officials continued to believe that *qigong* offered a means to wed the richness of China's traditional culture to a variety of utopian projects; at the same time, there had from the very beginning been *qigong* detractors who argued that *qigong* was nothing more than "feudal superstition" or clever parlor tricks. Still, *qigong* had considerable support among China's top leadership, especially after the student demonstrations of 1989, an indication that the politics of *qigong* were to some extent separate from debates over market reform and political control. *Qigong* continued to be broadly popular throughout much of the 1990s, even if the original "fever" may have diminished somewhat and media attacks against dubious *qigong* practices frequently appeared in official media.

FALUN GONG AND THE END OF THE *QIGONG* MOVEMENT

The Falun Gong demonstration outside of Communist Party headquarters in Beijing in late April 1999 marked the beginning of the end of official support for *qigong*. Although the Falun Gong began as a form of *qigong*, and Falun Gong founder Li Hongzhi was embraced by the *qigong* world when he "emerged from the mountains" to offer his teachings in 1992, from the outset Li claimed to teach *qigong* "at a higher level." While promising health and well-being like other *qigong* masters, Li accorded less importance to the Falun Gong exercises, and more to his spiritual teachings, which emphasized traditional morality and a Buddhist disdain for attachments, be they material, sentimental, or sensual. Li also presented himself as a godlike figure, able to care for his followers from afar, and demanded devotion from his followers which went beyond that demanded by most other *qigong* masters. Consequently, beginning from the mid-1990s, Falun Gong followers responded to media criticism with collective action, firmly if peacefully demanding equal time to respond to unfavorable newspaper or television reports. Motivated by their own self-righteousness and by the fact that *qigong* practice remained legal through the end of the

1990s, practitioners staged some 300 such demonstrations, culminating in the huge sit-in outside the gates of Zhongnanhai in 1999.

In the wake of the anti–Falun Gong campaign beginning in the summer of 1999, other *qigong* groups sought desperately to distinguish themselves from the Falun Gong, but to little avail. By the summer of 2000, the *qigong* movement was over, *qigong* organizations had disbanded, and most important *qigong* masters were in exile. Public security officials were ordered to keep a watchful eye on public parks so as to disperse groups of individual *qigong* practitioners. Nonetheless, *qigong* remains widely popular in Taiwan and elsewhere in the Chinese diaspora, and several *qigong* groups are currently positioning themselves to return to China should the campaign against Falun Gong come to a conclusion. Meanwhile, "health" *qigong*, which stresses the physical rather than the spiritual aspects of *qigong*, is being practiced in China, testifying to the ongoing popularity of *qigong*.

SEE ALSO *Falun Gong.*

BIBLIOGRAPHY
Chen, Nancy. *Breathing Spaces: Qigong, Psychiatry, and Healing in China.* New York: Columbia University Press, 2003.
Kohn, Livia. Quiet Sitting with Master Yinshi: The Beginnings of Qigong in Modern China. In *Living with the Dao: Conceptual Issues in Daoist Practice.* Cambridge, MA: Three Pines Press, E-Dao series, 2002.
Palmer, David. *Qigong Fever: Body, Science, and Utopia in China.* New York: Columbia University Press, 2007.

David Ownby

QING DYNASTY IN 1800

The last of the dynasties in the history of imperial China, the Qing dynasty, founded by the Manchus, a non-Han people, ruled over the country for 268 years (1644–1912). A dynasty of conquest noted for military exploits that turned the empire into the largest since the age of the Mongols and the world's largest land empire at the time, Qing governance simultaneously exemplified some of the highest ideals of Chinese political philosophy. While territorial expansion and commercial prosperity were among its prominent features, agriculture remained the core of state political and economic policies. Successful refinement of traditional political structures and statecraft created a government that was at once sophisticated and admired in many parts of the world, including the eighteenth-century West. The well-being of the general population with its aspirations for upward mobility and social justice continued to serve as the foundation for empirewide stability. Conversely, the ruler's failure to secure this foundation created conditions for upheaval and decline. In a dramatic

demonstration of the political dynamics of this era, Qing society by 1800 would exhibit both a zenith of social cohesion and an accumulation of social and fiscal liabilities. Forces at play in both domestic and interstate relations generated multiple challenges through which the Chinese polity transformed itself and defined its place, contributing in the process to the workings of global modernity in the Pacific Basin and beyond.

ESTABLISHING MANCHU RULE

As the Ming dynasty (1368–1644) entered its final stages, two forces readied themselves to seize power: rural rebels led by Li Zicheng (1606–1644), who captured Beijing in April 1644, forcing the Ming court to flee, and Manchu armies with dynastic ambitions under the leadership of Dorgon (1612–1650), regent to child emperor Shunzhi (r. 1644–1661). Ultimately, Chinese general Wu Sangui (1612–1678) opted to ally with the Manchu elite against the Chinese rebels, favoring Manchu military organization as well as a rudimentary administration that had developed in the Manchu capital in Liaodong. On June 6, 1644, General Wu and Dorgon entered Beijing, and the Manchus claimed the mandate of heaven, legitimizing their rule within the Chinese political system. Li Zicheng's forces were defeated by the summer of 1645. Rural rebels led by Zhang Xianzhong (1606–1647) to the south were routed by early 1647. Ming loyalists fueled by staunch anti-Manchu views continued to raise the possibility of a Ming restoration until 1662, when assassins killed the last claimants to the Ming throne.

A succession of three strong Manchu rulers brought the Qing to its fullest development, producing a pattern of central-government support for civil society unrivaled in early modern world history. The emperors Kangxi (r. 1661–1722), Yongzheng (r. 1723–1735), and Qianlong (r. 1736–1796) each played crucial roles in the state-building process, integrating aspects of Chinese political philosophy, Manchu statecraft, and military strategies deployed in the field of Eurasian politics.

EARLY QING REFORM EFFORTS

Kangxi was the first to tackle the problems of the domestic economy, including tax reform. His foray into a bureaucratic tangle of issues integral to problems of social justice proved daunting. In an effort to provide tax relief to a growing population, Kangxi froze the head tax (*ding*) quotas in 1712. Ultimately, however, fiscal inefficiency worsened and bureaucratic inertia impeded an empire-wide land survey that was necessary to realize his plans for more extensive reform.

Yongzheng committed himself with greater success to the reform of the head tax and customary fees. Under the existing terms of informal financing of local government, these fees were essential revenue for provincial and county operating costs but were also always a potential source of irregularity. To Kangxi's fixed tax quotas, Yongzheng added a fixed rate of surcharge intended as a subvention to replace the existing customary fees most prone to abuse and corruption. Yongzheng by imperial decree simultaneously prohibited collection of customary fees. These reforms contributed to rural prosperity under Qianlong's reign. The reform's lack of enforcement provisions regarding the prohibition of customary fees, however, gradually created a new buildup of bureaucratic corruption that became a major factor by 1800 in the mid-Qing rural decline.

Effective state-building depended on Manchu support for traditional Chinese scholarship, including calligraphy, poetry, and painting. Manchu emperors consistently modeled high-profile attention to literary cultivation. *The Four Treasuries*, a massive, multivolume scholarly compilation written over a ten-year period, was sponsored by Qianlong in an effort to continue a tradition begun by his father and grandfather of committing state resources for scholarly encyclopedic projects. The *Mustard Seed Garden* (1701), an exhaustive painting manual, the circulation of numerous anthologies of poetry written by women, and Cao Xueqin's *Dream of the Red Chamber* (1792), considered by many to be China's greatest novel, were also produced in an intellectual climate cultivated by Qing support.

RELATIONS WITH EURASIA

By 1800 Chinese dynastic rule had a long and extensive history of exchange with the Eurasian economic and cultural zones. The late Qing period, however, witnessed a new round of encounters that proved more intense and challenging to the country's political status quo. Eurasian politics included conflicts with Russian traders and nomadic groups along the northern borders, as well as with tribal groups to the southwest. Kangxi in 1689 negotiated the Treaty of Nerchinsk, setting a common border as well as terms of trade limited to exchange through merchants designated by the Qing government. In 1696 Kangxi successfully sent troops against Galdan (c. 1644–1697), leader of the Zunghar nomadic alliance, which had ties to the Dalai Lama of Tibet. In 1720 the Qing placed a new Dalai Lama loyal to itself in power in Lhasa. Campaigns to maintain the Qing position vis-à-vis the Russian Empire and the Zunghar continued through the reign of Yongzheng and into the period governed by Qianlong, who in 1755 ordered the slaughter of nomads in the western Mongol Empire of Zungharia as a final solution to the revival of major nomadic challenges on the Qing's northwest borders.

Relations with representatives from further west in the Eurasian ecumene developed initially over issues of authority pertaining to the work of Christian missionaries in China and later became embroiled with political and economic conflicts. In a 1692 decree, the Kangxi emperor affirmed a positive relationship with Jesuit missionaries in Beijing. He declared that, "The Europeans are very quiet... they do no harm to anyone.... Therefore, let no one henceforth offer them any opposition" (Neill 1964, pp. 189–190). However, a dispute fueled by contending orders within the Catholic Church raised the problem of possible conflicts between Chinese family practices of ancestor worship and papal interpretations of Catholic faith. In response, Pope Clement XI (r. 1700–1721) issued a decree in 1715 stating that, "As to exactly what customs should or should not be allowed to continue, the papal legate in China will make the necessary decisions....[C]ustoms and traditions that are not contradictory to Roman Catholicism will be allowed, while those that are clearly contradictory to it will not be tolerated under any circumstances" (Li 1969, p. 24).

Kangxi moved quickly and effectively to assert imperial dominion. In a 1721 decree, he made clear that, "I have concluded that the Westerners are petty indeed. It is impossible to reason with them because they do not understand larger issues as we understand them in China.... From now on, Westerners should not be allowed to preach in China, to avoid further trouble" (Li 1969, p. 22). Only the Jesuit order, at the expense of their relations with Rome, remained in good standing with Beijing. The court of Qianlong even employed a number of Jesuit artists and architects, including the Italian painter Giuseppe Castiglione (1688–1766).

In 1793 relations with far western Eurasia brought new economic issues into focus. Hoping to redress a growing imbalance of trade, a consequence of the British East India Company's outflow of vast sums of silver bullion, Lord George Macartney (1737–1806) arrived in Beijing representing King George III (r. 1760–1820) and England, a newly industrializing, aggressively expansive state. Desiring Chinese tea, silk, and porcelain, the English found themselves with nothing of sufficient value to support their growing volume of imports. The English were already shipping opium to China before Macartney's mission.

Received as a tribute emissary by the Qing court, Macartney brashly refused to perform the full ritual prostration, the kowtow, required for an audience with the emperor, and then proceeded to present his demands: abolition of the Qing *cohong* system that regulated foreign trade, the opening of new ports for commerce, and a standard of tariffs that would improve the market for foreign goods. While noting Macartney's decision to flaunt court rituals, Qianlong found his demands outrageous and proceeded to dismiss them. In response, Macartney wrote that the Qing was fated to fail in its efforts to ward off English terms of commerce, equated in his view with progress and civilization itself. Stressing that China could never build a free-trade state on its existing foundations, Macartney envisioned a world where "all the adventurers of all trading nations… would search every channel, creek, and cranny of China for a market" (Dawson 1967, p. 205). Macartney deemed what he saw as the pending collapse of the Qing system as evidence of the superiority of English authority and remained blind to the possibility of alternative routes to modernity and the question of whether or not China might pursue such a path.

PATTERNS OF DYNASTIC DECLINE AND RECOVERY

By 1800 the institutional strengths and weaknesses of the Qing dynasty operated in an arena of powerful new international developments emanating from industrial world centers. Patterns of dynastic decline and recovery would modulate in tandem as possibilities inspired by commercial and intellectual exchange among foreign and domestic groups grew. This had happened many times before in China's dynastic history, each period with its unique characteristics, creating the China that existed in 1800. The last long century of Qing rule between 1796 and 1912 demonstrated the tremendous achievements of the imperial political system, as well as its stubborn, chronic fault lines.

Population growth was itself a mark of social success, as well as a source of fiscal and political stress. Between 1573 and 1790, China's population doubled, growing from an estimated 150,000,000 to just over 301,000,000, with approximately 209,000,000 in 1767. Significant population growth with a fixed head tax as of 1712 meant a severe limitation on central government revenue, as well as an increase in corrupt practices related to customary fees. At the same time, a subbureaucracy of government agents beyond the discipline of official political channels increased dramatically to meet expanding local government workloads. Rural populations experienced the demoralizing affects of political corruption, followed by the strains of accumulating financial burdens. Central government graft associated with Heshen (1750–1799), Qianlong's favorite adviser, added to problems of corruption. Millenarian folk Buddhist groups known collectively as the White Lotus rebelled across vast areas of North China at the end of the eighteenth century. By 1800 China faced growing challenges from both domestic and international sources that would define its own historical passage to global modernity.

SEE ALSO *History: Overview, 1800–1860; History: Overview, 1860–1912.*

BIBLIOGRAPHY

Dawson, Raymond. *The Chinese Chameleon: An Analysis of European Conceptions of Chinese Civilization.* London: Oxford University Press, 1967.

Elliott, Mark, and Peter N. Stearns. *Emperor Qianlong: Son of Heaven, Man of the World.* Upper Saddle River, NJ: Pearson Longman, 2009.

Johnson, David, Andrew J. Nathan, and Evelyn S. Rawski, eds. *Popular Culture in Late Imperial China.* Berkeley: University of California Press, 1985.

Li, Dun J., ed. *China in Transition, 1517–1911.* New York: Van Nostrand Reinhold, 1969.

Naquin, Susan, and Evelyn S. Rawski, eds. *Chinese Society in the Eighteenth Century.* New Haven, CT: Yale University Press, 1987.

Neill, Stephen. *A History of Christian Missions.* Harmondsworth, U.K.: Penguin, 1964.

Perry, Elizabeth. *Challenging the Mandate of Heaven: Social Protest and State Power in China.* Armonk, NY: Sharpe, 2001.

Rawski, Evelyn S. *The Last Emperors: A Social History of Qing Imperial Institutions.* Berkeley: University of California Press, 1998.

Spence, Jonathan D. *The Search for Modern China.* 2nd ed. New York: Norton, 1999.

Roxann Prazniak

QING RESTORATION

Dynasties rise and fall. In Confucian thinking, the vicissitude of each dynasty depends on how well the rulers dispense their charge according to the mandate of heaven. An uncaring and corrupt administration results in decline, the prelude to final collapse. In some dynasties, amid the doom and gloom, observant and caring officials, sometimes even the emperors, would call for a restoration (*zhongxing*), a more-or-less concerted effort at restoring the purpose and energies that once brought the dynasty to its peak. As all dynasties must come to an end, the "restoration" is at best a holding operation, temporarily arresting the decline. Historically, most dynasties collapsed without the benefits of a restoration. As any restoration necessarily entails discussions of what went right for the dynasty in the first place, it tends to generate debates and dissention, unwittingly contributing to the sense of malaise that presages the final days of the ruling house.

Much misconception surrounds the Qing restoration in mid-nineteenth-century China. Even the date can be misleading. Chinese historians speak of a Tongzhi restoration (Tongzhi *zhongxing*) that, by definition, lasted the duration of the Tongzhi reign (1862–1874). This is an emperor-centered perspective, which is also the traditional perspective, pointing to the imperial person around whom ministers rallied. As a young boy dominated by a regency made up of his mother, Cixi (1835–1908), and the senior empress-dowager, Ci'an (1837–1881), the Tongzhi emperor could not effectively serve as the symbol of a restoration, in stark contrast to the young Meiji emperor, who would soon be made into an icon for a more dynamic restoration in Japan. In midcentury China, the signal from the imperial institution was weak. The initiatives to reinvigorate the government came mainly from the ministers, and mainly from the provinces, where restoration efforts began in the mid-1850s, depending on location.

We owe much of our understanding of the Qing restoration to the magisterial work of the American sinologist Mary Clabaugh Wright (1917–1970). Central to Wright's analysis is the notion that modern Chinese conservatism—a necessary part of any restoration—came into existence when its proponents were called upon to defend its core values against the challenges from the Taiping Uprising (1851–1864) and Western influence. Because the Confucian principles they were defending were not religious principles, which would be a matter of the heart, but social principles, which could only be preserved in social usage, "a Confucian society is of necessity an agrarian society: trade, industry, economic development in any form, are its enemies" (Wright 1965, p. 3). In the wake of the Second Opium War (1856–1860) and the suppression of the Taipings, a generation of leaders rose to the fore to tackle the twin problems of restoring social order and putting foreign aggression in check. The restoration agenda, therefore, comprised restoration of effective government along traditional lines and the implementation of new policies to ward off foreign and domestic threats. Initially, the Chinese were quite successful in dealing with modern diplomatic, military, and commercial problems. Nevertheless, extraordinarily favorable conditions notwithstanding, the restoration failed because, as Wright asserts, "the requirements of modernization ran counter to the requirements of Confucian stability" (p. 9).

RESTORING CIVIL GOVERNMENT

Restoring imperial authority and prestige entailed a broad range of activities, of which the restoration of civil government was critical. Informed by Confucianism, Chinese scholar-officials recognized that corrupt government was at the root of social disorder. Good government could only come with the nurturing and recruitment of men of talent—educated men with high moral qualities. Resumption of the civil service examinations thus received priority. Traditional learning and values were promoted, including the publication of the classics and histories by official printing offices. Both measures served to counter the influx of men who had entered government through military exploits or monetary contributions to war efforts. Vigorous officials like Ding Richang (1823–1882) used special examinations to keep such men from office. And if the civil examinations prescribed too narrow a curriculum, men with specialized skills and unusual talents were brought in by personal recommendation. The mathema-

tician Li Shanlan (1811–1882) found a berth in the Beijing Interpreters School (Tongwen Guan) on the strength of Guo Songdao's (1818–1891) support. From the mid-1860s, voices were heard to broaden the scope of the civil service examinations to include technology, mathematics, science, topography, foreign affairs, and so forth, presaging the reforms of the 1890s.

Restoration leaders also advocated modifying the government structure and the way it functioned. In 1867 Shen Baozhen (1820–1879) proposed that central government officials be given specialized responsibilities and that government should be restructured down to the subvillage level. In 1874 he called for centralized accounting and budgeting, while Ding Richang wanted to see sinecures abolished, terms of office lengthened, and the rule of avoidance lifted. He also proposed the use of newspapers to raise the people's awareness of foreign incursions and whip up their sense of loyalty.

THE ECONOMY

Economic recovery was an ongoing process since the mid-1850s. Efforts were often made soon after an area was cleared of rebels. Irrigation projects and tax breaks were standard fares to bring refugees back to their land. Zeng Guofan's (1811–1872) tax-reduction program for the lower Yangzi provinces in the late 1850s made taxes more realistic and yet produced a more reliable tax base to support government military expenditures. *Lijin*, the transit tax on goods introduced in 1853, was embraced, and its collection methods were refined to support new undertakings in the post-Taiping era. Looking beyond the traditional agrarian economy, some restoration leaders since the mid-1860s urged the exploitation of new resources, especially mining. The idea of commercial warfare (*shangzhan*), which Zeng Guofan first advanced in 1862, was given broader meaning in the next several decades, leading to enterprises designed to "retrieve lost economic rights" (*shouhui liquan*). This led directly to the founding of the China Merchants' Steam Navigation Company in 1872 and mechanized coal mines a few years later.

FOREIGN RELATIONS AND DEFENSE

In meeting the challenges from the West, restoration leaders were willing to break new ground. They began in 1861 with the founding of the Zongli Yamen, a quasi foreign office to handle new diplomatic affairs and the Western envoys resident in Beijing. The Beijing Tongwen Guan was established to train future interpreters and diplomats. Similar schools in Shanghai and Guangzhou followed. The Tongwen Guan soon included mathematics (a code word for modern science) in its curriculum. The acquisition of Western arms began much earlier. Zeng Guofan had attempted to secure steam warships in the 1850s. The Jiangnan Arsenal and Shipyard he helped establish in 1865 was the largest of its kind in Asia. Zuo Zongtang (1812–1885) then established the Fuzhou Navy Yard and Academy the next year. Shen Baozhen ably managed it for eight years, culminating in the halting of the Japanese advances on Taiwan in 1874 by the Fuzhou squadron.

Success on these fronts was marred by the incessant antimissionary riots from 1861, precipitated as much by aggressive missionaries as by recalcitrant gentry leaders and the ill-informed populace, sometimes with official encouragement. In 1870 the Tianjin riots took the lives of ten nuns, two priests, and several Westerners, with rioters burning a number of French, British, and American churches. The incident ended the era of the "cooperative policy," which, it has often been said, had given the Chinese a respite from the constant pressure of the West. In truth, the Chinese, having conceded extraterritoriality, traveling and evangelizing privileges, tariff autonomy, and so much more, should not have expected this much pressure so soon. Yet, the 1860s was a period when gunboat diplomacy reached new heights, signaled by the British show of force following the Yangzhou missionary incident of 1868. The British rejection in 1869 of the Alcock Convention, which would have raised import duties on opium and export duties on silk (measures favorable to China), underscores the limits of the cooperative policy, which nonetheless continued but only as an understanding among Western powers vis-à-vis China.

INTERNAL DISAGREEMENT AND FUTURE PROSPECTS FOR CHANGE

New and bold measures inevitably excited debate and opposition. Grand Secretary Woren (1804–1871) bitterly attacked the teaching of mathematics in the Tongwen Guan in 1867. The Princes of the Blood and Qingyi elements, a group of self-styled Confucian purists, hurled vitriol at the reformers in 1875. Their clamor would not subside until after the Sino-French War (1884–1885). But the restoration efforts continued right through the 1870s and early 1880s (or even later, some would argue).

The restoration began with the premise that it was possible to defend China's tradition with Western techniques, as Feng Guifen (1809–1874) articulated it in 1861. This idea was later popularized by Zhang Zhidong (1837–1909) as the *ti-yong* formula: "Chinese learning for fundamental structure (*ti*) and Western learning for practical use (*yong*)." Historians have argued that these two—Chinese *ti* and Western *yong*—are incompatible; any effort along these lines was doomed. In practice, however, restoration leaders like Feng, Ding Richang, and Shen Baozhen were more nimble in their understanding of the Chinese *ti*, enabling them to adaptively employ Western methods, even for administrative purposes.

As a result of the restoration, the China of the 1880s displayed many characteristics that were not present in the

1850s. It would have been too hasty and harsh to judge its effects within its first ten years (1861–1870) as some historians do. Restoration efforts continued into the 1880s and beyond. The restoration ended because it was expected to perform the impossible—it could not avoid the repeated diplomatic and military reverses inflicted by Western powers. It was eventually superseded by reforms of a different nature, to which it also contributed. The restoration was a part of a continuum.

SEE ALSO *China Hands; Defense, 1800–1912; Industrialization, 1860–1949.*

BIBLIOGRAPHY

Cohen, Paul A. Self-strengthening in "China Centered" Perspective: The Evolution of American Historiography. In *Qingji ziqiang yundong yantaohui lunwenji* [Papers from the Conference on the Self-strengthening Movement in the Late Qing], ed. Zhongyang Yanjiuyuan Jindaishi Yanjiusuo [Institute of Modern History, Academia Sinica], Vol. 1, 3–35. Taibei: Academia Sinica, 1988.

Liu Kwang-ching (Liu Guangjing). The Ch'ing Restoration. In *The Cambridge History of China*, Vol. 10: *Late Ch'ing, 1800–1911*, ed. John K. Fairbank, Pt. 1, 409–490. Cambridge, U.K.: Cambridge University Press, 1978.

Pong, David. The Vocabulary of Change: Reformist Ideas of the 1860s and 1870s. In *Ideal and Reality: Social and Political Change in Modern China, 1860–1949*, ed. David Pong and Edmund S. K. Fung, 25–61. Lanham, MD: University Press of America, 1985.

Pong, David. *Shen Pao-chen and China's Modernization in the Nineteenth Century.* Cambridge, U.K.: Cambridge University Press, 1994.

Wright, Mary C. *The Last Stand of Chinese Conservatism: The T'ung-chih Restoration, 1862–1874.* Rev. ed. New York: Atheneum, 1965.

David Pong

QINGDAO

Qingdao (Tsingtao) lies on the southern tip of the Shandong Peninsula (35°35′ ∼ 37°09′ N, 119°30′ ∼ 121°00′ E). It covers an area of 10,654 square kilometers, which includes sixty-nine islands. Qingdao's coastline is 862.64 kilometers long, with the continental coast accounting for 730.65 kilometers. The city center lies on a bay opening onto the Yellow Sea and extends to the east and north over hilly hinterland.

Qingdao has a moderate marine climate. Summer is influenced by monsoon and is humid with ample rainfall. In winter, cold, often stormy, winds from the northwest prevail. Spring (March till May) and autumn (September till November) are the most agreeable seasons, with dry sunny days and cool nights. The average mean temperature is 12.3° C. Average annual precipitation is 662.1

millimeters. Qingdao's natural resources include sea salt, minerals, grains, fruit, and livestock. Fisheries and the farming of abalone, oysters, prawns, scallops, and sea cucumbers contribute significantly to the economy.

EARLY DEVELOPMENT

The founding of the city of Qingdao is dated June 14, 1891, when the Qing government built fortified quarters for troops in an area hitherto called Jiao'ao. The urbanization of the area began with its occupation by Germany in 1897. An attack on German missionaries in Juye, Shandong, which cost two of them their lives, served as a pretext to send a German naval squadron to the area and deliver an ultimatum to China to grant Germany a territorial concession. Jiao'ao was handed over with no resistance by the Chinese troops stationed there. The treaty of concession, which granted Germany a ninety-nine-year lease over an area of about 550 square kilometers, was signed on March 6, 1898. The southern tip of the peninsula was chosen as the site of the new city and harbor given the name Qingdao, or Tsingtau in German, a name deriving from an offshore island. On September 2, 1898, Qingdao was declared a free port by Germany. Germany developed Qingdao into a naval base and placed the area under the jurisdiction of the Department of the Navy (as opposed to the Colonial Office).

The German occupation of Qingdao lasted for seventeen years (1897–1914). During this time, the German investment in Qingdao amounted to some 200 million gold marks. In addition to building the new city, Germany saw to the construction of the port and the railway link to Jinan, which came into service in 1904. With its European urban center and modern infrastructure, including hospitals and schools, Qingdao became a popular coastal resort. However, the German project of a "model colony" yielding ample financial returns for its investment did not become a reality.

After the outbreak of World War I (1914–1918), Japan conquered Qingdao on November 7, 1914. In 1917 China declared war on the German Empire. However, the outcome of the negotiations in Versailles was that Japan retained possession of Qingdao. The immediate consequence was a violent student demonstration in Beijing on May 4, 1919. This demonstration marked the inception of the Chinese patriotic "May Fourth movement" and led to the Chinese Republic's refusal to sign the Treaty of Versailles. Qingdao remained, with the "Shandong question," an international cause célèbre. Upon the insistence of the United States, Japan and China finally reached an agreement at the Washington Conference (November 12, 1921–February 6, 1922). Japan returned control of Qingdao and the Shandong railway to China on December 10, 1922. Japan was to occupy Qingdao once more during World War II (1937–1945).

HISTORICAL GEOGRAPHY AND DEMOGRAPHY

In 1897 the population of the German leasehold was estimated at 83,000. Toward the end of German rule, there were around 200,000 inhabitants, with Chinese accounting for more than 98 percent. About 56,000 people lived in Qingdao, the urban center of the leasehold.

The urbanization and industrialization of the area continued with the founding of the People's Republic in 1949, which led Qingdao to absorb neighboring centers, a process that continued till 1984. Now one of China's fifteen subprovincial cities, Qingdao encompasses seven urban districts (Shinan, Shibei, Sifang, Huangdao, Laoshan, Chengyang, and Licang) and five county-level towns (Jiaozhou, Jimo, Pindu, Jiaonan, and Laixi). By the end of 2006, Qingdao had 7,493,800 inhabitants, 2,710,000 of whom lived in the urban centers. More than 99.5 percent of the population is Han Chinese.

At the beginning of the 1990s, the authorities resolved to move the city center eastward to the Bay of Foshan, both to accommodate the pace of economic expansion and to preserve the European appearance of the Old City. As a result of this urban planning, two vibrant city centers exist side by side: the Old City, with its imposing structures from the colonial period and the tourist attraction of its seaside boulevard; and the new central business district, with its high-rise buildings that house banks, department stores, and government offices. In 2000 the city received the designation National Model City for Environmental Protection.

ECONOMY, TRADE, AND TRANSPORTATION

In official publications, Qingdao is styled a key textile, light industry, and chemical production center. In real terms, Qingdao is conspicuous for its industrial diversity. The production of mineral water and beer are legacies of the colonial period. Tsingtao beer is China's best-known brand. The many textile factories spin, weave, and process cotton fabrics and silks, make carpets, and produce clothing. The local rubber industry is the third largest in China. The firms Haier and Hisense play a dominant role not only in China's electronics and white-goods industry but also worldwide, while an important manufacturer of diesel locomotives and rolling stock has emerged from the former German railway repair yards in Sifang. Qingdao's diverse industries also produce machinery, automobiles, and ships. The city has become an important center for international trade, with goods worth $36.5 billion passing through it as imports and exports in 2006.

In November 2006, a World Bank study of investment climates ranked Qingdao as one of five leaders among the 120 Chinese cities surveyed. Foreign investment capital amounts to around $1.93 billion. The biggest foreign investor is South Korea.

Qingdao has an extensive road system (nearly 14,000 kilometers) and rail connections to the hinterland. It also has ferry links to Japan and South Korea and an international airport (Liuting). Qingdao is the home port of the Chinese Navy's Northern Fleet and the second busiest trading port for all of China. In 2006 some 224 million tons of cargo passed through it. Boasting three National Key Development Zones—Qingdao Economic and Technological Development Zone (QETDZ), Qingdao Free Trade Zone (QFTZ), and Qingdao Hi-tech Industrial Development Zone (QHIDZ)—Qingdao's aspiration for future development is to become an international center for logistics and high-tech industries.

CULTURE AND EDUCATION

Qingdao has thirteen universities and tertiary colleges and eleven research institutes and centers. The two most comprehensive universities are the Chinese Ocean University, a key national university with a strong focus on marine science and technology, and Qingdao University, the main provincial university. Qingdao is China's marine science research center with more than half of China's marine scientists working here. The Academy of Sciences of the People's Republic has its Institute for Oceanographic Research based in Qingdao.

The city has seven museums, five archives, two publishing houses, a radio, and a television station, as well as ten cultural-heritage sites of national significance. It hosts an annual series of fairs and festivals, including the China International Electronics and Household Appliances Expo and the Qingdao International Beer Festival. Qingdao was also the site of the 2008 Olympic sailing events.

SEE ALSO *Imperialism; Shandong; Treaty Ports; Urban China: Cities and Urbanization, 1800–1949; Urban China: Organizing Principles of Cities; Urban China: Urban Planning since 1978.*

BIBLIOGRAPHY

Biener, Annette. *Das deutsche Pachtgebiet Tsingtau in Schantung 1897–1914: Institutioneller Wandel durch Kolonialisierung* [The German leasehold Tsingtau in Shantung, 1897–1914: Institutional transformation through colonization]. Bonn, Germany: Matzat, 2001.

Bureau of Documentation and History, People's Government of Qingdao. *Qingdao nianjian 2007* [Qingdao yearbook 2007]. Qingdao: 2007.

Mühlhahn, Klaus. *Herrschaft und Widerstand in der "Musterkolonie" Kiautschau: Interaktionen zwischen China und Deutschland, 1897–1914* [Rule and resistance in the "model colony" Kiautschau: Interactions between China and Germany, 1897–1914]. Munich: Oldenbourg, 2000.

Yixu Lu

QINGHAI

Qinghai Province, formerly known by the Mongolian name Kokonor, meaning "blue lake," is located on the northeastern part of the Tibetan Plateau. Qinghai borders Gansu Province on the northeast, the Xinjiang Autonomous Region on the northwest, Sichuan Province on the southeast, and the Tibetan Autonomous Region on the southwest. Qinghai is administratively divided into one prefecture-level city (Xining), one prefecture (Haidong), and six autonomous prefectures (Haibei, Hainan, Huangnan, Golog, Yushu, and Haixi). In 2005 the population of Qinghai was approximately 5.2 million. Han Chinese accounted for 54.5 percent of the population and Tibetans 20.9 percent; other groups included Tu, Hui Muslims, Salar, and Mongols.

QINGHAI UNDER QING CHINA

Qinghai was incorporated into the territory of the Qing dynasty (1644–1912) in 1725, when, after the suppression of the Hoshot Mongols, the Yongzheng emperor (r. 1723–1735) appointed a superintendent for Qinghai Mongolian and Tibetan affairs in Xining and stationed troops in the region. The superintendent was responsible for overseeing local administrative and tributary affairs.

The Qing conquest of the Hoshot Mongols brought a different kind of ethnopolitics to Qinghai. Previously, the Mongols had dominated the Tibetans; now both groups were brought under Manchu governance and were kept segregated. This divide-and-rule policy kept these ethnic groups at bay and worked to ensure stability.

From the late eighteenth century onward, however, the weakened Mongols in the region provided the Tibetans with opportunities to cross the Yellow River from the south and occupy Mongol pasturelands in northern Qinghai, disregarding Qing administrative divisions. A massive migration then took place, leading to protracted conflicts and wars between Tibetans and Mongols. In 1822, in response to increasing tribal and ethnic conflict, the Qing court took military action to restore order. As conflicts increased, Beijing brought in more troops and built new fortresses. When peace was soon restored, a new kind of community of interacting Mongols and Tibetans evolved, and became a salient feature of Qinghai society.

THE FALL OF THE QING AND THE RISE OF THE MA FAMILY

More than a century of conflict between the Mongols and Tibetans had greatly weakened both parties by the 1820s, making room for more powerful contenders, the Hui Muslims. The Qing conquest of eastern Turkestan by the mid-eighteenth century also led to a more powerful Muslim presence in northwest China. In Shaanxi, Gansu, and Qinghai, between 1862 and 1873, major Muslim rebellions erupted against the Qing army, as well as the Mongols and

QINGHAI

■

Capital city: Xining

Largest cities (population): Xining (2,130,000 [2006])

Area: 721,000 sq. km. (278,000 sq. mi.)

Population: 5,200,000 (2005)

Demographics: Han, 54.5%; Tibetan, 20.9%; Hui Muslims, Tu, Salar, Mongol, others, 24.6%

GDP: CNY 64.1 billion (2006)

Famous sites: Great Mosque of Xining, North Mountain Temple, Kumbum Monastery, Qinghai Lake

Tibetans. During the Muslim rebellions and the Qing pacification that followed, Muslim rebel leaders from a local clan known as Ma eluded Qing forces. The Ma Muslims shrewdly surrendered and vowed to serve the Qing court. Some years later, the Ma Muslims in the Gansu and Qinghai areas emerged as an organized military power to defend the court and fight against anti-Manchu revolutionaries at the turn of the twentieth century. One Ma family member was appointed, in the 1880s, to be governor of Shaanxi and Gansu provinces (Qinghai was administratively part of Gansu). Subsequently, the Ma family achieved dominance in Chinese Inner Asia and established, in effect, a small dynasty of its own.

The 1911 revolution overturned the administrative system imposed on the non-Han Chinese peoples of the

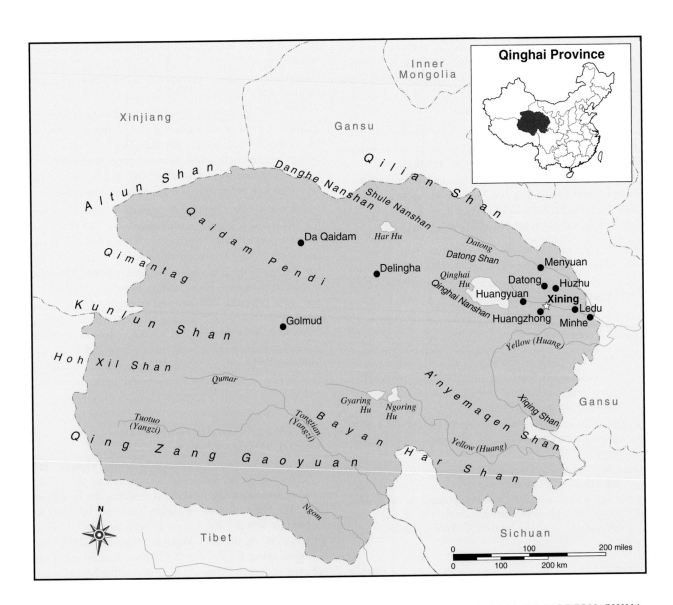

A Tibetan rider at the Qinghai Yushu Horse Racing Festival, Yushu Tibetan Autonomous Prefecture, Qinghai province, July 27, 2007. Located in western China, the province of Qinghai contains a large population of Tibetans, as well as Mongols, Hui Muslims, Salars, and Tu peoples. A remote province, Qinghai is important for its large natural gas, oil, and mineral deposits. CHINA PHOTOS/GETTY IMAGES

ethnic border regions. This political turmoil left Qinghai in local Muslim hands. Shortly after its inauguration in 1912, the new Chinese Republican government decreed that Qinghai become a special district within Gansu Province. After the Chinese Nationalists seized power in 1928 and established their central government in Nanjing, they mandated that Qinghai again be designated a province of the Chinese Republic. In spite of these efforts, the juggling of administrative systems to integrate Qinghai into the new Chinese Republican structure did not change the political reality that the entire northwestern Chinese region was still under the rule of the Ma Muslims. From the beginning of the Republican era until the end of the 1920s, the brothers Ma Qi (1869–1931) and Ma Lin (1876–1945) ruled the Gansu corridor and Qinghai, to be followed in the 1930s and 1940s by Ma Qi's sons, Ma Bufang (1903–1975) and Ma Buqing (1898–1977).

After coming to power, the Nationalists under Chiang Kai-shek (Jiang Jieshi) tried to break up the Ma Muslim bloc in Chinese Inner Asia. The Sino-Japanese War (1937–

1945) forced the Nationalists to retreat westward, giving the Ma Muslims an opportunity to extend their political power into Qinghai. Although Ma Bufang continued to rule Qinghai during World War II and the postwar period, Nationalist government personnel, institutions, and infrastructures began to appear in the region.

In the early 1950s, former Nationalist bureaucrats who had been sent to Qinghai during the war began mediating between the Chinese Communist authorities and local ethnic communities. In districts such as Golog, Yushu, and Choni, where power largely depended on local leadership, the political infrastructure created during the Nationalist era was still intact. The Chinese Communists extensively relied on these former Nationalist officials to help bring about a new sociopolitical order.

CURRENT ISSUES

In the early years of the twenty-first century, Qinghai under the People's Republic of China is trying to attract foreign investment. The province's undeveloped natural resource deposits, including potassium, chloride, magnesium, salts, gas, and oil, are among the largest in China. The opening of the Qinghai-Tibet Railway in July 2006 attracted tourism and brought prosperity to the region. Beyond the railway, Qinghai has felt the impact of the new infrastructure that the Great Western Development Scheme brought about since the late 1990s. New airports were constructed in such cities as Golmud and Xining, linking the province with major cities throughout China. In addition, newly installed hydropower stations in Qinghai have enabled the province to become an important hydropower base in northwest China. One of the key projects of the Great Western Development strategy is to deliver natural gas from the four major gas-reserve fields in the northwest, including the Qaidam Basin Gas Reserve in northwest Qinghai, to eastern China. In 2001 a new natural-gas pipeline linking Qinghai and Gansu provinces was completed. The pipeline runs 953 kilometers from the Qaidam Basin through Xining to Lanzhou, where it will be extended further east to major cities and provinces.

The unrest in Lhasa in March 2008 brought the world's attention to the ethnic tension between Han Chinese and Tibetans. In Qinghai, provincial security was tightened, and only a few minor protests by Tibetan monks against the Chinese Communist authorities were reported. After 1949, Han in-migration had increased significantly as the Chinese Communist authorities encouraged Han Chinese to settle in the region and engage in the new mineral industries. Given the current massive Han Chinese population in Qinghai, large-scale ethnopolitical turmoil and conflicts are less likely to happen there. Nevertheless, new issues confront the ruling Communist authorities: Environmental problems, such as soil erosion, water shortages, and deforestation, for example, are challenging the best minds among the officials and people of Qinghai.

SEE ALSO *Economic Development: Great Western Development Scheme; Minority Nationalities: Cultural Images of National Minorities; Minority Nationalities: Large National Minorities; Minority Nationalities: Overview; Tourism: Domestic; Tourism: Foreign.*

BIBLIOGRAPHY
Bulag, Uradyn E. *The Mongols at China's Edge: History and the Politics of National Unity.* Lanham, MD: Rowman & Littlefield, 2002.

Fletcher, Joseph. Ch'ing Inner Asia c. 1800. In *The Cambridge History of China*, ed. John K. Fairbank, Vol. 10, Pt. 1, 59–90. Cambridge, U.K.: Cambridge University Press, 1978.

Gladney, Dru C. *Ethnic Identity in China: The Making of a Muslim Minority Nationality.* Fort Worth, TX: Harcourt Brace, 1998.

Lipman, Jonathan N. *Familiar Strangers: A History of Muslims in Northwest China.* Seattle: University of Washington Press, 1997.

Lu Ding and William Allan Neilson, eds. *China's West Region Development: Domestic Strategies and Global Implications.* Singapore: World Scientific, 2004.

Yeung Yue-man and Shen Jianfa eds. *Developing China's West: A Critical Path to Balanced National Development.* Hong Kong: Chinese University Press, 2004.

Hsiao-ting Lin (Xiaoting Lin)

QIU JIN
1875–1907

As an emblem of twentieth-century nationalism and patriotism, the revolutionary woman martyr Qiu Jin is well known to Chinese people. Her story is intertwined with the origins of modern China. She was at times a school teacher, a feminist activist, an anti-Manchu patriot, a student in Japan, and a publisher of, and writer for, women's periodicals.

Qiu Jin was born in Fujian, though she was a native of Shaoxing, Zhejiang Province. Her original name was Guijin, and in the course of her life she used a number of other personal names, including Xuanqing (*zi*), Yugu (*xiaozi*), Jingxiong (later *zi*), and Jianhu nüxia (*hao*). Her family belonged to the scholar-official class, and she was the eldest of four siblings. Her arranged marriage to Wang Tingjun (1879–1909) produced two children, Wang Yuande (1897–1955) and Wang Canzhi (1904–1967), the latter of whom achieved fame as China's first woman pilot. Qiu Jin's marriage was unhappy, and in 1904 she took the unusual step of leaving her family to pursue her education in Japan.

Qiu Jin spent two periods in Japan between 1904 and 1906. Anecdotal evidence suggests she associated with the legendary figures Sun Yat-sen, Liang Qichao, and Chen Boping during these periods. Many of her revolutionary ideas developed in an environment of Japanese feminist activism that was fuelled by the example of Fukuda Hideko (1865–1927). The educator Shimoda Utako (1854–1936) had developed a teacher-training curriculum for Chinese women at the Jissen Women's University in Tokyo, and it was there that Qiu Jin was exposed to radical thinking.

The Japan experience was central to Qiu Jin's political and personal development, but her revolutionary fervor was not always welcomed in China. After training as a teacher in Tokyo she returned to her hometown, where she found short-term employment at schools including the Mingdao nüxue (Bright Path Girls' School). She also had an association with the Datong School in Shaoxing, which was used as a headquarters for revolutionaries. The building remains a national shrine to Qiu Jin and her compatriots.

Qiu Jin had more success in disseminating her revolutionary ideas through the written word. She was an accomplished poet and essayist, a fact that often has been overlooked in English-language scholarship. As a member of the privileged class she received training in the classics and elite arts, but she was also part of the contemporary movement to promote the use of the vernacular in women's publications. Her writings, from private letters to published essays, all exposed social, moral, and political injustices. While in Tokyo she had published the *Baihua bao* (Vernacular journal), and then in 1907 she set up and edited another periodical, the *Zhongguo nübao* (Chinese women's monthly). Both of these publications produced only a few issues, but they were an important part of the revolutionary feminist publishing milieu of the decade.

More fatefully, Qiu Jin became involved with anti-Manchu activists, including a male cousin, Xu Xilin (1873–1907), in a plot to overthrow the dynasty. After a planned uprising was sprung, she was captured, tried, and sentenced to death. She was beheaded at the public execution ground in Shaoxing on July 15, 1907. Court records of the case are scarce or incomplete, and Chinese biographies gloss over the precise nature of her crime. Available evidence of the case shows that her crime was judged to be treasonable. Four years after her execution, imperial rule ended and China embarked on its path to political modernization.

Given the timing of Qiu Jin's execution, it is not surprising that she has remained an enduring symbol of early Chinese feminism, heroism, and patriotism. Her image was used by various political groups throughout the twentieth century. In the first years after her death Qiu Jin was remembered as a family member or as a feminist. With the establishment of the new republic in 1912, her memory was appropriated by Sun Yat-sen's political machine and his followers before it could be established as anything other than nationalist. In the Communist period her reputation again was contested in working out what image best represented the identity of the nation.

Despite her fame, only one substantial English-language scholarly work about Qiu Jin was published between 1975 and 2000, though an abundance of Chinese research material on Qiu Jin is available. Scholarly research on Qiu Jin provides opportunities for cross-disciplinary analysis of gender, biographic writing, memory, and popular culture.

BIBLIOGRAPHY

Hamilton, Robyn. Historical Contexts for a Life of Qiu Jin (1875–1907). Ph.D. thesis, University of Melbourne, 2003.

Hu Ying. Writing Qiu Jin's Life: Wu Zhiying and Her Family Learning. *Late Imperial China* 25, no. 2 (2004): 119–160.

Hu Ying. Nine Burials of Qiu Jin: Building Public Monuments and Historical Memory. *Modern Chinese Literature and Culture* 19, no. 1 (2007): 138–191.

Mackie, Sue (later Wiles). Qiu Jin: Representative or Unique? B.A. Hons. thesis, University of Sydney, 1979.

Qiu Jin. In *Women Writers of Traditional China: An Anthology of Poetry and Criticism*, ed. Kang-I Sun Chang and Haun Saussy, 632–657. Stanford, CA: Stanford University Press, 1999.

Qiu Jin ji benshe 秋瑾集本社编 (eds.), *Qiu Jin ji* 秋瑾集 [Collected works of Qiu Jin]. Shanghai: Zhonghua Shuju Chubanshe 1960, 1962; reprint with revisions, Shanghai: Shanghai Guji Chubanshe, 1991.

Rankin, Mary B. The Emergence of Women at the End of the Ch'ing: The Case of Ch'iu Chin. In *Women in Chinese Society,* ed. Margery Wolf and Roxane Witke, 39–66. Stanford, CA: Stanford University Press, 1975.

Robyn Hamilton

R

RADIO

Visitors to the People's Republic of China during the height of the decade of the Cultural Revolution (1966–1976) often expressed their amazement (and occasional annoyance) at the sheer ubiquity of radio loudspeakers, blaring out a steady stream of revolutionary songs, political pronouncements, exercise drills, and entertainment, from city streets and village lanes, to factory floors and fields, schools, train carriages, and homes. Indeed, to a degree unheard of in the West, this highly centralized radio network had become by the late 1960s perhaps the most widely diffused mass medium in China. It also functioned on a fundamentally different basis from its Western counterparts, relying on line broadcasting (*youxian guangbo*) instead of wireless diffusion, and on collective rather than individualized and domestic listening. By 1973, China was quite literally wired for sound: 994 million speakers—one for every eight citizens—carried the voice of Radio Peking into the most remote recesses of the country by way of a system of provincial radio-receiving networks, linked in turn to nearly 2,500 local relay stations. Radio kept the nation on Beijing time, structured the rhythms of everyday life, and ensured that state power was not only visible, but also inescapably audible.

The development and particular characteristics of this system represented not only the ideological imperatives of Maoism and its emphasis on rural development and economic self-reliance, but also a reaction against the exigencies of the history of radio broadcasting in China. When the Chinese Communist Party (CCP) took power in 1949, there were only forty-nine government-owned radio stations in the entire country, broadcasting to approximately one million wireless radio receivers. The vast majority of these radios were owned by urbanites in the major cities of China's eastern seaboard, such as Shanghai, Beijing, Nanjing, and Tianjin. And while the ruling Nationalist Party (Guomindang, GMD) had taken steps before its military defeat and decampment to Taiwan to establish its own broadcasting system, the early development of radio broadcasting in China had been shaped less by government intervention than by foreign capital investment and local entrepreneurship in the colonial treaty ports.

Certainly, late Qing reformers and government officials as early as the first decade of the twentieth century had sensed the military and administrative importance of Guglielmo Marconi's (1874–1937) invention of radio telegraphy in the preceding decade. In 1905, as Marconi busied himself in constructing a system for transatlantic telegraphy, Yuan Shi-kai hired an Italian engineer to train Chinese naval officers in the new technology and to set up radio links between Beijing, Tianjin, Baoding, and Chinese military vessels.

The beginnings of commercial broadcasting in China date to 1923, just two years after the opening of the first licensed radio station in the United States, Pittsburgh's KDKA. Established by an American entrepreneur named E. G. Osborn, the Radio Corporation of China began broadcasting from the roof of a building on Shanghai's Bund under the call letters XRO. In 1924 Osborn's venture was followed by a second station run by the Kellogg Switchboard Supply Company, which worked closely with leading newspapers such as the *Shenbao*, and pioneered the live broadcast of popular music in association with the leading record company of the day, Pathé Orient. Early efforts by the GMD to harness the new medium also necessitated the importation from abroad of investments, equipment, and expertise, all of which were instrumental to the construction of official broadcasting stations in Beijing, Tianjin, and Shanghai in 1927, as well as the Central Broadcasting

243

System in the capital city of Nanjing (Zhongyang Guangbo Diantai) the following year. The colonial imprint was even stronger and more direct in Taiwan—where the first radio station was set up in one wing of the headquarters of the Japanese colonial government under the auspices of NHK (Nippon Hōsō Kyokai) in 1925—and in northeast China in the wake of the creation of the Japanese puppet state of Manchukuo in 1931. All of these official stations played pivotal roles in the diffusion of information and disinformation throughout World War II (1937–1945). Indeed, the CCP's first broadcasting venture was set up by the Xinhua News Agency in 1941 in Yan'an to counter the GMD's Central Broadcasting System.

The period from the late 1920s to the late 1940s was the heyday of commercial radio in China. The first locally owned and operated station in China was built in 1927 to help market Shanghai's Xinxin Company's own crystal radio receiver sets. By 1937, some fifty-five privately owned stations were broadcasting across the country, and that number had mushroomed to 108 by 1946. The boom, however, was overwhelmingly centered around the metropolis of Shanghai and its international settlements, where well over half of the stations were located. Some two hundred stations were known to have operated during this golden age, and the polyglot soundscape of news, advertising jingles, religious sermons, Mandarin popular song and foxtrots, and live performances of local opera, folk, and Western orchestral music with which they suffused the city helped shape Chinese music and culture in the Republican era. The arrival of the CCP in 1949, however, heralded a new era of nationalization, in which the broadcast medium was effectively rusticated in service of the revolution.

BIBLIOGRAPHY

Jones, Andrew F. *Yellow Music: Media Culture and Colonial Modernity in the Chinese Jazz Age.* Durham, NC: Duke University Press, 2001.

Liu, Alan P. L. *Communications and National Integration in Communist China.* Berkeley: University of California Press, 1971.

Yu, Frederick T. C. *Mass Persuasion in Communist China.* New York: Praeger, 1964.

Zhao Yuming, ed. *Zhongguo guangbo dianshi tongshi* [History of China's radio and television]. Beijing: Zhongguo Chuanmei Daxue Chubanshe, 2006.

Andrew F. Jones

RAPE

Rape, the forcing of sexual intercourse upon one person by another, usually by a man upon a woman, has been considered a serious crime since the early years of Chinese civilization (2000 BCE). In the law code of the Tang dynasty (618–907 CE), for example (c. 624 CE), the stated penalty for rape was exile (banishment to distant regions), a punishment graver than years of imprisonment. Laws in subsequent dynasties more or less adopted this position, so that by the turn of the nineteenth century, during the last imperial dynasty, the Qing (1644–1912), Section 366 of the Penal Laws stipulated that:

> Deliberate (sexual) intrigue with a married or unmarried woman shall be punished with 100 blows…and (sexual) violation of a married or unmarried woman, that is, rape, shall be punished with death by strangulation…and an assault with an intent to commit rape, shall be punished with 100 blows, and perpetual banishment to the distance of 3000 *lee* (miles). (Staunton 1966, p. 31)

MODERN CHINA

After the fall of the Qing and the end of the imperial system, the Chinese government developed a more modern legal system and the standard penalty for rape became less harsh in almost all Chinese communities, usually taking the form of years of imprisonment, while remaining much graver than for common physical assault. Yet, there could be exceptions if severe violence or homicide were involved. It was reported, for example, that in 1984 in Beijing, of fifty-two death-penalty cases, thirty-six were crimes related to sex, love, or marriage (Ruan Fangfu and Lau Manpang 2001). In Hong Kong, however, the death penalty was abolished in 1966.

The government of mainland China does not systematically or regularly publicize the number of rape cases, but academic and news reports from time to time suggest a rapid increase in the early periods of modernization and prosperous social development. On the mainland, the number of rapes was reported to have more than tripled from 1979 to 1983, and teenage rapists were no exception (Ruan Fangfu and Lau Manpang 2001). In Shanghai, with a population of around twelve million in which about 20 percent were adolescents, the reported numbers of adolescent rape cases were 150 in 1981, 192 in 1982, and 311 in 1983.

Rapid social and economic change in China has been advanced as a possible cause for the increase in the incidence of rape, but this cannot be proved (Ruan 1991). More-recent statistics suggest a slowing down or stabilization of the rates. In Heilongjiang Province in 2001, the total number of rape cases was 1,210, 13.6 percent lower than in 2000 (Heilongjiang Yearbook Editorial Committee 2002). In 2002 the number of rape cases nationally was 25,697, 4.01 percent lower than the previous year, although the total crime rate had increased by 14.04 percent (Wang W. 2004).

TAIWAN AND HONG KONG

During the same periods, increases in the number of rape cases were seen in Chinese communities outside mainland China. In Taiwan, for example, with a population of twenty million, the number of reported cases of sexual violence (including rape) was 4,478 in 2004, 4,900 in 2005, and 5,638 in 2006 (Xue Ling 2008). About 60 percent of the victims were under age eighteen, the youngest being three. In Hong Kong, with a population of about seven million, the number of rape convictions reported by the Hong Kong Police Force from 1980 to 1995 ranged from seventy to ninety per year. From 2002 to 2006, the number of rapes remained stable at an average of about ninety per year (Census and Statistics Department of Hong Kong 2008).

It was estimated that in Taiwan only one in seven to ten cases of sexual violence, and in Hong Kong, only one in ten, were reported to the police or the relevant agencies (Association Concerning Sexual Violence against Women 2005). No such estimation has been made in mainland China. But the reliability and value of these estimations is open to question, because such statistics are often compiled by organizations that work for rape prevention and aftercare services, using imprecise or unclear methodologies.

RAPE WITHIN MARRIAGE

In a 1989 national survey (Ng M. L. and Erwin Haeberle 1997), rape was reported to have occurred within 2.8 percent of marriages in China. As of 2008, however, the forcing of sex within marriage is not a crime in Chinese law. In cases brought to court, magistrates make differing judgments depending on circumstances. In both the PRC and Taiwan, it is a matter of controversy whether a law against marital rape should be adopted. The rape law in Hong Kong was amended in 2002 to specify that "unlawful sexual intercourse" does not exclude sexual intercourse that a man has with his wife, but no separate marital rape figures have been reported in Hong Kong's government crime statistics.

ATTITUDES AND SERVICES

In general, the Chinese public harbors no doubt that rape is a crime, but there are differences in attitudes toward the victim, who may be assigned a share of responsibility for the crime. Local governments, nongovernmental organizations (NGOs), and sex educators have attempted to correct this bias through public education, propaganda, and workshops, with some success (Association Concerning Sexual Violence against Women 2004).

Aside from criminal investigation and judiciary action, efforts have been made by the government, with the assistance of NGOs, to provide counseling and rehabilitation services to both victim and offender in many Chinese communities. For the victim, one-stop legal, forensic, medical, psychological, and social-work services have been organized to minimize the trauma of the sexual assault and the subsequent investigation, court procedures, and negative family and social reactions. For the offender, psychological treatment is given by professional counselors or psychiatrists when the offender is in prison. Treatment is continued if necessary during the observation or follow-up period after discharge, with the aim of reducing recidivism. As of 2008, Hong Kong provided the most advanced counseling and rehabilitation services, followed by Taiwan and mainland China.

SEE ALSO *Domestic Violence; Law on the Protection of Women and Children; Women, Status of.*

BIBLIOGRAPHY

Association Concerning Sexual Violence against Women (Hong Kong). *Rainlily Build-in Study Report, 2001–2003*. Hong Kong: Gender Research Centre, Chinese University of Hong Kong, 2004. http://www.hkabpw.org/app/webroot/files/1/RainLily_e.pdf.

Association Concerning Sexual Violence against Women (Hong Kong). *Newsletter* 18 (2005). http://www.rapecrisiscentre. org.hk/Newsletter18%20P1-7.pdf.

Census and Statistics Department, Government of the Hong Kong Special Administrative Region. Hong Kong Statistics. 2008. http://www.censtatd.gov.hk/hong_kong_statistics/statistics_by_subject/.

Heilongjiang Yearbook Editorial Committee. [Heilongjiang yearbook]. Harbin: Heilongjiang Nianjian Chubanshe (Heilongjiang Yearbook Publisher), 2002.

Ng M. L. and Erwin J. Haeberle. *Sexual Behavior in Modern China: Report of the Nationwide Survey of 20,000 Men and Women*. New York: Continuum, 1997.

Ruan Fangfu. *Sex in China: Studies in Sexology in Chinese Culture*. New York: Plenum, 1991.

Ruan Fangfu and Lau M. P. Sexuality in People's Republic of China. In *The International Encyclopedia of Human Sexuality*, ed. Robert Francoeur, Vol. 4, 182–210. New York: Continuum, 2001.

Staunton, George T., trans. *Ta Tsing Leu Lee, Being the Fundamental Laws, and a Selection from the Supplementary Statutes, of the Penal Code of China*. 1810. London: Cadell & Davies, 1966.

Wang W. Judiciary work in 2002. 2004. China Net. http://www.china.com.cn/zhuanti2005/txt/2004-06/02/content_5577958.htm

Xue Ling. *Taiwan xing qinhai fanzuide qingkuang* [The Situation of Sexual Assault Crimes in Taiwan]. 850 Boahunin [850 Protect You], 2008. http://webhost3.ly.gov.tw/11069/html/modules/tinyd01/index.php?id=1.

Emil M. L. Ng

RED GUARDS

The Red Guards (*hongweibing*), mainly high school and university students, were members of mass organizations that were used by Mao Zedong to help launch the Cultural Revolution (1966–1969). The first group, composed of a dozen students of the elite middle school attached to Tsinghua University, most of them being children of high-level cadres, was set up in Beijing on May 29, 1966. Inflamed by Mao's continuous calls, since 1964, to put politics—and his own ideology—above anything else, and well informed, thanks to their social status, about Mao's intentions to purge "revisionists" in the educational sphere, they dared confront their school's administration. In the first big-character poster, which they posted in their school on June 2, they wrote: "We pledge, in order to protect the Party Central Committee and our great leader Chairman Mao, to shed resolutely the last drop of our blood." This explains the meaning of the name they had chosen for their group (Red Guard). They used it again on June 5 to sign a big-character poster denouncing their school's leaders as "anti-Party and anti-socialist revisionists." During the following weeks, similar groups were formed in other Beijing schools and borrowed the name "Red Guards." They were later emulated throughout the country. At the same time, work teams had been sent by the Beijing Party Committee to universities and secondary schools to lead the implementation of the Cultural Revolution in these institutions. In some cases, they criticized and replaced the school Party Committee, in other cases they supported it. All the same, whereas most Red Guards accepted the leadership of the work teams, in other cases, a militant minority refused to obey and were then suppressed. When Mao came back to Beijing in mid-July, he estimated that the work teams were an obstacle to the full deployment of the Cultural Revolution and had them rescinded by the end of the month. The Red Guard movement developed rapidly after Mao openly disapproved of the work teams and, on August 1, 1966, replied to a letter from the first group of Red Guards, expressing his support and confirming that their action proved that "it is right to rebel against reactionaries."

In the Sixteen Points Notification adopted by the Central Committee of the Communist Party on August 8, 1966, the masses were exhorted to "liberate themselves" and the target of the Cultural Revolution was identified as "those within the party who are in authority and are taking the capitalist road." On August 18, Mao "reviewed" a crowd of one million from the Tiananmen rostrum, accepting a Red Guard armband from a member of the group, while next to him Lin Biao made an appeal for an attack on the old ideas, old culture, old customs, and old habits, subsequently known as the "Four Olds." The Red Guards, then, launched the Smashing of the Four Olds (*po si jiu*) campaign that resulted in the destruction of countless cultural objects and monuments, and in widespread brutality—often fatal—against teachers, school officials, and other "class enemies." In Beijing alone, the homes of 33,695 families of "bad" class background were looted, residents were beaten, 1,772 of them to death, books and paintings were burned, antiques and works of art destroyed, and tons of gold and silver were confiscated, as well as millions of yuan in cash. National treasures were destroyed, such as the Confucius temple in Qufu, Shandong. In Beijing, of 6,843 "places of cultural or historical interest," including many temples, shrines, and museums, 4,922 were destroyed at the end of the Cultural Revolution, most of them during this period of August to September 1966. At the same time, 397,000 persons of "bad" class background were ejected from the cities and forcibly repatriated in the villages whence their ancestors had come. Red Guards also took part in numerous meetings where "class enemies" in the educational, cultural, and political circles were humiliated and beaten. The most prominent figures targeted at that time included Peng Zhen, former Beijing mayor, Marshall Peng Dehuai, former defense minister, and Wang Guangmei, wife of Liu Shaoqi. The cruelty shown by these teenagers took its roots in the education they had received at school, which encouraged hatred for the "class enemies," and in the clear blessing received from Mao and his close associates during this period of "red terror," Mao continued to inspect Red Guard groups from across the country in seven mass rallies at which the Red Guards had the opportunity to express their fanatic adoration of the "Great Helmsman" (*weida duoshou*). During an operation called the "Great Networking" (*da chuanlian*) Red Guards from the provinces came to Beijing and Beijing Red Guards went to spread the revolutionary gospel throughout the country.

From January 1967 the Red Guards took part in the purging phase of the Cultural Revolution, when most party and government officials were toppled. During the process, Red Guard organizations divided into two factions, the old Red Guards and a newer, "rebel" faction. Former Red Guards and Sinologists have disagreed about the causes of the factionalism: Some point to social causes, emphasizing the domination of the older group by upper-class offspring of high-level cadres and the large number of lower-class members of the rebel faction; others explain the factionalism as a result of political infighting in a period when the objectives and consequences of the struggle were often unclear. Those divergent views can be explained partly by different situations prevailing in different cities and provinces.

Intervention by the People's Liberation Army and the encouragement to form new organs of power, the Revolutionary Committees, merely aggravated the conflicts, which became increasingly violent and brought the country to a state of chaos by early 1968. Finally, on July 27 Mao dispatched a workers' propaganda team led by army officers to the Tsinghua University campus. After the Red Guards opened fire on them, killing five, Mao called a meeting with Beijing Red Guard leaders and told them that he was determined to end the chaos in the country. Workers' propaganda teams took control of all educational institutions, and where Red Guards resisted, they were repressed by the military. The practice of sending educated youth "up to the mountains and down to the countryside" put an end to the Red Guard organizations by dispersing their members across the vast countryside.

During those two and a half years, the Red Guards were given a certain degree of autonomy of action and expression. They could choose which group to join, or even to stay idle at home; they could write posters and articles in their own journals; they could also choose to beat or even kill "class enemies." The only thing which they could not do was oppose Mao Zedong, but, as Mao's intentions and directives were rarely clear and detailed, they often needed to use their own judgment. Although most of the Red Guards used their autonomy unimaginatively, only trying to follow whatever trend seemed to get Mao's favor, others made good use of this unique opportunity for political autonomy in a country led by a Communist party. Some exceptional young people such as Yu Luoke (1942–1970) and Yang Xiguang (1948–2004) produced daring heterodox writings, which had a lasting influence, even though the leeway given to them was short-lived and the price they had to pay was very high. Years after the Red Guards had been disbanded, a significant number of them began a thorough reexamination of the Cultural Revolution, of Maoism, and of their own actions at the times. At the end of the 1970s, this generation was at the forefront of the Democracy Wall Movement, the first popular movement calling for democracy and the rule of law since 1949. Beginning in the 1980s some of them expressed regret for their behavior during the Cultural Revolution and asked their victims for forgiveness, but the official government policy of oblivion concerning the Cultural Revolution discouraged a thorough and widespread reexamination of this painful period. Early in the 2000s some former Red Guards called for public repentance (*chanhui*) and lamented that too many people from their generation preferred to forget the past.

SEE ALSO *Cultural Revolution, 1966–1969; Dissidents; Lin Biao; Liu Shaoqi; Peng Dehuai; Tiananmen Incident (1976).*

BIBLIOGRAPHY

Bu Weihua. *Zalan jiu shijie—Wenhua da geming de dongluan yu haojie* [Smashing the old world—the disorders and catastrophe of the Great Cultural Revolution]. Hong Kong: The Chinese University Press, 2008.

Song Yongyi, ed. *Wenhua da geming: lishi zhenxiang he jiti jiyi* [The Cultural Revolution: historical truth and collective memories]. 2 vols. Hong Kong: Tianyuan Shuwu, 2007.

Song Yongyi and Sun Dajin. *Wenhua da geming he tade yiduan sichao* [Heterodox thoughts during the Cultural Revolution]. Hong Kong: Tianyuan Shuwu, 1997.

Walder, Andrew G. Beijing Red Guard Factionalism: Social Interpretations Reconsidered. *Journal of Asian Studies* 61, 2 (May 2002): 437–471.

Xu Youyu. *Xingxing sese de zaofan—hongweibing jingshen suzhi de xingcheng ji yanbian* [Rebels of all stripes: a study of Red Guard mentalities]. Hong Kong: Chinese University Press, 1999.

Michel Bonnin

REFORM UNDER THE QING DYNASTY, 1800–1912

Between 1800 and 1912, the Qing dynasty passed from relative prosperity and stability to a state of virtually continuous crisis. Its collapse has sometimes been ascribed to its inflexibility and reluctance to act in the face of these crises, but this period in fact featured a sequence of reform efforts. Reforms went through a number of distinct, though overlapping stages, each with its signature characteristics. Here, the major reformers, their ideas and their efforts will be explored. The major foci will be the reforms and the mechanisms of reform, in the context of historical developments that are studied in detail elsewhere in these volumes.

Traditional notions of governance provided for periodic renewal and revitalization when signs of political dysfunction were noticed. These signs, when manifested in the forms of social disorder, such as frequent tax or rent resistance riots, rampant banditry, or open rebellion, could not escape official acknowledgement. Other signs could be more subtle, as when essential transport infrastructures, such as the Grand Canal, or vital distributive mechanisms, such as the salt monopoly, suffered degenerative systemic troubles, especially when such developments occurred incrementally over a prolonged stretch of time. When such malfunctions came to the notice of the government, either at the local or the imperial level, efforts might be taken to reinvigorate their administration. New management methods might sometimes result, but without jettisoning the basic principles on which the old or older methods and institutions were founded. These regenerative endeavors were present throughout Chinese history. In the modern era, the question is whether the font of ideas and methods of reform were adequate to inform the Qing government as it braced itself for the challenges of the time.

Confucian humanism insisted that the matters of government were nothing more than a human enterprise, free of divine intervention. Further, the purpose of government was good government. In Confucian parlance, this is reduced to the basic requirements of feeding, educating, and defending the people. These requirements were as simple as they were difficult to fulfill, as traditional methods and technologies were never equal to the vagaries of the natural elements, let alone when they were exacerbated by human (official) foibles. By insisting that government is an ethical concern—to feed, educate, and defend its people so that the traditional order of harmony and filiality be preserved—no government could escape the eventual fate of constant reforms in the struggle to maintain the Mandate of Heaven. Stronger governments might experience a more or less concerted and sustained effort at reform, often known as a dynastic restoration; lesser governments might simply slide straight down the path of perdition. Does the collapse of the Qing in 1912 then become the verdict on a long century of reforms? Or did the reforms in some tangible ways, albeit imperfectly, fashion China's transition from empire to nation?

FROM JIAQING TO LATE DAOGUANG, c. 1800–1839

Reforms were already overdue as the Qing dynasty (1644–1912) entered the nineteenth century. The new emperor, Jiaqing (r. 1796–1820), had inherited a court and a central bureaucracy bankrupted by the corruption of Heshen (1750–1799) and the senility of his father, the Qianlong emperor who, though officially retired in February 1796, continued to rule until his death on February 7, 1799. When Heshen was arrested and forced to commit suicide five days later, the empire was already in deep trouble. No sooner had the Miao Uprising (1795–1796) been put down in Guizhou and Hunan than the White Lotus Rebellion, provoked by official corruption, surged forth from Sichuan and Hubei, raging through several central provinces. The rebels were finally put down in 1804, but not before corrupt generals sent to suppress them had enriched themselves with government funds and extractions from the people. Jiaqing's response was to impose retrenchment at court. The gains were minor, but his stringent measures alienated many and took away the potential for more systematic reforms.

Jiaqing's reign was only half a century from the apogee of Qing power. It has been argued that the once mighty Manchu empire was not as prosperous as has been portrayed. If the court was not entirely unaware of the country's declining fortunes, it was certainly disconnected from the stirrings among scholars and officials in the provinces who hailed from the schools of Han learning and evidential research (*kaozhengxue*). Hong Liangji (1746–1809) and Gong Zizhen (1792–1841) were not only bemoaning the

rampant corruption in local government but also the problem of unbridled population growth as major factors of social unrest. Then, after years of effort, putting the methodology of evidential research to practical use, He Changling (1785–1848) published in 1826 a collection of the finest examples of official practices in practical statecraft (*jingshi*) under the title of *Huangchao jingshi wenbian*. It spawned a new genre of works on practical administration for the rest of the century. In that same year, Governor-general Ruan Yuan (1764–1849) of Guangdong and Guangxi founded the Xuehaitang (Sea-of-Learning Academy) in Guangzhou to promote his practical statecraft reformist agenda. It inspired the rise of many academies elsewhere and influenced reformers for decades to come. But this was already well into the reign of the Daoguang emperor (r. 1821–1850).

Having inherited a depleted treasury, Daoguang continued the practice of personal and public frugality, and he procrastinated as flooding of the Yellow River progressively worsened. Matters were brought to a head in 1824 when flooding blocked the Grand Canal and the flow of tribute rice to Beijing. Yinghe (1771–1839), president of the Board of Revenue with broad experience in several other ministries, including the Board of Works, advised sea transport of the grain tribute. Opinions from the provinces were solicited and the court was fortunate to have inputs from the experienced and able Governor Tao Zhu (1779–1839) of Jiangsu and He Changling, now Jiangsu finance commissioner. These men were in turn advised by Bao Shichen (1775–1855), another statecrafter who had studied the grain-transport system on the Grand Canal for nearly twenty years. For once, the court, the provinces, and the reformers were connected. They worked out a detailed system of sea transport, employing merchant cooperation. Adverse to the idea of expanding the bureaucracy—an expansion that would favor the provincial authorities at the expense of the court—and opposed by the vested interests of officials and laborers on the canal, the successful experiment of 1826 remained an experiment. Still, it foreshadowed the *guandu shangban* (government supervision, merchant management) practices of the 1870s. Further, Bao's essays on grain transport and the Grand Canal, and He's records of the sea-transport experiment, were quickly published, respectively, as *Zhongqu yishao* (Scooping out the thoroughfare) in 1826 and *Jiangsu haiyun quan'an* (The complete record of sea transport in Jiangsu) in 1827, for later reference.

The latter part of Daoguang's reign was beset by the nagging problem of opium. Confronted with the tricky issues of ethical government, public finance, and pragmatism, policy proposals were made and debated. Two rounds of debates, each lasting about six months, took place in 1836 and 1838. The first focused on the merits of legalizing the trade, not to condone a pernicious addiction, but to reverse the balance of trade and help solve the perennial revenue shortages that had been the bane of the Jiaqing reign since it began. The proponents of legalization lost the debate. Of interest, however, is that their leading members—Xu Naiqi, Lu Kun (1772–1835), Qigong (1777–1844), and Deng Tingzhen (1776–1846)—had all been either associated with or influenced by the faculty of the Xuehaitang of Guangzhou, and were supported in Beijing by none other than Ruan Yuan himself, who founded the academy, and was now a grand secretary. Their opponents, though coming from diverse quarters, also boasted among them Lin Zexu (1785–1850). Lin had been closely associated with a coterie of literati in the Spring Purification circle, one of many literary and poetry clubs in Beijing, but one that had become politicized and subscribed to the Song neo-Confucian reformism of the Tongcheng school. The sociopolitical networks for generating and promoting reforms (as well as opposing them) were in place.

The second debate dealt with prohibition and suppression of the opium trade and addiction. Reacting to a memorial advocating severe punishment of the user, the Daoguang emperor solicited opinions from the top central and provincial officials. The twenty-seven memorials that came in over a four-month period were then debated in a joint session of the Grand Secretariat and the Grand Council, reminiscent of the court conference of Han times, made famous by the debate on salt and iron in 81 BCE. The consultation, the debates, and the court conference (*tingyi*) in their various incarnations were to appear again in the history of reform.

Several points are noteworthy about this early phase of reform. First, early Qing dynasts had prohibited factions and cliques among literati and officials, yet the Jiaqing and Daoguang eras witnessed the rise of literary and poetry clubs that faintly recalled cliquism. Second, despite the Confucian proclivity of seeing social issues in cyclical terms, scholars like Gong Zizhen resuscitated the Gongyang commentaries and argued for a lineal view of history, a perspective that enabled him to see more clearly the dangers of unchecked population growth. He called for *gaige* (reform), a term that conveys a sense that something is ominously wrong, and he tried to provoke the literati into action by arousing their sense of shame (*chi*). Finally, what is also clear is the weak and vacillating imperial leadership of the Jiaqing and Daoguang reigns, and the power of vested interests; both are evident in the case of sea-transport of tribute grain in 1826. No one was encouraged to think outside the box.

ERA OF THE OPIUM WARS AND THE TAIPING WAR

With the dynasty plagued by foreign wars and internal upheavals, the reforms of the period understandably fell into two discrete areas: the production of modern armaments and military reforms on the one hand, and the raising of money to finance the wars on the other. During the first Opium War (1839–1842), Lin Zexu not only purchased Western guns but also a steamboat (soon captured by the British). Some efforts were made to manufacture Western firearms after the war. In 1843 Emperor Daoguang instructed Qiying (d. 1858) to secretly purchase foreign gunpowder for his inspection. Qiying dutifully obliged but also presented him with a gun and a revolver. Daoguang was pleased with the gadgets but, with an inexplicable sigh, exclaimed that it was beyond China's ability to imitate their manufacture. The creation of a Western-style navy with steamships, an idea offered by Wei Yuan (1794–1856), received little attention.

A significant innovation of the era was the rise of the provincial armies, notably those of Zeng Guofan (1811–1872) and his associates. Begun as adjuncts to the regular armies—the Banners and the Green Standards—the continued existence of the provincial armies after the Taipings and the Nians bespeaks their effectiveness, and put pressure on the reform of the standing armies. It was these provincial armies, too, that set up two arsenals in Hunan and Wuchang in the 1850s, and a third at Anqing in 1861, but none employed modern machinery. The most profound, long-term change in this era was the introduction of the *lijin* transit dues to fund rebel suppression. Their continuation significantly supplemented Qing revenue and helped finance numerous official undertakings and modernizing enterprises well into the twentieth century. Though these innovations enjoyed imperial sanction, the initiatives came essentially from the provinces. Even though Zeng Guofan was dispatched by the emperor to raise his army, the model and its subsequent transformation were provincial in origin. The wars had created some opportunities, but largely distracted the country from fundamental reforms.

THE ERA OF "SELF-STRENGTHENING," 1861–1895

Some of the endeavors after 1861, particularly those in the areas of military reform and defense modernization, were continuations of ideas and ambitions of the preceding decades, now made possible in an era of relative peace. Reforms in other areas, some truly fundamental, connected this period to the reforms of the late 1890s and the 1900s.

The reforms of this era may be said to have begun with the bugle call from Prince Gong (1833–1898), Guiliang (1785–1862), and Wenxiang (1818–1876)—leading members of the Zongli Yamen, the office for the management of foreign affairs, which was itself a product of reforms. The three called upon the government to "stir itself up" (*zizhen*) so that the country could become strong by its own efforts (*ziqiang*, literally, self-strengthened). In the next decade, provincial officials like Li Hongzhang (1823–1901) and Ding Richang (1823–1882) pointed up the new or unprecedented situation confronting the empire (*bianju* or *chuangju*) as they proposed reforms. "Self-strengthening" and "changed situation," ideas faintly heard in the 1840s, came into frequent usage.

The reforms of this era overlapped with aspects of Self-strengthening and the Qing restoration. This entry focuses on reforms, and will discuss the reinvigoration of the government or military modernization only when they bear upon reforms (to change ways of doing things for better results).

Opportunities for reform came on three particular occasions in 1866, 1867, and 1874 to 1875. The first came when the throne instructed eleven top officials from the coastal and Yangzi provinces to react to memoranda from Robert Hart (1835–1911), inspector-general of the Imperial Maritime Customs Service, and Thomas Wade (1818–1895), Chinese secretary of the British Legation. In these, Hart and Wade recommended reforms in China's management of foreign relations, public finances, and military affairs. The second opportunity was initiated by the Zongli Yamen in preparation for the forthcoming negotiations for treaty revision. Eighteen high provincial officials were asked to propose positions to be taken on issues likely to appear on the agenda. On the third occasion, following Japan's invasion of Taiwan, the Zongli Yamen asked the uncomfortable question: Why had the Chinese fallen short after fourteen years of self-strengthening? Again, fifteen high provincial officials were asked to respond.

Not all officials took advantage of these opportunities to press for reforms. In the case of the 1866 discussions, Zuo Zongtang (1812–1885) did seize the opportunity to put forward a proposal leading to the establishment of China's first modern naval dockyard and academy. The 1874–1875 discussions developed into a huge debate lasting more than six months, with the last two and a half months consumed by prolonged debates by court officials and imperial princes—a court conference—on the fifty-four memorials and memoranda that had been submitted. In the end, a program for defense modernization emerged: There was to be a northern and a southern navy, two modern coal mines, and the creation of a special maritime defense fund of four million *taels* per annum. It should be said, however, that defense modernization, narrowly conceived, had marginal bearing on reform. But the introduction of modern technology, production and resource management, support industries, education of new types of workers, technicians, and managers, not to mention public finance, had a deep impact on the Qing system.

The very nature of the 1867 round of discussions brought forth no concrete reform proposals but, along with the other two discussions, yielded a rich array of ideas for change. They included:

- Modifications of the civil service examinations, ranging from the incorporation of mathematics to science, foreign affairs, and languages.

- Specialization in government, including assigning specialized duties to presidents and vice presidents of the six boards, and practical training for Hanlin scholars.

- Centralized budgeting.

- Abolition of sinecures and redundant offices, such as the governorship in provincial capitals that also had a governor-general.

- Extension of local government to include new administrative units at the subvillage level.

- Establishment of government newspapers to create a more informed citizenry.

- Abolition of the rule of avoidance to allow officials to become more effective administrators.

This partial list attests to the richness of these policy discussions, anticipating some of the reforms of the next era. Why was more not accomplished before 1895?

The fate of the 1874–1875 debates provides much of the answer. After the fifty-four proposals came in, the throne turned them over to the princes of the blood, the grand secretaries, ministers of the six boards, and ministers of the nine courts. By including the last, the throne, while giving the impression of being inclusive, was in fact introducing to the debate the most conservative elements at court. The final debate then degenerated into a vitriolic attack on the persons of Li Hongzhang and Ding Richang, accusing them of trying to change China with barbarian ways. Sensing trouble, the Zongli Yamen presented a severely trimmed down reform proposal, which, after imperial scrutiny, became even more limited.

Qingyi (pure or disinterested opinion) refers to the lofty ideals of Confucianism and the officials who espoused them. In 1867, led by an archconservative neo-Confucian scholar, the Grand Secretary Woren (d. 1871), they attacked the introduction of mathematics into the curriculum of the Peking Language School (Tongwen guan). Defeated, they did not surface in force again until 1874 to 1875, when the Empress-dowager Cixi (1835–1908) found it convenient to give them free rein to check the rising modernizers. They and their successors continued to oppose any meaningful reforms throughout much of this period. Reformist ideas, particularly those suggesting any form of participatory government, would hence be restricted to mavericks like Guo Songdao (1818–1891) and the sojourners of the treaty ports or Hong Kong.

ERA OF THE HUNDRED DAYS' REFORM

The character of reform drastically changed following China's ignominious defeat at the hands of the Japanese in 1895. As the war set off a frenzied scramble for concessions, the sense of crisis heightened, fueling the drive for reforms. A much larger number and a far greater variety of people were involved in what could truly be described as a reform movement. A signature event was the ten-thousand-character memorial drafted by Kang Youwei (1858–1927) and Liang Qichao (1873–1929), and signed by 603 provincial degree holders who were then preparing for the metropolitan examinations in 1895. To promote their ideas, which included using the works of Gong Zizhen and other Gongyang scholars to support their advocacy of a parliamentary form of government, Kang and Liang founded study societies and newspapers, activities formerly denied to Chinese outside government. In the following years, these societies, newspapers, and magazines spread from Beijing to Shanghai, and to Hunan and Guangdong. Kang and Liang traveled and lectured. For the first time, reforms enjoyed the support of nonofficials drawn together from scattered parts of the empire in a common cause through study societies and newspaper readership.

Officials, too, supported reforms. In Hunan, Governor Chen Baozhen (1831–1900) was particularly active, while Governor-general Zhang Zhidong (1837–1909) promoted a milder version of reform. At court, the Guangxu emperor (r. 1875–1908) himself had been thinking along reformist lines for some time and adopted some of Kang Youwei's ideas.

The reform edicts of the Hundred Days' Reform for the first time proposed significant institutional changes, but fell short of broadening the decision-making processes. Still, the reform movement changed the face of China even as the Hundred Days' Reform itself was overturned. The study societies, newspapers, schools, and even contents of some of the provincial civil service examinations survived the crackdown, and would resurface one more time after 1900.

THE NEW POLICIES OR LAST-DITCH REFORMS, 1901–1912

In early December 1901, Cixi's court in exile finally took the initiative and asked for reform proposals from the high officials. While admitting that the methods of government should be changed (*bianfa*), a term used by the more daring of the reforming officials of the Self-strengthening era, she kept out of bounds the fundamental structure of Confucian sociopolitical relationships:

the "three bonds" (key Confucian relationships between ruler and ministers, father and son, and husband and wife) and the "five relationships" (the "three bonds" plus the relationship between elder and younger brothers, and elder and younger friends). By force of circumstance, this had to be a top-down reform, as the reformers of the Hundred Days' stripe had been exiled or silenced. Yet the reforms that resulted smacked heavily of the 1898 variety, some even harking back to the proposals of the 1860s and 1870s. Modern-sounding ministries were created, offices with overlapping responsibilities were abolished, students studying overseas were to be recruited for government service while more were sent abroad, the contents of both the military and the civil service examinations were modernized with the latter eventually abolished in 1905, Hanlin scholars were given further training, and so forth. There was also a new commercial code, and social reforms like the ban on footbinding and permission for marriages between Manchus and Chinese also became law. Like the Hundred Days' Reform, no change in decision-making processes was proffered. The most significant reform was the termination of the civil service examinations, which not only made room for the rise of modern education—a much-needed reform—but also let loose the hordes of young educated men to engage in the next round of reform, not to mention revolution.

The Japanese defeat of the Russians in 1904 to 1905 dealt the Qing a double blow: the shock of a rising Asian nation beating a major European power, and the insult of a foreign war conducted on Chinese soil and inflicting damage to Chinese nationals and property. Constitutional monarchy, thought to be the secret of Japanese success, was put on the table, admitting the need to change the decision-making processes. Constitutionalism is studied elsewhere in these volumes; it suffices to stress here that the movement toward constitutional government reopened the political playground to civilian associations and newspapers, suppressed since 1898. Slowed by an imperial court jealous of its power, some would say Manchu power, and undermined by the competing revolutionary movement, constitutional reforms got only as far as the convening of provincial assemblies—which were allowed only to advise but not legislate—as the dynasty collapsed.

SEE ALSO *Cixi, Empress Dowager; Grand Canal; Kang Youwei; Li Hongzhang; Liang Qichao; Lin Zexu; Opium Wars; Qing Restoration; Richard, Timothy; River Systems: Yellow River; River Systems: Water Control; Ruan Yuan; Shen Baozhen; Wei Yuan; Zeng Guofan; Zhang Zhidong; Zuo Zongtang.*

BIBLIOGRAPHY

Anthony, Robert J., and Jane Kate Leonard, eds. *Dragons, Tigers, and Dogs: Qing Crisis Management and the Boundaries of State*

Power in Late Imperial China. Ithaca, NY: Cornell University East Asia Program, 2002.

Chang Hao. Intellectual Change and the Reform Movement, 1890–1898. In *The Cambridge History of China*, Vol. 11, ed. John K. Fairbank and Kwang-ching Liu (Liu Guangjing), 274–338. Cambridge, U.K.: Cambridge University Press, 1980.

Ichiko Chuzo. Political and Institutional Reform, 1901–1911. In *The Cambridge History of China*, Vol. 11, ed. John K. Fairbank and Kwang-ching Liu (Liu Guangjing), 375–415. Cambridge, U.K.: Cambridge University Press, 1980.

Kwong, Luke. *A Mosaic of the Hundred Days: Personalities, Politics, and Ideas of 1898.* Cambridge, MA: Harvard University Press, 1984.

Lü Shiqiang. *Ding Richang yu ziqiang yundong* [Ding Richang and China's Self-strengthening]. Taibei: Institute of Modern History, Academia Sinica, 1972.

Polachek, James M. *The Inner Opium War.* Cambridge, MA: Harvard University Press, 1991.

Pong, David. The Vocabulary of Change: Reformist Ideas of the 1860s and 1870s. In *Ideal and Reality: Social and Political Change in Modern China, 1860–1949*, ed. David Pong and Edmund S. K. Fung, 25–61. Lanham, MD: University Press of America, 1985.

Pong, David. Shen Pao-chen and the Great Policy Debate of 1874–1875. In *Proceedings of the Conference on the Self-Strengthening Movement in Late Ch'ing China, 1860–1894*, 189–225. Taibei: Institute of Modern History, Academia Sinica, 1988.

Pong, David. *Shen Pao-chen and China's Modernization in the Nineteenth Century.* Cambridge, U.K.: Cambridge University Press, 1994.

Rankin, Mary Backus. *Elite Activism and Political Transformation in China: Zhejiang Province, 1865–1911.* Stanford, CA: Stanford University Press, 1986.

Thompson, Roger R. *China's Local Councils in the Age of Constitutional Reform, 1898–1911.* Cambridge, MA: Harvard University Press, 1995.

Wang Ermin. *Qing-ji binggongye de xingqi* [The rise of military industries in Late Qing]. Taibei: Institute of Modern History, Academia Sinica, 1963.

Wright, Mary C. *The Last Stand of Chinese Conservatism: The T'ung-chih Restoration, 1862–1874.* 2nd ed. Stanford, CA: Stanford University Press, 1962.

David Pong

REGIONALISM

Some scholars of modern Chinese history have used the term *regionalism* in discussing the period from the suppression of the Taiping Uprising in the early 1860s to the emergence of various warlord regimes in the 1910s and 1920s. They see the regional dominance of Qing-era provincial leaders with military responsibilities such as Zeng Guofan and Li Hongzhang as a harbinger of the final decentralization of power in the so-called warlord period (1916–1928). Implicit is a parallel argument that

the Chinese state, in the guise of both the Qing dynasty and the Republic of China to 1927, was deteriorating steadily to a final state of total ineffectiveness. Only with the rise of the Nationalist Party of Sun Yat-sen and his political heir Chiang Kai-shek, and then the Chinese Communist Party, were Chinese national leaders once again able to impose their wills and agenda on regional leaders.

THE TAIPING UPRISING

In a continental empire such as China in the centuries before 1900, the tension between region and center could not be avoided. Although a once-unified China did devolve into contending regional power bases after the fall of the Han dynasty in the third century CE, the political dream of unity remained and was finally realized by the Sui dynasty in the late sixth century. Never again would a period of disunion last as long as even a century. By the thirteenth century many of China's modern provincial boundaries had been drawn by its Mongol emperors, and in the succeeding Ming and Qing dynasties a set of administrative and fiscal measures ensured a dynamic and effective means for the central state to balance the contradictory principles of central control and regional autonomy. Chief among these were powers of appointment and the so-called law of avoidance that precluded imperial bureaucrats from serving in their home provinces. Moreover, officials were frequently moved from post to post so that affinities with local and provincial elites, with whom they could share common experiences such as participating in the imperial examination system, were less likely to develop. Beijing bureaucrats also controlled the disbursement of tax revenues. Although significant portions of these revenues were "retained" by local and provincial officials, this was done with Beijing's approval. In addition, Beijing could and did direct provinces to send tax revenues to other provinces as needed. A third way in which Beijing balanced control and autonomy was through the appointment of governors-general who supervised two or three provinces in conjunction with provincial governors. Not all governors shared jurisdictions with governors-general, but strategic areas often were administered by provincial officials with overlapping responsibilities.

During the first decade of the Taiping Uprising the Qing court relied on the command-and-control mechanisms just described. Not until 1860 did the court finally admit failure. At that point it authorized two innovations seized upon by advocates of the regionalism thesis: vesting civilian and military powers in one provincial official, and sanctioning the local collection and disbursement of a new transportation tax, the *lijin* tax, by provincial officials for provincial needs. Significantly, very little information about these tax revenues was communicated to Beijing. By these measures provincial officials such as Li

Hongzhang, who became responsible for the lower Yangzi region, could both command and fund regional armies that had been recruited from the myriad local militias first mobilized by elites to resist Taiping depredations.

Although there appears to be a similarity to the twentieth-century warlord period, a close investigation of the Taiping suppression and its aftermath does not support this thesis. Beijing still controlled appointments and budgets, even if it exercised less supervision of the *lijin* tax than it did of the land tax. The regional armies mobilized by Li Hongzhang and his colleagues provided a model for provincial forces in the post-Taiping era, and every province was urged to create such forces in light of the decreasing effectiveness of both the Green Standard and Manchu garrison units. After the crisis had passed, the usual division of civilian and military powers between two officials returned, in most cases, and even persons as well respected and powerful as Li Hongzhang and his protegé Yuan Shikai served at the pleasure of the imperial court. It was not until the 1911 Revolution that provincial military authorities usurped civilian control, and President Yuan Shikai soon reasserted central powers of appointment and fiscal management. His successors, however, were less successful, and his death in June 1916 is the conventional beginning of the warlord period in which, as Mao famously proclaimed, power grew out of the barrel of the gun. Not until the founding of the People's Republic of China in 1949 would civilian control of the military become paramount again. Moreover, Beijing regained central control over China's regions and, for the first time since the fall of the Qing, was able to project power into the Tibetan and Muslim regions of western China.

CULTURAL REGIONALISM

Although in political and administrative terms there are significant continuities in center-province relations in the nineteenth and twentieth centuries, notwithstanding the warlord period, it is important to consider also the social and cultural dimensions of regionalism in China. Not only were Qing bureaucrats unconcerned with expressions of regional identity and pride, they sometimes encouraged provincial elites to compile anthologies of regional poetry, essays, and histories. Beginning in the early nineteenth century in Guangdong in the south and evidenced as well in distant Shanxi in the north later in the century, sojourning officials encouraged and sponsored such scholarly endeavors. As long as this regional pride was divorced from political ambitions, none of these actions were seen as detrimental to central state power. This sanguineness lessened, however, in the late Qing as regional pride came to be politicized, first in the writings of Chinese students in Tokyo and then in pro-

vincial assemblies, to which some of these students were elected, that were seated in 1909. The epitome of the politicized province could be seen in the 1911 Revolution, when many provinces declared independence from the Qing. In the years leading up to the revolution a new generation of educated Chinese, especially those who were studying in Japan, reevaluated the meaning and significance of the province in the provincial associations they founded (e.g., students from Hubei, Hunan, Jiangsu, and Zhejiang) and the journals they published (e.g., *Jiangsu, Zhejiang Tide, Translations from [Hunan] Students Abroad, Zhili Speaks*).

These activities were not entirely unprecedented: Scholars in Beijing and merchants gathered in towns and cities across the empire often had established native-place associations where common dialects, cuisine, customs, and rituals created significant sociocultural bonds for sojourners far from home. Only at the end of the nineteenth century were there protopolitical activities in these merchant and scholar associations in cities such as Shanghai and Beijing. What was relatively new in the twentieth century, however, was the scope and scale of this politicization. In some cases, for example, Hunanese and Cantonese natives agitated for their provinces to lead a revolutionary surge that would sweep along the rest of China's provinces. This politicizing of provinces can also be seen as provincial assemblies began to challenge Beijing's provincial governors and to communicate their demands directly to the capital. After the dynasty fell, these civilian voices soon were overwhelmed by a new generation of regional militarists, the neutral label sometimes applied to warlords, who made appointments and controlled tax revenues without having to heed Beijing at all.

WARLORD ERA

Although the warlords of twentieth-century China do not appear to be descendants of the heroes of the Taiping suppression, they did share with Qing-era military leaders an ideological propensity to privilege the national over the local. There is little evidence, for example, that Li Hongzhang, Zeng Guofan, and Zuo Zongtang ever wavered from their support of the throne and Confucian ideology. Neither the imperial system nor Confucian ideology survived the 1911 Revolution, but a transregional ideological construct—nationalism—was shared by most warlords. A China unified by nationalism was a goal for them, even if few were willing to give up regional power without a fight and there were disagreements about what this nationalism meant. There are some exceptions to this generalization. In the 1920s a federalist movement conceptualized a China no longer bound by the legacy of unity bequeathed by the Han dynasty. Another exception, put forward by Stephen Platt using the methodology of the intellectual historian, posits that Hunanese intellectuals in the late Qing and early Republic were envisioning a Hunan no longer part of unified China and its heritage (Platt 2007). These "provincial patriots" imagined an even newer nation and a newer nationalism. Presumably, they conceived of the old continental empire shattered into pieces that would resemble the territories of the predynastic Warring States period that ended in the third century BCE. It was a vision obliterated, in the end, by the power of the centuries-old ideal of unity, now championed by the Chinese Communist Party. The question for the future is whether or not this is an ideal or an onus.

SEE ALSO *Elections and Assemblies, 1909–1949; Federalism; Li Hongzhang; Qing Restoration; Shen Baozhen; Taiping Uprising; Warlord Era (1916–1928); Yuan Shikai; Zeng Guofan; Zhang Zhidong; Zuo Zongtang.*

BIBLIOGRAPHY

Belsky, Richard. *Localities at the Center: Native Place, Space, and Power in Late Imperial Beijing.* Cambridge, MA: Harvard University Asia Center, 2005.

Duara, Prasenjit. Provincial Narratives of the Nation: Federalism and Centralism in Modern China. In *Rescuing History from the Nation: Questioning Narratives of Modern China,* 177–204. Chicago: University of Chicago Press, 1995.

Lary, Diana. *Region and Nation: The Kwangsi Clique in Chinese Politics, 1925–1937.* Cambridge, U.K.: Cambridge University Press, 1974.

Liu, Kwang-ching. Nineteenth-Century China: The Disintegration of the Old Order and the Impact of the West. In *China in Crisis,* vol. 1, bk. 1, ed. Ho Ping-ti and Tang Tsou, 93–178. Chicago: University of Chicago Press, 1968.

Michael, Franz. Introduction: Regionalism in Nineteenth-Century China. In *Li Hung-chang and the Huai Army: A Study of Nineteenth-Century Chinese Regionalism,* by Stanley Spector, xl–xli. Seattle: University of Washington Press, 1964.

Platt, Stephen R. *Provincial Patriots: The Hunanese and Modern China.* Cambridge, MA: Harvard University Press, 2007.

Pong, David. The Income and Military Expenditure of Kiangsi Province in the Last Years (1860–1864) of the Taiping Rebellion. *The Journal of Asian Studies* 26 (1966): 49–65.

Sheridan, James E. The Warlord Era: Politics and Militarism under the Peking Government, 1916–28. In *The Cambridge History of China,* vol. 12, ed. John K. Fairbank, 284–321. Cambridge, U.K.: Cambridge University Press, 1983.

Roger R. Thompson

RELIGIOUS ORGANIZATIONS

Religious organizations in China are in many ways different from those in the West. Organizations dedicated primarily or exclusively to religion and religious teachings, as well as lay devotional associations, tend to have blurry boundaries and a less clear concept of membership than do those of Western religions. For example, although many people in China regularly visit a temple, there is no real idea of formal temple membership or anything comparable to a parish, nor is one restricted from visiting a variety of temples or worshipping numerous deities. Because most people view the three main Chinese religions (Buddhism, Confucianism, and Daoism) as mutually compatible, one is not a member of any single teaching to the exclusion of others. There are notable exceptions, particularly Christianity and Islam, but generally speaking, organized religions in China place few concrete demands on their members.

On the whole, Chinese religions are weak as organizations. Although Buddhist monasteries and Daoist temples were built throughout China, most operated primarily as local institutions. Temples were organized hierarchically into parent-child networks, often through the practice of taking incense ashes from an existing temple to found a new one, a custom called "dividing the incense," but these networks were limited in scope. They never approached the level of coherence where China had anything like a national Buddhist or Daoist church. Overall, neither Buddhism nor Daoism had a large clergy. Some areas did have high concentrations of religious specialists. Putuo and Wutai mountains were associated with important Buddhist deities, and each was dotted with monasteries and supported thousands of Buddhist monks. Wudang and Tai mountains were similar centers of Daoism. Many other places, however, had few if any formally ordained Buddhists or Daoists. Especially in the countryside, Buddhism and Daoism existed with little or no influence of formally ordained clergy. In the late nineteenth-century city of Tianjin, there was one Buddhist monastery for every 1,700 adult residents. In the rural hinterland, the ratio was roughly 1 to 10,000.

In contrast, almost every type of organization had some religious component, particularly before 1949, and, as a result, the line between religious and secular organizations was never as firm as it often is intended to be in the West. Every Chinese family maintained an altar in the home and conducted regular rituals, both to worship ancestors and to pray for the welfare of the living. The same was true of most other organizations, such as businesses, trade guilds, and place-name associations, many of which had their own patron gods. Often this religious component had the function of holding a loose organization together and formalizing its leadership structure. Traditionally, most villages had some sort of temple or shrine, and held ceremonies on regular festival days, and occasionally to pray for protection from disasters such as drought or plague. These rituals were expressions of the collective identity and needs of the village, and every family in the community would visually participate,

Buddhists lighting butter-fueled lamps at the Dazhao Temple in Hohhot, Inner Mongolia, China, February 12, 2006.
Rather than prohibiting religious activity, Communist officials sought to maintain authority over religious institutions during the early
years of the People's Republic of China. In the 1980s, government attitudes toward religious independence softened, though certain
groups, such as Catholics and Tibetan Buddhists, remained under tight supervision. **FREDERIC J. BROWN/AFP/GETTY IMAGES**

either by taking part in the ceremony or by making a donation.

Certain religious organizations did make heavy demands on their members. Among these are the popular teachings known collectively as the *White Lotus*. This is not a single religion, but a tradition of independent teachings descended from lay Buddhist groups of the Song dynasty (960–1279) and characterized by a complex system of beliefs centering on a deity known as the Eternal Venerable Mother (*wu sheng laomu*). Reflecting the popular practice of blending religious traditions, White Lotus scriptures taught that this benevolent deity sent each of the great religious teachers of the past (Confucius, Laozi and the Buddha—this list would later expand to include Jesus and Muhammad, as well) into the world in order to save humanity from its own wickedness. Because the White Lotus tradition also featured vivid predictions of the apocalypse, it could easily become a seed for rebellion, when rebel leaders claimed to have been sent by the Eternal Venerable Mother to

raise an army and usher in a new era. Zhu Yuanzhang, the founder of the Ming dynasty (1368–1644) had come to power through an alliance with one such army, and from that time on, White Lotus scriptures were banned and the teachings energetically persecuted. White Lotus–style teachings did inspire a number of large rebellions (in particular, the mass movements of the nineteenth century), but the state was mistaken in believing them to be inherently seditious. In reality, only a small number of these teachings emphasized the apocalypse, or had any political ambitions. Most were small-scale organizations that served the daily religious needs of villagers, and were thus able to avoid government scrutiny. Descendants of White Lotus teachings remain active in many rural areas today.

Groups known collectively as *secret societies* also made heavy demands on members. These societies, such as the Heaven and Earth Society or the triads, are often associated with organized crime. While this characterization was in some cases accurate, secret societies were also organized to protect against bandits or as political cliques. What all of these groups shared was a religious element: a tradition of oaths and rituals that bound the group together and committed its members to secrecy.

During the nineteenth century, religious organizations in China underwent a number of changes. As the Qing state (1644–1912) grew increasingly weak and unable to realistically implement its policies, laws relating to the control of religion were poorly enforced. By law, Buddhist monks and Daoist priests were supposed to register with the government and receive an official certification, but with the declining ability of the state to enforce this rule, unregistered monks and priests began to move through society, often spreading teachings that an orthodox viewpoint would have considered heretical and dangerous. The weakness of the Qing state also eroded its ability to uncover White Lotus teachings and secret societies. At the same time, underground religious organizations grew in popularity. Increasingly frequent famines, natural disasters, and the general breakdown of domestic order made these organizations more attractive to new members, both because secret societies could offer some protection and because the apocalyptic predictions of White Lotus teachings seemed more realistic during times of crisis.

Small White Lotus–style uprisings, such as the 1774 rebellion of Wang Lun, began in the late eighteenth century and grew in size and intensity during the nineteenth. This trend culminated in the Taiping Uprising (1851–1864), a massive rebellion that was nominally Christian, but closely resembled White Lotus in its beliefs and organization. In the final years of the century, reaction against the proliferation of Christian missions led to a mass movement known in English as the Boxer Uprising (in reference to the martial arts practiced by the participants, known in Chinese as "Righteous and Harmonious fist" [Yihequan]). Scholars disagree over whether to call this event a White Lotus rebellion, but it did share many elements of White Lotus belief, and its rapid spread in the very shadow of the capital shows how completely the late Qing had lost the ability to control the proliferation of popular religious organizations.

CHANGES, 1911 TO 1948

The first half of the twentieth century was characterized by an unceasing call for political and social reform. This produced movements to eradicate popular religious practices, as well as to reform Chinese religion to suit the modern era. Chinese Buddhists began to organize themselves in emulation of the tactics used by successful Christian missionaries. The leading figure in this movement was the monk Taixu (1890–1947), who was tireless in his efforts to spark a Buddhist renaissance in China. At the same time, Chinese Christians, many of whom were beginning to feel restrained by the continued presence of foreign missions, began to think in terms of creating a Christian church unique to China.

While earlier White Lotus–style teachings remained strong in the countryside, new teachings in the same tradition were founded during this period. In contrast to the secrecy of earlier teachings, some of these new teachings, such as the Red Swastika Society (Hong Wanzi Hui), the Morality Society (Daode Hui), and the Way of Penetrating Unity (Yiguandao), strived for social recognition, and became very active as civic and charitable organizations. After the Japanese invasion of China, some of these teachings attracted members of the client governments of Manchukuo and the Wang Jingwei Nanjing government, giving rise to the claim that they had been complicit in the Japanese occupation.

CHANGES AFTER 1949

Having seen the difficulties created by Soviet attempts to destroy the Russian Orthodox Church during the 1920s, the officially atheist government of the People's Republic of China never attempted to destroy religion altogether. They were, however, determined to exert control over religious organizations. Five teachings (Buddhism, Daoism, Islam, and Protestant and Catholic Christianity) were officially recognized and reformed into government-run "patriotic" (*aiguo*) organizations. In the case of Christian churches, the policy was aimed at severing ties with foreign mission organizations; Chinese Christians were encouraged to join the officially recognized "three self" (self-governed, self-supporting, self-propagated) movement of the cleric Wu Yaozong (1893–1979). Other organizations were slated for destruction, first in the 1951 "suppress the counterrevolutionaries" (*zhenya fangeming*) movement, which targeted foreign Catholics and the very popular Way of Penetrating Unity, and later in similar campaigns throughout the 1950s. Fears of Tibetan separatism prompted a similar crackdown on Tibetan lamaseries in 1959. From the late 1950s through the late 1970s, illegal organizations existed only deep underground, and even official ones were hard-pressed to continue even the most basic operation.

By the late 1970s, the Chinese state was ready to begin loosening certain aspects of social policy, and religion made a rapid comeback. Official religious organizations led the way, serving as a diplomatic bridge to Christian, Muslim, and Buddhist countries. In the countryside, villages began to reconstruct temple networks and local religious teachings. Although these groups remained illegal, local cadres generally had little interest in policing such regulations, and often simply turned a blind eye to their resurgence. This tolerance had its limits. Tibetan Buddhism remained closely policed, and Chinese Catholics are still required to give fealty to the national Catholic Church, rather than to the Vatican. The lax attitude toward popular organizations changed quickly in 1999 with the campaign against Falun Gong, which revealed a new sensitivity of the Chinese state toward religious ideas and organizations.

SEE ALSO *Religious Policy; Secret Societies; White Lotus.*

BIBLIOGRAPHY
Bays, Daniel, ed. *Christianity in China: From the Eighteenth Century to the Present.* Stanford, CA: Stanford University Press, 1996.

DuBois, Thomas David. *The Sacred Village: Social Change and Religious Life in Rural North China.* Honolulu: University of Hawai'i Press, 2005.

MacInnis, Donald E. *Religious Policy and Practice in Communist China: A Documentary History.* London: Hodder & Stoughton, 1972.

Ownby, David. The Heaven and Earth Society as Popular Religion. *Journal of Asian Studies* 54, 4 (1995): 1023–1046.

Welch, Holmes. *Buddhism under Mao.* Cambridge, MA: Harvard University Press, 1972.

Yang Qingkun (C. K. Yang). *Religion in Chinese Society: A Study of Contemporary Social Functions of Religion and Some of Their Historical Factors.* Berkeley: University of California Press, 1961.

Thomas David DuBois

RELIGIOUS POLICY

China has long had an extremely varied religious landscape, with numerous forms of religious practice and organization embedded in local society and resistant to state control and standardization. When taking a long-term perspective, one can see how Chinese regimes have deployed efforts aimed at controlling and reforming this religious landscape, with results that rarely met their own standards. Some observers of the present situation, notably in mainland China, contend that it exhibits a fundamental continuity from imperial times, after the parenthesis of the Maoist years. According to them, present-day local officials, just like their Qing predecessors, despise popular religious culture but tolerate it unless it grows dangerous, in which case they repress it mercilessly. This line of analysis suggests that such continuity evidences a specificity of Chinese state and society in the management of religious pluralism.

On the other hand, there are also strong arguments in favor of rupture in the state-and-religion relationships between the late imperial period and the modern Republican and socialist regimes. The religious policy rupture initiated in 1898 ushered in an era of state nationalization of local temples and other religious institutions and resources. Within two decades, the imperial policy of

separating orthodoxy and heterodoxy was replaced with a policy of recognizing world religions while repressing all other practices branded as superstition. The first policy represents a project to reform Chinese religion from the inside, while the second amounts to managing religion from the outside.

LATE QING POLICIES

Religion as a category was introduced in China only around 1900 and was indeed used to redefine new policies. But if one starts from an anthropological definition of religion as including all institutions and practices dealing with death, gods, and destiny, then it appears that the late imperial state did have a coherent set of religious policies. Such policies were articulated with other issues of cultural policy, such as bans on operas and other performing arts, and with social control, as they overlapped to a great extent with the categories of "reforming the customs," *zheng fengsu*, or moral education, *jiaohua*.

These religious policies did not regulate beliefs so much as institutions and rituals—the Qing state, like its predecessors, being based on ritual orthopraxy as much as law. The state attempted to control who could perform which rituals, where, and when, and with what resources. These attempts were backed by a considerable number of restrictive laws, found in the Code (*Da Qing lüli*), imperial edicts and proclamations, Board of Rites and provincial regulations, jurisprudence, and proclamations by local officials. When reading these documents, one cannot fail to be impressed by the large array of practices that were banned. For instance, only state-supervised ordained and licensed individuals could act as Buddhist and Daoist clerics, and they could not engage in any activity outside their monastery, nor build any new monasteries. In addition, local cults were limited to those recognized by the state; all congregational groups (voluntary associations of people unrelated by blood or residence or profession) were banned, including so-called sectarians and Christians, as well as groups organizing temple festivals; family rituals were precisely regulated (mandatory burying, no cremation); prayers to heaven and the Big Dipper were illegal, as were spirit writing and possession; women were banned from entering temples; and so forth.

Starting from these prohibitions, one might agree with Dutch sinologist J. J. M. de Groot (1854–1921), who, in 1903, described the imperial state as fundamentally repressive and intolerant. Since then, many scholars have taken an opposite approach, focusing on actual practice rather than normative texts, and choosing to describe the Qing state and society as open, allowing subjects to believe and practice the religion they liked as long as they satisfied a certain set of demands for prescribed behaviors. And indeed, there certainly existed more religious diversity among both the governing elites and the population at large in Qing China than in other eighteenth- and nineteenth-century empires.

The normative texts describe a utopian project for building a society along the lines of fundamentalist Confucianism. The bottom line of the local officials' mission, as far as religion was concerned, was to enforce the basic distinction between the licit (patriarchal, ascriptive forms of religious organization: territorial communities, lineages, guilds) and the illicit (congregational religion based on common faith): "immoral temples have to be destroyed everywhere, temples to orthodox gods have to be supported everywhere" says a phrase found in the introduction to the section on temples in many local gazetteers.

GRAY ZONES OF TOLERANCE

The licit/illicit distinction expressed in sociological terms is convincing. On the ground, however, although the distinction was clear enough in some cases, such as with Christianity during the ban (1724–1842) or some congregational (sectarian) groups that turned violent—these being the best studied and the most violent aspects of Qing religious policy—in many other cases it was murky. Categories used to describe illegal religious practices, such as *xie*, "heterodox," or *yin*, "immoral," had different extensions according to the authors, genre, or context. Some officials used these categories broadly to label everything not expressly authorized, while others, probably the vast majority, used them to designate illegal religious activities they deemed particularly harmful, calling for suppression. Because of such distinctions, and also because in many cases the licit and illicit were intimately mixed, officials were, in practice, forced to devise compromises and open a gray zone between the allowed practices and the actively banned ones.

For instance, a cult such as Guandi (the deified hero Guan Yu, known as the "God of War" or "Martial saint," he was the official protector of the state and promoted as a paragon of loyalty) was official and state-supported, but there were many Guandi temples that were not authorized, many congregations (technically illegal) running Guandi temples (whether authorized or not), and a mixture of state-sanctioned rituals (spring and autumn sacrifices according to Confucian liturgy) and technically illegal rituals (processions with penitents and women, spirit-writing cults) taking place in such temples. Another case was Islam, which was deliberately although tacitly underregulated and left out of the purview of the bans on congregations.

In short, the gray zone resulted from a certain underregulation, in spite of the imposing number of laws, decrees, and official proclamations. For instance, the imperial state regulated which cults were authorized and which ones were banned, but it said practically nothing about how to manage a temple once it could legally exist, besides the basic principle that all religious property was inalienable and could not be sold or mortgaged. In this underregulated realm, local society developed contractual relationships (for instance, between lay leaders and religious specialists), and Qing magistrates upheld and enforced such contracts when they were asked to adjudicate conflicts.

The resulting interaction of local officials and local religion implied several modes of relationship: mutual ignorance, cooperation, negotiation (through intermediaries such as local gentry and clerical elites), and conflict (closing or destroying temples, banning festivals, arresting religious specialists), all of which were common. The actual combination of these modes went through huge variations in time (depending on occasional top-down campaigns of mobilization ordered by the emperor, combined with a general attempt at better controlling "popular" culture and religion in the post-Taiping years) and space (with different local religious systems having varying capacities to resist state encroachment). Another factor of difference was the degree of commitment of officials to religious policies, for reasons of both career strategy and personal belief and worldview. Elite religiosities informed religious policies and the way the policies favored certain institutions, cults, practices, and rituals over others.

A NEW PARADIGM

Paralleling the change of the political regime from an imperial state built on ritual orthopraxy and cosmological conceptions of power and order to a secular republic, twentieth-century changes in religious policy were informed by a paradigmatic shift in the way religion was conceived. The new paradigms of the political management of religion, of Western origin, all have in common a post-Enlightenment definition of religion as a churchlike institution separate from society, and include processes of negotiation between church and state for privileges and uses of the public sphere.

The effect on the Chinese world of these paradigms began at the turn of the twentieth century when the Western categories that underpin these paradigms were first introduced in China and then used by the dying empire and by the Republic of China to elaborate new religious policies. The bottom line of these policies was the recognition and limited support for those "religions" that could prove they fit a certain definition of this alien category, along with active suppression of anything else, which was categorized as "superstition." It is in this framework that the successive Chinese regimes conducted a policy branded as secular, even though this secularism should be considered a claim rather than a fact. The new religious policies of the Republican regime entailed the abandonment by the state of the imperial regime's religious prerogatives and the creation of a realm where "religions" could manage their own affairs within a framework of control and regulation set up by the "secular" state. Creating such a realm proved to be more complex than initially imagined by Republican leaders.

A 1901 article introduced into the Chinese language a word, *zongjiao*, destined to translate the Western notion of "religion" (see Bastid-Bruguière 1998). This word was from the start paired with its opposite, "superstition," *mixin*. Both were taken from Japanese, in which they had been coined some years earlier. These neologisms were part of a larger set of imported categories used to reclassify the whole of knowledge and social and political practices, including such words as *science* or *philosophy*. Chinese intellectuals initially debated the meaning of these notions, which were foreign to the late imperial Chinese world where religious life and social organization were deeply intertwined. During the first years of the century, *zongjiao* was almost synonymous with Christianity, but soon also included Islam, which was logical, in that *zongjiao* translated Western models of "religion." It was only gradually that *zongjiao* came to include Daoism and Buddhism. Heated arguments for or against the inclusion of Confucianism in this category raged for many years, before those arguing against inclusion gained the upper hand by the 1920s. For its part, most of Chinese religion remained excluded and is still categorized as "custom," "folklore," or "superstition," even though this has been changing since the beginning of the twenty-first century with the formation of new, more positive, official categories such as "popular faith" (*minjian xinyang*).

The notion of "religion" brought a theoretical justification to a vast project conducted by various sections of the late imperial and Republican political elite aimed at reconfiguring the religious field and drastically reducing the realm of legitimate religion. This project shrank the encompassing category of orthodoxy defined by the imperial regime to a few "religions" on a Christian-based model. One of the consequences of the drastic reduction was the confiscation and destruction of a large number of local temples, formerly orthodox but now labeled superstitious. This destruction was conducted in the name of antisuperstition, but also in order to appropriate the material and symbolical resources of local religious institutions for the purpose of state building. The emergence of this project can be traced to the 1898 reforms and the key figure of Kang Youwei (1858–1927).

The provisional constitution of the Republic of China, proclaimed on March 11, 1912, stipulates the "freedom of religious belief" (*xinjiao ziyou*). This text did not guarantee protection against destruction and violence in temples, but it encouraged legislators and thinkers to elaborate on the difference between legitimate "religion" and "superstition." This approach to religious policies was carried over and formalized by the Nationalist regime after 1927. After having rejected early temptations of an outright ban on religions, the regime decided to work with recognized, institutional religions along a corporatist model, while launching an all-out fight against "superstitions." This fight included bans on traditional festivals, a few of which (notably New Year) were given a modern meaning and incorporated into the new, Gregorian calendar; the invention and promotion of secular family rituals (weddings and funerals, including cremation); and the taxing or banning of superstitious activities (divination) and items (paper offerings and money). All of these policies, first launched by the Guomindang (GMD; Nationalist Party), were later carried out to greater effect under the People's Republic of China (PRC). Some GMD activists also trained students to vandalize temples, initiating a far-reaching destruction of religious art and memory (texts, archives).

The criteria by which the modern Chinese state decided whether to include or not a religious tradition within its list of recognized religions have mostly remained hazy, with few explicit guidelines. The Chinese state's attitude has been pragmatic: A religion was recognized if it could prove it was "pure" (spiritual and ethical in nature), well organized (with a national association), and useful (patriotic and contributing to social welfare and progress). Therefore, the official list of recognized religions was never closed, but encompassed those for which a national religious association was officially registered by the state; requests for such registration were always treated on a case-by-case basis. In practice, the current list of five recognized religions (Catholicism, Protestantism, Islam, Buddhism, and Daoism) appeared as early as 1912, but at various points in Republican history, other traditions, including the new religious groups known in recent scholarship as *redemptive societies*, were added to the list when their association was officially recognized. In the early twenty-first century, the world of religious-affairs officials is again caught in speculation about enlarging this list.

Taiwan, which was under Japanese rule (1895–1945), did not experience the 1898 reforms and the subsequent violent antisuperstition policies; it worked after 1945 with the Republican legislative framework and worldview that was highly distrustful of local "popular" religion. However, the religious structures of local society have survived there, and since the liberalization of the 1980s have flourished again, along with an extraordinary effervescence of new religious movements. Hong Kong, established along a colonial and postcolonial trajectory, and with less religious vibrancy, has always remained a religiously liberal and pluralistic society.

THE PEOPLE'S REPUBLIC OF CHINA

Meanwhile, the PRC went through religious repression of unprecedented scale, with the annihilation of various "sectarian groups" (notably the Yiguandao) as early as 1950, and the nationalization of all religious property (temple lands and buildings, lineage trusts). The only legal religious activities were the small-scale training and publications of the patriotic associations of the five recognized religions. Even this activity closed down during the Cultural Revolution, to operate anew after 1979. Since then, religious leaders have negotiated endlessly with many different state agencies to gradually recover their temples (but not their lands) and for the right to perform various rituals and activities. Alongside this realm of state-controlled, official religion, a gray zone has reemerged, with local temples being rebuilt and festivals reconvening (at a rate that varies considerably depending on the area) with tenuous legality. And the state now focuses its repression not so much on superstition (divination and spirit possession being increasingly ignored since the 1980s), as it did during the Maoist years, but on "evil cults," *xiejiao*, a reinvention of the old imperial concept, now used to label mass movements such as the Falun Gong or new Protestant sects.

SEE ALSO *Anti-Christian/Anti-Missionary Movements; Buddhism; Catholicism; Daoism; Falun Gong; Islam; Missionaries; Popular Religion; Protestantism; Religious Organizations; Religious Specialists since 1800; State Cult; Three-Self Patriotic Movement; White Lotus.*

BIBLIOGRAPHY

Bastid-Bruguière, Marianne. Liang Qichao yu zongjiao wenti 梁啟超與宗教問題 [Liang Qichao and the question of religion]. *Tôhô gakuhô* 東方學報 70 (1998): 329–73.

de Groot, J. J. M. *Sectarianism and Religious Persecution in China.* Amsterdam: Johannes Müller, 1903.

Goossaert, Vincent. 1898: The Beginning of the End for Chinese Religion? *Journal of Asian Studies* 65, 2 (2006): 307–336.

Overmyer, Daniel, ed. Religion in China Today. Spec. issue. *China Quarterly* 174 (2003): 307–520.

ter Haar, Barend. *The White Lotus Teachings in Chinese Religious History.* Leiden, Netherlands: Brill, 1992.

Yang, Mayfair Mei-hui, ed. *Chinese Religiosities: Afflictions of Modernity and State Formation.* Berkeley: University of California Press, 2008.

Yu, Anthony C. *State and Religion in China: Historical and Textual Perspectives.* Chicago: Open Court, 2005.

Vincent Goossaert

RELIGIOUS SPECIALISTS SINCE 1800

Due to its pluralistic nature, modern Chinese religion is characterized by the coexistence of several kinds of religious specialists who provide liturgical and spiritual services. Even if Muslim *ahong* and Christian priests are excluded, the variety of specialists who fulfill important liturgical functions is impressive, and includes Buddhists, Daoists, Confucians, spirit-mediums (also called shamans), diviners (including those specialized as geomancers), leaders and preachers of lay devotional or self-cultivational (sectarian) movements, and a whole array of ritual specialists and musicians, including actors, puppeteers, and storytellers reciting devotional literature. This variety is well documented for the nineteenth century and, in spite of century-long efforts at suppressing "superstitious occupations" and far-reaching recompositions of the division of religious labor in all parts of the Chinese world, these religious specialists are all still there.

CATEGORIES

The categories of religious specialist, ritual specialist, priest, cleric, monk, nun, and so forth are not standardized when discussing China, as these are simply heuristic categories. The different roles of religious specialists can in some cases be performed by the same person (e.g., Daoist and diviner, diviner and spirit-medium). It remains useful, however, to distinguish between clerical and nonclerical specialists. If *clergy* is defined as a body of professional religious specialists identified by a unified, supralocal written tradition (a canon), a liturgy, institutions, and rules of conduct, then there were three clergies in nineteenth-century China: the Confucians, the Buddhists (of both Chinese and Tibeto-Mongol traditions), and the Daoists of the two elite orders (Quanzhen and Zhengyi). By contrast, the other types of specialist—spirit-mediums, diviners, leaders of lay movements, and musicians—were not organized as clergies and did not define themselves through China-wide institutions. The three clergies had in common a certain degree of nationwide unification, though no overarching organization. They also had training and ordination centers—such as the Buddhist or Daoist monasteries or the Confucian academies (*shuyuan*)—where the canon was kept and specialists trained in exegesis and liturgy. These institutions defined the clerical traditions of Confucianism, Buddhism, and Daoism—known as the *Three Teachings*—from those other specialists who worked without such institutions.

The case of the Confucian clergy is very specific. Under a broad definition of *religious specialist*, it could be coherent to define the late imperial gentry (*shenshi*, a legal status that refers to all those who had passed at least the first degree of the imperial examinations) as the Confucian clergy, in the sense that they were the people responsible for the study, transmission, and interpretation of the sacred scriptures (the classics), and they had specific religious rights and duties (the bimonthly cult in the Confucius temple, which was closed to nongentry). In this sense, the Confucian examinations were the equivalent of Buddhist and Daoist ordinations (as Confucianism had no other form of ordination). However, the definition of *religious specialist* in the Confucian context can also, in a restrictive sense, be applied only to those performing paid ceremonial service. In contrast to Buddhists and Daoist clergy, who normally made a living, at least partly, from religion, only a small fraction of the Confucian clergy acted full time as religious specialists. Even though some *lisheng* (Confucian scholars who direct the proceeding of a ritual by reading aloud the prayers and instructing participants on how to perform their roles) were employed as full-time religious specialists by the state, most scholars provided paid liturgical or spiritual services for family rituals, state rituals, and communal sacrifices only occasionally, and many never did. Moreover, whereas the Buddhist and Daoist clergies adapted to the post-1911 era, the Confucian clergy disappeared with the end of imperial examinations in 1905, even though in some parts of China, *lisheng* (often hereditary) still act as priests to local communities.

It is possible to divide Chinese religious professionals into classes according to several criteria that place them on a scale of values: for example, whether they were paid for their services or performed such services free of charge, or whether they traveled or lived in a temple or at home. The status of Chinese religious professionals varied greatly, from that of socially valued scholars to that of semiliterate village specialists or illiterate spirit-mediums. This obviously led to a variety of attitudes and prejudices toward such specialists, and the premodern and modern intellectuals' contempt for ritual specialists or spirit-mediums was not often shared by the population at large, who typically respected people providing them with much-needed services. Gender distinctions were also critical; large numbers of female specialists were found among both clerics (Buddhist and Quanzhen Daoist) and nonclerics (e.g., spirit-mediums and female-dominated lay devotional-vegetarian traditions). Buddhist and Daoist nuns were numerous (probably in the range of one-third of the clergy before 1949; they have since become a majority in Taiwan) and enjoyed a large degree of autonomy, which made both the clergy and female religious sororities a first option for many estranged women, such as widows or orphans.

Religious specialists cooperated or competed with one another in an open religious field. Competition and cooperation played out in both of the areas where they offered their services—liturgy and spiritual teachings. Several types of clerics or specialists offered rituals for similar purposes (even though the rituals themselves were different), including death rituals, cures, and exorcisms. Similarly, the practice and transmission of self-cultivation techniques in the society encompassed a large range of teachers (including clerics, martial artists, doctors, and lay leaders), religious institutions, and social networks. Practitioners, who as disciples contracted a relation with a master but not with a religious institution, were interested not in confessional identity but in the reliability and efficiency of the techniques. All of these specialists transmitted a technical knowledge from master to initiate; many used to organize in professional corporations, which tried throughout the twentieth century and with varying degrees of success to morph into national associations.

CELIBACY AND ANTICLERICALISM

Whereas almost all specialists and indeed members of religious groups have to follow certain standards, only Buddhist and Quanzhen Daoist clerics are bound by strict rules of separation. Their ordination ritual entails "leaving the family" (*chujia*), which actually means changing one's family: Once in the clergy, Buddhists and Daoists, celibate or not, become part of a lineage (*zongpai*) organized very much like secular lineages; temple property and other assets and rights are transmitted from master to disciple like family assets are transmitted from parent to child.

Celibacy is not the only rule; with it comes prohibitions on meat (and some other "impure" foodstuffs) and alcohol. Observance of these rules (no sex, no impure food) guaranteed the ritual purity of Buddhist and Quanzhen Daoist clerics and qualified them to live within temples without desecrating them (religious specialists not living permanently within temples are rarely celibate and are not usually strict vegetarians) and to perform certain rituals in which the performer has to come into contact with deities. The twentieth-century transformations of traditional ethics (and therefore notions of purity) explain why it has now become more acceptable and common for Buddhist and Daoist clerics to be married.

That celibate clerics leave their families has long been an element in anticlerical discourse against them, at the same time that it qualifies them to fulfill certain ritual roles. Moreover, in late imperial times, a deep anxiety about the dangers of celibate clerics' sexual predation on women informed a popular lore exemplified in countless novels and actual bans (poorly enforced) on women visiting temples. Celibacy, however, was not imposed on all Buddhist and Daoist clerics. It was strictly enforced in large monasteries, where the clerical elite maintained harsh discipline and where abbots executed wayward monks or nuns. In small temples, where most clerics lived, it was possible to have a secret (or not-so-secret) sexual life. And many Buddhist and Daoist clerics who made a living from providing ritual services (notably funerals) in the countryside were married, a fact known and accepted by all.

Polemics about clerical sexuality declined in importance after 1900, to be replaced in anticlerical discourse by the issue of formal knowledge. A major argument of the modern anticlerical literature is the predominance of the lower classes in the clergy, which would explain their supposedly low level of education. While it is true that many clerics were adopted very young (a practice now banned) from poor families or for reasons of poor health, some of them made the best of clerical training to become highly literate. The seminaries now run by the Buddhist and Daoist associations attempt to systematically raise the level of formal education to fight public prejudice, a move seen by some as detrimental to spiritual training and clerical identity.

COUNTING AND CONTROLLING THE CLERICS

The various types of religious specialists all represented large numbers of people. The Buddhists alone numbered between 500,000 and 1 million during the late Qing period; the Daoists certainly numbered well over 200,000. Their combined total was thus in the range of 2 to 5 clerics per 1,000 inhabitants. The Confucian clergy was largest, with a post-Taiping estimation of 1.5 million degree holders, plus 2 million registered students, and approximately 5 million classically educated people, although only a small minority lived as *lisheng*. As for nonclerical specialists such as spirit-mediums and diviners, who were outlawed by both the imperial and post-1911 regimes, their numbers are impossible to estimate, but must have been higher than those of clerics. Precise numbers, however, are very hard to come by because they are directly related to the level of control the state exerts on clerics.

The late imperial state had little idea of the numbers of clerics because it had indirect control over them. A campaign to register all Buddhists and Daoists was carried out from 1736 to 1739 (with 340,000 clerics counted), but the effort was not sustained, resulting within a couple of decades in useless lists of dead clerics. Two parallel clerical administrations, one for Buddhists and one for Daoists, were set up, but functioned mostly as a link between local officials and the local elite clerics who provided the officials with ritual services.

In the Republican period, the legal status of ordained Buddhist or Daoist clerics (*sengdao*) was abolished, and so were the clerical administrations. National religious associations tried to take over some of their functions. When these associations were given a formal role in managing temples and in negotiating with the state in the 1929 law on temples, and to an even greater degree in the mainland after 1949, the Buddhist and Daoist associations became powerful institutions that worked to defend clerics' interests and to register and control (reform) all clerics, meeting in the process with much resistance. Such resistance meant that throughout the twentieth century and into the twenty-first, many Buddhists and Daoists have evaded registration. Available figures for the early twenty-first century suggest the numbers of Buddhist and Daoist clerics may be back to the absolute levels of the 1920s—thus in a lower proportion relative to the whole population. Because in the People's Republic these clerics are now subjected to much greater state control than a century ago, the situation has paradoxically, to some extent, empowered other specialists, such as spirit-mediums, diviners, and lay leaders of devotional groups, who have all been playing a major role in the religious revival throughout China.

SEE ALSO *Religious Organizations; Religious Policy.*

BIBLIOGRAPHY

Bruun, Ole. *Fengshui in China: Geomantic Divination between State Orthodoxy and Popular Religion.* Copenhagen: NIAS Press, 2003.

Chau, Adam Yuet. *Miraculous Response: Doing Popular Religion in Contemporary China.* Stanford, CA: Stanford University Press, 2006.

Clart, Philip. Confucius and the Mediums: Is There a "Popular Confucianism"? *T'oung Pao* 89, 1–3 (2003): 1–38.

Goossaert, Vincent. Resident Specialists and Temple Managers in Late Imperial China. Spec. issue on Religious Specialists and Local Communities. *Min-su ch'ü-yi* 153 (2006): 25–68.

Welch, Holmes. *The Practice of Chinese Buddhism.* Cambridge, MA: Harvard University Press, 1967.

Welch, Holmes. *The Buddhist Revival in China.* Cambridge, MA: Harvard University Press, 1968.

Vincent Goossaert

REN XIONG
1823–1857

Ren Xiong (*zi* Weichang, *hao* Xiangpu) was a woodblock-print designer and painter. Ren Xiong is first among the group of nineteenth-century painters known as the "Four Rens," whose style has come to be identified with an emergent "modern" Shanghai aesthetic. The four include his son Ren Yu (1853–1901), his brother, the Suzhou-based painter Ren Xun (1835–1893), and Ren Yi (1840–1895). Despite his early death from tuberculosis, Ren Xiong's work, particularly as circulated in his prints, had a powerful legacy in the later Shanghai school.

Self Portrait *by Ren Xiong, c. mid-nineteenth century.*
*Remembered as an important member of the early Shanghai
School of Painting, Ren Xiong remains well known for his
interest in depicting unusual aspects of common subjects, forcing
audiences to see familiar objects in a new way.* **REN XIONG/**
FOTOE

painter and poet, and later, with the town's instructor.
Many years later, it was recounted by a fellow painter that
Ren Xiong studied portraiture. When he was young, however, he liked to play with images, so that his pictures never
stayed within norms. They would show someone missing a
limb or blind in one eye, with a cleft palate or any number
of peculiarities (Chen Dingshan 1969, pp. 114–115; Erickson 2007, p. 30, note 1). Such interest in the strange—in
figures who populate the shadowy heterotopic social spaces
of a nation thrown into chaos through war and rebellion—
found expression in Ren's oeuvre throughout his life.

The late Ming–early Qing artist Chen Hongshou
(1599–1652) figured prominently in Ren's early education. Chen was a local hero in the neighboring town of
Zhuji, his birthplace. Two collectors, Zhou Xian and
Ding Wenwei, provided Ren with the opportunity to
study and copy Chen's paintings firsthand. And, like
Chen, Ren Xiong explored the woodblock-print medium
through several sets of prints, starting with the *Liexian jiupai*
(Immortals wine cards, 1854), published at his own expense
for the celebration of the birth of his son. His interest in
woodblock prints later extended to pictures of knights
errant in the *Jianxia zhuan* (1856), past worthies of the
Zhejiang region in *Yuyue xianxian zhuan* (1856), and lofty
scholars and hermits in the *Gaoshi zhuan* (1857).

A shared interest in the strange connected the brush of
Ren to Chen, and beyond that, they shared a distinctive and
self-consciously idiosyncratic style in which even the mundane appears distorted, new, reimagined. Ren's appreciation
for decorative motifs appears to have a further source in the
prints of the Japanese artist Hokusai Katsushika (1760–
1849). One album in particular, commissioned by Yao
Xie (1805–1864) in 1851, contains among its 120 leaves
illustrating poems by the patron, a notable emphasis on
patterned repetition of line and form, and, in a few cases,
quotation of Hokusai's figural work.

Ren's monumental self-portrait represents the crisis
of identity the artist felt as the Qing state, and the culture
and society around him, experienced chaos, war, and
rebellion at midcentury. The painter depicts himself
frontally, his gently rendered torso and head emerging
from jagged lines of the outer robe, which he seems to be
sloughing off much as a cicada sheds its shell. In the
inscription, Ren Xiong poignantly asks, "Who is the
ignorant one? Who the virtuous sage? I already am completely without any idea. In the flash of a glance, all I can
see is boundless void" (trans. Vinograd 1992, p. 129).

SEE ALSO *Chinese Painting (guohua); Ren Yi (Ren Bonian);
Shanghai School of Painting.*

BIBLIOGRAPHY
Chen Dingshan. *Dingshan lunhua qi zhong* [Seven discussions of
painting]. Taibei: Shijie wenwu chubanshe, 1969.

Ren Xiong was a native of Xiaoshan, Zhejiang Province. As a youth, he began to practice painting in his hometown, possibly under the guidance of his father, an amateur

Chou Ju-hsi (Zhou Ruxi) and Claudia Brown. *Transcending Turmoil: Painting at the Close of China's Empire, 1796–1911.* Phoenix, AZ: Phoenix Art Museum, 1992.

Erickson, Britta. Patronage and Production in the Nineteenth-Century Shanghai Region: Ren Xiong (1823–1857) and His Sponsors. Ph.D. diss., Stanford University, 1996.

Erickson, Britta. Zhou Xian's Fabulous Construct: *The Thatched Cottage of Fan Lake.* In *Art at the Close of China's Empire,* ed. Chou Ju-hsi (Zhou Ruxi), 67–93. Tempe: Arizona State University, 1998.

Erickson, Britta. Uncommon Themes and Uncommon Subject Matters in Ren Xiong's *Album after Poems by Yao Xie.* In *Visual Culture in Shanghai, 1850s–1930s,* ed. Jason C. Kuo, 29–54. Washington, DC: New Academia, 2007.

Vinograd, Richard Ellis. *Boundaries of the Self: Chinese Portraits, 1600–1900.* New York and Cambridge, U.K.: Cambridge University Press, 1992.

Lisa Claypool

REN YI (REN BONIAN)
1840–1895

Ren Yi (initially named Run, also *zi* Bonian, *hao* Xiaolou, and Ciyuan) was one of the most brilliant painters of the nineteenth-century Shanghai school. Ren Bonian was a native of Shanyin (modern Shaoxing) in Zhejiang Province. His father, Ren Hesheng (*zi* Songyun), a small-businessman dealing in grain, moved the family from Shanyin to Xiaoshan. Ren Bonian's son, Ren Jinshu, wrote in an inscription that his grandfather also practiced traditional Chinese portraiture and taught Ren Bonian this professional skill. Around 1861, the Taiping Uprising (1851–1864) swept through Zhejiang Province, and Ren Bonian's father died during the conflict. It is said that Ren Bonian himself was forced to join the troops as a flag bearer, but he managed to flee from the Taiping troops and return to Xiaoshan in early 1862.

There is a famous anecdote recorded by the modern master Xu Beihong (1895–1953), who credits it to the Shanghai artist Wang Yiting (1867–1938), about how Ren Bonian, with his humble background, became one of the most influential artists in Shanghai. Although recent research has disproved its veracity, its wide circulation among artists who admired him attests to the accuracy of its portrayal of Ren Bonian's precocious technical brilliance. The story relates that after his father's death, Ren Bonian made a living on the streets in Shanghai by selling painted folding fans to which he had added forged signatures of the famous painter Ren Xiong (1823–1857) (to whom he was unrelated, despite sharing a surname). One day Ren Xiong came upon Ren Bonian peddling his wares and was so impressed by his clever forgeries that he asked about the artist. Only after

Ren Bonian proclaimed that they were done by his uncle did Ren Xiong reveal his identity. Despite this awkward encounter, Ren Xiong is said to have appreciated Ren Bonian's talent and even sent him to study painting with Ren Xun (1835–1893), Ren Xiong's younger brother. The reliability of this anecdote, however, is brought into question by the fact that Ren Xiong died in 1857. If Ren Bonian went to Shanghai after his father's death in 1862, then it would have been impossible for him to have met Ren Xiong at that time. Regardless of this chronological discrepancy, Ren Bonian did in fact closely associate himself with Ren Xun in painting style, particularly during his early career.

Ren Bonian sojourned in the Ningbo area between 1865 and 1868, then traveled to Suzhou with Ren Xun in 1868 before finally moving to Shanghai in the winter of that year. Ren Xun introduced many prominent artists and patrons to him, including Yao Xiaofu (son of Yao Xie [1805–1864]) during his Ningbo period and Hu Gongshou (1823–1886), Sha Fu (1831–1906), Jiang Shinong, and others during his Suzhou period. These connections helped Ren Bonian tremendously in his early career in Shanghai. In particular, Hu Gongshou, as the leader of the art world in Shanghai at that time, introduced many opportunities to Ren and helped him find employment and lodging in the Gushangshi (Scent of Antiquity) fan shop when he first moved to Shanghai. In appreciation, Ren called his studio Yihe Xuan (literally, Studio of Relying on the Crane), which evoked the name of Hu's studio, Jihe Xuan (Studio of the Visiting Crane).

To compensate for his humble background and lack of proper literary training, Ren Bonian took the flower-and-bird literati painter Zhang Xiong (1803–1886) as his teacher on the advice of Hu Gongshou. Ren also made connections by means of his portrait skills. From the late 1860s and throughout his career in Shanghai, Ren produced approximately fifty portraits of fellow artists, friends, and patrons. In fact, it was quite fashionable in late nineteenth-century Shanghai to use portraits as a way of self-promotion. People would invite prominent figures to inscribe poems or colophons on their portraits to show off their social network and would sometimes even publish the inscriptions in the newly established media of the time—the newspaper. By contributing portraits to this trend, Ren participated in the social network-building of the mainstream art world in Shanghai, and he became quite famous in the early 1870s.

Living in Shanghai, one of the most cosmopolitan cities in the world at the time, Ren Bonian absorbed and transformed many different international stimuli into his art, including Western painting techniques, photography, and even Japanese woodblock ukiyo-e prints. He was said to have learned Western pencil sketch techniques from his friend Liu Dezhai, who worked in the Roman Catholic establishment in the Xujiahui area of Shanghai. Ren's art in the 1870s gradually evolved from the stiffer and more rigid forms and brushwork inherited from the style of the seventeenth-century artist Chen Hongshou via Ren Xun and Ren Xiong, to become more energetic and fluent in expression during the 1880s. His mature works from the late 1870s show a liberation of brushwork. By using impressionistic and quick brushwork along with unexpected compositions, he delivered a dramatic sense of movement that fit perfectly with the pace and content of urban life in Shanghai during this era of change.

SEE ALSO *Chinese Painting (guohua); Ren Xiong; Shanghai School of Painting; Wang Zhen (Wang Yiting); Xu Beihong.*

BIBLIOGRAPHY

Ding Xiyuan. *Ren Bonian: Nianpu, lunwen, zhencun.* Shanghai: Shanghai Shuhua Chubanshe, 1989.

Lai Yu-chih. Remapping Borders: Ren Bonian's Frontier Paintings and Urban Life in 1880s Shanghai. *Art Bulletin* 86, 3 (2004): 550–572.

van der Meyden, Hans. The Life and Works of Ren Bonian (1840–1896). *Oriental Art* 38, 1 (1992): 27–40.

Xu Beihong. Ren Bonian pingzhuan [Critical biography of Ren Bonian]. In *Ren Bonian yanjiu* [Studies on Ren Bonian], ed. Gong Chanxing, 1. Tianjin: Tianjin Renmin Meishu Chubanshe, 1982.

Lai Yu-chih

RESEARCH IN ENGINEERING

China's rise as an economic power has paralleled its gain in engineering prowess. Engineering, or applied science and technology, is a broad discipline that includes mechanical engineering, civil engineering, electrical engineering, chemical engineering, electronic engineering, biomedical engineering, and, by extension, the profession of those working in these disciplines.

EDUCATION AND RESEARCH INSTITUTIONS

Over 1 million new engineering undergraduates, half with bachelor degrees, have graduated in China every year since 2005, more than in any other country. Important engineering research is also being conducted in China's educational institutions, research institutes, and enterprises. The Chinese Academy of Sciences encompasses a number of engineering institutes. These include the Institute of Engineering Thermophysics, engaged in research related to power engineering, and the Institute

of Process Engineering, focusing on the motion, transfer, and reaction of substances in physical, chemical, and biological conversion processes. In fact, the Institute of Engineering Thermophysics is an offshoot of another engineering-related establishment, the Institute of Mechanics, which contributed to the development of China's strategic-missile program. Other Chinese Academy of Sciences institutes, especially those in high technology, also do engineering-related research. In addition, during the 1950s many research-and-development institutes were established within industrial ministries, and some later became parts of larger enterprises or became enterprises themselves.

China's leading engineering universities include Tsinghua, Shanghai Jiaotong, Zhejiang, and Tongji. Many of them have expanded the scope of their teaching and research to become more science-oriented and comprehensive by offering courses and programs in the natural sciences, social sciences, and humanities. Nevertheless, certain engineering fields remain strong in these universities: Tsinghua and Tongji are well known for their architecture and civil engineering programs, Shanghai Jiaotong is strong in shipbuilding, and Zhejiang in optical engineering, and so on. There also are universities that focus on specific engineering specialties, such as aeronautics and astronautics, mining, chemical engineering, information engineering, and agricultural and forestry engineering.

As of 2008, China had established 141 "national engineering research centers" at educational institutions and research institutes, integrating modern engineering technology into the solutions for problems in agriculture, information and communications, manufacturing, medicine and health, resource exploration, energy, light industry and textiles, materials, construction, and the environment.

At the top of China's engineering hierarchy is the Chinese Academy of Engineering, which is not only an honor society but also the nation's highest consultancy in engineering and technology matters. Unlike the Chinese Academy of Sciences, the Chinese Academy of Engineering does not have affiliated research entities; instead, it comprises only honorary members (*yuanshi*), who are elected every two years from among the entire engineering community. These outstanding engineers help draw the road map for the nation's engineering strategy and solve engineering-related problems.

ENTERPRISE-LEVEL RESEARCH

Much of China's engineering research is being carried out at the firm level. Enterprises operating in China—state-owned, private, and foreign-invested—conduct engineering research to manufacture new products, to improve production processes and capabilities, and to assimilate imported technologies. Such multinational companies as Sun Microsystems and Google have set up engineering research labs in China, not only to adapt technology developed in their home countries to the needs of China, but also to carry out innovative engineering research. In competing with these multinational establishments, Chinese domestic firms also devote significant financial and human resources to engineering research. As a whole, enterprises in China now spend more than two-thirds of the nation's research-and-development expenditure, much of which is engineering and application oriented, compared with less than half in the 1990s.

Thanks to its enhanced engineering and technology capabilities, China has become competitive in certain industries, including high-tech industries. Huawei, a non-state-owned telecommunications equipment maker founded in 1988, is an example. The company's charter mandates that the company devote 10 percent of its sales revenue to research and development and innovation, and increase the expenditure if necessary. Forty percent of the company's employees are engaged in research and development and engineering work, and the company is also involved in exploratory and precompetitive research. Huawei now leads in invention patents among China's domestic high-tech firms, and its intelligence network won China's Scientific and Technological Progress Award in 2002, a rare but impressive achievement for an enterprise.

Chinese engineers are extremely valued because of their roles in the economy and society. Since about the late 1980s, architects and civil engineers have designed and built numerous highways, bridges, railroads, and buildings. The construction boom leading to the 2008 Beijing Olympics set the stage for advances in Chinese engineering: Architectural projects such as the National Stadium (known as the "bird's nest"), the National Aquatics Center (known as the "water cube") involved sophisticated research in engineering to achieve such bold and novel structures.

MEGA ENGINEERING PROGRAMS

In early 2006, China released its Medium- to Long-Term Plan for the Development of Science and Technology. One significant aspect of the plan is its selection of four mega science programs and sixteen mega engineering programs to receive massive investment from the government between 2006 and 2020. The engineering programs identified in the Medium- to Long-Term Plan include the following (the plan indicates that the number of engineering programs is sixteen, but identifies only thirteen of them, the other three presumably national defense related):

1. Core electronic components, high-end generic chips, and basic software

2. Large-scale integrated-circuit manufacturing and technology

3. New-generation broadband wireless mobile telecommunications

4. Advanced numeric-controlled machinery and basic manufacturing technology

5. Large-scale oil and gas exploration

6. Advanced nuclear reactors

7. Water pollution control and treatment

8. Genetically modified organisms and the breeding of new varieties

9. Pharmaceutical innovation and development

10. Control and treatment of AIDS, viral hepatitis, and other major diseases

11. Large aircraft

12. High-definition observation systems

13. Manned aerospace and lunar exploration

Together, these programs represent China's ambition to achieve supremacy in science and technology, to become an innovation-oriented nation by the end of the plan period, and to sustain economic growth with the help of science, technology, and innovation. Major engineering programs, in particular, aim to make China internationally competitive in such industries as semiconductors, software, pharmaceuticals, and transportation, and to help solve China's problems in agriculture, resources and energy, the environment, and public health. Several initiatives, including the three engineering programs not identified in the Medium- to Long-Term Plan, will have significant implications for China's national security. One of the identified engineering programs—lunar exploration—began long before the initiation of the Medium- to Long-Term Plan, as China's first *Chang'e 1* satellite is now orbiting the Moon. Another program—the development of large aircraft—has passed its initial preparation stage and an enterprise has been formed to begin work.

SEE ALSO *High Technology; Research in the Sciences.*

BIBLIOGRAPHY

General Office of the Chinese Academy of Sciences. Nian Zhongguo Kexueyuan nianjian [Yearbook of the Chinese Academy of Sciences]. Beijing: Chinese Academy of Sciences, 2007.

Qiu Junping et al., comp. Nian Zhongguo yanjiusheng jiaoyu pingjia baogao [An evaluation report of postgraduate education in China]. Beijing: Science Press, 2006.

Cong Cao

RESEARCH IN THE SCIENCES

Although British sinologist and historian of science Joseph Needham (1900–1995) dated the origin of Chinese science to as early as the first century BCE, science in its modern sense was not introduced into China until the turn of the twentieth century with the return of scientists trained in the West and Japan. Through the efforts of these pioneers and their successors, science has gradually become institutionalized in China, and Chinese scientists have increasingly built international reputations and made important achievements in the understanding of nature.

THE CHINESE ACADEMY OF SCIENCES

The Chinese Academy of Sciences (CAS), headquartered in Beijing, is China's most important scientific establishment. It was formally founded as a government agency on November 1, 1949, one month after the People's Republic was proclaimed. The CAS took over all the research institutes in Peiping (now Beijing), Nanjing, and Shanghai that had been operating under the jurisdiction of the Academia Sinica and the Peiping Academy, both established by the Nationalist government in the late 1920s, with the exceptions of the Academia Sinica's Institute of History and Language and Institute of Mathematics, which retreated to Taiwan in late 1948 and early 1949.

The CAS merged China's science institutions into a new academy and gradually became the center and driving force of scientific work for the entire nation. CAS scientists played an important role in developing scientific enterprises in China and especially in contributing to the country's strategic-weapons programs. However, during the decade of the Cultural Revolution (1966–1976), CAS research was halted and many scientists were persecuted and deprived of their rights to work and teach; some even lost their lives.

The CAS resumed full operations after Mao Zedong's death in 1976. In the mid-1980s, when China reformed its science-and-technology management system, the CAS restructured under the rubric of "one academy, two systems," and began concentrating most of its efforts on research that directly benefits the Chinese economy, while continuing to function as a basic research entity. The CAS also began to spin off enterprises with marketable technology and products; and now the academy continues to hold shares in some of these enterprises, including Lenovo, a computer manufacturer that in late 2004 acquired IBM's personal computer business.

Into the 1990s, as the worldwide knowledge-based economy gained a foothold in China, the CAS faced the challenge of positioning itself in China's science-and-technology system. With "revitalizing the nation through science, technology, and education" becoming a new development strategy, the academy's leadership believed that the CAS could transform into a national knowledge-innovation center in the natural sciences, becoming a base for world-class state-of-the-art research fostering first-rate talent and promoting the development of high-tech industries. The resulting Knowledge Innovation Program, introduced in 1998, was a program that aimed to remake the academy in phases by 2010.

Among the goals of the Knowledge Innovation Program was gaining worldwide recognition and renown for thirty CAS institutes, including three to five with first-class standing internationally. In order to achieve this goal, the CAS introduced a "culture of innovation" in the academy and a redefinition of disciplinary orientations and missions at individual institutes. The academy also imposed a sharp reduction of redundant staff, and revitalized the human-resource base by recruiting a new generation of talented scientific leaders from among Chinese scientists working abroad, as well as from among promising young researchers in China through the One Hundred Talent Program. The Knowledge Innovation Program helped reinvigorate the CAS with eighty-four research institutes and a research staff of 45,000 scattered throughout the country.

In the meantime, the CAS serves as an honor society through its Academic Divisions (*xuebu*)—Mathematics and Physics, Chemistry, Life Sciences and Medicine, Earth Sciences, Information Technology Sciences, and Technological Sciences. These divisions elect eminent scientists *yuanshi* (academician), or China's highest designation in science and technology, signifying great academic authority.

OTHER PLAYERS

In addition to the CAS, China's basic science system includes government-supported research academies engaged in research-and-development activities related to such public interests as health, agriculture, and the environment. Most institutes focusing on applied research and development have become enterprises or been merged into enterprises.

Since the late 1970s, the research role of Chinese universities, especially "key" (*zhongdian*) institutions, has expanded dramatically, absorbing much work that had been left to the CAS in the 1950s, following the Soviet model. Their role has been further boosted with the implementation of the 211 Program, launched in 1993, to position approximately one hundred of China's universities as distinguished world-class academic institutions by the early twenty-first century, as well as the

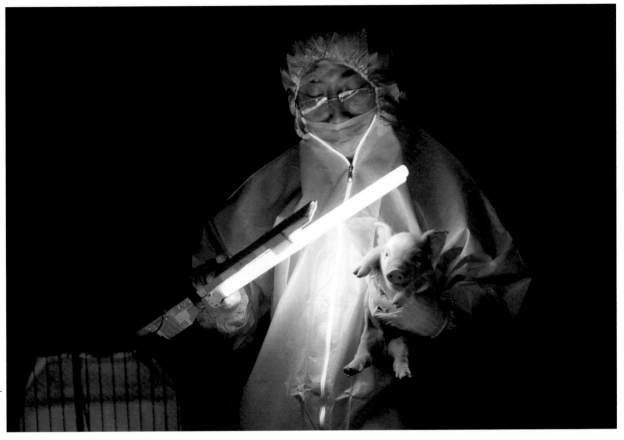

Researcher holding a piglet born to a genetically engineered mother, Harbin, China, January 11, 2008. *After the Cultural Revolution, during which many scientists suffered imprisonment or worse, China began investing heavily in science and technology, in hopes of strengthening the economy. In the area of genetic engineering, China has become a world leader, developing new applications for their cutting-edge research.* FREDERIC J. BROWN/AFP/GETTY IMAGES

985 Program, launched in May 1998, to reaffirm this effort. Beijing, Tsinghua (Qinghua), Zhejiang, Nanjing, Fudan, and Shanghai Jiaotong universities, the University of Science and Technology of China, Xi'an Jiaotong University, and the Harbin Institute of Technology have been selected as "keys" among the keys, or as potential world-class universities.

THE 973 AND MEGA-SCIENCE PROGRAMS

In the mid-1990s, China's scientific leadership argued that one of the consequences of the science-and-technology management-system reform, started in 1985, had been a change in orientation toward applications, causing scientists to ignore basic research. Many felt that China should make a greater commitment to basic research. Both the scientific and political leadership were also beginning to think that China should be operating in the top tiers of international science, that national prestige could be increased through significant scientific achievements, and

that the time had come for Chinese scientists, working in China, to be considered for Nobel Prizes.

Furthermore, elite scientists in the National People's Congress (NPC) and the Chinese People's Political Consultative Conference (CPPCC) lobbied for increases in the state's expenditure on research and development. This effort became strongest in March 1997 when the NPC and CPPCC held their annual session. The 973 Program, referring to its initiation in March 1997, originally called for the channeling of some 2.5 billion renminbi ($300 million), allocated over five years (1998–2002) through the Ministry of Science and Technology, to support projects falling within six broad areas relevant to the nation's economic and social development—population and health, information, agriculture, resources and the environment, energy, and new materials—at an average level of 30 million renminbi ($3.6 million) per project. The 973 Program was later extended.

Projects have to meet one of three criteria: (1) a project must solve major basic research problems with implications in China's social, economic, scientific, and technological development and have interdisciplinary and comprehensive significance; (2) a project must take advantage of China's special characteristics, especially its natural, geographic, and human resources; and (3) a project must help China occupy "an important seat" (*yixi zhidi*) in international research.

For each project, the Ministry of Science and Technology appoints one or two chief scientists who have the authority to decide the direction of the project and the addition of subprojects and the responsibility for administering budgets and personnel by working with a committee of experts. An approved project will receive stable funding for five years, with the addition of new researchers, new ideas, and new subprojects factored in. But continuous funding to a subproject for a further three years is not guaranteed and depends on a performance evaluation at the end of the second year (so-called 2+3 project management).

China set the ambitious goal of becoming an innovation-oriented nation by 2020, according to its Medium- to Long-term Plan for the Development of Science and Technology (2006–2020). China's leadership intended that the country would become a center of original research and indigenous innovations, thus lessening its dependence on foreign technology. Four basic science areas—development and reproductive biology, nanotechnology, protein science, and quantum research—were included in the plan's "mega-science" program and will receive substantial support.

CHINA'S STRENGTH IN THE SCIENCES

Although China lags behind the world's leaders in most areas of science, it has clearly shown with its nuclear and space programs its ability to mobilize the human and material resources necessary for sophisticated technological achievements. Chinese physicists, mathematicians, chemists, and life scientists have produced a number of remarkable accomplishments.

For example, Chinese life scientists successfully synthesized bovine insulin between 1958 and 1965; because they were the first to do so, some believe that this accomplishment could lead to China's first Nobel Prize in the sciences. Chinese life scientists enhanced their reputation when they joined counterparts in the United States, Germany, the United Kingdom, France, and Japan in an international effort to sequence the human genome at the turn of the twenty-first century. China is also a leader in the research and commercialization of genetically modified organisms. Also of note is China's research on nanotechnology. China is second only to the United States in papers published on nanotechnology, and nanoscale technologies have been incorporated into Chinese commercial products.

Since the late 1990s, China has made extensive investments in infrastructure related to science and technology, and many major science facilities are being constructed in China. These facilities may lay a foundation for international cooperation in science, and have the potential to produce first-rate achievements. For example, the Beijing Electron Positron Collider is acknowledged by the international community of high-energy physicists as having produced the most important experimental results in particle physics within this energy range. The collider is also serving as a stepping-stone for China's international collaboration in high-energy physics research.

Measured by the number of papers included in the *Science Citation Index* (*SCI*), a bibliometric database published by Thompson Reuters, China in 2006 ranked fifth in the world. With Chinese science moving toward the international frontiers of research, more and more foreign scientists have sought collaborative opportunities with their Chinese colleagues. Between 1996 and 2005, China's international collaborated papers doubled every 3.81 years, slightly faster than the total number of *SCI* papers authored by Chinese scientists, which doubled every 3.97 years. China's leading collaborators between 2001 and 2005, measured by the number of coauthored *SCI* papers, include the United States, Japan, Germany, the United Kingdom, Australia, Canada, France, and South Korea, all technologically advanced countries.

SEE ALSO *Academia Sinica (Zhongyang Yanjiuyuan); High Technology; Research in Engineering; Science and Technology Policy; Scientific Community; Scientific Exchanges.*

BIBLIOGRAPHY

Cong Cao. *China's Scientific Elite*. London and New York: RoutledgeCurzon, 2004.

Cong Cao, Richard P. Suttmeier, and Denis Fred Simon. China's 15-Year Science and Technology Plan. *Physics Today* 59, 12 (2006): 38–43.

Suttmeier, Richard P. *Research and Revolution: Science Policy and Societal Change in China*. Lexington, MA: Lexington Books, 1980.

Suttmeier, Richard P., Cong Cao, and Denis Fred Simon. "Knowledge Innovation" and the Chinese Academy of Sciences. *Science* 312 (2006): 58–59.

Cong Cao

RESEARCH ORGANIZATIONS

China has a comprehensive research network in the fields of the natural and social sciences. Of the approximately 2,000 organizations categorized as research organizations, the Chinese Academy of Sciences (CAS, Zhongguo Kexueyuan), which reports to the State Council, stands out as the best known. The CAS succeeded the Academia Sinica (Zhongyang Yanjiuyuan)—with the exception of the Institute of History and Philology (Lishi Yuyan Yanjiusuo) and part of the Institute of Mathematics, which fled to Taiwan—and the Peiping Academy (Guoli Beiping Yanjiuyuan) after the Communists took control of China in 1949. (Both the Academia Sinica and the Peiping Academy had been established during the Nationalist era, and the Academia Sinica still exists in Taiwan.) Since then, the CAS has evolved into a powerhouse of research in the natural sciences and high-technology. Headquartered in the nation's capital, the CAS has branches in Beijing, Shenyang, Changchun, Shanghai, Nanjing, Wuhan, Guangzhou, Chengdu, Kunming, Xi'an, Lanzhou, and Xinjiang, as well as some ninety affiliated research institutes.

There was a Division of Philosophy and Social Sciences within the CAS when the academy was founded, but because philosophy and social sciences were regarded as "politically incorrect," in 1957 research in these disciplines was suppressed or at least discouraged. Many social scientists had to work in jobs unrelated to their training, were criticized and sent to labor camps, or even lost their lives during various political campaigns, especially the Cultural Revolution (1966–1969). After the Cultural Revolution social science was revived, though there still are restrictions on what topics can be investigated. In 1977 the Division of Philosophy and Social Sciences was separated from the CAS to become the independent Chinese Academy of Social Sciences (CASS, Zhongguo Shehui Kexueyuan). Located in Beijing, it covers all the fields of social sciences and humanities as well as area studies.

In addition to carrying out research in their respective academic disciplines, the CAS and the CASS serve as China's "brain banks," advising government bodies at various levels on policy issues.

GOVERNMENT RESEARCH ESTABLISHMENTS

Various government-affiliated research establishments have been formed in response to the call for a more democratic and scientific policy-making process. In addition to its Research Office (Guowuyuan Yanjiushi), the State Council has an independent research organ, the Development Research Center (DRC, Guowuyuan Fazhan Yanzhou Zhongxin). Founded in 1981, the DRC is China's leading policy-oriented research and consulting institution because of its hierarchy and its access to the central government. Its most important function is the study of comprehensive and strategic issues confronting the nation and the organization of the nation's medium- and long-term economic and social development and regional development planning. It is particularly strong

in research of macroeconomic policy, development strategy and regional economic policy, industrial policy, rural economy, innovation, foreign economic relations, social development, enterprise reform and development, finance as well as international economy. The Party School (Dangxiao) and the Policy Research Office of the Chinese Communist Party (CCP) Central Committee also shoulder significant advising and consulting functions; the latter is a direct affiliate of the CCP Central Committee, just like its counterpart at the State Council. Within the People's Liberation Army, the Chinese Academy of Military Sciences (Zhongguo Junshi Kexue Yanjiuyuan) and the National Defense University (Guofang Daxue) are engaged in research on military modernization affairs.

Each government ministry and provincial government also has its own policy research office or similar organization responsible for investigating situations in its jurisdiction and providing policy recommendations. Some of the research institutions have become profit-driven and even listed companies. For example, CCID Consulting (Saidi Zixun), part of the China Center for Information Industry Development (Zhongguo Dianzi Xinxi Chanye Fazhan Yanjiuyuan), the research arm of the Ministry of Electronic Industry and later the Ministry of Information Industry (both predecessors of the Ministry of Industry and Information Technology), is the first Chinese consultancy listed on the Growth Enterprise Market (GEM) of the Hong Kong Stock Exchange. Leveraging its access to government and market information, CCID Consulting provides advice on policy, industry competitiveness, development strategy and planning, market research and entry strategy, and human resources management to industries as well as government.

Chinese universities are another driving force behind China's booming social science and policy research. One such example is the China Center for Economic Research (Zhongguo Jingji Yanjiu Zhongxin) at Peking University, founded by Lin Yifu (Justin Lin) in 1994, which integrates research with teaching and executive training. The Center for China Studies (Gongqing Yanjiu Zhongxin), a joint establishment of Tsinghua University and the Chinese Academy of Sciences, has produced research with significant implications in China's public policy formation.

NONGOVERNMENTAL AND SEMIGOVERNMENTAL THINK TANKS

After reform, a more open China saw the flourishing of quasi-governmental and nongovernmental think tanks. Among the most famous are the Chinese Institute of Politics and Public Administration (Zhongguo Zhengzhi yu Xingzhengkexue Yanjiusuo) and its successor, the Beijing Social and Economic Research Institute (Beijing Shehui Jingji Kexue Yanjiusuo), both now defunct. In the 1980s the institute was active in promoting political reform and a more pluralist society in China; it used *Jingjixue Zhoubao* (Economics Weekly), an institution journal, as the channel to disseminate research on the social consequences of China's economic reforms. This independent and liberal institute was shut down in the aftermath of the 1989 prodemocracy movement because its founders, Chen Ziming (b. 1952) and Wang Juntao (b. 1958), were accused of being the "black hands" behind the movement.

For several years after that, nongovernmental think tanks faded into the background if not disappeared. The further reform and opening of China advocated by Deng Xiaoping during his 1992 tour of South China accelerated the revival of such establishments. Now famous nongovernmental think tanks include China Development Institute (Shenzhen) (Zonghe Kaifa Yanjiuyuan [Shenzhen]), the China Institute of Reform and Development (Hainan) (Zhongguo Gaige Fazhan Yanjiuyuan [Hainan]), and the China Institute of Strategy and Management (Zhongguo Zhanlue yu Guanli Yanjiuhui Zhongguo).

The Unirule Institute of Economics (Tianze Jingji Yanjiusuo) is a well-known private nonprofit research institution. Founded in 1993 by five economists and the Beijing Universal Culture Corporation (Beijing Daxiang Wenhua Youxiangongsi), Unirule has directed its efforts to developing economic theories and finding solutions to China's economic and social problems. It also has a separate consulting arm to support its academic activities.

Although revenue at these nongovernment research organizations comes mainly from donations and provisional grants on a project basis from domestic and international organizations, their academics have formal appointments at leading universities, research institutes, and government. Moreover, some of these think tanks have connections with government through formal government officials, or their services are contingent on the government's request. Therefore, it is debatable whether they are genuinely private or independent.

INTERNATIONAL CONNECTION

International organizations such as the World Bank, the International Monetary Fund, and the Asian Development Bank, as well as foreign governments, have collaborated with China's governmental and nongovernmental research organizations in social and economic sciences, supporting and utilizing their services. For example, Peking University's China Center for Economic Research has been supported by the Ford Foundation, among others. Over the years, the Development Research Center of the State Council has forged extensive contacts with foreign governments, academics, and business communities as well as interna-

tional organizations by undertaking research projects and organizing high-level international events such as the annual China Development Forum. The external exchanges and cooperation have helped Chinese researchers draw on useful international experiences to advance China's reform, development, and opening to the outside world, and have helped the outside world better understand China.

SEE ALSO *High Technology; Research in Engineering; Research in the Sciences; Scientific Community; Social Sciences.*

BIBLIOGRAPHY

Gu, Edward X. Plural Institutionalism and the Emergence of Intellectual Public Spaces in China: A Case Study of Four Intellectual Groups. In *China and Democracy: Reconsidering the Prospects for a Democratic China*, ed. Suisheng Zhao, 141–172. London and New York: Routledge, 2000.

Shambaugh, David. Training China's Political Elite: The Party School System. *China Quarterly* 196 (December 2008): 827–844.

Sleeboom, Margaret. *The Chinese Academy of Social Sciences (CASS): Shaping the Reforms, Academia and China (1977–2003)*. Leiden, Netherlands, and Boston: Brill Academic, 2007.

Cong Cao

REVOLUTION OF 1911

The revolutionary movement that overthrew the Qing dynasty had a gestation period marked by nationalism, anti-Manchu sentiments, and republican aspirations, but this entry concentrates on the specific series of events that led to the fall of the Qing government in 1912.

In November 1908 the Emperor Guangxu (1871–1908) and the powerful Empress Dowager Cixi (1835–1908) had died, and there was a lack of leadership in the Qing court. In 1909 provincial assemblies were established in many provinces, and yet the gentry elite who were elected to the assemblies—the constitutionalists—were disappointed by the Qing court's decision not to open the National Assembly until 1913. In 1910 the court's attempts at centralization led to confrontations with the provinces over the railway issue, when it decided to buy up a line in Sichuan in which the local gentry had invested heavily. More confrontations followed in May of the next year, when it announced the nationalization of all trunk lines. In that same month the Manchu nobility, then in ascendance, formed a Manchu-dominated royal cabinet to replace the Grand Council. The court also faced a deeply dissatisfied populace in central China, where heavy floods in 1910 and 1911 climaxed years of bad harvests, sparking rice riots and antigovernment protests. Indeed, those years saw severe economic hardships in much of the middle and lower Yangzi River region. At the same time, rumors were rife that the foreign powers were about to carve up China like a watermelon.

WUCHANG UPRISING

The conditions were ripe for fresh uprisings against the dynasty after a series of previous attempts had failed. In April 1911 a section of the Guangdong New Army based in Guangzhou, which had been infiltrated by revolutionary elements, launched what Sun Yat-sen called "the ninth revolutionary attempt." Although the mutiny failed, the revolutionary momentum was sustained. On the night of October 10 another mutiny broke out, this time in Wuchang. The previous night, an accidental bomb explosion had occurred in the revolutionary soldiers' underground headquarters in Hankou's Russian Concession. Qing authorities then raided the premises, made a few arrests, and found the membership registers of the revolutionary soldiers, who were left with no option but to take immediate action. The uprising that followed was led by a noncommissioned officer named Xiong Bingkun, of the Eighth Engineer Battalion of the Eighth Division of the New Army, backed by the Twenty-ninth Infantry Regiment of the same division, the Forty-first Infantry Regiment of the Twenty-first Mixed Brigade, and other units, involving an estimated 4,000 men. Loyalist troops fled Wuchang after encountering the mutineers. The next night, the troops stationed in Hanyang across the river also rose in revolt, followed by those in Hankou the next morning. By then the entire tri-city of Wuhan had fallen into revolutionary hands.

The mutineers needed the backing of a prestigious public figure. They first approached the president of the provincial assembly, Tang Hualong (1874–1918). When Tang declined, they turned to a brigade commander, Colonel Li Yuanhong (1864–1928), forcing him at gunpoint to be the military governor of Hubei. Li was a good choice—he was popular with his troops, well liked by the provincial assemblymen, and he spoke English. His support, reluctant as it seemed, was important as a symbol of law and order around which the provincial assembly, the local elite, and the local population could rally, thus giving the uprising a good chance of success. As it turned out, Hunan was the first to respond, on October 22, by establishing a military government, followed a week later by Shanxi in the north. By the end of 1911 eight other provinces in central and south China were under revolutionary control of one kind or another. In all of them, the new military governments were a coalition of military and gentry elites. Meanwhile, most of east China north of the Yangzi River remained under imperial control. The imperial capital and adjacent provinces were defended by the Imperial Guard and the northern divisions of the New Army under the command of Yuan Shikai, who was recalled from the "retirement" to which he had been banished the previous year. Sun Yat-sen, newly returned from the United States, assumed the provisional presidency of the new republic in Nanjing on January 1, 1912. Fighting between the republican forces and Yuan's led to negotiations that averted a drawn-out civil war, especially after forty-four senior commanders of the Beijing Army, at the end of January, sent a telegram to the royal cabinet urging the formation of a republic. On February 12, the court announced the abdication of the six-year-old emperor Puyi and ordered Yuan to organize a provisional republican government, thus bringing the history of imperial China to a close.

INTERPRETATIONS AND SIGNIFICANCE

The 1911 Revolution has been interpreted in a variety of ways. The orthodox Nationalist school maintained that it was the work of Sun Yat-sen and the Revolutionary Alliance. In contrast, Chinese Marxist historians have long viewed it as a bourgeois-democratic revolution that was antifeudal, antidynastic, and anti-imperialist, while acknowledging the political and numerical weaknesses of the bourgeoisie. Both interpretations ignore the contributions of the constitutionalists. More recently, some Western scholars have characterized 1911 as an "upper-class revolt," or a revolt of the gentry, against the Qing, stressing the role and contributions of the constitutionalists and provincial assemblymen who sought political reforms and an expansion of their political role and influence. The commercial bourgeoisie was too small to have been the leading force, and only supported the revolution when it occurred. There is a consensus that 1911 was not a peasant revolt, despite widespread popular discontent prior to the revolution; the peasants simply were not mobilized.

The "upper-class" revolt interpretation, however, ignores the role and contributions of the rebellious troops of the New Army, especially those stationed in central and south China. The success of the Wuchang uprising was not fortuitous. But then the revolutionary troops would not have succeeded without the support of the provincial assemblies that collaborated with them in a military-gentry coalition that was to become a feature of provincial administration during the better part of the Republican period. Other social groups, such as the secret societies and nationalistic students recently returned from Japan, also participated in the revolution. Moreover, there were cleavages within each social class. In the final analysis, it was a coalition of forces rather than a particular class that undermined Manchu authority and eventually overthrew it.

The events of 1911 represented the first phase of China in revolution (1900–1913), followed by the Nationalist and Communist revolutions in the ensuing decades. In this first phase, the significance of 1911 lay in the overthrow of the two millennia-old imperial system. As a political revolution, it succeeded in achieving its immediate goal, but failed to bring about political reforms that were necessary to make the republic work. Instead, it brought the military to power, both in Beijing and in the regions. And it fell short of a social revolution in that its protagonists had few ideas about how Chinese society should be changed to meet the needs of a modern nation-state.

SEE ALSO *Constitutionalism; Sun Yat-sen (Sun Yixian); Wars and the Military, 1800–1912; Yuan Shikai.*

BIBLIOGRAPHY

Esherick, Joseph W. *Reform and Revolution in China: The 1911 Revolution in Hunan and Hubei.* Berkeley: University of California Press, 1976.

Fung, Edmund S. K. (Feng Zhaoji). *The Military Dimension of the Chinese Revolution: The New Army and Its Role in the Revolution of 1911.* Vancouver: University of British Columbia Press, 1980.

Hsieh, Winston. *Chinese Historiography on the Revolution of 1911.* Stanford, CA: Hoover Institution Press, 1975.

Liew, K. S. (Liu Jixiang). *Struggle for Democracy: Sung Chiao-jen and the 1911 Revolution.* Berkeley: University of California Press, 1971.

McCord, Edward A. *The Power of the Gun: The Emergence of Modern Chinese Warlordism.* Berkeley: University of California Press, 1993.

Rhoads, Edward J. M. *China's Republican Revolution: The Case of Kwangtung, 1895–1913.* Cambridge, MA: Harvard University Press, 1975.

Scalapino, Robert A., and George T. Yu. *Modern China and Its Revolutionary Process: Recurrent Challenges to the Traditional Order, 1850–1920.* Berkeley: University of California Press, 1985.

Wright, Mary Clabaugh, ed. *China in Revolution: The First Phase, 1900–1913.* New Haven, CT: Yale University Press, 1968.

Edmund S. K. Fung (Feng Zhaoji)

RICHARD, TIMOTHY
1845–1919

Timothy Richard was a missionary of broad theological vision and an advocate of Chinese national reform who influenced efforts late in the Qing dynasty (1644–1912) to combat China's domestic and international crises. Born on October 10, 1845, in Carmarthenshire, Wales, he was inspired by the Second Evangelical Awakening to become a missionary in China, which he considered the "most civilized of the non-christian nations" (Richard 1916, p. 29). In 1870 the Baptist Missionary Society sent him to Shandong in northern China.

Richard departed from traditional evangelistic methods by seeking to adapt Christianity to Chinese culture. To this end, he dressed in a scholar's gown and wore an artificial queue to gain access to local leaders, praised Confucian morality, taught that Christ was revealed in Mahayana Buddhism, mixed biblical quotations with Buddhist texts, and baptized converts in local temples. He also promoted proselytism through Chinese catechists, fought plague with Western medicines, and planted self-supporting congregations.

Richard's concept of mission was further broadened by his involvement in North China's "Great Famine" (1876–1879), which claimed as many as 13 million lives. Echoing Social Gospel activists in the West, Richard insisted that Christianity take "cognizance of all in this world as well as the next, in a word, of man—*body* and *soul*" (Richard 1907, vol. 2, p. 57). He saw famine relief as a mission imperative. After supplementing government food aid by distributing 60,000 English pounds solicited through the international press, he began searching for ways to prevent future famines.

Believing that China's deepening crises resulted from a crippling population explosion, destructive mid-century rebellions, and Western intrusion through the unequal-treaty system, Richard advocated economic-development measures to secure the well-being of the rural masses. In lectures and publications during the 1880s, he proposed Western-style agricultural modernization; industrial development through mining, railroads, and hydroelectric power; expanded commerce and international trade; education to foster scientific research, innovation, and entrepreneurialism; integration of science and technology into the civil-service examinations; and dissemination of new knowledge through learned societies, libraries, and newspapers.

Richard's blueprint appealed to such advocates of self-strengthening as Li Hongzhang (1823–1901), Zuo Zongtang (1812–1885), and Zhang Zhidong (1837–1909), who often consulted Richard on ways to enrich the nation and strengthen the military. But Richard's concerns for the rural poor resonated even more with treaty-port reformers such as Wang Tao (1828–1897) and Zheng Guanying (1842–1923). They incorporated Richard's ideas into their own recommendations to strengthen dynastic rule and enhance rural livelihood through the adoption of Western learning and political institutions, legal reform, a modern press, and a fair share for China in foreign commerce.

In September 1891 Richard became secretary of the Shanghai-based Society for the Diffusion of Christian and General Knowledge among the Chinese in the hope of stimulating reform thinking within China's intellectual community. Following Japan's upset victory in the first Sino-Japanese War (1894–1895), Richard focused the society's 250 publications (100 of which he authored, edited, or translated) on advocating change along the lines of Meiji Japan (1868–1912) and Peter the Great (r. 1682–1725) in Russia.

The reform leader Kang Youwei (1858–1927) incorporated Richard's ideas into his memorials to the Guangxu emperor (r. 1875–1908) urging institutional transformation. During the Hundred Days of Reform (Bairi Weixin; June 11–September 20, 1898), the emperor, who invited Richard to become his adviser, issued decrees mandating industrial and commercial development, Western-style schools, civil-service examination topics on practical subjects, public education through newspapers, and a constitutional monarchy.

After the Empress Dowager Cixi's (1835–1908) coup d'état aborted this effort, Richard became increasingly concerned that Manchu conservatism was making China vulnerable to further rebellion and international encroachment. In 1896 he advocated the creation of a League of Nations, in which the foreign powers would abandon their "scramble for concessions" in China, return tariff autonomy to the Qing government, and fund universal education in the country.

In 1900 Richard persuaded Britain to use its portion of the Boxer Indemnity to establish Shanxi University, which he hoped would become a beacon of modern higher education. In 1903 the Qing court ennobled Richard's ancestors for three generations. Two years later, the throne abolished the civil-service examination system, created Western-style schools (for which the Society for the Diffusion of Christian and General Knowledge among the Chinese was engaged to produce the textbooks), and took steps toward constitutional government.

In 1906 Richard attended the Lucerne Peace Conference to urge creation of a world peace federation and subsequently discussed the idea with President Theodore Roosevelt (1858–1919). Five years after Sun Yat-sen (1866–1925) led the overthrow of dynastic rule in China, Richard retired to London. At the time of his death on April 17, 1919, he was drafting a plan for a League of Religions to secure world peace and guarantee China's sovereignty.

China's May Fourth movement erupted two weeks after Richard's death and led China far beyond Richard's vision of gradual change. Richard's accommodationist approach to evangelism had earlier put him at odds with mainstream mission principles. Yet by the 1920s, half of the Protestant missionaries in China were involved in the kind of relief, medical, social, and educational work that Richard had pioneered.

SEE ALSO *Missionaries.*

BIBLIOGRAPHY
Bohr, P. Richard. *Famine in China and the Missionary: Timothy Richard as Relief Administrator and Advocate of National Reform, 1876–1884.* Cambridge, MA: East Asian Research Center, Harvard University, 1972.
Bohr, P. Richard. The Legacy of Timothy Richard. *International Bulletin of Missionary Research* 24, 2 (April 2000): 75–80.
Richard, Timothy. *Conversion by the Million in China: Being Biographies and Articles by Timothy Richard.* 2 vols. Shanghai: Literature Society, 1907.
Richard, Timothy. *Forty-five Years in China: Reminiscences.* New York: Frederick A. Stokes, 1916.
Wong Man-kong. Timothy Richard and the Chinese Reform Movement. *Fides et Historia* 31, 2 (Summer–Fall 1999): 47–59.

P. Richard Bohr

RIGHTS DEFENSE MOVEMENT

The Rights Defense movement (*weiquan yundong*) is not a structured organization, but rather a loose grouping of actors who have chosen a specific form of action. Its objective is to enforce the rights of citizens as guaranteed by the constitution of the People's Republic of China (PRC) and to redress violations. The expression *weiquan yundong* is usually translated as "Rights Defense movement," which is its literal meaning. However, because the goal of the movement is to enforce civil rights for all Chinese citizens, and many of its aspects recall the American civil rights movement, it is often referred to in English as the "Civil Rights Defense movement." The movement was made possible by the acknowledgement by the leadership of the party of the concept of human rights, which, until then, had been considered a bourgeois concept alien to socialism with Chinese characteristics. As is often the case in the PRC, the acknowledgement emerged during a period of leadership change. At the Sixteenth Party Congress in November 2002, Jiang Zemin ceded the secretariat general of the party to Hu Jintao, and in March 2003, Zhu Rongji left his position as premier to Wen Jiabao. Hu and Wen stated their commitment to the "rule of law," and in 2004 the protection of human rights was included in the constitution.

Chinese lawyers and legal scholars who supported aggrieved citizens decided to take the new leaders at their word (*jiaxi zhenchang*), as happens often in authoritarian regimes, and to denounce violations of human rights publicly. The Sun Zhigang case in 2003 symbolized the advent of the Civil Rights Defense movement in the public sphere. Sun Zhigang was a Hubei-born designer working in Guangzhou. He was taken to a custody and repatriation center because he could not show that he had a provisional residence booklet (*hukou*). During his detention, he was beaten to death, and his death sparked an uproar. This event triggered the first case of the Civil Rights Defense movement, which is characterized by the following aspects.

THE ROLE OF THE MEDIA

The death of Sun Zhigang was first reported in *Nanfang dushi bao* (Southern metropolis), whose reporter went to investigate the case by himself and showed that Sun's detention was illegal and violated the rules governing the functioning of custody and repatriation centers. The report referred to specific articles of the law to justify its denunciation of the authorities' behavior. The article was then republished by another newspaper. The Guangdong Party Committee ordered the media not to cover that story. Journalists obeyed, but it was already too late.

A great number of furious comments appeared on the Internet, and they did not cease with the party's reaction. The Sun Zhigang case had become a national *cause célèbre*. It provoked a string of discussions on the equal rights of migrants and residents, prompting some migrant workers to declare: "We are all Chinese, and some Chinese have beaten another Chinese to death."

THE ROLE OF THE LEGAL COMMUNITY

Legal scholars then seized on this case and three of them sent a letter to the National People's Congress asking for the abolition of the centers. Their reaction was based on a law (*lifa fa*) passed in 2000 that allowed citizens to propose the abolition of laws and regulations that they deemed unconstitutional. The legal scholars' objective was actually to use the constitution as an effective guarantee of citizens' rights.

On June 18, 2003, to the utter surprise of the signatories, Prime Minister Wen Jiabao announced the abolition of the detention and repatriation centers. Later, the agents who had beaten Sun to death were sentenced to heavy jail terms, with two receiving the death penalty (Jakes 2003). This was viewed as the first victory of public opinion since 1989: By challenging the legality of a well-established institution, legal scholars, helped by journalists who had denounced the scandal and supported by public opinion on the Internet, had succeeded in moving the government to make the decision for which they were asking. After that episode, many legal scholars, lawyers, and citizens alike were convinced that the law could be used to defend the rights of ordinary Chinese. This was the birth of the Rights Defense movement.

Then, many victims of abuse—villagers insufficiently compensated after land expropriation, peasants victimized by corrupt party secretaries, urban residents expelled from their homes to give way to developers—

began denouncing cadres' behavior by referring to their rights as guaranteed by the constitution. With the help of journalists and ordinary netizens, a network of lawyers and legal scholars specializing in rights defense emerged and is now considered as a tool to challenge abusive cadres. This network is informal, but it covers the entire country. It is different from the organizations that intellectuals created in the 1980s (see Béja 2004), but thanks to the Internet and new modes of communication (text-messaging, e-mail, etc.), the network can be relatively easily mobilized by people who fall victim to official bullies.

One notable characteristic of the *weiquan* network is that it cuts across social classes, allowing for collaboration between intellectuals (such as lawyers, journalists, and academics) and workers and peasants. In this, it differs from traditional forms of dissent and opposition in the PRC. Whereas during the 1980s, criticism of the party came mostly from intellectuals and students who had extensive contact with factions inside the apparatus and were pushing for the reform of the political system, the Civil Rights Defense movement originates in ordinary citizens who do not question the party political line or the nature of the regime, but openly and decidedly posit themselves within the system and try to solve concrete problems through official channels. Their demands are very different from those of their predecessors. For example, they do not ask for "freedom and democracy," nor do they denounce corruption in general. This new attitude is certainly a result of the repression of the 1989 prodemocracy movement.

Many of the scholars and journalists who constitute the bulk of the activists of the *weiquan yundong* were very young during the 1989 prodemocracy movement, but it impressed them strongly. In private, many of them acknowledge their debt to the students, but they also emphasize their differences. Xu Zhiyong, one of the legal scholars who appears as an important actor of the Rights Defense movement explains it clearly: "I have respect for those who raised human rights issues in the past," he said. "But now we hope to work in a constructive way within the space afforded by the legal system. Concrete but gradual change—I think that's what most Chinese people want" (quoted in Eckholm 2003).

In the early days of the *weiquan* movement, the authorities encouraged victims of abuse to seek redress in courts, rather than use traditional channels such as the *xinfang ju*, the network of official offices for complaints open to citizens. The authorities thought that this was a positive development that demonstrated the people's trust in the regime. In the early 2000s, the term *weiquan* was actually used in official language. It seemed that party leaders understood that civil rights activists did not challenge the legitimacy of the state but, on the contrary, took the state at its word and demanded that, in order to reinforce its legitimacy, the new team emphasize enforcement of the law.

GOVERNMENT CRACKDOWN

These hopes were soon disappointed. From 2005 onward, the party has taken numerous measures to curb the Civil Rights Defense movement by cracking down on its main actors. Luo Gan, then in charge of security and justice in the Politburo, declared that the movement harbored forces dedicated to overthrowing party rule (*International Herald Tribune* 2007). Afterward, courts acting in accordance with local governments condemned legal activists and lawyers who had played an important role in prominent *weiquan* cases, such as those of Chen Guangcheng, who protested forced abortions in Linyi, Shandong; Zheng Enchong, condemned in Shanghai for having assisted evicted residents; and Guo Feixiong, active in Taishi, Guangdong, who was sentenced to prison (see Human Rights Watch 2006).

In 2006 the National People's Congress passed a law providing for "New Guidelines on Lawyers," which restricted even further their independence and their ability to defend victims of abuses. The new guidelines explicitly state that "lawyers who handle mass cases should accept supervision and guidance by judicial administration departments" (Human Rights Watch 2006). Because lawyers must renew their licenses every year, it is easy to prevent those specializing in the defense of civil rights from continuing to practice. This is what happened to Gao Zhisheng in December 2005, to Li Jianqiang in Shandong in July 2007, and to Teng Biao in 2008 (see Chinese Human Rights Defenders).

In a continuing crackdown on the movement, many journalists have been either arrested or silenced, editorial boards have been restructured, netizens have been arrested and sentenced to jail terms, and books have been banned (see Béja 2007 and Chan 2007). The Rights Defense movement has then decreased in intensity, but it has continued to exist, even though it has adopted a low profile.

SEE ALSO *Household Registration; Internet; Migrant Workers; Prodemocracy Movement (1989); Rural Development since 1978: Three Rural Issues.*

BIBLIOGRAPHY

Béja, Jean-Philippe. *A la recherche d'une ombre chinoise: Le mouvement pour la démocratie en Chine, 1919–2004* [In search of a shadow: The movement for democracy in China, 1919–2004]. Paris: Seuil, 2004.

Béja, Jean-Philippe. La vie difficile des censeurs [The censors' hard life]. *Esprit* 336 (2007): 67–74.

Chan, Elaine. Pressing Issues. *South China Morning Post,* September 6, 2007.

Chen, Terrence. *Weiquan*, the Chinese People Rise Up to Defend Their Rights. *Chinascope* (October 2005). http://chinascope.org/main/content/view/396/130/.

Chinese Human Rights Defenders (CHRD): Human Rights News. http://crd-net.org/Article/Class9/Class10/Index.html

Eckholm, Erik. Petitioners Urge China to Enforce Legal Rights. *New York Times,* June 2, 2003.

Goldman, Merle. *From Comrade to Citizen: The Struggle for Political Rights in China.* Cambridge, MA: Harvard University Press, 2005.

Heuser, Robert. The Role of the Courts in Settling Disputes between the Society and the Government in China. *China Perspectives* 49 (2003). http://chinaperspectives.revues.org/document646.html.

Human Rights Watch. *"A Great Danger for Lawyers": New Regulatory Curbs on Lawyers Representing Protesters.* December 11, 2006. http://www.hrw.org/en/reports/2006/12/11/great-danger-lawyers.

International Herald Tribune. Chinese Official Urges Local Handling of Unrest. January 8, 2007.

Jakes, Susan. Hostages of the State. *Time Asia,* June 23, 2003.

Weiquan Online: An HRIC Backgrounder. *China Rights Forum* 3 (2006): 17–20.

Jean-Philippe Béja

RIVER SYSTEMS

This entry contains the following:

OVERVIEW

The rivers in China vary greatly in size and compose river systems of considerable variety. There are exterior drainage rivers flowing into the ocean and interior drainage rivers completely absorbed by the land in the inlands. About 50,000 rivers have drainage areas greater than 100 square kilometers (38.6 square miles), and about 1,500 rivers have drainage areas greater than 1,000 square kilometers (386 square miles) (Tang and Xiong). The Yangzi (Chang) River and the Yellow (Huang) River are the two longest rivers in continental China and are the third- and fifth-longest rivers in the world. The lengths of their main courses are 6,397 kilometers (3,975 miles) and 5,464 kilometers (3,995 miles), respectively.

Topographically, China's terrain descends in four steps from west to east. The top of this four-step staircase is the Qinghai-Tibet Plateau, averaging more than 4,000 meters (13,123 feet) above sea level. It is here that the major large rivers in China originate. Since China is climatically influenced by the monsoon, precipitation is concentrated mostly in summer and varies greatly from year to year. As a result, precipitation is unevenly distributed both temporally and spatially, and river runoff depth varies from zero in northwestern China to above hundreds of centimeters in southeastern and southwestern China.

The rivers of the nation are fed by various sources, including rainfall feeds throughout the country, snow and high-mountain glaciers feeds in northeastern and northwestern China, and abundant groundwater feeds found in the Karst regions of southwest China. All the large rivers originate from the Qinghai-Tibet Plateau and travel long distances, flowing through many provinces and regions. The Tarim River in the southern part of the Xinjiang Uygur Autonomous Region, one of the largest interior drainage rivers in the world, has a main-course length of 2,046 kilometers (1,271 miles) and a drainage area of 1 million square kilometers (400,000 square miles), including vast desert surroundings.

The Chinese government established the Ministry of Water Resources in 1950s, and the National People's Congress enacted the Water Law of the People's Republic of China in 1988 and revised it in 2002. It has also adopted laws for water development and water pollution.

Within the Ministry of Water Resources, the State Council set up the Office for Flood Prevention and Drought Control and also the State Flood Control and Drought Relief Headquarters. This latter department is in charge of organizing, coordinating, supervising, and directing nationwide flood control, carrying out flood control and drought prevention for major river basins and key water projects, monitoring for and warning of floods, and preparing basic information for dealing with emergencies.

The State Environment Protection Administration (the Ministry of Environmental Protection since March 2008), under the State Council, is in charge of monitoring and managing water quality, as well as making and enforcing policies for controlling water pollution. The Ministry of Land and Resources is in charge of monitoring and developing the nation's groundwater.

The river systems of the nation are integrally managed by river commissions under the Ministry of Water Resources. The commissions for the seven large drainage basins also coordinate the administration of adjacent smaller river systems so that all the river systems spread around the country are covered. In addition, the commissions play an integral role in river-basin development and governance, including water assessment, planning, protection, utilization, allocation, and management.

BIBLIOGRAPHY

Tang Qicheng, Xiong Yi, et al. *Zhongguo heliu shuiwen* [River hydrology in China]. Beijing: Kexue Chubanshe, 1998.

Changming Liu
Peng Liu

YANGZI RIVER

The Yangzi (Chang) River (between 90° 33′~112° 25′ E and 24° 30′~35° 45′ N) is the longest river in China and the third-longest river in the world. It originates from the glaciers of Geladandong in the Dangla (Tanggula) range on the Qinghai-Tibet Plateau. The river flows 6,300 kilometers through Southwest China, Central China, and East China to the East China Sea. The average annual runoff at its mouth amounts to 1,000 billion cubic meters and ranks third in the world after the Amazon and Congo rivers. The Yangzi flows through Qinghai, Tibet, Sichuan, Yunnan, Chongqing, Yunnan, Hubei, Hunan, Jiangxi, Anhui, Jiangsu, and Shanghai. Its drainage area of 1,820,000 square kilometers represents 19 percent of the total area of China. About 400 million people live in the Yangzi Basin, accounting for one-third of China's population. The Yangzi has more than 7,000 tributaries, with 8 tributaries whose watershed areas are more than 80,000 square kilometers—the Yalong, Min, Jialing, Wu, Xiang, Yuan, Han, and Gan rivers. The middle and lower reaches of the Yangzi River are dense with freshwater lakes, including Poyang (the largest freshwater lake in China), Dongting, Tai, and Chao.

CLIMATE

The Yangzi Basin lies in the East Asian monsoon zone. Other than its source region, which is located in the plateau cold zone of the Qinghai-Tibet Plateau, the basin has a subtropical monsoon climate. Most of the basin has an average temperature between 6 °C and 20 °C. However, the temporal variation of temperature in the basin is significant; it is hot and humid in the summer and dry and cold in the winter. The Yangzi Basin is rich in precipitation, with average annual precipitation of about 1,100 millimeters. Its average annual runoff is nearly 1,000 billion cubic meters, accounting for about 36 percent of China's total surface water runoff and twenty times that of the Yellow River.

DEVELOPMENT OF YANGZI RESOURCES

The Yangzi Basin is one of the cradles of Chinese civilization. The culture of the Yangzi River can be traced back 5,000 years by studying the ruins of the Sanxingdui sites and the ancient Shu culture. Waterway transportation on the Yangzi River may have started as early as the Neolithic period. During the Tang dynasty (618–907), transportation along the river underwent rapid development. The Yangzi River is now the most developed river transportation network in the country, with a total navigable length of more than 70,000 kilometers, accounting for 65 percent of the navigable river waters in China. The river thus facilitates trade between a large part of the country and the outside world. In addition, the Grand Canal, which had its beginnings in the Sui dynasty (581–618) and was extended many times subsequently, contributed greatly to the economic and cultural exchange between the Yangzi Delta and the North.

The development of irrigation using Yangzi waters has a long history. The Dujiangyan irrigation project, built before 256 BCE, is one of the world's oldest water projects and played a key role in flood control and irrigation on the Chengdu Plain. Since the beginning of the twenty-first century the irrigated areas of the Yangzi River Basin accounted for more than one-quarter of China's total irrigated land, and produced about one-third of the country's total grain output. In 2005, the Yangzi met the water demands of 0.44 billion people, accounting for more than 30 percent of China's population and 35.5 percent of China's gross domestic product.

The Yangzi River Basin is rich in water resources and is the source of China's South-North Water Transfer Project. This project includes three water-diversion routes: west, middle, and east. The west route transfers water from the Dadu, Yalong, and Tongtian rivers in the upper reaches of the Yangzi to the upper reaches of the Yellow River. The objective of the west route is to solve the water-shortage problem in Qinghai, Gansu, Ningxia, Inner Mongolia, Shaanxi, and Shanxi, and to mitigate drought and water shortage in northwestern China. The middle route transfers water from the Taocha sluice gate of the Danjiangkou Reservoir to the Tangbai River Basin, the upper and middle reaches of the Huai River, and the plain areas. The main objective of the project is to provide water for large and medium-sized cities along the route, and to meet the region's ecological and agricultural water demands. The east route will pump water from pumping stations near Yangzhou in Jiangsu Province, downstream of the Yangzi River to the eastern Huang-Huai-Hai Plain (the alluvial plain of the Yellow, Huai, and Hai rivers) and the Shandong Peninsula. The primary goal is to satisfy domestic and industrial water needs associated with developments in irrigation and ecology.

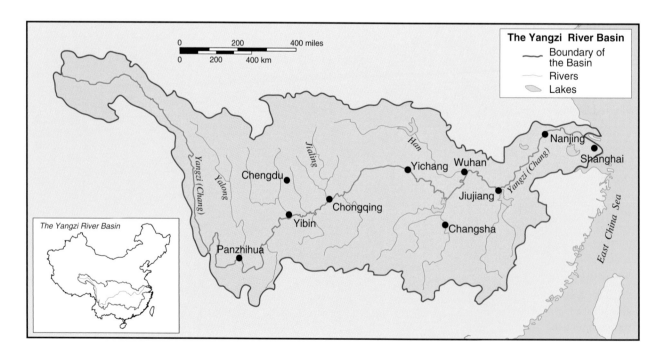

The Yangzi also has great hydropower potential, estimated at about 197,000 megawatts of installed capacity and one trillion kilowatt-hours of annual electricity supply. The Three Gorges Project, the largest hydropower project in the world, will be used for flood control, power generation, and navigation. The dam is 2,335 meters in length and 185 meters in height, and controls a drainage area of about one million square kilometers. The normal water-storage level of the reservoir is 175 meters and the total storage capacity is 39.3 billion cubic meters, more than half of which is used for flood control. The total installed capacity of the project is 18,200 megawatts, which consists of twenty-six hydropower units; the annual electricity generation is 84.7 billion kilowatt-hours.

Several other hydropower stations were under construction on the Yangzi River in 2008, including the Xiluodu Hydropower Station and the Xiangjiaba Hydropower Station. The Xiluodu station, the first large hydropower station on the Jinsha River, is due for commissioning by 2015. Its installed capacity is 12,600 megawatts, second only to the Three Gorges Project. The Xiangjiaba station is the last (in terms of location) large hydropower project on the Jinsha River, with a planned installed capacity of 6,000 megawatts. Construction began on the Xiangjiaba station in 2004, and it is scheduled for commissioning in 2015. These major hydropower projects will make tremendous contributions to flood control and economic development.

FLOODING

Although the Yangzi has nurtured China since the beginning of Chinese history, it has also been a frequent flood hazard. The rich precipitation throughout the basin has uneven temporal distribution, and mainly concentrates in the period from May to September. Some 210 floods were recorded during a span of about 2,000 years from the Han dynasty (206 BCE–220 CE) to the end of the Qing dynasty (1644–1912), and floods occur on average about once every ten years. Between 1860 and 1870, floods caused major damage to the affected basin areas. Since the People's Republic of China was founded in 1949, the Yangzi River experienced major floods in 1954, 1981, and 1998, causing great loss of property and lives. To mitigate the Yangzi flood problem, the Chinese government has strengthened levees, built flood-control reservoirs, restored wetlands that had been converted into farmland, and so forth.

ENVIRONMENTAL ISSUES

The baseline water quality of the Yangzi River is good, consistent with the abundance of its water resources, barring pollution. Due to rapid socioeconomic growth in the basin region, however, the water quality has worsened as a result of sewage. The amount of industrial wastewater discharged into the Yangzi has increased from fifteen billion tons a year in the 1980s to thirty billion tons in 2005. Monitoring indicates that wastewater discharge along the Yangzi accounts for one-third of the nation's total. As a result, about 30 percent of the river's water has deteriorated, creating stress on the water supply, which several major cities, including Shanghai, Nanjing, and Chongqing, rely on for drinking water. In addition, three large lakes in the basin—Dianchi, Chao, and Tai—have been experiencing "water blooms" of blue-green algae because of increasing nitrogen, phosphorus, and other nutrients being discharged into lakes.

Soil erosion along the upper reaches of the river has caused a serious sediment problem. Observation records indicate that about 400 million tons of sediment from the Yangzi flows into the sea each year. Although the power from the Three Gorges Dam will replace 50 million tons of coal annually, with an accompanying decrease of 100 million tons of carbon-dioxide emissions, the project will have adverse impacts on the environment. After the Three Gorges Reservoir reaches a level of 175 meters, the water flow will slow, and the dilution capacity will decrease significantly, leading to further water pollution in some segments of the river. The Three Gorges Project may result in changes to the ecosystem functions in the middle and lower reaches of the river, and the project may damage the living conditions of some rare and endangered species. In addition, the operation of the Three Gorges Reservoir will change the processes of erosion and sedimentation in the middle and lower reaches, causing soil incubation and swamps to develop in submerged regions upstream of the dam. Moreover, seawater intrusion may result in the formation of estuarial tides around the river delta.

Overall, the Yangzi River Basin is rich in resources and has a high population density, economic prosperity, and the highest level of urbanization in China. There are a number of important cities along the Yangzi River, including Chengdu, Chongqing, Wuhan, Nanjing, and Shanghai. The Yangzi Basin is also an important agricultural area. The Chengdu Plain, the Jianghan Plain, and the Dongting, Poyang, and Tai lake regions are major grain-producing areas in China. The Yangzi Basin is also an important industrial region of China: The Yangzi River Delta economic zone, for example, is located in an estuary of the Yangzi.

SEE ALSO *Grand Canal.*

BIBLIOGRAPHY
Chen Xiqing, Yixin Yan, Renshou Fu, et al. Sediment Transport from the Yangtze River, China, into the Sea over the Post–Three Gorge Dam Period: A Discussion. *Quaternary International* 86, 1 (2008): 55–64.

Liu Changming. China's South-North Water Transfer Project: To Solve the Water Shortage in North China on the Base of Efficient Use of Water. *Impact of Science on Society* 3 (2003):15–20.

Tang Qicheng. *China River Hydrology*. Beijing: Science Press, 1998.

Yangzi River Water Conservancy Committee. *Yangzi River Chronicle*. Beijing: Encyclopedia of China Press, 2007.

Changming Liu
Xiaomang Liu
Peng Liu

YELLOW RIVER

With a length of 5,464 kilometers and a drainage area of 795,000 square kilometers, the Yellow (Huang) River (between 96°–119° E and 32°–42° N) is China's second-largest river. It originates from the Qinghai-Tibet Plateau and travels through nine provinces and finally empties itself into Bohai Sea. As the mother river of China, the Yellow River has been seen as the cradle of Chinese civilization. Another description is "the sorrow of China," alluding to the frequency of its destructive floods on the country. Over the past 2,540 years, the Yellow River has spilled over its dikes 1,590 times and changed its course twenty-six times—that is, two dike breaches every three years and one course change every hundred years. The last shift of the river's main course from south to north was after a breach during a big flood in 1855 at Tongwaxiang, Henan province. At the beginning of the twenty-first century, about 150 million people rely on the Yellow River's water resources, and it serves as one of the main theaters for the ongoing national campaign to develop China's western hinterland.

PHYSICAL GEOGRAPHY

The bulk of the Yellow River basin is located in semi-humid and semiarid climatic zones. Its annual average precipitation is 447 millimeters, with evaporation of 388 millimeters. The temporal and spatial distribution of precipitation is very uneven, and about 70 percent of the precipitation comes from summer rainfall. In the Loess Plateau, along the middle reaches of the Yellow River, a one-day rainfall sometimes equals the average annual precipitation.

Hydrologically, the Yellow River's annual runoff depth is only 71 millimeters, accounting for just 16 percent of the precipitation. Moreover, the runoff varies greatly in time and space, is highly concentrated in the summer season, and fluctuates year to year. According to hydrological records from 1919 to 2006, the runoff in 1928 was only 25.7 billion cubic meters; runoff reached 97.3 billion cubic meters in 1964. There were, in particular, successive low-water years during the 1922–1932, 1969–1974, and 1991–2002 periods. The average natural annual runoff from 1956 to 2000 was 53.5 billion cubic meters, with the exploitable groundwater reaching 11.7 billion cubic meters. The largest flood discharge in the river's history was 33,000 cubic meters in the lower Yellow River in 1843. The river's annual average sediment load is 1.6 billion tons, according to records from 1919 to 1969.

EROSION AND SEDIMENTATION

The Loess Plateau, characterized by friable soil, a broken landscape, sparse vegetation, and torrential rain, is famous for its heavy soil erosion. The soil-erosion intensity in some parts of the Loess Plateau may reach 20,000 to 30,000 tons per year per square kilometers. Thus, after the Yellow River runs through the Loess Plateau, it harvests 1.6 billion tons of sediment, and its sediment concentration may reach 941 kilograms per cubic meter during the flood season. The river's annual average sediment concentration is 35 kilograms per cubic meter.

This huge quantity of sediment renders the lower Yellow River a suspended river with a stretching delta area. As of 2008, the riverbed in its lower reaches is generally three to five meters higher than the floodplain behind the levees—in some locations it is ten meters higher—making the Yellow River the most complicated and difficult to harness river in the world.

FLOOD CONTROL AND RIVER HARNESSING

The Yellow River's heavily silted flood waters and high-suspended riverbed produce the most difficult flooding situation in the world. Flood control in the lower Yellow River has been a major challenge for thousands of years, and many river experts have emerged throughout China's history, including the Great Yu (c. 2200 BCE), Jia Rang (c. 6 BCE), Wang Jing (69 CE), and Pan Jixun (sixteenth century).

Since 1949, China's government has made flood control a priority. The government's extensive efforts have included dike strengthening, reservoir construction, soil-erosion control, and river training, projects that have resulted in a successful avoidance of dike breaches and flooding for more than fifty years.

In order to halt the shrinking of the main channel in the lower Yellow River, in 2002 the Yellow River Conservancy Commission (YRCC) began to regulate flood and sediment by the reservoirs, achieving a higher efficiency of channeling sediment load measured that following year. Since 2003, the bank-full discharge of the main channel has been enlarged 50 to 100 percent. More

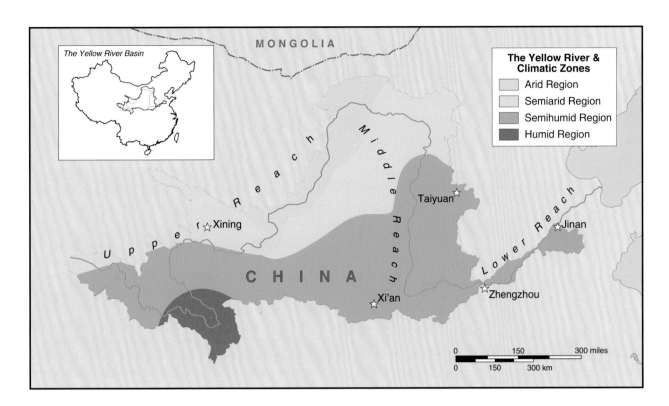

intensive soil-erosion control projects in the Loess Plateau region and sediment warping in the inner floodplain are also planned.

WATER RESOURCES DEVELOPMENT

The Yellow River basin is a water-short basin; its annual average runoff (53.5 billion cubic meters) only composes 2 percent of the entire country's runoff. But as the main water source for northern China, the Yellow River supplies water to 15 percent of China's farmland, fifty cities, and 12 percent of the population. Water per capita in the Yellow River basin is less than 450 cubic meters, which is much lower than the average level in China and in the world.

Water stress has become a serious concern in China. With intensive socioeconomic development, the country's rate of water consumption increases every year. Water consumption in the Yellow River basin increased from an amount of 12.2 billion cubic meters in 1950s to about 30 billion cubic meters since 1998. Most of the river-water withdrawal goes to the agricultural sector, which makes up about 85 percent of total utilized water in the basin. Over-withdrawal of water has caused the river downstream to dry up frequently since 1972, even though water-allocation plans have been issued by the Chinese central government since 1987. The drying-up ended in 1999, after the central government empowered YRCC to regulate runoff.

In the future, people's water requirements will certainly increase in line with the country's rapid economic development. In 2030 Yellow River runoff consumption is expected to reach about 40 billion cubic meters. This increase will put significant pressure on the water supply, because about 20 to 23 billion cubic meters of runoff must be left for sediment transportation and the sustainability of the river ecosystem. China is anticipating a "zero-growth" water consumption rate after 2030.

Along with the water shortage, since the 1980s China's water pollution situation has become increasingly serious. In 2000 the water in about 50 percent of the river was worse than IV degree, namely, COD > 30 milligrams per liter and NH3-N > 1.5 milligrams per liter, making the water-supply problem even more dire.

WATER MANAGEMENT

Because of its extreme importance and severe water problems, the government pays constant attention to the status of the Yellow River. Before the 1920s, the Yellow River was managed directly by the central government, and the main task was flood control. After YRCC was established in 1922, it became a vice-ministerial river-basin management organization and assumed responsibility for water management in the Yellow River basin. The agency is also charged with flood control and dike management in the lower Yellow River, as well as soil conservation in the Loess Plateau region.

This water-management model combines basin-level management with district-level management. YRCC is in charge of water-resources management at basin level, while provincial administrators, guided by YRCC, are responsible for water-resources management at the local district level.

BIBLIOGRAPHY

Brush, Lucien M., M. Gordon Wolman, and Huang Bingwei, eds. *Taming the Yellow River: Silt and Floods.* Dordrecht, Netherlands, and Boston: Kluwer, 1989.

Zhu Xiaoyuan, et al. *Huang he shuili weiyuanhui* [Study on water-resources changes in the Yellow River basin]. Zhengzhou: Yellow River Water Conservancy Press, 1999.

Changming Liu

HUAI RIVER

The Huai River, located between 111°55′ and 121°25′ E and between 30°55′ and 36°36′ N in the North China Plains of eastern Central China, is an ancient river with a long history. The Yangzi River (Chang Jiang) lies to the south of the Huai River, and the Yellow River (Huang He) is found to the north. Hence, the area south of the Huai River is generally referred as the Jiang-Huai region, while the area to the north is usually called the Huang-

Huai region. The Huai River basin has a wide drainage area extending from the Tongbai and Funiu mountains in the west to the Yellow Sea in the east, and from the Dabie Mountains and Jiang-Huai Hill Region in the south to the Yellow River and Mt. Yimeng in the north. The main course of the Huai River originates from the northern foot of the Tongbai Mountains in Henan Province, flows eastward through southern Henan Province and central Anhui Province, enters Hongze Lake in the middle of Jiangsu Province, and emerges from the lake to flow into the Yangzi River at Sanjiang Ying in Yangzhou, traversing a total length of 1,000 kilometers (620 miles) (see Figure 1).

Divided by the old course of the Yellow River, the basin separates into two major river systems, the Huai River and a system comprising the Yi, Shu, and Si rivers, encompassing a total watershed area of 270,000 square kilometers (104,000 square miles), of which 190,000 square kilometers (73,000 square miles) feed into the Huai River and 80,000 square kilometers (31,000 square miles) feed into the other system mentioned. There are numerous tributaries flowing into the main course of the Huai River, among them short southern tributaries coming from the mountains and long northern branches flowing over the Huang-Huai plain. There are also many large lakes, including Hongze, Nansi, and Luoma. Hongze Lake is the largest freshwater lake in the Huai River basin and is the fourth-largest in China.

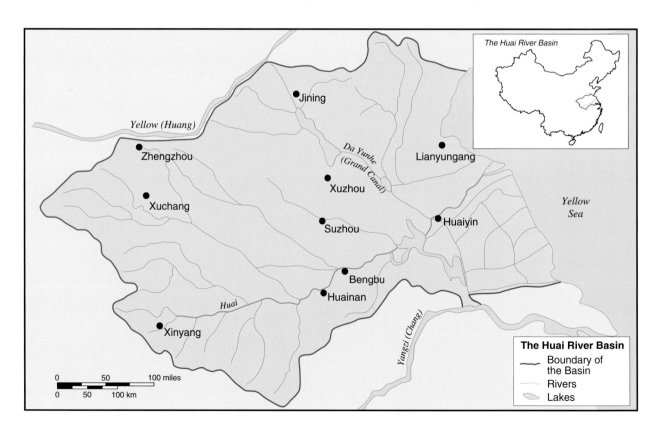

Since ancient times, the Huai River has been one of China's natural south-north dividing lines. Whether in geology, topography, hydrology, soil, climate, or biology, the two sides of the Huai River have significant differences. Especially in the climate, the Huai River basin is a transitional zone from South China's subtropical humid zone to North China's temperate subhumid areas, with the isoline for an average 95 centimeters (37 inches) of rainfall falling basically along the main course of the river. The Huai River basin has an average annual precipitation of 92 centimeters (36 inches), an average annual temperature of 11 to 16 degrees centigrade (52 to 60 degrees Fahrenheit), an average annual pan evaporation of 90 to 150 centimeters (35 to 59 inches), and a frost-free period of about 200 to 240 days a year. Temporal and spatial distribution of precipitation is very uneven, summer rainfall in most regions accounting for 50 to 80 percent of the annual total. The difference between low and high water runoff throughout the year reaches 3 to 4 times.

Before the Southern Song Dynasty (1127–1279), the Huai River was a good-quality river, with a good reputation for navigation and water quality. The Huai River used to enter the sea at Yuntiguan. Since the twelfth century, the Yellow River has captured and avulsed the Huai River, its intrusion bringing large quantities of sediment, upsetting the Huai River drainage system, and forcing the Huai River to enter the Yangzi River and became its tributary as a result. Hongze and Luoma Lakes were formed after the Yellow River captured the Huai River. This situation ended in 1855, when the Yellow River shifted its main course to the north and started flowing into the Bohai Sea. Since then the Huai River formed a pattern of much rain giving rise to great floods, less rain resulting in small floods, and no rain leading to droughts. Since the founding of the People's Republic of China, 11,000 sluices and dams have been built or repaired along the Huai River to prevent flooding and control drought. Drainage system has been preliminarily formed, so that Huai River water surges can enter sea through the North Jiangsu Irrigation Canal, the new Yi River, and other channels. In particular, the completion of the Huai River Ruhai Waterway allows the Huai River to empty into the Yellow Sea. Though these channels play a role in flood control and drought relief, the purification function of water bodies has greatly declined, and the water is seriously polluted toward the sea. Improving the Huai River system had become a key task for the country.

BIBLIOGRAPHY

Editorial Board of the Huai River Water Resources Commission. *Huaihe shuili guanli zhi* [Annals of water resources management for the Huai River]. Vol. 3. Beijing: Kexue Chubanshe, 2007.

Zhou, Yinkang, Zhiyuan Ma, and Lachun Wang. Chaotic Dynamics of the Flood Series in the Huaihe River Basin for the Last 500 Years. *Journal of Hydrology* 258 (2002): 100–110.

Suzhen Dang
Changming Liu

PEARL RIVER

The Pearl River (Zhu Jiang) is the largest river in South China. It originates in the Maxongshan Mountains in Zhanyi County, Yunnan Province. Its basin has an area of 453,690 square kilometers (175,170 square miles), extending across seven provinces in South China (Yunnan, Guizhou, Hunan, Jiangxi, Guangxi, and Guangdong), and it empties into the South China Sea. The upper reaches of the Zuo River, a small tributary of the Pearl River, is located in the northeast of Vietnam and has a drainage area of 11,590 square kilometers (4,474 square miles). The river system is formed by the convergence of numerous tributaries, mainly including the Xi (West), Bei (North), and Dong (East) rivers, along with the rivers in the Pearl River Delta area (Figure 1).

The Pearl River Basin is in the subtropics and has an average annual temperature between 14–22 degrees centigrade (57 and 72 degrees Fahrenheit). Annual precipitation ranges from 120–220 centimeters (47 to 87 inches), increasing gradually from west to east. The average annual runoff of the river is 336 billion cubic meters (11,865 billion cubic feet), with 238 billion cubic meters (8,404 billion cubic feet) coming from the Xi River, 39.4 billion cubic meters (1,391 billion cubic feet) from Bei River, 23.8 billion cubic meters (840 billion cubic feet) from Dong River, and 34.8 billion cubic meters (1,228 billion cubic feet) from the rivers of the Pearl River Delta area. Temporal variation of runoff is obvious and results in frequent floods and droughts in the basin.

In general, the Pearl River has plenty of water, a stable channel, and good navigation conditions. It is an important waterway from the Pacific Ocean toward the Indian Ocean. The Pearl River has 1,088 navigation channels and a total navigable length of 14,156 kilometers (8,796 miles), about 13 percent of China's total navigable length and second only to the Yangzi River. The Pearl River is also rich in hydropower potential, having 25,120 megawatts of installable capacity.

The Pearl River Delta, the large alluvial deltas formed by the Xi and Bei rivers, is located in the coastal area of eastern Guangdong Province. Clustered there are the large cities of Guangzhou, Shenzhen, Zhuhai, Shantou, Dongguan, Foshan, and numerous industrial townships. Before the Southern Song period (1127–1279)

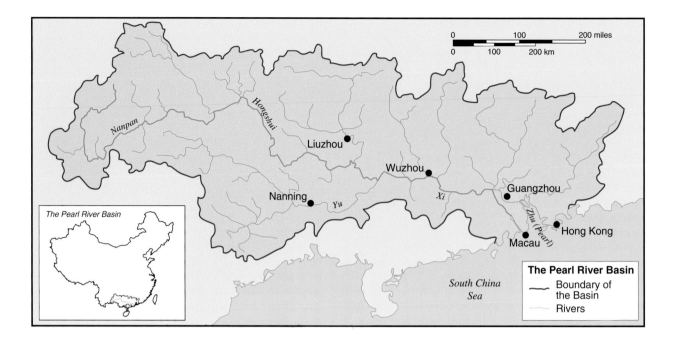

these regions were shallow wetlands and flood zones unsuited for agriculture and living, and the population in the area was scattered. Because of the expansion of the Yuan dynasty (1279–1368), many refugees from the central plains entered the area and engaged in silk production. The immigrants built up the levee system, lived peacefully, and developed the economy of the Pearl River Delta region.

During the Ming (1368–1644) and Qing (1644–1911) dynasties, the government paid great attention to the development of agriculture and the improvement of agricultural-production techniques. With the rapid development of the economy in the Pearl River Delta region, development of polder (low-lying land) and reclamation of land from marshes occurred on a large scale. During the 276 years of the Ming dynasty, more than 100 square kilometers (38 square miles) of land were opened up to cultivation, and the size of the Pearl River Delta region nearly doubled. During the Qianlong (1736–1796) and Jiaqing (1796–1820) reigns, a total of 53 square kilometers (20 square miles) of land were brought under cultivation, and another 80 square kilometers (30 square miles) were brought under cultivation during the Xianfeng reign (1851–1861). Polder development and land reclamation provided land for the development of agriculture, industry, transport, and foreign trade. In this way, it also brought enormous economic benefits and promoted social development. However, polder development and land reclamation conflict with flood routing and have adverse impacts on the ecology and environment of the Pearl River Delta region.

The Opium War (1839–1842) had a great impact on the region in that foreign aggression forced the Qing government to sign various unequal treaties consigning territories to foreign powers, including the delta's important harbors of Hong Kong and Macao. During the late Qing dynasty and the Republican period (1912–1949), the Pearl River Delta region was a major port for trade and developed rapidly. From the late 1970s, the region, with large amounts of foreign investment and its dynamic economy, was at the forefront of China's reform and opening up. In 2007 the Pearl River Delta Region is one of the most economically developed regions in the People's Republic, with a per capita gross domestic product of more than $7,000.

BIBLIOGRAPHY

Chen, C. T. A., H. K. Lui, X. X. Lu, et al. Hydrogeochemistry and Greenhouse Gases of the Pearl River, Its Estuary, and Beyond. *Quaternary International* 186 (2008): 79–90.

Pearl River Water Conservancy. *Zhujiang shuili jianshi* [A brief history of the Pearl River Water Conservancy]. Beijing: Shuili Dianli Chubanshe, 1990.

Changming Liu
Xiaomang Liu

RIVER COMMISSIONS

The Ministry of Water Resources of the People's Republic of China set up river commissions for the seven largest river basins in China: the Yangzi (Chang) River, Yellow

(Huang) River, Huai River, Hai River, Pearl River, Song-hua and Liao Rivers, and Lake Tai Basin. As for China's numerous other rivers, all the rivers in Southwest China are concurrently managed by the Yangzi River Water Resources Commission, all the rivers in Northwest China are the concurrent responsibility of the Yellow River Water Resources Commission, and all the rivers in Zhejiang, Fujian, and, nominally, Taiwan Provinces are concurrently under the direction of the Lake Tai Water Resources Commission. The river commissions solve issues regarding the allocation of water resources among different provinces and municipalities within the same basin. In the past, scattered water authorities had led to disagreements on water rights between upstream and downstream water users, so the river commissions were set up as centralized authorities for integrated water-resource management at the river-basin level to limit the power of provincial and local water-management authorities.

The river commissions coordinate water policy at the regional level. Their main tasks include, but are not limited to, administrative work; integrated water-resource management; river-basin planning; flood and drought control; river-channel management; survey, research, and design of major river junctions within the river basin; water-quality monitoring; and review and approval of engineering designs and river planning. Some of these river commissions have other specific and prioritized tasks related to their watersheds. For example, the Yangtze River Water Resources Commission is responsible for planning and designing the central route of the South-North Water Transfer Project, and the Yellow River Water Resources Commission governs issues related to soil conservation in the middle reaches of the Yellow River.

Four of the seven river commissions—the Songliao, Yellow River, Yangzi River, and Pearl River Water Resources Commissions—have been assigned to manage water rights for major watersheds straddling national borders. The administrative functions include quota management, approval of requests to withdraw water, and issuance of permits for water withdrawal.

Known as the Lancang River in China, the Mekong River is the eleventh-longest river in the world and the most important transborder river of China. In April 1995, Thailand, Laos, Cambodia, and Vietnam executed the Agreement on Cooperation for Sustainable Development of the Mekong River Basin, and as a result of the agreement, the Mekong River Commission was established. Commission member countries have collaborated on every aspect of development and management of the entire basin, including water resources, navigation, flood control, fishery, agriculture, hydropower, and environmental protection. From the date of its inception, the Mekong River Commission had been constantly inviting two upstream countries, Burma

and China, to join the commission, and it had initiated dialog between the member countries and Burma and China. According to its Web site, China's Ministry of Water Resources on April 1, 2002, entered into an agreement with the Mekong River Commission to provide hydrological data to the commission during flood seasons to help the downstream countries with flood control.

There are other water-management authorities outside the river commissions of the Ministry of Water Resources. Each of these agencies has different priorities and its own provincial- and municipal-level entities. These agencies include the State Environmental Protection Administration, which regulates water quality; the Ministry of Construction, which is responsible for municipal water supply; the Ministry of Agriculture, which handles irrigation; and the Ministry of Mines and Minerals, which has responsibility for groundwater.

BIBLIOGRAPHY

He, Daming, and Hsiange-te Kung. Southwest China and Southeast Asia: Towards Sustainability through Cooperative Development and Management of International Rivers. *Journal of Chinese Geography* 8, 3 (1998): 300–305.

Ministry of Water Resources. *Shuili Bu yu Meigong He weiyuanhui jianding baoxun xieyi* [Agreement concluded between the Ministry of Water Resources and the Mekong River Commission on reporting high water levels], 2002. http://www.mwr.gov.cn/tzgg/.

Xu Qianqing, ed. *Zhongguo shuili baikequanshu* [Chinese encyclopedia on water resources], p. 247. Beijing: Zhongguo Shuili Shuidian Chubanshe, 2006.

Changming Liu
Peng Liu

WATER CONTROL

According to legend, China's river-control practices can be traced back to 2037 BCE when the Great Yu conducted work on flood prevention on the Yellow (Huang) River. The earliest and largest irrigation system, on the Minjiang (Ming River), was established by Li Bing and his son in 256 BCE. In 468 BCE construction began on the 1,795-kilometer Grand Canal, the oldest and longest canal in the world, originally used for navigation and now utilized for water-transfer projects. Construction on the Grand Canal continued until 610 CE. China's rich history in water control has been inherited by successive generations. The Ministry of Water Resources (MWR) has been in operation since the founding of the People's Republic. By 2008 China had more than 84,000 dams or reservoirs of varying size, with a combined storage capacity of almost 500 billion cubic meters, making China the world leader in quantity of hydraulic structures.

The water supply for various sectors throughout the country has increased from about 100 billion cubic meters in the 1950s to about 560 billion cubic meters in the early twenty-first century. Embankment structures, including levees and dikes for prevention of floods and waterlogging, have reached a total length of more than 250,000 kilometers. China's total irrigation area in 1950 was 16 million hectares; by 2008 the figure was more than 56 million hectares. After many years of effort by the MWR, China has accomplished great feats of hydraulic engineering.

WATER-RESOURCES PLANNING

The first round of national water-resources assessment and development planning was conducted in the 1980s. Because of changing conditions, the MWR carried out another round of integrated national water-resources planning in 2002.

This effort was designed to clarify the quantity and quality, as well as the temporal and spatial distribution, of the country's water resources. The researchers also aimed to resolve key issues related to the development, utilization, allocation, conservation, protection, and pollution treatment of water resources. Their tasks included updated water-resources assessment, scientific forecasting of short- and long-term water demand, and optimized water-resources allocation based on the principles of water saving and water conservation. The 2002 integrated national water-resources planning work involved the Yangzi (Chang), Yellow River, Huai River, Hai River, Pearl River, Songhua River, Liao River, and Lake Tai, as well as other rivers in the southeast, southwest, and northwest. In addition, the MWR planned to establish an all-around program for flood control and hazard relief, a stable and efficient water-supply system, and a scheme for the protection of ecological integrity and water resources.

A passenger ship transitioning the locks at the Three Gorges Dam, Yichang, Hubei province, June 16, 2003. In an effort to control regional flooding and produce hydroelectric power, the Chinese began one of the world's largest building projects with the Three Gorges Dam. Originally proposed in the 1920s, the Three Gorges Dam has earned criticism from environmentalists. © REUTERS/CORBIS

LARGE-SCALE WATER PROJECTS

The Three Gorges Dam is one of the largest construction projects in the world. Beyond its massive hydropower capacity, the dam has an important role in flood prevention for vast downstream areas of the Jianghan Plain. This project was first proposed by Sun Yat-sen (Sun Yixian) in the 1920s. Since 1949 there have been frequent and intensive surveys of the dam site by the engineers of the Changjiang (Yangzi) Commission under the MWR. The National People's Congress approved the construction of the dam in 1992. The goals of the project include flood prevention, river navigation, and the generation of power for the surrounding communities. Construction was to be completed in 2009.

China's south-to-north water-transfer scheme was first proposed by Mao Zedong in the early 1950s. The Chinese Academy of Sciences organized an integrated survey on the feasibility of the project in the late 1950s, and the MWR has been responsible for engineering, planning, and design since the 1970s. There are to be three long-distance south-to-north water-transfer routes: the eastern route, the middle route, and the western route. Each route would divert water from a different reach of the Yangzi. In order to meet the water needs of accelerating economic development and population growth, as well as rapid urbanization, the Chinese government has decided to foster and speed up work on water-transfer planning and project design in the early twenty-first century. After twenty years of preparation, in 2005 the State Council adopted a plan to begin construction on both the eastern and middle routes. The expected amount of water to be diverted by the three routes from the Yangzi totals more than 40 billion cubic meters, which would make it the largest water-diversion system in the world.

WATER SAVINGS

Increasing water-use efficiency through technology is the most important measure for solving China's water-shortage problem. The Chinese government has enhanced its policy through the Resources Saving Society and Environment Friend Society, and water saving has been accomplished through legislation. In early 2008, the National Development and Reform Commission, along with the MWR and the Ministry of Construction, jointly released a plan to cut the nation's water use per unit of gross domestic product by 20 percent within five years. China's water-saving measures have been augmented by employing sprinkling-and-dropping irrigation in association with agronomic technologies. In the industrial sector, desalinized water has been utilized in the most water-consumptive industries, such as thermal power, petroleum, and chemistry enterprises. By 2008 the cost of desalinization had dropped to less than four Chinese yuan per cubic meter. In the domestic sector, the dissemination of water-saving facilities and the use of water-price elasticity have greatly reduced water consumption.

ENVIRONMENTAL PROTECTION

In China, there is a high level of competition among water users. Since the 1980s, industry and agriculture have increasingly drained water from the environment and ecosystems. A number of technologies have been developed to sustain and rehabilitate damaged eco-environment, including techniques to better determine water allocation and maintain necessary water levels, and engineering to dispatch water from wetlands to areas of need throughout the country. One of the key issues in ecosystem degradation in China is soil erosion and the consequent loss of soil and water. The National Compendia of Water and Soil Conservation Monitoring has been implemented for the 2006–2015 period to address this problem, and the Law of the People's Republic of China on Water and Soil Conservation, adopted in 1991, is under revision.

River water pollution is also a serious challenge being addressed by a number of relevant government bodies. The State Environmental Protection Administration (SEPA) and the MWR are the two major authorities jointly controlling China's water ecosystem and environment. SEPA mainly deals with environmental management and monitoring throughout the country, and the MWR handles water quantity and quality via its river commissions.

SEE ALSO *Irrigation and Management of Water Resources.*

BIBLIOGRAPHY

Wang Shucheng. 2003. *Resource-oriented Water Management: Towards Harmonious Coexistence between Man and Nature.* Beijing: China Water Conservancy and Power Publishing House, 2007.

Zhou Ying Zhubian, ed. *2007 Zhongguo shuili fazhan baogao* [China water development report 2007]. Beijing: China Water Conservancy and Power Publishing House, 2007.

Changming Liu

RONG ZONGJING
1873–1938

Rong Zongjing was the founder of one of China's most prominent family businesses and gained fame as the "cotton king" of Shanghai's textile industry in the early twentieth century. Although the majority of his textile mills were located in Shanghai, Rong Zongjing and his business fortune were closely linked to his hometown,

Wuxi, a commercial city famous for silk production in the prosperous part of Jiangsu Province. There the Rong family managed a silk cocoon trading company and had developed strong commercial and social ties over generations.

MAKING OF AN ENTREPRENEUR

Zongjing was the firstborn son in his generation, and in preparation for his future career in the family business, his father sent him to Shanghai for an apprenticeship that would allow him to study the business practices and operations in traditional banking institutions. At the time, Shanghai, a major treaty port, was becoming China's financial center for both Chinese and foreign banking institutions and investors. Rong Zongjing became an apprentice at the Yu Yuan Bank and the Sen Tai Bank in the early 1890s. With his newly gained expertise he founded his first business, the Guangsheng Bank, together with his father and younger brother Rong Desheng in 1896. Originally, the family wanted him to raise money in Shanghai to invest in their silk operations in Wuxi, but Rong Zongjing refused: His approach to business expansion and strategy differed from his family's, and this became a theme throughout Rong Zongjing's life as an entrepreneur. When his father died in 1896 Rong did not return to Wuxi and take over the family business as tradition dictated, but instead continued his banking operations in Shanghai and opened a branch in Wuxi run by his brother Rong Desheng. A few years later the two brothers joined the famous Yudaxiang commercial company in Shanghai through the connections of Rong Ruixing, a family member and comprador for Jardine, Matheson, and Company in Shanghai. Because Yudaxiang was also a major player in the remittance business from Shanghai providing capital for Wuxi's industries, Rong Zongjing decided to close his own banking operations in 1909, and from then on he concentrated on expanding the industrial side of the family business.

SHENXIN COTTON MILLS

By 1915 the Rong family had added two flour mills and the Shenxin cotton mill to its silk cocoon trading company in Wuxi—typical investments for commercial entrepreneurs exploring manufacturing opportunities during China's industrialization period in the early twentieth century. Rong Zongjing had a vision of expanding the Shenxin mill business into other cities in the lower Yangzi region, but senior members of his family wanted to keep the business a local, less risky operation, and opposed his plan vehemently. As a result, Rong Zongjing and his brother left Wuxi, the family business, and its network, and founded the first Shenxin mill in Shanghai in 1915. The two brothers personally provided more than half of the capital stock for the unlimited-liability company, which allowed them to control the firm in terms of financial and organizational management.

Because he was temporarily alienated from his family, Rong Zongjing was unable to raise money for new business ventures from his family network and had to turn to banks in Shanghai for capitalization. However, the late 1910s were a boom period for industrial ventures because foreign manufacturers had withdrawn from the China market during World War I, opening new opportunities for Chinese producers in the textile and consumer goods sector. Raising money was not a problem. The second Shenxin mill opened in Shanghai in 1919, and both mills showed excellent profits in the following years. By 1922 the capital of the Shenxin mills in Shanghai had risen to 16 million yuan, and Rong Zongjing and Rong Desheng owned 63 percent of the shares. In order to prevent influence from outside investors, Shenxin's bylaws stipulated that shareholders wanting to sell stock to investors outside the company first had to seek approval from all shareholders. This rule made financial and managerial control outside the Rong family impossible. In addition, Rong Zongjing established a holding company for all his businesses, the so-called General Corporation, which allowed him to manage the expanding enterprise through the headquarters in Shanghai.

BUSINESS EXPANSION

During the 1920s Rong Zongjing established six new cotton mills, four of them in Shanghai and one in Wuxi, and for the first time ventured into China's interior with a mill in Hankou. As China's transportation, financial, and commercial hub, Shanghai was the ideal place for the company headquarters to manage the growing business empire. Rong Zongjing paid particular attention to the distribution network, securing special shipping rates from the China Merchants' Steam Navigation Company that increased his profit margin vis-à-vis his competitors. An astute entrepreneur, Rong Zongjing adopted managerial methods for his enterprises that combined a progressive attitude toward shop-floor and company management with authoritarian, family-centered business practices. For example, he made every single factory manager call him at noon every day in order to give instructions. However, he also used the new technology of the telephone to gather better information on the harvest and prices of raw cotton nationwide, allowing him to purchase his raw material with a competitive advantage.

Although Rong Zongjing's business success was anchored in Shanghai, he also used the advantages of his family and social network in Wuxi to benefit his enterprises. This aspect of management became particularly obvious in terms of the workforce at Shenxin and other enterprises. Members of the Rong family and associates from Wuxi were employed as managers in the Shenxin mills and as supervisors on the shop floor, and they provided important business contacts in outside firms relevant to the Rong family's business interests. For example, due to his high position in the Shanghai branch of the Bank of China, Rong Zongjing's son-in-law Song Hanzhang brought important business and financial connections to Shenxin's business.

Rong Zongjing employed family members because they were trustworthy and promoted social cohesion, but he also actively tried to improve their educational and professional training to keep the business competitive. The family's sons and many sons-in-law were sent to study abroad, and Rong Desheng's son, Rong Yiren, obtained a bachelor's degree from the Lowell Textile School in Massachusetts. Rong Zongjing also recognized the need for more basic education of shop-floor supervisors and employees in their mills. Before their recruitment to Shanghai they were educated in primary schools sponsored by the Rong family and also received vocational training in company-owned institutes. In addition, employees from Wuxi were offered company housing and enjoyed certain social services through the company. These advantages were acts of social responsibility, but they were also practical means to avoid labor unrest in the mills. Shanghai was one of the centers of the strikes that affected the textile industry particularly in the late 1920s and early 1930s. But with a high number of loyal employees recruited from Wuxi (about 65%) who enjoyed better working and living conditions than Chinese workers in other textile enterprises, the Shenxin mills escaped serious labor unrest during those years.

POLITICAL INTERFERENCE

Yet, despite his cautious business and managerial strategies, Rong Zongjing and his enterprises were not able to avoid political interference, especially after 1927 when Chiang Kai-shek came to power under the new Nationalist government in Nanjing. Short of money and corrupt, Chiang resorted to unorthodox methods of coercion to fund his political agenda. For example, he forced Shanghai's businessmen and bankers to buy bonds issued by the Nationalist government. When Rong Zongjing refused, he was arrested on trumped-up charges and released only after Wu Zhihui, a family associate from Wuxi and a powerful member of the Nationalist Party, stepped in and negotiated the release. Unsurprisingly, Rong Zongjing had to purchase a large number of government bonds to settle the matter.

Despite this incident, Rong Zongjing maintained a prominent position in Shanghai's business community. He was head of the Association of Chinese Cotton Mill Owners, and took on active roles in government. In 1928 he was appointed adviser to the Ministry of Industry and Commerce, then became a member of the National Economic Council in 1933. Rong Zongjing's political and economic achievements in the national arena during the 1930s are disputed because he seemed to struggle with promoting his own business interests and following national economic policies at the same time, and consequently he fell out of favor with the Nationalist government. A devastating blow came in 1934 when the Shenxin mills, suffering from overextended loans, came close to bankruptcy. The government-controlled Bank of China forced Rong Zongjing to step down as Shenxin's manager, arguing that his enterprise did not have the necessary financial and strategic management to guarantee the company's recovery. Amazingly, Rong Zongjing managed to regain his position by once again utilizing his Wuxi family connections. After Wu Zhihui again lobbied Chiang Kai-shek and the government, the Bank of China and the Shanghai Commercial and Savings Bank issued new loans and Rong Zongjing was allowed to resume his position as general manager of the Shenxin mills.

Rong Zongjing's businesses were threatened again when Japan declared war against China in summer 1937. Because most of the Shenxin mills were located in Shanghai, close to where the Japanese invasion of the Chinese mainland began, the factories quickly suffered severe physical damage. By the end of 1937 two of the Shenxin mills had been completely destroyed by bombs and the rest of the mills had been expropriated by the Japanese occupation regime. Like other Chinese entrepreneurs trying to save their businesses and their livelihoods, Rong Zongjing considered seeking financial compensation in exchange for political support of the Japanese occupation authorities. However, because this course of action would have seen him labeled a collaborator, Rong Zongjing decided against this desperate step. Frustrated by a political situation that left him unable to run his businesses, he left Shanghai in January 1938 and moved to Hong Kong, where he died a few months later.

With the exception of the period of Japanese occupation, the Shenxin mills remained a privately held company until 1956, when it became a state-owned enterprise under the new socialist government of the People's Republic of China. After Rong Zongjing's death his brother Rong Desheng took charge of the family business, but he lacked the charisma and managerial talent of his elder brother, and was not able to unite the family and their business interests during the chaos of wartime China. Rong Hongyuan, Rong Zongjing's son, also could not align the interests of his brothers and cousins. A bitter succession dispute between him and one of Rong Desheng's sons finally led to the breakup of the central family business structure at the end of the war in 1945.

Rong Zongjing occupies an important place in the history of Chinese business. He was a remarkably talented progressive and charismatic entrepreneur who built one of China's largest and most successful modern textile enterprises. He skillfully incorporated the family and social networks from his hometown Wuxi into the business, thus securing a loyal workforce and trustworthy managers, and he cultivated business associates who were the only ones able to bail him out when political circumstances threatened him or his business. Rong Zongjing thus exemplifies the trajectory and fate of many industrial entrepreneurs of the Republican period who created successful new forms of Chinese business enterprises but faced an increasingly unstable political environment that produced dire socioeconomic consequences.

SEE ALSO *Industrialization, 1860–1949.*

BIBLIOGRAPHY

Bell, Lynda S. *One Industry, Two Chinas: Silk Filatures and Peasant-Family Production in Wuxi County, 1865–1937.* Stanford, CA: Stanford University Press, 1999.

Bergère, Marie-Claire. *The Golden Age of the Chinese* Bourgeoisie, 1911–1937. Cambridge, U.K.: Cambridge University Press, 1989.

Coble, Parks M. *Chinese Capitalists in Japan's New Order: The Occupied Lower Yangzi, 1937–1945.* Berkeley: University of California Press, 2003.

Cochran, Sherman. *Encountering Chinese Networks: Western, Japanese, and Chinese Corporations in China, 1880–1937.* Berkeley: University of California Press, 2000.

Eastman, Lloyd E. *Family, Fields, and Ancestors: Constancy and Change in China's Social and Economic History, 1550–1949.* New York: Oxford University Press, 1988.

Hao, Yen-P'ing. *The Comprador in Nineteenth-Century China: Bridge Between East and West.* Cambridge, MA: Harvard University Press, 1970.

Köll, Elisabeth. *From Cotton Mill to Business Empire: The Emergence of Regional Enterprises in Modern China.* Cambridge, MA: Harvard East Asia Center, 2003.

Köll, Elisabeth. *The Rong Family: A Chinese Business History.* Harvard Business School Technical Note N9-308-066. Cambridge, MA: Harvard Business School, 2007.

Rawski, Thomas. *Economic Growth in Prewar China.* Berkeley: University of California Press, 1989.

Elisabeth Köll

ROOT-SEARCHING LITERATURE

Between 1968 and 1975, some 12 million young urban Chinese were labeled "educated youth" and sent to live in the villages and border areas, in most cases with the intention that they would settle there and "learn from the peasants." Most found the experience a major ordeal, and after Mao Zedong's death and the fall of the gang of four in 1976, those who could do so returned to the cities.

Then during the liberalization that followed, the literary writers among them concentrated on showing the scars created by following political movements too dogmatically. Yet some of them began to reflect on their sojourns in the villages in a more nostalgic light.

In the mid-1980s talented young writers such as Liang Xiaosheng and Kong Jiesheng wrote tenderly about their adventures in the Great Northern Wastelands or the steamy forests on Hainan Island. Descriptions of the wonders of the more exotic areas of China soon turned into tales of self-discovery, and, in finding themselves, many of these writers claimed that they were uncovering the age-old roots of Chinese culture. They often experimented with unreliable narration, stream of consciousness, different language registers, and dialects to establish themselves in a loosely grouped school of writing known as root-searching literature (*xungen wenxue*). The published agenda of the root seekers, drafted by their main representative, the author Han Shaogong, announced their interest in exploring alternative Chinese cultures—including the culture of Chu (destroyed in 223 BCE)—as well as popular religions and the cultures of ethnic minorities, in an attempt to unearth roots that lay outside the mainstream Confucian tradition.

PRIMITIVE ROOTS

The weird and the bizarre thus became possible vestiges of embryonic civilizations of China. In Han Shaogong's stories of the period, for example, the lives, languages, and customs of remote communities are often described through the eyes of a young intellectual outsider. His story "The Homecoming" features a male protagonist who travels to a remote village, where he is eventually convinced that he is someone else, someone who stayed in the village years earlier and committed a crime there. Although the story has a dreamlike quality, the villagers and customs are described in detail, and there is no question that the protagonist is an educated youth who has returned to the city and later to the village in search of something or someone. Another emblematic root-searching story by Han Shaogong carefully documents the barbarity and outlandish superstitions of a primitive society that might have formed the roots of Chinese culture. The story "Ba Ba Ba," about two feuding villages and the fate of Bing, a severely handicapped child whose only words are "Ba Ba" and "*x* Mama," captures the horror many sent-down students must have felt when faced with primitive peasants.

The deliberately vague and misty quality of the environs described in the stories shows that the "roots" being sought had little to do with real historical Chinese cultural roots. They were—as Zheng Wanlong, one of the main exponents of this literature, explained—mainly the creations of their authors' imaginations. Zheng Wanlong spent his childhood among Oroqen huntsmen and Han gold miners in the remote forests of Heilongjiang. Although he moved to Beijing at the age of eight, his childhood experiences later provided a wealth of material for his fiction. When root searching became popular in the mid-1980s, Zheng Wanlong wrote a series of short stories and novellas under the title *Strange Tales from Strange Lands*, whose descriptions of the Oroqen tribes and their rites captured the imagination of critics and readers. The first ten stories from this series were published in 1986 in a collection titled *Shengming de tuteng* (The totems of life).

MORE REFINED ROOTS

In contrast to primitiveness, the roots of Chinese culture can be seen to emanate also from refined Confucian and Daoist philosophies. Such a characterization is provided by Ah Cheng, who was born and raised in Beijing. During the Cultural Revolution, he was sent to Inner Mongolia but managed to transfer to the semitropical Xishuangbanna region of Yunnan. He returned to Beijing in 1979 and his first attempt at fiction was "The King of Chess," written in 1984, which sparked a new interest in philosophical roots and created an Ah Cheng craze that lasted for two years. Two more king stories followed: "The King of Trees" and "The King of Children," both published in 1985. Ah Cheng also wrote a series of sketches titled *Biandi fengliu* (Romances of the landscape), which describe the scenery and customs of border areas far from civilization.

Other writers who have sometimes been included in the root-searching school include Wang Anyi, whose main contribution was a series of essays and short stories in the 1980s about young women in search of love and happiness. In fact, the so-called root-searching school was not a school in any formal sense. Some writers who were not educated youth but who wrote about the strange customs of rural or even urban China in the middle or late 1980s have also been discussed as part of this "school." For example, Mo Yan was only ten when the Cultural Revolution began, but his novels and stories, such as *Red Sorghum*, depicted village customs in such a sensational manner that they were quickly appropriated as examples of root-searching writing.

Many of the stories from this genre became even better known when they were made into internationally acclaimed movies. They appealed to an Orientalist fascination with the exotic in Chinese culture and, for a few years, received considerable attention both in China and abroad. In many ways the Nobel Prize–winner Gao Xingjian continued this style of writing. His most famous novel, *Soul Mountain*, written for the most part in China during the 1980s, exemplifies the typical combination of experimental techniques and root-searching themes. The protagonist of *Soul Mountain* travels through remote areas of China to record exotic languages and customs, features that are central to root-searching literature. This style of writing thus led to literature highly rated internationally.

SEE ALSO *Gao Xingjian; Jia Pingwa; Mo Yan; Wang Anyi.*

BIBLIOGRAPHY

Han, Shaogong. After the "Literature of the Wounded": Local Cultures, Roots, Maturity, and Fatigue. In *Modern Chinese Writers: Self-Portrayals*, ed. Helmut Martin, 147–155. Armonk, NY: Sharpe, 1992.

Li, Qingxi. Searching for Roots: Anticultural Return in Mainland Chinese Literature of the 1980s. In *Chinese Literature in the Second Half of the Twentieth Century: A Critical Survey*, ed. Pang-yuan Chi and David Wang, 110–123. Bloomington: Indiana University Press, 2000.

Louie, Kam. *Between Fact and Fiction: Essays on Post-Mao Chinese Literature and Society*. Sydney: Wild Peony, 1989. See pp. 91–102.

Kam Louie

RUAN LINGYU
1910–1935

Ruan Lingyu (Ruan Agen, Ruan Fenggen, Ruan Yuying), China's leading film actress during the silent era, is now remembered as much for her widely publicized suicide as for her incandescent performances in 1930s' hit films such as *The Goddess* and *The New Woman*. Ruan Lingyu dramatized through her life and work the rewards and challenges of modern society experienced by women in the Republican era.

The Cantonese Ruan was born and raised in Shanghai by her mother, who worked as a household servant. After attending a girls' school until age sixteen, Ruan screen-tested into China's largest movie studio at the time, Mingxing, earning roles in contemporary romance films and costume dramas. In 1929 she moved to Da zhonghua baihe (Great China Lilium Pictures), reorganized in 1930 into the larger Lianhua (United Photoplay). There, she played a wide range of roles, such as schoolgirls, revolutionaries, writers, mothers, prostitutes, spurned women, country girls, and rural craftswomen. The films that cemented her position as a star were generally contemporary melodramas, including *Lian'ai yu yiwu* (*Love and Duty*, 1930), *Taohua qixue ji* (*Peach Blossom Weeps Tears of Blood*, 1931), *Sange modeng nüxing* (*Three Modern Women*, 1932), and *Xiao wanyi* (*Little Toys*, 1933).

Ruan's best-known roles were tragic ones; her expressive yet restrained performance style often prompts comparisons with Greta Garbo. In less than a decade, she performed in nearly thirty films made by China's top film directors, including Sun Yu (1900–1990), Zhu Shilin (1899–1967), Bu Wancang (1903–1974), Cai Chusheng (1906–1968), and Fei Mu (1906–1951). Although only a fraction of these works are extant, several can be considered classics of world cinema. In *Shennü* (*The Goddess*, 1934) Ruan plays an anonymous streetwalker striving to be a virtuous mother. And in *Xin nüxing* (*The New Woman*, 1935) Ruan took on the role of the aspiring novelist Wei Ming, who supports herself as a music teacher at a girls' school in Shanghai until the combined challenges of manipulative men, single motherhood, media scandals over her "secret past," and the death of her daughter drive her to despair and suicide.

Weeks after the release of *The New Woman*, when Ruan was at the peak of her career, the actress seemed to reenact the film's tragic conclusion. Stardom had drawn attention to her private life, including her adopted daughter and a disastrous series of relationships with a common-law husband and a philandering businessman. Sensationalistic accounts erupted in a media scandal, culminating with the actress taking an overdose of sleeping pills on March 8, 1935—International Women's Day. Her funeral cortege drew tens of thousands of mourners to the streets of Shanghai. The influential author Lu Xun (1881–1936) published a eulogy indicting the press for profiteering and gossip, and lamenting that gender discrimination in contemporary society victimized young women like Ruan. Her despair also has been attributed to the challenges facing non-Mandarin speakers during China's gradual transition from silent to sound filmmaking in the early 1930s. The Hong Kong filmmaker Guan Jinpeng (Stanley Kwan, b. 1957) explores this theme in his semifictional, semidocumentary film *Ruan Lingyu* (also known as *Centre Stage*, 1992), interviewing filmmakers who knew Ruan, reconstructing her oeuvre through clips of extant films, and directing dramatizations featuring the Hong Kong star Zhang Manyu (Maggie Cheung, b. 1964) as the 1930s actress.

SEE ALSO *Women in the Visual Arts.*

BIBLIOGRAPHY

Harris, Kristine. *The New Woman* Incident: Cinema, Scandal, and Spectacle in 1935 Shanghai. In *Transnational Chinese Cinemas: Identity, Nationhood, Gender*, ed. Sheldon Hsiao-peng Lu, 277–302. Honolulu: University of Hawai'i Press, 1997.

Meyer, Richard. *Ruan Ling-Yu: The Goddess of Shanghai.* Subtitled DVD. Hong Kong: Hong Kong University Press, 2005.

Zhongguo Dianyingjia Xiehui Dianyingshi Yanjiubu, ed. *Ruan Lingyu.* Beijing: Zhongguo Dianying Chubanshe, 1985.

Kristine M. Harris

RUAN YUAN
1764–1849

Ruan Yuan was one of the most important and longest serving officials in the Qing field administration during the Jiaqing (1796–1820) and Daoguang (1821–1850) reigns. He was also an important patron of scholarship and literature, responsible for the compilation of many influential anthologies and for the founding of arguably the two most important Confucian academies during the Qing dynasty.

EARLY LIFE

Ruan Yuan was born into a socially ascendant family in the Yangzi River Delta city of Yangzhou, a center of wealth stemming from the city's role in the salt trade. The Ruan family's ancestors had settled in Yangzhou during the late Ming. Ruan Yuan's grandfather won a military *juren* (recommended man) degree in 1715 and campaigned against the Miao in Hunan Province. This man's wife, Ruan Yuan's paternal grandmother, was from the Jiang family. Ruan Yuan's father for a time worked with the Jiang family in the salt trade and acquired civil service examination titles available to merchants who donated money.

Although Ruan Yuan's grandfather had registered the family as residents of Yizheng County, in the lower portion of Yangzhou Prefecture, Ruan Yuan spent his childhood and received his education in the prefectural seat. While his father was often away from Yangzhou on business, Ruan Yuan received a thorough classical training. Ruan married a member of the Jiang family in 1783, and tested into the Yizheng county school in the following year. He subsequently moved through the higher levels of the examination system, passing the provincial examinations in 1786 and becoming a *jinshi* (presented scholar) in the metropolitan examination of 1789. In 1790 he was appointed a Hanlin Academy compiler. Ruan's wife died in early 1793; three years later he married Kong Luhua (1777–1833), a member of the Kong clan in Shandong. The clan were descendants of Confucius, and Luhua was the granddaughter of the duke representing the Kong clan. Ruan Yuan's early success in the civil service examinations and his strategic marriage into an ennobled family advanced the Ruan family's rise from the respectable fringes to the center of the local Yangzhou elite, and coincided with Ruan Yuan's first appointments to prestigious provincial posts.

POLITICAL CAREER

Ruan Yuan's first provincial appointment was as Shandong commissioner of education in 1793. In 1795 Ruan was transferred to the same post in Zhejiang. After three years of service in Zhejiang, Ruan returned to the capital, where he served in ministerial posts. During this time, he served as an examiner for the metropolitan examinations of 1799, which produced a notable class of *jinshi*-degree winners, including Wang Yinzhi (1766–1834), Zhang Huiyan (1761–1802), Chen Shouqi (1771–1834), and others who would become important scholars or officials. Ruan Yuan returned to the field administration late in 1799 as acting governor of Zhejiang Province; he fully held the position from 1800 until 1809, aside from a three-year period of mourning for his father during the middle of the decade. During his years as Zhejiang governor Ruan spent much of his time combating pirates, in particular Cai Qian (1761–1809). Ruan is credited with adequately defending the coast under his jurisdiction until the pirate threat subsided with Cai's death. In that same year, Ruan was removed from his post, charged with ignoring the malfeasance of a fellow graduate of Ruan Yuan's 1789 *jinshi* class who served under Ruan as commissioner of education in Zhejiang.

Nevertheless, Ruan Yuan was soon appointed to posts in the capital before once again being assigned to provincial posts. He was appointed governor of Jiangxi in 1814 and transferred to Henan two year later. Ruan was then promoted to the governor-generalship of Hunan and Hubei before being transferred in 1817 to the Guangdong-Guangxi governor-generalship, a post he held for eight years. In that post, based at Guangzhou, Ruan first turned his attention to shoring up coastal defenses against a growing English threat, even cutting off trade for a year in 1822. Ruan also made important contributions to the local infrastructure and economy, overseeing renovations of the crucial Mulberry Garden Enclosure (Sangyuanwei) in the Pearl River Delta in 1818 to 1819, and in 1823 successfully proposing that foreign ships importing rice to Guangzhou be allowed to export other commodities in turn, thus helping to ensure an ample supply of grain in the commercialized delta economy. Ruan Yuan's last provincial assignment was as governor-general of Yunnan and Guizhou, from 1826 to 1835. Thereafter, Ruan served in high-ranking posts in the capital until 1838, when he was allowed to retire to Yangzhou with the prestigious honorary title of "Grand Guardian of the Heir Apparent." After his death, Ruan was honored with the name *Wenda* (Accomplished in letters).

CULTURAL INFLUENCE

While serving in these provincial posts, Ruan Yuan emerged as the most important patron of scholarship and literature of his time, shaping numerous fields of cultural production for decades. Ruan is best known as an advocate of evidential research (*kaozheng*) and more narrowly, the tradition of Han Learning. In his first provincial assignment, as commissioner of education in Shandong during the early 1790s, Ruan erected a shrine in honor of the Han-era classical scholar Zheng Xuan (127–200), helping to promote the cult of this scholastic hero to Han Learning enthusiasts in the Qing. During his first year as full governor of Zhejiang Province, Ruan established in the provincial capital, Hangzhou, the Gujing jingshe (School of classical exegesis), which immediately became an important center of evidential research. He continued to promote the Zheng Xuan cult, enshrining Zheng in the new academy. In his widely read commemoration of the founding of the Gujing jingshe, Ruan argued that because they were older, Han-dynasty exegeses of the classics were more reliable than exegeses produced by Song-era neo-Confucians, including Zhu Xi (1130–1200).

In Guangzhou Ruan Yuan founded another academy, the Xuehaitang. Whereas the Gujing jingshe had been established in an area already closely associated with the eighteenth-century evidential research movement, the Xuehaitang is seen as having helped Guangzhou to emerge for the first time as a major center of classical scholarship. In his writings associated with the founding of the Xuehaitang, Ruan Yuan articulated a more eclectic approach to scholarship, and helped to set the stage for the emerging New Text and Han Learning–Song Learning Syncretism scholarly movements. In literature, Ruan was less eclectic, strongly promoting "literary prose" (*wen*) modeled on the sixth-century Wenxuan anthology over "utilitarian prose" (*bi*).

Aside from establishing academies, Ruan Yuan sponsored the compilation of several important anthologies. These include *Jingji zuangu*, a dictionary of the Confucian classics compiled during Ruan's term as Zhejiang commissioner of education; *Chouren zhuan*, a collection of biographies and brief summaries of the writings of mathematical astronomers, including some Europeans, produced at the same time; *Shisan jing zhushu*, a definitive edition of the Confucian classics, with commentaries by Han- and Tang-era Confucian scholars, produced while Ruan was Jiangxi governor; and *Huang Qing jingjie*, a large collection of Qing exegeses of the classics produced at the Xuehaitang. The disproportionate number of works by Yangzhou authors in this collection illustrates Ruan's effort to put Yangzhou on par with the recognized centers of evidential research in the eighteenth century, such as Suzhou and Hangzhou. Finally, Ruan Yuan produced several anthologies of local literature and studies of local metal and stone inscriptions; such texts mark the beginning of a trend that lasted through much of the nineteenth century.

SEE ALSO *Academies (shuyuan); Classical Scholarship and Intellectual Debates: 1800–1864; Qing Dynasty in 1800; Reform under the Qing Dynasty, 1800–1912.*

BIBLIOGRAPHY

Elman, Benjamin. *From Philosophy to Philology: Intellectual and Social Aspects of Change in Late Imperial China.* Cambridge, MA: Harvard University Press, 1984.

Finnane, Antonia. *Speaking of Yangzhou: A Chinese City, 1550–1850.* Cambridge, MA: Harvard University Press, 2004.

Meyer-Fong, Tobie. *Building Culture in Early Qing Yangzhou.* Stanford, CA: Stanford University Press, 2003.

Wei, Betty Peh-T'i. *Ruan Yuan, 1764–1849: The Life and Work of a Major Scholar-Official in Nineteenth-Century China before the Opium War.* Hong Kong: Hong Kong University Press, 2006. Readers should approach this otherwise useful book with caution, as there are some factual errors.

Steven B. Miles

RURAL COOPERATIVE MEDICAL SYSTEMS

Protection for China's rural population from the risk of ill health has since 1949 been provided primarily through the locally funded and organized "cooperative medical systems" (*hezuo yiliao zhidu*; CMS). This system was first established in the 1950s and then promoted more extensively in the 1960s and 1970s, but it collapsed in the early 1980s as rural agriculture was decollectivized and household farming introduced. From the late 1980s, the central government repeatedly promoted initiatives to reestablish CMS, and there were experiments with variations on the pre-1980s model. But comprehensive coverage of the rural population remained elusive, and only a minority participated in reform schemes. Since 2003 there has been particularly concerted support among the top leadership for, and central government investment in, a "new rural CMS," and it has been claimed that 80 percent of the rural population was participating as of late 2007.

SETTING UP THE SYSTEM,
1950s–1960s

Rural CMS was set up as communes were established, with the first experimental schemes developed from 1955 in Henan and Shanxi. They were promoted more widely during the Great Leap Forward of 1958 to 1959, but probably collapsed in the disastrous economic and social aftermath of that movement. The Maoist central leadership then promoted CMS again during the Cultural Revolution and its aftermath (1966–1976) alongside production-brigade health stations and "barefoot doctors" (*chijiao yisheng*).

Although driven by national policy, CMS in the pre-market reform period was organized and funded locally, and so consisted in reality of a variety of schemes across the countryside. A common arrangement, however, was that CMS funds were made up of contributions from production teams (*shengchan dui*, the lowest level of organization of agricultural production within the commune system) and from commune (*gongshe*) and production brigade (*shengchan dadui*) public-welfare funds (*gongyijin*). The precise balance in shares of funding varied from locality to locality, but by the 1970s there were two main types of scheme, one funded entirely by the commune, the other in which production brigades provided the majority of funds. Government budgetary subsidies also differed substantially across localities. There is at this time no reliable comprehensive data on cooperative or government spending on CMS health provision more broadly. However, budgetary investment appears to have been mainly confined to the provision of vaccines and contraception, health-campaign materials, and the training of local medical personnel.

CMS funds were then used to pay or reduce payments for commune members' treatment, immunizations, and medicine at the local health station. Sometimes CMS funds were also used to pay for more-expensive treatment or medicine at the nearest commune or county hospital. The quality and kind of treatment the system covered varied from place to place.

LIMITATIONS AND ACHIEVEMENTS

Accounts of China's rural CMS under collectivization often argue that by the late 1970s there was comprehensive provision delivering low-cost health services to a large majority of the population. The World Bank, for example, has argued that by 1975, 85 percent of the rural population was participating in CMS schemes that provided people with "access to cost-effective preventive and curative health services and some sharing of the risks of medically caused financial misfortune" (World Bank 1997, p. 2). It is unlikely, however, that such a large proportion of the population had access to anything more than very basic curative health services or that there was significant risk sharing. Despite the emphasis during the Cultural Revolution on redressing the urban bias in health services, in 1980 there were still more than four times more doctors per head of population in urban areas than in the countryside and more than three times the number of beds (Liu, Rao, and Hu 2002). Given the early accounts of problems with the systems, the degree of protection seems to have been limited in poor areas by lack of funding. This claim is backed up by figures on health spending. In 1980 rural collective funds accounted for only 17 percent of total health spending, even though 80 percent of China's population lived in the countryside. Private payments remained a significant share of total health spending in 1980 at 23 percent (Hossain 1997).

Because it was locally organized and funded, rural CMS in the era of collectivization provided access to only very basic services and suffered from many problems. Local schemes were poorly designed and were usually established with little expert input to ensure their financial sustainability. Many funds were soon bankrupted or were unable to pay for health treatment toward the end of each year. There are also reports of local officials abusing the funds and diverting them to other uses. Rural CMS provided a measure of basic health protection to rural dwellers, but while the national government wanted to see collective protection in the countryside, it did not commit state funding to the program. This decision contributed to the problems CMS encountered in meeting health needs, particularly when the collective sources of funding declined in the early 1980s.

Despite its limitations, rural CMS significantly extended access to health services in the countryside and is credited with contributing to dramatic improvements in infant mortality and life expectancy at a time when China's economic development level was still relatively low: the infant mortality rate improved from 200 per 1,000 live births in 1949 to 47 per 1,000 in 1973, and life expectancy rose from 35 to 65 (Liu, Rao, and Hu 2002).

THE COLLAPSE OF THE COOPERATIVE MEDICAL SYSTEM IN THE EARLY 1980s

Rural CMS was, however, soon to collapse in the post-Mao period, reportedly leaving only about 5 percent of villages with CMS by 1984. Although some localities may have provided assistance for the poorest, access to health care for most was now determined by ability to pay. This situation is thought to have contributed to stagnation in the health of the population on some indicators, notably the under-five mortality rate. Though there are no authoritative accounts, the collapse of CMS schemes seems to have been due to a combination of poorly designed and problematic plans, a shortage of government investment, and a decline in sources of collective funding following the decollectivization of agricultural production. At the same time, a political swing against the Cultural Revolution meant CMS lost the support of the Ministry of Health, which focused instead on generating income for health services from nonstate sources and encouraged their de facto privatization. And as part of this process, village-based barefoot doctors became private practitioners and sometimes moved out of poor areas, where it was difficult to make a living. This further reduced access to health care for rural dwellers on low incomes.

ATTEMPTS TO REFORM AND REVIVE COOPERATIVE SCHEMES

From the late 1980s and early 1990s, the central government put rural-health risk protection back on the agenda, but in 2002 it was still estimated that about 95 percent of rural Chinese were paying for their health care directly out of their own pockets and without any form of risk protection (Liu, Rao, and Hu 2002). And in late 2002, China's rural population (70% of the total) was said to consume only 20 percent of medical services and resources (*People's Daily* 2002).

Attempts to reintroduce some form of rural health protection—usually a form of CMS—from the late 1980s have been fraught with problems and until perhaps very recently resulted in no significant improvements in the shares participating in cooperative schemes. But since 2000, the reforms have had some new momentum, particularly from 2003 as the leadership of Hu Jintao and Wen Jiabao focused on rural areas and promoted the development of a "new socialist countryside." As part of this program, developing "new rural CMS" has been high on the agenda, and the central government began to commit resources for the first time from 2003. Whether it will be possible to overcome the enormous problems that have

so far prevented the widespread reintroduction of CMS remains unclear. But the central government claimed in late 2007 that 720 million rural dwellers, over 80 percent of the total, were participating (Xinhua News Agency 2007). If these figures are correct and current schemes are sustainable, then the Chinese government might be on track to achieve its target of extending CMS to all.

SEE ALSO *Epidemics; Rural Development, 1949–1978: Five Guarantees.*

BIBLIOGRAPHY

Anson, Ofra, and Sun Shifang. *Health Care in Rural China: Lessons from HeBei Province.* Aldershot, U.K.: Ashgate, 2005.

Carrin, Guy, Aviva Ron, Yang Hui, et al. The Reform of the Rural Cooperative Medical System in the People's Republic of China: Interim Experience in 14 Pilot Countries. *Social Science and Medicine* 48, 7 (1999): 961–972.

Feng Xueshan, Tang Shenglan, Gerald Bloom, et al. Cooperative Medical Schemes in Contemporary Rural China. *Social Science and Medicine* 41, 8 (1995): 1111–1118.

Hossain, Shaikh I. *Tackling Health Transition in China.* Washington, DC: World Bank, 1997.

Liu Yuanli, William Hsiao, Li Qing, et al. Transformation of China's Rural Health Care Financing. *Social Science & Medicine* 41, 8 (1995): 1085–1093.

Liu Yuanli, Rao Keqin, and Hu Shanlian. *Toward Establishing a Rural Health Protection System.* Manila, Philippines: Asian Development Bank, 2002.

People's Daily. November 21, 2002.

World Bank. *Financing Health Care: Issues and Options for China.* Washington, DC: Author, 1997.

Xinhua News Agency. October 18, 2007.

Jane Duckett

RURAL DEVELOPMENT, 1949–1978

This entry contains the following:

DAZHAI

■

The Dazhai Production Team in Xiyang County, Shanxi Province, was made a national model in 1964 when Mao Zedong issued the call, "In agriculture, learn from Dazhai." Dazhai's success story was based on its self-reliance in turning infertile soil into productive land by relying on manpower and hard work. Water was transported over many miles for irrigation, land was cleared in the mountains, and terraced fields were built that withstood drought and flood. Dazhai became an object of intense study.

The main driving force behind Dazhai's achievements was Chen Yonggui (1913–1986), a true Communist Party activist who represented the poor and lower-middle peasants of the village. Chen organized the less-productive villagers into teams with names such as "Oldsters and Youngsters" and "Iron Girls" to perform the backbreaking work that was needed to convert barren Dazhai into a "pacesetter in China's agriculture."

By the early 1970s, Dazhai had become the benchmark for all agricultural production in China. Some twenty-thousand visitors passed through daily to study this model of self-reliance. By late 1980, however, the Dazhai model was officially discredited. It transpired then that Dazhai's achievements were the result of extensive assistance from the People's Liberation Army. Even Dazhai's reliance on pure manpower and a clear understanding of proletarian politics turned out to be a hoax.

The influence of the Dazhai campaign proved tenacious. Even today, one can still see the faded slogans proclaiming "In agriculture, learn from Dazhai" in rural China. After the late 1990s, Dazhai's inhabitants no longer stressed self-reliance and hard work, but the goal of becoming as well off as the rest of the people. Not a single household was solely engaged in agriculture anymore, and more than 80 percent of the villagers now worked in industry and the service sector, in particular tourism. Most of the arable land had been turned into orchards and dense woods.

BIBLIOGRAPHY

China's Model Village: From Political Symbol to Brand Name. Xinhua News Agency, June 27, 2002. http://news.xinhuanet.com/english/2002-06/27/content_460077.htm.

Lu Xin-An. Dazhai: Imagistic Rhetoric as a Cultural Instrument. *American Communication Journal* 5, 1 (2001): http://www.acjournal.org/holdings/vol5/iss1/articles/lu.htm.

Tachai: Pacesetter in China's Agriculture. Beijing: Foreign Languages Press, 1978.

Wen Yin and Liang Hua. *Tachai: The Red Banner.* Beijing: Foreign Languages Press, 1977.

Zhao Jijun and Jan Woudstra. "In Agriculture, Learn from Dazhai": Mao Zedong's Revolutionary Model Village and the Battle against Nature. *Landscape Research* 32, 2 (2007): 171–205.

Stefan R. Landsberger

OVERVIEW

Rural development and its policies are the essential defining feature that separates the Maoist era from the reform policies launched by Deng Xiaoping in 1978. Chinese economic reforms started with rural reforms, and the peculiar structural conditions prevailing in the rural sector in 1978 explain much of the dynamics of the "China miracle," especially in the 1980s and 1990s. The flipside of this assessment is that Maoist development favored industrial development to the detriment of the rural sector, and that the explosion of growth after 1978 was very much the realization of a potential stymied for two decades.

PRINCIPLES OF RURAL DEVELOPMENT POLICY

Between 1949 and 1978 rural development was subordinated to two goals: state-led rapid industrialization and sociopolitical transformation in the countryside. In Chinese Communist Party (CCP) theory, the latter contributed to the former, because traditional elites wasted rural surplus for noninvestive purposes (e.g., luxury consumption, ritual expenditures, etc.), and because large parts of the rural labor force, particularly women, were idle. Thus, beginning with the land reforms of the late 1940s and early 1950s and culminating with the establishment of the People's Communes, rural development always was accompanied by political struggle. This had direct economic consequences because the issue of rural sideline activities and private enterprise loomed large in these conflicts, which were perceived as harbingers of a rebirth of capitalism in the countryside. Thus, during most of the period from 1949 to 1978 the opportunities for further developing rural sideline production remained very limited, and Chinese agriculture suffered from a lack of diversification and opportunity.

STATE FARMS

During the first thirty years of the People's Republic, state farms were a small part of the rural development equation. Even after their rapid growth in the 1950s, state farms made up less than 5 percent of the agricultural sector, a size that was maintained through the 1980s. Nevertheless, state farms played a nationally significant role in the rural development of border and remote regions, especially in Heilongjiang and Xinjiang, and in niche products, such as dairy and rubber, in which state farms were dominant until the 1990s.

China's state farms were modeled on the Soviet Union's *sovkhoz* farms. State farms are wholly owned by the government and were intended to be the most modern and socialist forms of agricultural production. The farms were to be set up on a large scale and to have processing, storage, and transport facilities on site. Additionally, state farms would provide a range of social welfare benefits to employees, who were to be paid wages, rather than with a share of the harvest as in the collective sector. The benefits of employment on a state farm were to include housing, medical care, and schooling for employees' children. The Soviet origins of China's state farms were attacked when the Russian approach to modernization was called into question by Mao Zedong and his supporters in the late 1950s. Yet, as in other sectors of the state-owned economy, the Soviet model remained in place as the dominant paradigm in which state farms were understood and evaluated.

The term *state farms* encompassed a wide variety of institutional and governmental affiliations. The farms that national statistics have typically been based upon were owned and run by the Ministry of Agriculture or the Ministry of Land Reclamation (1956–1982). Better-known farms, such as those of the Xinjiang Production and Construction Corps or the farms of the prison (*laogai*) system, were paid for, run, and assessed separately. Additionally, other national government ministries, provinces, counties, and municipalities all owned and ran state farms during the Mao years.

Beginning in the 1990s, most state farms underwent enterprise reforms that transferred managerial authority to production teams (contracting). In border regions, however, national government ownership and management of agriculture remained in place, particularly in Xinjiang. At the same time, and accelerating after 2000, many farms were privatized or taken public, with government entities maintaining majority or minority ownership stakes. In this way, their historical trajectory more closely followed the reforms of other state-owned enterprises. Some former state farms will likely become internationally competitive, publicly held agribusinesses, particularly in sectors such as dairy and food processing. In these cases, their heritage as state-owned enterprises will likely result in continued access to government financing and political clout.

Gregory Rohlf

This suppression of the division of labor in the Chinese countryside also reflected the absolute priorities of the CCP leadership in industrial development. Agriculture was a major source of industrial inputs, and increasing numbers of industrial workers had to be fed. In the growth model underlying Chinese economic policies under Maoism there was a fundamental trade-off between consumption and investment, and agriculture was tasked with minimizing consumption in order to maximize capital accumulation. This resulted in a price policy that favored industry in terms of both low-input prices and low-cost procurement of food for urban areas. The policy started with the implementation of the grain procurement system in 1954 and necessarily led to the establishment of increasingly repressive institutional structures in the countryside. This causal chain worked

via the weakening of incentives for agricultural production, followed by increasing shortages of agricultural produces. The political leadership reacted by stepping up pressure and resorting to command economy instruments. As a result, Chinese agriculture was geared toward supplying basic commodities to the industrial and urban segment in the economy.

ECONOMIC PERFORMANCE

The performance of agriculture between 1949 and 1978 clearly reflects these institutional and political conditions. The average growth rate of agricultural GDP during the period was only 2.2 percent (compared to 4.4% after 1978), and although this was a clear improvement over the pre-1949 era, it must be acknowledged that much of the first half of the twentieth century was marked by war and civil

WORK POINTS SYSTEM

With the advent of more advanced forms of rural collectivization in the mid-1950s, peasant labor became organized in work teams, which operated under production quotas issued from higher administrative levels and under guidance of a team leader. With different degrees of centralization, this system prevailed until 1978, when agricultural reforms were launched.

Within work teams the linkage between team output and individual labor contribution was determined by means of the work points (*gongfen*) system. Daily consumption was supported by a system of rations, so that after deducting this subsistence level and after fulfillment of procurement quotas, a surplus might have resulted. This surplus, measured in pecuniary values, was divided according to the work points that an individual had accumulated in the course of the agricultural year. Very often these claims were frozen on a forced savings account to support rural investment. Further, the actual worth of a work point could vary, according to the economic situation. There was a general trend of declining worth of work points, reflecting demographic conditions, as well as regional variation of the value of a work point, which reached from 4 to 5 fen in poor areas and 1.5 yuan in rich areas.

The work points system distinguished between time and piece rates, which were frequently applied conjointly. Time rates were based on an assessment of labor quality of types of workers, in terms of gender, age, qualification, etc. so that for example, an able-bodied male worker could earn between 9 and 10 points per day, whereas females would earn 7 to 8 points in the average. Piece rates were based on output. Time rates were the preferred approach, because they were seen to have a more equalizing effect. This system was modified with the political agitation for the Dazhai work points system, in which the labor contribution was assessed in regular self-assessment meetings. The Dazhai system also included aspects of work motivation and zeal, which, however, were mostly assessed in terms of the class status of the individuals. In many villages this factor contributed to increasing levels of tension and conflict, thus weakening the incentive functions of the work points system.

BIBLIOGRAPHY

Parish, William L., and Martin King Whyte. Material Equality and Inequality. In *Village and Family in Contemporary China*. Chicago: University of Chicago Press, 1978, pp. 47–72.

Carsten Herrmann-Pillath

strife. In the same period, industrial GDP grew an average of almost 10 percent, resulting in a major structural shift that saw the agricultural share shrinking from 59.7 percent in 1952 to 34.4 percent in 1978. At the same time, the employment share remained very high, moving only from 82.5 percent to 71.1 percent. This implies that agricultural labor productivity did not grow during the entire period—in fact, it declined below the 1952 level in the wake of the Great Leap Forward, and it recovered that level only in the mid-1970s. Similarly, according to some estimates, the growth of total factor productivity, a measure of total efficiency of the production process, was negative in the relevant period.

These performance indicators reveal that rural development in the Maoist era was a tragic failure, and became a nightmare during the Great Leap Forward, when distorted statistics and ideological frenzy caused one of the largest famines of the twentieth century, hitting the peasantry almost exclusively.

Rural development was also burdened by the effects of what can be seen as a massive pronatalist institutional setting in the countryside. Amid growing disillusion about the CCP leadership and the continuing tensions of political struggle, the family remained the essential core of peasant life. Within the arrangements of collectivization, the number of household members was a direct determinant of the few economic benefits a peasant could draw from the existing regime, such as the allotment of private plots. As a result, unfettered population growth put into perspective the growth of mandatory production of grain, cotton, and other agricultural commodities. For example, the production of oil-bearing crops shrank between 1958 and 1965, recovering to a mere 2.8 percent between 1966 and 1978. By comparison, it exploded with a 22.7 percent growth rate between 1978 and 1982. Grain production grew at a rate of 3.5 percent between 1953 and 1957 and again from 1966 to 1978 (with a catastrophic breakdown in between), just

PRODUCTION AND CONSTRUCTION CORPS

The first Production and Construction Corps (Shengchan Jianshe Bingtuan) (PCC) and the only one still in existence by 2009 is the Xinjiang PCC. This special economic and semimilitary organization was created in 1954 to maintain a strong Han and military presence in this border region inhabited by different ethnic groups (mainly Muslims) and to develop this backward region rich in mineral resources. The 175,000 members of the Xinjiang PCC were mainly former soldiers of the People's Liberation Army, which had taken over the Republic of East Turkestan in 1949. This organization was inspired by the traditional Chinese system of *tunken shubian* (settling soldiers to clear the land and protect the frontier). After ethnic problems in 1962, urban educated youth from the interior were sent in large numbers (including 100,000 Shanghainese from 1963 to 1965).

After the Sino-Soviet tension, Mao Zedong encouraged the creation of similar organizations in Heilongjiang. The Heilongjiang PCC was established in 1968, followed by others from 1969 to 1971 in such border regions as Inner Mongolia and Yunnan but also elsewhere (more than half of the provinces altogether). The military farms were mainly created by giving a military organization and adding military personnel to the former state farms or by transforming former labor camps. Their functions were more complex than before the Cultural Revolution (1966–1969), when a balance existed between the economic and military functions. Due to Mao's fears concerning a possible Soviet attack, the latter became prominent. Political and ideological objectives mingled: Large numbers of urban educated youth were sent as a way to disperse the former Red Guards, to alleviate the urban unemployment problem, and to "reeducate" a whole generation. The result was a bloating of the labor force, which could not be matched by a corresponding increase in production, especially in a context of prohibition of all "material incentives."

Relationships between educated youth and the uneducated and despotic military cadres were tense. Beatings and rapes of the former by some of the latter caused resentment among the youth and their parents. Because the dual leadership was costly and the military not expert in economic management, all the PCCs were losing money, including the Xinjiang PCC, which had been making a profit before the Cultural Revolution. All PCCs were then abolished between 1973 and 1975. Management of the farms was transferred to the local civil authorities. Most of the urban educated youth were able to go back home at the end of the 1970s, except the Shanghainese who had been sent to Xinjiang.

At that time, fear of Soviet encirclement and Uygur separatism, as well as a renewed interest in the economic capacities of Xinjiang, led the Chinese authorities to try and settle as many Han people as possible in the region. When the Xinjiang PCC was restored in December 1981, the collective-management system in Xinjiang, like the rest of the nation, gave way to economic reforms. It is now an integrated economic system of more than 2.5 million people (13 percent of the total Xinjiang population), including almost 1 million employed, comprising 14 divisions, 174 farms, and 4,391 industrial, construction, transport, and commercial enterprises, 13 of which are publicly traded. This special entity covering 74,500 square kilometers is mainly inhabited by Han people (almost 90 percent of the total) and is de facto only accountable to the center. Its annual output of around 43 billion yuan renminbi in 2007 made up 12.3 percent of that of the Xinjiang Autonomous Region. It has created its own cities, like Shihezi, and its own schools and universities, as well as hospitals and other public facilities.

Like all state farms, the PCCs made a real agricultural contribution in some places, but also had negative effects on the environment. They helped increase a military presence at the border in periods of tension, but on the whole they were more costly than useful. In the 1950s, the Xinjiang PCC was adapted to stabilizing a newly conquered territory. Today, its existence is a testimony of the quasi-colonial status of this region.

BIBLIOGRAPHY

He Lan and Shi Weimin. *Zhiqing beiwanglu: Shangshan xiaxiang yundong zhong de Shengchan Jianshe Bingtuan* [Memorandum for the educated youth: The Production and Construction Corps in the up to the mountains down to the villages movement]. Beijing: Zhongguo Shehui Kexue Chubanshe, 1996.

Heilongjiangsheng guoying nongchang jingji fazhan shi [History of the economic development of the state farms of Heilongjiang Province]. Harbin, PRC: Heilongjiang Renmin Chubanshe, 1984.

Liu Ke. *Xinjiang Shengchan Jianshe Bingtuan renkou qianyi yu kaifa yanjiu* [Study of the migrations of population and development in the Xinjiang Production and Construction Corps]. Ürümqi, PRC: Xinjiang Renmin Chubanshe, 1997.

McMillen, Donald H. Xinjiang and the Production and Construction Corps: A Han Organization in a Non-Han Region. *Australian Journal of Chinese Affairs* 6 (1981): 65–96.

Xinjiang Production and Construction Corps. http://www.bingtuan.gov.cn.

Michel Bonnin

barely supporting the growing population and limiting the qualitative change in food consumption, particularly meat production.

THE LEGACY OF MAOIST RURAL DEVELOPMENT

Faced with massive underemployment in the rural sector, the CCP leadership already had mobilized rural labor for industrialization directly; the result was the disastrous failure of small-scale steel production during the Great Leap Forward. Nevertheless, during the 1970s this approach to rural industrialization was revived. The aim was to relieve the shortages of industrial goods in the countryside, while also exploiting locational advantages and low transport costs of the decentralized industrial structure. Agricultural development was severely hampered also by the lack of industrial inputs such as fertilizers and construction material for infrastructure development. Thus, especially in the more advanced regions closer to urban centers, the People's Communes began to establish rural enterprises, sometimes also reviving the sideline production traditions of pre-1949 rural China. After a shakeout following the demise of Maoist policies, many of those enterprises helped to launch the tremendously successful township and village enterprises in the 1980s. In the late 1970s the increasing availability of industrial inputs, together with the importation of large-scale chemical-production facilities made possible by the thawing of political relations with the West, contributed to boost agricultural growth that was triggered by the 1978 reforms.

Rural development after 1949 did manifest very positive features in terms of general population indicators, in particular health and life expectancy and distribution of wealth and income. These effects were mainly the result of the internal pacification of the countryside (the Cultural Revolution spilled over from the cities only to a limited degree), and the efficacy of mass mobilization in improving basic living conditions, such as the famous campaigns against rats and other carriers of infectious diseases. However, this does not invalidate the assessment that between 1949 and 1978 China's peasants faced massive economic discrimination, which was further heightened by increasing social discrimination that resulted from the institutionalization of a status system that put urbanites into a privileged position in every respect.

BIBLIOGRAPHY

Ash, Robert. Squeezing the Peasants: Grain Extraction, Food Consumption and Rural Living Standards in Mao's China. *China Quarterly* 188 (2006): 959–998.

Maddison, Angus. *Chinese Economic Performance in the Long Run: 960–2030 AD.* 2nd ed. Paris: Organization for Economic Cooperation and Development, 2007.

Perkins, Dwight H. China's Economic Policies and Performance. In *The People's Republic, Part 2: Revolutions within the Chinese Revolution, 1966–1982.* Vol. 15 of *The Cambridge History of China,* ed. Roderick MacFarquhar and John K. Fairbank. Cambridge, U.K., New York, and Melbourne: Cambridge University Press, 1991.

Carsten Herrmann-Pillath

LAND REFORM OF 1950

The Agrarian Reform Law of 1950 was an essential legal building block of the development strategy of the "new democracy" that was propagated by the Chinese Communist Party (CCP) during the period of radicalization after the mid-1950s. The law had the following objectives:

- Redistributing land (and complementary property such as tools and draft animals) from the landlord class to the poor peasant class to achieve a more equitable distribution of land,

- Increasing the productivity of agriculture by suppressing unproductive uses of funds and enhancing individual incentives,

- Fostering the emergence of advanced forms of production, and

- Suppressing and eradicating traditional ("feudal") social structures in the countryside.

The law protected private ownership of land, including the rights of members of the rich peasant class, who hired additional labor for cultivation. Furthermore, commercial and industrial enterprises enjoyed protection, even if they were owned by landlords, because they were regarded to be advanced economic formations. Thus, formally speaking, the law was mainly focused on economic development.

In the first months after the Agrarian Reform Law was promulgated in June 1950, for the most part these precepts were followed. However, with China's entry into the Korean War, as ideological frenzy and fears of counterrevolutionary activities considerably intensified during winter 1950/1951, implementation of the law was hampered by heightened conflict and aggression.

SOCIOECONOMIC CONTEXT AND CCP STRATEGY

The Land Reform of 1950 was the formal conclusion of a protracted and complicated process of land reform that had started already in areas occupied by Communist forces in the 1930s, especially the Jiangxi Soviet. Before 1949 it had proceeded successfully in the so-called Old Liberated Areas—parts of north, northeast, and east China, home to roughly a quarter of the Chinese population. In these areas the Agrarian Reform Law simply consolidated the accomplishments.

But after 1949, the Communist Party was faced with the very demanding challenge of expanding Communist rural administration to all parts of China, including vast geographical areas such as the entire region of South China, where there had been no land reform measures and Communist power was almost nonexistent. Thus, in many areas of Guangdong, for example, land reform was completed only in 1952. Against this backdrop, land reform also has to be seen as a crucial element in the CCP's strategy to win legitimacy. Land reform was accompanied by a revolution in the structure of village hierarchies, because poor peasants not only were the main recipients of redistributed land, but also were supposed to be the main source of the new socialist cadre stratum. With this approach, land reform continued in the tradition of class struggle in the war against the Guomindang forces before 1949. In these years, it was inextricably linked with the process of mobilizing support for the CCP, and in recruiting for the People's Liberation Army (PLA).

The Agrarian Reform Law marked a major change in CCP strategy with regard to the implementation of land redistribution. Before 1949 the CCP had relied mainly on the "mass line" to push land reform: Land redistribution was conducted by villagers organized in peasant associations, often supported by external work teams sent in by the CCP. This approach produced many outbreaks of violence. Villagers had to be mobilized to speak out against their former elites, who played vastly different roles in different places, from respected lineage elder to local bully. Where Communist power was not perceived as being consolidated unmistakenly, peasants feared the revival of the old system. As a result, when political agitation reached a certain height, villagers killed and destroyed property indiscriminately to make a return of the old elites physically impossible. With the transition to national power, the CCP intended to constrain this brutality, but in the end, land reform was a violent process: at least one million people were killed, mostly former landlords and rich peasants, and almost the same number were imprisoned.

A major problem in implementing the land reform law was the existing rural class structure. This structure was analyzed methodologically by Mao Zedong's famous 1927 "Report on an Investigation in the Peasant Movement in Hunan." A "landlord" in traditional China was usually an absentee owner or a manager of a lineage estate. In many Chinese villages the landlord class was physically absent. In some areas of China, the so-called dead landlords, or lineage estates, were by far the most important landholding institutions. According to the traditional understanding, the corporate estate managers earned a considerable private profit from managing the estates, but were not included in the landlord class. Furthermore, in less productive agricultural regions the surplus was too small to maintain a sustainable landlord class, so the boundaries between rich peasants and landlords tended to be fuzzy. Thus, a major aim of land reform was the final destruction of the economic foundations of the traditional rural social structure, excluding the nuclear family, and less a substantial redistribution of a limited pool of land. All traditional institutions, such as lineage halls and temples, relied on estates, which were annihilated.

RESULTS OF LAND REFORM

Land reform did succeed in equalizing the distribution of land, but it did not succeed in equalizing the distribution of income. According to some estimates, after land reform poor and middle peasants owned more than 90 percent of China's land, but rich peasants' plots were still twice the average size of poor peasants'. Furthermore, poor peasants often suffered from a lack of complementary capital and labor power to make the best economic use of their land. In addition, in the more developed regions of China land reform resulted in the conversion of estates into shares, because division was not feasible in holdings such as orchards and fish ponds. In the end, rural inequalities increased again, with middle and rich peasants emerging as the main beneficiaries of land reform. This was a major impetus for collectivization, supported by the growing disillusionment of the poor peasant stratum, which included a growing number of newly coopted rural cadres.

SEE ALSO *Peasantry since 1900.*

BIBLIOGRAPHY
Riskin, Carl. State Power and the Foundations of Socialism. In *China's Political Economy: The Quest for Development since 1949.* Oxford, U.K.: Oxford University Press, 1987.
Shue, Vivienne. *Peasant China in Transition: The Dynamics of Development Toward Scoialism, 1949–1956.* Berkeley: University of California Press, 1980.
Tang, Anthony M. *An Analytical and Empirical Investigation of Agriculture in Mainland China, 1952–1980.* Taibei: Chung-Hua Institution for Economic Research, 1984.
Teiwes, Frederick C. Establishment and Consolidation of the New Regime. In *The People's Republic, Part 1: The Emergence*

of Revolutionary China 1949–1865. Vol. 14 of *The Cambridge History of China*, ed. Roderick MacFarquhar and John K. Fairbank. Cambridge, U.K., New York, Melbourne: Cambridge University Press, 1987.

Carsten Herrmann-Pillath

COLLECTIVIZATION

Collectivization refers to the process of socialist transformation of Chinese rural society after 1949, culminating in the establishment of People's Communes at the end of the 1950s. In spite of the abolishment of the communes in 1982, this process left a lasting legacy for China: In 2008 land property rights in rural areas still were owned by rural collectives that correspond to the grassroots-level administrative units. In addition, collectivization prepared the institutional setting for the emergence in the 1980s of township and village enterprises, which also were managed mainly by the local administrations, and which have undergone a privatization process since the mid-1990s.

Collectivization built on the land reform of the late 1940s and early 1950s, responding to perceived failures in equalizing peasant incomes. At the same time, the adoption of a heavy-industrialization strategy along the lines of the Soviet model required agriculture to become a major source of surplus that could be channeled into capital accumulation. Hence, collectivization became the crucial institutional device to extract resources from the rural sector. This caused endemic incentive problems in collectivized agriculture, which were tackled by increased reliance on ideological mobilization and mass campaigns, first in the Great Leap Forward, and later in the Socialist Education Campaign and the Cultural Revolution.

In the 1950s collectivization began with "mutual aid teams" in which peasants were supposed to cooperate by means of reciprocal labor exchange, mutual lending of tools and draft animals, and so forth. But given the inequality of means among poor and rich peasant households, further collectivization of land and capital was necessary to achieve a stable institutional solution. At first, collectivization preserved rental claims by the original owners, but allowed for further centralization of decision-making power. With the strengthening of the poor peasant class in rural society, an interest group emerged that was highly responsive to Mao Zedong's policy turn toward more radical collectivization. Within only two years the development from advanced cooperatives to People's Communes

was hammered through, resulting in almost complete collectivization of agriculture at the end of 1958.

Whereas lower forms of collectivization often had corresponded to natural social units in the countryside (such as hamlets, lineages, and so forth), the communes moved toward a much higher level of aggregation, encompassing traditional marketing areas and beyond. After the failure of the Great Leap Forward and a downsizing of the communes, rural collectives stabilized in a decentralized form that renewed the correspondence between socialist institutions and traditional social structure, thereby paving the way for the vigorous revival of peasant traditions after 1978.

A rural collective of the 1960s and 1970s typically consisted of four layers: the household, the production team, the production brigade, and the People's Commune. Households (not individuals) were the units assigned tasks, work points, or private plots, and they were led by male household heads. The production team was the pivotal economic decision-making unit, and each had a team leader, an accountant, a work point recorder, and so on; most teams consisted of about fifty households, which constituted an entire village or hamlet in many parts of China. The production team was the owner of the collective land, tools, draft animals, and other capital goods, and managed all the tasks assigned from above, particularly production quotas related to state procurement of agricultural products. The team also controlled individual labor (apart from work on private plots). Sometimes team members were delegated to work in brigade enterprises, where they earned collective income for the team.

The production brigade was the base unit delivering most of the social services to the peasant economy and for managing larger-scale complementary units such as repair shops and food-processing factories. Brigade cadres were collective cadres, but the brigade did not play a separate role in the rural ownership system. In comparison, the People's Commune was a Janus-faced unit that already contained state-level organizational units. As the central linkage of financial flows between the rural sector and the other, urban sectors of the economy, the communes and their state cadres were able to pursue partly autonomous economic objectives, particularly with regard to rural industries.

To a large degree, collectivization supported social involution of rural society, because the collective units became increasingly insular, even in terms of kinship relations across different settlement units. Only the dynamics of rural reforms after 1978 broke this trend.

BIBLIOGRAPHY

Potter, Sulamith Heins, and Jack Potter. *China's Peasants: The Anthropology of a Revolution.* Cambridge, U.K., and New York: Cambridge University Press, 1990.

Riskin, Carl. *China's Political Economy: The Quest for Development since 1949*. Oxford, U.K.: Oxford University Press, 1987.

Carsten Herrmann-Pillath

PEOPLE'S COMMUNES

The People's Communes (*renmin gongshe*) were the main organizational structure in the Chinese countryside under Maoist rule. First launched in 1958 in preparation for the organizational prerequisites for the Great Leap Forward (GLF), they were abolished again between 1982 and 1984, when the new constitution of 1982 reinstated the old rural administrative structure below county level.

In the first stage of their development, communes were all-inclusive administrative units encompassing several *xiang* (administrative villages), that is, the former administrative unit between the county (*xian*) and the village (*cun*). By 1961 they already had been sized down, mostly to the level of a *xiang* or a market town (*zhen*). This measure illustrates the two very different roles communes played in rural development.

FIRST STAGE: MAOIST MILLENARIANISM AND FORCED INDUSTRIALIZATION

During the GLF the communes were large-scale units of mass mobilization heralding the millenarian calls of Communism. Their organization was quasi military, and they centralized decision making in agricultural production in order to release as much peasant labor as possible for the purposes of infrastructure construction (especially irrigation) and small-scale industrialization (small-scale steel furnaces). At the same time, they were intended to be spearheads of social transformation, especially in dissolving the family as a unit of consumption. Until the disastrous consequences of the GLF became evident, communes provided free meals and other services that were supposed to free women from traditional household chores. In the first months, the commune ideal resonated with the millenarian tradition in Chinese peasant culture, and heralded a fundamental cultural transformation in substituting the family stove with the mass-scale canteen. Communes triggered a mania of "eat it up," finally depleting even the emergency grain reservoirs.

Yet, the first-stage communes constituted part and parcel of the Maoist industrialization strategy, which aimed at maximizing the rural contribution to industrial accumulation. The step-by-step introduction of state procurement of agricultural products and of collective organizations resulted in serious disincentives for peasant producers. This also aggravated the problem of rural surplus labor. Full-scale collectivization and mass mobilization aimed at finally resolving these contradictions. This was bolstered by the establishment of the household registration system (*hukou*), which turned the communes into the basic cells of Maoist rural society, from which peasants could never escape except by enrolling in military service.

SECOND STAGE: LOCAL STATE AND ECONOMIC DEVELOPMENT

The resulting havoc rapidly led to a thorough restructuring of the communes. Foremostly, this included a decentralization of decision making in production and a reconstitution of the household as the basic socioeconomic unit, including the limited use of private plots. Communes adopted a three-level administrative structure, with the team as the basic level and the brigade as the intermediate.

Notwithstanding the considerable regional variations across China, the major functions of a second-stage commune can be summarized as

1. acting as the bottom level of state administration, such as branches of the State Procurement Organization, the Credit Cooperative; and the Tax Bureau;

2. providing social services such as education and health care to the rural communities; and

3. managing rural industrial enterprises.

The third function became increasingly important in the 1970s, gradually creating a dualist economic system in which the rural sector also became increasingly self-reliant in basic industrial goods such as cement and textiles. A well-developed commune at the end of the 1970s owned several basic industrial units catering for the immediate needs of the local economy, as well as some enterprises that continued with pre-1949 local manufacturing traditions such as wood processing, handicrafts, or scrap steel works. These local industries prepared the ground for the upsurge in the 1980s of the township and village enterprises, which became a major factor of growth.

The second function reflected a fundamental tension in the socioeconomic fabric of communes, and may be regarded as the historically essential one. In pre-1949 China, state administration ended on the county level. With the fusion of village and townships in the communes, and after the introduction of the household registration system, the population of a commune typically included both peasants and urbanites, intermingling at the headquarters, often in a traditional market town. Townspeople enjoyed urban household status and its corresponding privileges. The urban unit became the spearhead of the state's further intrusion into rural society, supported by the instruments of mass communication and improving logistics. At the core of this were the group of state cadres, who had a status different from collective cadres, especially on the lower administrative levels of the communes. State cadres had responsibility for fulfilling the obligations to the state (e.g., grain quotas), but they also mediated between the rural population and upper-level administrative units. Very often, state cadres had been relocated from other places.

The paradoxical result of this advance by the state was that, with the simultaneous emergence of a dualist economic structure, a cleavage opened up between the local government and the central government. On the one hand, state cadres represented the encroachment of formal power structures into peasant life, which provided the government's massive infrastructural capacity in, for example, population policies. On the other hand, there were strong incentives to pursue autonomous goals, especially in the local economy. Hence the contradictory picture of post-Mao society, with the central government able to interfere in even the most intimate aspects of peasant life, but at the same time unable to control the dynamism of the rural economy.

After the abolishment of the communes, the old functions had to be reassigned to the new (and old) entities. This resulted in neglect of the communes' second function, the provision of social services to the rural population, because they were not represented by any interest group among the new rural elites. Over the years, the demise of the communes caused the collapse of the unique rural health care system, which had integrated commune hospital services with essential and simple services delivered by legions of "barefoot doctors" at the village level. In some parts of rural China, collectivist ideals were revived later in some villages with strong rural industries. In other places, a vacuum was created that has never since been filled.

BIBLIOGRAPHY

Madsen, Richard. The Countryside under Communism. In *The People's Republic, Part 2: Revolutions within the Chinese Revolution 1966–1982.* Vol. 15 of *The Cambridge History of China*, ed. Roderick MacFarquhar and John K. Fairbank. Cambridge, U.K., New York, and Melbourne: Cambridge University Press, 1991.

Potter, Sulamith Heins, and Jack Potter. *China's Peasants: The Anthropology of a Revolution.* Cambridge, U.K., and New York: Cambridge University Press, 1990.

Unger, Jonathan. *The Transformation of Rural China.* New York: Sharpe, 2002.

Carsten Herrmann-Pillath

GREAT LEAP FORWARD

The Great Leap Forward emerged from the experience of the First Five-Year Plan, in which China attempted to apply Soviet methods of administrative central planning. Although the First Five-Year Plan was generally successful in generating industrial growth, it was unable to solve some deep-rooted problems and its structure and methods alienated Mao Zedong.

ROOTS IN THE FIRST FIVE-YEAR PLAN

First, agriculture could not meet the demands of rapid industrialization for more food and agricultural materials to feed China's growing nonagricultural workforce and light industries, and to exchange for imported capital goods. Second, the industries being built with Soviet aid and embodying Soviet capital-intensive technology created few new jobs for China's growing labor force. Only a small fraction of the thirty-odd million net new entries to the working-age population over the plan years (1953–1957) could be absorbed outside of agriculture. Third, with the state takeover of virtually all nonagricultural production after 1956, the burden of central administrative planning severely overtaxed the new and underprepared planning apparatus. Although a Second Five-Year Plan was drawn up to cover 1958 to 1962, it quickly became a dead letter in the emerging campaign of the Great Leap Forward.

The First Five-Year Plan's centralized, top-down methods of planning learned from the Russians were sharply criticized by Mao. He argued that such methods created an elite of bureaucrats who would regard themselves as superior to the masses and demand privileges, and that they ignored the creative potential of ordinary people, who were reduced to a passive role in carrying out directives from above. The material incentives required by such a system were also alien to Mao, who preferred the egalitarian distribution and motivational approaches of the revolutionary era.

The road to the Great Leap Forward was paved in part by the collectivization of agriculture in 1955 and 1956, during which private farming virtually disappeared, and in part by the decentralization of the system of economic planning and management in 1957 and 1958, which passed control of much economic activity to provincial and local governments. The political conditions for the Great Leap Forward were established by the harsh anti-rightist campaign of 1957, which severely punished people bold enough to accept Mao's invitation (in the Hundred Flowers campaign of 1956 to 1957) to criticize the party. This campaign ensured that there would be little resistance to the sharp change in economic policy.

GREAT LEAP CAMPAIGNS AND POLICIES

The immediate objective of the Great Leap Forward was to lift China onto a qualitatively higher level of development by means of three years of unrelenting and superhuman effort. In the winter of 1957 to 1958, a huge farmland capital construction campaign was launched in the countryside to build dams and reservoirs and extend the irrigated acreage. The agents of this campaign were the 740,000 agricultural collectives that had emerged from the "socialist high tide" of 1955 to 1956 and that averaged 164 households each. With too few people and resources to meet the demands put on them, these collectives began joining forces and thus formed what came to be called *rural people's communes.* Central party guidelines for the communes were published in the Beidaihe Resolution of 1958, and by December of that year the entire countryside was organized into some 26,000 communes containing an average of 5,000 households each. This size, corresponding to several townships (*xiang*), was excessively large from both a management and an economic standpoint, and the communes were soon broken into smaller units. By 1963 their number had grown to 74,000, averaging some 1,800 households each. They had a three-tier structure, with the commune itself at the top, the production team (*shengchan xiaodui*) at the bottom, and the production brigade (*shengchan dadui*) in between. The brigade corresponded roughly to the administrative village, with several hundred households, and the team to a neighborhood or "hamlet" of anything from fifteen to thirty or forty households.

The Great Leap Forward personified Mao's resistance to both markets and central planning as institutions to coordinate the economy. Lacking a coordinating mechanism, economic activity devolved down to self-sufficient units with minimal external links. Industrial ministries and even individual enterprises took this route in industry, whereas in agriculture the "self-reliant" unit was the commune. The commune was to be a vehicle for overcoming what Mao called the *three great differences*—between industry and agriculture, city and countryside, and mental and manual labor. Income distribution was egalitarian; for a time, much of farmers' income, including basic food, was distributed "free," without regard to work done. Enterprises and communes were managed by "revolutionary committees" of ordinary workers or farmers, managers, and technicians. Managers of enterprises were expected regularly to spend time doing manual work. Planners, administrators, and intellectuals of all kinds, condemned as "bourgeois experts," were "sent down" (*xiafang*) to do ordinary labor. Statistics became a motivational vehicle, and objective information dried up. Central planning collapsed, and a campaign style of administration was practiced.

"Walking on two legs" was perhaps the most characteristic slogan of the Great Leap Forward. It meant using all available resources and technology to develop more quickly. Thus, small, simple, and indigenous technologies would be used in the countryside alongside the urban large-scale, complex, and modern ones on which the First Five-Year Plan had concentrated exclusively. A great campaign to produce iron and steel in small rural "backyard furnaces" was launched in 1958. Tiny "factories" sprouted everywhere in the villages. Such work kept millions of farmers preoccupied during the harvest season of 1958, and an unknown portion of that year's large harvest was accordingly left in the fields. Water conservancy projects were carried out without assistance from "bourgeois" experts, with the result that widespread salinization of the North China Plain (China's largest agricultural area) damaged soil fertility for many years.

Although industrial output soared in 1958 and 1959, much of it was of poor quality, especially the crude iron and steel produced in rural furnaces and foundries. Many areas lacking iron ore melted down good-quality iron tools and implements to feed the furnaces. Even Mao was to refer to this episode as "a great catastrophe." In July of 1959, the policies of the Great Leap Forward were challenged by the defense minister, Peng Dehuai, at a party meeting in Lushan. Mao purged Peng from the leadership. He then reinstated the radical policies of the Great Leap Forward, which had been in the process of amelioration. This prolonged and deepened the disaster already in progress.

FAMINE

In agriculture there was no "great leap." The 1958 grain crop was an excellent one, but it was unevenly harvested, and by spring of 1959 there was hunger in many parts of China. The next three years' harvests were disastrously low, reaching a trough of 143.5 million metric tons in 1960 and 147.5 million tons in 1961 (compared with 1958's estimated 200 million tons). The result was massive famine. In those three years (1959–1961), the national mortality rate climbed to 14.6, 25.4, and 14.2 per thousand, respectively, compared to 10.8 in 1957. Excess mortality due to the famine is estimated to have ranged from fifteen to thirty million people. Most scholars agree that the principal cause was the policies of the Great Leap Forward, which destroyed work incentives, lowered productivity, harmed the land, wasted vast amounts of resources, and confiscated grain from the rural population to shield urban residents from the full impact of the famine. The Chinese government has never frankly acknowledged that what they refer to as the "three hard years" actually constituted a huge famine. Research on it continues to be officially discouraged in China.

Grain exports to the Soviet Union continued during the famine, in repayment of development loans taken before Sino-Soviet relations soured in 1960. The government finally

Woodcut illustrating peasants learning to read. *Much of Mao Zedong's plans during the Great Leap Forward involved improving the living standards for millions of rural Chinese through government administration of the nation's economy. However, life for many citizens became desperate, as agricultural production shrank in favor of industrial output, leading to a period of extreme starvation throughout the countryside.* **MARY EVANS PICTURE LIBRARY/EVERETT COLLECTION**

began to import grain to feed the coastal cities in 1961, taking some procurement pressure off the rural population. Although per capita grain supplies remained very low in 1962, crude mortality rates had fallen below 1957 levels.

AFTERMATH

With the collapse of the Great Leap Forward, rural markets were restored, and in some areas family farming was permitted again, although the shell of the commune structure was retained. Elsewhere, farming was done by small work groups within the production team. In most places, the team, rather than the much larger brigade or commune, was now the "basic accounting unit." This meant that most income earned within the team stayed at that level, rather than being passed up to higher levels to be redistributed, as earlier in the Great Leap Forward. Team members received work points for their labor and were paid in grain and cash according to their work point accumulations. Team level organization of production

and income distribution proved to be a stable approach that lasted until collective farming was abandoned in the early 1980s. Grain output (but not output per capita) recovered to the 1957 level by 1965 and to the 1958 level a year later. The Third Five-Year Plan, due to begin in 1963, was postponed until 1966. The interim three years of recovery were deemed a period of "readjustment, consolidation, filling out and raising standards." Agriculture was to be taken as the "foundation" of the national economy, meaning that industrial development would have to conform to agriculture's ability to provide a surplus. For the moment, magic bullets such as the Great Leap Forward were off the table.

SEE ALSO *Agricultural Production; Famine since 1800; Five-Year Plans.*

BIBLIOGRAPHY

Ashton, Basil, Kenneth Hill, Alan Piazza, and Robin Zeitz. Famine in China, 1958–1961. *Population and Development Review* 1, 4 (1984): 613–645.

Banister, Judith. *China's Changing Population*. Stanford, CA: Stanford University Press, 1987.

China Economic Review 9, 2 (1998): 103–166. Spec. issue on the Chinese famine of 1959 to 1961.

Coale, Ansley. *Rapid Population Change in China, 1952–1982*. Committee on Population and Demography Report No. 27. Washington, DC: National Academy of Sciences Press, 1984.

Kane, Penny. *Famine in China, 1959–61: Demographic and Social Implications*. London: Macmillan, 1988.

MacFarquhar, Roderick. *Origins of the Cultural Revolution*, Vol. 2: *The Great Leap Forward, 1958–1960*. New York: Columbia University Press, 1983.

Meisner, Maurice. *Mao's China and After: A History of the People's Republic*. 3rd ed. New York: Free Press, 1999.

Peng Xizhe. Demographic Consequences of the Great Leap Forward in China's Provinces. *Population and Development Review* 13 (1987): 639–670.

Riskin, Carl. *China's Political Economy: The Quest for Development since 1949*. Oxford and New York: Oxford University Press, 1987.

Riskin, Carl. Seven Questions about the Chinese Famine of 1959–1961. *China Economic Review* 9, 2 (1998): 111–124.

Walker, Kenneth R. *Food Grain Procurement and Consumption in China*. Cambridge, U.K.: Cambridge University Press, 1984.

Yang Dali (Dali L. Yang). *Calamity and Reform in China: State, Rural Society, and Institutional Change since the Great Leap Famine*. Stanford, CA: Stanford University Press, 1996.

Carl Riskin

CREDIT COOPERATIVES

The first credit cooperatives were created in Chinese Communist Party (CCP) controlled areas already in 1945, building on a long tradition of mutual-aid associations in the Chinese countryside. The main goal of these institutions was to protect peasants from widespread usury. There were also credit departments in the supply and marketing cooperatives, which reflects the important function of rural credit to bridge the time between planting and harvest. After 1949, the CCP policy with regard to the rural sector vascillated for a couple years, with the brief existence of an Agricultural Cooperative Bank and later the establishment of the Agricultural Bank of China, which was merged with the People's Bank of China during the Great Leap Forward. Thus, credit cooperatives remained the central and most stable part of the rural financial system until 1978, with the number of such cooperatives reaching roughly sixty thousand at the end of the Maoist era. However, their functions changed in an important way, concomitant to collectivization and the introduction of mandatory planning in agriculture.

The new functions of the credit cooperatives emerged as a result of increasing imbalances between the rural supply of agricultural goods and the supply of industrial goods to the countryside. With the establishment of mandatory planning in grain and oil production and distribution in late 1953, farm households obtained cash inflows from the state that they could not adequately spend on industrial goods. Thus, credit cooperatives took on the role of rural savings banks that absorbed the surplus liquidity. Excess liquidity had been a major concern for CCP policy makers since the successful suppression of inflation in the early years of the People's Republic of China.

As a result, the number of credit cooperatives exploded within a few years, reflecting the active role of rural cadres in their creation and thus jeopardizing the principle of voluntary membership and self-management, which is inherent in the notion of a cooperative. With the establishment of the people's communes, credit cooperatives were merged with the commune organization. At the same time, the cooperatives were declared to be local offices of the People's Bank, thus fully integrating them into the national system of monetary policy and financial control.

During collectivization, credit cooperatives obtained the important function of channelling government credit into the countryside, providing farmers with a major incentive to join the new collective institutions. This function became obsolete after the creation of the communes. From that time onward, credit cooperatives emerged as the centerpiece of a mostly self-contained and localized rural financial system, in which farmers accumulated small savings on cooperative accounts, and commune authorities decided the allocation of credit. Between 1958 and 1978, the volume of loans given by the cooperatives grew with a rate of increase almost double the growth of bank credits. Funds even flowed out of the rural sector via redeposits at the People's Bank, as the rural economy was demonetized to a large degree. Demonetization was the effect of the work-point system of the communes, by which farmers accumulated work points, with balances calculated only at the end of the agricultural production cycle. Typically, given the few possibilities to spend cash in the countryside, positive cash balances were deposited with the credit cooperatives. During this period, the rate of growth of rural deposits was even higher than the rate of growth of loans by cooperatives. The total volume of loans permitted a cooperative was also capped far below its volume of credits, so that the banking function of the cooperatives was severely curtailed.

Typical credit cooperatives would include both state and rural cadres, thus reflecting the two faces of a commune organization and a bank branch. They would operate small branches in every village, which mainly managed the savings transactions. Farmers could only borrow a limited amount of money from the cooperatives, without collateral. The family was responsible for repayment, such that, for example, sons could be required to pay back loans taken by their fathers. The major role of credit in farmers' everyday lives was a form of social security, because loans could be used for emergency treatments in urban hospitals, for example. Under the austere conditions of Maoist China, conspicious consumption on such occasions as weddings was almost entirely suppressed. Thus, the main role of cooperatives was the funding of commune projects, of which small-scale industries became the most important in the 1970s.

After 1978, the institutional features of agricultural credit cooperatives changed only slowly, revealing the continuity of the Chinese industrialization strategy, which had discriminated against the rural sector systematically. Discriminatory redeposit rates with the state banking system and low access of farmers to credit remained central features for many years.

SEE ALSO *Banking: Overview; Microfinancing.*

BIBLIOGRAPHY

Potter, Sulamith Heins, and Jack Potter. Maoist Society: The Brigade. In *China's Peasants: The Anthropology of a Revolution*, 129–142. Cambridge, U.K., and New York: Cambridge University Press, 1990.

Xiao Huang Huiying (Katharine H. Y. Huang Hsiao). *Money and Monetary Policy in Communist China*. New York and London: Columbia University Press, 1971.

Carsten Herrmann-Pillath

FIVE GUARANTEES

The five guarantees, a system of rural social relief initiated in the 1950s, has survived into the reform era, the latest official document being "Nongcun wubao gongyang tiaoli" (Regulations concerning the work of providing the "five guarantees" in rural areas), promulgated by the State Council in March 2006. The five guarantees have remained the same over the years, initially including food, clothing, housing, health care, and burial expenses; later also primary schooling. They can be enjoyed by the elderly, disabled people, and minors in rural areas who fall into the category of the "three *no*'s": no offspring or parents able to care for them, no working ability, and no source of income (*White Paper* 2004). From 1958 to 1982, the period of collective agriculture, the power to allocate welfare funds lay in the hands of leaders of the production teams (Oi 1989, p. 141). Assistance was given as a cash subsidy, a free supply of essential goods, or a combination of both (Dixon 1981, p. 192). The welfare system was thus highly decentralized, with responsibility for provision resting at the lowest level of state administration. The central state did not allocate fund-

ing for rural welfare and insisted that rural communities be self-reliant, frugal, and mutually helpful in welfare matters (Wong 1994, pp. 312–313; *White Paper* 2004). The support offered under the five guarantees was generally of low quality, and only the most destitute qualified. Recipients generally felt humiliated by the assistance, and the system did not function everywhere (Potter and Potter 1990, p. 227; Thøgersen 2002, pp. 2, 5).

The introduction of a market economy since 1978 led to a rapid decrease in the social security enjoyed by the rural poor. The abolition of the people's communes in 1982 destroyed the meager protection that the team could provide and in reality transferred the responsibility for elders and other needy persons back to the family as agricultural production and welfare provision both became privatized. The responsibility for the five guarantees was transferred to the Ministry of Interior. In some places, taxes were levied on land-use rights or labor power to provide for welfare, but these strategies were not universally adopted. Health and pensions are the most important welfare items. In the early 1980s, the rapid collapse of the cooperative medical system left 90 percent of peasants without any health insurance (Ge and Gong 2005, p. 4). In 2002 the Chinese Government began to set up a new rural system of cooperative medical service supported by funds from the government, collectives, and individuals. For elderly support, welfare homes for the elderly were encouraged to initiate income-generating activities to enable the elderly to earn their own living. From the 1990s the Chinese government began to try out an old-age insurance system in some rural areas, but most elderly are not covered. In May 2007 the State Council announced the expansion of a system of subsistence allowances for the poor into the rural areas. Local governments will be responsible for allocating and distributing subsidies to people living under the official poverty line.

SEE ALSO *Family: Roles of the Elderly; Social Policy Programs.*

BIBLIOGRAPHY

Dixon John. *The Chinese Welfare System, 1949–1979*. New York: Praeger Publishers, 1981.

Ge Yanfeng and Gong Sen. *An Evaluation of and Recommendations on the Reforms of the Health System in China*. Beijing: Project Team of the Development Research Center, 2005. *China Development Review* (supplement) 7, 1 (2005): 1–259.

Nongcun wubao gongyang gongzuo tiaoli [Regulations concerning the work of providing the "five guarantees" in the rural areas]. Adopted by the State Council on January 11, 2006, effective from March 1.

Oi, Jean. *State and Peasant in Contemporary China*. Berkeley: University of California Press, 1989.

Potter, Shulamith Heins, and Jack M. Potter. *China's Peasants: The Anthropology of a Revolution.* Cambridge, U.K.: Cambridge University Press, 1990.

Thøgersen, Stig. *The Elderly in Rural China: A Research Report.* Copenhagen: Centre for Development Research, 2002.

White Paper on China's Social Security and Its Policy. Beijing: Information Office of the State Council, 2004.

Wong, Linda. Privatization of Social Welfare in Post-Mao China. *Asian Survey* 34, 4 (April 1994): 307–325.

Hatla Thelle

RURAL DEVELOPMENT SINCE 1978

This entry contains the following:

OVERVIEW
Jonathan Unger

AGRICULTURAL POLICY
Lynette H. Ong

AGRICULTURAL BANKING
Lynette H. Ong

RURAL INDUSTRIALIZATION
Delia Davin

THREE RURAL ISSUES
Heather Xiaoquan Zhang

OVERVIEW

Rural China has undergone an extraordinary transformation since 1978. In the late 1970s, villagers worked together in groups in a collectivized agriculture, whereas starting in the early 1980s farming was transformed into a private family endeavor. In the late 1970s, poverty prevailed across almost all of rural China, whereas since the early 1990s major regional variations have become evident, with some districts very prosperous and others still impoverished. In the late 1970s, the great majority of rural men were restricted by government regulations to remain for life in the village of their birth, whereas starting in the 1980s and accelerating in the years since, vast numbers have been leaving the countryside to seek their livelihoods elsewhere.

DECOLLECTIVIZATION AND HOUSEHOLD FARMING

Starting after the failed Great Leap Forward of 1958–1960 and lasting until the early 1980s, village residents all belonged to so-called production teams that each contained ten to fifty families. The member households owned the land in common, worked the fields together under the leadership of the production team head, and shared in the harvest yields. This was by way of "work points" that each individual worker earned each day and that were converted into cash and grain after the harvest.

In the early 1980s, this system was disbanded and plots of land were distributed to each family, usually on a per capita basis. The official news media reported that this shift to family farming (to what officially is called the *Household Responsibility System*) was a spontaneous bottom-up initiative by farmers, and most English-language authors have accepted this claim. But this was the case only with the first moves to family farming in a poor, remote part of China, where impoverished farmers of Fengyang County in Anhui Province in 1978 secretly began to work the land independently as families. This was approved by the province's Communist Party secretary, Wan Li (1916–), who in 1980 was elevated to the post of national deputy premier in charge of agriculture. Interviews with villagers from across China reveal that in almost all cases the subsequent shift to family farming that swept rural China between 1980 and 1983 was implemented by county governments, not at the farmers' own initiative. As a result, in almost every village in China exactly the same system of household farming has been installed.

Under this system, families separately cultivate the land and sell their own crops, but the landholdings are not strictly private. The former production teams (today normally titled "villager small groups," *cunmin xiaozu*) retain ownership, and a household cannot sell its fields or forfeit them to its creditors. The central government insists that each household should have a land contract that has now been extended to thirty years, during which time the family's plots of land are not to be redistributed. However, surveys show that most farmers prefer for their villager small group to reallocate the farmland periodically among households. They want this so as to take account of the changes over time in the size of families and to ensure that each household has enough land. By 1997, according to a report by the Ministry of Agriculture, 80 percent of the villager small groups had secretly readjusted landholdings at least once, and 66 percent had done so more than once. Even though illegal, the practice has continued. In villages that still rely largely on agriculture, a readjustment of landholdings normally occurs once every three to seven years, each time re-creating a near-equal per capita land distribution.

RISES IN PRODUCTION AND DIFFICULTIES IN LIVELIHOODS

Agricultural productivity and living standards both rose dramatically in the first half of the 1980s. In part this was due to a government policy to increase the prices offered to farmers for their produce. In part, too, it was due to farmers being allowed to use some of their land to diversify into crops that were well suited to their soil and climate, in place of the Maoist policy that had forced the agricultural collectives to concentrate almost entirely on grain. The big gains of the 1980s were also due to the families' more efficient application of labor and fertilizer once farming was freed from the often cumbersome management of the teams. Villagers also were allowed to use their spare labor to engage profitably in cottage industry and other endeavors outside of agriculture. Throughout the 1980s, farmers increasingly were able to produce for a free market, as private traders were permitted, and as the government's purchase quotas on agricultural produce began to recede, except on specialty crops like tobacco.

However, the gains in farmers' living standards were undermined starting in the mid-1980s. From about 1985 up to the early 2000s, as production increased, the real prices the farmers received for their crops progressively declined, while the prices charged for fertilizer and industrial inputs rose. Exacerbating their financial difficulties, increasingly high fees began to be charged in the countryside for public services like education and health care. At the same time, local taxes and charges rose, as inefficient rural bureaucracies became bloated with officials' relatives and cronies.

The hardships faced by many farmers contributed to a massive outpouring of migrant labor from the poorer parts of the countryside, composed largely of unmarried young people who remitted a portion of their earnings home. By the 2000s, more than 100 million migrant workers were laboring in factories and as hired hands in the richest rural districts.

Starting in the early 2000s, the financial difficulties of farm families began to ease as crop prices, after dropping for a decade and a half, began rising. At about the same time, the Chinese government, worried about the prospects of rural unrest, implemented measures in 2001 to force rural county and township governments to reduce the farmers' tax and fee burdens. Going a step further, in 2006 agricultural land taxes were entirely eliminated nationwide, and a very small per-acre subsidy was granted to grain farmers. Giving further relief to village families, at the beginning of 2007 rural school tuition fees (though not textbook fees) were abolished nationwide up through grade nine.

RICH AND POOR REGIONS

Since the mid-1980s, different parts of the countryside fared very differently. Farmers in the agricultural heartlands of central China had been worst affected by tax burdens and by the price squeezes on agricultural commodities. Some of the farmers in the heartlands specialize in tobacco, cotton, and other commercial crops, but most inhabit a grain belt that stretches from the northeast (Manchuria) down through the provinces of Hebei, Henan, Hubei, Hunan, Anhui, Jiangxi, and across into Chongqing and Sichuan. Farmers in these areas had good reason to resent the local officials' levies of high taxes and fees and poor services, and most rural protests have erupted there.

China's most poverty-stricken districts lie mostly in the southwest and west and the mountainous reaches of north-central China. These areas contain large stretches of marginal agricultural land, with poor soils and inadequate rain. The farmers of the southwest and west include the bulk of China's ethnic-minority peoples, some of whom are particularly impoverished. Many of the families here are subsistence farmers. They have not suffered from high taxation, since there is little to tax. In fact, the central government provides grants of aid to these districts. The almost insurmountable cause of persisting poverty in these areas is a depressing combination of remoteness, thin soils, climatic dryness, overpopulation, and ecological degradation.

These regions stand in sharp contrast to the rural districts along the coast and within striking distance of cities. Since the 1980s, these rural areas have greatly prospered, in part from high vegetable prices but far more from off-farm entrepreneurship and a surge in rural industrialization. Most of this small industry was initiated and owned by township and village governments up through the mid-1990s. At that point, local private factories began to outstrip public industry, much of which began to be sold off. Rural counties in the coastal regions also have attracted a massive influx of factory investment by Taiwanese, Hong Kong, and Korean companies, which transferred much of their own labor-intensive export industry to China. The rural Chinese populace in some of these industrialized districts has benefited from substantial land-rental income, distributed to them by way of mini-welfare states established by village and township governments to benefit the villagers. (Migrant workers and other newcomers to these districts have been excluded from access to any local public goods whatsoever.)

However, there are wide variations in the industrializing districts in the performance of local governments toward the local villagers. A large number of cases have been reported where self-seeking and corrupt village, township, and county authorities have confiscated the farmers' land, have inadequately compensated them, and have resold the land at high prices for redevelopment. This was the most common single cause of mass rural protests in China during the 2000–2008 period.

COERCION AND DEMOCRATIZATION

A separate cause of discontent has been the draconian birth-limitation program. In much of rural China since

An ethnic Naxi farmer at work in a terraced plot of land, Baishuitai, Yunnan province, May 30, 2006. *Rural areas in China underwent a significant transition at the end of the twentieth century as government officials phased out collective farming and allowed citizens to maintain allocated plots of land. While this switch improved the lives of many, millions of rural Chinese continue to endure lives of poverty, particularly in isolated areas with large populations of ethnic minorities.* © MICHAEL REYNOLDS/EPA/CORBIS

the early 1980s, a couple is not permitted to have a second child if their first child is a son. If the first child is a daughter, the couple is allowed to try again for a boy, but they are legally limited to a second child. A hefty monetary penalty for violations is imposed for each extra child above that. Pressures have been placed on township and village officials to enforce the program—their salaries and promotions often are dependent on keeping the local birth rate under control. Wives wanting extra children sometimes circumvent the cadres' efforts by going into hiding during pregnancy with relatives in other villages. Whereas other sources of rural discontent have involved local officials imposing local taxes and fees in defiance of central government regulations, stringent birth limitation is very much a central policy.

To reduce rural disgruntlement and unrest over the former types of impositions, the central government passed a law in 1987 requiring rural authorities to implement elections for the selection of village officials. In some villages, the elections involve vigorous multicandi-

date competition. In many others, incumbent village officials, often with the connivance of township and county officials, ensure their own reselection through their complete domination of election procedures. In all cases, the most powerful position in a village—that of the Communist Party secretary, who handles the most important local decisions—is not up for election, as this choice remains exclusively within the hands of the party. In addition, there are no elections for officials above the village level. The national leadership thus far has been adamant that political participation should be restricted to the grassroots village level.

COMMUNITY ORGANIZATION AND FAMILIES

In some villages where local public services are poor, religious temple organizations and lineage groups have stepped forward to provide welfare services and to raise funds to improve village roads and other infrastructure. But these organizations rarely organize farmers against the local officials. They more often support one local cadre or another on the basis of common lineage or hamlet, and in turn become the cornerstones of patronage systems, to the benefit of some parts of a village and the detriment of other parts.

Family mores have changed considerably since the late 1970s. Whereas during the Maoist period, one of the adult sons normally continued after marriage to live in his parent's home with his wife and children in what anthropologists call a stem family, daughters-in-law did not appreciate the arrangement. It has now become normal for all sons to establish separate households immediately after their weddings and to give a greater priority to their own conjugal relationship than to their obligations toward their parents. Nonetheless, especially in the poorer regions of the agricultural heartlands, the older people today often bring up their grandchildren, since many of the young couples are away from home year round as migrant workers.

SEE ALSO *Household Responsibility System (baogan daohu); Land Use, History of; Population Policy: Birth-Planning Policy.*

BIBLIOGRAPHY
Bernstein, Thomas, and Xiaobo Lü. *Taxation Without Representation in Rural China.* New York: Cambridge University Press, 2003.

Bossen, Laurel. *Chinese Women and Rural Development: Sixty Years of Change in Lu Village, Yunnan.* Lanham, MD: Rowman & Littlefield, 2002.

Chan, Anita, Richard Madsen, and Jonathan Unger. *Chen Village, from Revolution to Globalization.* Berkeley: University of California Press, 2008.

Chen Guidi, and Wu Chuntao. *Will the Boat Sink the Water? The Struggle of Peasants in 21st-Century China.* New York: HarperCollins, 2006.

Christiansen, Flemming, and Zhang Junzhuo, eds. *Village Inc.: Chinese Rural Society in the 1990s.* Richmond, U.K.: Curzon, 1998.

Fan Jie, Thomas Heberer, and Wolfgang Taubmann. *Rural China: Economic and Social Change in the Late Twentieth Century.* Armonk, NY: Sharpe, 2006.

Friedman, Edward, Paul G. Pickowicz, and Mark Selden. *Revolution, Resistance, and Reform in Village China.* New Haven, CT: Yale University Press, 2005.

Gao Mobo. *Gao Village: A Portrait of Rural Life in Modern China.* London: Hurst, 1999.

Ku Hok Bun. *Moral Politics in a South Chinese Village: Responsibility, Reciprocity, and Resistance.* Lanham, MD: Rowman & Littlefield, 2003.

Liu Xin. *In One's Own Shadow: An Ethnographic Account of the Condition of Post-reform Rural China.* Berkeley: University of California Press, 2000.

Murphy, Rachel. *How Migrant Labor Is Changing Rural China.* Cambridge, U.K.: Cambridge University Press, 2002.

Oi, Jean C. *Rural China Takes Off: Institutional Foundations of Economic Reform.* Berkeley: University of California Press, 1999.

Riskin, Carl, Zhao Renwei, and Li Shi, eds. *China's Retreat from Equality: Income Distribution and Economic Transition.* Armonk, NY: Sharpe, 2001.

Ruf, Gregory A. *Cadres and Kin: Making a Socialist Village in West China, 1921–1991.* Stanford, CA: Stanford University Press, 1998.

Unger, Jonathan. *The Transformation of Rural China.* Armonk, NY: Sharpe, 2002.

Vermeer, Eduard B., Frank N. Pieke, and Chong Woei Lien. *Cooperative and Collective in China's Rural Development: Between State and Private Interests.* Armonk, NY: Sharpe, 1998.

Yan Yunxiang. *Private Life Under Socialism: Love, Intimacy, and Family Change in a Chinese Village, 1949–1999.* Stanford, CA: Stanford University Press, 2003.

Jonathan Unger

AGRICULTURAL POLICY

Rural China has undergone dramatic development since the launch of market reforms in 1978, but many challenges still remain. Starting from Xiaogang village in Anhui Province, agricultural decollectivization, particularly the household responsibility system, abolished collective farming and restored day-to-day farming decisions to rural households. The policy raised farmers' productivity and pulled millions of them out of poverty during the 1980s.

Meanwhile, agricultural decollectivization also released surplus farm labor and stimulated growth of *xiangzhenqiye* (township and village enterprises, TVEs), which are rural enterprises located in peri-urban areas. Rapid development of the TVEs during the 1980s and early 1990s helped to absorb surplus farm labor and supplemented farming income with wage income.

Growth in rural income tapered off in the second half of the 1990s after a robust increase in the first fifteen years of economic reform. Rural development became more challenging after the low-hanging fruits—agricultural decollectivization and development of rural enterprises—had been harvested. Moving forward, China's central policy makers realized that they needed to make deeper reforms, in the rural credit sector, land ownership rights, and the household registration system.

The magnitude of rural savings was as large as three trillion yuan in 2007. Traditionally, rural savings have been channeled to finance urban development and industrial growth, leaving little much-needed capital for the expansion of private rural entrepreneurship. Beginning in 2003, *nongcunxinyongshe* (rural credit cooperatives, RCCs), the primary credit institutions in rural China, underwent ownership and corporate governance reforms in order to better serve the credit demands of rural residents. Furthermore, the central bank began to liberalize the rural financial sector in 2007 by issuing licenses for the establishment of private township-and-village banks and credit companies as part of its efforts to restructure the rural credit market. This market liberalization was a turning point in the rural financial sector.

Since 1978 farmers have enjoyed user rights to land though the ownership rights still formally reside with the collectives. The lack of property rights was not an issue in the 1980s, but it has prevented farmers from making long-term investment in the land, reducing the ecological sustainability of the farmland. Rural land issues are a constant source of social clashes between peasants and local government officials. As urbanization and industrialization proceed rapidly in China, land in this densely populated country has risen tremendously in value. Local government officials convert farmland to industrial and commercial uses in order to sell them to real estate developers and industrialists for lucrative prices. These transactions often are conducted without proper public consultation or compensation to the peasants whose livelihoods depend exclusively on farmland. Thousands of land-related rural protests are staged annually, manifesting the serious sociopolitical implications of ambiguous land ownership rights. Nonetheless, if the central government were to allow for private ownership of farmland, economic downturns and layoffs from urban industries may leave no social safety net for many migrant workers. Because farmland is the only life support for rural residents, the issue of privatizing land ownership is treated with extreme caution by central policy makers in China.

After nearly three decades of reforms, 70 percent of the country's population (900 million people) still resides in the countryside. To lift the living standards of the large rural population, the central policy makers know they need to allow some rural residents to migrate to the cities. The household registration (*hukou*) system that divides the population into rural and urban and binds them to their places of birth has been relaxed gradually during the 1990s to allow rural residents to find jobs in urban factories. However, with the sluggishness in global demand that began in 2008, many factories in the coastal cities have closed down and laid off migrant workers. The ability of the cities to absorb migrant workers is being challenged for the first time since the launch of reform in 1978. Hence, sustainable rural development in China remains a key policy challenge.

SEE ALSO *Township and Village Enterprises.*

BIBLIOGRAPHY

Byrd, William, and Qingsong Lin, eds. *China's Rural Industry: Structure, Development, and Reform.* New York: Oxford University Press, 1990.

Jinqing Cao. *China Along the Yellow River.* Trans. Nicky Harman and Huang Ruhua. London and New York: RoutledgeCurzon, 2000.

Nyberg, Al, and Scott Rozelle. *Accelerating China's Rural Transformation.* Washington, DC: World Bank, 1999.

Ong, Lynette. The Political Economy of Township Government Debt, Township Enterprises, and Rural Financial Institutions in China. *China Quarterly* 186 (2006): 377–400.

Zhou, Kate Xiao. *How the Farmers Changed China: Power of the People.* Boulder, CO: Westview, 1996.

Lynette H. Ong

AGRICULTURAL BANKING

Agricultural banking provides essential banking services to about 800 million rural residents living in western and central China as well as peri-urban locales in the eastern coastal region. For the period beginning in 1978, agricultural banking in China can be divided into banking for retail consumers and policy banking for state agricultural procurement. Retail banking serves the credit demands of rural households, individual household businesses (*getihu*), and small and medium-sized enterprises in rural areas, whereas policy banking provides loans to enterprises specializing in state agricultural procurement.

The Rural Credit Cooperatives (RCCs) or *nongcunxinyongshe*, which collectively account for more than an 80 percent share of total rural deposits and loans, are the backbone of household finance in rural China. Owing to their monopoly position in rural China, the RCCs are critical to lifting household income, stimulating the growth of small and medium-sized enterprises. Beginning in 1979 the central government required the RCCs to report to the Agricultural Bank of China (ABC) (*zhongguo nongye yinhang*). For a decade-and-a-half the credit cooperatives functioned as the state bank's grassroots branches and were required to place low-interest-yielding reserve at the bank. This resulted in historic financial losses at the RCCs. Their relationship with the ABC was formally severed in 1996 as part of the central government's move to restructure the rural financial system around three institutions entrusted with distinctive tasks: the ABC for commercial loans, the Agricultural Development Bank of China (ADBC) (*nongye fanzhan yinhang*) for agricultural policy loans, and the RCCs for household finance. The credit cooperatives were managed indirectly by the central bank between 1996 and 2003. Since 2003 they have been managed by the provincial unions (*shenglianshe*), which are effectively controlled by the provincial governments. Provincial unions are the bodies managing all credit cooperatives that exist within the provinces. They are strictly administrative organizations that do not take savings or issue loans.

The central government has been trying to make the RCCs, in their various institutional forms, more responsive to the needs of rural households. Nonetheless, their loans are often reallocated to local government-related projects that tend not to be repaid. In the early 2000s almost half of the 35,000 RCCs nationwide were technically insolvent. Because they were the only formal credit providers in the countryside, the central government could not allow the RCCs to fail and injected some 650 billion yuan to help them write off enormous historic losses. In addition, the central bank has also introduced various lending schemes with subsidized interest rates to boost lending to rural households and to improve the RCCs' profitability.

The Agricultural Bank of China was established by the central government in the 1950s to support agricultural production and to manage the RCCs. The ABC took over the People's Bank of China's rural branches in 1979 and assumed a range of policy and commercial functions, including lending to rural industries, financing state procurement of agricultural products, and managing the RCC system. During the 1980s it functioned largely as a state policy bank to finance the central government's projects in the agricultural sector. Before the agricultural policy bank was set up in 1994, the ABC was responsible for financing all state agricultural purchases.

Despite its name, the Agricultural Bank of China has been largely divorced from agricultural households. Since the mid-1990s the ABC has become increasingly commercially oriented; its loans are mostly allocated to large-scale agricultural and industrial enterprises. In the late 1990s it closed down all grassroots branches in rural townships and villages to improve profitability. Meanwhile, the ABC centralized lending decisions to the county and higher administrative levels, resulting in fewer loans for agricultural household borrowers. Since 1998 the ABC has been responsible for administering the poverty loan program (*fupin daikuan*), intended to alleviate poverty by providing loans at a subsidized interest rate to rural households in poor counties. Nonetheless, the program is widely known to have extremely low repayment rates and suffers from widespread abuse of funds.

The Agricultural Development Bank of China is a policy bank specializing in providing loans to enterprises purchasing grain, cotton, and consumption oil for the purpose of national food security. Unlike the RCCs or ABC, the capital of ADBC comes from the central bank instead of household savings or enterprise deposits. Partly owing to its nonprofit orientation and the absence of supervision mechanisms, the ADBC is afflicted with chronic financial losses. Because its capital is heavily subsidized by the central government, the bank has frequently misallocated loans for nonofficial purposes.

SEE ALSO *Banking: Big Four; Banking: Nonperforming Loans; Financial Markets.*

BIBLIOGRAPHY

Findlay, Christopher, Andrew Watson, Cheng Enjiang, and Zhu Gang, eds. *Rural Financial Markets in China.* Canberra, Australia: Asia Pacific Press, 2003.

Ong, Lynette. Multiple Principals and Collective Action: China's Rural Credit Cooperatives and Poor Households' Access to Credit. *Journal of East Asian Studies* 6, 2 (2006): 177–204.

Lynette H. Ong

RURAL INDUSTRIALIZATION

Rural industrialization has formed part of China's rural development strategy since the 1950s, and rural industries were already making a minor but significant contribution to total rural output value by the end of the Maoist period. Rural industry underwent sharp changes in organizational form, ownership, and performance in the reform period from 1978. Its expansion in the 1980s and 1990s was so extraordinary that it became the major driver of growth in the national economy. Rural industry has brought about enormous economic, social, and physical change in China's rural areas.

ORIGINS OF RURAL INDUSTRY

Many parts of China had a rich tradition of rural handicrafts at the time of the Communist takeover. Some items for everyday use in the villages, such as furniture, farm implements, bricks, and utensils, were produced in every region, while specialized activities such as textile production, coal mining, or oil processing took place where there were locally available resources. Although individual handicraft enterprises were suppressed after agricultural collectivization in the 1950s, many were reorganized into cooperatives. It was hoped that rural industry, developed partly on the basis of the old handicrafts, could supply agriculture and local rural families with the everyday articles they needed. This policy was intended to free large-scale industry to concentrate on producer goods and the needs of the urban consumer and to relieve pressure on the overstretched transport infrastructure.

The mistakes of the Great Leap Forward (1958–1960) included an overambitious program for the expansion of rural industrialization. Cutbacks and closures followed. When the economy recovered, rural industrialization continued with a focus on village enterprises that supplied everyday local needs, and on county- and commune-level plants that produced key inputs for agriculture. Five industries were especially favored: cement, chemical fertilizer, electric power, farm machinery, and iron and steel. Although many enterprises were inefficient, producing at high cost and resulting in serious pollution, they filled real gaps in the rural economy. By the late 1970s, for example, they supplied around half of China's total cement and chemical fertilizer output. In 1978 there were around 1.5 million rural enterprises employing 28 million rural people.

RURAL INDUSTRY UNDER THE ECONOMIC REFORMS

The rural reforms after 1978 provided an economic climate in which rural industry could flourish, and for fifteen years the sector grew by almost 25 percent per annum. Under the reforms, agricultural production was devolved completely to peasant households, and the restrictions on small-scale non-agricultural production by rural households were removed. Small-scale private enterprises began to emerge. Free markets were permitted in which the surplus agricultural and nonagricultural production could be sold and inputs purchased. As rural incomes increased, so did demand for the cheap products of rural industry. With the decollectivization of agriculture, communes replaced townships as the lowest level of government, and production brigades gave way to village committees. Rural enterprises that had previously belonged to the communes or production brigades became the town and village enterprises—TVEs—that have played a prominent part in China's economic miracle.

An official 1984 decision to encourage TVE growth was followed by large-scale loans from state banks. Fiscal decentralization gave local officials greater autonomy in economic management. At the same time, new evaluation criteria linked the remuneration and promotion of local officials to the success of rural industry. This provided important new incentives to officials to adopt more entrepreneurial behavior. By mid-1996, the 23 million TVEs employed 135 million laborers, and produced 20 percent of China's total gross domestic product. They proved effective at absorbing rural surplus labor and lifted many millions out of poverty. TVEs also contributed to the dramatic growth of China's exports. By the 1990s, about one-third of all exports, predominantly textiles, light industrial goods, machines, food, and chemicals, were produced by TVEs. Their cheap, labor-intensive products were competitive on the international market. TVEs also contracted with urban industrial enterprises to supply parts or to undertake labor-intensive processing. Increasingly, TVEs attracted significant foreign investment.

Local governments, increasingly dependent on rural enterprises for revenue, and aware of their role in providing employment and raising rural living standards, did all they could to promote them. This stage of TVE development is sometimes referred to as local state corporatism, meaning that local governments behaved like profit-seeking corporations in bearing the risks of investment in industry.

EVOLUTION

Although TVEs are usually regarded as having developed from the rural industries of the Maoist era, they have become markedly different in terms of ownership and organization. The official definition of a TVE is vague, but it embraces all industrial enterprises located in the countryside, regardless of whether they are owned collectively or privately. Collective ownership means ownership by the township or village, while private ownership includes ownership by individual households or shareholders, as well as joint ventures between TVEs and state-owned or private enterprises, including those funded by foreign or Hong Kong or Taiwanese capital.

Some collectively owned enterprises developed from commune industries, while others were set up by township or village officials in the wake of the economic reforms. Some were run by local governments, others by a single manager. As time went on, local officials often raised capital by selling shares or indeed entire enterprises. Many began effectively to operate as private enterprises, while retaining the collective label for the period when private enterprise was still regarded as politically dubious. This practice, known as "wearing the red hat," allowed enterprises to gain access to land, credit, government, and tax breaks through close contacts with local government. On the other hand, it perpetuated a "fuzzy" system of property rights, which could have a negative impact on business confidence and constrained enterprises from making decisions on a purely business basis.

There has been considerable regional diversity in TVE structure and ownership. TVEs in some areas, such as Guangdong Province, were early associated with private entrepreneurship and capital, whereas collective enterprises remained dominant well into the 1990s in other areas, such as the Yangzi Delta.

PROBLEMS OF TVE DEVELOPMENT

Although TVEs have undeniably made an enormous contribution to China's development, their effect has not been wholly positive. They have been associated with a growth of official corruption. At the time of decollectivization, local officials in charge of the distribution of former collective property were in a strong position to benefit from it. Many of them or their relatives emerged as TVE managers and used the enterprises both to raise revenue and to line their own pockets. Even TVEs owned or managed by nonofficials were highly dependent on the good will of local officials and often paid bribes.

TVEs have contributed to a loss of control by the central government. It has proved very difficult to raise

taxes from these enterprises because the growth of localism has facilitated tax evasion by entrepreneurs connived
at by local officials. Rural industries are often highly
polluting, and local officials are often reluctant to enforce
antipollution measures on them. Health and safety regulations tend to be poorly observed in TVEs, and working conditions are generally much worse than in urban
industry. Anxious to protect the interests and competitiveness of their own local industries, local officials are
again unwilling to take action on these problems.

TVEs are unequally distributed geographically. In
Jiangsu and Zhejiang, they provide approximately half
of all rural employment, compared with 19 percent in
Sichuan and 12 percent in Guizhou. About two-thirds of all
TVEs are in the coastal regions. Although their rural locations have boosted rural incomes and thus reduced the
urban-rural divide within these regions, their geographical
concentration has meant increasing economic disparities
between the coastal regions and the interior. Government
efforts to promote the development of TVEs in the interior
provinces have met with only limited success.

DEVELOPMENTS SINCE
THE MID-1990s

TVEs have undergone considerable change in parallel with
more general changes in the political and economic environment favoring private entrepreneurship. From 1995 to
1997, fiscal, banking, and legal reforms intended to constrain the power of local officials created a less comfortable
climate for TVEs. The immediate result was a slight reduction in the number of enterprises and in employment and
production in the sector. A general retrenchment even
forced some enterprises to go bankrupt. Once the benefits
of public ownership were reduced, TVEs were less protected, had difficulty in obtaining credit, and were more
exposed to competition. By the end of the decade, growth in
the restructured rural industrial sector had resumed, but the
size of the collectively owned sector had been reduced by a
wave of privatization. Large-scale restructuring also included
enterprise consolidation and vertical integration. By 2002,
only a quarter of all TVE workers were employed in collectively owned enterprises.The majority of TVEs were in
private hands, and their ties to local officials and local
communities were less close.

The extraordinary success of China's rural industries
and their contributions to economic growth and poverty
reduction have attracted considerable attention from
development specialists who debate whether the model
is transferable.

SEE ALSO *Township and Village Enterprises.*

BIBLIOGRAPHY
Bramall, Chris. *The Industrialization of Rural China*. New York:
    Oxford University Press, 2007.

Byrd, William A., and Lin Qingsong, eds. *China's Rural Industry:
    Structure, Development, and Reform*. New York: Oxford
    University Press, 1990.
Oi, Jean. *Rural China Takes Off: Institutional Foundations of
    Economic Reform*. Berkeley: University of California Press,
    1999.
Sigurdson, Jon. *Rural Industrialization in China*. Cambridge,
    MA: Harvard University Press, 1977.
Whiting, Susan H. *Power and Wealth in Rural China: The
    Political Economy of Institutional Change*. Cambridge, U.K.:
    Cambridge University Press, 2001.

Delia Davin

THREE RURAL ISSUES

The market-oriented reforms and decollectivization in
the late 1970s returned land use rights and the autonomy
of agricultural production to China's farming households. The central government also repeatedly increased
the official procurement prices for grain and other agricultural produce in the early 1980s. The impact of these
policies on agricultural production and farmers' income
was very positive, but by the late 1980s the initial effects
of the rural reform started to diminish. According to the
China Statistical Yearbook farmers' per capita income
grew 15.2 percent per annum between 1978 to 1985
and only 3.7 percent in 1997 to 2000, while China's
GDP grew at about 8 percent per annum for the same
period (National Bureau of Statistics of China 1986;
1990; 2001), suggesting that Chinese farmers benefited
disproportionately less from the country's rapid economic
growth. As China's rural sector increasingly lagged behind
after the mid- to late 1990s and the problems became more
acute, the situation was termed *san nong wenti* (the "three
rural issues") in the official discourse, in the popular press,
and in academic research. The Chinese character *nong* trans-
lates as "rural"; the "three nongs" refer to *nongye* (agriculture), *nongcun* (rural areas), and *nongmin* (farmers). In other
words, the "three rural issues" are problems related to
agriculture, rural areas, and farmers.

Apart from farmers' stagnant incomes, the rural issues
also include widening regional disparities, that is, between
the eastern coastal (more urbanized) and the central and
western inland (more rural) regions, between the urban and
rural sectors, and within rural areas. Chinese official sources
show that the urban-rural income disparity increased to
3.2:1 in 2003. When taking into account other factors such
as urban welfare advantages in education, health care, and
housing, the real urban-rural income ratio could be 5: 1 or
6:1—considerably worse than the ratio of 1.8:1 in 1985,
and poor compared with the developing countries' average
of 1.7:1 (Wang 2004). The widening urban-rural gap
aggravates rural poverty. The renowned sociologist Lu

Xueyi at the Chinese Academy of Social Sciences found that in 2001, 58 percent of the rural population's annual per capita income was below the national rural average of 2,366 Chinese yuan, and 13 percent was below 1,000 yuan. Lu estimated that some 10 percent of Chinese farmers fell into the category of the poor relative to urban dwellers, and about 14 percent of them (20 to 30 million rural people) were in absolute poverty, with an annual per capita income of less than 625 yuan (Lu 2005, p. 63).

Rural poverty was partly attributable to the heavy burdens of tax and levies imposed on farming households by different levels of the government. Li Xiande at the Chinese Academy of Agricultural Sciences showed that farmers' tax burdens included, for example, the agricultural tax paid to the central state; a wide range of financial "obligations" paid to local authorities under different names, including the so-called public accumulation fund or public welfare fund; and administrative fees at the village level for education supplement, social help, family planning, collective transportation maintenance, and cultural activities at the township level; and many arbitrarily levied taxes and charges. These can total as many as 100 separate taxes in extreme cases, and at least ten in most places. These combined, can account for nearly 20 percent of the net income of a farming household, despite the official policy that the combined taxes should not exceed 5 percent of a rural household's net income (Li 2003, pp. 46, 49, 72).

Poverty in suburban areas also has been exacerbated during the rapid urbanization process, where the imbalance of power between the urban and rural sectors, and between the local authorities and urban developers on the one hand and the farmers on the other, has seriously skewed the process of reallocation of scarce resources such as agricultural land in favor of the state and developers. It is estimated that some 40 to 50 million farmers have lost their land and their livelihoods due to urban expansion. Most of them have not received adequate financial compensation, and as a result have joined the ranks of the so-called four withouts—without land, without job, without social security, and without means to seek justice (Lu 2004, pp. 177–178). These landless farmers are struggling on the brink of unemployment and poverty.

These rural issues are also manifestations of political corruption and therefore become sources of mounting tensions between local government and farmers. Social discontent and even unrest is demonstrated in often violent protests launched by rural people and in their petitions to the upper-level authorities (Chen and Wu 2004). These issues have been a serious cause for concern for President Hu Jintao and Premier Wen Jiabao after their assuming office in 2003. Every year between 2004 and 2008 the central government's first annual policy document, dubbed the No. 1 Central Document, has focused on rural problems, signalling the high priority given to agricultural and rural development. Since 2006 new emphasis has been placed on holistic and balanced development between urban and rural areas, on the "construction of the new countryside," and on "industry subsidizing agriculture." New policy initiatives introduced in 2007 include a pilot program of urban-rural integrated development in southwestern China's Chengdu and Chongqing, and various social protection schemes for rural-urban migrants across the country. In October 2008, the Communique passed at the 17th Central Committee of the Chinese Communist Party's Third Plenum stressed the need for strict regulation of land use and land management, as well as for finance and welfare provision in rural areas.

Specific policy measures include:

abolition of agricultural tax in 2006, with increased state regulation of local authorities in respect of local levies and fee charges;

substantial increases in central government fiscal transfers to subsidize local government and promote rural development;

increased state subsidies to grain farmers and tightened control over the rise in prices for agricultural input to tackle the adverse terms of trade for the rural sector;

accelerated regulations on land requisition, compensation to farmers, and protection of farmers' livelihoods, rights, and interests; and

substantially increased state investment in a wide range of public services in rural areas, such as rural education (e.g., enforcement of free compulsory education and improvement of school quality of rural schools), health care services (e.g., expansion of the new rural cooperative medical care system to cover all rural residents), pensions, and other social safety nets.

At this stage, however, it is too early to assess the effects of these policy measures on resolving the three rural issues.

SEE ALSO *Poverty; Taxation since 1978.*

BIBLIOGRAPHY

Chen, Guidi, and Chuntao Wu. *Zhongguo nongmin diaocha* [A survey of Chinese peasants]. Beijing: Renmin wenxue chubanshe (People's Literature Publication Company), 2004.

Li Xiande. Rethinking the Peasant Burden: Evidence from a Chinese Village. In *Rural Development in Transitional China: The New Agriculture*, ed. Peter Ho, Jacob Eyferth, and Eduard B. Vermeer, 45–74. London: Frances Cass, 2003.

Lu Xueyi. Readjusting the Urban-Rural Relations and Satisfactorily Resolving the Problems Related to Farmers and the Countryside. In *Blue Book of China's Society: Analysis and Forecast on China's Social Development 2005*, ed. Ru Xin, Lu Xueyi, Li Peilin, et al., 175–186. Beijing: Zhongguo shehui kexue wenxian chubanshe (Social Science Academic Press), 2004.

Lu Xueyi. *San Nong Xin Lun* [New perspectives on the "Three Rural Issues"]. Beijing: Zhongguo shehui kexue wenxian chubanshe (Social Science Academic Press), 2005.

National Bureau of Statistics of China. *China Statistical Yearbook, 1986; 1990; 2001*, Beijing: Zhongguo tongji chubanshe (China Statistical Publishing House).

Wang Mengkui. The Two Main Problems in China's Modernisation Process—The Urban-Rural Gap and Regional Discrepancies. *Chinese Rural Studies*, 2004. http://www.ccrs.org.cn.

Heather Xiaoquan Zhang

RUSSIA, RELATIONS WITH

The Soviet Union became the first country to recognize the People's Republic of China after it was established on October 1, 1949. But the Soviet relationship with the Chinese Communist Party was long-standing. Soviet representatives were present at the creation of the Communist Party and maintained close contacts with the Communists throughout their turbulent Stalin-imposed partnership with the Guomindang (Nationalist Party) until 1927. Soviet connections with the Chinese Communist Party never ceased, even as Chiang Kai-shek (Jiang Jieshi) violently suppressed the party's activities in 1927. Joseph Stalin had several agents at Mao Zedong's base in Yan'an in the 1930s. The Soviet Union also assisted the Communist forces with material supplies. The Soviet dictator thought that the Chinese Communist Party could not succeed in a military contest with the vastly superior and internationally recognized Guomindang. His best hope was for a coalition government that included the Chinese Communist Party, a party susceptible to Soviet influence. But with Japanese incursions into China in the late 1930s, even that long-term goal was superseded by Stalin's more immediate imperative to achieve a united front between the Chinese Communist Party and the Guomindang to create a credible opposition to Japanese expansion in East Asia.

After August 1945, when the Soviet forces swept across Manchuria and Inner Mongolia in the final chapter of World War II, the Chinese Communist Party maneuvered itself into a strategic position in Manchuria, where the Soviets allowed Japanese weapons to fall in the Communists' hands. Throughout the Chinese civil war (1945–1949), the Soviet Union maintained cross-border trade with the Chinese Communists in Manchuria. Yet Stalin hedged his bets with a Soviet treaty with the Guomindang in 1945, which guaranteed quasi-imperial Soviet interests in Manchuria. Stalin was content with his position in China and was not in a hurry to support Mao Zedong's revolution until it became blatantly clear that the Chinese Communist Party would prevail. It has been argued that until 1948 Stalin did not rule out a division of China similar to that of Germany or a coalition government between the Chinese Communist Party and the Guomindang.

POSTLIBERATION

After some hesitation, Stalin agreed in January 1950 to give up his 1945 treaty with the Republic of China to sign a new treaty of alliance with the People's Republic of China. Yet he still placed Soviet geopolitical interests above communist solidarity with China. Stalin wrestled from Mao new concessions in China, even as he gave up some of his old gains acquired in 1945. The Soviet Union obtained a stake in a number of industrial enterprises in China and a sphere of special influence in Manchuria and Xinjiang. Soviet troops—having been at the warm-water base of Port Arthur (Lüshun) since 1945—remained there, though Stalin promised to take them back at a future date. Mao swallowed his pride, for the Sino-Soviet alliance promised him great dividends: Soviet economic aid, a security guarantee, political legitimization of the Communist regime, and, of course, a substantial increase in Mao's personal prestige. For this reason Mao chose to ally China with the Soviet Union when he wrote, in June 1949, that in the Cold War China would henceforth "lean to one side": the Soviet side.

In 1954 the Soviet leader Nikita Khrushchev, on his first visit to China, not only renounced Stalin's special interests in China (to Mao's relief), but substantially increased Soviet economic aid to the People's Republic of China. In the 1950s, thousands of Soviet specialists worked in China in all economic spheres. Moscow provided blueprints and equipment for the construction of dozens of industrial enterprises, which churned out everything from trucks to MIG airplanes. China coordinated its economic planning with the Soviet Union to facilitate this unprecedented transfer of expertise and technology. Soviet universities welcomed scores of Chinese students in all disciplines, including nuclear physics. The first Chinese nuclear bomb, detonated in 1964, was in many ways a brainchild of Sino-Soviet scientific collaboration. In return, China supplied the Soviet Union with strategic raw materials, foodstuffs, and some consumer goods, often at heavily subsidized prices. Yet in the 1950s, it is fair to say, China received more than it gave.

Despite growing economic, cultural, and scientific ties between China and the Soviet Union in the late 1950s, tensions were brooding under the surface of communist solidarity. Mao felt that the Soviet leadership looked down

318

Chinese Communist marchers holding posters of Joseph Stalin on the anniversary of the founding of the People's Republic of China, October 1, 1951. *Prior to the founding of the People's Republic of China, the Soviet Union provided support to the Communists during their fight against the Nationalist government. Relations between the two countries deteriorated in the 1960s, however, as China feared future domination by the more developed country.* © **CORBIS**

upon China. He was right. Khrushchev considered the Soviet Union the flag bearer for the socialist camp. The Soviet Union, he believed, was the cradle of the communist revolution: It defeated Germany in World War II; it was the most industrially developed socialist country; it held a nuclear umbrella. Khrushchev, for all his lip service to the idea of equality among socialist states, thought that he was communist number one. But the role of a junior partner in an alliance of "cat and mice," as Mao put it, was simply unacceptable to China.

Mao considered himself to be a far more experienced revolutionary than Khrushchev. He was unhappy with Khrushchev's posturing as the final authority in ideological matters. Mao was particularly upset when in February 1956 Khrushchev, without a prior consultation with

China, condemned Stalin's crimes in a secret speech to the Soviet Party Congress. The "secret speech," leaked to the wider world, caused uncertainty and upheaval in the communist world, none more serious than the 1956 crises in Poland and Hungary. In view of Stalin's record in China, it was strange that Mao would choose to defend him, yet Mao was China's Stalin, and Khrushchev's criticism of Stalin was also criticism of Mao. In any case, Mao could not accept such sharp ideological rhetoric from an upstart like Khrushchev. It was up to him, Mao thought, to render the judgment that Khrushchev had abandoned Stalinism ("a great sword"), betrayed the revolution, and "revised" Marxism-Leninism.

In the early 1960s Sino-Soviet polemics flared up in the open. To sum up this bizarre exchange of accusations,

Chinese propaganda stressed class struggle within the nation and tensions in foreign affairs, while the Soviets responded by defending Khrushchev's "thaw" (de-Stalinization) at home and his policy of peaceful coexistence with the West. In reality, ideology was not at the center of the Sino-Soviet split. It was the inequality of the Sino-Soviet alliance that brought it to ruin. Yet ideological squabbles contributed to the rising tensions. Mao used his ideological disagreements with the Soviet Union to consolidate his position and eliminate his real or imagined enemies in China. Thus, in 1966 Mao engineered the overthrow of his potential rival Liu Shaoqi because Liu, "China's Khrushchev," followed "revisionist" policies and, like Khrushchev, took the "capitalist road."

The alliance suffered from what policy makers in Beijing interpreted as Khrushchev's arrogant attitude. In 1958 tensions were exacerbated by the Soviet proposal to build a long-wave radio station for military purposes on China's soil, and a joint submarine fleet. To the Chinese leaders, such proposals were reminiscent of the imperialist encroachment China suffered in the nineteenth century. In 1959 Khrushchev refused to supply China with a prototype atomic bomb, nervously backing out of a previous agreement in light of Mao's militant statements and unpredictable foreign policy. The same year the Soviet Union took a neutral stand in the Sino-Indian border conflict, when, in Mao's opinion, it should have supported China, its ally, over capitalist India. In 1960 Khrushchev, angry with China's criticism of his policies, recalled all Soviet specialists in China, giving Mao a convenient excuse to blame the failure of the Great Leap Forward on the Soviet sabotage.

Worsening of Sino-Soviet relations translated into tensions along their long border. In 1962 China accused the Soviet Union of inciting ethnic Uygurs and Kazakhs in Xinjiang to cross the border into the Soviet Union, and some 60,000 nomads fled China that year. Soviet involvement in this incident was probably minimal (these minorities had their own grievances against the Chinese authorities), but sour sentiments remained on both sides. In 1964 Mao announced that in the nineteenth century, Czarist Russia unfairly annexed large parts of China in Siberia and East Asia, and that the country still had not paid its bill. Mao could not, of course, be seriously claiming millions of square miles of territory, and in fact he later admitted that he was simply firing "empty cannons." But his remarks were met with apprehension by the Soviet leaders, ever haunted by a sense of insecurity about the Soviet Union's exposed eastern frontiers.

In response to a looming Chinese "danger," especially pronounced during the Cultural Revolution, when even the Soviet Embassy in Beijing came under siege by the revolutionary Red Guards, the Soviet Union built up massive forces along its border with China and, by a special arrangement, stationed an army in neighboring Mongolia. In Beijing these moves were inevitably interpreted as a threat to China's security, all the more real after the Soviet invasion of Czechoslovakia in 1968 to "save" socialism. China also stationed a huge army at the border. In March 1969 hostilities erupted at Zhenbao Island on the Ussuri River. As war fever gripped Beijing, both sides took steps to diffuse the situation in a meeting between Prime Ministers Zhou Enlai and Aleksey Kosygin in September 1969.

With the Soviet Union now ranked as China's number-one enemy, Mao sought to relax tensions with the United States, and this move resulted in a Sino-U.S. rapprochement in 1972. Relations with the Soviet Union remained cool for the rest of the decade, with minimal trade and endless border talks, which failed to reach any agreement. In the meantime, China called for a united front against Soviet hegemony and participated in various third-world proxy wars in Africa and Asia on the side against the Soviet enemies.

AFTER CHINA'S REFORM AND OPENING UP

Mao's death and the launching of Deng Xiaoping's reforms did not immediately lead to any obvious improvements in Sino-Soviet relations. Maintaining a huge army was a drain on China's economy, and Deng understood this. Yet China did not depend on the Soviet Union for its four modernizations. It depended on American, West European, and Japanese investments, and on access to Western markets.

But in 1981–1982 Deng Xiaoping began to reevaluate China's relationship with the United States. Strains in the Sino-U.S. relationship over President Ronald Reagan's commitment to supply weapons to Taiwan and restrictions on the supply of certain technologies to China made Deng think that his quasi alliance with the United States against Soviet hegemony was not working as planned. Deng also felt that the Soviet Union—bogged down in Afghanistan, exhausted from the arms race with the United States, and suffering from endemic economic difficulties—was a lesser threat to China than before. In 1982 Deng decided that China would no longer inevitably oppose Soviet hegemony, but that it would oppose any power that had hegemonic pretensions, including the United States.

Sino-Soviet political consultations began in October 1982, but became deadlocked over Deng Xiaoping's "three obstacles" to normalization. Deng insisted that the Soviet Union withdraw its troops from the border and Mongolia, make Vietnam pull out troops from Cambodia (Vietnam, the Soviet ally, had invaded Cambodia in 1978 to overthrow the China-backed Pol Pot regime),

Russian President Vladimir Putin (right) with Chinese leader Hu Jintao, Moscow, Russia, March 26, 2007. *After tense relations during the previous decade, China began cultivating a closer relationship with the Soviet Union in the late 1980s. Upon the Soviet Union's collapse, the Chinese entered a trade relationship with the new Russian Federation, exporting inexpensive consumer goods and importing technological products from more scientifically advanced Russian industries.* © **MISHA JAPARIDZE/POOL/EPA/CORBIS**

and pull back from Afghanistan. The Soviet leaders, although willing to normalize relations with China, were not willing to pay for it so dearly. Political consultations dragged on inconclusively for the rest of the decade, yet Sino-Soviet relations still improved markedly. Despite the three obstacles, trade, cultural, and scientific ties between China and the Soviet Union grew substantially even before Mikhail Gorbachev came to power in the Soviet Union.

Gorbachev's "new thinking" in foreign policy had a positive impact on Sino-Soviet relations. Gorbachev was eager to reduce tensions along the Sino-Soviet border. He also withdrew Soviet forces from Afghanistan and Mongolia, and pressured Vietnam to find a peaceful resolution to its involvement in Cambodia. In May 1989 Gorbachev traveled to China to meet with Deng Xiaoping. This meeting, in Deng's words, "closed the past and opened the future" of Sino-Soviet relations. The new relationship was much different from that of the 1950s. China and the Soviet Union were now on equal terms, no longer enemies, and not allies but simply good neighbors. In the meantime, Sino-Soviet border talks resumed, and a comprehensive border agreement was signed in May 1991.

The demise of the Soviet Union opened a new era in China's relations with Russia. Cross-border trade boomed, just as a deep recession hit the Russian economy. In the 1990s thousands of traders made regular cross-border trips to China for cheap consumer goods, bringing back as much as they could carry to supply rapidly growing street markets in Russia. From Russia China imported raw materials (especially fuels), but also aerospace equipment, nuclear reactors, advanced weaponry, and machine tools. In addition to consumer goods, China exported telecommunications equipment, electronics, and automobiles. Between 1992 and 2006, official (and somewhat underestimated) Sino-Russian trade grew almost sixfold to US $35 billion. In 2006 China was Russia's third-largest trading partner, though this relationship was not reciprocal, as China's trade with the United States and Japan still vastly dwarfed its trade with Russia.

The most remarkable transformation of Sino-Russian relations occurred in the political sphere. Building on the political consultations of the 1980s and successful border talks, China, Russia, and the Soviet successor states—Kazakhstan, Kyrgyzstan, and Tajikistan (all bordering on China)—in 1996 concluded an agreement on confidence building in the border area. This agreement, signed in Shanghai, signaled the beginning of the "Shanghai process" and led to the establishment of Shanghai Cooperation Organization in 2001, with the five earlier participants plus Uzbekistan. In the same year China and Russia signed a friendship and cooperation treaty.

Both the Shanghai Cooperation Organization and the newly established Sino-Russian "strategic cooperative partnership" are subtly anti-American, inasmuch as China and Russia both strive to promote a multipolar world order in place of a U.S.-centered unipolar one. Sino-Russian relations of the early twenty-first century are in line with the conception, first articulated by Deng Xiaoping in 1981–1982, that both countries will cooperate to oppose hegemony of whatever form (perceived since the Iraq War as U.S. unilateralism). Beyond this strategic conception, the underlying principles of the Shanghai Cooperation Organization and Sino-Russian relations include mutual appreciation of each other's struggle with terrorism (mainly understood in the context of Russia's problems in Chechnya and China's efforts to contain Uygur separatism in Xinjiang), mutual noncriticism of each other's internal policies and human-rights record, and development of economic, cultural, and scientific cooperation.

SEE ALSO *Central Asian States, Relations with; Communist Party; Five-Year Plans; Foreign Trade since 1950; Harbin; International Relations; Mao Zedong; Sino-Soviet Schism.*

BIBLIOGRAPHY

Heinzig, Dieter. *The Soviet Union and Communist China, 1945–1950: The Arduous Road to the Alliance.* Armonk, NY: Sharpe, 2004.

Lukin, Alexander. *The Bear Watches the Dragon: Russia's Perceptions of China and the Evolution of Russian-Chinese Relations since the Eighteenth Century.* Armonk, NY: Sharpe, 2003.

Lüthi, Lorenz M. *The Sino-Soviet Split: Cold War in the Communist World.* Princeton, NJ: Princeton University Press, 2008.

Westad, Odd Arne, ed. *Brothers in Arms: The Rise and Fall of the Sino-Soviet Alliance, 1945–1963.* Washington, DC: Woodrow Wilson Center Press, 1998.

Wilson, Jeanne L. *Strategic Partners: Russian-Chinese Relations in the Post-Soviet Era.* Armonk, NY: Sharpe, 2004.

Wishnick, Elizabeth. *Mending Fences: The Evolution of Moscow's China Policy, from Brezhnev to Yeltsin.* Seattle: University of Washington Press, 2001.

Sergey Radchenko

RUSSIAN ÉMIGRÉS

Of the 2.5 million people who left Russia during the Russian civil war of 1918–1922 (pitting the Bolshevik Red Army against the White Army), some 250,000 fled to China. Most found their first shelter in Harbin on the Chinese Eastern Railway, built by Russia in 1898–1903. This remnant of ambitions to create a Yellow Russia had transformed the small river port of Harbin into an administrative and commercial center of Russian interests in China. By the early 1920s, the influx of White military, gentry, intelligentsia, merchants, workers, and peasants swelled Harbin's Russian population of 43,000 railway employees and settlers to 165,000. Settlements at stations along the Chinese Eastern Railway drew some émigrés, and 13,000 Cossacks settled in the Three Rivers region (Hulunbuir). By the mid-1930s, Tianjin became home to 6,000 émigrés; some 2,000 lived in Shenyang (Mukden); Changchun, Jilin, Dalian, and Qingdao sheltered several hundred each; and close to 1,000 Russians served in the armies of Chinese warlords. Over 300 found refuge in the Beijing Ecclesiastical Mission and in the Legation Quarter. Remnants of the White Army sailed to Shanghai, were reluctantly admitted, and dispersed. A small community formed in Hankou, the former center of Russian tea concessions. Over 13,000 fled across the border to Xinjiang.

HARBIN

The largest concentration of Russians settled in Harbin. Its quasi-Russian administration, lifestyle, and language offered opportunities for economic and cultural survival during an interlude away from home. In their self-absorbed isolation, the émigrés were indifferent to China, its culture, and its plight at the time. In their Russian enclave, they formed White political organizations; expanded the existing Russian school system; and opened a law school with economic and oriental departments, a polytechnic institute, a teachers' college, a theological school, and trade schools. They set up a theater, an opera, a symphony orchestra, libraries, and literary societies, and by 1945 they had published over 3,500 books and 530 periodicals. The Russian Orthodox Eparchy, established in 1922 in Harbin, looked after fifty churches and two monasteries. Lutherans, Byzantine-Slavic Catholics, Old Believers, Molokane Spiritual Christians, Evangelic Christians, Seventh-day Adventists, Baptists, Pentecostals, and Methodist Episcopalians spread their beliefs. The émigrés joined small Russian-speaking communities of Poles, Jews, Ukrainians, Turkic-Tatars, Germans, Georgians, Armenians, Latvians, Lithuanians, Estonians, Czechs, and Yugoslavs, most having houses of prayer, clubs, charities, publications, and elementary schools. Some émigrés found work at the Chinese Eastern Railway and its auxiliary enterprises; others managed to bring out money and run flour mills, soybean-oil factories, distilleries, tobacco factories, mechanical workshops, dairies, and companies offering services. Others survived by working outside of their professions. Charities helped the poor, but some people fell between the cracks or succumbed to alcohol and drugs, and Harbin newspapers reported many suicides. Along the Chinese Eastern Railway, there was work in forestry, coal mines, dairies, and husbandry; in the Three Rivers area, Cossacks set up over twenty villages and engaged in agriculture and hunting.

POLITICAL PAWNS, 1920–1932

From September 1920, China no longer recognized czarist diplomats and deprived Russians of extraterritoriality rights. The former zone of the Chinese Eastern Railway became a Special Region of the Eastern Provinces, where China regained sovereignty in court, police, and municipal matters. In 1924 the Soviet Union signed treaties with China and with the warlord Zhang Zuolin on the joint Sino-Soviet administration of the Chinese Eastern Railway and demanded that it employ only Soviet and Chinese citizens. Many émigré employees took Soviet passports, some patriotically, others as "radishes" (Red outside, White inside); a small number became Chinese citizens; the rest were dismissed. To the dismay of the Whites, the Soviet administration celebrated Soviet holidays and established workers' clubs, schools, youth organizations, and periodicals. This Sovietization led to Chinese protests and an armed conflict in 1929, with the Soviet Union emerging victorious. A thousand Russian émigrés, including children and elders, were massacred by Soviet troops in the Three Rivers region.

PUPPETS IN MANCHUKUO, 1932–1945

In 1931–1932 Japan occupied Northeast China and turned it into a puppet state, Manchukuo (Manzhouguo). By 1935 Japan forced the Soviet Union to sell its share of the railway, and 25,000 Soviet citizens left for the Soviet Union, where many perished in purges. The remaining 60,000, some seeing the Japanese as White allies, were ruled by the Japanese Military Mission and its collaborationist Bureau for the Affairs of Russian Émigrés, set up in 1934 and headed by appointed White generals, with branches in all major settlements and ethnic communities. The Russian Fascist Party played a prominent role in the bureau. Every Russian individual and organization had to be registered with the bureau, which controlled all Russian financial, economic, cultural, and religious activities, all jobs for Russians, and wartime rations. Outside Manchukuo, émigrés were subject to collaborationist Anti-Comintern Committees, set up by the Japanese. In Manchukuo, by 1941 the Japanese established Russian branches of the Manshūkoku Kyōwakai (Manchukuo Cooperation Association), closed all postsecondary Russian schools except for the theological school, reorganized schools on a Japanese model, took over many Russian businesses and enterprises, required citizens to study Japanese, and instituted endless glorification of Manchukuo and Japan. Defiance was squashed, prominent opponents were deported, and others disappeared in the Japanese gendarmerie or in the laboratories of Unit 731 as victims of biological experimentation.

SHANGHAI

Toward the end of 1930s, the steady exodus of émigrés from the Northeast increased the Russian population of Shanghai to over 25,000 and made it the largest European community there. Shanghai also had active communities of Jews, Ukrainians, Georgians, and Turkic-Tatars. Émigrés worked in foreign enterprises, in a special detachment of the Shanghai Volunteer Corps, and in the police. They scabbed in Chinese strikes. Many dancing girls were Russian. Émigrés formed several contending political, charitable, and cultural organizations, and they published periodicals. On the Red side, the Soviet Consulate found sympathizers, especially among the young and among some Russian Jews, and the Soviet Club opened in the late 1930s. In 1938–1941, Jews from Germany, Austria, Czechoslovakia, and parts of Poland, Lithuania, Latvia, and Estonia were able to flee to China, but only some of them were Russian Jews; most formed their own networks. While it was suicidal to be pro-Soviet in Manchukuo, in Shanghai the Japanese permitted Soviet broadcasts (in Russian and English), films, wartime chronicles, and periodicals.

LEAVING CHINA

After the war, many émigrés believed in a changed Russia under the Soviets. The Russian Orthodox Church in China, except for the defiant Shanghai Cathedral, went over to the Moscow Patriarchate. In Shanghai, 10,000 émigrés took Soviet passports and 8,000 were repatriated in 1947, some to end in camps. In 1949 the International Refugee Organization evacuated some 5,500 Shanghai Russians to Tubabao, in the Philippines, and then to Australia, the United States, South America, and South Africa. Northeast China was occupied by the Soviet Army, and some 20,000 émigrés were arrested and taken to the Soviet Union to be shot or sent to camps. The rest were pressured to take Soviet passports, though not everyone did. Glorification switched from Manchukuo to the Soviet Union, portraits of Stalin were hung in place of those of the Manchu emperor, the Society of Soviet Citizens replaced the Japanese Bureau for the Affairs of Russian Émigrés, and children went to Soviet-type schools. In the early 1950s, these new Soviet citizens from various cities in the Northeast accepted being sent to the virgin lands of Kazakhstan. Many Jews went to Israel; Poles, Czechs, and Yugoslavs were repatriated to their homelands. Other Harbin Russians succeeded in immigrating to Australia, Brazil, Argentina, Chile, and the United States. The Russian émigrés, who in many cases lived in China for three generations, are now dispersed all over the world. Prominent Russian émigrés include the Shanghai-born conductor Elijah Moshinsky; professors V. A. Riazanovskii and G. K. Gins of California; scholar V. V. Ponosov of Australia; poets Arsenii Nesmelov, Mary Custis Vezey,

and Valerii Pereleshin; and the actor Yul Brynner, who spent much of his youth in Harbin.

SEE ALSO *Harbin; Jewish Communities and Refugees; Russia, Relations with; Shanghai.*

BIBLIOGRAPHY

Bakich, Olga. Charbin: "Rußland jenseits der Grenzen" in Fernost. In *Der grosse Exodus*, ed. Karl Schlögel, 304–328. Munich: C. H. Beck, 1994.

Bakich, Olga. Émigré Identity: The Case of Harbin. In Harbin and Manchuria: Place, Space, and Identity, ed. Thomas Lahusen. Spec. issue, *South Atlantic Quarterly* 99, 1 (Winter 2000): 51–73.

Bakich, Olga. *Harbin Russian Imprints: Bibliography as History, 1898–1961.* New York: Norman Ross, 2002.

Balakshin, Petr. *Final v Kitae* [Finále]. 2 vols. San Francisco: Sirius, 1958–1959.

Li Xinggeng et al., ed. *Fengyu fuping: Eguo qiaomin zai Zhongguo, 1917–1945* [Trials and tribulations: Russian émigrés in China, 1917–1945]. Beijing: Zhongyang Bianyi Chubanshe, 1997.

Ristaino, Marcia Reunders. Shanghai: Russische Flüchtlinge im "gelden Babylon." In *Der grosse Exodus*, ed. Karl Schlögel, 329–345. Munich: C. H. Beck, 1994.

Ristaino, Marcia Reunders. *Port of Last Resort: The Diaspora Communities of Shanghai.* Stanford, CA: Stanford University Press, 2001.

Stefan, John J. *The Russian Fascists.* New York: Harper & Row, 1978.

Wang Zhicheng. *Shanghai eqiao shi* [A history of Russian émigrés in Shanghai]. Shanghai: Shanghai Sanlian Shudian, 1993.

Olga Bakich

RUSTIC REALISM IN ART

Rustic realism (*xiangtu xieshi*) is a school of painting that emerged from China's art academies in the early 1980s and is considered by critics to parallel the root-searching (*xungen*) school of literature. Through its naturalistic style and down-to-earth subject matter, it overturned the emphasis on class struggle and the socialist realist paradigm of art that dominated the decade of the Cultural Revolution (1966–1976). Following the death of Mao Zedong in 1976 and the arrest of the Gang of Four, who were blamed for his policies, the visual arts experienced a gradual shift in tone. Artists began to explore a new realism, seeking to discard the artificiality and heroic optimism promoted by Cultural Revolution authorities, particularly Mao's wife, Jiang Qing, which had yielded a mode of painting they now denigrated for its falsity and vulgarity as "red, bright, and vivid" (*hong, guang, liang*). Although the continued adherence of Mao's successor, Hua Guofeng, to Mao's ideals prevented dramatic changes in the kinds of art publicly exhibited and discussed in 1977 and 1978, within the art academies the techniques of socialist realist and academic painting that had been mastered during the first three decades of the People's Republic of China were increasingly turned to new purposes. Particularly after the rise to power of Deng Xiaoping in 1979, and his slogan, "seek truth from facts," the young artists of the emerging rustic realism school took the lead in forging a new kind of painting that was striking in the context of its time.

In the vigorous ideological debate that eventually overturned Mao's condemnation of "humanism," artists found further intellectual and political support for their revulsion against the overblown socialist realist depictions of workers, peasants, and soldiers that were mandatory during the Cultural Revolution. Instead of stereotypes based on Mao's concept of class struggle, they sought to directly depict the human qualities of their subjects in everyday situations. It was as if "art had returned from Heaven to the mundane world" (Galikowski 1998, p. 203).

The first generation of art school graduates in the post-Mao era took many approaches to convey the spirit of the times. Whereas scar painting, which began in 1978, deployed a realist vocabulary enlivened by melodrama to expose the devastation caused by the Cultural Revolution and the Red Guard movement, rustic realist artists drew inspiration from their experiences laboring in the countryside during the latter half of the Cultural Revolution. Beginning in 1968 almost all of China's urban young people had been "sent down" to rural areas or factories to be reeducated. Some moved directly into rural villages, while others worked on large military farms or even in compounds that had previously served as labor reform camps for political criminals. Almost all art students accepted by China's art academies from the late Cultural Revolution into the 1980s, therefore, had spent years laboring as rusticated youth. Many were also former Red Guards. In their varied experiences far from their urban homes, they had all witnessed and lived the unidealized reality of China's peasant or proletarian class, coming to know well the backbreaking labor, rugged conditions, and rural poverty that were obscured by propaganda. Having themselves served as tools in the implementation of Mao's utopian policies, many appeared to possess a wisdom beyond their years.

Rustic realism depicts the same rural subjects that might have been seen in the work of socialist realist propagandists, but the artists apply their technical skills to explore the humanity of individual farmers. Such work looked old-fashioned to Western observers at the time and was not of great interest to the international art community; but in the context of its day, its unvarnished realism of surface and the ambiguity of the artists' attitude toward their subjects were shockingly powerful rejections of the practice of art as propaganda.

Scar painting and rustic realist painting were closely related in terms of technique and their rejection of socialist realist content. Several artists who had previously been part of the scar movement, such as He Duoling (b. 1948), Cheng Conglin (b. 1954), and Ai Xuan (b. 1947), became rustic realist painters in the early 1980s. However, whereas scar painting was confrontational, focusing on the experiences that had disillusioned a generation—primarily the violence unleashed by Mao Zedong in the early years of the Cultural Revolution—rustic realism was more contemplative. Works in this vein reflected the deep impact of artists' experiences in the countryside by portraying everyday people like those they had known there. Their attempts at faithfully realistic depictions of farmers and herders, both Han Chinese and minorities, aimed to capture the humanity of their subjects. Thus their art was taken as a hopeful sign in a period of great uncertainty.

ARTISTS

Many of the first rustic realist painters, such as Luo Zhongli (b. 1948) and He Duoling (b. 1948), lived in the western province of Sichuan, where they spent years in extremely remote mountain villages or among the several minority groups of their home region. Sichuan's distance from the capital and from east-coast urban centers gave artists the freedom to develop their own vision. The most influential rustic realist painting may have been that of Luo Zhongli, who was then a student (and subsequently a teacher and director) at the Sichuan Academy of Fine Arts. The awarding of top honors to his striking photorealist oil painting *Father* (*Fuqin*) sparked controversy at the Second Chinese Exhibition for Young Artists in Beijing in 1980, but its innovations were ultimately accepted by the official art establishment.

Unlike Luo's unflinching realism, the work of He Duoling and Ai Xuan tended more toward the romantic, magical-realist style and compositions of the American painter Andrew Wyeth (1917–2009), whose work was widely known in China at that time. He's idyllic *Revival of Spring*, which portrays a peasant girl sitting in a field and staring anxiously off into space, was highly regarded by Chinese art circles when it was first exhibited in 1982. The Beijing artist Ai Xuan, who spent years in Tibet and Sichuan during the Cultural Revolution, is known for his somber depictions of Tibetans. For some later practitioners, particularly younger artists who may lack the rural experiences of their elders, rustic realism has become a vehicle for demonstrating technical virtuosity in realist painting.

Other seminal examples of rustic realist painting emerged from the Central Academy of Fine Arts (CAFA) in Beijing. Chen Danqing's (b. 1953) dark and brooding *Tibetan Series* (*Xizang xuhua*), seven pieces of which were shown at the CAFA graduation exhibition in Beijing in

LUO ZHONGLI'S *FATHER*

Luo Zhongli's iconic *Father* (*Fuqin*) is a large painting, measuring roughly 63 inches by 94 inches (160 x 240 cm), that meticulously depicts in the photorealist manner the head of an aged, wrinkled Sichuan peasant. The anonymous man stares intently at the viewer while holding high, in his gnarled, rough hands, a bowl half full of tea. Every pore and crease on the man's face and every nick in his fingernails are clearly visible. Despite the ambiguity of the man's expression, and indeed of the artist's purpose in painting him, the work is both powerful and compelling. This old man, with a lifetime of labor etched on his face, was not the artist's actual father, but with his identity left obscure he could be understood as anyone's father.

Before 1979 an image of this size, particularly in the format of a bust-portrait, was usually reserved for important political figures, particularly Mao. Party officials reacted viscerally against this startling, ambiguous image of a peasant, most likely seeing it as an appropriation of the format of the Mao cult. Indeed, if rendered in such a manner a decade earlier, the painting would have been condemned as blasphemy.

Luo admired the American photorealist painter Chuck Close (b. 1940), whose postmodern format he borrowed here, as well as Jean-François Millet, the nineteenth-century French painter of peasants. Although *Father* is commonly compared to Close's portraits, which endeavor to alienate the sitter from the viewer through the objectivity of the photorealist lens, Luo's similarly imposing painting is instead rather inviting because of the care and sensitivity in which he chooses to render the old peasant. Luo's approach encourages the viewer to wonder about and sympathize with the aging and impoverished subject and at the same time to appreciate the integrity of his essential humanity.

The father of this huge image is not the iconic Mao but instead a simple man who represents dignity and honesty in the face of life's suffering. By implication, then, Luo's *Father* may be read as questioning the efficacy of Communist economic and social policies that have left this old peasant still so poor. Indeed, the veteran revolutionary artist Li Shaoyan, who reviewed the painting in Sichuan, is said to have remarked that one cannot see how this is a peasant of postrevolutionary China. Thus Li suggested that the artist add a ballpoint pen tucked behind the peasant's ear to signify that the old man was at least literate. Luo complied with this idea, but the ballpoint pen does not clarify the ambiguity of his situation, which was exactly the artist's point.

Vivian Y. Li
Julia Andrews

the fall of 1980, were widely acclaimed for their technical skill and sensitivity to their subject matter. Chen had been sent to the countryside in 1970, spending eight years based in rural Jiangxi and Jiangsu. During that time he taught himself to paint, and at the end of the Cultural Revolution he traveled to Tibet to depict its people. As the artist has explained, he was in Tibet when news of Mao's death arrived; his painting *Tears Flooding the Autumnal Fields* is based on a scene he witnessed of Tibetans weeping over the news. After exhibiting this and a second Tibet-themed painting at national exhibitions in 1977, he was admitted to the graduate painting program of CAFA in 1978. The school retained him as a teacher in 1980, but two years later he moved to New York, where he spent eighteen years before returning to Beijing in 2000. Unlike those of He Duoling, Chen's figures were not overtly sentimental, but they possess a slight flavor of exoticism that may appear old-fashioned to Western observers. Nevertheless, in their own time they were remarkable for their directness and their sensitive rendering. His paintings, with their dark palette, are appreciated in China for their combination of sympathy and acute observation, for avoiding the idealization of their subjects, and for suggesting through a portrait-like rendering of weathered faces the real hardships of people's lives.

Rustic realism was created by disenchanted artists who lived through the highly political Mao years to challenge socialist realist conventions and express their own understanding of China's people. In addition to their art historical significance in the early 1980s, the imagery and compositions of rustic realist works also influenced some Fifth-Generation Chinese filmmakers, such as Chen Kaige (*Yellow Earth*, 1984) and Zhang Yimou (*Red Sorghum*, 1987).

SEE ALSO *Film Industry: Fifth Generation Filmmakers; Oil Painting (youhua); Root-Searching Literature; Scar (Wound) Art.*

BIBLIOGRAPHY

Andrews, Julia F. *Painters and Politics in the People's Republic of China, 1949–1979*. Berkeley: University of California Press, 1994.

Cohen, Joan Lebold. *The New Chinese Painting, 1949–1986*. New York: H. N. Abrams, 1987.

Galikowski, Maria. *Art and Politics in China, 1949–1984*. Hong Kong: Chinese University Press, 1998.

Gao, Minglu. *The Wall: Reshaping Contemporary Chinese Art*. Buffalo, NY: Albright-Knox Art Gallery, 2005.

Vivian Y. Li
Julia F. Andrews

S

SAI JINHUA

1874–1936

Sai Jinhua is one of China's most famous courtesans. Late Qing and Republican writers and playwrights saw in her a powerful cipher to explore and express the plight of modernity as China stood on the cusp of great changes. Writing about her thus became an easy way to indulge in nostalgia for the lost late imperial courtesan culture, but also to come to terms with the turbulent landscape of late nineteenth- and early twentieth-century Chinese history, when traditional gender roles began to change and China clashed with the West.

It is almost impossible to distinguish fact from fiction in most retellings of Sai Jinhua's life story, which are often informed by fictional representations. Still, the basic narrative that keeps seducing readers and audiences in China and abroad is as follows. A native of Suzhou, hailing from an impoverished family of merchants, Sai Jinhua started her career in her early teens, when she was tricked into prostitution by a relative as a way to cope with her family's declining finances. When she was twelve years old, she became the third concubine of the *zhuangyuan* (the highest rank in China's examination system) Hong Jun (1840–1893), a man many years her senior. When he was appointed ambassador, she followed him to Europe and spent three years abroad, between Berlin and Saint Petersburg, during which time she gave birth to a daughter. After Hong Jun's death, Sai Jinhua was expelled from the Hong household (and had to leave her daughter with them) and resumed her old profession under the name of Cao Menglan. Capitalizing on her fame and using the connections she had established among powerful officials during her

marriage to Hong Jun, she became one of the most popular stars in the courtesans' quarters and worked in Beijing, Shanghai, and Tianjin.

In 1900, during the Boxer Uprising, she escaped from Tianjin to Beijing, where she supposedly had a liaison with Count Alfred Waldersee (1832–1904), the commander in chief of the foreign troops that arrived in Beijing to stamp out the antiforeign movement. In the aftermath of the Boxer Uprising, Sai Jinhua supposedly played an active role in bringing aid to the populace of Beijing and also in the peace talks. During this time, she was also running her own establishment, and in 1905 she was arrested after Fengling, a prostitute working for her, killed herself. Accused of having driven the girl to suicide, Sai Jinhua was exiled to her native Suzhou. Between 1906 and 1922, she was twice married and twice widowed, and moved to and from Beijing, where she died, an opium addict, in extreme poverty. Her only sources of income by this time were old patrons and journalists. Indeed, she managed to exploit her fame by selling her story to newspapers almost until her dying day.

Perhaps the most important question to explore when examining the protean figure of Sai Jinhua is the rationale behind her continuing fortunes, especially given the fact that courtesans had been part of the entertainment and leisure culture of the upper classes in China since the Tang dynasty (618–907). In fact, the heyday of their role as cultural icons was the late Ming (1368–1644) period, a time where different socioeconomic factors contributed to the creation of a vast community of scholars and merchants in the Jiangnan region who became fundamental in patronizing, supporting, and weaving courtesans into a complex network of cultural and emotional exchanges. At that time, courtesans were well-trained performers with a high level of literacy and artistic skills, and they were often prolific poets and writers. Later, because of the various historical changes that brought about the fall of the Ming dynasty and the abrupt reduction in the quantity and quality of literati patronage of courtesans, this category of women became increasingly more specialized in sex work.

By the late Qing, when Sai Jinhua began her career, brothels still retained their important function as a social space of male bonding and social display. The quality of courtesans' training had dramatically declined, however, and as Sai Jinhua herself had occasion to say, she was not a talented performer in any area. The opening of the treaty ports as a result of the Opium Wars, and especially the emergence of Shanghai as a new center of economic, industrial, and cultural production, drew countless men and women in search of employment. Sai Jinhua was able to acquire visibility and to engage the growing media networks in this changing urban landscape. She never left behind her work or her status as a sex worker, but thanks to her savvy manipulation of the attention she had attracted as the wife of a prestigious official, her entrepreneurial skills, and the appeal of her life story, she emerged as one of the first icons in a growing star-driven entertainment culture centered in Shanghai.

Because of her very peculiar and public career, her fame extended well beyond China: Chinese and Western authors and scholars alike have been under her spell since the end of the last century. And her journey retains its market appeal in different media: Rumors have floated since the late 1990s that Sai Jinhua's life story would become the center of a multimillion-dollar Sino-American film project.

SEE ALSO *Prostitution, History of.*

BIBLIOGRAPHY

Chang Hsin-hai. *The Fabulous Concubine: A Novel.* New York: Simon and Schuster, 1956.

Henriot, Christian. *Belles de Shanghai: Prostitution et sexualité in Chine aux XIXe–XXe siècles.* Paris: CNRS, 1997.

Hershatter, Gail. *Dangerous Pleasures: Prostitution and Modernity in Twentieth-century Shanghai.* Berkeley: University of California Press, 1997.

Li Wai-yee. The Late Ming Courtesan: Invention of a Cultural Ideal. In *Writing Women in Late Imperial China*, ed. Ellen Widmer and Kang-i Sun Chang, 46–73. Stanford, CA: Stanford University Press, 1997.

McAleavy, Henry, trans. *That Chinese Woman: The Life of Sai-Chin-hua, 1847–1936.* New York: Crowell, 1959.

Ropp, Paul S. Ambiguous Images of Courtesan Culture in Late Imperial China. In *Writing Women in Late Imperial China*, ed. Ellen Widmer and Kang-i Sun Chang, 17–45. Stanford, CA: Stanford University Press, 1997.

Paola Zamperini

SALT, 1800–1949

During the Qing dynasty (1644–1912), the salt trade was run as a government monopoly. The Qing government divided the country into eleven salt-production areas and assigned each the responsibility of supplying salt to a certain area.

In devising this production and distribution scheme, the Qing government had taken geographical constraints and transportation routes into consideration. It made sense, for instance, that salt from Fujian would supply Fujian and part of Zhejiang bordering Fujian, and that salt from Lianghuai would supply Hubei with the Yangzi River as the main transportation route. Nevertheless, problems among different salt-consumption areas almost certainly arose along the artificial administrative boundaries. Society's response was smuggling, if not outright resistance to the government's monopoly. For example, Hunan and Jiangxi were required to consume salt transported from Lianghuai. However, it was much less costly to supply the area with salt from Guangdong, their neighboring province. Not surprisingly, Guangdong salt was smuggled into the area, much to the dismay of Lianghuai salt officials and merchants.

In terms of financial contribution to the Qing government, the Lianghuai area was the most important salt-production area. Lianghuai contributed the largest portion of salt revenue for the Qing government because it had access to the Grand Canal and virtually the entire middle to lower course of the Yangzi River.

ADMINISTRATION

The Qing salt administration consisted of a three-tier hierarchy of salt-tax supervisorates (*yanke tiju si*), subcommissions (*fensi*), and salt-distribution commissions (*yanyun si*). All major salt-production areas came under the jurisdiction of the salt-distribution commissions. The Lianghuai Salt Distribution Commission, for instance, commanded three subcommissions, which, in turn commanded twenty-three salt-tax supervisorates. A commission was headed by a salt-distribution commissioner (*yanyun shi*), ranking 3b; a subcommission by a second assistant salt controller (*yunpan*), ranking 6b; and a salt-tax supervisorate by a supervisor, ranking 8a. On top of the salt-distribution commission was an annually rotated salt censor (*xunyan yushi*) sent from the central government. The three-tier salt-administrative hierarchy much resembled the three-tier local-government hierarchy within a province: a circuit (*dao*) headed by a circuit intendant (*daotai*), ranking 4a; a prefecture (*fu*) headed by a prefect (*zhifu*), ranking 4b; and a county (*xian*) headed by a county magistrate (*zhixian*), ranking 7a (Zhao et al. 1977, pp. 3349, 3352–3357). However, a salt-tax supervisorate was a much smaller geographical unit than a county. Typically overseeing a few dozen salt-production households, a salt-tax supervisorate was a salt-production unit serving political, military, and social functions.

THE ROLE OF SALT MERCHANTS

To guarantee that salt from a certain area reached the designated sales area, the Qing government issued salt tickets (*yanyin*) and organized salt merchants into salt syndicates (*gang*). The salt ticket was both a salt-trade license and a salt-tax bill. Originated in 1617, late in the Ming dynasty, the syndicate system was a government patronage through which chosen salt merchants were granted the hereditary and exclusive privilege of trading salt in return for a hereditary obligation to pay the salt tax (Huang 1974, pp. 220–221). More specifically, syndicate merchants were annually issued a certain number of salt tickets, for which they paid the tax, and they then sold the tickets to subcontractors in the salt trade.

Once a family was made syndicate merchants, bankruptcy or death was its only exit. In the eighteenth century and first half of the nineteenth century, being a lifelong syndicate salt merchant was considered a rare stroke of good fortune and never a problem. The Lianghuai syndicate salt merchants, for example, reaped enormous profits and stunned the country with their luxurious way of living and their quest for literati taste (Ho 1954). They were also well known for their "voluntary" donations to the government during military campaigns, natural disasters, and auspicious occasions. An official estimate put the total donation of salt syndicates at "no less than 30 million taels (2.4 million pounds) of silver" from Yongzheng to the early Jiaqing era (1723–1804) (Zhao Erxun 1977, p. 3613). Seeing the huge profits to be had, the Imperial Household Department (Neiwu Fu), the private investment arm of the emperor, sought a share in the salt trade by tendering loans to syndicate salt merchants in return for handsome interest and profits. In 1703, for instance, the Lianghuai syndicate salt merchants were promised a loan of 1 million taels (80,000 pounds) by Emperor Kangxi during his official visit to the south (Gugong bowuyuan Ming-Qing dang'anbu 1975, p. 26; Zhao Erxun 1977). By the late eighteenth century, however, legal surcharges and illegal extortion had combined to cut the profit margin of the salt monopoly to

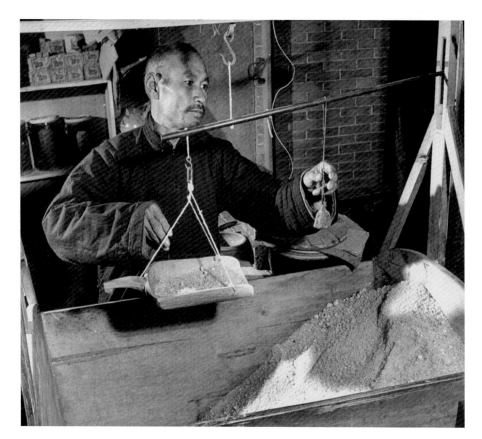

Chinese salt merchant, May, 1947. *Early experts at refining natural resources into useable salt, the Chinese employed this knowledge to add considerable wealth to their country. Leaders throughout Chinese history have treasured the precious commodity, controlling the trade of the substance and levying taxes on its sale.* **MARK KAUFFMAN/TIME LIFE PICTURES/GETTY IMAGES**

the bone. Syndicate salt merchants found it more and more difficult to fulfill their tax obligations.

By the 1830s, attention of the Qing government was brought to the inconvenient fact that the cumulative tax in arrears in Lianghuai had reached a glaring 63 million taels (5.2 million pounds) of silver. Tao Zhu, then governor of Jiangsu, memorialized the emperor with a radical plan: break the monopoly of the syndicate. In 1831 Tao Zhu's plan was approved but was restricted to the northern part of the Lianghuai area, known as Huaibei. Under Tao Zhu's plan, the old salt tickets and their ownership by the syndicate salt merchants were invalidated. In their place new salt tickets (*yanpiao*) were issued, and anyone who could pay the tax was eligible to apply for a ticket and engage in the salt trade. By 1833 Tao Zhu's plan was fully implemented in the entire northern part of Lianghuai. The southern part of Lianghuai, known as Huainan, together with its vast and profitable market stretching from Jiangsu to Hubei, remained unaffected. In 1849 a great fire broke out and devoured many of the salt ships anchoring in Wuhan, the wholesale terminal for the entire Huguang salt market. Lu Jianying, the governor-general of Huguang, proposed carrying out Tao Zhu's plan in the market area for salt from Huainan. After the emperor gave his permission, Lu's reform achieved initial success. However, in less than two years, in 1851, the Taiping Uprising broke out. For a decade the entire Yangzi River area was turned into a battlefield, and the Lianghuai salt monopoly totally collapsed (Zhao Erxun 1977, pp. 3617–3620). After the Taiping war, the Qing government partially restored the Lianghuai monopoly with Li Hongzhang's system of "return tickets" (*xunhuan piao*) and levied more and more surcharges. In the 1880s the tax per ticket was raised from 1 tael (1.3 ounces) to almost 7 taels (9.2 ounces) (Zhao Erxun 1977, pp. 3629–3630).

Both the late Qing dynasty and the abortive early Republican government relied heavily on salt revenue as surety for foreign loans. In 1913, as part of the conditions of the reorganization loan from Britain, France, Germany, Russia, and Japan to Yuan Shikai, then-president of the Republic of China, a Sino-foreign inspectorate for salt administration (*yanwu jihe zongsuo*) was formed, with Sir Richard Dane (Ding En) as its foreign inspector (*yang huiban*) and advisor (*guwen*). For five years during his term of service, till 1918, Dane contrived to rationalize the salt administration and to centralize the salt revenue, winning compliments from within China and without (Adshead 1970). Yuan's abortive attempt to return China to a monarchy and his death in 1916 were followed by civil war and instability well until 1927, when the Guomindang (Nationalist Party) managed with difficulty to establish a Nationalist government with its capital in Nanjing. Dane's reform of the salt administration was thus not sustained.

Salt production and distribution

Production areas	Designated sales areas
Changlu	Zhili (Hebei) and part of Henan
Fengtian	Fengtian, Jilin, and Heilongjiang
Shandong	Shandong and parts of Henan and Jiangsu
Lianghuai	Anhui, Jiangxi, Hubei, Hunan, and parts of Jiangsu and Henan
Zhejiang	Zhejiang and parts of Jiangsu, Anhui, and Jiangxi
Fujian	Fujian and part of Zhejiang
Guangdong	Guangdong, Guangxi and parts of Fujian, Jiangxi, Hunan, Yunnan, and Guizhou
Sichuan	Sichuan, Tibet, Guizhou, and parts of Hubei, Hunan, Yunnan, and Gansu
Yunnan	Yunnan
Hedong	Shanxi and parts of Henan and Shaanxi
Shaanxi and Gansu	Shaanxi and Gansu

SOURCE: Zhao Erxun et al., ed. *Qingshi gao* (Manuscript on Qing History). Beijing: Zhonghua Shuju, 1977, pp. 3603–3604.

Table 1

METHODS OF PRODUCTION

Salt from Changlu, Fengtian, Shandong, Lianghuai, Zhejiang, Fujian, and Guangdong was produced by heating seawater (either with fire or through solar evaporation). Salt from Sichuan and Yunnan was produced by boiling brine raised from deep wells. Salt from Hedong and from Shaanxi and Gansu was produced by directly dredging the playa for salt (Zhao Erxun 1977, p. 3604; Chiang 1983, p. 199).

Production of sea salt (whether by boiling or by solar evaporation) and of playa salt involved relatively little capital. Comparatively speaking, it was in the salt-mining industry of Sichuan that the most advanced technological sophistication and the most intensive capital pooling were realized in the history of the salt trade in premodern China. To gain access to black brine lying as deep as 3,000 feet underground, substantial capital was needed to develop sophisticated well-drilling equipment. Merchants therefore formed partnerships through which shares of a salt well were issued, bought, and sold. Wells were known to be drilled for decades without profitable return, and share ownership was known to pass through generations and to change hands among strangers (Zelin 2005).

BIBLIOGRAPHY

Adshead, Samuel. *The Modernization of the Chinese Salt Administration, 1900–1920.* Cambridge, MA: Harvard University Press, 1970.

Chiang, Tao-chang. The Salt Trade in Ch'ing China. *Modern Asian Studies* 17, 2 (1983): 197–219.

Gugong bowuyuan Ming-Qing dang'anbu [Ming-Qing Archives Bureau, Old Palace Museum], ed. *Guanyu Jiangning zhizao Caojia dang'an shiliao* [Archives of the Cao family: The Jiangning textile intendant]. Beijing: Zhonghua Shuju, 1975.

Ho, Ping-ti. The Salt Merchants of Yang-chou: A Study of Commercial Capitalism in Eighteenth-Century China. *Harvard Journal of Asiatic Studies* 17, 1–2 (1954): 130–168.

Huang, Ray. *Taxation and Governmental Finance in Sixteenth-Century Ming China.* Cambridge, U.K.: Cambridge University Press, 1974.

Zelin, Madeleine. *The Merchants of Zigong: Industrial Entrepreneurship in Early Modern China.* New York: Columbia University Press, 2005.

Zhao Erxun et al., eds. *Qingshi gao* [Manuscript on Qing history]. Beijing: Zhonghua Shuju, 1977.

Wing-kin Puk

SANMIN ZHUYI

SEE *Three Principles of the People (Sanmin zhuyi).*

SCAR (WOUND) ART

Scar art (*shanghen*), sometimes translated as "wound art," was an important trend beginning in 1978 that reflected on the decade of the Cultural Revolution (1966–1976) with striking negativity. Its name was derived from the contemporaneous literary movement, scar literature, which also criticized the Cultural Revolution as a period of chaos and repression by revealing the miserable lives of ordinary people who lived through it. Although the Cultural Revolution administrators known as the Gang of Four were arrested in 1976, the autocratic administration of the Chinese Communist Party did not begin liberalizing until 1978, when a series of policies made during the Cultural Revolution were discarded or altered. *Shishi qiushi* ("seeking truth from facts") became one of the most widely adopted slogans of the day. Young painters, reacting against the many false representations in Cultural Revolutionary art, set out to reveal "true reality" in their work. At the 1979 national art exhibition in Beijing, an emerging group of scar artists showed many works that contrasted with the "red, bright and vivid" (*hong guang liang*) revolutionary art of the previous era. This younger generation redeployed socialist realist styles, the only art vocabulary approved by the party before and during the Cultural Revolution—and the one in which they had been trained—to reveal the facts of the past and present. Among the first group of works of scar art were paintings about the April Fifth movement that arose at the time of the Tiananmen Incident of 1976. In April of that year, the government suppressed public mourning in Beijing of the recently deceased premier Zhou Enlai, leading to riots. The government's decision was blamed on the Gang of Four, who used the unrest as an excuse to dismiss Zhou's successor, Deng Xiaoping. Defined as a counterrevolutionary event at that time, the movement was redefined as patriotic in 1977, following the demise of the Gang of Four. The scar paintings dealing with this episode, like their predecessors in the Mao era, were grounded in political attitudes rather than aesthetic concerns; the artists simply changed the iconography to suit the new ideological situation. However, gaining the courage to criticize, scar artists worked against the utopianism of Cultural Revolutionary art, seeking to unmask the damage caused by the Gang of Four, expose the public to the authentic history of the Cultural Revolution, and depict the true status quo. This art movement raised a key issue: What truth or reality should art depict?

ART AND TRUTH

One of the strongest expressions of this dilemma was *Feng* (Maple), a *lianhuanhua* (literally, "serial pictures," a graphic novel or comic) that was widely discussed and debated but, owing to political censorship, remained unresolved. Published in 1979 in the monthly magazine *Lianhuan huabao*, *Feng* is one of the earliest representative works of scar art. Organized as a series of thirty-two small paintings and based on a short story of the same title by Zheng Yi, the *lianhuanhua* narrates a tragic tale set in the early Cultural Revolution from the viewpoint of a middle school teacher. A pair of young lovers, his students Lu Danfeng (whose name means Crimson Maple) and Li Honggang, are impelled to break ties when their Red Guard groups become enemy factions. After a particularly bloody clash, Danfeng follows the dictates of revolutionary heroism by plunging to her death from the roof of a building rather than surrender to Honggang's victorious troop. The story closes, as red maple leaves fill the scene, with Honggang's arrest and execution for Danfeng's murder. In a practice established in the late Cultural Revolution, the *Feng* paintings were a collaborative by Chen Yiming, Liu Yulian, and Li Bin, a group of "rusticated youth" (*xiaxiang zhiqing*) illustrators in Heilongjiang. By depicting a tragedy featuring familiar elements of the Cultural Revolution, the artists invited viewers of that time to recollect the frenetic past decade, during which the definition of truth was blurred, human relations distorted, factionalism reigned paramount, and the future of the younger generation was forfeited.

After the publication of *Feng* some critics began to raise questions regarding the function of art, specifically its obligations to reality. The banning of distribution of the *Feng* issue of *Lianhuan huabao* further stimulated this debate. Although many agreed that art should disclose the true facts of history, opinion as to the best approach to this goal diverged: some favored persuasive distortion—for example, caricaturing villains like the Gang of Four so as to unmask their evil—whereas others favored naturalistic representation—presenting villains in their real times and circumstances. Advocates of the naturalistic approach feared that exaggeration would only facilitate artistic expression at the cost of historical facts. The scar painters took the path of representing real scenes from the Cultural Revolution to stimulate the recollection of past suffering. In the words of *Feng*'s authors, "in order to show the purity, the loyalty, the love and the tragedy of our generation, we want to represent these beautiful things destroyed by naked brutal reality" (Gao 2005, p. 88).

The female protagonist in *Feng* serves as an emblem of beauty. In the context of the Cultural Revolution, in which beauty and love were both taboo, the love between the couple, like the artists' own passion for art, could never be directly revealed but only demonstrated through work and the proletarian revolution. Adopting a plain, naturalistic style, marked by such authentic but shocking touches as a background poster of the violently purged Cultural Revolution leader Lin Biao, *Feng* reminds its audience of the disorders of that decade and implicitly cautions them to reject any movement that so devastates beauty, love, and humanity. The work, which touched a nerve among its sympathetic readers, urged them to break through the barriers of narrow-minded political categories.

LEADING ARTISTS OF THE MOVEMENT

Some of the bloodiest Red Guard battles, resulting in great loss of life, took place in Sichuan province, and Sichuan artists emerged as the most powerful practitioners of scar art. Their work was first displayed nationally at the Chinese National Art Gallery (now the National Art Museum of China), in the 1979 national art exhibition celebrating the thirtieth anniversary of the founding of China. This first nationwide art exhibition after the Cultural Revolution attracted great attention. Viewers accustomed to seeing idealized works depicting the happy lives of citizens of Socialist China were shocked by the oil paintings of Sichuan Academy of Art students. These paintings, though still utilizing socialist realist techniques, depicted distressing subjects never seen in Maoist art.

Two of the most eminent members of the group are Cheng Conglin and Gao Xiaohua. Cheng Conglin (b. 1954), a native of Chengdu, Sichuan, entered the Sichuan Art Academy in 1977. In the 1979 exhibition, his oil painting *A Certain Snowy Day in 1968* (*1968 nian mouyue mouri xue*, 1979), depicting the aftermath of an armed fight between two factions of Red Guards, was among the works that defined the phenomenon of scar art. As noted by Lü Peng in his 2006 study, the painting's naturalistic style was heavily influenced by Soviet prototypes, especially those in *Morning of Streltzi's Execution* (1881) and *Feodosia Morozova* (1883), by Vasily Ivanovich Surikov (1848–1916). The work illustrates a type of tragedy—the

violence of factionalism, of Chinese against Chinese—that was experienced by many of Cheng's fellow Sichuanese and that was unique to the Cultural Revolution. Deploying the vocabulary of Cultural Revolution socialist realism, including its melodrama, to attack the movement that produced it, the artist depicts cheering winners, humiliated losers, and puzzled elderly onlookers. The painting encourages viewers to ponder the intentions of the movement's backstage manipulators, suggesting that the strong passions of the day—a self-righteous zeal to implement narrow notions of right and wrong, and the hatred of those presumed to be enemies—are the result of ignorance.

Gao Xiaohua (b. 1955) was born in Nanjing and traveled all over China with his parents, who both worked in the army. Aware of fierce battles during the Cultural Revolution, he was driven to question what seemed to him the disorder of life. Gao began painting *Why* (*weishenme*, 1978) soon after his entrance into the Sichuan Art Academy. Eschewing the socialist realist convention of presenting exalted leaders from the perspective of their optimistic subjects looking upward, Gao's painting depicts a group of wounded Red Guards from a bird's eye view. The central figure sits on the curb with his head wrapped in bandages, looking lost and helpless, possibly wondering what happened to his missing comrades and why events have brought him to this point. The painting, from composition to content, is a complete contradiction of "red" art and the standards of Mao's Yan'an Forum. The scene of despair expresses the pessimism of many members of the artist's generation and demonstrates the Cultural Revolution's catastrophic consequences. Another oil painting by Gao, *Catching the Train* (*ganhuoche*, 1981), a realistic illustration of the scene at a crammed railway station, implicitly criticizes socialist realist images of joyful, well-organized workers, peasants, and soldiers. The tableau shows a moment in which the crowd is out of control, with many figures appearing worried and disheartened. The dark palette, like that in *Why*, also denies the Maoist aesthetic of painting with bright colors.

Recovering from the trauma of the Cultural Revolution, young artists of the period sought to express their feelings and opinions. Under the banner of scar art, they recorded with their brushes what they had seen and were seeing, exploring a new reality with the inherited vocabulary of socialist realist styles. With the consolidation of the post-Mao government under Deng Xiaoping in 1979, art that was overtly critical of the Communist regime was once again seen as politically problematic. Many veteran scar artists, including Gao Xiaohua and Cheng Conglin, shifted their attention outward, to rural or minority subjects, and joined the ranks of the rustic realists who emerged in 1980.

SEE ALSO *Oil Painting (youhua); Scar (Wound) Literature.*

BIBLIOGRAPHY

Andrews, Julia F. *Painters and Politics in the People's Republic of China, 1949–1979.* Berkeley: University of California Press, 1994.

Gao, Minglu, ed. *The Wall: Reshaping Contemporary Chinese Art.* Buffalo, NY: Albright-Knox Art Gallery, 2005.

Lü Peng. *Ershi shiji Zhongguo yishushi* [A history of art in twentieth-century China]. Beijing: Peking University Press, 2006.

Yanfei Zhu

SCAR (WOUND) LITERATURE

When Mao Zedong died in 1976 his wife, Jiang Qing, and her colleagues, the so-called Gang of Four, were arrested. Policies of the previous ten years were immediately reversed. By 1977 the Cultural Revolution was over, and its cultural products were attributed to the discredited Gang of Four and thus open to repudiation. Between 1977 and 1979 there was a determination by many political and literary actors to investigate and right the wrongs that had led to the chaos of the Cultural Revolution. The rehabilitation of former politicians and bureaucrats came first. In July 1977 Deng Xiaoping was for the second time restored to his former posts, and many other disgraced politicians, bureaucrats, and intellectuals also were reinstated. As well as enlarging his power base by restoring personnel whose sympathies were akin to his own, Deng consolidated his support by encouraging intellectuals to denounce Cultural Revolution policies.

Literary intellectuals responded quickly and vehemently. The first new kind of writing to emerge, "scar literature" (*shanghen wenxue*, also translated as "wound literature"), which lasted from the end of 1977 to 1979, was new only in terms of its themes. It retained the "socialist realist" method of writing, and few of its writers or works lasted beyond the short period when it was in vogue. One of the few who did survive was Liu Xinwu (b. 1942), who played a significant role in departing from the orthodox socialist revolutionary writing—which depicts happy workers and peasants and nasty capitalists and landlords—that had dominated the mainstream literary scene since the Yan'an Forum on Literature and Art in 1942. The keynote for this new literature was struck with the publication of Liu's "Class Teacher" (*Ban zhuren*) in *People's Literature* (Renmin Wenxue) in November 1977. "Class Teacher" was pioneering in its condemnation of the educational and cultural policies of the previous decade, complemented by its praise for intellectuals.

It is not surprising that the first story officially published in China that exposed the damage inflicted by the Cultural Revolution was about education. The main concern for the leaders of the Cultural Revolution had been nurturing "revolutionary successors," and education was considered the way to ensure the continuation of their policies. "Class Teacher" exposed the scars left by these policies. The story's teacher, Zhang Junshi, agrees to admit a young hooligan into his class but is opposed by another student, Xie Huimin, the party secretary of the Youth League branch. Zhang Junshi discovers that whereas the new student's delinquency is due to no more than lack of parental care, the real problem is Xie Huimin, who has been so indoctrinated with Communist dogma that she cannot think beyond slogans. Zhang Junshi fails to persuade her to be more flexible, and the story ends with a call to "save the children." Readers enthusiastically received this plea for less rigid education, and a spate of stories attacking previous policies followed.

"Class Teacher" was followed in August 1978 by "Scar" (*Shanghen*) by a university student, Lu Xinhua (b. 1953). Also about intellectuals, "Scar" deals with the emotional stress and domestic tragedies caused by the Cultural Revolution. The protagonist follows political campaigns so faithfully that she renounces her mother, who was labeled a rightist. By the time she realizes that her mother was wrongfully denounced, her mother has died and it is too late for reconciliation. The story thus went beyond the political and educational spheres, exposing a system that destroyed natural bonds such as those between mother and daughter, and it inspired the name for the writing that explored the wounds created by the Cultural Revolution: "scar literature." Although their analyses were superficial, Liu Xinwu and Lu Xinhua became overnight celebrities. Many critics defended their exposés of problems in socialist China, and nothing was published attacking them.

The overwhelmingly enthusiastic reception of these stories encouraged other writers to discover other "scars" inflicted by the Cultural Revolution. Most were inexperienced authors who produced little of artistic value, but what they lacked in literary talent they made up for in enthusiastic criticism of the Cultural Revolution. They were encouraged by the Communist Party, whose Central Committee declared a party policy of greater openness at its Third Plenum in December 1978. This was illustrated most vividly in the promulgation of two new principles—"practice is the sole criterion of truth" and "seek truth from facts." These principles encouraged writers to become even more daring in their work. Throughout 1979 it was fashionable to break into "forbidden areas," including love and sex, as well as reevaluations of the campaigns of the 1950s.

Some ideologies that had been sacrosanct since 1949 were exploded. For example, the myth that workers were all working happily toward socialist construction under enlightened party leadership came under scrutiny. In September 1979 the relatively unknown worker-writer Jiang

Zilong wrote "Manager Qiao Assumes Office" (*Qiao changzhang shangren ji*) which is about industrial management and the stagnation of industry under the "Gang of Four" and the difficulties of economic reform. This story held the attention of Chinese readers for months: Hundreds of people wrote about it and many work units held seminars on its significance. China was no longer seen as the workers' paradise where laborers selflessly and happily made useful products while busily uncovering class enemies. More "scars"—such as inertia, incompetence, and corruption—were being revealed.

Scar literature became more thematically diverse, and more experienced authors joined the author ranks. Gao Xiaosheng was among the most accomplished. Gao had been labeled a rightist in 1957 and spent most of the next twenty-two years in his home village. He reentered the literary arena in 1979 with the short story "Li Shunda Builds a House," which quickly established his reputation as a chronicler of the problems faced by ordinary peasants. Adopting a traditional story-telling narrative persona, he tempered his indignation with humor. This story of one man's attempts to improve his life is narrated in the context of political changes in China since 1949. It shows that, for poor peasants, the Cultural Revolution was not the only period with disastrous consequences: Every political movement since 1949 brought nothing but more hardship.

In this way, the exposure of social ills in China uncovered origins that stretched beyond the Cultural Revolution. Literature was still used as a political tool, but the political analysis was less superficial and simplistic than it had been. By the early 1980s scar literature, a phenomenon that lasted only couple of years, had given way to writing that was intended to help the reform program.

SEE ALSO *Poetry: Misty Poetry; Propaganda Art: Scar (Wound) Art.*

BIBLIOGRAPHY

King, Richard. "Wounds" and "Exposure": Chinese Literature After the Gang of Four. *Pacific Affairs* 54, no. 1 (1981): 92–99.

Kinkley, Jeffrey, ed. *After Mao: Chinese Literature and Society, 1978–1981.* Cambridge, MA: Harvard University Press, 1985.

Louie, Kam. *Between Fact and Fiction: Essays on Post-Mao Chinese Literature and Society.* Sydney: Wild Peony, 1989.

Kam Louie

SCIENCE AND TECHNOLOGY POLICY

The progress of science and technology (S&T) in China during the twentieth century witnessed many bright moments as well as some severe setbacks. In the twenty-first century,

Gross domestic expenditure on research and development in China, 2000–2005

	2000	2001	2002	2003	2004	2005
GERD (billion yuan)	89.57	104.25	128.76	153.96	196.63	245.00
GERD/GDP (%)	0.90	0.95	1.07	1.13	1.23	1.34

GERD = gross domestic expenditure on research and development.

SOURCE: Ministry of Science and Technology of the PRC, 2007.

Table 1

China has substantially increased its investments in research and development (R&D), currently spending almost 1.5 percent of gross domestic product as of 2007. Having carried out its first manned space flight in 2003 and a lunar mission in 2007, China demonstrated advanced technological capabilities and can claim membership in an exclusive club of nations so far comprising only the United States, Russia, and China. China is now an emerging technological superpower, and the Chinese leadership's strategy for 2020 is to achieve this status through the promotion of indigenous innovation (*zizhu chuangxin*).

Reforms carried out since 1980 have introduced three major changes. First, the open-door policy has enhanced China's access to a global pool of technologies and gradually reoriented Chinese developmental efforts. Second, extensive reforms introduced through S&T policies have successfully mobilized economic incentives for technological development and diffusion. Third, there has been a shift in focus from state-sponsored research projects toward a broader framework of support for technological innovation, including a clear recognition of the role that businesses play in innovative processes.

HISTORY

During the first decades of the People's Republic, founded in 1949, S&T were considered of strategic value for defense and industrial development, and the leadership annually invested more than 1 percent of national income in support of S&T activities. These activities were carried out in state-run research institutes and helped China to develop atomic bombs and satellites. The radical policies of the Cultural Revolution undermined the system, however, and it was revitalized only after the launch of an ambitious ten-year plan to catch up with advanced industrialized countries at the National Science and Technology Conference in 1978. This event and the establishment of the State Science and Technology Commission as the highest government authority for the sector marked the return of S&T policy to center stage, but it was the Communist Party Central Committee's Decision on the Reform of the Science and Technology Management System, passed in March 1985, that ultimately created the framework for a major restructuring of the institutional and regulatory framework for S&T policy.

Commercialization of Technology This policy document introduced such new concepts as commercialization of technology and mobilization of scientists to generate a stream of technology transfer and the creation of new spin-off technology ventures in China during the 1980s and 1990s. As the policy opened up new sources of finance for research institutes and universities, the government reduced its allocation of funding for operating expenses and introduced more competitive procedures for public funding of research projects. As opportunities for making money in the market on the basis of new knowledge and technology opened up, scientists and engineers started to enter the business world.

The 1980s also witnessed the introduction of other policies promoting the commercialization of technology and measures to protect intellectual property rights, such as the Patent Law, adopted in 1984. The 863 High Technology Plan, approved by China's paramount leader Deng Xiaoping in March 1986, injected RMB 5.9 billion into high-technology projects in the civilian and defense sectors from 1986 to 2001. The Torch Program, established in 1988 to support the commercialization of high technology, led to a proliferation of new high-technology development zones in China, where both domestic and foreign high-tech firms set up in great numbers. Furthermore, a number of state-run venture-capital companies were created to help finance the new technology firms. Also in 1986, the National Natural Science Foundation of China was set up to finance basic research projects on the basis of academic excellence.

An Innovation Policy for a Knowledge-Based Economy The 1990s became a decade of rapid economic growth in coastal regions largely fueled by foreign investors encouraged by policies that promised access to the Chinese market in return for injections of advanced technology. Yet universities and research organizations such as the Chinese Academy of Sciences appeared to be marginalized, and apart from a few successful high-technology firms, such as Legend Computer Company (later renamed Lenovo), most enterprises in China paid scant attention to the need for research and innovation. The fragmented structure of the S&T system revealed the need for integration of activities, linkages between key actors, and a more decisive approach to policy making—all in order to provide a more encouraging environ-

ment for indigenous Chinese innovation. The situation called for evaluating and upgrading China's national innovation system, taking into account the prospects for increased market competition as a result of joining the World Trade Organization and the need for competitiveness in the global knowledge economy. This became the cornerstone of the new policy for "revitalizing the nation through science and education" adopted at the National Conference on Science and Technology in 1995, and the new policy framework became streamlined with the establishment of the Ministry of Science and Technology and a high-level Steering Group for Science and Technology and Education in 1998.

The New Innovation Drive of the Twenty-first Century Subsequently, China's leadership committed itself to increasing investments in research and development by both government and business sectors, as emphasized in policy statements presented in January 2006 at the National Congress on Science and Technology, which also adopted a fifteen-year "Medium- to Long-Term Plan for the Development of Science and Technology." The plan formulated topics of strategic research and a range of specific projects in key economic areas, advanced high technology, and frontier sciences such as nanotechnology. The policies aimed to develop an enterprise-centered technology-innovation system in China. As shown in Table 1, the increased support for innovation has caused the proportion of gross domestic product spent on R&D to grow at a rate of between 5 and 10 percent annually since 2000, and it is expected to continue expanding during the next decade to reach an internationally comparable rate of 2.5 percent in 2020.

With the quantitative output of Chinese scientific publications and patents escalating since the 1990s, the effects of the reforms are becoming apparent. In 2005 China was ranked fifth among nations in terms of quantity of scientific publications registered by the Science Citation Index, publishing 6.5 percent of the world's scientific output, in contrast to only 2 percent in 1995. However, Chinese academic papers still receive fewer citations than other nations (3 citations on average, in comparison to 12 citations for U.S.-authored papers). Hence, there is a need to raise the quality of publications in the future. Similarly, the quantity of applications by domestic Chinese organizations to register for Chinese patents has also grown from fewer than 100,000 in 1995 to almost 400,000 in 2005. The vast majority of granted domestic patents are related to less-sophisticated utility models or appearance designs, but the domestic share of more advanced invention patents has increased to almost 40 percent of all invention patents granted in China in 2005.

CHINA'S INNOVATION SYSTEM: STRUCTURE AND ACTORS

In catching up with advanced industrialized economies since the 1980s, the Chinese leadership has transformed the institutions and organizations dominating scientific and technological activities. However, the innovation system is still heavily influenced by a gap between research and production, inherited from a Soviet approach to planning and executing technological development, and by weaknesses inherent in China's developing economy, such as a lack of qualified human resources and vast regional and social inequalities.

Policy-Making Agencies Although policies have called attention to the need for decentralized decision making, the state still prevails in the system. The key policy-making Ministry of Science and Technology is also involved in executing the priorities of five-year plans and long-term strategies through a number of programs, such as the National Key Technologies Research and Development Program, the 863 National High Technology Research and Development Program, and the 973 National Program on Key Basic Research Projects. For the defense and aeronautic sectors, the Committee of Science, Technology, and Industry for National Defense is in charge of a portfolio of projects, some of which are coordinated with civilian high-technology R&D projects. Other ministries and provincial or local governments are also setting their own priorities and investing in projects. Subnational agencies are currently estimated to contribute more than 40 percent of government appropriations for S&T.

Public Research Institutes and Universities The core of the national innovation system is still a large number of government-sponsored public research institutes and universities, though the domestic business sector and foreign multinationals have recently come to play an important role. The Chinese Academy of Sciences is the country's most advanced research organization, with 108 scientific-research institutes, over 200 S&T enterprises, and a university and graduate school, altogether, with other supporting units, employing almost 60,000 persons. In many fields of basic and applied research, it occupies a leading position and employs some of the best scholars in China. Only recently has it been challenged for this position by key universities. The Chinese Academy of Sciences is also active in commercializing research and has been the source of a substantial number of high-technology firms. The Knowledge Innovation Program, initiated in 1998 and allocated RMB 20 billion from 2001 to 2005, seeks to create centers of excellence, with the aim that at least five research institutes will become world leaders by 2010.

In the pre-reform era, the mission of most universities in China hardly included research, but newly established graduate education, an influx of Chinese scholars trained overseas, a new research culture, and additional financial resources (more than RMB 15 billion for R&D expenditures at Chinese universities in 2004) have enabled key universities to became strong in basic research.

Business Firms Emerging as R&D Sponsors From 1998 to 2003 a group of 1,050 research institutes engaged in applied research and technological development under various industrial ministries were transformed into business units, becoming contractors and/or consultants for state-owned enterprises that they had previously served in the industrial sector. This organizational change fostered new commercial linkages between research and production and had the effect of increasing the proportion of R&D performed by the business sector in the national statistics on R&D. In the performance of R&D, the business sector in China has raised its share from 40 percent at the beginning of the 1990s to nearly 70 percent in 2005. In some sectors, such as computers and telecommunications, leading Chinese firms such as Lenovo, Huawei, and ZTE (Zhong Xing Telecommunication Equipment Company) spend up to 15 percent of their turnover on R&D in laboratories in China as well as overseas.

Although more than 90 percent of R&D by business firms suffers from weak human resources and a lack of managerial know-how, it is encouraging that a larger number of firms are becoming engaged in innovation. With the development of high-technology zones, science parks, and incubators, a particularly promising group of small technology-based firms has emerged. These firms contribute significantly to R&D investments and patent applications for inventions in major urban centers in China, as well as to exports of high-technology products. Such firms are often spin-offs from technical research work at research institutes and universities, and have formed a base for the emergence of successful Chinese high-technology firms.

Foreign R&D Laboratories An additional component of China's innovation system that scarcely existed before 1995 is foreign R&D organizations established by multinational firms. As a result of the open-door policy of the 1980s, foreign direct investments have introduced many new technologies, though most of the joint ventures seek to take advantage of cheap manufacturing opportunities, with the result that foreign-owned firms currently contribute more than 60 percent of China's high-technology exports.

In the 1990s multinational firms became increasingly engaged in R&D activities in China, initially to ensure that new products were adapted to the expanding and progressively more sophisticated Chinese market, but subsequently as a platform for development of new technologies for global markets. In 2007 foreign R&D has been estimated to account for more than a quarter of business R&D in China, and the country has attracted investments in more than a dozen new R&D laboratories by multinational firms eager to exploit the availability of highly qualified, but less expensive, R&D personnel. A number of showcase laboratories set up by firms in the information-and-communications-technologies sector such as Microsoft and Motorola bear witness to China's new status as a source of new technology for global markets.

Strengths and Weaknesses The progress achieved by S&T policy reform since the 1980s demonstrates that China can become an important future player in terms of scientific research and technological innovation. Various programs have been launched to attract overseas Chinese scientists and engineers to return to China to set up technology-based firms.

Nevertheless, the emerging strengths of the innovation system are concentrated in relatively few locations in coastal and major urban centers such as Beijing and Shanghai, with large regions such as the Western provinces of China and important economic sectors such as agriculture and public health experiencing little sustained progress. Moreover, a great number of industrial enterprises are still operating with wasteful and polluting technology, and even if the business sector has increased its R&D investments, the vast majority of enterprises have limited capabilities and a low propensity to innovate. China's innovation system suffers from limited supplies of well-trained scientists, engineers, and technicians, with the most-talented people seeking opportunities abroad or outside S&T. Business firms are still averse to taking the risk of investing in major innovations, and the financial system does not support innovation to a sufficient degree. From a long-term perspective, China needs to strengthen its capabilities in basic scientific research (currently only 5.4% of gross domestic expenditure on R&D is devoted to basic science) in order to provide a fountain of new discoveries and research at the frontiers of technological development.

POLICY ISSUES

The successes of China's S&T policy reforms must be viewed against a range of continuing challenges that cast a shadow on the future implementation of ambitious goals to make China a technological superpower based on indigenous innovation. One of these challenges is how to govern S&T effectively. Another is how to promote creativity and raise the level of scientific and technological competence in the nation as a whole. Ultimately, challenges include wider issues of the social and environmental implications of the Chinese leadership's priorities.

S&T Governance The current system of governance for S&T suffers from two important shortcomings. For one, initiatives to promote scientific research and technological innovation tend to be designed and implemented in a top-down manner, and this reduces the scope for other stake-holders to participate and contribute. Also, a diversified mix of policies to support innovation, including components such as tax incentives and financial-system reform, requires stronger interagency coordination and cooperation between regional and central bureaucracies.

The first problem, a legacy of the planned economy in China, tends to favor programs that rely on pick-the-winner approaches, where the winner is either a winning technology or a favorite actor (such as a research institute, university, or firm). Even where Chinese policy makers pay lip service to the principle that market demand is a central input for selecting future technologies, or the principle that autonomous scientific interest is essential for selecting research topics at the frontiers of knowledge, they tend to overestimate the ability of scientific committees and government officials to identify future trends and priorities.

The second problem is the perennial issue of lack of coordination among central government agencies and between central and regional governments in China. Tax incentives and the regulation of venture-capital funds involve government agencies for finance at both the central and provincial/municipal levels, and their work needs to be aligned to the priorities of the Ministry of Science and Technology. Moreover, training scientists and engineers requires coordination with agencies regulating education at the central and local levels. The issue of coordination is unlikely to be resolved merely by setting up another high-level committee. Rather, agencies and their staffs have to adopt more flexible and open approaches to communication and decision making.

Education and Creativity With the expansion of higher education in China, the basis for future indigenous innovation is emerging. Chinese enrollments in science and engineering departments are large compared with those of other nations (at least 50 percent of university enrollments, with more than 1 million engineering graduates in 2005), and the quality of training at key universities has risen for both undergraduate and graduate students. It is widely acknowledged, however, that education in China hardly encourages creativity, and the most entrepreneurial and skilled graduates tend to go abroad for further training, or they are hired by foreign multinational firms. For indigenous innovation and creativity to increase in China, a new culture needs to develop among Chinese domestic firms. Knowledge and innovation has traditionally been dominated by practical and political agendas in China. A more exploratory approach is called for in the future. Furthermore, China needs to continue to attract returnees from abroad to help the economy grow a viable sector of creative firms.

Technology fair, Beijing, June, 2001. *Beginning a program of economic reform in the 1970s, China continues to devote considerable resources to developing an innovative science and technology industry, encouraged by foreign businesses looking to capitalize on China's low labor costs.* © **BOB SACHA/** CORBIS

Social and Environmental Sustainability The Chinese leadership appears, for better or worse, to have become infatuated with high technology. The benefit is that a strong commitment to S&T in development and to investments in innovation has created an environment more conducive to innovation and technological competition.

The problem is that when priorities and policies are excessively focused on prestigious projects, such as manned space travel or the production of advanced integrated circuits, the more mundane but critical issues of employing S&T to solve pressing problems of poverty, public health, and environmental sustainability tend to be ignored. It is essential that innovation not only benefit the emerging middle class in the relatively well-off urban areas of the coastal provinces but also reach into the backward western provinces and help lift the rural population out of poverty. If China can broaden its innovative efforts to encompass these marginalized segments of the population and lift them out of poverty, it will greatly contribute to global innovation and economic development.

SEE ALSO *High Technology; Research in Engineering; Research in the Sciences; Scientific Community.*

BIBLIOGRAPHY

Baark, Erik. Knowledge and Innovation in China: Historical Legacies and Institutional Reform. *Asia Pacific Business Review* 13, 3 (July 2007): 337–356.

Cao, Cong, Richard P. Suttmeier, and Denis F. Simon. China's 15-Year Science and Technology Plan. *Physics Today* 59 (December 2006): 38–43. http://www.physicstoday.org/vol-59/iss-12/p38.html.

Gu, Shulin. *China's Industrial Technology: Market Reform and Organizational Change.* London: Routledge, 1999.

Organisation for Economic Co-operation and Development. *OECD Reviews of Innovation Policy. China. Synthesis Report.* Paris: Author, 2007.

Segal, Adam. *Digital Dragon: High-Technology Enterprises in China.* Ithaca, NY: Cornell University Press, 2003.

Sigurdson, Jon. *Technological Superpower China.* Cheltenham, U.K.: Edward Elgar, 2005.

Varum, Celeste, Can Huang, and Borges Gouveia. *China: Building an Innovative Economy.* Oxford: Chandos, 2007.

Erik Baark

SCIENTIFIC COMMUNITY

The Western concept of "scientific community" was not introduced into China until the early 1980s when *The Structure of Scientific Revolutions* (1962) and *The Essential Tension: Selected Studies in Scientific Tradition and Change* (1977), both by Thomas Kuhn (1922–1996), were translated into Chinese. But it is with the Chinese publication of Robert K. Merton's (1910–2003) *Science, Technology, and Society in Seventeenth Century England* (1938) in 1986 that Chinese researchers started to embrace the concept. Such terms as *invisible college, paradigm,* and *scientific community* have become part of the discourse in the social studies of science and technology in China.

KEJIJIE

A term similar to "scientific community," *kejijie,* had been known in China for a long time. In fact, *kejijie* and the China Association for Science and Technology (CAST), an umbrella organization for science and technology professionals in China, have been separate functional groups participating in the Chinese People's Political Consultative Conference, China's political advisory body, since the founding of the People's Republic in 1949.

The so-called *kejijie,* literally meaning "circles of science and technology," is more concerned with the institutional organization of science and technology in China. In particular, *kejijie* included five fronts (*dajun*), dating back to the PRC establishment. The first was the Chinese Academy of Sciences, established in 1949 to be the center and the driving force of scientific work for the entire nation. In the meantime, following the Soviet model, China set up research academies in various ministries. For example, the Ministry of Health established and still has under its jurisdiction the Chinese Academy of Medical Sciences and the Chinese Academy of Traditional Chinese Medicine; the Ministry of Agriculture founded the Chinese Academy of Agricultural Sciences and research institutes of agricultural sciences in the provinces; and each of the industrial ministries also set up its own specialized research institutes and laboratories in many of the major industrial enterprises. Universities had focused their mission on training after the adjustment of colleges and departments in the 1950s. Military-focused research institutes and universities were usually treated as a different category. And lastly, there were various kinds of research institutes associated with enterprises.

The institutional organization of Chinese science did not experience dramatic changes in terms of the "fronts" engaged in research activities until the late 1970s when the reform and open-door policy was initiated. Since then, China's universities and colleges, especially "key" (*zhongdian*) institutions, have seen their roles in research expanded and enhanced dramatically. Institutions of learning have been encouraged to better serve the nation's economic development through spinning off enterprises with products and technologies developed there. Some applied research-oriented institutes have become enterprises themselves or research-and-development arms of large enterprises.

Parallel to the institutional organization of science in China is the web of professional societies, represented by CAST and its affiliated societies. However, these societies have until recently not played an important role. There were few professional-development activities and academic exchanges, and professional societies were, and in many instances are still, the places where retired scientists and officials from science- and technology-related government agencies are able to extend their influence. With the introduction of the norms and practices of international science, Chinese scientists have realized the value of the "invisible college," and are more willing to participate in academic exchanges and even urge professional societies to organize such activities so that peers can learn from each other, discuss various issues concerning their professions, and share their research. Therefore, in recent years, more activities aimed at stimulating academic exchanges among scientists and engineers have been initiated. In fact, CAST has since 1999 held its annual conference around the country, following the practice of its international counterparts, such as the American Association for the Advancement of Science. The annual conference has become a platform bringing together scientists to exchange their research and promote the role of science and technology in a society that has become technologically sophisticated.

CHINA'S CONNECTION TO THE INTERNATIONAL SCIENTIFIC COMMUNITY

For many years, Chinese scientists were not actively engaged in international academic exchange, although many of the older generation used to be closely linked with the interna-

tional scientific community due to their study and research stints overseas in the pre-PRC period or the early years of the PRC. After China restored its position in the United Nations in 1971, its scientists started slowly to enter the international arena. Finally, China's opening to the world since the late 1970s has seen its scientists becoming active members of the international scientific community.

An increasing number of Chinese scientists getting advanced training and research experience overseas are returning to China. As a result, Chinese science has been influenced by what has been done at the frontiers of international science, despite a gap that is yet to be narrowed. They also collaborate with their former mentors, classmates, and colleagues and are sought after in such endeavors. In fact, between 1996 and 2005, more than 20 percent of publications by Chinese scientists in international journals were coauthored by at least one counterpart from a foreign institution. There is little doubt that Chinese scientists are well connected in the international scientific community.

Scientists at work in the laboratories of Central South University, Changsha, Hunan province, June 19, 2006. *After years of relative isolation, many Chinese scientists rejoined the international community in the 1980s, as Deng Xiaoping looked to modernize China's economy by encouraging the study of science and technology. By the 2000s, many Chinese who had studied abroad returned home to share their acquired knowledge with a new generation and assume leadership positions on multi-national research projects.* GUANG NIU/ GETTY IMAGES

In addition, Chinese scientists have participated in activities organized by major international organizations in science and technology and even led such organizations through government and institutional arrangements or through CAST and its affiliated societies. For example, while conducting Antarctic research as early as 1980, Chinese earth scientists became involved in the Scientific Committee on Antarctic Research, among the earliest such organizations in the world. Chinese scientists also have joined the Integrated Ocean Drilling Program, an international partnership of scientists and research institutions organized to explore the earth's structure and history through scientific ocean drilling, and Chinese scientists have been active members of the International Geosphere-Biosphere Program to study global climate change.

As a whole, CAST and its affiliated societies are members of more than 200 international science and technology organizations, with more than 350 Chinese scientists holding leadership positions in these organizations, including two of the world's most influential: the International Council for Science, a nongovernmental organization representing a global membership that includes both national scientific bodies and international scientific unions, and the World Federation of Engineering Organizations, an international nongovernmental organization that brings together national engineering organizations from more than ninety nations and represents some fifteen million engineers from around the world. In addition, the Chinese Academy of Sciences is a leading member of the InterAcademy Council, a multinational organization of science academies created to mobilize the world's best scientists, engineers, and medical experts to provide knowledge and advice to national governments and international bodies.

CAST also has organized international science and technology conventions in China, including the World Engineers' Convention in 2004 and the International Council for Science General Assembly in 2005. Other important international science and technology conferences held in China and organized by the affiliated societies of CAST include the International Congress of Mathematicians in 2002, the International Zoological Conference in 2004, and the International Plant Protection Conference in 2004.

SEE ALSO *Research in the Sciences; Science and Technology Policy.*

BIBLIOGRAPHY

China Association for Science and Technology. http://www.cast.org.cn

Cong Cao. *China's Scientific Elite.* London and New York: RoutledgeCurzon, 2004.

Cong Cao

SCIENTIFIC EXCHANGES

International cooperation in science and technology has long been central to China's development. As a developing country, China must absorb knowledge from other countries, especially advanced countries; as Chinese science advances to the frontiers of international research, foreign scientists will be more willing to collaborate with their Chinese counterparts. In fact, international cooperation in science and technology has become a strategy in China's overall foreign policy.

After the establishment of the People's Republic in 1949, and until the early 1960s, China's main partners in scientific endeavors were the Soviet Union and the Eastern bloc countries. Such cooperation shaped China at a time when the nation badly needed assistance in developing its industries and education system. The Soviet Union assisted with 156 construction projects in China during this period, many with significant scientific content, and laid the foundation for the development of the Chinese economy. Scientists from the Soviet Union also helped launch China's nuclear weapons program, although they withdrew when relations between the countries deteriorated.

China virtually closed its door on international cooperation in science and technology thereafter, except for a few small-scale exchanges of students and scholars with some Western European countries. This period witnessed major achievements in high technology elsewhere, while China engaged in ten years of a political campaign, the decade of the Cultural Revolution (1966–1976), during which scientists and other professionals became targets.

That situation changed in the late 1970s when China initiated its reform and open-door policy. China has since dispatched an enormous number of students and scholars to developed countries for advanced studies and research, many of whom now lead China's scientific enterprises, hold posts in higher education, and have even become part of the technocracy. Some of those who settled overseas have helped build bridges for Sino-foreign exchange and collaboration in science and technology.

The decade since the mid-1990s also has seen a rapid growth in the number of joint publications by collaborating Chinese and foreign scientists. Such collaborations account for a quarter of the Chinese papers published in journals catalogued by the *Science Citation Index.*

Along with collaborations based on the interests of individual scientists, China also cooperates with other countries through government-sanctioned programs. The Framework Programs of the European Union, the world's largest government-sponsored research-and-development initiative aimed at solving scientific problems with global impact, was launched in 1984 and began inviting Chinese participation in 1998. In return, China agreed to open its State High-Tech Research-and-Development Program (the 863 Program) and the State Basic Research-and-Development Program (the 973 Program) to scientists from the European Union.

China has signed science-and-technology cooperation agreements with more than one hundred countries and has actively participated in international projects, such as ITER, a joint international research-and-development project that aims to demonstrate the scientific and technical feasibility of fusion power. Chinese scientists have also been involved in the Galileo global navigation satellite system project and the Human Genome Project, among others.

The emphasis on indigenous innovation as stipulated in China's Medium- to Long-Term Plan for the Development of Science and Technology does not discourage China's collaboration with foreign counterparts. The establishment of a cross-ministry coordination mechanism in late 2007—involving the Ministry of Science and Technology; the Ministry of Education; the Commission for Science, Technology, and Industry for National Defense; the Chinese Academies of Sciences and Engineering; the National Natural Science Foundation of China; and the State Administration of Foreign Experts Affairs—is aimed at integrating domestic resources, enhancing international cooperation, and better serving China's national interests. For that purpose, China is now pursuing comprehensive, multidimensional, high-level international collaborations in science and technology in a wide range of fields.

SEE ALSO *Chinese Overseas; Research in the Sciences; Science and Technology Policy.*

BIBLIOGRAPHY

Suttmeier, Richard P. Scientific Cooperation and Conflict Management in U.S.-China Relations from 1978 to the Present. In *Scientific Cooperation, State Conflict: The Roles of Scientists in Mitigating International Discord*, eds. Allison L. C. de Cerreño and Alexander Keynan, 137–164. New York: New York Academy of Sciences, 1998.

Xu Ang. China Looks Abroad: Changing Directions in International Science. *Minerva* 46 (2008): 37–51.

Cong Cao

SCRAMBLE FOR CONCESSIONS

Japan's emergence from the Sino-Japanese War (1894–1895) as an East Asian power forced the Western nations to reassess and safeguard their interests in the region, especially in Qing-dynasty China (1644–1912). Russia quickly mobilized the Triple Intervention (with France and Germany) to forestall Japan's possession of Liaodong Peninsula in southern Manchuria as a ceded colony and secured China's agreement in 1896 to extend the Trans-Siberian Railway through Manchuria to Vladivostok. The lure of financial gain also fueled fierce competition in floating the three major loans (one Franco-Russian and two Anglo-German) for Beijing's indemnity payments to Japan. All this, and more, presaged the escalation of foreign rivalries in postwar China that peaked in the "scramble for concessions" from 1897 to 1899.

The frantic race began when Germany acquired compensations for two German priests who had been murdered in Juye, Shandong Province, in November 1897: the lease of Jiaozhou Bay and the adjoining Qingdao area for ninety-nine years and Shandong as a "sphere of influence" with exclusive railway and mining rights. Russia followed with the concession of the southern end of Liaodong for twenty-five years, including Lüshun (Port Arthur) as a naval base and Dalian as a trading port, with the right to connect both by a railway with the Trans-Siberian extension in the north. Meanwhile, France consolidated its penetration into China's southwest by securing Qing assurances not to alienate Yunnan, Guangxi, and Guangdong provinces to other powers, the right to construct railways joining this region with French Vietnam, and the lease of a naval base in Guangzhouwan in Guangxi for ninety-nine years. In addition, China agreed to seek French assistance if a new postal service was to be established in the future.

In parallel action, Britain obtained comparable concessions: China's retention of a British subject as inspector-general of the Maritime Customs for as long as British trade with China surpassed that of other countries, a ninety-nine-year New Territories leasehold contiguous to its colonial holdings in Kowloon and Hong Kong Island, and the promise not to alienate any of the Yangzi Valley provinces to other powers. (This last concession prompted the German response that, unlike Germany's primacy in Shandong, nonalienation did not actually give Britain a foothold and did not, therefore, preclude the Yangzi Valley, a so-called British sphere of influence, from remaining "unreservedly open to German enterprise." As such, not all "spheres of influence" were the same insofar as the interests of individual powers were concerned.) Finally, Britain leased, with German understanding, Weihaiwei in northern Shandong as a naval base for twenty-five years, a strategically inferior gain justified by London as a "cartographic consolation" in view of German and Russian preponderance in North China.

Italy was the only country that tried but failed to benefit from the scramble; its attempt to lease Sanmenwan in Zhejiang was rejected. Japan also joined the fray by getting Chinese assurance not to alienate Fujian Province opposite its colony, Taiwan, to another power. Distracted by the Spanish-American War (1898), the United States advanced no claim but communicated the Open-Door Note (originally, a British idea) in 1899 to Germany, Russia, Britain, Japan, Italy, and France, pleading for the "perfect equality of treatment" of all countries within the various "spheres of influence." Hailed by the American press as a diplomatic coup that possibly saved China, the note elicited only lukewarm responses from the recipient states. Wariness about the financial, military, and political burdens of colonizing China's vast, populous territory deterred the powers from actually partitioning the Qing empire.

The overseas quest for naval bases and for mining, loan, and railway projects signaled the importance of sea power and financial imperialism in late nineteenth-century global politics. The Qing court was too weak to resist most of the foreign demands and managed only to modify some of the harsh terms. As the sense of doom thickened, the search for relief by both the government and the educated elite culminated in the throne's inauguration in June 1898 of what became the Hundred Days' Reform.

SEE ALSO *Foreign Concessions, Settlements, and Leased Territories; Imperialism.*

BIBLIOGRAPHY

Morse, Hosea Ballou. *The International Relations of the Chinese Empire.* 3 vols. London: Longmans, Green, 1910–1918.

Otte, Thomas G. *The China Question: Great Power Rivalry and British Isolation, 1894–1905.* Oxford: Oxford University Press, 2007.

Schrecker, John. *Imperialism and Chinese Nationalism: Germany in Shantung.* Cambridge, MA: Harvard University Press, 1971.

Luke S. K. Kwong (Kuang Zhaojiang)

SCULPTURE AND PUBLIC ART

The most important Chinese sculptures traditionally served religious and funerary purposes, furnishing temples with images of the gods for worship and tombs with figures to attend the deceased in the afterlife. Such work was often anonymous, and despite its long tradition and stylistic evolution, before the twentieth century Chinese sculpture was not a subject of particular scholarly interest or artistic value to Chinese art connoisseurs. Instead, they focused their attention on the high arts of painting and calligraphy. As China opened its ports to foreign settlement and trade in the mid-nineteenth century, European residents began constructing public spaces and, just as they did in their home countries, commissioning the erection of public sculptures. Therefore, sculptures displayed in public spaces were typically European-style works by Western sculptors. Beginning in the 1910s and 1920s, as the notion of modernization spread, art students sought up-to-date knowledge of Western art abroad, and a few, overcoming the Chinese prejudice against it, studied sculpture. Upon their return to China, some artists taught at the newly launched art schools, thus contributing to the establishment of the art education system in modern China.

Western-style Chinese sculpture, characterized by Western techniques and European academic approaches, began to appear in such a context in the late 1920s. Most early productions were small statues and busts that directly copy Western examples. In 1929 more than fifty works of sculpture, the majority of them portraits, academic nudes, or other relatively naturalistic figural depictions, were put on view at the first National Fine Art Exhibition. In the 1930s the first major public sculptural campaign began with the Republican government's campaign to produce bronze statues in memory of its founder, Sun Yat-sen (Sun Yixian, 1866–1925). From then on, most sculptures were made to honor political leaders, generals, historic figures, and heroic martyrs who died in revolutionary battles. Perhaps because of the narrow subject matter and limited public demand, it was difficult to make a living as a sculptor at the time, and few sculptors remained committed to the art. Those who did supported themselves as teachers.

THE FORERUNNERS

Li Jinfa (1900–1976), one of the founders of modern sculpture education in China, was educated in France. He entered the École Nationale des Beaux Arts de Dijon in 1919 and later transferred to the École Nationale Supérieure des Beaux-Arts in Paris. After returning to China in 1925, Li participated in establishing and directing the sculpture departments in several prominent modern art institutes, including the Shanghai Art Academy, the National Academy of Art in Hangzhou, and the Guangzhou Municipal Art School. Besides his contributions to art education, Li was recognized nationwide for his naturalistic and subtle works of sculpture. He created sculptured images of notables like Sun Yat-sen, Cai Yuanpei (1868–1940), Wu Tingfang (1842–1922), Deng Zhongyuan (1886–1922), and Li Pingshu (1854–1927). In 1928 he produced a 39-foot-long decorative relief to install above the main entrance of the Nanjing Grand Theater in Shanghai (the present Shanghai Concert Hall). The huge stone tablet, featuring male and female nude performers, shows influences of ancient Greek art and the late-nineteenth-century European symbolist movement.

Liu Kaiqu (1904–1993), another significant sculptor and art educator of the Republican era, was also trained in France, between 1929 and 1933, where he studied with Jean Boucher (1870–1939) in Paris. Upon his return Liu was hired to teach sculpture at the National Academy of Art in Hangzhou. Many of his works of the 1930s and 1940s were sculpted to accompany monuments in memory of political leaders and anonymous war heroes. His famous 1934 stone sculpture, the *Battle of Shanghai (January 28 Incident) Monument*, commemorating the soldiers who sacrificed their lives defending China against Japan, was erected beside West Lake in Hangzhou, as Chinese monumental sculpture began to come into its own. Chinese sculpture historians considered the work, which no longer survives, to be a success, and its two main images, an officer and a soldier, inspired reverence from the viewing public.

Jiang Xin (1894–1939) and Zhang Chongren (1907–1998) are among those artists who practiced both painting and sculpture. Jiang graduated in oil painting from the Tokyo School of Fine Arts and then studied sculpture in France. Zhang Chongren, initially trained at the Catholic Tushanwan orphanage and painting school at Xujiahui in Shanghai, went to the Royal Academy in Brussels in 1931. After returning to China, they each started private sculpture studios, teaching art students and producing sculptures on commission. Jiang's works primarily included portraits of contemporary notables and designs for monuments, such as his portrait of Shao Xunmei, exhibited in the 1929 National Art Exhibition. The bronze sculpture *Martyr Chen Yingshi*, also created for public display by West Lake in Hangzhou, is a good example of Jiang's equestrian statues. The uplifted front legs of the horse, the tension of the human figure, and the floating robes created heroic momentum. Zhang Chongren mainly created portrait statues for notables of the day, including his grandfather Ma Xiangbo (1840–1939). In Belgium, Zhang Chongren became a friend of the writer and artist Hergé (the pen name of Georges Prosper Remi, 1907–1983), best known for the comic *The Adventures of Tintin*. Zhang helped him conceive and illustrate *The Blue Lotus: Tintin in China*, which features a character, Chang, based on the Chinese artist.

SOCIALIST REALISM

During the first two decades of the People's Republic of China, under Soviet influence there was a boom in public art in the form of monuments and sculptures eulogizing leaders, heroes, and the people. Although the subjects and contents were commonly patriotic and didactic, the styles were deeply influenced by Soviet socialist realism, a combination of Western naturalism and ideologically controlled Soviet realism, the latter of which focuses on politically appropriate thematic choices as well as purposeful exaggerations and distillations.

The magnificent *People's Heroes Monument*, standing in the center of Tiananmen Square, is representative of public art of the early Maoist era. It took six years, from 1952 to 1958, to finish the project. The monument itself was designed by the architect Liang Sicheng, with titles and inscriptions written by Chairman Mao Zedong and Prime Minister Zhou Enlai. A tribute to the heroes of the Chinese revolution, the 125-foot-high monument rests on a pedestal on which appear ten marble relief carvings, each depicting a revolutionary campaign or historic moment in China's modern history. The themes of the reliefs were chosen by the historian Fan Wenlan, and Liu Kaiqu directed the group of artists who sculpted them. They appear in chronological sequence, proceeding in a clockwise direction: Lin Zexu Burning Opium at Humen (1839), Jintian Uprising (1851), Wuchang Uprising (1911), May Fourth Movement (1919), May Thirtieth Movement (1925), August 1 Nanchang Uprising (1927), Anti-Japanese Guerrilla Wars (during the Second Sino-Japanese War, 1937–1945), Crossing the Yangzi River (1949), the last of which is flanked by two auxiliary bas-reliefs on the subjects of "Supporting the Frontline" and "Welcoming the People's Liberation Army." Chinese critics praised the reliefs as a successful example of integrating Western artistic conventions, particularly a naturalistic approach to subject matter, and Chinese conventions, particularly the use of multiple perspectives, a feature of traditional Chinese painting. The use of Western techniques to depict Chinese nationalistic subjects was certainly noteworthy, though the use of multiple perspectives is part of an international vocabulary of sculpture.

Another upsurge in the making of public art came with the commissions for Ten Great Buildings in Beijing to celebrate the tenth anniversary of the new China. *Celebration of the Bumper Harvest* (1959), adjacent to the Agriculture Exhibition Hall, includes two groups of human figures and animals. In rather propagandist fashion, it shows the joyfulness of farmers during the Great Leap Forward (1958–1960). On the periphery of the Military Museum are sculptures of groups of workers, farmers, and soldiers, symbolizing the heroic spirit of the Chinese people. Works of revolutionary romanticism, these group sculptures became exemplars for later works. The artists who created them cooperated on an unprecedented scale; as John T. Young notes in his 1999 book, of the 108 sculptors summoned to participate in the project of creating group sculptures around the Mao Memorial Hall in 1978, not one signed his work.

THE CULTURAL REVOLUTION

In the early 1960s, a brief period of cultural liberalization, Chinese sculptors had begun to evaluate the merits and shortcomings of both the Soviet mode and Western

Time of Jurassic, *by Chinese sculptor Sui Jianguo, on display at Perth, Australia, March 17, 2005.* *Variety in sculptures rebounded in China after the Cultural Revolution, as artists experienced new, though not complete, freedom in selecting themes for their creations. More of the resulting art has become available to a global audience as well, as evidenced by this brightly colored sculpture on display at an art show in Australia.* **PAUL KANE/GETTY IMAGES**

modernism. They were tiring of the heroic topics and exaggerated expressions typical of the Soviet prototypes; yet they were not ready to abandon realism and representation for the abstraction pursued by their peers in the West. The French sculptor Auguste Rodin (1840–1917) was among the romantic masters the Chinese looked to for sources of inspiration. During this period another group of sculptors kept themselves abreast of modernist trends, thereby planting the seeds for future diversification of methods.

The iconoclastic decade of the Cultural Revolution (1966–1976) brought China into a long nightmare, in which all art was scrutinized by the Gang of Four for formal and ideological purity. The development of sculpture was hindered, if not pushed backward. Senior sculptors were persecuted and humiliated, sculpture departments in art institutes were shut down, and many sculptures—anything deemed to be related to feudalism, capitalism, or imperialism—were demolished. Ironically, in the grandiose campaign of tearing down the statues of the old "gods," many images of the new idol thrived. As the veneration of Chairman Mao grew into a cult, numerous statues of Mao were erected in the most significant locations in squares, parks, and schools, and indeed in any public space. Although some of these sculptures are high-quality artistic achievements, most of them look mass-produced and exist only as the marks left by a political tragedy.

POST-MAO ERA

The end of the Cultural Revolution allowed Chinese society to return to a normal developmental trajectory. Sculpture as public art, now called "urban sculpture," was supported by the government in the establishment of two institutes, the National Urban Sculpture Planning Group and the National Urban Sculpture Art Committee, both headed by Liu Kaiqu, in 1982. Most provinces and cities also set up local organizations for planning and public arts administration. In 1984 the first National Urban Sculpture Planning and Design Exhibition was held to facilitate communication among sculptors and arts administrators. Throughout the 1980s and early 1990s, administrators emphasized the creation of sculptures that popularize revolutionary history, instill patriotism, and facilitate urbanization. In 1985 the first government-sponsored sculpture park, Shijinshan Park, opened in Beijing, and sculpture-themed parks then began to flourish all over the country. As a result, the public developed an awareness of the correlation between sculpture and its environment.

DIVERSIFICATION

Sculpture and public art entered a new phase of diversification in the mid-1990s. In 1993 the National Urban Sculpture Art Committee reissued certificates to sculptors and refined the team of artists working on urban sculpture projects. In 1994 the second National Sculpture Art Exhibition served as a retrospective of the past ten years' explorations in urban sculpture. Chinese sculptors since then have been exploring the possibilities of subject matter, materials, and techniques, as well as pursuing their interests in searching for sculpture's functions and meanings in the public space.

Contemporary Chinese sculptors face both challenges and opportunities. Because of language barriers, many of them remain unaware of cutting-edge international art. The government still serves as the major patron of public sculpture projects, thus placing limitations on artists who must comply with official regulations. However, as Young observes, more and more artists have had the chance to exhibit and travel globally, and privately funded public commissions afford them the freedom of artistic exploration. Successful sculptors like Sui Jianguo (b. 1956) and Zhan Wang (b. 1962) have been able to adjust their works according to different needs. In his 1990 piece, *Structure*, for the Olympic Center, Sui Jianguo adopts abstract forms not only to suit the surrounding architectural styles, but to avoid controversies that can be caused by figurative sculpture. *Sidewalk* (1990), Zhan Wang's contribution to the same sports complex in Beijing, is a progressive work that integrates sculpture into public space and addresses 1990s cultural issues. In 2000 an exhibit held in both Shanghai and Paris showed the works of these two leading figures of Chinese public art.

The contemporary Chinese sculpture and public art scene also includes artists who might be regarded as marginalized, namely "diaspora" and women sculptors. Wang Keping (b. 1949), one of the "Star Artists" of the early 1980s, created such politically provocative works as *Silence* (1979) and *Idol* (1980). Although he left for France in the mid-1980s and is less well-known in China, he has continued to create idiosyncratic sculptures, remaining a significant star internationally. As public sculptors, Chinese women such as Jiang Bibo (b. 1939), Wu Huiming (b. 1944), and Shi Hui (b. 1955) face sexism in the general culture, yet they are as successful as their male counterparts in domestic competitions and active on the international stage.

SEE ALSO *Art Schools and Colleges; Influences Abroad: Maoism and Art; Propaganda Art; Socialist Realism in Art; Stars (Xingxing) Painting Group, 1979–1983; Women in the Visual Arts.*

BIBLIOGRAPHY

20 shiji Zhongguo chengshi diaosu [Twentieth-century Chinese urban sculpture]. Nanchang, China: Jiangxi Meishu Chubanshe, 2001.

Young, John T. *Contemporary Public Art in China: A Photographic Tour.* Seattle: University of Washington Press, 1999.

Yanfei Zhu

SECRET SOCIETIES

Chinese society has long been characterized by a plethora of voluntary associations, which, since the beginning of the twentieth century, scholars have divided into two broad categories: (1) transmitted teachings, sects, and religions, known as *jiao*; and (2) popular, secular organizations, associations, or brotherhoods, known as *hui*. Some took the form of simple informal pacts, established by small groups of people for such purposes as watching crops or burying parents. Others, under the leadership of community or lineage elites, served a variety of local ritual or organizational needs.

Secret society, a Western term introduced into China from Japan in the early twentieth century, has been variously rendered into Chinese as *mimi shehui*, *mimi xiehui*, *mimi huidang*, and *mimi banghui*. Within China, secret societies have usually taken the form of clandestine organizations devoted to religious, social, or political activities whose leaders employed special argot, symbols, and rituals to bind members together and distinguish them from outsiders. Their penchant for crime and violence, along with rituals commonly drawn from popular religion, frequently drew the ire of Chinese rulers, who perceived them as challenges to the cosmic power of the son of heaven, and banned them as heterodox.

THE HEAVEN AND EARTH ASSOCIATION

One of the most influential and long-enduring Chinese secret societies is the Heaven and Earth Association (Tiandihui, also known as triad or TDH). From earliest times, the TDH was characterized by secret initiation rituals in which new members swore oaths of brotherhood before burning incense, passed under crossed swords, imbibed mixtures of wine and the blood of sacrificial cocks, and smeared their own blood by pricking each other's fingers. The oaths—simple compositions of a sentence or two—called for initiates to come to the aid of each other and implored heaven to witness their ceremonies by bringing down on those harboring bad intentions the crossed swords under which they were about to pass.

Thereupon, initiates were taught the society's secrets in the form of code words and gestures that helped members identify themselves to one another and universalized the association so that speakers of one dialect could communicate with those of another. One of the TDH's earliest pass words was "five dots twenty-one" (*wudian ershiyi*), a coded reference to the name "Hong." Common gestures called for extending the three middle fingers to heaven when reaching for tea or tobacco and coiling queues or fastening shirts in certain ways.

Eventually, these simple initiations evolved into elaborate rituals as initiates enacted the deaths of their former selves and their rebirth as "brothers" into new Hong "families." Complex oaths of thirty-six articles prescribed how members should regard one another. New couplets, rhymes, and incantations were recorded in registers that served as the repositories of society lore and whose possession became the most important criterion of subsequent society formation and leadership. Modern groups were further linked by strictly maintained hierarchies of ranked officials, each designated by a symbolic number such as 489, 438, or 426, derived from coded symbols for the name "Hong" or combinations of the sixty-four hexagrams or other auspicious numbers in Chinese mythology.

THE ORIGINS CONTROVERSY

The origin of the TDH is still a controversial topic among historians of China who, depending on the sources they use, have tended to regard it as either a Ming loyalist or mutual-aid association. Scholars of the Ming loyalist persuasion argue that the TDH was a proto-national political group created by Zheng Chenggong (Koxinga, 1624–1662) or his counterparts in the seventeenth century for the purpose of overthrowing the Qing dynasty of China's Manchu conquerors and restoring the native Ming. Histories espousing Ming loyalism as the raison d'être of the TDH tend to be based on internally generated sources, such as the society's creation myth, which are read as coded references to anti-Manchu resistance on the part of Chinese elites and their politically conscious followers.

Basing their views on more recently opened Qing dynasty archives in both Taiwan and mainland China, scholars of the "mutual-aid" persuasion argue that the TDH was founded in Fujian Province at Gaoxi township's Goddess of Mercy Pavilion in 1761 or 1762 by Monk Ti Xi (given name: Zheng Kai, also known as Monk Wan and Monk Hong Er) and that it was but one of several societies or *hui* to appear at this time.

Like their counterparts elsewhere, the founders of the TDH drew inspiration from a milieu characterized by overpopulation, social dislocation, and collective violence exacerbated by lineage feuding, from which they created an organization capable of responding in a variety of ways. As priests, medical practitioners, exorcists, conjurers, and cloth sellers, these individuals, hailing from the lowest and most marginal ranks of Chinese society, were preoccupied with the issues of survival, where some of their most important needs were protection against extortion and support networks to which they could resort in times of trouble. Brotherhoods based on fictive kinship extended the personal networks of such people more widely.

TDH HISTORY AND ACTIVITIES

Regardless of their origins, by the late eighteenth century, society members organized for one purpose often found themselves mobilized for different ends that involved them in activities where the distinctions between legal/illegal, protection/predation, and orthodox/heterodox blurred. Such was also the case for the TDH, as elements of extortion, racketeering, and criminal entrepreneurship emerged almost immediately within its ranks. Aspiring leaders quickly took advantage of moneymaking opportunities inherent in its transmission, as the prospect of charging new members small initiation fees and pocketing the proceeds provided compelling motivation for society formation from the beginning. Once formed, societies could be readily mobilized for a variety of purposes. Some leaders founded societies with the specific intent of carrying out armed robberies, piracy, local feuding, or even rebellion.

Few regions of China were as insurrection-prone as the southern coast, and the society had barely been in existence seven years before the first of what would become a tradition of society-inspired uprisings was launched. In light of the origins controversy, the nature of these uprisings is crucial to one's understanding of the early TDH and in answering the question of the extent to which the TDH was inspired by Ming restoration rhetoric. These initial rebellions, however, seem to have been wholly free of such rhetoric, for the appeal was instead to a scion of the Song, not the Ming, dynasty. Despite the fact that nowhere do archival documents mention the Ming restoration or loyalty to Zheng Chenggong as a cause for any of the uprisings of the Qianlong era, the TDH clearly did adopt restoration ideology. Since written records were not kept for the first thirty years of its existence and the society spread exclusively through oral transmission, it may never be known when the idea first appeared, but archival documents suggest its emergence in written form during the Jiaqing era in response to the government crackdown that came during the Lin Shuangwen uprising, for it was during this uprising, in 1787, that the existence of the TDH first came to the attention of the Qing government. This discovery marked a turning point for the TDH, which was immediately banned.

Five years later (1792), the government incorporated a new provision into the legal code that mentioned the TDH for the first time and sentenced to immediate decapitation anyone who founded a chapter. Once proscribed, TDH members quickly responded by changing or disguising the name of their individual groups in the hopes of avoiding detection and producing propaganda that may have been more political and hence more anti-Manchu in their fight for survival.

During the nineteenth century, as the society spread throughout South China, TDH members, now commonly known as triads, continued to be involved in local insurrections, uprisings, and underworld activity that increasingly revolved around opium smuggling. By the 1840s, Chiu Chau

(Chaozhou) speakers from Shantou (Swatow), long associated with the Chinese underworld, were moving into Shanghai at the center of the Chinese trade. A few years later, the Red Turban Uprising in the Pearl River Delta was instrumental in the launching of the Taiping Uprising (1851–1864), and TDH cooperation with the pirates of Guangxi and Guangdong enabled the Taipings to survive early sieges in 1851 and 1852. The aftermath of the Taiping rebellion sent a wave of triads to Hong Kong, Southeast Asia, and the United States, while in China the slogan "armies protect the emperor; secret societies protect the people" increasingly represented reality in the face of a deteriorating dynasty.

The apex of triad power can perhaps be said to have come during the Republican era through association with Sun Yat-sen (Sun Yixian or Sun Zhongshan) and the toppling of the Manchu regime. Thereafter, the center of underworld activity gradually shifted to Shanghai as Green Gang member Du Yuesheng (1887–1951), under the patronage of Chiang Kai-shek (Jiang Jieshi), was allowed to consolidate his position as the opium king of China in return for his role in suppressing Communists during the Canton Massacre of April 12, 1927. With the encouragement of Chiang Kai-shek, China became the first modern country where secret criminal societies were able to play a fundamental role in legitimate administration of government as triads, infiltrating both the military and the police. The triads became Chiang Kai-shek's strongmen, and few criminal enterprises in China were without triad protection, oversight, and acquiescence.

World War II (1937–1945) and the Japanese occupation that began in 1941 gave the triads an unprecedented opportunity to solidify control over the black market and vice trade in Hong Kong. With the elimination of British administrators and police, triads often reached accommodation with the occupation forces: In return for giving the Japanese information and helping them maintain order, the triads were allowed to run Hong Kong's illegal businesses. As the war ended, the Japanese, destroying police records of triad activity in Hong Kong, made it difficult for the British to restore order as criminal bosses solidified their power by gaining control of construction, transportation, and government workers. Triads also "helped" the police by turning in expendable "brothers" for what would become police raids on competitors' gambling and opium dens. Triad infiltration of police and government made British administration ineffective in either countering or curtailing these activities.

Upheaval and dislocation characterized the triads of the late 1940s and 1950s. As the civil war on the mainland intensified, the British in Hong Kong adopted an open-door policy for refugees who came flooding in and made new targets for triad recruiters as the center of the Chinese underworld gradually shifted from the mainland to Hong Kong. Once again at the core were thousands of Chiu

Chau speakers, many of whom also infiltrated the police department.

However, rifts soon arose within the Chinese underworld as the refugees from the mainland brought their own societies, which challenged the Hong Kong triads' domination of the underworld. Gang wars between rivals proliferated throughout the 1950s, and one of the most interesting, between Du Yuesheng's Green Gang, now exiled to Hong Kong, and the triads from Chiu Chau, took place without the firing of a single shot as gang members on both sides bribed Hong Kong police to crack down on their rivals.

Although the Chiu Chau triads succeeded in ousting the Green Gang from Hong Kong, the conflict left them weakened and the door open to yet another rival: the 14K from Canton (Guangzhou). Founded in 1947 as an outgrowth of a Nationalist army officer's military association, the group's avowed purpose was to reconquer the mainland, but upon the officer's death, members embarked on a campaign of extortion and intimidation that marked their emergence into criminality. Between 1953 and 1956, they made a bid to monopolize control over the Hong Kong underworld, an endeavor supported from Taiwan by Chiang Kai-shek, who wanted them to wrest control away from the British and open the door for the Chinese Nationalists to seize power. Their plan backfired as the riots of 1956, which saw attacks on foreigners, torched buildings, and looted retail shops, resulted in the dispatching of the British army to quell the disturbances. The 14K threat was repelled, and thereafter the British police organized a Triad Society Bureau, which resulted in the arrest and deportation of several thousand members, many of whom were sent to Taiwan, where they joined the Nationalist-supported United Bamboo Society. They helped the society establish new branches in Hong Kong as crucial links in the developing heroin trade between Hong Kong and Taiwan.

The upheavals of the 1950s made perfectly clear that no single group could dominate the Chinese underworld and that to expand their business, the various syndicates would have to work together. As a result, the same groups who dominated the Hong Kong underworld during the 1950s—the 14K, the Wo syndicate, and the Sun Yee—are still major players today. The new prosperity of the 1960s meant that there was more money to be spent on vice, and by then the triads were in a position to become key players in the worldwide narcotics market.

The 1960s and 1970s also witnessed a second wave of migration from Hong Kong to the West, which coincided with a significant rise in the international heroin traffic, along with increases in more traditional triad activities, such as gambling, prostitution, loan-sharking, racketeering, and blackmailing. Since then, the most revolutionary change has been the entrance of the triads into legitimate businesses that range from home decoration firms to fancy hotels and licensed casinos. With so much profit from illicit enterprises, triads needed new places for investment and money laundering.

The late 1970s and 1980s saw an expansion of triad activity from the Golden Triangle to the Golden Shopping Arcade and the black market of Hong Kong's pirated electronics and software. The triads' next move was into white-collar crime, where young, highly educated men with technical skills in computer hacking, accounting, legal services, banking, and stock markets engage in sophisticated crimes of stock manipulation, securities counterfeiting, bond and money laundering, and credit-card fraud. The return of Hong Kong (1997) and Macau (1999) to the People's Republic of China has only increased the triads' capacity for interaction, to the point where some regard their bids for dominance as the most frightening new development in international crime since the mafia ceased to be a patriotic Sicilian organization. Others have succumbed to fascination with the exoticism, heroism, and glamour of bad-boy culture that is prevalent throughout Chinese popular culture and film.

SCHOLARLY PERCEPTIONS

Almost as interesting as the history of the TDH itself is the way it has been understood by those who have come into contact with it. Depending on their particular worldview and the resources at their disposal, different generations of scholars and administrators have come to significantly different understandings of the nature and essence of the TDH and, in the process, have generated a vast and complex historiography that can be divided into four schools.

Officials in the employ of colonial governments in Southeast Asia were the first to regard the triads as a topic of research interest, and they transmitted, annotated, and published many of the society documents discovered within their administrative jurisdictions. The nineteenth-century environment of these officials was one in which secret societies, especially the Freemasons, dominated the landscape. Their discovery of secret societies among the Chinese at a time when Masons in the West were under suspicion caused many of these officials, who were themselves Freemasons, to focus on the similarities between secret societies of the East and West and to propound the idea that the Chinese and Masonic orders were descendants of a common mythic ancestor.

Scholarship of the Republican period was an outgrowth of the political needs of Sun Yat-sen, who discovered that aid from local societies was essential in mobilizing overseas support for political revolution. After 1911, scholars began combing the historical record for evidence to substantiate Sun's claims and validate the national posture of their depiction. This scholarship, which gave rise to the

Ming loyalist view of the society's origins, is most frequently identified with works of Xiao Yishan (1902–1978) and Luo Ergang (b. 1903).

Scholarship in the West during the 1960s and 1970s featured attempts to study history from the bottom up in terms of class struggle and peasant uprisings on the Chinese mainland, as well as primitive revolutionaries, popular organizations, and social mobility as expressions of popular opposition to state and elite oppression. This perspective is most closely associated with French scholar Jean Chesneaux (1922–2007) and his colleagues in the Annales school.

Scholarship on the basis of archival materials that depict the TDH as a fraternal mutual-aid association, begun during the 1970s and 1980s, has given rise to new information making possible a fuller narrative of the history of all Chinese secret societies, along with a discussion that now includes popular and heterodox religions in ways that have blurred the boundaries between groups previously referred to as either "sects" or "societies."

BIBLIOGRAPHY

Booth, Martin. *The Triads: The Growing Global Threat from the Chinese Criminal Societies*. New York: St. Martin's Press, 1990.

Bresler, Fenton. *The Chinese Mafia*. New York: Stein and Day, 1981.

Chesneaux, Jean, ed. *Popular Movements and Secret Societies in China, 1840–1950*. Stanford, CA: Stanford University Press, 1977.

Luo Ergang. *Tiandihui wenxianlu* [Bibliographic studies of sources on the Tiandihui]. Shanghai: Zhengzhong Shuiju, 1943.

Morgan, W. P. *Triad Societies in Hong Kong*. Hong Kong: Government Press, 1960.

Murray, Dian, in collaboration with Qin Baoqi. *The Origins of the Tiandihui: The Chinese Triads in Legend and History*. Stanford, CA: Stanford University Press, 1994.

Ownby, David. *Brotherhoods and Secret Societies in Early and Mid-Qing China: The Formation of a Tradition*. Stanford, CA: Stanford University Press, 1996.

Posner, Gerald L. *Warlords of Crime Chinese Secret Societies: The New Mafia*. New York: Penguin, 1988.

Xiao Yishan, ed. *Jindai mimi shuihui shiliao* [Historical materials on modern secret societies]. 1935. Taibei: Wenhai Chubanshe, 1970.

Dian Murray

SENT-DOWN EDUCATED YOUTH

In the People's Republic of China (PRC), young educated urbanites, commonly known as "educated youth" (*zhishi qingnian,* abbreviated *zhiqing*), were sent down to the countryside from 1955 onward, and this practice became part of the regular functioning of the administration in 1962. However, the numbers involved were not high: probably less than 1.5 million "educated youths" were sent down from 1955 to 1966. Most of them, relocated in the 1960s, were young people from "bad families," who, because of their political stigma, were disadvantaged in their efforts to obtain jobs or further their studies after lower middle school.

"UP TO THE MOUNTAINS AND DOWN TO THE COUNTRYSIDE" MOVEMENT

This practice was temporarily interrupted in 1966, because of the disorders of the Cultural Revolution. But it was revived with quite different characteristics and on a much larger scale in 1968. From that year until 1980, almost seventeen million young, urban, lower and higher middle-school graduates took part in the "Up to the Mountains and Down to the Countryside" movement (*shangshan xiaxiang yundong*), launched by Mao Zedong on December 22, 1968. This Rustication movement (as it is also known in English) had different purposes, with short-term and long-term objectives. In 1968 it was used by Mao to put an end to the Red Guards movement and to solve the problem of their employment after more than two years of chaos and economic stagnation, but it was also part of Mao's long-term anti-intellectual objective of "revolution in education." Students were to be "reeducated" by poor peasants, possibly for life, and when universities eventually reopened on a small scale in 1970, the sent-down educated youths could only be selected from among other "workers, peasants, and soldiers" on political, rather than academic, criteria. This movement was also supposed to help bridge the gap between city and countryside, and between intellectual and manual labor.

Some scholars argue that the main rationale of the movement was to solve the urban unemployment problem, but statistics do not support this assertion, since over the whole period the number of peasants who migrated to urban areas to get a permanent job is roughly the same as the number of educated youths excluded from these areas. In fact, although the system of residence control (*hukou*) could have prevented it, there was during this period a large exchange of population and of labor between urban and rural areas.

The first wave of educated youths was composed of a large majority of the 1966, 1967, and 1968 graduates of lower and higher middle schools (called the "three older" classes, or *laosanjie*) and of the 1969 graduates. Most of them were sent somewhere inside their own province, but some large cities sent students to remote parts of the country. Although some of the youths were real volunteers, there was in effect no possibility to resist assignment to the countryside. Some young people were sent to the military farms of the Production and Construction Corps, where they received a fixed, albeit low, salary, but where political control was strict. In the mid-1970s these farms were transferred to the civilian administration and became state farms. From 1968 to

1980, around 2.5 million educated youths went to these farms. The majority were sent to villages (called "production teams of people's communes"), where they had to rely on work-points earned by their labor to receive a share of the collective production. Many among these *chadui* ("inserted into teams") youths were unable to be self-sufficient and had to receive help from their parents. Although, after some time, a minority were given nonmanual jobs as school teachers, accountants, or "barefoot doctors," most of them were confined to manual labor.

DISAFFECTION WITH THE MOVEMENT AND THE RETURN HOME

Material difficulties and moral problems prevented the sent-down educated youths from accepting their new fate, especially since the peasants saw them mainly as a burden. During the 1970s, disaffection was ripe, especially when the offspring of high-level cadres were able to go back home in large numbers "through the backdoor." After Li Qinglin, a primary-school teacher from Fujian Province, wrote a letter to Mao to denounce this situation and to complain about the problems facing him and his children, a national conference was convened in 1973 and some remedial measures decided, which improved somewhat the conditions of life for the youths. Although these were not sufficient to modify the widespread social dissatisfaction with this movement, authorities were able to maintain this "new-born policy of the Cultural Revolution," even when Hua Guofeng succeeded Mao in 1976. Only when Hua's power began to weaken in 1978 could doubts concerning this policy be heard in official circles.

During a new national conference that ended in December 1978, it was decided that the movement would slow down gradually and that educated youths already in the villages would be allowed to return home, if they had real difficulties. But, educated youths working in farms would be considered farm employees and would not be allowed to go back to the cities. The young people concerned would not accept this decision, however. Taking advantage of the new political atmosphere surrounding the emergence of the reformists and of the preparations of a limited war with Vietnam, the educated youths in Yunnan farms resorted to all methods of resistance (petitions, strikes, hunger strikes, sending of a delegation to Beijing, etc.) to express their determination to go back home. And, in these special circumstances, they were able to obtain the first victory of a grassroots movement against the Chinese Communist Party since 1949. They were allowed to return home, as were almost all other educated youths installed in farms, with the exception of the Shanghai youths who had been sent to the Xinjiang Production and Construction Corps before the Cultural Revolution.

Those who were in villages were also swept up by the "wind of going back to the cities" (*fan cheng feng*). They left the countryside en masse, saying that they all had "difficulties." Although the authorities tried hard to send a sizeable number of new educated youths to the countryside in 1979, resistance was strong and, in 1980, the policy was terminated. The sudden return of around eight million young people in about three years (1978–1980) posed a real problem of employment, but in a new era when economic development had taken precedence over ideological dogmas, the costs of the Rustication movement in terms of economic inefficiency and of social dissatisfaction were considered unsustainable.

LONG-TERM IMPACT

From 1968 onward, this movement was an important element in Mao's struggle against "revisionism." Probably fearful of a postmortem fate similar to Joseph Stalin's, Mao had attempted to forge "revolutionary successors" devoted to his own brand of socialism. Their exceptional experience has indeed left its mark on the generation of sent-down educated youths, but the result was the contrary of Mao's expectations. They became realistic, conscious of the necessity to defend their own rights, and suspicious of all ideologies and grand phrases. Although their feelings of belonging to a specific group have always been strong, their attitudes toward their past experience are diverse. On the whole, this "lost generation," as it has been called, lost not only its illusions but also the right to decent schooling, and this had a permanent effect on their individual destinies. Some of them remain bitter, but many prefer to express nostalgia about their youth and to stress the value of their experience, in spite of—or maybe because of—its apparent irrelevance in the new era. Due to their unique experience, the small minority among them who were able to pass the university entrance examinations, restored and opened to them in 1977 to 1978, made important contributions, especially in the fields of literature, arts, and social science.

SEE ALSO *Cultural Revolution, 1966–1969; Education; Mao Zedong; Tiananmen Incident (1976); Xiafang.*

BIBLIOGRAPHY

Bernstein, Thomas. *Up to the Mountains and Down to the Villages: The Transfer of Youth from Urban to Rural China.* New Haven, CT: Yale University Press, 1977.

Bonnin, Michel. *Génération perdue: Le mouvement d'envoi des jeunes instruits à la campagne en Chine, 1968–1980* [The Lost Generation: The rustication of educated youth in China, 1968-1980]. Paris: Éditions de l'école des hautes études en sciences sociales, 2004.

Ding Yizhuang. *Zhongguo zhiqing shi: Chulan, 1953–1968 nian* [History of the Chinese educated youth: The first waves, 1953–1968]. Beijing: Zhongguo Shehui Kexue Chubanshe, 1998.

Gu Hongzhang and Hu Mengzhou, eds. *Zhongguo zhishi qingnian shangshan xiaxiang shimo* [From beginning to end: The

rustication of Chinese educated youths]. Beijing: Zhongguo
Jiancha Chubanshe, 1996.

Liu Xiaomeng. *Zhongguo zhiqing shi: Dachao, 1966–1980 nian*
[History of the Chinese educated youth: The big wave,
1966–1980]. Beijing: Zhongguo Shehui Kexue Chubanshe, 1998.

Rosen, Stanley. *The Role of Sent-Down Youth in the Chinese Cultural
Revolution: The Case of Guangzhou.* Berkeley: University of
California, 1981.

Scharping, Thomas. *Umsiedlungsprogramme für Chinas Jugend, 1955–
1980* [Relocation programs for China's youth, 1955-1980].
Hamburg, Germany: Institut für Asienkunde, 1981.

Michel Bonnin

SERVICE SECTOR (TERTIARY INDUSTRY)

With the progression of economic development, the service sector becomes more and more important and finally emerges as the largest sector in the economy. This structural regularity, however, conceals the fact that services include a very wide variety of different economic activities, reaching from the peddler to the huge global bank. In fact, services also play a significant role in creating employment in less developed countries, especially in the informal economy, and include petty trading, personal services such as repairs, and restaurants. In the most advanced economies, banking and finance, education, health-care services, and tourism become the generators of high added value. This correlation between sector structure and economic development is of particular importance for China, as Chinese economic reforms after 1978 initially built on the dynamics of the small-scale service sector in both the cities and the countryside to create employment and to improve the livelihood of the population. Reform of the more advanced sectors such as finance and complex transport services such as aviation were slow until the mid-1990s, speeding up only after China's entry to the World Trade Organization (WTO) in 2001.

Typically, services are tightly regulated in many countries, especially with regard to foreign investment and external trade. This is a result of the much closer interaction between domestic regulations and the external trade and investment regime, because services, as opposed to trade in goods, often require the domestic presence of service providers. Therefore, trade in services is the object of a special WTO agreement, the General Agreement on Trade in Services (GATS), to which China acceded in 2001, with substantial concessions that surpass those of many other developing and even industrialized countries. With the increasing liberalization of services trade, China will see very dynamic growth of the service sector in the future, and this will be the main driver of maintaining its high-growth pattern in the 2010s.

SERVICE STATISTICS IN CHINA

As compared with industry and agriculture, services pose special challenges to statistical measurement. This is particularly true for China because the Chinese statistical system had to shift from a central planning system to modern national accounting. In 1985 a separate "tertiary industry" (*di san chanye*) category was introduced, assigning construction to industry (the secondary sector) and distinguishing between "circulation" (*liutong bumen*) and "services" (*fuwu bumen*). The latter was conceived very broadly, including even public services such as the police. Although the definition was streamlined in 2003, a fundamental vagueness persisted because many public services underwent a process of marketization (*chanye hua*), switching from the status of a public institution (*shiye danwei*) to an enterprise (*qiye danwei*). Furthermore, the large sector of small-scale services at the fringes to the informal and shadow economy defies exact methods of measurement, especially in the rural areas.

As a result, in 2005 the government undertook a major revision of gross domestic product (GDP) data because the first national economic survey had shown that the tertiary sector had been seriously underestimated. For 2004, the sector share in GDP was revised from 31.9 percent to 40.7 percent, and GDP was adjusted by a whopping 16.8 percent. However, comparing China with India reveals a still lower share of services, which demonstrates the pivotal role of manufacturing in China's development strategy, especially in the context of China's integration into global supply chains. This is also is reflected in Chinese statistics that offer an alternative calculation of the tertiary industry share with "comparable prices," that is, real values. From that viewpoint, the tertiary sector rose only from 24 percent to 27.7 percent share in GDP. However, the assessment of this kind of data is extremely difficult, because the quality and scope of services has changed tremendously since the 1980s.

In sum, Chinese national statistics do not offer a systematic and coherent picture of the sector, because more detailed data are dispersed across the different subsectoral categories such as finance, transport, and education, and they cannot be easily compared given their different organizational and institutional features.

THE MAOIST ERA AND THE FIRST WAVE OF SERVICE LIBERALIZATION

According to Marxist economics and its corresponding national accounting system, most services are regarded as unproductive because they merely redistribute production, or deal with immaterial items. Consequently, services in China remained severely underdeveloped until 1978, and the tertiary sector share even shrank. In fact, many service activities were automatically supplanted by organizational mechanisms of the planned economy, such as the system of financial control by state banks, which therefore did not assume the role of a service provider, or the mandatory purchasing system that substituted for a wide range of trading activities and their complementary services. The Maoist industrialization strategy went a big step further, suppressing even small-scale businesses such as restaurants in its control of almost all flows of agricultural goods in the state procurement system. As a result, in 1978 China had a service sector that was substantially smaller than those of even low-income economies; it shrank between 1952 and 1980 from 28.3 percent to 20.6 percent. This underdevelopment of services aggravated the disguised unemployment in the rural sector, which therefore suffered from stagnant productivity.

In the first years after 1978, old ideological prejudice remained strong. Policy makers recognized that the tertiary sector offered the solution to the very serious unemployment problem in China, because many services are labor intensive. However, there was a backlash against these "capitalist practices" for several years, and the service share in GDP hovered between 20 and 25 percent until the mid-1980s. In 1992 the Chinese Communist Party promulgated the "Decision on the Acceleration of Tertiary Sector Development," which set the framework for the years to come. The tertiary sector received renewed attention in a special document released by the State Council in March 2007 ("Some Opinions about the Acceleration of Service Sector Development").

The result of this initial political stalemate was that in the first decade of reform, the most dynamic field in service development was the so-called individual enterprises (*getihu*), which were limited in size (fewer than eight employees) and therefore did not count as genuinely capitalist enterprises. This was the organizational framework appropriate for small-scale transport companies, restaurants, repair shops, and retail shops, which mushroomed in Chinese rural townships and urban places. These were highly fluid family-owned companies that typically fell below the threshold of formal government taxation but faced arbitrary interference from local administrations. The institutional obstacles for service sector development in more complex services have remained strong, especially in the countryside. A case in point is the lack of an adequate response to the vigorous demand for more flexible financial services for small-scale business and farmers in the countryside. This situation led to the rapid growth of rural credit foundations and other forms of private credit for a brief time in the late 1990s, followed by a crackdown on supposedly destabilizing financial misbehavior. Thus the state maintained financial repression in the rural sector.

Regulatory impediments, limited access to credit, and other discriminatory determinants of business dynamics reveal the lasting impact of China's past policy approaches. A good indicator is the employment shares of different kinds of ownership. In 2005 the nongovernmental sector (including collective units and all other types of private units) had a share of roughly 80 percent of employment in the catering business and almost 70 percent in retail trade, whereas in wholesale trade it had just a 50 percent share. In education and health care almost 90 percent of employees work in state-owned units. In the financial industry, the share of the nongovernmental units is about 40 percent; this includes the large sector of urban cooperative banks, which are owned by local governments. In newly emerging services the legacy of the past can be overcome more easily. Thus, in real estate, for example, the share of nongovernmental units has already reached almost 70 percent. The overall picture of the tertiary sector still reveals a fundamental dualism between market-oriented small-scale services on the one hand and advanced services in nationally sensitive sectors on the other.

LIBERALIZATION, DEREGULATION AND OPENING-UP: THE WTO AND BEYOND

Following the big push of the almost complete liberalization of small-scale services, sector growth faltered in the 1990s, when further development would have depended on the liberalization of the more advanced services, such as banking, insurance, health care, and education. Against this background, WTO entry can be regarded as a lever to regain domestic dynamics in service development.

Service growth is driven by demand, and requires innovative attitudes on the part of both service providers and users. Correspondingly, service development is particularly strong in the coastal provinces of China and lags behind in other regions: In 2006 about 60 percent of value-added in the tertiary sector was produced in the coastal provinces, whereas the share of the central and western provinces had shrunk to about 20 percent each. Chinese citizens in the coastal areas use the threefold level of per-capita service volume than citizens in the other regions. These differences reflect a divergent dynamics of urbanization, as demand for services is particularly strong in urban regions. Structural changes also clearly affect service demand, with education and health-care services showing the strongest expansion since the late 1990s. It is important to note that the role of urbanization also refers to the structural transformation of the countryside. A good indicator is the employment in the subsector of leasing and business services, a newly emerging service field less hampered by past policies and structural legacies. In 2005 in most advanced urban regions such as Beijing, almost 10 percent of total employment was in that subsector. By comparison, its employment figure was almost 3 percent for Guangdong Province; 2.5 percent for Zhejiang Province; about 1.5 percent in provinces such as Shandong,

Jiangsu, and Fujian; and about 1 percent in provinces such as Jiangxi, Guizhou, and Anhui.

This modernization trend is reflected also in the main areas of small-scale business, retail trade and catering services. With the easing of ideological reservations about larger scale private companies, in the 2000s Chinese cities saw an upsurge of chain stores and chain restaurants, posing a formidable challenge for small-scale businesses. By comparison, in advanced services, sector reforms can be technologically and institutionally very complex, because there is no simple way to privatize and open up markets, and because they often take place in a rapidly evolving technological setting. A case in point is telecommunications. Within little more than a decade, China grew from an underdeveloped country to the global lead market in telecommunications. As in other high-tech services such as air transport, in telecommunications this first required the splitting up of monopolistic government agencies such as China Telecom into at least two competing entities (here, China Telecom and China Netcom). In China, a standard approach is to define regional boundaries of the new units but allow for cross-regional competition (this approach was also applied in airtransport services). While new competitors are allowed market access, the government unit previously responsible for service provision must transform itself into a regulatory body. In the case of telecommunications, a Ministry of Information Industry was created by merging the Ministry of Post and Telecommunications, the Ministry of Electronics Industry, and parts of other administrative units.

This example shows the need for large-scale deregulation measures, especially in banking and finance, telecommunications, and transport, to further boost service growth. In this regard, China does not differ substantially from many other countries, including industrialized ones, as these sectors are often government monopolies or feature very high barriers to entry. At the same time, China had to increase substantially the knowledge transfer in the service industries in order to achieve competitiveness. A case in point are the large state banks, which have been overloaded with bad credits, and have to maintain a nationwide net of branches, which have been managed as state administrations, but not as a modern finance business.

WTO entry was also conceived as a trigger for the modernization of these outmoded business structures and organizations. In 2000 the Chinese services sector was one of the most protected in the world: The tax equivalent to the barriers to establishment was calculated as 250 percent, compared with 37 percent in Malaysia and 22 percent in Korea. With its WTO commitments, China opened up almost all service industries to a substantial degree. However, the market entry of foreign service providers has been hampered by zigzags in regulatory procedures, as in the detailed capital requirements to set up insurance ventures,

and the specific regional sequence of opening up (which was limited to a few cities during the transitional period). Foreign investment in the Chinese service sector increasingly takes the form of stakes in Chinese companies, especially in finance industries, after the corporatization of the Chinese banks and insurance companies. However, sensitive areas such as telecommunications and air transport have caps of 49 percent of foreign-invested capital.

Without a doubt, further modernization, liberalization, and transformation of the service sector are at the center of China's transition to a knowledge economy. New technologies have a great impact on the provision of services, affecting even the rural areas by linking farmers to the export business via new forms of integrating trade and production. The crucial determinant of a successful transition is expanding investment in education.

BIBLIOGRAPHY

Findlay, Christopher, Mari Pangestu, and Roy Chun Lee. Service Sector Reform Options: The Experience of China. In *China: Linking Markets for Growth*, ed. Ross Garnaut and Ligang Song, 95–117. Canberra: Asia Pacific Press, Australian National University, 2007.

Naughton, Barry. Growth and Structural Change. In *The Chinese Economy: Transitions and Growth*, 139–160. Cambridge, MA: MIT Press, 2007.

Carsten Herrmann-Pillath

SERVILE STATUSES

Marxist historians in the People's Republic of China, following Mao Zedong, have characterized China after the Opium War (1839–1842) as semifeudal (and semicolonial), which implies some degree of serf-like conditions among the tenants of landlords. Nevertheless, although slavery existed throughout the history of imperial China, by the late Qing dynasty (1644–1912) most of the Han Chinese population of the empire was generally free of bonds that might be described as servile.

Plantation slavery of the kind that used to exist in European colonies and in the southern United States appears to have been unknown in China. At the time of the Manchu conquest (1616–1644) and immediately after, the Manchu bannermen acquired estates cultivated by servile or near-servile labor, but this form of exploitation later disappeared, and in the late Qing period the servile dependents of bannermen were mostly domestic servants. In the late Qing the vast majority of the peasantry were free commoners, at least from a legal point of view. Master-employee relationships were not equal, but tended to be contractual rather than based on coercion, and traditional custom did not oblige tenants or laborers to work for any particular master.

Even then, both the state and wealthy private individuals had dependents with some of the characteristics associated with servile status or slavery: They were subordinate to masters, forced to labor, traded like property, and cut off from normal kinship ties. In some places hereditary servants were attached to wealthy families and performed unpaid labor. It is impossible to estimate the number of slaves or hereditary servants in Qing dynasty China. It is safe to assume, however, that the share of slaves in the population was much lower than in countries with plantation slavery. Servile dependents were mainly household servants or provided services at ritual occasions. They enhanced the comfort and prestige, but not necessarily the wealth, of their masters.

SLAVERY IN TRADITIONAL CHINESE LAW

The most common Chinese words that roughly correspond to "slave" are *nu* and *nubi*, the latter specifically referring to "male and female slaves." These words occur, for instance, in the traditional penal code. Other expressions were used for people with servile status in legal texts and in other official documents, as well as informally (e.g., *nupu*, "bondservant").

The criminal justice system imposed punishments that were in some cases similar to slavery. Two of the main five categories of punishment (*wu xing*) were penal servitude for periods varying from one to five years, and different kinds of exile for life. A special form of the latter was deportation (*faqian*), which involved slavery in a military garrison in Manchuria or Xinjiang. None of these punishments were hereditary, penal servitude had a specific time limit, and even deportation could be brought to an end in a general amnesty or sometimes by redemption. Enslavement as *nu* was not an ordinary punishment; instead, it was inflicted on the children and female family members of rebels and traitors. Those who were enslaved in this way were given to meritorious officials. Close adult male relatives of rebels and traitors, however, were not enslaved but executed.

The law was somewhat ambiguous in regard to the legality of commoners keeping slaves. Legally a distinction was made between ordinary commoners, who were known as "good" or "honorable" (*liang*), and people with inferior status known as "mean" or "base" (*jian*). The latter included slaves, as well as people with dishonorable occupations such as entertainers (including prostitutes) and some lowly government employees, so-called yamen runners. In principle it was a punishable offense to sell good people into slavery. However, the law did not prohibit people from selling themselves into slavery or the sale of those who were already slaves. Furthermore, Qing law recognized that the destitute could not be prohibited from selling their children or wives into slavery. A large proportion of those who were sold into private slavery were probably children, especially girls. Sales

of people might be registered with the authorities, but it was not compulsory. Those who became slaves through unregistered transactions had the right to redeem themselves. Kidnapping and selling "good" people into slavery was treated as a serious crime, but may have been an important source of new slaves.

The master-slave relationship in criminal law was in certain respects similar to that of fathers and sons. If slaves were disrespectful or committed crimes against their masters or masters' family members, they were given a much heavier punishment than that applicable to individuals who committed the same offense against their social equals. The law provided that a son murdering his father, or a slave murdering his master, should be sentenced to death by slicing, the most severe degree of punishment. In contrast, masters were entitled to punish their slaves, although the intentional killing of a slave was a punishable offense. There was no legal obstacle to masters having sexual intercourse with unmarried slave women, whereas sexual relations between a male slave and his master's female relatives were treated as a serious crime.

Long-term employees had an intermediate position between the free and the unfree. Laborers hired on a yearly basis were in a servile relationship to their masters as long as their contracts lasted, but were legally equal to other commoners. Those who worked for the same master for several years and were given a wife acquired the same legal status as a person who had been sold in an officially registered sale.

SOCIAL STATUS OF SLAVES

The terms for people in servile relationships varied from place to place. "Hereditary servants," for example, were known as *shipu*, but also as *ximin* and *xiafu* (Cantonese: *sai-man* and *ha-fu*) in South China and the New Territories of Hong Kong.

The treatment of servitude also varied. Children who were sold to well-off households appear to have been used predominantly as domestic servants, but children were also purchased or indentured to be trained as entertainers or work as prostitutes. It was probably much more common to buy girls than boys for work as household servants. Female servitude normally was not lifelong, and the owners had a moral and legal obligation to marry off their maidservants when they had grown up. They could also be sold as concubines, and trading concubines was not uncommon among the rich. It was in any case common for women to be given a way out of servitude, although it also happened that slave women were given as wives to male slaves. Male slaves were less likely to be manumitted, and their treatment was harsher, as in the case of the *ximin* in the New Territories of Hong Kong.

It should be noted that people with no male heirs also purchased boys to adopt. Such designated heirs eventually became full members of their new families and were in a

Workers freed from slave-like conditions at an illegal brick manufacturing facility, Linfen, Shanxi province, May 27, 2007.
While plantation-style slavery did not exist in China, many wealthy families purchased slaves to assist in running a household. At the end of the Qing dynasty, slavery officially became illegal, though modern-day instances of citizens being forced against their will to work continue to exist, as seen in the above photo. © EPA/CORBIS

very different position from slaves. Young girls likewise were purchased to be brought up as daughters-in-law, but their status could easily be changed to that of servants.

Debt was a reason for adults to sell themselves into slavery. There were also those who found it advantageous to accept a mild form of dependency in order to gain the protection of a powerful family. One purpose of such an action, if it was taken freely, might be to escape from responsibility for tax payments.

Male slaves when they grew up might be given wives and be allowed to set up their own homes. In many places such people and their descendants continued to perform unpaid labor for their masters, but lived with their families in houses of their own. Hereditary servants and household slaves both were required to behave very respectfully. They used very deferential language when speaking to members of their masters' families, and they could not eat at the family tables. Members of servile households typically were called upon to provide customary services designed to enhance the prestige of their master, such as playing music

and carrying sedan chairs at weddings and funerals. That sort of servile condition appears to have been in decline by the late Qing era, but still persisted in some places, notably Guangdong. Discrimination against such people continued into the middle of the twentieth century.

In some cases social reality was very much at variance with legal status. People who were legally servile but served the emperor or other powerful and wealthy people held influential positions. A well-known example is the bondservants of the merchants of Huizhou Prefecture in Anhui. Some of these bondservants were trusted business managers who handled their masters' affairs without close supervision. They had little in common with ordinary household slaves.

In China as in other countries some powerful servants of the state were formally servile. The bondservants (*baoyi*) of the imperial household and Manchu princes could sit government examinations and serve as officials. Some were trusted advisers of the emperors. Keeping eunuchs was an imperial prerogative, and many eunuchs served at the court and in special administrative agencies. Although eunuchs can be said to have been in a servile position, those who were close to the emperor or served in administrative posts exercised influence and enjoyed comfortable lives.

Other groups that were traditionally treated as inferior to commoners included the above-mentioned "mean" categories of entertainers and yamen runners, as well as the boat people (*danmin* or "Tanka") of the southern coasts and waterways. Members of these groups did not all have masters and should not be labeled uniformly as "servile."

ABOLITION AND REPUBLIC OF CHINA (1911–1949)

There was no significant abolitionist movement during the Qing, at least not before the last few years of the dynasty. However, after the Boxer Uprising in 1900, conservative political forces were weakened and radical reforms of many kinds were instituted in the last decade of the dynasty. As government officials prepared legal and constitutional reforms, enslavement as a punishment was abolished in 1905. In the following year it was proposed to phase out private slavery, which was seen as incompatible with good government and a prosperous modern nation. It was noted that slavery had been abolished in the countries of the West. It took several years of further deliberation before abolition was eventually approved in 1910, the year before the Republican revolution. Generally, slaves were supposed to be transformed into hired laborers. At the same time the legal distinction between the "good" and the "mean" also was eliminated.

The Republic adopted laws based on the German civil code. Slavery and servile conditions were illegal and probably declined in most places. Although hereditary servants or slaves continued to serve wealthy masters in some parts of rural China, there was no legal way of forcing their return if they left. Evidence from the New Territories of Hong Kong and elsewhere in South China suggests that hereditary servants mainly performed domestic chores for their masters, but keeping them usually did not yield any economic profit. Such servants were a luxury for the well-off.

Vestiges of old servile relationships persisted beyond the end of Qing. Termination of the inferior status of the so-called fallen people (or "lazy people") in parts of Zhejiang had been attempted as early as 1723. The writer Lu Xun has described how some of the fallen people still offered customary services to their patrons at the time of the Republican revolution.

The purchase of girls to serve as household servants continued as a common practice among the wealthy in the Republican period. As in earlier times, young girls from poor families were sold, or kidnapped, and put to work as maidservants. In Hong Kong the sale and keeping of *mui-jai*, as they are known in Cantonese, caused considerable controversy in the 1920s and 1930s, and the custom was suppressed only gradually under pressure from antislavery campaigners in both Hong Kong and Britain.

BIBLIOGRAPHY

Huang Shuping and Gong Peihua. *Guangdong shipuzhi yanjiu* [A study of the Guangdong hereditary servants]. Guangzhou, China: Guangdong Gaodeng Jiaoyu Chubanshe, 2001.

Jaschok, Maria. *Concubines and Bondservants: A Social History.* London and New Jersey: Zed Books, 1988.

Jing Junjian. *Qingdai shehui de jianmin dengji* [The status of mean people in Qing society]. Hangzhou, China: Zhejiang Renmin, 1993.

Lu Xun. Wo tan "duomin" [Talking about the "fallen people"]. In *Lu Xun quanji* [Complete works of Lu Xun], vol. 5. Beijing: Renmin Wenxue, 1982.

Meijer, Marinus J. Slavery at the End of the Ch'ing Dynasty. In *Essays on China's Legal Tradition*, ed. Jerome Alan Cohen, R. Randle Edwards, and Fu-mei Chang Chen, 327–358. Princeton, NJ: Princeton University Press, 1980.

Watson, James L., ed. *Asian and African Systems of Slavery.* Oxford, U.K.: Blackwell, 1980.

Wei Qingyuan, et al. *Qingdai nubi zhidu* [The Qing system of slavery]. Beijing: Zhongguo Renmin Daxue, 1982.

Anders Hansson

SEVERE ACUTE RESPIRATORY SYNDROME

Severe acute respiratory syndrome (SARS) is a respiratory disease in humans that is caused by the SARS coronavirus (SARS-CoV). The SARS epidemic began in Foshan in Guangdong Province in November 2002. A Chinese physician who attended the ill inadvertently became the index case for a global chain of transmission when he travelled to Hong Kong in late February 2003 and unknowingly infected other travelers, who then spread the disease to Vietnam (February 23), Canada (February 23), Singapore (February 25), Taiwan (February 25), and other countries. By July 31, 2003, the virus had caused 8,096 known cases of infection and 774 deaths worldwide. Among the affected countries, China was hit particularly hard, with 5,327 cases and 349 fatalities.

The SARS epidemic triggered the most serious socialpolitical crisis in China since the 1989 Tiananmen crackdown. An information blackout characterized the initial government response to SARS. Indeed, until early April 2003, the government authorities were essentially in denial, sharing little information with the World Health Organization (WHO) and even barring WHO experts from visiting Guangdong, the epicenter of the outbreak. The government's failure to publicize the outbreak in a timely and accurate manner, coupled with the general medical and epidemiological uncertainty, caused fear, anxiety, and panic

Workers disinfecting an elementary school classroom, Shanxi province, April 23, 2003. *In November 2002, an outbreak of SARS (severe acute respiratory syndrome) began in northern China and spread to other countries by spring of the following year. Only after threats by the world health community to isolate China did the central government begin to participate in open campaigns to rid the country of the illness.* © **XINHUA/XINHUA PHOTO/CORBIS**

nationwide. At the height of the epidemic in Beijing, a sea of people in white masks—most of them scared migrant workers and university students—flocked to train and bus stations and airports in the hope of fleeing the city. By late April, an estimated one million people, around 10 percent of the population in Beijing, had fled the city for other parts of China. In the countryside, worried villagers set up roadblocks to keep away people from Beijing. A series of riots against quarantine centers was also reported in May.

The World Health Organization became involved on February 10, 2003, after receiving an e-mail rumor about the presence of the atypical pneumonia in Guangdong. On March 15, WHO issued its first SARS-related emergency travel advisory. Ten days later, the Chinese government for the first time acknowledged the spread of SARS outside of Guangdong. Despite government media control, the news about SARS circulated via mobile phones, e-mail, and the Internet. On March 31, the *Wall Street Journal* published an editorial calling for other countries to suspend travel links with China until it implemented a transparent public-health campaign. Meanwhile, 110 countries with which China had

diplomatic relations placed at least some restrictions on travel to China. As the international pressure mounted, the State Council held its first ad hoc meeting on SARS on April 2. The same day, WHO issued the most stringent travel advisory in its fifty-five-year history, advising people not to visit Hong Kong and Guangdong, prompting Beijing to hold a news conference in which the health minister Zhang Wenkang promised that China was safe and SARS was under control.

Enraged by the minister's false account, Dr. Jiang Yanyong, a retired surgeon at Beijing's 301 Military Hospital, sent a letter to two television stations, reporting the actual situation in Beijing. *Time* magazine picked up the story and posted it on its Web site on April 9. The letter generated a political earthquake in Beijing, leading to the removal of the mayor of Beijing Meng Xuenong and the minister of health on April 21. After that, the central government leaders began to address the epidemic in a more open and decisive manner. On April 23, a task force known as the SARS Control and Prevention Headquarters of the State Council was established to coordinate national efforts to combat the disease, while at the same time a national fund of two billion yuan ($242 million) was created for SARS prevention and control. In part because of the momentous government measures, the epidemic started to lose its momentum in late May. On July 5, 2003, WHO announced that the SARS epidemic had been effectively contained.

The SARS debacle also justified the central leaders' efforts to reinforce their control over lower-level officials. As part of a nationwide campaign to mobilize the system, the State Council sent out inspection teams to twenty-six provinces to scour government records for unreported cases and to fire officials for lax prevention efforts. It was estimated that by the end of May, nearly one thousand government officials had been disciplined for their "slack" response to the SARS epidemic.

SEE ALSO *Epidemics; Migrant Workers.*

BIBLIOGRAPHY
Kleinman, Arthur, and James L. Watson, eds. *SARS in China: Prelude to Pandemic?* Stanford, CA: Stanford University Press, 2006.
Knobler, Stacey, et al., eds. *Learning from SARS: Preparing for the Next Disease Outbreak.* Washington, DC: National Academies Press, 2004.
World Health Organization. Summary of Probable SARS Cases with Onset of Illness from 1 November 2002 to 31 July 2003. http://www.who.int/csr/sars/country/table2004_04_21/en/index.html.

Yanzhong Huang

SEX EDUCATION

In ancient times, medical and religious writings were the main source of sexual knowledge for the Chinese; for the illiterate majority, such knowledge was transmitted by drawings, sculptures, and word of mouth. Sex dolls or painted scrolls were placed by tradition at the bottom of newlyweds' luggage as sex-education gifts from parents. This tradition lasted up to the early decades of the twentieth century.

During the Republican era, magazines and newspapers occasionally published factual medical information about reproduction. Some famous authors also wrote books introducing Western ideas and theories about sex (Zhang Jingsheng [1926] 1967; Ellis 1946), bringing the Chinese their first contact with modern sex education.

In the early decades of the People's Republic of China, Premier Zhou Enlai lent his support to the systematic provision of sex education, with initiatives undertaken in 1954, 1963, and 1975 (Hu Peicheng 2008). This program was mainly meant to meet the need for population control. Moreover, for about a decade beginning in 1965, specially trained "barefoot doctors" in rural areas propagated basic knowledge about sex to illiterate peasants, with an emphasis on the physiology of reproduction and methods of contraception. Efforts and publications covering other areas of sex education were rare (Ruan Fangfu 1991).

At the beginning of the 1980s, with the onset of the reform era, a revised edition of a basic sex-education book written in 1957 was published (Wang Wenbin et al. 1980) and soon became a best seller. Since then, numerous other sex-education books, covering a wide range of topics, have been published. These publications are comparable to those available elsewhere in the contemporary world, though in general they are less explicit or permissive in tone. The open-door policy also exposed China's younger generation to new sexual attitudes, behaviors, and lifestyles, requiring a long-term national policy on comprehensive sex education to counteract the threat of sexually transmitted diseases (especially AIDS), teenage pregnancies, premarital and extramarital sex (by promoting sex within marriage), and other sex-related problems.

China's first high-school sex-education course was introduced experimentally in Shanghai in 1981. This program became the prototype for sex-education courses that were offered in many schools in all major cities in subsequent years. In 2002 China passed a Law on Population and Planned Parenthood (Guojia Renkou Yu Jihua Shengyu Fa), which requires all schools to implement formal sex education for adolescents for a minimum number of teaching hours every year, to be decided by individual schools (CRI Online 2004; Hu Peicheng 2008). Most primary and secondary schools conduct a minimum of five to ten hours of sex education per year.

China has tried to strike a balance between the educational needs of the general public and the need to control pornography and sexual exploitation. The working principle is that, as long as messages about sex are delivered in the proper language for the purpose of health or serious discussion, they are permitted within as wide a margin as possible. Hence, in contemporary Chinese cites, sex shops, advertisements for sex-related products, sculptures and paintings depicting nudes or erotic imagery, explicit government sex-education posters, and the like are often clearly visible in major public areas. Adults can buy contraceptive pills, condoms, potency drugs, and sex toys over the counter practically everywhere in China. The government's Family Planning Association runs "sex bars" or "sex tea houses" where members of the public can meet and socialize surrounded by contraceptives, condoms, sex-education books, posters, and artistic displays of a sexual nature.

A popular sex-education magazine, *Ren zhi chu* (The beginning of man), began publication in 1990 in Guangzhou. It has a large national circulation, selling about one million copies per issue, as well as an online edition. The

Guangzhou government, collaborating with the commercial sector, also started an annual "Sex Cultural Festival" in 2002. It consists of three or four days of public activities with sex-education themes, including lectures, exhibitions and product displays, plays and shows, carnival stalls, and other forums. The festival has been well received by the public, and has been imitated by other cities in China, including Beijing, Hong Kong, and Macau (Ng M. L. 2006).

SEE ALSO *Homosexuality; Sexuality.*

BIBLIOGRAPHY

Ellis, Havelock. *Xing xin li xue* [Psychology of sex]. Trans. and adapted by Pan Guangdan. Pan Kwangtan Chongqing, PRC: Commercial Press, 1946.

Hu Peicheng. Zhongguo dalu xing jiankang jiaoyu de lishi [Sexual health education in mainland China: Its history, present, and future]. *Huaren xing yanjiu* [Chinese sexuality research] 1 (2008): 21–24.

Landsberger, Stefan R. Stefan Landsberger's Chinese Propaganda Poster Pages: Barefoot Doctors. International Institute of Social History. http://www.iisg.nl/landsberger/bfd.html

Ng M. L. The Transformation of a Sexual Culture: The Chinese Paradigm. *Sexual and Relationship Therapy* 21, 2 (2006): 137–141.

Ren zhi chu zazhi zaixian [*Ren zhi chu* online]. http://www.rzc.com.cn

Ruan Fangfu. *Sex in China: Studies in Sexology in Chinese Culture.* New York: Plenum, 1991.

Wang Wenbin, Zhao Zhiyi, and Tan Mingxin. *Xing de zhishi* [The knowledge of sex]. 1957. Rev. ed. Beijing: Popular Science Publishing House, 1980.

Zhang Jingsheng (Chang Ching-sheng). *Sex Histories: China's First Treatise on Sex Education.* 1926. Trans. Howard S. Levy. Yokohama, Japan: Bai Yuan Society, 1967.

Emil M. L. Ng

SEX RATIO

Sex ratio (SR) is the most popular of several indexes of sex composition used in scholarly analyses (Hobbs 2004, p. 130). It is defined as the number of males for every one hundred females, as follows:

$$SR = (Pm/Pf)*100$$

An SR above 100 indicates an excess of males, and an SR below 100 indicates an excess of females. This is the formula used by most demographers and by such international bodies as the United Nations, particularly in their analyses of China. In some Eastern European countries and in India, Iran, Pakistan, Saudi Arabia, and some other countries, the sex ratio is calculated as the number of females per one hundred males (Poston 2005). On average, "national sex ratios tend to fall in the narrow range from about 95 to 102, barring special circumstances, such as a history of heavy war losses (less males), or heavy immigration (more males); national sex ratios outside the range of 90 to 105 should be viewed as extreme" (Shryock, Siegel, et al. 1976, p. 107).

CHINA'S SEX RATIO FROM THE QING ERA TO THE 1980s

Preferential treatment toward males is part of the Confucian value system. During the Qing dynasty (1644–1912), female infants were sometimes killed, often by drowning, or their births would not be reported, resulting in higher than average SRs (Jiang 1998). Official population data indicate that in 1746 the SR for adults was 135 and for children 128; from 1776 to 1859 the mean SR for all ages was 122. Population statistics from the late Qing are unreliable due to disruptions caused by the Taiping Uprising (1851–1864) and wars, and the SR for this period is not known (He Bingdi 1959).

The establishment of the Nationalist government in Nanjing in 1927 inaugurated a new era in China, but the sex ratio remained high, mainly because of female infanticide. However, the sex ratio declined after the Communist revolution, and the gender imbalance was greatly reduced. This occurred for two main reasons. First, after 1949, efforts were made to alter the traditionally low status of women. Although discrimination against female children still existed, the situation of women improved. Second, Mao Zedong rejected traditional Malthusian arguments that population growth would eventually outrun the food supply, and he regarded China's huge population as an asset. As a consequence, China's sex ratio in the 1960s and the 1970s was near normal (Baculiano 2004). This situation changed dramatically in the 1980s.

CHINA'S SEX RATIO AT BIRTH

Since the late 1980s, China has had an unexpectedly high imbalance in its SR, due almost entirely to a much higher than average sex ratio at birth (SRB). Most societies have SRBs between 104 and 106, that is, 104 to 106 boys are born for every 100 girls. This biologically normal SRB is probably an evolutionary adaptation to the fact that females have higher survival probabilities than males at every stage of life. As a consequence, more males than females are required at birth for there to be approximately equal numbers of males and females when the groups reach their marriageable ages. Biology thus dictates that the age-specific SR will be highest among the very young, and should then decline with age, attaining a value of around 100 for persons in their late twenties. SRs continue to decline to levels of around 50 or 60 among the oldest people.

These SR patterns should occur in most populations, barring extreme forms of disturbance or human intervention. One such intervention is female-specific abortion, which results in an SRB well above 105. This is the cause of China's current high SRB. Unlike earlier times, there is little evidence that female infanticide or the non-enumeration of female babies is causing China's high SRBs (Zeng Yi et al. 1993; Eberstadt 2000, p. 228; Chu Junhong 2001).

The SRB in the United States is invariant at about 105 for every year. In contrast, China had an SRB slightly above 107 in 1980, but China's SRB began to increase in the late 1980s, reaching 115 in 1990, 120 in 2000, and 118 in 2005. This has occurred in China for three main reasons. First, fertility has declined rapidly in China, from 6 children per woman in the 1960s to around 1.7 at the start of the new millennium. Second, China is characterized by a Confucian patriarchal tradition where son preference is strong and pervasive. In the past, when Chinese women had six children on average, the probability was very low (less than 2%) that none of the six children would be male. By comparison, when a woman has between one and two children, the probability is between 25 and 50 percent that she will not have a son (Pison 2004). Third, ultrasound technology that enables prenatal determination of sex has been widely available in China since the 1980s. Many Chinese couples use this technology to identify the sex of the fetus, and some couples may choose to undergo abortion if the fetus is female.

POTENTIAL SOCIAL PROBLEMS RESULTING FROM CHINA'S HIGH SRB

One study estimated that by 2006 there would be approximately thirty-two million Chinese males born who will ultimately not be able to find Chinese women to marry (Poston and Glover 2006). These males may never marry and will have little choice but to develop their own lives and livelihoods. Some experts predict that they will settle in "bachelor ghettos" in Beijing, Shanghai, Tianjin, and other big cities, where commercial sex outlets would be prevalent. They may also be more prone to crime than if they had married (Laub and Sampson 2003, pp. 41–46; Hudson and den Boer 2004). In addition, a broad HIV/AIDS epidemic could develop if China's commercial sex markets expand to accommodate the millions of surplus males (Parish et al. 2003; Tucker et al. 2005).

SEE ALSO *Family: Infanticide; Family: One-Child Policy; Gender Relations; Women, Status of.*

BIBLIOGRAPHY

Baculiano, Eric. China Grapples with Legacy of Its "Missing Girls": Disturbing Demographic Imbalance Spurs Drive to Change Age-Old Practices. NBC News/MSNBC, September 14, 2004. http://www.msnbc.msn.com/id/5953508

Chu Junhong. Prenatal Sex Determination and Sex-selective Abortion in Rural Central China. *Population and Development Review* 27, 2 (2001): 259–281.

Clarke, John I. *The Human Dichotomy: The Changing Numbers of Males and Females.* New York: Pergamon, 2000.

Eberstadt, Nicholas. *Prosperous Paupers & Other Population Problems.* New Brunswick, NJ: Transaction, 2000.

Guttentag, Marcia, and Paul F. Secord. *Too Many Women? The Sex Ratio Question.* Newbury Park, CA: Sage, 1983.

He Bingdi (Ho Ping-ti). *Studies on the Population of China, 1368–1953.* Cambridge, MA: Harvard University Press, 1959.

Hobbs, Frank. Age and Sex Composition. In *The Methods and Materials of Demography,* eds. Jacob S. Siegel and David A. Swanson, 2nd ed., 125–173. San Diego, CA: Elsevier Academic, 2004.

Hudson, Valerie M., and Andrea M. den Boer. *Bare Branches: The Security Implications of Asia's Surplus Male Population.* Cambridge, MA: MIT Press, 2004.

Jiang, Tao. *Zuo Wei She Hui Zhu Ti De Xiang Cun Ren Kou Jie Gou* [Rural population structure as the principal part of a society]. In *Zhong Guo Jin Dai Ren Kou Shi* [China's Modern Population History], 319–367. Taipei: Nan Tian Bookstore, 1998.

Laub, John H., and Robert J. Sampson. *Shared Beginnings, Divergent Lives: Delinquent Boys to Age 70.* Cambridge, MA: Harvard University Press, 2003.

Parish, William L., Edward O. Laumann, Myron S. Cohen, et al. Population-Based Study of Chlamydial Infection in China: A Hidden Epidemic. *Journal of the American Medical Association* 289 (2003): 1265–1273.

Pison, Gilles. Fewer Births, but a Boy at All Costs: Selective Female Abortion in Asia. *Population and Societies* 404 (Sept. 2004): 1–4.

Poston, Dudley L., Jr. Age and Sex. In *Handbook of Population,* eds. Dudley L. Poston Jr., and Michael Micklin, 19–58. New York: Kluwer Academic/Plenum, 2005.

Poston, Dudley L., Jr., and K. S. Glover. China's Demographic Destiny: Marriage Market Implications for the 21st Century. In *Fertility, Family Planning, and Population Policy in China,* by Dudley L. Poston Jr. et al., 172–186. London: Routledge, 2006.

Shryock, Henry S., Jacob S. Siegel, et al. *The Methods and Materials of Demography.* Condensed ed. by Edward G. Stockwell. New York: Academic Press, 1976.

Tucker, Joseph D., Gail E. Henderson, T. F. Wang, et al. Surplus Men, Sex Work, and the Spread of HIV in China. *AIDS* 19, 6 (2005): 539–547.

Zeng Yi, Tu Ping, Gu Baochang, et al. Causes and Implications of the Recent Increase in the Reported Sex Ratio at Birth in China. *Population and Development Review* 19, 2 (1993): 283–302.

Dudley L. Poston, Jr.
Yu-Ting Chang
Danielle Xiaodan Deng

SEXUAL DYSFUNCTION

Chinese medical lore considers inadequacies in sexual function to result from kidney, liver, or spleen diseases due to humidity, heat, or energy depletion, causing a deficiency in *yang* elements (Xu S. K. 1990), the male (in contrast with the female) or the light (in contrast with the dark) essence of the universe. The treatment for such a condition is lifestyle changes, such as diet supplements, herbs, exercise, and acupuncture or moxibustion, aimed at correcting any imbalance. Building on these concepts, the Chinese find crucial linkages between the genitals and the other bodily organs. When, for any reason, the genitals or other bodily organs or the linkages between them bring about worries in a person, specific patterns of fear about the body or the mind, with both bodily and sexual symptoms, are provoked. *Suoyang* (or Koro) and *shenkui* are examples of syndromes exhibiting these symptom patterns. *Suoyang* ("retraction of *yang*") is an acute panic aroused by the perceived retraction of a man's penis or a woman's nipple or vagina, causing a feeling of impending death. *Shenkui* ("weakness of the kidney") is a feeling of sexual inadequacy provoked by bodily symptoms that are believed to be signs of kidney deficiency. These conditions have at times occurred as epidemics in Chinese communities (Tseng Wen-shing et al. 1992).

China was quick to adopt the Western concepts of sexual dysfunction at the beginning of the reform period in the early 1980s and included sexual dysfunction as a disease category in the first version of the *Chinese Classification of Mental Disorders* (1981). However, reliable figures on the rates of each type of dysfunction have not been collected. A 1989 sexuality survey covering 7,602 married adults in fifteen major Chinese cities (Liu D. L. et al. 1992) reported that 76 percent of husbands and 60 percent of wives were satisfied with their sex lives. Thirty-seven percent of wives complained of pain during sexual intercourse. The Shanghai Committee of Rehabilitation of Male Dysfunctions estimated in 1989 that at least 20 percent of China's adult population was suffering from some type of sexual dysfunction (Ruan Fangfu 1991). A mid-1990s survey of six hundred couples found 70 percent of them were unhappy with their sex lives (Pan S. M. 1995). Another group of researchers interviewed 7,697 couples who had been married for six years and found that 5 percent of the wives and 2 percent of the husbands did not reach orgasm during sex (Guo Y. N. et al. 2004).

More precise and reliable figures are available on erectile dysfunction among Chinese men. A random-sample survey of 1,506 males aged twenty-six to seventy, performed by the Family Planning Association of Hong Kong (2001), indicates that among respondents who had sexual partners, 61.4 percent reported no erectile problems in the previous six months. Researchers believed, however, that most who complained about erectile problems were actually suffering from low sexual desire. Thus, the true prevalence of erectile dysfunction in China, taking into account all major studies, was about 5 to 6 percent (Liu J. T. et al. 2005; Chen C. et al. 2004).

The adoption of the concept of sexual dysfunction has led to the establishment of Western-style sex clinics in China. By the mid-1990s, there were more than thirty such clinics, concentrated in major cities (Liu D. L. and Ng M. L.1995). Ten years later, such clinics existed in nearly every large city in China (Ruan Fangfu and Lau M. P. 2004). On average, the most common disorders diagnosed in these clinics

Vending machine selections, including counterfeit Chinese Viagra, condoms, and corn snacks, Jinan, July 27, 2004. *While traditional Chinese medicine generally attributed sexual dysfunction to kidney, liver, or spleen problems, in the late twentieth century many patients turned to Western treatments, such as erectile-enhancing drugs, to address sexual performance difficulties.* **AP IMAGES**

were erectile and ejaculatory dysfunctions for males and inhibited sexual desire and orgasmic dysfunction for females. The pattern varies from clinic to clinic, however, perhaps reflecting differences in help-seeking behavior rather than the true incidence of dysfunction (Ng M. L. [Wu Minlun] et al. 2001).

SEE ALSO *Medicine, Traditional; Sexuality.*

BIBLIOGRAPHY

Chen C (Chan C)., He K (Ho K)., Xiang L (Heung L)., (Chen W) Chan W. Study on Knowledge, Attitude, and Sexual Behaviour among the Chinese Elderly Males in Hong Kong. *Hong Kong Practitioner* 26 (2004): 64–73.

Chinese Society of Psychiatry. *Chinese Classification of Mental Disorders* (CCMD1). Beijing: Author, 1981.

Family Planning Association of Hong Kong (FPAHK). *Men's Health Survey 2001*. Hong Kong: Author, 2001.

Guo You Ning, Wu Minlun (Ng Manlun), and Chen K (Chan K). Foreplay, Orgasm, and After-play among Shanghai Couples and Its Integrative Relation with Their Marital Satisfaction. *Sexual and Relationship Therapy* 19, 1 (2004): 65–78.

Huang M. H. and Xu S. K. The Conceptualisation and Treatment of Koro in Traditional Chinese Medicine. In *Sexuality in Asia*, 231–238. Hong Kong: Hong Kong College of Psychiatrists, 1990.

Liu J. T. (Lau J. T.), Jin J. H. (Kim J. H.), and Xu H. Y.(Tsui H. Y.). Prevalence of Male and Female Sexual Problems, Perceptions Related to Sex and Association with Quality of Life in a Chinese Population: A Population-based Study. *International Journal of Impotence Research* 17, 6 (2005): 494–505.

Liu D. L. and Wu Minlun (Ng Manlun). Sexual Dysfunction in China. *Annuals of the Academy of Medicine of Singapore* 24 (1995): 728–731.

Liu D. L., Wu Minlun (Ng Manlun), and Chou Liping, eds. Zhongguo Dangdai Xing Wenhua (*Sexual Behavior in Modern China: A Report of the Nationwide Sex-Civilization Survey on 20,000 Subjects in China.*) Shanghai: Joint Publishing, 1992.

Pan Suiming. Sexuality and Relationship Satisfaction in Mainland China. *Journal of Sex Research* 7, 4 (1995): 1–17.

Ruan Fangfu. *Sex in China: Studies in Sexology in Chinese Culture.* New York: Plenum, 1991.

Ruan Fangfu and Lau M. P. China: Sexual Dysfunctions, Counseling, and Therapies. In *The Continuum Complete International Encyclopedia of Sexuality*, eds. Robert Francoeur and Raymond Noonan, 200. New York, Continuum, 2004.

Tseng Wen-shing, Mo Kan-ming, Li Li-shuen, et al. Koro Epidemics in Guangdong, China: A Questionnaire Survey. *Journal of Nervous and Mental Illness* 180 (1992): 117–123.

Wu Minlun (Ng Manlun), Gao Xinin (Ko Seknin), and Feng Shuzhen (Fung Sukching). Xianggang Daxue Mali Yiyuan Xing Zhensuo Fuwu Jin Wunian Huigu (A five-year review of the sex clinic service in Queen Mary Hospital of the university of Hong Kong). *International Chinese Sexology Journal* 1, 1 (2001): 19–22.

Xu S. K. Treatment of Impotence by Traditional Chinese Herbal Medicine. In *Sexuality in Asia*, 225–230. Hong Kong: Hong Kong College of Psychiatrists, 1990.

Wu Minlun (Ng Manlun)

SEXUALITY

As revolution brought an end to imperial rule in China, the rapid spread of Western medical science heralded another, just as radical, end to authoritative understandings of human sexuality. Frank Dikötter notes in his 1995 study that social reformers increasingly linked China's national weakness to antiquated views about sexuality and reproduction, hailing scientific sex education, the control of sexual desire, and attention to sexual hygiene as key factors contributing to national strength. Disseminated through the new print media, scientific journals, and sex education primers, the traditional idea of sexual difference as the physical expression of the cosmological order gave way to definitions of sex as a series of natural physiological distinctions. Male and female bodies were no longer described as an idealized complementarity between *yin* and *yang*; instead, as Charlotte Furth observes

in her 1994 essay, the concept of gender differences, rooted in scientific evidence, yielded hierarchical notions of "normal" male activity and female passivity oriented toward reproduction.

Although medical science applauded the eugenic benefits of sexual satisfaction and contraception, it was also used to identify "perverse" practices such as masturbation, prostitution, and homosexuality, thus establishing sexuality as an instrument of social control and, frequently, female subordination. During the political struggles between the 1920s and the 1940s, many sex-related issues, such as maternal health, the appropriate form and age of marriage, female celibacy, and so on, became topics of heated, often ideologically driven, debate. However, the modern distinctions between normative reproductive sexuality and non-normative sexual identities set the parameters for subsequent conceptualizations, including those of the Mao era.

The Mao years are commonly characterized as a period of sexual puritanism. Medical experts attempting to disseminate information about sex could not compete with the official exponents of "socialist morality"; with its potential incitement to individual desires, sexual knowledge was anathema to an ideology that stressed the collective good. Individual expressions of sexual interest were commonly described as signs of "bourgeois immorality"; with little access to sex education and relevant information, young people grew up in a sexual culture that, as one study from the 1950s put it, was "shrouded in mystery and shameful secrecy" (Wang et al. 1956, pp.1–2). Nevertheless, throughout the 1950s official journals and medical advice pamphlets published numerous articles establishing the official view on sex-related issues, shoring up the view of sex as a hierarchy of natural instincts and practices, as Harriet Evans observes in her 1997 study. The government, thus established sexuality as an arena of social control and, implicitly, sexual inequality, contradicting the Maoist slogan that "whatever men can do, so can women."

In twenty-first-century China, sex is an omnipresent feature of popular culture, from advertisements and popular magazines, to sex counseling centers, clinics treating sexual dysfunctions and sexually transmitted diseases (STDs), television debates encouraging parents to talk with their children about sex, advice hotlines about sexual violence and prostitution, and online discussions of gay and lesbian topics. Sociological surveys have indicated a rapid diversification of sexual behavior, which some, as Suiming Pan (2008) reports, describe as a "sex revolution." Yunxiang Yan's 2003 study of private life in a Chinese village notes that romantic desire has become a significant component of young people's sense of personal identity. Sex education has become more common in schools, in acknowledgment that children who will have unprecedented access to choice in their sexual activities need to be given appropriate information. Much of this public discussion of sex has been sponsored by government agencies concerned with the spread of HIV/AIDS and the

Female impersonators between performances, Chengdu, Sichuan province, June 2, 2006.
Once persecuted in the early days of the People's Republic of China as a symbol of decadence, homosexuals in China during the early twenty-first century enjoy greater acceptance by the government. Clinics aimed at stopping the spread of HIV have begun to open, and in 2001, China's national psychiatric association stopped listing homosexuality as a mental disorder. **AP IMAGES**

increased incidence of premarital sex and teenage pregnancy. The discussion is also the product of activist efforts to seek recognition for gay and lesbian rights.

The term *sexuality*, deriving from post-Mao women's studies debates about how to conceptualize sex and gender, is variously articulated as *xingcunzai, xingyishi*, or *xingxiang*. Theoretical reflections on sex, gender, and sexuality continue to take new and exploratory dimensions. However, standard academic, medical, and popular opinion continues to define sex in terms that draw on ideas from the early twentieth century and that were maintained throughout the Mao years. Thus the common assumption that today's sexual culture is the liberating result of China's Westernization and globalization ignores a continuity with the recent past. The notion of progress in understandings of sexuality overlooks the often discriminatory implications of changing sexual practices and attitudes; it also ignores the constraints placed on individuals whose sexual orientation is outside what is accepted as "normal" and who face discrimination when attempting to gain recognition for their minority status. Although the absence of specific legal clauses against homosexuality is widely explained as the legacy of China's historical tolerance toward homosexuality, gays and lesbians continue to struggle for recognition in an ideological and moral climate that at best gives grudging acknowledgment to their existence. Increasing individual self-expression still runs up against the institutions of heterosexual marriage and reproductive sexuality.

SEE ALSO *Homosexuality; Sex Education; Sexual Dysfunction.*

BIBLIOGRAPHY

Dikötter, Frank. *Sex, Culture and Modernity in China: Medical Science and the Construction of Sexual Identities in the Early Republican Period.* London: Hurst & Company, and Honolulu: University of Hawaii Press, 1995.

Evans, Harriet. Defining Difference: The "Scientific" Construction of Female Sexuality and Gender in the People's Republic of China, 1949–59. *SIGNS: Journal of Women in Culture and Society* 20, 2 (1995): 357–394.

Evans, Harriet. *Women and Sexuality in China: Dominant Discourses of Female Sexuality and Gender since 1949.* Cambridge, MA: Polity Press, 1997.

Furth, Charlotte. Rethinking Van Gulik: Sexuality and Reproduction in Traditional Chinese Medicine. In *Engendering China: Women, Culture, and the State,* ed. Christina K. Gilmartin et al., 125–146. Cambridge, MA: Harvard University Press, 1994.

Hinsch, Bret. *Passions of the Cut Sleeve: The Male Homosexual Tradition in China.* Berkeley: University of California Press, 1990.

Pan, Suiming. *China Sex Revolution Reports.* Gaoxiong, Taiwan: Universal Press, 2008.

Rofel, Lisa. *Desiring China: Experiments in Neoliberalism, Sexuality, and Public Culture.* Durham, NC: Duke University Press, 2007.

Wang, Wenbin, Zhiyi Zhao, and Mingxin Tan. *Xing de zhishi* [Knowledge about sex]. Beijing: Renmin weisheng chubanshe, 1956.

Yan, Yunxiang. *Private Life under Socialism: Love, Intimacy, and Family Change in a Chinese Village, 1949–1999.* Stanford, CA: Stanford University Press, 2003.

Zhang, Everett Yuehong. The Birth of Nanke (Men's Medicine) in China: The Making of the Subject of Desire. *American Ethnologist* 34, 3 (August 2007): 491–508.

Harriet Evans

SHAANXI

Modern Shaanxi takes its name from an ancient geographical reference: It is the area west of a region called *Shan* in Henan. The name *Shaanxi*—with a double *a*—was adopted to distinguish this province from Shanxi, its neighbor to the east. (The first character in both names is *shan* in pinyin, with Shaanxi's *shan* in the third tone. In the earlier postal spelling, "Shensi" was used for Shaanxi, and "Shansi" for Shanxi.)

GEOGRAPHY

Even in modern times, Shaanxi has not been able to escape its history—and perhaps its people have not cared to do so. Shaanxi's capital, Xi'an, was China's capital for thirteen dynasties, and a visitor touring the Xi'an area sees one tomb mound after another as reminders of Shaanxi's ancient history. Xi'an, historically known as Chang'an, sat just below the Wei River, waterway of the ancient Qin state, life-giver to this central plain for generations of Shaanxi people. These ancient sites are spread over an area of more than 100 kilometers around Xi'an, from Lintong, home of the tomb of the Founding Qin Emperor (Qin Shi Huangdi), to Xianyang, his capital city—and site of today's Xi'an airport.

Shaanxi is divided into three parts, a feature captured in its nickname *san Qin*—"the three parts of Qin," a continuing reference to the ancient state of Qin. South of the mountains is Qin-nan, an area that belongs geographically with Sichuan. This southern part of the province produces fine tea (a product not well known outside the province). It is more widely known that the Qin-nan region is a giant panda habitat and the site of a panda preserve.

The central plain of Shaanxi ranges from the mountains south of Xi'an to about 100 kilometers north of the capital city. Its productivity determined that the center of Qin would be located in this breadbasket area. The Wei River remains a major resource but also serves as a local example of the limited water supply in northern China.

The most storied part of Shaanxi in modern times is Shaanbei, the proud but poor northern region. Besides Yan'an, the "Red capital" of the 1930s and 1940s, Shaanbei's other cities include Mizhi, home of the anti-Ming rebel leader Li Zicheng (1606–1644); Qingjian, center of the haunting folk music of Shaanbei; and Yulin, a Great Wall town that flourishes thanks to natural gas resources in the area. This is the "yellow earth" of the Northwest Loess Plateau (*Xibei huangtu gaoyuan*). Extending from south of Yan'an to Yulin in the

north, Shaanbei is the broadest stretch of this vast region that has contributed much to China's history and culture.

Appropriately, the tomb—or perhaps simply *a* tomb—of the legendary Yellow Emperor is also located in Shaanxi, at Huangling (the Yellow Emperor's tomb), near the margin of Shaanbei and the central plain. Other provinces have similar sites, all claiming to have been the birthplace (or the death place) of the Yellow Emperor (*Huang di*), China's mythical founder. Shaanxi also boasts a site supposed to be the origin of *Yan di* ("Emperor of Incandescent Virtue," an alternative name for *Shen nong*, "the Divine Farmer"), a parallel figure to the Yellow Emperor. Recently constructed, this Yan di site is at Baoji, the railroad junction and Shaanxi's second-largest city, located about 160 kilometers west of Xi'an.

SHAANXI TO 1949

Despite its pivotal position in early Chinese history, by the Qianlong reign of the Qing period (late eighteenth century), Shaanxi had deteriorated into a backwater with its old capital city a regional administrative center, quite down-at-the-heels. The nineteenth century ravaged Shaanxi: Remnants of the Nian rebel movement took refuge in the Qinnan region in the 1860s and 1870s. The Muslim rebellions then followed, leaving Shaanbei devastated, impoverished even beyond the usual level of hardship there.

The circumstances of revolutionary political struggle contrived to bring Shaanbei front and center in the mid-1930s. The Red Army arrived in Shaanbei in October 1935 at the end of the epic Long March. The army settled at Yan'an, which then served as the center of the Chinese Communist movement through the end of the War against Japan in 1945. In gaining administrative control in Shaanbei, the Communists had to assimilate earlier local Communist leaders such as Liu Zhidan (1903–1936), and to pacify a variety of bandit groups in this desperate part of China. The party leadership achieved these goals gradually while pressing their larger purpose of leading China's national resistance against Japan.

In 1936, Shaanxi served as the stage for a pivotal episode in the emergence of a modern Chinese state. The Xi'an Incident (or Xi'an Coup) in December of that year produced a new balance of tensions between Chiang Kai-shek's Nationalists and Mao's Communists. At issue was whether Chiang would lead a coalition in resisting Japanese aggression in north China or would concentrate his efforts on the Communists, whom he always saw as his arch rivals. The result, after intensive negotiations in which Zhou Enlai played a key role, was that China's two most influential political movements resumed cooperation against the invading Japanese forces—at least formally.

The standard view of the Xi'an Incident is that Zhang Xueliang (1901–2001) of Manchuria, son of the warlord Zhang Zuolin (1875–1928), set out to maneuver Chiang Kai-shek into renewed cooperation with the Chinese Communists in fighting the Japanese. It generally passes without notice that Zhang was joined in his efforts by Yang Hucheng ("Tiger City" Yang; 1893–1949). Yang Hucheng was a Shaanxi man, from Pucheng County northeast of

A temple on Hua Shan, one of five sacred Daoist mountains in China, 2006. The political center of China for thirteen dynasties, the province of Shaanxi features an assortment of historical attractions, including the Terracotta Army of the first Qin emperor and Hua Shan, one of the five mountains most revered in Daoist teaching. © FRANK LUKASSECK/CORBIS

Xi'an. He began his revolutionary career as a local activist during the 1911 Revolution and controlled the provincial government by the 1930s. Unlike Zhang Xueliang, Yang was not well educated, but he worked hard to develop Shaanxi. His political views were progressive and populist. When Zhang and Yang were prosecuted for perpetrating the Xi'an Incident, this difference in status was clearly recognized in the punishments. Zhang had better credentials and so was placed under house arrest by Chiang Kai-shek for as long as Chiang lived. Yang Hucheng, the less impressive figure, was sent on a "world inspection tour," but was arrested upon his return and later secretly executed (1949).

THE YAN'AN MODEL

Until relatively recent developments in scholarship outside China, the "Yan'an model" was regarded as the prototype for the People's Republic established in 1949. The idealistic populism of Yan'an, the "Red capital," provided a great contrast to Chiang Kai-shek's Nationalist capital in Chongqing. The American journalist Edgar Snow wrote enthusiastically of the Communist movement in his classic *Red Star over China* (1937), and many Chinese intellectuals went to Yan'an to contribute their talents to the movement. Their experiences perhaps made it easier for other intellectuals to remain in China after 1949. Yan'an lent appeal to the ultra-Maoist movement, the Cultural Revolution that began in 1966. Thus many foreign idealists continued to believe Beijing propaganda during the Cultural Revolution, and continued to admire the "Yan'an model" until they met individuals who described their personal hardships, or read the memoirs that began to appear in the 1980s. Although Yan'an provided popular mobilization and exemplified socialist culture, it also was the environment in which Mao Zedong's autocratic tendencies took shape in party organs and mass discipline. Recent scholarship outside China has reflected this more balanced appraisal.

REFORM PERIOD

Since about 1980, economic development has continued apace in Shaanxi as elsewhere. Despite its revolutionary role, Shaanxi people have regarded their province as backward and seriously underdeveloped. A visit to Xi'an today belies such a negative judgment, and the same can be said for many of the province's smaller cities. Much of the recent development is solidly based, featuring joint ventures and high-tech projects. Tourism has been important too, with Xi'an serving as the base for pilgrimages by hordes of visitors to the Qin founding emperor's mausoleum, with its terra-cotta warriors and horses (*bingma yong*) that date from 210 BCE. (This site is located in Lintong, about 40 kilometers east of Xi'an.) Some who come to see the terra-cotta army also visit the neolithic village site at Banpo, which previously had been Xi'an's major attraction.

SHAANXI

Capital city: Xi'an
Largest cities (population): Xi'an (7,530,000 [2006])
Area: 205,800 sq. km. (79,500 sq. mi.)
Population: 37,350,000 (2006)
Demographics: Han, 99.5%; Hui, 0.4%
GDP: CNY 452.3 billion (2006)
Famous sites: Famen Temple, Yangling Mausoleum Museum, Qian Mausoleum (Qianling), Yan'an, Banpo Neolithic village, Daqin Pagoda, Mount Hua, Mount Taibai, Qin Founding Emperor's Mausoleum

---

Yan'an is a secondary tourist destination, as are the other Shaanbei towns and cities and the region's eerily beautiful countryside. Highways have been vastly improved so that these places are less remote than before. Railways now link Xi'an and Yulin in the far north, with stops at most of the other larger places in Shaanbei. A new rail link southeastward from Xi'an has cut travel times to the southern city of Ankang and onward to eastern Sichuan and Hubei. Infrastructure developments such as these provide hope and a solid basis for development in the more remote parts of Shaanxi.

Mao Zedong greatly admired the Founding Qin Emperor. Mao and the Chinese Communists led a reunification of China too, albeit by force but also by balancing a set of communities and interests in ways perhaps not so different from those used by the Qin emperor. Shaanxi people rightly remain proud of their ancient heritage and culture. As modern development gains momentum in this formerly backward part of China, local people seek to retain the best of the past in their newer, more comfortable environment.

CONTEMPORARY SHAANXI
CULTURE

Much in the cultural life of Shaanxi today is related to the traditional earthbound culture. Peasant paintings from Hu County (*Hu xian*) west of Xi'an have attracted national and international attention. These paintings featured political themes in efforts to build socialism during the 1960s and 1970s; more recently they have displayed rural life in simple, colorful styles. Shaanxi also features a variety of other traditional folk arts, including papercuttings, many in a primitive folk style, which have made some older Shaanbei women famous throughout China. Other traditional arts such as bread sculpture are carried forward in marriage customs in Shaanbei.

The music of Shaanbei travels with natives when they leave home. The melodies and simple lyrics of this music resonate with foreigners who appreciate the folk music of their own cultures. Shaanxi also has its own regional style in traditional Chinese opera, known as *Qin qiang*; this is a shrill, even grating style that many natives adore, but is an acquired taste for foreigners. Some Shaanxi music features the *suona*, a simple wind instrument that produces sound at once shrill and plaintive.

One of China's most highly admired film directors, Zhang Yimou, got his start at the Xi'an Film Studio in the early 1980s. Zhang was among the first directors to draw world attention to Chinese cinema.

Shaanxi has produced several fiction writers with national and even international followings. Best known is Jia Pingwa, who achieved success with his early short stories on peasant life. During the 1990s he turned to longer novels. The first of these was *Fei du* (*The Abandoned Capital*; 1993), an obscene satire ostensibly about life in Xi'an, though many regarded it as the expression of the author's outrage at the government's leaders after June Fourth 1989 (the Tiananmen Square massacre).

Two other historical novels from the mid-1990s have attracted a nationwide readership. Gao Jianqun's *Zui hou yige Xiongnu* (*The Last Xiongnu*; 1993) linked the experiences of Shaanbei revolutionaries with the spirit of the ancient Xiongnu people who marauded in that area. Chen Zhongshi's *Bailu yuan* (*White Deer Plain*; 1993) followed the history of a small place in Shaanxi through the Republican era and its political vicissitudes, suggesting that change is difficult and might never have had much effect on village China. Both these novels have been reprinted, Chen's in the prestigious Mao Dun reprint series.

SEE ALSO *Jia Pingwa; Snow, Edgar; Xi'an; Yan'an.*

BIBLIOGRAPHY

Johnson, Ian. *Wild Grass: Three Stories of Change in Modern China.* New York: Pantheon, 2004.

Keating, Pauline. *Two Revolutions: Village Reconstruction and the Cooperative Movement in Northern Shaanxi, 1934–1945.* Stanford, CA: Stanford University Press, 1997.

Selden, Mark. *China in Revolution: The Yenan Way Revisited.* Armonk, NY: M. E. Sharpe, 1995.

Snow, Edgar. *Red Star over China.* 1937. New York: Grove Press, 1994.

Vermeer, Eduard B. *Economic Development in Provincial China: Central Shaanxi since 1930.* Cambridge, U.K.: Cambridge University Press, 1988.

Edward S. Krebs

SHANDONG

This coastal province of Shandong is 156,700 square kilometers, about the size of Mexico. Since the 1980s, Shandong has participated in the remarkable economic growth so thoroughly transforming China. This new prosperity reverses the

---

SHANDONG

Capital city: Jinan
Largest cities (population): Qingdao (8,178,500 [2005]), Jining (8,118,000 [2006]), Yantai (6,500,000 [2006]), Jinan (6,030,000 [2006])
Area: 156,700 sq. km. (60,500 sq. mi.)
Population: 93,670,000 (2007)
Demographics: Han, 99.3%; Hui, 0.6%
GDP: CNY 2.18 trillion (2007)
Famous sites: Yellow River, Grand Canal, Mount Tai, Qufu (home of Confucius), Dai Temple at Taian, Penglai Pavilion, Mount Lao near Qingdao

---

province's previous reputation as the home of poverty-stricken farmers. A triangle connecting Jinan with Yantai and Qingdao on the Shandong Peninsula is the richest section both agriculturally and industrially.

The 2000 census recorded Shandong's population as 90.8 million, making it the second most populous province after Henan, its western neighbor. Many poor farming families still live in western Shandong, often on land that has been rendered alkaline by the lowering of North China's water table. In 2007 Shandong's estimated population was 93.67 million, giving it a population density of 592 per kilometer.

GEOGRAPHY

Sixty-five percent of Shandong's land is part of the broad alluvial North China plain. A limestone massif lies in the center, and includes the sacred peak Taishan. The long thumb of the Shandong Peninsula projects eastward and contains low rounded hills and small fertile basins. The peninsula divides the shallow Bohai Gulf from the Yellow Sea. The weather on the peninsula is much more temperate than the main part of the province, where a continental climate prevails, with hot, humid, rainy summers and cold, dry winters.

Over the past two millennia, the mighty Yellow (Huang) River flooded regularly, producing different river courses across Shandong. Sometimes the Yellow River flowed, as it now does, north into the Bohai Gulf, and at other times it flowed south of the Shandong Peninsula into the Yellow Sea. Today, the river is a shallow shadow of its former self. The combination of diversions and irrigation projects, along with

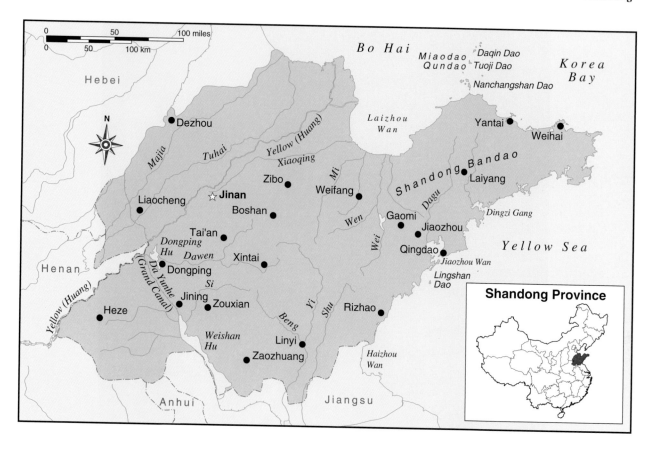

the steady depletion of the North China water table, has mostly ended the flood threat.

The Shandong Peninsula has long presented a challenge to coastal navigation. Consequently, until the steamship era, the movement of surplus grain from the Yangzi River Valley to the Chinese political capital at Beijing was accomplished by means of an inland canal, the famous Grand Canal that runs across the western part of Shandong Province. By the mid-twentieth century, the Grand Canal had ceased to function as a significant transport system. Today, it is only in use south of Jining and is of little economic importance.

Navigation across the Bohai Gulf proved much easier. In fact, during the Ming dynasty (1368–1644), Shandong administered parts of Liaoning Province. After the mid-nineteenth century, streams of emigrants from Shandong peninsular ports traveled across the Bohai Gulf to China's northeast, then known as Manchuria.

Prior to 1900, Shandong had a well-developed agricultural economy producing winter wheat, cotton, sorghum, and tobacco, as well as tussah silk cloth and handicraft specialties of embroidery and glass. The Yellow River proved too treacherous for shipping, but the Grand Canal was useful. Smaller rivers carried considerable trade, as did primitive roads.

IMPERIALISM IN SHANDONG

Shandong was of minor importance to Western imperialism until the Sino-Japanese War of 1895 brought a surge of interest. In 1898 the British had taken Weihaiwei as a naval base, while the Germans occupied a colony at Qingdao. The Germans also developed Qingdao as a naval base while building a railroad connecting with the provincial capital, Jinan.

The Boxer Uprising, in which armed rural residents attacked Chinese Christians and foreign missionaries, began in western inland Shandong in 1899 and spread across large parts of North China. The tide of violence passed quickly, and by the time of the Qing dynasty's collapse in 1911, Shandong was connected to the world by modern railways, ports, and telegraph. The Germans developed coal mines around the present-day city of Zibo for their railway and navy. Farther south, along the Beijing-Shanghai line, the mines at Zaozhuang began producing high-quality coal suitable for coking. Modern communication fed an increasing flow of settlers from overcrowded Shandong into Manchuria, while also stimulating internal commerce.

Early in World War I (1914–1918), the Germans lost their colony at Qingdao to the Japanese. The Treaty of Versailles confirmed the Japanese claim. Japanese businesses developed export industries in Shandong, including cotton-spinning mills at Qingdao. Even after returning

Visitors climbing Mount Tai, Shandong, June, 1981. *While much of Shandong features flat land well suited to cotton and wheat crops, a group of mountains rise in the center of the province. One of these mountains, Mount Tai, pictured here, is recognized as one of the five most sacred mountains in the Dao tradition.* © **LOWELL GEORGIA/CORBIS**

Qingdao to Chinese administration in 1922, the Japanese retained financial control of the railroad, as well as major industrial and commercial interests in eastern Shandong. In the first half of the twentieth century, Shandong prospered modestly through a combination of its traditional agricultural output of wheat, cotton, and sorghum, as well as handicraft silk and embroidery, plus new export lines such as straw hats, peanuts, and coal.

Shandong's government during the Republican period (1911–1949) lay in the hands of warlords, most of whom rapaciously extracted taxes and conscripted men to support their armies. Chiang Kai-shek's (Jiang Jieshi's) Nationalist government never gained control of the province after 1927.

In 1937 Japan occupied Shandong, holding the cities, railroads, and major roads until Japan's surrender in 1945. During those years, there were Chinese Communist guerrilla bases in Shandong, especially in the remote parts of the province. These bases formed part of the Shanxi-Hebei-Shandong-Henan base area, where Deng Xiaoping served as political commissar.

SHANDONG AFTER 1949

Building on earlier guerrilla activities in Shandong, the Communist Party placed dedicated leaders in the province, including the infamous Kang Sheng (1898–1975), during the Civil War and the subsequent period of land reform in the early 1950s. The province lost most overseas trade connections through the American-led trade embargo imposed on China. The province's two main cities, Qingdao and Jinan, developed several major industries, including the manufacturing of automobiles, railway equipment, and other heavy machinery. The area around the present-day city of Zibo also became home to many industries, including electrical generation, chemicals, aluminum, ceramics, and glass. In 1961 the Shengli (Victory) oilfield was discovered near the mouth of the Yellow River. This oilfield is now China's second largest and is centered around Dongying city.

Rural reforms beginning in 1980 freed Shandong farmers from collective agriculture and eased poverty. After twenty-five years of liberal economic reform, Shandong thrives on a combination of domestic industry and sizable foreign investment, especially investment on the Shandong Peninsula from nearby South Korea and Japan. The eastern corridor includes the four largest municipalities—Jinan Qingdao, Zibo, and Yantai—all with populations of two to three million people. Railways throughout the province have been modernized, and Shandong claims to have the most extensive network of modern freeways in China. Major industrial companies, both domestic and international, are found in all major cities. Data from 2004 set Shandong's gross domestic product at 2.18 trillion renminbi (about $23.7 billion) and its per capita income at 23,546 renminbi (about $3,000).

SEE ALSO *Jinan; Qingdao.*

BIBLIOGRAPHY

Buck, David D. *Urban Change in China: Politics and Development in Tsinan, Shantung, 1890–1949.* Madison: University of Wisconsin Press, 1978.

Chang Liu. *Peasants and Revolution in Rural China: Rural Political Change in the North China Plain and Yangzi River Delta, 1890–1949.* London: Routledge, 2007.

Chengrui Mei and Harold E. Dregne. Silt and the Future Development of China's Yellow River: A Review Article. *Geographical Journal* 167, 1 (2001): 7–22.

Cohen, Paul. *History in Three Keys: The Boxers as Event, Experience, and Myth.* New York: Columbia University Press, 1997.

Goodman, David S. G. Jinjiluyu in the Sino-Japanese War: The Border Region and the Border Government. *China Quarterly* 140 (1994): 1007–1024.

Jae Ho Chung. A Sub-provincial Recipe for Coastal Development in China: The Case of Qingdao. *China Quarterly* 160 (1999): 919–952.

Jinghao Sun. City, State, and the Grand Canal: Jining's Identity and Transformation, 1289–1927. Ph.D. diss., University of Toronto, 2007.

Pomeranz, Kenneth. *Making of a Hinterland: State, Society, and Economy in North China, 1853–1937.* Berkeley: University of California Press, 1993.

David D. Buck

SHANGHAI

The city of Shanghai is located on the western coast of the Pacific Ocean and right at the T-junction of the mouth of the Yangzi River and the central section of China's coastline. Geologically, Shanghai is part of the alluvial plain that makes up the Yangzi Delta, and the Huangpu River (a branch of the Yangzi) and the Suzhou River (a branch of the Huangpu) run through the city. It is part of the North Asia subtropical monsoon climate region, and has four distinct seasons and ample sunshine and rainfall.

Shanghai Municipality, which is administered directly by the Chinese central government, occupies an area of 2,448 square miles (6,341 square kilometers), nearly ten times the size of Singapore. It includes ten urban districts that make up the city proper or central area, eight suburban districts, and one county. The central area covers 794 square miles (2,057 square kilometers)—about twice the size of the land area of New York City—of which more than 116 square miles (300 square kilometers) is built-up and densely populated. This area has been rapidly expanding in recent years as a result of a construction boom. The newest and most dazzling urban district is Pudong (literally, "east of the Huangpu River"), which developed at the turn of the twenty-first century from an area of factories, warehouses, and farmland into an advanced business and financial center. The municipality also encompasses about thirty islands in the Yangzi River and along the coast of the East China Sea, including China's third-largest island, Chongming Dao.

Shanghai's port, unfrozen all year around, is one of the largest in China, accounting for nearly one-fifth of the

Chinese immigrants from the Jiangnan region and Canton (Guangdong) generally did well in the city, whereas people from Subei (north of Jiangsu Province) typically worked as poor laborers. Migration came to a halt in the early 1950s, and since then virtually all members of the city's younger generation were Shanghai-born. Beginning in the late 1990s, however, new waves of migration have increased the population markedly. A "floating population" of over six million were living in the city in 2008, which means one in three people in Shanghai have moved from another province (Dong Hui 2008).

The Shanghai dialect, which linguistically belongs to the Wu dialect, was originally a branch of the dialect of Songjiang Prefecture, of which Shanghai was a subordinate county. In the first few decades of the treaty-port era, the Shanghai dialect essentially retained its original form. To this day this dialect is still spoken by people in the vicinity of Shanghai, especially in the districts of Nanhui, Fengxian, and Songjiang. The modern Shanghai dialect, the one spoken in Shanghai proper, diverged from its source by absorbing influences from the dialects of Suzhou and Ningbo, two areas that provided many immigrants early in the twentieth century. This makes the Shanghai dialect the youngest in China. Most residents also speak Putonghua (Mandarin), which is the language of instruction in all schools from kindergarten to university. English is the most common second language; those aged forty and younger are more likely to speak English with a certain level of fluency.

"GOOD OLD SHANGHAI"

Shanghai began more than 1,000 years ago as a small market town. The name *Shanghai* literally means "upper sea," which was originally the name of a branch of the Wusong River (now known as the Suzhou River). Shanghai also is known commonly by two epithets: *Hu* and *Shen*. Both have historical roots: *Hu* was an ancient bamboo fishing instrument that was widely used along the Wusong River, and *Shen* is derived from Lord Chunshen (d. 238 BCE), a noble of the state of Chu who governed the Wu area, of which Shanghai was a part, and helped develop the local irrigation system. Shanghai became a county seat in 1292 during the Yuan (Mongol) dynasty (1279–1368) and enjoyed centuries of prosperity as a cotton and textile-based commercial center up to the Opium War (1839–1842).

Following the provisions of the Treaty of Nanjing (1842) that ended the Opium War and a supplementary agreement signed in 1843, the ruling Qing (Manchu) dynasty opened Shanghai to British trade and residence. Other Western countries demanded and received similar privileges. Modern China's largest foreign concessions, known as the International Settlement, which was controlled by the British and Americans, and the French Concession, were set up north of the original walled Chinese city

country's total cargo volume handled in coastal ports. Major highways and railroads radiate from Shanghai to all of China's major cities and towns. The city's subway system, launched in 1995, was being expanded in 2008; it had well over two million riders on an average day in 2007. In 2000 a state-of-the-art and fully modern international airport in Pudong started operation (giving Shanghai a second airport, in addition to the Hongqiao International Airport in the southwest suburb), further elevating the city to the status of an advanced modern metropolis. A maglev train service began in 2004; in 2008 there were plans to extend it to nearby cities such as Hangzhou.

POPULATION AND DIALECT

In 2008 the permanent, registered population of the Shanghai urban agglomeration, including migrants who stayed in the city for six months or more, reached 18.58 million, making it China's largest city. The population of Shanghai increased tenfold from about half a million in 1842 to five million in 1949. Before 1949, approximately 80 percent of Shanghai's residents were immigrants from elsewhere in China and about 3 percent were foreign-born.

NANJING ROAD

Nanjing Road (Nanjing Lu), Shanghai's main commercial street, served in different periods as a symbol of colonial grandeur, imperialist intervention, and postsocialist consumerism. It originated in 1851 as Park Lane and was popularly known as the Great Horse Road (Da Maloo). Paved with elegant wood bricks in 1908, Nanking Road became the retail center of the International Concession by the 1910s. The establishment of department stores—first Lane Crawford and Whitelaws, later Sincere (Xianshi) and Wing On (Yong'an)—introduced Western shop-window dressing and marketing strategies. A visitor to Nanjing Road could enjoy a display of modish couture and world-class architecture, such as the Cathay Hotel (now Peace Hotel, built in 1926–1928), the Continental Emporium Building (now Donghai Building, built in 1931–1932), and Da Sun Department Store (now Shanghai No. 1 Department Store, built in 1934–1936). People came to Nanjing Road not only to buy but also to watch and be watched.

Situated between the Bund to the east and Horse Race Club to the west, and the site of international enterprises such as the British-American Tobacco Company, Nanjing Road was associated with foreign control over China's resources. After the Communist takeover in 1949, the road was transformed, together with the adjacent horse racetrack, which was converted into the People's Square and People's Park in 1952. A political campaign that peaked in 1963, Emulating the Good Eighth Company of Nanjing Road (Xiang Nanjing Lu Shang Hao Balian Xuexi), targeted the street, with its jazz bars and neon lights, as a den of counterrevolutionary recalcitrance. Since the economic reforms of the 1980s, Nanjing Road once again became a bustling center of shopping and tourism. In 1999 Nanjing East Road was redesigned as a pedestrian mall 1 kilometer (0.6 miles) long. Nanjing West Road, Bubbling Well Road of the colonial period, is home to landmarks such as the Broadcasting and TV Building, the Plaza GG and Tomorrow Square malls, and the Portman Ritz-Carlton Hotel.

BIBLIOGRAPHY

Braester, Yomi. "A Big Dying Vat": The Vilifying of Shanghai during the Good Eighth Company Campaign. *Modern China* 31, 4 (October 2005): 411–447.

Cochran, Sherman, ed. *Inventing Nanjing Road: Commercial Culture in Shanghai, 1900–1945*. Ithaca, NY: East Asia Program, Cornell University, 1999.

Yomi Braester

and practically became a state within a state. Over the next eighty years Shanghai developed a distinctly Western character and underwent a period of important commercial, industrial, and political development, earning for itself nicknames such as "Pearl of the Orient," "Paris of the East," and "Chinese New York." During this time there emerged in Shanghai a distinctive urban culture known as *Haipai* (Shanghai school, or Shanghai style).

The term *Haipai* was coined in the late nineteenth century to refer to Shanghai-style painting and Shanghai-style Peking Opera. Later, it was used in literary circles and figured prominently in a debate over literature and politics in 1933 and 1934 between hinterland-based authors, represented by Shen Congwen (1902–1988), and writers in Shanghai. Since the 1930s the terms *Jingpai* (Beijing school) and *Haipai* have been used broadly to refer to the general cultural differences between Shanghai and the hinterlands (represented by Beijing). Haipai culture is generally perceived as open, liberal, and receptive to Western influences. Shanghai's lead in fashion, publishing, journalism, avant-garde arts, modern drama, and motion pictures enhanced its image as China's most Westernized city.

Shanghai reached its zenith in the 1920s and 1930s. Trade and industries prospered and a modern urban culture flourished. Politically, the city was the "backyard" of the Nationalist government, which set the capital in Nanjing, as most top government leaders, including Chiang Kai-shek (1887–1975), had residences in Shanghai and often held behind-closed-doors decision-making meetings there before official announcements were made to the public. Japan bombarded the Chinese part of the city in 1937 and soon occupied it. But Shanghai's foreign concessions were protected by the Western powers and became a safe haven for business and refugees in the vast Japanese-occupied areas, earning the city the name *Solitary Island*. Among the refugees were about 30,000 Jews who fled from Nazi Germany, because at this time Shanghai was the only port in the world that did not require an entry visa or a passport. Japan finally occupied the entire city during the Pacific War (1941–1945), ending Shanghai's wartime boom. After the war

Shanghai reemerged as China's major domestic and international trading, banking, and shipping center, but the Chinese civil war (1946–1949) interrupted Shanghai's growth.

UNDER COMMUNISM

The Communists took over Shanghai in May 1949 with minimal bloodshed and little damage to the city. Shanghai, which had about five million residents at the time, was designated as one of the three municipalities (the other two were Beijing and Tianjin) that would be directly administered by the central government. The new regime described Shanghai as the "birthplace of the Communist Party" and a city with a "glorious revolutionary tradition," but it also viewed the city as a "bridgehead of Western imperialism," strongly imbued with a capitalist economy and bourgeois culture that conflicted with Communist ideology. Nonetheless, Shanghai continued to be China's leading industrial center, satisfying China's domestic needs and providing a substantial portion of its national revenue. In 1978 the Shanghai Municipality outranked all of China's provinces, accounting for 8 percent of total national income, 13 percent of gross industrial output, and 30 percent of exports. The city was indeed a cash cow, with 87 percent of the revenues it generated between 1949 and 1983 being taken by the central government, a figure higher than anywhere else in China. Up to the early 1980s, on average, Shanghai contributed nearly one-sixth of China's total revenue. As a result, many much-needed investments in infrastructure and urban development in the city were delayed (Lu 2004, p. 255).

In 1984 Shanghai, together with thirteen modestly developed coastal cities and towns, was designated an "open city," that is, open to foreign investment. But the designation of Shanghai as an economic development zone rather than a special economic zone (SEZ) downplayed the role of Shanghai at the national level. Overall, Shanghai took a backseat in China's economic reform during the 1980s, when southern cities such as Guangzhou and the SEZs in Guangdong and Fujian became the sites of huge foreign investments and trade.

But by the early 1990s the revitalization of Shanghai as China's economic powerhouse had already started. In the wake of the Tiananmen Incident of 1989, Jiang Zemin (b. 1926) rose from mayor of Shanghai to general secretary of the Chinese Communist Party (CCP). Premier Zhu Rongji (b. 1928), the prime mover of China's economic reform in the 1990s, also had served as Shanghai's mayor. The rise of these Shanghai officials to national leadership apparently accelerated the development of Shanghai. But the architect of Shanghai's growth was Deng Xiaoping (1904–1997) himself. In his 1992 "inspection tour of the south," Deng urged the further opening of Shanghai and expressed his regret that Shanghai had not been designated a SEZ in the early 1980s.

THE RESURGENCE OF A GREAT CITY

The opening of Shanghai's Pudong area in the early 1990s for investment and development signaled the city's return to the forefront of Chinese economic reform. Plans were underway to make Shanghai the "dragonhead" of development of the Yangzi River Basin and beyond. These plans have developed the city into an international center of finance, export processing, business services, and high-tech industries. The Shanghai Stock Exchange, reestablished in 1991, is the largest in mainland China, the third largest in Asia (after Tokyo and Hong Kong), and the fifth largest in the world. Along with its reemergence as China's financial center, the city also is working toward regaining its position as China's leading industrial base. The Baosteel Group Corporation, made up a number of state-owned companies merged in 1998 to form China's largest iron and steel conglomerate, is ranked among the world's top 500 companies by *Fortune* magazine. China's superscale petrochemical industrial center, the Shanghai Chemical Industrial Park, is located in Shanghai's Jinshan District near the Hangzhou Bay. Other industries, such as electronics and information technology, automobile manufacturing, and power generation, are also undergoing tremendous growth.

Since the mid-1990s Shanghai has been one of the world's fastest-growing metropolitan economies. The building frenzy of the 1990s and early 2000s has physically changed the city at a rate rarely seen in urban history. In the early 1980s the twenty-four-story Park Hotel that had towered over Shanghai for half a century was the tallest building in the city, and there were only four other buildings in the entire city that reached the height of twenty stories. By 1999 Shanghai had 1,350 buildings that were higher than twenty stories, nearly all of which were built in the 1990s. The reshaping of the landscape of Shanghai was such that in the late 1990s, every three months on average the authorities had to print a new version of the city map. Nearly 1,000 high-rise buildings were added to Shanghai's landscape in the first eight years of the twenty-first century. As a result of the building frenzy, much of the old city was literally destroyed. In particular, the *shikumen*, a type of row house unique to Shanghai, which throughout much of the twentieth century housed about 80 percent of Shanghai residents, succumbed to the bulldozer at an alarming rate.

One of the most important advantages of Shanghai is its human resources. For more than a century, the city has been China's leading intellectual powerhouse and the cradle of modernity. Although this tradition was suppressed during Mao's times, in the 2000s it was undergoing a renaissance, implementing a comprehensive strategy of revitalizing the city by promoting science and education. The number of university students increased steadily during the 1990s and by the early twenty-first century was more than double that of the late 1980s. Nearly half of all

Nanjing Road, Shanghai, c. 2002. *One of the largest port cities in China, Shanghai served as an important center of international trade before the establishment of the People's Republic of China. As the government reopened the city to foreign investment in the 1990s, Shanghai has once again become a prosperous business hub, undergoing a radical building boom to accommodate the new prosperity and population growth.* © LIU LIQUN/CORBIS

university graduates in the 2000s were from science and engineering programs.

Shanghai is often seen as the primary competitor of Beijing. Shanghai's successful bid for the World Exposition in 2010, the first registered expo in a developing country, was widely viewed as the central government's way of assuaging Shanghai's envy of Beijing's hosting the Summer Olympics in 2008. Politically, Shanghai has been under the shadow of Beijing since the establishment of the Communist regime, but Shanghai-based leaders frequently have played significant roles in the central government, giving rise to the epithet *Shanghai clique.* The best-known Shanghai faction was the Gang of Four, headed by Mao's wife, Jiang Qing (1914–1991), which rose to power from Shanghai during the Cultural Revolution (1966–1976). More

recently, a group of top Communist leaders led by Jiang Zemin were promoted from Shanghai to key positions in the central government after the Tiananmen Incident of 1989. Since then it is said that some leaders in Beijing harbor ill will against the Shanghai clique.

The rivalry between Shanghai and Hong Kong for status (particularly in the economic arena) is another tale of two cities in modern China. Both cities are situated in China's richest delta areas and are important gateways to the mainland. Both cities have extensive experience with the West and are known for their busy ports and other links to world trade. Both cities have a distinguished commercial culture that has been nourished in large measure by a modern Western entrepreneurial spirit. Historically, Shanghai was more prominent than Hong Kong in the pre-Communist era, but it became virtually closed off from the rest of the world after 1949, allowing Hong Kong to enjoy a monopoly on trade and business in the region for decades prior to the 1990s. The resurgence of Shanghai in the early years of the twenty-first century encouraged some to think that Hong Kong's dominance as a trading and financial center might diminish. More sober-minded assessments hold that the two cities can have a mutually beneficial relationship.

In comparison to other major cities in the developed world, Shanghai has yet to establish firmly the rule of law, which is a prerequisite to institutionalized accountability, transparency, and the free flow of information. These are essential to conducting business and forming a culture that will make Shanghai a first-class world city.

SEE ALSO *Jiangsu; Special Economic Zones; Treaty Ports; Urban China: Cities and Urbanization, 1800–1949; Urban China: Organizing Principles of Cities; Urban China: Urban Planning since 1978.*

BIBLIOGRAPHY

Cochran, Sherman, ed. *Inventing Nanjing Road: Commercial Culture in Shanghai, 1900–1945.* Ithaca, NY: Cornell University East Asia Program, 1999.

Dong Hui. Census Will Update Population Records. *Shanghai Daily,* October 31, 2008.

Farrer, James. *Opening Up: Youth Sex Culture and Market Reform in Shanghai.* Chicago: University of Chicago Press, 2002.

Goodman, Bryna. *Native Place, City, and Nation: Regional Networks and Identities in Shanghai, 1853–1937.* Berkeley: University of California Press, 1995.

Honig, Emily. *Creating Chinese Ethnicity: Subei People in Shanghai, 1850–1980.* New Haven, CT: Yale University Press, 1992.

Lee, Leo Ou-fan. *Shanghai Modern: The Flowering of a New Urban Culture in China, 1930–1945.* Cambridge, MA: Harvard University Press, 1999.

Leung Yuen-sang. *The Shanghai Taotai: Linkage Man in a Changing Society, 1843–90.* Honolulu: University of Hawaii Press, 1990.

Lu, Hanchao. *Beyond the Neon Lights: Everyday Shanghai in the Early Twentieth Century.* Berkeley: University of California Press, 1999.

Lu, Hanchao. Nostalgia for the Future: The Resurgence of an Alienated Culture in China. *Pacific Affairs* 75, 2 (Summer 2002): 169–186.

Lu, Hanchao. Shanghai Rising: Resurgence of China's New York City? In *Urban Transformation in China,* 250–265. Aldershot, U.K.: Ashgate, 2004.

Shanghai Nianjian Bianzuan Weiyuanhui, comp. *Shanghai nianjian* [Shanghai yearbook]. Vols. 1996–2007. Shanghai: Shanghai Renmin Chubanshe, 1996–1997; Shanghai Nianjian She, 1998–2007.

Wakeman, Frederic, Jr., and Wen-hsin Yeh, eds. *Shanghai Sojourners.* Berkeley: University of California Institute of East Asian Studies, 1992.

Xiong Yuezhi, ed. *Shanghai tongshi* [Shanghai general history]. 15 vols. Shanghai: Shanghai Renmin Chubanshe, 1999.

Yatsko, Pamela. *New Shanghai: The Rocky Rebirth of China's Legendary City.* Hoboken, NJ: John Wiley and Sons, 2000.

Yeh, Wen-Hsin. *Shanghai Splendor: Economic Sentiments and the Making of Modern China, 1843–1949.* Berkeley: University of California Press, 2007.

Hanchao Lu

SHANGHAI MIXED COURT

Famous at the time as the largest court in the world, the International Mixed Court of Shanghai was created in 1864 and brought to an end in 1927. It spanned a succession of national and local governments in China and survived several rounds of calls for its abolition. The court was controversial because it typified the foreign intrusion into China's politics, economy, and society that was rampant in the late nineteenth and early twentieth centuries. Created by an agreement that was forced upon the Chinese emperor by British and American military officers, the court then went on to assume powers over Chinese defendants that went well beyond what was contemplated in the agreement. At the same time, the court's multinational character made it a pioneer of a genre of tribunal with a multinational judicial bench, variations on which were later founded in the French Concession of Shanghai, Tianjin, Ningbo, Hankou, and then beyond China, in Egypt and the Hague, and among which can be counted today's international commercial arbitration tribunals.

The International Mixed Court of Shanghai provided an important beachhead for foreign activities in China during this semicolonial period and a model for later tribunals with multinational jurisdictions. In addition, it served as the linchpin of the legal system of Shanghai as the city evolved from a Chinese fishing port to an international financial, trading, and investment center. The court reinforced the city's autonomy from national government as it resisted efforts by Chinese officials to draw it into a hierarchical system of appeals up to the Chinese capital. By deciding lawsuits related to Shanghai's growing infrastructure and burgeoning real estate market, the court facilitated the commodification of the city's land. The urban landscape was transformed by a skyline of skyscrapers, and streets were busy with motorized transport and lined with world-class factories, imposing civic institutions, elegant apartment buildings, and state-of-the-art telecommunications. By deciding contract disputes, the court eased barriers to entry to business during a period of expansion of the local economy and its opening to the international economy. And, by enforcing the local foreign government's regulations, the court strengthened foreign control over Shanghai.

CREATION

Starting with the signing of the Treaty of Nanjing in 1842, a series of bilateral treaties between China and sixteen foreign governments granted the foreign governments limited rights over their own nationals while in China. In that same year Shanghai's new International Settlement was created by British consul-general Captain George Balfour, who obtained consent from the Chinese government for British consular officials in Shanghai to act as sole leasor of all the land within that territory, and in 1853 British consul-general Rutherford Alcock turned the International Settlement into an autonomous municipality with the backing of the British navy and collaboration by Americans and other foreign consuls.

Dissatisfied with the original set-up of Shanghai's court, which conceded greater power to the Chinese, Balfour and the Shanghai *daotai* (prefect) signed an agreement on April 20, 1869, that set up a tribunal in which Chinese and British officials would jointly try lawsuits in the International Settlement. The Chinese name of the court was the *Yangjingbang* (formerly *Yangkingpang*) *sheguan*—"the official installed (north of) the Yangkingpang creek," after the creek that divided the International Settlement from the French Concession, a similar zone carved out of an area just outside the city wall by French diplomats in 1849. The English name of the agreement was the "Mixed Court Rules." The agreement contained many limits on the court's jurisdiction, and reserved to other Chinese authorities in the area some jurisdiction over Chinese in the International Settlement, such as the right to arrest Chinese there without permission or assistance from the settlement's foreign police. The Zongli Yamen, which functioned as the emperor's foreign affairs department, approved the agreement, though Prince Gong (1833–1898), who headed the Zongli Yamen, withdrew his recognition of the court by 1880.

INTERNATIONAL BENCH

The English name of the court, the "International Mixed Court," referred to the character of its bench, which was composed of one Chinese judge and another judge—an "assessor"—who was a citizen of one of the treaty powers that enjoyed extraterritorial rights. The agreement that established the court excluded France, which set up its own Mixed Court for Shanghai four years later, but over the years it did not impede the participation of Americans, Germans, Japanese, Italians, Portuguese, Austro-Hungarians, Dutch, Russian, and Spanish on the bench of the court. The Chinese judge handed down decisions in cases involving only Chinese parties, whereas the foreign judge handed down decisions in cases where one of the parties was foreign. The foreign member of the bench was called an "assessor" in a bow to the original plan to keep his status below that of a judge. The assessors usually were drawn from the ranks of vice-consuls. Chosen mainly for their fluency in Chinese,

many of them lacked legal training and often lacked even the motivation to work hard on the Mixed Court's bench, owing in part to a dim view of the court by the diplomatic corps. Assessors enjoyed lengthy lunch hours, annual vacations back home, and short tours of duty at the court. The judge and assessor were supposed to deliberate together in each case, but defer to the one who was going to hand down the decision. This rule did not prevent tensions on the bench, nor did it shield the bench from tensions among the assessors' bosses, the foreign consuls-general stationed in Shanghai.

In the first few decades the prefect of Shanghai, who was then a part of the Chinese imperial bureaucracy, appointed the Chinese judge, and the appointment was ranked lower than the lowest-level judges in that bureaucracy. This process continued after relations between the imperial government and the Mixed Court soured in 1905, and even after the imperial government was overthrown in 1912, but beyond the formalities, foreign officials' influence over the appointments grew.

This growing foreign influence at the court finally prompted an objection from the Shanghai prefect in 1905. Spurred by the British judge's decisions to send all female Chinese convicted at the court to a prison controlled by the foreign government of the International Settlement, known as the Shanghai Municipal Council, the Chinese prefect ordered the Chinese judge at the court to maintain control over the custody of one such woman, the widow of a wealthy mandarin official from Sichuan province. The police force of the Shanghai Municipal Council had arrested her while she was passing through the International Settlement and charged her with kidnapping for having in her retinue several young girls whom she had purchased to be her slaves. The assistants to the Chinese judge came to blows with the police, and the police emerged victorious. The foreigners who appointed the court's judges used this incident as a pretext for increasing their control of the operations of the court. Thereafter, Municipal Police officers watched all court hearings, and all revenues from the court flowed into the budget of the Shanghai Municipal Council, which since 1898 had bankrolled the salaries of the court's employees and the overhead to operate its facilities.

After the end of imperial rule in China in 1912, foreign consuls in Shanghai extended even further their control over the court, finding ways to exert more influence on the choice of the Chinese judge at the Mixed Court. World War I unleashed a round of efforts to remove Germans from the triumvirate known as the "major treaty powers"—Great Britain, the United States, and Germany—who had monopolized the judicial work of the court.

JURISDICTION AND CASELOAD

The treaties of the mid-nineteenth century granted immunity from Chinese law to foreigners. Thus the principle that defendants are sued in their own courts became the cornerstone of the system of extraterritoriality. Though this principle on its face treated Chinese and foreigners equally, the operation of two court systems—the consular courts and the mixed courts—in Shanghai and most of the other treaty ports led to inequity in the application of the principle. Whereas foreigners had to be sued in the consular courts, Chinese did not have to be sued in courts established and run solely by the Chinese government, but could be dragged into the Mixed Court as defendants. For them, the Mixed Court in Shanghai, and its counterparts in other cities and in the French Concession of Shanghai, had to be counted as a "Chinese" court for this purpose. There was no real reciprocity.

Did treatment of Chinese defendants in the International Mixed Court actually fail to give them the home-field advantage enjoyed by foreign defendants in the consular courts? The Mixed Court was supposed to apply Chinese law in its decisions involving Chinese plaintiffs suing Chinese defendants, and there is little evidence to suggest that foreign law was applied in such decisions. Where Chinese did not enjoy the advantage they might have gained from familiar law was when foreigners sued them at the Mixed Court. Then a foreign judge handed down the decision and in practice departed from Chinese law in arriving at that decision.

Criminal prosecutions at the Mixed Court put Chinese defendants at the greatest disadvantage. Serving time in one of the prisons attached to the court meant doing hard labor in a chain gang, a term that may have been invented by the Shanghai Municipal Police. Some convicts were sentenced to humiliating and painful corporal punishments, such as a certain number of days in the *cangue*, a Chinese-style stock or large wooden cuff for the neck, on a public street. By contrast, foreigners could be sentenced to punishments for crimes only by their consular courts and were confined usually to small jails run on the property of the consulate. Such facilities were relatively lax, and the grounds were on tree-lined streets in one of the loveliest sections of town.

The court's broad subject matter and collaboration with a zealous local police force led to a caseload that reached one million or so cases filed over sixty-three years, prompting the French scholar Jean Escarra to call it the largest court in the world. The caseload grew steadily throughout that period, possibly influenced by the growth of Shanghai's population and by the Shanghai Municipal Police's paranoia about Communism.

The court heard criminal cases, civil cases, and cases in which the defendants were charged with minor violations of municipal regulations passed by the Shanghai Municipal Council, a foreign body made up of members elected by foreign "ratepayers" in the International Settlement of Shanghai. Ratepayers were those who held title to land in the Settlement, title which functioned as close to ownership as was possible in a system where the entire settlement was leased (albeit forcibly) by the Chinese government to the foreigners for their long-term but not indefinite use. The vast majority of the court's cases involved enforcement of the municipal regulations.

Civil cases were divided into two categories, those involving at least one foreigner, and those involving only Chinese parties. The latter far outnumbered the former. Chinese residents outnumbered foreign residents in the International Settlement, and residence determined where in the city a Chinese had to be sued. The procedures of the court slightly favored plaintiffs, and therefore both foreigners and Chinese might have felt encouraged to litigate there.

PRO-PLAINTIFF PROCEDURE

Plaintiffs went to little expense or trouble to secure a judgment from the Mixed Court. All lawsuits were supposed to begin with the plaintiff's filing a short, boilerplate petition with the register of the court. Even this simple requirement was eased, in practice, by Chinese judges accepting petitions during hearings, by the registrar accepting petitions forwarded from foreign consulates, and by judges dispensing with petitions altogether in land and rent cases. In the latter circumstances, all the landlord had to do was to ask the court for an order to board up the rented premises, providing little more than the names and addresses of the renters. In the last few decades of the court's operation, the landlord then took the order to the police station nearest the property in question, and the police there immediately boarded up the premises. The speedier this process, the more advantageous to the landlord, because the tenant was thereby prevented from moving out his personal possessions. Once the landlord had separated the tenant from his possessions, the landlord gained greater leverage to extract payment from the tenant, or he could sell the possessions himself.

Plaintiffs were fairly well assured that the judgment would be enforced. Cases, once filed, did not have much time to settle because judgment usually came swiftly, so those who wanted to use the threat of litigation to spur settlement could do so. Before 1905, Chinese imperial staff called "runners" delivered the orders of the court and were responsible for executing them. In 1905 the British and American-run Shanghai Municipal Police took over this function and performed it enthusiastically and efficiently.

The effectiveness of the court favored plaintiffs because the speed of the process gave defendants little or no time to prepare their defense, and the truncated nature of the process, especially in landlord-tenant cases, required little expenditure of time or effort for the plaintiff to supply what the court deemed necessary to rule in its favor. Though plaintiffs at the Mixed Court were sometimes foreign, defendants there were never foreign, so foreigners never suffered the burden of swift judgments against them (except as losing plaintiffs, failing to get anything from victorious defendants). By contrast, a defendant who lost could go to debtors prison, where he also was kept during the period from the serving of the summons upon him through any hearing or trial that was conducted by the court. Defendants, even in civil cases, expended considerable sums to hire lawyers just to try to persuade the court to let them out on bail until judgment. Any third party who promised to put up the bail money, but then failed to do so, also was imprisoned.

Chinese and foreign plaintiffs were treated differently. The court provided a more summary process to Chinese civil litigants than it did to foreigners. For example, compared to cases brought by foreigners, two to three times as many "purely Chinese" cases were squeezed into a single court session. Nonetheless, Chinese litigants had to wait about two times longer than foreign litigants to get their cases heard once they had filed a petition.

ROLE IN THE ECONOMY AND LOCAL POLITICS

The International Mixed Court played an important role in expanding foreign control over the use of land in Shanghai during a period of intensive development. From its inception, the court considered land-rights questions raised by Chinese with claims to land within the International Settlement because it performed essential functions in the transfer of ownership of local land. Before parties could transfer ownership, the Mixed Court's Chinese judge had to issue a formal order to the current owners declaring a transfer of ownership. The foreign judges channeled applications for these orders from foreign lawyers to the Mixed Court magistrate. The *dibao*, usually an elderly, respected Chinese person living in the neighborhood where the land was situated, then had to chop the bill of sale and witness the transfer between buyer and seller of the *fangdan*, a document that provided evidence of ownership during the Qing dynasty. In some cases, *dibao* were recalcitrant and the only way to secure their chop on bills for sale of land tracts was for Mixed Court runners or municipal police officers forcibly to bring the *dibao* before the court. The Mixed Court also forwarded applications for foreign title deeds to the respective consulates. In considering claims to land, the court recognized the validity of indigenous legal devices such as the *dibao*, the *fangdan*, the *hongqi* (sealed title deeds for land), and tax receipts, alongside the foreign title deeds created by and registered in the consulates of Shanghai, but accorded the foreign documents more weight.

In its decisions in land disputes, the court defined, individualized, and secured land ownership and made land rights easily transferable, and so facilitated raising capital. In land disputes, the court settled questions of ownership and control. In land transactions, the court assured notice of the transfer of various rights to land through public documents authorizing the transfers.

The court enforced contracts, and in doing so undermined the strength and exclusivity of networks of Chinese merchants that were based on family and native-place ties. Many Chinese merchants in Shanghai at the time were organized into guilds, which enforced agreements between guild members by threatening or executing expulsion. For agreements between guild members and non-guild members, they threatened the withdrawal of the guilds' goods or services from the non-guild member. Not just foreign businesses, but Chinese businesses as well, took advantage of the different kind of leverage that the Mixed Court afforded them in negotiating their affairs. Merchants engaged in trades in which guilds existed in Shanghai chose not to invoke their affiliations with guilds, and the guilds themselves brought lawsuits at the court. Hundreds of Chinese sued one another for unpaid debts, or to liquidate Chinese banks, and even instigated criminal charges against business associates with pending civil claims for misappropriation of goods, damage from nonpayment of debt, and defamation.

The Shanghai Municipal Council passed dozens of regulations that the Shanghai Municipal Police enforced on anyone living in or doing business in the International Settlement. Seeking fines for violators, the police prosecuted at the International Mixed Court all Chinese and foreigners who were not represented by any consuls in Shanghai. License cases comprised over half of the court's docket, and they accounted for the largest share of any type of case, criminal or civil. Licensing proved so successful a strategy for raising revenue for the municipal council that the Chinese municipal government of Shanghai copied it and sold licenses to Chinese enterprises within its jurisdiction.

RENDITION

Throughout the 1910s and 1920s, Chinese critics of the court published books and articles in Chinese and English attacking it and demanding that foreigners give up control over it. Feelings against it intensified in 1925, when the Shanghai Municipal Police shot at protestors amassed outside a precinct station and then prosecuted some of them. The Ministry of Foreign Affairs negotiated with the Assessors of the International Mixed Court to devise a future for the court with gradually lessening foreign control.

From 1927 to 1930 the court passed through an interregnum in which the foreign assessor was present at all hearings involving a foreigner, but was not permitted to sit on the bench or rule. The appearance of foreign lawyers was curtailed and limited to those who had purchased expensive licenses from the Ministry of Justice in China's new capital,

Nanjing. During this time, the foreign personnel who kept track of the court's records trained Chinese to take over this work. These measures were part of a compromise to induce the foreigners to give up their control, but it did little for the court's reputation. Chiang Kai-shek personally tried to bolster his efforts to undermine the Chinese Communist Party by influencing the decisions of the Mixed Court. The Municipal Council found tax collection more difficult. Still, the court processed about the same number of cases as at the peak of its caseload in the mid-1920s.

In 1930 the Nanjing government convened negotiations with the representatives of the United States, Great Britain, the Netherlands, Norway, and Brazil to wrest control of the court away from local Chinese and foreign authorities. Thereafter, the court was called the First Special District Court of Shanghai, and it operated with that moniker until it was dismantled in 1941 when Japanese troops took control of the International Settlement. During its final decade, its cases were appealed up through China's reinvigorated national court system, ending more than sixty years of local autonomy for the court.

SEE ALSO *Extraterritoriality; Foreign Concessions, Settlements, and Leased Territories; Imperialism; Law Courts, 1800–1949; Shanghai; Treaty Ports.*

BIBLIOGRAPHY

Escarra, Jean. *Le droit chinois: Conception et evolution.* Peking, 1936.

Huayang susong li'an huibian [Collection of foreign lawsuits]. 2 vols. Shanghai: Shanghai Shangwu Yinshuguan Chuban, 1915.

Kotenev, Anatol M. *Shanghai: Its Mixed Court and Council.* 1925. Taipei: Ch'eng-wen, 1968.

Kotenev, Anatol M. *Shanghai: Its Municipality and the Chinese.* 1927. Taipei: Ch'eng-wen, 1968.

Lee, Tahirih V. Law and Local Autonomy at the International Mixed Court of Shanghai. Ph.D. diss., Yale University, 1990.

Lee, Tahirih V. Risky Business: Courts, Culture, and the Marketplace. *University of Miami Law Review* 47 (May 1993): 1335–1414.

Sifabu duiyi Shanghai zujie huishengongtang [The Ministry of Justice on the International Mixed Court of the Shanghai International Settlement]. *Falu zhoukan* [Law weekly] 11 (1923): 17.

Stephens, Thomas B. *Order and Discipline in China: The Shanghai Mixed Court, 1911–1927.* Seattle: University of Washington Press, 1992.

Tahirih V. Lee

SHANGHAI SCHOOL OF PAINTING

The rise of the Shanghai school of painting in the later nineteenth century was a direct result of catastrophe and opportunity. After China's losses in the Opium War (1839–1842),

Shanghai had been designated one of five treaty ports under the 1842 Treaty of Nanjing and opened to foreign residents and trade. Because of this strong foreign presence, Shanghai remained relatively unscathed by the destructive passage of the Taiping Uprising (1851–1864) through the Jiangnan area. Although many of the great Jiangnan cities and cultural centers such as Suzhou and Hangzhou were devastated by the uprising, Shanghai profited from the region's losses, attracting refugees and establishing itself as a cultural and economic center. The majority of painters and calligraphers active in Shanghai in this period were not natives of the city, but part of a flood of sojourners whose hometowns had been ravaged by the events of the Taiping Uprising, and who came to Shanghai for its prosperous markets and many opportunities. These artists were not united by any formal or institutional bonds, but the dynamic and lively art world they created in later nineteenth-century Shanghai often is referred to as the Shanghai school (*Haishang huapai* or *Haipai*), forged from the trials of the uprising and the rich possibilities of the cosmopolitan treaty port.

CHARACTERISTICS

The hundreds of artists who flocked to the city from the 1860s onward served a large and prosperous middle-class market. The rapid growth of the art market was intertwined with the urban dweller's vigorous investment in pleasure and leisure; Shanghai's merchant classes were avid consumers of art made to decorate, entertain, and amuse. Functional in purpose, paintings and calligraphy were used as decorations in domestic and business interiors, as gifts, and also as personal adornment in the fashionable format of the painted fan. At the same time, artists soon developed distinctive styles that catered to a Shanghai taste for the flamboyant and intensely visual, with large-scale works of engaging subjects that were brightly colored and vividly composed. Because of their location in international Shanghai, artists were exposed to new forms of art such as photographs and oil painting, yet most preferred to work in the classic brush-and-ink media of Chinese painting (referred to in the twentieth century as *guohua* or "national painting"). The subjects of Shanghai painting also were traditional, and reveal the middlebrow tastes of clients who preferred ornamental and diverting genres such as animal, bird-and-flower, and figurative painting over more scholarly genres, such as landscape painting, which faded in importance during this period. Although the subject matter reveals the popular and commercial orientations of Shanghai painting, its sophistication, vigor, and glamour demonstrates the energy of a city and culture moving into a modern era.

EARLY DEVELOPMENT

Shanghai painting of the 1860s and 1870s builds on trends from the earlier half of the century, particularly in the emphasis on beautiful women (*meiren hua*) and bird-and-flower subjects. Developments in the latter genre were especially significant, and bird-and-flower specialists such as Zhang Xiong (1803–1886), Zhou Xian (1820–1875), Wang Li (1813–1879), and Zhu Cheng (1826–1899) painted attractive, elegant works notable for their charming subjects and bright coloring. The innovation of these works lay in their fusion of the sophisticated and the accessible: The subjects are freshly observed and at the same time, often chosen for their auspicious and popular associations. In addition, these artists frequently heightened the visual appeal of their works with dynamic compositions and spontaneous, vivacious brushwork. Intimate formats such as album leaves and fans were common in this period (painted fans by Zhang Xiong and Zhu Cheng were especially in demand), yet began to give way to larger, splashier formats better suited to display, such as the multiscroll sets that could effectively cover a wall with as many as twelve matching hanging scrolls.

SHANGHAI SCHOOL AT ITS HEIGHT

The painter Ren Xiong (1823–1857) often is considered a forerunner of the Shanghai school. His monumental life-sized *Self-Portrait* (c. 1850s, Beijing Palace Museum) is a searing image of the individual confronting the chaos and confusion of the late Qing era. Ren's powerful originality and inventive range of subjects had a potent impact on later artists, including his clansman Ren Yi (1840–1895). Although many Shanghai artists specialized in specific genres, Ren Yi (also known as Ren Bonian) was known for his mastery of nearly every genre, and his astonishing technique and visual wit give his works a startling immediacy. Ren Yi's influential figural works often were drawn from popular myth, history, and legend; his large-scale *Su Wu Tending Sheep* (1880, National Art Museum of China, Beijing) depicts a first century BCE paragon of loyalty, and also alludes to contemporary issues of nationalism and conflicted transcultural contact. Like Ren Xiong, Ren Yi was a brilliant portraitist, and his images of his art-world colleagues are remarkable explorations of the artist's changing roles in modern society. Ren's portrait of Wu Changshi (1844–1927) as *A Miserable and Shabby Official* (1888, Zhejiang Provincial Museum, Hangzhou), one of numerous portraits painted at his friend's request, is a sharp and mocking look at the humiliations of the petty bureaucrat at the exhausted end of the Qing dynasty. In addition, the example of Ren Yi highlights several developments in the period, such as the rise of the celebrity-artist publicized in newspapers and magazines. His close connections to the Shanghai fan shop also underscore the growing professionalization of the art world, which relied on these businesses for art supplies, as places to gather and to serve as informal art dealers. Like many other prominent artists in Shanghai, Ren was also a participant in Shanghai's new photolithographic illustrated book industry that made Shanghai school works

A Miserable and Shabby Official *by Ren Yi, 1888.* *One of the most notable artists in the Shanghai School of Painting, Ren Yi remains known not only for his abilities in a variety of genres, but also for the humor evident in his works. In this portrait of Wu Changshi, Ren depicts the diminished status of imperial bureaucrats at the end of the Qing dynasty.* **REN YI/FOTOE**

available to a large viewing public. The artist most associated with modern mass media was Wu Jiayou (d. 1893), whose Western-influenced journalistic illustrations for popular pictorials such as the *Dianshizhai Illustrated Magazine* (*Dianshizhai huabao*, 1884–1898) and *Feiyingge Illustrated Magazine* (*Feiyingge huabao*, 1890–1893) depicted news events and human interest stories from China and abroad for a fascinated urban readership.

The very different styles and themes of Ren Yi's contemporaries and friends Xugu (1824–1896), Hu Yuan (1823–1886), and Wu Changshi reflect the diversity of the artists active in Shanghai. The monk-painter Xugu is known for his crystalline and coolly contemplative images of animal, bird, and plant subjects, whereas Hu Yuan was enormously respected as an artist working in the literati tradition, as highly regarded for his calligraphy and poetry as his painting. Hu Yuan's abstracted landscapes and simple scholarly still-life paintings have a visual pithiness and panache that situated them securely within the Shanghai tradition. Wu Changshi, a latecomer to painting, extended the influence of the Shanghai school well into the twentieth century. Trained as a seal carver and calligrapher, he folded the aesthetic of these traditional literati art forms into his plant and flower paintings, boldly brushed and colored works that sought to capture the essence of China's visual traditions, as well as formally new and abstract compositions. Wu's works enjoyed great popularity in Japan, and serve as an example of the lively interchange between Shanghai artists and Japanese scholars, artists, and patrons.

The deaths of many of these masters by 1900 marked the end of the Shanghai school. However, their revitalization of traditional Chinese painting styles and subjects, and their creation of a new art world adapted to the modern metropolis helped usher Chinese art into a new century and era; their innovations were continued and developed by later artists such as Pan Tianshou (1897–1971) and Cheng Shifa (1921–2007).

SEE ALSO *Art Societies since 1800; Chinese Painting (guohua); Pan Tianshou; Ren Xiong; Ren Yi (Ren Bonian); Taiping Uprising; Wu Changshi (Wu Junqing).*

BIBLIOGRAPHY

Brown, Claudia, and Chou Ju-hsi. *Transcending Turmoil: Painting at the Close of China's Empire, 1796–1911.* Phoenix, AZ: Phoenix Art Museum, 1992.

Chou, Ju-hsi, ed. *Art at the Close of China's Empire.* Phoebus 8. Tempe: Arizona State University, 1998.

Chung, Anita, and Shan Guolin. *Chinese Paintings from the Shanghai Museum, 1851–1911.* Edinburgh: National Museums of Scotland, 2000.

Kuo, Jason, ed. *Visual Culture in Shanghai, 1850s–1930s.* Washington, DC: New Academia, 2007.

Lai, Yu-chih. Remapping Borders: Ren Bonian's Frontier Paintings and Urban Life in 1880s Shanghai. *Art Bulletin* 86, 3 (September 2004): 550–572.

Shan, Guolin. Painting of China's New Metropolis: The Shanghai School, 1850–1900. In *A Century in Crisis: Modernity and Tradition in the Art of Twentieth-Century China*, ed. Julia F.

Andrews and Kuiyi Shen, 20–63. New York: Guggenheim Museum, 1998.

Vinograd, Richard. Portrait and Position in Nineteenth-Century Shanghai. In *Boundaries of the Self: Chinese Portraits, 1600–1900*, 127–155. Cambridge, U.K.: Cambridge University Press, 1992.

Roberta Wue

SHANXI

Shanxi Province, located in North China to the southwest of Beijing and to the northeast of Xi'an, has emerged as a key province in modern China's industrial development. Blessed with extensive deposits of coal and iron, the connection of landlocked Shanxi with the rest of China via railroads first built in the early twentieth century has contributed to the reemergence of Shanxi as an economic center of China.

During much of the Qing dynasty, before the creation of a modern transportation network, Shanxi's merchants had become wealthy for several reasons, including their dominance of China's trade with Mongolia and Russia, much of which was transported along the great north-south trade route that bisected the province and ran through Datong in the north and the provincial capital, Taiyuan, at the center of the fertile and populous Taiyuan Basin. The Fen River runs in a southwestern direction through the basin on its way to the Yellow River, which defines the border between Shanxi and Shaanxi to the west. Shortly after the waters of the Fen River join the Yellow River, the waters of the Wei River (which runs near Xi'an to the west) flow into the Yellow River as it makes its great turn to the east, the river now defining the border between Shanxi and Henan to the south on its way to the North China Plain. This nexus of trade routes in Shanxi helped connect its famous network of bankers to branches throughout China and elsewhere in Asia. This private banking network was used by the Qing government for public finance, allowing provincial governors to remit tax monies with written financial instruments.

The importance of this economic activity (which also included young men who clerked outside the province and handicraft production) meant that mountainous Shanxi, with arable land comprising only 20 percent of its territory, could support a population in excess of what the land itself could support. Wheat, barley, and millet were crops sown in nineteenth-century Shanxi, but significant imports of rice and wheat from Shaanxi, as well as grain from what is now Inner Mongolia (which had been developed extensively by Han Chinese peasants) and northern Shanxi, were needed to sustain the population of the Taiyuan Basin.

SHANXI

Capital city: Taiyuan

Largest cities (population): Taiyuan (3,490,000 [2006]), Datong, Yangquan

Area: 156,800 sq. km. (60,500 sq. mi.)

Population: 33,750,000 (2006)

Demographics: Han, 99.5%; Hui, Manchu, Mongol, 0.5%

GDP: CNY 475.2 billion (2006)

Famous sites: Yungang Buddhist cliff sculptures, Mount Wutai, Fogong Temple Pagoda, walled city of Pingyao, Qiao Family Mansion, Hukou Waterfall

THE "INCREDIBLE FAMINE" AND ITS AFTERMATH

The economic prosperity of mid-nineteenth-century Shanxi was relatively unaffected by the great rebellions that wracked other parts of China, and the province was called on repeatedly to help finance Qing suppression efforts. In the late 1870s, however, Shanxi suffered a stunning reversal of fortune from which it would not recover for almost a century. Shanxi and other provinces in north China were struck by successive droughts in 1876 and 1877. Shanxi was hit the hardest, and this natural disaster, exacerbated by an inadequate government response compounded by an inefficient transportation network, spelled disaster. According to one estimate, "the province lost between one-third to one-half of its pre-famine population of between fifteen and seventeen million people to starvation, diseases, and flight" (Edgerton-Tarpley 2008, p. 1). Not until after 1950 did Shanxi's population return to the pre-1877 level. The "Incredible Famine" transformed Shanxi and "had local, national, and global implications" (Edgerton-Tarpley 2008, p. 1).

News of the Shanxi famine reached national and international audiences, including Protestant missionaries already in China such as Timothy Richard (1845–1919). Richard's efforts to help Shanxi's people subsequently opened the province to Protestant missionaries who joined the handful of Catholic missionaries already at work in the province. These missionaries and their Chinese converts became targets of anti-Western and anti-Christian violence in 1900, in the latter part of the Boxer Uprising.

There was great loss of life in Shanxi and in the districts just beyond its northern boundary in present-day Inner Mongolia. Almost two hundred Western missionaries and their family members, and about 5,000 Chinese Christians, perished in 1900. Also targeted in this period were Westerners and associated Chinese who were seeking to exploit

Shanxi's rich coal resources. The British Pekin Syndicate was a leader of this effort, and both before and after 1900 there were indigenous efforts to thwart these designs. Finally, in 1908, after a prolonged campaign that involved both students and merchants, the Pekin Syndicate sold its rights to Shanxi's coal to Shanxi's first Chinese-owned modern-style mining enterprise. The industrial might of Shanxi today is rooted in part in this achievement.

REPUBLICAN-ERA SHANXI

Shanxi's industrial and economic development in the Republican period is closely associated with Yan Xishan (1883–1960), the son of a bankrupt Shanxi banker from the Datong region who rose to prominence in the years after the 1911 Revolution, especially 1918 to 1937, on the basis of his military credentials and prowess. Shifting his alliances in the fluid world of warlord China, Governor Yan finally gained the support of Chiang Kai-shek, whose own Nationalist regime was inspired by Yan's experiments in local administrative, educational, and social reforms in his "model province." Although staunchly anti-Communist, Yan cooperated with the Communists on the basis of national United Front policies during the Sino-Japanese War, when most of Shanxi was under Japanese control. Communist grassroots organizing took place in Shanxi's Taihang Mountains on its eastern boarder with Hebei Province. This guerrilla presence was also seen elsewhere in Shanxi. Yan Xishan, like Chiang Kai-shek, turned on his wartime ally as civil war recommenced in China after Japan's defeat in 1945. Back in Taiyuan, defended in part by surrendered Japanese troops, Yan Xishan waged an unsuccessful battle again the Communists, and by April 1949 Yan had been pushed from the province.

SHANXI IN POST-1949 CHINA

Yan's modernizing goals for the province's economy, which had been shared by the Japanese, were reprised by the economic planners of the People's Republic of China, who envisioned Shanxi as a focus of development during the First Five-Year Plan (1953–1957), which emphasized development of heavy industry. Shanxi, with one-third of China's known coal deposits, and much of its most easily accessible deposits, needed only capital investments for mining operations, mills, and rail lines.

Farming continues in Shanxi in the midst of its industrialization, and millet, sorghum, wheat, oats, buckwheat, corn, and potatoes are among the crops grown by its farmers. A wide variety of noodles and pancakes are made with these ingredients, and this county-by-county diversity can also be found in the different types of vinegar and spirits Shanxi produces. There is also cultural diversity in Shanxi, even though the overwhelming percentage of the population is Han Chinese, with Hui, Manchu, and Mongol, according to the 2000 census, comprising collectively less than .5 percent of Shanxi's thirty-two

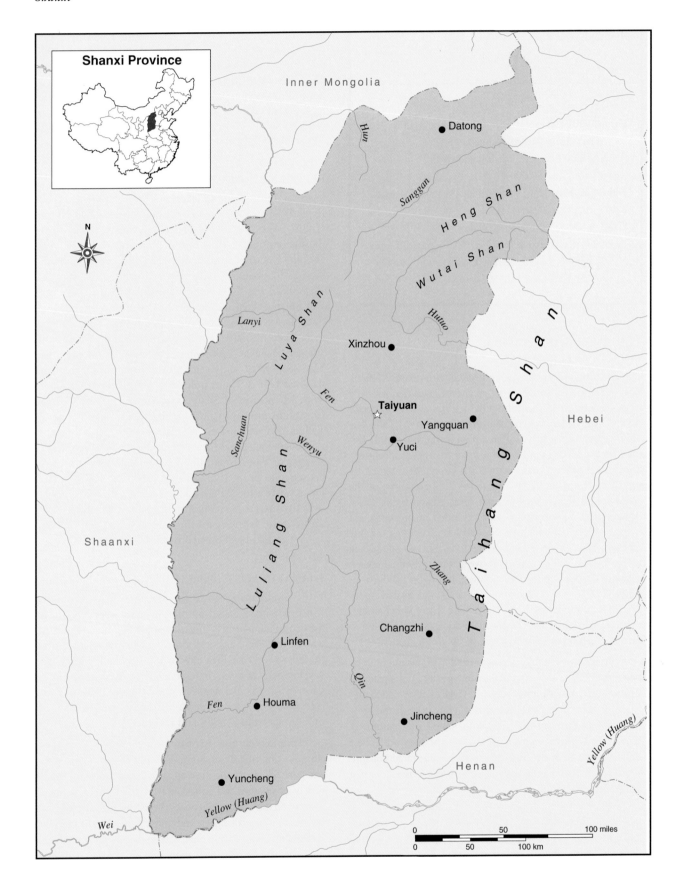

million citizens. Nevertheless, there are linguistic differences within this homogenous population as well as broad regional differences defined in part by geography. In addition to the central Shanxi Taiyuan Basin, there are four other regional cultures: Datong, in the north in the area by the Great Wall; the southeast region, which includes Zhangzhuang, the "village of Longbow" made famous by the American writer William H. Hinton (1919–2004), who chronicled the Communist-led land revolution that took place in 1947, and by the films of his daughter, Carma Hinton (b. 1949), and her husband, Richard Gordon; the southwest quadrant of the province, which is dominated by the salt lake and the salt works that had been so important in Shanxi's imperial-era economy; and the poor areas of the Luliang Mountains that run along the Yellow River as it divides Shanxi from Shaanxi to the west.

SHANXI'S CULTURAL HERITAGE

Shanxi's long history, which dates to the earliest dynasties, contributes to a rich cultural heritage that has been preserved at internationally acclaimed sites. Shanxi's Buddhist sites include the Yungang Buddhist cliff sculptures near Datong, the Buddhist monasteries at Mount Wutai, and the largest examples of wooden pagodas of any province of China, including the 220-foot-high pagoda of the Fogong Temple, built in 1056. The walled city of Pingyao, one of the main centers of the Shanxi banking network, is graced by thousands of Ming- and Qing-era residences. This UNESCO World Heritage Site (1997) in central Shanxi is near another famous group of Qing-era buildings, the Qiao family mansion compound in Qixian that was filmed by Zhang Yimou in his *Raise the Red Lantern* (*Da hong denglong gaogao gua*, 1991).

SEE ALSO *Zhang Yimou.*

BIBLIOGRAPHY

Edgerton-Tarpley, Kathryn. *Tears from Iron: Cultural Responses to Famine in Nineteenth-Century China.* Berkeley: University of California Press, 2008.

Gillin, Donald G. *Warlord: Yen Hsi-shan in Shansi Province, 1911–1949.* Princeton, NJ: Princeton University Press, 1967.

Harrison, Henrietta. *The Man Awakened from Dreams: One Man's Life in a North China Village, 1857–1942.* Stanford, CA: Stanford University Press, 2005.

Hinton, William. *Fanshen: A Documentary of Revolution in a Chinese Village.* New York: Monthly Review Press, 1966.

Thompson, Roger R. *Twilight of the Gods in the Chinese Countryside: Christians, Confucians, and the Modernizing State, 1861–1911.* In *Christianity in China: From the Eighteenth Century to the Present,* ed. Daniel H. Bays, 53–72. Stanford, CA: Stanford University Press, 1996.

Thompson, Roger R. *Military Dimensions of the "Boxer Uprising" in Shanxi, 1898–1901.* In *Warfare in Chinese History,* ed. Hans van de Ven, 288–320. Leiden, Netherlands: Brill Academic, 2000.

Roger R. Thompson

SHAO XUNMEI
1906–1968

Shao Xunmei (Zinmay Zau) was born into a wealthy aristocratic family in Shanghai. His paternal grandfather was a high-ranking diplomat of the Qing court, and his maternal grandfather was Sheng Xuanhuai, a dominating businessman, official, banker, and industrialist of the late Qing period. Upon graduating from what is now the Shanghai Jiaotong University (founded by Sheng Xuanhuai), Shao Xunmei went to study at Cambridge University, England, at the age of seventeen. Before his departure he was engaged to his cousin, a granddaughter of Sheng, for whom he wrote a love poem in free verse that later was published in the *Shun Pao.* On his voyage to Europe, he stopped in Naples and was enchanted with an image of Sappho that he saw in a museum. This encounter unleashed a libidinally charged creativity in teenage Shao and the sensual Greek poetess would be invoked as his muse for a long time to come.

In 1926, after two and a half years abroad, Shao Xunmei sailed back to Shanghai and, supported by his considerable financial resources, devoted himself to poetry and began an active role in publishing. His first poetry collection, *Paradise and May,* containing thirty-three experimental poems, was published in January 1927. By then he had befriended Xu Zhimo, Liu Haisu, and many other artists and editors active in Shanghai. Not satisfied with being a stakeholder of the newly created Crescent Moon Press, in spring 1928 Shao launched Golden House Press, through which he published a collection of his translated poems as well as a slim volume of literary essays. In May 1928 Shao put out his second poetry collection, *Flower-like Evil,* which was described as a daring and indulgent literary work "redolent with the breath of spring and the aroma of flesh, containing the magnificent magic of overwhelming seduction" (quoted in Lin 2002, p. 48). Many of the same poems appeared in his two poetry collections and they led to Shao being labeled a sensualist and decadent poet, distinguishing him from his contemporaries such as Xu Zhimo, Guo Moruo, and Wen Yiduo.

In July 1928 Shao helped to finance the revival of the *Roaring Lion* bimonthly, beginning his long involvement in journal publications. (His only short story, "Removal," was published in its fifth issue.) *Roaring Lion* was short-lived, and in 1929 Shao started, with the assistance of the translator Zhang Kebiao, the *Golden House* monthly. They set out to resist a left-wing, instrumentalist understanding of literature and art, and sought to create a pure, transcendent art. Shao's many contributions to the monthly included poems, translations, and critical essays. In spite of his and his associates' efforts, the journal remained mostly an insiders' publication and ceased to exist after seven issues.

A more successful venue soon opened up when Shao was contacted by the financially insolvent publishers of the *Modern Pictorial* bimonthly, a cartoon magazine. After making a considerable investment, Shao joined the editorial board in

November 1930 and offered to bankroll the acquisition of advanced printing equipment from abroad to produce a premium publication with ample coverage of current events. The series of changes introduced by Shao revitalized the *Modern Pictorial* and helped turn it into a serious competitor of *The Young Companion*, the leading pictorial of the time. The success of the pictorial led to the 1933 reorganization of *Modern Pictorial*'s press, the China Fine Arts Publisher, as the Shanghai Modern Book Company, with Shao as one of its five shareholders.

Through his involvement with the China Fine Arts Publisher and then the Shanghai Modern Book Company, between 1932 and 1934 Shao Xunmei published five new journals, the most important of which was *The Analects* bimonthly, edited by Lin Yutang. In 1934 the *Modern Sketch* was launched to feature cartoons because the *Modern Pictorial* had begun to carry more photographs.

As he became more successful and influential as a publisher, Shao continued to write poetry. "I for one have never for a moment left poetry behind," he said in 1934, "I have accumulated thousands of lines of poetry in my memory" (quoted in Lin 2002, p. 162). In 1931, at Xu Zhimo's invitation, Shao participated in the preparation of the *Poetry* quarterly and published in its inaugural issue, "Xunmei's Dream," which was widely regarded as his most representative work. In 1936 Shao published his third and last poetry collection, *Twenty-five Poems*, as part of a ten-volume series of modern poetry that he sponsored.

When the Sino-Japanese War broke out in 1937 Shao Xunmei stopped writing modern poetry altogether and sought to contribute to the resistance effort. In September 1939, in cooperation with his American lover Emily Hahn (whom he had met in 1935), Shao started a monthly, *Free Talk*, with an English-language counterpart, *Candid Comment*, for an international audience.

The establishment of the People's Republic in 1949 moved Shao Xunmei further away from his roles as a poet and publisher. He never gained the full trust of the new regime; indeed, he was imprisoned and reduced to dire poverty. For a while he earned a meager living by translating the poems of Shelley and Byron but none of his translations was published before his death.

SEE ALSO *Literary Societies; Pictorial Magazines since 1880.*

BIBLIOGRAPHY

PRIMARY WORKS

Xunmei wencun [Selected writings by Shao Xunmei]. Ed. Chen Zishan. Shenyang, China: Liaoning Education Press, 2006.

SECONDARY WORKS

Lee, Leo Ou-fan. *Shanghai Modern: The Flowering of a New Urban Culture in China, 1930–1945*. Cambridge, MA: Harvard University Press, 1999.

Lin Qi. *Haishang caizi Shao Xunmei zhuan* [Biography of Shao Xunmei, a talented man from Shanghai]. Shanghai: Shanghai People's Press, 2002.

Xiaobing Tang

SHEN BAOZHEN
1820–1879

Shen Baozhen, distinguished official, patriot steeped in Confucian values, modernizer, reformer, and Qing restoration leader, was born into a scholarly family of modest means in Fuzhou (Fujian Province). Brought up as one of eight children, two of whom died in infancy, and by a father who had to eke out a living by teaching (he did not pass the *juren* or provincial examination until Shen was twelve), the family was nonetheless well-connected. His father was married to Lin Zexu's (1785–1850) sister, when Lin, later immortalized by the Opium War (1839–1842), was then only a staff member (*muyou*) in the provincial governor's yamen. Shen's education, formal or otherwise, was influenced by his father and mother, his father's colleagues at the Aofeng Academy (noted for their pragmatic interpretation of Confucianism), a teacher known for his reformist bent and anti-British slant, and his uncle, Lin Zexu, who was gaining a reputation as a reformer in Shen's formative years.

Shen earned his *juren* degree in 1839, placing third, and married Lin Zexu's second daughter, Puqing, the same year. He failed the metropolitan examinations three times before gaining the *jinshi* degree in 1847, but was placed forty-second (out of 231), high enough to be dispatched to the Hanlin Academy. Successive promotions there resulted in his appointment in 1852 as associate examiner in the Zhili provincial examinations and, in 1854, as one of six supervisory censors for the Jiangnan Circuit, a region with which he was to be associated for much of the next ten years and again in the last four years of his life.

SHEN'S RISE DURING THE TAIPING YEARS

Shen distinguished himself in the fateful years of the Taiping Uprising (1851–1864). In an era when countless local officials fled in the face of rebel attacks, Shen returned from an official errand to defend his prefectural seat at Guangxin (Jiangxi Province), while his wife stood firm, wrote with her own blood an appeal for reinforcements, and challenged the troops to defend the city until death. Guangxin's defense became an instant legend, and Shen, after a year as prefect (1856–1857), was quickly promoted to a circuit intendancy (*daotai*), also based at Guangxin, then, in 1862, following two-and-a-half years mourning his mother's death, to the governorship of Jiangxi.

Many a Qing official had recommended Shen for the Jiangxi governorship, but none was more eager than Zeng Guofan (1811–1872), who wanted Shen to turn Jiangxi into a supplier of his military needs. As the province was still recovering from the worst of the Taiping war, and was periodically threatened by defeated rebels from neighboring provinces as well as its own rebels—a sure sign of the province's continuing instability—Shen had a difficult task on hand.

Shen's top priority was to restore the scholar-gentry's faith in the Confucian order and popular faith in the government. He resuscitated the civil service examinations after a decade-long hiatus, fought bureaucratic corruption, and increased official efficiency. He also attempted to stamp out female infanticide. Financially, he successfully implemented a tax surcharge-reduction program Zeng had initiated in 1861. Combined with a budgeting system—his most innovative administrative reform—Shen generated extra monies for Zeng's campaign, but not nearly enough to avert a bitter dispute between them. Further, the benefits of these reforms failed to trickle down to the common people, as hoped. In foreign affairs, Shen handled an aggressive French missionary with firmness but, needing to maintain gentry support, erred in letting the gentry-led antimissionary riots run their course. In handling other diplomatic disputes, however, he was evenhanded. Jiangxi was a much better place when he left in 1865 to mourn his father's death.

A SELF-STRENGTHENER

In 1867 Shen became a leading "self-strengthener" when summoned to serve as director-general of China's first fully fledged naval dockyard and academy near his native Fuzhou. Widely perceived as an unworthy career move for one with his distinguished accomplishments—he was the highest-ranking official in the entire late Qing to have personally managed full-time a self-strengthening project—his willingness to assume its leadership attests to his patriotism. For eight years, aided by a team of French and British experts led by Prosper Giquel (1835–1886), he oversaw the construction of sixteen wooden steamers, plus a small gunboat designed and built by the academy's graduates, a testimony to its success even in the face of severe financial stringency. When Shen left the Fuzhou Navy Yard in 1875, it was ready to move on to the building of the next generation of warships as its students were sent to Europe for further studies.

In his last year at Fuzhou (1874–1875), Shen played a critical role in the defense of Taiwan when the Japanese invaded the island on the pretext of the maltreatment of shipwrecked Liuqiuans (Ryukyuans). A strong military buildup stalled Japanese progress, but inept negotiators at Beijing resulted in a treaty that implicitly conceded to the Japanese claim over the Liuqius. While on Taiwan, Shen initiated modernization projects—China's very first telegraph lines and modern coal mine—and upgraded the island's administration, more fully integrating it into the Qing empire.

THE GOVERNOR-GENERAL SHEN

In late 1875 Shen became the governor-general of Liang-Jiang, a territorial appointment second in importance only to that of Zhili, then held by Li Hongzhang (1823–1901). Shen's administration was reminiscent of the approach and vigor he demonstrated in Jiangxi. He dedicated much energy to reviving the region's agriculture, but the efforts were largely foiled by revenue shortages, the Great North China Drought and Famine (1876–1879), and plagues of locusts in successive years. His dismantling of the Wusong Railway, built by the British without Chinese authorization, was a manifestation of "Confucian patriotism" but often misunderstood as a conservative reaction. He collaborated with Li Hongzhang on many defense-modernization efforts, and was instrumental in acquiring the shipping interests of the American Russell & Co. to strengthen the nascent China Merchants' Steam Navigation Company. Ill health plagued Shen's last year. He died in office on December 20, 1879.

Truly a man in an age of transition, Shen adhered rigidly to Confucian values, favoring the scholar-gentry's interests, trusting them to pass on the benefits of his reforms to the lower social classes. Yet he was willing to fundamentally transform the scholar-gentry by advocating a modern curriculum for the civil service examinations, and he promoted the rise of a new elite based on technical know-how and the centralization of budgeting as well as specialization among officials. Some of his reformist ideas foreshadowed those of the Hundred Days' Reform of 1898.

SEE ALSO *Giquel, Prosper; History: Overview, 1860–1912; Li Hongzhang; Lin Zexu; Qing Restoration; Reform under the Qing Dynasty, 1800–1912; Taiping Uprising; Zeng Guofan; Zuo Zongtang.*

BIBLIOGRAPHY

Lin Chongyong. Lin Jingren yu qiyuan xueshu [Lin Puqing's letter of blood begging for military help]. *Zhongyang yanjiuyuan jindaishi yanjiusuo jikan* [Bulletin of the Institute of Modern History, Academia Sinica] 7 (1978): 287–308.

Lin Chongyong. *Shen Baozhen yu Fuzhou chuanzheng* [Shen Baozhen and the Fuzhou Navy Yard]. Taibei: Lianjing Chubanshe, 1987.

Lin Qingyuan. *Fujian chuanzhengju shigao* [A draft history of the Fuzhou Navy Yard]. Fuzhou, PRC: Fujian Renmin Chubanshe, 1999.

Pang Baiteng (David Pong). *Shen Baozhen pingzhuan: Zhongguo jindaihua de changshi* [A critical biography of Shen Baozhen: China's venture in modernization]. Shanghai: Guji Chubanshe, 2000.

Pang Baiteng (David Pong). Shen Baozhen yu Liang-Jiang nongye de fuxing [Shen Baozhen and revival of the agrarian economy in the Liang-Jiang provinces, 1875–1879]. In *Shen Baozhen yanjiu* [Studies on Shen Baozhen], ed. Lu Meisong, 102–117. Fuzhou: Haifeng Chubanshe, 2001.

Pang Baiteng (David Pong). Zhongguo de di-yi-tiao dianbao xianlu yu 1874–1875 Taiwan de kang-Ri junshi xingdong [China's first telegraph lines and the defence of Taiwan against the Japanese in 1874–1875]. In *Jindai Zhongguo haijun-shi xinlun* [Modern Chinese naval history: New perspectives], eds. Lee Kam-keung, Mak King-sang, So Wai-chor, and Joseph S. P. Ting, 270–280. Hong Kong: Hong Kong Museum of Coastal Defence, 2004.

Pong, David. The Income and Military Expenditure of Kiangsi Province in the Last Years (1860–1864) of the Taiping Rebellion. *Journal of Asian Studies* 26, 1 (1966): 49–66.

Pong, David. Confucian Patriotism and the Destruction of the Woosung Railway, 1877. *Modern Asian Studies* 7, 4 (1973): 647–676.

Pong, David. The Vocabulary of Change: Reformist Ideas of the 1860s and 1870s. In *Ideal and Reality: Social and Political Change in Modern China, 1860–1949*, eds. David Pong and Edmund S. K. Fung, 25–61. Lanham, MD: University Press of America, 1985.

Pong, David. Li Hung-chang and Shen Pao-chen: The Politics of Modernization. *Chinese Studies in History* 24, 1–2 (Fall–Winter 1990–1991): 110–151.

Pong, David. *Shen Pao-chen and China's Modernization in the Nineteenth Century*. Cambridge, U.K.: Cambridge University Press, 1994.

Pong, David. Salt for the Tables of Hubei: The Battle for Salt Sales in the Aftermath of the Taiping Rebellion. In *Wang Ermin jiaoshou bazhi gaoshou rongqing xueshu lunji* [Festschrift in celebration of Professor Erh-min Wang's eightieth birthday), ed. Bingren Sung, et al. Taibei: Guangwen shuju, 2009.

David Pong

SHEN CONGWEN
1902–1988

Shen Congwen (born Shen Yuehuan), one of China's finest and most influential writers of the twentieth century, was a founder of China's New Literature (*xin wenxue*), which favored the contemporary vernacular instead of classical Chinese and subjective, modern subject matter rather than classical models. As a writer of stories, novels, essays, travelogues, and memoirs, he was best known for his exquisite style. For political reasons he stilled his pen just prior to the Communist revolution of 1949 and turned his attention to art history. Many in his literary cohort turned to programmatic social and political themes by the 1930s; but Shen Congwen remained dedicated to unbounded linguistic, sty-

listic, and intellectual exploration of the literary revolution of the 1910s and 1920s and its May Fourth literature, which embraced social criticism but regarded didacticism as old-fashioned. Shen wrote memorably of West Hunan (Xiangxi), his native region in southern China, as a realm of frontier autonomy. Hence he became known retrospectively, in the 1980s, as a major writer of *xiangtu* (native-soil; regionalist; rural; homeland) literature, with values implicitly reproving, in a non-Marxist way, the profit seeking, power politics, and militarism of modern urban society. His success in sidestepping the politicization of art in successive eras when it was ever more subordinated to propaganda came to epitomize independence of mind and endurance of spirit.

RUDE BEGINNINGS

Shen Congwen was born into a declining military family in Fenghuang, Hunan, at a cultural frontier between lowlander Han Chinese and nonliterate but fiercely independent, pre-urban, tribal montagnards such as the Miao, Tujia, and Gelao. Shen's mother was an assimilated Tujia, his blood paternal grandmother a Miao. The Han despised the Miao, using them as servants, but respected their martial skills after centuries of Miao uprisings against Han encroachment and taxation. The upland peoples' alien customs, colorful women's costumes and crafts, sexual freedom, and rich oral culture of extemporized mountain love ballads and ceremonial songs captured the imagination of Shen Congwen's young student readers when later he put this exotic culture into his short stories. He depicted local maidens in ethnic attire in *Congwen zizhuan* (Congwen's autobiography; 1931); represented Miao folk songs and adapted folklore plots in "Long Zhu" (named after a Miao singing master; 1929), *Shenwu zhi ai* (The shaman's love; 1929), and "Yuexia xiaojing" (Under moonlight; 1933); and titillated young urban readers with tales of trysts among teenage lovers unhindered by Confucian and bourgeois ideas of chastity, in *Ahei xiaoshi* (The story of Ahei; 1928).

Shen Congwen's father was originally an officer in the local military colony, whose century-old forts had been built to contain the Miao (in Shen's vision they were ruins of a more heroic age). Absent from home during most of Congwen's childhood, he was an unsuccessful anti-Qing and then anti-Yuan Shikai revolutionary. Congwen entered the local warlord armies as an adolescent without an inheritance. On his marches he got to know river ports and border villages he would make famous in his future works, such as Chadong, the setting of *Bian cheng* (translated as *Border Town* or *The Frontier City*; 1933). Contrary to that novel's pacific images, warlord-era West Hunan was a bloody place, with mass executions and uprisings by fanatical "spirit soldiers." The dark pathos and mindless brutality, the camaraderie, swagger, and peculiar codes of ethics of local soldiery, and the amazing stories told around army campfires later entered Shen's "Ruwu hou" (After entering the ranks; 1927), "Wo de jiaoyu" (My education; 1929), and "San ge nanren he yi ge nüren" (Three men and a woman; 1930). Shen gained literary, calligraphic, and antiquarian skills as librarian and curator, from 1922 to 1923, of local warlord Chen Quzhen ("King of West Hunan," 1919–1935), which allowed him to seek his future as a new intellectual in Beijing and, thirty years later, to pursue a career in art history.

MASTER LITERARY CRAFTSMAN

Arriving in Beijing in 1923, Shen Congwen was unable to enter a university by the examination or self-financing routes, so he wrote short pieces for newspaper feuilletons while auditing classes at Peking University. His publications captured the attention of the writers Xu Zhimo, Hu Shi, and Chen Yuan (1896–1970). In poetry and prose, Shen poured out his complaints against materialistic and traditional urban society in the voice of a poor student. His other persona was an iconoclastic storyteller and rough ex-soldier from China's Southwest tribal frontier who shocked urban audiences with tales of "the real China," a backward place of brutality, outlandishly primitive and ancient customs, yet also freedom and multiethnic vigor. As the prolific young "Dumas of China," Shen Congwen wrote in several vernacular idioms: local (West Hunanese dialect), national (Modern Standard Chinese, which was just then developing from Beijing dialect), and "foreignized" (borrowing syntax from translations of foreign literature). In time he blended Western influences with the spontaneous word pictures, rather than the clichés, aphorisms, and set rhythms, of classical Chinese lyricism, developing a new literary register for vernacular Mandarin.

Though an autodidact who never graduated from primary school, Shen Congwen became a literary editor (notably, of the *Dagongbao* or *L'Impartial* Literature Supplement, 1933–1935), critic, and college teacher, first at the Wusong China Institute (1929; there he met Zhang Zhaohe, whom he married in 1933), then at Wuhan University (1930), Qingdao University (1931–1933), Southwest Associated University (1939–1947), and Peking and Furen universities (1947–1949). Eschewing the overtly political advocacies of his early confederates and biographical subjects Ding Ling and Hu Yepin (1903–1931), and leftist literary polemicists of the 1930s, Shen proudly and anachronistically proclaimed that he wanted his literature to be a "little Greek temple" for the worship of humanity. The lyric, pastoral prose of *Border Town* embodied that ideal; it became a modern classic and Shen's representative work. That and later novels also set in West Hunan, most of them unfinished and with ever darker themes of decadence and despoliation of the countryside, later won Shen a reputation as his generation's great *xiangtu*

writer. These include *Fengzi* (Phoenix; 1933–1937), *Xiaozhai* (Little stockade, 1937), *Chang he* (Long river; 1938–1943), and *Xue qing* (Clearing after the snow; 1945–1947), together with his subjective travelogues *Xiang xing san ji* (Recollections of West Hunan; 1934) and *Xiangxi* (West Hunan; 1938).

His short fiction, too, celebrated humble provincial folk, but more often shopkeepers, mill owners ("Sansan," 1931), rural rebels, and the dispossessed, such as boatmen, prostitutes ("Baizi," 1928), and hired workers ("Guisheng," 1937), than ordinary peasants. The beauty of the rural settings, Shen's devotion to craftsmanship, nuance, and understatement in his classic works, and opposition to oppressive modern forces of commerce, fascism, Communism, and neotraditionalist Confucianism, cemented his reputation as a rural regionalist, even a Daoist. Shen Congwen in the 1930s and 1940s turned toward path-breaking modernist explorations touching on psychological, philosophical, and religious questions. In "Caiyuan" (Vegetable garden; 1929) and "Sheng" (Living; 1933), he wrote of the domestic conflicts and gentle hypocrisies of urban bourgeois society and the pathos of everyday life in the old neighborhoods of Beijing. Despite his provincial origins, Shen Congwen, who polemicized against the cultural pretensions of Shanghai and Nanjing (the new national capital), was seen in the 1930s as the head of a Beijing school or academic school dedicated to a new aesthetic of the vernacular.

SILENCE AND REDIRECTION AFTER COMMUNISM

Under attack as a bourgeois, reactionary, even pornographic writer as the Communist revolution neared Beijing in 1948, Shen withdrew from writing and attempted suicide in 1949. He devoted the rest of his life to research in Chinese artifacts and art history. Beginning as a common docent in the palace museum, Shen parlayed his knowledge of porcelains and other art objects (which he collected before the revolution) into employment as a researcher at the National History Museum, where work was relatively protected from political campaigns. Besides books on historical Chinese mirrors, lacquerware, ceramics, textiles, brocades, and design motifs, he finally published, after Mao's death, his massive *Zhongguo gudai fushi yanjiu* (Researches into ancient Chinese costume; 1981). Specialists considered these works perceptive but not requiring the linguistic genius of a Shen Congwen. By avoiding propaganda work, Shen Congwen escaped entrapment as a rightist, unlike Communist former friends such as Ding Ling. The abuse he suffered in the Cultural Revolution was mild for a high intellectual.

As literature recovered from "politics in command" after the death of Mao, Shen Congwen's literary legacy reemerged. The effective banning of his old creative works was lifted in mainland China by 1980 and in Taiwan in 1986 (authors who resided in the mainland had been generally banned in Taiwan regardless of the content of their writings), resulting in a 1980s "Shen Congwen craze" among intellectual readers in both societies. His impact on students and protégés who survived the revolution, notably Wang Zengqi (1920–1997), was celebrated, and young writers drawn to rural and psychological motifs outside the passé Maoist rural revolutionary formulas took inspiration from Shen, including Hunanese like He Liwei (1954–), Gu Hua, Han Shaogong (1953–), Ye Weilin (1934–), and Sun Jianzhong (1957–), and possibly even the avant-garde writers Gao Xingjian and Can Xue. In the Taiwan orbit, Bai Xianyong (1937–) acknowledged Shen's influence. Shen Congwen's example, with that of Wang Zengqi as intermediary, was credited by some critics with energizing the "root-seeking" movement of the mid-1980s, in which young authors searched for a Chinese cultural essence in localities outside the political power center of North China and independent of fads from abroad. Shen Congwen's backbone and perspicacious detachment from revolutionary politics were universally honored outside China but remained controversial in China's literary establishment.

SEE ALSO *Literary Societies.*

BIBLIOGRAPHY

Kinkley, Jeffrey C. *The Odyssey of Shen Congwen.* Stanford, CA: Stanford University Press, 1987.

Liu Hongtao. *Shen Congwen xiaoshuo xin lun* [New views on Shen Congwen's fiction]. Beijing: Beijing Shifan Daxue chubanshe, 2005.

Peng Hsiao-yen. *Antithesis Overcome: Shen Congwen's Avant-Gardism and Primitivism.* Taipei: Institute of Chinese Literature and Philosophy of the Academia Sinica, 1994.

Shen Congwen. *Imperfect Paradise: Stories by Shen Congwen.* Ed. and trans. Jeffrey Kinkley. Honolulu: University of Hawai'i Press, 1995.

Shen Congwen. *Shen Congwen quan ji* [The complete works of Shen Congwen]. 30 vols. Taiyuan: Beiyue wenyi chubanshe, 2002.

Wang, David Der-wei. *Fictional Realism in Twentieth-century China: Mao Dun, Lao She, Shen Congwen.* New York: Columbia University Press, 1992.

Jeffrey C. Kinkley

SHENYANG

Shenyang in Liaoning Province is one of Northeast China's major industrial centers. It lies approximately 500 miles (or some 740 kilometers) northeast of Beijing in the middle of the vast plains of Manchuria, and is mostly known today for undergoing a deep economic crisis as a result of the restructuring of its large state enterprises. But one cannot reduce Shenyang to its unemployment or urban poverty rates and workers' strikes. It is still a city of considerable importance, both in terms of its 7.2 million population and its economic weight. Using coal extracted in places such as Fushun, Liaoyang, Fuxin, or Anshan, Shenyang factories turn the steel produced in cities such as Benxi or Anshan into vehicles, machine tools, or military hardware. Lying at the center of one of China's most industrial and urbanized regions, Shenyang is no mere provincial capital: Under the names of Fengtian and then Mukden, it once lay at the heart of international conflicts for the control of Manchuria, with its large mining resources fueling the greed of both the Russian and the Japanese empires from the end of the nineteenth century. Shenyang's recent history thus remains intimately tied to that of iron ore and nonferrous metals, coal, and heavy processing industries. Shenyang used to be also the capital of the Qing dynasty until its relocation in Beijing in 1644 after the fall of the Ming dynasty.

INDUSTRIAL DEVELOPMENT

Shenyang's industrial development dates from the late nineteenth century, when the first modern industrial enterprises were founded. The turn of the century saw the creation of two large arsenals and the construction of the Shenyang-to-Beijing railway with the help of both British funds and engineers. These first efforts at modernization were entirely motivated, however, by military considerations aimed at securing the empire's northern borders from both Russian and Japanese territorial claims.

The Mukden Incident on September 18, 1931, signaled the formal political and military takeover of the whole region by the Japanese, who had already been playing an important role in the region since their 1906 takeover of the railway line from the Russians. Far from being a simple railway company, the South Manchurian Railway had become a tool for the economic exploitation of Manchuria. Japan used it to launch a number of infrastructural works, and then to support or develop the exploitation of raw materials (mining and agricultural products) and half-finished products, with the aim of furthering the expanding Japanese economy.

The formal annexation of Manchuria did mark a new stage, however, and the setting up of its modernizing project served the purpose of legitimizing its recent colonization. It was mostly during the war that Japan started to develop *in situ* machine tool and military hardware industries: Manchuria was transformed from being a mere source of raw materials for Japan's mighty industries to being a supplier itself of transformed goods through its progressive mastery of the necessary technological means. Placed at the receiving end of such massive investments, Mukden was thus able to develop and profoundly diversify its industrial infrastructure (Schumpeter 1941). It must be acknowledged that, beyond the harshness of its colonization, Japan managed to establish and develop during the 1930s what remains today the basis of the city's industrial fabric in both public and private modes. And it is during this period that Mukden established itself as the industrial center of a dozen medium-sized steel and mining cities surrounding it.

INVESTMENT AND RESTRUCTURING AFTER 1949

At the time of the Communist takeover, Shenyang counted the greatest number of heavy industries of any site in the whole of China. This heritage had, however, been partly damaged in the meantime by the civil war and the Red Army's industrial plundering. The new Chinese authorities targeted Shenyang as one of the main beneficiaries of the new regime's investment policies. Shenyang thus became the largest production center for Chinese steel, but also the center of China's most advanced economic region. Because of its strategic importance, Soviet influence was stronger there than elsewhere.

Although the part played by heavy industry remained the most important in terms of employment (60% of the active population in 1980) and production value (42.6%) up to the reforms, some light industry had also been developed since 1949 in Shenyang. Its industrial base is thus more diversified than that of the smaller surrounding cities such as Anshan, Fushun, Benxi, or Panjin, where 80 to 90 percent of wage earners are employed in mining and heavy industry.

The Maoist period allowed Shenyang to develop the industrial base it had inherited from the Japanese, but at the cost of a great squandering of human and natural resources. While it lacked competition, the city played a leading role in "socialist" industrialization, but this marvelous layout was particularly vulnerable to the change in the rules of the game that would be brought about by the reforms since 1978. From one day to the next, goods that were highly sought after in a shortage economy suddenly became unsalable. Once raw materials, energy, and labor came to have a market price, wasting them threatened not only the region's ecosystem but

Workers at a coal processing plant near Shenyang, November 25, 2007. Located in a region rich in coal reserves, the city of Shenyang remains an industrial center, home to numerous manufacturing facilities. Many workers in Shenyang became unemployed, however, at the end of the twentieth century, as state-run businesses struggled to become competitive during China's transition to a market-based economy. © MARK/EPA/CORBIS

also the profitability of the enterprises themselves. Without being the sole factor explaining why the reform of the state enterprises failed, there is little doubt that Shenyang's discovery of the market economy was all the more brutal since socialist construction had been very advanced there.

In the reconfiguration of China's economic geography engendered by the reforms, this large industrialized city has progressively lost its importance with the second phase of the reforms since 1992, despite its well-trained labor force and favorable situation within one of China's richest provinces and not far from a major seaport. When it was only a question of establishing a small trading fringe within a still largely state-owned economy, Shenyang firms were able to take up the challenge by increasing their production. But with the deepening of the reforms, Shenyang's state economy ran into an increase of competition that it was badly equipped to confront, unable as it was to reform its internal functioning or to improve control over its investments. The awakening was both late and brutal.

Of course, the slowness of the reform of the state enterprises did not prevent a degree of economic diversification in services. Since the beginning of the reforms, but more markedly since the beginning of the 1990s, a private sector has managed to develop and thus create numerous jobs. This developing private sector is in some ways an economy of resourcefulness, as it has become the only way to scrape out a living at a time when the social cost of the transition is being strongly felt. Unemployment affects between 30 and 40 percent of the active population, at least if beneficiaries of early retirement and the "working" population of idle enterprises are added to the official unemployment statistics. Concretely, the progressive privatization of the economy rhymes with its progressive deindustrialization.

Although Shenyang, like Chinese cities in general, has diversified its economy by allowing a new private sector to develop, it has not become a new pole of growth. Being too off-center in relation to most of the Chinese market, Shenyang has not managed to attract foreign capital or develop any new sector by its own means. Because it did not enjoy geographic or political advantages in any way comparable to those of the southern coastal regions, Shenyang could not succeed in its transition simply by authorizing the development of a private sector, rural industry, and foreign investments. The transition could have been successfully effected in Shenyang only by restructuring the state enterprises. But this reform came up against a number of difficulties, not merely economic and social but political as well. Despite the fact that the municipality has had a reformist bent and has experimented since the middle of the 1980s with different types of conversion of the ownership status of the state enterprises, the very preponderance of the state economy in Shenyang has strongly determined the form the transition has taken there (Kernen 2004).

Since the turn of the present century, and in particular since the Liaoyang demonstrations, Shenyang is at the center of an ambitious project for revitalizing the entire northeastern economy. Substantial financial assistance has been granted by the central authorities to ensure the development of new infrastructure, as well as the payment of pensions and unemployment benefits. Although this increase in assistance to the Northeast does have a positive impact, it is too early to judge whether it will ensure a new development of industry in the region. In any case, national and international migrations from the Northeast have not stopped for the moment.

SEE ALSO *Liaoning; Urban China: Cities and Urbanization, 1800–1949; Urban China: Organizing Principles of Cities; Urban China: Urban Planning since 1978.*

BIBLIOGRAPHY

Kernen, Antoine. *La Chine vers l'économie de marché: Les privatisations à Shenyang.* [China Toward Market Economy: The Privatization in Shenyang]. Paris: Karthala, 2004.

McCormack, Gavan. *Chang Tso-lin in Northeast China, 1911–1928: China, Japan and Manchurian Idea.* Stanford: Stanford University Press, 1977.

Schumpeter, E. B., ed. *The Industrialization of Japan and Manchukuo, 1930–1940. Population, Raw Materials, and Industry.* New York: Macmillan, 1941.

Antoine Kernen

SHOPS

The shop was a ubiquitous feature of Chinese urban life, attesting to a highly developed consumer culture well before the nineteenth century. The location, business practices, and management styles of these commercial establishments reflected the social and economic structures that gave shape to them over the centuries, most notably during the Tang dynasty (618–907) when trade and productivity exponentially increased, and monetization and innovations in financial instruments capable of servicing rapid economic growth occurred. The market served the state, and merchants were expected to pay for the privilege; thus commerce was controlled and practices were regulated through craft (producer), service, and commercial guilds, or *hang*, organized by merchants according to trades or place of origin.

BEFORE THE TWENTIETH CENTURY

The term *hang* originally designated a street block within the walled ward of the city market consisting of shops in the same trade, replete with requisite signage. This fixed spatial organization facilitated quality control, standardization of weights and measures, and tax collection. The *hang* also diminished cutthroat competition, and brought some comparative shopping convenience to the consumer. By the Song dynasty (960–1279), shops had dispersed throughout the city outside of the designated "official" markets and even beyond the walls into the suburbs (*guan*). Mixed shopping streets appeared, although some shops selling similar goods did regroup in other parts of the city. This dispersal may have been a driver in establishing the guild as the foremost and abiding commercial entity in China before the mid-twentieth century.

Membership in the commercial guilds was based on the shop unit, with fees payable according to the value of shops' sales. Fees were used to pay various government exactions or to secure permits necessary to the continuation of a trade, a reflection of the low status of the merchant class and the state's perpetual search for revenues. Fees were also raised for the welfare of guild members, though commercial shops with interests firmly located *in situ* often contributed to local festivals, street repairs, and poor relief.

Shop employment was based on the apprentice system, with recruits coming from the countryside or the shop owner's native place. Apprentices were often relatives (clan members), since a guarantor for good behavior was mandatory. The shop master served *in loco parentis*; food, lodging, and clothes were provided, as well as a small salary when the trainee was adequately numerate and adroit in haggling with customers. Working hours were not fixed, but shops usually closed when the city gates were shut.

By the mid-nineteenth century and the opening of the treaty ports to foreign trade and residence, distinctive aspects of this preindustrial and protocapitalist retailing persisted, though retailing and consumption in China's rapidly growing urban centers began to be transformed as a result of new markets (and new consumers), competition with foreign goods and firms, the introduction of new management and business techniques, innovations in transportation (railway) and communications (the telegraph), and by 1895 the right granted to foreigners to open manufacturing and industrial enterprises in China.

By 1897 in Guangzhou, for example, there were reportedly ninety thousand shops scattered over two thousand streets, a commercial density unmatched except by the most modern cities in the West. Shops or *dian* were located on the ground floor of two- or three-story buildings with signage and banners to advertise the business. Brand names or "branding" of products either to designate the place of origin famous for particular products—such as cotton cloth from Shanghai, silks from Suzhou, or wine from Zhejiang—or increasingly manufacturing firms that used trademarks as a pledge of quality became widespread as competition intensified.

Imported goods or goods manufactured locally with their own trademarks and advertising styles were often viewed as superior, which was another goad to improve quality. Shops with closed fronts that sold valuable items such as silver or gold did not display their products but fetched them from the back of the shop after sizing up their customers' wants or needs. Open-fronted shops (with removable doors or gates) usually displayed their goods behind glass-fronted counters, but fruit or inexpensive items often spilled out toward the street to attract passersby—that is, if the streets were wide enough. In Guangzhou, building density was such that two sedan chairs could not pass each other on some streets, making shopping difficult. To lure customers, merchants paid for rattan matting to be slung from the tops of opposing buildings, covering and thereby cooling the narrow lanes during the hot summer months. Shopkeepers, their families, and their employees often lived on the premises to better secure their property.

THE RETAILING REVOLUTION OF THE REPUBLICAN PERIOD

With the overthrow of the Qing dynasty (1644–1912) and the transformation of China into a modern republican state, retailing underwent its own "revolution." Guilds and their control of trade began to give way to general chambers of commerce, although noncommercial guilds retained their autonomy, with only commercial guilds joining up under some restrictions. The new Republican government attempted to regulate the guilds in 1929 by issuing an industrial and trade association act aimed at the registration of existing guilds and the licensing of new trade associations, mediation in trade or labor disputes, tax collection, and other issues affecting business practices. Shops not affiliated with any guild continued with little governmental interference, as did the small street shops that supplied the neighborhood with daily necessities.

New modes of retailing were modeled on the "universal providers," after department stores like those in the West were introduced in colonial Hong Kong and the treaty ports of Guangzhou and Shanghai in the early twentieth century. These stores—in Shanghai the "big four" were Sincere (1917), Wing On (1918), Sun Sun (1926), and Dah Sun (1936)—were owned, capitalized, and managed by Chinese entrepreneurs hailing from the same native place (Xiangshan) in South China. The "one hundred goods" stores (*baihuo shangdian*) sold everything under one roof for a "fair" fixed price in well-designed buildings with grand facades. The buildings were constructed to stream customers from the streets through the glass-countered displays to the top floor. The large-scale retailing of daily articles, luxury goods (both foreign and Chinese-made), food stuffs, and so on was profitable and convenient, and had a substantial impact on the business of traditional retail shops nearby. However, small

Bead shops on a street in Beijing, May 22, 1933. *In early Chinese history, officials designated specific areas of the market for the sale of a singular product. While this practice ended during the Tang dynasty, influences of the tradition appear in this 1933 photo of bead shops in Beijing.* © BETTMANN/CORBIS

neighborhood shops and local markets continued to coexist with this new type of retail institution, and many people were aware of but rarely visited these grand emporiums.

COLLECTIVIZATION IN THE PEOPLE'S REPUBLIC

With the establishment of the People's Republic in 1949 and the systematic elimination of private property and capitalism, large and medium-sized retail shops were collectivized and former shop owners became shop employees—of the state. The socialist transformation of society and the economy entailed a move toward production rather than consumption. Shops may have physically remained in the same locations, but names and essences changed to reflect their state-owned status.

By the time of the Cultural Revolution in the mid-1960s (during the "destroy the Four Olds" campaign—old

ideas, culture, customs, and habits), traditional shop names with historical or literary allusions became either utilitarian monikers or revolutionary slogans. Access to state-controlled resources became dependent on centralized planning, procurement, and supply linked to rationing of vital commodities (rice, cooking oil, grain, cloth, and other goods) channeled through neighborhood shops to legally registered households (*hukou*) or to laborers at their place of work (*danwei*). Small shops (licensed to individuals) that sold less-vital commodities, such as sundries, tobacco, or snacks, were tolerated, but access to state-controlled goods remained problematic.

MARKET REFORM

With the reforms of 1978 and 1979 and the shift to the so-called socialist market economy—that is, from state-owned and managed enterprises to state-owned but enterprise-managed entities—foreign investment, as well as a resurgence of private-sector retailing, brought back profit as an incentive. Modernization of marketing, supply chains, and management in line with international standards affected large and small retail shops. Gleaming shopping malls were megaprojects anchoring urban development as China "opened up to the outside world." The humble shop, however, continued in its quotidian way to adapt to the social, political, and economic changes inherent in China's transformation into a modern nation state. In Hong Kong, now a Special Administrative Region of the PRC, this can be seen in the survival of shops, *dian,* or *hang* (like their Tang-dynasty predecessors, shops selling similar products located on the same street) or the lowly *shiduo* (pronounced *si-door* in Cantonese dialect and used as a homophone for the English word *store*), which can still be found among the glittering high-rises of "Asia's world city."

SEE ALSO *Commercial Elite, 1800–1949; Sincere Department Stores; Wing On Department Stores.*

BIBLIOGRAPHY

Burgess, John Stewart. *The Guilds of Peking.* New York: Columbia University Press, 1928.

Kato Shigeshi. On the *Hang* or the Associations of Merchants in China. *Memoirs of the Research Department of the Toyo Bunko* 9 (1936): 45–83.

Lu Hanchao. *Beyond the Neon Lights: Everyday Shanghai in the Early Twentieth Century.* Berkeley: University of California Press, 1999.

MacPherson, Kerrie L., ed. *Asian Department Stores.* London: Curzon, 1998.

Kerrie L. MacPherson

SICHUAN

Until 1997, when the easternmost parts of Sichuan became the province-level municipality of Chongqing, Sichuan was China's most populous province. Even divested of Chongqing, Sichuan ranks third among China's provinces in population (87.5 million in 2005) and fifth in area (485,000 square kilometers).

Long known as "heaven's storehouse" (*tianfu*), Sichuan contains some of China's most productive farmland. Separated from neighboring provinces by high mountain ranges and internally united by convenient river transportation, Sichuan has developed a strong regional identity. The province in its present form can be divided into two main parts: the fertile, densely populated Sichuan Basin and the mountainous west. The Sichuan Basin in its turn consists of the Chengdu Plain, sometimes referred to as Shu, and the hill country along the Yangzi (Chang) River, known as Ba. The irrigated Chengdu Plain is the historical heart of the province and the earliest part of southwest China to be integrated into the Chinese polity. The hills of Ba attracted

---

SICHUAN

■

Capital city: Chengdu

Largest cities (population): Chengdu prefecture (11,034,000 [4,971,500 within urban districts, 2007])

Area: 485,000 sq. km. (187,000 sq. mi.)

Population: 87,500,000 (2005)

Demographics: Han, 95% Yi, 2.6% Tibetan, 1.5% Qiang, 0.4%

GDP: CNY 863.7 billion (2006)

Famous sites: Dazu Rock Carvings; Huanglong Scenic and Historic Interest Area; Jiuzhaigou Valley Scenic and Historic Interest Area; Mount Emei Scenic Area

---

substantial Chinese immigration only in the Song era (960–1279), and it was not until the early twentieth century, when rising demand for Sichuan silk, *tong* oil, and opium triggered an export boom, that population densities in the eastern basin began to approach those in the Chengdu Plain.

Western Sichuan consists of three distinct regions that differ in geography and ethnic composition, though they are all characterized by high elevations, geographical isolation, predominantly non-Han populations, and relative poverty. In the north lie the mountains and grasslands of Aba (Ngawa) Autonomous Prefecture, inhabited by Qiang, Jiarong, and Amdo-speaking Tibetans, with a large pocket of Han Chinese near Songpan. Ganzi (Garzê) Autonomous Prefecture, along the Sichuan-Tibetan border, is mainly inhabited by Khampa Tibetans. Liangshan Yi Autonomous Prefecture, in the southwest of the province, is home to the Nosu Yi people. It also contains the industrial city of Panzhihua with its mainly Han-Chinese population.

HISTORY

Home to the Shu and Ba kingdoms in the fifth century BCE, Sichuan was conquered by the state of Qin in 316 BCE. Around 250 BCE, the Qin governor Li Bing established the Dujiangyan irrigation system, a network of canals that transformed the Chengdu Plain into one of China's most productive agricultural regions. Sichuan's inaccessibility (the road to Sichuan was said to be "harder to travel than the road to heaven") was a blessing in times of war, but also attracted armies that used Sichuan's natural defenses to rebuild their strength. Sichuan became a battleground in the Song-Yuan, Yuan-Ming, and Ming-Qing transitions, each time suffering catastrophic population losses. Having lost almost all of its

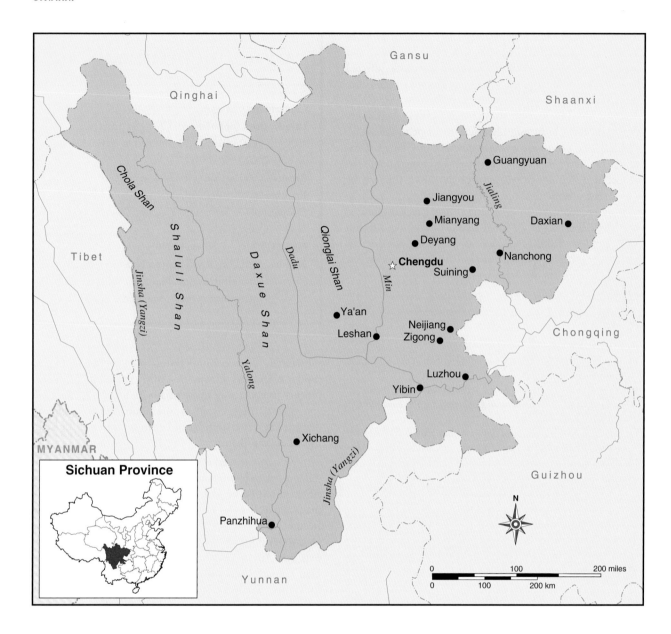

population in the Ming-Qing transition, Sichuan was repopulated from Hubei and Hunan in the seventeenth and eighteenth centuries. For almost two centuries, Sichuan was the largest recipient of transprovincial migration, but by about 1840 the province had filled up and large numbers of Sichuanese began to move into neighboring provinces.

The growing pressure on the land was also reflected in increased violence. In the 1860s, the arrival of a Taiping army under Shi Dakai (1831–1863) sparked the Li-Lan rebellion, but both the Taipings and the Li-Lan rebels were easily defeated by the Qing. By and large, nineteenth-century Sichuan remained a backwater, almost untouched by the rapid socioeconomic changes that transformed coastal China at that time. Despite a succession of reformist governors in the late Qing, the province saw the rise of a separatist movement under the slogan "Sichuan for the

Sichuanese." Anti-Qing agitation culminated in the 1911 railroad-protection movement and the subsequent collapse of the Qing. The resulting vacuum was filled by military rulers who fought hundreds of mostly small-scale wars between 1917 and 1935.

Republican Sichuan was notable above all for the rapaciousness of its military rulers, some of whom collected taxes for eighty years in advance. In 1935 the Chongqing-based warlord Liu Xiang (1890–1938) defeated his uncle and rival, Liu Wenhui (1895–1976), and united the province. At the same time, the growing presence of the Communists—in 1932 the Fourth Route Army under Zhang Guotao (1897–1979) had established a Soviet government in northern Sichuan, and in 1935 the Red Army on its Long March crossed the western part of the province—provided Chiang Kai-shek (Jiang Jieshi) with a pretext to sideline Liu Xiang

A river flowing through the city of Kangding, Sichuan, October 10, 2007. *The province of Sichuan remains a productive agricultural region, featuring a fertile interior, sub-tropical climate, and navigable rivers to transport crops to other areas of China. Rich in natural resources, Sichuan contains a large amount of the heavy industry and light manufacturing sectors of the Chinese economy.* © RYAN PYLE/CORBIS

though local rulers usually sought recognition from Beijing. It was only in the closing years of the Qing dynasty that the Sichuan governor-general Zhao Erfeng (1845–1911) invaded the Tibetan kingdom of Batang and established the short-lived province of Xikang, covering most of the Kham region of traditional Tibet (merged back into Sichuan and Tibet in 1955). In 1950 the People's Liberation Army (PLA) crossed Xikang on its march to Lhasa, defeating weak Tibetan forces on its way. From the Chinese point of view, Tibetan areas in Sichuan were not part of Tibet and did not come under the Seventeen-point Agreement (1951) between Beijing and the Dalai Lama, which promised the protection of the old order in Tibet. The Chinese government therefore pursued more radical land reforms and religious policies in the Tibetan areas of Sichuan than in Tibet proper, which explains why these regions saw some of the greatest militancy and most severe repression during the 1956 uprising. In recent years, Tibetans in Aba and Ganzi Autonomous Prefectures appear to enjoy more cultural autonomy and religious freedom than Tibetans in the Tibet Autonomous Region.

Sichuan was one of the last provinces to come under Communist control, and the People's Liberation Army encountered strong resistance until 1951—longer in the Yi and Tibetan borderlands, where rebellions continued to flare up until 1960. The 1950s saw a greater integration of Sichuan into the national economy thanks to the completion of the Chengdu-Baoji railroad and improved navigation through the Yangzi River gorges. Throughout the 1950s, Sichuan subsidized China's industrialization with massive grain exports. Sichuan's leftist leadership continued to export grain in the midst of the 1959–1962 famine, leading to an estimated excess mortality of eight million people, more than in any other Chinese province (Bramall 1993, p. 298).

Mao Zedong's ambitious Third Front program, designed to prepare China for a Soviet invasion, led to improvements in the railroad network and the establishment of heavy industries and defense industries, many of them in remote areas. Sichuan was briefly on the forefront of economic reform in the late 1970s, when the party secretary Zhao Ziyang pioneered the return to household farming that became national policy in the 1980s. When the focus of China's reforms shifted to urban and coastal China, the province, with its loss-making Third Front industries and limited access to foreign markets, fell behind.

Since 1985, Sichuan has become China's largest source of migrant labor, with an estimated six million migrants working outside the province in 2006. In 1997 Chongqing and twenty-one surrounding counties split off from Sichuan to form an independent provincial-level unit. Since 1999 the central government's "Great Western Development scheme" has led to infrastructural investments and a building boom

and bring Sichuan under Guomindang control. Once in control, the Guomindang government began to develop Sichuan as a resource base for the anticipated war with Japan. When the war broke out, Chongqing became the wartime capital, and much of the nation's institutional and industrial infrastructure was moved to Sichuan. While Chongqing suffered heavily from Japanese bombing, the province saw substantial investment and an influx of skilled labor between 1937 and 1945. These gains were reversed, however, when the government returned to Nanjing in 1945.

Western Sichuan needs to be considered separately. Despite the costly Jinchuan wars against the Jiarong Tibetans (1744–1749 and 1771–1776), the Tibetan and Yi populations of the area remained de facto independent,

that has benefited Chengdu and the surrounding counties but has exacerbated inequality within the province.

CLIMATE, AGRICULTURE, AND INDUSTRY

With a humid, subtropical climate and fertile soil, the Sichuan Basin is one of the most productive agricultural areas in the world. Major products are rice, wheat, rapeseed, and vegetables. The Dujiangyan irrigation system, kept in constant repair for more than 2,000 years, made the provincial core immune to floods and droughts. The province is also a major producer of silk, tea, fruit, and other cash crops. Western Sichuan is home to large stands of timber, which were rapidly depleted until catastrophic flooding along the Yangzi River led to a total logging ban in 1998. Environmental degradation in the uplands is one of the major problems facing the province.

Despite its geographical isolation, Sichuan was home to China's largest premodern industry: the Zigong salt yards, which employed close to 100,000 workers and sustained a host of auxiliary industries. To reach the underground reservoirs of brine and natural gas, Zigong workers drilled wells more than 1,000 meters deep, using hand-operated percussion drills until the mechanization of the industry in the early twentieth century. Today, Sichuan is one of the major industrial bases in western China, with heavy industry (coal, energy, steel), light manufacturing (wood and food processing, textiles, electronics), and a rapidly growing tertiary sector. Western Sichuan contains some of the most spectacular scenery in China, and tourism has become an important source of income in some mountain areas, such as the world heritage site of Jiuzhaigou.

CULTURE AND EDUCATION

Most Sichuanese claim descent from Hubei (in particular Macheng County) and Hunan. Linguistically and culturally, Sichuan shares traits with the Middle Yangzi region, as well as with the southwestern provinces of Yunnan and Guizhou that were also resettled from Hubei and Hunan in the early Qing. The Sichuanese speak a form of southwestern Mandarin, related to dialects spoken in Hubei,

Earthquake survivors searching through debris for personal possessions, Sichuan province, May 21, 2008. *Though known throughout Chinese history as a fertile agricultural region, Sichuan also remains home to a large population of rural poor in the mountainous west, many of whom lived in substandard housing that collapsed after a 2008 earthquake, killing more than 68,000 people.* © **MICHAEL REYNOLDS/EPA/CORBIS**

Yunnan, and Guizhou. Sichuan's claims to cultural prominence stem mainly from the Han (206 BCE–220 CE), Tang (618–907), and Song dynasties, when Chengdu served as a refuge for scholar-poets (Du Fu, Li Bai) in times of unrest. In later dynasties, Sichuan lost its prominence, though Chengdu retained a reputation for refined living, and local art forms from opera to embroidery continued to flourish. In the twentieth century, Sichuan produced several famous writers and artists (Ba Jin, Guo Moruo, Zhang Daqian) and CCP leaders (Deng Xiaoping, Nie Rongzhen, Liu Bocheng, Chen Yi). The province today has some forty institutions of higher learning, mainly concentrated in Chengdu. Illiteracy rates are still high, especially in remote mountain areas.

SEE ALSO *Chengdu; Chongqing; Earthquakes since 1800.*

BIBLIOGRAPHY

Bramall, Chris. *In Praise of Maoist Economic Planning: Living Standards and Economic Development in Sichuan since 1931.* Oxford, U.K.: Clarendon Press, 1993.

Hosie, Alexander. *Szechwan: Its Products, Industries, and Resources.* Shanghai: Kelly and Walsh, 1922.

Kapp, Robert A. *Szechwan and the Chinese Republic: Provincial Militarism and Central Power, 1911–1938.* New Haven, CT: Yale University Press, 1973.

Stapleton, Kristin Eileen. *Civilizing Chengdu: Chinese Urban Reform, 1895–1937.* Cambridge, MA: Harvard University Asia Center, 2000.

Zelin, Madeleine. *The Merchants of Zigong: Industrial Entrepreneurship in Early Modern China.* New York: Columbia University Press, 2005.

Jacob Eyferth

SILK SINCE 1800

Silk has been the quintessential Chinese product since ancient times, and in the period after 1800, it was China's major export and played an important role in the agricultural economy and a lesser role in the modern industrial sector. In the ancient Roman world silk became known as "seres," the Greek word for China. Silk was a source of wealth for the imperial court, and was part of the peasant household's tax obligation, at least in principle. From the sixteenth century, Chinese silk was carried to the New World by Spanish traders, and also to Japan, where it was highly prized. In the early nineteenth century, silk was one of the commodities in the British-dominated Canton trade. After the Treaty of Nanjing (1842) and the opening of treaty ports, the center of trade shifted to Shanghai, which had easy access to the sources of silk production in the adjacent districts of Zhejiang Province. Exports of raw silk more than doubled between 1868 and 1900. By the turn of the twentieth century, silk had surpassed tea as China's leading export, and even with the diversification of China's overseas trade, silk continued to be China's major export commodity until the 1930s.

OLD AND NEW TECHNOLOGY

Silk production comprised four basic stages: the cultivation of mulberry leaves, the raising of silkworms (sericulture), the reeling of silk thread from cocoons, and the weaving of silk fabrics of many varieties. Farmers cultivated mulberry trees, usually amid grain and other crops, and harvested the leaves to feed the silkworms in the spring. The silkworms grew rapidly over a period of about a month and a half. The process required constant attention, usually from the women in the household. After its fourth molting, the mature silkworm spun its cocoon. After sorting, the fresh cocoons were reeled at home using machines operated either with a treadle or by hand. The reeled silk, known as raw silk, then underwent intermediate processes such as twisting to form warp and weft threads. In the final stage, the threads were prepared for weaving, a step often performed outside the farm household in urban workshops, the most important of which were the Qing Imperial Silk Factories in Nanjing, Suzhou, and Hangzhou.

In the mid-nineteenth century, steam filatures for the reeling of silk were introduced in the Guangzhou (Canton) area and in Shanghai. The reeling machines employed Italian or French techniques. This step separated reeling from sericulture. Households sold their fresh cocoons to local cocoon hongs, which were equipped with large ovens. The hongs in turn would sell the dried cocoons to the filatures. Filature silk was more suitable for export because it was more reliable in quality, and could meet the standardization required by the power looms of silk-weaving factories in the United States and Europe. By the 1910s, virtually all export white silk was machine-reeled. For the domestic market, however, home-reeled silk maintained a constant level of output.

SILK-PRODUCING REGIONS

The traditional methods of sericulture and reeling were concentrated in the old silk districts in Zhejiang Province, extending from Hangzhou to Huzhou, near Lake Tai. The highest grade of white silk from this area was known to Western traders as *Tsatlees*. There was a moderate rate of growth from 1880 to the 1920s. By contrast, new silk-producing areas in adjacent Jiangsu Province to the north doubled their output in the same period, and their cocoons were sent to steam filatures for reeling. The devastation caused by the mid-century Taiping rebellion (1851–1864) provided an opportunity for new crop choices. Local entrepreneurs created new marketing networks to procure cocoons from farm households. The city of Wuxi became

Processing silk cocoons, Chengdu, China. *Known for the production of silk since ancient times, China continues to be a leading exporter of the material. Much of the traditional silk industry centered around small farms until the 1980s, when the Communist government looked to profit from the export of silk and began modernizing the manufacture of the textile.* © TOM NEBBIA/CORBIS

the center of the cocoon trade, which supplied both Shanghai and local filatures. Officials supported the initiatives of local businessmen, but private and state interests were often in conflict, particularly over taxation of the cocoon trade.

The Guangzhou delta region of South China also experienced rapid growth in silk production due to the export market. Although silk piece goods played a role in the early years of the Canton trade, from the mid to late nineteenth century, steam-filature raw silk came to dominate the export trade. Due to its favorable climate, Guangdong Province was able to support six or seven crops of worms and leaves per year—compared with one or two crops in Jiangsu and Zhejiang provinces. Sericulture was a year-round, rather than seasonal, occupation for most peasant households in Guangdong. In the main districts—Shunde, Nanhai, and Xiangshan—most of the land was devoted to mulberry cultivation, and most of the households specialized in sericulture. In some localities, sericulture was combined with fish farming, following a "four water six land" method of land use and fishponds.

Other regions also produced silk. Sichuan Province experienced growth similar to that of Guangdong and Jiangsu—its cocoon output doubled between 1879 and 1926. However, its industry remained unmodernized, and its predominantly yellow variety of silk was directed toward domestic and non-Western foreign markets, such as India. Hubei Province produced an inferior grade of yellow silk, some of it destined for India and the Middle East. Shandong Province and Manchuria produced wild silk, spun from silkworms that fed on oak leaves. *Tussah* silk and the *pongees* woven from them were much in demand from the 1910s to the 1930s.

THE MODERN SECTOR AND WORLD COMPETITION

Despite this rapid growth, and the importance of silk in China's foreign trade, by 1909 Japanese silk exports overtook the Chinese, capturing an ever larger share of the expanding world market. This was a signal achievement for Japan since its silk technology and output had traditionally lagged behind China's. Japan's silk outstripped Chinese silk because its industry could manufacture a more consistent and reliable raw silk that met international standards. The highest grades of Chinese silk were still the best in the world, but ordinary grades of Chinese silk did not compete favorably with Japanese silk.

There were a number of reasons for the weakness of China's silk exports relative to Japan's. The silk business was particularly subject to risks of various types. Silkworms were disease-prone, and infestation could quickly wipe out a season's investment in leaves, land, and labor. Filatures had difficulty obtaining a steady and reliable supply of cocoons each season, and volatility and speculation characterized the cocoon trade. Because sericulture was seasonal, the filatures at Shanghai did not operate all year around. Most firms rented facilities on a short-term basis rather than having direct ownership of physical plants. Even at Guangzhou, where seasonality was not an issue, there was a separation of ownership and management. Silk workers, mostly women and children, worked under harsh conditions, and staged strikes on several occasions.

Filatures in Shanghai and Guangzhou had difficulty raising capital and relied on short-term loans from native banks, *qianzhuang*. A few Chinese firms operated under nominal foreign ownership to gain legal and tax advantages. Although foreigners were reluctant to invest in the manufacturing side, foreign trading companies controlled the export business. Since they did not directly engage in export, Chinese silk manufacturers did little in the way of research into foreign markets and tastes until the 1930s.

Although some blame may be assigned to the domination of foreign capital at Shanghai, weak leadership by the Chinese government was a larger factor. Unlike the Japanese Meiji government, which promoted the development and modernization of the Japanese silk industry as a national economic goal, the Qing officials had no national policy. Not until the 1920s and 1930s did the Republican-era authorities, both national and provincial, take steps to support the reform of the industry and research into international markets. But the timing was bad. The world depression seriously endangered the silk market, and in the 1930s the introduction of synthetic fibers, rayon and nylon, cut into the world demand for silk.

SILK IN THE PEOPLE'S REPUBLIC OF CHINA

In the late twentieth century, by contrast, the PRC government took an active role in promoting silk production and exports of raw silk, silk fabrics, and silk garments. Zhejiang and Jiangsu provinces were by far the largest producers. Growth in the 1980s and early 1990s led to overproduction and losses in some years. China was the world's largest silk producer. In 2005 it accounted for 74 percent of global raw silk production, and 80 to 90 percent of the

world export market. However, quantity was not matched by quality and responsiveness to high-end markets. Aggressive marketing led to accusations of dumping by India, a chief competitor. Domestically, the silk business experienced volatility and speculative practices.

SEE ALSO *China Merchants' Steam Navigation Company; Lu Zuofu; Piracy, Maritime.*

BIBLIOGRAPHY

Bell, Lynda S. *One Industry, Two Chinas: Silk Filatures and Peasant-Family Production in Wuxi County, 1865–1937.* Stanford, CA: Stanford University Press, 1999.

Eng, Robert Y. *Economic Imperialism in China: Silk Production and Exports, 1861–1932.* Berkeley: Institute of East Asian Studies, University of California, 1986.

Li, Lillian M. *China's Silk Trade: Traditional Industry in the Modern World, 1842–1937.* Cambridge, MA: Council on East Asian Studies, Harvard University, 1981.

Moore, Thomas G. *China in the World Market: Chinese Industry and International Sources of Reform in the Post-Mao Era*, chap. 4, pp. 98–110. Cambridge, U.K.: Cambridge University Press, 2002.

Shi Minxiong (Shih Min-hsiung). *The Silk Industry in Ch'ing China.* Trans. E-tu Zen Sun. Ann Arbor: Center for Chinese Studies, University of Michigan, 1976.

Lillian M. Li

SINCERE DEPARTMENT STORES

The first Sincere Department Store opened in Hong Kong in 1900, launching modern retailing and service business in China. Its founder, Ma Yingbiao (1864–1944), embarked on the venture after seeing how one such business, Anthony Hordern & Son, had grown into the largest department store in Sydney. Ma had gone to Australia around 1883 from Zhongshan County, near Macau, to seek employment. In less than ten years, he rose from laboring as a miner to the position of partner in the Yongsheng Company in Sydney, trading in fruits, seafood, and sundries among Fiji, China, and Australia. His five other partners, all fellow Zhongshanese, would later either join him in Sincere or found their own department stores.

MA YINGBIAO'S VISION AND FIRST STORE

Ma's vision to launch such a business in Hong Kong, and soon thereafter in Shanghai, was not only trailblazing but also daring. It was nothing less than creating a new market in China by forging new forms of organization and new practices in selling upscale, mostly Western, imported household goods in a new way. He had a difficult time convincing his friends and partners to pool their financial resources for such a venture.

Ma left Sydney in 1894 and moved to Hong Kong, where he set up a business that allowed him to maintain contact with fellow emigrants in Australia, as well as kin and friends at home. Meanwhile, he studied the business and social climate in Hong Kong while refining his understanding of the retail and management models he had learned from his many visits to the Sydney department store. It took him five years before he succeeded in winning eleven partners and a paid-up capital of HK$25,000 (Hong Kong dollars). Ma found the store's location on 172 Queen's Road, Central, at the center of the island's commercial district. It occupied one storefront on three floors, and had a staff of twenty-five.

The partnership almost fell apart just before the store opened on January 8, 1900, when Ma's partners found out that he had spent four-fifths of his capital on elegant glass display counters and other refined décor for Sincere's shopping floor. A second near-disaster occurred during its first year when a typhoon toppled the store's two upper floors and forced it to move to temporary quarters. In 1904 the original store reopened, and Sincere quickly established its name as a world emporium selling high-quality imported goods, with each item categorized and clustered into different sales departments, and sold at a clearly marked and fixed price. Customers were impressed by the open display of high-end articles, the courteous service, and the individual receipts for each item they purchased. Only Ma's attempt to introduce young girls as salespeople failed to take hold; the store was swamped by gawking men who milled around them unceasingly. It was not until the 1930s that salesgirls could be regularly employed by Sincere and the other department stores.

All these practices ran counter to the customs of traditional Chinese businesses. But Ma's timing could not have been better. First, both Hong Kong and Shanghai became China's premier urban centers with the largest Western presence and cultural influence. By the mid-1890s, Hong Kong's population had reached 250,000, while Shanghai's International Settlement was considerably larger, at around 350,000. Both cities enjoyed modern municipal amenities, such as large boulevards, piped-in water, and streetlights. Through waves of internal migrations of wealthy Chinese seeking the comparative political security of these two foreign-controlled enclaves, large numbers of their residents were ready to accept such items of everyday use as soap, perfumery and cosmetics, and knitted and other woolen clothing. Such goods clearly reflected a modern style of living. In addition, influential Confucian scholars such as Liang Qichao (1873–1929) had begun to advocate giving merchants and their businesses greater support so that the Chinese nation could better engage the West through "busi-

ness warfare" (*shangzhan*). The Chinese elite's new interest in the role and status of the merchant class had great impact in these urban areas, for these sentiments resonated with the presence of Western merchants who clearly enjoyed high social prestige in their own community and managed modern businesses in grand office buildings.

Ma injected this aura of respectability into Sincere from its beginning. Besides its efficient management style and its display of opulent goods in elegant settings, he carefully cultivated other images of modernity. He set up regular working hours for his employees, including lunch breaks and Sunday mornings off to attend Christian church services, and he did away with apprenticeships and began a training program for newly hired junior clerks. Because Sincere's clerks mostly came from Zhongshan, he provided dormitory-style housing with facilities for sports, social activities, reading, and classes in English and accounting.

Ma was equally anxious to adopt a modern corporate structure. As sales took off, Sincere became very profitable. Between 1904 and 1907, profits grew quickly. In 1909 several of Ma's old partners from Australia were added to the Sincere partnership. Their infusion of new capital, combined with the plowback of undistributed earnings, allowed the company to raise its capital to $200,000. Sincere then registered with the Hong Kong government as a limited-liability company.

EXPANSION

By 1907 Sincere was poised to expand. It had outgrown its existing space, and Ma proved his boldness in choosing a two-acre land tract at a newly reclaimed area on the fringe of the commercial district. He also leased a new four-floor store nearby that took up six contiguous lots. By the time the leased store opened in 1909, the area had street trams and many new offices and shops. This led to a fivefold increase in profits by 1912. The following year, the company's capital was increased to $800,000, and the store moved again, this time to a newly completed six-story building on the two-acre site Ma had bought earlier.

This success allowed Sincere to launch capital-subscription campaigns to open new stores in Guangzhou in 1911 and in Shanghai between 1914 and 1917. All three stores included new kinds of service-oriented businesses, including rooftop entertainment parks and, on the lower floors, modern hotels, elegant tea rooms and restaurants, and Western-style barber shops. The Shanghai store on Nanjing Road became a national landmark, known for being the most opulent Western-style building housing a Chinese-owned business when it first opened.

By 1918 the Sincere stores in Hong Kong and Shanghai had $2 million in paid-up capital, while the Guangzhou store had $400,000. Ownership, however, remained largely in the hands of a small group of old partners, while the small shareholders, about one thousand in number, were mostly fellow Zhongshanese and Ma's friends or relatives. To further centralize control and strategy, Ma and his partners decided to pool the individual boards and the separate capital accounts into one. On this united board of directors, Ma remained as managing director. He reorganized the company's upper management by setting up several divisions headed by a general administration that included accounting, personnel, numerous sales departments, and a department of inspectors who functioned like censors of traditional Chinese bureaucracy, with special powers to investigate any suspected malfeasance or unethical behavior.

Besides adding more department store branches, Sincere also expanded in other directions. In 1915 and 1923, Ma and his partners founded two affiliated companies in Hong Kong: the Sincere Insurance and Investment Company and the Sincere Life Insurance Company. They also set up purchasing offices in London, Kobe, and Singapore, for 80 to 90 percent of the company's goods were imports. By the early 1930s, this high percentage was reduced because, beginning in the 1920s, Chinese students and factory workers staged demonstrations to boycott foreign goods and encourage the use of domestic goods. However, since around 1911, Ma had been recruiting skilled craftspeople and had set up ten factories in Guangzhou to produce cabinets and other home furnishings, ironworks, varnish, and cosmetics. Although only the cosmetics factory survived the 1910s, Ma opened similar factories in Shanghai, starting in the late 1910s. This time, the company's backward-integration policy paid off, and helped Sincere weather the campaigns in favor of domestically produced goods.

In 1925, the Sincere Company celebrated its twenty-fifth anniversary with much fanfare. From its modest beginnings of $25,000 in paid-up capital, twelve partners, and twenty-five employees, it now had $7 million, three thousand shareholders, over two thousand employees, and several thousand factory workers. This period marked the company's high point.

COMPETITION AND OTHER CHALLENGES

By then, the Wing On Department Stores, which followed a similar path of development but started later, in 1907, had overtaken Sincere in size and reputation. When Wing On opened its Shanghai store in 1918, a keen sense of competition, spurred on by the founders' common backgrounds as fellow Zhongshanese, former colleagues in Australia, and kinsmen through marriage, seemed to favor Sincere. But the Wing On stores turned out to be grander than Sincere's, while Wing On's sales soon exceeded its competitor's. Furthermore, Wing On expanded into modern industry and went on to become one of China's largest textile manufac-turers, while Sincere's factories rarely broke into modern industry. And Sincere had a more difficult time responding to the labor strikes and political conflicts that affected Chinese business throughout the 1920s and 1930s.

Ma's strengths as a visionary leader were not matched by his skills as a manager. In 1922 bickering among the directors forced Ma to give up his position as managing director. His long-term associate and senior manager for the Shanghai store, Liu Xiji (1881–1926), resigned several months later after he and Ma disagreed over how dividends and bonuses were to be distributed between the Hong Kong and Shanghai operations. This dispute was a forecast of greater accounting problems to come. In the mid-1930s, a financial crisis forced Sincere's overextended capital resources to fall short, and bank creditors took control of the company for a period. This was followed by the full-scale Japanese invasion in 1937, and Sincere ceased operation from 1941 until the end of World War II in 1945. After 1949, all of Sincere's operations on mainland China closed while the Hong Kong store reconstituted itself. The store in Hong Kong continues to operate as of 2008.

SEE ALSO *Chinese Overseas: Returned Overseas Chinese; Shops; Wing On Department Stores.*

BIBLIOGRAPHY
Chan, Wellington K. K. "Selling Goods and Promoting a New Commercial Culture: Shanghai's Four Premier Department Stores on Nanjing Road, 1917–1937." In *Inventing Nanjing Road: Commercial Culture in Shanghai, 1864–1949*, ed. Sherman Cochran, 19–36. Ithaca, NY: Cornell East Asia Publications, Cornell University, 1999.

Lee Chengji. *Shi dagongsi* [The four premier companies]. No. 59 of *Zhongshan wenshi*. Guangdong, PRC: Historical Materials Committee of Zhongshan Municipality, 2006.

Ma Yingbiao. *Jiating biji* [Family notes]. Unpublished manuscript, n.d.

Sincere Company. *Xianshi gongsi ershiwu zhounian jiniance* [The Sincere Company: Twenty-fifth anniversary commemorative issue]. Hong Kong: Author, 1925.

Sincere Company. *The Sincere Company, Limited, Hong Kong: Diamond Jubilee, 1900–1975*. Hong Kong: Author, n.d.

Wellington K. K. Chan (Chen Jinjiang)

SINO-FRENCH WAR, 1884–1885

The Sino-French War was Qing China's first war against a major European power after it adopted Western-style weaponry. The war emerged from the Sino-French dispute over Annam (Vietnam), one of China's major tributary states.

In 1859 France invaded Saigon (present-day Ho Chi Minh City) under the pretext of punishing antimissionary incidents. With treaties signed in 1862 and 1874, France gained a territory in the south known as Cochin-China and reduced Annam to protectorate status. However, China refused to accept the treaties. In 1875 Prince Gong (1833–1898), chief minister of the Grand Council and the Zongli Yamen (foreign ministry), reiterated China's suzerainty over Annam, which continued to pay tribute to China and requested military aid in suppressing local rebels in 1879.

By 1882, French troops had entered Tongking (Tonkin), in north Annam, and occupied Hanoi. Their expedition met skirmishes from the Black Flag Army, a Chinese militia led by Liu Yongfu (1837–1917), a former rebel. China responded to French aggression by sending troops to Tongking and protesting to France. However, attempts at negotiations between Li Hongzhang (1823–1901), governor-general of Zhili Province, and the French minister in China in November 1882, and later with the French minister in Japan in June 1883, failed to settle the dispute.

In the process of negotiation, China became increasingly belligerent. Officials of the Qingyi faction, who held the high ideological ground, advocated war and accused Li Hongzhang of appeasement. The Empress Dowager Cixi (1835–1908) ordered preparations for war. France was also aggressive. French admiral Amédée Courbet (1827–1885) defeated the combined Chinese–Black Flag forces and captured the strategic cities of Son Tay in December 1883 and Bac Ninh in March 1884. Enraged, Cixi executed troop commanders and dismissed Prince Gong. Yet, both sides opted for peace because China could no longer launch attacks and France was involved in other disputes in Egypt and Madagascar. However, before Li Hongzhang's agreement with the French could be ratified, in June 1884 Chinese and French troops clashed in Bac Le, and the French side suffered a setback. France issued an ultimatum, demanding an indemnity and the immediate withdrawal of Chinese troops.

To force Chinese concessions, Courbet's fleet bombarded Jilong in northern Taiwan in August. In October, he attacked the Fuzhou Shipyard in Fujian Province, one of China's most important modern shipyards, and overwhelmed the Fuzhou fleet in an hour. Hoping to establish a commercial foothold on north Taiwan, Courbet moved from Fuzhou to capture Jilong, blocked the island's west coast and, briefly in January 1885, blocked Ningbo in Zhejiang Province. In late March 1885, Courbet seized the Pescadores Islands. However, in Tongking, Chinese troops defeated the French in Lang Son in March. The French premier was forced to resign, and France offered China an armistice. Cixi accepted it, fearing that Russia and Japan might attack China. In June, Li Hongzhang and the French minister in China signed a treaty: China recognized all French-Annamese treaties, and France withdrew its troops from Taiwan and the Pescadores.

The impact of the war was far-reaching. The downfall of Prince Gong meant the dominance of Cixi in court

politics. Qing officials sensed the urgency of building a modern navy, and established the Admiralty (Haijun Yamen) in 1885. Moreover, the war accelerated the collapse of the ancient tributary system. In 1885 Britain secured a treaty from China, making Burma (Myanmar) a British protectorate but permitting it to pay tribute to Beijing. Japan, which had already annexed the Ryukyu Islands in 1879, finally ended Chinese suzerainty over Korea after the Sino-Japanese War (1894–1895).

The war also provoked a rise in nationalism. News from the front line stirred antiforeign sentiment. Common people attacked churches and foreigners, especially French missionaries. Local gentry organized militia for coastal defense and donated money for the war effort in Taiwan. Furthermore, young radicals such as Sun Yat-sen (Sun Yixian) saw the final settlement as an act of humiliation for China and proof of the Qing dynasty's incompetence. They later used it as an argument against Qing rule in their revolutionary propaganda.

SEE ALSO *Defense, 1800–1912; France, Relations with; Vietnam, Relations with.*

BIBLIOGRAPHY

Cady, John F. *The Roots of French Imperialism in Eastern Asia.* Ithaca, NY: Cornell University Press, 1954.

Eastman, Lloyd E. *Throne and Mandarins: China's Search for a Policy during the Sino-French Controversy, 1880–1885.* Cambridge, MA: Harvard University Press, 1967.

Long Zhang. *Yuenan yu Zhong Fa zhanzheng* [Vietnam and the Sino-French War]. Taibei: Taiwan Shangwu Yinshuguan, 1996.

Rawlinson, John L. *China's Struggle for Naval Development: 1839–1895.* Cambridge, MA: Harvard University Press, 1967.

Wang Hsien-chun (Wang Xianqun)

SINO-JAPANESE WAR, 1894–1895

The first Sino-Japanese War reversed the traditional East Asian balance of power, with Japan supplanting China. It began as a contest for control over Korea that escalated, ending with Japan's destruction of Chinese sea power for the next century.

The causes and outcome of the war reflected long-term domestic trends. Since the Industrial Revolution, China had been declining relative to the industrializing nations, whereas Japan had Westernized in the late nineteenth century and become a great power capable of self-defense. Meanwhile, Russia's plans to build a Trans-Siberian Railway, announced in 1891, heralded its East Asian ambitions.

This changing power balance and competing Japanese and Russian ambitions were the underlying causes of the war. The specific events that triggered the conflict were

Korea's escalating instability from debilitating infighting within the ruling dynasty, and the outbreak of the greatest peasant rebellion in Korean history. China and Japan both sent troops to restore order, China at Korea's request and Japan over Korea's objections.

Japan began the war as soon as Britain recognized Japan's Westernization by renegotiating their treaties on the basis of juridical equality on July 16, 1894. Nine days later, Japan turned to the foreign policy phase of its national-security strategy by initiating the Sino-Japanese War in order to preempt Russian expansion.

Japan organized its military forces along Western lines under a general staff and unified command. Japanese soldiers had a standard kit, including Japan's first-rate Murata rifle. Chinese land forces had no hospital, commissariat, or engineering organizations. Many soldiers were armed with only pikes. Chinese forces were an aggregation of banner forces responsible for upholding Manchu minority rule, provincial Green Standard forces proficient at constabulary functions rather than conventional warfare, and the Westernized forces of Li Hongzhang, China's quasi foreign minister in the last quarter of the nineteenth century, and the nation's most famous self-strengthener and main military strategist.

The Chinese and Japanese navies ranked among the best in the world, and experts considered them roughly comparable. What Li Hongzhang's Beiyang Fleet lacked in speed it made up for in firepower and armament. Japan had no counterpart for China's two largest, heavily armored battleships.

Fighting was concentrated in four theaters: Korea, Manchuria, Shandong, and Taiwan. Although Li Hongzhang tried to avoid war, Japan sought out his Beiyang Fleet in the waters off Seoul, attacking three vessels near Feng Island on July 25 and later that day sinking *Kowshing*, a British-owned, Chinese-leased troop transport. The Japanese army then engaged Chinese forces south of Seoul, winning at Sŏnghwan on July 29. These events precipitated formal declarations of war on August 1, but troop buildup took the next month and a half.

Then in a three-day period in September, Japan defeated China decisively on land and sea, accomplishing its primary objective to expel China from Korea. China failed to contest the dangerous Japanese river crossing at P'yŏngyang, or to attack their vital but vulnerable troop and supply ships. After P'yŏngyang fell on September 16, Chinese forces fled to Manchuria.

On September 17 the Japanese navy found the Beiyang Fleet near the mouth of the Yalu River, where Japan sank four Chinese vessels, losing none of its own. Thereafter, Chinese ships never crossed the Weihaiwei-Yalu line, allowing Japan to deploy troops and furnish supplies at will. Had China sunk troop transports or interrupted Japanese supplies by sea, the outcome of the war might have changed.

After that, hostilities concentrated in Manchuria. Japan deployed troops by sea to the Liaodong Peninsula to take China's naval base at Lüshun (Port Arthur), which had China's only facilities for repairing capital ships. Japan took the peninsula's narrow neck in the Battles of Jinzhou (November 5–6) and Dalian (November 7–9). Lüshun then fell on November 22. A Japanese massacre of Chinese civilians ensued.

Meanwhile, at the Battle of Juliancheng on the Manchuria bank of the Yalu, again China failed to contest the Japanese river crossing. The city fell on October 26. Japanese forces pursued ever deeper inland. The strategic city of Haicheng fell on December 13 but Chinese counterattacks continued until March 2, 1895. Haicheng was the war's most bitterly contested city because it lay at the geographic gateway from the mountains on the Korean border onto the ancestral plains of the Qing dynasty.

Simultaneously, Japan opened the Shandong campaign to take China's second naval base at Weihaiwei. It blockaded the Beiyang Fleet and soon sank China's only significant modern naval force, which China never used for any offensive purpose. Weihaiwei fell on February 12.

On February 20 Japan ordered its navy to take the Pescadore Islands off Taiwan. They fell on March 20. In the ensuing Taiwan campaign, Taibei fell on June 6, Taizhong on August 26, and Tainan on October 21, with Japan proclaiming victory on November 20, although an insurgency persisted for a year.

Immediately after the fall of Lüshun, China opened negotiations as a delaying tactic in the hopes of an eleventh-hour European intervention that never materialized. Japan rejected China's first two diplomatic missions for lack of proper negotiating credentials. Meanwhile, China lost its navy at Weihaiwei. The properly accredited third mission under Li Hongzhang arrived in Japan on March 19 and concluded the Treaty of Shimonoseki, terminating the war on April 17. Japan's campaign to take Taiwan coincided with these negotiations.

The treaty ceded to Japan Taiwan, the Pescadores, and the Liaodong Peninsula. On April 23, the Triple Intervention of Russia, Germany, and France forced Japan to return the Liaodong Peninsula to China in exchange for a higher indemnity. The European powers did not want Japanese troops so close to Beijing. The indemnity more than covered Japan's war costs and funded a massive postwar rearmament program.

Russia, concluding that Japan threatened its own territorial ambitions, made an unprecedented postwar redirection of its foreign policy from Europe to Asia. In 1898 Russia took the Liaodong Peninsula for itself. Its Manchurian railway concessions, acquired between 1896 and 1898, were China's largest foreign concessions. Japan and Russia remained locked in a spheres of influence contest until Japan's defeat in World War II.

Engraving of the Battle of Port Arthur, c. 1894. *Looking to counter Russian influence in the region, Japan pushed Chinese forces out of Korea in 1894, starting the Sino-Japanese War. In a little over one year, Japanese troops routed the poorly equipped Chinese army, destroying the country's attempts at self-modernization and eroding the legitimacy of the Qing emperor.* **THE BATTLE OF PORT ARTHUR, C. 1894 (COLOURED ENGRAVING), CHINESE SCHOOL (19TH CENTURY)/BIBLIOTHEQUE NATIONALE, PARIS, FRANCE/THE BRIDGEMAN ART LIBRARY INTERNATIONAL**

The Western powers concluded that China's dismal military performance proved it incapable of reform. Therefore, they created an alternative to Chinese administration by vastly expanding their concessions areas. This scramble for concessions entailed French domination of China's three southernmost provinces, German domination of Shandong, Russian domination of Manchuria, British domination of central China, and Japanese domination of Fujian Province across from Taiwan.

The war and the scramble for concessions fatally undermined the legitimacy of Manchu minority rule. Japan's rejection of Sinification for Westernization and military victory overturned the myths of China's primacy and the universality of Confucianism. Unlike the Opium Wars, which entailed small coastal forces, the Sino-Japanese War went deep inland, demonstrating the unprecedented failure of the Manchus to defend China from Japan. The war signaled the failure (and end) of the Self-strengthening movement and led directly to the short-lived Hundred Days' Reform (1898). The war also marks the divergence of Chinese and Taiwanese economic and political development and the origins of the two-China problem as well as the origins of Korea as a festering international security problem.

SEE ALSO *Defense, 1800–1912; History: Overview, 1860–1912; Imperialism; Wars and the Military, 1800–1912; Wars since 1800.*

BIBLIOGRAPHY

Elleman, Bruce A. The Sino-Japanese War and the Partitioning of China. In *Modern Chinese Warfard, 1795–1989*, 94–115. London: Routledge, 2001.

Kuwada Etsu. *Kindai nihon sensō shi*. Tokyo: 同台経済懇話会, 1995.

Ōei Shinobu. *Sekaishi toshite no nichi-ro sensō*. Tokyo: 立風書房, 2001.

Paine, S. C. M. *The Sino-Japanese War of 1894–1895: Perceptions, Power, and Primacy*. Cambridge, U.K.: Cambridge University Press, 2003.

Qi Qizhand, ed. *Zhongri zhanzheng*. 11 vols. Beijing: Zhongua Shuju, 1989–1996).

Sun Kefu. *Jiawu zhongri luzhan shi*. Harbin: Heilongjiang Renmin Chubanshe, 1984.

S. C. M. Paine

SINOLOGY

According to the *Oxford Dictionary of the English Language*, the word *sinology*, a Greek and Latin hybrid, came into common usage sometime after 1860. Today, although scholars are not always clear about what they mean by *sinology*, this term may be regarded as the study of pre-modern Chinese civilization through philological and literary analysis. During the nineteenth and early twentieth centuries, the sinology curriculum in European and North American universities consisted of reading Chinese texts using techniques from Western classical scholarship, comparative philology, and, to a certain extent, Chinese annotated textual commentaries. Confusion about the term *sinology* arises if one defines the word as the study of all matters related to China, from its economy, to its history, to its literature. But the recognition that sinology might be interdisciplinary came only in the decades after the Second World War, when interest in hitherto neglected topics of Chinese culture and society first developed. By then the excesses of sinology were well known. As the eminent French sinologist Étienne Balazs (1905–1963) noted in 1960, "Sinology at this time has become nothing more than philological hair-splitting" (p. 196).

As a field of academic research and teaching, sinology was first given formal status in France, where in 1814 Jean-Pierre Abel Rémusat (1788–1832) took up the inaugural chair in Chinese created at the Collège de France. Abel Rémusat was the first in a line of distinguished French scholars who set high standards for learning about China in that country. His lecture notes were published in French in a compilation that became the first systematic exposition of the Chinese language in a European language.

One of the hallmarks of China studies in the nineteenth century was the distinction made between learning of the classical Chinese language, confined to elitist academic institutions, and education in the modern, spoken variant for practical reasons—commerce, diplomacy, missionary work—in specially funded professional schools for these purposes (e.g., l'École des langues orientales vivantes in Paris, established in 1843, or Berlin's Seminar für orientalischer Sprachen, created in 1887). While one might suppose that these latter institutions were integral to the contemporary needs of Western imperialistic ventures in China, academic sinologists engaged in imperialism as well, albeit of an intellectual kind. Because their scholarly discourse centered on uncovering philosophical truths embedded in the "unchanging" philosophy of Confucianism, they lent credence to popular conceptions of China's static nature and its incapacity to partake in the "progress" of history. They also reinforced this tendency through their method of study, which focused almost exclusively on the translation and annotation of texts. Moreover, because Western scholars were "subservient to the Chinese literati self-image" embedded in traditions of Chinese scholarship, they

also perpetuated what this status group considered important and relevant (Wright 1960). Thus, these sinologists did not write about China, as Edward Said has accused, in mythical and stereotypical terms. Rather, in their thrall to the literary and cultural traditions of the Chinese elite, Western sinologists upheld the privileged status of this group and denied Chinese studies exposure to the nascent disciplines of social anthropology, archaeology, epigraphy, and ethnology.

Perhaps the most ambitious expression of the exegetical mode of study was James Legge's (1815–1897) translation of the Chinese classics, which appeared between 1861 and 1872. Nowadays while China specialists may find Legge's corpus of work "basically sound . . . and still useful" (Barrett 1989, p. 75), in its heyday it too gave weight to Chinese literati scholastic preferences, which idealized the classics as timeless repositories of moral ideas and institutions. Legge had been a missionary in China, but in 1876 he was appointed to the first chair of Chinese established at Oxford University. As a missionary-turned-academic, Legge was not all that unlike his Cambridge University counterpart Sir Thomas Wade (1818–1895), a diplomat-turned-academic. Wade is probably best remembered for his romanization of Chinese, with which his Cambridge successor, Herbert Giles (1845–1935), another former diplomat, is also associated. Despite their important contributions, the activities of these three men and other sinologists of their generation (e.g., the Leiden sinologist Gustav Schlegel [1840–1903] and the Berlin scholar Wilhelm Schott [1807–1889]) were, in the view of their contemporaries, "not much more than exotic ornaments in their universities" (Franke 1995, p. 14). In Italy, sinology did not fare much better. Although that country had a head start owing to the Jesuit monopoly on China studies until the early nineteenth century, sinology there still remained within the missionary tradition for the next 150 years. In sum, an established program of China studies in Western academic institutions would have to wait until the twentieth century.

THE INTEGRATION OF SINOLOGY INTO ACADEMIC CURRICULA IN THE EARLY TWENTIETH CENTURY

By the 1890s there were significant changes in sinology. China researchers began to pursue their studies in China itself and to collaborate with Chinese intellectuals. Prominent among this group was the Frenchman Édouard Chavannes (1865–1918), who may be credited as the first true modern China scholar. Not only was he a master of a wide range of primary sources, he was also an intellectual innovator. After several years of residence in Beijing, he was appointed professor of Chinese in 1892 at the Collège de France, where he became the first instructor to periodize Chinese history into specific eras, each with distinctive characteristics. His translation of the *Shiji* (Records of the historian), part of which was published in six volumes as *Les mémoires de Se-ma Ts'ien* (1895–1905), remains indispensable even today for anyone studying this text. Chavannes furthered the study of Chinese Buddhism with his literary translations, and he pioneered the use of epigraphy and ethnography with textual analysis and historical criticism in his meticulous interpretive examination of the Daoist cult associated with the pilgrimage to the sacred mountain Mount Tai (*Le T'ai Chan*, 1910). Chavannes was also among the first Western scholars to access and utilize the documents discovered at Dunhuang. Among his students were four other eminent French sinologists: Paul Pelliot (1878–1945), Marcel Granet (1884–1940), Henri Maspero (1883–1945), and Paul Demiéville (1894–1979).

Although the origins of Russian sinology may be traced to eighteenth-century scholars, it was V. P. Vasil'ev (1818–1900) who first transformed China studies there. After residing in Beijing with the Russian clerical mission from 1840 to 1850, Vasil'ev established sinology programs first in Kazan University and then in Saint Petersburg University. He also initiated the study of Chinese religions, and published in a compendium on world literature, the first essay on the history of Chinese literature written by a European. V. M. Alekseev (1881–1951) took Vasil'ev's work a number of steps further, displaying an expertise in a wide range of topics from Chinese phonetics and epigraphy to classical poetry and folklore. Alekseev was the first European scholar to attempt to work out the meanings of popular Chinese New Year pictures (*nianhua*), which he discovered on a journey accompanying Chavannes through North China.

In Germany, Otto Franke (1863–1946), who also trained in China after university study in Europe, became professor of Chinese first in Hamburg in 1910 and then in Berlin in 1923 and made major contributions to the development of modern sinology. His forte was historical synthesis. He wrote the first political narrative of the Chinese state, *Geschichte des chinesischen Reiches* (A History of the Chinese Dynasties, five volumes, 1930–1952), and thereby freed China from the "stultifying dogma" that it had no history (Honey 2001, p. 141). Besides leaving a large corpus of publications, Franke also taught an entire generation of sinologists, including Balazs, Rolf Stein, Karl Bünger, Wolfram Eberhard, Walter Fuchs, Walter Simon, and the American George A. Kennedy.

SINOLOGY AT MID-CENTURY: THE TRANSITION TO MODERN CHINA STUDIES

The study of China took on new aims and methodologies in the course of the twentieth century. Until the Second World War, sinology in the United States was a limited affair—there was no major China center in any American university, and where some teaching was done, it was usually conducted by a European. Examples of this trend include the Germans Paul Carus and Bernard Laufer, both at the University of Chicago, Frederic Hirth at Columbia University, and the British scholar John Fryer at the University of California at Berkeley. And it was another European scholar, the Russian-born, French-naturalized Serge Elisséef (1899–1972), who helped lay the foundations for one of America's best-known institutions for the study of China, the Harvard-Yenching Library at Harvard University.

At Harvard in the late 1930s, John K. Fairbank (1907–1991), America's most eminent China scholar, began his career as an instructor in the history department and initiated a new phase in China studies with the first course on modern Chinese history. After the war, Fairbank again broke new ground with a regional-studies program on China and peripheral areas that allowed students to combine language study with training in history or one of the social sciences. Fairbank's endeavors helped stimulate more interest in China studies beyond Harvard and into the curricula of American colleges and universities. In his lectures and well-known books, Fairbank proclaimed that modernization in East Asia was impeded by traditional Chinese culture, and that China's modern development occurred only in response to external stimuli. Such thinking caused controversy, and led other specialists to reconsider contemporary trends in China study.

By the 1960s a number of eminent scholars, including the British sinologist Denis Twitchett, became concerned that "the heavy linguistic burden which sinology imposes" might somehow get lost in the demands of disciplinary training, especially in the social sciences (Twitchett 1964, p. 112). By this time sinology had fallen victim to the Cold War, and many American scholars abandoned Fairbank's multidisciplinary approach altogether and focused on the politics of Communist China. Other academics chose to follow Japanese scholarship on traditional China.

Japan had a very long history of sinological study. For hundreds of years before the twentieth century Japanese scholars of China, known as *kangakusha*, had learned about China through textual exegesis of the Confucian canon. Although Meiji era reforms in education brought Western specialists to Japan, such as the German Ludwig Reiss (1861–1928), who inspired new forms of historiography that made China part of Oriental history, the sinology curriculum in Japan basically remained committed to the tradition of commentary. Prewar Japan's most famous sinologist was Naitō Konan (1866–1934). His analysis of Chinese history, which traced the rise of modern China to the Song era (960–1279), became so influential that leading textbooks in English and French published in the 1960s incorporated his periodization. In postwar Tokyo, Marxism dominated China studies, while in Kyoto scholars continued to endorse Naitō's ideas, especially those concerning the centrality of local society to China's development in the long term.

RECENT DEVELOPMENTS IN CHINA STUDIES

In the last decades of the twentieth century, as more and more American, European, and Japanese scholars and students gained easier access to archival sources in East Asia, the study of China was once again transformed. Improved language training both in and outside China has also helped facilitate learning both modern and classical Chinese. In addition, the study of Manchu has attracted those wanting to understand better the empire-wide dimensions of China's last dynasty, the Qing (1644–1912). But it is the subdiscipline of Chinese archaeology that has made the greatest impact on the study of China by revising chronologies, redating texts, and expanding the pool of material artifacts. Newly discovered treasures dating from thousands of years ago link early China to regions as far away as Central and Southeast Asia, India, and Burma (Myanmar). For example, the bronzes unearthed at Sanxingdui in Sichuan Province have revamped the received notion that the Chinese people descended in a single direct line from one core region in the middle and lower reaches of the Yellow River. Other excavations in Tarim, Xinjiang, have uncovered the remains of Caucasian peoples, in the form of mummies wrapped in textiles similar to those found in ancient tombs in what is now central Europe. Thus, as research continues to intensify on texts found on oracle bones or on bamboo slips or silk fragments unearthed in newly discovered grave sites, it is likely that the threads linking China to the rich tapestry of global history will be unraveled. The new documentary finds will need ever more precise philological scrutiny and sophisticated textual analysis, which should boost the significance of sinology study both within and outside China.

BIBLIOGRAPHY

Balazs, Étienne. The Birth of Capitalism in China. *Journal of the Economic and Social History of the Orient* 3 (1960): 196–216.

Barrett, Timothy H. *Singular Listlessness: A Short History of Chinese Books and British Scholars.* London: Wellsweep, 1989.

Fogel, Joshua A. *Politics and Sinology: The Case of Naitō Konan (1866–1934).* Cambridge, MA: Council on East Asian Studies, 1984.

Franke, Herbert. In Search of China: Some General Remarks on the History of European Sinology. In *Europe Studies China*, ed. Ming Wilson and John Cayley, 11–25. London: Han-Shan Tang Books, 1995.

Honey, David B. *Incense at the Altar: Pioneering Sinologists and the Development of Classical Chinese Philology.* New Haven, CT: American Oriental Society, 2001.

Said, Edward. *Orientalism.* New York: Vintage Books, 1978.

Twitchett, Denis. Comments on the "Chinese Studies and the Disciplines' Symposium": A Lone Cheer for Sinology. *Journal of Asian Studies* 24, 1 (1964): 109–112.

Wilson, Ming, and John Cayley, eds. *Europe Studies China.* London: Han-Shan Tang Books, 1995.

Wright, Arthur. The Study of Chinese Civilization. *Journal of the History of Ideas* 21, 2 (1960): 235–255.

Zurndorfer, Harriet T. *China Bibliography: A Research Guide to Reference Works about China, Past and Present.* Leiden, Netherlands: Brill, 1995.

Zurndorfer, Harriet T. Orientalism, Sinology, and Public Policy: Baron Antoine Isaac Silvestre de Sacy and the Foundation of Chinese Studies in Post-Revolutionary France. In *Images de la Chine: Le contexte occidental de la sinologie naissante*, ed. Edward J. Malatesta and Yves Raguin, 175–192. Paris: Institut Ricci, 1995.

Zurndorfer, Harriet T. Not Bound to China: Étienne Balazs, Fernand Braudel, and the Politics of the Study of Chinese History in Post-War France. *Past and Present* 185 (2004): 189–221.

Harriet T. Zurndorfer

SINO-SOVIET SCHISM

The emergence and rapid escalation of the Sino-Soviet conflict in the late 1950s and early 1960s was not only belatedly grasped in the West, it also surprised the participants themselves. Many factors have been noted: state interests, nationalism and national dignity, contrasting international strategies, exaggerated ideological differences, rivalry in the international communist movement, different domestic policies, and personality clashes of headstrong leaders (Mao Zedong and Nikita Khrushchev). All played their part.

CHINA'S RISE FROM SUBORDINATE PARTY TO COLEADER OF INTERNATIONAL COMMUNISM

The background to the schism was decades of participation in the international communist movement, the Communist Party of the Soviet Union (CPSU) as undisputed leader, and the Chinese Communist Party (CCP) as one of its most successful offspring. The relationship was marked by a fervent sense of being part of the world revolution and by hierarchical deference, but as Mao developed an independent organization, tensions emerged. Nevertheless, Mao always intended to "lean to one side" and concluded the Sino-Soviet alliance in 1950, notwithstanding resentment over Joseph Stalin's (1879–1953) terms, which made it China's last unequal treaty. The post-Stalin Soviet leadership headed by Khrushchev (1894–1971) sought to repair the relationship, and by 1954 voided the most galling aspects of the 1950 treaty, stepped up concrete aid to China, and declared the PRC coleader of the movement. Beyond this, Soviet management of the international movement became more flexible generally, as seen in the rapprochement with Yugoslavia, a development the CCP strongly approved, and Soviet and Chinese foreign policies were highly compatible. The relationship was never better, but Stalin's death left Mao with an opposite number in Khrushchev who did not inspire deference.

Major developments in the Sino-Soviet Schism

Date and event	Nature of development
2/1956: CPSU Twentieth Congress	Khrushchev's denunciation of Stalin
10–11/1956: Polish and Hungarian crises	CCP concern with clumsy Soviet handling of crises, active role in moderating tensions
11/1957: Moscow conference of ruling communist parties	Chinese support of Soviet leadership but different views on international strategy
1958: military cooperation issues	Mao interprets Soviet proposals for joint facilities as impinging on PRC sovereignty
7/1958: Middle East crisis	USSR proposes diplomatic settlement in UN where PRC is unrepresented
8–10/1958: Taiwan Straits crisis	Conducted with little consultation, PRC resentment over tepid Soviet support
1958–1959: Soviet criticism of Great Leap Forward	CPSU reacts to Chinese claims of rapid progress to communism
Mid-1959: USSR reneges on nuclear aid	Soviets tear up 1957 agreement to assist Chinese nuclear weapons program
9–10/1959: Khrushchev meetings with Eisenhower and Mao	Tense visit to Beijing after U.S. summit emphasizing peaceful coexistence
10/1959: Sino-Indian border skirmishes	Soviets adopt neutral stance, seen as violating fraternal obligations by PRC
4/1960: Lenin anniversary polemics	CCP comprehensively indicts Soviet theory, strategy, and tactics
Mid-1960: withdrawal of Soviet experts from China	USSR pulls out experts at time of severe PRC economic collapse
From 1960: border clashes and dispute	Incidents along 4,500-mile border, in 1963; China raises territory lost to czarist Russia
11/1960: Moscow conference of 81 communist parties	Both sides compromise but only paper over fundamental differences
10/1961: CPSU Twenty-second Congress	Khrushchev attacks Albania, Zhou Enlai walks out
10–11/1962: Sino-Indian border war	Soviet military aid provided to India
10/1962: Cuban missile crisis	China accuses Soviet Union of adventurism and capitulationism
8/1963: nuclear-test-ban treaty	U.S.-USSR-UK treaty bans testing while China prepares for own test (successful in 10/1964)
1963–1964: Sino-Soviet polemics	CCP open letters attack Soviet domestic as well as foreign policy revisionism
From 1965: Soviet military buildup	Major shift of Soviet forces from Europe to Chinese border areas
8/1968: invasion of Czechoslovakia and Brezhnev doctrine	PRC alarm after invasion and Soviet claim of right to intervene in socialist countries
3/1969: Zhenbao (Ussuri) border clash	Major clash raises fears on both sides, leads to PRC preparations for full-scale USSR attack
8/1971: Soviet-Indian treaty	Chinese fear of Soviet encirclement increases
2/1972: Nixon visit to PRC	Sino-U.S. rapprochement heightens USSR fears
Mid-1970s: Soviet involvement in Africa	PRC reacts to Soviet backing of revolutionary movements with support of rightwing groups
1975–1979: Sino-Vietnam conflict	PRC reacts to growing Vietnamese alignment with USSR culminating in early 1979 war
1977–1978: U.S.-China normalization	PRC spurns post-Mao Soviet offers of better relations to focus on U.S. ties
12/1979: invasion of Afghanistan	Confirms PRC view of Soviet expansionism
5/1989: Gorbachev visits Beijing	Formal CPSU-CCP ties restored two and a half years before collapse of USSR

Table 1

IDEOLOGICAL SPLIT AND STATE THREATS

The first issue in the series of events leading to the split (see Table 1) was Khrushchev's denunciation of Stalin at the 1956 Soviet Twentieth Party Congress, which left the Chinese upset by the lack of prior consultation and concerned that Khrushchev had undermined the legitimacy of communism everywhere. Unease with CPSU leadership was further heightened by Soviet handling of the Polish and Hungarian crises in fall 1956, and China moved to mediate between Moscow and the Eastern Europeans. Mao fundamentally sought to shore up Soviet leadership but, as in the Yugoslav case, in a less hierarchical sense, and in the process China's confidence in its own role grew.

At the November 1957 Moscow conference, China again strongly supported the Soviet Union but in an altered manner that called for tighter control of the Soviet bloc, backed the new Soviet attack on Yugoslavia, and joined Moscow in a more aggressive international strategy toward the West, with Soviet gratitude reflected in prom-

ises to assist the PRC's nuclear weapons program. Yet at the same conference, portentous differences emerged, with Mao having a more optimistic view of the international balance of forces.

These differences began to manifest themselves in various developments over the next few years. Given the more optimistic view of the balance of forces, the Chinese felt the Soviets should have adopted a stronger posture in specific crises and international strategy generally. Specifically, despite ongoing efforts to pressure the United States, Moscow adhered to peaceful coexistence over CCP objections, notably concerning Khrushchev's 1959 summit with President Dwight D. Eisenhower (1890–1969), which was quickly followed by a tense meeting with Mao in Beijing. Given the nature of the regimes, these differences were formulated in increasingly polemic ideological prescriptions—the CCP emphasizing support for wars of national liberation in the third world in contrast to peaceful coexistence. While the arguments on both sides were overblown, they reflected an underlying reality: The Soviet Union was a nuclear superpower engaged with the United

States on a worldwide basis, while China was partially ostracized internationally, without diplomatic relations with the United States or a United Nations seat; and the Soviet Union's primary focus was Europe, with the result that the PRC's regional interests had a lower priority in Moscow.

A range of other issues emerged from 1958. An ideological issue concerning domestic policy was Soviet criticism of Mao's Great Leap Forward and the accompanying claim of a special path for building communism, producing resentment in Beijing. Arguably the most important conflict at this early stage concerned Soviet plans for joint military facilities in China, plans that ironically both enhanced PRC defenses and were consistent with Mao's call for a tougher communist posture, but which, given the detail, Mao interpreted as an effort to exert Soviet control and offensive to national dignity. An issue combining national interests with expectations of fraternal support was the border conflict with India in 1959 (when Moscow tried to stay neutral) and the larger war in 1962 (when the Soviet Union provided military supplies to India). Soviet actions can be seen as part of a strategy of building ties with the nonaligned movement, but from Beijing they appeared a betrayal of internationalist duty.

While incessant CCP criticism can arguably be seen as the main factor driving the conflict to schism, Soviet actions from 1959 to 1963 played a major role: tearing up the 1957 nuclear agreement in 1959, withdrawing experts in 1960, openly attacking Albania, which had defied Moscow and developed ties with China in 1961, and concluding the 1963 nuclear-test-ban treaty with the United States and United Kingdom at a time when China had not yet achieved nuclear status. For its part, China denounced Soviet actions during the 1962 Cuban missile crisis as both adventurism in putting the missiles in, and capitulationism in taking them out. This was followed by open polemics not only attacking Moscow's foreign policy, but (à la Yugoslavia) declaring the Soviet domestic structure revisionist.

In the early 1960s, two contradictory tendencies emerged in Mao's thinking and in PRC policy—a less revolutionary foreign policy that focused more on building a broad array of anti-U.S. and anti-Soviet forces than simply emphasizing third-world revolution, and an obsession with preventing Soviet-style revisionism in China. The latter led to the Cultural Revolution, which in turn prevented the PRC from pursuing a coherent foreign policy, but this changed in 1968 with the Soviet invasion of Czechoslovakia and the Brezhnev Doctrine claiming the right to intervene in other socialist countries. This, together with border skirmishes since the early 1960s that became more ominous since 1965 with the massive buildup of Soviet troops on the border, shifted Chinese attention to strategic threats as reflected in the rhetorical change from "Soviet revisionism" to "Soviet social imperialism." Any doubt was removed by the major armed clash at Zhenbao Island on the Ussuri River in March 1969, an attack that immediately led to PRC war preparations in anticipation of a full-scale Soviet attack. The key policy adjustments were pursuit of Sino-U.S. rapprochement and Mao's "one-line" policy of opposition to the Soviet Union and, by extension, Soviet allies. By the mid-1970s, this included Vietnam and liberation movements in Africa, notably the revolutionary regime in Angola. In this realpolitik approach, Deng Xiaoping faithfully carried out Mao's wishes, much as he had when denouncing Soviet revisionism in the early 1960s.

THE POST-MAO ALLEVIATION OF THE SCHISM

Following Mao's death in 1976, China maintained hostility toward the Soviet Union as Soviet efforts to reduce tensions were rebuffed. Deng placed priority on normalizing relations with the United States, a priority reflecting continuing concern with the Soviet strategic threat, as well as a calculation that U.S. ties were crucial to China's modernization and would be facilitated by conflict with Moscow. The hostility underlay the brief war to "teach Vietnam a lesson" in early 1979, while the strategic concern was confirmed by the Soviet invasion of Afghanistan at the end of the year. But as the 1980s unfolded, China concluded that the Soviet Union was overextended by its adventure, and its threat reduced. Normalization of Sino-Soviet relations was finally achieved in May 1989 with Mikhail Gorbachev's visit to Beijing and the reestablishment of CPSU-CCP relations.

The irony was that the restoration of fraternal ties had little to do with settling the ferocious ideological exchanges of the 1950s and 1960s, nor was there any compelling strategic need for normalization with the Soviet empire crumbling, and the regime itself having only another two-and-a-half years to survive. Chinese scholars today acknowledge CCP errors in the conduct of the ideological polemics and later in overestimating the Soviet strategic threat. A second irony was that Gorbachev's visit came during the 1989 Tiananmen demonstrations, even as his own empire was fracturing. The lesson learned by Chinese leaders from this conjunction of events was that Gorbachev's loss of political control in the Soviet Union could not be tolerated in China.

SEE ALSO *Chinese Marxism: Overview; Deng Xiaoping; Lin Biao; Mao Zedong; Peng Dehuai; Russia, Relations with.*

BIBLIOGRAPHY

Brzezinski, Zbigniew K. *The Soviet Bloc: Unity and Conflict.* Rev. ed. New York: Praeger, 1960.

Dittmer, Lowell. *Sino-Soviet Normalization and Its International Implications, 1945–1990.* Seattle: University of Washington Press, 1992.

Gittings, John. *Survey of the Sino-Soviet Dispute: A Commentary and Extracts from the Recent Polemics, 1963–1967.* New York: Oxford University Press, 1968.

Lieberthal, Kenneth. *Sino-Soviet Conflict in the 1970s: Its Evolution and Implications for the Strategic Triangle.* Santa Monica, CA: Rand, 1978.

Lowenthal, Richard. *World Communism: The Disintegration of a Secular Faith.* New York: Oxford University Press, 1964.

Westad, Odd Arne, ed. *Brothers in Arms: The Rise and Fall of the Sino-Soviet Alliance, 1945–1963.* Washington, DC: Woodrow Wilson Center Press, 1998.

Zagoria, Donald S. *The Sino-Soviet Conflict, 1956–1961.* New York: Atheneum, 1964.

Frederick C. Teiwes

SMUGGLING

Smuggling, defined as the evasion of taxes on trade, or the contravention of an official embargo on trade, has been significant in modern Chinese history. Smuggling took many forms. Salt was smuggled to break the government monopoly on its trade of that commodity. A great deal of illicit activity over the centuries also consisted of traders' evasion of local levies on goods shipped within and between regions. In addition, regional authorities were responsible for food security in their jurisdictions, and in times of shortages they imposed restrictions on the extra-regional shipment of foodstuffs.

Three areas of smuggling were particularly significant to the late Qing and early Republican regimes. A century of opium smuggling into China began in the late eighteenth century in association with British empire-building in Asia. Later, the smuggling of Japanese-manufactured goods accompanied the expansion of Japanese military and economic power in China in the 1930s. During both periods, the smuggling of armaments enriched those who flouted Chinese and foreign embargoes on the arms trade.

BRITISH-BACKED OPIUM SMUGGLING

Opium imports into China became contraband goods when an imperial edict of 1729 prohibited the importation, sale, and consumption of opium. The trade in opium continued to expand despite the ban, spurred by the British control of abundant supplies in colonial India and by the willingness of Chinese traders and officials to cooperate in shipping and distributing the drug. The opium business grew rapidly, leading to a series of military conflicts and diplomatic confrontations between Qing China and a British-led group of Western states. As the business expanded after the end of the Opium War in 1842, Shanghai became a major emporium largely on the basis of the lucrative illicit trade. Reluctantly authorizing legalization of the opium trade in 1860, the Qing state developed a centralized tax-collection system in which tariffs and transit taxes on opium shipments became a major source of revenue. Opium smuggling continued, however, as many dealers evaded official control. As a British colony, Hong Kong was a free port, and the colony's economic importance rested largely on its role as a transshipment center for large quantities of opium smuggled into South China. This role continued even after a set of opium ordinances designed to halt the flow of opium through Hong Kong took effect in 1887. Authorities often turned a blind eye to the misconduct of local dealers who shipped large quantities of opium into China under cover of their official licenses as brokers supplying limited quantities of the drug to consumers in Hong Kong. On one occasion in 1894, the governor of Hong Kong overturned a ruling of the colony's supreme court in a case in which a large illicit shipment of opium had been confiscated. Contracts for the opium brokerage business were due to be renewed at the time, and the governor feared that would-be bidders would be deterred by enforcement of the ordinances (Wright 1950, p. 589).

Inward smuggling operations are inevitably balanced by outward smuggling. Following the opening of the treaty ports, Chinese and foreign interests cooperated in the "coolie trade," exporting labor in contravention of Chinese law. Although emigration became legal in 1893, smuggling continued in this business when merchants kidnapped or tricked villagers in order to sell them into servitude overseas. From 1842 to the 1930s the southern port of Xiamen became a particularly important transit point for both smuggled opium imports and labor exports, which were carried in British-owned ships, mainly to Southeast Asia but also as far as the Caribbean and Peru.

The special privileges in China that Westerners had gained through war included exemption from internal transit taxes, and this encouraged a new kind of smuggling during the 1840s: Unscrupulous foreigners sold protection from taxation to Chinese traders by collecting fees to register their businesses under foreign flags or renting space for their cargoes on foreign ships. Despite their privileges in China, foreigners operating in the treaty ports sought reductions in their taxes on foreign trade and demanded regularity in the administration of trade from one part of China to the next. Foreign business interests and the sovereign authority of the Qing state were gradually reconciled in the 1860s by the creation of a central agency: the Chinese Imperial Maritime Customs Administration. Thereafter, the customs authorities took responsibility for rationalizing national tariff regulations and for preventing tariff evasion. In addition, the customs agency became responsible for the enforcement of embargoes on arms imports. Earlier systems of revenue collection were not immediately displaced by customs, however, occasionally resulting in claims by local authorities that duties should be paid on goods that had cleared customs. Until it began to build up its own preventive fleet in 1928, the customs agency's enforcement of regulations and embargoes depended on the cooperation of the armed forces and other authorities in particular locations in recognizing and checking smuggling activity.

SMUGGLING IN ARMAMENTS

The most significant embargo on armaments imports in Chinese history resulted from an international agreement in May 1919. Fearful of the repercussions of civil war in China, Britain, France, the United States, and nine other countries jointly declared that they would ban the export to China of arms, munitions, and materials used to make weapons, and would prohibit their nationals from serving as intermediaries in such exports. This embargo was lifted in 1929 in recognition that it had not been effective, had diverted business to countries that were not party to the agreement such as Japan and the Soviet Union, and might in fact have fuelled an arms race between China's regional military commanders as they sought the restricted goods to equip and modernize their forces. The northern general Zhang Zuolin (1875–1928) was one of the militarists who imported contraband goods during the 1920s, employing as his agent a former British military officer named Francis ("Frank") Sutton (1884–1944).

JAPANESE-BACKED SMUGGLING

Just as Hong Kong's status provided opportunities to smugglers in South China, Japan's leaseholds and the Japanese military occupation of territory in North China after 1895 produced waves of illicit trade. The Japanese occupation of Manchuria in 1931 immediately created a serious smuggling problem, one that became critical in 1934 when the U.S. Silver Purchase Act led to large outward shipments of the silver coins upon which China's national monetary system was based. To balance outward flows, Japanese dealers smuggled manufactured goods into China, working with many Korean runners as well as Chinese partners in these operations. Prohibited and restricted goods, particularly armaments and morphine, along with consumer goods such as rayon cloth and white sugar, were smuggled in large quantities through the Japanese-occupied Northeast. The cloth and sugar were imported in contravention of the high tariffs that had been imposed on them by the central government in Nanjing beginning in 1928, after China gained freedom from the tariff restrictions of the Qing era.

Japanese-backed smuggling in North China became an international crisis in 1936. This followed the establishment of a Japanese-sponsored regional government in coastal territory south of the Great Wall adjacent to Manchuria. Called the East Hebei Anti-Communist Autonomous Government

Smuggled cars packed in a shipping container, Fuzhou, Fujian province, December 18, 2004. Smuggling of goods into China has persisted for centuries, with merchants sneaking salt and opium shipments into the country to avoid taxation imposed by imperial officials. In the 2000s, automobiles have become a favorite import of smugglers, despite government efforts to increase security at Chinese ports. AP IMAGES

(*Jidong fangong zizhi zhengfu*), the territory was administered by a chairman, Yin Rugeng (1885–1947), who repudiated the authority of China's government in Nanjing and established a separate customs regime. His low tariffs, set at one-quarter of Nanjing's rates, encouraged a wave of smuggling of rayon, sugar, and kerosene in such massive quantities that Chinese authorities, foreign governments, and the general public became alarmed, fearing a collapse of China's industrial sector if tariff protection were lost and damage to China's creditworthiness if reduced customs revenue delayed the repayment of foreign loans secured on customs revenue. When Japanese officials responded stubbornly to protests against the smuggling in North China, claiming that the trade through East Hebei was legitimate, antipathy toward Japan and sympathy for China's national cause increased, both in China and in the West. Despite the close attention of journalists and governments, however, large quantities of Japanese goods continued to flow through eastern Hebei to other regions. After Japanese armies occupied North China from July 1937, the flow of goods continued uninterrupted across the wartime borders between Japanese-occupied zones and Free China.

SMUGGLING SINCE 1949

After historical experiences of foreign smuggling activity as a prelude to assaults by foreign armies, Chinese authorities since 1949 have viewed smuggling as a threat to national security. Serious offenders are subject to the death penalty. Smuggling in the People's Republic of China is generally a form of official corruption. During the 1980s, for instance, many government units in South China and beyond purchased automobiles illicitly imported through the island of Hainan. Foreign nationals have been only minor players in smuggling since 1949, however, as China has successfully defended its territorial sovereignty. Nonetheless, separate trade regimes in Taiwan, Hong Kong, and Macau have provided opportunities for smugglers along the southern coast. With China's recent commercial expansion, the surveillance capacity of its coastal fleet has not kept pace with flows of unregistered trade crossing the South China Sea. Piracy, inevitably associated with smuggling, has become a problem in the region.

SEE ALSO *Salt, 1800–1949.*

BIBLIOGRAPHY

Adshead, Samuel Adrian M. *The Modernization of the Chinese Salt Administration, 1900–1920.* Cambridge, MA: Harvard University Press, 1970.

Chan, Anthony B. *Arming the Chinese: The Western Armaments Trade in Warlord China, 1920–1928.* Vancouver, Canada: University of British Columbia Press, 1982.

Drage, Charles. *General of Fortune: The Story of One-armed Sutton.* London: Heinemann, 1963.

Hill, Emily M. Japanese-backed Smuggling in North China: Chinese Popular and Official Resistance, 1935–1937. In *Resisting Japan: Mobilizing for War in Modern China, 1935–1945,* ed. David Pong, 20–54. East Norwalk, CT: EastBridge, 2008.

Kwan, Man Bun. *The Salt Merchants of Tianjin: State-making and Civil Society in Late Imperial China.* Honolulu: University of Hawaii Press, 2001.

Qi Chunfeng. *Zhongri jingji zhanzhong de zousi huodong, 1937–1945* [Smuggling activities during the Sino-Japanese economic war, 1937–1945]. Beijing: Beijing Renmin Chubanshe, 2002.

Trocki, Carl A. *Opium, Empire, and the Global Political Economy: A Study of the Asian Opium Trade, 1750–1959.* New York: Routledge, 1999.

Wakeman, Frederic, Jr. Shanghai Smuggling. In *In the Shadow of the Rising Sun: Shanghai under Japanese Occupation, 1937–1945,* Wen-hsin Yeh and Christian Henriot, 116–155. New York: Cambridge University Press, 2004.

Waldron, Arthur. *From War to Nationalism: China's Turning Point, 1924–1925.* New York: Cambridge University Press, 1995.

Wright, Stanley F. *China's Struggle for Tariff Autonomy, 1843–1938.* Shanghai: Kelly and Walsh, 1938.

Wright, Stanley F. *Hart and the Chinese Customs.* Belfast, U.K.: William Mullan, 1950.

Emily M. Hill

SNOW, EDGAR
1905–1972

Edgar Snow was the first Western reporter to visit the blockaded "Red capital" of the Communist-controlled part of the Republic of China (ROC) in 1936. During his visit, Snow, a respected American journalist and writer, interviewed a group of top Chinese Communist leaders, including future party chairman Mao Zedong. His detailed interviews resulted in several eye-opening books and articles, which depicted Mao and his followers in a favorable light as idealistic revolutionaries who advocated radical agrarian reform and were defending China against Japanese imperialism and colonialism.

EARLY LIFE

Edgar Parks Snow was born on July 17, 1905, in Kansas City, Missouri. He attended the University of Missouri's School of Journalism before moving to New York in 1924 to pursue a career in advertising. In 1928 Snow traveled to China, where he stayed for the next thirteen years, reporting on East Asian affairs for the *Chicago Tribune, New York Sun, New York Herald Tribune, London Daily Herald,* and other major newspapers and magazines. He learned Chinese, became assistant editor of Shanghai's *China Weekly Review,* and lectured at the Yenching University in Beijing, one of the leading Christian colleges founded by American missionaries. His first book dealing with the Japanese invasion of Manchuria, *Far Eastern Front,* was published in 1933 and was followed by other authoritative books that made him world-renowned.

In June 1936 Snow sneaked through the Guomindang's blockade to reach Bao'an, the temporary capital of the "Chinese People's Soviet Republic" in the northern province of Shaanxi, and spent the next five months with Mao Zedong and other top Communist leaders. Snow gave a very sympathetic firsthand account of how the little-known Chinese Communists and their Red Army were fighting against Imperial Japan's brutal aggression and occupation, while trying at the same time to improve the lives of local landless peasants. His famous book-length report, *Red Star over China,* traces the rise of the Chinese Communist Party from its obscure beginning in 1921 to the epic Long March (1934–1935) and the temporary retreat to Yan'an in the 1930s. Published in 1937, Snow's best seller became a classic of modern journalism and remains to this day a primary source on the early history of China's Communist revolutionary movement. In 1939 he paid a second visit to Mao and his followers in Yan'an, which was under attack by the government forces of Chiang Kai-shek (Jiang Jieshi) and the advancing Japanese armies.

LATER YEARS

Snow returned to the United States in 1941 with his first wife, Helen Foster Snow, whom he had met and married in China. During World War II he was dispatched as a war correspondent for the *Saturday Evening Post* to Hong Kong, the Philippines, India, China, and the Soviet Union to write about their role in the fight against fascism and Nazism—experiences that became the basis for his books *Battle for Asia* (1941) and *People on Our Side* (1944). He reported with anguish how Chiang Kai-shek's forces had attacked and massacred Red Army units instead of jointly resisting the Japanese invaders. Because of his status as a lifelong "friend of China" and his efforts to win American diplomatic recognition for the recently established People's Republic of China (PRC), Snow was accused of being a Communist and was questioned by the Federal Bureau of Investigation during the Joseph McCarthy (1908–1957) witch-hunt era. Snow was never called before the congressional committees investigating un-American activities, but the Red Scare of the late 1940s and early 1950s eventually forced him to flee to Switzerland, although he retained his U.S. citizenship and passport.

Snow returned to China in 1960 and again in 1964 to 1965 to interview Chairman Mao and Premier Zhou Enlai. In his books *The Other Side of the River: Red China Today* (1962) and *The Long Revolution* (1972), he described Communist-ruled China in a positive light, refusing to criticize Mao's "Great Proletarian Cultural Revolution" (1966–1969). As the Cold War hysteria waned, his writings reappeared in the American print media due to his extraordinary personal access to the most important figures in Communist China's ruling elite. During his final trip to China in August 1970, Chinese government officials told him that they would welcome an official visit to Beijing by President Richard Nixon (1913–1994), a piece of information that Snow made known to the White House. Although eager to normalize relations with mainland China, the Nixon administration would not entrust Snow with any mediating role because of his reputed pro-Communist leanings. When he was stricken with pancreatic cancer on the eve of President Nixon's historic trip to China, the Chinese authorities sent a medical team to Switzerland to help with his treatment. Snow died on February 15, 1972, in Geneva, but his remains are buried on the campus of Peking University in Beijing under a headstone that reads: "Edgar Snow, an American friend of the Chinese people."

SEE ALSO *Mao Zedong; United States, Relations with.*

BIBLIOGRAPHY

Farnsworth, Robert M. *From Vagabond to Journalist: Edgar Snow in Asia, 1928–1941.* Columbia: University of Missouri Press, 1996.

Hamilton, John M. *Edgar Snow: A Biography.* Bloomington: Indiana University Press, 1988.

Snow, Edgar. *Red Star over China.* Rev. ed. New York: Grove Press, 1968.

Snow, Helen Foster. *My China Years: A Memoir.* New York: Morrow, 1984.

Thomas, S. Bernard. *Season of High Adventure: Edgar Snow in China.* Berkeley: University of California Press, 1996.

Rossen Vassilev

SOCIAL AND COMMUNITY ORGANIZATIONS

Social organizations are vital for China's development as a society. The rise of associations and organized interest groups played an important part in the civic revolutions in Europe and North America. As in China, in the beginning European associations (such as associations of entrepreneurs, guilds, and other interest associations) were weak and just advised the bureaucracy. Only with increasing power did they turn against the absolutistic state and become an instrument of democracy. Even such nonpolitical hobby associations as sports clubs and choral groups played an important political role in Western political life of the nineteenth century. Early on, Alexis de Tocqueville (1805–1859) described the function of such associations in the process of democratization, expressing ideas that apply to China today: Public life, business transactions, and cooperative ventures require regulation of common actions, the right of assembly, and freedom of association. Such associations act in the interstices between the individual and the state.

Social-interest organizations, that is, associations for organized expression and the enforcement of social interests, are an important factor in the process of democratization. Such groups, in the interest of their members, seek to articulate common interests and influence society. This is a political process, though, as in China, it starts with professional associations. Associations and organizations of a broad spectrum of interests form an important basis for social competition. Functional organizations—such as associations of entrepreneurs, producers, professionals, and peasants—can articulate their interests. They contribute to a multitude of ideas and attitudes and thus support the development of pluralistic thinking.

NEW INTEREST GROUPS

In China, the rise of new strata and new social actors have led to the development of new social groups, and new group interests have spawned the formation of professional and social associations and organizations. Since the late 1980s it has been permitted by law to establish scientific, entrepreneurial, professional, academic, artistic, and hobby associations. At first most such associations were formed in rural areas. This concentration in rural areas was because peasants for decades lacked channels to articulate their interests and resolve conflicts.

DEVELOPMENT OF ASSOCIATIONS

According to the Ministry of Civil Affairs, which is responsible for registering associations, by the end of 2005 the ministry had registered 320,000 nonstate organizations from the county level upward, that is, associations, federations, and other organizations such as nongovernmental organizations (NGOs) and government-organized NGOs (GONGOs). These figures do not include associations at the township and village level, as they are not required to register. The term *association*, however, is rather imprecise, as it encompasses organizations founded by the central government as well as those set up by citizens. One has to differentiate among various categories of organizations: government-run organizations (*guanban*), whose leaders are appointed by party and state organs and which get their financial means from the state; half-government-run organizations (*banguan*), whose leaders come from institutions to which the half-government-run organizations belong and whose finances come from the state or are self-procured; and privately run organizations (*minban*), which are founded by citizens with official permission and which procure their own finances.

LIMITED ROOM TO MANEUVER

All such organizations must operate under the control of the party and state and are not autonomous. Although the Chinese government officially encourages citizens to set up social organizations and NGOs, their aims and activities are subject to strict official supervision. This is why so far there are no genuine pressure groups in China. Yet Chinese organizations have a certain freedom to act, and in particular are free to advocate to the government for their members (be they individuals, entrepreneurs, or professionals).

Furthermore, unlike in democratic systems, in China such organizations cannot be set up autonomously. They have to be registered, and the Regulations concerning Registration and Administration of Social Organizations of 1989 stipulate that registration is possible only with the help of a patron institution or sponsoring agency. For every registration, an official institution (office, state or party institution, or public enterprise) needs to sponsor the association and

assume responsibility for formal patronage, monitoring, and performing legal functions. Moreover, only one NGO may operate in a specific sector in each region. Yet these restrictions do not mean that associations primarily represent the interests of the party-state.

The events of the June 1989 prodemocracy movement show, however, how the party-state reacts when political structures begin to form parallel to the power system. Especially during the urban protest movements in spring 1989, one of the central questions was whether the Chinese Communist Party was willing to tolerate autonomous organizations of intellectuals, students, and workers confronting the party. Various interest organizations came into existence and even official associations, such as the Chinese Union of Writers, tried to become autonomous of the party. Party leaders recognized the danger resulting from the rise of parallel power structures and consequently suppressed the newly formed organizations after June 4, 1989. The urban protest movement thus stood for autonomous organizations that could stand up to the authoritarian state.

Prior to 1989, social organizations emerged spontaneously and were not monitored and controlled by the central government. An autonomous space began to exist within which such organizations could act rather independently. After 1989 the central authorities pursued a double strategy: They suppressed associations that could challenge the power monopoly of the Communist Party, and they attempted to incorporate important organizations into the government. Accordingly, in 1998 new regulations were passed, Regulations concerning Registration and Administration of Social Organizations, and the somewhat nebulous clauses of pre-1989 regulations became more precise and more restrictive.

ENVIRONMENTAL MOVEMENT

Although most associations are concerned with sports, health, recreation, professions, culture, science and technology, and similar activities, since 2000 there has emerged a broad range of social organizations and foundations active in politically more sensitive fields. For instance, an environmental movement is gradually evolving, and environmental NGOs are coming into being. The latter originate mainly in larger cities and areas affected by evident ecological crises, and are locally organized and oriented. According to official Chinese data, in 2005 more than 2,000 such NGOs existed, most of them emerging after 1990. They are involved with protecting the environment and endangered animal species; aiding fringe groups, AIDS patients, and ethnic minorities; protecting cultural relics; advocating on consumer issues; and preserving nature and the landscape. There are also NGOs involved in extending and enhancing grassroots elections, participating in urban neighborhood communities, providing legal advice, and improving the labor conditions of rural migrant workers.

Students viewing donated books, Changchun, Jilin province, September 12, 2006. *In the late 1980s, the Chinese government began allowing the formation of organizations based around a common interest, such as a trade, social concern, or hobby. Many of these groups have provided services on a local level, such as donating supplies to schools, preserving green space in urban areas, or assisting migrant workers, filling needs often unmet by the central government.* **CHINA PHOTOS/GETTY IMAGES**

Successful social and environmental movements since 2000 have been movements against hydroelectric power plants in Yunnan Province, against dismantling Beijing Zoo, and for air conditioning set at 26 degrees Centigrade (79°F), to mention just a few. Moreover, network organizations composed of a larger number of individual organizations have evolved, for example, Friends of Nature (China's first environmental NGO), Green Earth Volunteers, the China Wildlife Protection Organization, the China NPO (nonprofit organization) Network, and the Chinese Association of NGO Cooperation. Networks operating over the Internet have proved most effective for NGO work. Additionally, an increasing number of student groups perform monitoring functions. According to reports in 2006, such student groups existed at 176 universities in 26 provinces.

SOCIAL ASSOCIATIONS AND THE GOVERNMENT

As long as such organizations do not pursue political or politically sensitive objectives, the central government takes a benevolent attitude toward them, since they address issues at the local level that the central government is unable to solve. Both government officials and the wider public see them as benefiting society. In May 2006 *Renmin Ribao* (People's Daily) asserted that without public participation of citizens, there would be no improvement of environment protection. A survey of *China Development Brief* in 2002 in Beijing revealed that 80 percent of the respondents held that NGOs support or complement the work of the government. Most respondents conceived social organizations not as independent bodies but as entities serving to amend governance. Yet such organizations frequently come into conflict with local authorities, particularly if they take up issues that infringe upon the financial or political interests of local authorities.

In addition to official local associations, also cropping up are traditional independent or semi-independent organizations, such as clan associations, hometown associations, secret societies, and beggar's guilds, as well as occupational associations, and artists' societies. In urban areas, peasants with common interests unite in hometown associations (*tongxiang bang*), which comprise people from the same township, county, or province and act as interest organizations. Members live together in common living quarters and are obliged to mutually support their peers. Active in China's larger cities, they partially control entire markets. They function as self-protecting organizations of worker migrants and sometimes even as rudimentary trade unions. There are even illegal trade unions of migrant workers that organize strikes and demonstrations.

Thus far, peasant interest organizations do not yet exist. To fill this gap, in rural areas informal "opinion leaders" and "peasant lawyers" are emerging. These are persons assigned by peasants of one or several villages or even a township to convey problems to higher echelons, to draft and submit petitions (a legally confirmed right). Peasants even establish "economic associations" and cooperatives to advocate for the social rights of the rural population. As long as the central government is reluctant to allow official interest organizations of peasants, peasants' grievances will continue to manifest themselves in informal organizations and collective action.

Religion is a contested field. Officially recognized religious communities are strictly controlled by the state. More traditional ones, such as temple associations, sects, and underground churches, often function as social pockets of resistance to government authorities and hence are not tolerated by the central government. They are thus unable to affect the development of civil society.

With respect to autonomy, Chinese associations and NGOs clearly differ from their counterparts in Western societies. Yet in a society like China, connections between social associations and government authorities are helpful, as they contribute to solving problems through informal channels and by informal bargaining. The negotiation of interests in fact requires such connections to enforce interests more easily. Such semiautonomous associations also function as precursors of genuine autonomous economic and political associations. In present Chinese society (2008), associations have a rather ambiguous character. On the one hand, they are subject to the supervision and control of the central authorities. Yet on the other hand, they exhibit certain elements of independence as long as they do not challenge the powers that be.

With growing economic liberalization, the government is no longer in a position to control all social activities. Furthermore, the government does not think it necessary to interfere as long as such bodies do not start to become parallel entities challenging the power monopoly of the party. The emergence of autonomous horizontal associations represents the rise of new social groups and group interests that the government, with its traditional institutional structure, is unable to bind, that are developing according to their own systematic dynamism. This societal corporatism (contrasting

with state corporatism) encompasses sectoral organization from below and the formation of interests at the grassroots level and their incorporation. As it is still not possible to establish parallel political structures in China, the alternative can only be to develop independent ad hoc zones of autonomy that do not provoke the state politically. A less important economic role for the state in the future, combined with social change, will certainly enhance the power of autonomous groups.

While in Western democratic societies, corporatism involves the incorporation of autonomous social associations in official politics, it has a totally different meaning in China. Here the central authorities decide everything. These authorities integrate existing associations into bargaining and discussion processes while strictly controlling them. This kind of corporatism bans the rise of parallel associations wanting to act autonomously from the government.

The inclusion of social associations and NGOs in bargaining processes with the central government allows those organizations (via various networks, interrelationships, and links) to affect the central government. This has the effect of partially neutralizing the separation between state and society. Social problems can thus be more easily solved. Incorporating social organizations into the political system by means of bureaucratic and instrumental interrelations with the central government and its players also serves to strengthen the legitimacy of those organizations.

INFILTRATION OF THE PARTY-STATE

Additionally, society, via associations and interest groups, infiltrates state and party and thus initiates processes of change. Ding Xueliang sees such groups as institutionally amphibious. They are closely connected to party-state structures, going as far as to be institutionally parasitic in that their interests and financial means are bound to the central government. Yet party and state institutions can be infiltrated and changed by these organizations. Since party members are based in all social institutions, there is mutual interweaving and penetration. Ding is right in criticizing a concept of civil society that is based on an antagonism between state and society and is unable to interweave the two.

It is open to debate whether more independently operating social movements, such as the environment movement, will have a greater impact in the future. Some argue that such movements are prone to come into conflict with the central authorities and thus might become proponents of political change. Others argue that because of rigid state control, their political effect will be rather limited and that confrontational behavior would just provoke tighter control from the center.

Developments in the former Soviet Union and other former socialist countries has shown that during phases of political change, alternative structures can quickly be formed with the help of interest associations. They may even develop into parties or as ad hoc groups that gain local influence in realms no longer dominated by the party. Even party organizations eventually turn against the party to offer themselves as alternatives to these interest associations and to regain confidence among the population.

SEE ALSO *Government-Organized Nongovernmental Organization; International Organizations, Relations with, since 1949; Prodemocracy Movement (1989).*

BIBLIOGRAPHY

Cooper, Caroline M. "This Is Our Way In": The Civil Society of Environmental NGOs in South-West China. *Government and Opposition* 41, 1 (2006): 109–136.

Ding Xueliang. Institutional Amphibiousness and the Transition from Communism: The Case of China. *British Journal of Political Science* 24 (1994): 298–300.

Ho, Peter. Greening without Conflict? Environmentalism, NGOs, and Civil Society in China. *Development and Change* 32 (2001): 893–921.

Ma, Qiusha. *Non-governmental Organizations in Contemporary China: Paving the Way to Civil Society?* London: Routledge, 2006.

Saich, Tony. Negotiating the State: The Development of Social Organizations in China. *China Quarterly*, no. 161 (2000): 124–141.

Yang, Guobin. Environmental NGOs and Institutional Dynamics in China. *China Quarterly*, no. 181 (March 2005): 46–66.

Thomas Heberer

SOCIAL CLASSES BEFORE 1949

The idea of social classes was introduced into China from Marxist ideology, and it became very influential as class analysis became a guiding principle for building the "New China" in the 1930s and 1940s. Thus, for example, the violent transformation of rural society was grounded in the analysis of class structure in the villages. Nevertheless, the Western idea of social classes does not fit readily into Chinese realities. China did not have a large "working class" in the cities, or even a "landlord class" in many villages. An understanding of class structure in pre-1949 China, therefore, has to take account of the difference between the "longue durée" of Late Imperial society (1368–1912) and the "short century" of structural disruption following the Opium Wars that formed the background to the social revolution in the 1930s and 1940s. Some long-term structural determinants from Late Imperial society continued into the late Qing dynasty and the Republic, but major social changes were also coming about during that last century.

BASIC STRUCTURAL PRINCIPLES OF LATE IMPERIAL SOCIETY

According to Confucian state ideology, Late Imperial society consisted of the four strata (listed here in a sequence of declining social prestige) of scholar-officials, peasants, artisans, and merchants. With this *simin* (four classes of people) categorization, the Confucian elite referred to the legitimate functional groups in Chinese society without implicating the modern notion of a "social class." This idea of the functional groups in society survived until Republican times, when the notion of constituency (*jie*) was first used as an alternative concept to social class to describe the landslide changes in Chinese social structure, and at that time women and workers were identified as new forces of social change.

The long-run determinants of social change in China on the eve of revolution were shaped by several factors.

1. Chinese social structure was state-centered in the sense that social elites depended on the legitimacy provided by the state, and on access to cultural and social capital controlled by the state. This state-dependency was epitomized in the system of imperial examinations. The abolishment of the exam system in 1905 represented a truly revolutionary rupture between Late Imperial society and twentieth-century China.

2. State-dependent social structure included a growing stratum of "brokers," that is, local elites who mediated state power and arranged a balance between local interests and the state bureaucracy. As brokers, their exalted sociostructural position depended on recognition by the local society as well as their access to the official stratum through personal networks of clientilism, *guanxi*, and marriage ties. The emergence of brokers was driven mainly by economic and population growth without a corresponding growth in formal state institutions.

3. Related to this, Chinese social structure was deeply shaped by cultural repertoires, particularly those based on literacy. Beyond the tiny stratum of government officials who had succeeded in the imperial examinations, the social elite defined itself mainly by its capacity to handle the cultural capital reflected in the written traditions of China.

4. Rooted in cultural traditions reaching back two millenia, Late Imperial society manifested a fusion of rural and urban society in the sense that there were no fundamental cleavages between the two spheres, and elite status was perceived to be reflected in a rural-centered lifestyle. This fusion was mainly supported by the integrating forces of extended kinship, in particular lineage and clan organizations. From this, in

GENTRY

Variously translated also as *literati, scholar-bureaucrats,* and *scholar-officials,* the Chinese term for *gentry* (*shenshi*) refers to an elite group of learned men who acquired their status as gentry by passing the Confucian-based civil-service examinations. By the twentieth century, the meaning of *gentry* broadened to include those community leaders who managed services neglected by the increasingly inept Qing government.

In late imperial China, gentry status was inseparable from the civil-service-examination system. One became regarded as lower gentry as a result of success at the prefectural level (the *xiucai,* or cultivated-talent, degree), and one was esteemed as upper gentry upon success at the provincial level (the *juren,* or provincial-graduate, degree) and the metropolitan level (the *jinshi,* or presented-scholar, degree). Although the lower gentry acquired prestige and power in their local communities and assumed leadership positions in village governance, the examination degree they acquired did not make them eligible for official posts within the imperial bureaucracy. Those highly coveted positions were reserved for holders of higher degrees obtained at the provincial or metropolitan level.

By the late Qing, gentry status became more readily accessible to a growing number of merchants, by either marrying into a gentry family or purchasing an examination degree from the financially pressed Qing government. Like the gentry who acquired their status through examination success, the merchant-gentry (*shangshen*) based their power on office holding and landownership, and assumed leadership positions in the community.

Even before the abolition of the civil service examination system in 1905, then, the gentry as a cohesive group united by a shared set of Confucian ideals and defined by their success on the civil service examinations had already begun to break down. However, as a social class with political clout and economic wealth, the gentry persisted well into the twentieth century, and the Chinese term *shenshi* came to acquire the more general meaning of "elite". No longer tied to success in the examination system, elite status in the Republican period (1912–1949) became determined by wealth, whether in the form of landholdings or capital. Severance from state endorsement also meant that the Republican elite was much larger, more diverse, and also more autonomous. A weak central government further allowed these locally prominent men to take over duties neglected by the state: managing village affairs and directing local projects to benefit their community, foster village solidarity, and enhance their own prestige. In contrast to the late imperial gentry, the Republican elite not only acted independently of the state but also, more significantly, increasingly felt no allegiance to it.

BIBLIOGRAPHY

Chang, Chung-li. *The Chinese Gentry: Studies on Their Role in Nineteenth-Century Chinese Society.* Seattle: University of Washington Press, 1967.

Rankin, Mary Backus. *Elite Activism and Political Transformation in China: Zhejiang Province, 1865–1911.* Stanford, CA: Stanford University Press, 1986.

Lisa Tran

earlier sociostructural analyses, the notion of "gentry" as the dominant class had emerged.

5. Finally, Late Imperial society was extremely mobile and included various regional "frontier societies" with weak or almost absent government representation. This contributed to a great sociostructural diversity across the regions of China that lasted into the twentieth century, and it bolstered the central role of brokerage by local elites in social structure.

In analyses since the 1980s of Late Imperial society, old notions of the "gentry" or the "scholar-officials" have been discarded in favor of the more general notion of "elites," with fuzzy boundaries prescribing the role of local power brokers, who, in the case of rural strongmen, did not participate in the "great tradition" of Confucian culture. The defining structural characteristics of Late Imperial society was not class, but status, which was embedded in the political order.

SOCIAL CHANGE AND RESILIENCE OF TRADITIONAL STRUCTURES

Late Imperial society was the most prosperous period in Chinese history, but it was achieved under the growing strain of relentless population growth, which drove social involution and compression at the bottom level of society. As the Chinese government remained almost fixed in size (in terms of both personnel and fiscal resources), society grew beyond its reach. The most important effect of this was the rise of the merchant within the traditional social structure. In Late Imperial society merchants became respected members of local elites and assumed many functions in civic self-organization. In the emerging urban centers they became brokers between the state and local society, a position they began to share with the traditional brokers, the literati who had retired from office, temporarily or otherwise, or had failed to gain a government position in the first place. This implied that merchants increasingly defined themselves in terms of literati cultural values, a process that was strongly backed during the nineteenth century, when the Qing government increasingly relied on the sale of official status for government funding. From this, a fusion of the merchant and literati groups emerged in elite structures, inverting the classical hierarchy of status.

The interaction among elites in local society was dominated by the principles of extended kinship. There were regional variations, depending on the size of the agricultural surplus that could maintain socioeconomic differentiation; generally, the pivotal role of kinship was strengthened in the frontier societies, where the role of government was weak. Chinese lineage organization allowed for a pronounced economic inequality between lineage segments and individual households, which was sometimes hidden behind the structures of corporate landholdings managed by elite families. Yet, lineage defined an in-group/out-group boundary that also fostered the image of lineage solidarity, especially in the often strained competitive relations between lineages, but also against outsiders in general, including even the representatives of the state. Therefore, socioeconomic class distinctions became blurred in the context of a local "moral economy," and idealized collective memories tell the tales of poor peasant boys working their way up to the elevated stratum of scholar-officials.

In spite of these notions of upward social mobility, Late Imperial society also featured a strong conception of heredity of status, but with the peculiar twist of accentuating micro-status, particularly of occupational groups. The notion of a nobility was absent, given the merit-based examination system. The emperor's family was the only structural equivalent to the contemporary Western notion of nobility, merged with the conception of ethnic dominance under Manchu rule. As China was a multiethnic society with a non-Chinese ruling stratum, the Manchus retained a hereditary status because of intentional measures of ethnic separation, such as protecting the Manchu homelands. Thus, the Manchu military (the Banners and the Green Standards) were a large hereditary status group. But hereditary status also played a strong role at the bottom levels of society, where groups of servile people—slaves, in fact—were bound to their roles across generations. Many occupations were family-based, thus resulting in a hereditary status, with different levels of social esteem and reputation. With the internal colonization of many frontier regions, ethnic differences also coalesced with distinctions of social status, such as with the emergence of Hakka identity.

Beyond these distinctions, Late Imperial society was structurally very homogenous; the most numerous group were the peasants, with the household as the basic unit. Rural society did not have pronounced structural disparities—the economic unit was the small-scale family farm, worked by owners in North China and by quasi-permanent tenants in the more developed southeastern regions. Large landholdings were fragmented into those units, which often formed a part of hereditary assets. Landlords were mostly absentee owners.

This homogenous social structure implied high risks of downward social mobility in case of economic distress, which was the sad normal state of nineteenth-century China. Chinese social structure always included a segment of outcasts, often in the sense of the "social bandit" imbued with popular legitimacy. Other forms of outcast social organization were sects and secret societies, some of which aimed to subvert the reigning social structure (such as the prescribed gender roles). In the nineteenth century these mechanisms erupted into the Taiping Uprising (1851–1864).

THE TRANSITION TO REVOLUTION

The period between the Opium Wars and 1949 manifested many new trends in social structure that were mainly the result of the weakening and final collapse of the state—the imperial state, but also the failed Republican state.

A common thread of sociostructural change is the role of merchants, who formed the core of an emerging "bourgeoisie" stratum in Republican China. A special group in this merchant group were the brokers between foreigners and Chinese society, who emerged from their role of compradores in the last decades of Qing rule. Merchants had organized themselves into lodges that became chambers of commerce, and they increasingly adopted functions of urban government during this transitional period. This was bolstered by a strengthening political awareness driven by a growing nationalist sentiment. Civic culture was supported by the emergence of a modern press and the spread of modern lifestyles made possible by educational modernization. However, these structural trends were finally crushed by the Guomingdang, which claimed political supremacy and again imposed the principle of state-centered social structure. Similarly, Nationalist forces suppressed any political representation of the small new class of urban workers, who were still stuck between traditional workplace paternalism and a growing awareness of exploitation and social injustice.

Porters transporting a seated woman, c. 1936. *Throughout the centuries, the majority of China's population has been composed of rural farmers, leading to a great disparity of wealth between landowners and peasants.* **GENERAL PHOTOGRAPHIC AGENCY/HULTON ARCHIVE/ GETTY IMAGES**

The most important trend in social-structural evolution was the expanding role of the military at the national and local levels. The Qing government had to rely increasingly on regional military forces, which were still embedded in the traditional elite structure. Endemic unrest fostered a rapid militarization of local elites, too, mostly in self-defense, but increasingly also as exploiters. These two strands culminated in the rise of the regional warlord systems after 1911. Republican China introduced an entirely new structural principle into Chinese society—the legitimate dominance of the military, which was supported by an elite system of military schools from which a stratum of military officers emerged, underpinned by the notion of military citizenship. This sociostructural supremacy of the military was broken only after 1949, when the Chinese Communist Party principle of party dominance over the military reinstated the primacy of the political order.

With the abolishment of the imperial examination system, the organizational foundation of elite selection in traditional China collapsed. Education remained a core defining feature, though, and in early twentieth-century China an education abroad became important. Nationalist elites were increasingly foreign-educated, especially in Western countries, whereas the emerging Communist elites often had a Japanese, Russian, or European education. Although the numbers of these foreign-educated elites were relatively small, they assumed a pivotal role in the modernization of China.

A major effect of all these social-structural changes was the appearance of a stratum in Chinese society that had lost its connections to rural society. The split between the rural and the urban was further deepened by the growing role of foreign communities in the treaty ports, which shifted the focus of social life toward cultural norms imported from the Western countries, such as Western consumerism.

In Chinese local society, the violent environment of the twentieth century engendered the final collapse of the traditional moral economy. Militarization contributed to the emergence of local societies empowered by the force of sheer physical threat and abuse, epitomized in the role of the local bully. Where extended kinship ties remained strong, basic order could be maintained. Chinese villages turned into small worlds under constant threat from marauding bandits, ransacking Guomindang forces, and, later, Japanese invaders with "burn and kill" tactics. In some places, social involution involved the literate groups in society, who sometimes embarked on collective action, or just joining the growing group of "bandits." These were the strata from which Mao Zedong's revolutionary forces were recruited after they had been expelled from the urban centers of social change.

SEE ALSO *Commercial Elite, 1800–1949; Peasantry, 1800–1900; Servile Statuses.*

BIBLIOGRAPHY

Eastman, Lloyd E. *Family, Fields, and Ancestors: Constancy and Change in China's Social and Economic History, 1550–1949.* New York and Oxford, U.K.: Oxford University Press, 1988.

Naquin, Susan, and Evelyn Rawski. *Chinese Society in the Eighteenth Century.* New Haven, CT, and London: Yale University Press, 1987.

Rankin, Mary B., John K. Fairbank, and Albert Feuerwerker. Introduction: Perspectives on Modern China's History. In *Republican China, 1912–1949, Part 2.* Vol. 13 of *The Cambridge History of China,* 1–73. Cambridge, U.K., and New York: Cambridge University Press, 1986.

Carsten Herrmann-Pillath

SOCIAL CLASSES SINCE 1978

Chinese social stratification has undergone profound changes since 1978 as a result of the economic reforms, in particular the decollectivization of agriculture and the rise of private industry and private property. The clearly defined status hierarchy of the planned economy has been replaced by a system of stratification based on control over resources, wealth, occupation, and salary. In turn, these determinants are influenced by factors such as educational level, social networks and gender, and registration as an urban or rural resident.

As China became more urbanized after the economic reforms, new groups emerged. The middle class grew, entrepreneurs flourished and many professionals acquired

greater independence from the state. Urban workers have lost status compared with the past, but they still enjoy better living standards and more security than the rural migrant workers who form a demographically significant underclass in the cities. The gap between the urban and rural population has widened. Average rural per capita incomes by the mid-2000s were only about one-third of those in urban areas. Inequality within the countryside has also increased. Those who depend on raising crops have lower incomes and status than those involved in rural industry.

Chinese social stratification still has special features that go back to the Maoist era. The most important of these are ascribed status as an urban or rural resident, party membership or other forms of social capital, and the system of ownership and control of land. All these factors contribute to the social status of each individual and family and their chances of social mobility. Although new pathways to social mobility have developed, the most important determining factor of the status an adult is likely to attain is still the family into which he or she is born.

THE RURAL AREAS

Prior to the economic reforms, there were two major social groups in the countryside: peasants who tilled the soil or worked in rural collective industry, and rural cadres (officials) who were responsible for local government and for managing collective agriculture and who controlled all substantial economic activity in the countryside. Rural residents were tied to the land. They had no right to seek nonagricultural employment in the urban areas. The income of each rural household depended on the success of the collective and on the amount of labor its members contributed to the collective. Thus, although there was considerable inequality between rich and poor rural areas, income differences within each village were small.

After 1978, the economic reforms transformed the rural society by giving control of land back to the peasant household, encouraging nonagricultural household sidelines, and promoting collectively owned and later private rural industry. By the early 1990s, the more successful rural areas were leaving poorer ones far behind, and the differentiation between households within villages had greatly increased. Leasing and subletting of land allowed some peasant families to gain control of larger areas. Others moved out of cultivation to concentrate full time on specialist livestock, manufacturing, trading, or transport enterprises.

Many rural cadres were able to benefit from the dissolution of the communes. They supervised the dispersal of collectively owned property and the award of new production contracts. Usually slightly better educated than the average peasant, and with contacts and horizons that extended beyond the village, they were especially well placed to take advantage of the new opportunities in the

Attendees of a real estate exhibition, Shanghai, October 3, 2005. *As many urban Chinese enjoy greater levels of prosperity at the turn of the twenty-first century, few of these benefits have reached the countryside. Improved wages have allowed many city-dwellers the opportunity to enjoy modern accommodations, while millions of rural residents continue to endure poor living conditions.* © QILAI SHEN/ EPA/CORBIS

countryside. Many became the managers or even owners of the "town and village enterprises" that played such an important part in China's economic growth. Rural industrialization has led to widening income inequalities in the countryside as workers tend to earn much more than those who rely on raising crops, and the new rural entrepreneurs do better still. The gap between the wealthiest rural regions and poorer ones where there is still very little rural industry has also widened.

From the early 1980s, increasing numbers of rural residents took advantage of the relaxation of restrictions on movement to seek temporary employment in the cities. It is estimated that 150 million peasants now work in construction, petty trading, and manufacturing, mostly in the prosperous coastal regions. The money they remit to their families may be used to build a house, set up a small business, or keep a child in school, all ways in which rural families seek to improve their social and economic status. However, although rural migrants are now permitted to work in the urban areas, they remain at a considerable disadvantage compared to urban residents. They are

excluded from the better jobs and have lesser entitlements to welfare, health care, and education. This discourages long-term urban settlement. It continues to be common for migrants to return to the rural areas after a few years in the city and to be replaced by other younger migrants.

URBAN AREAS

Before 1978, approximately 20 percent of the Chinese population was urban. By the mid-2000s, the figure exceeded 40 percent. Both in the Maoist and in the reform era, urban incomes were higher and more secure than rural incomes, and urban people had better access to subsidized education and health care. Before the economic reforms, the great majority of the urban employed worked for state or collectively owned enterprises. The former offered better pay and conditions than the latter. The urban population was classified either as workers or cadres, that is, blue collar or office workers. Cadres as a group were somewhat better paid than workers. Both cadres and workers were graded and paid according to skill and seniority. Better-off enterprises had more employees in high grades than poorer

Contestant on a cosmetic surgery reality show, Changsha, Hunan, December 1, 2006. *With the introduction of market reforms in the late 1970s, many citizens in urban areas began to earn higher incomes as the economy expanded. Accordingly, some Chinese began to spend this newfound wealth on goods and services, such as automobiles, cosmetics, and plastic surgery, previously out of reach for an average citizen.* AP IMAGES

enterprises, and provided better housing and other non-monetary benefits. However, income differences were small compared to those in the reform era.

State-owned enterprises continued to dominate the urban economy until the mid-1990s, but stratification grew within the state-owned sector with the reforms. Bonuses became an important element in the pay of workers in the 1980s, increasing the reward for qualifications and hard work but also enriching those who happened to work for successful enterprises. The expansion of private enterprise in the urban areas in the 1990s brought the rapid growth of material inequality. Managers and business people became the new economic and social elite. In the cities, as in the countryside, some of the new entrepreneurs made private fortunes by finding their own niche in the market. Others enriched themselves by using their official positions to their own advantage.

Cadres who had control over scarce resources could benefit from privatization. They took cuts from sales of state property, used their access to subsidized materials and transport facilities to do deals, and accepted bribes or levied fees when signing contracts and arranging the transfer of land. The so-called princelings, children and relatives of top Communist Party leaders, were particularly notorious for their corrupt behavior both in the privatization of state enterprises and in the establishment of joint enterprises with foreign companies. The greed of this elite was replicated down the social scale as the transition from the state-controlled economy provided opportunities for graft to corrupt cadres at all levels.

The privatized economy also gave rise to legitimate wealth earned from business and professional activities. The owners or managers of both Chinese and foreign-invested enterprises, often former cadres, as well as accountants, lawyers, and doctors who practice privately, earn incomes many times larger than those of the average worker. Increasingly, the richest purchase their own houses, live in gated communities, drive cars, favor top-brand goods, and send their children to the best schools, constructing lives that are very different from those of ordinary urban citizens.

ELITE GROUPS

The term *elite groups* comprises a complex and changing reality. There are two major elite groups in China: the *political elite* and the *socioeconomic elite*. The first group, which forms the party-state *nomenklatura*, although long-standing and stable since 1949, suffered—along with other social categories—from political campaigns and purges in the 1950s, during the Cultural Revolution (1966–1969), and after June 4, 1989.

Since the launching of the reform process in 1978, diversification within the Chinese society has led to a progressive renewal of China's political elite. Thus, even though the majority of leading cadres (*lingdao ganbu*) in China today received training in science, often in engineering, at the local level, more and more officials are trained in economics, law, or public administration. The promotion of Hu Jintao, a graduate of Tsinghua University, to the position of general secretary of the Chinese Communist Party (CCP) at the Sixteenth Party Congress in November 2002 symbolizes the rise of this new generation of party leaders.

Marked by the Cultural Revolution but promoted under the reform era, the "fourth generation" of leaders differs from those in power under Mao Zedong, Deng Xiaoping, and Jiang Zemin in terms of educational criteria, technical expertise, and political experience. Attendance at the party schools' regular sessions remains required training for any cadre who seeks career advancement within the ruling elite, which is estimated to number around 80,000. Although most officials seek legitimacy through institutional channels, they continue to rely at the same time on informal networks (*guanxi*): nepotism and favoritism are still factors in elite recruitment and promotion. Indeed, a significant number of China's leaders are either princelings (*gaogan zidi* or *taizi*) or were aides (*mishu*) to top officials. For example, Wen Jiabao, after assisting Zhao Ziyang (1919–2005) in a time of crisis in 1989, earned respect from other political leaders, despite factional struggles. Xi Jinping, a graduate of Tsinghua University, is the son of Xi Zhongxun (1913–2002), a former Politburo member, and was also the *mishu* of a former minister, Geng Biao (1909–2000).

Made up of members of socio-professional categories that have either emerged or been rehabilitated since 1978 (academics, entrepreneurs, managers in the private sector, journalists, artists, lawyers, etc.), the social elite are mainly urban dwellers of coastal China. Although relatively well-off, they have differing social, cultural, and economic backgrounds. While some private entrepreneurs run successful businesses and have accumulated impressive fortunes, despite having their education cut short by the Cultural Revolution, a large portion of this group was trained in the mainland's universities and an increasing number received part of their education abroad, some in major Western universities. More than China's middle class, this socioeconomic elite forms a community with strong and influential positions, typified elite roles, and behavior.

In July 2001, the CCP reached a turning point in its history by inviting China's new socio-professional elite to become party members. In doing so, the party hoped to renew its social base and thus strengthen its legitimacy and authority. Although entrepreneurs remain a minority within the CCP (around 200,000 out of 73.36 million members in October 2007), this policy has borne fruit. Indeed, while some members of this elite are truly cosmopolitan, liberal, and even democrats who have profited from the reforms and been increasingly consulted by the ruling power, many more are driven by patriotic, if not nationalistic, feelings, often manipulated by the same power.

The endemic corruption of China's political system is nurtured by the weakness of the administrative and judicial institutions. The majority within these groups fear social instability above all and thus favor the preservation of the CCP's undisputed rule.

Some predict that the diversification of Chinese society and the increasing autonomy of the superior socioeconomic strata will divide the political elite, thus eroding the CCP's monopoly and leading, little by little, to the liberalization of the regime. However, since the Tiananmen crackdown in 1989, the strengthening allegiance of the socio-professional elite to the country's political leaders suggests that an authoritarian and elitist regime will remain in power.

BIBLIOGRAPHY

Bo Zhiyue. Political Succession and Elite Politics in Twenty-First Century China: Toward a Perspective of "Power Balancing." *Issues and Studies* 41, 1 (2005): 162–189.

Cao Cong. *China's Scientific Elite*. New York: RoutledgeCurzon, 2004.

Dickson, Bruce J. *Red Capitalists in China: The Party, Private Entrepreneurs, and Prospects for Political Change*. New York: Cambridge University Press, 2003.

Hong Yung Lee. *From Revolutionary Cadres to Party Technocrats in Socialist China*. Berkeley: University of California Press, 1991.

Li Cheng. *China's Leaders: The New Generation*. Lanham, MD: Rowman and Littlefield, 2001.

Li Cheng. The Status and Characteristics of Foreign-Educated Returnees in the Chinese Leadership. *China Leadership Monitor* 16 (fall 2005).

Tran, Emilie. From Senior Official to Top Civil Servant: An Enquiry into the Shanghai Party School. *China Perspectives* 46 (March–April 2003).

Zang Xiaowei. *Elite Dualism and Leadership Selection in China*. London: RoutledgeCurzon, 2000.

Zang Xiaowei. Institutionalization and Elite Behavior in Reform China. *Issues and Studies* 41, 1 (2005): 204–217.

Emilie Tran

SOCIAL CAPITAL AND STRATIFICATION

Social capital—in the sense of social networks in which norms of reciprocity and trust are observed—are important to the understanding of Chinese social stratification. Social capital was characterized by a high degree of politicization in Maoist China. Revolutionary pedigree was important. To have worked for the revolution early or to have a parent who had done so might qualify an individual for preferment at work. Even when "old revolutionaries" had not risen very high in the hierarchy themselves, they were likely to have contacts, direct or indirect, with senior cadres who could be asked for help. Similarly, party membership both enhanced an individual's chances of preferment within the bureaucracy and gave access to a network of useful contacts.

Class labels awarded at the time of the establishment of the People's Republic created a system of status inheritance that also played a role in stratification. Candidates from the "good" social classes—workers or poor and lower-middle peasants—were supposed to be preferred for selection and advancement over those from bourgeois, rich peasant, or landlord families. However, the ascendancy of the revolutionary families was not complete. The pre-revolutionary elite or their children were often able to use their cultural capital—superior education or qualifications—to maintain their status, especially within the professions and the cultural sphere.

After 1978, the old class labels were abolished. Education, qualifications, and competence are now supposed to be the sole criteria for advancement. However, social and cultural capital remains important. Those who are related to people with status or who can make use of influential social connections are more likely to climb the social ladder. Family, kin, classmates, and colleagues may all be mobilized in the personalized use of networks or *guanxi*, as this form of social capital is termed in Chinese. Party membership remains helpful to promotion within the bureaucracy.

SOCIAL MOBILITY, EDUCATION, AND STATUS SECURITY

The market reforms, the rise of labor markets, the crumbling of the boundaries between status groups, and the rapid growth of cities and the middle class have created unprecedented opportunities for social mobility in China. Rural migrants seek opportunities in the towns, and urban people migrate to the areas of greatest development. In contrast with the Maoist past, it is now possible to move from job to job or firm to firm in pursuit of advancement.

A college education became almost a prerequisite for an administrative or managerial job from the 1990s, and at all levels of employment, job status is closely related to educational attainment. The rising return to education and the intense competition for entry-level posts in high-status occupations has created an intense demand for good schools, and parents are prepared to pay for the best that they can afford. The stratification of education tends to mirror that of society. Urban school provision is variable; the best staffed and equipped schools charge the highest fees and have strict entry criteria. The worst urban conditions are found in schools set up for migrants, where fees are much lower. Provision in the countryside is poorer still, and the dropout rate is higher. Urban children average four more years of schooling than rural children. The children of intellectuals, cadres, and managers are much more likely to go to senior middle school and college than the children of workers or peasants. Thus, in China as in other societies where the market economy predominates, there is a potential for social mobility, but middle-class groups are advantaged by their ability to pass on both economic and cultural capital to their children.

China's rapid development has produced much upward mobility, but downward mobility is a much-feared possibility. Parents push their children at schools so that they will be able at least to maintain the status of their natal families. Examination failure apart, many circumstances may pull people down the social hierarchy. Business failures, redundancy, and the closure of enterprises all claim their victims. In the absence of comprehensive social security or medical-insurance coverage, illness, accidents, or the loss of a wage earner can impoverish whole families.

GENDER AND STRATIFICATION

The gender gap is everywhere apparent in Chinese occupational stratification. Girls are more likely to leave school early and less likely to reach senior middle school or university. In the cities, women generally receive lower wages than men, even when they do the same jobs. They have more difficulty in finding jobs and are more likely to be found in the comparatively low-paid sectors, such as office work, teaching, and health care. In the rural areas, women are often left to till the fields while the men in the family take up better-paid work in rural industry or in the towns. The considerable emphasis on the appearance and attractiveness of young women may relate to the fact that marriage to a higher-status man is seen as an alternative way for a woman to achieve higher status for herself.

SEE ALSO *Social Classes before 1949.*

BIBLIOGRAPHY

Bian Yanjie. Chinese Social Stratification and Social Mobility. *Annual Review of Sociology* 28 (2002): 91–116.

Li Yi. *The Structure and Evolution of Chinese Social Stratification.* Lanham, MD: University Press of America, 2005.

Oi, Jean C., and Andrew G. Walder, eds. *Property Rights and Economic Reform in China.* Stanford, CA: Stanford University Press, 1999.

Stockman, Norman. *Understanding Chinese Society.* Cambridge, U.K.: Polity Press, 2000.

Wang Feng. *Boundaries and Categories: Rising Inequality in Post-socialist Urban China.* Stanford, CA: Stanford University Press, 2008.

Delia Davin

SOCIAL POLICY PROGRAMS

This entry contains the following:

OVERVIEW
Heather Xiaoquan Zhang

SMALL WELFARE
Wong Chack-kie

FOOD-FOR-WORK SCHEME
Hatla Thelle

MINIMUM LIVING STANDARD GUARANTEE SYSTEM
Joe Leung

OVERVIEW

Social policy comprises a set of social provision programs aiming at protecting social rights and meeting a range of social needs of citizens through targeted allocation of resources (Titmuss 1976). These programs deal with education, health care, housing, pension, employment and income maintenance, poverty alleviation, disaster relief, other public services, and so forth. Together they should provide social security and protection for all citizens. Based on such an understanding, we often use terms such as *social policy, social security, social protection,* and *welfare* interchangeably.

SOCIAL POLICY IN THE PRE-REFORM PERIOD

China's social policy has changed substantially since the initiation of market reforms in the late 1970s. During the pre-reform period, China adopted a so-called state and collective welfare model (Guan 2000). In urban areas, the state was the principal welfare provider, directly allocating the necessary resources to state-owned enterprises (SOEs), government organizations, and other state sectors, which distributed the funds among their employees. For the urban minority who were not attached to any work unit (*danwei*), including the *sanwu renyuan* (the "three nos"—those with no income, no work ability, and no family support), the state provided resources for poverty relief allocated from the central government to the local authorities at the district level. Despite China's low per capita income level, the urban welfare programs provided basic security for urban residents and a rather generous package for public-sector employees,

including, for example, life-long employment known as the "iron rice bowl" (*tie fanwan*), free health care introduced during the Cultural Revolution in the 1970s, low-cost education, heavily subsidized housing, basic state pension, paid maternity leave for women, and paid sick leave.

In rural areas, agricultural collectives were mainly responsible for welfare and public service provision for rural residents whose entitlements were linked to their universal membership in the collectives. The welfare programs covered the main areas of health care and education, including a free rural cooperative medical care scheme implemented during the Cultural Revolution and expanded primary education through locally funded village schools (*minban xuexiao*). Most rural people had their own housing but did not have pensions, relying instead on their sons for old-age support. A "five guarantees" (*wu bao*) scheme was established by which rural collectives met the basic needs of the members who were not able to work or did not have children to support them in old age, through guaranteeing food, clothing, shelter, health care, and a burial after death. The state provided direct funds for special poverty reliefs such as emergency relief after natural disasters and for those in extreme hardships or destitution (Lin 2007).

Despite its many problems (e.g., low quality of services, ineffective use of resources, and a salient urban-rural gap in welfare financing and provisioning), this system nonetheless provided most Chinese with basic social welfare—an achievement that most other low-income countries largely failed to attain. Life expectancy increased from thirty-five in 1952, just after the Communists took national power, to sixty-eight in 1982, shortly after the start of the post-Mao reforms in 1979; the infant mortality rate declined from 250 to 40 per 1,000 live births during the same period (Feng 2007, p. 96). The public or collective ownership of the means of production and the state's tight control over key resources, combined with economic central planning and the official Marxist egalitarian ideology, allowed the central government to mobilize and allocate the necessary resources to its priority areas, particularly welfare for Chinese people.

SOCIAL POLICY IN THE ERA OF MARKET REFORMS

The post-Mao market reforms and the accompanied institutional change radically altered these conditions. In rural areas, agricultural decollectivization in the late 1970s and early 1980s dismantled rural collectives, together with their function of welfare provision. The ensuing fiscal decentralization considerably weakened the ability of the new village and township governments to provide basic social services such as education and health care. At the same time, the family planning program significantly reduced the number of children for each farming household, decreasing the role of the family in welfare production and provision, including its ability to care for the elderly and the sick. In urban areas, market reforms and the open-door policy brought about diversification in the ownership structure and intensified competition in the industrial sector. The previous *danwei*-based welfare regime was considerably undermined, with SOEs attempting to reduce production costs and survive the new market competition from foreign-owned and/or private firms, which did not shoulder social responsibilities such as providing welfare for their employees. Urban industrial reforms and restructuring that accelerated in the mid-1990s as China became increasingly integrated into the international economic system led to massive layoffs in SOEs, resulting in unprecedented unemployment and the emergence of new forms of poverty (e.g., relative poverty and deprivation) in Chinese cities.

Deepening of the market reforms and relaxation of restrictions on population and labor mobility, combined with widening income discrepancies between urban and rural areas, have prompted large-scale rural-urban migration. According to China's official estimate, the number of migrants seeking jobs in Chinese cities reached 120 to 200 million nationwide early in the twenty-first century (State Council of the People's Republic of China 2006, pp. 3–4), representing about one-sixth of the country's entire population. This huge and heterogeneous group, though most vulnerable to poverty and insecurity, has been left uncovered by existing social security programs.

Nationally, the market reforms have gone hand in hand with greater inequalities between regions and sectors, and among different social groups, leading to increased vulnerabilities, marginalization, and socioeconomic disadvantage for those who have not benefited proportionately from the reforms, including the rural population, SOE laid-off workers, the unemployed, rural-urban migrants, and the elderly. Although this scenario called for strengthened social policy intervention, this did not happen until the early 2000s. Before then, the development strategy placed overwhelming emphasis on economic growth while systematically minimizing "unproductive" welfare expenditures. The consequences were a serious erosion of the existing social security system, long-term underinvestment in developing new welfare schemes, new or higher user fee charges for public services (particularly education and health care, rendering such services inaccessible for the majority), and a failure to protect Chinese citizens against a plethora of emerging uncertainties and risks associated with the market economy. For example, once a model of equitable health care provision in the developing world, by 2000 China was rated 144 out of 191 countries in terms of health care performance, and 188, or third from the bottom, in terms of the fairness of its health system (WHO 2000, pp. 202, 191).

IMPROVEMENTS IN THE 2000s

All this has led to growing social discontent that poses serious threats to the societal and political stability of the country. Since the early 2000s the new leadership of Hu Jintao and Wen Jiabao has begun paying greater attention to equity and social justice by improving social security and welfare for the Chinese people. Discourses such as "people-centered development" (*yirenweiben*), "building harmonious society" (*goujian hexie shehui*), and the "scientific development outlook" (*kexue fazhanguan*) have signaled a new emphasis on the role of the state in addressing worsening problems of polarization of wealth and uneven development through central government fiscal support and improving welfare and public good provision. The government has accelerated its pace of establishing, expanding, and enhancing a wide range of social security programs, including new social insurance schemes that combine social pooling and personal accounts with contributions from both employers and employees, and means-tested social relief programs such as the Minimum Living Standard guarantee (*zuidi shenghuo baozhang zhidu*), medical assistance, housing subsidies, continued support for the "five guarantees" scheme, legal aid, and disaster and poverty reliefs.

Most recently, social policy development has attached greater importance to statutory social protection and institutionalization of various welfare schemes. In 2004, China's "social security year," saw social security as a basic social right formally incorporated into the country's constitution. In the same year, the State Council published a white paper that detailed the state's responsibilities for supporting and improving a range of social insurance and welfare schemes under its social security system (State Council of the People's Republic of China 2004). The *danwei*-based welfare regime has been gradually replaced with a so-called socialized welfare system, by which citizens' social welfare is managed, operated, and monitored by the designated government ministries and their local bureaus and departments. The Ministry of Labor and Social Security is responsible for the range of social insurance schemes, whereas the Ministry of Civil Affairs oversees the various means-tested social relief programs, services, and benefits. Today, China's emerging social security system can be deemed a "welfare mix," where many agents—state, market, and civil society, communities, and households—have roles in welfare production, provision, and management.

State intervention in social welfare has been consolidated further since 2007, when new stress was placed on urban-rural integration (*cheng xiang yitihua*), particularly in the field of social security, to address the unequal entitlements, rights, and access to welfare provision and resources between urban and rural areas. This initiative was piloted in Chengdu and Chongqing in 2007, followed by other large cities such as Beijing, Shanghai, and Tianjin in 2008. The rural cooperative medical service system that was rolled out in 2002 has been rapidly expanded recently; its nationwide adoption is scheduled for 2009, with a three-tiered health care network at the county, township, and village levels established by 2010. The government, which neglected the issue for too long, has just seriously started considering how to protect the social rights of the large mobile population within the framework of urban-rural integration, equal rights, and universal entitlement.

The Chinese leadership is expected to continue to push ahead social policy reforms. The global financial crisis that began in 2008 and the havoc it has visited on developing countries serve as a rigorous test for the foundation, feasibility, functions, and robustness of the social safety nets being built in China.

SEE ALSO *Poverty; Social Welfare; Standard of Living.*

BIBLIOGRAPHY

Feng, Zhiqiang. Marginalisation and Health Provision in Transitional China. In *Marginalisation in China: Perspectives on Transition and Globalisation*, ed. Heather Xiaoquan Zhang, Bin Wu, and Richard Sanders, 97–116. Aldershot, U.K.: Ashgate, 2007.

Guan, Xinping. China's Social Policy: Reform and Development in the Context of Marketisation and Globalisation. *Social Policy and Administration* 34, no. 1 (2000): 115–130.

Lin, Ka. Institutional Responses to the Changing Patterns of Poverty and Marginalisation in China since 1949. In *Marginalisation in China: Perspectives on Transition and Globalisation*, ed. Heather Xiaoquan Zhang, Bin Wu, and Richard Sanders, 117–131. Aldershot, U.K.: Ashgate, 2007.

State Council of the People's Republic of China. *Zhongguo Shehui Baozhang Zhuangkuang he Zhengce* [China's social security and its policy]. Government White Paper, September 2004. http://china.org.cn/e-white/20040907

State Council of the People's Republic of China. *Zhongguo Nongmingong Diaoyan Baogao* [Research report on migrant workers in China]. Beijing: Zhongguo Yanshi Chubanshe, 2006.

Titmuss, Richard. *Commitment to Welfare.* London: Allen and Unwin, 1976.

World Health Organization (WHO). *The World Health Report 2000—Health Systems: Improving Performance.* http://www.who.int/whr/2000/en

Heather Xiaoquan Zhang

SMALL WELFARE

The Chinese term "small welfare" or "small well-being" (*xiaokang*) originally referred to an integrated society based on the institution of rituals known in Confucian literature as *li* (Wang Yubo 1992, p. 62; He Ziquan 2003, p. 20). In its modern usage, the term means that a person is moder-

ately well-off, leading a life above the subsistence level without being really wealthy.

Small-welfare and social-welfare societies have gained currency in China since Deng Xiaoping met the visiting Japanese prime minister Ohira Masayoshi (1910–1980) in 1979. Deng Xiaoping remarked that China's Four Modernizations were aimed at a small-welfare living standard for the people. Deng also set the target of attaining small welfare in China as measured by a gross national product (GNP) per capita of $1,000 (in U.S. dollars) by the end of the twentieth century. This would amount to quadrupling the 1979 GNP per capita of $250. In 1984 Deng also predicted that once China was a small-welfare society, it would be another thirty to fifty years before China approached the economic standards of developed countries. At that stage, China would have the resources to tackle regional disparities and the rich-poor gap. Small welfare, in Deng's thinking, was a dynamic concept for national social and economic development.

Since 1979, building a small-welfare society has become a national development goal. At the Thirteenth Party Congress of the Chinese Communist Party (CCP) in 1987, a three-stage approach was adopted for building a small-welfare society (Zhao Ziyang 1987). Stage one was to double China's 1980 GNP and provide the material foundation for the satisfaction of basic survival needs. This was not yet small welfare but was achieved in 1987. Stage two was to double China's GNP again by 2000; then, China would have reached an economic level comparable to small welfare. Stage three was to attain GNP per capita comparable to medium-income countries by the mid-twenty-first century. Then, people would be relatively well-off, and China would basically have achieved modernization.

Stage three was more explicitly elaborated at the Sixteenth Party Congress of the CCP in 2002, when the building of a small-welfare society was conceptually modified to the building of a *comprehensive* small-welfare society. Not only were higher levels of economic development targeted, but also higher levels of democracy, culture, science and education, social harmony, and people's standard of living (Jiang Zemin 2002). The target date was set at 2020.

In 1991 national, urban, and rural indicators were established by a small-welfare study team under the State Statistical Bureau. However, indices to progress toward the goal of a small-welfare society were far from all systematically reported, and data is not fully accessible by the public. From the disclosed information, it is known that only three thresholds of the sixteen national indicators—per capita rural net income, per capita protein intake, and rural primary basic health care—were not attained in 2000. The total achievement rate was 96.6 percent (He Qiang 2003, p. 25). Obviously, there were significant regional and rural-urban disparities in terms of small-welfare measures across the country (He Qiang 2003, p. 26).

The State Statistical Bureau established twenty-five indicators in six areas for measuring the progress of a comprehensive small-welfare society (Jin Zhong 2006). The six areas are: (1) *economic development*, measured by four indicators, including per capita GNP at 28,000 yuan and a tertiary sector exceeding a 50 percent share; (2) *social harmony*, measured by five indicators, including a Gini coefficient between 0.3 and 0.4, and an urban-rural income disparity of less than 2.8:1; (3) *quality of life*, measured by five indicators, including per capita disposable income at 13,000 yuan and an Engels coefficient of less than 40 percent; (4) *democracy and the legal system*, measured by two indicators, including citizens' satisfaction with democratic rights and an indicator of security larger than 100; (5) *science and technology*, measured by five indicators, including research-and-development investment at 2 percent of GDP and 10.5 average years of education; and (6) *resources and environment*, measured by four indicators, including aggregate fuel consumption at less than 0.84 standard coal tons per 10,000 yuan of GDP, and water consumption at less than 200 cubic feet per 10,000 yuan of GDP. Many of these indicators are objective, but some are subjective and imprecise, especially in the case of democracy and the legal system. In 2006 progress toward the comprehensive small-welfare society nationwide was assessed at 69.05 percent, or by area: 63.82 percent in economic development, 67.89 percent in social harmony, 64.60 percent in quality of life, 88.18 percent in democracy and the legal system, 76.25 percent in science and technology, and 69.05 percent in resources and environment (Study Team of the Statistical Science Research Institute 2007).

In summary, small welfare in modern China is a complex concept, and encompasses more than economic wealth. Deng Xiaoping set the target for building a small-welfare society in stages; the overarching strategy is economic growth first, followed by social equity and other national concerns.

BIBLIOGRAPHY

He Qiang. Suo you xiao kang shui ping he quan mian xiao kang she hui [All *xiaokang* level and comprehensive *xiaokang* society]. *Journal of Beijing Normal University* (Social Science Edition) 2 (2003): 23–27.

He Ziquan. Quan mian jian she xiao kang she hui [Comprehensively building *xiaokang* society]. *Journal of Beijing Normal University* (Social Science Edition) 2 (2003): 20–23.

Jiang Zemin. Quan mian jian she xiao kang she hui: yin ling you zhong guo te se de guo you qi ye de xin shi dai [Comprehensively building *xiaokang* society: Spearheading the new era of Chinese socialist enterprise with special characteristic]. Report at the Sixteenth Party Congress of the Chinese Communist Party. November 8, 2002.

Jin Zhong. Quan mian xiao kang de mu biao li wo men hai you duo yuan? [How far is the goal of comprehensive *xiaokang* from us?]. South China Net. 2006. www.southcn.com.

Study Team of the Statistical Science Research Institute, State Statistical Bureau. Zhong guo de quan mian jian she xiao kang she hui 2006 nian jin zhan jian du bao gao [Monitoring report on the progress of China's comprehensively building *xiaokang* society 2006]. Xinhua Net. 2007 www.news.xinhuanet.com

Wang Yubo. Xiao kang li shi yan jiu [*Xiaokang* historical study]. *Sociological Research* 2 (1992): 62–68.

Zhao Ziyang. Yan zhe you zhong guo te se de she hui zhu yi dao lu qian jin [Marching along the socialist road with Chinese Characteristics]. Report at the Thirteenth Party Congress of the Chinese Communist Party. October 25, 1987.

Wong Chack-kie

FOOD-FOR-WORK SCHEME

The food-for-work program is one of a large number of poverty-alleviation policies that the Chinese government has set up since the 1980s under different agencies and through different funding channels. It is mainly related to government investment in construction of rural infrastructure in poor areas. The program was initiated in 1984 and was organized and run by the State Planning Commission at central and local levels. It has developed in two stages and is still being implemented in the 592 designated poor counties as of 2008. Until the mid-1990s the focus of the program was to satisfy poor farmers' basic needs or provide relief to victims of natural disasters by providing households with daily necessities in return for labor. Surplus agricultural labor power was used for building roads, building water-conservancy facilities, or developing local industry on a small scale. The focus was on relief, not on construction. The local government financed purchase of materials and tools, and the central government provided commodities like grain and cotton, which were distributed to the farmers. During this period, basic needs for food and clothing were satisfied for a great majority of the poor by this and other poverty-reduction programs.

The guiding ideology changed with introduction of the "8.7" poverty-alleviation plan of 1994. The name referred to the program's primary aim, which was to lift 80 million people out of poverty in seven years. Focus was shifted to generating jobs and improving conditions for farmers to become self-employed. The target became poor areas more than individual farmers or households. Investments were channeled into bigger infrastructural projects, including power grids, and social development, such as primary education, cultural activities, and health care. The central government contributes by designing projects, providing technical support, hiring experts, and buying materials, while village and township committees organize the input. Participation is not voluntary at the individual level. According to official and other sources, farmers are remunerated for their time (Guojia Jihua Weiyuanhui 2005, Tao and Liu 2007), but not always, as other sources claim that the "labour input of farmers is basically unpaid" (Zhu and Jiang 2004). In any case, farmers share the benefits derived from improvements to infrastructure, with the more productive and active farmers naturally gaining more than the less industrious.

The program is organized as a top-down process from the National Development and Reform Commission (earlier, the State Planning Commission or State Development Planning Commission) down to food-for-work offices under the county development-planning commissions. The provincial level determines the type of construction activity, the county level selects villages to participate, and village committees decide on household contribution of labor. Villagers cannot refuse participation without having to pay a fine. According to central stipulations, the annual unpaid labor must not exceed 30 days per person, but this provision is not always strictly adhered to. Yet the program seems generally to have been supported by poor farmers because it adds value to their land-use rights acquired during the reform period, has generated new jobs in agricultural production, and has allowed farmers to secure more stable income, which has enabled poor families to cover travel expenses for one member to go out and seek employment elsewhere.

The program is evaluated as having played an important role in alleviating poverty in the poorest regions of China. Official figures from 2005 show that government sources have invested RMB 80 billion through the food-for-work program since 1984. Of this amount, RMB 15 billion has come from the central government, while the rest consists of matching funds from local sources. Workers on average received RMB 120 annually through participation. Furthermore, figures indicate that 70 percent of public-infrastructure construction in poverty-stricken counties during this period was done under this program. As a combined result of all poverty-reduction programs implemented since the beginning of the reform period, the number of people in China living in absolute poverty has decreased from 250 million in 1978 to 29 million in 2003—a drop in the poverty rate from 31 percent to 3 percent. Figures showing exactly how much of this drop can be attributed to the food-for-work program have not been found.

BIBLIOGRAPHY

Guojia Jihua Weiyuanhui (State Planning Commission). Quanguo yigongdaizhen gongzuo zongjie (1984–1995) [Summary of Food for Work Program (1984–1995)]. 1996. http://www.ndrc.gov.cn/

Guojia Jihua Weiyuanhui (State Planning Commission). Xin xingshi xia de yigongdaizhen chengxiao xianzhu [Outstanding results of the Food for Work Program under the new circumstances]. 2005. http://www.ndrc.gov.cn/

National Bureau of Statistics. Rural Survey Organization. *Poverty Statistics in China.* 2004. http://www.nscb.gov.ph/

Tao, Rao, and Mingxing Liu. Poverty Reduction, Decentralization, and Local Governance in China. In Yang, 2007, pp. 193–221.

Yang, Dali L., ed. *Discontented Miracle: Growth, Conflict, and Institutional Adaptations in China.* Hackensack, NJ: World Scientific, 2007.

Zhu Ling and Jiang Zhongyi. The Food-for-Work Policy and Expansion of Rural Employment in Poor Areas in Western China. Geneva: International Labour Office, 2004. http://www.ilo-mirror.cornell.edu/

Hatla Thelle

MINIMUM LIVING STANDARD GUARANTEE SYSTEM

Under the traditional socialist system, the limited role of the government was to take care of the "three no's": those with no family support, no ability to work, and no sources of income. Social assistance, known as the Minimum Living Standard Guarantee System (Zuidi Shenghuo Baozhang Zhidu) in China, is a means-tested social-protection program where eligibility depends on a test of incomes. Introduced first in Shanghai in 1993, the program has provided assistance of last resort to poverty-stricken urban residents with household-registration status. As the market-oriented reforms of the retirement, medical-care, and unemployment-insurance programs have been riddled with the problems of low coverage, inadequate funding, and poor management, social assistance has gained growing significance in recent years, with increasing numbers of recipients and government financial allocations (Leung 2006). In 2006 the number of recipients was 22.3 million. The average assistance need was RMB 170 per person per month, and the average actual benefit received was RMB 92 per person per month (Ministry of Civil Affairs 2007). Total expenditures amounted to RMB 22.4 billion, and about 61 percent of the expenditures came from the central government (table 1).

Minimum Living Standard Guarantee System

Year	Recipients (millions)	Expenditures (billions RMB)	Contribution, central govt. (billions RMB)	Avg. need per person per month (avg. benefit) (RMB)
1999	2.66	1.54	0.4 (26%)	
2000	4.03	2.96	0.8 (27%)	
2001	11.71	5.42	2.3 (42%)	
2002	20.65	10.86	4.6 (42%)	155 (52)
2003	22.47	15.10	9.2 (61%)	149 (58)
2004	22.05	17.27	10.2 (59%)	152 (65)
2005	22.34	19.19	11.2 (58%)	156 (72)
2006	22.41	22.40	13.6 (61%)	170 (92)

SOURCE: China Civil Affairs Development Report 2007. http://www.mca.gov.cn.

Table 1

The assistance line is calculated according to a minimum standard of living that relies on a budget standard, often based on expenditure surveys of low-income households, and is limited by the financial capacity of the local government. At a subsistence level, the benefit received would merely cover basic food and clothing costs. Assistance lines set up by local governments vary significantly across cities. Higher rates are found in coastal cities. Since this welfare is community-based in operation, neighborhood cadres are responsible for receiving and processing applications, delivering benefits, and periodically reviewing recipients' situations.

According to the government classification, in 2006, 4 percent of the recipients were low-income; 16 percent, layoffs; 2 percent, retirees; 19 percent, unemployed; 4 percent, the three no's; and 50 percent, family members (dependents of the main claimant).

Over the years, the proportion of family members has increased significantly, whereas the proportions of low-income recipients, layoffs, retirees, and the three no's have registered declines. In contrast with the traditional three no's, the majority of the new urban poor can work. In addition, poverty is often associated with disability and poor health. A survey by the government in 2002 indicated that 34 percent of recipient households had disabled persons, and 65 percent had chronically sick members (Leung 2006).

Future issues include the need to raise assistance lines to compensate for soaring food prices, provide incentives to encourage able-bodied recipients to become reemployed, and institutionalize the management process. More important, the effectiveness of the Minimum Living Standard Guarantee System hinges on integration with other means-tested assistance for the poor, including medical care, education, and housing. In 2007 the program was extended to rural areas, and it is hoped that the program will soon include migrant workers working in cities as well.

BIBLIOGRAPHY

Leung, Joe. The Emergence of Social Assistance in China. *International Journal of Social Welfare* 15 (2006): 188–198.

Minzheng Bu (Ministry of Civil Affairs). *Zhongguo Minzheng Shiye Fazhan Baogao 2007* [China civil affairs development report 2007]. http://www.mca.gov.cn

Joe Leung

SOCIAL RITUALS

Chinese society has long emphasized rituals as central elements in the reproduction of shared cosmologies; of the legitimate authority of the imperial state and Confucian elites; and of cultural bonds between the center and periphery, urban areas and the countryside, and elites and peasants. One of the early instigators of this tradition is the *Book of Rites* (*Liji*), a compilation of funeral rites and other religious practices that forms one of the Five Classics, which aspirants for the imperial bureaucracy had to study. As James Watson demonstrates in his historical anthropology "Rites or Beliefs?" (1993), long-standing patterns of social mobility and pedigree fostered standard religious and ritual practice across the empire. Rites could thus incorporate historical and contextual variations while maintaining the same basic structure throughout China. As repetitive practices that acted as carriers of traditional cosmology, they centrally shaped China as a civilization. As a result, Chinese elites and commoners historically stressed "orthopraxy" over "orthodoxy" (Watson 1993). In sum, rituals can give room to creativity while reproducing shared subjectivities, cultural configurations, and social bonds. The emphasis on ritual propriety (*li*) in China can thus be contrasted with the concomitant stress on individual expression and obedience to the law in Western civilizations.

Social rituals as standardized patterns of everyday interactions that create social bonds and are backed up by concepts of politeness, propriety, and etiquette have only more recently become a focus of scholarly attention. The reasons for this attention are manifold: new possibilities for sociological and anthropological studies in China, a new interest in the reproduction of the social in the midst of radical structural and cultural change, a new perspective on Chinese kinship as a process, and (coming from contemporary mainland China itself) a new political emphasis on creating a "civilized citizen." Maoist China was a revolutionary society that sought to destroy the Four Olds (Si Jiu; namely, old customs, old habits, old culture, and old thinking) in order to radically alter personal and collective subjectivities, political relations, and the nature of social bonds. The state outlawed many old religious rituals and replaced them with new, revolutionary, and secular forms centering on the socialist state.

Post-Maoist Chinese society, as Taiwan before, was then again radically altered by its engagement with global markets. Most relevant in changing the "fabric of Chinese society" (Fried 1969) were new status markers, inequalities, and the promotion of the self-reliant, urbane, and entrepreneurial citizen against the old altruistic collective citizen (in a Maoist sense). Although the old rules and cosmologies have radically changed, new cultural elements have been incorporated into daily life through mundane social rituals that define Chinese civilization in contemporary terms. This entry will focus on three sets of social rituals as representative of the expressive nature and materiality of Chinese relations: (1) gifts, emotions, and personal relations (*guanxi*); (2) hosting, commensality, and banquets; and (3) the cycles of visits, separation, and reunion.

GIFTS, EMOTIONS, AND PERSONAL RELATIONS

It has been argued that Chinese society and the Chinese person is neither individualistic nor collective, but relationship-based. Confucianism spoke of the five cardinal relationships (*wulun*; namely, sovereign-subject, father-son, husband-wife, elder brother–younger brother, and friend-friend), which formed the blueprint for all other relationships within society. According to Morton Fried (1969), the fabric of Chinese society is woven together by behavioral configurations that, when not based on the five cardinal relationships, are based on feelings of closeness (*ganqing*). Feelings of closeness describe the intensity of nonfamilial relationships, often bridging class differences. Fried distinguished between friendship and "feelings of closeness." For him, the latter are more formal, based on common interests and often including a recognized degree of exploitation. This view was later echoed in a very different corner when business-school circles discovered the Chinese propensity to establish networks of personal connections as the basis for a more flexible, more successful, "Confucian capitalism." Although the concept of Confucian capitalism was largely intellectually obsolete in 2008, was contributed to a new interest in the active production and management of social relations in China.

Scholars (as well as ordinary people) distinguish between more instrumental personal networks (which are manipulated to get things done, to go through the back door, or to pull favors [a pattern that in mainland China carries the name *guanxixue*, the art of social connections]) and actively cultivated social bonds, good feelings, and relatedness. Mayfair Yang (1994) draws a strong contrast between instrumental urban connections and an expressive rural gift economy. In contrast, Yunxiang Yan (1996) sees the difference determined more by social and/or geographical distance. Clearly, however, personal relations (*guanxi*) are not simply social connections, but are part of Chinese civilizatory practices directly related to important concepts such as *ganqing* (feelings of closeness), *renqing* (human feelings and moral propriety), and *mianzi* (face). Both Yang and Yan show how face can be actively accumulated in developing personal relations. A focus on social rituals has thus changed the older Western perception of Chinese society as rule-bound, stressing instead flexibility and the importance of individual and collective practice.

Andrew Kipnis (1997) explicitly stresses the communicative aspects of personal relations (*guanxi*). For him, the language of personal relations consists of exchanges of gifts and labor, etiquette, and bodily postures. These serve to foreshadow relationships, rather than simply to reenact social rules. Kipnis also stresses that in the practice of personal relations, material interests and the production of emotions are not necessarily opposed (as is often assumed in the West). As Alan Smart (1993) argues most concisely, it is the form and timing that determines what kind of relationship is produced. Comparing bribery and gift exchange, he shows that whatever the original intentions of the initiator of a personal relation, it is the etiquette of the exchange that eventually determines the meaning and nature of the resulting relationship.

HOSTING, COMMENSALITY, AND BANQUETS

A Chinese family is defined, among other things, through commensality. It is a group of people who eat from the same stove, and any official family division (*fenjia*) always implies that the stove is divided. Should a family separate before one or both parents are deceased, the sons' responsibility of caring for the parents, as dictated by filial piety (*xiao*) and by law, often involves an arrangement called meal rotation (*chi huotou*). Here the surviving parent rotates among the different households of the sons, sharing meals first with one family, then with another. This practice has clear economic reasons, but it also symbolizes the ongoing familial relationship between parent and sons after separation.

In a context where commensality is part of the making of families, receiving guests and hosting visitors is an important social ritual for creating or renewing social bonds. Because of the variety of possible relations and statuses, hosting also exerts major demands on social etiquette. Seating arrangements, for example, are given considerable attention. To express particular respect and politeness, the host will assign the guest the place of honor facing the door, with the host seated to the left. In family homes, meals are typically taken in the central guest room (*keting*). Seating arrangements here might reflect the status differences among the family members and guests and their respective social distance from the host. Such consciousness of etiquette and status is extended to the food and its presentation. As a standard, a table receiving a guest is decked out with at least four plates of food, but the quality of the food will vary according to the status of the guest (Liu 2000, pp. 95, 111). At first a guest might politely decline an invitation, but as the other relevant party of this social ritual, he is eventually obliged to accept if he does not want to refuse the relationship.

Typically, during the dinner the host will repeatedly fill the guest's bowl with the delicacies laid out on the table and keep his glass always filled to the brim, while at the same time making excuses for the simplicity of the meal. The guest, for his part, will praise its tastiness and the hospitality he enjoys. Yang (1994, p. 138) describes how an "invitation" can take on the form of a ritualized contest where the host tries to drag the resisting guest into his house or into a restaurant and the question of who pays the bill in a restaurant might turn into a struggle for the bill.

Banquets are major moments of status negotiation and an important vehicle for making or renewing social bonds. This is as true for meetings of businessmen or officials today as it was for the eleven heroes of the Song-dynasty classic *Outlaws of the March* (*Shuihu zhuan*), who reorganized their leadership by rearranging banquet seating (Kipnis 1997, p. 47). Banquets were also always central elements of Chinese weddings and funerals. Banquet hospitality thus expresses not so much kindness but differential forms of inclusion that renegotiate relationships between host and guests. Not surprisingly, the nouveaux riches of contemporary China are associated in the popular mind with lavish banquets (*dachi, dahe*; literally, "big eating," "big drinking").

VISITS, SEPARATION, AND REUNION

The Chinese use expressive culture to demonstrate feelings of closeness (*ganqing*), culture (*wenhua*), and civility (*wenming*). The last item is looked upon as a central asset of modern Chinese citizens and society, but it often differs from feelings of closeness and culture as embodied in social rituals. An important element of social rituals is the etiquette involved in visits, in receiving and sending off family members, friends, and officials. The central ideas here are *laiwang* (literally, comings and goings), which describes the cycle of visits, and *Li shang wanglai* (etiquette requires reciprocity) (Stafford 2000). Yan has likened the flow of gifts to the creation of a Chinese community as a small moral world. Stafford shows how the comings and goings of visits—the coming together on mundane occasions; on state holidays, weddings, and funerals; and on Chinese New Year—weave together the fabric of Chinese society. In addition, to continue with Fried's original metaphor, it is the changing forms of etiquette—the different material elements that accompany visits, reunions, and separations—bring about the changing patterns of Chinese sociality.

Historically, more formal visits marked by elaborate rituals of arrival and departure were linked with the annual cycle of calendrical festivals, whose central days were (and, especially in rural China, still are) framed by greeting (*jie*) and sending off (*song*) gods and ancestors (Stafford 2000, p. 32). These rituals of greeting and sending away again thus link humans with the spirits, family members with ancestors, while already anticipating a future reunion. In the past they also linked commoners to the state, as in the Qing dynasty (1644–1912) grand sacrifices, which were built around moments of arriving, parting, and returning (of the emperor, the ancestors, and the spirits). Such rituals were ultimately ascribed the function of uniting, whether it be a family, a lineage, a village, or the entire realm (Stafford 2000, p. 78).

Social rituals might also offer a sense of history and time different from the grand narratives of modernization

and historical conservatism. Especially in the countryside, this is evident in the jumbling together of apparently unrelated cultural elements: aerobics performances at funerals, depictions of U.S. dollar bills on posters of Chinese deities, disco balls illuminating local opera performances, or the use of pop music and brass bands at temple festivals. Social rituals such as these can integrate different cultural elements into a single narrative of reunion, reassembling, and renewal, despite being unrelated in the dominant understanding of history and culture. Social rituals are thus central elements in actively appropriating change from below and integrating local livelihoods with the larger historical narratives of modernity, globalization, and Chinese national culture.

BIBLIOGRAPHY

Fried, Morton. *Fabric of Chinese Society: A Study of the Social Life of a Chinese County Seat.* New York: Octagon Books, 1969.

Kipnis, Andrew. *Producing* Guanxi: *Self, Sentiment, and Subculture in a North China Village.* Durham, NC: Duke University Press, 1997.

Liu, Xin. *In One's Own Shadow: An Ethnographic Account of the Condition of Post-Reform Rural China.* Berkeley: University of California Press, 2000.

Smart, Alan. Gifts, Bribes, and *Guanxi:* A Reconsideration of Bourdieu's Social Capital. *Cultural Anthropology* 8, 3 (1993): 388–408.

Stafford, Charles. *Separation and Reunion in Modern China.* Cambridge, U.K.: Cambridge University Press, 2000.

Watson, James L. Rites or Beliefs? The Construction of a Unified Culture in Late Imperial China. In *China's Quest for National Identity,* ed. Lowell Dittmer and Samuel S. Kom. Ithaca, NY: Cornell University Press, 1993.

Yan, Yunxiang. *The Flow of Gifts: Reciprocity and Social Networks in a Chinese Village.* Stanford, CA: Stanford University Press, 1996.

Yang, Mayfair M. *Gifts, Favors, and Banquets: The Art of Social Relationships in China.* Ithaca, NY: Cornell University Press, 1994.

Susanne Brandtstädter

SOCIAL SCIENCES

Although there was no lack of elaborated approaches to govern the human world in imperial China, social science as an instrument to conceptualize and regulate the social realities created by the global system of nation-states and industrial capitalism did not exist in China until the turn of the twentieth century. Since then, the development of Chinese social sciences has been inseparable from the country's turbulent history and its rapidly changing political scenes.

THE ARRIVAL OF MODERN SOCIAL SCIENCE

The first and foremost change took place at the turn of the twentieth century, when China found itself engulfed by domestic unrest and foreign encroachments. Specifically, increased contacts between China and the industrial West as a result of war, diplomacy, and trade since the second half of the nineteenth century had subjugated the country to the European colonial gaze, making China appear to be lacking social order and social facts in the eyes of Western observers.

The idea of social science presumes the social world as an objective or independent reality with its own laws and mechanisms waiting to be discovered and examined. As this view of the human world became increasingly prominent in the West, European and American social scientists also believed that the differences and complexities of foreign societies such as China could be made familiar using the same social scientific analysis that privileged standardization, abstractions, modeling, comparison, and numbers. Meanwhile, as social science was increasingly being upheld as the universal language to make sense of the human world, many Chinese intellectuals, feeling humiliated because of their inability to conceptualize and represent their own society using this new framework, also began to advocate the importance of social scientific thinking.

At the start of the twentieth century, Yan Fu (1854–1921) was the most influential person in bringing ideas of social science into China through his translations of major European social science treatises, such as Herbert Spencer's *Study of Sociology* (1873) and Adam Smith's *Wealth of Nations* (1776). Early Chinese interest in social science was further augmented by Chinese students returning from Japan, where social science was fast becoming an important part of the intellectual and political landscape. And like its European, American, and Japanese counterparts, early Chinese social science was heavily colored by the ideologies of progressivism, nationalism, and social Darwinism.

Still, there were hardly any large-scale or concerted efforts to develop social science into academic disciplines or techniques of government at this time. The most noticeable attempt to adopt some elementary social statistical methods to study the Chinese population was the national census conducted by the Qing government (1644–1912) in 1909, just a few years before the abdication of the dynasty. As part of a series of institutional and political reforms, including especially the proposed constitutional monarchy, this was China's first modern census aimed at enumerating the entire Chinese population using a standardized template based on the Meiji Japanese model.

SOCIAL SCIENCE AS A NEW CONCEPTUAL FOUNDATION FOR THE EMERGING NATION

The collapse of the Qing in 1912 was followed by a period of political disintegration and warlord rivalries. The failure of the revolution of 1911 to establish a stable and function-

ing republic convinced many Chinese intellectuals that China's problems rested upon its inability to get rid of the plague of tradition. Many of them therefore began to look for a new knowledge foundation capable of filling the vacuum left behind by the bygone neo-Confucian scholarship and statecraft techniques. Social science, because of its professed qualities of being able to transcend histories, cultures, ideologies, and politics, was quickly regarded as the new paradigm for reconceptualizing and rebuilding the nation. This impulse to understand and describe human society in terms of natural science reached its height during the iconoclastic May Fourth movement of 1919. During this time, the commitment to the social science idea was mostly articulated as scientism, and the social sciences as disciplinary knowledge inquiries and training remained undeveloped.

The rise of the Nationalist state and the rebuilding of the Republic in the second half of the 1920s marked a period in which the development of the social sciences became institutionalized, specialized, professionalized, and systematic. Unlike the previous self-taught social thinkers who learned about the ideas of social science primarily through their experience in Japan or through translated works, the new generation of Chinese social scientists, who were prominently political liberals, was mostly trained in the United States and Europe. The most prominent among them included Chen Da (1892–1975) in sociology, Fei Xiaotong (1910–2005) in ethnology and sociology, Fu Sinian (1896–1950) in history and linguistics, Li Ji (1896–1979) in archaeology and physical anthropology, Li Jinghan (1894–1987) in sociology, Pan Guangdan (1899–1967) in sociology, Sun Benwen (1891–1979) in sociology and social psychology, and Tao Menghe (1887–1960) in sociology. The heavy presence of sociology in this group was especially driven by the belief that sociology as a science of society held the key to social reform projects that would rescue China from decline. Not surprisingly, many of these social scientists were affiliated with research institutions and universities that were directly or indirectly connected to the ruling Nationalist regime.

The most prominent state-sponsored research institution was the Academia Sinica, which included institutes specializing in ethnology, linguistics, and general social sciences. Meanwhile, disciplinary social sciences such as sociology, ethnology, linguistic, archaeology, physical anthropology, economics, and psychology also mushroomed in major universities across the country, even though their developments were uneven. There were also social survey research and social engineering projects supported by foreign institutions and existing independently from the state. The most noticeable sponsoring institution was the Rockefeller Foundation from the United States, which invested heavily in the development of public health as well as social science research and education. Although the American social scientific involvement in China was cut short as a consequence of the outbreak of full-scale war between China and Japan in 1937 and the eventual victory of the Communists in the Chinese civil war in 1949, the experience and programs it generated during the process eventually played an important role in social engineering projects in other parts of the world, including even that of the United States.

Finally, there were also Marxist social thinkers, many of whom did not affiliate with the mainstream academic institutions, carrying out social science research. Because of their overt political activism, they were often not regarded as professional social scientists by the liberal establishment. Qu Qiubai (1899–1935), Mao Zedong (1893–1976), and Chen Hansheng (1897–2004), among others, were the most famous of this group. Mao, who would eventually became the leader of the Communist movement, even used the findings of his own social investigations to justify his theory of peasant revolution. In this sense, in spite of their limited academic influence at the time, the ideas and social surveys developed by these Marxist social scientists were pivotal in creating the theories of the Communist revolution that would shape the course of Chinese history in much of the twentieth century.

THE ROLE OF SOCIAL SCIENCE IN THE EARLY PEOPLE'S REPUBLIC

The rise of the Communist regime after World War II (1937–1945) and the Chinese civil war introduced a different context for the development of the social sciences in China. Whereas social science was earlier used to search for a new knowledge foundation to save the Chinese nation and civilization, it was now being used to reinforce the revolutionary undertakings of the ruling regime. Not surprisingly, liberal social science disciplines such as sociology, political science, and economics were deemed "bourgeois" and were therefore eliminated from university curriculums. Ethnology and linguistics survived the purge and were incorporated by the Communist state into projects on taxonomy and the classification of ethnic minorities. They indeed occupied a crucial role in constructing and maintaining the narrative of China being a multiethnic nation-state made up of fifty-six nationalities.

Meanwhile, the Academia Sinica, including many of its social science researchers and programs, was relocated to Taiwan along with the defeated Nationalist government. Those social scientists who chose to stay in the mainland, subsequently, were compelled or forced to pursue research agendas that embraced a dogmatic social and economic analytical framework to study and affirm the narratives of class struggle, historical materialism, and revolution. Furthermore, during this period, the so-called Marxian social science in China was drawing heavily from Maoist and Soviet ideas, rather than the broader Marxist tradition.

Subsequently, the social sciences sanctioned by the state became nothing more than lip service for the regime.

THE DEVELOPMENT OF SOCIAL SCIENCE FOR SOCIALIST MODERNIZATION PROJECTS

The death of Mao Zedong and the end of the decade of the Cultural Revolution in 1976 marked the close of the revolution era and the beginning of the reform era. The emphasis on economic development through scientific methods and expertise under the leadership of Deng Xiaoping (1904–1997) particularly entailed a different kind of social science research. The Chinese Academy of Social Sciences was established in 1977 to promote and coordinate the development of the social sciences for socialist modernization projects. The Shanghai Academy of Social Sciences, founded in 1958 but shut down during the Cultural Revolution, was also reopened in 1978. Indeed, during this period, numerous academies of social sciences were founded across the country. They included academies established in Beijing (1978), Tianjin (1979), Fujian (1978), Guangdong (1980), Hubei (1978), Hunan (1978), Jiangsu (1980), Shanxi (1979), and Sichuan (1978), as well as those in other provinces. Some of these academies were reorganized from existing economic, historical, and philosophical research institutes founded in the 1950s, but their arrival no doubt pointed to the renaissance of the social sciences in China.

In the early days of the market reform, the intellectual agenda of the Chinese social sciences was still carefully defined as the study and promotion of Marxism-Leninism, Mao Zedong Thought, and Deng Xiaoping Theory. Political science, for instance, was promoted under the framework of socialist democracy. Still, liberal social science disciplines and subfields that were once deemed "bourgeois" were reinstated and again being taught at universities. In fact, rapid industrialization and privatization has even put many new social and economic problems, such as migrant workers, unemployment, juvenile delinquency, welfare, housing, property rights, inflation, income disparity, and so forth, on the forefront, demanding new services from social scientific disciplines that are inherently connected to the neoliberal social order. In addition, the further integration of China into the global economy since the 1990s also made other previously unavailable disciplines such as international relations, political science, and law, as well as public relations and opinion surveys, increasingly indispensible. In addition, in light of the rising economic disparities resulting from China's inexorable policy of economic development and authoritarian rule, the government increasingly used nationalism to foster national solidarity, political stability, and state legitimacy in order to dampen the growing social discontents. Consequently, ethnology, anthropology, archaeology, and history remain a significant force in the construction of Chinese national identity.

Although the development of the social sciences remains partially monitored and regulated by the state, it is also heavily dictated by the imperatives of globalization. As a result, social science research in China is more diverse than ever. In addition to quantitative research in traditional social science disciplines, interdisciplinary research, postcolonial studies, and critical social theory have also been gaining traction in major universities. At the same time, Chinese social scientists are enjoying an unprecedented level of exchange and collaboration with their colleagues around the world.

CONCLUSION

The history of the social sciences in China has gone through three distinct phases. The most dramatic shift occurred at the turn of the twentieth century, when social science replaced neo-Confucian scholarship and statecraft techniques as a new conceptual foundation for China's national and civilizational survival. But even in the later phases, when the social sciences were mobilized for constructing new theoretical grounds for the deepening of the revolution during the Communist era and the modernization projects of the reform era, the shift in conceptual categories and research paradigms was no less profound. Moreover, in spite of foreign influences, Chinese social scientists, regardless of their ideological inclinations, all strived to adapt the social sciences into the Chinese environment. As such, the development of the social sciences in China, not unlike elsewhere in the world, shows that there is an inherent connection between the political order and the structure of social scientific knowledge, and that the production of social scientific knowledge is inseparable from the local cultural and political contexts.

BIBLIOGRAPHY

Chiang Yung-chen. *Social Engineering and the Social Sciences in China, 1919–1949.* Cambridge, U.K.: Cambridge University Press, 2001.

Gransow, Bettina. The Social Sciences in China. In *The Cambridge History of Science*, Vol. 7: *The Modern Social Sciences*, ed. Theodore M. Porter and Dorothy Ross, 498–514. Cambridge, U.K.: Cambridge University Press, 2003.

Wong Siu-lun. *Sociology and Socialism in Contemporary China.* London: Routledge and Kegan Paul, 1979.

Tong Lam

SOCIAL WELFARE

This entry contains the following:

OVERVIEW

When the People's Republic of China (PRC) was established in 1949, social welfare was all but nonexistent. After years of civil war and foreign occupation, there was grave economic disruption, hyperinflation, and population displacement. The next eight years (1949–1957) brought a high growth rate, rapid reconstruction, and the introduction of social-welfare schemes, most still surviving. Soon after, however, China entered the turbulent twenty years of the Great Leap Forward and the Cultural Revolution (1966–1969). These two decades saw the most severe famine ever, with tens of millions of deaths. The living standard of the population increased little, if at all, and ad hoc changes were made in labor insurance that would create future problems. However, one positive development during this turbulent period was the extension of primary health care to most of the countryside.

China entered the reform period in December 1978 with most of the population still classified as rural. The rural economy was fully collectivized, as it has been since 1958, and the urban economy was dominated by the state sector. Daily life and provision for social needs were structured in urban areas by work units (*danwei*) and in the countryside by rural collective units. However, the prevalent living standard was barely discernible from poverty, and up to a third of the rural population lived below the poverty line.

INTRODUCTION OF SOCIAL WELFARE IN THE PRC

Article 45 of the first Constitution of the PRC (1954) recognized that "Citizens of the People's Republic of China have the right to material assistance from the state and society when they are old, ill, or disabled. The state develops the social insurance, social relief, and medical and health services that are required to enable citizens to enjoy this right." The 1949–1978 period saw the introduction of a range of social-welfare schemes that can be classified as follows:

1. contributory labor insurance for the urban labor force

2. means-tested assistance

3. natural-disaster relief

4. health-care insurance

These schemes did not constitute a coherent whole, and were characterized by two features. First, conforming to a pattern that still holds, each scheme applied to either the urban or the rural population, but not to both. Second, the schemes were embedded into an economy that gave particular importance to providing the rural labor force with access to land and the urban labor force with jobs. This second characteristic accounts for much of China's success in reducing destitution among its population.

LAYING THE FOUNDATIONS OF RURAL AND URBAN SOCIAL SECURITY

In 1949 and throughout the thirty years leading up to the start of the reform period, the overwhelming majority of the population was rural. The new regime, recognizing that rural well-being depended on access to land, ruthlessly promoted land reallocation. This policy was aimed at providing land to poor peasants who had little or no land, allocating it according to the size of the household and including individuals who were not farmers but part of the rural economy, such as peddlers. Land reallocation reduced poverty, but did not eliminate it; relative to the population, land was limited, and the yield of a plot of land was further limited by the low level of agricultural technology.

Land reform was a transitory phase on the path to collectivization. Within nine years (1949–1958), Chinese agriculture went from family farming to full-scale collectivization, combining distribution according to need and distribution according to work, with the first having primacy over the second. The collective organization of the rural economy ensured that each household had enough for basic needs. Need was restrictively interpreted in terms of grain per capita, a convention surviving well into the 1980s. When assessing the role of collective agriculture in providing social protection, its impact on economic incentives also requires consideration. It is said that the collective organization functioned well in only a third of units. In most cases, collective agriculture provided security but at a low living standard—secure, but poor.

In urban areas, the cornerstone of social security was employment. But the underdevelopment of the economy severely limited the ability of the government to provide jobs. Over the period of the First Five-Year Plan (1952–1956), the pace of development was rapid, with free movement of labor from rural to urban areas. The latter could not be sustained for long, given the magnitude of surplus labor in the countryside. To keep the employment guarantee within manageable limits, stringent restrictions on rural-to-urban migration were introduced, based on the household registration system (*hukou*). This restriction, introduced in 1958, has cast a long shadow on the lives of the population by institutionalizing a division between rural and urban inhabitants. Urban registration has conferred a privileged economic status, with the possibility of a comparatively higher living standard. Rural inhabitants have had guaranteed access to land, but because economic opportunities vary widely with the locality, this access has not ruled out poverty, and in some areas severe poverty. The control on migration proved remarkably successful in achieving its aim. Aside from minor fluctuations, the ratio of the urban population to the total remained constant for twenty years between 1958 and 1978.

The control on migration went in tandem with a glaring disparity in the social security provision for the urban and rural populations. In principle, though not always in practice, urban residents benefited from a complementary combination of comprehensive labor insurance and a wide range of goods, such as housing and grain, at subsidized prices. In contrast, social security provision in rural areas was sparse and remained so over the reform period.

URBAN LABOR INSURANCE

Labor insurance, the precursor of what from the 1990s began to be called "social insurance," was introduced in 1951 but for the urban labor force only. It covered retirement pensions, medical care, occupational injury and disability compensation, maternity expenses, and funerals, but not unemployment benefits. Unemployment was regarded as a category specific to capitalism. However, it was recognized that placement into jobs may take time; the hiatus between becoming available for work and finding a job was known as "waiting for a job," and an allowance was provided to cover basic needs over the period. For a developing economy, especially one that had just emerged from a long period of civil war, labor insurance was generous. Its introduction was not a response to current problems; rather, it was intended to mark the position of workers in the urban-industrial economy that was taking shape.

Labor insurance was financed solely by work units, and no contributions were made by employees. The premium was set at 3 percent of the wage bill. Of this amount, 30 percent was allocated to the labor-insurance general fund of the All-China Federation of Trade Unions (ACFTU) at the national and provincial level. The remaining 70 percent went to the labor-insurance fund of the enterprise branch of the ACFTU, and was used to fund pensions, medical care, and funeral expenses. In the event of a shortfall, the gap was financed by a higher level of the ACFTU (the city or province level). In this way, the labor-insurance scheme maintained a uniform nationwide system for collecting premiums and paying out benefits.

The scheme underwent a fundamental change with the start of the Cultural Revolution. The ACFTU stopped functioning and its responsibilities were transferred to enterprises, which stopped paying contributions, financing benefits from their current expenditure. The pooling of social security expenditure across enterprises, previously ensured by the 30 percent of contributions paid to the national and provincial branches of the ACFTU, stopped altogether, and the scheme became completely decentralized. Labor insurance, previously a national scheme, became an enterprise scheme. This introduced a variation in the level of provision because the financial position of the enterprises varied widely. As the number of pensioners rose in the 1970s, many enterprises could not meet their social security obligations, and in response postponed retirement. China entered the reform period with a huge backlog of workers who were past retirement age but still working. One of the first measures of the reform period was to restore retirement at the prescribed ages, and the number of retirees increased sharply, creating a huge problem for labor insurance. The problem was not new, just hidden because the system was not operating.

THE ROLE OF THE WORK UNIT

Another salient feature of the social-welfare regime in urban areas was the central role of work units, a role that would continue well into the reform period. Historically, Chinese state enterprises have operated as semi-enclosed communities, more akin to the army than to firms in market economies. Along with producing goods or services for sale, they also provided, either free or at low prices, a wide range of goods and services to their current and retired employees and often their families as well. Prominent among these goods and services were housing, inpatient and outpatient medical treatment, schooling for children, and in some cases even public utilities. A cash wage was just one component of a package with an array of benefits in kind. The extended social role of Chinese state enterprises tethered most urban laborers to their respective work units for not merely their working lives but also retirement. Over the reform period, this role was increasingly perceived as a major barrier in enterprise reform.

Labor recruitment in state enterprises and government organizations was geared less toward meeting the labor demand and more toward preventing the emergence of unemployment in urban areas. As it were, the labor supply created its own demand, and this had two consequences. First, the work-unit-based social provision covered a large majority of the urban population. In 1978, 78.3 percent of the urban labor force was employed in state enterprises and government organizations, and the rest were employed in collective enterprises, which tended to emulate state enterprises. Second, because of the large excess of job seekers relative to vacancies in urban areas, most work units had more employees than they needed. State enterprises were the mainstay of the urban social-welfare system and the supplier of a wide range of services

that in market economies would be provided by the government, civil associations, or firms. Preempted by the extensive social role of work units, government provision of social services tended to be sparse, and largely for government employees.

THE EXTENSION OF MEDICAL CARE TO VILLAGES

A notable achievement of the decade of the Cultural Revolution (1966–1976) was the extension of primary medical care to villages. This involved dispatching medical personnel from urban areas to villages, establishing village health stations, training a large number of paramedics (the so-called barefoot doctors), and developing the rural cooperative medical-insurance schemes. These initiatives addressed two issues central to the provision of primary health care in developing economies. The first was training medical personnel in sufficient numbers and, more important, deploying them in the countryside. On the eve of decollectivization in 1979, around 85 percent of the rural population was covered by some form of rural cooperative medical insurance, which was jointly financed by contributions from the participants and subsidies by the local government. Both the rural cooperative medical-insurance schemes and the rural health care network suffered from major shortcomings, but they represented a massive improvement over what previously existed. Following the division of the land among rural households, these disappeared from much of the countryside.

MEANS-TESTED SCHEMES

In response to natural calamities and personal mishaps and contingencies, there developed a number of means-tested schemes. Some were targeted at individuals and households, and others were targeted at localities. Prominent among the first were the "five guarantees" (*wubao*) and assistance to poor households (variously termed *kunnan hu* or *tekun hu*). Schemes directed at localities or regions included natural-disaster relief and assistance to revolutionary base areas—localities that were under Communist control during the civil war.

The "five guarantees" scheme, introduced in 1956, referred to five basic needs: food, health care, shelter, clothing, and funeral expenses. Over time, the term has come to designate persons with "three no's": those lacking the physical capacity to work, relatives to depend on, and savings or assets. The recipients of *wubao* relief have predominantly been elderly persons without family support. The scheme was formalized and put on a sounder financial footing in 1994. The number of *wubao* recipients is small, but it has a special significance in China because of the tradition of looking after parents in old age.

CONCLUSION

The years from 1949 to 1957 constituted a formative period for social welfare. Taken together, the schemes were a disparate assortment and segmented into urban and rural, a division that still persists in 2009. Labor insurance, which was modeled on social-welfare schemes in welfare states, started off on a good footing in 1951. Had the scheme kept to its original structure, it could have developed into the centerpiece of a modern social security system. However, as a result of ad hoc changes in operation and financing in 1961, labor insurance had a troubled history over much of the reform period. It was only in 1998 that the scheme was overhauled and transformed into social insurance.

SEE ALSO *Rural Cooperative Medical Systems; Rural Development, 1949–1978: Five Guarantees; Urban Employment and Unemployment since 1949.*

BIBLIOGRAPHY

Ahmad, Ehtisham, and Athar Hussain. Social Security in China: A Historical Perspective. In *Social Security in Developing Countries*, eds. Ehtisham Ahmad, Jean Drèze, John Hills, and Amartya Sen, 247–304. Oxford: Oxford University Press, 1991.

Dixon, John E. *The Chinese Welfare System: 1949–1979.* New York: Praeger, 1981.

Athar Hussain

FAMILY-BASED CARE

Whereas social welfare in the West is often associated with the welfare state or welfare policies or programs for the well-being of the citizen, welfare in China is commonly connected with the family as the main social institution providing care and support to its members in time of need.

THE FAMILY AS A WELFARE INSTITUTION

Providing welfare within the family accords with Confucian doctrines. Parents are to teach and care for the young (Zhan and Bradshaw 1996); children are to respect and care for their parents in old age (Ikels 1993). In filial piety and ancestor worship, filial responsibilities for aging parents are emphasized to the point of attaining a religious dimension (Fairbank, Reischauer, and Craig 1978; Granet 1975).

Since the establishment of the People's Republic of China in 1949, the government has continued to emphasize the importance of familial intergenerational care. The normative expectation and practice is for grandparents to help take care of grandchildren. Likewise, adult children are expected to provide direct care for aging parents at home (Zhan 2004, Davis 1983). Although the government has established welfare centers for orphans and childless elders

since the 1950s (Chen 1996, Sher 1984), disabled children and frail elders who have family depend on familial care. Care patterns are typically patrilocal: Grandparents provide care to their adult sons' children; sons and daughters-in-law provide care for aging parents. Prior to the 1980s, living arrangements were also typically patrilocal (Lavely and Ren 1992). Retirement pensions are available only for urban elders who worked in state-owned enterprises. The vast majority of rural elders (over 95%) have neither pensions nor medical care for their old age (Feng and Xiao 2007, Giles and Mu 2007); most completely depend on their children to provide funds for living. Hence, most people in rural China continue to believe the old Chinese saying "Yangzi fanglao" (Raise children for the benefit of old age).

CHANGING DYNAMICS OF FAMILY WELFARE

The heavy reliance on the family for the welfare of its members faces severe challenges in China in the early twenty-first century. Several factors jointly contribute to these challenges. First, the economic reforms and free-market system since the 1980s have dramatically reduced the number of state-owned enterprises. So workers as well as retirees experience tremendous insecurity in employment, health-care access, and pension benefits. Yet reliance on adult children is increasing as families become more fragile.

Second, the one-child policy is creating an inverted pyramid where one couple, both from one-child families, have to care for as many as four aging parents, along with their own single child. This dependency ratio is creating an unprecedented squeeze on this first generation of adult single children sandwiched between aging baby boomers and their own children. The expectation that this middle generation of workers with no siblings can financially support and physically care for the old and young is increasingly untenable for millions of families.

Third, there is an ongoing process of urbanization in China. Millions of rural workers are migrating to urban China in search of better opportunities, leaving aging parents at home, oftentimes alone. Decreasing numbers of children and lack of a social-welfare system mean that aging adults in rural China face challenges unprecedented in Chinese history.

Finally, at a time of industrialization and globalization, low fertility rate and longer life expectancy are causing China's population to age. As a result of economic reforms, the one-child policy, urbanization, and population aging, the family is becoming more mobile, more fragile, and smaller in size.

While the family continues to be the core welfare institution in Chinese society, it is becoming less able to provide for all the needs for its well-being. These challenges raise concern as to the future feasibility of relying exclusively on the family as the sole welfare institution in rural China. Societal and governmental programs of assistance are necessary to ensure the welfare of future Chinese families.

BIBLIOGRAPHY

Chen, Sheying. *Social Policy of the Economic State and Community Care in Chinese Culture: Aging, Family, Urban Change, and the Socialist Welfare Pluralism.* Brookfield, VT: Avebury, 1996.

Davis, Deborah. *Long Lives: Chinese Elderly and the Communist Revolution.* Cambridge, MA: Harvard University Press, 1983.

Fairbank, John K., Edwin O. Reischauer, and Albert M. Craig. *East Asia: Tradition and Transformation.* Boston: Houghton Mifflin, 1978.

Feng, Nailin, and Ning Xiao. Population Aging in China as Reflected by the Results of the 2005 Population Sample Survey. Paper presented at the 23rd Population Census Conference: Utilization of the 2000 and 2005 Rounds of Asia-Pacific Censuses, 2007. http://www.ancsdaap.org/cencon2007/Papers/China/China_Feng.pdf

Giles, John, and Ren Mu. Elderly Parent Health and the Migration Decisions of Adult Children: Evidence from Rural China. *Demography* 44, 2 (2007): 265–288.

Granet, Marcel. *The Religion of the Chinese People.* New York: Harper and Row Publishers, 1975.

Ikels, Charlotte. Chinese Kinship and the State: Shaping of Policy for the Elderly. *Annual Review of Gerontology and Geriatrics* 13 (1993): 123–146.

Lavely, William, and Xinhua Ren. Patrilocality and Early Marital Co-residence in Rural China, 1955–1985. *China Quarterly* 127 (1992): 594–615.

Sher, Ada Elizabeth. *Aging in Post-Mao China: The Politics of Veneration.* Boulder, CO: Westview Press, 1984.

Zhan, Heying Jenny. Willingness and Expectations: Intergenerational Differences in Attitudes toward Filial Responsibilities. *Marriage and Family Review* 36, 1–2 (2004): 175–200.

Zhan, Heying Jenny, and R. W. Bradshaw. Texts and Contexts: The Book of Analects for Women. *Journal of Historical Sociology* 9, 3 (1996): 261–268.

Zhan, Heying Jenny, and Rhonda J. V. Montgomery. Gender and Elder Care in China: The Influence of Filial Piety and Structural Constraints. *Gender and Society* 17, 2 (2003): 209–229.

Heying Jenny Zhan

SOCIAL CARE

After the establishment of the People's Republic of China in 1949, the responsibility for providing care and support to the country's older people, orphans, and others in need rested primarily with the family, whose efforts were supplemented by the work unit–based social welfare system. The government only took care of the "three no's": those with no family support, no working ability, and no sources of income were cared for in welfare institutions operated by local governments.

Like other countries, China is facing the formidable and mounting challenge of providing social care to its vulnerable populations, particularly older people. Due to its rigorous family-planning policy and an increase in life expectancy, China has become an aging society. Yet it is still a developing economy. The key features of its aging population are its large size, rapid aging process, and significant regional, female-male, and rural-urban differences (Information Office 2006). According to a 2006 national survey on disability, more than half of China's eighty-three million disabled persons were over the age of sixty.

Family support for older people is a long-standing and cherished Chinese tradition. However, the capacity of the family to provide care to its needy members has been eroded by the increased participation of women in the economy, smaller family size, and higher residential mobility. "Empty-nest" families have become more common, particularly in rural areas, from which more young people have migrated to cities for jobs (Leung 2006).

According to a longitudinal survey, the proportion of older people that requires full social care increased from 6.6 percent in 2000 to 9.8 percent in 2006 (China National Commission on Aging 2007). In 2006 there were approximately 42,000 residential welfare institutions with 1.87 million beds catering to a total of 1.47 million residents, a growth from the 1.1 million beds catering to 0.85 million residents in 2000. Thus, the residential care services sector has been expanding rapidly (Ministry of Civil Affairs 2007). The majority of residents in such institutions are older people. Overall, the institutionalization rate of older people was less than 1 percent in 2006. Admission to these institutions is largely based on one's being classified as among the "three no's" or having the ability to pay the market-level fees, rather than on social and health-care needs. Since the early 2000s, the utilization rate has been consistently around 75–78 percent. Among these welfare institutions, there are approximately 250 children's homes serving 45,000 orphans (Ministry of Civil Affairs 2007). With 0.6 million orphans in China, even with the rapid development of foster care, the service can hardly meet the need.

About 75 percent of residents are placed in welfare institutions operated by the collectives, referring to the township governments in rural areas and the street (neighborhood) offices in urban districts. About 20 percent are received in institutions operated by the city-level governments. Around 5 percent of residents are living in institutions operated by the "society," including those operated by nonprofit organizations and the business sector (Ministry of Civil Affairs 2007). Only those homes operated by the city-level government receive partial government subsidies, whereas most other homes finance their operation with fees paid by residents. Under the policy of "socialization" (having a pluralistic welfare), the government has pledged to facilitate the establishment and provision of residential welfare institutions operated or managed by the private and the nongovernmental sector. Preferential policies include exemptions or reduction in taxes and utility charges, as well as the provision of land and premises. In practice, these preferential policies have not been fully implemented. Being poorly equipped and staffed, non-state-operated residential institutions face low utilization rates and unstable incomes.

Since the late 1990s, the central government and some local governments have enacted guidelines and regulations prescribing the desired quality standards for welfare institutions. These standards cover staffing, premise size, physical environment, and personal-care services. With regard to staff quality, there is an explicit requirement that institutions employ trained social workers and registered personal-care workers. However, monitoring performance and enforcing compliance have been difficult. In some large cities, such as Shanghai and Beijing, the government carries out annual inspections to ensure that welfare institutions meet standards. Personal-care workers in the cities may be provided with in-service training on basic care skills. Based on public examinations, around 20,000 personal-care workers in the cities have obtained basic qualifications by 2006. Still, China's welfare institutions are largely staffed by insufficiently qualified and trained workers.

There is substantial variation in quality between welfare institutions. The government-operated institutions are usually better financed, have quality staff and facilities, maintain higher standards, and are more appealing to older people and their families. But because institutional care services are costly and not acceptable to many of China's older people, mainly due to the high fees and for cultural reasons, the government has promoted the development of community-based home care. The new policy direction for the development of services for older people includes the following elements: family care is the foundation; community care provides the necessary support; and residential care is supplementary. Community-based services for the elderly may include day care, meal delivery, home care, and escort services. However, service development has been uneven, with community services largely concentrated in economically better-off cities and districts. Support from the central government for the development of such community services, particularly in economically deprived areas, has been limited (Leung 2006).

The heavy reliance on the government in the provision of welfare services, even though it is patchy and insufficient in places, is related to the still fledgling development of charitable, nongovernmental organizations in China. By 2003 there were around 1,200 charitable foundations in China engaged in the field of poverty alleviation, education, and environmental protection. They have limited total assets of about five billion yuan. A survey of nongovernmental organizations in China revealed that their development is hindered by the lack of a culture of public donation,

domineering control from the government, and weak leadership (Leung 2005). Charities that are independent of the government remain rare.

With growing economic prosperity, the social-care market operated by the for-profit sector should have great potential for development. To further the policy of socialization, local governments have attempted to purchase services from nongovernmental organizations, or have allowed them to operate governmental welfare institutions.

In summary, social-care services are mostly remedial and government-operated, and meant for the destitute only. Because China is facing an aging society, institutional care services have emerged as a major form of social care. Providers have become more diversified to include the private and nongovernmental sector. Being market-driven, needy older people may have difficulty receiving support. Looking ahead, there is an urgent need for the government to develop and enforce minimum standards for social-care services. The training and recruitment of qualified social-care staff is a priority. Specialized social-care services should be developed to cater to the needs of elderly people with mental illness or dementia. Finally, the interface between community services, family care, and institutional care should be strengthened.

BIBLIOGRAPHY

China National Commission on Aging (Zhongguo Laoning Gongzuo Weiyuanhui Bangongshi). *The Longitudinal Study on the Demographic Situation of Older People in Urban and Rural China* [*Zhongguo chengxiang laolian renkou zhuangkuang diaocha*]. http//www.cnca.org.cn.

Information Office of the State Council of the Peoples Republic of China. *The Development of China's Undertakings for the Aged.* 2006. http://www.china.org.cn/english/aged/192020.htm

Leung, Joe. Social Welfare Reform in China: From Employment-based Welfare to Social Welfare. In *Eastern Asian Welfare Regimes in Transition: From Confucianism to Globalization,* eds. Alan Walker and Chack Kei Wong, 49–72. Bristol, U.K.: Policy Press, 2005.

Leung, Joe. Community Services for the Elderly in China. In *Handbook of Asian Aging,* eds. Hyunsook Yoon and Jon Hendricks, 405–430. New York: Baywood, 2006.

Ministry of Civil Affairs of the People's Republic of China (Zhongguo Minzheng Bu). *China Civil Affairs Development Report 2007* [*Zhongguo minzheng shiye fazhan baogao*].http://www.mca.gov.cn

Joe C. B. Leung

CARE AND AID FOR THE DISABLED

Welfare policies and programs began in the West in the late nineteenth century, but chronic war and social upheaval delayed China's development of even a limited welfare system until the early years of Communist rule in the 1950s. Since the 1980s China has developed more extensive welfare programs for the care of the disabled. While certain welfare programs offer direct government assistance, benefits, or services, others may direct resources to support institutions concerned with providing welfare, such as the family, the private sector, or nonprofit organizations.

Disability occurs for three reasons: birth, accident, or aging. Types of disability may be physical, mental, or aging-related. People may suffer different levels of disability; some are not considered disabled. Here "the disabled" refers to those who have lost the ability to perform without assistance one or more activities of daily living because of physical, mental, or age-related impairment by birth, accident, or aging; and who are unable to make a living or earn an income to allow them to live independently.

CARE FOR DISABLED YOUTH

From 1950 to the 1980s, most disabled youth were exclusively cared for by family members in family settings. The government took care only of orphans and childless elders, housing them in orphanages and elder homes (Chen 1996). The social stigma of these institutions was strong. In 1990 the Chinese government formally adopted a law guaranteeing the rights and interests of the disabled. By 1994 thousands of community rehabilitation centers opened to provide services for those with sight, hearing, and speech disabilities. More than 1,000 schools and 5,000 classes opened to serve 210,000 special-education students with physical and mental disabilities (China State Council, Information Office 2003). The Special Olympics held in Shanghai in October 2007 evinces China's enhanced attention to the disabled. As government attention increased and the stigma lessened, there has been more willingness to identify mental disability. In Shanghai, mental illness was reported at 0.32 percent in the late 1970s, but at 1.55 percent in 2006 (Dalby 2006). The disabled in China were recently reported as numbering 83 million, among them 9.8 million intellectually disabled (Xinhua News Agency 2007). Care for the disabled has been a joint effort of the government, private or nonprofit groups, and families. Growing numbers of care facilities for people with mental disabilities have started up, especially in major cities, but many lack adequate funding or trained medical and professional staff members (Dalby 2006). Even with the growth in social awareness and governmental attention to the care of the disabled, large numbers of severely disabled children and adults continue to be at risk. When families are no longer able to provide proper care, many of the disabled are left on the streets to fend for themselves. Some live in squalid conditions; others are abused (Hallett 2006).

CARE FOR ADULTS WITH WORK-RELATED DISABILITIES

The 1990 law protecting the disabled included a provision of equal rights in education, employment, and treatment to persons disabled in accidents. This offers protection to those who become disabled at work, but only applies to urban workers, specifically to those working in state-owned enterprises. Those disabled due to military or "patriotic" causes are also eligible for medical treatment, financial assistance, and prioritization for social and educational services.

Since 1980 labor practices in China have changed so that most workers are employed in nonstate sectors, including the private sector, joint ventures, or foreign-capitalized enterprises. These nonstate-sector employees were not covered by the 1990 disability law. In addition, workers from the countryside who flooded into urban areas for manufacturing and construction jobs have had no protection under the law. Consequently, millions of Chinese workers have worked without disability protection despite long work hours and unsafe working conditions. Based on the Chinese rural labor rights protection network, there were 35.2 million Chinese workers who were permanently or temporarily disabled at work (Brown 2002).

In 2003 the Chinese government adopted legal regulations expanding protection and welfare to those who become disabled at work in both the public and private sectors. These regulations clearly obligated both state enterprises and private-business owners to pay for work-related-injury insurance to the local labor protection bureau for new employees before they are legally hired. When disabled, a worker is eligible to receive different levels of financial compensation from the work-related-injury fund, based on estimations of the disability for work and living. Financial compensation to disabled employees is provided jointly by employers and local provincial governments. These regulations, however well conceived, have been implemented unevenly. More than 90 percent of rural migrant laborers, including temporary workers in the dangerous construction and mining sectors, still have no injury insurance.

CARE FOR THE AGED

Care for the aged, stemming from Confucian teachings of filial piety, has long been a Chinese cultural value. Children have been expected to provide financial, emotional, and physical care for their parents in old age (Zhan and Montgomery 2003). The government reinforced this tradition by requiring adult children to provide care for dependent elderly parents by law (Gu and Liang 2000). Care for the aged in China since the 1950s can be divided

446

An autistic boy undergoing physical therapy at school, Beijing, May 9, 2008. *Prior to the 1980s, most care for disabled or elderly family members occurred in the home. At the end of the twentieth century, however, the Communist government began establishing schools for special needs children, nursing homes for the aged, and rehabilitation centers for adults injured in the workplace.* **CHINA PHOTOS/GETTY IMAGES**

into three domains: financial provision, medical care, and physical care.

Financial provision for the aged has not been widely available in China because of a rural-urban divide in government programs. In rural China, where a vast majority of the Chinese population resides (roughly 60 percent in 2007), no central- or local-government programs existed to provide finances for older adults. In the early twenty-first century, as in times past, elders rely on adult children for financial support (Goldstein and Ku 1993, Ikels 1989). In urban China prior to the 1980s, most workers worked in state-owned enterprises, which provided retirement pensions (Davis 1993, Sher 1984). Since the economic reforms of the 1980s, financial provision for urban workers has depended on funding from the government, workers, or employers. But decentralization and privatization have reduced the percentage of urban retirees covered by these pensions to only 43 percent in 2000 (Chow and Xu 2003, p. 134). Since the 1990s, the Chinese government has

started to distribute minimum social assistance to urban dwellers whose "household income falls below a locally determined minimum standard" (Bloom, Lu, and Chen 2003, p. 160). The amount varies by region and by rural or urban residence, and assistance is means-tested (recipients have to provide evidence of need) (Leung 2006).

Medical care for the aged is similarly affected by the urban-rural divide. From the 1950s to the 1980s, most urban workers and retirees enjoyed medical benefits, while rural elders had to rely on families to pay for their medical care. The system of "barefoot doctors" prior to the 1980s provided basic community care to rural families and elders (Davis-Friedmann 1983, Liu et al. 1995). After the 1980s, community clinics of barefoot doctors were dissolved as countywide hospitals became more professional. Medical costs have gone up while affordability and access have gone down (Liu et al. 1995). Families are shouldering the high cost of medical care. In urban China, medical care for the disabled has become more disparate, and access to medical care has become more uneven, according to geographic location, type of employment, and income (Grogan 1995, Henderson et al. 1995). Medical costs for the aged and disabled are high and rapidly rising with age.

Physical care for the aged has largely depended on the family. Not until the late 1990s were there any institutions available for the care of older adults with children (Zhan et al. 2005). Since 1950 childless elders have been provided and cared for in institutions supported by the government (Chen 1996, Sher 1984). For elders with adult children, familial care typically follows a patrilocal pattern, whereby sons and daughters-in-law provide physical care (Lavely and Ren 1992). Recent studies, however, reveal a different pattern in urban China: Daughters are just as involved in the care for aging parents as sons (Zhan and Montgomery 2003). After welfare reforms in the late 1990s, welfare institutions were decentralized, and new, for-profit institutions were opened to care for elders with family members. Recent studies found that there has been rapid growth of elder-care institutions in urban China (Zhan, Liu, and Guan 2006; Zhan, Liu, and Bai 2006). As adult children are becoming fewer in number, institutional care seems to be becoming a more accepted alternative for elder care.

Demographic and health trends are resulting in a larger elderly population. Urbanization and the market economy are unintentionally placing the disabled at greater risk. Longer life expectation, the one-child family policy, and greater geographic mobility are putting great strains on Chinese families' ability to care for the disabled. Jointly, these forces will present an unprecedented challenge to all citizens in China in the coming decades.

BIBLIOGRAPHY

Aspalter, Christian. *Democratization and Welfare State Development in Taiwan.* Burlington, VT: Ashgate, 2002.

Bloom, Gerald, Yuelai Lu, and Jiaying Chen. Financial Health Care in China's Cities. In *Social Policy Reform in China*, ed. Catherine Jones Finer, 155–168. Burlington, VT: Ashgate, 2003.

Brown, Garrett D. The Global Threats to Workers' Health and Safety on the Job. *Social Justice* 29, 3 (2002): 12–26.

Chen, Sheying. *Social Policy of the Economic State and Community Care in Chinese Culture: Aging, Family, Urban Change, and the Socialist Welfare Pluralism.* Brookfield, VT: Avebury, 1996.

Chen, Yunying. Organizational Partnership for Supporting the Disabled in China. Paper presented at the 26th Asia-Pacific International Seminar on Education for Individuals with Special Needs, 2007. http://www.nise.go.jp/kenshuka/josa/kankobutsu/pub_d/d-252/d-252_6.pdf

China State Council. Information Office. The Rights and Interests of the Disabled. In *Progress in China's Human Rights Cause in 2003.* White Paper. http://www.china.org.cn/e-white/20040330/7.htm

Chow, Nelson, and Yuebin Xu. Pension Reform in China. In *Social Policy Reform in China: Views from Home and Abroad*, ed. Catherine Jones Finer. Burlington, VT: Ashgate, 2003.

Dalby, Chris. Private Centers Give Lifeline to Chinese Mentally Disabled. China.org.cn, 2006. http://www.10thnpc.org.cn/english/news/186794.htm

Davis, Deborah S. Financial Security of Urban Retirees. *Journal of Cross-Cultural Gerontology* 8 (1993): 179–195.

Davis-Friedmann, Deborah. *Long Lives: Chinese Elderly and the Communist Revolution.* Cambridge, MA: Cambridge University Press, 1983.

Finer, Catherine Jones, ed. *Social Policy Reform in China.* Burlington, VT: Ashgate, 2003.

Goldstein, Melvyn C., and Yachun Ku. Income and Family Support Among Rural Elderly in Zhejing Province, China. *Journal of Cross-Cultural Gerontology* 8 (1993): 197–223.

Grogan, Colleen M. Urban Economic Reform and Access to Health Care Coverage in the People's Republic of China. *Social Science and Medicine* 41 (1995): 1073–1084.

Gu, Shengzu, and Jersey Liang. China: Population Aging and Old Age Support. In *Aging in East and West: Families, States, and Elderly*, ed. Vern L. Bengtson, D. D. Kim, and K. S. Eun, 59–94. New York: Springer, 2000.

Hallett, Stephen. One Eye on China: Learning Disability in the People's Republic. 2006. http://www.bbc.co.uk/ouch/closeup/china/010606.shtml

Henderson, Gail, Shuigao Jin, John Akin, et al. Distribution of Medical Insurance in China. *Social Science and Medicine* 41 (1995): 1119–1130.

Ikels, Charlotte. Becoming a Human Being in Theory and Practice: Chinese Views of Human Development. In *Social Structure and Aging: Age Structuring in Comparative Perspective*, ed. David I. Kertzer and K. Warner Schaie, 109–134. Hillside, NJ: Lawrence Erlbaum Associates, 1989.

Ikels, Charlotte. Chinese Kinship and the State: Shaping of Policy for the Elderly. *Annual Review of Gerontology and Geriatrics* 13 (1993): 123–146.

Lavely, William, and Xinhua Ren. Patrilocality and Early Marital Co-residence in Rural China, 1955–1985. *China Quarterly* 127 (1992): 594–615.

Leung, Joe C. B. The Emergence of Social Assistance in China. *International Journal of Social Welfare* 15 (2006): 199–198.

Liu, Yuanli, William C. Hsiao, Qing Li, et al. Transformation of China's Rural Health Care Financing. *Social Science and Medicine* 41 (1995): 1085–1093.

Quadagno, Jill. *Aging and the Life Course.* 4th ed. Boston: McGraw-Hill, 2008.

Sher, Ada Elizabeth. *Aging in Post-Mao China: The Politics of Veneration.* Boulder, CO: Westview Press, 1984.

Wong, Joseph. *Healthy Democracies: Welfare Politics in Taiwan and South Korea.* Ithaca, NY: Cornell University Press, 2004.

Xinhua News Agency. China to Train 1 Million Intellectually Disabled Athletes. 2007. http://en.chinagate.com.cn/medicare/2007-10/10/content_9026199.htm

Zhan, Heying Jenny, G. Y. Liu, and H. G. Bai. Recent Development of Chinese Nursing Homes: A Reconciliation of Traditional Culture. *Ageing International* 30, 2 (2005): 167–187.

Zhan, Heying Jenny, G. Y. Liu, and H. G. Bai. Recent Development in Chinese Institutional Elder Care: Changing Concepts and Attitudes. *Journal of Aging and Social Policy* 18, 2 (2006): 85–108.

Zhan, Heying Jenny, G. Y. Liu, and X. Guan. Availability and Willingness: Compare Attitudes toward Institutional Care between Chinese Elderly Parents and Their Adult Children. *Journal of Aging Studies* 20, 3 (2006): 279–290.

Zhan, Heying Jenny, and Rhonda J. V. Montgomery. Gender and Elder Care in China: The Influence of Filial Piety and Structural Constraints. *Gender and Society* 17, 2 (2003): 209–229.

Zhongguo nongmingong weiquan wang (The Chinese Rural Labor-rights Protection Network). 2004. Cong gaige "Gongshang baoxian tiaolo" rushou, tuijin nongmingong gongshang wenti tuoshan jiejue [Properly solving issues concerning work-related injuries of migrant workers by reforming "work-related insurance regulations"]. http://www.zgnmg.org/zhi/dybg/bg005_1.htm

Heying Jenny Zhan
Baozhen Luo

PENSIONS

China has two public pension schemes. One is largely confined to the urban labor force and is a component of social insurance, which also covers health care, unemployment benefits, and disability compensation. The other is a rural scheme, which was still in its trial phase in 2009 in that the government had yet to decide on the final shape of the scheme and its extension to the whole rural population. The rural-urban separation is not particular to the pensions system; it runs through the Chinese social security system.

TWO SCHEMES FOR AN EXPANDING ELDERLY POPULATION

The first, largely urban, scheme (hereafter, the social-insurance pension scheme) has 187.7 million participants, consisting of 141.3 million contributors and 46.4 million pensioners, which makes it the largest pension scheme in the world. However, the contributors to the scheme constitute less than half of China's entire urban labor force. The rural scheme is smaller, with 53.7 million contributors and 3.6 million beneficiaries. The two schemes' 50 million or so pension recipients constitute only a minority of the elderly population: 29.6 percent of people over sixty, or 42 percent of people over sixty-five. A vast majority of elderly in China depend on family, usually male descendants, for financial support. There are questions concerning the sustainability both of the pension schemes and of dependence on family members.

The ratio of elderly in the population has been rising and will likely continue to rise during much of the twenty-first century. Defining the elderly population as those aged sixty-five and above, the percentage more than doubled from 4.9 percent in 1982 to 9.1 percent in 2006. This trend is caused by the lowering of fertility rates due to birth control and by rising life expectancy at retirement. The lowering of fertility rates reduces the percentage of children

initially, and later of working-age adults. Rising life expectancy directly increases the percentage of elderly in the population. Under current arrangements, most of the extra cost of supporting the elderly population will fall on families, which may not be able to sustain such support. With rising life expectancy at retirement, each succeeding cohort of the elderly would need to be supported for a longer period than did the preceding. Moreover, because of the use of birth control, the future cohorts of elderly will have fewer offspring to depend on than the present cohort does. A hypothetical example is a family of two earners and five dependents, consisting of a working couple (both single children themselves), their single child, and their four elderly parents.

The social-insurance pension scheme was introduced in 1998 to replace a scheme that dated back to 1955. The pension is made up of two parts (referred to as *pillars*): a flat-rate basic pension financed from the social pool and a variable pension paid out of the accumulated contributions in individual accounts. The first pillar, set at 25 percent of the average wage in the locality, aims to provide basic subsistence, and is paid in full to everyone with a contribution record of at least fifteen years. The variable pillar links pension to income in employment and consists of a ten-year annuity paying out 1/120th of the accumulated sum per month in the individual account. Upon the exhaustion of the individual account, the variable component continues to be paid out of the social pool, which is replenished by employer contributions and the residual government contribution. There is also a third pillar, which is voluntary and is left to the commercial sector and intended as a supplement to the second pillar. It was not yet fully operational in 2009.

CONTRIBUTIONS AND PAYOUTS

The pension scheme is jointly financed by employee and employer contributions. Since 2006, these have been set at 8 percent and a maximum of 22 percent of the wage bill respectively. The total contribution rate is high by international standards. The employee contributions are, in principle, deposited into respective individual accounts, but not in practice. Of the employer contribution, 19 percent goes into the social pool that pays out current pensions, and the remaining 3 percent is paid into the National Social Security Fund, which is intended to cover future pension payments. The financial integrity of the system is maintained by the government's commitment to cover any excess of the current pension payments over available funds. The government contribution to the pension scheme has been substantial.

Since 1998, when the current system began operating, pensions paid out to retirees were to be at least in part determined by their entitlements under the superseded (pre-1998) system, which left behind no funds to honor these entitlements. By default, these entitlements became liabilities of the current system and are too large to finance from the social pool replenished by employer contributions. This has led to a diversion of funds in individual accounts to pay current pensions, and the need for subsidies from the government budget. The diversion of funds has forced a suspension of the second pillar and raises the question of the status of individual accounts and how these are going to be honored when the account holders retire. The current system has yet to be fully implemented and will remain unimplemented until a mechanism to finance the future liabilities of the pre-1998 system is found and the status of individual accounts is settled.

A significant step toward expanding the sources for financing pensions was the establishment in 2000 of the National Social Security Fund, which receives a part of employer contributions (3 percent since 2006), occasional contributions from the government, and an allocation of shares in state-owned enterprises when floated on the stock market. The fund is controlled by the Central Ministry of Finance and is allowed to invest part of its funds in equities, including foreign equities.

Although social insurance is based on regulations issued by the State Council and the Ministries of Labor, Personnel, and Social Security, many of the details of the schemes are left to the discretion of the provincial or municipal governments. More consequential, the budgetary units for social insurance are 269 cities (excluding county-level cities and towns), and generally cities are expected to cover from their own budget any social-insurance deficit in their jurisdiction.

This highly decentralized budgeting creates a wide variation in the financial positions of city-level schemes and thereby weakens the financial foundation of China's social-insurance system.

For example, in the case of pensions, the current financial position depends on the balance between the inflow of contributions and outflow of pensions. Generally, this balance varies across cities. As a result, decentralized budgeting creates a situation in which some cities run a deficit and others a surplus, even though taken together the budget is in balance.

There are ad hoc transfers from the central and provincial governments to cities with strained finances to ensure that they meet their pension obligations. But there is as yet no regular framework for fiscal transfers from higher to lower government tiers to cover expenditure responsibilities. An overhaul of the system of intergovernmental finances has been high on the reform agenda for years, but remains unrealized. A pooling of pension contributions and expenditures at the provincial level is the policy aim.

RETIREMENT AGE

The mandatory retirement age is low and varies with occupation and gender, as follows:

Men (except heavy duty manual workers): 60

Women in professional work: 55

Heavy duty male workers: 55

Women, manual workers: 50

Many retire earlier than the already-low mandatory retirement age. Early retirement has been a frequent remedy for dealing with unemployment among older workers. The principal barrier to raising the retirement age is the fear of worsening an already serious unemployment problem. However, there are strong arguments in favor of announcing a stepwise rise in the retirement age when the number of working-age adults starts declining around 2020.

PORTABILITY

China's pension entitlements are not fully portable. The principal barrier is the fragmented financing and management of the scheme, which goes together with lack of easy transferability of data on subscription and a mechanism for financial settlement across jurisdictions.

SEE ALSO *Family: Roles of the Elderly; Leisure and Culture for the Elderly; Life Cycle: Old Age.*

BIBLIOGRAPHY

Feldstein, Martin, and Jeffrey Liebman. Realizing the Potential of China's Social Security Pension System. In *Public Finance in China: Reform and Growth for a Harmonious Society*, eds. Lou Jiwei and Wang Shuilin, 309–313. Washington, DC: World Bank, 2008.

Mukul Asher, Nicholas Barr, Peter Diamond, et al. Social Security Reform in China: Issues and Options. China Economic Research and Advisory Program, October 2004.

National Bureau of Statistics of China. *China Labor Statistical Yearbook, 2007.* Beijing: China Statistics Press, 2007.

State Council of the PRC. China's Social Security and Its Policy (2004). *People's Daily Online*, September 7, 2004.

Athar Hussain

SOCIAL WELFARE SINCE 1978

Before 1978, China's record in raising the well-being of its population was generally creditable and in some respects outstanding. A major blemish is the great famine of 1959 to 1961, which claimed tens of millions of lives and was due in part to mistaken policies. Aside from this catastrophe, China managed to protect its population from destitution and starvation. Notably, it achieved a substantial reduction in the incidence of parasitic and infectious diseases and built a network of primary health care that covered almost all of its rural population.

In the pre-1978 period, a policy of ensuring basic income was woven into the fabric of economic organization, a feature that would turn out to be incompatible with a market economy. Those able to work were, if urban residents, sooner or later provided with a job, or, if rural residents, assigned a remunerative task by the collective unit of which they were a part. Once employed, a worker could confidently expect to remain employed until retirement. The payment of an allowance in cash and kind was confined to a very small group unable to work. The employees of the state sector and larger collective enterprises, constituting most of the urban labor force, received a range of benefits in kind (work-unit welfare) and were covered by *labor insurance*, the precursor of what from the second half 1990s would be termed *social insurance*. On the eve of the reform period, the labor-insurance system was not fully functional. In particular, there was a massive backlog of employees past retirement age who had yet to retire.

Since the launch of reforms in 1978, four developments in the social-welfare field stand out. The first is the dramatic fall in rural poverty in tandem with the decollectivization of the rural economy. Over thirty years, the percentage of the poor in the rural population fell from 30.7 percent in 1978 to 1.6 percent in 2007. The downward trend in poverty has proceeded in tandem with rising inequality within and between rural and urban areas. As measured by the ratio of average household per-capita incomes, the income gap between urban and rural areas, which narrowed substantially between 1978 and 1984, has since been widening, and by 2000 exceeded the level in 1978. Added to this, interpersonal income inequality in both rural and urban areas has also risen, particularly sharply since the early 1990s.

The second development is the loosening and then the abolition from 2000 to 2007 of all formal restrictions on rural-to-urban migration. Large-scale migration began in the late 1980s, and a sizeable population of migrants has since been a regular feature of Chinese cities, especially large cities. Regardless of their length of stay in destination, migrants are treated as residents of a locality other than where they have actually been living and working. Only a small percentage of them are covered by social insurance, and none is entitled to means-tested social assistance. Numbering between 130 to 200 million, China's migrant population represents a huge blind spot in the social security cover.

The third development is the combination of the steady erosion of the inherited social security regime, a massive retrenchment of labor from the state sector, and the appearance of urban poverty as a major social issue. The fourth is the setting-up of a new social security regime, first, in urban areas and, with a lag, in rural areas, a process that is still under way.

Reform of the social security regime, particularly of the schemes covering the urban population, has been a running strand of the transition since 1978. Until the middle of the 1990s, these reforms consisted mostly of piecemeal measures to prop up the inherited schemes, particularly the old-age pension scheme. The reforms since 1995 have been aimed at instituting a new system in urban areas to replace the existing one. Among these reforms, the salient ones can be grouped under five headings: (1) extending social security schemes, previously confined to state and urban collective-sector employees, to the whole of the labor force; (2) divesting enterprises of their social-welfare responsibilities and transferring the administration of the five social insurance (previously labor insurance) schemes in the Ministry of Labor (renamed the Ministry of Labor and Social Security) and its territorial subsidiaries, provincial and city Labor and Social Security bureaus; (3) replacing the financing of social insurance by employers alone with joint financing by employers, employees, and the government, along with proposing to raise the budgetary unit for social insurance from the city to the provincial level; (4) reappraising and formalizing entitlements under social-insurance schemes (the introduction of employee contributions has been accompanied by the introduction of individual accounts for old-age pensions and medical-care insurance); and (5) introducing Minimum Living Standard Assistance (MLSA), a comprehensive social-assistance scheme for urban households falling below the poverty line.

A by-product of the withdrawal of the employment guarantee has been the appearance of urban unemployment, which since the second half of the 1990s has been both open and substantial. This has gone together with the emergence of poverty as a salient feature of the urban landscape, which previously was regarded as an almost exclusively rural phenomenon. The combination of urban unemployment and poverty brought to the fore the issue of income maintenance for the urban population. This prompted the government in 1998 to extend unemployment insurance to the whole urban labor force and to introduce MLSA, providing a means-tested cash allowance to urban households falling below the poverty line.

Previously regarded as a task for the distant future, the reform of the rural social security system has risen higher on the government's agenda. The period since 2000 has seen a series of initiatives to extend the percentage of the rural population covered by social security schemes and to fill gaps in the social security cover. These include iterative modifications of the rural cooperative medical-insurance scheme and assistance with medical costs and the introduction of means-tested MLSA for the rural population.

OVERVIEW OF CHINA'S SOCIAL SECURITY SYSTEM

A social security system with its own administration, with regular sources of finance, and separated from the organization of economic activity is largely a development from the second half of the 1990s, one that is still under way. The current system consists of an assortment of schemes aimed at the following: poverty alleviation; income maintenance in the event of unemployment, occupational injury, sickness, and retirement; and subsidized or free medical care as and when needed.

These schemes divide into the familiar categories of "social insurance" and "social assistance" (social safety net). Whereas social insurance is principally financed by contributions, and where the benefits it provides depend on the individual contribution record, social assistance is financed from government revenue and benefits are means-tested.

In China, the contributory and noncontributory schemes, taken together, are characterized by two salient features: (1) segmentation and striking differences in provision across groups; and (2) highly decentralized financing and management. All social security schemes are earmarked either for the urban or the rural population; as yet, there is none that covers the whole population. From the point of view of social security, the population is divided along two lines: (1) rural and urban; and (2) in an urban setting, permanent residents and immigrants.

The difference in the social security provision for the urban and for the rural population is glaring. In principle, urban residents (excluding migrants) benefit from a complementary combination of a comprehensive social insurance and MLSA, which bridges any shortfall of household per-capita income up to the local poverty line. In contrast, social security provision in rural areas is sparse. Apart from two limited contributory schemes, all rural schemes fall under the category of "social assistance," aimed at relieving severe poverty only. Social insurance does not apply to the rural labor force, not even to wage-employees of town and village enterprises, who number 147 million.

There are two professed rationales for the limited social-protection cover in China's rural areas. One is that each rural household is assigned a plot of agricultural land that serves as a floor to household income. The other is the high cost of introducing a social security regime comparable to the one in urban areas relative to the limited capacity to collect taxes and social security contributions in rural areas. Both need to be qualified. The protection provided by land plots is highly variable and has diminished over time because of the combination of the increase in the rural population and the diversion of land to nonfarm uses. Besides, since the 1994 tax reform, public finances have improved dramatically and the budgetary constraint has loosened considerably.

Both rural and urban social security systems are highly decentralized. In the case of the urban schemes, for both social insurance and MLSA, the budgetary units are 269 cities (excluding county-level cities and towns); generally cities are expected to cover from their own budgets any

deficit on social insurance and the cost of MLSA in their respective jurisdictions. The balance between contributions and expenditures varies across cities, depending on the unemployment rate and the number of pensioners relative to contributors. Apart from a few large cities, most cities constitute too small a budgetary unit to provide sufficient risk-pooling to ensure the sustainability of social insurance.

Decentralization in rural areas runs deeper than in urban areas. Apart from a few schemes run by national and provincial governments, most social security schemes are organized at the grassroots level of villages. Such schemes include assistance to poor households and the rural pensions and cooperative medical-insurance schemes.

A pooling of social insurance contributions and expenditures at the provincial level is the policy aim. In most cases, this would be sufficient to put the urban social security system on a sound financial footing, because many of the Chinese provinces are as populous as sizeable countries. But the aim has not progressed beyond trial schemes and partial pooling.

TRENDS

The most notable trend is the progressive erosion in the distinction between urban and rural, which has cast a long shadow on the Chinese social security system and on a wide range of other institutions and social phenomena. The driving forces behind the trend are two developments since the late 1990s. One is the emergence of a large population of immigrants, who find themselves in "no man's land," excluded from social security at their destination and also at their place of origin by virtue of their absence.

The second development eroding the distinction between rural and urban inhabitants is the appearance of a sizeable population of landless rural households, which is an anomaly in the context of the Chinese social security system. Classified as "agricultural," they are excluded from the social security cover for "urban" households on the grounds of having a plot of land, which they no longer possess. Until the late 1990s, there were few such households, and most of them had given up their land voluntarily. Since the late 1990s, however, the number of landless rural households has grown rapidly, due mostly to the requisition of land for "development zones" in return for a derisory level of compensation. Regarding such households as a potential source of social instability, the government has extended MLSA for "non-agricultural" households to rural households with no land or insufficient land. This constitutes a major breach of the separation of social security schemes for the rural and urban populations. Extrapolated over time, such extensions of the urban schemes will not mean an end of the distinction between "rural and urban" per se, but rather a progressive shrinkage of the category "rural."

SEE ALSO *Social Classes since 1978; Social Policy Programs; Urban Employment and Unemployment since 1949.*

BIBLIOGRAPHY

Hussain, Athar. Social Welfare in China in the Context of Three Transitions. In *How Far across the River: Chinese Policy Reform at the Millennium*, eds. Nicholas Hope, Dennis Tao Yang, and Yang Li Mu, 273–312. Stanford, CA: Stanford University Press, 2003.

State Council of the PRC. China's Social Security and Its Policy (2004). *People's Daily Online*, September 7, 2004.

Athar Hussain

SOCIALISM

In mainland China, "socialism" (*shehui zhuyi*) has come to connote Marxism or Communism, and the role of socialism in social democracies is mostly overlooked in general discussion. The ascendancy of Marxism and Communism over various other types of socialism took place in China as early as the 1920s and 1930s. Although China had its own traditions of utopian and egalitarian philosophies, often with a Daoist coloring, which fueled peasant wars and uprisings throughout Chinese history, these were largely discredited in the closing years of the Qing dynasty (1644–1912) by the carnage brought about by the Taiping Heavenly Kingdom and the utter failure of its original egalitarian and "pseudo-Christian" ideals. Although the Communist insurgency from the late 1920s onward would link up in the twentieth century with many of the secret societies that drew on this utopian tradition of the knight-errant and brotherhoods of equals, these were usually temporary strategic relationships based on contingency.

THE INTRODUCTION OF WESTERN SOCIALISM TO CHINA

Knowledge of socialism in its nineteenth-century European sense was introduced into China from Japan in the closing decade of the Qing dynasty, largely through the medium of students living there, and indeed the Chinese word for *socialism* was originally a Japanese neologism. The context of Western socialism was little understood when it was introduced as a doctrine to Chinese readers, and it was perhaps not as significant intellectually as anarchism, with which it was often linked, in the period prior to the May Fourth movement of 1919.

Although Kang Youwei's philosophy of *datong* (great unity) drew heavily on traditional Chinese utopian philosophy, latent in a "Confucian" *Liyun* cosmogony of three ages (*sanshi*) of human social development, it was his prominent student Liang Qichao who first acquainted Chinese readers with socialist ideas in a series of essays

published in Japan in his journal *Qingyi bao*, beginning with an article titled "Lun qiangquan" (On power) that appeared in 1899. By 1901 the term *shehui zhuyi* (Japanese: *shakaishugi*) was used by Liang in some of his essays. In a 1904 article titled "Zhongguo zhi shehui zhuyi" (Chinese socialism), Liang wrote that socialism was essentially the public ownership of land and capital and concluded that the ancient Chinese ideal of the "well-field" (*jing tian*) system was based on the same principle as modern socialism.

Before 1905 there were at least four Chinese-language journals that frequently included articles on socialism: Liang Qichao's *Xinmin congbao* (New people's miscellany), as well as *Shiwu bao* (Current affairs) and *Yishu huibian* (Collected translations), all published in Japan and circulated in China, and *Xin shijie xuebao* (New world), published in Shanghai. The Chinese study of socialist ideas was inspired in the main by Japanese, not Russian, writers. The latter were more influential in the development of Chinese modern anarchistic thought.

Although the "reformist" Liang Qichao was the most important "public intellectual" in the first decade of the twentieth century, it would fall to Sun Yat-sen (Sun Yixian) to lead the Chinese revolution and head, for a short time, the state ushered in by the events collectively referred to as the 1911 revolution. The revolution was suppressed in 1913 by Yuan Shikai. There was no clear-cut division between reformers and revolutionaries in the final decade of the Qing dynasty. Sun Yat-sen's ideas on socialism and land nationalization developed during his stay in Japan from 1897 to 1900, and through his companion Miyazaki Torazō (1870–1922) he was introduced to the socialist ideas of the American political economist Henry George (1839–1897), whose speeches had been translated into Japanese as early as 1887.

DEVELOPMENT OF SOCIALIST IDEAS IN A CHINESE CONTEXT

In the late-Qing debates that circled around issues of socialism, the term *minsheng zhuyi* (literally, "people's life-ism") existed side by side with the term *shehui zhuyi*, and Sun Yat-sen and the Chinese revolutionaries were able to resolve the Western ambiguity between state socialism and the beliefs of the socialist parties. The foundation of the Revolutionary Alliance (Tongmenghui) and the establishment of *Min bao* (The people's journal) by Chinese in Japan in 1905 provided reformers and revolutionaries with an organizational and ideological focus, and marked a new stage in the development of socialist ideas in a Chinese intellectual context.

Hu Hanmin (1879–1936) was one of the leading Chinese advocates of socialism. He conducted a debate through the journals with Liang Qichao, in which socialism featured as a major topic. Hu's ideas were significant because he later served as an adviser to Sun Yat-sen, and many of Hu's ideas were incorporated into the program of the Revolutionary Alliance that Sun headed in the years before the 1911 revolution. Speaking for the Revolutionary Alliance, Hu Hanmin wrote in *Min bao* in March 1907 that "our socialism" (*minsheng zhuyi*) was different from foreign socialism (*shehui zhuyi*), for the first time making official the break between Western-style "socialism" and his party's Chinese *minsheng zhuyi*.

After 1907, the social democracy and state socialism projected in the earlier period became irrelevant. However, after the fall of Western socialism in China, the movement was not obliterated without trace. Sun Yat-sen continued to proclaim his land policies. Although interest in social democracy was dead at the center, its ideas continued to spread among the middlebrow and the young. Elements persisted in the later anarchism and in the vague ideas promoted by Jiang Kanghu (1883–1954) in the years following the 1911 revolution. Jiang established a Socialist Research Society (Shehui Zhuyi Yanjiu Hui) in May 1911 and later in the year reorganized it as the China Social Party (Zhongguo Shehui Dang), the first political organization in China to be a called a *dang* (party). The Chinese Socialist Party, which endorsed a diluted mixture of socialism and anarchism, had more than two hundred branches and perhaps as many as 400,000 members. Jiang Kanghu was active in education, and this also facilitated the exposure of Chinese intellectuals to non-Marxist socialist ideas. In 1922 Jiang founded Shanghai Southern University (Shanghai Nanfang Daxue), and in 1934 he traveled to Taiwan as nominal head of the Canada China Academy (Kannatai Zhongguo Xueyuan) and as a consultant to the U.S. Library of Congress, where he lent support to nationalist causes. His China Social Party remained active in politics until it was eventually subsumed within Wang Jingwei's left-wing Japanese puppet government in 1937. At the end of World War II (1937–1945), Jiang was tried as a traitor and given a life sentence; he died in prison in Nanjing in 1954.

SOCIALISM UNDER THE CHINESE COMMUNIST PARTY

By and large, from the Northern Expedition (1926) onward, the Chinese Communist Party (CCP) and the Guomindang (GMD) were both Leninist-style political organizations, although the GMD under Chiang Kai-shek (Jiang Jieshi) paid only lip service to some socialist ideals. After 1949, eight "democratic" political parties continue to maintain a nominal existence in the People's Republic of China under the aegis of the CCP's New Democratic policy, and all of these preserve some elements of the socialist programs of the former GMD within their political "agendas." Together with the CCP, the democratic parties maintain the rump form of a multiparty socialist

state. However, the CCP acknowledges alternate forms of socialism, as exemplified by its celebration of the one-hundredth birthday of George Bernard Shaw in 1956, when Shaw's Fabian socialism was cited as evidence of "the superiority of socialism over capitalism," although meaning in this context Chinese Communism.

Since the beginning of the opening and reform in 1978, political reform has remained on the agenda to a lesser and greater extent, and to this end the CCP Party School keeps abreast of developments within socialism in a worldwide context, being addressed by representatives from European and other social democracies.

SEE ALSO *Communist Thought in China, Origins of; Democratic Parties: Overview.*

BIBLIOGRAPHY

Bauer, Wolfgang. *China and the Search for Happiness: Recurring Themes in Four Thousand Years of Chinese Cultural History.* Trans. Michael Shaw. New York: Seabury Press, 1976

Bernal, Martin. *Chinese Socialism to 1907.* Ithaca, NY: Cornell University Press, 1976.

Li Youning (Li Yu-ning). *The Introduction of Socialism into China.* New York: Columbia University Press, 1971.

Bruce G. Doar

SOCIALIST MARKET ECONOMY

The term *socialist market economy* is the official designation of the current Chinese economic system in the documents of the Chinese Communist Party and the Chinese government. It was adopted at the fourteenth congress of the Communist Party in 1992 and further specified in a Central Committee decision of 1993, followed ten years later by another resolution that continued in the same spirit but further elaborated on details. In 1993 the term was also adopted in an amendment to the constitution. The 1992 decision was a comprehensive treatment of all important aspects of the economic system of China, presaging most institutional changes adopted thereafter. The notion of the market was broad in scope, including all goods and factor markets and external economic relations.

There is a long tradition in Chinese socialism of attempts to synthesize the market mechanism with socialist ideology and socialist ideas about political organization. In many earlier approaches, this resulted from the recognition that China was in a state of underdevelopment that would not allow the transition to communism because it lacked an industrial basis and hence also a strong working class. In political practice, these socialist ideas were expressed in the theory of New Democracy, which was crafted by Mao Zedong as a transitional concept for the early stage of socialism in China and was briefly guiding policies in the first years of the People's Republic. These ideas have to be seen against the historical background of competing ideologies, especially Sun Yat-senism, as all these ideas converged on the notion of state-led industrialization. Almost all Chinese reformers in the twentieth century agreed on some core principles of economic and social policies of modernization that assigned a pivotal role to the government, including national planning of pillar industries and external economic relations.

In the late 1950s, the increasing ideological confrontation between the Soviet Union and China was also related to questions of economic policies. In China, a split emerged between Maoist approaches to development and conceptions inspired by an adapted Soviet system of planning, including use of incentives and indirect levers to steer the economy and allowance of some flexibility for market allocation, especially in agriculture. Radical Maoism eschewed both policy tools as triggers of a capitalist restoration and relied almost exclusively on campaigns and moral pressure to solve incentive problems in the economy. Until the demise of the Gang of Four, this ideological outlook prevailed over attempts to combine planning and local markets after the disaster of the Great Leap Forward, attempts supported precisely by those leaders that assumed a critical role in the post-Mao transition, such as Deng Xiaoping and Chen Yun.

Conceptually, *socialist market economy* was the endpoint of a stepwise evolution of terms designating the target of economic reforms after 1978, an evolution that included such terms as *planned commodity economy*. The 1992 decision prepared the ground for a systematic shift toward economic policies that not only completed the transition to market allocation in the economy, but also allowed for significant changes in the system of property rights, especially the gradual dismantling of collective ownership in rural industries and the launch of the corporatization of the state-owned sector. Since 2004 private ownership had enjoyed the protection of the constitution. Yet in the context of the promulgation of the new Property Law in 2007, there was also strong opposition by some leading intellectuals, who denounced its capitalist nature.

The socialist market economy is sometimes deliberately conflated with the social market economies of Western and Northern Europe, yet there are important differences. The original practice of the socialist market economy did not emphasize welfarism, and in fact led to an almost complete destruction of rudimentary welfare systems in the countryside, as well as of the cradle-to-grave

danwei (work unit) system in the cities. Welfarism emerged as a political issue in the context of the propagation of the "harmonious society" under the current leadership of Hu Jintao, reflecting increasing concerns about the rapidly increasing inequality in Chinese society. Welfarism also emerges as a response to the dramatic demographic changes induced by the one-child policy, in particular with regard to the need to build pension systems and to set up comprehensive health insurance.

The main ingredients of the socialist market economy, abstracted from actual political practice, are as follows:

- Maintaining a significant and controlling stake of the central government in pillar industries, while at the same time implementing competition between the corporatized units

- Transitioning to a regulatory state, in the sense of implementing a stronger role for the government in standardizing and enforcing institutions, and reducing the extent of intervention in the economy by governmental directives

- Building advanced systems of industrial-policy design on the different levels of government

- Rejecting the proposition that Western-style democracy is a necessary complement of the market economy

- Viewing the state as the avant-garde of social change and modernization, with broad scope, including authority over demography and population quality, technological and scientific advance, and civilizational endeavors such as religion

From the viewpoint of many advanced industrial countries, *socialist market economy* is an oxymoron, because the term *socialist* implies excessive government intervention. The political consequence is that, for example, the European Union still does not recognize China as a market economy and raises many objections to Chinese economic practices in the context of the World Trade Organization. As a result of the stability of the Chinese political system and the tremendous economic growth and development of China, China emerges as a new systems challenge to established notions of the globalization of liberal values rooted in the European and American intellectual tradition. At the same time, Marxists of the early twenty-first century reject the Chinese development as a betrayal of the idea of communism.

BIBLIOGRAPHY

Clarke, Donald C. Legislating for a Market Economy in China. *China Quarterly* 191 (2007): 567–589.

Greenhalgh, Susan, and Edwin A. Winckler. The Hu Era: From Comprehensive Reform to Social Policy. In *Governing China's*

Population: From Leninist to Neoliberal Biopolitics. Stanford, CA: Stanford University Press, 2005.

Naughton, Barry. Market Transition: Strategy and Process. In *The Chinese Economy. Transitions and Growth.* Cambridge, MA: MIT Press, 2007.

Carsten Herrmann-Pillath

SOCIALIST REALISM IN ART

Socialist realism is an ideologically driven theory, originating in the Soviet Union and adopted by the Chinese leadership in the 1950s, that sought to delineate the norms governing artistic creativity and thereby ensure the ideological purity of all creative production. Its key aims, thoroughly didactic in nature, were to reflect the struggles of the working classes in forging a new socialist society, to inculcate in the masses a high level of social awareness, and to instill in the masses a sense of purpose and optimism as they sought to attain the goal of Communism. It also served as a vehicle to bring to public attention shifts in official policy and, less explicitly, as a means to reform intellectuals' thinking, by enforcing the disciplined practice of socialist-realist methods. Debates on socialist realism in both the Soviet Union and China highlighted issues such as the class nature and social function of art, the social obligations of artists, and the correct relationship between art and politics. Socialist-realist art was seen as an antidote to the idea of art for art's sake, as an attempt to move away from the elitist nature of art, and as a way to make "high art" more accessible to the broad mass of people.

SOVIET ORIGINS

The term *socialist realism* was credited to Soviet leader Joseph Stalin in 1932, and was formally adopted by the first Congress of Soviet Writers two years later. It subsequently became the orthodoxy for all cultural realms in the Soviet Union, thus uniting poets and painters, writers and dramatists, within one theoretical framework. Several core concepts, such as the need for art to serve the people and genuinely reflect the lives of the working classes, are evident in the work of nineteenth-century Russian theorists such as Vissarion Belinsky, Nikolai Chernyshevsky, and Nikolai Dobrolyubov, and prominent early Russian Marxists, such as Georgi Plekhanov and Vladimir Lenin. In art, the antecedents of Soviet socialist realism can be traced back to Ilya Repin, Vasily Surikov, and other social realists in the late nineteenth and early twentieth centuries. Known as the Wanderers or Itinerants (*Peredvizhniki*), these artists were strongly influenced by the formal realism of the European academies, though their work usually also displayed a critical edge, reflecting their sense of social responsibility. Themes of human poverty and hardship were common, but many works also revealed the beauty, strength, and fortitude of peasants and workers. Socialist realism incorporated many of the formal aspects of Itinerant paintings, but its content was based squarely on the Marxist premise that art should "evaluate life from the heights of Communist ideals."

DEVELOPMENT IN CHINA

From the late 1920s on, Chinese Marxist theoreticians, most notably Qu Qiubai, and a number of left-wing writers and artists, explored the issue of the class nature of art, concluding that art should be utilized as an important component of class struggle, and artists should be redirected to reflect in their work the lives of the laboring classes. Mao's Yan'an talks in 1942 crystallized these earlier ideological strands, entrenching them in party policy. It was, however, in 1951 that the first major official pronouncement was made in China on the theory of socialist realism, when cultural czar Zhou Yang called Soviet socialist-realist literature and art "beneficial spiritual food" for the Chinese people, and advocated that in cultural matters China should learn from other countries, especially the Soviet Union. In elucidating the theoretical foundations of socialist realism, Zhou and other Chinese cultural theorists highlighted the theory of reflection (*fanying lun*), on which the Marxist view of art is based. It consists of two strands. The first is the material-realist approach adopted by the eighteenth-century French encyclopedia school and based on the empirical tradition in Western philosophy, which in art is associated with such scientific techniques as perspective and shading for producing an objective likeness of the external material world. The second is objective idealism, based on Plato's universal forms or Hegel's abstract categories or absolute ideas. This approach is similar to the materialist approach in that it aims to project a mirror image of the world, but of the ideal world, not of the material world. Socialist realism synthesizes these two strands. Images in socialist-realist art—whether of peasants tilling fields, workers tending furnaces, or party leaders strategizing on the next stage of the revolution—are clearly derived from the material world and based on objective reality, while the idealized element is seen in such features as dramatic gestures and facial expressions, inordinately large muscles in male (and sometimes female) figures, and the use of bright colors, especially red. The precepts of socialist realism could be most comfortably accommodated in figurative oil painting, monumental sculpture, and propaganda posters, all of which, to the Chinese, were foreign, mainly Soviet, imports.

While the adoption of socialist realism in the Soviet Union was, in many ways, the simple act of giving official sanction to a movement in art already well established for half a century, Chinese artists, most of whom were steeped in the ink-painting tradition, found it a greater challenge to incorporate the new approach in their work (Chinese ink painters generally achieved only limited success in this respect.) In addition, China, unlike the Soviet Union, did not have a strong tradition of social critique in art, though a small group of avant-garde artists who formed an art group known as the Juelan She (Storm society) for a brief period in the 1930s did occasionally imbue some of their work with sympathetic renderings of the poor and downtrodden. The introduction of socialist realism into China in the early 1950s was facilitated to some extent by prominent artists like Xu Beihong, head of the Central Academy of Fine Art (Zhongyang Meishu Xueyuan), who studied classical realism in Western art academies in the 1920s. But particularly significant in disseminating the concept of socialist realism was the two-way exchange in the 1950s of artists and art theorists from China and from the Soviet Union and Eastern Europe. Prominent figures like Alexander Gerasimov, president of the Soviet Academy of Arts, gave lectures in China, while Chinese art establishment officials Jiang Feng, Cai Ruohong, Luo Gongliu, and others visited their counterparts in the Soviet Union and Eastern Europe, and received instruction from them. Between 1955 and 1957 the Soviet oil painter Konstantin Maximov held training classes in Beijing and promoted the ideas of the nineteenth-century Russian art theorist Pavel Chistiakov, who stressed the need for artists to depict objects as our eyes see them, using the scientific method of fine drawing. In addition, exhibitions of work from the Soviet bloc were overwhelmingly in the socialist-realist mode, and many official Soviet tracts on socialist realism were translated into Chinese for dissemination among the Chinese art community.

Despite this substantial input from the Soviets, however, the limitations placed on artistic content as prescribed by socialist realism, coupled with highly circumscribed modes of expression that had to accord with fixed "scientific" criteria, often led to repetition and stultification, particularly in oil painting.

During the Great Leap Forward (1958–1960), the idea of socialist realism in China was taken a step further with Mao's exhortation that art should comprise a combination of revolutionary (in essence, socialist) realism and revolutionary romanticism. The concept of revolutionary romanticism did not originate with Mao; Andrei Zhdanov, Soviet Politburo member and hard-line ideological leader in the 1930s, mentioned it in political speeches, and it could be found, in embryonic form, in the work of nineteenth-century Russian theorists like Dimitri Pisarev. The difference between socialist realism and revolutionary romanticism is mainly one of degree—the latter involves an inordinate emphasis on the romantic dimension, often to the point of excessive exaggeration. Revolutionary romanticism is philosophically more deeply rooted in objective idealism than in materialism, and

was particularly well suited to conveying the grandiose vision of the Great Leap.

Mao's call for a combination of socialist realism and revolutionary romanticism in art, incorporating strong elements from China's folk art tradition, essentially resulted in a more pronounced melding of Soviet-inspired cultural theories with "Chinese characteristics," thus enabling socialist realism to endure in China beyond the Sino-Soviet schism of the late 1950s, until the end of the Cultural Revolution period.

SEE ALSO *Oil Painting (youhua); Propaganda Art; Sculpture and Public Art.*

BIBLIOGRAPHY

Andrews, Julia F. *Painters and Politics in the People's Republic of China, 1949–1979.* Berkeley: University of California Press, 1994.

Galikowski, Maria. *Art and Politics in China, 1949–1984.* Hong Kong: Chinese University Press, 1998.

James, C. Vaughn. *Soviet Socialist Realism: Origins and Theory.* London: Macmillan Press, 1973.

Valkenier, Elizabeth. *Ilya Repin and the World of Russian Art.* New York: Columbia University Press, 1990.

Maria Galikowski

SOCIALIZATION AND PEDAGOGY

In pre-twentieth-century China, most village and community schools—known generically as *sishu*—had no fixed schedules or curriculum. Students of all ages tended to be seated together rather than being divided into distinct classes or allocated differentiated space. Students memorized the key texts of the classical Confucian canon (at their own individual pace), as well as reading morality books (*shanshu*) that emphasized the importance of virtues such as filial piety. Although these schools catered principally to boys, this did not mean that female education was regarded as unimportant in traditional China. Since the inner sphere (*nei*) of the household associated with the female gender was perceived as the ethical and behavioral training ground for the outer world (*wai*) of public and official life associated with the male gender, it was considered essential that women receive the appropriate moral instruction. Daughters—at least of the upper classes—were taught the Confucian classics and histories within the household, mainly by fathers or private tutors, from the age of four or five alongside their brothers. It was only from the age of eight that boys were removed from the "inner quarters" to participate in more formal schooling at a *sishu*. Instruction for girls, meanwhile, after the age of ten, tended to become more narrowly focused on the teaching of specific "womanly skills" (*nügong*), such as needlework or weaving.

EDUCATIONAL REFORM IN THE TWENTIETH CENTURY

With the growing enfeeblement of the ruling dynasty in the wake of internal and external challenges at the end of the nineteenth century, however, a number of officials and scholars began in the 1890s to argue that a more structured school system (utilizing a wider curriculum) aimed at a wider constituency was necessary to guarantee national survival. After the disaster of the Boxer Uprising in 1900, the Qing government itself sanctioned a reform program that included the abolition of the traditional civil service examination system in 1905 and its replacement by a national three-tiered school system that incorporated both Chinese and Western learning. In the view of the Qing government, the new school system would cultivate loyal and disciplined subjects and hence shore up the foundations of dynastic rule. For the reformist scholar-gentry elite, the modern schools would also train a hardworking, frugal, and skilled citizenry shorn of its "superstitious" beliefs and practices and dedicated to the enhancement of national prosperity in an increasingly competitive world.

Such expectations underpinned the educational aims promulgated by the newly created Board of Education (Xuebu) in 1906. Insisting that education henceforth had to focus on training the majority of the populace rather than cultivating a talented few, the Board of Education noted that it had to inculcate in the minds of pupils the five principles of loyalty to the dynasty, reverence for Confucius, concern for the public welfare, respect for a martial outlook, and the prioritizing of practical study.

Although initially the Qing government had been reluctant to sanction *public* schooling for girls, it sanctioned the creation of separate primary and teacher-training schools for girls in 1907. In providing a certain amount of modern knowledge while also instilling the "feminine virtues" of chastity, obedience, modesty, and self-sacrifice, the new public schools for girls aimed to cultivate future "worthy mothers" (*xianmu*) capable of educating patriotic sons and maintaining a harmonious and prosperous household as the foundation of a strong state. Public girls' schools, in fact, had already begun to be opened privately by reformers and educators—the first such school appeared in Shanghai in 1896—and since the turn of the century, these schools had responded to this new phenomenon by producing "new-style" textbooks specifically aimed at girls' schools. Although such textbooks reinforced the official rationale for female education—insisting that girls were the future "mothers of the nation" (*guomin zhi mu*) supervising well-run households—they also lauded the example of Western heroines

such as Joan of Arc and Madame Roland to emphasize the importance of women being actively engaged in public and national affairs.

A new school system was established in 1912 following the overthrow of the monarchy and its replacement by a republic. Coeducation was now allowed at the primary level, and a more unified curriculum (that eliminated instruction in the Confucian classics) was prescribed that would train citizens to be aware of both their rights and duties. The modern schools, the first of which had often been located in appropriated traditional buildings, such as Confucian academies and Buddhist temples, increasingly differed from their late imperial forebears. They adopted standard timetables and schedules, distributed and classified students in space (e.g., by placing students of the same age and similar abilities in one class), and imposed elaborate and strict rules designed to regulate student behavior.

Even a revolutionary such as Mao Zedong (in 1921) wistfully harked back to more "traditional" times when, he believed, teachers and students in Confucian academies had more personal rapport and the environment was not so formal. An emphasis on regulation was even more pronounced under the Nationalists in the late 1920s and 1930s, when schools devoted increasing amounts of time to military-style drills and training (primarily for boys) as a means to instill habits of discipline, cleanliness, and simplicity. It was often assumed at this time that social and moral training was just as important as the transmission of specialized knowledge.

POST-1949 DEVELOPMENTS

During the early Maoist period in the 1950s, pupils were especially made aware of their duties to the broader community, while textbooks insisted that any personal ambitions had to be subordinated to the goal of contributing selflessly to the new society. This was part of Mao's grand scheme to "transform" the people through the creation of a "virtuocracy," in which an individual's moral worth was the principal criterion determining job allocations and promotions (Shirk 1982, p. 4). Ironically, it led to fierce political competition within schools as students sought to demonstrate their ideological fervor and activism. Such competition culminated in physical violence during the Cultural Revolution in the 1960s as middle-school and college students formed rival Red Guard organizations that fought each other on the streets, each claiming to be the true champions of Mao's thought.

By the end of the 1960s, when schools reopened after having been closed from 1966 to 1968, academic achievement took second place to political loyalty (to Mao's "line") and enthusiasm for manual labor. An attempt was also made at this time to streamline the education system by unifying primary and secondary schools and prescribing a uniform ten-year curriculum.

Since the death of Mao in 1976 and the Chinese Communist Party's support for market-oriented reform, education has undergone enormous change. The Maoist emphasis on egalitarianism, class struggle, and commitment to the collective has been replaced by valorization of academic standards, competition, and diversity (and a corresponding acceptance of inequality). Downplaying the importance of ideology, schools are now expected to foster individual talents and skills considered necessary for the development of science and technology. The school system itself has also become more variegated, with elite "key-point" schools and colleges existing alongside less well-endowed primary, secondary, and vocational schools. Since the early 1990s there has also been a revival of private schools; by 2003, China had over seventy thousand such schools, enrolling fourteen million students (Jing Lin 2007, p. 45). In another echoing of the past, most schools, in addition to equipping students with the skills to compete in a market economy, also instill "traditional" values such as filial piety—perceived as a positive aspect of Chinese culture and thus a core element of the "patriotic education" the party has been promoting since the Tiananmen protests of 1989.

SEE ALSO *Education: Moral Education.*

BIBLIOGRAPHY

Bailey, Paul J. *Reform the People: Changing Attitudes towards Popular Education in Early Twentieth Century China.* Edinburgh, U.K.: Edinburgh University Press, 1990.

Bailey, Paul J. *Gender and Education in China: Gender Discourses and Women's Schooling in the Early Twentieth Century.* London: Routledge Curzon, 2007.

Bastid, Marianne. Chinese Educational Policies in the 1980s and Economic Development. *China Quarterly* 98 (1984): 189–219.

Culp, Robert. *Articulating Citizenship: Civic Education and Student Politics in Southeastern China, 1912–1940.* Cambridge, MA: Harvard University Press, 2007.

Hannum, Emily, Albert Park, and Cheng Kaiming. Market Reforms and Educational Opportunity in China. In *Education and Reform in China*, eds. Emily Hannum and Albert Park, 1–23. London: Routledge, 2007.

Jing Lin. Emergence of Private Schools in China. In *Education and Reform in China*, eds. Emily Hannum and Albert Park, 44–63. London: Routledge, 2007.

Pepper, Suzanne. *Radicalism and Education Reform in 20th-century China: The Search for an Ideal Development Model.* Cambridge, U.K.: Cambridge University Press, 1996.

Rosen, Stanley. Recentralization, Decentralization, and Rationalization: Deng Xiaoping's Bifurcated Education Policy. *Modern China* 11, 3 (1985): 301–346.

Shirk, Susan. *Competitive Comrades: Career Incentives and Student Strategies in China.* Berkeley: University of California Press, 1982.

Unger, Jonathan. *Education under Mao: Class and Competition in Canton Schools, 1960–1980.* New York: Columbia University Press, 1982.

Paul Bailey

SOCIOECONOMIC INDICATORS

By the beginning of the twenty-first century, researchers were able to cite with confidence a wide range of standard socioeconomic indicators in China: population, gross domestic product, per capita income, life expectancy at birth, literacy rates, urbanization, income inequality. They could also break down such figures by gender, by region, and by rural versus urban. All these indicators—with the possible exception of income inequality pre-1949—were unarguably at levels unprecedented in Chinese experience. Earlier dates are more ambiguous.

APPROACHES

Identifying socioeconomic indicators for earlier times involved moving backward from the present to the past—a procedure that almost inevitably involves combining inferences from limited (and imperfect) quantitative data with guesses about the impact of natural disasters, political change, and military conflict. Angus Maddison's studies (1998, 2001) are the most systematic attempt to do this for China as a whole. Profoundly skeptical of studies by those suffering from "sinophilia" (e.g., Pomeranz 2000), Maddison concludes that western Europe's per capita gross domestic product (GDP) surpassed that of China in the fourteenth century; thereafter, the latter remained unchanged until the early nineteenth century. Per capita GDP then fell (by just over 25 percent) between 1820 and 1950, doubled between 1950 and 1973, then almost quadrupled again between 1973 and 1998 (Maddison 2001, pp. 44–47, 264).

Those who see the Ming (1368–1644) and Qing (1644–1912) as eras of modest but real per capita growth—resulting in conditions in the most prosperous regions of China equaling or surpassing those of western Europe (in Maddison's terms, approximately $1,200)—must posit (1) an even more substantial rise in incomes as result of China's medieval economic revolution in the Song (960–1279); (2) a more severe decline between 1820 and 1950; (3) a more modest rise between 1950 and 1973 (the doubling of income under Mao Zedong reflecting improved statistics as much as or more than economic expansion); or (4) some combination of the three.

Maddison's technique problematically leads him to posit an *average* per capita GDP for Italy of $676 in 1500 and $777 in 1600, as opposed to an unchanging $600 for China. How this is to be reconciled with the glowing reports about conditions in China of Marco Polo in the late thirteenth century or Matteo Ricci at the end of the sixteenth is unclear.

A second approach is to divide the estimated GDP by the population at some earlier point. China's rich historical tradition provides us with what would seem, at first blush, to be a wealth of data. Critical evaluation has long since made clear that the quality of these numbers varies wildly.

None can be used without careful analysis of how they relate to underlying realities. G. William Skinner (1987) has shown that the long-accepted figure for China's population in 1850 (430 million) is some fifty million too high. If we divide Zhang Zhongli's estimate of China's GDP in the 1880s with a corrected post-Taiping population of 350 million, we obtain a per capita product of 8 *taels* (rather than Zhang's 7.4). This would translate to $11.75 at the then-current exchange rate (in 1933 dollars, $35.25). Since the per capita income for 1933 was $46, the growth would have been 24 percent, not 30 percent (Zhang Zhongli 1962, p. 324). A population of 439 million and Maddison's conversion of Liu Dazhong and Ye Gongjia's (1965) reconstruction of the 1933 GDP to 1990 constant dollars (Maddison 1998, p. 158) yields $673 per capita. The 1880s figure, in 1990 dollars, works out to $511.50.

The former is higher than Maddison's estimate of per capita income in either 1913 or 1950; the latter is lower than his estimate for 1870 or 1913. In both absolute terms, and in the trajectory they describe, these studies imply substantially different trajectories. Nonetheless, Zhang Zhongli noted that 7.4 *taels* "could buy at the wholesale price an amount of rice about twice the need of rice consumption of an average Chinese" (1962, p. 297). Unless one argues for an extremely skewed distribution of wealth, this suggests that most Chinese had a substantial cushion separating them from bare subsistence.

A third approach is to examine the experience of well-documented groups—such studies have been particularly significant in reconstructing vital statistics over time (see Wolf and Huang 1980; Lee and Wang 1999; Harrell 1995). These have provided extremely precise figures—but, as their authors have been quick to warn, records for even the best-documented populations are incomplete (Telford 1990). Moreover, well-documented populations are almost certainly atypical rather than representative. Attempts to use social biographies can provide us with much information about elites—but there is ample reason to believe that, in all but the worst of times, elite experience was substantially different from that of the population as a whole, even in a particular area (see Marmé 2005).

There are finally studies that attempt to use proxy variables to provide indications of overall conditions—whether of literacy rates (Rawski 1979), of diet (Fang Xing 1996), or of cloth production per capita (Pomeranz 2000). A recent attempt to summarize the results is aptly subtitled "Regional Differences, Temporal Trends, and Incomplete Evidence" (Pomeranz 2005). Such studies inevitably rely on anecdotal evidence and arguable inference. They almost always describe regions, if not particular localities, rather than China as a whole. The degree to which they provide

sound bases for comparisons across time or over space is also open to question. Take the claim that some 40 percent of males and 10 percent of females achieved basic literacy in the Qing period. Was mastery of a few hundred characters "literacy" remotely comparable to literacy rates in early twenty-first-century China (or in other societies)?

A TENTATIVE SYNTHESIS

Drawing on these various approaches, one would suggest that China's average per capita income in the late eighteenth century was slightly lower than that of western Europe as a whole (with favored regions like the Lower Yangzi core approximating that of western Europe). Between 1800 and 1850, the populations on the peripheries of the empire's macroregions grew, while those in the cores remained stable, leading to a modest decline in average per capita GDP. The midcentury rebellions led to short-lived but significant disruption of the cores. These rapidly recovered, then grew at significantly higher rates (especially from 1895 on). Such growth in the cores statistically overwhelmed the growing number of poor on the peripheries—until the cores were again disrupted by war in the 1930s and 1940s.

Given the rate of population expansion during the Maoist era (plus heavy investments in defense), it is unlikely that living standards per capita did more than recover levels attained in the early 1930s between 1949 and 1976. Income was, however, more equally distributed; the 1960–1962 period apart, the population was less subject to localized but severe fluctuations in basic necessities; investments in public health led to substantial gains in average life expectancy; after a sharp increase in the 1950s, urbanization rates stabilized; and mass literacy campaigns resulted in unprecedented degrees of basic literacy.

Mao's death in 1976 was initially followed by a rise in rural incomes. Especially since 1992, there has been a dramatic shift of population from rural to urban areas, a sharp rise in per capita incomes (especially in the urban areas), and a marked increase in income inequality (more dramatic between regions than within regions). Nonetheless, gains in basic education and in life expectancy appear thus far to have been maintained.

SEE ALSO *Illiteracy; Income; Population Policy: Demographic Trends since 1800; Urban China: Urbanization since 1949.*

BIBLIOGRAPHY

Fang Xing. "Qingdai jiangnan nongmin de xiaofei [Expenditures of Jiangnan peasants in the Qing]." *Zhongguo Jingji Shi Yanjiu* 11.3 (1996).

Harrell, Stevan, ed. *Chinese Historical Micro-demography.* Berkeley: University of California Press, 1995.

Lee, James Z., and Wang Feng. *One Quarter of Humanity: Malthusian Mythology and Chinese Realities.* Cambridge, MA: Harvard University Press, 1999.

Lee, James Z., and Wang Feng, with Li Bozhong. "Population, Poverty, and Subsistence in China, 1700–2000." In *Population and Economy: From Hunger to Modern Economic Growth*, eds. T. Bengtsson and O. Saito, 73–109. Oxford, U.K.: Oxford University Press, 2000.

Liu Dazhing (Liu Ta-Chung) and Ye Gongjia (Yeh Kung-Chia). *The Economy of the Chinese Mainland: National Income and Economic Development, 1933-1959.* Princeton, NJ: Princeton University Press, 1965.

Maddison, Angus. *Chinese Economic Performance in the Long Run.* Paris: Organization for Economic Cooperation and Development, 1998.

Maddison, Angus. *The World Economy: A Millennial Perspective.* Paris: Organization for Economic Cooperation and Development, 2001.

Marmé, Michael. *Suzhou, Where the Goods of All the Provinces Converge.* Stanford, CA: Stanford University Press, 2005.

Pomeranz, Kenneth. *The Great Divergence: China, Europe, and the Making of the Modern World Economy.* Princeton, NJ: Princeton University Press, 2000.

Pomeranz, Kenneth. "Standards of Living in Eighteenth Century China: Regional Differences, Temporal Trends, and Incomplete Evidence." In *Living Standards in the Past: New Perspectives on Well-Being in Asia and Europe*, eds. Robert C. Allen, Tommy Bengtsson, and Martin Dribe, 23–54. Oxford, U.K.: Oxford University Press, 2005.

Rawski, Evelyn Sakakida. *Education and Popular Literacy in Qing (Ch'ing) China.* Ann Arbor: University of Michigan Press, 1979.

Skinner, G. William. "Sichuan's Population in the Nineteenth Century: Lessons from Disaggregated Data," *Late Imperial China* 8.1 (1987), 1–79.

Telford, Ted A. Patching the Holes in Chinese Genealogies, *Late Imperial China* 11.2 (1990), 116–135.

Wolf, Arthur P., and Huang Jieshan (Chieh-Shan). *Marriage and Adoption in China, 1845–1945.* Stanford, CA: Stanford University Press, 1980.

Zhang Zhongli (Chang Chung-li). *The Income of the Chinese Gentry.* Seattle: University of Washington Press, 1962.

Michael Marmé

SONG QINGLING
1893–1981

Song Qingling (Soong Ching-ling, Suzie Soong) was the wife of Sun Yat-sen (Sun Yixian or Sun Zhongshan), revolutionary and founder of the Republic of China. When Sun died in 1925, Song Qingling's position as his widow made her a significant public figure for the rest of her long life. Groups claiming the mantle of the "father of republicanism" vied for his widow's support. Qingling herself believed that her primary duty was to remain faithful to Sun's radical principles. She opposed Chiang Kai-shek (Jiang Jieshi) when he assumed leadership of her husband's party, the Guomindang (GMD; Nationalist Party), and became an advocate of civil rights and resistance to the Japanese occupation. The drama of her position was heightened when Chiang Kai-shek became her brother-in-law in 1927 upon marrying her younger sister, Song Meiling (Soong Mei-ling, 1898–2003). After 1949 Song Qingling became a vice chair of the new People's Republic of China.

EARLY LIFE AND EDUCATION

Song Qingling was the second daughter of devout Christian parents. Her mother had received a Western education and her father, Charlie Song (usually known as Charlie Soong, Chinese name Song Jiashu, 宋嘉樹, born Han Jiaozhun [韓教準] 1866?–1918), was a Shanghai businessman who had sojourned in the United States, where he had been ordained as a Southern Methodist minister. Her elder sister, Song Ailing (Soong Eling, 1890–1973), married Kong Xiangxi (H. H. Kung, 1881–1967), later a GMD government minister, and became a wealthy businesswoman in her own right. The girls were educated at the leading missionary school in Shanghai and then at Wesleyan College in Macon, Georgia. Only fifteen when she left China and twenty when she returned, Song Qingling acquired near-native English skills, an excellent Western education, an understanding of other cultures, and a sophistication unusual even in young Shanghai women of the time.

PUBLIC ROLE AS WIFE OF SUN YAT-SEN

Charlie Song was a close associate of Sun Yat-sen. In 1913 the Song family accompanied Sun into exile in Japan. First Ailing and subsequently Qingling worked as Sun's secretary. The Song parents were too modern to expect to arrange their children's marriages, but they were shocked by Song Qingling's announcement in 1915 that she was going to marry Sun. He was forty-nine and she was twenty-two, and he had a wife of many years (his marriage had been arranged by his family) and three children. Divorce was unthinkable and Sun did not wish Qingling to be considered a concubine. In the end he announced that he considered himself divorced, his first wife retired to Macau and the wedding to Qingling took place. For the remaining ten years of Sun Yat-sen's life, he was accompanied everywhere by Song Qingling, whose public role as his wife was a new phenomenon in Chinese society.

The couple returned to China in 1917. In the following six years, Sun headed three different Republican governments based in Guangzhou and was twice forced to resign and retreat to Shanghai. Disappointed by the limited interest shown by the Western powers in his ideas for China's development, he turned to the Soviet Union.

With the help of Russian advisors, he reorganized the GMD along the lines of the Soviet party, and he established an alliance with the Chinese Communist Party (CCP). Song Qingling was made head of the GMD Women's Department.

Sun went with Song Qingling to Beijing in January 1925 to negotiate with the military government there. However, he became ill, and in March he died of cancer. His political testament asked that the GMD remain committed to its new radical policies. Henceforth, Song Qingling devoted her life to promoting his legacy. She developed an unadorned though elegant appearance appropriate to her position as Sun's widow. Like her sisters, she wore the *qipao,* the close-fitting, high-collared garment then considered to be the national dress for women, but hers were always simply styled in plain colors. Her hair was pulled back into a severe bun and she wore little jewelry.

BREAK WITH FAMILY AND GMD

In 1926 a split emerged in the GMD. Song Qingling was a member of a government dominated by the left of the party in Wuhan. In Shanghai, Chiang Kai-shek emerged as the leader of the right-wing faction. After a massacre of left-wing activists, he eventually emerged as the victor.

Qingling and other members of the Wuhan group fled to Moscow in September 1927. In the same month, Chiang Kai-shek married Song Meiling in a highly publicized Christian ceremony. Despite Song Qingling's bitter opposition to the match, Chiang's legitimacy in the GMD was strengthened by the family connection to Sun Yat-sen that the marriage conferred, while Meiling's beauty, the apparent modernity of their relationship, and her excellent English were all useful in consolidating Chiang's presentation as a modern leader for China. For Song Qingling, the marriage resulted in a political break with her family.

In 1929 Song Qingling returned to China from Europe to attend Sun Yat-sen's official interment in Nanjing. Anxious to avoid political exploitation of her presence, she issued a statement declaring, "my attendance at the burial is not to be interpreted in any sense as implying a modification or reversal of my decision to abstain from any direct of indirect work of the Guomindang so long as its leadership is opposed to the fundamental policies of Dr. Sun" (Chang Jung 1986, p. 69).

From 1931 Song Qingling lived in the French concession in Shanghai. She campaigned against the GMD's policy of nonresistance to Japanese encroachment on Chinese territory and raised money for welfare projects, she set up the

Song Qingling, broadcasting on "The Voice of China" radio station XGOY, Chongqing, 1940s. *In 1915, twenty-two-year-old Song Qingling married Sun Yat-sen, founder of the Republic of China. Upon his death, she sided with the left wing of the revolutionary movement against Chiang Kai-shek, eventually becoming a People's Republic of China vice president after the Chinese Civil War.* PICTORIAL PARADE/HULTON ARCHIVE/GETTY IMAGES

China League for Civil Rights in 1932 and headed the National Salvation Association set up in 1936 with the educator Tao Xingzhi (1891–1946) and the banker Zhang Naiqi (1897–1977), the association that campaigned for the GMD and the CCP to join forces to resist the Japanese and which became China's third-largest political grouping. Though some of her associates were imprisoned or even killed, her position as Sun's widow protected Qingling from direct attack. As other radicals were increasingly silenced, her voice became particularly important. She opposed the neo-Confucian philosophy of Chiang's New Life movement, arguing that China needed revolution, not Confucian revival.

WARTIME ACTIVITY AND PRC ROLE

Song Qingling's position was transformed by the formation of a United Front between the GMD and the CCP, closely followed in 1937 by open war between China and Japan. As the Japanese moved toward Shanghai, she fled to Hong Kong, where she spent three years organizing medical supplies for hospitals in the Communist-controlled areas of China. Her associates in these activities included the veteran GMD leader He Xiangning, the young Ding Cong, later to become a famous cartoonist, and American journalist Edgar Snow. In 1941 she left Hong Kong for Chongqing, the seat of the GMD refugee government, on the last plane out before the Japanese occupation. In Chongqing, partially reconciled with her sisters, she engaged with them in war and welfare work.

At the end of the war, Qingling appealed for a coalition government between the GMD and the CCP. When civil war broke out, she became honorary president of an anti-Chiang group, the Revolutionary Committee of the Chinese Guomindang. In 1949 her siblings and their families left China, but Qingling remained to welcome the new People's Republic, of which she became a vice chair, a largely honorary post. Qingling devoted herself to making speeches in support of the new regime, working for the All-China Women's Federation, of which she was honorary president, and heading her China Welfare Institute, which carried out welfare work for children and also published the English-language magazine *China Reconstructs*. She abandoned the role of social and political critic that she had played for so long under the Republic of China.

Honored in the early years of the new regime, Qingling was provided with a former prince's mansion in Beijing in addition to her Shanghai house. It is now a museum, with displays on her life. However, during the Cultural Revolution her house was looted and her parents' graves desecrated. Premier Zhou Enlai then issued an order that she should be protected. She made some attempts to help friends who were in trouble and to defend her husband's reputation from the criticism of the ultraleft. After Mao Zedong's death in 1976, she offered warm support to the new reform leadership. She died in 1981, succumbing to the leukemia that had been diagnosed twenty years earlier.

SEE ALSO *All-China Women's Federation; Song Ziwen (T. V. Soong); Sun Yat-sen (Sun Yixian).*

BIBLIOGRAPHY

Bergère, Marie-Claire, *Sun Yat-sen.* Stanford, CA: Stanford University Press, 1998.

Chang Jung with Jon Halliday. *Mme Sun Yat-sen (Soong Chingling).* Harmondsworth, U.K.: Penguin, 1986.

Epstein, Israel. *Woman in World History: Life and Times of Soong Ching Ling (Mme Sun Yatsen).* 2nd ed. Beijing: New World Press, 1995.

Hahn, Emily. *The Soong Sisters.* New York: Doubleday, 1941.

MacKinnon, Stephen, and Janice Agnes Smedley. *The Life and Times of an American Radical.* London: Virago, 1988.

Song Qingling. *Song Qingling Xuanji (Selected Works of Song Qingling).* Beijing: People's Publishing House, 1984.

Soong Ching Ling Foundation, ed. *Soong Ching Ling (Mme Sun Yat-Sen).* Beijing: *China Reconstructs Magazine*, 1984.

Delia Davin

SONG ZIWEN (T. V. SOONG)
1894–1971

Song Ziwen (T. V. Soong) was a prominent businessman and politician in the Republic of China during the first half of the twentieth century. Born into a wealthy family of Shanghai Christians in December 1894, the son of Song Jiashu (Charles Soong; 1863–1918) and a brother to the eminent Song sisters, Song Ziwen obtained a bachelor's degree in economics from Harvard University in 1915 and undertook graduate studies at Columbia University from 1915 to 1917. In 1917 he returned to China and became a secretary in the famous Hanyeping Iron and Coal Company.

In 1923 Song Ziwen joined his brother-in-law Sun Yat-sen (Sun Yixian or Sun Zhongshan) in his revolutionary campaign to unify China, thus beginning his political career. After serving as Sun's private secretary, Song held high positions in Sun's Guangzhou (Canton) government, including Central Bank manager and finance minister. After Chiang Kai-shek (Jiang Jieshi) completed his Northern Expedition in 1928, Song joined the Guomindang (GMD)-led Nationalist government, serving as minister of finance (1928–1933), governor of the Central Bank of China (1928–1934), and acting president of the Executive Yuan (1930–1933).

During the early years of Nationalist rule, Song Ziwen simplified China's tax system, increased government tax

Song Ziwen signing the 1942 lend lease agreement between the United States and China. *After earning a degree in economics from Harvard University, Song Ziwen returned to China and began working at a large industrial company. The brother-in-law of both Sun Yat-sen and Chiang Kai-shek, Song used his connections to join the Republican government, acting as an economic reformer and a foreign minister who cultivated diplomatic ties with the United States.* **MYRON DAVIS/TIME & LIFE PICTURES/GETTY IMAGES**

revenue, and established modern China's first bond and stock markets in Shanghai. In 1931 he helped establish the National Economic Council (which in 1934 became the China Development Finance Corporation) to supply credit for China's industrialization and attract foreign capital to China. But in 1934, Song resigned from most of his government positions. Rumor had it that Song and Chiang Kai-shek (who had married Song's sister Meiling in 1927) had quarreled over government spending levels. Chiang wanted more state funds to expand his military campaigns against the Chinese Communists while putting the Japanese military threat on hold.

After four official resignation attempts from the Nationalist government between 1928 and 1934, it became obvious that Song Ziwen could no longer agree with Chiang Kaishek's policies. During the early 1930s, Song took the strong position that China should ally itself with the United States and Britain to block Japan's growing military power. But Chiang and many high GMD officials preferred a policy of subduing the Communists before fighting the Japanese. Song thus gradually became a solitary, dissident warrior in GMD political circles, setting the stage, perhaps, for his departure from the political arena in 1934.

In the summer of 1940, three years after the Marco Polo Bridge incident, Chiang Kai-shek dispatched Song to Washington, D.C., as his personal representative to the U. S. government. Chiang wanted him to work with the United States and win President Franklin D. Roosevelt's support for China's war with Japan. Until late 1943, Song negotiated substantial loans from the United States to support the Chinese war effort. In December 1941, immediately after the attack on Pearl Harbor, Chiang Kai-shek appointed Song minister of foreign affairs (though he remained in Washington) to manage China's alliance with the United States and Great Britain. In this capacity, Song developed access to the center of power, namely, the White House, and he was able to convince President Roosevelt to factor China into the U. S. strategic thinking. Song remained in Washington until October 1943, when he returned to China's wartime capital in Chongqing.

In December 1944, while continuing to serve as foreign minister, Song was appointed deputy president of the Executive Yuan. In April 1945 he led the Chinese delegation to the first United Nations conference in San Francisco, where, by virtue of China's position as an Allied Power, he was one of four cochairmen. Song visited Moscow twice in mid-1945 and negotiated a treaty with Soviet Russia to clarify China's boundaries in Central and North Asia. Song resigned as foreign minister in July 1945 because he could not prevent the de facto independent (since 1924) Mongolian People's Republic from being legally detached from China.

In 1946 Song Ziwen fought hyperinflation and tried to revive China's war-ravaged economy. The government under him accepted labor's demand for automatic wage adjustments corresponding to the rise in the cost of living in postwar China. But the decision not only accelerated the upward wage-price spiral; it also compromised the GMD's long-standing alliance with business and industry and roused the resentment of entrepreneurs, who felt the concession to labor was contributing to their own rising production costs. In early 1947, he left the Executive Yuan and served in his last official post as governor of Guangdong Province. With the defeat of the Nationalists in 1949, Chiang Kai-shek and his GMD administration withdrew to Taiwan, while Song moved to New York, where he lived in retirement. He passed away in San Francisco in 1971 at the age of seventy-seven.

For a long time Song was being described as privileged, corrupt, and money-hungry, and his unique family relationship with Sun Yat-sen and Chiang Kai-shek earned him much censure for Nationalist China's defeat in 1949. With the release of his personal papers at the Hoover Institution in Stanford University, California, scholars have begun to reevaluate his role in modern China history. In 2006 Fudan University and the Hoover Institution jointly convened a symposium called T. V. Soong and Wartime Nationalist China, 1937–1945. The conference papers, since published in a conference volume (Wu Jingping 2008), attest to Song's standing as a politician of unusual capability, talent and integrity.

SEE ALSO *Chiang Kai-shek (Jiang Jieshi); Song Qingling; Sun Yat-sen (Sun Yixian).*

BIBLIOGRAPHY
Seagrave, Sterling. *The Soong Dynasty.* New York: Harper & Row, 1985.

Tuchman, Barbara W. *Stilwell and American Experience in China, 1911–1945.* New York: Macmillan, 1970.

Wu Jingping, ed. *Song Ziwen yu zhanshi Zhongguo (1937–1945)* [T. V. Soong and wartime Nationalist China, 1937–1945]. Shanghai: Fudan Daxue Chubanshe, 2008.

Hsiao-ting Lin (Xiaoting Lin)

SOUTH CHINA SEA

The South China Sea is the geostrategic heart of Southeast Asia. Controlled by outlets in the north through the Luzon Strait and Taiwan Strait and in the south through the narrow Strait of Malacca and Singapore, the South China Sea is the primary seaway through which vital natural resources and merchandise are shipped to and from Southeast Asian states, China, Japan, and Korea. The ongoing disputes over the many islands in the South China Sea are a major potential flashpoint for conflict in the region.

The disputes involve hundreds of small uninhabitable islands, coral atolls, reefs, shoals, and submerged rocks scattered across the South China Sea. Although oil is an important factor, strategic considerations and concerns about control over the sea-lanes are also at the heart of the dispute. China and Vietnam both claim the Paracel (Xisha) Islands about 150 miles southwest of Hainan Island. The Spratly (Nansha) Islands dispute is more complex, involving claims by the People's Republic China (PRC), Vietnam, the Philippines, Malaysia, and Brunei, with the added complication of claims by Taiwan. China claims all islands in the Spratly group, while Vietnam claims most of them. The Philippines claim a few islands off the coast of Palawan Island; Malaysia claims the Tsengmu Reef off the coast of Borneo; and Brunei claims the Louisa Reef, located northwest of Brunei within its exclusive economic zone. Each party to the dispute occupies several islands within the Spratly group.

On January 19, 1974, PRC forces occupied the Paracel Islands that were held by the collapsing South Vietnamese regime. Following the fall of South Vietnam in 1975, the Socialist Republic of Vietnam took possession of several of the Spratly Islands that had been held by the Saigon regime and asserted claims to numerous islands in the area. In 1976 China reacted by asserting "indisputable sovereignty" over the Spratly Islands and their "adjacent sea areas" and declaring that the islands have always been part of China's territory since ancient times.

The 1982 Law of the Sea Convention complicated the South China Sea disputes by prescribing economic rights over vast areas surrounding islands, initiating a scramble by the states in the region to assert claims and establish special economic zones. The possibility of the existence of oil and natural gas reserves and marine life resources around the islands raises the economic stakes and compounds the difficulty of finding a resolution. China began to aggressively assert its claims to South China Sea islands, and on March 14, 1988, China wrested control of several islands in the Spratly group from Vietnam, the first islands in the Spratly group actually occupied by PRC forces.

While China maintains that all the islands of the South China Sea have been Chinese territory since ancient times, these "historical claims" were first asserted on a modern Nationalist Chinese government map published in 1947 that included a U-shaped line encompassing the entire South China Sea. Although the PRC continues to publish maps showing the U-shaped line, this is only a "customary line" that was initially drawn without careful consideration and no clear understanding of its legal significance. China does not claim the entire South China Sea, only the islands and surrounding exclusive economic zone allowed by the Law of the Sea.

All of the other claimants, including Taiwan, occupied an estimated twenty-one islands, shoals, and reefs before China gained a foothold in the Spratly archipelago by taking control of six islands in 1988. Vietnam's claim is based on French control during colonial times. Following its independence in 1947, the Philippines claimed some of the Spratlys that Japan had occupied during World War II. The Philippines' claim is based on the assumption that Japan enjoyed sovereignty over the islands, but after the war Tokyo abandoned the islands, and the Philippines assumed ownership. Manila has undertaken various acts, such as naval inspections tours and diplomatic notes, to assert its ownership. In 1971 a brief conflict with Taiwan occurred when Filipino troops attempted to land on Taiping Island (Itu Aba) but were repulsed by the Nationalist Chinese forces. In 1974 the Philippine navy took control of five islands. In 1978 a presidential decree declared the "Kalayaan Islands" an integral part of the Philippines and strategically important for national defense.

In early 1995 tension between China and the Philippines flared up when a group of Filipino fishermen was detained by the Chinese navy while working around Mischief Reef, territory claimed by the Philippines. The

Philippine navy also detained five Chinese fishing boats and arrested sixty-two Chinese fishermen for "illegal entry" and "poaching." After three days of negotiations in March 1995, no resolution was reached. In mid-1999 conflict again erupted over an island in the Pratas (Zhongsha) Islands. The Philippines asserted a claim to an island that was within its 200-mile territorial waters, but China rejected the claim.

Malaysia asserted a claim to the continental shelf in 1979 and then established an exclusive economic zone adjacent to Borneo in 1980, claiming several islands in the Spratly group and actually occupying three atolls. This contrasts with others' claims, which are all premised upon prior occupation or discovery. In March 1995 Malaysian patrol boats opened fire on a Chinese trawler off the coast of Sarawak, injuring several Chinese fishermen.

China has indicated willingness to compromise and proposed setting aside the question of sovereignty while pursuing joint development and seeking a resolution to the dispute with all claimants. Indonesia stepped forward as an honest broker in 1990 and hosted several sessions of a "Workshop on Managing Potential Conflicts in the South China Sea." In 1992 the Association of Southeast Asian Nations (ASEAN) issued a declaration on the South China Sea that called on disputants to exercise self-restraint and eschew the use of force when settling territorial claims. The improved atmosphere in the South China Sea disputes can also be attributed to the improvement in Sino-Vietnamese relations after the settlement of their other bilateral territorial differences during the 1990s. This opened the door for progress on the more complicated, multilateral South China Sea disputes. In October 2003 China signed the 1976 ASEAN Treaty of Amity and Cooperation, which requires all states in the region to peacefully settle differences or disputes "by rational, effective and sufficiently flexible procedures, avoiding negative attitudes which might endanger or hinder cooperation."

The basis for a multilateral settlement has been established. If the ASEAN states as a group progress toward some mode of formal cooperation for resource development, China should not be expected to remain a bystander. China would try to prevent an anti-China coalition by seeking settlements of these disputes and to thwart involvement by outside powers like the United States. While any resolution of the South China Sea disputes is complicated by historical and legal questions, it is likely that the involved states will eventually seek a compromise settlement to ease cooperation on more fundamental economic and security issues where military force has little or no utility.

SEE ALSO *ASEAN, Relations with; Geographical Regions, Natural and Human; Natural Resources; Southeast Asian States, Relations with; Vietnam, Relations with.*

BIBLIOGRAPHY

Chen Jie. China's Spratly Policy: With Special Reference to the Philippines and Malaysia. *Asian Survey* 34, 10 (1994): 893–903.

Heinzig, Dieter. *Disputed Islands in the South China Sea: Paracels, Spratlys, Pratas, Macclesfield Bank.* Wiesbaden, Germany: Harrassowitz, 1976.

Hyer, Eric, ed. *The South China Sea Territorial Disputes.* Spec. issue. *American Asian Review* 12, 4 (1994).

Hyer, Eric. The South China Sea Disputes: Implications of China's Earlier Territorial Settlements. *Pacific Affairs* 68, 1 (1995): 34–54.

Li Laito (Lee Lai To). *China and the South China Sea Dialogues.* Westport, CT: Praeger, 1999.

Lu Zijian (Chi-kin Lo). *China's Policy towards Territorial Disputes: The Case of the South China Sea Islands.* New York: Routledge, 1989.

Samuels, Marwyn S. *Contest for the South China Sea.* New York: Methuen, 1982.

Eric Hyer

SOUTHEAST ASIAN STATES, RELATIONS WITH

China's relations with the ten countries of Southeast Asia—Brunei Darussalam, Myanmar (Burma), Cambodia, Indonesia, Laos, Malaysia, the Philippines, Singapore, Thailand, and Vietnam—have varied greatly over time since the establishment of the People's Republic of China on October 1, 1949.

DIPLOMATIC RELATIONS

On January 18, 1950, Vietnam—that is, the Vietminh—became the first Southeast Asian country to establish diplomatic relations with China. China established diplomatic relations with Burma on June 8 and with Indonesia on June 9 that same year. Cambodia and China established diplomatic relations on July 19, 1958. China established diplomatic relations with Laos on April 25, 1961.

When the Association of Southeast Asian Nations (ASEAN) was established in 1967, none of its member-states—Indonesia, Malaysia, the Philippines, Singapore, and Thailand—had diplomatic relations with China. Indonesia had cut off diplomatic relations in October 1966 following the failed coup in Indonesia in 1965. However, on May 31, 1974, China and Malaysia established diplomatic relations. China and the Philippines did likewise on June 9, 1975, and China and Thailand did so on July 1, 1975. The normalization of relations between China and Indonesia on August 8, 1990, paved the way for expanded relations between China and ASEAN. When diplomatic relations were established with Singapore on October 3, 1990, and with Brunei Darussalam on September 30, 1991, China had full diplomatic relations with all of the ASEAN member-states.

THE DIVERSITY OF CHINA'S RELATIONS WITH THE SOUTHEAST ASIAN COUNTRIES

The diversity in China's relations with the ten Southeast Asian countries is more pronounced than is displayed by the diplomatic relations. China's relations with Indonesia and Vietnam, in particular, have been marked by dramatic changes. The changes in relations between China and the Southeast Asian countries can often be explained by domestic changes in the Southeast Asian countries, coupled with shifts in China that have an impact on foreign policy, such as the Cultural Revolution in the 1960s and the initiation of economic reforms in the latter half of the 1970s.

In the 1950s, China maintained relations with only three Southeast Asian countries: Burma, Indonesia, and Vietnam (i.e., the Vietminh during the First Indochina Conflict [1946–1954] and the Democratic Republic of Vietnam [DRV] from 1954). China's relations with both the DRV and Indonesia were very good during the decade, and this situation persisted into the 1960s. Relations with Indonesia took a turn for the worse with the coup in 1965.

In the late 1950s and early 1960s, relations also expanded with Cambodia and Laos when China's strategy was to resist the United States, as reflected in its actions during both the Korean War (1950–1953) and in the first and second Indochina conflicts. Consequently, China gave extensive support to the DRV, and eventually to the Pathet Lao in Laos. After the overthrow of Prince Norodom Sihanouk in Cambodia in 1970, China lent its support to a front led by the prince that included Communist forces. Despite the gradual rapprochement between China and the United States in the early 1970s and the deepening conflict between China and the Soviet Union, China continued to support its allies in the Second Indochina Conflict up to the end of this conflict in 1975.

The second half of the 1970s saw major changes in China's interaction with the Southeast Asian region. The establishment of diplomatic relations with Malaysia, the Philippines, and Thailand in the mid-1970s signaled growing relations with non-Communist-ruled countries, while a sharp deterioration in relations with Vietnam and Laos displayed the growing rift between the former allies. Relations with Cambodia, however, were diametrically opposite, with a close and expanding collaboration and with increased support to Cambodia in its conflict with Vietnam. The Vietnamese military intervention in Cambodia in late 1978 and the initiation of economic reforms in China led to further expansion of relations with the ASEAN member-states, with the exception of Indonesia. China also gradually abandoned its support for armed Communist movements in non-Communist states of Southeast Asia, including Malaysia and Thailand.

The Cambodian conflict brought China's strategic interests and its opposition to intervention in line with the official policy of ASEAN. In particular, collaboration with Thailand increased. Economic relations strengthened with the deepening of China's reform process and the simultaneous growth of a number of Southeast Asian economies in the 1980s and especially during the first half of the 1990s.

The restoration of diplomatic relations with Indonesia in 1990 paved the way for diplomatic relations with the smaller regional powers of Singapore and Brunei. The resolution of the Cambodian conflict and the full normalization of relations with Vietnam in late 1991 brought about a state of normal diplomatic relations between China and all countries of the region. Normalization paved the way for expanding economic interaction, deepening political relations, and a closer relationship between China and ASEAN. With the expansion of membership in ASEAN during the second half of the 1990s, all ten Southeast Asian countries were brought into the framework of China-ASEAN collaboration. China's response to the Asian financial crisis in the late 1990s—in particular its decision not to devalue its currency—was much appreciated by the affected countries in Southeast Asia, and further strengthened relations. China's relations with the Southeast Asian region have continued to expand in the 2000s.

China's influence in Southeast Asia varies considerably from country to country. Influence is stronger with the countries bordering China in mainland Southeast Asia, and gradually weakness as one moves into maritime Southeast Asia, that is, Brunei, Indonesia, Malaysia, the Philippines, and Singapore. Thus, China's economic presence is more obvious in northern Myanmar, Laos, and Vietnam—regions that could have a direct impact on China's territory and where cross-border relations exist. China's influence is also in evidence in Cambodia. Political relations are also very close with Vietnam and Laos, where party-to-party relations with the Chinese Communist Party prevail. China also maintains strong relations with ruling elites in Myanmar, Cambodia, and Thailand. With Singapore, the economic dimensions of collaboration are apparent. In Malaysia, although the economic dimension is important, mutual efforts have been directed at expanding political collaboration. The relationship with Indonesia is strengthening, but the legacy of decades of animosity remains. Relations with the Philippines have at times—in particular, the second half of the 1990s—been negatively affected by disputes involving the South China Sea, that is, the overlapping claims to the major parts of the Spratly archipelago. In fact, disputes over island groups and/or maritime zones in the South China Sea loom as a potential

Defense Chief Orlando Mercado with photographs of sea coral harvested by Chinese fisherman in disputed waters, Quezon City, Philippines, February 3, 2000. *For centuries, China has extended its influence in the region, particularly among border nations. Some of the more remote island countries of Southeast Asia, however, dismiss China's dominance, as demonstrated by the Philippines insistence of ownership of the Spratly Islands against Chinese objections.* **AP IMAGES**

renewed source of conflicts between China and the following countries of Southeast Asia—Brunei, Indonesia, Malaysia, the Philippines, and Vietnam—if they are not managed successfully.

THE MOST RADICAL CHANGES IN RELATIONS: THE CASES OF INDONESIA AND VIETNAM

China enjoyed privileged relations with Indonesia under the presidency (1945–1967) of Sukarno (1901–1970), as evidenced by the early establishment of diplomatic relations and China's strong support for Indonesia's anticolonial foreign policy, which stood in opposition to the interests of major Western powers, such as the United States and the United Kingdom. The positive nature of China-Indonesia relations was demonstrated by negotiations in 1955 on the possibility of dual nationality for Chinese nationals in Indo-

nesia. The two countries signed a treaty on dual nationality in Bandung on April 22. During the Sukarno era, Indonesia's Partai Komunis Indonesia (PKI) was the third-largest Communist party in the world, a factor that made collaboration with China stronger.

China's strong relations with Indonesia came to an end with the rise to power of General Suharto (1921–2008) after the failed coup in Indonesia in 1965. The coup was blamed on left-leaning military officers, and sparked widespread persecution of members of the PKI and against ethnic Chinese in the country, resulting in at least 500,000 deaths and the repatriation of some 200,000 Chinese to China. Diplomatic relations with China were broken off by Indonesia in October 1966 and reestablished only in August 1990. Since then, relations have been expanded both politically and economically, but China's claims in the South China Sea have been a source of concern for Indonesia.

After the DRV was established in 1954, relations with China became very close. China provided the DRV with extensive economic and military assistance, and sent thousands of advisers to assist in various fields. China also provided the DRV with considerable assistance during the Vietnam War against the Republic of Vietnam and the United States in the 1960s and the first half of the 1970s. However, problems developed owing to different perceptions of the Soviet Union and divergent views on relations and negotiations with the United States.

After the end of the Vietnam War in 1975, relations between China and Vietnam went through dramatic changes, from seemingly good and normal relations in 1975 to war in 1979. Relations deteriorated over the following issues: (1) differences in opinion concerning the Soviet Union and China's uneasiness about Vietnam's relations with that country; (2) conflicting interests in Cambodia and China's gradually increasing support for Cambodia in the conflict between Vietnam and Cambodia; (3) territorial disputes between China and Vietnam; and (4) the situation of ethnic Chinese in Vietnam and the way in which the Chinese minority was treated. In fact, it was the mass migration of ethnic Chinese from Vietnam in the spring of 1978 that officially led to public deterioration of bilateral relations between the two countries. The overall deterioration of relations led to a militarized conflict that escalated into China's attack on Vietnam in February and March 1979.

The normalization process between China and Vietnam began with low-level contacts in the mid-1980s that eventually led to full normalization in November 1991. Since then, the relationship between China and Vietnam has been characterized by two contradictory trends, one positive with expanding contacts and cooperation in many fields, and the other negative with continued differences relating primarily to territorial disputes. The positive trend has been prevalent since full normalization, but has at times been weakened by fluctuating levels of tension relating to border disputes, in particular those in the South China Sea area.

IMPLICATIONS FOR THE UNITED STATES

Relations between China and the United States have been influenced by developments in Southeast Asia. The 1950s and 1960s were characterized by confrontation, as displayed by the Chinese and American involvement in the first and second Indochina wars. Both countries perceived the other as an antagonist, and although they did not confront each other militarily, as they had in Korea, the conflict was deep. As relations with the Soviet Union deteriorated sharply in the late 1960s, China began reappraising its foreign policy, and with the Soviet Union emerging as China's main enemy, improving relations with the United States became attractive.

The United States wanted to disengage from Vietnam and was also amendable to improved relations with China. The rapprochement process gained momentum after 1975, and particularly in 1978, when a major realignment took place after China's relations with Vietnam deteriorated. Vietnam moved into an alliance with the Soviet Union, and China and the United States fully normalized their relations. In response to Vietnamese military intervention in Cambodia in late 1978, both China and the United States pursued similar policies of opposing the Vietnamese presence in Cambodia and seeking to isolate Vietnam regionally and internationally. This situation prevailed until the Cambodian conflict was resolved in October 2001 and the Cold War ended. The Cambodian conflict was resolved through a conflict resolution process that was characterized by negotiations among the major powers, among the regional powers, and among the Cambodian parties.

Developments during the 1990s and 2000s indicate that policies pursued by China toward Southeast Asia have at times been in line, and at times in contradiction, with the policies of the United States. In other words, there is an interplay of collaboration and competition in the two countries' policies toward Southeast Asia. China's influence is strongest where the United States' influence and presence is more limited, implying that there might be disagreements—for example, over relations with Myanmar—but not a sharp competition for influence. China's influence is limited in countries with which the United States is a close ally (e.g., Singapore and the Philippines), thus reducing the risk for confrontation over influence. China pursues policies that enhance whatever benefits it can generate from Southeast Asia, and not necessarily to curtail the influence and presence of the United States. Furthermore, the economic clout of China is considerably more limited than that of the United States, and consequently China does not seek to compete directly with the United States for economic influence in Southeast Asia.

SEE ALSO *ASEAN, Relations with; United States, Relations with; Vietnam, Relations with.*

BIBLIOGRAPHY

Evans, Grant, Christopher Hutton, and Kuah Khun Eng. *Where China Meets Southeast Asia: Social & Cultural Change in the Border Regions.* Singapore: Institute of Southeast Asian Studies, 2000.

Ho Khai Leong and Samuel C. Y. Ku, eds. *China and Southeast Asia: Global Changes and Regional Challenges.* Singapore: Institute of Southeast Asian Studies; Gaoxiong, ROC: Center for Southeast Asian Studies, National Sun Yat-sen University, 2005.

Percival, Bronson. *The Dragon Looks South: China and Southeast Asia in the New Century.* Westport, CT: Praeger, 2007.

Xinhua News Agency, Home News Library, comp. *China's Foreign Relations: A Chronology of Events (1949–1988).* Beijing: Foreign Languages Press, 1989.

Yee, Herbert, and Ian Storey, eds. *The China Threat: Perceptions, Myths, and Reality.* London and New York: RoutledgeCurzon, 2002.

Ramses Amer

SOVIET UNION

SEE *Russia, Relations with.*

SPACE PROGRAM

Fewer than ten years after the establishment of the People's Republic of China (PRC) in 1949, China launched its space program. By 2003 China had sent its first *taikonaut* (astronaut) into space, joining the ranks of the world's major space powers and becoming the first space power in Asia.

HISTORICAL BACKGROUND

In 1955 Chinese rocket specialist Qian Xuesen returned to China from the United States to build China's space technology and industry in cooperation with the Soviet Union. In 1956 Moscow agreed to transfer rocket technology to the PRC, with the R2 (Raketa 2) rocket. In 1960 China launched its own model of the R2, the DF1 (Dong Fang 1), the first of the Long March launcher series.

Further progress was slowed by the Sino-Soviet conflict in 1960 and the turmoil of the Cultural Revolution. China nevertheless launched its first satellite in 1970, playing the song "Dongfang hong" (The East Is Red) around Earth. China deployed its first intermediate-range ballistic missile, the DF3, in 1971. During this period, China's space program was exclusively military and closely linked to its nuclear program.

In 1979 Deng Xiaoping launched China's policy of reform and opening up. For a while, the space program, which was strongly linked to China's military capability, lost precedence to economic modernization and development. During the 1980s, therefore, China put more stress on becoming a significant player in the civilian commercial launch market. From 1985 to 2000, China launched approximately twenty-five foreign satellites. After several launching failures and the loss of satellites, as well as the decision by the United States to halt its collaboration with China under suspicion of spying, the military dimension once again took priority in China's space program. Accord-

Manned Chinese spacecraft **Shenzhou V** ***at launch, October 15, 2003.*** *In 2003, China sent its first* taikonaut *to space. Developing a space program for both commercial and military interests, China looks to send a manned space mission to the moon after 2020.* AFP/GETTY IMAGES

ing to China, however, the decision in 2007 to build a new heavy launch vehicle is linked both to its lunar program and China's desire to play a larger role in the commercial launch market. Cooperation with Russia was renewed at the beginning of the 1990s with the launching of Project 921, the manned space program, in 1992.

China's space program accelerated in the early 2000s with an increase in the number of launchings. There were five launchings in 2002, six in 2003, including the first manned space flight, ten in 2004, and five in 2005, including the second manned space flight. China's State Council also published two white papers on space development, in 2000 and 2006. Both insist on the independent and peaceful nature of China's space program.

COMPLEX OBJECTIVES

China's space program answers complementary objectives. First, the space program brings prestige; since the beginning, it has contributed to the perception of China, both inside and outside the country, as at least a potential great power. More recently, the commercial dimension has been another important incentive. However, in spite of its official peaceful nature, China's space program must also contribute to the country's comprehensive capability and national security. Furthermore, dual-use technology developed through space-related research contributes to China's overall military capability in significant sectors like missile development. The space program also helps the Chinese military develop its capabilities in communications, observation, mapping, tracking, and global positioning. All these technologies are essential to the development of missile capability.

China is developing its own still-rudimentary Beidou Global Positioning System (GPS). In 2007 Chinese authorities announced an acceleration of a GPS program called Compass. China's objective is to build its own permanent and stable "all-conditions" observation and guiding capability on which modern, high-tech warfare is based.

In apparent contradiction to the professed peaceful use of space as the official basis for China's space program, in January 2007, apparently in answer to the U.S. antiballistic missile program, China proceeded to test its first antisatellite missile, destroying an old satellite with a high level of accuracy using a ballistic missile. A few months earlier, China had tested a laser beam to blind an American satellite.

China's civilian space program evolved from its military space program, and both remain strongly intertwined. At the organizational level, the Ministry of Science and Technology and the China National Space Administration are officially in charge of the program. However, the People's Liberation Army and its armament department play a leading role in all aspects of the space program.

As in all sectors linked to defense, the space program budget is not completely transparent. According to official Chinese sources, the budget for 2007 amounted to fewer than $2 billion, less than 10 percent of the U.S. space-program budget. The total budget for the five Shenzhou launchers reached only $2.4 billion between 1999 and 2006, according to official sources.

THE FIRST STEPS OF AN AMBITIOUS PROGRAM

In 1992 China launched an ambitious manned space-flight program, Project 921. The first flight, *Shenzhou 5,* successfully took place in October 2003, and the second one, *Shenzhou 6,* occurred in October 2005. The next step was to be a spacewalk mission in 2008. China also plans to establish its own space station.

In 2004, shortly after the success of *Shenzhou 5,* China launched a lunar-exploration program that may result in a manned lunar expedition after 2020. In October 2007, *Chang'e* satellite successfully embarked on its first observation mission. The objective of this program is to send, first, an unmanned vehicle to the Moon around 2017, and then possibly a manned expedition.

In order to achieve these ambitious objectives, and make a comeback on the big launcher market, China decided to build a new series of heavy-lift launch vehicles, the Long March 5. This launcher will be built near Tianjin, in a new high-tech hub, as a symbol of China's emergence as a high-tech power. It will be launched from a new site built on Hainan Island and transported from the building site to Hainan by sea. This Hainan launch site will complement the three inland sites of Jiuquan, Xichang, and Taiyuan.

China's progress in space technology has been impressive. In order to improve its capabilities, China is counting on cooperation with established space powers like Russia and the European Union (EU). In Europe, France has been identified as an important partner in space research. Cooperation with the United States ceased at the end of the 1990s with accusations of spying, and the debate about the renewal of this cooperation continues. As of 2008, the United States remained opposed to China's participation in the international space-station program.

INTERNATIONAL COOPERATION

Historically, the Soviet Union has been the first partner of the PRC. After almost three decades of interruption, cooperation with Russia on the manned space-flight program was renewed at the beginning of the 1990s, after the fall of the Soviet Union. China also built an extensive network of partnerships with state agencies and research institutions in France, Great Britain, and Canada, as well as, more recently, in developing countries like Nigeria and Brazil.

China was interested in participating in Europe's Galileo project—a satellite navigation system—in the hope of gaining access to important technologies. However, China's participation since 2005 has been reduced, due in part to an EU embargo on arms sales to China, and China's access to some types of technology has been limited. In 2007 China's financial participation in the Galileo project was reduced from a promised 200 million euros to 64 million euros.

In the meantime, the European Space Agency (ESA) and Chinese research centers have established joint training and research programs. Other joint programs are run by the European Commission and the Chinese Ministry of Science and Technology. In 2003 a China-Europe Global Navigation Satellite System Technical Training and Cooperation

Taikonaut waving a Chinese flag during a spacewalk, September 27, 2008. While China initiated research into space exploration in the mid-1950s, development slowed during the Cultural Revolution. As China looked to improve their international reputation in the late 1970s, government funding of the space industry increased, leading to the first manned Chinese space flight in 2003 and hopes of reaching the moon in subsequent decades. © ZHA CHUNMING/XINHUA PRESS/CORBIS

Center was established in Beijing to improve the participating countries' ability to prevent natural disasters. Starting in 2003, ESA and the Space Research Center of the Chinese Academy of Science cooperated on the Double-Star Program—Chuang Xing in China and Cluster II in Europe—with the launching of four European satellites and two Chinese satellites.

China's space program plays an important role in the perception of China as a great technological power. In terms of prestige, it helps China to distinguish itself from other developing countries. The visibility of a manned space program, the only one in Asia, plays an important role in building that perception.

SEE ALSO *Heavy Industry; High Technology; Research in the Sciences.*

BIBLIOGRAPHY
Harvey, Brian. *China's Space Program: from Conception to Manned Spaceflight.* New York: Springer, 2004.

Valérie Niquet

SPECIAL ADMINISTRATIVE REGIONS

When Deng Xiaoping emerged as the Chinese leader at the end of 1978, Beijing began to formulate a new policy for "peaceful reunification" with Taiwan and avoided statements of liberating it by force. A series of peaceful initiatives was launched, starting with "A Message to Compatriots in Taiwan" in January 1979, by the Standing Committee of China's National People's Congress (NPC). On September 30, 1981, Ye Jianying (1897–1986), chairman of the Standing Committee of the NPC, announced a nine-point proposal for resolving the Taiwan issue.

This nine-point proposal offered autonomy for Taiwan and the retention of Taiwan's own armed forces, as well as the retention of Taiwan's capitalist economy in the event of reunification. Chinese leaders also promised that Taiwan could maintain its economic and cultural relations with foreign countries, and the people's way of life would remain unchanged. This proposal was probably the foundation of the "one country, two systems" model, which was later said to be a major contribution of Deng Xiaoping.

472

China's new Constitution, promulgated in December 1982, provides the constitutional basis for special administrative regions (SARs). Article 31 of the Constitution states: "The state may establish special administrative regions when necessary. The systems to be instituted in special administrative regions shall be prescribed by law enacted by the National People's Congress in the light of specific conditions." In line with this, the Constitution grants the NPC the power "to decide on the establishment of special administrative regions and the systems to be instituted there." The term *special administrative region* was first made known to the world when the draft Constitution was released for commentary earlier in April in the same year.

FUTURE OF HONG KONG

Meanwhile, the issue of Hong Kong's future came into the picture. Murray MacLehose (1917–2000), then the governor of Hong Kong, visited China in March 1979 and raised the question of land leases in the New Territories that would expire in 1997. No concrete agreement was reached, and Deng Xiaoping simply asked the governor to tell investors in Hong Kong "to put their hearts at ease." In 1982 the British government pushed China to clarify its policy on Hong Kong's future. To this end, a British minister, Humphrey Atkins (1922–1996), visited Beijing to seek to begin formal negotiations.

The following April, former British Prime Minister Edward Heath (1916–2005) visited China. Deng Xiaoping met him and offered an outline of China's plans for Hong Kong's future. Hong Kong was to become a special zone under Chinese sovereignty, governed by its own inhabitants, and retaining its existing capitalist way of life and its legal system, but without any continuing British presence in the territory's administration. At this juncture, the draft Constitution was released, and the Taiwan issue and Hong Kong's future were linked by the concepts of "one country, two systems" and the SAR.

It was soon clear that the first SAR was intended to be Hong Kong, which would then generate a positive demonstration effect on Taiwan. In the mid-1980s, there was a thaw in the relations across the Taiwan Strait, but there were neither formal contacts nor negotiations. Many

Pro-democracy demonstrators in Hong Kong on the ninth anniversary of Chinese rule, July 1, 2006. Before Britain's lease on Hong Kong ended in 1997, government officials negotiated with the People's Republic of China (PRC) over the colony's status after the handover. In response, the PRC designated Hong Kong as a Special Administrative Region, allowing the new territory to operate under a different set of laws than mainland China, thereby preserving some of Hong Kong's autonomy. © PAUL HILTON/EPA/CORBIS

Taiwanese businesspeople set up manufacturing operations in mainland China to exploit the cheap land and labor there.

Formal negotiations on Hong Kong's future began with the visit of the British Prime Minister Margaret Thatcher to Beijing in September 1982. The negotiations led to the conclusion of the Sino-British Joint Declaration in September 1984. This document, together with its three annexes, defined the way Hong Kong would be run after 1997 as an SAR according to the model of "one country, two systems." The outcome of the diplomatic negotiations then had to be stipulated in Hong Kong's Basic Law, that is, its "mini-constitution." The crucial question was the trustworthiness of the Chinese leadership regarding the subsequent honest implementation of the pledges made.

At the same time, the Chinese authorities were concerned about tendencies of Hong Kong becoming an "independent political entity." The Basic Law was designed to allow the Chinese authorities to retain ultimate political control. The powers to amend and interpret the Basic Law are in the hands of the NPC and its Standing Committee. The appointments of Hong Kong's chief executive and principal officials by the central government are said to be "substantial," meaning that the latter can refuse to make the appointments. Finally, the electoral systems were designed in such a way that the chief executive would be someone trusted by the Chinese leadership and accepted by the local business community, while the prodemocracy movement would not be able to capture a majority of the legislative seats even though it could secure an absolute majority of votes in direct elections.

MACAU

The case of Macau, China's second SAR, was different from that of Hong Kong. After the 1974 military coup in Portugal, the new Portuguese government tried to return Macau to China. Beijing declined because it did not want to destabilize Hong Kong. In April 1987 the Sino-Portuguese Joint Declaration was signed, following the Hong Kong model. The joint declaration stipulated that Macau would become an SAR on December 20, 1999, about two-and-a-half years after Hong Kong. The Portuguese colonial administration had already lost control of Macau from 1966 to 1967 during the Cultural Revolution, and the local people welcomed the departure of the Portuguese administration because of its corruption and incompetence. In 1998 and 1999 the law-and-order situation deteriorated so badly that the local community explicitly wished that the return to China would have occurred sooner.

The Chinese leadership certainly hoped that the SARs would be successful because it was eager to show the world that the Chinese could do better than the British in governing Hong Kong; the successful return of Hong Kong and Macau would contribute to its status in Chinese history. Failure of the SARs, in turn, would affect the international community's confidence in China's modernization efforts. The Chinese authorities therefore poured money into Hong Kong in the final years of the British administration to ensure its stability and prosperity. They again supported Hong Kong financially when economic difficulties in 2003 and the incompetence of the administration of Chief Executive Tung Chee-hwa (Dong Jianhua) triggered a massive protest rally on July 1 in response to the proposed Article 23 legislation, which was perceived to restrict the cherished freedoms of the people of Hong Kong.

THE TWENTY-FIRST CENTURY

In the decade following its return to China, the Hong Kong SAR continued to function as an international financial center and an international business services center. Hong Kong has been able to maintain fruitful economic and cultural ties with foreign countries. Its economic challenges are similar to those of Singapore and Taiwan: a high-cost structure and keen competition from neighbors. But the demand for democracy has not been met. Chinese authorities are reluctant to give up their ultimate political control, and it does not appear that genuine democracy will be realized soon. Without the legitimacy bestowed by democratic elections, Hong Kong's SAR government will find it difficult to tackle the demand for better social services and the cleavages generated by the widening gap between the rich and poor.

The administration in the Macau SAR of Chief Executive Edmund Ho Hau-wah (He Houhua), though, has been popular because the economy has been performing well since Ho took office in 1999 and the law-and-order situation has improved greatly. The demand for political participation has not been strong in Macau.

Meanwhile, political liberalization initiated in the final years of the Jiang Jingguo (Chiang Ching-kuo) presidency led to full democracy in Taiwan in the mid-1990s. The prospect of becoming an SAR under Chinese sovereignty obviously has no appeal to the Taiwan people, who cannot accept any erosion of their democratic rights. The demand for democracy in Hong Kong has been exploited by the administration of Taiwanese president Chen Shui-bian to discredit Beijing's appeal for peaceful reunification with Taiwan.

SEE ALSO *Deng Xiaoping; Foreign Policy Frameworks and Theories: One-China Policy and "One Country, Two Systems"; Hong Kong; Macau.*

BIBLIOGRAPHY
Chen Mingqiu (Chan, Ming K.), and Su Yaochang (Alvin Y. So), eds. *Crisis and Transformation in China's Hong Kong.* Armonk, NY: Sharpe, 2002.

Cheng Ming (Sing Ming), ed. *Hong Kong Government and Politics.* Hong Kong: Oxford University Press, 2003.

Lu Zhaoxing (Lo Shiu-hing). *The Politics of Democratization in Hong Kong.* London: Macmillan; New York: St. Martin's Press, 1997.

Ten Years of the Basic Law. Spec. anniversary issue. *Hong Kong Law Journal* 37, 2 (2007).

Zheng Yushuo (Cheng, Joseph Y. S.), ed. *The Hong Kong Special Administrative Region in Its First Decade.* Hong Kong: City University of Hong Kong Press, 2007.

Joseph Y. S. Cheng (Zheng Yushuo)

SPECIAL ECONOMIC ZONES

The term *special economic zone* (SEZ) refers to five geographic territories in China that served as economic experimental laboratories as part of Deng Xiaoping's economic reforms of 1978 and the subsequent "open-door" policy. The objective was for these zones to function like the many export-processing zones found all over the world in being able to attract foreign capital, transfer technology, earn foreign revenue from exports, and generate employment. At the same time, these zones allowed China to experiment with market mechanisms and engage global capitalism on a limited scale, while the rest of the country was mostly closed to foreign trade and investment.

In 1980 four SEZs—located in Shenzhen, Zhuhai, Shantou, and Xiamen—were established, with a fifth, in Hainan, launched in 1988. In 1990 the Pudong New Area, an SEZ in all but name, was developed in Shanghai. Due to the initial success of the SEZs in attracting foreign investment and driving economic growth, from 1984 onward the zones program was expanded, with different types of zones introduced, including economic and technological development zones, free-trade zones, and even tourism development zones. These new zones were usually developed by local authorities with approval from Beijing.

Although there were more than five hundred such zones by 1997, the SEZs had the widest range of preferential economic policies, giving them a unique competitive advantage within China. For example, between 1984 and 1997, foreign investors in SEZs paid an income tax of only 15 percent, compared to 33 percent in other zones. However, by the time China joined the World Trade Organization (WTO) in 2001, many such preferential policies had been eliminated. The few remaining preferential policies, such as those to encourage investments in high technology, would apply uniformly to all zones, including the SEZs. This led some observers to suggest that China's special economic zones were no longer "special."

POLICIES

The SEZs were economically innovative in three respects. First, not only could industrial investors qualify for a series of tax incentives and investment benefits—including tax holidays and exemptions, duty-free privileges, and preferential fees for land or facility use—overseas ethnic Chinese businesspersons investing in SEZs could qualify for additional benefits. To encourage such investments, all five SEZs were located in the southern provinces of Guangdong and Fujian, which were geographically close to Hong Kong, Macau, and Taiwan.

Second, in order to operate within an SEZ, enterprises were required to form equity joint ventures with a Chinese firm, so as to assist Chinese firms with capital injection, as well as to foster technology and managerial skills transfer. At the same time, new joint ventures in the SEZs had to conform to China's national labor laws. Hence, these firms were obliged to continue such labor practices as providing all meals and medical coverage for Chinese workers.

Third, economic policy in the SEZs allowed for foreign investments not just in industrial production, but also in the agricultural, animal husbandry, tourism, and housing sectors. This was a significant departure from the worldwide export-processing zone model, which usually only catered to industrial investors.

Lastly, the authorities managing the SEZs enjoyed some economic and political autonomy. For example, SEZ authorities were given the power to approve foreign investment applications, without having to seek clearance from Beijing or from provincial authorities. SEZ authorities were also allowed to retain some earnings from foreign investments for expansion plans or other municipal uses.

While there were some adjustments to the SEZ policy—such as tariff "rationalizations" in 1994 and 1995—the most

SHENZHEN

Shenzhen covers an area of 780 square miles (2,020 square kilometers) on the coast of South China, lying immediately north of Hong Kong across the Shenzhen River. The name *Shenzhen* means "deep drains," demonstrating the city's close relationship with farming activities. Residents here have long made their livelihoods from farming and fishing.

In May 1980 Shenzhen was officially made the site of experiment for the special economic zone (SEZ) model attributed to Premier Deng Xiaoping. The Shenzhen SEZ was created by combining the four districts in Baoan County that shared the border with Hong Kong—Nanshan, Futian, Luohu, and Yantian—which had a population of around 30,000, mostly involved in fishing and farming, and covered an area of about 126 square miles (327.5 square kilometers). Since 1993, another 618 square miles (1,600 square kilometers) has been added, including the Baoan and Longgang districts, the more rural part of Shenzhen. Although the location of the SEZ in Shenzhen was chosen to take advantage of its proximity to Hong Kong, the boundary was made very explicit—a high protective fence along the Shenzhen and Shatoujiao rivers separates Shenzhen and Hong Kong. Across this boundary came foreign investments from the south through Hong Kong. The SEZ and the rural sections of the city are separated by another boundary called the *erxian* (literally, "second border") that served to control the number of mainland workers arriving from different parts of China. The importance of this second border has dwindled with the increasing urbanization of the rural section of the city. Shenzhen SEZ was the boomtown of the 1980s where capital, labor, and know-how met. Symbolized as the window through which new technology, knowledge, management, and foreign policy entered China, the SEZ contributed much to the Four Modernizations program launched in the 1970s. "Shenzhen speed" became the model of development for other parts of China.

Shenzhen's population grew from 314,000 to 1.5 million in the first decade of its existence. Many of the new residents were party cadres with a pioneer spirit and young graduates who filled jobs at the high-tech factories in the Shekou Industrial Zone. Peasant *mingong* (migrant workers) flocked to the rest of the SEZ, filling places in its manufacturing and entertainment industries. Today there are nine million people living in the city, excluding daily commuters from Dongguan and Hong Kong. Around 20 percent hold Shenzhen *hukou* (permanent residency). As a migrant city, the overall population is young, averaging thirty years old, but education and income levels are polarized. Individuals lacking proof of identity, work, and fixed residence (*sanwu*, literally, "three lackings") are the socially underprivileged. Before 2003 they were repatriated, and in 2008 still suffered from police harassment.

The cheaper living cost in Shenzhen has attracted Hong Kong consumers to its many restaurants, massage and beauty parlors, photo salons, and retail shops; at the same time, pirated goods, prostitution, and illegal drugs have proliferated. Then again, the establishment of Shenzhen University and other academic institutions and research centers, as well as improvements in urban infrastructure including highways, an airport, and numerous skyscrapers, have made this city a social and economic miracle that competes with Hong Kong and Guangzhou as a major city of the Pearl River Delta. The rise of the Shenzhen *ren* (Shenzhen people) identity points to the culture that has developed gradually among a diverse population that shares the same dream of upward social mobility.

BIBLIOGRAPHY

Lei, Guang. Rural Taste, Urban Fashions: The Cultural Politics of Rural/Urban Difference in Contemporary China. *Positions: East Asia Cultures Critique* 11, 3 (2003): 613–646.

Lin Yuru. *Zhongguo jingjitequ jianzhi* [Introduction to Chinese special economic zones]. Guangzhou: Guangdong Renmin Qubanshe, 1990.

Tam, Siumi Maria. The Structuration of Chinese Modernization: Women Workers of Shekou Industrial Zone. Ph.D. diss., University of Hawaii, 1992.

Siumi Maria Tam

significant change occurred when China formally joined the WTO in 2001 and had to abide by the principle of "national treatment." This not only meant that rules and laws limiting foreign investment to specific cities or zones would not be permissible under WTO standards, it also meant that if any preferential economic policies were allowed, they had to be uniformly applied across the country. As a result, the SEZs' preferential tax rate of 15 percent was aligned to the new uniform national tax rate of 25 percent.

GDP in Special Economic Zones (in U.S. dollars, billions)

SEZ	1979	1994	2001
Shenzhen	0.02	6.71	17.5
Zhuhai	0.03	1.96	4.0
Shantou	0.08	2.33	5.7
Xiamen	0.08	2.24	6.4
Hainan	0.7 (1987)	4.8	6.8

SOURCE: "China's Island Province Has Booming Economy." Xinhua News Agency, 11 February 2001; "Fujian Sees 9.5 Per Cent GDP Growth." *China Daily*, 11 January 2001; Gao, Guanjian, and GuoQiang Long. "Special Economic Zones (SEZs) and Economic and Technological Development Zones (ETDZs) in China," in S. P. Gupta (ed.) *China's Economic Reforms: The Role of Special Economic Zones and Economic and Technological Development Zones.* Singapore: ISEAS, 1996, pp. 129–167; Park, J. D. *The Special Economic Zones of China and Their Impact on Its Economic Development.* Westport: Praeger, 1997; "Shenzhen Sniffs after GDP High." *China Daily*, 28 March 2001; "Twentieth Anniversary of Shantou SEZ Celebrated." Xinhua News Agency, 22 October 2001; "Zhuhai Zone has been in Shenzhen's Shadow." *Economist Intelligence Unit,* 27 June 2001.

Table 1

Cumulative foreign direct investment in the Special Economic Zones (SEZ) (in U.S. dollars, billions)

SEZ	Up to 1985	Up to 1993	2000s
Shenzhen	2.8	14.8	30.5
Zhuhai	1.6	5.3	18.4
Shantou	0.2	4.9	10
Xiamen	0.5	9.3	18.5
Hainan	n.a.	10.7	11

SOURCE: "China's Island Province Has Booming Economy." Xinhua News Agency, 11 February 2001; "Fujian Sees 9.5 Per Cent GDP Growth." *China Daily,* 11 January 2001; Gao, Guanjian, and GuoQiang Long. "Special Economic Zones (SEZs) and Economic and Technological Development Zones (ETDZs) in China," in S. P. Gupta (ed.) *China's Economic Reforms: The Role of Special Economic Zones and Economic and Technological Development Zones.* Singapore: ISEAS, 1996, pp. 129–167; Park, J. D. *The Special Economic Zones of China and Their Impact on Its Economic Development.* Westport: Praeger, 1997; "Shenzhen Sniffs after GDP High." *China Daily,* 28 March 2001; "Twentieth Anniversary of Shantou SEZ Celebrated." Xinhua News Agency, 22 October 2001; "Zhuhai Zone has been in Shenzhen's Shadow." *Economist Intelligence Unit,* 27 June 2001.

Table 2

PERFORMANCE

Between 1980 and 1994, the five SEZs accounted for only 0.35 percent of China's total land area, and their population was only 0.8 percent of China's total population. Yet, by 1994, the SEZs accounted for more than 20 percent of all foreign investment in China, and 15 percent of all exports from China. Driven by growth in its four SEZs, Guangdong's gross domestic product (GDP) per capita, which was ninth highest in the country in 1958, rose to fifth highest in 1994. Similarly, Fujian's GDP per capita, driven by growth in Xiamen SEZ, rose from sixteenth highest in 1978 to tenth highest in 1994.

Of the five SEZs, the Shenzhen SEZ is considered to be the most economically dynamic and successful (see Table 1). Its dynamism was fueled by foreign investment, mainly from neighboring Hong Kong. Hong Kong firms relocated much of their industrial production to Shenzhen for the purposes of cost savings and profit maximization. Finished and semifinished products from these factories were mostly exported to the rest of the world through Hong Kong. Between 1980 and 1995, Shenzhen was one of the largest exporting cities in all of China (see Table 2).

While most investments were in the industrial sector, there were many other projects, including some in the commerce and tourism sectors. To further boost the development of the SEZ, the Shenzhen Stock Exchange was launched in 1991. Economic growth in the zone averaged 30 percent per annum between 1980 and 1997, and over

20 percent between 1997 and 2007. By 2008, Shenzhen's GDP per capita rose to almost $10,000 (in U.S. dollars), which ranked as the highest among cities in China.

The Xiamen SEZ, located in Fujian Province, was designed to attract Taiwanese investments. In 1980, 2.5 square kilometers of the Huli district of Xiamen were chosen as the site of the SEZ. Foreign-investment inflow was fairly high (see Table 2), leading to an expansion of the zone to 131 square kilometers in 1984, incorporating the whole of Xiamen and the neighboring district of Gulangyu. In 1980 there were fewer than 500,000 people employed within the SEZ; by 1989, the number had risen to over 600,000. Xiamen's overall resident population increased from one million in 1995 to over 2.6 million in 2004.

Although most investors in the Xiamen SEZ were from Hong Kong, between 1980 and 1989, Taiwanese investment averaged 25 percent, which was the highest for all the SEZs. Between 1990 and 1997, the proportion increased to around 40 percent. Growth in Xiamen, although not as rapid as Shenzhen, has been higher than in the other SEZs. In 2000 Xiamen's GDP per capital stood at over $4,500, which is seventeenth highest among Chinese cities. Also, while industrial production is the largest component and the main driver of the Xiamen SEZ's economic growth, the zone has seen a rapid expansion of financial services, especially in the 1990s.

The Zhuhai and Shantou SEZs have always been smaller projects. The Zhuhai SEZ was established along

Exports from the Special Economic Zones (SEZ) (in U.S. dollars, billions)

SEZ	1986	1994	2000
Shenzhen	0.72	14.0	16.1
Zhuhai	0.07	1.4	2.9
Shantou	0.07	1.8	2.0
Xiamen	0.16	1.9	4.7
Hainan	0.43 (1990)	0.4	0.8

SOURCE: "China's Island Province Has Booming Economy." Xinhua News Agency, 11 February 2001; "Fujian Sees 9.5 Per Cent GDP Growth." *China Daily*, 11 January 2001; Gao, Guanjian, and GuoQiang Long. "Special Economic Zones (SEZs) and Economic and Technological Development Zones (ETDZs) in China," in S. P. Gupta (ed.) *China's Economic Reforms: The Role of Special Economic Zones and Economic and Technological Development Zones*. Singapore: ISEAS, 1996, pp.129–167; Park, J. D. *The Special Economic Zones of China and Their Impact on Its Economic Development*. Westport: Praeger, 1997; "Shenzhen Sniffs after GDP High." *China Daily*, 28 March 2001; "Twentieth Anniversary of Shantou SEZ Celebrated." Xinhua News Agency, 22 October 2001; "Zhuhai Zone has been in Shenzhen's Shadow." *Economist Intelligence Unit*, 27 June 2001.

Table 3

the border with Macau. It began operations in 1980 with a land area covering 6.1 square kilometers, later expanding to 121 square kilometers in the 1990s. The Zhuhai SEZ's main investors were from Hong Kong and Macau, combining to account for over 90 percent of all foreign investments. Most of the investments were in labor-intensive and light manufacturing, with almost all products destined for Hong Kong first, and then out to the rest of the world. Since the late 1990s, Zhuhai has also attempted to develop its tourism sector, mainly to take advantage of Macau's development. Due to its modest economic growth, the Zhuhai SEZ's urban population growth increased from 300,000 in 1979 to only around 500,000 in 1999.

The Shantou SEZ, which began operations in 1981, originally covered an area of 1.6 square kilometers within Shantou (Swatow) city. The logic of situating an SEZ in this city was to take advantage of the large number of overseas Teochiu (the Chaozhou diaspora) that had migrated to Hong Kong, Taiwan, and Southeast Asia. However, while Shantou's level of foreign investments and economic growth was generally higher than the rest of China, it was lower than the other four SEZs. Despite this, in 1984 the Shantou SEZ expanded to 52.6 square kilometers, and enlarged again in 1991 to cover the whole city of Shantou, with a total area of 234 square kilometers.

Although economic growth in Shantou has been high when compared to other Chinese cities, it can only be described as modest by SEZ standards. Like the Zhuhai SEZ, the Shantou SEZ has been involved in labor-intensive and light manufacturing. Employment grew from 2,500 in 1980 to over 36,000 in 1989. Shantou's overall resident population grew moderately from almost four million in 1994 to around five million in 2007.

The Hainan SEZ was established in 1988, not only in response to the encouraging performance of the original four SEZs, but also as a response to Hainan's economic backwardness and overreliance on agriculture. In 1987 Hainan's GDP was $700 million, which was nineteenth out of twenty-nine major cities in China. It became the largest zone, encompassing the entire Hainan Island, which is around 34,000 square kilometers. To help attract foreign investments, the Hainan SEZ had the most liberal investment conditions. It was also elevated to the status of a province in 1988 to give it the autonomy to implement developmental policies. The local authorities thus chose to introduce nonagricultural economic activities, including industrial production and tourism, to supplement its existing economy. For example, the Yangpu Economic Development Zone, near Haikou, was established in 1992 as a purpose-built industrial estate to attract foreign investment. At the same time, foreign investors were invited to develop the tourism potential of the city of Sanya in southern Hainan.

While Hainan's economy has been fairly turbulent, it has still seen some growth, which was mainly driven by foreign investments in agriculture and tourism. The island's population has grown steadily, from six million in 1987 to eight million in 2004. More importantly, between 1989 and 2001, the GDP per capita rose from $100 to over $1,000. Unlike in the other SEZs, there was a significant presence of investors—accounting for 16 percent—from Southeast Asia, including Thailand and Singapore.

CHALLENGES AND PROSPECTS

The main challenges faced by the SEZs were uneven regional development and a "race to the bottom" competition for foreign investments. While the GDP of the SEZs grew more than 25 percent per year between 1980 and 2001, the other zones grew less than 15 percent per year over the same period. The sudden wealth in the SEZs thus generated large-scale labor migration, especially headed toward the Shenzhen SEZ and Shanghai's Pudong New Area. This created a new problem in China: the emergence of sweatshops. Initially, since most workers in the SEZs were locals, their residency status ensured that they had access to the full range of social-welfare entitlements under China's socialist system. However, due to the rapid growth in the SEZs, there was a massive labor shortage, especially in the Shenzhen SEZ. As a solution, the zones turned to temporary migrant labor, particularly less-educated female workers from rural areas. This practice has led to the problem of the "dormitory labor regime," where female workers are housed at dormitories owned by either the factories or the local authorities. These female workers were subjected to strict controls over movement and behavior, as well as corporal punishment, physical assaults, body searches, and other unlawful abuses by their employers. However, since the 1990s, such abusive practices have been reduced significantly, mainly due to greater monitoring by both the state and activist groups.

Another challenge faced by the SEZs was "zone fever." Not only were there many zones within China that were competing to attract foreign investors, many other countries in the Asia Pacific region adopted "zonal" strategies for growth and development. Some countries, including Vietnam, India, and North Korea, opted to follow the Chinese SEZ model, as opposed to the more generic export-processing zone model. This ultimately created additional competition for China's SEZs.

The competition, local and international, had some benefits, in that it pushed the SEZs to improve their efficiency; however, it also led to other zones adopting "undercutting" as a tactic. With preferential policies of the SEZs effectively removed, they have had to compete on a more level playing field against other Chinese cities. Under these conditions, Shenzhen and Xiamen, with long-standing links to Hong Kong and Taiwan respectively, are in a favorable position to retain their economic dynamism. Hainan has carved a niche for itself in the tourism sector, while improving its agricultural yield. Shantou and Zhuhai will probably continue with modest growth and development.

The SEZs and the wider national-level SEZ strategy will be remembered as a struggle over China's economic soul. Indeed, the semiretired Deng Xiaoping used his visit of the SEZs in 1992—the "southern tour"—to reestablish the momentum he had started toward market liberalization in the face of mounting pro-socialist political and economic conservatism. The SEZs have today become integral components of China's economy and significant nodes within the global economy. The zones have fulfilled their promise of transitioning China from socialism to market socialism.

SEE ALSO *City and Regional Planning; Companies: Joint Ventures; Economic Reform since 1978; Foreign Investment since 1949; Socialist Market Economy; Urban China: Development Zones; Urban China: Urban Planning since 1978.*

BIBLIOGRAPHY

China Daily. Fujian Sees 9.5 Per Cent GDP Growth. January 11, 2001.

China Daily. Shenzhen Sniffs after GDP High. March 28, 2001.

Crane, George T. *The Political Economy of China's Special Economic Zones.* Armonk, NY: Sharpe, 1990.

Economist Intelligence Unit. Zhuhai Zone Has Been in Shenzhen's Shadow. June 27, 2001.

Gao Guanjian and Long Guo Qiang. Special Economic Zones (SEZs) and Economic and Technological Development Zones (ETDZs) in China. In *China's Economic Reforms: The Role of Special Economic Zones and Economic and Technological Development Zones,* ed. S. P. Gupta, 129–167. Singapore: ISEAS, 1996.

Park Jung-Dong. *The Special Economic Zones of China and Their Impact on Its Economic Development.* Westport, CT: Praeger, 1997.

Pun Ngai. *Made in China: Women Factory Workers in a Global Workplace.* Durham, NC: Duke University Press, 2005.

Wu Weiping. *Pioneering Economic Reform in China's Special Economic Zones: The Promotion of Foreign Investment and Technology Transfer in Shenzhen.* Aldershot, U.K.: Ashgate, 1999.

Xinhua News Agency. 20th Anniversary of Shantou SEZ Celebrated. October 22, 2001.

Xinhua News Agency. China's Island Province Has Booming Economy. February 11, 2001.

Alexius A. Pereira

SPORTS

The influence of the Western powers following the Opium War (1839–1842) with the British instituted the era of modern sports in China. Before the war, Confucianism, with its emphasis on hierarchy and ritualized performance, pushed traditional competitive athletic games such as Chinese football (*cuju*), archery, and polo into obsolescence. A major exception to this decline was martial arts (*wushu*). Offensive and defensive martial arts were based on the fighting methods of five animals: the crane emphasized balance; the dragon, spirit and agility; the leopard, strength; the tiger, power; and the snake, the ability to hit vital points of the body. Gradually, as Chinese society militarized, practitioners of *wushu* employed weapons, including the sword, spear, and knife. Martial arts fit well into a Chinese society that combined modernity with a traditional emphasis on absolute patriarchal loyalty and a student's obedience to a master. *Wushu* also appealed to warlords and, eventually, to such national leaders as Chiang Kai-Shek (Jiang Jieshi). Martial arts played a key role in the Boxer Uprising of 1900, and thereby won support from conservatives and patriots.

THE LATE QING ERA

After the Opium War and foreign encroachments, Qing dynasty (1644–1912) leaders strove to accommodate Westernization through sports. Mass military exercises were based on successful Western models and included gymnastics and marching drills to create good soldiers.

Western-style schools and academies were established, including the Tianjin Weaponry Engineering College (founded in 1885), the Guangdong Navy Academy (1887), and the North Western Navy Academy (1881), among many others. The physical education curriculum at these schools included compulsory military exercises and such sports as fencing, boxing, soccer, high and long jump, swimming, skating, and gymnastics. Top achieving boys were sent to the United States for advanced training. The Westernization movement coincided with the belief that China had been a "sick and weak man" and needed physical exercise to become a strong nation.

That belief, reinforced by China's humiliating defeat in the first Sino-Japanese War (1894–1895), became ideology as China strived for a stronger state through the promotion of Western patterns of physical exercise. Gymnastics and newer sports (often introduced by YMCA missionaries), including basketball, baseball, volleyball, tennis, badminton, and track and field, became mandatory parts of school curriculums. In 1910, one sports star, Sun Baoxin, a high jumper from Tianjin, frustrated because his long queue (the braid of hair that in Manchu law gave him identity) knocked the high bar off its stand, cut his hair and returned the next day to become the high-jump champion of China.

THE REPUBLICAN ERA

Following the Republican overthrow of the Qing dynasty, the view of sports as nation-building became standard. Mao Zedong observed in 1917 that physical education was key to physical health, that a healthy body was the basis of moral and intellectual development, and physical fitness must be based on a positive mind. Traditional cultural exercises were useless, he declared, but to participate in exercise was to participate in revolution. The influential writer Lu Xun (1881–1936) agreed that modern sports could push aside outmoded traditions.

The Nationalist government of the 1920s borrowed the pragmatic ideas of the American educator John Dewey (1859–1952) to foster social evolution and individualism among male *and* female students. New schools, such as the Zhejiang Women's Physical Education Institute (founded in 1920), among many others, trained teachers of physical education. Regional sports associations arose in the 1910s and 1920s to organize athletic competitions and to sponsor Chinese athletes at international meets in Australia, New Zealand, Japan, and Europe. The China National Amateur Athletic Federation (founded in 1924 in Nanjing) supervised China's national and international athletic competitions and represented the nation on the International Olympic Committee. Forms of competition, rules, and regulations were derived from Olympic models, and traditional Chinese

sports were not included in such competitions as the Far Eastern Championships, in which China took part four times between 1924 and 1948, and the Olympics, which China joined three times between 1932 and 1948. China thereby modernized its sports culture through national and international competitions. Additionally, Western military exercises were dropped as hindrances to personal development and as symbols of conformity.

In 1929 the Nationalist government issued the Law of Sports (*Tiyu fa*) which mandated that boys and girls take part in physical education to develop their bodies for the good of the country. Other than *taijicao*, a slow-moving version of martial arts, modern sports now dominated Chinese athletics and performances.

This transition brought controversy. After Liu Changchun (1909–1983), the national sprint champion, failed in the first heat of the Olympic competition in Los Angeles in 1932, the newspaper *Dagong Daily* editorialized that modernization had only created inferior imitations of Western sports and that China should rely on its athletic traditions. After a heated debate, the Nationalist government acknowledged the importance of martial arts. After the Japanese invasion of China in 1937 instigated a national crisis, the debate ended, and a combination of martial arts and modern sports became the favored model. This fusion of Western sports, physical education, and culture with traditional Chinese forms including martial arts, chess, *qigong*, mountain climbing, and military training, became known as *tiyu*, "physical culture."

With this nationalist and somewhat ambivalent combination, China ventured forth to the Olympic games. After the disappointment of the 1932 Olympics (though the games legitimized the Nationalist state's position against the Japanese), China sent a forty-two-person delegation to the 1936 Berlin games. The team won no medals, but the martial artists excelled, and the swimmer Yang Xiuqiong (1918–1982) cemented her status as a sports idol back home.

After World War II (1937–1945) and during the turmoil of the civil war, China took part in the 1948 Olympics in London. Once again, the team won no medals. Conditions were so bad that the team stayed in an elementary school, cooked its own meals, and had to borrow money for passage home.

THE PRC PERIOD

After the establishment of the People's Republic of China (PRC) in 1949, the Chinese team took part in the 1952 Olympics in Helsinki, but disputes over Taiwan's status kept the PRC out of subsequent Olympics until the 1980s.

During the 1950s, the PRC enunciated a policy of "friendship first, competition second" in international play. After an overwhelming Chinese victory in a Ping-

Chinese badminton player Lin Dan at the World Badminton Championships, Anaheim, California, August 18, 2005. As Western influences became stronger after the Opium Wars, many Chinese began partaking in group and individual athletics, in part to create a nation of strong, healthy citizens better suited to defend China. This sports tradition has continued under Communist rule, with many Chinese athletes involved at the highest levels of competition. © LUCY NICHOLSON/REUTERS/CORBIS

Pong competition with North Korea and Japan, Premier Zhou Enlai apologized to the North Korean leader Kim Il Sung (1912–1994). Kim replied that, although he appreciated Zhou's gesture, "no country wants to intentionally lose to the other country's team. It does not sound right." Later, in the Olympic qualifying round in 1979, the Chinese soccer team plotted to create a tie with the North Korean team. After reaching a score of 3–3, the Chinese relaxed, but the Koreans scored again and then played hard defense to defeat their opponents. Xu Guoqi cites an article quoting the The Chinese as realizing that "there is no such thing as friendship in games, even with a socialist brother country like North Korea" (Xu Guoqi 2008, p. 51). In 1972, Ping-Pong competitions helped thaw relations between the United States and China.

Domestically, Mao's influence on sports was profound. His slogan, "Develop physical culture and sports, strengthen the people's physiques," appeared on the sides of gymnasiums and became a standard fixture in placard sections at sports meets. Mao also demonstrated his fitness by swimming about a mile across the Yangzi (Chang) River near

Wuhan (where the river is narrower) in 1966, which inspired a national swimming craze. Such symbolism continued, as indicated by a 1984 article in which Premier Zhao Ziyang, aged sixty-four, was reported to jog forty minutes every morning and to take a half-hour walk every evening.

The Chinese Communist Party established a system of sports schools based on the Soviet model. The Chinese sports hierarchy forms a pyramid structure from local (county, township, and city) sports commissions to provincial and municipal (Beijing, Shanghai, and Tianjin) units, to the State Sports Commission, all designed to recruit promising athletes, who move up the levels to the national team. Superior athletes, as in the Nationalist era, perform at the National Sports Games. Beginning in 1959, the tenth anniversary of the revolution, the National Games took on sharp ideological themes. Following the disaster of the Great Leap Forward, no games were held until 1965. Then, the themes of the Second National Games indicated the onset of the Cultural Revolution, with calls to Lift High the Revolutionary Torch, Rely on Our Own Effort and Work Hard for the Prosperity of the Country, Tightly Grip the Gun in Your Hand, and Carry the Revolution through the End. By the 1983 games, softer images of springtime, used in the 1959 competitions, reappeared.

As Maoist culture lapsed in the 1980s, the ideology of Western-style competition, with a much heavier emphasis on winning, gained strength, whether in local games or the Olympics. China is no longer a loser in the Olympics and won one hundred medals at the 2008 Beijing Olympics, including fifty-one gold medals. Despite China's wishes, however, Chinese martial arts were not on the program. Western-style sports celebrities have also emerged in China, a phenomenon epitomized by the basketball star Yao Ming.

In 1994 Chinese soccer became the first sport to professionalize, followed by basketball, volleyball, and table tennis. The professionalization process led to commercialization as sports associations became profit-making entities, and as a club system developed, professional leagues formed, and commercial management systems took shape. Professionalism has encouraged the emergence of a sports-management market and business-structured systems. Sports club operations now cover ticket sales, advertising, club transfers, commercial matches, television broadcasting, and other commercial activities. These developments have moved Chinese sports far from their traditional origins.

SEE ALSO *Olympics; Physical Education; Sports Figures.*

BIBLIOGRAPHY
Brownell, Susan. *Training the Body for China: Sports in the Moral Order of the People's Republic.* Chicago: University of Chicago Press, 1995.

Brownell, Susan. *Beijing's Games: What the Olympics Mean to China.* Lanham, MD: Rowman & Littlefield, 2008.

Fan Hong and Tan Hua. Sport in China: Conflict between Tradition and Modernity, 1840s to 1930s. In *Sport in Asian Society: Past and Present,* eds. J. A. Mangan and Fan Hong, 189–212. London: Cass, 2003.

Gao Yunxiang. Sports, Gender, and Nation-State during China's "National Crisis" from 1931–1945. Ph.D. diss. University of Iowa, 2005.

Morris, Andrew. *Marrow of the Nation: A History of Sport and Physical Culture in Republican China.* Berkeley: University of California Press, 2004.

Xu Guoqi. *Olympic Dreams: China and Sports, 1895–2008.* Cambridge, MA: Harvard University Press, 2008.

Gao Yunxiang

SPORTS FIGURES

The democratization of fame occurred later in sports than in other areas of entertainment. The film stars Hu Die and Ruan Lingyu, the Peking opera actor Mei Lanfang, and the writer Lu Xun were national figures before major sports celebrities emerged. Chinese sports were generally mass amateur calisthenics, and since China only recently adopted Western sports, the fame of standout players was limited. Not until China's first Olympic participation was there a famous athlete.

China's first Olympic entry in 1932 was not auspicious. Liu Changchun, China's best short-distance runner, was the nation's sole participant. Arriving exhausted after a lengthy sea voyage, he failed to advance beyond the first round. Still, when Liu boarded a ship bound for Los Angeles, a huge crowd turned out at Xinguan Pier in Shanghai to bid him farewell. In Los Angeles, the American and world press hailed him as the "lone representative of four hundred million people." Athletes from around the world embraced Liu. His celebrity stemmed from his loyalty to the nation and his presence at the Olympics and among the world's athletic champions. Similar accolades were given to the female Chinese swimmer Yang Xiuqiong when she competed in the 1936 Berlin Olympics. Magazine images of Yang portrayed her in bathing suits. Yang also gained notoriety from her rumored affair with Chu Minyi (1884–1946), the secretary general of the Executive Yuan, the vice chairman of the National Games, and the leading Guomindang spokesman for mass physical education (Chu later became infamous as a key sports official for the Japanese sponsored Wang Jingwei regime and was executed by the Nationalist government for treason).

Athletic celebrity coalesced with film celebrity for the 1930s actress Li Lili. A former athlete, Li starred in a number of Chinese films, including *Tiyu huanghou* (Queen of sports), *Xiao wanyi* (Little toys), *Huoshan qingxue* (Revenge by the Volcano), and *Dao ziran qu* (Return to nature). She was generally clad in sports gear, demonstrating physical education and modern sports fitness. Her strong limbs and torso represented the New Woman, while her curvaceous figure allowed sensuous display. Li's stardom conjoined Chinese visions of fitness and fame. Fame for Yang and Li meant emphasis on their physical beauty, as opposed to the national pride engendered by their male counterparts.

The early decades of the People's Republic were not conducive to personal athletic fame. In the years just before the Cultural Revolution (1966–1969), Zhuang Zedong excelled at Ping-Pong, winning three consecutive men's singles championships at the World Table Tennis Championship between 1961 and 1965. His total number of titles exceeded all those won by other members of the Chinese national teams combined. Nationalism was always at the heart of his efforts. Zhuang Zedong recalled that every shot he took at a Japanese opponent in table-tennis matches was revenge for past national suffering, and that he strove to "win honor for the whole nation and for

Chairman Mao." Premier Zhou Enlai reopened table tennis competition in 1969. Such competitions lapsed during the Cultural Revolution. Two years later Zhuang initiated Ping-Pong diplomacy by giving the American player Glenn Cowan a silk-screen portrait of the Huang Mountains when the American accidentally got on the Chinese-team bus.

While athletic fame and glory were downplayed on the Chinese mainland, in Taiwan athletes gained global popularity in the late 1960s. Yang Chuanguang (C. K. Wang) became known as the "iron man of Asia" for his decathlon feats. After winning gold medals in the event at the 1954 and 1958 Asian games, Yang had a memorable competition with the American Rafer Johnson at the 1960 Rome Olympics. Yang won seven of the competitions, but Johnson squeaked by to win the gold medal by winning the other three by large margins. Yang settled for the silver medal. He competed again in the 1964 Tokyo Olympics, finishing fifth in the decathlon. Another popular Taiwan athlete was the female runner Ji Zheng, who represented Taiwan in the 1968 Olympic Games at Mexico City and won a bronze medal in the 80-meter hurdles. Ji was known as the "flying antelope."

In the reform years after the death of Mao Zedong in 1976, Olympic glory became the best path to athletic fame in China. Li Ning won six medals at the 1984 Olympics, including three gold medals in the floor exercise, pommel horse, and rings. Li retired from competition in 1988 and became a highly successful entrepreneur in athletic clothing and footwear, thereby leveraging athletic stardom into business success. He remains chairman of the board of directors of Li-Ning Company. Male Olympic competitors continue to hold international appeal. Liu Xiang won the first-ever gold medal for China in a track-and-field event by winning the 110-meter hurdles at the 2004 Olympics. Since then Liu has maintained the world record in this event and is the first Chinese triple-crown winner: Olympic champion, world record holder, and world champion. He has been best in the world at the 110-meter hurdles at many events over the past four years. Sadly, Liu developed a chronic inflammation of his right Achilles tendon, which forced him to withdraw from the 2008 Beijing Olympics, much to the sorrow of millions of Chinese fans, who had regarded a triumph by Liu as essential to a successful Chinese showing at the Olympics. Cuba's Dayron Robles won the event, though he did not break Liu's record, and he later commented that his victory lacked the thrill of competing with Liu.

National Basketball Association player Yao Ming (center), competing for Team China in the International Basketball Federation World Championship tournament, Sapporo, Japan, August 20, 2006. With the exception of a few gold medal-winning Olympic athletes, nationally known sports figures remained uncommon in China until the end of the twentieth century. The development of professional sports leagues in China and the success of athletes in overseas competition, however, have led to increased recognition of some participants, such as NBA All-Star Yao Ming. © FRANCK ROBICHON/ EPA/CORBIS

China's investments in the Olympic games brought fame to some women Chinese athletes. Lang Ping was a member of the Chinese women's volleyball team that won the gold medal at the 1984 Summer Olympics in Los Angeles. Known as the "iron hammer," Lang led the Chinese team to the championship at the World Cup in 1981 and 1985. Lang later became head coach of the Chinese Olympic team in 1995 and guided the squad to a silver medal in the 1996 games in Atlanta, Georgia, and to second place at the World Championships in Japan in 1998. After retiring for health reasons, she returned as a professional coach first in Italy and, since 2005, as head coach of the U.S. Women's national volleyball team. Fu Mingxia, another woman, won Olympic gold medals in diving competitions in 1992 and 1996. In the 2004 Olympic games, Guo Jingjing subsequently won a gold medal in the women's 3-meter-springboard synchronized diving event with Wu Mingxia and an individual gold medal in the women's 3-meter springboard diving event. Known as the "princess of diving" and notorious for her fashions and for her relationship with the scion of a wealthy Hong Kong business family, Guo won an individual gold medal in the 3-meter-springboard diving event and won another gold medal with Wu in the 2008 Olympics.

Since China professionalized some sports in the 1990s and allowed its athletes to join international sports leagues, by far the most famous player has been the basketball star Yao Ming. After playing several years for the Shanghai Sharks, Yao was the first overall selection in the 2002 National Basketball Association draft and was awarded to the Houston Rockets. Yao became an All-Star in his first year and, though hampered by injuries, gradually developed into the top center in the league, a feat that brought him global fame never before achieved by a Chinese athlete. Yao's fame has brought him annual earnings of US $55 million in salary and endorsement fees of such products as Pepsi-Cola, Visa, Apple Computers, and McDonalds, and he has written a best-selling autobiography. Yao's emergence into global fame is analogous to China's rise to superpower status, and his earnings are analogous to the commercialization of Chinese sports.

SEE ALSO *Olympics; Olympics, 2008 Beijing Olympic Games; Physical Education; Sports.*

BIBLIOGRAPHY

Brownell, Susan. *Beijing's Games: What the Olympics Mean to China.* Lanham, MD: Rowman and Littlefield, 2008.

Morris, Andrew. *Marrow of the Nation: A History of Sport and Physical Culture in Republican China.* Berkeley: University of California Press, 2004.

Xu Guoqi. *Olympic Dreams: China and Sports, 1895–2008.* Cambridge, MA: Harvard University Press, 2008.

Gao Yunxiang

STANDARD OF LIVING

The *standard of living* is a measure of economic welfare that is most often captured by per capita gross domestic product (GDP). GDP is a less-than-perfect measure, and other indicators of the quality of life, including household consumption expenditure, educational attainment, and health, nutrition, and life expectancy are equally important. Any assessment of the standard of living must also concern itself with the distributive dimension of each of these measures.

Since the late 1970s, the Chinese economy has grown at an impressive annual rate of nearly 8 percent per capita. By 2007, this growth had lifted per capita GDP in China, measured in U.S. dollars, to nearly $2,500. More meaningful is a comparison of purchasing power parity (PPP), which reflects differences between countries in the costs of goods and services not captured by exchange rates. On a PPP basis, China's per capita GDP in 2007 was between $5,500 and $6,000—depending on the PPP converter one uses—or between one-seventh and one-eighth of per capita GDP in the United States.

An examination of long-run trends in the standard of living in China since 1800 is handicapped by significant data limitations, especially for the nineteenth century and the first decade or so of the twentieth century. Many of these difficulties relate to measuring output, and consumption and incomes tied to agriculture, which even as late as the early 1950s remained the source of 60 percent of GDP. Compounding the difficulty is a lack of historical price data needed to convert nominal estimates of welfare in *yuan* into measures of real purchasing power over goods and services. These converters are essential to making valid comparisons over time, as well as between China and the rest of the world.

Angus Maddison (1998, 2001) provides the most widely cited estimates of per capita GDP in China over time, measured in 1990 international dollars. For both 1700 and 1820, estimated per capita GDP is $600. This drops to $530 by 1870, recovers slowly over the next sixty years to $578 in 1933, but falls sharply again to $439 in 1950. It is not until 1957 or so that a per capita GDP of $637 surpasses the level of 1820 (and 1700). Maddison estimates that per capita GDP rises thereafter, hitting $978 and $3,117 in 1978 and 1998, respectively.

A useful assessment for China must be situated in the context of concurrent changes in the standard of living of the world's most advanced countries. It is widely agreed among economic historians that the early nineteenth century marks a critical turning point in the rate of development of the world's most advanced countries. After rising only negligibly, if at all, in previous centuries, per capita incomes in western Europe and North America experienced an acceleration in growth during the nineteenth century that continued through the twentieth century. This momentous shift has two important implications. First, over the course of two centuries, growth contributed to a fifteen- to twentyfold improvement in per capita incomes in the most successful of these countries (e.g., the United States, France, Sweden, etc.), which was accompanied by equally important improvements in other indicators of the standard of living, such as health and life expectancy. Second, growth contributed to a massive widening of the gap between the world's richest and poorest countries. If this ratio was on the order of 4 or 5 to 1 in 1800, by 2000 it had increased to nearly 20 to 1.

CHINA IN 1800

Until the publication of Kenneth Pomeranz's *The Great Divergence* (2001), conventional wisdom among historians was that the standard of living in China in the late eighteenth century was significantly below that of the most advanced countries in Europe. Madisson's estimates for China for 1820 reflect much of this received wisdom, and put per capita GDP in China at one-third of that in the United Kingdom or the Netherlands. Drawing on a variety of data to estimate consumption and income levels during the mid-Qing (1644–1912), and building on earlier work of such scholars as Susan Hanley and Yamamura Kozo (1978) on Japan, Pomeranz provocatively argues: "It seems likely that average incomes in Japan, China and parts of southeast Asia were comparable to (or higher than) those in western Europe even in the late eighteenth century" (Pomeranz 2001, p. 49). This reassessment of the economy must be viewed in the context of a much larger and ongoing reinterpretation of mid-Qing demographic, social, and political history carried out by James Lee and Cameron Campbell (1997), R. Bin Wong (1997), Li Bozhong (1998), and others.

An important implication of Pomeranz's estimate is that it was only in the nineteenth century (and not much earlier) that the standard of living in China and, for that matter, other parts of Asia diverged with that of Europe. He attributes much of the divergence to differences in the ability of these two parts of the world to deal with increasingly binding resource constraints, notably, land. His estimates, as well as those he cites in support regarding agricultural productivity, household demographic behavior, and so forth, have not gone uncontested, and they are the source of lively academic debate. Serious questions exist over their accuracy and representativeness for the Lower Yangzi, which is the focus of much of Pomeranz's work, let alone for all of China.

A cross-country comparison by Robert Allen et al. (2007) using real wages provides an alternative basis of comparison. The real wage is the ratio of the wage a worker is paid to a price index, and is a measure of a worker's purchasing power over goods and services. These estimates are not without their own shortcomings, and for China they do not automatically generalize to a population in which 60 to 70 percent derived their livelihood directly from agriculture. However, they suggest a significantly lower standard of living in China than in Europe, with real wages in China conservatively at a third or so of those in London or Amsterdam, and much more in line with wage levels estimated for southern Europe.

CHINA SINCE 1800

The nineteenth century is currently an empirical black box for China. It is also a tumultuous period in Chinese history, during which China was forcibly opened up to the world economy, experienced a significant loss of life and devastation in the course of the Taiping and Nian rebellions after 1850, and witnessed the end of the Qing dynasty (1644–1912). Climate shifts may also have affected agriculture. Maddison's per capita GDP estimates for these years largely reflect current historiography on the impact of these shocks. It is important to remember, however, that the underlying data for these estimates are very thin, a point that Maddison readily acknowledges.

Sufficient data exist that allow for more credible estimates of GDP in the 1930s, which can be linked to other countries, as well as to the 1950s. The starting point for estimates in the 1930s is T. C. Liu and K. C. Yeh's classic 1965 study, which provides an analysis of GDP between 1933 and 1959. Fukao Kyoji, Ma Debin, and Yuan Tangjun (2007) have provided improved estimates of PPP converters for the United States, Japan, and China in the 1930s, enabling them to revise real per capita GDP comparisons across these countries. In absolute terms, their estimates for China are slightly higher than Maddison's (1998) and put per capita GDP in China in the 1930s at one-ninth that of the United States and one-third that of Japan. These may be lower bounds. Their estimates of PPP converters are based exclusively on urban price data; however, other studies suggest that the cost of living is typically much lower in rural than in urban areas. China was the most rural of the three countries, by a wide margin.

Average per capita GDP can be a misleading indicator in a country such as China that by the 1930s had a population of over 500 million. Significant regional differences in economic development and standard of living quite likely existed. Ma Debin (2008), for example, estimates for the 1930s that per capita GDP in the Lower Yangzi, a region of sixty million, was more than 50 percent higher than the national average. He attributes a significant portion of this to the more rapid growth in the region in the early twentieth century. Some corroborating support for this interpretation is provided by Stephen Morgan's (2004) examination of the regional behavior of heights (an anthropometric measure that can be linked to living standards) of railroad workers in China.

Estimates of the rate of growth of per capita GDP in the early twentieth century by Ma Debin for the Lower Yangzi and Thomas Rawski (1989) at the national level raise the possibility that the standard of living for a significant portion of the Chinese population may have risen through the first few decades of the twentieth century. These estimates, especially at the national level, remain a source of debate, which existing data sources cannot easily resolve. Data limitations, notably for agriculture, make extending estimates back to the last half of the nineteenth century even more tenuous.

Slightly more can be said about the distribution of welfare in the 1930s. With only 10 to 15 percent of the population living in cites, distribution is largely a rural story. Overall, agriculture was the source of two-thirds of GDP, and the entire rural economy, which includes farm and nonfarm sideline activities, accounted for an even higher percentage. Although off-farm labor markets, land rental, and nonagricultural sideline activities helped to offset differences in land endowments among households, land ownership remained an important determinant of material well-being. Nearly half of the GDP coming from agriculture, or nearly a third of total GDP, represented the return to ownership of farmland.

Landholding data collected by the National Land Commission (Tudi Weiyuan Hui) for 1.75 million rural households suggest that a quarter of all households were landless in the 1930s. Utilizing household income estimates collected as part of the same survey, Loren Brandt and Barbara Sands (1992) put the Gini coefficient for rural inequality of per capita household income in the vicinity of 0.40. (The Gini coefficient is a commonly used measure of inequality, which is equal to zero when there is perfect equality, and equal to one if one individual receives all of the income or possesses all of the wealth.) By comparison, the Gini coefficient for land, also measured on a per capita household basis, was around 0.65 to 0.70.

For the entire economy, inequality was probably higher, but with only 10 to 12 percent of the population living in cities and the portion of GDP going to urban residents twice this, at most, there is an obvious upper limit on how high inequality may have been. Charles Roll (1980) argues that wages received by individuals working in factories and the service sector—the bulk of the population in the cities—were in fact tightly linked to opportunity costs in the farm sector. Examples can be provided of Chinese families in the cities that enjoyed enormous wealth, but back-of-the-envelope calculations by Brandt and Sands suggest a Gini coefficient for the entire economy no higher than 0.45. This is high by international comparison, but on par with current estimates for China, which are discussed in more detail below.

There are no estimates of poverty in China in the 1930s using, for example, the World Bank's popular one dollar per day per capita. But one stark reminder of the low absolute standard of living for a significant portion of the Chinese population is George Barclay et al.'s (1976) estimate of average life expectancy in rural China, which they put at only twenty-four years.

LIVING STANDARDS UNDER THE PEOPLE'S REPUBLIC, 1949–1978

The standard of living in China benefited from the end of nearly a decade and a half of hostilities in 1949, and then rapid economic recovery in the early 1950s. Even with the huge economic setback associated with the Great Leap Forward (1958–1960), and a loss of life estimated to be upward of twenty-five to thirty million, the Chinese economy still managed to grow in per capita terms at an annual rate of nearly 4 percent over this thirty-year period. Nonetheless, a case can be made that many of the gains registered over this period in the standard of living of the People's Republic of China (PRC), especially in such indicators as life expectancy, can be attributed as much to a new set of institutions that achieved a more equal distribution of society's output as to economic growth that increased the size of the pie on a per capita basis.

In the countryside, where more than 80 percent of China's population lived, land reform followed by the collectivization of agriculture in the mid-1950s contributed locally to a highly egalitarian distribution of income and consumption that significantly benefited the poor (Roll 1980). Equality at this level was reinforced by the introduction of and expansion in the collective provision of basic health services and education. In most areas, enrollment in primary school became nearly universal, and by the late 1970s was probably slightly in excess of 90 percent.

In the cities, the socialization of industry and trade, the establishment of an egalitarian wage system, investment in public health and sanitation, and "public" provision of education, housing, and medical care, often through an individual's *danwei* or unit, played a role similar to that of the new collective institutions in the countryside. Any differences in income that did emerge in the cities were further dampened by the rationing of important consumer durables and key food items, such as grain.

Maddison's estimates suggest that per capita GDP rose significantly over this period. Only a small amount of this growth likely translated into improvements in incomes and personal consumption, especially after 1957. Estimates of per capita consumption of major consumer items reported by Nicholas Lardy (1984) show, for example, a decline between 1957 and 1978 in grain and vegetable consumption that was only modestly offset by increases in consumption of pork and cloth. Throughout much of the

1960s and 1970s, the Chinese economy was plagued by rising inefficiency and falling productivity growth. Growth rates were only maintained by allocating an increasing proportion of GDP to investment; overall, the share of GDP going to consumption fell, and per capita consumption levels languished.

E. B. Vermeer (1982) has suggested that, on the eve of economic reform in 1978, average personal consumption levels in the countryside were probably similar to those in the 1930s. Chris Bramall (1989) has made a similar finding for rural Sichuan. Charles Roll (1980) and Thomas Rawski (1982) argue the same for urban China. This behavior does not preclude improvement in the standard of living on other margins, such as infant mortality, life expectancy, and educational attainment. At the national level, estimates compiled by Andrew Mason and Wang Feng (2008) show a rise in life expectancy from 42.2 for males and 45.6 for females in 1950 to 66.5 for males and 69.4 for females in 1982. Over the same period, infant mortality fell by nearly a factor of four. Using the PRC's 2000 population census, Emily Hannum and her coauthors (2008) document a fall in the percentage of the population without formal education from 51 percent for men and 88 percent for women in the oldest age cohort of eighty and above, to 2 percent for men and 4 percent for women among people twenty-five to twenty-nine years old. On the other hand, rates of lower-secondary and above attainment increased from 12 percent for men and 2 percent for women among the eighty and above cohort, to 78 percent for men and 68 percent for women in the younger cohort. The keys to reconciling these two contrasting pictures are the more egalitarian institutions described above and investment in basic public goods in both the cities and the countryside.

SOURCES OF INEQUALITY IN THE PRE-1978 PERIOD

A new set of socialist institutions helped to reduce differences between individuals and households at the local level, and likely reduced overall inequality. Still, significant differences in the standard of living persisted in China, especially between the urban and rural populations. China's development strategy discriminated against agriculture and the rural sector in many ways and had a marked pro-urban, pro-industry bias (Naughton 1995). For example, prices received by agricultural collectives for grain and other farm produce were kept artificially low as part of a policy of extracting "forced" savings out of the countryside to help finance state investment. Moreover, much of this investment was directed toward industry and the cities rather than agriculture and the countryside. These policies helped to maintain levels of welfare in the countryside well below those enjoyed by favored urban residents. Elements of this bias persist today.

There are few estimates of the urban-rural gap for the pre-1978 period, and those that have been made are hampered by incomplete information on a number of important components of income—for example, income earned by rural households from small private plots, and the value of in-kind subsidies and transfers in the cities. Thomas Rawski (1982) estimates that per capita incomes may have differed by a factor of 3 to 4, excluding the value of urban subsidies households received, and may have been as high as 6 to 1 with urban subsidies added in. Of course, the rationing of key consumer goods in cities during this period implies that differences in actual consumption were much smaller, and a significant component of the differences in income simply translated into much higher per capita accumulated savings in cities. Nonetheless, huge differences in living standards between the countryside and cities explain the household registration system and the tight restrictions the government imposed on migration between the countryside and the cities in China over this period.

Regional differences in the countryside may have also widened. The Maoist policy of local self-sufficiency in grain production disrupted historical patterns of specialization in farming, and forced many localities to reduce production in more lucrative cash crops and sidelines in favor of increases in cultivated area in grain (Lardy 1983). The policy was especially costly in poorer areas. These disparities were reinforced by restrictions on migration, as well as a policy of fiscal decentralization after 1957 that limited the amount of redistribution between rich and poor rural areas. Significant differences emerged in the pre-1978 period in local expenditure on public goods, as well as investment in commune- and brigade-run enterprises. By the late 1970s, upward of 250 to 300 million individuals living in rural China found themselves below China's own stark poverty line. Among the poorest and most highly concentrated of these populations were those living in the central and southwest parts of the North China Plain, the northwestern Loess Plateau, the Yunnan-Guizhou Plateau, and the Northwest Guangxi Mountains (Vermeer 1982).

In the cities, regional differences may have narrowed. As part of China's Third Front development strategy in the 1960s and 1970s, upward of 80 to 90 percent of capital formation in industry was directed toward the less developed and poorer cities in the interior. This likely helped to reduce income differences between China's historically richer coastal urban centers and those in inland areas.

POST-1978

The onset of economic reform in the late 1970s had a profound impact on economic growth and the standard of living in China (Brandt and Rawski 2008). These reforms originated in the agriculture sector and marked a return to family farming after nearly a quarter of a century of collectivized agriculture. The boom in agriculture production, combined with the rapid growth of off-farm nonagricultural opportunities, had a sizeable and immediate impact on average incomes and consumption levels. With nearly 80 percent of the population living in the countryside, the effect was especially pronounced in rural households, and these reforms were instrumental in quickly pulling a third or more of China's poorest rural households above the poverty line.

Since the late 1970s, reforms have spread to nearly every corner of the economy, and helped to sustain rates of per capita growth in GDP in the vicinity of 8 percent annually. By the wonders of compounding, this growth has translated into an eightfold increase in average per capita incomes, with growth in per capita consumption slightly less. This growth also underlies the sharp reduction in the percentage of the population living in poverty, as well as the rapid narrowing in the gap in material consumption between China and the more advanced countries.

There were also marked improvements in other measures of the standard of living. Estimates compiled by Andrew Mason and Wang Feng (2008) show that between 1982 and 2000 life expectancy for both males and females rose by five years to 71.0 and 74.8, respectively. Infant mortality also continued to fall, and by 2000 was 20.8 per 1,000 live births compared to 36.5 in 1982. By comparison, the 2000 infant mortality rate was 5.8 in the European Union and only 2.9 in Hong Kong. Estimates reported by China's Ministry of Education also show rising school enrollment rates: Between 1980 and 1998, the percentage of school-age children enrolled in primary schools rose from 93.9 to 98.9 percent, while the percentage of primary-school graduates entering junior high increased from 75.9 percent to 94.3 percent. Since the late 1990s, university enrollment has also exploded.

Although inequality fell early in the reform period, there are numerous indications of a reversal in this trend in the case of consumption and income inequality in China (Ravallion and Chen Shaohua 2007). Official estimates using survey data from China's National Bureau of Statistics suggest a Gini coefficient in 2001 of 0.45 and slightly lower, 0.40, if cost-of-living differences between localities are factored in. By comparison, both measures were in the vicinity of 0.30 in the late 1970s. Academic opinion, however, is that estimates for later years are probably too low and exclude both high-income households at the top and low-income households at the bottom. The actual Gini coefficient is probably between 0.45 and 0.50, implying levels of inequality higher than those of the 1930s. Rising inequality has become a major concern for the Chinese leadership.

Much is often made of the role of rising interregional differences as well the gap between urban and rural households in China's inequality, but the contribution of these sources to the rapid rise in inequality may be much less than commonly believed (Benjamin et al. 2008). Moreover, even the highest estimates of the urban-rural gap are significantly lower than estimates for the period prior to economic reform. The migration of nearly 150 million people, much of it rural to urban, as well a growing interprovincial trade, have likely played an important equalizing role.

Much more important is the rising inequality between neighbors. In rural areas, this increase can be tied to differences in the ability of households to take full advantage of emerging sources of nonagricultural income and the laggard growth of farming income, especially beginning in the mid-1990s. In the cities, on the other hand, a decline in the role of subsidies and entitlements such as housing and health care, an increase in wage inequality related to labor-market and enterprise reform, and the effect of the restructuring of state-owned enterprises on some cohorts and households through layoffs have all played a part in widening the income distribution. Endemic corruption also likely skews the distribution of the benefits of economic growth. More generally, in urban and rural areas alike, there has been lingering and possibly rising inequality in overall educational achievement, the impact of which has been exacerbated by rapidly rising returns to education in the labor market. The causal relationship between incomes and education can be tricky to sort out, but the experience of other countries is that both of these trends may be a portent of rising income inequality in the future.

SEE ALSO *Poverty; Social Policy Programs.*

BIBLIOGRAPHY

Allen, Robert C., Jean-Pascal Bassino, Ma Debin, et al. Wages, Prices, and Living Standards in China, Japan, and Europe, 1738–1925. Working Paper No. 316. Department of Economics, Oxford University, 2007.

Barclay, George W., Ansley J. Coale, Michael A. Stoto, and James Trussell. A Reassessment of the Demography of Traditional Rural China. *Population Index* 42 (1976): 606–635.

Benjamin, Dwayne, Loren Brandt, John Giles, and Wang Sangui. Income Inequality during China's Transition. In *China's Great Economic Transformation*, eds. Loren Brandt and Thomas G. Rawski, 729–775. New York: Cambridge University Press, 2008.

Bramall, Chris. *Living Standards in Sichuan, 1931–1978.* London: Contemporary China Institute, School of Oriental and Asian Studies, University of London, 1989.

Brandt, Loren, and Barbara Sands. Land Concentration and Income Distribution in Republican China. In *Chinese History in Economic Perspective*, eds. Thomas G. Rawski and Lillian M. Li, 179–206. Berkeley: University of California Press, 1992.

Brandt, Loren, and Thomas G. Rawski, eds. *China's Great Economic Transformation.* New York: Cambridge University Press, 2008.

Fukao Kyoji, Ma Debin, and Yuan Tangjun. Real GDP in Pre-War East Asia: A 1934–36 Benchmark Purchasing Power Comparison with the U.S. *Review of Income and Wealth* 53, 3 (2007): 503–537.

Hanley, Susan, and Yamamura Kozo. *Economic and Demographic Change in Preindustrial Japan,* 1600–1868. Princeton, NJ: Princeton University Press, 1978.

Hannum, Emily, Jere Behrman, Wang Meiyan, and Liu Jihong. Education in the Reform Era. In *China's Great Economic Transformation,* eds. Loren Brandt and Thomas G. Rawski, 215–249. New York: Cambridge University Press, 2008.

Lardy, Nicholas. *Agriculture in China's Modern Economic Development.* New York: Cambridge University Press, 1983.

Lardy, Nicholas. Consumption and Living Standards in China, 1978–1983. *China Quarterly* 100 (1984): 849–865.

Lee, James, and Cameron Campbell. *Fate and Fortune in Rural China: Social Organization and Population Behavior in Liaoning, 1774–1873.* New York: Cambridge University Press, 1997.

Li Bozhong. *Agricultural Development in Jiangnan, 1620–1850.* New York: St. Martin's Press, 1998.

Liu, T. C., and K. C. Yeh. *The Economy of the Chinese Mainland: National Income and Economic Development, 1933–1959.* Princeton, NJ: Princeton University Press, 1965.

Ma Debin. Economic Growth in the Lower Yangzi. *Journal of Economic History* 68, 2 (2008): 355–392.

Maddison, Angus. *Chinese Economic Performance in the Long Run.* Paris: Organization for Economic Cooperation and Development, 1998.

Maddison, Angus. *The World Economy: A Millennial Perspective.* Paris: Organization for Economic Cooperation and Development, 2001.

Mason, Andrew, and Wang Feng. The Demographic Factor in China's Transition. In *China's Great Economic Transformation,* eds. Loren Brandt and Thomas G. Rawski, 136–166. New York: Cambridge University Press, 2008.

Morgan, Stephen. Economic Growth and the Biological Standard of Living in China, 1880–1930. *Economic and Human Biology* 2, 2 (2004): 197–217.

Naughton, Barry. *Growing out of the Plan: Chinese Economic Reform, 1978–1993.* New York: Cambridge University Press, 1995.

Pomeranz, Kenneth. *The Great Divergence: China, Europe, and the Making of the Modern World Economy.* Princeton, NJ: Princeton University Press, 2001.

Ravallion, Martin, and Chen Shaohua. China's (Uneven) Progress against Poverty. *Journal of Development Economics* 82, 1 (2007): 1–42.

Rawski, Thomas. The Simple Arithmetic of Chinese Income Distribution. *Keizai Kenkyu* 33,1 (January 1982): 12-26.

Rawski, Thomas. *Economic Growth in Prewar China.* Berkeley: University of California Press, 1989.

Roll, Charles R. *The Distribution of Rural Incomes in China: A Comparison of the 1930s and the 1950s.* New York: Garland, 1980.

Vermeer, E. B. Income Differentials in Rural China. *China Quarterly* 89 (1982): 1–33.

Wong, R. Bin. *China Transformed: Historical Change and the Limits of the European Experience.* Ithaca, NY: Cornell University Press, 1997.

Loren Brandt

STARS (*XINGXING*) PAINTING GROUP, 1979–1983

The Stars Painting Group (*Xingxing huahui*) is often considered the first unofficial art group to openly challenge Communist Party arts policies and practices in the period after the Cultural Revolution. While recent research suggests that they were just one of many such unofficial groups, and perhaps not the very earliest, there is no doubt that they attracted the greatest media attention, and thus had the greatest long-term impact.

The first Stars exhibition (*xingxing meizhan*), which was unofficial and unapproved, was hung outdoors in the yard adjacent to the east wing of the National Art Museum of China (then called the China Art Gallery, (Zhongguo Meishuguan) in Beijing on September 27, 1979, just before the opening of the National Art Exhibition inside the same gallery. Twenty-three artists participated, displaying 150 artworks on a 40-yard-long stretch of the museum's iron fence. The works included oil paintings, ink paintings, pen drawings, woodblock prints, and sculptures in various modernist styles.

THE FIRST STARS EXHIBITION (SEPTEMBER TO DECEMBER 1979)

Although different artists recall the events slightly differently, the participants Huang Rui (b. 1952) and Wang Keping (b. 1949) agree that the Stars Exhibition aimed to demonstrate that art could be made outside the official art establishment, and that the exhibitors were artists despite their lack of recognition by the state. Under the institutional system of art in the People's Republic of China (PRC) at that time, the Stars Group had no professional or social stature and no authorization to organize an exhibition in an official gallery. Nevertheless, they were activists eager to be the very first group to hold an unofficial exhibition without formal approval, thereby drawing enormous attention and making the point that art was for all the people. The organizers intended to display their artworks from September 27 to October 3, 1979, to coincide with the Fifth National Art Exhibition held in the China Art Gallery. The audience for their event included other artists from unofficial art groups, art students particularly from the attached middle school of the Central Academy of Fine Arts (Zhongyang meishu xueyuan) and certain curious and initially supportive government officials. Among those supporters from literary and artistic circles were Liu Xun (1923–2007), vice chairman of the Beijing Artists Association (Beijing meishujia xiehui) and Jiang Feng (1910–1982), chairman of the Chinese Artists Association (Zhongguo meishujia xiehui). The first day of the exhibition was deemed a success, and the exhibition was later reviewed in the party organ *Meishu* (Art) by the art critic Li Xianting (b. 1949) who was then the reporter of *Meishu*. The exhibition may be seen as marking the emergence of modernist Chinese art after more than ten years of strict art censorship during the Cultural Revolution.

The police intervened when the Stars Group began hanging their artworks on the fence on the second day, September 28. In response, the artists drafted two letters of protest, one of which they posted on the Xidan democracy wall and the other at the exhibition site. Liu Xun (himself a painter) agreed to let them continue their exhibition in a space at Beihai Park, the Huafang Studio, in mid-October, but representatives of unofficial journals then on the ascendant urged the Stars to fight for their rights rather than compromise. Although the artists were divided on the issue, the more radical among them prevailed. Thus, despite Liu Xun's attempt to negotiate with the Stars on September 30, they demanded an official apology from the authorities and threatened to demonstrate if it had not arrived by the morning of the October 1 National Day holiday. Having received no apology, they assembled at the Xidan democracy wall on October 1. Ma Desheng (b. 1952) and representatives of the unofficial journals gave speeches. Over 1,000 demonstrators, only a few of whom were Star Group artists, started the march from Chang'an Avenue, holding banners reading "Maintain the constitution" on the front and "Demand political democracy, demand artistic freedom" on the back. After the police obstructed them at Liubukou, the crowd dispersed, and only around twenty people remained in the demonstration. Instructed by the police to change their route, they continued to march to the Municipal Committee Headquarters, where representatives of the different groups presented speeches. An official at the compound received their letters of protest, and the authorities then declared the rally and demonstration over. Various spectators were attracted along the way, including overseas students, foreign specialists, and diplomatic personnel. As the Stars protest was raised with other political issues, it drew foreign press attention and suddenly made the Stars Exhibition a spectacle. This protest for freedom of artistic expression was seen by some as unprecedented in the history of the PRC.

Despite their earlier radical position, the Stars Group resumed their first exhibition in an official venue at Beihai Park, from November 23 to December 2, 1979. There were 31 artists with 170 artworks. A seminar on November 30 led to a contentious debate between the Stars Group and the New China News Agency (Xinhuashe) concerning the foreign press reports of the Stars Group as dissident, underground, and rebellious. This quasi-official exhibition, a continuation of the unofficial one at the park, signified success in the artists' fight for a formal exhibition space and recognition for their artworks. The total attendance at the exhibition was estimated at 20,000.

LATER EXHIBITIONS

In summer 1980 the Stars Painting Group, by then formally registered in the Beijing Municipal Artists Association, applied for its next exhibition through Jiang Feng. The second official Stars exhibition was held at the China Art Gallery from August 24 to September 7, 1980, with total attendance estimated to be over 80,000. Before the exhibition opened the group enjoyed support from two officials, Liu Xun, who had taken charge of the Beijing Municipal Artists Association, and Jiang Feng. This exhibition effectively marked the end of their group activities in China.

The Stars tried in vain to organize a memorial activity near the China Art Gallery in 1981, but it was banned. Three of the group's members, Huang Rui, Ma Desheng, and Wang Keping, planned to hold an exhibition in the Beijing Jixing Elementary School from August 7 to August 14, 1983, but it too was banned. In November 1984 the members Yan Li (b. 1954), Yang Yiping (b. 1947), and Ma Desheng planned a painting exhibition in Beijing that was cancelled by the authorities one day before its opening. Most of their major events since that time have been outside mainland China and have been retrospective exhibitions in Hong Kong, Taibei, and Paris in 1989, and in Tokyo in 1993 and 2000. A retrospective also was held in Beijing in 2007.

THE STARS ARTISTS

The backgrounds of the members of the Stars Group were diverse. Most were self-taught artists who had worked in factories during the Cultural Revolution, but some came from families that had enjoyed high status before or during the Cultural Revolution and thus understood the ins and outs of Chinese politics. Some members resumed academic training after the Cultural Revolution. Bao Pao graduated from the Sculpture Department in the Central Academy of Fine Arts; Bo Yun (b. 1948) graduated from the Art History Department in the Central Academy of Fine Arts; Ai Weiwei (b. 1957) also undertook formal study at Central Academy of Drama (Zhongyang xiju xueyuan). Shao Fei (b. 1954) was a professional artist in the Beijing Painting Academy (Beijing huayuan); Yin Guangzhong (b. 1945) was an artist in the Guiyang Painting Academy (Guiyang huayuan). He Baosen (b. 1938) taught in Beijing Workers' Cultural Center and Central

Academy of Arts and Crafts (now the College of Art at Tsinghua University), and taught two of the main organizers of the Stars exhibitions, Huang Rui and Ma Desheng.

Some group members moved abroad in the 1980s, which contributed to the group's disbanding. Wang Keping (b. 1949), renowned for his sculptures with vivid sociopolitical messages, moved to Paris in 1984 and remains focused on making wooden sculptures of the body. Ma Desheng, who wrote poetry and drew illustrations for the underground literary journal *Jintian* (Today) in addition to making woodblock prints for the Stars exhibitions, moved to Switzerland in 1985, then to Paris in 1986, New York in 1989, and back to Paris in 1994. He continues to write poetry and create artworks in different media. Li Shuang (b. 1957) was jailed from September 1981 to July 1983 in Beijing for her relationship with a French diplomat. She left for Paris in December 1983 and continues to create oil paintings. Qu Leilei (b. 1950) moved to London in 1986. His work focuses on the Chinese ink painting tradition and the subject of memory. A few of the Stars have returned to China after living abroad for some time. Huang Rui left for Osaka in 1984 and returned to China in 2002. He has been active in organizing retrospective group exhibitions abroad and creating artworks in different media. Ai Weiwei left for the United States in 1981 and returned to China in 1993. He has multiple roles: artist, curator and juror in the contemporary Chinese art field. Yan Li became a freelance artist and writer before leaving for the United States in 1985. He established the Chinese-language poetry journal *Yi hang* (First Line) in New York in 1987. He wrote extensively and published four novels in the 1990s, and continued to paint in a surrealist style. He lives in Shanghai. Shao Fei (b. 1954), who moved abroad in the 1980s and returned to China in the 1990s, addresses female and national themes in ink and oils. Mao Lizi (Zhang Zhunli, b. 1950) left for Paris in 1990 and worked as a guest teacher in an art institute for a year. He now lives in Beijing. His work portrays everyday objects in a meticulous manner. Some Stars artists continued their artistic careers in China throughout this period. Yin Guangzhong, a native of Guiyang, has been active in creating pottery masks, oil paintings, and prints in his southwestern hometown. Yang Yiping has developed a nostalgic style of painting figures and scenery of the revolutionary era in gray tonalities. Bo Yun (Li Yongcun, b. 1948) has been teaching Western art theory in the Tsinghua University College of Arts (formerly the Central Academy of Arts and Crafts) and creating artworks in various media. Gan Shaocheng (1948–1996), who participated in the Stars exhibitions of 1979 and 1980, as well as the Stars demonstration in 1979, set up his own sculpture studio in June 1995. He died in a car accident in 1996, leaving behind a lifetime's work of 50 paintings, 250 wood sculptures, and 11 stone sculptures.

In the end, the real significance of the Stars Group may have been their success in breaking through the official-unofficial boundary, and in fostering the perception of young artists who followed that organizing artists groups was an effective way to claim their artistic freedom. Many artists of the '85 New Wave movement saw themselves as inheritors of the Stars.

SEE ALSO *New Wave Movement, '85.*

BIBLIOGRAPHY

Blaine, Julien, ed. *Poemes & art en Chine, les "non-officiels." Doc(k)s* 114f no. 41 (winter 1981).

Blaine, Julien, and Anna Gipouloux. The Stars: A New Art Movement in China. Trans. H. F. Ashworth. *Libération,* (September 21, 1981).

Demand for Artistic Freedom: Stars 20 Years. Tokyo: Tokyo Gallery, 2000.

Fok, Siu Har Silvia. The Development of the Stars Artists, 1979–2000. Masters thesis, University of Hong Kong, 2002.

Fok, Siu Har Silvia (Huo Shaoxia). Xingxing yishujia: zhongguo daidang yishu de xianfeng 1979–2000 [The Stars artists: pioneers in contemporary Chinese art, 1979–2000]. Taibei: Artists Publishing, 2007.

Hui Ching-shuen, ed. *Stars 10 Years.* Hong Kong: Hanart 2, 1989.

Koppel-Yang, Martina. *Semiotic Warfare: The Chinese Avant-garde, 1979–1989, a Semiotic Analysis.* Hong Kong: Timezone 8, 2003.

The Stars 15 Years. Tokyo: Tokyo Gallery, 1993.

Silvia Siu Har Fok

STATE CULT

All the ritual activities performed in the name of the Qing dynasty (1644–1912), whether intended for the welfare of the emperor's sole person or family or for the entire empire and all its subjects, were predicated on a shared cosmology and a common empirewide ritual culture. The emperor, as the son of heaven, gained his legitimacy from his ancestors, who had been promoted as heavenly deities. He maintained his legitimacy by properly performing rituals to his ancestors and to other stellar deities. The state governed by "instructing the people through the worship of the gods" (*yi shendao shejiao*), therefore authorizing, controlling, and presiding (in theory) over all types of worship. The emperor enjoyed absolute religious authority, deciding on the promotion of the gods and the orthodox or heterodox nature of any teaching—Confucian, Buddhist, Daoist, or otherwise.

COURT AND STATE

Religion and ritual around the Qing emperors hinged on a fundamental opposition between state ritual and court ritual. State ritual was mandated by the Statutes (*Da Qing huidian*) and was minutely described in various normative texts. Court ritual was the private domain of the emperor and his family, and was neither mandated by any code nor consigned into official record. Court ritual was much less constrained by rules than state ritual, and much more inclusive and pluralistic.

The emperors' personal interest in religious traditions varied, some being more inclined toward Tibeto-Mongol Buddhism (the Qianlong emperor established the label *Lamaism*, a problematic term that has stuck), others more toward Daoism or Chinese Buddhism, notably until the long Cixi regency. A highly petrified form of "shamanism" was also practiced in order to maintain a Manchu ethnic identity. But it is difficult to ascertain what exactly the emperors believed; whatever their beliefs, court ritual remained pluralistic and cumulative by nature.

Daoist, Confucian, Chinese Buddhist, Tibeto-Mongol Buddhist, and shamanist services continued to be performed at court up to 1911. This was a costly affair, with dozens of full-time salaried priests for each of these various ritual traditions (many more priests were called from Beijing temples for the largest celebrations). Many temples, altars, and shrines were maintained within the palace, around it in the Imperial City, and in the various parks around Beijing. The dwindling of court revenues from the 1830s onward necessitated reducing the scale of the intense yearly program of rituals, but the rituals remained impressive nonetheless up to the end. The major junctures in the court's liturgical calendar—notably the emperor's birthday, as well as funerals and times of emergency (natural disasters or wars)—were marked by simultaneous Chinese Buddhist, Tibeto-Mongol Buddhist, and Daoist services in many temples.

THE REGISTER OF SACRIFICES

State cults were more narrowly Confucian in liturgy and theology than court rituals, even though Daoists and Buddhists

Temple of Heaven, Beijing, constructed in 1420. *According to Chinese custom, the power of an emperor descends from the spirits of his predecessors. In order to maintain legitimacy, emperors paid special attention to honoring the deceased, following proscribed rituals at specially constructed temples, such as the Temple of Heaven, used during the Ming and Qing dynasties.* © **WANG SONG/XINHUA PRESS/ CORBIS**

were involved in certain marginal aspects. State cults were divided into three tiers. The top tier (*shangsi*) involved the emperor himself performing as chief sacrificer, and was aimed at the highest deities protecting the emperor and the empire: heaven, earth, and other stellar deities. These sacrifices, performed with the help of Daoist (up to 1742) and Confucian ritual specialists, happened once a year, such as the famed sacrifice to Heaven on Winter solstice. Ordinary folk were in no way involved in these very sacred, elaborate rituals.

The second tier (*zhongsi*) involved sacrifices performed in the capital city, with the emperor delegating an official to perform in his name. Second-tier sacrifices were aimed at the most revered saints of official religion, such as Confucius (with two sacrifices a year, on the first *ding* days of the second and eighth month), Guandi, or Wenchang (with one sacrifice each on their birthday). The lower tier (*qunsi*), by far the largest, encompassed all local gods recognized by the state and for whom sacrifice was authorized. At this level one found both local heroes and Confucian worthies, and local gods with their festivals and a history of exorcist and spirit-possession practices (occasionally disguised under more orthodox pretenses). Local officials had to be either present or represented by another official during the yearly sacrifice of each of these gods (as a rule, on the god's birthday), but the temples were left to local communities or to clerics to manage, and usually received no public funding. The list of local gods recognized by the state in each district (the list can be found in the relevant local gazetteer, *difangzhi*) could run to several tens; adding that to those temples (Confucius temple; City God, Chenghuang temple) with which local officials had close contact, means that officials had to visit temples and officiate at sacrifices several times a month on average.

The process of canonization, whereby local cults were integrated into state sacrifices—that is, listed in the register of sacrifices (*sidian*), almost always in the lower tier—was a major aspect of imperial religious policy. The *sidian* also specified the details of the liturgy, including the texts of the prayers and the details of the offerings (notably the sacrificial animals; only Heaven and Confucius received beef, the other gods receiving various amounts of pork and lamb, or in a few cases of Buddhist or Daoist gods, no meat at all), putting each detail in its place in the larger cosmological hierarchy. The list and the ranks were continually changing. Many local cults were granted canonizations (inscription in the *sidian*) in the wake of the Qing victory against the Taipings in 1864, but the flow of grants had been reduced as early as 1875. In 1904 a string of requests by provincial governors met with a blanket rebuttal by the Ministry of Rites, which made it clear that it would no longer deal with local cults. An important symbolic link between the state and the religious organization of local society was thus severed. The ministry's decision should be understood in a larger context where prepara-

tions for a constitutional state marginalized the state rituals, a progressive desacralization in the conceptions of the state since the nineteenth century, and a sharp decline in ritualistic studies among Confucians made issues such as the canonization of local cults irrelevant to most central government officials.

SEE ALSO *Cosmology; Emperors, 1800–1912.*

BIBLIOGRAPHY

Naquin, Susan. *Peking: Temples and City Life, 1400–1900.* Berkeley: University of California Press, 2000.

Rawski, Evelyn S. *The Last Emperors: A Social History of Qing Imperial Institutions.* Berkeley: University of California Press, 1998.

Vincent Goossaert

STATE-OWNED ENTERPRISES

The state-owned enterprise (SOE) is a peculiar institutional and organizational form in the industrial sector of socialist economic systems. Typically, and certainly in China, the agricultural sector has been collectively owned. However, the ownership regime is insufficient to fully describe organizational patterns and performance, because state ownership can be embedded in different types of economic systems. This is especially important to understanding the role of SOEs in China, which have faced substantial changes in the systemic environment since the mid-twentieth century.

THE RISE AND DECLINE OF THE SOE

In the early years, SOEs emerged in part from the direct takeover by the Chinese Communist Party (CCP) of the nationalized industries of the Republican era and of foreign-owned companies, in particular Japanese companies. During the 1950s, the scope of SOEs rapidly expanded due to the Soviet-aided buildup of a modern industrial sector, which was accompanied by the establishment of a central-planning apparatus and by further nationalizations, in particular of medium-scale companies. By the end of the 1950s, SOEs had become the dominant institutional form in China's industrial sector, and this form was transferred into the urban collective sector when these entities were integrated into the command economy.

During the 1960s and 1970s, SOEs also became the main social-structural unit in urban society. At the heyday of Maoism, an SOE would not only control the economic aspects of the life of its employees (such as workplace assignments or the allotment of ration coupons), but would interfere with their private lives (e.g., marriage) and would

IRON RICE BOWL

The term *iron rice bowl* (*tiefanwan*) refers to the system of lifetime employment and comprehensive social security in Chinese state-owned enterprises (SOEs) and other forms of government employment that emerged in the late 1950s and was dismantled step by step after the launch of urban industrial reforms in 1984. It was complementary to the *danwei* (unit) system in social organization and to the system of household registration, and was created to stabilize the organizational core of the industrialization strategy of the Chinese Communist Party. With the iron rice bowl, state-employed workers emerged as a privileged stratum in Chinese society, although they faced tight constraints in wage policy that aimed at maximizing accumulation in state industry.

In fact, the iron rice bowl did not equalize living conditions across China, even within the SOE sector. Depending on the administrative status of a SOE, the actual quality of the social services in a unit varied widely. Because access to the scarcer, more valuable consumption goods was very limited, the system allowed for differentation in living standards through clientelism and political favoritism. In this sense, the iron rice bowl boils down to an employment guarantee. This guarantee slowly transformed many SOEs into organizations tightly integrated by relationships of clients and even kin, as many workers married within the unit, and the

informal practice of sons inheriting work from their fathers prevailed.

The iron rice bowl was broken by a series of measures beginning in 1984. One was the devolution of organizational units into other forms of ownership, including forced employee buyouts and other types of organizational spin-offs, which effectively changed the claims to lifetime employment. Another was the practice of *xiagang* (layoff), by which employees effectively were laid off but formally were retained by the company, supported far below subsistence needs. Finally, the gradual development of labor contract law enabled SOEs to offer new forms of contracts without employment guarantees. All this changed the Chinese labor system into an almost free labor market with weak regulatory standards, because the system of unemployment benefits evolved in a regionally fragmented and incomplete fashion. In 2008 the promulgation of a new labor law reintroduced much stronger worker protections, including tighter constraints on layoffs.

BIBLIOGRAPHY

Whyte, Martin King, and William L. Parish. *Urban Life in Contemporary China*. Chicago: University of Chicago Press, 1984.

Carsten Herrmann-Pillath

exert tight political control. These features were summarized in the term *danwei* (work unit).

By the end of the 1970s, the SOE had become a closed social structure with many functions that went far beyond the core task of production. The lack of labor mobility further accentuated this closure. This supported a tendency countering the deprivation of formal employee rights, because paternalism also created interlocking interests between employees and leaders. For example, in Chinese SOEs of the 1980s, kinship ties greatly interfered with enterprise organization, as in the widespread informal practice of a son inheriting a workplace from his father.

In this systemic setting, the traditional SOE was operating with two primary goals: maximizing output and maximizing employment. SOE reforms were launched in 1984, mainly in two areas. First, the systemic framework underwent gradual changes, particularly in increasing the scope of market allocation and the entrepreneurial decision-making powers of the enterprise. Second, steps were taken to break up the high degree of vertical integration, especially in order to eliminate the burden of social services and of hidden unemployment

resulting from the lifelong-employment guarantee. The government exerted its ownership rights mainly via the "responsibility system," which was a system of contractual obligations between the enterprise, its general manager, and the supervisory government authority. Until the mid-1990s, these measures only contributed to a marginal improvement of SOE performance.

Thus, new major policy initiatives were adopted, the most important being a drive toward corporatization, which was described as a transition to a modern enterprise system, and the decision to focus government control on 500 to 1,000 larger-scale and key companies, a policy referred to as *zhua da fang xiao* (keep control of the big ones, let the small ones go). The legal basis for the corporatization drive was a new company law that was promulgated in 1993. This law provided a foundation for the gradual transformation of all SOEs into either joint-stock corporations or limited-liability companies. In such sectors as construction, this policy resulted in a major change in ownership structure: In 1995 there were only 613 companies listed in the "other" category of the *China Statistical*

Yearbook, against 7,531 SOEs; by 2007 this number had exploded to 49,294, compared to 5,319 SOEs. The policy also resulted in the emergence of a new kind of SOE, epitomized in the rise of global, internationally listed companies that pursue aggressive growth strategies. Today, there is a distinction between *state-owned* and *state-controlled* enterprises, with the latter referring to enterprises for which the government is the majority and controlling shareholder.

A large number of small and medium-scale SOEs underwent a privatization process, often via employee buyouts, with incumbent managers taking a leading role, thus realizing a model of insider control. The process was triggered by the concentration of inefficient, below-optimum-scale SOEs on the lower levels of government, which were facing hard budget constraints in the fiscal system and were thus motivated to get rid of loss-making enterprises. These efforts resulted in a substantial shift of operating goals regarding SOEs on the part of the superordinate governments: The employment goal was replaced by financial goals and local developmental goals. Even in the case of privatization, local governments continue to be stakeholders in the transformed SOEs, because a good economic performance ranks very high on the list of political priorities.

The gradual change in the role of SOEs is also reflected in structural changes in the Chinese economy (see Table 1). In 2007 traditional SOEs turned into ordinary players in Chinese industry, existing alongside other kinds of corporations. Only 9 percent of total industrial output was produced by traditional SOEs (another 10 percent was produced by joint-stock corporations). The SOE share of urban employment was 8.2 percent. However, SOEs still have a disproportionately large share of fixed assets, 15.5 percent, which reveals their strategic role in the Chinese economy. Further, there is considerable regional variation in the significance of SOEs, reflecting different historical backgrounds in Maoist development policies. For example, in

northeastern Liaoning Province, once an industrial heartland of China, the SOE sector was responsible for 44 percent of gross industrial output and 58.6 percent of total assets in 2007, whereas in southeastern Zhejiang Province, one of the newly emerging industrial powerhouses of the country, the respective shares were 12.6 and 15.6 percent. Most SOEs are still the larger (i.e., more capital-intensive) and often the leading companies in the Chinese economy. Thus, further improvement of SOE performance remains an important task. This came to the fore when the SOE sector emerged as a major obstacle to further reforming the Chinese banking sector after China's entry into the World Trade Organization in 2001. SOE need for credit refinancing and ongoing investment expansion was the most important single reason for the burden of bad credit in Chinese state banks.

REFORM AND RESTRUCTURING IN THE NEW MILLENNIUM

The Chinese SOE sector was very different from the SOE sector in other socialist economies, reflecting the fundamental differences between the Chinese planning system and Soviet-style central planning. These differences included the fragmented and regionalized structure of the system of superordinate government agencies, the looseness of mandatory plans, and the central role of bargaining and exchange among SOEs and other organizations.

After a wave of decentralization during the Great Leap Forward, the SOE ownership structure emerged as a complex system of assignments to regional authorities on different levels. These assignments were bolstered by informal rules that secured control rights resulting from investments in an SOE. Thus, SOEs were closely related to certain supervisory departments in the government, which minimally owned entitlements to control the enterprises, coalescing into a "regional property-rights system." As a result, SOEs manifested multifarious relations with different

---

National and sectoral shares of SOEs in employment, gross output, and fixed assets, 2007

	National	Industry	Construction	Domestic trade Wholesale	Retail
Number of units	n/a	3.0	8.6	13.1	9.8
Employment	22.0 (urban sector only)	8.2	15.0	26.8	9.3
Gross output	n/a	9.0	20.8	6.9 (total sales volume)	6.9 (total sales volume)
Fixed assets	28.2 (investment into social fixed assets)	15.5	25.8	n/a	n/a

All figures are percentage shares of the respective total.

SOURCE: Calculations by Carsten Herrmann-Pillath, based on data published in the *China Statistical Yearbook, 2008.*

Table 1

---

government agencies. Whereas such SOEs as large-scale energy producers were sometimes clearly assigned to one powerful government agency, many SOEs manifested the phenomenon of "multiple principals" or "many mothers-in-law"—that is, SOEs faced demands and orders from different government agencies, such as for-profit remittances from the finance bureau of the local government, procurement plans from the material-allocation bureau, and wage plans from the labor bureau. These different demands did not integrate into one coherent plan, so that production quotas had to be set so as to simultaneously match the directives of different principals. Thus, the typical SOE in China did not face tight production plans on the eve of reforms.

In other regards, SOEs manifested the characteristic features of a planned economy, such as the tendency toward vertical integration—that is, toward developing comprehensive production systems. Including most supplies under the control of an SOE was a strategy to increase plan certainty and autonomy from outside interference. This tendency also reflected the aforementioned trend toward organizational closure. This had important consequences for the behavior of factory directors and general managers: Far into the 1990s, many SOE managers actually maximized the interests of the collective, because their internal power position was built on their maintaining a paternalistic relation with employees. The increasing pressure of market competition, first through township and village enterprises (TVEs) in the 1980s and since the mid-1990s through foreign-investment enterprises (FIEs), enforced a breakup of this pattern of mutual interests, triggering a substantial change in the corporate culture of SOEs. Transitional phenomena in this process included the massive relocation of the workforce into spin-offs, which resulted from the strategy of breaking up vertically integrated companies.

Through the 1980s and 1990s, an important political strategy in the restructuring of the SOE sector was the establishment of enterprise groups. One major motivation was to overcome the obstacles to sectoral restructuring that resulted from the regional property-rights system and from the legacy of Maoist regional policies. A major weakness of the Chinese SOE sector was its low degree of industrial concentration and its dispersed sectoral structure, leading to a large number of enterprises operating without economies of scale. Enterprise groups were expected to support the restructuring by, for example, transforming small producers into specialized suppliers.

The crucial political step toward the completion of the transition of the SOE sector was the establishment of State Asset Supervision and Administration Commissions (SASACs) on different levels of government in 2003. An SASAC is intended to be an independent public body with the task of

operating and divesting state assets with the highest economic benefit. Typically, the SASAC would become a shareholder in a transformed SOE, both majority and minority, depending on the optimal strategy. On the central level, the SASAC keeps control of key industrial enterprises in sectors that have been identified by the government as leading sectors, such as energy, metals, telecommunications, and the automotive industry. However, the functioning of SASACs is plagued by intergovernmental conflicts of interest, especially with the Ministry of Finance. On the central level, the companies subordinate to the SASAC are often restructured former ministries and very large corporate holdings consisting of numerous dependent companies, which in turn may have a composite ownership structure.

The modern Chinese SOE is typically a listed company with limited liability and a standardized governance structure. It is highly centralized under the leadership of the chief executive officer and the board of directors. Government representatives dominate the board of directors, as the majority of the shares are not traded publicly. The network of stakeholders adds to this formal governance structure. For example, a central SOE might foster close relations with local government authorities, whose support it needs in case of site expansion. Employees have a weak voice in the SOE structure, although they are included in the supervisory board. Finally, the control of the *nomenklatura* by the CCP looms large over the careers of top executives. Beyond reform and restructuring, the role of the party committee in managing and supervising SOEs is a historical constant. All SOEs manifest a parallel organizational structure in terms of party cells and lead units at the top of the hierarchy. In traditional SOEs, the roles of the party secretary and the director were often fused. Corporatization of SOEs notwithstanding, the role of the CCP in economic life has not been weakened substantially, and may have become strengthened as a result of the co-optation of new social elites into the CCP, a development emerging as a major issue in further reforms of the corporate governance structure.

The future of SOEs depends on their ability to meet the challenge of globalization. Today, Chinese SOEs in banking and petrochemicals are already among the world's largest corporations. They have adopted modern management practices and even include foreign expertise in their top-level management. They enjoy substantial government support in the context of technology and industrial policy. They are likely to continue to be major players in the Chinese economy for the foreseeable future.

SEE ALSO *Labor.*

BIBLIOGRAPHY

Garnaut, Ross, Ligang Song, and Yang Yao. Impact and Significance of State-Owned Enterprise Restructuring in China. *China Journal* 55 (2006): 35–66.

Granick, David. *Chinese State Enterprises. A Regional Property Rights Analysis*. Chicago and London: Chicago University Press, 1990.

National Bureau of Statistics of the PRC. *China Statistical Yearbook 2008*. Beijing: China Statistics Press, 2008.

Naughton, Barry. *The Chinese Economy: Transitions and Growth*, chap. 13. Cambridge, MA: MIT Press, 2007.

Organization for Economic Cooperation and Development. *OECD Economic Surveys: China* (vol. 2005, no. 13), chap. 2. Paris: Author, 2005.

Tenev, Stoyan, Zhang Chunlin, and Loup Brefort. *Corporate Governance and Enterprise Reform in China: Building the Institutions of Modern Markets*. Washington, DC: World Bank and International Finance Corp., 2002.

Carsten Herrmann-Pillath

STATISTICS

Official statistics in China are compiled by the National Bureau of Statistics (NBS, Guojia Tongji Ju) and by other institutions with approval from the NBS. The NBS regularly publishes a wide range of statistical data in approximately two dozen statistical yearbooks. The prime publication is the comprehensive *China Statistical Yearbook*, published around October of each year with data through the previous year. It is preceded by a "Statistical Communiqué" in February and the *China Statistical Abstract* in May.

The data reported in the *China Statistical Yearbook* are available online at the NBS Web site, free of charge, from the 1996 issue. The Web site also has quarterly and monthly data on selected indicators since 2001 (since 2002 in English). The Chinese Web site provides yet further data, including data from recent censuses, as well as links to the statistics Web pages of other government organizations and provincial statistical bureaus. Provincial statistical bureaus, as well as a few municipal/prefectural statistical offices, issue their own statistical yearbooks and some also provide data online.

The coverage of statistical yearbooks is for many indicators limited to the previous year or to data since 1978. The NBS at regular intervals publishes compendia that go back to 1952 but cover only a limited set of indicators. The most recent volumes are *China Compendium of Statistics, 1949–2004* and *Data of Gross Domestic Product*, both comprising national and provincial data, with the latter limited to (revised) national income and product accounts data.

PRIOR TO THE REFORM PERIOD

The NBS was established in August 1952 as a successor to the statistics division of the Central Finance and Economics Commission, created in October 1949. Its immediate task was to coordinate statistical work at lower adminis-

trative levels (provinces and below), as well as within other central departments, in order to create a uniform nationwide reporting framework. Statistical bureaus at all administrative levels were to provide planning departments with the data needed to design five-year and annual plans and to supervise their implementation.

Statistical work was severely disrupted during the Great Leap Forward (especially in 1959–1961), as well as in the last ten years of Mao's rule (1966–1976). Nationwide data for 1967–1969, the beginning of the Cultural Revolution, were not compiled at the time (but only retrospectively), and the NBS was disbanded in late 1969. From May 1970, a limited reporting system was maintained by a newly created department of the State Planning Commission, but compilation of statistical data remained incomplete through 1977. The NBS was reestablished in March 1978. Personnel of the statistics administration at the county level and above numbered 200,000 in 1955, 7,000 in 1976, 16,000 in 1980, and approximately 90,000 in the early 2000s.

THE NATIONAL BUREAU OF STATISTICS DURING THE REFORM PERIOD

The NBS is an institution directly under the State Council, with a rank half a level below that of a ministry. It consists of a dozen functional departments (such as a national-income-accounts division), a dozen administrative facilities (such as a publishing house), and the national-survey-team headquarters. This headquarters maintains survey teams in approximately one-third of all counties and municipal- or county-level cities. The NBS exercises professional leadership over provincial statistical bureaus and provides guidance to statistical departments in close to 100 other central-government institutions (from which the NBS also receives data).

Statistical departments at all levels enjoy only limited independence. The Statistics Law of 1996 (a revision of the 1983 law) states, "The leaders of localities, government departments, or other units may not order or ask statistical departments and statistical personnel to change or falsify statistical data" (Article 7). While not mentioned in the law, key data compiled by a local statistical bureau need to be approved by the local government leader before they can be reported up to the next-higher-level statistical bureau, and the National Development and Reform Commission has access to NBS data before their publication. Hence, regular channels for political interference exist, and there can be little doubt that political considerations shape the work of statistical bureaus at all levels.

This became explicit when the NBS created the new category "state-owned and state-controlled enterprises" in response to Jiang Zemin's redefinition of public ownership in 1997, and when an NBS "work regulation" (of 1995) stated that the NBS was to implement "important decisions and instructions of the Chinese Communist Party Central Committee and the State Council." While the NBS regularly makes available to the public a large body of data, it also responds to discretionary requests of the central leadership and submits special reports to the offices of the Chinese Communist Party Central Committee and the State Council.

DATA COMPILATION METHODS

According to the revised Statistics Law of 1996, "Statistical investigation should collect and compile statistical material in regular census as a foundation; in routine sample surveys as a mainstay activity; and in required statistical reports, key investigations, and comprehensive analyses as supplemental activity."

The shift away from the traditional reporting system has been limited. Industrial enterprises that are either state-owned or have an independent accounting system and annual sales revenue in excess of RMB 5 million report directly to the statistical authority every month; this group of enterprises currently accounts for more than 90 percent of industrial value added, which in turn accounts for almost half of the gross domestic product (GDP). The largest 5,000 industrial enterprises send their data through an online reporting system to the NBS. Similar arrangements apply to other sectors of the economy.

NBS departments and survey teams conduct at least a dozen different types of regular surveys, ranging from agricultural-production surveys to household-income-and-expenditure surveys. Survey quality varies, and the data only gradually find their way into the compilation of major statistical indicators. For example, since 2004, price indexes obtained through surveys are used to deflate industrial-output value—an innovation over the previous practice of adjusting values by applying product-specific base-year prices.

A stable schedule of censuses is yet to emerge. The latest censuses are the fifth population census of 2000 (every ten years); the first economic census of 2003 (every five years, to cover the whole economy except agriculture), with implementation postponed to 2004 because of the outbreak of severe acute respiratory syndrome (SARS); the second agricultural census of 2006 (every ten years); and the second census of basic statistical units of 2001 (supposedly every five years). The tertiary-sector census (first conducted in 1993) and the industrial census (conducted for the third time in 1995) have been merged into the first economic census. Other government departments conduct their own statistical censuses or quasi censuses, examples being the first national census of the sources of environmental pollution by the State Environmental Protection Administration at the end of 2007, and the second

national survey of land use in 2007–2009 by the Ministry of Land and Resources.

DATA QUALITY

There is general agreement that data published at the time of the Great Leap Forward are problematic but that falsification of pre-reform statistical data was otherwise improbable (Perkins 1966). In the reform period, data compiled at lower levels of the statistical system are often considered to be of questionable quality, but the bias is ambiguous (Cai 2000). Thus, local leaders may face incentives to overreport to gain promotion or to underreport to avoid paying taxes, but most local data do not find their way into provincial or national statistics.

Thomas Rawski suspects significant falsification of GDP at the national level around 1998, but Carsten Holz (2003) argues that the evidence of data falsification is not compelling, and Nicholas Lardy argues that official GDP growth rates are confirmed by trends in related time series. Harry Wu and Angus Maddison question the quality of Chinese data in the long run. Wu created an alternative industrial-output series, and Maddison an alternative GDP series. Holz (2006) contests these alternative series. Internal consistency checks on GDP growth conducted via the expenditure approach to the calculation of GDP (Keidel 2001) or via the income approach do not yield systematically different results.

Chinese data come with a substantial margin of error. During the reform period the NBS has faced considerable challenges, such as rapid growth in the number of productive units outside the traditional reporting system and changes in statistical concepts and indicators (in particular, the adoption of the United Nations' System of National Accounts in 1993). The level of data accuracy is perhaps best captured by the size of the benchmark revisions to GDP after the 1993 tertiary-sector census and the 2004 economic census, revisions upward by 10 percent and 17 percent in those years respectively.

Official Chinese data are poorly understood when official explanations omit to provide a precise definition of a particular indicator, to report its coverage, or to point out statistical breaks. Consequently, a considerable literature has developed explaining specific Chinese data. A nonexhaustive list of areas and authors includes industry statistics (Holz and Lin 2001), energy statistics (Sinton and Fridley 2001), transport statistics (Huenemann 2001), household-income statistics (Bramall 2001), population statistics (Scharping 2001), migration and household-registration statistics (Chan and Liu 2001), unemployment statistics (Solinger), farm-labor statistics (Rawski and Mead 1998), rural-poverty statistics (Park and Wang 2001), and irrigation measures (Nickum 1995).

SEE ALSO *Central State Organs since 1949: State Council, Commissions, Ministries, and Bureaus; Cultural Revolution, 1966–1969; Economic Reform since 1978; Five-Year Plans; Labor: Unemployment; Rural Development, 1949–1978: Great Leap Forward.*

BIBLIOGRAPHY

Bramall, Chris. The Quality of China's Household Income Surveys. *China Quarterly*, no. 167 (September 2001): 689–705.

Cai Yongshun. Between State and Peasant: Local Cadres and Statistical Reporting in Rural China. *China Quarterly*, no. 163 (September 2000): 783–805.

Chan, Kam Wing, and Ta Liu. National Statistics on Internal Migration in China. *China Information* 15, 2 (2001): 75–113.

China Compendium of Statistics, 1949–2004 [Xin Zhongguo wushiwu nian tongji ziliao huibian]. Beijing: Zhongguo Tongji Chubanshe, 2005.

China Statistical Abstract [Zhongguo tongji zhaiyao]. Beijing: Zhongguo Tongji Chubanshe, 1984–.

China Statistical Yearbook [Zhongguo tongji nianjian]. Beijing: Zhongguo Tongji Chubanshe, 1981–. http://www.stats.gov.cn.

Dangdai Zhongguo de tongji shiye [Statistics in contemporary China]. Beijing: Zhongguo Shehui Kexue Chubanshe, 1990.

Data of Gross Domestic Product of China, 1952–2004 [Zhongguo guonei shengchan zongzhi hesuan lishi ziliao 1952–2004]. Beijing: Zhongguo Tongji Chubanshe, 2007.

Holz, Carsten A. "Fast, Clear, and Accurate": How Reliable Are Chinese Output and Economic Growth Statistics? *China Quarterly*, no. 173 (March 2003): 122–163.

Holz, Carsten A. China's Reform Period Economic Growth: How Reliable Are Angus Maddison's Estimates? *Review of Income and Wealth* 52, 1 (March 2006): 85–119.

Holz, Carsten A., and Yi-min Lin. Pitfalls of China's Industrial Statistics: Inconsistencies and Specification Problems. *China Review* 1, 1 (Fall 2001): 29–71.

Huenemann, Ralph W. Are China's Recent Transport Statistics Plausible? *China Economic Review* 12, 4 (2001): 368–372.

Keidel, Albert. China's GDP Expenditure Accounts. *China Economic Review* 12, 4 (2001): 355–367.

Lardy, Nicholas. Evaluating Economic Indicators in Post-WTO China. *Issues and Studies* 38, 4–39, 1 (December 2002–March 2003): 249–268.

Maddison, Angus. *Chinese Economic Performance in the Long Run.* Paris: Development Centre of the Organisation for Economic Co-operation and Development, 1998.

Nickum, James E. *Dam Lies and Other Statistics: Taking the Measure of Irrigation in China, 1931–91.* Honolulu, HI: East-West Center, 1995.

Organisation for Economic Co-operation and Development. *National Accounts for China: Sources and Methods.* Paris: Author 2000.

Park, Albert, and Sangui Wang. China's Poverty Statistics. *China Economic Review* 12, 4 (2001): 384–398.

Perkins, Dwight H. *Market Control and Planning in Communist China.* Cambridge, MA: Harvard University Press, 1966. See appendix A.

Rawski, Thomas G. What Is Happening to China's GDP Statistics? *China Economic Review* 12, 4 (2001): 347–354.

Rawski, Thomas G., and Robert W. Mead. On the Trail of China's Phantom Farmers. *World Development* 26, 5 (May 1998): 767–781.

Scharping, Thomas. Hide-and-Seek: China's Elusive Population Data. *China Economic Review* 12, 4 (2001): 323–332.

Sinton, Jonathan E., and David G. Fridley. A Guide to China's Energy Statistics. *Journal of Energy Literature* 8, 1 (2002): 22–35.

Solinger, Dorothy. Why We Cannot Count the "Unemployed." *China Quarterly*, no. 167 (September 2001): 671–688.

Wu, Harry X. How Fast Has Chinese Industry Grown?— Measuring the Real Output of Chinese Industry, 1949–97. *Review of Income and Wealth* 48, 2 (June 2002): 179–204.

Carsten A. Holz

STILWELL, JOSEPH
1883–1946

Joseph Warren Stilwell served as commanding general of U.S. Army forces in the China-Burma-India theater during World War II (1937–1945). His recall from China by President Franklin D. Roosevelt (1882–1945) remains a historical controversy.

Raised in Yonkers, New York, Stilwell was sent by his banker father to the U.S. Military Academy at West Point to curb his rebelliousness. He graduated thirty-second in a class of 124 cadets in 1904, and was known for his athletic competitiveness. He served in the Philippines before becoming an intelligence officer in France during World War I (1914–1918).

Fearing that peacetime would be tedious, Stilwell enrolled in Chinese-language training at the University of California, Berkeley, from 1919 to 1923, followed by service as a training officer at Fort Benning, Georgia, where he earned the nickname "Vinegar Joe" for his unbending discipline. The army then posted Stilwell to Tianjin (Tientsin) with the Fifteenth Infantry, the famous "Old China Hands" commanded by George Marshall (1880–1959). As a military attaché in the 1930s, Stilwell scouted China's terrain, analyzed battles of the Sino-Japanese War (1894–1895), and mixed with common Chinese soldiers and local officials.

After the Japanese attack on Pearl Harbor in December 1941, Marshall named Stilwell commanding general of the U.S. forces in the China-Burma-India theater. His directive was to keep China in the war with little promise of support until victory was achieved in Europe. When Stilwell arrived in Chongqing in March 1942, Chiang Kai-shek (Jiang Jieshi) gave him command of Chinese troops in Burma (Myanmar) originally under British control. The Japanese took Rangoon (Yangon), cutting the Burma Road supply route to Kunming, but Stilwell refused

General Joseph Stilwell meeting with an injured Chinese soldier, Assam, India, March 29, 1944. *In the early 1940s, Stilwell led the U.S. military effort in China, attempting to coordinate the movements of Chinese, British, and American troops against the Japanese. Failing to wrestle control of Chinese forces from Chiang Kai-shek, Stilwell lost his post in China and ultimately served as a commander during the Battle of Okinawa.* **AP IMAGES**

British offers to evacuate him by air. Instead, he made a grueling overland trek to India, where he told reporters "we took a hell of a beating."

Stilwell's Yankee bluntness appealed to the American public but not to Chiang or the British, who distrusted American motives only slightly less than each other's. Stilwell's priority was to attack Japan, and he suspected the British were more concerned with regaining the empire their incompetence had lost. They saw him as ineptly aggressive, vengeful, and distracted by his efforts to replace the Burma Road with a tortuous Ledo Road, instead of further developing modern air power to bring supplies over the "Hump."

Stilwell's relations with Chiang were even testier. The common Chinese soldier, Stilwell maintained, if given proper training and support, would match any in the world, but he railed at Chiang's officer corps for their stupidity, corruption, and cowardice. Stilwell initially got along well with Madame Chiang (Song Meiling, 1898–2003), but privately called Chiang "Peanut," originally his military code name, and soon fumed over Chiang's micromanagement, crony politics, and refusal to risk his armies against the Japanese.

The clash was more than personal. Chiang demanded American matériel but resisted American control because he felt little obligation to a country brought into the war by Pearl Harbor, not friendship, and was insulted by the Allies' "Europe first" strategy. While tactically he fought a low-cost holding action against a superior but familiar power, strategically he needed to rebuild his armies for postwar confrontation with the Communists. Stilwell, a lifelong Republican, saw the Communists as a force to be used against the Japanese and pressured Chiang to allow a liaison mission to Yan'an. Claire Chennault (1890–1958), commander of the American Flying Tigers, convinced Chiang that long-range bombing from bases in China would knock Japan out of the war. Stilwell countered that such raids, even if successful, would simply provoke a Japanese ground offensive to seize the airfields, a prediction that played out in the spring of 1944. At Marshall's behest, Roosevelt sent Chiang an ultimatum: Put both Chinese and American forces under American command. Chiang gave in but in return demanded Stilwell's recall. In October 1944 Roosevelt acceded, and Stilwell was withdrawn. Ironically, the land-based strategy that had required Chinese support then shifted to an island-hopping strategy in which China and its domestic politics were irrelevant.

Stilwell commanded U.S. forces in the Battle of Okinawa in 1945, then returned to California. He died of stomach cancer in 1946.

500

SEE ALSO *Anti-Japanese War, 1937–1945; Chiang Kai-shek (Jiang Jieshi).*

BIBLIOGRAPHY

Stilwell, Joseph. *The Stilwell Papers.* Ed. Theodore White. New York: Sloane, 1948.

Stilwell, Joseph. The World War II Diaries of General Joseph W. Stilwell (1941–1945). Hoover Institution Library and Archives. http://www.hoover.org/hila/collections/6977902.html

Romanus, Charles F., and Riley Sunderland. *Stilwell's Mission to China.* Washington, DC: Department of the Army, Historical Division, 1953.

Romanus, Charles F., and Riley Sunderland. *Stilwell's Command Problems.* Washington, DC: Department of the Army, Historical Division, 1956.

Romanus, Charles F., and Riley Sunderland. *Time Runs Out in CBI.* Washington, DC: Department of the Army, Historical Division, 1960.

Tuchman, Barbara. *Stilwell and the American Experience in China, 1911–45.* New York: Macmillan, 1970.

Van de Ven, Hans J. *War and Nationalism in China, 1925–1945.* London and New York: RoutledgeCurzon, 2003.

White, Theodore, and Annalee Jacoby. *Thunder Out of China.* New York: Sloane: 1946.

Charles W. Hayford

STOCK MARKET

SEE *Financial Markets.*

STRIKES

The notion of strikes in China was consolidated, undermined and developed, in both popular consciousness and official discourse (or the lack thereof), during the Prodemocracy Movement in Beijing in May–June 1989. Andrew Walder and Gong Xiaoxia characterize the Prodemocracy Movement as representing "the emergence of a new species of political protest in the People's Republic" that diverged from the kind of worker activism previously seen in the Cultural Revolution "where factions of political leaders mobilized their local followers for political combat" (Walder and Gong 1993, pp. 3–4). Jack Goldstone argues that "unlike other confrontations that involved mainly intellectuals, such as the Hundred Flowers Movement, or other events that were in some sense orchestrated by the regime, such as the Cultural Revolution, Tiananmen marked the first time that intellectuals and popular elements acted independently to challenge the regime" (quoted in Perry 1994, p. 3).

SHANGHAI'S STRIKE WAVE IN 1957

However, one must also take note of the labor unrest in 1957, which Elizabeth Perry notes has been largely overlooked in the English-language literature covering the period and conveniently forgotten by the Chinese who fondly "point to the 1950s as a kind of golden age—a period of unusual harmony and goodwill marked by a special closeness between the Chinese people, particularly the working class, and their new socialist government" (Perry 1994, p. 2). Perry observes that studies of dissent in China have primarily focused on the treatment of and by intellectuals, and argues that the labor unrest rampaging Shanghai in 1957, in which the intelligentsia were notably not involved, highlighted "the importance of the relationship between workers and intellectuals" (p. 4) and "revealed deep divisions within the Chinese working class itself" (p. 2). As Perry notes (pp. 7–9), the Shanghai strike wave was also significant as it coincided with the uprising in Hungary against the Soviet Union, Mao Zedong's Hundred Flowers Movement, and the elimination of private firms and their replacement with "joint-ownership enterprises" in which around 90 percent of the more than 1,300 incidents took place. Half of the disputes arose from demands for improved income or welfare, one-third from a recent State Council directive that apprenticeship training be extended, 7 percent from actions by cadres, and the rest from the new household registration system (pp. 9–10).

THE ROLE OF WORKERS IN THE PRODEMOCRACY MOVEMENT IN 1989

The independence between intellectuals and "popular elements" in the Prodemocracy Movement that Goldstone observes was, however, blurred and indeed caused by the discord between workers and students. While workers due to their lack of education looked to students for advice on legal and technical matters, workers in the Prodemocracy Movement focused from the beginning on economic issues and "displayed an acute sense of alienation not only from the political system but to a considerable extent also from the student leaders and intellectuals" (Walder and Gong 1993, p. 15). Workers' demands revolved in particular around price stabilization, employment security, freedom of employment, cessation of gender discrimination in employment, better work conditions, and, above all, the right to strike (Walder 1991; Walder and Gong 1993; Howell 1997).

Throughout the Prodemocracy Movement, workers regarded students as the epitome of the elitist class that oppressed them. Meanwhile, students preferred to focus on political issues and to assert exclusive control over the course and aims of the Movement. Walder and Gong observe that:

These differences, and the students' growing attraction to the elite's factional struggle, underlined a sharp class distinction in the politics of dissent: the students understood elite political discourse, were themselves a tiny elite, and many would probably become officials in the future....From the outset of their movement, and continuing well into martial law, the students made a self-conscious effort to maintain their "purity" (*chunjiexing*). This meant, in practice, that they limited their politics to moral questioning of the authorities, seeking to speak as the conscience of the nation, striving to maintain public order and production, while keeping off to one side any "narrow" economic and group interests that might potentially disrupt their quest (Walder and Gong 1993, p. 23).

Walder and Gong note that students went so far as to exclude workers from Tiananmen Square proper, until military action appeared imminent when workers were finally allowed onto the square to protect students. Moreover, it was only on June 3, 1989, that students finally sought the collaboration of workers in staging a general strike. Afterward, workers received much harsher penalties than did students, including the death penalty, for participating in the Prodemocracy Movement (Walder and Gong 1993, pp. 24–25).

POST-1989 DEMANDS FOR LABOR STANDARDS AND WORKERS' RIGHTS

As Virginia Leary has pointed out, workers' rights are a good indicator of a country's level of protection of human rights in general, because workers constitute the bedrock of a society and if their rights are not recognized and protected then it is improbable that human rights in general are recognized and protected in that country (Leary 1996, p. 22). In her study on labor standards and human rights under China's market socialism, Anita Chan demonstrated that the labor rights of tens of millions of Chinese workers were systematically ignored, undermined, or violated, often physically through forced and bonded labor, control of bodily functions including toileting, corporal punishment, and violence (Chan 1998, pp. 890–891, 894–897).

Violations of labor rights and standards are particularly acute for citizens who seek to take part in China's economic development by moving to China's major cities such as Beijing, Shanghai, and Guangzhou, as they are subjected to "immigration" controls under China's household registration system and are viewed by the bureaucracy and the existing urban populations as both a threat to stability and a source of criminality and diseases. In addition, it was the injustice and corruption of their managers, which many workers felt resembled the state bureaucracy,

that led workers to find resonance with and join the student movement that culminated in the tragic Tiananmen Square suppression (Walder 1991). Leary asserts that the Chinese government was in fact more alarmed at the demands of workers for the right to organize and participate in labor unions than at the students' call for democracy per se (Leary 1996, p. 23). Walder and Gong likewise argue that the military crackdown on June 4, "launched despite the rapidly dwindling numbers of students and citizens on the square, was probably motivated in large part by these officials' mortal fears of a workers' insurgency" (Walder and Gong 1993, pp. 27–28).

However, Marc Blecher observes that despite the subsequent climate where "a political atmosphere of intense surveillance and repression prevailed" (Blecher 2002, p. 284), workers remained undaunted in their demands, and hundreds of strikes involving tens of thousands of workers occurred in most of China. Blecher notes that:

> Four Xi'an cotton mills were shut down as early as 6 June 1989. During the second half of the year, over 15,000 workers engaged in over 700 incidents of industrial action in state and collective firms throughout the country, protesting against management's "failure to guarantee basic living conditions"—and that counts only those outbreaks that made it into official reports. The working class thus succeeded in challenging the state even at the moment the state was most intent on intimidating society. As the political situation began to relax after 1992, worker protest intensified. In 1992, official statistics reported more than 540 demonstrations, 480 strikes and 75 assaults on government offices. In 1993, strike activity in Fujian tripled over the previous year....in 1996, the number of protests rose 50 percent over the previous year (Blecher 2002, pp. 284–285, references omitted).

Feng Chen notes that due to continual subsistence crises and managerial corruption, 3.6 million workers had been involved in strikes and demonstrations by 1998 (Chen 2000, p. 41). Jude Howell observes that the Chinese media have generally focused on labor protests in foreign-invested enterprises, despite the higher incidence in state-owned enterprises,

> to deflect attention from the highly controversial attempts to reform state-owned enterprises and defuse the potential wider impact of such unrest. Moreover, by focusing on the grievances of workers in foreign enterprises the leadership could both rally support along nationalist lines for tighter regulation of foreign companies, in relation to employment practices and more general matters such as taxation, and introduce labour legislation, which not only included protective measures for

workers but also confirmed the legitimacy of bank-ruptcy and dismissal (Howell 1997, p. 164).

Despite its large-scale and violent military crackdown on Tiananmen Square in 1989, the government subsequently was reluctant to suppress workers' demonstrations as long as they remained localized and did not escalate into general strikes. Chen discerns that:

> the government is afraid that such incidents thwart one of its paramount goals—social and political stability. But on the other hand, crackdowns against people who make no political claims and only demand a minimum livelihood would place the government in a morally and politically indefensible position. Suppressing these protests would make the government look indifferent to the condition of the working class, and cause even greater resentment among workers. Thus, the government has adopted a policy of conciliation and has emphasized the use of "persuasion" and "education" to resolve the conflicts…defused through the state's effective implementation of modest compensatory measures aimed at temporarily alleviating the economic plight of laid-off workers (Chen 2000, pp. 61–62).

Ching Kwan Lee (2000) observed that, in the reform era, labor protests in China discarded the banner of class struggle and began to revolve around notions of the rule of law and of rights.

LABOR LAW IN CHINA

Workers in China do not have a legal right to strike, which was eliminated when the 1982 Constitution was promulgated. The Trade Union Law of 1992 did not revive the right to strike. Any demonstration or assembly in China requires the prior approval of the local public security bureau, which is rarely granted (Chen 2000, pp. 60–61). However, Howell argues that the Labor Law of 1994, which became effective on January 1, 1995, marked a crucial change in labor relations in China, in particular through the All-China Federation of Trade Unions (Howell 1997, p. 167). The Labor Law introduced arrangements for collective bargaining premised on tripartite representation of trade unions, foreign investors, and the state.

The Labor Law, which governs all employment relationships in China (Art. 2), is organized into thirteen chapters with 107 articles. Article 3 in Chapter 1 guarantees, among other things, the rights of workers to equality in employment, freedom of employment, labor safety and sanitation protection, and remuneration for work, rests, holidays, and leaves of absence. Article 7 guarantees "the right to participate in and organize trade unions in accordance with law" and states that trade unions "shall represent and safeguard the legitimate rights and interests of

laborers, and stage activities independently in accordance with law." Article 8 provides that workers "shall take part in democratic management through workers' congress, workers' representative assembly, or any other forms in accordance with law, or consult with the employer on an equal footing about protection of the legitimate rights and interests of laborers."

Chapter 2 of the Labor Law prescribes that the state shall create and expand employment opportunities and encourage enterprises to do the same. Gender discrimination in employment is specifically outlawed (Chap. 2, Arts. 12–13), and special protection for female and juvenile workers is laid out in Chapter 7. Prominent attention is paid to the role of contracts in employment, with Chapter 3 devoted to the nature and requirements of contractual stipulations, including collective contracts. Chapter 4 is devoted to work conditions, with Article 36 stipulating a maximum of eight work hours a day and forty-four work hours a week, Article 38 guaranteeing one day of rest per week, and Article 44 stipulating remuneration for overtime work. Articles 48 and 49 in Chapter 5 guarantee and stipulate standards on minimum wages, while Chapter 6 stipulates the standards and requirements for labor sanitation and safety. Chapter 8 provides for professional training. Chapter 9 governs the requirements of social insurance and welfare treatment. Chapter 10 stipulates the standards and processes for the settlement of labor disputes. Chapter 11 lays out the requirements for supervision and inspection of compliance with the Labor Law, and Chapter 12 details the legal consequences for noncompliance. Hilary Josephs argues that "the Law appears to acknowledge that the same inequality of bargaining power between employer and employee which prevails in market economies can also exist in a transitional economy, and therefore the worker requires added legal protection, including the ability to enforce his rights as a private litigant" (Josephs 1995, p. 570).

SEE ALSO *Labor; Migrant Workers; Prodemocracy Movement (1989).*

BIBLIOGRAPHY

Blecher, Marc J. Hegemony and Workers' Politics in China. *China Quarterly* 170 (2002): 283–303.

Chan, Anita. Revolution or Corporation? Workers and Trade Unions in Post-Mao China. *Australian Journal of Chinese Affairs* 29 (1993): 31–61.

Chan, Anita. Labor Standards and Human Rights: The Case of Chinese Workers under Market Socialism. *Human Rights Quarterly* 20 (1998): 886–904.

Chen, Feng. Subsistence Crises, Managerial Corruption and Labour Protests in China. *China Journal* 44 (2000): 41–63.

Howell, Jude. The Chinese Economic Miracle and Urban Workers. *European Journal of Development Research* 9 (1997): 148–175.

Josephs, Hilary K. Labor Law in a "Socialist Market Economy": The Case of China. *Columbia Journal of Transnational Law* 33 (1995): 559–581.

Lau, Raymond W. K. Socio-Political Control in Urban China: Changes and Crisis. *British Journal of Sociology* 52 (2001): 605–620.

Leary, Virginia A. The Paradox of Workers' Rights as Human Rights. In *Human Rights, Labor Rights, and International Trade*, eds. Lance A. Compa and Stephen F. Diamond (22–47). Philadelphia: University of Pennsylvania Press, 1996.

Lee, Ching Kwan. The "Revenge of History": Collective Memories and Labor Protests in Northeastern China. *Ethnography* 1 (2000): 217–237.

Perry, Elizabeth J. Shanghai's Strike Wave of 1957. *China Quarterly* 137 (1994): 1–27.

Walder, Andrew G. Workers, Managers and the State: The Reform Era and the Political Crisis of 1989. *China Quarterly* 127 (1991): 467–492.

Walder, Andrew G., and Gong Xiaoxia. Workers in the Tiananmen Protests: The Politics of the Beijing Workers' Autonomous Federation. *Australian Journal of Chinese Affairs* 29 (1993): 1–29.

Wright, Teresa. The China Democracy Party and the Politics of Protest in the 1980s–1990s. *China Quarterly* 172 (2002): 906–926.

Phil C. W. Chan

STUDENT ORGANIZATIONS AND ACTIVISM, 1900–1949

Officially recognized and less-formal associations of varying kinds played key roles in structuring the daily life, educational experiences, and political activities of college and university students in early twentieth-century China. Students with common interests (studying a foreign language, sharing a hobby, loving poetry, etc.) routinely formed organizations. Campus associational life was structured around a mix of groups, some formed spontaneously by like-minded pupils and others created in a top-down manner (called into being by faculty, for example, or a political party). In the Republican era (1912–1949), some Chinese student groups went for long stretches (or their entire existence) without becoming involved in oppositional politics, while others figured centrally in protests (whether or not formed to do so).

In all these respects the Chinese experience is similar to that of modern countries around the world, but there are distinctive features of the Chinese case. These relate to the especially powerful roles students played in protests (partly an outgrowth of the unusual centrality of campus unrest in mass movements in China throughout the last century) and the importance of certain kinds of groups (especially native-place societies, which were formed by youths from the same hometown, region, or province).

EARLY TWENTIETH-CENTURY ASSOCIATIONS AND PROTESTS

The history of modern Chinese institutions of higher education can be traced back to the late nineteenth century, which saw the founding of missionary institutions such as Shanghai's St. John's College (established in 1879) as well as the Chinese-run Peking University (established in 1898). These earliest modern Chinese campuses had reading societies, drama groups, and other kinds of associations from the start. But it was only at the beginning of the 1900s that the entwining of campus associations and political activism began in earnest.

The 1903–1919 period saw the eruption of a series of urban protests, most of which were linked to real or feared infringements on Chinese sovereignty. Faculty members and students at colleges and universities often played active roles in these protests, as sometimes did their counterparts at secondary schools. Important early events included: the 1903 Shanghai demonstrations against czarist Russia's encroachments into northern China; the 1905 gatherings in Guangzhou (Canton) and elsewhere calling for a change in discriminatory U.S. immigration policies; the 1915 marches fueled by anger at Japan's infamous "Twenty-one Demands"; and the May Fourth movement of 1919, which began with Beijing student demonstrators calling for the ouster of officials seen as corrupt and too willing to allow former German territories in North China to be ceded to Japanese control in the postwar settlement being negotiated in Paris, and which reached its high point with a general strike in Shanghai. Accompanying most of these agitations were boycotts of the goods of an individual country—and students often took the lead in organizing and trying to gain compliance for these boycotts, even though members of other social groups took part in all of these protest waves.

In each of these early large-scale student (or student-led) movements, as well as in the many small-scale protests that erupted at individual schools, previous ties between youths and existing organizations served as building blocks for activism. As the struggles unfolded, new groups were founded, often including both students and faculty, which were designed purely to oversee protests and coordinate activities at different campuses. Typically, though, the leaders of these new groups were the same individuals who had taken active roles in less explicitly political campus associations. Often, for example, they were class monitors or members of school councils. There was, in other words, considerable continuity between the roles that students played in ordinary times and those they took on in extraordinary moments of political mobilization, though

504

mass movements tended to introduce novelties, such as providing increased opportunities for leaders on different campuses to interact.

The most detailed information about how the pattern just described played out is provided by memoirs and other materials dealing with the May Fourth struggle. Accounts of Beijing activism in 1919 reveal that many educated youths involved in the May Fourth movement had formed ties and gained leadership skills through the plethora of study societies, literary societies, lecture brigades, and reading groups that had sprouted during the preceding year on local campuses. These campus organizations, which often included radical young faculty members as well as students, frequently had explicitly political orientations.

In both Beijing and Shanghai, however, the May Fourth movement engaged a broad spectrum of the student population, not only groups already disposed toward radicalism. Consider, for example, the case of the Shanghai Student Union (SSU) and steps taken to maintain order during a demonstration in China's biggest treaty port.

The SSU was established right after the first local protest of 1919, a "citizen's assembly" held on May 7— an event designed to express outrage over the proposed terms of the Treaty of Versailles and call for the release from custody of Beijing students who had been arrested because of their role in the May 4 march for which the movement was named. Not all delegates attending the first meeting of the SSU were students, for some campuses sent teachers or professors to represent their interests. But of the students who attended, some had previous experience in explicitly political organizations and knew one another already. The Fudan University student who served as the SSU's first temporary chairman, for example, had earlier been a leading figure in the Students' Self-Governing Society of his school. Another Fudan University student who assumed various positions of authority within the SSU had helped found a short-lived antimonarchical association in 1917. The Tongji University representatives to the SSU, on the other hand, presumably all came from the ranks of a different sort of organization: the school's Association of Class Monitors, meaning they were no strangers to exercising authority nor to one another. And to keep participants in line during the marches of 1919, a third type of preexisting organization figured centrally: Boy Scout troops. Some of these troops were linked to another nonpolitical association, the YMCA.

PROTESTS OF THE 1920s to 1940s

The decades stretching from May Fourth to the end of the Republican period saw a continuation of the patterns described above, both in the frequency of student movements and the roles that explicitly political and other kinds of campus associations played in those struggles. There were, however, some changes, the most important of which had to do with political parties. Throughout this period, the Communists and the Nationalists continually founded student organizations (generally underground ones in the former case, often officially recognized ones in the latter case), while also trying to infiltrate independent groups and those established by the rival party. This gave a significantly different complexion to campus political life in post–May Fourth upheavals such as the anti-imperialist May Thirtieth movement of 1925, the 1931 protests triggered by the Japanese invasion of Manchuria, and 1935's December Ninth movement— during which students called on Chiang Kai-shek (Jiang Jieshi), as they had in 1931, to go to war against Japan.

The Shanghai mobilization against American imperialism of late 1946 and early 1947 illustrates the complex ways that student protests were shaped by and built upon preexisting and newly formed student groups, including groups that had close ties to the Communist and Nationalist organizations and groups that were independent of the parties. This protest began in late December 1946 as word spread that two American soldiers stationed in Beijing had raped a female Chinese student. It culminated on New Year's Day of 1947 with a large march.

The Shanghai school that took the lead in the agitation was Ji'nan University. On December 27, the day that reports of the Beijing rape first appeared in Shanghai newspapers, dorm rooms were transformed into impromptu debating halls, as students and progressive professors gave speeches about the need to take action. Two days later, a meeting of representatives of all local clubs and student organizations was convened. The more than one hundred youths in attendance formed a new umbrella society, the Ji'nan Anti-U.S. Brutality Alliance. This group called for a schoolwide strike and mass actions throughout the city, and selected nineteen delegates to spread the news of Ji'nan's plans to other campuses. This liaison team quickly established links to many local schools, aided in doing so by the variety of multicampus organizations already in existence. For example, group-singing societies at more than a dozen schools belonged to a citywide New Music Club.

At other schools, things unfolded a bit differently than they had at Ji'nan. At Jiaotong University, for example, representatives of departments, rather than organizations, met to plan collective action, while at Fudan University, the Female Students' Association took the lead. But the end result was similar: the founding of a campuswide protest organization devoted to this issue. Then, thanks to liaison efforts such as that spearheaded by Ji'nan students, a citywide protest group (a successor to the SSU) was founded that oversaw the organization of the New Year's Day march.

Within this larger group, there were students whose paths had crossed at earlier points, whether because they were known to each other via their secret membership in a Communist youth group or because they were part of a nonpolitical citywide organization such as the New Music Club.

Memoirs by former student activists detail the many ways that, during that 1947 protest and others preceding and following it, activities on individual campuses and coordination between groups based at different schools was facilitated by preexisting and often overlapping ties established via membership in associations. For example, a disproportionate number of members of one school's literary society known for its involvement in radical causes hailed from the same province, and hence brought together people who already knew each other via membership in a native-place organization before they became part of that more politically oriented club. Sometimes a nonpolitical organization would morph into a protest group, as occurred in the 1930s when a sports team, whose most charismatic member happened to be an underground Communist organizer, evolved into a march-security team that helped maintain order during demonstrations. And there were loyalist student movements as well, aimed at generating support for the Nationalists or voicing antagonism toward the Communists, in which similar patterns unfolded—except that members of youth groups with ties to that party, such as the Three People's Principles Youth League, took the lead.

CONCLUSIONS

The frequency with which Chinese students took to the streets during the first half of the twentieth century sets them apart from the youth of many other countries. So, too, does the range of protest activities in which they became involved, including everything from multiclass rallies decrying the oppressive and corrupt nature of domestic authorities, to boycotts of the goods of foreign imperialists, to classroom strikes, to the mass pilgrimages to Nanjing in the 1930s.

One other distinctive feature about Chinese campus politics, though, is the degree to which student activists gained experience through participation in a broad cross-section of clubs and societies. Scholars of student politics primarily interested in other parts of the world have argued for the importance of separating campus groups that serve a "socializing" function (that is, preparing youths to take on conventional roles in society) and those that are "transgressive" in nature (that is, oriented toward challenging the status quo). The presumption in this literature is that associations such as fraternities, sports teams, and mainstream student councils steer youths in one direction (away from rather than toward radical action), while protest leagues and radical study groups take them in another (into the realm of

the counterculture or even revolutionary militancy). The Chinese case suggests, however, that this kind of divide is not always as relevant as it seems. In events such as the May Thirtieth movement, as perhaps in patriotic agitations in other settings where anger over imperialism inspires a large number of students to take to the streets, a mixture of "socializing" groups (such as native-place societies) and "transgressive" associations (such as clubs formed to study or spread the word of radical thinkers) can be seen facilitating campus mobilization.

SEE ALSO *Liberalism; May Fourth Movement; Nationalism.*

BIBLIOGRAPHY

Borthwick, Sally. *Education and Social Change in China: The Beginnings of the Modern Era.* Stanford, CA: Hoover Institution Press, 1983.

Israel, John. *Student Nationalism in China, 1927–1937.* Stanford, CA: Stanford University Press, 1967.

Li, Lincoln. *Student Nationalism in China, 1924–1949.* Albany: State University of New York Press, 1994.

Lipset, Seymour Martin, and Philip Altbach, eds. *Students in Revolt.* Boston: Houghton Mifflin, 1969.

Peng Ming. *Wusi yundongshi* [A history of the May Fourth movement]. Beijing: Renmin Chubanshe, 1984.

Perry, Elizabeth J., and Jeffrey N. Wasserstrom, eds. *Shanghai Social Movements, 1919–1949.* Spec. issue of *Chinese Studies in History: A Journal of Translations* (Fall–Winter 1993–1994). Trans. Zhu Hong, with Thomas Peterson.

Wasserstrom, Jeffrey N. *Student Protests in Twentieth-century China: The View from Shanghai.* Stanford, CA: Stanford University Press, 1991.

Weston, Timothy B. *The Power of Position: Beijing University, Intellectuals, and Chinese Political Culture, 1898–1929.* Berkeley: University of California Press, 2004.

Ye Wenxin (Yeh Wen-hsin). *The Alienated Academy: Culture and Politics in Republican China, 1919–1937.* Cambridge, MA: Harvard University Press.

Jeffrey N. Wasserstrom

STUDY ABROAD

Although it had opened its schools for students from foreign lands for centuries if not millennia, China started to send a large number of students to foreign countries for formal education and training only in the mid-nineteenth century. Since then study abroad has kept evolving and expanding to meet China's needs for modernization. Between 1847 and 2007, about 1.3 million Chinese students went abroad for education. The vast majority of those who pursued education overseas before the end of the 1980s returned to China shortly after completing their educational program abroad. Equipped with updated knowledge, cutting-edge skills, and fresh ideas, these returnees, popularly known as overseas students (*liuxuesheng*), made unparalleled contributions to China's modernization.

THE INCEPTION YEARS

Initiated as part of missionary endeavors in China, study abroad in the nineteenth century remained mostly a private enterprise, involving a relatively small number of students who usually pursued secondary education overseas. Rong Hong and two of his classmates who arrived in the United States with their missionary teacher in 1847 were the first students from China engaged in study abroad in modern Chinese history. Though missionaries and private institutions played a dominant role, the Qing government sent scores of students to Western nations to be trained as military officers and warship builders in the 1870s. The first and largest group of government-sponsored students, 120 in total, were sent to the United States in four installments between 1872 and 1875. However, the Qing Court terminated the experiment and recalled all the students in 1881. As a result, China's study abroad continued functioning mostly as a private enterprise with a small number of male students predominantly from coastal areas.

Most returnees, including both self- and government-sponsored students, had to face tough conditions, especially in the early years, since Western learning was neither recognized nor accepted by the Qing government and most Chinese intellectuals during this period. Despite the difficult environment, returned students made remarkable contributions to China's early modernization effort. Rong Hong, who returned to China after graduating from Yale University in 1854, helped Zeng Guofan, one of the reform-minded high-ranking officials of the Qing Court, build the Jiangnan Arsenal (Jiangnan Zhizao Zhongju), China's first modern factory, in Shanghai in the mid-1860s. Zhan Tianyou, one of the 120 child students brought to the United States by Rong Hong in the 1870s, completed the railroad between Beijing and Zhangjiakou, the first railroad independently designed and built entirely by Chinese. Sun Yat-sen, who attended elementary and middle schools in Hawaii and received his college education in Hong Kong, began in the 1890s to organize a revolution that eventually led to the overthrow of the Qing dynasty and the establishment of the Republic of China.

EXPANSION UNDER THE VISIBLE HAND OF THE GOVERNMENT

Study abroad from China changed fundamentally and expanded drastically in the first half of the twentieth century under direct and extensive intervention from the central government. Under increasing internal and external pressure, Chinese regimes from the collapsing Qing Court to the short-lived Nationalist government were forced to intensify their modernization effort. The Qing Court finally terminated the civil-service examination and began to establish modern schools and colleges in 1905. This and many other modernization efforts created a huge demand for experts and professionals trained in modern colleges and universities. With limited higher-education resources in China, sending students abroad for undergraduate and graduate levels of education became a popular policy shared by all Chinese regimes of the period. Tapping its own financial resources and taking advantage of the Boxer Indemnity returned by the United States and other countries, a sum totaling tens of millions of U.S. dollars, the Chinese government could provide full or partial financial support for tens of thousands of students, including a small but increasingly larger number of female students, to pursue education abroad. As a result, the vast majority of Chinese students seeking higher education went abroad, and most of them chose the United States and other Western nations instead of Japan. The establishment of effective control over passport issuance and foreign-currency exchange in the mid-1930s allowed the central government to set higher qualifications and stricter regulations for both government- and self-sponsored students.

With their higher levels of education and larger numbers, overseas students during this period left much broader and deeper marks on almost every aspect of China's modernization. Although all Chinese regimes tried to have the vast majority of students, 80 percent, study science, engineering, mining, medicine, agriculture, and business, about half of them managed to focus in the social sciences, humanities, arts, and law. As a result, in the 1910s they could introduce not only "Mr. Science" but also "Mr. Democracy" to the Chinese people for the first time. While many returnees—such as Du Kezhen, Mao Yisheng, Sa Bendong, Hu Shi, Lu Xun, Zhao Yuanren, and Wen Yiduo—became prominent scientists, engineers, philosophers, and artists, others rose as top political leaders, including such Nationalists as Chiang Kai-shek (Jiang Jieshi), Kong Xiangxi, Song Ziwen, and Chen Lifu, and such Communists as Zhou Enlai, Zhu De, and Deng Xiaoping. Their actions and interactions greatly determined the direction and pace of China's modernization in the twentieth century.

CONTRACTION DURING THE COLD WAR

The Communist victory in 1949 brought government control over study abroad to its fullest extent. Established early in the Cold War, the new People's Republic of China cut off its educational ties with all Western nations. To meet its need for highly trained experts, the Communist government sent over ten thousand students to the Soviet

Union and other Communist countries in Eastern Europe between 1950 and 1965. As the sole sponsor for all students sent abroad, the government was finally able to make sure that almost all students focused on science and technology. The split between China and the Soviet Union and the intense struggles among Chinese Communists themselves brought already limited study abroad to a complete stop. With the beginning of the Cultural Revolution in 1966, China stopped sending any students abroad. It resumed sending only a small number of language students abroad after its return to the United Nations in October 1971. Fewer than 2,000 students were sent abroad between 1972 and 1978.

In its early years the Communist government tried to get as many students stranded abroad back to China as possible, yet most foreign-trained experts and professionals suffered tremendously in numerous political movements launched by the Communist Party since the mid-1950s. While most returned students could not make full use of their talents and expertise, those involved in the development of nuclear bombs, missiles, and satellites were able to make extraordinary contributions in the Cold War years. Some returnees, such as Jiang Zemin and Li Peng, also later rose to be top Communist leaders. During this period thousands of Chinese students chose to stay permanently overseas, mostly in the United States, a development that made the brain drain a new issue in China's study abroad.

PRIVATIZATION IN THE REFORM ERA

Study abroad entered a new era as China started to reform and open up to the outside world in the late 1970s. As part of its effort to shift the nation's focus from class struggle to the Four Modernizations, China, under the leadership of Deng Xiaoping, started to send a large number of students abroad in 1979. In that year, about 1,700 students were sent to 32 countries. By 2007 the number had increased about 90 times, reaching 150,000. Between 1979 and 2007 China sent over 1.2 million students abroad, about ten times as many as the previous 130 years. While most students sent abroad in the early years received financial support from or through the Chinese government, self-sponsored students began to dominate the scene in the mid-1980s as the central government relaxed its control over passports and foreign currencies. Since the late 1990s, self-sponsored students accounted for about 90 percent of all Chinese students pursuing education abroad. Unlike their government-sponsored counterparts, self-sponsored students were more likely to choose practical fields of study, take a longer time to complete their education, seek employment after graduation, and change their legal status for extended or even permanent stays in their host countries. As a result, about 75 percent of those who

went abroad for education during this period are still studying or working in foreign countries. In response to this new phenomenon, the Chinese government revised its study-abroad policy in the 1990s. While continuing to support study abroad and to encourage students to return to China, it gave students the freedom to get in and out of the country, hoping that they would provide their services for the motherland in diverse ways.

Although only about 25 percent of Chinese students have returned to China since 1979, the absolute number, about 320,000 in total, is still about three times greater than the number in the previous 130 years. Recent returnees, going back to China within a relatively short period, have been able to form a critical mass in almost all fields and to help China narrow its gap with developed nations. Besides their knowledge and skills obtained through college education, many in this new generation of students returned with rich work experience, new products, cutting-edge research projects, generous foreign investment, broad business and academic contacts, sophisticated management skills, and better understanding of foreign cultures and peoples. While many have accepted state-assigned positions in government, universities, and state-owned-enterprises, a large percentage of recent returnees have chosen to set up their own businesses or work for other private enterprises or international companies in China. Taking advantage of advances in transportation and communication technology, more Chinese students have found new ways to keep themselves deeply involved in China's economic and social development without completely giving up their own careers or business interests in foreign lands. The constant expansion and evolution of study abroad has generated a most dynamic force for the rise of China as a modern nation.

SEE ALSO *Education.*

BIBLIOGRAPHY

Hayhoe, Ruth, and Marianne Bastid, eds. *China's Education and the Industrialized World: Studies in Cultural Transfer.* Armonk, NY: M. E. Sharpe, 1987.

Li, Hongshan. *U.S.-China Educational Exchange: State, Society, and Intercultural Relations.* New Brunswick, NJ: Rutgers University Press, 2008.

Li Xisuo. *Jindai liuxuesheng yu zhongwai wenhua* [Modern foreign-educated students and cultural exchange between China and foreign countries]. Tianjin: Tianjin Renmin Chubanshe, 1991.

Liu Zhen, ed. *Liuxue jiaoyu shiliao* [Historical records of study abroad]. 4 vols. Taibei: Guoli Bianyi Guan, 1977.

Wei Daozhi, ed. *Zhongwai jiaoyu jiaoliu shi* [A history of educational exchange between China and foreign nations]. Changsha: Hunan Jiaoyu Chubanshe, 1998.

Ye Weili. "Nü liuxuesheng": The Story of American-Educated Chinese Women, 1880s–1920s. *Modern China* 20, 3 (July 1994): 315–346.

Hongshan Li

SUN DAOLIN

1921–2007

Sun Daolin, one of the most popular actors in twentieth-century China, was born in Beijing to a Zhejiang family. His original name was Sun Yiliang. His father, Sun Wenyao, a graduate of Louvain University, Brussels, was an engineer, but early on Sun showed an inclination for the arts. He published his first short story, "Muzi liang" (The Mother and the Son), at the age of fifteen. In 1938 he enrolled as a philosophy student at Yen-ching University (the predecessor of Peking University), where he came under the influence of Huang Zongjiang (b. 1921), who later became a famous theatrical actor and playwright. Sun joined the Yen-ching Drama Society (Yanjing jushe), studied Constantin Stanislavski's acting methods, and ultimately embarked upon a career dedicated to theater and film.

With the eruption of the Pacific War and the dissolving of Yen-ching University, Sun became a theatrical actor, working with the China Traveling Drama Troupe (Zhongguo Lüxing Jutuan) led by Tang Huaiqiu (1898–1954), Guohua Drama Society in Shanghai, and the South-North Drama Society in Beijing between 1943 and 1944. He performed in productions of Cao Yu's *Leiyu* (*The Thunderstorm*, 1934), Ba Jin's *Jia* (*The Family*, 1933), and Alexandre Dumas fils's *La dame aux camélias* (*The Lady of the Camelias*; Chinese: *Chahua nu*, 1847).

After the war, Sun finished his college education and soon was invited to join the Shanghai film industry, which led to a six-decade film career of over twenty films. His best known pre-1949 films include *Da duanyuan* (*The Great Reunion*, dir. Ding Li, 1948) and *Wuya yu maque* (*Crows and Sparrows*, dir. Zheng Junli, 1949). In the latter film, Sun's portrayal of a cowardly intellectual undergoing politicization on the eve of the New China won him the Individual First film award. He played a similar character in *Zaochun eryue* (*Threshold of Spring*, dir. Xie Tieli, 1963), an adaptation of a 1929 novel depicting the political awakening of an intellectual. Criticized during the Cultural Revolution (1966–1969) as a "poisonous weed" because of its bourgeois sentiment, the film later was reinstated as a rare example of artistic achievement and subtle humanism. In 2006 it was adapted into a Shaoxing opera, for which Sun served as art consultant.

After 1949, inspired by his experience during the Korean War, Sun played revolutionary figures in war films including *Dujiang zhencha ji* (Reconnaissance across the Yangtse, dir. Tang Xiaodan, 1954) and *Yongbu xiaoshi de dianbo* (The Eternal Wave, dir. Wang Ping, 1958). Sun was interested in not only reprising a character type, but also revisiting literary works. As a college student, he had played the younger brother in the play *Leiyu*; later he played the elder brother, and finally the father in the 1984 film version that he directed himself.

As a director, Sun's last film was *Zhan Tianyou* (2001), a biopic about the early twentieth-century pioneer of Chinese railroad construction—a project Sun had planned for nearly four decades. Coming from a theatrical background, Sun also was a voice actor for more than twenty foreign-language films, including *Hamlet* and *The Idiot*.

Sun's contribution to Chinese cinema and theater was acknowledged in a 1983 British Channel Four documentary, *Visions: Shanghai Cinema* (dir. Ron Orders). In early 2007 he was present at the opening of the Sun Daolin Film Museum (Sun Daolin Dianying Yishu Guan) in his ancestral town, Jiashan, Zhejiang Province. He died in December that year, and was survived by his wife, the opera singer Wang Wenjuan (b. 1926), and his daughter Sun Qingyuan (b. 1964).

SEE ALSO *Film Industry.*

BIBLIOGRAPHY

PRIMARY WORK

Sun, Daolin. *Stepping into the Sunshine* (Zoujin yangguang). Shanghai: Shanghai Renmin Chubanshe, 1997.

SECONDARY WORKS

Clark, Paul. Film-Making in China: From the Cultural Revolution to 1981. *China Quarterly* 94 (1983): 304–322.

Shen Feide, and Zhang Xin. Sun Daolin zhidao yingpian *Zhan Tianyou* [Sun Daolin Directs *Zhan Tianyou*]. *Shiji* [The Century] 2 (2001): n.p.

Sun Daolin wei yueju Zaochun eryue yanyuan shuoxi [Sun Daolin Explains *Early Spring* to the Shaoxing Opera Actors]. February 12, 2003. http://www.jfdaily.com/logo/mingren/sdl/x2.htm (Jiefang wang or Liberation Network).

Wang, Yongyun. "Sun Daolin at China Traveling Drama Troupe" (Sun Daolin zai zhonglu). *Shanghai Theater* (Shanghai xiju) 2 (2008): 37.

Xiao Gao. Sun Daolin dianying yishuguan luocheng [Sun Daolin Film Museum Erected]. *Dazhong dianying* [*Popular Film*] 5 (2007): 37.

Yiman Wang

SUN YAT-SEN (SUN YIXIAN)
1866–1925

Sun Yat-sen (Sun Yixian), the revolutionary and founder of the Republic of China that overthrew the Qing dynasty, was born in the farming village of Cuiheng (Ts'ui-heng) in 1866. Despite his modest background, adhering to traditional customs and studying classical texts, from a young age Sun was influenced by Western thought and culture that encroached in nearby Hong Kong and Macao.

Sun Yat-sen made a profound impact on China through his revolutionary leadership and his political writings designed to create a modern democratic republic. He is revered by both the Nationalist and Communist Parties, which have different interpretations of his political philosophy. To honor Sun, elaborate memorials were constructed in Nanjing and Taibei, and smaller statues and portraits of Sun abound in China and in Chinese communities throughout the world. Since World War II, scholarly interest in Sun has spurred the publication of many books and articles about every aspect of his life.

WESTERN EDUCATION

Sun's revolutionary path was shaped by the opportunity to follow his elder brother, Sun Mei, to Hawaii, where he received a Western education. In 1879 at age thirteen Sun Yat-sen enrolled in the Iolani School, an Anglican institution, to learn English. After a brief period of attendance at Oahu College, an American Congregationalist school, Sun returned to Cuiheng. After four years in Hawaii Sun had become increasingly skeptical of Chinese traditional beliefs. He left his home village for Hong Kong in June 1883, and in November he entered the Diocesan School, sponsored by the Church of England, for further Western studies; in the following year he entered Queen's College. In 1884 Sun was baptized a Christian, but conforming to Chinese tradition, he agreed to an arranged marriage to Lu Muzhen (1867–1952), a native of Cuiheng.

Having decided on a medical career, in 1887 Sun entered the College of Medicine in Hong Kong, where he studied under Dr. James Cantlie (1851–1926), dean of the college. After graduating in 1892 with a distinguished record, Sun was qualified to practice medicine and perform surgery, but when he went to Macao he could not obtain a license to practice because his degree from the General Medical Council of Great Britain was not recognized. Instead, Sun opened the China-West Pharmacy, which provided free service to the poor, and performed surgery at the Kian Wu hospital until he was stopped by the Portuguese authorities.

SEEDS OF REVOLUTION

Sun's familiarity with Western ideas and his concern about the Qing dynasty's failure to deter Western imperialism on Chinese soil led him to consider revolutionary activities. In 1894 he wrote to an influential official in charge of foreign affairs, Li Hongzhang, advocating a massive modernization strategy for China that included educational programs, new technologies, expansion of the economy, and development of agriculture, while emphasizing China's independence. Preoccupied with Japan's incursion into Korea, Li did not respond to Sun's proposals.

After returning to Hawaii in the same year, Sun organized the Xingzhonghui (Revive China Society) in November 1894 with the objective of overthrowing the Manchu rulers and setting up a republican government. Back in China, the plot to start an uprising in Guangzhou (Canton) in October 1895 failed, and Sun escaped to Hong Kong. For the next sixteen years, Sun traveled to Japan, Southeast Asia, the United States, and Europe, recruiting supporters and seeking financial backing for future revolutionary activites.

Sun's Marriages and Consorts During Sun's revolutionary activities and foreign travels his wife, Lu Muzhen, dutifully took care of his parents, following Chinese tradition. The couple had a son, Sun Ke (Sun Fo, 1891–1973), who received an education in the United States and became a political conservative in the Nationalist Party. In 1895 the family moved to Honolulu, where they lived with Sun's brother Sun Mei. Lu Muzhen gave birth to two girls in Hawaii before returning to China in 1907.

When Sun was away from Lu Muzhen he had relationships with other women. When he was in medical school he had an affair with Chen Cuifen (1873–1960), and during a stay in Japan he secretly married a much younger Japanese woman, with whom he had a daughter he never saw. His most significant relationship was with Song Qingling, one of the three famous Soong sisters—daughters of the prominent businessman and missionary Charles (Charlie) Jones Soong (c.1863–1918). Qingling, a graduate of Wesleyan College in Macon, Georgia, became a fervent supporter of Sun's revolution. Although Sun was never formally divorced from Lu Muzhen, he married Qingling, twenty-six years his junior, on October 25, 1915. She became closely involved with Sun's political activities, and after Sun's death became active in Chinese Communist affairs.

Capture in London and Fugitive Status During Sun's trip to London in October 1896 he renewed his friendship with Dr. Cantlie. While going to meet him and his wife, Sun was invited by two strangers to stop at their residence, which turned out to be the Qing legation; they captured

Sun Yat-sen with his advisors, China, c. 1910s–1920s. *With his presidency of the Republic of China short-lived, Sun Yat-sen later established a government in the south of China, laying plans to gain control of the north. While Sun died in 1925, his efforts set the foundation for Chiang Kai-shek's successful campaign to create a united, modern republic.* © CORBIS

Sun and planned to send him to China for execution. With the help of a servant, Sun sent a message to Dr. Cantlie, who publicized the kidnapping in the *London Globe*. Embarrassed by the incident, the legation released Sun, and he became internationally recognized as a leading revolutionary figure in China.

Now regarded as a fugitive by the Manchu government, in July 1897 Sun went to Japan, where he disguised himself by cutting off his queue, growing a mustache, wearing Western clothing, and adopting the Japanese name *Nakayama*. Significant during his sojourn in Japan was his meeting with Miyazaki Torazō (Tōten) (1871–1922) and his brother Miyazaki Yazō (1867–1896), who shared Sun's views on overthrowing the Manchus and introduced him to influential people such as Inukai Tsuyoshi (1855–1932), later Japan's prime minister, who helped Sun with funds and housing. After returning to China in 1899 and planning a series of uprisings that failed, Sun went back to Japan for another three years, gaining support from Chinese students.

By 1903 Sun had begun to advocate for establishing a republic in China and creating a revolutionary army. In the next two years Sun expanded his following in Southeast Asia, the United States, and Europe, uniting rival parties and several student groups into a new central revolutionary organization, the Tongmenghui (United League, or Revolutionary Alliance). With young intellectuals part of Sun's revolutionary movement, he established the journal *Minbao* in 1905. It was in *Minbao* that his ideological principles of Sanmin zhuyi (Three Principles of the People) were first discussed.

Under pressure from the Qing government in 1906, Japan expelled Sun. Undaunted, Sun took advantage of the sympathetic French in Indochina and set up a military training base with the help of his loyal supporters Hu Hanmin (1879–1936) and Wang Jingwei (1883–1944), and he continued to establish branches of the Tongmenghui abroad, seeking support and funding. Despite his success in expanding his revolutionary movement, and clear indications in 1909 that the Qing government had weakened, further uprisings in China failed.

1911 REVOLUTION

Success finally came on October 10, 1911, at the tricity of Wuhan, where many revolutionaries had infiltrated the Qing army. On the day before, while revolutionaries were making explosives for a planned uprising, an accidental explosion occurred in the basement of a building in the Russian concession in Hankou. When it was revealed that local police had discovered a list of revolutionaries in the area, the Tongmenghui decided to begin a major uprising in Wuchang and set up a government at Nanjing. At the time, Sun Yat-sen was in the United States seeking funding, and he read about the uprising in a newspaper while traveling by train from Denver to Kansas City. Sun decided to continue his travels to Washington, D.C., London, and Paris, where he was largely unsuccessful in securing loans and diplomatic recognition.

When Sun returned to China on December 25, 1911, the revolutionaries controlled the southern half of China and had established a provisional Republican government at Nanjing. Four days later Sun Yat-sen was made provisional president, and on January 1, 1912, the Republic of China was formally proclaimed.

Yet, the revolution was not complete because the northern half of China was controlled by Yuan Shikai, who was supported by the Manchu government. To unite China, Sun offered Yuan the presidency on the condition that the emperor abdicated and Yuan supported the Republican government. Yuan agreed, and on April 1, 1912, Sun Yat-sen relinquished his title and presidential duties. Seeking greater control, Yuan moved the government to Peking (Beijing). In response, Song Jiaoren (1882–1913) brought the various parties in the National Assembly together and established the Guomindang (GMD, Nationalist Party). To counteract this potential opposition, Yuan called Sun Yat-sen and Huang Xing (1874–1916) to Beijing. Sun was appointed director of his own ambitious plan to modernize China by expanding railroad development throughout the country.

Despite his effort to placate Sun with a government appointment, Yuan saw his power slipping and resorted to bribery, threats, violence, and assassination of rivals. When Sun's supporter Song Jiaoren (1882–1913) was murdered at the railroad station in Shanghai on March 20, 1913, Yuan was implicated. Sun and Huang Xing considered retaliating against Yuan with military force.

THE SECOND REVOLUTION AND CIVIL WAR

As Yuan and the Guomindang fought over control of the National Assembly, Yuan sent his Beiyang Army south. When the military governor of Jiangxi Province, Li Liejun (1882–1946), declared the independence of his province, the Second Revolution (1913) began. In the safety of Japan, Sun reorganized and strengthened the Guomindang, naming it Zhonghua Gemingdang (China Revolutionary Party). Members were required to take an oath of obedience to Sun, but Huang Xing refused and broke from Sun.

Meanwhile, Yuan took dramatic steps to enhance his power. He dissolved the parliament in January 1914, making himself a virtual dictator, then declared himself emperor in December 1915. Yuan died on June 16, 1916, ending his farcical attempt at reviving the monarchy.

After the death of Yuan, a power struggle ensued between Premier Duan Qirui (1864–1936) and Vice-Premier Li Yuanhong (1864–1928). Duan eventually gained control in Beijing. Sun then attempted to ally with Zhang Zuolin (1873–1928) in Manchuria to launch a northern expedition against Duan, but the situation was complicated by the fight for control of Beijing by Cao Kun (1862–1938) and Wu Peifu (1874–1939), leaders of the Zhili clique, who challenged Duan Qirui, the recognized leader of the Anhui clique.

To revive the old parliament, Sun began the *hu-fa* (constitution protection movement) and organized a rump parliament in Guangzhou on August 31, 1917. This act plunged China into civil war. Dissension among the southern leaders paralleled those in the north, and Sun was forced by his once loyal military commander, Chen Jiongming (1878–1933), to leave Guangzhou. Sun fled to the French concession in Shanghai on August 14, 1922, and began to plan further military action.

The Nationalist-Communist Alliance When Chen Jiongming was driven out of Guangzhou by superior provincial armies, Sun returned to the city in January 1923 and sought ways to reorganize and strengthen the Guomindang. Enamored by Communist discipline, organization, and economic developments in the Soviet Union, Sun sought assistance from the Communists. The alliance forged by Sun and Adolf Joffe (1883–1927), a Soviet diplomat, was set out in a manifesto on January 26, 1923.

Mikhail Borodin (alias Gruzenberg, 1884–1951) was sent by the Comintern in October 1923. As Sun's adviser Borodin was instrumental in reorganizing the Guomindang, establishing a structure, regulations, and manifesto similar to those of the Communist Party of the Soviet Union. These principles were adopted on January 20, 1924 at the First National Congress of the Guomindang. Emphasizing his position and power, Sun took the titles *zongli* (head of government and party) and *dayuanshuai* (generalissimo). In May 1924 he created the Huangpu (Whampoa) Military Academy to prepare army officers for a northern expedition, and Chiang Kai-shek (Jiang Jieshi) (1887–1975), who had trained in the Soviet Union, was made commandant. Despite his cooperation with the

Sun Yat-sen, July 1, 1923. *Sun Yat-sen made his first attempt at overthrowing the imperial Chinese government in 1895, fleeing to Hong Kong after the plot failed. After several more false starts, Sun's revolutionary forces finally disposed the Qing emperor in 1911, establishing the Republic of China on January 1, 1912.* **TOPICAL PRESS AGENCY/GETTY IMAGES**

Communists, though, Sun fundamentally disagreed with Marxist ideology that denied materialism as a primary motivating force in history and the inevitability of class struggle.

The Unfinished Revolution While these events took place in South China, Duan Qirui emerged to dominate the northern government. Working with Zhang Zuolin, Duan invited Sun Yat-sen to Beijing to discuss a possible accord. Sun traveled via Shanghai and Japan, and when he reached Tianjin on December 4, 1924, very ill and in pain, he was brought to the Union Medical College Hospital and treated for liver cancer. Unable to negotiate with Duan and seeking comfort, he went to the home of Gu Weijun (Wellington Koo, 1888–1985), where he died on March 12, 1925, aged fifty-nine.

Sun left two "wills"—one leaving his modest personal effects to his second wife, Song Qingling, and another, drafted by Wang Jingwei, urging Sun's followers to complete the unfinished revolution.

SUNISM

Among the various treatises written by Sun, the most prominent was the *Sanmin zhuyi* (The Three Principles of the People). Sun's ideas for the Principles had taken form by 1905, but he revised them in 1919 and his work

was interrupted again in 1922. After making additional changes, in 1924 he finished the project except for two chapters of the third principle, livelihood (*minsheng*), which were written later by Chiang Kai-shek.

Sun's first principle, nationalism (*minzu*), emphasized ridding China of Manchu rule and foreign privilege while uniting Han Chinese and ethnic minorities. An independent, sovereign China, Sun contended, could be accomplished only after all foreign domination was eliminated. Despite his desire to eliminate indebtedness to foreign bankers, Sun's railway reconstruction program also was essential to unifying China, and he recognized the need for foreign loans.

The second principle, democracy (*minquan*), was to take the form of a republic that would guarantee against autocratic and tyrannical leadership. Sun cautioned against excessive liberty that could lead to anarchy; he favored a strong government and was not concerned that it would become despotic. In developing China's version of a republic, Sun conceived of a Five-Power Constitution that included executive, legislative, and judicial branches of government, as well as two from China's experience, examination and censorial branches, the latter of which would have impeachment powers. Seeking social changes, Sun proposed laws forbidding the sale of women into concubinage, cruel punishment, physical torture, and forced confessions.

In the third principle, livelihood (*minsheng*), Sun promoted a more equitable distribution of wealth, and his economic reforms focused on construction, industrialization, regulation of capital, and the equalization of land ownership. Large private industries such as banking, railways, and navigation were to be nationalized to prevent private capital from controlling economic life. Regarding land reform, Sun favored a single tax system, equating it with the "single whip method" (*yitiaobian*) of the Ming dynasty. Sun's plan was influenced by the tax theory of Henry George (1839–1897), a nineteenth-century American economist who supported land nationalization. Departing from George, Sun advocated a universal tax rate of 1 percent with future increases in land value to be appropriated by the government.

Western historians have questioned whether Sun's ideas were innovative or a synthesis of different schools of thought. Considering the structure of the democratic government he proposed and his social and economic views, Sun's ideology suggests a combination of traditional cultural heritage stemming from his early Chinese education and his Western ideas from his studies and experiences in Hawaii, Hong Kong, and Macao. Although Sun is generally admired by Chinese historians because of his contribution to China's modernization, some Western historians have criticized his writings as less sophisticated than those of the prominent reformers Kang Youwei and Liang Qichao. Nevertheless, some of the extensive and detailed proposals Sun outlined in *The International Development of China* had an impact on China's modernization in later years; for example, his program for railroad development and water control, which seemed unrealistic during his lifetime, have largely come to fruition under the Communist regime. In the twenty-first century, because Sun is admired in both China and Taiwan, his ideology has been considered as a possible basis of agreement for unification.

SEE ALSO *Revolution of 1911; Song Qingling; Wang Jingwei.*

BIBLIOGRAPHY

PRIMARY WORKS

Sun Yat-sen. *The International Development of China.* [1922]. 2nd ed. New York: Da Capo Press, 1975.

Sun Yat-sen. *Memoirs of a Chinese Revolutionary: A Programme of National Reconstruction for China.* [1927]. New York: AMS Press, 1970.

Sun Yat-sen. *The Three Principles of the People: San min chu i/by Sun Yat-sen; with Two Supplementary Chapters by Chiang Kai-shek.* Taibei: China Publishing Company, c.1989.

SECONDARY WORKS

Bergère, Marie-Claire. *Sun Yat-sen.* Trans. Janet Lloyd. Stanford, CA: Stanford University Press, 1998.

Chang, Sidney H., and Leonard H. D. Gordon. *All Under Heaven: Sun Yat-sen and His Revolutionary Thought.* Stanford, CA: Hoover Institution Press, 1991.

Chang, Sidney H., and Leonard H. D. Gordon, eds. *Bibliography of Sun Yat-sen in China's Republican Revolution, 1885–1925.* 2nd ed. Lanham, MD: University Press of America, 1998.

Schiffrin, Harold. *Sun Yat-sen and the Origins of the Chinese Revolution.* Berkeley: University of California Press, 1970.

Schiffrin, Harold. *Sun Yat-sen: Reluctant Revolutionary.* Boston: Little, Brown, 1980.

Wei, Julie Lee, Ramon Myers, and Donald Gillin, eds. *Prescriptions for Saving China: Selected Writings of Sun Yat-sen.* Stanford, CA: Hoover Institution Press, 1994.

Wilbur, C. Martin. *Sun Yat-sen, Frustrated Patriot.* New York: Columbia University Press, 1976.

Leonard H. D. Gordon

SUZHOU

This southern Jiangsu metropolis, a key hub on the Grand Canal, has long been celebrated as a paragon of cultural sophistication, refined natural beauty, and wealth, not only in China but throughout East Asia. Its renown is exemplified by the well-known Southern Song saying, "Above is heaven, below are Suzhou and Hangzhou." Founded as the capital of Wu in 514 BCE, Suzhou was only fleetingly the capital of a state, yet the city and its hinterland have been central to the political and economic fortunes of numerous kingdoms and dynasties due to its bounty of rice, cotton, and tea, the fame of its manufactured products such as silk textiles, and the wealth and power of its elites. During the Qing, 600 local men secured the *jinshi* degree (the highest degree in the civil service examinations), and about twenty secured the status of *zhuangyuan* (top scorers in the examination), a level of dominance unmatched by any other locality. This scholarly hegemony afforded Suzhou inordinate influence in politics and culture.

In the early nineteenth century Suzhou's urban population reached its imperial period apogee, estimated at 700,000 to one million, among the world's largest at that time. The city was devastated during the 1860 Taiping siege and the 1863 Qing recapture. It lost one-half to two-thirds of its inhabitants and was slow to rebuild. Shanghai, theretofore a small regional city, permanently usurped Suzhou's former role as dominant urban center, despite the efforts of Suzhou's officials, literati, and business elites to best their rival. Nonetheless, late nineteenth- and early twentieth-century city leaders implemented ambitious modernization schemes that aimed to deploy Western-style city planning to transform the city into a commercial and industrial metropolis.

TWENTIETH-CENTURY CHALLENGES

Following the 1911 Revolution the city lost its status as co-capital of Jiangsu Province; the outflow of provincial officials and their retinues again led to a severe depletion of the population and local economic activity. Urbanist development efforts nonetheless bore fruit, especially during the period of municipal government from 1927 to 1930, when the provincial government bore the exorbitant cost of intensive infrastructural reconstruction with an eye to making Suzhou a showcase city for the province and nation as a whole.

Throughout the Republican period, leftist writers depicted Suzhou as a redoubt of benighted feudalism dominated by wealthy landlords and Guomindang officials pursuing luxurious dissipation amid the city's many famed scenic spots. After 1949 officials attempted to reorient the city from a "consumer" to a "producer" city by bolstering textile production and reviving some handicraft industries, among other economic reforms. The new state also strove to redeem the celebrated scholar gardens, symbols of elite privilege. Beginning with the Liuyuan in 1954, a number of these were nationalized and opened to the public. By 1964 the Garden Bureau had reconstructed and opened twelve key gardens, which were reinterpreted as monuments to the labor, talent, and ingenuity of working-class people. Many historic and cultural sites, including the gardens, were damaged or fully destroyed by the Red Guards.

City planning and urban economic development, almost entirely neglected during the Cultural Revolution (1966–1969), were revived during the Reform Era. In light of the pervasive destruction of Suzhou's cultural properties and the possibility of future losses due to economic development, the central government successively designated Suzhou a Scenic Tourist City and Historic Cultural Capital in 1981 and 1982, and developed a comprehensive plan for the preservation of the historic Pingjiang quarter in the city's northeast. In 1986 the State Council approved a comprehensive city plan with the goal of "completely protecting Suzhou's ancient appearance while simultaneously constructing modern new areas."

BALANCING HERITAGE WITH DEVELOPMENT

Although complete protection of the traditional urban fabric proved untenable, the city's store of historic architecture marks it as increasingly unique in present-day China. Preservation efforts have been furthered by the growth of domestic and foreign tourism. Since 1996, through the efforts of local and national authorities, nine paradigmatic scholar gardens have been listed as UNESCO World Heritage Sites to augment their protection. An I. M. Pei (b. 1917) design for a new Suzhou Museum generated controversy in 2003 when it emerged that the construction required the demolition of a tatty section of a nineteenth-century palace, the Taiping Zhongwangfu. The museum, a graceful modernist interpre-

tation of Jiangnan garden architecture, eventually opened in 2006 and has become a Suzhou icon.

In an effort to preserve the historic city center, authorities have designated two new industrial economic zones as the city's major growth areas. To the west is the municipally managed Suzhou New Area Industrial Zone, established in 1990. To the east is the much larger Suzhou Industrial Park, originally named China-Singapore Industrial Park, which was established in 1994 as a joint venture with the Singapore government. Based on the planned Singapore industrial-residential community of Jurong, the park was originally projected to attract US$ 20 billion in investment, support a population of 600,000, provide employment for over 360,000 people, and cover an area of 70 square kilometers (27 square miles) once fully developed. Both have exceeded expectations and are among the most successful special economic zones in China, prompting discussion in management circles of a "Suzhou model of development." Foreign direct investment in Suzhou has, at times, exceeded that of Shanghai, and the city has become a center of light industry, pharmaceuticals, and electronics manufacturing. Per capita GDP for 2006 was 79,406 yuan (about US$ 10,087), fifth among 659 Chinese cities. Toward the end of 2005, the official population of Greater Suzhou was approximately six million registered permanent residence holders, of whom more than two million live within the city itself, and nearly four million immigrants.

In addition to raising living standards, this rapid development has fostered corruption. In fall 2008 Jiang Renjie, a former vice mayor in charge of urban development, transportation, and real estate, was found guilty of receiving a total of 108.67 million yuan, 50,000 Hong Kong dollars, and 4,000 U.S. dollars in bribes, and sentenced to death. At the time of writing, it was still unclear whether others might yet be implicated. The affair rocked the city and raised new concerns regarding the unforeseen effects of development.

SEE ALSO *Jiangsu; Urban China.*

BIBLIOGRAPHY

Carroll, Peter J. *Between Heaven and Modernity: Reconstructing Suzhou, 1895–1937.* Stanford, CA: Stanford University Press, 2006.

Marme, Michael. *Suzhou: Where the Goods of All Provinces Converge.* Stanford, CA: Stanford University Press, 2005.

Shi Jianhua, et al. *Suzhou gucheng de baohu yu gengxin* [The protection and renewal of Zuzhou's ancient city]. Nanjing, China: Dongnan Daxue Chubanshe, 2003.

Shi Yonghong. Suzhishi yuan fushizhang Jiang Renjie shouhui guoyi yishen beichu sixing [Suzhou City former Vice-Mayor Jiang Renjie who accepted more than a hundred million in bribes receives a death sentence]. http://news.xinhuanet.com/newscenter/2008-10/23/content_10238383_1.htm October 23, 2008.

Peter J. Carroll

T

T. V. SOONG

SEE *Song Ziwen (T. V. Soong).*

TAIBEI (TAIPEI)

Taibei, the capital of Taiwan, is unusual in that it is located in a basin surrounded by volcanoes and mountains. Some parts of the Datun (Tatun) Volcano Group dominating the northeastern skyline of the city still emit sulfur gas every day, even though their last eruption occurred an estimated two hundred thousand years ago. The sunken basin was previously a lake in different phases of topographic transformation, and after the water receded for the last time during the Kangxi period (1662–1722) of the Qing dynasty, the fertile catchment area nourished by four major rivers (the Jilong [Keelung], Dahan, Xindian, and Danshui [Tamsui], into which the others converge) soon became the foundation of the city. Such landscape antecedents not only mark the boundary and watersheds of the present city but also nurture Taibei's environmental resources (prominently the hot spring in the Beitou area) and irreplaceable urban characteristics that coincide with the association of the volcano, which is volatile, restless, and energetic.

The major rivers played a vital role in Taibei's irrigation and agriculture and led to the formation of trade routes and port towns. Early settlers of the Lowland Tribes (Pingpuzu) paddled their canoes (pronounced *mankah* in the aboriginal language) along the rivers for small-scale fishing and farming, and when the first-generation Han immigrants arrived in the early eighteenth century and built their first row of shop-houses by the Danshui River

quay (Guiyang Street of today), the image of canoe trading soon elicited a name for Taibei's first port town: Mankah. This port's strategic location at the confluence of the Xindian and Dahan rivers gained for the port the great advantage of extended trade with mainland Chinese merchants, and by 1740 it had already evolved into a significant township where merchant guilds operated businesses and built temples and shop houses.

Internal conflicts between Han clans and guilds of different immigrant origins led to bloodshed and consequential "exile development" in Dadaocheng (Tuatiutia), farther downstream the Danshui River. Dadaocheng developed by leaps and bounds owing to its flourishing tea trade with foreign merchants operating through the comprador system. Dadaocheng enjoyed wealth accumulated from foreign sources and became the most densely populated area in Taiwan of the late nineteenth century.

Taibei's morphological evolution took an unprecedented turn when Imperial Commissioner Shen Baozhen proposed to the Qing court in 1874 to build a city wall in the heart of the Taibei basin to secure an increased tea and camphor economy and satisfy demands for fortification. Taibei's inner city would be the last square city in Chinese history according to the rules of cosmology and its city wall one of the most short-lived before its demolition by the Japanese colonial regime at the turn of the twentieth century. But Taibei was also the first modernized city in China to have electric street lamps and other civil engineering and streetscape upgrades under the administration of the first provincial governor of Taiwan, Liu Mingchuan. The formal planned city drew private capital from Mankah and Dadaocheng to build up regular shop-houses along well-lined streets and boost market vitality. The tripod coordination of Taibei's three city blocs (Mankah, Dadaocheng, and the inner city gave rise to remarkable commercial prosperity and a vigorous street life, and allowed Taibei to emerge as a political and economic hub of northern Taiwan.

TAIBEI UNDER JAPANESE COLONIAL RULE

The Japanese colonial authorities, after they took control in 1895, reconfigured the inner city. The colonial planners ushered in baroque planning based on functional rationality and the Western "City Beautiful" concept. Accordingly, the symbolic city walls of the Qing period were torn down to yield their ramparts to tree-lined boulevards. An eclectic Renaissance-style architecture dominated most public buildings and street facades, while the old city gates were peculiarly preserved as landmarks inside the novel spatial form of grand boulevard circles. By imposing building codes, Japanese measurement standards, urban infrastructure, public parks, and public facilities, the Japanese refashioned Taibei into a crossover of Western urban planning superimposed on a traditional Chinese city scheme.

Under the Japanese, urban planning became an effective tool for building modern industrial cities in Taiwan to serve the purposes of Japan's imperial capitalism. Nonetheless, its implementation improved the living quality of common housing and the city as a whole, helping to improve sanitation and reduce riots in the colonial cities. During the period of colonial pacification, the Japanese—in three stages of urban-rectification planning and implementation in 1899, 1901, and 1905—modified the fabric of the existing city of around 61,221 and, despite demolitions of temples and houses on designated public domains, peacefully transformed the regional seat of Qing-dynasty administration into a modern city.

Prewar Japanese economic prosperity spilled over from Japan to its colony through Japanese merchants and administrative officials who brought their families and businesses to Taiwan. The population of Taibei reached 264,420, with the rate of increase peaking at 34.18 percent in 1931. Subsequently the comprehensive Urban Plan for Greater Taibei, drastically modifying the original plan, was announced in 1932. The 1932 plan incorporated the outlying areas of the Taibei basin and demarcated the boundary of the present-day city. The plan, covering an area of 25.7 square miles, 9.5 times the scale of the 1905 plan, was projected to the year 1955 when the population was expected to be 600,000.

During the Japanization phase of the colonial period, the planned development of Taibei manifested the Japanese determination to further modernize the colonial city even during wartime. The implementation of the influential Taiwan Urban Planning Ordinance (Taiwan Dushi Jihua Ling) started at 1937. This ordinance, the first complete regulation of physical planning, introduced

land-use zoning to Taiwan, a practice that increased the segregation of urban landscapes by use, by land rent, and by class and ethnic distinctions. It is still followed, as of 2008, by the Taibei Bureau of Urban Development and dictates urban patterns of most formal sector development. The ordered and modernized city of colonial Taibei manifests the Japanese intention to build a regional center featuring an integrated economy that merges the monopolistic state with private capital.

TAIBEI UNDER THE GUOMINDANG

Japan's fifty-year-long (1895–1945) colonial rule of high-handed measures and ostentatious conciliation had a tremendous impact on all aspects of Taibei's urban life and institutions and left an array of cultural legacies. After World War II, Taibei proved to be more advanced and modernized than most Chinese cities. When Chiang Kai-shek's Guomindang (Nationalist) regime resumed rule over Taiwan, it conveniently adopted Taibei's colonial planning and zoning codes with little reinterpretation. For nearly two decades after the war, Taibei developed by gradual spatial expansion based on the well-established colonial plan.

After Chiang Kai-shek's complete retreat in 1949, Taibei became the "temporary" capital of the Republic of China as well as the regime's political, economic, and judicial center. The tremendous amount of U.S. aid between 1950 and 1965 enabled the Guomindang to extensively develop Taiwan. In return, Taiwan strengthened its dependent affiliation with the United States and allowed itself to be absorbed into the world system of capitalism. The government instituted policies to move surplus capital and labor out of the agricultural sector into industrial production. Intensive industrialization fostered rapid urbanization. Predictably, Taibei and its surrounding regions absorbed the largest share of immigrants from rural areas all over the island. As a result of the influx of Mainlanders and rural immigrants, Taibei's population surged to a record-breaking half million by 1950. In 1967 Taibei was promoted as a Special Municipality, and most surrounding cities and towns in the Taibei basin east of the Danshui River were incorporated into the growing metropolis. The city's area increased to nearly 105 square miles, while the population jumped to 1.55 million.

The total population of the Taibei basin (including Taibei City and part of Taibei County) climbed from 2.62 million in 1970 to 4.07 million by 1980. Transportation became a critical issue, and the bridges connecting both sides of the Danshui River, originally built as escape routes in case of war, became directly responsible for the sprawl of Taibei's satellite cities. After its completion in 1957, the Songshan International Airport gradually assumed its key role as the new gateway of the capital and impelled the development of Taibei's northeast corner.

Taibei 101, the world's tallest occupied building, Taibei, Taiwan, June, 2004. *Set in a basin, surrounded by mountains, the capital city of Taiwan grew considerably after Chiang Kai-shek took control of the nationalist government on the island in the 1950s. Taibei quickly became a leading economic force in the region, initially producing simple manufactured goods before becoming known as a major exporter of high tech items since the 1980s.* © **LOUIE PSIHOYOS/CORBIS**

In the 1960s and 1970s the grand Dunhua Boulevard, extending from the entrance of the airport, was an impressive showcase of civil works to greet the visitor. It crossed Ren'ai Boulevard, of the same scale and meticulously cultivated landscape, and at the far end of Ren'ai Boulevard stood the symbolic Presidential Hall. But during the same period a brief detour from the boulevards into the back alleys and old districts of the city revealed activities and informal-sector constructions that told a different urban tale.

Nestled in small openings between buildings or sprawling out into the arcade spaces directly from private living rooms were subcontracting laborers engaged in piecework to help achieve and sustain the Taiwan miracle. Behind the facade of Taiwan's economic miracle of the early 1970s hid many a humble family working together as a nameless unit, so many that "the living room as factory" became a state slogan.

The economic takeoff since 1964 produced double-digit growth in Taiwan's gross national product. With a national saving rate higher than 25 percent, both developers and buyers were able to accumulate the capital necessary to stir-fry the housing market, particularly walk-up apartments. The inflation of land prices in Taibei since the 1970s made housing development costly and created an investment environment favoring capital-rich corporations and those who hoarded land from an earlier period. Housing became an unaffordable commodity for a large number of salary earners, and this situation evolved into a serious social problem in Taibei. In the 1980s one of the most significant social movements in the capital city was the Shell-less Snail Movement (Wu Ke Woniu Yundong), which, on the night of August 26, 1989, summoned more than 10,000 "snails without shells" (or people who could not afford housing) to take over and sleep on the street as a demonstration against the Guomindang's poor housing policy.

The lifting of martial law in 1987 was a turning point in Taiwan's grassroots movements. Ever since, protests and street demonstrations occupying the streets of the capital and paralyzing traffic have became common street scenes. Social movements transformed into many nongovernmental organizations, which advocated democratic participation at all levels. In the 1990s the concept of community empowerment prevailed in social discourse and action projects, and those who were disempowered learned to organize themselves or find like-minded citizens to advocate and initiate social action. Voices calling for preservation of historical heritage and landscape conservation began to challenge the predominant ideology of Taibei's urban development. Slogans jelled into policies and ordinances.

In 1994 Chen Shuibian, representing the Democratic Progressive Party, became the first directly elected mayor of Taibei. The 2000 direct election sent him to the presidency of Taiwan and toppled the long rule of the Guomindang. Taibei witnessed the incredible process of Taiwan's democratization. The city government was relocated to Xinyi Special District in 1994, which propelled the rapid development of the immediate neighborhood. With special design guidelines and zoning ordinances, the Xinyi District vied to establish itself as a regional business center for the global market and as a financial center for East Asia. Especially with the rise of Taibei 101 as the tallest building in the world in 2003, at 1,670 feet, the west-side historical cores of Mankah and Dadaocheng were further marginalized under its shadow. Yet the historical traces of the old city survived, including such sites as the West Gate area (Ximending), the squatter village at Baozangyen, and Dihua Street, and are irreplaceable.

But most of Taibei's 2,630,000 citizens (along with many urban commuters from Taibei County) would probably agree that the uniqueness of the capital city lies not in having the tallest building or a clean subway system in a bustling financial hub, but in having a liberal metropolitan atmosphere, a vibrant and nonstop nightlife, and a firm middle class society that likes to patronize numerous good bookstores, coffee shops, and teahouses at street corners. Some of the most distinctive urban experiences of Taibei can be explored by wandering into the crevices between Taibei's different historical layers: its beginning as a progressive Qing administrative city, its undeniable colonial past, overlaid with Westernization, democratization, and modernization. This distinctive city, which happens to preserve some of the most traditional traits of Chinese culture, such as the treasures in the National Palace Museum and traditional Chinese characters, is also the most liberal, heterogeneous, and open-minded of all Chinese cities.

SEE ALSO *Taiwan, Republic of China; Urban China: Cities and Urbanization, 1800–1949; Urban China: Organizing Principles of Cities; Urban China: Urban Planning since 1978.*

BIBLIOGRAPHY
Chen, Zheng-xiang. *Taiwan di zhi* [Taiwan's geographic records]. Taibei: Nan-tien, 1993.
Huang, Shih-meng, ed. and trans. *Taiwan dushi jihua Jiangxi lu* [Taiwan urban planning seminar records of 1937]. Taibei: Hu-Shih, 1992.
Wang Guofan, Chen Sanjing, and Huang Yuyuan, eds. *Taibei-shi fazhan shi* [A developmental history of Taipei]. Vols. 1–4. Taibei: Taibei Wenxian Weiyuanhui, 1981.
Zhang, Jingsen. *Taiwan de dushi jihua (1895–1988)* [Taiwan urban planning (1895–1988)]. Taibei: Yeqiang, 1993.
Zhuang, Yong-ming. *Taibei laojie* [Old streets of Taipei]. Taibei: China Times Press, 1991.

Min Jay Kang

TAIPING UPRISING

The Taiping Uprising (1851–1864) was the largest and, in terms of human lives, most costly armed conflict worldwide during the nineteenth century. The Taipings set out to establish a "heavenly kingdom of great peace" (*taiping tianguo*) under Christ returning in the shape of his younger, this time Chinese, "brother," Hong Xiuquan (1814–1864). The Taipings challenged the Qing court and its Manchu (not Han-Chinese) rulers as "of the devil" and set out to replace the Confucian state-examination system with a new canon made up of the Taiping testament and Christian testaments brought by Protestant missionaries.

The uprising is associated with three different and linked trajectories, including the Second Great Awakening, a highly energized outpouring of religious enthusiasm that began around 1800 in Europe and the United States. The Second Great Awakening was transnational in character,

HONG XIUQUAN

Hong Xiuquan (1814–1864) was the messianic leader of the Heavenly Kingdom of Great Peace. Born near Guangzhou (Canton) into a modest Hakka clan, he pursued education instead of emigration or rebellion as a way up, thus, like his eventual opponents, gaining familiarity with the Confucian canon. Failing to make the diminutive Hakka examination quota, in 1837 he fell into a mental crisis and experienced a vision, which became the blueprint for its later reenactment on earth: Brought to heaven on a "direct road," he was cleansed inside and out, and then brought before an "old man" with a blond beard and an unfamiliar outfit. This man complained that the Chinese had forgotten even the name of the creator and had sided with the devils. He ordered Hong to drive out the devils and redeem mankind, the first such effort having been made earlier by his first son. Hong was supported in his battle by the old man and his son, who referred to Hong as his "younger brother." After Confucius sided with the devil and drew many "brothers and sisters" with him, he was whipped on the old man's orders. After driving the devils back into their hell, Hong was ordered to go back to Earth and do the same, a mandate he reluctantly accepted. A promised explanation and proof for the authenticity of the vision failed to materialize, and he returned to teaching.

Not until 1843 did the proof turn up: the compilation *Good Words to Admonish the Age*, by the Protestant convert Liang Afa. Its excerpts from the Christian testaments explained the old man, his son, the devil, the battle, and Hong himself. In a strictly scriptural way, Hong concluded that he was God's second son, and that his was the Second Coming beginning with the apocalyptic battle. Unsure of this reading, he sought confirmation in Canton in 1847 from the American revivalist missionary Issachar Jacox Roberts (1802–1871), who rejoiced in the conversion of this untutored "Cornelius soul." Like many other new religious movements at the time, Hong's dispensation formed in a contact zone with a missionizing Christian religion. The Christian testaments, together with his own vision testament, became the fundaments of Taiping faith. After he began rallying supporters to destroy religious "idols" as counterparts to the "devils" of his vision, government persecution set in. In a dramatic turn, two of Hong's associates, Yang Xiuqing (d. 1856) and Xiao Chaogui (d. 1852), started acting as mediums for the old

man and his son respectively and were installed as military commanders. Such mediums of gods are familiar in south Chinese temples. After the Taiping had established the New Jerusalem in Nanjing, Hong assumed the title "King of the Heavenly Kingdom of Great Peace." The old man gave him that title rather than *di* (emperor) because that was the Qing emperor's blasphemous abuse of God's name.

Hong's main concern was to restore China to its belief in the one God from pre-imperial times and to guide the deluded "brothers and sisters" with a new orthodox Taiping canon and the iron rod of a Moses to become true "humans." He pruned the Chinese classics and wrote new songs, prayers, poems, and doctrinal works. At the same time, he was willing to absorb the best from the Christian "overseas brethren." Firmly convinced that God's support alone secured victory, he looked in vain for other signs after the death of the two mediums. Even during the final siege of Nanjing in 1864, the soldiers on the city wall were heard day and night reciting the new prayer written by Hong for the purpose. While the city fell, Hong took his own life.

An approach that treats religious fervor as a medical condition has long dismissed Hong as a mentally ill man; another approach has described him as cleverly disguising his anti-imperialist and antifeudal aims with religion. Research focused on the relative importance of the transcultural element in Taiping thought and practice has established links between the Second Great Awakening, an early-nineteenth-century Protestant revival movement in the United States, while others focused on elements of Chinese popular religion.

BIBLIOGRAPHY

Spence, Jonathan. *God's Chinese Son: The Taiping Heavenly Kingdom of Hong Xiuquan.* New York: Norton, 1996.

Teng, Yuan Chung. Reverend Issachar Jacox Roberts and the Taiping Rebellion. *Journal of Asian Studies* 23, 1 (1963): 55–67.

Wagner, Rudolf G. *Reenacting the Heavenly Vision: The Role of Religion in the Taiping Rebellion.* Berkeley: Institute of East Asian Studies, University of California, 1982.

Weller, Robert P. *Resistance, Chaos and Control in China: Taiping Rebels, Taiwanese Ghosts, and Tiananmen.* Seattle: University of Washington Press, 1993.

Yap, P. M. The Mental Illness of Hung Hsiu-ch'uan, Leader of the Taiping Rebellion. *Far Eastern Quarterly* 13, 3 (1954): 287–304.

Rudolf G. Wagner

critical of the established churches, and linked to "dissident clergy." It led to a dramatic increase in missionary activity organized by newly formed independent missionary bodies to convert the heathen before the impending millennium, and to numerous new religious movements in the contact zones between these missionaries and locals. The Taiping Uprising can also be linked to the social and political upheavals across the globe that accompanied the rise of modernity. These were epitomized by the 1848 upheavals across Europe and the 1857 Sepoy Mutiny in India, and were followed by a conservative backlash. A third trajectory was formed by the deepening internal crisis of a Chinese state challenged by a population explosion, low revenue, a clogged system of state-society communication, and assertive Western powers. A residual narrative from the historiography of the People's Republic of China (PRC) claims that the Taipings' "struggle against big landlords" and "against imperialism" was a precursor to China's revolution. No historical evidence supports this view, however.

ORIGINS

The Taiping Uprising originated near Guangzhou, at the time China's only gateway to the overseas world. The area had resisted the Manchu conquest, and was notorious for violent conflicts between "locals" (Punti) and immigrants purportedly from the north, known as "guests" (Hakka). During the 1830s and 1840s, numerous candidates claimed a mandate for opposing the Manchu court and restoring the Han-dominated Ming dynasty (1368–1644). Hong Xiuquan was the only claimant accepted beyond his clan and village, and he eventually challenged the dynasty altogether.

In 1837 Hong experienced a vision in which he was transported to heaven, where he encountered an old man and his son. The old man ordered him to drive out the "devils" who had conquered the lower layers of heaven and had found support among the Chinese "brothers and sisters" as well as Confucius himself. The old man ordered Hong to return to the earth and do the same battle. A book that had been announced in the vision to authenticate its truthfulness only materialized in 1842. It helped Hong understand his vision: The Chinese tract *Good Words to Admonish the Age*, which included excerpts from the Christian Bible and other religious writings, identified the "old man" that Hong had seen in heaven as God, as well as the old man's son, Jesus. The book also described a battle with the devil, and announced the return of the son, which Hong read as a reference to his own coming. Although reluctant, Hong decided to take up the battle against the devil. The divine support his cause seemed to receive, even in the direst of circumstances, might have prompted many to side with him.

To learn more about the teaching behind this tract, Hong and his cousin Hong Rengan (1822–1864) traveled to Guangzhou to visit the American revivalist missionary Issachar Jacox Roberts (1802–1871), who had followed the appeal of the German missionary Karl Friedrich August Gützlaff (1803–1851) to help in the rapid conversion of the Chinese. Despairing at his mission's lack of success, Roberts saw the arrival of the two men in 1847 as the hopeful "commencement of the outpouring of the Holy Spirit upon this benighted country." Many years of close interaction between evangelical missionaries and the Taipings followed. For these missionaries, the Taipings were part of the same worldwide outpouring of the Holy Spirit that had prompted them to come to China, and, given the preparatory work of the Spirit, they hoped for the "Blitzconversion of entire regions." The Taipings' success confirmed their dreams. The missionaries reckoned—in vain—that patient teaching might overcome the Taipings' "Socinian" and other theological "deviations," deviations that were to be expected among a people lacking previous exposure to true doctrine. They shared with the Taipings the belief that before the establishment of a unified imperial rule in 221 BCE, commoners and princes had believed in the one god. Thereafter, China had fallen victim to the devil with the eager support and agency of the Confucian literati. The Christian and Taiping message was designed to bring them back to the original Chinese belief in the one god that was also the Christian belief.

OPEN REBELLION

When Manchu forces intervened against the destruction of devilish village "idols" by Hong and his friends, Hong defined the Manchu rather than these sculptures as the true "devils" of his vision, and rose in open rebellion in 1851 in Jintian, Guangxi Province. Taiping action was seen as an effort at translation and reenactment of the heavenly scenario of the vision, enriched by references to authenticated precedents, especially the march of the children of Israel through the desert under Moses's stern leadership, St. John's Revelations, and the frequent divine interventions through Taiping mediums.

Battling the devil in the vision in heaven, Hong had been supported by the old man and his first son, who were translated into the earthly form of Yang Xiuqing (d. 1856), who became the medium for god, and Xiao Chaogui (d. 1852), through whom Jesus spoke. Both were installed as military leaders, with their trance utterances carefully recorded. After a swift and victorious campaign that also convinced their opponents of their divine support, the Taipings conquered faraway Nanjing in the rich Yangzi Valley, the "new Jerusalem," which became the capital of a large section of Central and South China. Manchus were killed wherever possible as "devils." The inability of the Manchu court to hold the Taipings at bay, together with the Taipings' strength and pro-Western orientation, led London to consider recognizing the Taipings as China's legitimate government.

522

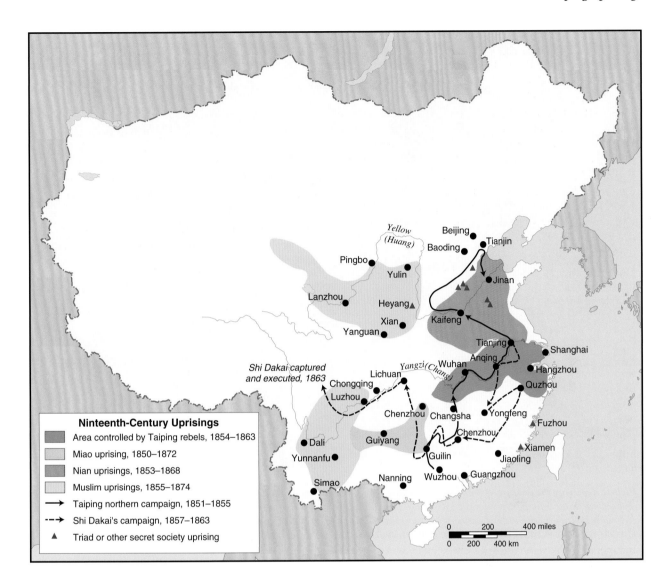

Ninteenth-Century Uprisings

- Area controlled by Taiping rebels, 1854–1863
- Miao uprising, 1850–1872
- Nian uprisings, 1853–1868
- Muslim uprisings, 1855–1874
- → Taiping northern campaign, 1851–1855
- --→ Shi Dakai's campaign, 1857–1863
- ▲ Triad or other secret society uprising

Once the "devils" were driven back into their "hell" (the Taipings designated as hell the region around Beijing where the Manchus exerted their power over the rest of China), the "heavenly kingdom of great peace" would be established. Confucian examinations were abolished and the Ten Commandments were ruthlessly enforced, following the model of Moses's rule with the "iron rod," to make the Chinese into "humans" once again. Unity among the "brethren and sisters" was stressed, and animosity between the Hakka and Punti denounced. The Taipings set out to establish a social environment that would encourage their brand of Christian behavior. It was to include hospitals, railways, schools, newspapers, and other elements taken from missionary reports about the West, along with a land system based on the *Ritual of Zhou*, with poorer regions receiving supplements from the surplus of their wealthier neighbors, the difference being that men and women received equal allotments. There was to be no separation between the professional army and civilians. In foreign policy, the Taipings' China was to join the "overseas brethren" as a Christian nation. They nevertheless steadfastly retained their doctrinal independence, with their direct mandate from god, and continued banning the opium imported by their overseas brethren. After the death, in an internal fight in 1856, of Yang, who had turned out to be a gifted strategist, the Taipings lost their strategic orientation. A march north to Beijing was halted in sight of the deserted city walls because no heavenly order had been received to proceed.

The increasingly conservative political climate in Europe after the upheavals of 1848 and the shock of the Sepoy Mutiny brought an end to the public sympathy that had supported the Greek struggle against the Ottoman Empire. Britain sold arms to the Qing court, and permitted its employment of British officers such as Charles Gordon (1833–1885). At the same time, a new generation of

Picture depicting the capture of Nanjing by Taiping rebels. *Many Chinese held deep sentiments against the Qing dynasty, displeasure that erupted in the Taiping Uprising of 1850. Led by Hong Xiuquan, a Christian convert who amassed an unorthodox following, the rebels eventually controlled large areas of southern China before collapsing in 1864 to Qing forces supported by Great Britain and France.*
THE ART ARCHIVE/SCHOOL OF ORIENTAL & AFRICAN STUDIES/EILEEN TWEEDY/THE PICTURE DESK, INC.

missionaries from the official churches arrived. They had little sympathy for their enthusiastic brethren either at home, where they cursed them as "Mormons" or "sectarians," or in the field, where they denounced their tolerance of "Mohammedan" polygamy and "heathenish" ancestor worship. The new missionaries dismantled the Association to Convert the Chinese by Means of Native Evangelists set up by Gützlaff in the late 1840s, many members of which had joined the Taipings in Nanjing.

The efforts of Hong Xiuquan to stem the tide by inviting his cousin Hong Rengan—the "most enlightened Chinaman" (as described by James Legge) with close links to missionaries in Hong Kong—to become prime minister in 1859 did result in a dramatically modern government program, but did not achieve its goal. The British government gained the concessions it wanted with the Beijing Convention in 1860, and then unequivocally sided with the Qing court. In the most radical exchange, one of the new missionaries claimed in 1861 that rather than being a part of the outpouring of the Holy Spirit, "the mission of the Taipinites is one of Judgement alone" for the Chinese refusal to adopt what he considered the true faith. Roberts, who by then was the Taiping "foreign minister," saw the Holy Spirit going to extremes: "Would it not be better in the highest sense of the word for half the nation to be exterminated than go on as they have been, if the other half should thereby learn righteousness?" (Roberts 1861).

FORCES OPPOSED TO THE TAIPING

A sense of crisis had begun brewing in China in the 1830s, although there was little understanding of the economic, demographic, or structural problems that might have been responsible. The crisis was instead attributed to a departure from the enlightened political ideals of the distant past, including the practice of remonstrance. The point of reference was the golden age in pre-Qin antiquity, mediated through writings on political reform by Gu Yanwu (1613–1682). This assessment of the crisis and its possible remedy

INSTITUTIONAL LEGACIES OF THE TAIPING UPRISINGS

The Taiping advanced into the Yangzi River valley, culminating in the establishment of the Taiping capital in Nanjing in 1853, endangered the Qing government, and undermined its revenue base. To raise funds for the Qing army, a transit tax on trade called *lijin* was instituted in Yangzhou in the same year and later quickly adopted throughout the provinces. The *lijin* tax was an extra duty for imported goods. Unlike maritime customs, which was fixed at 5 percent of the value of imported goods and collected by the Chinese Custom House on behalf of the imperial government, provincial governments collected the *lijin*, and the tax rate varied between provinces.

The introduction of the *lijin* tax allowed provincial governments to have additional funds to sponsor local militia groups known as *tuanlian*. Such militias in essence meant local militarization, posing a threat to the authority of the imperial government as well as a risk to social stability. However, facing the challenge of suppressing the Taiping rebels, the court gave its approval in the early 1850s.

Like the provincial governments, the Qing imperial government desperately needed further sources of revenue at this time. In 1858, with the help of the British, U.S., and French consuls, the government established the Imperial Maritime Customs Service, in which a British official was appointed as inspector general, to take charge of all maritime customs in treaty ports. Since the Qing government could not collect much land tax in the empire, the duties handed over by the Customs Service became a mainstay of revenue for the imperial government.

In sum, militias, the transit tax, and the Imperial Maritime Customs Service with its Western inspectors general were all institutions adopted by the Qing court in the 1850s. They helped the Qing court tide over its financial and military difficulties of the time, but increased the power of the provinces and gave foreigners an opportunity to interfere in the administration of Chinese maritime customs. The Taiping Uprising was finally suppressed in 1864, but as provincial leaders and Western countries refused to relinquish their power, these three institutional legacies and their impacts survived well into the Republic.

BIBLIOGRAPHY

Beal, Edwin George. *The Origin of Likin, 1853–1864*. Cambridge, MA: Harvard University Press, 1958.

Brunero, Donna. *Britain's Imperial Cornerstone in China: The Chinese Maritime Customs Service, 1854–1949*. London: Routledge, 2006.

Kuhn, Philip A. *Rebellion and Its Enemies in Late Imperial China: Militarization and Social Structure, 1796–1864*. Cambridge, MA: Harvard University Press, 1970.

Luo Yudong. *Zhongguo lijin shi* [A history of the *lijin* tax]. 2 vols. Taipei: Wenhai Chubanshe, 1970.

Willoughby, Westel W. *Foreign Rights and Interests in China*. 2 vols. Baltimore, MD: Johns Hopkins Press, 1927.

Wright, Stanley F. *Hart and the Chinese Customs*. Belfast, Ireland: Wm. Mullan and Son, 1950.

Sui-wai Cheung

was shared by the Taipings, with their constant reference to early monotheistic China; by ethnic Han officials such as Zeng Guofan (1811–1872), who campaigned against the Taipings after most Manchu units had been defeated; by intellectuals such as Feng Guifen (1809–1874), who wrote a daring critical appraisal of the state of the nation in 1862; and by the Protestant missionaries.

Defense of the embattled dynasty and of Confucianism was shouldered by Han Chinese officials led by Zeng Guofan and Li Hongzhang (1823–1901). They recruited local militias and drew on a newly imposed *lijin* transit tax in central Chinese provinces devastated by the Taiping march and Manchu vengeance. They cut into the Taiping recruitment base and were able to sustain a long war without central government financial support. Although the Taiping stood their ground and won many battles even in 1862 and 1863, their loss of strategic orientation and of perceived direct guidance from god put them into a passive position. Eventually, in 1864, the imperial army conquered Nanjing in a huge looting spree. The surviving Taiping leaders were flayed. The fourteen years of civil war left large parts of Central China depopulated, with the loss in human lives estimated by some at thirty million. Hardly a building of traditional religion or learning was left standing.

The Manchu managed to hold the throne until 1912, and the victorious Han Chinese generals kept their leadership positions. While they opted for a restoration after the Taiping demise, their extensive private staffs also provided new career options for innovative persons who originated many of the bolder reform proposals, ushering in the end of the dynasty. The hypothesis that the use of militias during the war militarized society and provided the backdrop for the warlordism of the early Republic has been disputed (Kuhn 1970).

THE AFTERMATH

Besides a few commemorative articles in a Chinese periodical in 1873, little energy was wasted overcoming the trauma of the civil war. The huge quantities of Taiping documents were destroyed, and today mostly survive only in rare copies carried abroad by missionaries. Stray Taiping units remained active as late as 1884, when Liu Yongfu's (1837–1917) Black Flags sided with the Qing against the French in Annam in present-day Vietnam. By 1900, revolutionaries such as Sun Yat-sen (Sun Yixian) dared to claim inspiration from Hong Xiuquan, and the Taiping myth started to develop with novels and document collections. By the 1930s, Taiping utopian dreams, stripped of their religious element, were read as forerunners of modern socialist aspirations, and eventually the Taipings were inscribed into official PRC historiography as early revolutionaries who failed only because they lacked the Communist Party leadership or ideology. The Monument to the People's Heroes in Tiananmen Square, completed in 1958, includes a succession of rungs illustrating the long revolutionary struggle leading up to Communist victory in 1949. The Taiping rebels, together with Lin Zexu's (1785–1850) burning of foreign opium, constitute the earliest "revolutionary" and "anti-imperialist" episodes depicted on the monument, followed by the 1911 Wuchang Uprising that led to the Republic and the 1919 May Fourth movement that brought about the founding of the Chinese Communist Party.

SEE ALSO *Giquel, Prosper; Gordon, Charles; Li Hongzhang; Qing Restoration; Zeng Guofan; Zuo Zongtang.*

BIBLIOGRAPHY

Callery, J. M., and Melchior Yvan. *History of the Insurrection in China, with Notices on the Christianity, Creed, and Proclamations of the Insurgents.* Trans. John Oxenford. New York: Harper, 1853.

Edkins, Jane R. *Chinese Scenes and People, with Notices of Christian Missions and Missionary Life in a Series of Letters from Various Parts of China with a Narrative of a Visit to Nanking by Her Husband the Rev. Joseph Edkins of the London Missionary Society.* London: Nisbet, 1863.

Hamberg, Theodore. *The Visions of Hung-Siu-Tshuen, and Origin of the Kwang-si Insurrection.* 1854. New York: Praeger, 1969.

Jian Youwen (Jen Yuwen). *Taiping tianguo dianzhi tongkao* [The institutional structures of the Taiping kingdom of heavenly peace: An investigation]. 3 vols. Hong Kong: Jianshi Mengjin Shuwu, 1958.

Jian Youwen (Jen Yuwen). *Taiping tianguo quanshi* [A complete history of the Taiping kingdom of heavenly peace]. 3 vols. Hong Kong: Jianshi Mengjin Shuwu, 1962.

Jian Youwen (Jen Yuwen). *The Taiping Revolutionary Movement.* New Haven, CT: Yale University Press, 1973.

Kuhn, Philip A. *Rebellion and Its Enemies in Late Imperial China.* Cambridge, MA: Harvard University Press, 1970.

Meadows, Thomas Taylor. *The Chinese and the Rebellions, with an Essay on Civilization and its Present State in East and West.* London: Smith and Elder, 1856.

Michael, Franz, ed. *The Taiping Rebellion: History and Documents.* 3 vols. Seattle: University of Washington Press, 1971.

Roberts, Issachar Jacox. For the Banner and Pioneer. *Baptist Banner and Western Pioneer* 30 (14 July 1847): 118.

Roberts, Issachar Jacox. Letter dated Nanking May 23, 1861. *Overland China Mail* 239 (12 July 1861).

So Kwan-wai and Eugene Boardman. Hung Jen-kan: Taiping Prime Minister, 1859–1864. *Harvard Journal of Asiatic Studies* 20, 1/2 (1957): 262–294.

Teng Yuan Chung. Reverend Issachar Jacox Roberts and the Taiping Rebellion. *Journal of Asian Studies* 23, 1 (1963): 55–67.

Wagner, Rudolf G. *Reenacting the Heavenly Vision: The Role of Religion in the Taiping Rebellion.* Berkeley: Institute of East Asian Studies, Center for Chinese Studies, University of California, 1984.

Wagner, Rudolf G. God's Country in the Family of Nations: The Logic of Modernism in the Taiping Doctrine of International Relations. In *Religion and Rural Revolt: Papers Presented to the Fourth Interdisciplinary Workshop on Peasant Studies, University of British Columbia, 1982,* ed. János M. Bak and Gerhard Benecke, 354–372. Manchester, U.K.: Manchester University Press, 1984.

Wagner, Rudolf G. Operating in the Chinese Public Sphere: Theology and Technique of Taiping Propaganda. In *Norms and the State in China,* eds. Huang Chun-chieh (Huang Junjie) and Erik Zürcher, 104–138. Leiden, Netherlands: Brill, 1993.

Wagner, Rudolf G. Understanding Taiping Christian China: Analogy, Interest, and Policy. In *Christen und Gewürze: Konfrontation und Interaktion kolonialer und indigener Christentumsvarianten* [Christians and spices: confrontation and interaction among colonial and idigenous variants of Christianity], ed. Klaus Koschorke (Hg.), 132–157. Göttingen, Germany: Vandenhoeck und Ruprecht, 1998.

Xiang Da, ed. *Taiping tianguo.* 8 vols. Shanghai: Shanghai Renmin Chibanshe, 1957.

Xie Xingyao. *Taiping tianguo zh Shehui zhengzhi sixiang.* 1935. Minguo congshu 4/79. Shanghai: Shanghai Shudian, 1992.

Zhang Dejian. *Zeqjing huizuan* [A compilation with information on the rebels]. 1932. In *Jindai Zhongguo shiliao congkan,* vol. 215. Taibei: Wenhai Chubanshe, 1968.

Rudolf G. Wagner

TAIWAN, REPUBLIC OF CHINA

This entry contains the following:

OVERVIEW

Historical narratives about Taiwan conflict sharply, illustrating the elusive nature of objectivity and underscoring the truism that history is among the victor's spoils. Chinese nationalists and Taiwanese nationalists view Taiwan's past differently. Characterizations of the island—including such factors as geological and genetic evidence that may verify a link between the island and the Chinese mainland—are freighted with implications for the political legitimacy of rival regimes.

Although Chinese nationalists claim that Taiwan has been part of China since antiquity, a preponderance of historical evidence suggests that Taiwan—like Mongolia, Xinjiang, and Tibet—was among those territories into which the Manchu rulers of the Qing dynasty (1644–1912) extended political control as part of imperialist conquest. Taiwan was represented on Qing maps and in its annals as a prefecture of Fujian Province beginning in 1684, before which there is no evidence of control by previous rulers of China.

Located approximately 80 to 100 miles off China's southeastern coast, Taiwan is far enough offshore to have been long perceived by Chinese as remote, but close enough to provide a bridgehead for potentially menacing foreign powers. For that reason, Taiwan has repeatedly figured in the geostrategic calculations of Chinese rulers and their adversaries abroad.

QING CONTROL

The Qing impulse to control Taiwan may have reflected an understanding that the island had served as a base for Dutch traders who established settlements along the southwest coast (1624–1661), Spanish who settled in the northwest (1626–1646), and an independent Chinese kingdom (the Zheng regime, 1661–1683) that took the island from the Dutch, allied with forces in southeast China loyal to the former Ming dynasty (1368–1644), and resisted Qing rule. Taking control of Taiwan offered the Qing hope that it could prevent the island from being used again as a redoubt by Chinese rebels or hostile foreign powers.

Yet, the Qing did not manage to exert control over the entirety of Taiwan. The central mountain range and the slender eastern seaboard remained home to non-Chinese aboriginal tribes that had once been the dominant population of the island. Qing authority extended along the western coastal plains, where the regime endeavored to accommodate both the claims to tribal lands by aboriginal peoples and the expanding demand for access to arable territory by Chinese migrants from the mainland, who pursued the cultivation of sugar, rice, and eventually tea.

To impede use of the island by rebels and ne'er-do-wells, as well as to maintain stability on what was a strategic frontier, the Qing quarantined Taiwan, forbidding Chinese from migrating to Taiwan at will and greatly regulating commerce and travel between the island and the mainland. Yet, friction between the aboriginal population and the Chinese migrants over access to land, as well as other forms of communal strife, led to rebellion and turmoil. The Qing sought to divide the island, establishing a north-south boundary beyond which Han Chinese were not permitted to reside. Over time, pressure by mainland settlers to turn more land to the tiller pushed that boundary deeper into what had been aboriginal territory. Conflict persisted.

By the end of the nineteenth century, the limits of Qing control over Taiwan's aboriginal population became a strategic liability when foreign governments protested to Beijing about the savage treatment their mariners faced when they fell into the hands of non-Chinese tribesmen—including some headhunters—after ships wrecked off Taiwan's shores. At first, the Qing court disavowed responsibility for what occurred beyond the boundary it established between its own jurisdiction and the wilds of aboriginal Taiwan. In 1867 and 1872, the court turned aside the grievances of American and Japanese envoys seeking protection from the Qing court for their citizens who came ashore on Taiwan.

In 1874, after Japan's protest was deflected by the Qing, Tokyo sent a punitive naval expedition to Taiwan to exact retribution from aboriginals for the killing of Japanese sailors, as well as fifty-four men from a Ryukyuan ship (the Mudanshe Incident). Japan, then in an expansionist mood, had both the Ryukyu Archipelago (annexed in 1879) and Taiwan in its sights. The Qing denial of jurisdiction east of the aboriginal boundary signaled to Japan—and other foreign rivals—that Qing sovereignty over Taiwan was contestable.

During the Sino-French War (1884–1885) for influence over Vietnam, France blockaded Taiwan and briefly occupied the northern port of Jilong as part of a naval campaign to ensure Qing compliance with the Li-Fournier agreement, a pact that greatly increased France's influence in Vietnam. This galvanized the Qing court to bolster its defense of and assert its sovereignty over the entirety of

Taiwan, which it then designated as a province in 1885 and over which it upgraded administrative control.

JAPANESE RULE

During the Sino-Japanese War (1894–1895), Japan successfully challenged Qing suzerainty over Korea, imposing in the Treaty of Shimonoseki a raft of punitive conditions, including the demand that the Qing cede Taiwan. Hence, from June 1895 until Japan surrendered at the end of World War II in August 1945, Taiwan was administered as a Japanese colony, despite a failed effort by Chinese elites to establish an independent Republic of Taiwan.

Fifty years under Japanese rule left indelible impressions on Taiwan's infrastructure, economy, social organization, culture, and relationship to China. Chinese nationalists tend to frame the period as an extension of the narrative of foreign imperialist oppression, emphasizing episodes of popular resistance on the island to Japanese colonial rule. Taiwanese nationalists tend to emphasize how Japan was just one in a succession of foreign regimes that came to govern, each contributing to a cosmopolitan identity rooted on the island that prompts Taiwanese to view themselves as distinct from Chinese.

Indeed, there was both considerable—and bloody—resistance to Japan and consequential assimilation of Japanese influence. Taiwan was integrated into the Japanese economy as a source of rice, sugar, camphor, and other agricultural products and later was developed by Japan to engage in light industry. Japan endeavored to modernize Taiwan, extending rail lines and roadways, introducing a telephone network, hydroelectricity, modern banking and accounting systems, improvements to public health and sanitation systems, hospitals, and schools. Strict social control was maintained by the Japanese who established a fierce system of laws, taxation, policing, justice, and punishment. Taiwan's Han Chinese and aboriginal peoples were highly regulated as Japanese subjects, but as second-class citizens in Japan's model colony.

Wartime mobilization prompted Japan to develop heavy industry on Taiwan. During World War II, Tokyo used Taiwan to stage operations elsewhere in Asia. At war's end, pursuant to the Cairo Declaration (1943) and the Potsdam Declaration (1945), "all the territories Japan has stolen from the Chinese," including Taiwan, were "restored to the Republic of China," even though that republic was established sixteen years after Taiwan was ceded to Japan and had never governed the island.

THE REASSERTION OF CHINESE GOVERNANCE

Taiwan's population was bitterly disappointed that the return of Chinese governors in 1945 did not feel like liberation from colonial rule. Chinese administrators sent by the government of Chiang Kai-shek (Jiang Jieshi) on the mainland mismanaged the island's affairs and its populace, giving rise to intense irritation that erupted in popular protest against the administration on February 28, 1947. China's forceful suppression of what it perceived as rebellion and its inclinations to totalitarian rule ensured decades of hostility between "Mainlanders," who dominated the political apparatus of the island as a minority, and the majority population that imagined itself as more "Taiwanese" than Chinese. This friction intensified after the Chinese Communist Party (CCP) established the People's Republic of China (PRC) on the mainland in 1949,

impelling the rump Republic of China government and its loyalists to take refuge on Taiwan.

BIBLIOGRAPHY

Campbell, William. *Formosa under the Dutch, Described from Contemporary Records.* London: Kegan Paul, 1903.

Davidson, James W. *The Island of Formosa: Past and Present.* New York: Macmillan, 1903.

Knapp, Ronald G. *China's Island Frontier: Studies in the Historical Geography of Taiwan.* Honolulu: University of Hawai'i Press, 1980.

Rubinstein, Murray A., ed. *Taiwan: A New History.* Expanded ed. Armonk, NY: Sharpe, 2007.

Shepherd, John Robert. *Statecraft and Political Economy on the Taiwan Frontier: 1600–1800.* Stanford, CA: Stanford University Press, 1993.

Teng, Emma Jinhua. *Taiwan's Imagined Geography: Chinese Colonial Travel Writing and Pictures, 1683–1895.* Cambridge, MA: Harvard University Press, 2004.

Alan M. Wachman

POLITICS SINCE 1945

Following Japan's defeat at the end of World War II, Taiwan was handed over to the Republic of China (ROC) government in October 1945. After a fifty-year gap, Taiwan was once again a Chinese province. Although most Taiwanese initially welcomed Guomindang (Kuomintang) (GMD) troops, corruption and misrule soon soured relations between the Taiwanese and their new GMD rulers.

Tensions reached a climax in the spring of 1947 following what became known as the February 28 Incident. An accidental shooting of a bystander in a scuffle over the attempted arrest of a vendor selling contraband cigarettes in Taibei sparked riots and led local Taiwanese to take over the running of most of the island's towns and cities. Although the GMD governor held negotiations with the Taiwanese Settlement Committee, he had secretly telegrammed for troop reinforcements from mainland China. When these troops arrived, thousands of the islanders were massacred, particularly educated members of the elite who had been involved in trying to keep order and negotiate. After the crushing of this uprising, the February 28 Incident became a taboo subject for over forty years. The legacy of the initial period of GMD rule in Taiwan was ethnic injustice and the creation of a cleavage between native Taiwanese and mainland Chinese identity that remains significant to this day.

Following the GMD's defeat in 1949 in the Chinese Civil War, martial law was declared on Taiwan in January 1950 and remained in effect until 1987. There was a massive wave of immigration from the mainland in 1949 and 1950 as the ROC's forces, civil servants, and institutions evacuated to Taiwan. This group and their descendants became known in Taiwan as *Mainlanders* and were to dominate the top positions in the ROC state for the next four decades.

In late 1949, few expected the GMD regime to survive long; however, it was saved by the outbreak of the Korean War in 1950. As a result, the United States protected Taiwan with its Seventh Fleet, and in 1954 the United States signed a Mutual Defense Treaty with the ROC. The GMD had initially set up a provincial government structure in Taiwan, but after the ROC central government arrived from the mainland, the two bodies began to administer completely overlapping territory. Since the ROC still claimed to be the sole legitimate government of all China, it was unacceptable to remove either layer of government. Therefore, a system of government was established in accordance with the 1947 ROC constitution, which was designed to cover all of China but from 1949 could only be applied in Taiwan. The government included two national elected bodies, the National Assembly and the Legislative Yuan. The former was responsible for electing a president and revising the constitution, while the latter functioned as the lawmaking institution. The Executive Yuan, headed by the premier, handled the day-to-day running of the government. In theory, this meant that there were two heads of state, the president and the premier. However, since Chiang Kai-shek (Jiang Jieshi), and then his son Jiang Jingguo (Chiang Ching-kuo), held the presidency for almost all of the martial-law period, political reality dictated that Taiwan had a presidential system.

Although Taiwan did not hold its first multiparty democratic election until 1991, it has a long history of conducting competitive nonpartisan elections. In 1946, soon after the GMD took control of Taiwan, elections were held for city, town, and district consultative councils. By 1955 the government offices opened to direct election included town, city, and county councillors, county magistrates, city mayors, and provincial assemblymen.

Although the ROC pointed to local elections to justify its claim to be "Free China," in reality the system fell far short of being fully democratic. Firstly, under martial law, it was forbidden to form political parties, and there were severe restrictions on constitutionally guaranteed freedoms of speech and assembly. The two permitted opposition parties, the Young China Party and the Democratic Socialist Party that had been formed on mainland China before 1949, played no more than a token role, becoming known as "flower vase parties." An attempt was made in the late 1950s by Mainlander intellectuals and Taiwanese politicians to form a Chinese Democratic Party. However, following the imprisonment in 1960 of its key instigator, Lei Zhen, the movement collapsed.

The GMD dominated elections throughout the first three decades of ROC rule on Taiwan. Elections were actually very competitive, with competition occurring between GMD-affiliated local factions rather than between political parties. When the GMD regime moved from the mainland to Taiwan, it lacked grassroots support; therefore, it chose to establish a patron-client relationship with local elites, which involved an exchange of economic privileges for political support. As a result, until the 1990s the majority of GMD candidates were from local factions. Although there was often room for independent candidates in multimember constituencies, the GMD did not face even a semi-organized opposition until the late 1970s.

The second democratic weakness of early elections was that only local elections were held. The highest elective offices were seats in the Provincial Assembly, while the members of the Legislative Yuan and National Assembly elected in 1947 on the Chinese mainland remained frozen in office. The justification was that national elections would have to wait until the recovery of the Chinese mainland; it was argued that if such bodies were elected solely in Taiwan, they would cease to represent all of China. Therefore, though Taiwan had regular elections, the central government and parliamentary bodies remained insulated from local public opinion.

Although in theory there was a separation of party and state under martial law, in reality the two overlapped. Therefore, it became a prerequisite for anyone seeking high office in the central and provincial governments, the military, and the civil service to be a GMD party member. Moreover, the GMD's total political domination enabled it to accumulate a vast real estate and business empire that became known as the *party assets*. Finally, even if candidates wished to challenge the GMD regime, they found it difficult to get their message out because the GMD dominated Taiwan's media.

ELECTORAL REFORM AND THE RISE OF OPPOSITION PARTIES

This situation only began to change in the 1970s. A combination of diplomatic, political, social, and economic developments contributed to the rise of an opposition movement that eventually became the Democratic Progressive Party (DPP). First, in 1969 the government began to open for election a limited number of supplementary seats in the national parliament, though the subsequent pace by which such seats were opened up for direct election was exceedingly slow. In the final supplementary election in 1989, only 30 percent of seats were contested, with many parliamentarians who had been elected on the mainland in the 1940s still in office. These limited national-level elections provided the opposition a platform

President of Taiwan Chen Shui-bian (center) campaigning with vice president Annette Lu (right), during a 2004 election, Kaohsiung, Taiwan, March 19, 2004. *After their defeat in the Chinese Civil War, thousands of Guomindang supporters poured into Taiwan, establishing control of the island and declaring martial law. Led by President Chiang Kai-shek, the Guomindang retained a firm grip on Taiwan until the 1980s, when martial law ended, fully democratic elections began, and native Taiwanese attained more positions in national government.* © **THOMAS WHITE/REUTERS/CORBIS**

from which to attack the GMD during election campaigns that became known as *democratic holidays.*

Another factor was the diplomatic setbacks of the 1970s, which damaged the GMD's claim to be the sole legitimate government of all China. Particularly harmful was the ROC's expulsion from the United Nations in 1971 and the loss of U.S. diplomatic recognition when the United States established full diplomatic relations with the People's Republic of China (PRC) in 1979. In addition, after Jiang Jingguo succeeded his father as president in the 1970s, there was a slightly more relaxed political environment, permitting the development of the opposition. One writer described this as a transition "from hard to soft authoritarianism" (Winkler 1984).

During the martial-law years, Taiwan experienced rapid economic growth, with an average growth rate of 8.9 percent

between 1951 and 1984, a phenomenon that has become known as the *Taiwan economic miracle.* These economic trends resulted in the creation of a much-expanded middle class. When the new opposition emerged, its strongest support initially came from the urban middle class.

In the late 1970s and early 1980s, an opposition movement involving anti-GMD figures began to coalesce. The movement became collectively known as the Dangwai (Tangwai), meaning "outside the party." The Dangwai movement began to openly challenge the GMD, and following a human rights march in 1979 that became known as the Gaoxiong (Kaohsiung) Incident, Jiang Jingguo reacted harshly by rounding up and putting on trial nearly all the leading opposition figures. The movement soon recovered, with the wives or defense attorneys of the prisoners standing for election. Gradually, the disparate

Main parties' vote percentage in Taiwan's parliamentary elections

	1986	1989	1991	1992	1995	1996	1998	2001	2004	2005
GMD	69.2 (80.8)	60.2 (71.3)	71.2 (78.2)	53 (59.6)	46.1 (51.8)	46.9 (54.8)	46.4 (54.7)	28.6 (30.2)	32.8 (35.1)	38.9 (39.4)
DPP	22.2 (16.7)	28.3 (20.8)	23.9 (20.3)	31 (31.1)	33.2 (32.9)	29.9 (29.6)	29.6 (31.1)	33.4 (38.7)	35.7 (39.6)	42.5 (42.8)
NP	—	—	—	—	13.0 (12.8)	13.7 (14.7)	7.1 (4.9)	2.9 (0.4)	0.1 (0.4)	0.9 (1)
PFP	—	—	—	—	—	—	—	18.6 (20.4)	13.9 (15.1)	6.1 (6.1)
TIP	—	—	—	—	—	—	1.5 (0.4)	0 (0)	0 (0)	—
TSU	—	—	—	—	—	—	—	8.5 (5.8)	7.8 (5.3)	7.1 (7.1)
CSDP	—	—	0 (2.1)	0.6 (1.6)	—	—	—	—	—	—

Note: Guomindang (GMD), Democratic Progressive Party (DPP), New Party (NP), People First Party (PFP), Taiwan Independence Party (TIP), Taiwan Solidarity Union (TSU), Chinese Social Democratic Party (CSDP). Party seat shares are shown in parenthesis.

SOURCE: National Chengchi University Election Study Center election database; Schaferrer 2003.

Table 1

groups moved from setting up associations toward founding a political party, nominating a slate of candidates, and presenting voters with a common policy platform.

By the mid-1980s, it had become increasingly difficult for the GMD to crack down on the opposition, as it had done in 1979. When the DPP was formed illegally in 1986, instead of mass arrests, Jiang tolerated the move and talked of ending martial law. The DPP was able to gradually expand its support base on a platform of democratization, self-determination, and ethnic justice.

By the time martial law ended in 1987, the GMD had also become a fundamentally different party. The Mainlander domination of party and government positions had gradually eroded under Jiang Jingguo, a process described as *Taiwanization*. The number of non-Mainlander politicians in the party's central standing committee rose from zero in 1952 to more than 57 percent in 1993. In addition, the party had largely ceased to pay lip service to the notion of recovering the Chinese mainland; instead, it increasingly based its legitimacy on its economic record, democratic reforms, and electoral performance.

When Jiang Jingguo died in 1988, his vice president, Li Denghui (Lee Teng-hui), succeeded him to become the ROC's first non-Mainlander president. Although Jiang had initiated democratic reforms, their speed and scope increased under Li. During the 1990s, a series of constitutional revisions radically altered the structure of the ROC government. First, there was a huge expansion in the number of offices opened for direct election, a process that culminated in the first direct presidential election in 1996. The first fully democratic elections were held for the National Assembly in 1991, the Legislative Yuan in 1992, and the provincial governorship in 1994. In addition, the overlapping government structure was radically streamlined. In the late 1990s, the entire provincial gov-

ernment structure was abolished; then, in 2000, the National Assembly was frozen, with the power for constitutional reform moving to the Legislative Yuan.

The smooth and peaceful democratization that occurred under Li Denghui in the 1990s led to international praise of Taiwan's democracy. Unlike many other new democracies, Taiwan's parties became institutionalized, elections were highly competitive, and parties debated important political issues during the campaigns. Moreover, Taiwan's parties moved from their initially polarized positions on core issues to moderate centrist stances during the 1990s. When in 2000 Taiwan experienced its first change in ruling parties, some observers claimed that Taiwan had become a consolidated democracy. However, since 2000, appraisals of the state of Taiwan's democracy have been increasingly critical. Key factors in the changing mood include the 2001–2002 economic recession, increasing party polarization, and political violence.

ELECTORAL TRENDS

An examination of electoral trends reveals the patterns of change and continuity in Taiwan's party politics since the first multiparty elections in 1986. Table 1 shows the main parties' share of the vote and seats in parliamentary elections between 1986 and 2005.

Although a large number of political parties were formed following the termination of martial law, the GMD and DPP were the only two relevant political parties in the first four elections. During this period, Taiwan had a system dominated by one party, as the GMD won absolute majorities in both vote and seat shares. During the mid-to-late 1990s, the party system became more competitive, with the arrival of a third important party, the New Party (NP). Although the GMD retained its seat-majority in

The main parties' vote percentage in Taiwan's first three presidential elections

	1996	2000	2004
GMD	54	23.1	49.9
DPP	21.1	39.3	50.1
NP	14.9	0.1	—
PFP	—	36.8	—
Others	10	—	—

SOURCE: National Chengchi University Election Study Center election database.

Table 2

both the National Assembly and Legislative Yuan, it could no longer garner a majority of the vote share.

After 2000 the party system became both more complex and more competitive, with no single dominant party and four relevant parties. The DPP replaced the GMD as the largest party in terms of both vote and seat shares but could not gain a parliamentary majority, and two new parties emerged, the Taiwan Solidarity Union (TSU) and the People First Party (PFP). In 2001 the PFP challenged the GMD's position as the largest opposition party. In parliament, the PFP allied with the GMD to form a legislative majority that could block DPP government bills, an alliance known as the *Pan Blue bloc*. Similarly, the TSU and DPP became known as the *Pan Greens*.

In 2008 Taiwan planned to implement a new single-member district, two-vote electoral system for legislative elections. Under the new system, only one candidate will be elected in each constituency, and voters will have one vote for their preferred candidate and a second for a political party. This system was expected to favor the two largest parties, the GMD and DPP, leading to the development of a two-party system. The trends in election results indicate that, compared to neighboring democracies such as South Korea or Japan, Taiwan's party system has been much more stable—the GMD and DPP have remained Taiwan's major political parties since 1986.

Table 2 shows the results of the first three presidential elections in Taiwan.

The overall trend is the exact reverse of that seen in parliamentary elections; in presidential elections, there has been a progressive reduction in the number of relevant parties compared to the move toward multiparty politics in parliamentary elections. The first direct presidential election was held in 1996, and was the GMD and Li Denghui's greatest victory. Li won with 54 percent of the vote against two GMD rebel candidates and an official DPP candidate.

The Li Denghui era came to an end in the second direct presidential election in 2000. This time, there were three relevant candidates, including one rebel GMD candidate, the former provincial governor, Song Chuyu (James Soong). The election was disastrous for the GMD when its candidate, Lian Zhan (Lien Chan), took third place with only 23 percent of the vote, while Song almost won with 36 percent. But it was the DPP's Chen Shuibian (Chen Shui-bian) who emerged victorious with 39 percent of the vote. Thus, the 2000 election brought about Taiwan's first change of ruling parties through elections.

In the third presidential election in 2004, Lian and Song stood as a joint GMD/PFP ticket against the DPP incumbent in a two-horse race. Despite Lian and Song holding a huge initial lead in opinion polls, the DPP was able to gradually narrow the gap until Chen Shuibian overtook the GMD in some polls the week before voting day. Chen won the election by a slim margin of thirty thousand votes, but the GMD challenged the legitimacy of the election result, accusing the DPP of electoral fraud. In the aftermath of the contested election, Taiwan experienced its worst political violence since the late 1980s when pro-GMD protestors demanded that the election be nullified. The disputed election has led to the increasing polarization of the island's parties and constant legislative gridlock. Both trends have contributed to growing disillusionment and cynicism among voters over the state of Taiwanese democracy.

Since the GMD's second presidential defeat it has achieved a remarkable recovery in its fortunes. After the Taipei mayor Ma Yingjiu (Ma Ying-jeou) became party chairman the GMD became increasingly popular, winning a series of local elections in 2005 and 2006. In contrast, the sluggish economic growth, perceived DPP extremism and corruption scandals all contributed to rising voter dissatisfaction with the DPP government. As a result of these developments and the new electoral system, the GMD won landslide victories in both the legislative and presidential elections in 2008.

SEE ALSO *Chen Shuibian; Chiang Kai-shek (Jiang Jieshi); Li Denghui (Lee Teng-hui).*

BIBLIOGRAPHY

Corcuff, Stéphane, ed. *Memories of the Future: National Identity Issues and the Search for a New Taiwan.* Armonk, NY: Sharpe, 2002.

Fell, Dafydd. *Party Politics in Taiwan: Party Change and the Democratic Evolution of Taiwan, 1991–2004.* London: Routledge, 2005.

National Chengchi University Election Study Center election database. http://esc.nccu.edu.tw/eng/data/data01.htm

Rigger, Shelley. *Politics in Taiwan: Voting for Democracy.* London: Routledge, 1998.

Roy, Denny. *Taiwan: A Political History*. Ithaca, NY: Cornell University Press, 2003.

Schaferrer, Christian. *The Power of the Ballot Box: Political Development and Election Campaigning in Taiwan*. Lanham, MD: Lexington, 2003.

Tien Hung-mao. *The Great Transition: Political and Social Change in the Republic of China*. Stanford, CA: Hoover Institution Press, 1989.

Tien Hung-mao, ed. *Taiwan's Electoral Politics and Democratic Transition: Riding the Third Wave*. Armonk, NY: Sharpe, 1996.

Winkler, Edwin A. Institutionalization and Participation on Taiwan: From Hard to Soft Authoritarianism? *The China Quarterly* 99 (September 1984): 481–499.

Dafydd Fell

ECONOMIC DEVELOPMENT SINCE 1945

Taiwan's economic rise since 1945 has been miraculous. When Taiwan reverted to China in 1945, the former Japanese colony was an agricultural economy. After trade ties with the mainland were severed when the Communists took power in 1949, Taiwan was barely able to produce basic products to meet the demands of its population of eight million. This situation changed completely over the following decades. Per capita gross domestic product (GDP) rose from $146 in U.S. dollars in 1951 to $14,519 in 2000, a hundredfold increase within fifty years. Taiwan was transformed from an agricultural exporter to a major global producer of industrial products, and in 2000 Taiwan ranked as the fourteenth-largest exporter in the world.

THE STATE'S ROLE IN TAIWAN'S ECONOMIC DEVELOPMENT

Both intentionally and unintentionally, the state was a critical player in Taiwan's economic development. In the late 1950s, as the small domestic market became saturated, the government adopted an export-oriented strategy. Measures to encourage exports included devaluing the currency, providing preferential loans and tax rebates for exporting firms, providing exporting firms with foreign exchange to import the necessary equipment, materials, and technology, and building export-processing zones. Hundreds of export-processing zones throughout the island contributed to exportation in the way of direct exporting and a demonstrative effect for exportation. In addition, the development of education provided a basis for the growth of a qualified labor force: 95 percent of primary-school-age children attended school in 1964, and 80 percent of junior-high-school-aged children attended school in 1970.

The government economic planning agency, whose name changed over time, played a leading role in economic development by formulating and executing important industrial policies. By the mid-1980s, two economic officials had become the architects of Taiwan's economy. Yin Zhongrong (1903–1963), empowered by Chiang Kai-shek (Jiang Jieshi), initiated most of the crucial economic policies. Later, Li Guoding (K. T. Li, 1910–2001), known as the "godfather of Taiwan's high-tech industries," became associated with the growth of the semiconductor and computer industries. In addition, the government's industrial policy contributed to the success of Taiwan's petrochemical and semiconductor industries, although government efforts to develop the automobile industry ended in failure. Due to the substantial government intervention in the economy, Taiwan was labeled a "developmental state."

Evidence shows that the Guomindang's (GMD's) top priority was to maintain its rule on Taiwan. Therefore, economic policies were often based on political, rather than economic, considerations, and economic goals were subject to political goals. For example, although a number of measures were taken to boost exports between the late 1950s and the early 1960s, state-owned banks continued to lend money to large firms that were not involved in exporting, thus undermining the government's efforts to boost exports. This occurred because the government needed to secure the support of large firms that had been fostered by the GMD regime.

In the beginning, capital consisted mainly of fixed assets left by former Japanese colonists and equipment and capital relocated from Chinese mainland. U.S. aid played a critical role in the 1950s in Taiwan's development. Entering the 1960s domestic savings emerged as Taiwan's primary source of capital.

LAND REFORMS

Learning from its bitter experience on the mainland, the GMD conducted land reforms to win the support of peasants, to foster independent farmers, and to secure a supply of grain for the armed forces. Between 1949 and 1961, a total of 107,000 *jia* (one *jia* equals 9,699 square meters, or about 2.4 acres) of state-owned land that was formerly owned by Japanese colonialists was transferred to 203,500 farming households, and a total of 143568 *jia* of land was bought from 106,049 landlords and sold to 194,823 farming households. Due to the land reforms, the proportion of rented land to total farming land dropped from 41 percent in 1949 to 10 percent in 1961. The political and economic consequences for the GMD were that it won the support of the farmers, most of whom had never expected to own their land. In addition, the increased agricultural output met the demand for food on the island. With the rise in the farmers' purchasing power,

Workers operating lathes in a ceramics factory, Taipei, Taiwan, 1977. *Though previously an agricultural colony of Japan, Taiwan quickly became an economic powerhouse after the 1949 takeover by the Republic of China. Initially supported by the United States to counter Soviet influence in the region, Taiwan became home to a large number of small to medium-sized businesses that provided the country with a lucrative flow of manufactured goods for the export market.* © PIERRE BARBIER / ROGER-VIOLLET / THE IMAGE WORKS

the domestic market for industrial products expanded. Agricultural taxation was an important component of government revenue during the 1950s and 1960s. A number of former landlords became industrialists after they were paid for their land with shares in the privatized state-owned companies.

PRE-1980s DIVISION OF LABOR

Until the mid-1980s, there was a clear division of labor between state enterprises and private-sector companies. This division was characterized by a "dual market" and a "tripartite market." The dual market comprised the domestic market, which was jointly monopolized by state enterprises and large private enterprises, and the export market, which was dominated by small and medium-sized enterprises (SMEs). The tripartite market comprised state enterprises, large private enterprises, and SMEs. State enterprises, including those owned by the central and provincial governments, as well as the military and the GMD, monopolized upstream sectors like petrol refining and steel, the financial sector, infrastructure, transportation, and basic industries, as well as monopoly sectors like tobacco. Large private firms were entrenched in the intermediate stream industries, such as petrochemicals, and SMEs had a free run in the downstream sectors. This unique division of labor was an unintended consequence of the state's policy toward the private sector, according to which the state protected and restricted large firms while neither encouraging nor restricting SMEs. The division was also the result of the state's political strategy for managing societal forces.

LEADING COMPANIES

The success of a number of companies typifies the emergence of Taiwan's economy. Formosa Plastics Corporation and Taiwan Semiconductor Corporation represent traditional industries and high-tech industries respectively. Formosa Plastics was founded in 1954. By the 1970s, it had become the largest company in Taiwan and the world's largest producer of polyvinyl chloride. Taiwan Semiconductor, a state-private joint venture initiated by the government in the early 1980s, became one of the most successful global producers in the semiconductor industry. Two other companies, Acer and Hon Hai (Foxconn), display Taiwan's strength in the computer and electronics industry.

SMALL AND MEDIUM-SIZED COMPANIES

Taiwan's economic experience is distinctive in the success of its SMEs. SMEs have formed the backbone of Taiwan's rise as a competitive global exporter, which in turn has been the engine of Taiwan's industrialization. For example, SMEs accounted for 44.9 percent of the entire value of production in 1976, and 47.6 percent in 1984. SMEs employed 61 percent of all workers in 1976 and contributed over 60 percent of the value of exports.

However, the government's contribution to the success of the SMEs was limited. By the time the government began to pay attention to SMEs in the mid-1970s, they had already become the island's major exporters. Even though a number of SME policies and measures were initiated after the mid-1970s, their impact was limited. Nevertheless, Taiwan's SMEs benefited from the division of labor between the state-owned enterprises, large enterprises, and SMEs. This marketplace structure provided space for SMEs to operate. In general, the success of the SMEs came about through their own efforts, including their flexible production, low labor costs, international linkages, and cooperative networks that resolved problems ranging from capital to marketing, management, and technology. Cultural traits, such as being one's own boss, diligence, family values, and close family relationships, also played an important role in the success of Taiwan's SMEs.

UPGRADE AND RELOCATION

Due to the rapid rise in costs and environmental pressures on the island, in the mid-1980s Taiwan was no longer a desired location for producers of labor-intensive products. The SMEs began to move their operations to Southeast Asia and the Chinese mainland, with Taiwanese investments in these regions reaching over $200 million, making Taiwan the region's second-largest investor, after Japan. Outsourcing opened a much larger stage for Taiwan's companies to flourish, as Taiwan became the second-largest provider of parts and components in Asia. Beginning in the mid-1980s, Taiwan upgraded to a capital and technology-based economy. As manufacturing activities moved to the mainland, Taiwan's economy hollowed, and services rapidly rose from 55.1 percent in 1991 to 73.44 in 2006.

INFRASTRUCTURE, ENERGY AND ENVIRONMENT

As the economy developed, infrastructure continuously improved. There were six main infrastructure projects during the late 1960s and mid-1970s: Taizhong Port, Suao Port, Taibei (Taipei) International Airport, a highway to connect Taibei and Gaoxiong (Kaohsiung), a north-south electric railway, and an east-west Tropic of Cancer railway across the island. These projects greatly enhanced Taiwan's level of infrastructure. A second highway was built in the 1980s. In the 1990s and 2000s, subway systems were built in Taibei and Gaoxiong, and in 2006 a high-speed 300-kilometer-per-hour railway connected Taibei and Gaoxiong, a distance of 345 kilometers, reducing travel time from four hours to one and a half hours. This was the first public project in Taiwan's history that was invested and built by private companies. It was also the world's largest public BOT (build-operate-transfer) project. Taiwan now also boasts a well-developed air network that connects all major cities on the island, as well as the offshore cities.

Taiwan lacks energy resources and in 2007 was 95 percent dependent on imports to meet its energy demands. Petroleum and gas make up 69 percent of the island's energy consumption, while coal and nuclear sources account for 32 percent and 8.5 percent respectively. The government has attempted to increase energy production in order to meet the needs of the country's rapid industrial growth. Beginning in the late 1960s, the development of nuclear power became part of the energy strategy. The first nuclear power plant was built in 1978, and two others were completed in the early 1980s. The construction of a fourth plant that was interrupted by political dispute is supposed to be completed in 2012.

Rapid industrial growth in the 1960s and 1970s was achieved at the expense of the environment. There was little attention to pollution until the 1980s. An Environmental Protection Administration (EPA) was established in 1987, and thereafter a number of laws and regulations were promulgated, including regulations that require polluters to pay fines. In the early 1990s, the government encouraged private investment in the environmental sector, and shifted emphasis from encouraging investment to boosting industrial upgrades aimed at controlling pollution. Tax exemptions and subsidies were provided for companies that procured environment-related equipment and technologies. The government has also implemented a strategy to increase the supply of clean energy and to

Workers producing air conditioning units, Nanchang, China, June 12, 2007. *In the 1980s, many of Taiwan's labor-intensive industries left the island for the People's Republic of China, replaced by firms engaged in the manufacture of high-tech goods. By the 2000s, many of these companies began shifting the production of high tech products to the mainland, while keeping business offices and research and development centers in Taiwan.* © **ADRIAN BRADSHAW/EPA/CORBIS**

diversify the composition of energy. In 2007 renewable energy amounted to 5.9 percent of the total energy supply.

ECONOMIC TIES ACROSS THE TAIWAN STRAIT

The Chinese mainland has become Taiwan's most important investment destination and trading partner. The mainland is also a major recipient of Taiwan's outsourced industries. After Taiwan's government opened the door to the mainland in 1987 and allowed residents to visit families and relatives there, economic ties across the strait grew considerably. In 2006 trade with the mainland was $88.12 billion, with a $38.54 billion Taiwan surplus. The mainland has become Taiwan's biggest export destination and the biggest source of its trade surplus. But the rapid increase in trade with the mainland has led to Taiwan's trade dependence on the mainland. The share of Taiwan's exports to the mainland (including Hong Kong) as a proportion of its total exports increased from 26.6 percent in 2001 to 39.8 percent in 2006.

The sum of Taiwan's investments in the mainland that were approved by the government reached $47.25 billion in 2005, representing 53.28 percent of Taiwan's total accumulated foreign investment, with some 35,000 Taiwanese firms holding investments on the mainland. But the true numbers may be much higher than those provided by Taiwanese authorities. Many companies invested in the mainland through a third location in order to avoid restrictions imposed by Taiwan's government. According to official statistics provided by the mainland, there were 70,256 Taiwanese firms on the mainland. The sum of Taiwan's investments represented 71 percent of its total foreign investment in 2005 and 63.9 percent in 2006.

Forty percent of Taiwan's industrial exports were produced on mainland China, but in the communications and information-technology sectors, the figure had reached 73 percent by 2005. The focus of Taiwan's investment on the mainland has undergone a shift from SMEs to business groups, from labor-intensive industries to technology-based industries, and from manufacturing to services. As a result, a new economic pattern has emerged: Business groups are maintaining their operational centers and core research-and-development activities in Taiwan, are moving manufacturing activities and some research and development to the mainland, and are exporting products to North America, Europe, and Japan.

STANDARD OF LIVING AND TWENTY-FIRST-CENTURY CHALLENGES

Taiwan's standard of living steadily increased with economic growth. The share of household spending on food and clothing relative to total spending decreased from 44.8 percent in 1984 to 31.0 percent in 1996. The most noteworthy achievement was the relatively equal distribution of income among the citizenry. Between 1964 and 2000, the income of the top 25 percent of the population was 4 to 5.5 times that of the lowest 25 percent of the population. After 2001, this gap doubled.

Entering the twenty-first century, Taiwan's economy faces a number of problems: its aging population, fewer children, slow industrial upgrading, energy supply, and the conflict between industrial development and environmental protection. Between 2001 and 2006, economic growth was 3.4 percent, lower than that of Singapore, South Korea, and Hong Kong, the other three Asian "tigers." The political divisions between the ruling DPP government (2000–2008) and the opposition GMD, along with cold cross-strait relations, exacerbated the situation. In the late 1990s, cross-strait relations replaced the ruling party's focus on power as the major political factor influencing economic development. Taiwan's future economy will be largely dependent on how it deals with its relations with mainland China.

BIBLIOGRAPHY

Berger, Suzanne, and Richard K. Lester, eds. *Global Taiwan: Building Competitive Strengths in a New International Economy.* Armonk, NY: Sharpe, 2005.

Greene, J. Megan. *The Origins of the Developmental State in Taiwan: Science Policy and the Quest for Modernization.* Cambridge, MA: Harvard University Press, 2008.

Lin Jingyuan (Lin Ching-yuan). *Industrialization in Taiwan, 1946–72: Trade and Import-Substitution Policies for Developing Countries.* New York: Praeger, 1973.

Wade, Robert. *Governing the Market: Economic Theory and the Role of Government in East Asian Industrialization.* Princeton, NJ: Princeton University Press, 1990.

Wu Yongping. *A Political Explanation of Economic Growth: State Survival, Bureaucratic Politics, and Private Enterprises in the Making of Taiwan's Economy, 1950–1985.* Cambridge, MA: Harvard University Press, 2005.

Xue Limin (Hsueh Li-min), Xu Zhenguo (Hsu Chen-kuo), and Dwight H. Perkins. *Industrialization and the State: The Changing Role of the Taiwan Government in the Economy, 1945–1998.* Cambridge, MA: Harvard University Press, 2001.

Wu Yongping

SOCIAL CHANGE SINCE 1945

At the end of World War II (1937–1945), the victorious Allied powers agreed that Taiwan should be returned to the Republic of China (ROC). The Nanjing-based ROC government declared Taiwan a province of the ROC in 1945, citing the unsigned Cairo Declaration (1943) as justification. The Cairo Declaration was a result of the Cairo Conference of November 27, 1943, where Franklin Roosevelt of the United States, Winston Churchill of the United Kingdom, and Chiang Kai-Shek (Jiang Jieshi) of the ROC were present. One of the main points of the declaration was that all territories Japan had stolen from China, including Manchuria, Taiwan, and the Pescadores, shall be restored to the ROC.

Four years later, the ROC government under Chiang Kai-shek and the Nationalist Party (Guomindang or GMD) was defeated by the Communists in the Chinese civil war. The GMD government took refuge on Taiwan in 1949, and the ROC was thereby downsized from a vast territory to one that comprises only Taiwan and a few small islands. The lost mainland territories became the People's Republic of China (PRC), established in 1949 by the triumphant Chinese Communist Party under Mao Zedong.

When Taiwan became part of the ROC, people on Taiwan were looking forward to more political autonomy after fifty-one years of colonial rule. But they were soon disappointed because: (1) the troops sent by the GMD government to take over Taiwan in 1945 were poorly trained and undisciplined, while the major force remained on the mainland battling the Communists; (2) most administrative and managerial posts at various levels of the provincial government were staffed by personnel from the mainland, which made Taiwan's natives feel that they were being treated like colonial subjects; and (3) high inflation, shortages of daily necessities, unjust appropriation of personal property, and rampant corruption in the provincial government intensified hostility among Taiwanese (*benshengren*) whose families had settled on the island several generations earlier toward Mainlanders (*waishengren*) who immigrated to Taiwan only after 1945.

FEBRUARY 28 INCIDENT

On February 28, 1947, two GMD policemen beat up a Taiwanese woman selling contraband cigarettes on the streets of Taibei (Taipei). A passerby intervened and was shot dead, news of which triggered a protest in Taibei, which quickly spread across Taiwan. The "incident" almost became a revolution as Governor Chen Yi (1883–1950) ignored demands for reform. Many Mainlanders became victims of street violence during the riots, but the Taiwanese paid a harsh price in the aftermath. Chen Yi proclaimed martial law and requested military reinforcements from the mainland to suppress the protestors. In the succeeding weeks and months, tens of thousands of Taiwanese people were killed, imprisoned, and tortured. A generation of the island's educated elite was wiped out.

The February 28 Incident, commonly known as "2–28" in Taiwan, became a taboo subject until martial law was lifted in 1987, although the incident has defined the development of modern Taiwan's social and political life. It soured the relationship between *benshengren* and *waishengren* for many decades. It also became an emotional platform for Taiwanese dissidents to appeal to voters during elections. By the 1990s, the process of democratization had finally enabled different groups of people on Taiwan to reexamine "2–28" in a more open manner and to seek reconciliation. In 1995 Taiwanese president Li Denghui (Lee Teng-hui) made the first formal apology on behalf of the GMD government for the atrocity and the decades-long repression that followed. During the 2000 presidential election, the Democratic Progressive Party (DPP) ended the GMD's political domination. In 2003 President Chen Shuibian (Chen Shui-bian) presented rehabilitation certificates to the victims of the February 28 Incident and their families. The victims included the families of the man and the woman involved in the initial incident on February 28, and in the ensuing protest and suppression ending May 16, 1947.

LANGUAGE POLICIES AND IDENTITIES

Chiang Kai-shek brought with him to Taiwan approximately 1.5 million soldiers and civilian refugees from all over the Chinese mainland. Although an overwhelming majority of the population in Taiwan in the late 1940s spoke only regional languages (including Taiwanese, Hakka, and many aboriginal languages) and, because of the occupation, some Japanese, Mandarin was established as the official language. The GMD government suppressed local languages in the public sphere, including the media, in order to strengthen the use of Mandarin and a GMD-oriented national identity. Although the government recognized that Taiwan had regional particularities, it "assiduously promoted the idea that the island was the repository and guarantor of Chinese tradition as well as the mainland's rich diversity. . . . Popular culture stressed mainland roots, addressing history and life on the mainland, not the island. Politically and to some extent culturally, then, Taiwan became a microcosm of pre-1949 mainland China as interpreted by the KMT" (Gold 1993, pp. 171–172).

The suppression of local languages and Taiwanese identity in the media became a thorny issue after the process of social, cultural, and political democratization began on the island in the early 1980s. For example, the original regulation prohibited the use of local languages in

films. But the 1983 film *Erzi de da wanou* (The Son's Big Doll, released abroad as *The Sandwich Man*), directed in part by Hou Xiaoxian (Hou Hsiao-Hsien), used Taiwanese dialect in one third of the film. All the major presses in Taiwan were united in supporting the film as it awaited the approval of the Government Information Office (GIO). Cultural and social elites appealed to the government to loosen the ban on local languages in films, and the government obliged. Later that year, the GIO approved Hou's *Fenggui lai de ren* (People from Fenghui, released abroad as *Boys of Fenggui*, 1983/1984), which used Taiwanese in half of the film. Since the 1990s, there have been no restrictions on the use of local languages in Taiwanese films. Moreover, freedom of the media in general and the equality of languages in Taiwan have made substantial progress. The DPP-led government passed the Language Development Law in 2003 to address the balance, equality, and importance of regional languages and local cultures. The freedom of Taiwan's press was ranked forty-third out of 168 countries worldwide in 2006 by Reporters without Borders, and twentieth out of 194 countries in 2007 by Freedom House.

Taiwan underwent a very successful Mandarin campaign in the 1960s, until Mandarin become embedded in the daily lives of all parts of the society. The 2008 population of twenty-three million is generally said to comprise 73 percent Taiwanese, 13 percent Mainlanders, 12 percent Hakkas, and 1.7 percent indigenous peoples. Most people on Taiwan are fluent in both Mandarin and one local language. Mandarin proficiency is especially widespread among those who received formal education since the late 1940s.

For the generation that experienced the Mandarin campaign in the 1960s and for younger speakers, Mandarin has become their daily and most-familiar language, even though many of them identify a local language as their mother tongue. In other words, Mandarin is widely used across ethnic boundaries in Taiwan, although the standard Mandarin widely spoken in Taiwan, *guoyu* (literally, "national language"), is different from the Mandarin of the People's Republic of China, *putonghua* (literally, "common language"), in terms of accent, slang, and certain terminologies. While the languages used in the Taiwanese media during the 1980s and the 1990s could be associated with certain ideologies or political motivations (e.g., Taiwanese consciousness versus GMD-oriented Chinese ideology), it is increasingly difficult to make such distinctions today.

The differences in identities between the Taiwanese and the Mainlanders have also become less pronounced. The second-generation Mainlanders were either born or grew up in Taiwan, and their descendants had never visited China until the two sides agreed to permit contact across

Immigrant brides learning about life in Taiwan from a social worker, Taipei, March 5, 2003. Since the 1990s, a record number of cross-cultural marriages have occurred in Taiwan, as many men import brides from other countries in the region. While the majority of these immigrant spouses hail from mainland China, thousands of others come from Southeast Asian countries, adding another dimension to the cultural diversity on the island nation. **AP IMAGES**

the Taiwan Strait in the late 1980s. In 1998 Li Denghui proposed the term *New Taiwanese* to include all residents on Taiwan who share five decades of common cultural, social, and political experiences, as well as democratic aspirations, on the island. Although the national identity of the ROC on Taiwan remains a contentious issue, the concept of New Taiwanese has gained significant support, which contributed to the victory of Ma Yingjiu (Ma Yingjeou) in the 1998 Taibei mayoral election, as well as the 2008 presidential election.

ECONOMIC TRANSFORMATION AND ITS IMPACT

Over the second half of the twentieth century, Taiwan transformed itself from a predominantly agrarian economy into a vigorous industrialized society. As a consequence, Taiwan's social trends have undergone great changes. For example, extended farming families have been replaced by nuclear urban families. From the 1970s onward, the birthrate has been declining, while both the divorce rate and average age of marriage have been rising. The average age

of marriage for men was 27.1 in 1975, rising to 32.6 in 2006, while for women it rose from 22.8 to 29 during the same period. Meanwhile, the divorce rate increased from 1.1 percent in 1985 to 2.8 percent in 2006. The average number of births per woman was 5 during the 1960s, falling to 2 in the 1980s and to 1.12 in 2006.

Several key elements contributed to Taiwan's economic success and each had a direct or indirect impact on the islanders' daily lives. First, an effective land-reform program, launched in 1949, laid the foundation for future development.

Second, the government adopted an import-substitution policy in the 1950s aimed at making Taiwan self-sufficient by producing inexpensive consumer goods and processing imported raw materials. This brought a large number of Taiwan's women into the labor market in cities.

Third, the government promoted an export policy from the late 1950s throughout the 1960s, which meant that Taiwan quickly became known internationally as an exporter of manufactured products.

Fourth, the implementation throughout the island of compulsory education from six years to nine years in 1968 increased the competitiveness of Taiwan's human resources. This policy also gradually redefined gender roles as an increasing number of Taiwan's women pursue higher education, embrace professional careers, gain financial independence, and compete with men in all walks of life. Nowadays, almost half of Taiwan's adult women are regular wage earners. It is common for both parents to work full-time outside the home and for the school system to care for children. As the numbers of children, handicapped, and senior citizens who require assistance from nonfamily sources are growing, demands for government services and private organizations that provide welfare services have increased sharply.

Fifth, one of the major objectives in the government's economic planning was equitable distribution of income, which provided social stability for further economic transformation, and contributed to the rise of the middle class in the 1980s and the process of political and social reform. Statistics show that the average income of the top 20 percent of the population was twenty times that of the bottom 20 percent in 1953. In the 1980s, this ratio was reduced to a range of between one to five and one to four.

Beginning in the 1980s, the government implemented a series of measures to internationalize the economy and privatize state-run enterprises. Labor-intensive industries gave way to technology- and capital-intensive industries. Electronics and information technology businesses grew rapidly in the 1990s and became the leading industries in Taiwan's manufacturing sector. As a result, the government legalized the practice of bringing in blue-collar guest workers in the early 1990s. This policy, together with an increase in marriages between citizens of Taiwan and foreign nationals, resulted in the number of foreign nationals living in Taiwan increasing from 30,000 to 424,000 between 1991 and 2006. By 2006, marriages of Taiwanese to immigrants accounted for one in every six marriages, and children of these marriages made up 11.7 percent of all new births.

Another significant economic trend beginning in the 1980s was the rise of investment in the PRC by Taiwan's business community. After martial law was lifted in 1987, private contacts between Taiwan and China were permitted, and the flow of business across the Taiwan Strait became vibrant. Although there was increasing concern that massive outflows of China-bound investment and Taiwan's growing dependence on China as an export market would ultimately hurt Taiwan's national security, the GMD government led by President Ma Yingjiu, elected in 2008, decided to embrace further contact with the PRC, in contrast to the previous DPP government's cautious attitude toward the mainland.

In addition, Taiwan is now home to an aging population. To counter the impact of an aging society on national development and in response to the demands of other social trends, the government has implemented policies that focus on social welfare, social integration, environmental protection, and sustainable development. For example, several laws have been enacted to promote gender equality, especially the protection of women's rights in the home and at work. Seven public day-care centers for the elderly were established by 2005. In 2006 a bill was drafted for the National Pension Act, which proposes that anyone aged twenty-five to sixty-four not covered by another form of social insurance can be included in the program. Disabled people are encouraged to take advantage of standard educational institutions whenever possible, with many regular schools offering special classes. The Indigenous Peoples Basic Act of 2005 stipulates that the government should provide resources to help indigenous peoples develop a system of self-governance, formulate policies to protect their basic rights, and promote the preservation and development of their languages and cultures. Finally, as Taiwan has experienced an immigration boom composed largely of spouses from China and Southeast Asian countries, the government has recognized the importance of helping these immigrants assimilate. Counseling services, education, and other assistance are provided for foreign spouses, more than 90 percent of whom are female, totaling more than 360,000 in 2006, making them the fifth-largest demographic group in Taiwan.

BIBLIOGRAPHY

"2-28" Incident Research Committee of the Executive Yuan (Xingzhengyuan yanjiu "2-28" shijian xiaozu). *A Report of the "2-28" Incident Research* ["2-28" shijian yanjiu baogao]. Taibei: Shibao, 1994.

Gold, Thomas B. Taiwan's Quest for Identity in the Shadow of China. In *In the Shadow of China: Political Developments in Taiwan*, ed. Zeng Ruisheng (Steve Tsang), 169–192. London: Hurst, 1993.

Government Information Office of the Republic of China. *A Brief Introduction to Taiwan*. Taibei: Author, 2004. http://www.gio.gov.tw/taiwan-website/5-gp/brief/

Government Information Office of the Republic of China. *Taiwan Yearbook 2005*. Taibei: Author, 2006.

Government Information Office of the Republic of China. *Taiwan Yearbook 2006*. Taibei: Author, 2007.

Government Information Office of the Republic of China. *Taiwan Yearbook 2007*. Taibei: Author, 2008. http://www.gio.gov.tw/taiwan-website/5-gp/yearbook/

Rawnsley, Gary D., and Cai Mingye (Ming-Yeh T. Rawnsley), eds. *Critical Security, Democratisation, and Television in Taiwan*. London: Ashgate, 2001.

Rawnsley, Gary D., and Cai Mingye (Ming-Yeh T. Rawnsley). Chiang Kai-shek and the 28 February 1947 Incident: A Reassessment. *Issues & Studies* 37, 6 (2001): 77–106. http://blog.chinatimes.com/mingyeh/archive/2008/01/15/236312.html

Wachman, Alan M. *Taiwan: National Identity and Democratization*. Armonk, NY: Sharpe, 1994.

Ming-Yeh T. Rawnsley (Cai Mingye [Tsai Ming-Yeh])

FOREIGN RELATIONS SINCE 1949

The Republic of China (ROC) was formally established in 1912 and at least nominally governed mainland China until 1949. At the time of its inception, the ROC maintained official and unofficial relations with the United States, Japan, and the European powers that had been established by the previous Qing imperial government.

Defeated by the Chinese Communists in the 1946–1949 civil war, the Nationalist government of the ROC retreated to the island of Taiwan from 1947 to 1949. After the establishment of the People's Republic of China (PRC) in October 1949, the United States was on the verge of switching diplomatic recognition from the ROC to the PRC when hostilities broke out on the Korean peninsula in June 1950. With the onset of the Korean War, the United States changed its policy from dropping the ROC to defending it. European countries that maintained formal relations with the ROC were Belgium, France, Greece, the Vatican, Italy, and Portugal. Twelve other countries—Albania, Bulgaria, Czechoslovakia, Denmark, Finland, Hungary, Norway, Poland, Romania, Sweden, Switzerland, and East Germany—adopted a one-China policy that recognized the PRC as the sole representative of China. Two nations, the United Kingdom and the Netherlands, established diplomatic links with the PRC without taking a stance on the one China principle. These losses were minimally offset by recognition in 1952 by Spain, which had recognized Wang Jingwei's pro-Japanese government during World War II.

During the 1950s and 1960s, the ROC's most important foreign-policy goal was to discourage its diplomatic partners from switching formal relations from the ROC to the PRC. Despite the loss of Denmark, the Netherlands, Sweden, and the United Kingdom (which switched from the ROC to the PRC in 1950), of Norway (1954), and of Yugoslavia (1955), the ROC was largely successful in retaining its diplomatic allies from 1950 until the early 1970s. The exception was France, which in 1964 became the first major country to switch diplomatic recognition from the ROC to the PRC. The one-China policy of ROC President Chiang Kai-shek (Jiang Jieshi) prohibited Taiwan from allowing France concurrent recognition of both the PRC and the ROC, so Taiwan terminated its relationship with France. With Chiang's one-China policy forcing nations to choose between the ROC and the PRC, the ROC began to lose European allies. Although Malta established formal ties with the ROC in 1967, Italy and Canada switched from the ROC to the PRC in 1970. The ROC was becoming increasingly isolated.

The watershed event in Taiwan's increasing diplomatic isolation occurred in October 1971, when the PRC replaced the ROC in the United Nations' China seat. The ROC was one of the five founding members of the United Nations and was a permanent member of the Security Council from 1945 until 1971. The establishment of the PRC in 1949 created challenges for Taiwan's membership in the United Nations. In particular, the ROC needed to defend its occupation of the Chinese seat on the U.N. Security Council. Despite the PRC's mounting challenge to the ROC's occupation of the China seat in the 1950s and 1960s, the United States was able to keep the PRC out of the United Nations by branding it an aggressor nation for its role in the Korean War and arguing that the PRC did not meet the U.N. requirement that member nations be "peace-loving states."

As the PRC worked to collect supporters for a U.N. seat, Chiang Kai-shek refused to consider concurrent recognition in the United Nations, citing his one-China policy. Challenges to the ROC's U.N. membership became more serious in the 1960s as U.N. membership expanded to include countries more sympathetic to the PRC. In 1961 the U.N. General Assembly adopted Resolution 1668 stating, "In accordance with Article 18 of the Charter, any proposal to change the representation of China is an important question." This meant that any change to China's representation would require a two-thirds vote by the General Assembly. In October 1971 the General Assembly rejected the notion that China's representation was "an important question," and approved Resolution 2758, calling for the transfer of the China seat in the United Nations from the ROC to the PRC and the expulsion of the "representatives of Chiang Kai-shek." The United States moved that a separate vote be taken on Taiwan's expulsion. The U.S. draft resolution would have allowed the PRC to join the United Nations as China's representative and the ROC to retain a seat in the General Assembly. The motion failed, and rather than be expelled from the United Nations, the ROC delegation walked out of the world body. The fallout for Taiwan was severe. In the 1970s, forty-six countries switched diplomatic recognition from the ROC to the PRC, including the United States, Japan, and Canada.

Despite its loss of diplomatic partners, the ROC in 2008 enjoys unofficial relations with nearly 60 countries. Specifically, it maintains 92 representative and branch offices that perform the functions of embassies in the capitals and major cities of 59 countries. Moreover, 48 countries that do not have formal diplomatic relations with the ROC have established 58 representative or visa-issuing offices in Taiwan. In the absence of official ties, Taiwan promotes "people's diplomacy" (*quanmin waijiao*), in which private citizens participate in various international activities to broaden the ROC's diplomatic space. Most people's diplomacy activities are undertaken in conjunction with efforts by domestic nongovernmental organizations and international nongovernmental organizations.

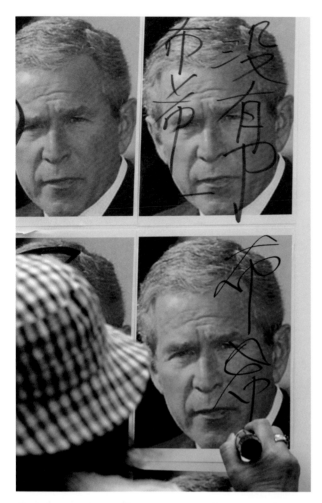

Protestor writing graffiti on a picture of U.S. President George W. Bush at the American Institute in Taiwan, May 5, 2006. *A traditional supporter of Taiwan since the People's Republic of China (PRC) supported North Korea during the Korean War, the United States began to normalize relations with the PRC during the 1970s. In partial response to Taiwan's insistence to be recognized as the only legitimate government of China, many nations have instead sided with the increasingly powerful PRC, further marginalizing the island on the world stage.* **AP IMAGES**

Taiwan's international nongovernmental organizations engage in democracy building, humanitarian relief, cultural exchanges, trade, and economic cooperation. According to ROC government statistics, from the 1970s to the end of 2005 Taiwanese citizens had participated in activities organized by 2,077 international nongovernmental organizations. These include the Taiwan Foundation for Democracy, an international nongovernmental organization dedicated to strengthening democracy and human rights in Taiwan and abroad by organizing more events to discuss the advancement of democracy; the World Forum for Democratization in Asia, an international

forum that offers a regional mechanism for discussing and coordinating the work of Asian democracy groups and activists; and the Democratic Pacific Union, a nongovernmental organization dedicated to consolidating democratic values, fostering economic development, and protecting the security of Pacific countries. The Democratic Pacific Union maintains the Pacific Disaster Prevention Center and the Pacific Center Disaster Reduction International Training Program for Typhoon and Flood Reduction, an election monitoring group, fellowships, and scholarships.

Since the turn of the twenty-first century, the PRC has used various tools to blunt Taiwan's official and unofficial diplomacy and to further isolate Taiwan. China offers foreign aid and debt relief to Taiwan's mostly impoverished allies to switch allegiance to the PRC. This strategy has been quite successful. Between 2000 and 2007 the ROC lost eight diplomatic partners to China and gained only one. The greatest challenge for the Ministry of Foreign Affairs, the ROC's key foreign-policy institution, is retaining relations with its remaining twenty-four diplomatic partners.

ROC REPRESENTATION IN THE UNITED NATIONS

Since 1993 Taiwan has initiated annual campaigns for U.N. membership. Although the campaigns have varied in strategy, the goal is the same: to challenge the U.N.'s exclusion of Taiwan and gain representation for its people. The ROC government argues that U.N. Resolution 2758 dealt with the representation of the people of mainland China, but not those of Taiwan, in the United Nations.

In the early campaigns, a dozen or so of the ROC's U.N. allies petitioned the U.N. General Assembly to appoint an ad hoc committee to consider concurrent representation for the PRC and the ROC. They argued that historical precedent allowed concurrent representation, and that Taiwan's exclusion was an "exceptional situation" in the international context. Later proposals dropped reference to the Republic of China and instead called for representation of the people living on Taiwan, as opposed to the people living on the Chinese mainland. For example, the 2004 petition argued that U.N. Resolution 2758, which admitted the PRC to the United Nations, did not address the issue of the representation of "the twenty-three million people of Taiwan" in the United Nations. Another difference was the use of "Taiwan," as well as the "Republic of China," to refer to the nation. The 2005 proposal referred to the island as the "Republic of China (Taiwan)." Previous proposals referred to it merely as the "Republic of China." In 2007 Taiwan for the first time applied directly for new membership. Undeterred by the U.N. Secretariat's rejection of the application, ROC President Chen Shuibian

CROSS-STRAIT RELATIONS

In 1895 China ceded Taiwan to Japan following China's defeat in the first Sino-Japanese War (1894–1895). In 1945 Taiwan was returned to China after the Japanese defeat in World War II (1937–1945). The Communist takeover of China in 1949 started the cross-strait confrontation between the People's Republic of China (PRC) on the mainland and the defeated Guomindang (GMD) government of the Republic of China (ROC) in Taiwan.

With the outbreak of the Korean War in 1950, the United States reversed its policy of nonintervention in the Taiwan Strait by dispatching its Seventh Fleet to the region. In 1954 the U.S. government signed a Mutual Security Treaty with Taiwan. Antipathy between the PRC and the United States continued until the 1970s. On January 1, 1979, the United States recognized the PRC as the sole legal government of China, but passed the Taiwan Relations Act as a guide for its unofficial relations with Taiwan.

The confrontation between the PRC in the mainland and the ROC in Taiwan continued throughout the Mao Zedong era of the 1950s to 1970s, when China was determined to liberate Taiwan through force. However, in the mid-1950s, the PRC began launching peaceful initiatives by proposing negotiations with Taiwan. Taiwan dismissed these initiatives as propaganda. Nevertheless, the two sides did establish contact through secret channels and worked out some tentative proposals and arrangements for reunification. However, the Cultural Revolution, which began in China in 1966, brought these talks to an end.

At the start of the Deng Xiaoping era in late 1978, Beijing formed a new policy of "peaceful reunification." It put forward a nine-point proposal to Taiwan on September 30, 1981, including a plan for establishing "three direct links" across the Taiwan strait. On February 22, 1984, China officially announced the "one country, two systems" formula for reunification, and from the mid-1980s there began a thaw in cross-strait relations. In November 1987 Taiwan lifted its ban on travel to the mainland. Most impressive of all was the fast development in cross-strait economic relations, with rapidly increasing investment in and trade with the mainland by Taiwanese businesspeople.

In September 1990 Taiwan set up the National Unification Council and the Mainland Affairs Council to make overall plans for handling mainland affairs and, in early 1991, adopted the Guidelines for National Unification. It set up a semiofficial organization, the Strait Exchange Foundation (SEF), to handle cross-strait affairs with its mainland counterpart, the Association for Relations across the Taiwan Strait (ARATS). The two sides had several informal meetings in 1992, which led to a groundbreaking meeting in Singapore between Taiwan's Gu Zhenfu (Koo Chen-fu, 1917–2005), chairman of SEF, and Wang Daohan (1915–2005) of ARATS, known as the Wang-Koo meeting. A second Wang-Koo meeting was scheduled for July 20, 1995. But the visit of Taiwanese president Li Denghui (Lee Teng-hui) to the United States in June 1995 and Beijing's subsequent angry response led to tensions across the strait and plunged cross-strait relations to their lowest point since the late 1970s.

From mid-July 1995 to early 1996, the PRC conducted military exercises and "missile tests" around the Taiwan Strait. Warning the PRC of "grave consequences," the United States sent two aircraft carrier groups to the strait. In defiance of China's pressure, Li Denghui, after winning Taiwan's presidential election in 1996, continued his uncompromising stance toward the mainland. On July 9, 1999, he came out with a "two states" theory, which for the first time openly defined the relations between the mainland and Taiwan as "between two states, at least a special relationship between two states."

This development sent cross-strait relations into another crisis. For the first time, the pro-independence Democratic Progressive Party (DPP) won Taiwan's presidential election in 2000. While Taiwan under the GMD accepted the notion of "one China but free interpretations (of this one China)," as well as the so-called 1992 consensus regarding the "one China principle" as reached by ARATS and SEF in 1992, the new president, Chen Shuibian (Chen Shui-bian), challenged both the "consensus" and the "one China" principle. The mainland refused to deal with the DPP government unless it accepted the "one China" principle, and the PRC began working more closely with Taiwan's opposition parties and businesspeople for closer economic ties across the strait (the "three direct links"). The PRC also worked with the United States and other countries to prevent a radical move by Taiwan toward de jure independence.

Sheng Lijun

pledged to put the question of U.N. membership before the Taiwanese people in a referendum. The referendum, held with the March 2008 election, failed.

BIBLIOGRAPHY

Charter of the United Nations. New York: United Nations, 1945. http://www.un.org/aboutun/charter/

Government Information Office. *Taiwan Yearbook 2007.* Internet edition. http://www.gio.gov.tw

Hickey, Dennis Van Vranken. *Foreign Policy Making in Taiwan.* London: Routledge, 2007.

Larus, Elizabeth Freund. Taiwan's Quest for International Recognition. *Issues and Studies* 42, 2 (June 2006): 23–52.

Wu Chi-chung. One China Policy Review Series (Part 4). *Taiwan Daily,* August 1, 2004.

Elizabeth Freund Larus

EDUCATION

Taiwan has been strongly influenced by Confucianism, which emphasizes both the family unit and the value of education to society (Smith 1991). Since gaining independence from Japanese colonial rule in 1945, Taiwan's educational achievements have been remarkable. By 2002 the literacy rate had reached 96 percent, over 95 percent of students continued in education beyond the school-leaving age, and 69 percent of senior high-school graduates gained admission to an institution of higher education (Guo Yugui 2005). In addition, student performance in mathematics and science outstripped that of many other countries. Alongside Japan and Korea, Taiwan is viewed as a model of educational success (Stevenson and Stigler 1992; Reynolds 2000; Guo Yugui 2005).

CENTRALIZATION AND EDUCATIONAL EXPANSION, 1945–1987

Educational expansion helped to fuel the economic transformation from the 1960s (Tien 1996). Under the ruling Guomindang (Nationalist Party), which represented the interests of Chinese Mainlanders (those who fled to Taiwan from mainland China in the wake of the Communist revolution in 1949, about 13 percent of the population), Mandarin became the official language of instruction, replacing colonial Japanese and superseding Taiwanese (van den Berg 1985; Oladejo 2006). The 1947 constitution of the Republic of China centralized the control of education through three tiers of government: the Ministry of Education, the provincial departments of education, and the local city or county education bureaus (Smith 1991; Law 1995).

In 1968 compulsory education was extended to nine grades, covering the ages six to fifteen: six years in elementary school and three in junior high school. Further pro-

gression depended on passing competitive examinations for admission to a senior high school or senior vocational school, and beyond that for admission to a college or university. Private schools were crucial to this educational expansion, especially in providing preschool places, post-compulsory education for students rejected by the state system, and cram schools (*buxiban*) to help students succeed in examinations. The school curriculum allocated almost a third of the timetable to science and mathematics; other subjects included languages, physical education, music, and social studies in elementary schools, and civic and moral values, history, and geography in junior high schools. From 1966, when the Taiwanese government adopted a manpower development plan, more emphasis was placed on vocational and technical education to meet the manpower needs of economic expansion, although this trend has come to a halt since the mid 1990s.

A typical daily program in all schools normally runs from 7:30 a.m. to 4 p.m., bolstered by extracurricular activities, homework, or supplementary classes running until 8 or 9 p.m. Strict discipline in senior high schools has been the responsibility of military officers, but the system has been criticized for the excessive pressure placed on students.

Tertiary education offered various routes, with senior high-school graduates normally preparing for university, and graduates of senior vocational schools seeking admission to two-year junior colleges or four-year institutes of technology.

REFORM AND LIBERALIZATION, 1988–2008

After the lifting of martial law in 1987 and the emergence of democracy, the 410 Demonstration for Educational Reform (1994) marked a turning point. Textbooks became subject to scholarly review rather than government approval, and teacher training became more diversified. Both the national curriculum and systems of student assessment have become more flexible. Students in senior high school are offered more study electives and can defer their choice of a specialist route of study (between social sciences/humanities and life/natural sciences) until their final year.

Beginning in 1996, several experimental bilateral schools were introduced to offer more flexibility of provision by combining both academic and vocational programs. Steps were also taken to reduce the importance of the competitive examination system and provide fairer access for students. Pilot comprehensive junior-senior high schools were introduced to allow students access to further education without having to pass entrance examinations. Similarly, a multiple-channel entrance system for admission to university was introduced in 2001 so that students are no longer solely dependent on examinations. Discipline in postcompulsory educational establishments is also being liberalized, and by 2010 it is expected that the use of military personnel to enforce discipline in schools will have been phased out. Students continue to work under pressure, but dropout rates are low, running only 0.071 percent of the student population in December 2007 (*China Post* 2008) and still falling as a result of improved monitoring and student counseling.

Under a policy of decentralization, universities have been granted more autonomy. Since 2005 universities have been permitted to appoint their own presidents without Ministry of Education approval. In addition, universities now control their own budgets; they are no longer fully funded by the central government and must therefore generate at least 20 percent of income from alternative sources. Such fiscal decentralization can be partly explained by the rapid expansion of higher education; between 1985 and 2005, the number of students in four-year institutions of higher education tripled, with a gross enrollment rate of 67.7 percent. In the process, many junior colleges have been upgraded to the status of a university or a four-year institution of technology to meet the employment needs of the rapidly expanding high-tech economy. Amendments to the University Act (1994) have allowed student representation at faculty conferences and the appointment of foreign university presidents. However, liberalization has been accompanied by directives, implemented in 2005, to improve the quality of higher education through more systematic evaluation under the Higher Education Evaluation and Accreditation Council of Taiwan. Through the Top Universities and Research Centers Project, the government has also concentrated additional funding (about $1.5 billion annually from 2006 to 2008) to help Taiwan's top universities build into world-class institutions.

Promoting lifelong learning beyond functional literacy is important to maintaining a skilled workforce and sustaining Taiwan's competitive edge into the twenty-first century. Studies have identified five main groups whose needs should be more specifically targeted: adults aged fifty-plus who missed out; younger adults who dropped out of school; ethnic minority groups whose knowledge of Mandarin is limited; foreign laborers with limited language skills; and professional groups seeking career enhancement (Lee Chuan 1997; Ho Ching-jung 1997). Opportunities for further study have been extended through Taiwan's Open University and open junior colleges, while further provision has been made for professional groups to add to their qualifications through part-time postgraduate study and in-service training. In the teaching profession, for example, by 2005, 16.59 percent of junior high and 12.14 percent of elementary-school teachers had acquired higher degrees, figures set to rise with a further investment of $120 million from 2006 to 2009 in the teacher-qualification program (Government Information Office 2006).

EDUCATIONAL PRIORITIES FOR THE FUTURE

Three priorities identified at the National Education Development Conference in 2003 have yet to be fully realized. The first is to secure social equity and justice by improving educational opportunities for disadvantaged groups, including indigenous peoples (Chou Hui-Min 2005; Tu Cheng-sheng 2007). The second is to further enhance the quality of higher education in the face of global competition, especially by improving the status of institutes of technology and strengthening partnerships with industry (Tu Cheng-sheng 2007). The third is to continue to improve schooling by phasing in twelve years of compulsory education and reducing class size, where numbers remain in excess of forty in senior high schools, thirty-five in junior high schools, and twenty-nine in elementary schools (Government Information Office 2006). In the wake of democratization, moral and civic education will also need to cultivate modern citizens with a capacity for critical thinking and a sense of national identity, coupled with a global perspective and a concern for human rights (Lee Chi-Ming 2004).

BIBLIOGRAPHY

The China Post. Taiwan's School Dropout Rate Continues Falling. January 25, 2008. http://www.chinapost.com.tw/

Chou Hui-Min. Educating Urban Indigenous Students in Taiwan: Six Teachers' Perspectives. Ph.D. diss., University of Maryland, 2005.

Government Information Office. Education. In *Taiwan Yearbook 2006*, chap. 18. http://www.roc-taiwan.org.uk/taiwan/

Guo Yugui. *Asia's Educational Edge: Current Achievements in Japan, Korea, Taiwan, China, and India.* Lanham, MD: Lexington Books, 2005.

Ho Ching-jung. Lifelong Learning and Basic Literacy: Adult Literacy Education in Chinese Taipei. In *Lifelong Learning: Policies, Practices, and Programs,* ed. Michael Hatton. Toronto: Humber College, 1997: 140–153

Law, Wing Wah. The Role of the State in Higher Education Reform: Mainland China and Taiwan. *Comparative Education Review* 39, 3 (1995): 322–355.

Lee Chi-Ming. Changes and Challenges for Moral Education in Taiwan. *Journal of Moral Education* 33, 4 (2004): 575–595.

Lee Chuan. From Supplemental Education to Lifelong Learning in Chinese Taipei. In *Lifelong Learning: Policies, Practices, and Programs,* ed. Michael Hatton. Toronto: Humber College, 1997: 316–326

Oladejo, James. Parents' Attitudes Towards Bilingual Education Policy in Taiwan. *Bilingual Research Journal* 30, 1 (2006): 147–170.

Reynolds, David. School Effectiveness: The International Dimension. In *The International Handbook of School Effectiveness Research,* eds. Charles Teddlie and David Reynolds, 232–256. London: Falmer Press, 2000.

Smith, Douglas C., ed. *The Confucian Continuum: Educational Modernization in Taiwan.* New York: Praeger, 1991.

Stevenson, Harold W., and James W. Stigler. 1992. *The Learning Gap: Why Our Schools Are Failing and What We Can Learn from Japanese and Chinese Education.* New York: Summit, 1992.

Tien, Flora F. How Education Drove Taiwan's Economic Development. *Economic Reform Today* 4 (1996): 13–18.

Tsurumi, E. Patricia. *Japanese Colonial Education in Taiwan, 1895–1945.* Cambridge, MA: Harvard University Press, 1977.

Tu Cheng-sheng. Taiwan's Educational Reform and the Future of Taiwan. Paper presented at the London School of Economics and Political Science, January 10, 2007.

van den Berg, Marinus Elisa. *Language Planning and Language Use in Taiwan: A Study of Language Choice Behavior in Public Settings.* Taipei: Crane, 1985.

Michael D. Wilson

MILITARY FORCES

The military forces of the Republic of China in Taiwan were established by and with the personnel that retreated to Taiwan with the Guomindang (GMD) and the Nationalist armed forces (*guo jun*; approximately 800,000 troops) under Chiang Kai-shek's (Jiang Jieshi's) leadership in 1949. The major branches of the military include the army, navy, marine corps, air force, military police, combined logistics command, and reserve command. Among the unique strategies of the Ministry of National Defense (Guofang Bu) was the establishment of the General Political Warfare Department (Zong Zhengzhi Zuozhan Ju) with divisions in all military branches. This department was charged with the responsibilities of propaganda campaigns, the policing of the loyalty of military personnel, and military intelligence against mainland Chinese infiltrators. Chiang's son Chiang Ching-kuo (Jiang Jingguo) presided over this unit.

From this time through the 1970s, Chiang Kai-shek and the military strategists defined the primary mission of the military to be retaking mainland China (*fangong dalu*) and reuniting China (*tongyi Zhongguo*), as exemplified by the speeches and programs of annual National Day military parades (October 10) and fueled by full-scale military conflicts with the People's Liberation Army (PLA) in Taiwan's Quemoy (Jinmen), a group of offshore islands just eight miles off the coast of mainland China, from 1954 to 1955 and 1958 to 1959. Hao Po-tsun (Hao Bocun), then commander of the Army's Ninth Division, played a major role in defending Quemoy in 1958 and became the first, albeit controversial, instance of an active-duty military member to be involved in the political scene (he served as premier of the Executive Yuan from 1990 to 1993).

The ROC troops worked closely with the Seventh Fleet of the U.S. Navy, sent as part of the U.S. blockade during the Korean War (1950–1953) to prevent conflicts across the Taiwan Strait. Officers in Taiwan's military have also been regularly sent to the United States for training. In regard to regional collaborations, Taiwan's military has helped to train thousands of Singaporean soldiers since 1975. There had been no other serious conflict until the so-called third Taiwan Strait crisis from 1995 to 1996, when the PLA conducted a series of missile tests in the waters in the vicinity of Taiwan and live-ammunition exercises to warn Taiwan's president Lee Teng-hui (Li Denghui) against his departure from the one-China policy. The ROC military did not respond in kind and remained low key.

After Chiang Kai-shek's death in 1975, Chiang Ching-kuo paid lip service to the ideology of recovering mainland China, but gradually shifted the military's primary mission from offense to defense. Since 1990, multiple armament upgrade programs and proprietary technologies have replaced dated weapons, with an emphasis on self-defense and a strategic focus on the heavily urbanized environment of the western side of the island. The new mission of the navy, for example, is to defend Taiwan against a blockade or invasion by the PRC. Traditionally, most equipment was purchased from the United States, but since the late 1980s Taiwan's military has relied more on European suppliers due to tensions in the triangular relationship between Taiwan, the United States, and China. The shift in military thinking has been exemplified by such purchases as the MIM-104 Patriot from the United States (a surface-to-air missile system deployed around Taibei), the Kang Ding (La Fayette) class light multimission frigates from France, the Hai Lung class submarine (Zwaardvis class) from the Netherlands, Mirage 2000-5 fighter aircraft from France, and F-16 A/B fighter jets and AH-1W Super-Cobra attack helicopters from the United States. However, procurement has remained a sensitive issue throughout Taiwan's military history, and since the late 1990s Taiwan has witnessed more locally designed and manufactured weapon systems. A fighter jet designed and manufactured in Taiwan, the Indigenous Defense Fighter (IDF), nicknamed Ching-kuo in honor of Taiwan's former president, entered active service in 1994.

Accompanied by major reforms to streamline the military (the *jingshi* program), the current strategy has evolved into one that emphasizes "offshore engagement" (*jingwai juezhan*). From the 1950s to the 1980s, male citizens of Taiwan were obliged to perform compulsory military (*yiwu yi*) service of two to three years (for a total of approximately 430,000 active-duty military members). The downsizing effort, with a refocus on the island rather than the mainland, was initiated in July 1997. By 2008, the compulsory service period had been reduced to one year (for a total of approximately 270,000 active-duty military members). Minister of National Defense Chen

Taiwanese soldiers at attention during training exercises, Tsoying, Taiwan, September 26, 1995. *The role of Taiwan's military shifted in the late 1970s from regaining mainland China to defending the island from invasion by the People's Republic of China. While a major importer of equipment from the United States since the 1950s, Taiwan has looked to other Western countries for weapons in the twenty-first century, purchasing French fighter jets and Dutch submarines for self-defense.* TAO-CHUAN YEH/AFP/GETTY IMAGES

Chao-min (Chen Zhaomin) announced on May 21, 2008, a new strategic plan to replace compulsory military service with a voluntary recruitment system (*mubing zhi*) to build a fully professional armed force of 200,000. The 2008 military budget of $10.5 billion consists of 2.5 percent of Taiwan's gross domestic product.

Closely connected with military ideology throughout this period was the issue of accommodating veterans and mainland soldiers who were forced to settle in Taiwan. Numerous residential compounds known as military villages (*juan cun*) were set up throughout the island to accommodate demobilized soldiers and their families and to sustain the military's claim of sovereignty over China. These residential compounds and their unique culture remain an inalienable part of the military and cultural history of Taiwan.

SEE ALSO *Chen Shuibian; Chiang Ching-kuo (Jiang Jingguo); Chiang Kai-shek (Jiang Jieshi); Foreign Policy Frameworks and Theories: One-China Policy and "One Country, Two Systems"; Li Denghui (Lee Teng-hui).*

BIBLIOGRAPHY

Edmonds, Martin, and Michael Tsai, eds. *Defending Taiwan: The Future Vision of Taiwan's Defence Policy and Military Strategy.* London: RoutledgeCurzon, 2003.

Edmonds, Martin, and Michael Tsai, eds. *Taiwan's Defense Reform.* London: Routledge, 2006.

Liang Likai. *Kua shiji de guofang liliang: Cong chuantong dao xiandai de Zhonghu Minguo guojun* [An armed forces for the twenty-first century: The modernization of the R.O.C. military]. Taibei: Qingnian ribao, 1998.

Tucker, Nancy Bernkopf, ed. *Dangerous Strait: The U.S.-Taiwan-China Crisis.* New York: Columbia University Press, 2005.

Alexander C. Y. Huang

DEMOCRATIC PROGRESSIVE PARTY

Taiwan's Democratic Progressive Party (DPP) was formed in September 1986. It was the first genuine opposition party to challenge the ruling Guomindang (Kuomintang,

GMD). At the time, Taiwan was still under martial law, and the formation of opposition parties was illegal. However, President Jiang Jingguo (Chiang Ching-kuo) opted for tacitly tolerating the new party. Despite its lack of preparation, the DPP managed to win a respectable 22 percent of the vote in its first election in December 1986.

The party was formed out of a disparate collection of opposition groups collectively known as the Dangwai (Tangwai, "outside the party") that shared only a hatred of the GMD and a belief in the need for democratization. Initially, the DPP took a moderate position on national identity, calling for Taiwanese self-determination rather than outright independence. However, during the party's first five years it became increasingly radical, culminating in the 1991 Taiwan Independence Clause, which called for the establishment of a "Republic of Taiwan."

The DPP's extremist position during the first direct national elections in 1991 is often blamed for its poor performance, with the party winning only 18 percent of the seats. Following this defeat, moderate DPP leaders such as Xu Xinliang (Hsu Hsin-liang), Shi Mingde (Shih Ming-teh), and Chen Shuibian (Chen Shui-bian) inaugurated a gradual transformation of the party that culminated in its presidential election victory in 2000. Critical components of the DPP's electoral rise include moderation on the issue of Taiwan's independence, a new emphasis on social policy, improvements in political communication, and an effective candidate-selection process.

After 1991, the DPP began stressing the more moderate and electorally popular elements of the independence issue. For instance, DPP leaders dropped the party's references to a "Republic of Taiwan," instead attacking proposals for unification and repackaging independence with appeals for United Nations membership. This approach culminated in the passing of the Resolution on Taiwan's Future, which recognized the "Republic of China" as the nation's name and stated that there was no need to declare independence because Taiwan was already independent.

The DPP also stressed alternative policy areas, particularly social welfare, political corruption, and environmental protection. Throughout the 1990s, the DPP won much support as a result of its call for old-age pensions, causing the GMD to consider adopting the policy by the late 1990s. In addition, the DPP's antinuclear stance and its calls for stricter environmental standards appealed to urban voters and enabled the party to cement a useful alliance with the environmental movement. The DPP also benefited from attacks on the GMD's political corruption. In fact, during the 1990s, the DPP stressed anticorruption more than any other political issue. The DPP's accusations of vote buying, contract corruption, and embezzlement were to prove severely damaging for the GMD.

The DPP also attempted to improve the quality of its political communication after its amateur efforts in early elections. The party's employment of younger advisers in the preparation of propaganda ensured a more innovative style of political advertising. By 2000 the DPP had developed the most professional political marketing among Taiwan's parties.

Another factor that contributed to the DPP's rise was its candidate-nomination system. The DPP adopted an institutionalized selection system with regular party primaries that enabled the DPP to avoid the repeated splits that led to the GMD's fall from power.

Since winning the presidency in 2000, the DPP has struggled to make the transition from opposition party to governing power. Although it became the largest parliamentary party in 2004, the DPP failed in both 2001 and 2004 to gain a majority in the Legislative Yuan, which remains dominated by the Pan-Blue parties (GMD and its allies). However, the DPP remains skilled at election campaigning. Its 2004 Hand-in-Hand Rally, which involved a human chain across the island, was the most effective mobilization event of the presidential campaign. Therefore, despite an economic recession, the DPP was able to win the 2004 presidential election and reach record vote and seat shares in parliamentary elections.

In contrast to the DPP's move toward a more moderate and multi-issue approach in the 1990s, since 2000 voters perceive that the DPP has become increasingly extreme. Since coming to power, the DPP has faced difficulty fulfilling its social welfare and anticorruption pledges. Instead, it has often fallen back on the divisive national-identity issue.

During the DPP's second term in office its popularity declined significantly. It suffered from a string of corruption scandals and a reputation for poor economic management. In addition the party failed to cope with the new electoral system used in the 2008 legislative elections. As a result of the new electoral system and voter dissatisfaction the DPP lost both legislative and presidential elections in 2008.

SEE ALSO *Chen Shuibian; Taiwan, Republic of China: Politics since 1945.*

BIBLIOGRAPHY

Fell, Dafydd. *Party Politics in Taiwan: Party Change and the Democratic Evolution of Taiwan, 1991–2004.* London: Routledge, 2005.

Kuo, Julian. *Minjindang zhuanxingzhitong.* Taibei: Commonwealth Publishing, 1998.

Rigger, Shelley. The Democratic Progressive Party in 2000: Obstacles and Opportunities. *China Quarterly* 168 (2001): 944–959.

Rigger, Shelley. *From Opposition to Power: Taiwan's Democratic Progressive Party.* London and Boulder, CO: Rienner, 2001.

Dafydd Fell

TAN DUN
1957–

Tan Dun, composer and conductor, was born on August 18, 1957, near Changsha, in Hunan, and lives in New York. He grew up in the Hunan countryside with his grandparents. Tan describes his childhood environs as "naturally musical." Music was part of everyday life. It did not employ specific musical instruments, necessarily, but made use of all kinds of materials: paper, pots, and bamboo among them. When Tan came across a violin one day, it seemed to him no different from these "musical instruments" he had encountered earlier.

EDUCATION AND EARLY COMPOSITIONS

In 1974 Tan was sent to live among the peasants of a commune in the vicinity of his hometown Changsha, sharing their daily work, rice-planting, for two years. While he thought he would be forever committed to agricultural life, music offered a "way out." Tan began to collect folk songs and became a "village conductor," leading musical celebrations and rituals. Some of his first compositions—such as the string quartet *I Dream of Mao Zedong*, which would later, in 1978, open the doors to the Central Conservatory in Beijing for him—date to this time. When a boat carrying the local Peking opera troupe capsized in 1976, drowning many musicians, Tan was asked to join the troupe, and worked with them for a year and a half.

Between 1978 and 1983, Tan studied composition at the Central Conservatory in Beijing under Li Yinghai (1927–2007) and Zhao Xingdao (b. 1921). He was part of a legendary class of thirty, chosen from thousands of applicants, that produced many composers now internationally renowned, including Su Cong, Guo Wenjing, and Qu Xiaosong. This so-called Chinese New Wave of composers was destined to change, radically, China's musical universe. A number of guest lecturers, including Alexander Goehr, George Crumb, Hans Werner Henze, Toru Takemitsu (1930–1996), Isang Yun (1917–1995), and Chou Wen-chung, visited the conservatory at this time, exposing the students, who had hitherto been trained exclusively on styles from the nineteenth century and earlier to the sounds and theories of New Music.

Tan Dun was quick to learn. In 1983 he won his first international prize at the Carl-Maria von Weber Music Contest in Leipzig for his string quartet *Feng-Ya-Song* (风雅颂), named after the sections of the ancient Chinese *Book of Songs*. Praised as the "pride of our country," he would soon be attacked as a "running dog of capitalism" during the anti–spiritual pollution campaign, which began in the waning months of 1983. During this time, Tan's music could not be played in public venues. However, the campaign ran out of steam by the spring of 1984. As Tan Dun's international fame and success continued to soar (arguably his most popular recent international prize is the 2001 Academy Award for his score to Ang Lee's film *Crouching Tiger, Hidden Dragon*), he was courted by China's government and commissioned to write for official celebrations, such as those for Hong Kong's reunification with China in 1997 (*Heaven Earth Mankind: Symphony 1997*) and the 2008 Beijing Olympics.

Tan Dun left China in 1986 to study in New York at Columbia University with Mario Davidovsky, George Edwards, and Chou Wen-chung. Like other Chinese composers from his generation, folk music, as well as the whole range of China's ancient musical, literary, and philosophical culture, would serve him as an inspirational source. One of his most radical "Chinese" compositions is his 1985 piece *On Taoism* for voice, bass clarinet, contrabassoon, and orchestra, which superscribes Chinese instrumental and vocal techniques onto an extraordinary instrumental ensemble. Tan continued along this line in his ritual opera *Nine Songs* (1989), composed for fifty ceramic instruments that Tan created in collaboration with potter Ragnar Naess. Struck, blown, and bowed, the instruments are meant to echo the Chinese philosophical idea of the primacy of earth (i.e., clay) among the "five elements."

MUSICAL ECLECTICISM AND INTERNATIONALISM

Yet, Tan's music is not restricted to Chinese traditions. His musical eclecticism spans the world; he employs African rhythms, Indian melodies, Tibetan instruments, jazz and medieval chant, rock 'n' roll and Chinese *kunqu* (昆曲), and he combines oratorio and ritual. In reverence to his childhood musical experiences, Tan's compositions also include the sounds of paper and water, and of stone, clay, and electronics. Visual impressions, too, have left a significant imprint on his music, from *Eight Memories in Watercolour* (1978) to *Death and Fire: Dialogue with Paul Klee* (1992). These efforts to read visuals musically have culminated more recently in his *Visual Music*, a 2005 multimedia exhibition in which he attempts, in a distinctly Daoist gesture, to make sounds visible and colors audible with an installation made of pianos.

In 1992 Tan had been the youngest composer to receive the prestigious Suntory Prize commission (Japan), joining John Cage (1912–1992), Takemitsu, Henze, Iannis Xenakis (1922–2001), and others. In 1998 he became the youngest winner of the Grawemeyer Award for Music Composition, the world's most prestigious prize for composers. The prize was awarded for his opera *Marco Polo* (1995), which incorporates Eastern and Western operatic traditions, varied musical styles, and multiple languages, cultures, and time periods to create a music that has been described as "authentically international" music. The story is told simultaneously through two different perspectives: that of Marco (action), the strong young adventurer engaged with life and travel, and that of Polo (memory), who plays out Marco's inner thoughts and reflections on his past journeys. *Marco Polo* is a typical example of Tan Dun's interest in exploring transcultural structural parallels. In *Orchestral Theater III: Red Forecast* (1996), for example, he presents several different views of the 1960s through the Maoism of the Chinese Cultural Revolution, the atrocities of the Vietnam War, and the American flower-power movement. In *Orchestral Theater IV: The Gate* (1999), Tan introduces three types of female performers, one Japanese, one Chinese, one European. In *Orchestral Theatre I: Xun*, written in 1990, he thrice transforms the classical orchestra: The performers, in addition to playing their own instruments, triple as vocalists and *xun* players (a Chinese mouth organ).

Structural balance and counterpoint are the compositional elements that also determine Tan Dun's series of *Yi* (i.e., change) concertos, beginning with *Intercourse of Fire and Water: Yi1* (1995), for cello and orchestra. Here, the cello soloist borrows performing techniques from the Chinese *erhu* and the Mongolian fiddle. *Yi2* (1996) for guitar blends and contrasts the different traditions, relationships, and characteristics of two plucked instruments: Spain's flamenco guitar and China's lute *pipa*. Tan's *Concerto for Pizzicato Piano and Ten Instruments* (1995) examines the myriad ways in which four pitches, C-A-G-E, can be articulated and resonate. The piano, plucked on the inside strings throughout, presents in all different registers the four notes of this motive. Each is developed further through the soloist's use of fingering techniques borrowed from the Chinese *pipa*.

Ghost Opera (1995) for string quartet and *pipa* sums up Tan's eclectic artistic language by juxtaposing various art forms, including the European classical concert tradition, Chinese shadow-puppet theater, visual art installations, folk music, drama, and shamanistic ritual. Tan reflects on China's ghost operas, through which shamans would communicate with spirits of the past and the future, establishing dialogues between the human soul and nature. His piece does precisely that by invoking spirits from the past, including Johann Sebastian Bach's *Well-Tempered Piano*, William Shakespeare's *Tempest*, and the Chinese folk song "Little Cabbage." It also includes sounds made with water, stones, metal, and paper to symbolize nature and eternity.

SEE ALSO *Music, Western and Russian Influence on; New Wave Movement, '85.*

BIBLIOGRAPHY

Frank, Kouwenhoven. Composer Tan Dun: The Ritual Fire Dancer of Mainland China's New Music. *China Information* 6, 3 (1991–1992): 1–24.

Mittler, Barbara. *Dangerous Tunes: The Politics of Chinese Music in Hong Kong, Taiwan, and the People's Republic of China since 1949.* Wiesbaden, Germany: Harrassowitz, 1997.

Utz, Christian. *Neue Musik und Interkulturalität: Von John Cage bis Tan Dun.* Stuttgart, Germany: Steiner, 2002.

Yu Siu Wah. Two Practices Confused in One Composition: Tan Dun's *Symphony 1997: Heaven, Earth, Man.* In *Locating East Asia in Western Art Music,* eds. Yayoi Uno Everett and Frederick Lau, 57–71. Middletown, CT: Wesleyan University Press 2004.

Barbara Mittler

TAN KAH KEE

SEE *Chinese Overseas: Tan Kah Kee.*

TAXATION AND FISCAL POLICIES, 1800–1912

During the last century of the Qing, from 1800 to 1912, the dynasty was passé. Its state taxation and fiscal policies had two distinctive features. First, there was a hangover of old, well-entrenched policies that had been handed down from previous generations. Second, there was a range of contingent, ad hoc measures that aimed to address changes.

DIRECT AND INDIRECT TAXES

The Qing maintained a balanced state budget thanks to its adherence to the Confucian moral economy. But due to the perpetual physiocratic state-peasant alliance, the direct tax on the agricultural sector in the form of a land-poll (*diding yin*) was low. The per capita tax burden in 1766 was a mere 8 percent of that in 1381 under the Ming dynasty. Much of the lowering of the tax burden can be attributed to Emperor Kangxi's (r. 1661–1722) edict in 1712 to freeze the total tax revenue extracted from agriculture (*yongbu jiafu*, literally, "never increasing tax"), despite China's swelling population, enlarged land reclamation, and enhanced yield level. This policy was carefully observed until 1840. Overall, the direct tax was collected in a combination of goods and cash at the level of 30 million to 35 million *taels* of silver per annum (1,125 to 1,312 metric tons). The regional burden was relatively even (Liang Fangzhong 1980).

For indirect tax, the situation varied, and the tax rates were elastic. The Qing commercial taxes on ordinary domestic trade were low. There was hardly any tax on rural grassroots markets. Formal tax checkpoints (*queguan, chaoguan,* or *changguan*) were maintained at transportation hubs to collect duties (*guanshui, guanchao*) on goods in transit at 5 percent of the goods' prices. Long-distant traders were eligible for these duties. Before 1840, the empire had about three dozen such checkpoints.

The lion's share of indirect taxes came from the salt tax (*yanke*) and tea tax (*chake*). Both were under government licensing control (*yan yin, cha yin*). The taxes on salt and tea were collected by merchants who functioned as tax farmers. The government set up only a revenue target. The actual tax rate was in the hands of individual merchants. This was a low-cost operation for the government but created a loophole for rent-seeking by merchants. Indeed, the Qing salt merchants had the reputation of living most extravagantly. But even so, tax revenue was limited. In the 1840s, only 10 million *taels* of silver (375 tons) were collected per year from the salt tax and internal customs duties (*guan shui*) (Zhou Bodi 1981). The ratio between direct and indirect taxes was roughly three to one. The empirewide tax burden was about 0.1 *taels* per head.

TRIBUTE GRAIN

However, the lightness and fairness of the Qing taxes ended with the tax called "annual stipend rice for Beijing" (*cao mi, cao liang*). During the nineteenth century, the amount to reach Beijing was fixed at 4 million *dan* (289,960 tons) a year. It was a hard-budget, nonnegotiable tax (*zheng-e*) on top of the universal land-poll tax. Although only about 5 grams per capita, this tax was not imposed evenly. Eight provinces out of China's eighteen were subject to this tax: Shandong, Henan, and Anhui in the north; and Hubei, Hunan, Jiangsu, Zhejiang, and Jiangxi in the south.

If this were not bad enough, many agents were able to take a cut from rice collection to rice transport and final delivery. It was documented that at least 10 million extra *dan* were routinely collected from villages just to ensure the final 4 million *dan* for Beijing. So, the total tax burden was 14 million *dan* (over 1 million tons), 350 percent of the original amount (Chen Longqi 1992).

In addition, there were numerous fees to be paid on the way to Beijing at the rate of about ten *taels* of silver per *dan*. In lump sum, the total tax burden was over 60 million *taels* per year (2,250 tons). Given that the total population of the eight provinces was 206.3 million in 1820, the per capital tax burden was 0.3 *taels*, 300 percent of the normal burden elsewhere. Furthermore, powerful families were often exempted from this tax. The stipend rice tax was thus the source of social tension because of the whole category of abuse and inequality. In this context, Beijing's balanced budget alone did not spell popular contentment.

CUSTOMS HOUSES AND TRANSIT LEVIES

After 1842, two changes occurred. The first was the institution of customs houses to collect duties on post–Opium War (1839–1842) foreign trade. It began with five treaty ports under the 1842 Treaty of Nanjing. By 1908, China had forty-two Imperial Maritime Customs Houses (*haiguan*), plus 103 branches. A flat duty rate of 5 percent was applicable to all imports and exports. The income from the duties not only paid for China's war reparations and foreign debts (17.9% of the revenue) but also supported the day-to-day running of the bureaucracy (53.5% of revenue).

Unlike the new tariff on foreign trade, which went well with the general population, the second change—the introduction of the transit levy (*lijin* or *likin*), at 1 to 2 percent of the value of goods marketed—was deeply unpopular. The measure was originally taken as a contingency during the empirewide social unrests in the 1850s to the 1870s. The troublemakers, especially the Taipings, effectively cut large chunks from the Qing state's usual revenue sources: 41.6 percent of the land-poll tax and 78 percent of the tribute grain (Liang Fangzhong 1980). Under such circumstances, the large-scale transit levy was the only option for the survival and revival of the Qing sate.

For the majority of ordinary Chinese who regularly engaged with market exchange without paying taxes, this was hard to accept, not to mention that foreigners were all exempted from this levy according to their treaty privilege. In the beginning, the transit levy was imposed by provincial governors in the "frontline" regions to finance a desperate war against rebels. For example, Zeng Guofan had 480 transit-levy checkpoints in Hubei Province, where the fighting was fierce (Zhao Erxun 1986). After the social unrests were suppressed, the levy stayed in effect until 1931. As a decentralized provincial tax free from interference from Beijing, local strongmen had powerful incentives to keep it going after its original mission to raise money for the war was long accomplished.

BUSINESS DONATIONS AND SALES OF OFFICIAL TITLES

The last two categories of the Qing state revenue were irregular business donations (*juanxiang*) and sales of official titles (*juanguan*). Prior to 1840, business donations mainly came from the "chartered maritime trades" (*hangshang*) in Guangzhou (Canton) and licensed salt merchants (*yanshang*) who made monopolistic fortunes at the mercy of the Qing state. A large proportion of the chartered maritime trades were rendered bankrupt as a result of forced business donations. The purchased official titles had only vanity value, as the titleholders were not allowed to take office. So, the supply was unlimited from the state's point of view. The trade was clearly income and price elastic for buyers. But buying a title was commonly considered as a donation to help the state finance. The income of both categories went straight to the Qing coffers.

THE COSTS OF WAR AND MILITARY MODERNIZATION

In terms of government expenditure, 1842 represented a turning point, after which a balanced budget was no longer feasible due to China's chronic war reparations to the foreign powers and the costs of combating rebellions. In addition, there was the urgent need for military modernization (including new weapons and arsenals, ships and shipyards, armies and navies, and the hiring of foreign technicians and mercenaries). From 1842 to 1911, China's reparations totaled 274.2 million *taels* of silver (10,280 tons) (Tang Xianglong 1992). The social unrests in the 1850s to 1870s cost well over 900 million *taels* (33,750 tons) (Peng Zeyi 1990).

The Qing military modernization cost far less than one might imagine. From 1866 to 1907, forty large home-constructed ships cost 8.5 million *taels*, and their maintenance another 1.5 million *taels*. Shipbuilding and maintenance thus totaled about 10 million *taels*. From 1874 to 1911, the aggregate cost of imported ships was 16 million *taels* minimum (Zhao Erxun 1986). If the new armies had the same price, China's total extra military budget was likely to be in the region of 50 million *taels* (1,875 tons). These extras totaled 1,224.2 million *taels* (45,900 tons). This was 17.5 million *taels* per year for seventy years (1840–1910), 39 to 44 percent of the pre-1840 revenue. Now, budget deficits and foreign borrowing were inevitable. From 1853 to 1911, China's cumulative governmental foreign debts were in the region of 592.1 million *taels* (22,200 tons), railway investments included (Li Yunjun 2000).

THE QING'S SLOWNESS TO ADAPT

The essential problem for China's taxation and fiscal policies was the political center's slowness in adapting to the changing environment. Fundamentally, China was under-governed because the state was too small, too cheap, and too weak for too long. In total only 30,000 officials and officers ran the single largest empire in Asia, a factor that had benefited the public in the past, but reduced China's administrative, financial, and military abilities from around the time of the first Opium War. China paid a heavy price for this lack of governance.

SEE ALSO *Chinese Maritime Customs Service; Foreign Loans, 1800–1949; Taiping Uprising.*

BIBLIOGRAPHY

Bao Shichen. Ti caobi [To eliminate malpractices in tribute-grain shipping]. In *Huangchao jingshi wenbian* [Collection of documents of the Qing administration], ed. He Changling and Wei Yuan, 1097 Reprint. Beijing: Zhonghua, 1992.

Chen Longqi. Caoyun [Tribute-grain shipping]. In *Huangchao jingshi wenbian* [Collection of documents of the Qing administration], ed. He Changling and Wei Yuan, 1089 Reprint. Beijing: Zhonghua, 1992.

Deng Gang (Kent G. Deng). *The Premodern Chinese Economy: Structural Equilibrium and Capitalist Sterility.* London and New York: Routledge, 1999.

Deng Gang (Kent G. Deng). State Transformation, Reforms, and Economic Performance in China, 1840–1910. In *Nation, State, and the Economy in History*, ed. Alice Teichova and Herbert Matis. Cambridge, U.K.: Cambridge University Press, 2003.

He Changling. Caozheng yi [On tribute-grain shipping administration]. In *Huangchao jingshi wenbian* [Collection of documents of the Qing administration], ed. He Changling and Wei Yuan. Reprint. Beijing: Zhonghua, 1992.

Li Yunjun, ed. *Wan Qing jingji shishi biannian* [A chronicle of late Qing economic history]. Shanghai: Shanghai Classics Press, 2000.

Liang Fangzhong. *Zhongguo lidai huko tiandi tianfu tongji* [Dynastic data of China's households, cultivated land, and land taxation]. Shanghai: Shanghai People's Press, 1980.

Peng Zeyi. *Shijiu shiji houbanqide Zhongguo caizheng yu jingji* [China's finance and economy during the second half of the nineteenth century]. Beijing: Chinese Finance Press, 1990.

Tang Xianglong. *Zhongguo jindai haiguan shuishou he fenpei tongji* [Statistics of customs revenue and its distribution in modern China]. Beijing: Zhonghua, 1992.

Wang Mingyue. Caobi shu [Memorial to the throne on malpractices in tribute-grain shipping]. In *Huangchao jingshi wenbian* [Collection of documents of the Qing administration], ed. He Changling and Wei Yuan, 1093 Reprint. Beijing: Zhonghua, 1992.

Wang Yejian (Wang Yeh-chien). *Land Taxation in Imperial China, 1750–1911* Cambridge, MA: Harvard University Press, 1973.

Xu Ke. *Qing bai lei chao* [Collection of anecdotes of Qing times]. Shanghai: Commercial Books, 1917.

Yin Jishan. Liti caoshi shu [Memorial to the throne on tribute-grain shipping reform]. In *Huangchao jingshi wenbian* [Collection of documents of the Qing administration], ed. He Changling and Wei Yuan, 1099. Reprint. Beijing: Zhonghua, 1992.

Zhao Erxun. *Qingshi gao* [Draft history of the Qing dynasty]. Vol. 125: Shihuo liu. In *Er-shi-wu shi* [Twenty-five official histories]. Shanghai: Shanghai Classics Press, 1986.

Zhao Gang (Chao Kang). *Man and Land in Chinese History: An Economic Analysis.* Stanford, CA: Stanford University Press, 1986.

Zhou Bodi. *Zhongguo caizheng shi* [A history of state finance in China]. Shanghai: Shanghai People's Press, 1981.

Kent G. Deng

TAXATION SINCE 1978

At the start of its period of economic reform in 1978, China was bequeathed an overly simplified tax system. This occurred because under the planned economy the Chinese government obtained revenues mainly through profit remittances from state-owned enterprises (SOEs). Simplification of the tax system reached such an extent that SOEs, the main taxpayers at that time, paid only one tax—an industrial-commercial tax.

In the 1980s, several taxes were introduced. First, the corporate income tax (CIT) for SOEs was introduced in 1984, replacing remittance of all profit to the government. This reform, described as "changing profit into tax" (*li gai shui*), was meant to provide SOEs with incentives for increasing efficiency. The CIT system was modified by the contract system in 1988. The contract specified a profit level that was subject to the standard tax rate, regardless of whether the enterprise achieved profits reaching this level. On profits above this level, a lower tax rate was imposed. This contract system aimed to provide enterprises with an incentive to increase profitability. Second, different systems of CIT were introduced for each ownership type: joint venture, foreign, collective, and private enterprises. Third, an individual income tax was introduced in 1980 to tax both foreigners and Chinese citizens but it was mainly designed for foreigners because its high levels of exemption would have excluded most Chinese. In 1988 a personal income adjustment tax was introduced, targeting Chinese citizens with high incomes. Fourth, the industrial-commercial tax was replaced by a product tax, a value-added tax (VAT), and a business tax in 1984 (World Bank 1990).

By the end of 1980s, China had a complicated tax structure, which hampered tax administration. Moreover, the coexistence of multiple CIT systems impeded equal competition among enterprises. Reforms in 1994 revamped the tax system to address these problems. The tax structure was simplified, reducing the number of tax types from thirty-four to eighteen. First, the product tax was abolished, and instead the VAT covered all manufactured goods. In addition, a VAT invoice system was introduced. Second, CIT for domestic enterprises was unified at the flat rate of 33 percent. For foreign-invested firms, a different CIT system was applied and generous tax holidays at the beginning of operation were still offered. Third, old taxes levied on personal income, the individual income tax, and the personal-income adjustment tax were consolidated into a single personal income tax. After the 1994 reform, China still levies the personal income tax on different sources of income, rather than on total income.

FISCAL RELATIONS

During the Maoist era, the central government allocated fiscal revenues to provinces according to its assessment of provincial expenditure needs. In 1980 revenue-sharing reform, dubbed "eating from separate kitchens" (*fenzao chifan*), was conducted. This reform drew a division of revenues and expenditures between the central and provincial governments so that each level of government was responsible for balancing its budget. In 1985 fiscal reform was performed to address the problem of surplus and deficit provinces. Revenues were divided into three categories: the fixed revenue of the central government, the fixed revenue of local governments, and shared revenue. If

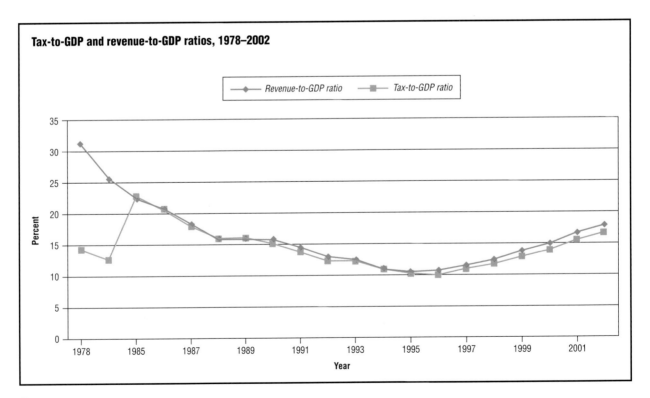

Tax-to-GDP and revenue-to-GDP ratios, 1978–2002

Figure 1

provincial fixed revenue exceeded the province's expenditure needs, excess revenue had to be transferred to the center. If provinces could not meet their expenditure needs by fixed revenue, they were allowed to retain some shared revenues. This fiscal system helped provinces meet their expenditure needs, but it did not create incentives to collect more tax revenue. In 1988 the central government introduced the contract system to provide local governments with incentives to collect taxes. The contract specified a sharing proportion for a basic level of revenue. For revenue exceeding this level, provinces were allowed to keep a higher proportion.

Against the backdrop of declining tax revenues, in 1994 the central government introduced a tax assignment system. The main goal of this reform was to increase tax revenues, particularly those of the central government. By assigning separate tax types to the central and local governments, central leaders intended to redress the problems associated with the prior fiscal regimes. Until 1994, local governments were charged with collecting all taxes and sharing a percentage of tax revenues with Beijing. Pre-1994 revenue-sharing systems were perceived to be undermining local governments' tax-mobilization efforts. Since the local governments had to share tax revenues with the central government, they tried as much as possible to hide these revenues from Beijing. In 1994 Beijing established a national tax bureau in order to prevent local governments from hoarding central taxes.

On the one hand, in the 1994 tax assignment, consumption taxes, customs, VAT on imports, and CIT from enterprises owned by the central government all belonged to the central government. On the other hand, business taxes, personal income taxes, CIT from local enterprises, and other minor taxes belonged to the local government. The VAT, the dominant source of tax revenue, was assigned as a shared tax, with the central government returning 25 percent of VAT proceeds to local governments. From 2002, CIT and the personal income tax became shared taxes.

TAX COLLECTION OUTCOMES

Figure 1 shows the tax-to-GDP (gross domestic product) and revenue-to-GDP ratios. In 1978 there was a huge gap between the two ratios, indicating that considerable revenues were flown from profit remittance of SOEs. The gap narrowed almost to zero after implementing the "changing profit into tax" reform in 1984. The tax-to-GDP ratio fell from 23 percent in 1985 to 12 percent in 1993, leaving China with taxation levels lower than those in both the average developed country (37%) and undeveloped country (16%). The 1994 tax reform initially failed to deter the downward curve of the tax-to-GDP ratio, which further declined from 12 percent in 1993 to 10.5 percent in 1996. But the tax-to-GDP ratio increased from 11 percent in 1997 to 17 percent in 2002.

In order to understand the sources of the change in the tax-to-GDP ratio since 1994, this ratio is divided into various tax types. Table 1 shows the tax-to-GDP ratio by eight major tax types, grouped into three categories of shared, central, and local taxes. The domestic VAT, a shared tax, initially declined slightly as a percentage of

Tax-to-GDP ratio by major tax type, 1994–2003

| | Shared tax | Central taxes | | | Local taxes | | | | | |
	Domestic VAT	VAT on imports	Consumption tax	Central CIT	Business tax	Local CIT for domestic firms	CIT for foreign invested firms	Personal income tax	Sum of these taxes	Total taxes
1994	4.8	0.7	1.1	0.9	1.5	0.6	0.1	0.2	9.9	11
1995	4.6	0.7	1.0	0.7	1.6	0.6	0.1	0.2	9.5	10.3
1996	4.5	0.7	1.0	0.6	1.6	0.5	0.2	0.3	9.4	10.2
1997	4.8	0.7	1.0	0.4	1.8	0.7	0.2	0.4	10	11.1
1998	4.8	0.7	1.1	0.4	2.1	0.7	0.2	0.4	10.4	11.8
1999	5.0	1.3	1.1	0.5	2.1	0.7	0.3	0.5	11.5	13.0
2000	5.3	1.7	1.0	0.8	2.1	0.8	0.4	0.7	12.8	14.1
2001	5.7	1.7	1.0	0.8	2.2	1.3	0.5	1.0	14.2	15.7
2002	6.0	1.8	1.0	0.9	2.4	1.0	0.6	1.2	14.9	16.8
2003	6.3	2.4	1.0	1.0	2.5	1.0	0.6	1.2	16	17.6
Diff.	1.5	1.7	−0.1	0.1	1.0	0.4	0.5	1.0	6.1	6.6

Note: *Diff.* refers to the difference of the tax-to-GDP ratio from 1994 to 2003.

SOURCE: Author's calculations. Data on taxes are from *Zhongguo shuiwu nianjian* (China taxation yearbook), various years. Data on domestic VAT collection from 1994 to 1998 are from Su Xiaohua (2001). Data on the GDP are from *Zhongguo tongji nianjian* (China statistical yearbook), various years.

Table 1

the GDP, and then increased. Among three major central taxes, VAT on imports increased rapidly, while the consumption tax and central CIT remained stagnant as a percentage of the GDP. All four major local taxes increased significantly as a percentage of the GDP.

RURAL TAXATION

In the 1990s, the payment of taxes and fees put heavy burdens on peasants, a situation that often led to rural unrest. Peasants faced six types of charges: (1) state taxes, such as the agricultural tax; (2) township and village levies (*jiti tiliu* and *tongchou fei*); (3) arbitrary collection of fees, apportionments, and fund-raising (*sanluan*); (4) fines; (5) compulsory labor service, often monetized; and (6) compulsory grain sales to the state at below-market prices. State taxes comprised 1.8 percent of net per capita income of rural residents in 1998. The 1993 national regulation stipulated that township and village levies should not exceed 5 percent of net per capita income. However, in many localities, the levy exceeded this level. It is difficult to estimate the burdens resulting from arbitrary fee collection. According to the Ministry of Agriculture, this burden comprised 2.3 percent of net per capita income in 1991.

To relieve the burden on peasants, the central government adopted a two-stage measure. At the first stage, starting from 2002, local fees levied on peasants were abolished and the rate of agricultural tax increased to compensate revenue loss. At the second stage, the agricultural tax was abolished by 2006. Fiscal transfers from the central government were made to local governments to compensate for the revenue loss. It appears, however, that such fiscal transfers are not sufficient to compensate all revenue loss, and local governments have coped with this problem through underprovision of public goods.

SEE ALSO *Central-Local Relationships; Standard of Living.*

BIBLIOGRAPHY

Agarwala, Ramgopal. *China: Reforming Intergovernmental Fiscal Relations.* World Bank Discussion Papers, China and Mongolia Department, no. 178. Washington, DC: World Bank, 1992.

Bahl, Roy. *Fiscal Policy in China: Taxation and Intergovernmental Fiscal Relations.* South San Francisco, CA: 1990s Institute, 1999.

Bernstein, Thomas P., and Xiaobo Lu. *Taxation without Representation in Contemporary Rural China.* Cambridge, U.K.: Cambridge University Press, 2003.

Dangdai zhongguo congshu bianji weiyuanhui. In *Dangdai Zhongguo caizheng* [Contemporary fiscal system in China]. Beijing: Zhongguo Shehui Kexue Chubanshe, 1988.

Kennedy, John James. From the Tax-for-Fee Reform to the Abolition of Agricultural Taxes: The Impact on Township Governments in North-west China. *China Quarterly* 189 (2007): 43–59.

Lee, Pak K. Into the Trap of Strengthening State Capacity: China's Tax-assignment Reform. *China Quarterly* 164 (2000): 1007–1024.

Li, Linda Chelan. Working for the Peasants? Strategic Interactions and Unintended Consequences in the Chinese Rural Tax Reform. *China Journal* 57 (2007): 89–106.

Oksenberg, Michel, and James Tong. The Evolution of Central-Provincial Fiscal Relations in China, 1971–1984: The Formal System. *China Quarterly* 125 (1991): 1–32.

Su Xiaohua. Zengzhishui shuifu fenxi yu zhengce tiaozheng jianyi [Analysis of the value-added tax burden and policy recommendations]. In *Zhongguo shuiwu nianjian 2002* [China taxation yearbook 2002]. Beijing: Zhongguo Shuiwu Chubanshe, 2001.

Wang Chuanlun. Some Notes on Tax Reform in China. *China Quarterly* 97 (1984): 53–67.

Wang Shaoguang and Hu Angan. *The Chinese Economy in Crisis: State Capacity and Tax Reform.* Armonk, NY: Sharpe, 2001.

Wong, Christine P. W., Christopher Heady, and Wing T. Woo. *Fiscal Management and Economic Reform in the People's Republic of China.* Hong Kong: Oxford University Press, 1995.

World Bank. *China: Revenue Mobilization and Tax Policy.* Washington, DC: Author, 1990.

Zee, Howell H. Empirics of Crosscountry Tax Revenue Comparisons. *World Development* 24, 10 (1996): 659–671.

Zhang Le-Yin. Chinese Central-Provincial Fiscal Relationships, Budgetary Decline, and the Impact of the 1994 Fiscal Reform: An Evaluation. *China Quarterly* 157 (1999): 115–141.

Zhongguo shuiwu nianjian [China taxation yearbook]. Beijing: Zhongguo Shuiwu Chubanshe, 1994–2004.

Zhongguo tongji nianjian [China statistical yearbook]. Beijing: Zhongguo Tongji Chubanshe, 1994–2004.

Eun Kyong Choi

TEA SINCE 1800

For more than two thousand years, tea has played a conspicuous cultural and economic role in Chinese civilization. During this period, numerous centers of specialized tea production sprang up as scattered enclaves punctuating the extensive humid uplands of central and southern China. Methods of processing the leaves of the tea plant, generically designated as *Camellia sinensis,* were reinvented and subtly refined over the centuries to meet a wide range of indigenous and foreign consumer tastes (tea consumers in China as a rule being more discriminating than foreigners are). The result was a bewildering variety of product classifications and subtypes. These are based upon a wide range of factors, such as the varieties of the plant itself, the shape of the leaves, time of plucking, region of production, and most significantly, the method of manufacture and the degree of fermentation or oxidation involved in that process. By the beginning of the nineteenth century, the three major classifications of tea widely known today had been firmly established: the fully fermented black teas (*hongcha*) that became so popular throughout the British Empire; semifermented teas (*qingcha*), such as the famed oolongs, long preferred in North America; and the unfermented green teas (*lucha*), much favored by tea connoisseurs in China and Japan.

CHINA'S PRE-1842 TEA TRADE: BY LAND AND SEA

Along with porcelain and silk, tea was one of the most valuable native Chinese products to penetrate the international market over the last few centuries of the imperial era. Under the Qing dynasty (1644–1912), a specialized overland tea trade developed that was initially dominated by well-organized Chinese caravan traders. The compressed blocks of tea (brick tea) constituting the unusual staple of

this trade were long-lasting as well as portable, and became so valued in inner Asia that they were commonly accepted as a form of currency. In the early nineteenth century, increasing amounts of brick tea and other types of black tea reached expanded markets further west in Russia, and during the second half of the century a few Russian firms set up their own tea-processing businesses in Hankou (Hankow) and a few other locations to service what emerged as a profitable, highly distinctive trade.

The bulk of China's tea trade after 1800 was centered upon the maritime export of tea via the southern coastal metropolis of Guangzhou (Canton). All legitimate Sino-Western commerce at that port took place under the bureaucratic constraints of the so-called Canton system. Qing regulations punctiliously delimited the parameters and timing of this trade, and defined its protocols by devices

Workers refining tea leaves, China, c. 1885. *Tea has endured as a valuable Chinese export for over two thousand years. While competition from British colonies in the nineteenth century diminished China's monopoly on tea, a renewed interest in tea cultivation began in the late twentieth century as growers looked to regain the country's status as world leader in exporting the traditional beverage.* TEA INDUSTRY PHOTOGRAPH COLLECTION. BAKER LIBRARY, HARVARD BUSINESS SCHOOL, HISTORICAL COLLECTIONS

such as the *co-hong* merchants' licensed trade monopoly. Recent scholarship suggests that, regardless of its restrictions, the Canton system institutionalized stability by reducing commercial risks, thereby facilitating the successful long-term expansion of Sino-Western business dealings.

Several European trading companies, as well as American merchants, participated in the lucrative export of black and green teas, but the English East India Company easily eclipsed any of its competitors. Until the 1830s, when country traders took over, the company controlled 25 to 30 percent of Canton's foreign commerce, fostering a trilateral trade between its own colonial domains in India, China, and the United Kingdom. Tea formed the linchpin of this intricate exchange, joined by silver and eventually opium as imports offsetting the considerable expenditure involved in funding annual tea shipments.

Demand for European goods in Canton remained very limited, while the world market for China's tea, silk, and porcelain grew steadily over the eighteenth century. Settlements in cash sustained the trade, as silver specie flowed to Canton and north into the interior, where it was often tied up for lengthy periods in the form of contractual capital advances to provincial tea merchants. Western traders confronted a persistent balance-of-payments problem, one unfortunately resolved by China's rising tide of opium imports over the first three decades of the nineteenth century. Belated but determined Qing emergency measures to curtail opium addiction and importation led to open warfare and China's humiliation in the one-sided Opium War with Great Britain (1839–1842). The diplomatic settlements ending that conflict inaugurated a much less restrictive phase of Sino-foreign commerce, and a more dynamic, innovative, and competitive era in the international tea trade.

EXPANDED EXPORTS AND GLOBAL COMPETITION

Five Chinese treaty ports were opened to foreign trade and residence after 1842, and dozens more followed over the next half-century. Coastal and riverine ports—Shanghai, Fuzhou (Foochow), and Hankou being the most significant—emerged as new centers of a booming tea-export trade from the late 1840s to the 1880s. The trade was greatly facilitated by new types of fast maritime cargo vessels (the celebrated British and American clipper ships, and soon thereafter, regular steamship services), and the inauguration of reliable global telegraph networks, greatly reducing the risks and costs of long-distance commercial transactions.

Tea, bread, and jam became daily convenience foods sustaining the energies of the industrial working class in mid- to late-nineteenth-century Great Britain, the professed "workshop of the world." Per capita average consumption of tea in that country rose from 1.41 pounds in the 1801–1810 period to 5.70 pounds in the 1891–1900 period. Regardless of whether it took place in London, Melbourne, Saint Petersburg, or Boston, teatime was synonymous with the worldwide consumption of Chinese teas, often favoring stronger, cheaper varieties of black teas. Chinese exports continued to monopolize world tea markets until late into the second half of the nineteenth century. The well-documented historical experience of Fujian (Fukien), which alone generated 40 percent of China's total tea exports (and 50 percent of its black tea exports) from the 1860s to the 1880s, suggests the considerable economic impact of this expanded global trade upon a major tea-producing province.

Tea growing and preliminary processing (into crude tea, which was then sold and commercially reprocessed to suit the demands of domestic or export markets) was traditionally a village enterprise in China. Rather than expend additional funds and labor to concentrate upon tea cultivation, farmers commonly regarded tea as a sideline cash crop. Production was overwhelmingly small-scale, frequently haphazard, and widely dispersed among countless villages and local market towns in China's central and southern provinces. While China's post-1842 treaty system largely precluded direct forms of foreign investment in any forms of tea growing and processing, foreign firms typically continued to dominate the trade's overseas financial, shipping, and marketing sectors long into the twentieth century.

After decades of false starts and experimentation, mid-nineteenth-century British colonial entrepreneurs in northeast India (especially Assam) and Ceylon (Sri Lanka) and the Dutch in the East Indies (Indonesia) successfully established the plantation cultivation of tea in tropical zones where (unlike the subtropical regions of China) year-round production was feasible. Plantations could now achieve economies of scale with the centralized, quasi-militarized control of large labor forces constantly engaged in cultivation and tea picking. Pioneering the large-scale, increasingly mechanized and standardized processing of black tea, Anglo-American corporate capitalists launched vigorous, sustained, and successful mass-marketing campaigns. This advertising made brands such as Lipton and Brooke Bond internationally recognized household words by the early twentieth century. China's traditionally structured, hitherto complacent tea trade now struggled against emerging waves of overseas organizational and technological competition. The corporate plantation model of black tea production was quickly extended to British tropical colonies in eastern and southern Africa (Kenya and Nyasaland or Malawi), while Chinese overseas markets were further undercut by the Japanese empire's determined efforts to promote exports of its own green and semifermented teas.

REVIVAL OF TEA PRODUCTION AND TRADE IN THE MODERN ERA

Even though the large domestic tea trade continued to serve as an insulating buffer for many tea farmers and merchants, the painfully rapid decline of a valuable export trade challenged and perplexed economic reformers over the first half of the twentieth century. Efforts to revitalize the tea trade in the late Qing and Republican eras, if only modestly successful, did include a wide spectrum of proposed remedies or panaceas ranging from reduced taxation, marketing reforms, improved methods of growing and processing, and state-sponsored radical reorganization of the entire tea industry.

Following the inauguration of the People's Republic in 1949, for almost three decades Chinese tea production and distribution were closely regulated by a hierarchy of local, provincial, and national agencies. The Maoist system of rural collectivization led to the establishment of large-scale tea farms (including a number operated as *laogai* or penal institutions), and a significant degree of advancement in tea growing and processing. With the abandonment of collective agriculture after 1978, a complex hybrid system embracing a majority of small-scale tea growers and producers as well as large state farms has emerged. Tea production for both domestic and foreign markets has increased steadily, with the prospect that China may soon surpass India and reassume its traditional role as the world's leading tea exporter.

BIBLIOGRAPHY

Etherington, Dan M., and Keith Forster. *Green Gold: The Political Economy of China's Post-1949 Tea Industry.* Hong Kong and New York: Oxford University Press, 1993.

Gardella, Robert. *Harvesting Mountains: Fujian and the China Tea Trade, 1757–1937.* Berkeley: University of California Press, 1994.

Lyons, Thomas P. *China Maritime Customs and China's Trade Statistics, 1859–1948.* Trumansburg, NY: Willow Creek Press, 2003.

Mui Hoh-cheung and Lorna H. Mui. *The Management of Monopoly: A Study of the English East India Company's Conduct of Its Tea Trade, 1784–1833.* Vancouver: University of British Columbia Press, 1984.

Ukers, William H. *All about Tea.* 2 vols. New York: *Tea and Coffee Trade Journal* Company, 1935.

Van Dyke, Paul A. *The Canton Trade: Life and Enterprise on the China Coast, 1700–1845.* Hong Kong: Hong Kong University Press, 2005.

Robert Gardella

TEACHER EDUCATION

Teacher training (*shizi peixun*), also known as normal education (*shifan jiaoyu*), first emerged in China around the turn of the twentieth century. Before this time, teach-ers were educated but were not formally trained in pedagogy by subject matter. The terms *normal education* and *teacher training* refer to education and professional development of teachers for basic education, including kindergarten (*you'eryuan*) for three- to five-year-olds. However, these terms were long used in a narrow sense to mean simply pre-service teacher training. In 1997 *teacher education* (*jiaoshi jiaoyu*) was officially adopted to mean all teacher-related educational activities, such as pre-service training, on-the-job training, probation employment, qualifying examinations, and in-service professional development. Teacher education in China has evolved through approximately four periods since the early twentieth century.

ESTABLISHMENT (1897–1918)

In the late nineteenth century, domestic and international crises in China, combined with a burgeoning capitalist economy, gave rise to movements for mass education. Teacher training in its modern sense first emerged in Shanghai in 1897 and in Beijing in 1902. A number of missionary-run nursery teacher classes became available between 1898 and 1905, and the first Chinese-run nursery teacher school was created in Shanghai in 1907.

In 1905 the Qing imperial government was compelled to abolish the imperial examination system for selecting officials and began to promote school education. After the fall of the Qing in 1912, the new Republican government introduced pre-service teacher training for basic education (as opposed to kindergartens). This government-run system offered tuition waivers for teachers in training, and a number of teacher-training schools were introduced by regional and local governments. At the time, missionary-run colleges and universities supplied teachers for private, and a few public, kindergartens in China.

EARLY DEVELOPMENT (1919–1949)

The May Fourth movement spread the Western ideas of democracy and science along with Marxist ideas in China. In 1922 the Beijing government adopted the U.S. education model and relocated secondary- and elementary-school teacher training in the education departments of universities and in vocational high schools. This reorganization meant the dismantling of the government-run normal-education system. But the U.S.-inspired system deteriorated. In 1927 the Nationalist government reunified China and largely restored government-run normal education through the restoration and establishment of normal schools and colleges. Chinese-run programs for training kindergarten teachers were established in different provinces, reversing the dominance of missionary schools in the kindergarten teacher market.

In the ensuing two decades, the reorganized system and the government-run system coexisted, due partly to wartime necessity and partly to the heated debate over the value of the U.S. model for China. Behind the lines during the Anti-Japanese War (1937–1945), the number of teacher-training institutions and their enrollment grew remarkably. The Nationalist government made substantial advances in teacher training in terms of administrative structure, curricular activities, faculty composition, and management. At the same time, in the regions that the Chinese Communist Party governed, teacher-training schools were created to help fight the Japanese invasion, to produce food and supplies, and to promote democratic political awareness among peasants. By 1949, China had twelve normal universities or colleges with a total enrollment of 12,039. Additionally, three university-affiliated normal colleges enrolled 4,363 students. At the secondary level, there were 610 normal schools with 151,750 students.

SUBSTANTIAL GROWTH (1950–1979)

After the People's Republic of China (PRC) was founded in 1949, the government strove to rid the country of poverty and to create an educated socialist labor force. Teacher training became central to the national educational system. The planned centralized economy based on the Soviet model and the prioritization of education for manual workers and peasants reinforced the government-run normal-education system to train teachers for elementary, secondary, and vocational schools. China had only two elementary schools offering diplomas for kindergarten teachers in 1952. These were replaced by nineteen training schools at the secondary-education level by 1965. Within the teachers colleges and normal universities, pre-service programs were divided into general and specialized training. Specialized training included arts, music, sports, and vocational skills. Professional-development institutions were also created to provide continuing in-service education for teachers.

During this period, the teachers colleges and normal universities initiated curriculum and pedagogy reform in elementary and secondary education. But overall, their influence was weak because of the narrow curricular needs in basic education. In comprehensive universities, an undergraduate major that combined teacher training with education in a subject area like physics or Chinese during the last two years of the program often resulted in inadequate training in both areas for would-be teachers. At the time, continuing in-service education for teachers focused on meeting diploma requirements for the job, rather than on research-based explorations of teaching and learning. During the decade of the Cultural Revolution (1966–1976), teacher-training institutions faced staff reductions, the brutal persecution of teachers, and even closure. Despite these setbacks, the early years of the PRC saw substantial growth in teacher training at all levels of basic

education, and a large number of teachers and teacher educators became trained.

PROSPERITY AND TRANSITION (1980–PRESENT)

After the Cultural Revolution, China entered an unprecedented period of economic, political, and legal reform accompanied by a long-standing open-door policy. Normal education has since shown great growth. By 2005, there were 506 normal institutions nationwide, with a total enrollment of 2,487,600, without taking into account continuing in-service education. At around the turn of the century, the global economy also ushered in a maturing market economy in China. In this context, nine-year compulsory education was introduced. Educational reforms in early childhood education and basic education began to promote lifelong learning. In parallel, the system of pre-service teacher training began to transition toward education for both pre-service and in-service teachers. This transition prioritizes the quality rather than the quantity of teacher education, with the goal of improving education at all levels.

Two policy documents issued by the China State Council were critical for teacher education and professionalization during this transitional period: the Action Scheme for Invigorating Education Toward the Twenty-first Century (1998), and the Decision on Basic Education Reform and Development (2001). These policies resulted in four changes. First, teacher education has moved from a closed system to an open system that encourages universities that are not strictly normal universities to offer teacher education programs, while making multidisciplinary education available within normal universities. Second, pre-service and in-service teacher education have been aligned, as have early childhood and basic education, with the aim of developing a lifelong education system. Third, the professionalization of teachers has been reinforced by a series of legislative measures, such as the Teacher Law (1993) and Regulations on Teacher Qualifications (1995), together with the Implementation of the Regulations on Teacher Qualifications (2000), which specifies a teacher-certification process. Fourth, teacher education has undergone a curriculum overhaul, with the addition of a two-year teacher diploma program to the four-year subject-area major, the development of a new curriculum to emphasize the professional goals of prospective teachers, and the promotion of group learning among teachers, with a focus on case studies and clinical diagnoses.

Past experiences in teacher training lend two shared insights into today's teacher educators in China. One is that teacher education needs to be one step ahead of the rest of the educational system. The government "has set education as the utmost priority in China's strategic development," but "the quality of education lies in teachers' hands and, thus, excellent teacher education promises a bright future of China" (Wen Jiabao 2007, p. 4). As a result, the government restored the tuition-waiver policy for all teacher-education students in 2007. The second insight is that teacher-education reform should extend from the historical development of such education programs in the Chinese context.

For more than one hundred years, two issues in teacher education have been hotly debated: whether or not teacher education should occur *only* in specialized teacher-education institutions, and whether or not scholarly accomplishments should be prioritized over professional skills. On the first issue, a consensus has settled on the demand-supply notion of the teacher market. Rapid and uneven development in China demands both specialized teacher-education institutions and other types of teacher education to meet diverse needs. On the second issue, there is a consensus that recognizes the importance of integrating scholarship and professionalism in all types of teacher education. In kindergarten teacher education, however, a critical insight is widely acknowledged: the way that kindergarten teachers learn will become the way that children learn. This understanding has become a thrust in kindergarten curriculum reform that emphasizes showing respect for children, valuing children's interest, and joining children in their learning. The curriculum reform has been aligned with reform efforts in basic education to promote lifelong learning for all future citizens.

RURAL TEACHER EDUCATION

In contrast to urban areas, education for rural teachers in China continues to face poverty-related challenges. The shortage of rural teachers is tenacious. China's rural population shrank from 84 percent in 1978 to 56 percent in 2007, but more than twenty million people still live in extreme poverty. During the first decade of the twenty-first century, China strategically approached the problems of rural teacher education by stimulating agricultural development and increasing investment in basic education and teacher education in rural areas. Policies were issued, for example, to establish standards for compulsory education, to increase teachers' salary and benefits, and to enhance the quality of teacher-education colleges in rural areas. This approach was meant to establish a virtuous circle of enrollment, career choice, teacher quality, and teacher retention.

Most rural teachers attend teachers colleges, focusing on four-year and two-year programs. In some regions, schools at the secondary level train teachers for local kindergartens, elementary schools, and, in some cases, middle schools. All students receive tuition waivers, free room and board, and a stipend. In order to retain teachers for local needs, these teacher-education institutions try to meet the common professional standards for teachers, and adjust their curriculum to integrate the specific needs and aspirations of rural teachers.

The government has sought innovative ways to replenish rural teachers, ensure their full-time employment, encourage volunteers to teach in poor western regions, and develop programs that award a master's degree in rural education. In addition, an increasing number of urban teachers and administrators have been going to rural areas to work with rural teachers. Nationwide, more than a million rural teachers have participated in professional development programs offered by the government to elementary, middle, and high school teachers.

SEE ALSO *Education.*

BIBLIOGRAPHY
Chen Hancai. *Zhongguo Gudai You'er Jiaoyushi* [The history of early childhood education in ancient China]. Guangzhou, PRC: Guangdong Gaodeng Jiaoyu Chubanshe, 1996.

Gu Mingyuan. *Jiaoyu Dacidian: Shifan Jiaoyu* [Education dictionary: normal education]. Shanghai: Shanghai Jiaoyu Chubanshe, 1990.

Jin Changze. *Shifan Jiaoyushi* [The history of normal education]. Hainan, PRC: Hainan Chubanshe, 2002.

Liu Zhanlan and Liao Yi, eds. *Cujin You'er Jiaoshi Zhuangye chengzhangde Lilun he Shijiancelue* [Theories and practical strategies for sustaining early childhood teachers professional growth]. Beijing: Jiaoyu Kexue Chubanshe, 2006.

Ma Xiaofeng. *Zhongguo Shifan Jiaoyushi* [The history of China's normal education]. Beijing: Shoudu Shifan Daxue Chubanshe, 2003.

Song Silian and Han Lixue. *Zhongguo Shifan Jiaoyu Tonglan* [General introduction to China's normal education]. Changchun, PRC: Dongbei Shifan Daxue Chubanshe, 1998.

Wen Jiabao. Jiaoshi shi taiyangxia zuiguanghuide zhiye [Teacher's career is most glorious under the sun]. *Renmin Ribao* [People's Daily]. September 10, 2007.

Wen Jiabao. Zai dishiyijie Quanguorenmin Daibiaodahui Diyicihuiyishang zuo *Zhengfu Gongzuo Baogao* [The government's work report to the first meeting of the eleventh National People's Congress]. *Renmin Ribao* [People's Daily]. March 3, 2008.

Zhongguo Jiaoyu Nianjian Editorial Board. *Zhongguo Jiaoyu Nianjian 2006* [China education yearbook, 2006]. Beijing: Renmin Jiaoyu Chubanshe, 2006.

Zhou Ji. Dalibanhao Nongcunjiaoyu, *Zhongguo Jiaoyubao* [Strive to advance rural education]. *China Education Daily*. October 23, 2008.

Ma Xiaofeng
Hsueh Yeh (Xue Ye)

TECHNICAL AND VOCATIONAL EDUCATION AND TRAINING

SEE *Vocational Education.*

TELEVISION

Television is subject to the same regulation applied to all media in China: a heavy-handed control and censorship exercised by the party-state, and in particular by the State Administration of Radio, Film, and Television (SARFT). Easily controlled in the production and broadcasting stages, television is a medium of propaganda that reaches most Chinese households, and no other medium, not even the Internet, can match the depth and scope of the audio-visual impact it has on the Chinese population. At the same time, television is both a product of and embodiment of modernity and must be accommodated by sometimes outdated government ideologies, particularly in light of market-economy reforms.

At the end of the 1970s in China there were fewer than one TV set per 100 inhabitants, and only about 10 million people had access to TV programs; in 2008 there were more than forty TV sets per 100 inhabitants, and Chinese television boasted 1 billion viewers a day. In the mid-1960s there were twelve TV stations; in 2008 there were more than 4,000 stations, both national and local, with hertzian, cable, and satellite broadcasts.

National broadcasting is still in the hands of China Central Television (CCTV, created in 1958), with sixteen stations. CCTV-1 is the flagship station, offering news, TV dramas, and documentaries that have been sanitized by the party-state. More daring programs can be found on the stations serving international audiences, such as CCTV-4 in Chinese (since 1992), CCTV-9 in English (since 2000), and CCTV-E&F in French and Spanish (since 2004). Two other important "local" groups are the Shanghai Media Group, with fourteen stations, and the Beijing Television Station, with ten stations. The only semiprivate station authorized to broadcast news programs in Chinese is Phoenix, a Hong Kong–based satellite station launched in 1996 by the savvy businessman Liu Changle (b. 1951). Although Phoenix often is praised by economic and political urban elites in China, and has grown from a single station into an integrated group with five stations broadcasting in Mandarin and reaching 150 countries, it is subject to intense scrutiny by the censorship apparatus.

One of the most salient changes in Chinese television that has occurred since the 1990s is the progressive, irreversible shift from a broadcaster-centered model to an audience-based model, and from a conception of TV as only hieratic, edifying, and educational to one that is both informative and entertaining. In addition, content has been broadened from dealing with just local and national issues to include more global perspectives, and it is now broadcast beyond China's borders, acquiring an international reach able to compete with the most important foreign broadcasts. Many examples illustrate these changes. Some news programs and documentaries such as *Jiaodian Fangtan* (Focus), *Xinwen diaocha* (News probe), and *Jinri shuofa* (Law today), all broadcast by CCTV, have become popular because they deal sympathetically with the people and their day-to-day lives. In addition, there are more "live" programs, though in China "live" programs carry a thirty-second signal delay (just in case something has to be censored). Rules on joint production of non-news programming have been relaxed. In 2008 there were two news-only stations, one broadcast by Phoenix and launched in 2001, the other one by CCTV and launched in 2003. The popularity of some non-news programs borders on insubordination. In August 2005, for example, the finale of the reality show *Chaoji nüsheng* (Super voice girls, the Chinese equivalent of *American Idol*) broadcast by Hunan Satellite TV garnered a larger audience than the Chinese New Year's Eve gala show of CCTV-1, the usual record holder for audience numbers (and advertisement receipts). Since then, air time for reality show programs, denounced as "vulgar" in the state national media, has been reduced by official regulations issued by the SARFT.

Despite instances of Falun Gong hacking into provincial TV broadcasts, government control of TV in China is still pretty much intact. New developments, whether profit-oriented because of the huge revenues generated by TV advertising or technology-driven with the advent of Internet broadcasting and HDTV (since 2005), do not threaten the state's control. The coverage of the terrible earthquake that struck Sichuan on May 12, 2008, killing more than 69,000, illustrates that the state control over television broadcasting: In less than a week all TV stations had returned to the carefully staged and tightly "directed" reporting of the news as it was happening.

SEE ALSO *Censorship; Internet; Propaganda.*

BIBLIOGRAPHY

Boyd-Barrett, Joseph Oliver, and Shuang Xie. Al-Jazeera, Phoenix Satellite Television and the Return of the State: Case Studies in Market Liberalization, Public Sphere and Media Imperialism. *International Journal of Communication* 2 (2008): 206–222.

Ying Zhu. *Television in Post-reform China: Serial Dramas, Confucian Leadership and the Global Television Market.* London: Routledge, 2008.

Yuezhi Zhao. *Media, Market, and Democracy in China: Between the Party Line and the Bottom Line.* Chicago: University of Illinois Press, 1998.

Yuezhi Zhao. *Communication in China: Political Economy, Power and Conflict.* Lanham, MD: Rowman & Littlefield, 2008.

Eric Sautedé

TEXTILES

In the late nineteenth and early twentieth centuries, China's textile industry slowly became important in the country's modernization efforts. Hundreds of thousands of people were employed in the textile industry, from silkworm rearing and the reeling of cocoons, to cotton cultivation, yarn spinning, the making of thread, fabric weaving and knitting, yarn and fabric dyeing, and fabric finishing.

The textile industry has always been an important industry in China. By the early twenty-first century, it was one of the country's largest employers and an important export-oriented industry, providing China with a good source of foreign-exchange and tax revenue. Most countries in their initial stages of economic development are heavily dependent on textiles for growth. In contemporary times, China has become the world's largest textiles and clothing trader, with over $171.2 billion worth of clothing and textile products being exported in 2007.

THE IMPACT OF INDUSTRIALIZATION ON CHINESE TEXTILES

China's modern textile industry was started by a returned overseas Chinese, Chen Qiyuan, in 1873 in southern China's Guangdong Province, where silk was produced for export. Subsequently, in 1876, the governor-general of Shaanxi and Gansu provinces, Zuo Zongtang, established the Gansu General Woolen Textile Factory, equipped with German machinery under a German technician. In 1890 Li Hongzhang set up the Shanghai Cotton Mill, China's first cotton-textile factory. The factory was organized into two sections, yarn spinning and fabric weaving, and had American- and British-made yarn-spinning machines with 35,000 spindles and 530 looms. American technicians also worked in the factory.

The use of machines in Chinese textile manufacturing continued to grow; by the end of 1895, China had 175,000 yarn spindles and 1,800 looms in its comprehensive textile mills (excluding small-scale fabric mills and traditional handlooms). The Chinese textile industry in its early mechanized days was heavily protected, and only

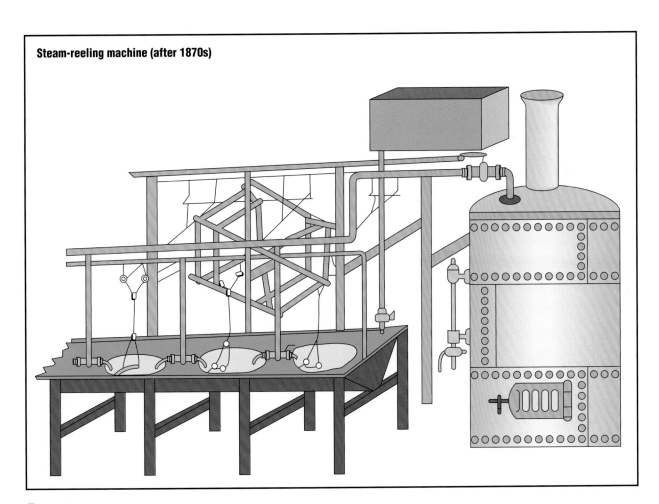

Steam-reeling machine (after 1870s)

Figure 1

approved Chinese traders were allowed to set up factories. The situation changed after the first Sino-Japanese War (1894–1895), when the defeated Chinese were forced to sign the Treaty of Shimonoseki, granting the Japanese the right to build factories in China, including mills for its lucrative textiles market.

In response, the Qing government encouraged private Chinese citizens to invest and set up textile factories. There were two waves of euphoria. In the first, from 1896 to 1899, there was a rush to set up textile factories; a total of 153,000 yarn spindles and 216 looms came into operation within these four years. The second wave ran from 1905 to 1908, when a further nine factories with an additional 128,000 yarn spindles were added. Shanghai alone added 9,000 more spindles to its yarn-spinning capacity. Many local governments in China were keen to encourage new textile-related operations because the industry was a good source of revenue and the supply of native cotton was abundant.

Along with the Japanese, Britain, Germany, and the United States were attracted to the Chinese textile industry, and by 1897 these three countries had set up a total of five factories (Japan had five). By 1913, right before the start of World War I (1914–1918), eight foreign textile factories had been set up with a total of 339,000 yarn spindles and 1,986 looms.

From 1914 to 1931, World War I and its aftereffects resulted in a shortage of imported cotton into China. Because the amounts of domestic cotton and other materials were limited, the price of Chinese textiles rose, and the industry boomed. In addition, American and British investments in the Chinese textile industry were greatly reduced after the war; the Japanese took over and monopolized most of China's foreign-invested textile interests, occupying almost half of the industry.

During the Chinese civil war period (1927–1949) and the gradual Japanese encroachment beginning around 1931 leading to the Second Sino-Japanese War (1937–1945), many Chinese textile-related facilities were badly damaged, causing the industry to fall into decline. Of those factories that did survive the conflict, fifty-four were forcefully taken over by the invading Japanese forces, and put under "military management." The Japanese controlled 70 percent of all yarn spindles and 66 percent of all looms in China at that time.

At the end of World War II in 1945, with the Japanese gone, the Chinese textile industry was dominated by three remaining players: British-invested textile firms; Chinese private textile enterprises; and state-owned textile enterprises that were predominantly controlled by the Nationalist (Guomindang) government.

Under China's First Five-Year Plan (1953–1957), priority was given to developing China's cotton-textile industry, and painstaking efforts were made to transform privately run textile factories into socialist-oriented enterprises. During this period, China's textile industry grew.

However, during the period covered by China's Second Five-Year Plan (1958–1966), which was extended due to disruption caused by the disastrous Great Leap Forward (1958–1960), cotton production was greatly reduced and textile factories began producing inferior fabric. By the second half of the 1960s, most existing textile-related projects were forced to stop.

During the 1967–1977 period, China introduced the large-scale synthesis of oil-based raw materials into its textile industry. The 1970s and 1980s saw renewal and revitalization for the industry. Foreign technologies and know-how were readily welcomed into China, more machines were introduced, and the labor-intensiveness of the industry was reduced. Much of the foreign technology and know-how came to China via investments from elsewhere in Asia, including textile enterprises based in Hong Kong, Taiwan, South Korea, and Japan, where manufacturing costs were rising rapidly.

DOMESTIC AND INTERNATIONAL TRADE

According to official Chinese records, before 1949 the total amount of cotton fabric consumed in China annually was about 2.8 billion meters. Prior to 1949, the market for domestic textiles in China was not large because the Chinese were generally poor after so many years of war. Despite the country's low per capita textile consumption, the Chinese textiles market was huge, due to China's large population size. Living standards improved tremendously after 1949, and by 1952 the total amount of cotton fabric sold annually was 3.1 billion meters.

However, the early 1960s saw a drastic reduction in the volume of textiles consumed, partly because of the failed Great Leap Forward campaign, but also because of overcapacity problems in the industry. Overcapacity did not directly lead to lower consumption. During the Great Leap, people were starving and food was the main concern and getting new clothing, a secondary concern; excess textile production could not be sold and this subsequently led to a reduction in the volume of textiles consumed. By 1961 the total amount of cotton textiles consumed domestically had fallen to about 1.9 billion meters. The situation began improving by 1964, and in 1965 the total amount of cotton fabric consumed domestically increased to 4.4 billion meters.

Since the 1970s, the Chinese textile industry has continued to expand. Textiles were China's leading export item from 1977 to 1978, after which textile exports fell below oil and other chemical products. In 1982 total textile sales reached 46.6 billion yuan ($6.9 billion), eight times the 1952 figure.

A Hand-reeling machine (before 1870s)

Figure 2

From the 1930s to 1940s, China's average annual export of textiles was valued at slightly more than $40 million. The story of the internationalization of the Chinese textile industry can be broken into three stages.

The first stage occurred after the founding of the People's Republic in 1949. Economic sanctions were put in place by the global community against China at this time, with the result that China could, for the most part, export only to the Soviet Union and Eastern Europe. By the late 1950s, these countries accounted for 70 percent of China's textile exports. During the 1950s China underwent a period of nation building, and had a limited supply of goods to export. Textiles continued to be exported, however, and became an important foreign-exchange earner. China's total export earnings in 1950 reached $530 million, of which textiles comprised about 5 percent (or $26.5 million). By 1960, the respective figures for textile exports were $1.9 billion and 29 percent ($549 million), more than a twenty-fold increase since 1950.

During the second stage, from 1960 to 1963, textile export earnings reached $1.7 billion, 30 percent of the total export earnings of China. These increased exports took place in the immediate aftermath of the Great Leap Forward, when China was picking up the pieces.

The third stage of development of the Chinese textile industry was from the 1970s to the early 1980s. In 1971 China rejoined the United Nations, after which trade relations improved tremendously with Japan, the United States, and some Western European countries.

By the beginning of the twenty-first century, China's textile industry had entered its fourth stage of development. In 2000 the value of Chinese textiles amounted to one-quarter of the global total, and Chinese textile exports stood at 14.7 percent, with imports of textiles at 3.7 percent. China's accession into the World Trade Organization in late 2001 opened more export opportunities for Chinese textiles.

THE IMPACT ON WORLD MARKETS AND INTERNATIONAL TRADE RELATIONS

From 1993 to 1998, China's textile industry underwent a period of low quality and low standards, characterized by huge losses at state-owned textile enterprises. The worst year was 1996, when the industry lost 10.6 billion yuan ($1.6 billion). Consolidation of the industry was completed only at the end of 2000, when restructured state-owned textile companies finally made a profit of 6.7 billion yuan (just under $1 billion). Restructuring at that time involved attracting the more technologically advanced Hong Kong, Taiwanese, Korean and Japanese textile companies into China as well as consolidating the bigger existing Chinese domestic textile firms.

China's dominance of the global textile and garment trade is slowly being eroded as rising costs of labor and raw materials are making it tougher to compete with rival Asian producers. Other Asian countries, including Bangladesh, Cambodia, Pakistan, India, Indonesia, and Vietnam, will increasingly nibble away at China's global market share.

China accounted for almost one-third of world garment exports in 2007. However, a slowdown in shipments of textiles and garments may reduce China's trade surplus, which surged 52 percent in the first eleven months of 2007. Textiles and apparel accounted for about 15 percent of China's total exports in 2007.

The Chinese government has cut export-tax rebates and tightened lending. In addition, with average wages rising by more than 50 percent since the early 2000s and the Chinese yuan gaining about 18 percent against the American dollar since the end of the currency peg in 2005, it is projected that China can remain a textile export juggernaut only until 2015 to 2020.

Industry production costs, including raw materials, labor, energy, and environmental protection, have increased, as have the effects of rising interest rates and capital shortages. Vietnam is one of the main beneficiaries of the drop in American textile imports from China. In the first quarter of 2008, sales of Vietnamese-made apparel in the United States were up by over 30 percent compared to the first quarter of 2007.

Chinese exporters were expected to enjoy a brief resurgence in the U.S. market in the first quarter of 2009, after safeguard quotas have been removed by U.S. authorities on December 31, 2008. Although the quotas affect only thirty-four product categories, many of these products sell in large volumes and China has proven in the past that it is particularly good at supplying them. The growth in Chinese exports of apparel may slow after 2010, and its purchases of clothing from overseas may rise as domestic consumers become more affluent. The expected rise in China's domestic consumption may be offset by declines in developed countries.

SEE ALSO *Silk since 1800.*

BIBLIOGRAPHY

Bi, William. China's Textile Industry Becoming Less Competitive. *Bloomberg News,* January 8, 2008.

Dangdai Zhongguo congshu. *Dangdai Zhongguo de fanzhi gongye* [Contemporary textiles industry of China]. Beijing: Zhongguo Shehui Kexue Chubanshe, 1984.

Fangzhi gongye shi wuguihua [The Tenth Five-Year Plan of the textiles industry]. In *Ru-Shi de Zhongguo fangzhiye* [China's textiles industry after WTO entry]. Beijing: Zhongguo Fangzhi Chubanshe, 2002.

Findlay, Christopher, ed. *Challenges of Economic Reform and Industrial Growth: China's Wool War.* North Sydney, NSW, Australia: Allen & Unwin, 1992.

Haig, Paul, and Marla Shelton. *Threads of Gold: Chinese Textiles, Ming to Ch'ing.* Atglen, PA: Schiffer, 2006.

Hutt, Julia. *Understanding Far Eastern Art: A Complete Guide to the Arts of China, Japan, and Korea: Ceramics, Sculpture, Painting, Prints, Lacquer, Textiles, and Metalwork.* Oxford: Phaidon, 1987.

Su Yaochang (Alvin Y. So). *The South China Silk District: Local Historical Transformation and World-System Theory.* Albany: State University of New York Press, 1986.

Textiles Intelligence: Business and Marketing Analysis for the World's Fibre, Textile, and Apparel Industries. http://www.textilesintelligence.com.

World Trade Organization. *Yu Zhongguo fangzhi gongye* [WTO and China's textiles industry]. Beijing: Zhongguo Fangzhi Chubanshe, 2001.

Siow Song Teng

THREE PRINCIPLES OF THE PEOPLE (SANMIN ZHUYI)

Sanmin zhuyi (pinyin), the ideological basis of Sun Yat-sen's political program, is often translated as the Three Principles of the People, and less often as the Three Great Principles or the Three People's Principles. Generally, it was the first major ideological platform to fully abandon China's traditional, feudal order and define a modern nation-state. Specifically, the three principles are *minzu zhuyi* (nationalism), *minquan zhuyi* (democracy, or people's rights), and *minsheng zhuyi* (socialism, or people's welfare).

The principle of *minzu* sought to unify Han Chinese, Mongols, Tibetans, Manchus, and Muslims—China's five major ethnic groups—into a single grand nation, free of imperialist and Qing dynasty influence. The principle of *minquan* aimed to empower China's citizens with political representation via a national assembly, and political participation via the rights to elections, initiative, referendum, and recall. *Minquan* also outlined a government system of five branches. Three of the five were inspired by the Western liberal political institutions: legislative, executive, and judicial. The remaining two (control and examination) stemmed from the traditional Confucian order; the control (or censorate) branch oversaw government offices with the powers of consent, impeachment, censure, and audit, whereas the examination branch focused on qualifying individuals for civil service. Of the three principles, the third, *minsheng*, was the least carefully defined, and particularly vulnerable to ranging interpretations. It highlighted the need to create a viable socioeconomic system via industrialization, equalized land ownership, and a just tax system, although the means to these ends remained somewhat unclear.

BIRTH OF THE PHILOSOPHY

Sanmin zhuyi evolved over several years as a blueprint for a prosperous, stable, and modern sociopolitical order. Its creator, Sun Yat-sen, the father of modern China, spent most of his revolutionary career abroad, and drew heavily from U.S. political ideals as well as traditional Confucian concepts. Combining the best of both worlds, he believed, would negate the social pressures spawning labor unrest in Europe and the United States during the late nineteenth century. In 1897, only two years after his revolutionary society, the Tungmenghui (Revolutionary Alliance or United League), first began engaging the Qing dynasty, Sun floated a prototype of his revolutionary vision. By 1905 the principles of *Sanmin zhuyi* had taken form and become the ideological backbone of his movement. The collapse of the Qing dynasty in 1912 gave Sun a chance to put his ideals into practice, and he began readying the foundations for a new state: the Republic of China. His dreams were soon dashed, however. Shortly after its founding in January 1912 the Republic fell victim to the dictator usurper Yuan Shikai and a series of warlord overlords after him. Political control fell apart, dividing China into a smattering of independent warlord territories.

China's fragmented state prompted Sun to organize a new revolutionary party, the Guomindang (GMD or Nationalist Party), launch another round of revolutionary action, and tighten his vision of Chinese modernity. Political maneuverings kept him busy but gave him a clearer understanding of what China needed. In late 1922 and through 1923, Sun secured control over Guangzhou (Canton) and aligned with Russia. Capitalizing on the revolutionary momentum he had gained, he set about cementing his ideals in the minds of his revolutionary followers. In early 1924, encouraged by Russian advisers, Sun delivered a series of lectures on *Sanmin zhuyi*, giving his revolutionary party and posterity the most definitive account to date. His published notes became canon. Nevertheless, even in this comprehensive form they remained incomplete. Sun delivered six lectures each on *minzu* and *minquan*, but only four lectures on *minsheng*. (For that reason, Chiang Kai-shek, Sun's follower and successor in the Nationalist Party, later added two additional *minsheng* lectures based on his understanding of Sun's original ideas.)

SANMIN ZHUYI AFTER SUN

After Sun's death in March 1925, *Sanmin zhuyi* became a focus of intense political and ideological rivalries. Eager to seize Sun's legacy, subsequent regimes in China claimed to champion his platform but then contorted it to suit their own particular needs. In 1928 Chiang Kai-shek and Wang Jingwei, rival Nationalist leaders, both claimed to be heirs to Sun's vision, but predominantly emphasized the principle of *minzu* defined in anti-imperialist terms. During China's involvement in World War II (1937–1945), Japan's occupation governments employed their own particular reading of *Sanmin zhuyi*, spun to mean collaboration with the Japanese. Meanwhile, Communist Party (CCP) leaders highlighted the principle of *minsheng* defined in Marxist, socialist terms. Before 1949, however, despite governments' strongly announced commitments, widespread war, corruption, rival ideologies, and entrenched social hierarchies ensured that no government paid much more than lip-service to Sun's full vision.

In 1949 Communist forces established the People's Republic of China (PRC) and drove Chiang's regime into retreat to Taiwan. Subsequently, *Sanmin zhuyi* in the PRC faded under the ascending influence of Marxism and Mao Zedong Thought. Nevertheless, in Taiwan *Sanmin zhuyi* found new life as the Republic of China government adapted to new geostrategic conditions. It became a vital and potent symbol of the Republic of China and its ruling Nationalist Party, inspiring the names of new streets, businesses, buildings, and babies. Throughout Taiwan, institutes for the study of *Sanmin zhuyi*, university departments, and educational curricula kept academic and popular attention on the nation's founding principles. From elementary school books to mandatory university courses, educational curricula in the Republic of China on Taiwan emphasized the lessons of *Sanmin zhuyi*. Nationalist publishers, meanwhile, produced a mountain of volumes on the political ideals.

Before 1975, when Chiang Kai-shek died, *minsheng* and *minzu* principles enjoyed full attention but *minquan* principles were limited. Government structures followed Sun's five-branch model, but citizens of the Republic of China enjoyed none of the democratic rights Sun had outlined. Cold War conflict kept the country under martial law. After Chiang Kai-shek's death in 1975, however, his son Chiang Ching-kuo (1910–1988) initiated political reforms aimed at democratization. By the end of the 1980s, when elections became commonplace, Sun's vision enjoyed its fullest expression to date. During the 1990s, after democratization allowed Taiwan's opposition party greater control, government endorsements of *Sanmin zhuyi* declined. Nevertheless, the principles remain an important component of political discourse in Taiwan.

SEE ALSO *Sun Yat-sen (Sun Yixian).*

BIBLIOGRAPHY

Shihlien Hsu, Leonard. *Sun Yat-Sen: His Political and Social Ideals.* Whitefish, MT: Kessinger Publishing, 2007.

Sun Yat-Sen. *The Three Principles of the People: The Great Bright Way for China.* Taipei: China Publishing Company, 1981.

Sun Yat-Sen. *Sanmin Chui: The Three Principles of the People.* Taipei: China Cultural Service, 2003.

Wells, Audrey. *The Political Thought of Sun Yat-Sen: Development and Impact.* Palgrave Macmillan, 2002.

Michael G. Murdock

THREE-SELF PATRIOTIC MOVEMENT

The Three-Self Patriotic Movement was a mass organization that was part of the Communist Party's United Front policy. It was launched by the party to politicize the religious sphere and control China's Protestant communities. The term *Three-Self*, originally coined in the nineteenth century by Rufus Anderson (1796–1880) of the American Board of Commissioners for Foreign Missions and Henry Venn (1796–1873) of the Church Missionary Society, refers to a mission policy that organized native Christians in Africa and Asia into self-supporting, self-governing, and self-propagating churches. After the Communist revolution of 1949, the Chinese government replaced the "Three-Self" slogan with the "Three-Self Patriotic Movement" (Sanzi Aiguo Yundong) to legitimatize the state's takeover of the Protestant church.

THE MAO YEARS

On June 28, 1949, Wu Yuzong (Y. T. Wu, 1893–1979), general secretary for publications of the National Committee of the Young Men's Christian Association (YMCA) in China, acted as a middleman between the Communist Party and the National Christian Council. He urged church leaders to support the Communist movement. Many leaders of the YMCA and Young Women's Christian Association (YWCA) assisted Wu in pursuing a pro-Communist agenda in the Protestant circle.

The collaboration between the Communist Party, the YMCA, and the YWCA dates back to the revolutionary movement, between the 1920s and 1940s, when the Communist Party co-opted some YMCA and YWCA leaders. The major YMCA and YWCA leaders in Shanghai came from the Episcopal Church. An institutional link between the Episcopal Church and the Three-Self Patriotic Movement was St. John's University in Shanghai, a Christian university noted for its emphasis on liberal theology, foreign-language skills, and social and political activism. Several St. John's-educated Episcopalian pastors left the church and joined the Communist Party. During the Sino-Japanese War (1937–1945), St. John's was the only higher educational institution to operate in Japanese-occupied Shanghai after the other colleges moved to the interior. The chief organizer of the YMCA training program in Shanghai was Ding Guangxun (K. H. Ting), a St. John's graduate and an Episcopalian pastor, who was elected bishop by the clergy and laity of the Zhejiang Diocese in March 1955 and became the leader of China's Three-Self Patriotic churches in the 1980s and 1990s. By accommodating their Christian faith with Mao's revolution, many YMCA and YWCA leaders were eager to work for the new socialist state.

In July 1950, Wu Yuzong led a delegation of nineteen Protestant church leaders to meet with Premier Zhou Enlai and draft a public statement, known as "The Christian Manifesto," which expressed Chinese Christians' loyalty to the Communist state. The manifesto urged Christians to support "the common political platform under the leadership of the [Communist] government," and formally established the Three-Self Patriotic Movement. On the surface, the movement called for the indigenization of Protestant churches. But its goal was to force the Christians to sever their institutional ties with foreign missionary enterprises.

Change in global politics affected the Chinese Christians. After the outbreak of the Korean War (1950–1953), the government expelled all foreign Catholic and Protestant missionaries from China. The state confiscated all the mission properties, and forced Christians to cut ties with foreign churches. In the midst of the Korean War, the state founded the "Preparatory Committee of the Oppose America and Aid Korea Three-Self Reform Movement of the Christian Church" to conduct denunciation campaigns against Western missionaries. After a series of denunciations, the first National Christian Conference was held in the summer of 1954, in which Wu Yuzong was elected chairman and assigned to take charge of the Three-Self Patriotic Movement. Officials of the Bureau of Religious Affairs served as "advisers" to the movement and kept an eye on Chinese church leaders.

Within less than a decade, the Three-Self Patriotic Movement ended the missionary era in China and marked the beginning of the Communist takeover of Protestant church affairs. The leaders of the Three-Self Patriotic Movement had served as mere agents of the state to control and reshape Protestant churches according to the Communist Party's designs. Under the tremendous pressure for absolute loyalty to the Maoist state, political neutrality was not an option, and the churches could exist only precariously. The Three-Self Patriotic Movement was clearly in conflict with the missionaries' initial goal of creating self-supporting, self-governing, and self-propagating churches on Chinese soil.

At the same time, the Communist state launched denunciation campaigns to co-opt Protestant church leaders into the socialist order. The church leaders were required to accuse foreign missionaries whom they had known for many decades. This was a regular procedure throughout China. While the state appeared to have co-opted the urban church leaders in the Three-Self Patriotic Movement, the socialist transformation of rural China threatened Christian villages. The land reform designed to break landlords' dominance had the added impact of undermining the socioeconomic basis of Christian villages. The Christian villages failed to protect their properties, and all the rural congregations ceased to function after the land reform. Church buildings were converted into local schools, warehouses, village factories, and government offices.

Besides controlling all the Protestant churches and institutions, the Three-Self Patriotic Movement sought to politicize Protestant doctrines and practices. The movement subordinated the religious mission of the church to the political agenda of the Communist Party. Many Protestant ministers and congregants were forced to attend political study sessions in which they had to express their support for the socialist state. The Christian ideas of pacifism, universal love, and salvation by faith were dismissed as imperialist opiates, while anti-imperialism and class struggle were glorified as Christian virtues.

In 1958 the movement imposed a unified liturgy on all Protestant denominations and banned religious texts that

568

PATRIOTIC RELIGIOUS ASSOCIATIONS

After the Communists came to power in 1949, the Maoist state succeeded in registering all Catholics, Protestants, Buddhists, Daoists, Muslims, and other religious followers across the country. It also founded a number of patriotic religious associations as part of a complex bureaucratic mechanism to regulate religious activities, control religious doctrines and institutions, and undermine the autonomy of religious groups, all in the name of patriotic nationalism and revolutionary socialism. These associations were called "patriotic" because of the Chinese government's concern that religious organizations should be independent of foreign influence. During the turbulent period of the Cultural Revolution (1966–1976), all churches, monasteries, temples, and mosques were closed, and there were no public religious activities. Since the 1980s, under Deng Xiaoping's leadership and subsequently, religious practices have once more been permitted. To monitor and control the reviving religious communities, the state established eight national religious organizations:

- Chinese Buddhist Association (Zhongguo fojiao xiehui; 中国佛教协会)
- Chinese Daoist Association (Zhongguo daojiao xiehui; 中国道教协会)
- Chinese Islamic Association (Zhongguo yisilanjiao xiehui; 中国伊斯兰教协会)
- Chinese Catholic Patriotic Association (Zhongguo tianzhujiao aiguo weiyuanhui; 中国天主教爱国委员会)
- National Administrative Commission of the Chinese Catholic Church (Zhongguo tianzhujiao jiaowu weiyuanhui;中国天主教教务委员会)
- Chinese Catholic Bishops College (Zhongguo tianzhujiao zhu jiao tuan; 中国天主教主教团)
- National Committee of the Three-Self Patriotic Movement of the Protestant Churches in China (Zhongguo jidujiao sanzi aiguo yundong weiyuanhui; 中国基督教三自爱国运动委员会)
- China Christian Council (Zhongguo jiaodujiao xiehui; 中国基督教協会)

These control devices not only legitimized the state's interference in religious activities but also integrated organized religions into the dominant political, social, and ideological order.

BIBLIOGRAPHY

Kindopp, Jason, and Carol Lee Hamrin, eds. *God and Caesar in China: Policy Implications of Church-State Tensions.* Washington, DC: Brookings Institution Press, 2004.

MacInnis, Donald E. *Religion in China Today: Policy and Practice.* Maryknoll, NY: Orbis, 1989.

Joseph Tse-Hei Lee

contradicted political unity and socialism. The denunciation campaigns purged large numbers of respected and experienced church leaders and replaced them with leaders of the Three-Self Patriotic Movement who had little theological training and ministerial experience. But the most intense period of persecution was the 1960s. The Socialist Education movement (1962–1965) and the decade of the Great Proletarian Cultural Revolution (1966–1976) put tremendous pressures on Protestants. All the church leaders, including the leaders of the Three-Self Patriotic Movement, were severely persecuted. If the church leaders happened to come from landholding and merchant families, they would be labeled as landlords and capitalists. There was no future for them and their children. This explains why many young Protestants voted with their feet by escaping to Hong Kong throughout the 1960s and 1970s. Because China was almost totally shut off from the outside world during the Cultural Revolution, people in the West assumed that Christianity had totally disappeared. When China was opened again in the late 1970s, people were surprised to see that the Chinese church was still alive.

THE REFORM ERA

Deng Xiaoping's economic reform after 1978 departed from the antireligious ideology of the Maoist era. Many Protestant church leaders released from labor camps and prisons took advantage of the new political climate to organize religious activities. They received visitors from Hong Kong and the West, answered religious questions from faith-seekers, and provided pastoral services to their followers. An explosive growth of Christianity was reported across the country, especially in areas not previously visited by missionaries.

Coinciding with the "Christianity fever" in the 1980s, the Communist state founded two parallel ecclesiastical structures with offices at the national, provincial, and district levels to regulate public religious activities. In 1980 the Bureau of Religious Affairs appointed Bishop Ding to revive the Three-Self Patriotic Movement. In the same year, Ding was instrumental in forming the China Christian Council to manage the internal affairs of the Protestant church. He chaired both organizations from 1981 to 1996. In reality, both organizations served as the state's arm in ecclesiological affairs. In opposition, the autonomous Protestant groups, known as "house churches," that refused to join the Three-Self Patriotic Movement and the China Christian Council remained critical of the state's interference in the church.

Nevertheless, there is a mixture of the different denominational traditions of Protestant liturgy within the Three-Self Patriotic churches across China. Members of the pre-1949 independent Chinese churches, such as the Little Flock, the Jesus Family, and the True Jesus Church, often worship in officially registered churches. The Little Flock still practices the breaking of bread on Sunday evenings and requires women to cover their heads during services. And members of the True Jesus Church and the Seventh-day Adventists observe the Sabbath on Saturday instead of attending Sunday services.

The Three-Self Patriotic churches and the autonomous Protestant groups are pragmatic in dealing with each other. For example, in the early 1980s, several respectable Protestant ministers from the Chaozhou-speaking region of Guangdong Province joined the Three-Self Patriotic Movement after their release from labor camps. Since then, these church leaders have mediated between the local authorities and autonomous Protestant groups in the region. As their memories of religious persecution during the Maoist era fade, most of the Three-Self Patriotic and autonomous church leaders have refrained from attacking each other. This sense of pragmatism has shaped the interactions between the state-controlled churches and the autonomous Protestant communities in China today.

SEE ALSO *Catholicism; Protestantism; Religious Policy.*

BIBLIOGRAPHY

Bays, Daniel H., ed. *Christianity in China: From the Eighteenth Century to the Present.* Stanford, CA: Stanford University Press, 1996.

Bays, Daniel H. Chinese Protestant Christianity Today. *China Quarterly* 174 (2003): 488–504.

Harvey, Thomas Alan. *Acquainted with Grief: Wang Mingdao's Stand for the Persecuted Church in China.* Grand Rapids, MI: Brazos Press, 2002.

Hunter, Alan, and Chan Kim-Kwong. *Protestantism in Contemporary China.* Cambridge, U.K.: Cambridge University Press, 1993.

Kindopp, Jason, and Carol Lee Hamrin, eds. *God and Caesar in China: Policy Implications of Church-State Tensions.* Washington, DC: Brookings Institution Press, 2004.

Lee, Joseph Tse-Hei. Christianity in Contemporary China: An Update. *Journal of Church and State* 49, 2 (2007): 277–304.

Luo Zhufeng, ed. *Religion under Socialism in China.* Trans. Donald E. MacInnis and Zheng Xi'an. Armonk, NY: Sharpe, 1991.

Wickeri, Philip L. *Seeking the Common Ground: Protestant Christianity, the Three-Self Movement, and China's United Front.* Maryknoll, NY: Orbis, 1988.

Wickeri, Philip L. *Reconstructing Christianity in China: K. H. Ting and the Chinese Church.* Maryknoll, NY: Orbis, 2007.

Joseph Tse-Hei Lee

TIANANMEN INCIDENT (1976)

The first Tiananmen Incident of April 5, 1976, while vastly different in crucial respects, shared important similarities with the more famous events of June 4, 1989: discontent with Communist Party policies, perceived disrespect toward a popular recently deceased leader (Zhou Enlai in 1976, Hu Yaobang in 1989), and elite mishandling of the situation, which inflamed popular passions and culminated in violence.

FACTORS LEADING TO TIANANMEN

Unhappiness with the radical resurgence since late 1975 fueled the popular discontent that exploded on Tiananmen Square in April. While this involved sentiment in support of Deng Xiaoping in his conflict with the gang of four, interpretations of the incident as an outcome of this struggle are misplaced. Deng had been effectively removed from power by Mao Zedong in late 1975, and he accepted his fate and played no role in the events of April. The gang had little impact on Mao's turn against Deng (the key influence being that of Mao's nephew Mao Yuanxin), and relatively few demonstrators on Tiananmen Square raised Deng's name. Yet distaste for the radical turn underpinned the passions released, and reflected implicit backing for Deng.

The central motivating factor was disrespect toward Premier Zhou following his death in January by restrictions on mourning activities, the refusal to declare Zhou a "great Marxist," and an abrupt ending to the mourning period. This was determined by Mao, who believed Zhou was unsympathetic toward the Cultural Revolution and regarded mourning activities as a cover for dissatisfaction with the movement. With the resulting sense of grievance widespread, the coming Qingming festival to honor the dead provided the populace with an opportunity to make amends, while at the same time creating official nervousness.

THE EVENTS OF APRIL

The Tiananmen Incident drew sustenance from the Nanjing Incident in late March. A clumsy March 25 article in

Shanghai's *Wenhuibao* that was erroneously interpreted as an attack on Zhou enraged Nanjing students; demonstrations erupted, leading radicals Jiang Qing (Mao's wife, 1914–1991) and Zhang Chunqiao (1917–2005) were denounced by name, and news of these events spread to Beijing. Politburo members led by Hua Guofeng (1921–2008), who had been chosen by Mao to succeed Zhou as premier, worried about possible "counterrevolutionary" aspects of this "incident," but refrained from labeling it as such. Similar nervousness surrounded management of events on Tiananmen Square, with a command post established on the edge of the square on April 2, and warnings issued against reactionary activities.

A small number of wreathes mourning Zhou had been placed on the square since mid-March, but with news of the Nanjing Incident reaching the capital, they began to proliferate from March 30. As this outpouring of grief for Zhou gathered force, poems, posters, and speeches critical of radicalism grew and, most distressing to the leadership, a small number of oblique statements attacking Mao appeared. From the end of March to April 3, more than 1 million people visited the square, but at the same time order prevailed, and the authorities showed great restraint. On Sunday, April 4, Qingming itself, 1 million to 2 million people representing a cross section of Chinese society came to Tiananmen to honor Zhou. There are differing accounts of the precise mix, but the poorest of peasants, ordinary workers and cadres, rusticated youths back from the countryside, and expensively clothed higher-level cadres were all represented, while the Politburo radicals subsequently claimed intellectuals and the children of high-ranking cadres were the real troublemakers. Clearly, however, top leaders played no role in organizing or encouraging the masses.

Events heated up as elements in the large crowd articulated views critical of the radicals and particularly Jiang Qing. These views were reported to the Politburo, and Jiang demanded action, specifically to remove the wreathes. Beijing Mayor Wu De (1914–1995), who had informally agreed that wreathes could stay another two days, sought without success to deflect this demand, and the wreathes were removed overnight. When this was discovered on the morning of April 5, several tens of thousands of outraged citizens gathered on the square, demanded the return of the wreathes, overturned a police van, and set alight the temporary command post. Still, the authorities continued to exercise restraint, seeking to end disruptions by warnings rather than force, with Wu De's prerecorded speech demanding that people leave the square. As numbers dwindled, Wu again tried to delay in the hope that a violent clash could be avoided, but around 11 P.M. several hundred remained who were beaten and arrested. Despite rumors, and in dramatic contrast to 1989, relatively little physical damage was done, and no one died.

Throughout these events, two impulses dominated Politburo discussions. One was to defend Mao's prestige, the other was restraint. Mao was briefed throughout by Mao Yuanxin, and made the crucial decision on April 5 that the square would have to be cleared—by mouths (persuasion) if possible, by fists (not lethal force) if necessary. But for most of the crisis, the Politburo exercised an unusual amount of initiative given Mao's fragile health. None of the participants dissented from the need to enforce Mao's line, while of the gang of four only Jiang Qing—in sharp disagreement with the other three—pressed for more violent action.

THE IMMEDIATE AFTERMATH AND POST-MAO CONSEQUENCES

The immediate outcome of the crisis was to make official Mao's apparent January choice of his successor—Hua Guofeng became first vice chairman of the Chinese Communist Party, as well as premier. Deng was officially accused of manipulating the incident, and formally removed from his official posts but not, on Mao's orders, expelled from the party. This solidified Hua's position during the process of removing the gang after Mao's death, a process in which, despite belief to the contrary, he was the decisive actor. But as the post-Mao leader, Hua had to manage two contradictory consensus positions—protecting Mao's prestige and bringing Deng back, and the Tiananmen events impinged on both. Mao had authorized the crackdown, and Deng was seen as its victim, even though he had lost power earlier and Mao took measures to guarantee his safety immediately afterward.

With many in the elite and society calling for a "reversal of verdicts" on the Tiananmen Incident, the issue festered over the next two years before being reversed just before the Third Plenum at the end of 1978. It had become intertwined with a range of matters from the Cultural Revolution decade, and leaders such as Wu De who were ousted from power in 1978, and eventually Hua, suffered from having been in authority during this chaotic period *and* lacking sufficient revolutionary seniority to be forgiven for their missteps. The irony was that during the Tiananmen Incident they had done their best to minimize harm to demonstrators on the square.

SEE ALSO *Deng Xiaoping; Zhou Enlai.*

BIBLIOGRAPHY

Garside, Roger. *Coming Alive! China after Mao.* New York: McGraw-Hill, 1981.

Teiwes, Frederick C., and Warren Sun. *The End of the Maoist Era: Chinese Politics during the Twilight of the Cultural Revolution, 1972–1976.* Armonk, NY: Sharpe, 2007.

Yan Jiaqi and Gao Gao. *Turbulent Decade: A History of the Cultural Revolution.* Trans. and ed. D. W. K. Kwok. Honolulu: University of Hawai'i Press, 1996.

Frederick C. Teiwes

TIANANMEN SQUARE PROTESTS, 1989

SEE *Prodemocracy Movement (1989).*

TIANJIN (TIENTSIN)

Tianjin's origins can be traced to 1404, when a walled guard station was established on the city's present site. Now one of the four municipalities reporting directly to the State Council, it is one of the largest cities in China, with an area of 4,364 square miles and a population of over 10 million in 2008.

EARLY HISTORY

The city was strategically located in that it protected the approach to Beijing from the sea and also served as a transportation terminal on the Grand Canal for the tribute-grain system. Situated at the confluence of the major navigable rivers on the North China plain and the Hai River, which drains into the Bohai gulf, the city became a center for trade along the coast and to the interior, and for the administration of customs duties and the salt monopoly in Hebei and Henan provinces. In recognition of its economic importance, the city was elevated from a guard station to an autonomous department in 1725, and became the seat of Tianjin Prefecture in 1731. By the nineteenth century, if not earlier, Tianjin, in addition to being an administrative center, had became the economic center of North China (supporting Beijing, the cultural and political center), with a commercial hinterland that stretched from the coastal plain, over the Taihang mountains, and into the steppes beyond. Trade was the lifeblood of the city, since Tianjin produced little of its own (except for salt) and relied on grain supplied from Henan, Shandong, and the northeastern provinces.

ARRIVAL OF THE WEST

The arrival of the Western powers in China altered Tianjin's developmental path and layout. The key battles of the Second Opium War (1856–1860) centered on the Dagu Fort at the mouth of the Hai River, the gateway to Tianjin. The Treaty of Tianjin, signed in 1858 at the conclusion of the first phase of the war, gave the foreign powers rights to establish legations in Beijing. With the Convention of Beijing, concluded at the end of the war, Tianjin became a treaty port. Charles Gordon (1833–1885) laid out the boundary of the British concession south of the Chinese walled city. American (1860) and French (1861) concessions were established soon afterward. Among the early landmarks established in the foreign concessions was a Catholic cathedral, Notre Dame des Victoires, completed in 1869 but extensively damaged during antiforeign riots in 1870. The deaths of twenty-one (mostly French) foreigners during these riots have gone down in history under the rubric of "the Tianjin Massacre," an event held to have marked a distinct downturn in Sino-Western relations.

The Germans and Japanese established concessions in Tianjin in 1895 and 1896, respectively, followed by the Russians (1900), Belgians (1902), Italians (1902), and Austrians (1903). The expanding foreign population developed the area south of the walled city along both sides of the Hai River, an area almost eight times the size of the Chinese walled city. Foreign investments in the concessions between 1860 and 1948 totaled over $110 million, though the Boxer movement (1900) left parts of the city in ruins.

Foreign presence also stimulated Tianjin's early Westernization. The Self-strengthening movement (1861–1894) and the post-Boxer reforms led to the establishment of various state-owned industrial enterprises—including the Beiyang Arsenal, telegraph service, and mint—concentrated northeast of the city across the Hai River. Exploitation of natural resources such as coal resulted in publicly traded enterprises, including the Kailuan Mining Administration and Yongli Chemical Industries. Processing of native products for export led to the industrial development of leather tanning, wool spinning and weaving, carpet weaving, bristle manufacture, and egg products. Light industries also prospered as the city became home to North China's first modern factories for milling flour, rolling cigarettes, spinning and weaving cotton, and manufacturing soap. Before World War II, the city was, in terms of paid-up capital, the country's second-largest industrial center, behind Shanghai, and the largest in North China.

Tianjin played a pioneering role in education, from a kindergarten for girls to institutions of higher learning, including Charles D. Tenney's Anglo-Chinese School and Beiyang University. Nankai School, founded by Zhang Boling (1876–1951) in 1904, was reorganized as Nankai University, again at Zhang's initiative, and grew into one of China's foremost institutions of higher education. During the Anti-Japanese War (1937–1945), Nankai University was evacuated first to Changsha and then to Kunming. It was integrated for the duration of the war with Peking (Beijing) and Tsinghua (Qinghua) universities, the three uniting to form the historic National Southwest Associated University (Guoli Xinan Lianhe Daxue).

The city's size and location gave it advantages and disadvantages as an administrative center. It served as the provincial capital for Hebei Province from 1870 to 1911 (sharing that responsibility with Baoding). After a short period as an independent municipality (*zhixia shi*) under the Nationalist government, it was the provincial capital again from 1930 to 1935, after which its status as an independent municipality was restored. This trajectory would be repeated after 1949. During the Anti-Japanese War, the city was governed from Beijing by a puppet government under Japanese control.

POST-1949 DEVELOPMENTS

After 1949 Tianjin came under Beijing's shadow. As a result, from 1950 to 1975 state investment in the municipality lagged behind the capital and Shanghai at an average ratio of 1:3.2:2.75, respectively. As state strategy shifted, Tianjin's economy went through three transformations. From 1949 to 1957, its economy recovered from the civil war, the city completed the socialist transformation of private enterprise, and the state emphasized heavy industries in its investments. As a result, the city's economy grew almost fivefold at an average annual rate of 23 percent, outpacing the national average and Shanghai.

Human and natural disasters disrupted Tianjin's growth from 1958 to 1978. From 1958 to 1966 Tianjin was incorporated with Hebei Province and served as the provincial capital until the upheaval of the Cultural Revolution led to a relocation of the capital's functions first to Baoding and then permanently to Shijiazhuang. During the Great Leap Forward the pace of growth slowed to 4 percent, picking up only slightly during the decade of the Cultural Revolution to reach an average of 6.7 percent between 1966 and 1976. The tertiary sector remained underdeveloped in this period as a result of the continued emphasis on industrial production. The earthquake of 1976, resulting in almost RMB 4 billion in property damage and over 20,000 deaths, dealt another blow to the city.

Economic reforms since 1978 widened the gap between Tianjin and the other growth poles such as Shanghai, Guangzhou, and Shenzhen. State investment in the city amounted to less than RMB 3 billion each year between 1978 and 1985. Even so, light, consumer-oriented industries grew at an annual rate of 9.9 percent, in contrast to the low pace of 6 percent between 1953 and 1978. In part, this shift can be attributed to the influx of foreign direct investment from Hong Kong, Taiwan, and Japan. From a beginning of two contracts worth less than $3 million signed in 1979, over eight thousand contracts had been signed by 1994, involving over $7 billion in foreign direct investments, led by Otis (1984), Motorola (1992), and other household names such as Coca-Cola, Pepsi, Samsung, Yamaha, Novo Nordisk, and Nestle.

In 1994, as part of the state's strategy to develop the coastal area east of Tianjin, the Tianjin People's Congress established the New Coastal District (Binhai Xinqu), encompassing the port at Xingang, the salt fields of Hanggu, the oil field and refinery at Dagang, the Tianjin Economic and Technological Development Zone, and a free-trade zone. The district absorbed one-third of the municipality's investments, the state increased its investment from RMB 20 billion to RMB 50 billion per year, and these sources were supplemented by investment from foreign companies and former state-owned enterprises, which, as a result of economic reforms, became publicly traded conglomerates. By 2005 almost half of the municipality's gross domestic product came from the district.

The New Coastal District also plays a central role in the 2006 master plan for Tianjin. Sea, highway, and rail, including a new high-speed rail link between Tianjin and Beijing, will link a ring of cities to form the Greater Bohai Economic Region. Conceived of as a third growth pole after Shenzhen and Pudong (Shanghai), the district in 2008 received such privileges as the authority to experiment with new land-use and financial policies. A new exchange for over-the-counter trading of equity securities and corporate bonds has received state approval. Through the local branch of the Bank of China, individual investors will also be able to invest directly in Hong Kong's stock market. Tianjin will thus reclaim its place as the economic and financial center of North China, while Beijing will continue as the political and cultural center of the country.

SEE ALSO *Foreign Concessions, Settlements, and Leased Territories; Opium Wars; Treaty Ports; Urban China.*

BIBLIOGRAPHY

Guojia Tongji Ju [National Bureau of Statistics], comp. *Quanguo gesheng zhizhiqu zhixiashi lishi tongji ziliao huibian, 1949–1989* [A compilation of historical statistical materials on provinces, autonomous regions, and centrally administered municipalities, 1949–1989]. Beijing: Zhongguo Tongji Chubanshe, 1990.

Hershatter, Gail. *The Workers of Tianjin, 1900–1949.* Stanford, CA: Stanford University Press, 1986.

Rogaski, Ruth. *Hygienic Modernity: Meanings of Health and Disease in Treaty-Port China.* Berkeley: University of California Press, 2004.

Tianjinshi Defangzhi Bianxiu Weiyuanhui [Committee for Editing Tianjin Annals], comp. *Tianjin Tongzhi* [Tianjin annals]. Tianjin: Tianjin Shehui Kexueyuan Chubanshe, 1996.

Tianjinshi Tongji Ju [Tianjin Bureau of Statistics], ed. *Tianjin wushinian* [Tianjin over half a century]. Beijing: Zhongguo Tongji Chubanshe, 1999.

Kwan Man Bun (Guan Wenbin)

TIBET

Tibet is the indigenous home of the Tibetan people. It is located on the Tibetan Plateau, the highest region on Earth, with an average elevation of 4,900 meters (16,000

```
┌─────────────────────────────────────────┐
│                                           │
│                 TIBET                     │
│                                           │
│                   ■                       │
│  ───────────────────────────────────────  │
│                                           │
│  Capital city: Lhasa                      │
│  Largest cities (population): Lhasa       │
│      (475,500), Shigatse,                 │
│      Chamdo                               │
│  Area: 1,202,230 sq. km. (471,000 sq. mi.)│
│  Population: 2,810,000 (2006)             │
│  Demographics: Tibetan, 92.8%; Han, 6.1%; │
│      Hui, 0.3%; Monpa, 0.3%; other, 0.2%  │
│  GDP: CNY 29.1 billion (2006)             │
│  Famous sites: Potala Palace, Jokhang     │
│      Temple, Namtso Lake, Tashilhunpo     │
│      Monastery                            │
│                                           │
└─────────────────────────────────────────┘
```

feet). The definition of Tibet in administrative terms remains divisive and controversial. The People's Republic of China equates Tibet with the Tibet Autonomous Region (TAR), a province-level entity that includes Arunachal Pradesh, now under India's effective jurisdiction. The Tibetan government-in-exile and the Tibetan refugee community in India under the Fourteenth Dalai Lama refer to a much broader geographical range, encompassing not only the TAR but also ethnographically Tibetan areas of present-day Qinghai, Gansu, Sichuan, and Yunnan provinces under China. By the end of 2001, the TAR had a population of 2.63 million, of which 92.2 percent were Tibetans, 5.9 percent were Han Chinese, while other ethnic peoples accounted for 1.9 percent.

EARLY QING CHINA AND TIBET

The current debate over Tibet's political status and its relations with China has deep roots going back to the empire building of the Qing dynasty (1644–1912). When the Qing forces penetrated Qinghai in the mid-1640s, an alliance between the Qing and the Tibetans was in the interest of both parties. The Tibetans wished to establish a friendly relationship with the new dominant power in China and Inner Asia, and the Qing court sought to use Tibetan Buddhism to strengthen its ties with the Mongols. The visit of the Fifth Dalai Lama (1617–1682) to Beijing in 1653 demonstrates this unusual relationship between the early Qing and the Tibetans.

With the consolidation of Qing control in China, and the decline of Mongol power in Inner Asia, the Qing was able to intervene in Tibet without regard for Tibet's role in Inner Asian affairs. From 1720 to the late eighteenth century, the Qing gradually increased its authority in Tibet, intervening in the case of third-party invasions of Tibet (1720 and 1792) and internal disorders (1728 and

1750). Each intervention resulted in an increase in Qing administrative control over Tibetan affairs. Two permanent *ambans*, Qing imperial residents, were installed in Lhasa in 1727 to closely superintend Tibetan affairs. This arrangement was reinforced by the presence of a Qing garrison force in Tibet, which indicated the strengthened Qing military authority there.

In 1792, after successfully repelling the invading Gurkhas in Tibet, the Qing court took the occasion to extensively restructure its protectorate over Tibet. The status of the *ambans* was elevated above that of the Dalai Lama. They not only took control of Tibetan defense and foreign affairs, but were also put in command of the Qing garrison and the Tibetan army. The Qing also required that the incarnations of the Dalai and Panchen Lamas be chosen with the supervision of the *ambans*. This meant that the final authority over the selection of reincarnations, and thus over political succession in the Tibetan system of combined spiritual and temporal rule, would henceforth belong to the Qing government.

THE DECLINE OF QING POWER IN TIBET

The measure put into effect in 1792 represented the height of Qing influence in Tibet. Thereafter, the Qing became increasingly preoccupied with problems in the interior, and officials in Beijing found it less and less easy to intervene in Tibetan affairs. When the Gurkhas again attacked Tibet in 1855, the Qing was so preoccupied with the Taiping Uprising (1851–1864) that it was unable to respond to the Tibetans' request for assistance. Thus, the Tibetans were forced to pay tribute to Nepal and grant judicial extraterritoriality to Nepalese subjects in Tibet. By the second half of the nineteenth century, the Qing *ambans*, who represented the Qing emperor and Qing authority, could do little more than exercise ritualistic and symbolic influence.

In 1895 Qing China suffered defeat in the war with Japan, thus beginning the final decline of the dynastic order. The final years of the dynasty witnessed the rise of Han Chinese nationalism, in reaction to both foreign imperialism and the alien rule of the Manchus. Meanwhile, competition between the British and Russian empires over influence in Central Asia began to transform Tibet into an object of international interest. In order to ward off possible threats from the north and thus protect its position in India, the British regarded it essential to maintain a sphere of influence and a military buffer in Tibet. In 1904, in order to counteract growing Russian activity in Tibet, the British launched a military expedition to the region. As a result of this invasion, the British secured certain trade privileges and were allowed to open three trade marts at Gyantse, Yatung, and Gartok. In

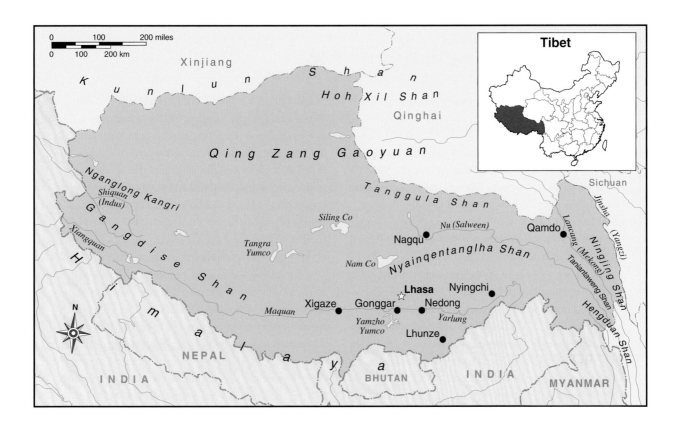

subsequent treaties, the British further secured the guarantee that Qing China would exclude all other foreign powers from Tibet, thus preventing Russian interference in Tibet. In terms of the concept of international law, these treaties signed between Britain and Qing China also affirmed Qing overlordship in that region.

LATE QING REFORMS IN TIBET

The British invasion of Tibet in 1904 had far-reaching implications in terms of contemporary Tibetan issues. It ended Tibet's century-long international isolation. It also established direct relations between the British and the Tibetans, upon which Tibet might theoretically have built a case for international recognition as an independent state. Meanwhile, the growth of British interest and activity in Tibet caused Qing China to attempt to restore its precarious position in Lhasa. In 1905 the Qing initiated a series of new programs to consolidate central authority in southwest China. These programs included eliminating local autonomous Tibetan chiefdoms in the Kham (Eastern Tibet) area, and reducing the number of monks in monasteries.

Beijing's new deals caused wide disaffection locally, and in one uprising a Qing *amban* was killed. In swift retaliation, the Qing sent an army to suppress the rebellion and reinforce its authority over Tibet. The Qing reforms

shocked the Thirteenth Dalai Lama (1876–1933). Frustrated that the Qing troops were sent to Tibet to ensure China's control over him, in 1910 the Dalai Lama decided to flee into exile in India. Beijing responded by deposing him. However, the Qing in the 1900s was by no means comparable to the Qing in the 1700s. With the outbreak of the Chinese revolution in 1911, the Qing's proactive policies over Tibet became unsustainable. Taking advantage of the chaotic situation in China proper, the Tibetans demanded the withdrawal of all Chinese soldiers and officials from Tibet. Chinese troops were finally removed from Tibet in late 1912.

REPUBLICAN CHINA AND TIBET

With the ousting of Qing troops, along with Chinese authority, from Tibet, the status of Tibet as part of China's frontier territory became a highly controversial issue that would remain unresolved throughout the subsequent Republican era (1912–1949). Immediately after its foundation on January 1, 1912, the Chinese Republic began to show interest in transforming the Inner Asian dependencies of the defunct Qing into integral parts of the Chinese state. Yuan Shikai, president of the new Republic, propagated a doctrine of equality among the "five nationalities" of China—the Han, Manchu, Mongols, Tibetans, and Hui Muslims—the major component peoples of the

LHASA

Lhasa, literally "place of the Buddha," is the capital of Tibet and residence of the Dalai Lamas. As of 2006, Lhasa's population was about 255,000. The city is part of Lhasa Prefecture and the terminus of the Qinghai-Tibet railway. The total population of Lhasa Prefecture was 521,500, among which 81 percent were Tibetans and 17 percent were Han Chinese, excluding the People's Liberation Army (PLA) troops stationed there. The opening of the railway on July 1, 2006, connected Lhasa and Beijing, and accelerated the Han influence in Tibet.

In the seventh century, Songtsen Gampo unified Tibet and first established his political center at the site of present-day Lhasa. From the fall of Songtsen Gampo to the accession of the Fifth Dalai Lama (1617–1682), the center of political power in Tibet was not always situated in Lhasa. However, the importance of Lhasa as a religious center became increasingly significant as time passed. By the fifteenth century, Lhasa had risen to prominence after the founding of three large Gelupa monasteries—Ganden, Sera, and Drepung—by Tsongkhapa (1357–1419). The scholarly achievements and political astuteness of the Gelupa sect restored Lhasa to center stage once again.

During the reign of the Fifth Dalai Lama, Lhasa was both the religious and political capital of Tibet. In 1645 the Potala Palace, first constructed during Songtsen Gampo's reign, was rebuilt to a height of about 120 meters. It became the residence of the Dalai Lamas, who made the capital their seat of political and religious rule, and a landmark on the Lhasa skyline. In 1987 to 1989, several major demonstrations were launched by monks and nuns in Lhasa to reject Chinese rule. The Chinese government responded by tightening control over the monasteries and reeducating their leaders. Many monks who refused to accept reeducation were imprisoned and others fled their monasteries and escaped into India. In 2008, the year of the Beijing Olympics, further demonstrations led to violent conflict between Tibetans and security forces, and to attacks on Han and Hui businesses, with loss of life on both sides.

Agriculture and husbandry had been Lhasa's way of economic life. By the second half of the twentieth century, new industries were steadily improving Lhasa's living standard. After the opening of the Qinghai-Tibet railway, the tourism industry brought new business opportunities to the region. To maintain the balance between humans and their environment, Tibetan local officials also emphasize tourism and services, hoping these will lead to improvements in Tibet's welfare. Once considered the "forbidden city" and having its unique traditions, Lhasa has been undergoing complex and unpredictable changes.

BIBLIOGRAPHY

Barnett, Robert. *Lhasa: Streets with Memories*. New York: Columbia University Press, 2006.

Chapman, F. Spencer. *Lhasa: The Holy City*. 1938. Delhi: Bodhi Leaves, 1992.

Hsiao-ting Lin (Xiaoting Lin)

former Qing empire. This five-nationality doctrine was premised upon the Han Chinese belief that border peoples only wanted equal treatment under a Chinese administration, not freedom from Chinese control altogether. However, the Dalai Lama, who in 1912 returned to Lhasa with British patronage, was no longer prepared to accept Chinese authority over his territory.

In 1913 and 1914, the British proposed that a tripartite conference on Tibet's status be held at Simla, India, and Beijing was forced to accept the participation of Tibetan delegates at this event on an equal footing. No consensus concerning Tibet's status was reached at the conference. The Tibetans claimed independence from Chinese authority, whereas the Chinese uncompromisingly insisted on maintaining China's sovereignty over Tibet. China's verbal sovereignty over Tibet continued after the Nationalists under Chiang Kai-shek (Jiang Jieshi) came to power in 1928. Throughout the Republican period, against a backcloth of British patronage, a relatively weak Chinese central regime, and a chaotic situation in China proper, the Tibetans enjoyed an independent status free from Chinese dominance, even if such independence was de facto, not de jure.

TIBET UNDER COMMUNIST CHINESE RULE

After defeating Nationalist forces in the Chinese civil war (1946–1949), the Communist People's Liberation Army (PLA) invaded Qamdo, crushing the ill-equipped Tibetan army, which offered little resistance. In May 1951, Tibetan representatives in Beijing were forced to sign a Seventeen-point Agreement with the Communist leadership. The accord acknowledged China's sovereignty over Tibet. A few months later, the Fourteenth Dalai Lama ratified the agreement.

At the initial stage of Communist rule, the Dalai Lama was assured that his status, along with Tibet's traditional dual political-religious system, would remain intact. However, Beijing's ultimate goal was to integrate Tibet into China through Chinese administration and other reforms. In March 1955, the preparatory committee to rule the TAR was first established. Meanwhile, land redistribution and "democratic" reforms were introduced outside the political boundary of the TAR in the ethnic Tibetan areas of Qinghai, Yunnan, and Kham, which caused local revolts to erupt. By late 1958, the PLA was instructed to pacify the revolts in Kham and Qinghai. Local Tibetans began moving into the TAR, toward Lhasa.

In Lhasa, tensions also reached a critical point by the middle of 1958. The Chinese Communists accused the Dalai Lama and his government of sympathizing with anti-Chinese resisters and of supplying them with arms. The tensions finally reached a climax in March 1959. No longer able to control the situation in Tibet, the Dalai Lama fled from Lhasa to India with U.S. covert aid. In 1960 the Indian government permitted the Dalai Lama and his followers to establish a "government-in-exile" in Dharamsala, which continues today.

By May 1959, the Tibetan revolt was over. The absence of the Dalai Lama facilitated Chinese Communist control over Tibet. Beijing abolished the Dalai Lama's administration system and replaced it with Communist control. Tibet was reorganized into more than seventy rural counties and special districts to replace the feudal governing structure. In urban areas, street and local committees were established to

A Tibetan monk and nomads play basketball near Zoige, Tibet, August 30, 2007. Chinese dominance over Tibet began in the mid-1600s, as Qing rulers supported the Tibetans to defeat Mongol invaders. While Chinese influence has fluctuated in centuries since, the People's Liberation Army reasserted control of the region in the early 1950s, sparking an ongoing struggle for Tibetan independence. © MARTIN RUETSCHL/KEYSTONE/CORBIS

manage local security, hold public meetings, and regulate population movement. In rural areas, Communist-dominated peasant associations also regulated local affairs. Although these administrative changes helped Beijing control Tibetan society, tensions and conflicts between the Han Chinese and the Tibetans continued. In March 1989, tension in Lhasa reached a new height, forcing the Chinese to impose martial law over the next twelve months.

CHINA-TIBETAN TANGLES

Since 1959, the self-exiled Tibetan government in Dharamsala has attracted thousands of Tibetan refugees to join its Free Tibet movement. Yet the Dalai Lama's exiled leadership could not agree on goals. On the one hand, the Dalai Lama extolled the virtues of being ready to return to Tibet. On the other hand, in order for refugees to raise themselves above bare subsistence, it is essential that the government-in-exile deepen its social foundation in its governed communities and interact more closely with its Indian neighbors. For several decades after 1959, the Dalai Lama and his advisers were unable to reconcile these goals.

Beginning in the late 1970s, the Chinese government initiated a dialogue with the Dalai Lama to have him return to China and achieve the final legitimation of Chinese rule in Tibet. The Dalai Lama responded in his 1988 Strasbourg address by formally accepting Chinese sovereignty over Tibet in exchange for genuine and well-defined autonomous rights for Tibetans. By proposing Tibetan autonomy, the Dalai Lama implied a Tibet governed by the Tibetans themselves under China's legal and territorial framework, rather than seeking Tibet's political independence from Chinese jurisdiction. Yet his proposal was ignored by the Chinese to whom it was directed, and by Tibetans who rejected it. His proposal only impressed the international community, for whom the fundamental issues of sovereignty and independence were not as important as the Dalai Lama's spirit of concession toward resolving an international conflict.

In the 1990s, Beijing was little disposed to compromise on Tibet, because a solution to that problem seemed finally within its grasp. Beijing was convinced that any autonomy, cultural or political, would only revive Tibetan nationalism and encourage Tibetan demands for greater autonomy, including independence. After the riots of 1987 to 1989, Beijing formulated a new strategy to resolve the Tibet issue. It offered a program of colonization under the guise of Tibet's separate development. This strategy was accompanied by continuous education and ideological indoctrination to win over Tibetans. Beijing's 1994 decision to revive its long-delayed plan to complete a railroad link via Golmud to Lhasa also demonstrates a policy of colonial flexibility that uses both traditional Chinese frontier policy and an admission that the Communist promise of national minority autonomy was only meant to achieve assimilation. The building of the new railroad, which is part of the Great Western Development Scheme launched in 2000, has generated a hostile response from Tibetans, both in the TAR and in exile, who perceive it as a potential threat of further Han dominance, politically, religiously, and culturally. Whether China's policy will effectively settle its Tibet issue and Beijing's relations with the Dalai Lama remains to be seen.

SEE ALSO *Buddhism; Dalai Lama.*

BIBLIOGRAPHY

Goldstein, Melvyn C. *A History of Modern Tibet, 1913–1951: The Demise of the Lamaist State.* Berkeley: University of California Press, 1989.

Grunfeld, A. Tom. *The Making of Modern Tibet.* Rev. ed. Armonk, NY: Sharpe, 1996.

Lin Hsiao-ting. *Tibet and Nationalist China's Frontier: Intrigues and Ethopolitics, 1928–49.* Vancouver: University of British Columbia Press, 2006.

Smith, Warren W., Jr. *Tibetan Nation: A History of Tibetan Nationalism and Sino-Tibetan Relations.* Boulder, CO: Westview, 1996.

Tsering Shakya. *The Dragon in the Land of Snows: A History of Modern Tibet since 1947.* New York: Columbia University Press, 1999.

Lin Hsiao-ting (Xiaoting Lin)

TOURISM

This entry contains the following:

OVERVIEW
Pál Nyíri

DOMESTIC
Alan A. Lew

FOREIGN
Alan A. Lew

TRAVEL ABROAD
Wolfgang Georg Arlt

OVERVIEW

China is both one of the world's top tourist destinations and tourist-sending countries. This tourism in the modern Western sense is a recent phenomenon, but China has a premodern tradition of leisure travel.

LITERATI TRAVEL IN IMPERIAL CHINA

Leisure travel became a popular activity for the educated gentry in the sixteenth century. It involved travelling to both nature sites (mountains, lakes, rivers) and architectural monuments (temples, pavilions, towns) known for their literary or artistic associations; some were also popular Buddhist or Daoist pilgrimage destinations. The main objective of literati travel was to experience the sights and emotions immortalized by literary heroes of the past, some of whom engraved or painted the sites with calligraphy. Accounts from the seventeenth century testify to a well-developed "tourism business," with inns at famous sites such as Mount Tai offering sedan chairs and "postsummit receptions" to gentry travelers as well as pilgrims.

Sets of views (*jing*) of famous sites were well known from woodblock prints. These views became so established that artists could paint, and poets dedicate poetry to, famous sites without visiting them. *Jing* encompassed not only a particular angle of viewing a site but also the circumstances of viewing (season, time of day, weather, and the spectator's mood). Educated viewers were immediately able to identify the best-known sites by their accepted iconography: thus, "scholars in a boat beneath a cliff inevitably signified journeying to Red Cliff" (Strassberg 1994, p. 7) as described in Su Shi's (1037–1101) famous eponymous ode.

THE RISE OF MODERN TOURISM

In the first half of the twentieth century, Western-style tourism made very limited inroads into the lifestyles of China's affluent classes (Dong 2007). The first Chinese travel agency opened in Shanghai in 1927, but it had only a few customers every year before the Japanese invasion forced it to close. Meanwhile, under the Nationalist government of Chiang Kai-shek (Jiang Jieshi), canonical sites of literati travel were recast as sites of national memory. The tomb of Song dynasty hero Yue Fei (1103–1142) in Hangzhou (Wang 2000), built at this time, remains a key "patriotic education site" today.

After assuming power in 1949, the Chinese Communist Party, unlike its Soviet mentor, did not develop tourism. Soviet-style sanatoria (*liaoyangyuan*, a cross between a resort and a hospital) were open only to cadres, while sightseeing tourism was treated as a tool for showcasing the achievements of socialism for "foreign friends" and overseas Chinese (China International Travel Service was subordinated to the Overseas Chinese Affairs Bureau). For the few who were familiar with the idea of leisure travel, it was constrained by poverty, the need for government permission for movement between cities, and ideological suspicion. From the late 1950s to the late 1970s, leisure activities that were not explicitly associated with carrying out the party's teachings risked being labeled counterrevolutionary. Despite a law on the protection of "cultural relics," pre-1949 architecture was neglected or destroyed as representing "feudal culture." The Red Guards' "pilgrimages" to revolutionary sites during the Cultural Revolution were the only large-scale form of domestic tourism.

TOURISM AFTER MAO

After 1978, the government restored many classical palaces, temples, imperial tombs, classical gardens, museums, and sections of the Great Wall as citizens were once again encouraged to take pride in the famed cultural and natural sights of antiquity. After 1994, many of these were designated "patriotic education sites." At first, however, tourism development focused exclusively on incoming tourism as a means of earning foreign currency. Although Deng Xiaoping wanted to target primarily American and Japanese visitors, ethnic Chinese from Hong Kong, Taiwan, and Southeast Asia accounted for the majority of incoming tourists. Reflecting this fact, the government approved the development of twelve new holiday zones in the southern and coastal regions, targeting primarily overseas Chinese tourists.

As incomes rose in the late 1980s to early 1990s, domestic tourism began to emerge, mostly in the form of collective sightseeing trips organized by state-sector employers for their employees. Lack of leisure time (apart from the Spring Festival, traditionally spent in the ancestral home, only Sundays were free from work) and government ambivalence (some leaders were concerned that tourism encouraged prostitution, gambling, and other vices) constrained individual travel. But an estimated 2,000 to 2,500 amusement and theme parks, most of them showcasing China's cultural traditions or ethnic customs, sprang up in the cities in the 1990s, encouraged by the government as aiding patriotic education.

It was not until 1998 that the government began promoting tourism as a way to stimulate slack domestic consumption. To this end, in the following year, it introduced three weeklong public holidays around the October 1 and May 1 state holidays and the Spring Festival. Tourism during these "golden weeks" rapidly became part of the emerging urban middle-class lifestyle. In a 2002 survey of big-city residents, a quarter of respondents said they had traveled at least once during the golden weeks in the previous year. In 2008 the golden weeks were broken up into six shorter periods. Ideologically, the promotion of tourism is seen as beneficial for the creation of a modern, patriotic citizenry.

THE STRUCTURE OF TOURISM

Most of China's tourists travel in groups—organized by an employer, a travel agency, or a group of friends. Although

Swimming area of a five-star resort, Jiuzhaigou, Sichuan, March 28, 2008. *Prior to the late 1970s, the Communist government curtailed tourism opportunities by limiting the movement, earnings, and leisure time of citizens. As these restrictions became relaxed, large numbers of newly prosperous Chinese began to take advantage of domestic tourism destinations, encouraging the growth of a previously neglected industry.* © **DIEGO AZUBEL/EPA/CORBIS**

backpacking is becoming fashionable among young urbanites, the continued dominance of organized tourism seems assured, as first-time tourists will remain the mainstay of the market for some years. The most popular destinations continue to be those known from the *jing* of literati travel: famous mountains, Buddhist grottoes, lakes, and gardens. But some newly developed nature sites and new archaeological finds (such as the terracotta soldiers in Xi'an), as well as destinations associated with the exotic culture of ethnic minorities (including a prefecture in Yunnan Province renamed Shangri-la), are rapidly catching up. The government has made an effort to promote "red tourism" to sites associated with the history of the Communist Party and its leaders, but these (except Mao Zedong's mausoleum in Beijing) have not become truly popular. Nowadays, revolutionary, nationalistic, religious, and literary meanings are allowed to coexist, such as at Mount Tai, where viewing inscriptions by former party leaders are as much part of sightseeing as burning incense to gods. Rather than conflicting, these various meanings all fit into the official narrative of China's ancient cultural history

leading seamlessly into its present as a modern multiethnic nation under the party's leadership.

Sites awarded the World Heritage designation by UNESCO attract particularly many tourists, and the list expands annually thanks to China's active nomination efforts. Most of the famous nature and ethnic tourism sites are in the poorer, less accessible western part of the country, and the government has made tourism a central element of its Great Western Development strategy. In many regions of Sichuan, Yunnan, Guangxi, and Tibet, tourism is now the main source of income.

Despite a policy of "state withdrawal" from the management of tourism announced in 1998, government bodies are involved in all tourism development projects. The infrastructural development of tourist attractions—whether nature sites, old town quarters, or monasteries—is undertaken either by private contractors or in cooperation between an investor and the local government. The investment is recouped from ticket income and licenses to private entrepreneurs operating hotels, restaurants, or shops on or outside the site. Competition between local

WORLD HERITAGE SITES

The People's Republic of China in 1985 ratified the UNESCO Convention on World Heritage Sites, properties deemed by the World Heritage Committee (part of the United Nations Educational, Scientific and Cultural Organization) to be of universal cultural value. China's move came as part of a broader effort toward fuller engagement with the international community in the years following the abandonment of hard-line Maoism in the late 1970s. An enthusiastic campaign to obtain official UNESCO recognition for key sites has been part of efforts on the one hand to raise China's international prestige, and on the other to position the Communist regime as the champion and custodian of the nation's cultural and natural heritage.

As with its renewed participation in the Olympic movement (starting with the 1984 Los Angeles games), and an almost obsessive pursuit of Nobel prizes, the government was motivated in large part by a desire to secure international recognition for China's status. The amassing of UNESCO-accredited World Heritage Sites began with the "inscribing" of the Great Wall in 1987 and went on to include unusual built sites in the provinces, such as the walled city of Pingyao in Shanxi, and the *diaolou* of Kaiping in Guangdong province, as well as nature reserves or scenic spots such as Mount Huangshan in Anhui. This drive to gain the official UNESCO designation has acquired, both at an official and a popular level, something of the flavor of a heritage Olympics, as is reflected in a 2008 statement by the China National Tourist Office in Canada noting that "as of November 2007, among the 845 World Heritage Sites ... China has 35, ranking the third in the world. These sites comprise the most essential part of China's valuable and rich tourism resources."

Besides raising China's international profile, and helping to promote both domestic and international tourism, the designation of "Chinese" World Heritage Sites has also, as with many other aspects of state policy, become intertwined with assertions of China's territorial claims in its border regions. Thus Taiwan so far lacks a single officially recognized World Heritage Site (though Taiwan's Council for Cultural Affairs has designated several "potential" candidates) because the cross-strait stalemate over the island's sovereignty precludes a legitimate application for UNESCO recognition for any sites there. No such problem is faced by Macau, whose return to the motherland in 1999 was followed in 2005 by World Heritage status for its "historic center." Lhasa, the Tibetan capital, meanwhile boasts two World Heritage Sites, the Potala Palace and the Jokhang Temple (designated in 1994 and 2000 respectively).

One of the ironies of China's pursuit of World Heritage status for some of its totemic locations of historical interest or natural beauty is that increasing celebration of heritage has been accompanied by accelerated destruction of old town- and cityscapes and rapidly worsening environmental degradation. The imperial palaces of Beijing were granted UNESCO recognition in 1987, but the *hutongs* [lanes] of the old city that surrounded them then have since been almost entirely demolished. A similar pattern has been witnessed in Lhasa, and in a host of cities across China (the case of Macau, with its densely packed, soaring skyscrapers, speaks for itself). Meanwhile, rapid growth in domestic tourism has increased pressure on natural sites such as Jiuzhaigou in Sichuan, despite notional curbs on daily visitor numbers.

Such tensions arising from conflicting factors— heritage protection, increased tourism, economic growth, urban development, environmental pollution—though far from unique to China have manifested themselves there in a particularly stark manner. This has been noted, albeit diplomatically, in UNESCO reports on the condition of Chinese World Heritage Sites, but it has also increasingly prompted expressions of popular and official anxiety within China itself. So far, however, a no-holds-barred drive for economic growth has in practice generally tended to trump both heritage and environmental concerns.

BIBLIOGRAPHY

China National Tourist Office, Toronto, Canada. World Heritage Sites in China. http://www.tourismchina-ca.com/wheritage.html

Council for Cultural Affairs, Taiwan. World Heritage Website. http://english.cca.gov.tw/ct.asp?xItem=12711&ctNode=4172

Waldron, Arthur. *The Great Wall of China: From History to Myth.* Cambridge, U.K., and New York: Cambridge University Press, 1990.

Xu, Guoqi. *Olympic Dreams: China and Sports, 1895–2008.* Cambridge, MA: Harvard University Press, 2008.

Edward Vickers

governments in attracting investors often results in large-scale development even at remote nature sites, leading to increasing concerns with environmental sustainability and conservation. Although national cultural relics (*wenwu*) and tourism authorities, as well as international bodies and environmental organizations, are pressing for more conservation in tourism development, the dominant model remains mass tourism with more interest in modern infrastructure than material authenticity.

For example, the World Natural Heritage site of Jiuzhaigou in Sichuan, inhabited by a few thousand Tibetans, attracts over three million tourists annually. While tourism has improved the livelihoods of many people, the contracting of entire villages to private developers often results in conflicts over the distribution of profit. Entrepreneurs from more developed areas who flock to newly developed tourist destinations accelerate cultural change brought about by rapid modernization. This is a particularly contentious issue in the case of Tibet, where Western human rights groups accuse the Chinese government of using tourism development to further a deliberate policy of Sinification. Yet many Tibetan and other ethnic minority entrepreneurs have also benefited from the tourism boom.

Overseas tourism from China has been growing rapidly since 1990, when the government allowed Chinese travel agencies to organize tours to Southeast Asia. By 2008 agencies could organize tours to most popular destinations in the world. Thirty million PRC citizens traveled abroad in 2005, compared to five million in 1997. The World Tourism Organization expects China to become the largest source of tourists in the world by 2020, with 100 million.

SEE ALSO *Minority Nationalities: Cultural Images of National Minorities; Prostitution, History of; Service Sector (Tertiary industry).*

BIBLIOGRAPHY

Arlt, Wolfgang. *China's Outbound Tourism.* New York: Routledge, 2006.

Dong, Madeleine Yue. Shanghai's China Traveler. In *Everyday Modernity in China,* eds. Madeleine Yue Dong and Joshua Goldstein, 195–226. Seattle: University of Washington Press, 2007.

Lew, Alan A., Lawrence Yu, John Ap, and Zhang Guangrui, eds. *Tourism in China.* Binghamton, NY: Haworth Hospitality Press, 2003.

Naquin, Susan, and Chün-Fang Yü, eds. *Pilgrims and Sacred Sites in China.* Berkeley: University of California Press, 1992.

Nyíri, Pál. *Scenic Spots: Chinese Tourism, the State, and Cultural Authority.* Seattle: University of Washington Press, 2006.

Oakes, Tim. *Tourism and Modernity in China.* New York: Routledge, 1998.

Strassberg, Richard E., trans. and ed. *Inscribed Landscapes: Travel Writing from Imperial China.* Berkeley: University of California Press, 1994.

Wang Liping. Tourism and Spatial Change in Hangzhou, 1911–1927. In *Remaking the Chinese City: Modernity and National Identity, 1900–1950,* ed. Joseph Esherick, 107–120. Honolulu: University of Hawai'i Press, 2000.

Pál Nyíri

DOMESTIC

Domestic tourism in modern China did not become a major phenomenon until the 1990s. In the first decade after the Mao Zedong era, leisure travel was considered a hedonistic bourgeois activity that was contrary to Communist ethics and reflected poorly on the individual. Cost was also a major barrier to leisure travel at a time (1970s) when the three material symbols of success were a watch, a bicycle, and a sewing machine, though that was later upgraded to a television, a refrigerator, and a motorcycle in the 1980s. Leisure trips were primarily made to visit relatives and to shop in larger cities. In addition, other than in Beijing, tourist attractions in these early years were limited and poorly developed.

GROWTH OF DOMESTIC TOURISM

The earliest estimate of domestic tourism was made by the China National Tourism Office (CNTO) for 1985 when some 240 million individual trips were taken. This increased to 639 million trips in 1996 and 1.5 billion trips in 2006. Over 90 percent of urban residents and about 50 percent of rural residents take at least one trip a year. (In addition, over 34.5 million Chinese travelled outside of China in 2006.) The CNTO expects that domestic tourist expenditures will account for 70 percent of the projected US $128.6 billion in travel industry revenues for the country in 2007.

The growth in domestic tourism in the 1990s was the result of growing incomes, and an increasing demand by urban workers for leisure and recreation. Demand for tourist attractions greatly expanded when the five-day workweek was adopted in May 1995, and in the 1990s the central government designated and developed twelve major resort destinations (eleven were coastal beach resorts, one was a mountain resort). But possibly the biggest tourism phenomenon in China in the 1990s was the development of recreational theme parks. Over two thousand theme parks—two hundred of them based on the sixteenth-century novel *Journey to the West (Xiyouji)*—were built between 1989 and 1998. Most, however, were poorly planned and were losing money or had closed by the end of the 1990s.

Surveys of Chinese domestic tourists reveal that they are overwhelmingly interested in recreational activities, escaping from the pressure of work, and shopping. This

Chinese tourists in costume at the Forbidden City in Beijing, May 3, 2005. *Due in part to improvements to the national transportation system, increased incomes, and fewer government restrictions on travel, the number of Chinese citizens taking domestic vacations has increased considerably at the turn of the twenty-first century. Historic Chinese sites, such as Beijing's Forbidden City, and other areas known for their natural beauty have become popular destinations for Chinese tourists.* © **CLARO CORTES IV/REUTERS/CORBIS**

is often done in organized tours that involve relatively long bus rides on China's growing highway system. For rural residents, these trips are usually to larger cities, while urban residents seek out resorts outside of the city. Domestic vacation travel in China often takes place through the workplace, with workers having special access to employer- and union-owned resort facilities. Mainland Chinese also comprise the majority of tourists to Hong Kong (for shopping) and Macau (for gambling). Chinese tourists are among the biggest spenders when they travel overseas, making them a highly desired market.

DESTINATIONS AND STYLES OF TRAVEL

The online travel economy in China is relatively small, though as the growing middle class becomes more comfortable with credit-card use, this could change rapidly. One use of the Internet is for the creation of "donkey friend" travel groups. These are small groups of mostly younger, metropolitan Chinese that form online to plan a trip together. The preferred method of travel is with a backpack and comfortable clothing, and they seek out the more remote and ethnically diverse destinations in China's south and west.

For most of China, however, mass tourism is the standard form of tourism to most of the country's more popular destinations. While the conservation of cultural and natural heritage sites has been a major challenge, the transformation of China's urban consumer landscape has been dramatic. In two decades, the Chinese consumer has evolved from a "preconsumer" (in the Mao era) to a member of a consumer-based society, to a postmodern or hypermodern consumer.

Urban areas compete for tourist dollars by developing international-standard "shoppertainment" and "eatertainment" venues and districts. This is best seen in the recreational shopping street, which is a retail street or district that is closed to most vehicular traffic either all or part of the time. Such pedestrian streets serve as regional recreation destinations and are often promoted as tourist destinations.

Family portrait at Hong Kong Disneyland, May 20, 2006. *Until the 1990s, the Chinese government discouraged citizens from taking tourist vacations to other areas of the country. Domestic tourism only gained popularity at the turn of the twenty-first century as family income increased and employees began to receive more government-mandated vacation time during which to travel.* © ATLANTIDE PHOTOTRAVEL/CORBIS

Nanjing Road in Shanghai, renovated in the 1980s, is one the older examples. Newer examples include the hypermodern Wangfujing Street in Beijing, renovated in the 1990s; the gentrified Xintiandi shopping area in Shanghai and Shangxiajiu Road in Guangzhou, both renovated in 2003; and Beijing Road in Guangzhou, pedestrianized in 2005.

The biggest boost to domestic tourism came in October 1999 when China's first "golden week" was celebrated during China's National Day. Three annual golden weeks were subsequently adopted to promote travel and consumer spending to both boost the economy and further modernize the Chinese citizenry. The three golden weeks included the Spring Festival (the Lunar New Year in January or February), May Day (May 1), and National Day (October 1). During these weeks most employees received three days of holiday and had two weekend days shifted to midweek, giving them seven days off from work (followed by a seven-day workweek when they returned).

An estimated twenty-eight million domestic travelers took advantage of the first golden week in 1999. During National Day in 2007, more than 120 million Chinese travelers overwhelmed the country's transportation infrastructure and tourist attractions. Beijing alone received an estimated 4.32 million visitors, and sites such as Tiananmen Square presented serious crowd-management challenges. Following several years of calls to cancel the golden weeks, they were changed in 2008 to create more three-day and four-day weekend holidays throughout the year.

Chinese perceptions and experiences of attractions in China differ significantly from that of foreign tourists. This is mostly a reflection of the culture of the Chinese language. The traditional approach to learning Chinese writing is rote memorization of Chinese characters from books that recount the great stories and people from China's history. This inculcates cultural knowledge that is applied to the Chinese landscape, and is an integral part of the Chinese tourist experience. The Chinese characters carved in the face of a mountain and the names given to a cave or river bend touch a deep cultural knowledge that can only be superficially appreciated by anyone raised in a non-Chinese culture.

This cultural knowledge extends to the more recent past as well, which is often displayed in the same cultural manner as the ancient past. "Red tourism" (or "patriotic tourism") and related cultural artifacts and souvenirs have become popular in China, though sometimes in a kitsch manner. Recognizing this, the central government established a 700 million yuan (US $86.4 million) fund in 2005 to develop and promote red tourism. Twelve destination areas and thirty red routes were identified for development between 2005 and 2010. China has the largest domestic tourism market in the world, and it has proven to be a driving force in the modern Chinese economy.

SEE ALSO *Shops.*

BIBLIOGRAPHY
China National Tourism Office (CNTO). 2007. China Tourism Statistics. http://www.cnto.org/chinastats.asp

Lew, Alan A., Lawrence Yu, John Ap, and Guangrui Zhang, eds. *Tourism in China.* Binghamton, NY: Haworth Press, 2003.

Wen, Julie Jie, and Clement Allan Tisdell. *Tourism and China's Development: Policies, Regional Economic Growth, and Ecotourism.* Singapore: World Scientific Publishing, 2001.

Alan A. Lew

FOREIGN

Like much of China's economy, the growth of the country's tourism industry in the post-Mao era has been nothing short of phenomenal. From almost no leisure tourism of any kind during the Cultural Revolution, China in 2006 was the fourth most visited country in the world, receiving 41.8 million international overnight visitors (this figure is used by the World Tourism Organization for international comparisons). The World Tourism Organization has projected that China's international tourism will continue to grow by 8.7 percent annually through the next decade, making it the most visited international destination in the world by the year 2020.

Unlike the data used by the World Tourism Organization, China's official tourism numbers (collected by the China National Tourist Office) includes day visitors. This gave the country 124.9 million cross-border visitors in 2006, of which 102.7 million were compatriots from Hong Kong, Macau, and Taiwan, and the remaining 22.2 million were foreign visitors from elsewhere. The following discussion is based on data provided by China National Tourist Office.

In the years of the Cultural Revolution (1966–1969) and its aftermath (to 1976), international and domestic tourists in China were almost nonexistent. The objectives of tourism at that time were diplomatic and educational, and were limited to small delegations from other communist states, socialist states, and sometimes, communist parties in noncommunist states. After the Cultural Revolution, tourism was still viewed as a highly suspect "bourgeois" pursuit, and while the number of foreign visitors grew to around thirty thousand per year (including day visitors), they were still largely tied to political objectives. A year after Mao Zedong's death in 1976, China's central government for the first time embraced international tourism as a tool for economic development under Deng Xiaoping's Four Modernizations.

Tourism development was slow in the 1980s, with foreign tourist arrivals not reaching one million until 1984. Including Chinese compatriots, mostly from Hong Kong, China's total number of international visitors reached over ten million for the first time in 1984.

***Tourists crowding the Badaling Great Wall, Beijing, May 3, 2007.** Since the 1990s, the Chinese government has encouraged the development of the tourism industry, taking advantage of numerous sites of historical importance to attract foreign visitors. Consequently, money spent by tourists has become a significant source of foreign revenue for the Chinese economy.* © CHEN XIAODONG/XINHUA PRESS/ CORBIS

International tourism today is one of China's major sources of foreign currency earnings, with receipts from international visitors contributing $29.3 billion (1.1 percent of the gross domestic product) to China's economy in 2005. (Domestic tourism expenditures reached 528.6 billion renminbi [$67.7 billion] in that same year.) The World Travel and Tourism Council has estimated that in 2006 these expenditures supported 17.4 million jobs that were directly related to China's travel and tourism industries, accounting for 2.3 percent of the country's total employment. Including indirect employment associated with public and private investments supporting travel and tourism brings those numbers up to 10.2 percent, or 77.6 million jobs.

INTERNATIONAL TOURIST SOURCES

The three compatriot territories of Hong Kong, Macau, and Taiwan are the largest sources of international visitors to China. Hong Kong and Macau have been formally part of China since 1997 and 1999, respectively. As special administrative regions, they maintain a high level of political autonomy from China, as well as international border formalities with the mainland. Because of this, their borders are considered international for tourism data-collection purposes.

Beyond these territories, the largest sources of international tourists are South Korea and Japan (almost 4 million each in 2006), Russia (2.4 million), the United States (1.7 million), and Malaysia and Singapore (almost 1 million each). These are followed by the Philippines, Mongolia, and Thailand in Asia (about 600,000 visitors in 2006), and then the United Kingdom, Australia, Germany, and Canada from outside of Asia (about 500,000 visitors).

These patterns reflect a source country's geographic proximity to China, its business relationships with China, its Chinese ethnic affinities, and the economic well-being of the source country. The majority of China's tourists from Southeast Asia are ethnic Chinese whose motivations and travel behavior are distinct from that of nonethnic

Chinese visitors. The result is three patterns of international visitation to China (data for 2006): (1) compatriot tourists—82 percent of international tourists; (2) Asian intraregional or short-haul foreign tourists—11 percent; and (3) interregional or long-haul tourists—7 percent. A fourth travel pattern that is difficult to quantify is that of ethnic Chinese foreigners, who mostly come from Southeast Asia and compose 10 to 20 percent of foreign tourists to China.

Compatriot tourists have the strongest familial and business relationships with China. Their family travels mostly take them to Guangdong Province (adjacent to Hong Kong and Macau) and Fujian Province (across from Taiwan). Visa regulations make Hong Kong and Macau compatriots' access to China much easier than that of foreign visitors, and compatriots are the largest source in foreign direct investment in China. As such, they dominate international business travel to China. They are also more likely to make repeated trips to China, to take short-break tours to dispersed destinations throughout the country, and to take purely recreational trips to China

(such as a beach vacation). In this way, their travel patterns are similar to domestic Chinese, who are drawn to destinations that are well-known nationally and regionally within China, but largely unknown among interregional long-haul tourists.

In the 1980s, the early years of modern tourism's return to China, the impact of compatriot Chinese tourism was mostly seen in the hotel landscapes of Beijing, Shanghai, and Guangzhou. The first large modern hotels in these cities were built as joint ventures by compatriot entrepreneurs. Those hotels, such as Guangzhou's White Swan Hotel, stood in dramatic architectural contrast to the drab existing skyline, and were made off-limits to local Chinese because of their potentially capitalist influences.

Asian intraregional tourists include all of China's major tourist source countries, except for the United States. Their primary motivations in traveling to China are visiting places where they have friends, family, historical or ancestral ties, or a shared language, culture, and religion. Russians, Mongolians, and Central Asians, for

Hotel guests enjoying a swim and movie, Beijing, October 21, 2007. *Tourism opportunities remained small in China until the 1990s when government officials began encouraging overseas visitors. In the 2000s, China has experienced increasing numbers of tourists exploring the country, leading to the development of a thriving hospitality industry and expectations to become the largest tourist destination by 2020.* © ROBERT WALLIS/CORBIS

example, mostly visit Heilongjiang (formerly Manchuria), Inner Manchuria, and Xinjiang; South Koreans concentrate in Beijing and Northeast China, which is close to the Korean Peninsula and where some ethnic Korean communities are found; Japanese travel to Shanghai more than any other city in China; Thais are drawn to nearby Yunnan Province, while other Southeast Asians visit Fujian Province, where many of them have ancestral roots. In addition to the ethnic and historical ties that influence these travel patterns, proximity and a large growing middle-class allow intra-Asian tourists to take short-break leisure and business trips to China.

Ethnic ties to home villages (*xiangxia*) have had real economic impacts in parts of China with overseas Chinese ties. This has been especially true of Guangdong and Fujian provinces, where remittances from relatives residing in compatriot territories and overseas helped sustain many communities through the Maoist era. Today, almost every township in these two provinces has a local Overseas Chinese Affairs Office that facilitates overseas Chinese visits, donations, and investments, and publishes magazines that are sent throughout the world with articles about visits by relatives who love their home villages. Hospitals, schools, bridges, and parks are the most popular facilities that have been built in small towns and villages by overseas donations.

Interregional long-haul visitors from the rest of the world spend more time, visit more places, and spend more money in China than most of the other visitor segments. They are less likely to be business travelers, are less likely to be repeat visitors, and are more likely to focus on China's four best-known attractions and destinations: Beijing, Shanghai, Xi'an, and Guilin. Repeat interregional tourists will visit other well-known destinations on subsequent visits, such as Kunming, Hangzhou, and the Three Gorges region of the Yangtze River (Changjiang). In addition to overseas ethnic Chinese, some long-haul tourists also have special tourism ties to China that shape their visits. Jews are drawn to Shanghai's Hongkou Ghetto, where some twenty-thousand European Jewish refugees resided under Japanese rule during World War II (1937–1945), and Germans are drawn to Qingdao in Shandong Province, which they held as a protectorate from 1897 to 1914.

TOURISM INVESTMENT

China's entry into the World Trade Organization in 2001 required it to open its economy to international investment and competition, and regulations were changed in 2005 to allow foreign travel agencies and hotel companies to operate in China without a local joint-venture agreement. While foreign travel agencies did not rush in after the change, hotels did. The earlier period of hotel development had resulted in a small number of high-end hotels

serving international tourists and business travelers in the major cities, along with a large number of older and smaller hotels owned by a wide range of local and central government agencies. Since 2005, most of the major international hotel chains from Europe and the United States have been rapidly building to fill the void in mid-range hotels. This construction has taken place throughout China, taking advantage of the country's growing highway network. Five-star hotels have also been built, though these were mostly in Beijing, Shanghai, and Guangzhou in the lead-up to the 2008 Beijing Olympic Games.

Compared to the number of domestic tourists in China (1.5 billion person trips in 2006), international and foreign tourism is relatively limited. However, international tourism to China has had a significant impact on the Chinese landscape, especially in the country's major cities and at its best-known international destinations. This was probably most apparent in Beijing's hosting of the 2008 Olympic Games. This event not only intensified international scrutiny of China's internal and external diplomacy but it also prompted the government to address quality issues in its hospitality, transportation, and tourism services. As China further opens to international businesses and as its tourism industry matures, the influence of the global tourism economy is likely to become even more pervasive throughout China.

SEE ALSO *Chinese Overseas: Diaspora and Homeland.*

BIBLIOGRAPHY

China National Tourist Office. China Tourism Statistics. 2007. http://www.cnto.org/chinastats.asp

Lew, Alan A., Lawrence Yu, John Ap, and Zhang Guangrui, eds. *Tourism in China*. Binghamton, NY: Haworth Press, 2003.

Wen, Julie Jie, and Clement Allan Tisdell. *Tourism and China's Development: Policies, Regional Economic Growth, and Ecotourism*. Singapore: World Scientific, 2001.

Alan A. Lew

TRAVEL ABROAD

The aphorism "traveling for one thousand *li* equals reading ten thousand books" has been a commonly accepted truth for many centuries in China. In imperial China, however, there was no tradition of outbound travel to areas beyond the realm of the Han culture, with the exceptions of some monks who traveled to India to fetch Buddhist scriptures in the first millennium CE and the voyages of Zheng He (1371–c. 1433), the "Chinese Columbus," to Africa in the fifteenth century. China had neither a Herodotus nor a Marco Polo or Ibn Battuta.

Civil wars and Japanese occupation constrained outbound tourism between 1911 and 1949. For Chinese living in the former British colony of Hong Kong and on Taiwan, outbound tourism has been a part of daily life for many decades. The last restrictions on foreign travel were removed for Taiwanese passport holders in 1979. In the People's Republic of China, however, tourism even within China was considered a wasteful, bourgeois practice before 1978. With the beginning of the "reform and opening" policy in 1978, inbound tourism came to be promoted as a fast and easy way to earn foreign currency. Domestic tourism reemerged against the wishes of the Chinese government, and became acknowledged only in the 1990s as an important part of the service industry. Domestic tourism was a crucial element in the ideological switch from rural socialism to urban consumerism. With more than 1.6 billion domestic tourism trips in 2007, China has become the largest national tourism market in the world.

The gates to outbound travel were opened only reluctantly in several stages. Three distinguishable phases of China's outbound tourism development can be identified.

The first phase started in 1983 with so-called "family visits," first to Hong Kong and Macau and later to several Southeast Asian countries, with the receiving side ostensibly paying for the trips. At the same time, the beginning of China's integration into the world economy resulted in a growing number of delegations traveling to leading economic countries to attend fairs, business talks, training programs, and so forth. Almost all of these trips comprised a touristic element, while many were in fact simply pleasure trips in disguise, with expenses paid with public or government money.

The second phase started in 1997 with the official recognition of the existence of outbound leisure tourism (as opposed to family reunions and business trips) with the passage of the Provisional Regulation on the Management of Outbound Travel by Chinese Citizens at their Own Expense and the signing of the first Approved Destination Status (ADS) agreements with Australia and New Zealand. The ADS system is based on bilateral tourism agreements whereby a government allows self-paying Chinese tourists to travel for pleasure to its territory in guided groups and with a special visa. By 2009 more than 130 countries enjoyed ADS agreements with China, with the United States added in 2008. The regulations for visits to Hong Kong and Macau were also relaxed in several steps after 1997.

As the number of outbound travelers rose from eight million in 1997 to twenty-nine million in 2004, a chaotic and mostly unregulated situation developed. Many travel groups were organized by nonauthorized agencies in the form of "zero-dollar tours," in which inbound travel companies receive no payment for providing food, local transport, and accommodation, but earn their money by coercing tourists into buying goods and additional services for inflated prices at the destination.

The third phase of China's outbound tourism development began in 2005. With growth rates falling, governments in many host countries reinforced visa procedures to hinder illegal immigration. At the same time, the tourism industry exchanged its overoptimistic estimates of Chinese visitor numbers for frustrated stories about demanding, unruly, and hard-bargaining customers. The outbound travel market also became more fragmented as more destinations became available, and a split developed between organized high-end tours like golf trips or cruises, self-organized small groups, and the bargain-driven ADS mass market.

The Chinese government changed its official stance on the question of outbound tourism in 2005. Instead of trying to limit the total number of outbound travelers, the government now takes measures to control outbound travel through more detailed regulations. Improvement of the quality of options offered to prospective Chinese tourists is a major issue. In 2008 the China Outbound Tourism Research Institute (COTRI) accordingly introduced a "China Outbound Tourism Quality Label."

Chinese outbound tourism statistics are unreliable. Chinese customs exit statistics, which record only the first port of call, and the national statistics of host countries often differ widely. Of the approximately forty-one million outbound trips made in 2007, about twenty-seven million had Hong Kong and Macau as a final destination, with another seven million headed for border areas, mostly for the purpose of retail trading, gambling, or prostitution. Of the remaining seven million outbound trips, three million were to Asia (mainly Japan, Vietnam, and other parts of

Chinese outbound tourism 1995–June 2008 (in million persons)

	Travellers	Growth in %	Total growth in %
1995	7,139.0	—	
1996	7,588.2	6.3	
1997	8,175.4	7.7	1995–1999
1998	8,425.6	3.1	29.3
1999	9,232.4	9.6	
2000	10,472.6	13.4	
2001	12,133.1	15.9	
2002	16,602.3	36.8	2000–2004
2003	20,221.9	21.8	275.5
2004	28,852.9	42.7	
2005	31,003.0	7.5	
2006	34,520.0	11.3	2005–2007
2007	40,950.0	18.6	32.1
2008 Jan–June	21,800.0	6.5	

SOURCE: China National Tourism Administration.

Table 1

China outbound tourism 1995–2007 in million border-crossings

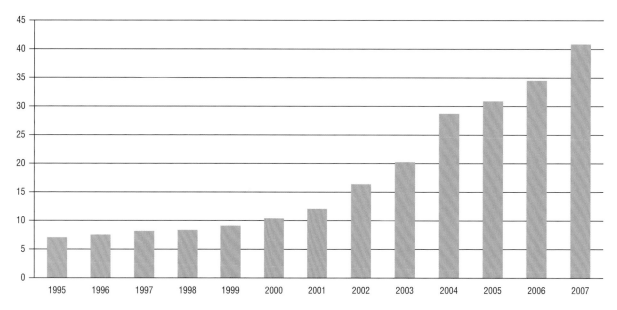

SOURCE: China National Tourism Administration.

Figure 1

Southeast Asia), two million to Europe (including 800,000 to Russia), one million to the Americas (mainly the United States), 500,000 to Oceania, and 300,000 to Africa (mainly Egypt and South Africa), with the remaining 200,000 not specified.

Travel motives are often mixed. Status enhancement is the top priority for leisure trips, especially those to destinations outside Asia. Business trips and visits to friends and family often include a leisure element. Shopping and gambling are important activities, along with sightseeing.

Gender and age distribution differ between destinations, with the proportion of male and middle-aged travelers generally rising with the distance of the destination. Sixty percent of all outbound travelers live in Beijing, Shanghai, or Guangdong Province.

The outlook for China's outbound tourism is bright. By 2009 China had become responsible for about 4 percent of the global international tourism market, in terms of both money and travelers. With tourism deeply rooted in the behavior patterns of Chinese consumers but only 3 percent of the Chinese population crossing the border in 2007, this proportion is bound to rise in the coming decades, notwithstanding any short-term economic downturn or a change in the political system.

SEE ALSO *Prostitution, History of.*

BIBLIOGRAPHY

Arlt, Wolfgang Georg. *China's Outbound Tourism.* New York: Routledge, 2006.

China Outbound Tourism Research Institute (COTRI). http://www.china-outbound.com/

Lew, Alan A., et al., eds. *Tourism in China.* New York: Haworth, 2003.

National Tourism Administration of the People's Republic of China (CNTA). http://en.cnta.gov.cn/

Ryan, Chris, and Gu Huimin, eds. *Tourism in China: Destination, Cultures, and Communities.* New York: Routledge, 2009.

World Tourism Organization (UNWTO), ed. *Study into Chinese Outbound Tourism.* Madrid: Author, 2003.

Wolfgang Georg Arlt

TOWNSHIP AND VILLAGE ENTERPRISES

Township and village enterprises (TVEs; *xiang zhen qiye*) have been an important part of economic reform in China since the late 1970s. Although post-1978 economic reform began in agriculture, TVEs represented an important early reform effort in China's business enterprises. TVEs grew rapidly in the 1980s in both absolute terms and relative to other parts of the industrial economy, particularly state-owned enterprises. That growth, absolute and relative, slowed in the 1990s.

Both the early rapid success of TVEs and their later slowdown present puzzles. The early growth of TVEs occurred despite poorly defined property rights governing the control and division of surplus, even though standard economic theory suggests that property rights are essential to economic development. Over time, through a succession of economic reforms, property rights within TVEs became more sharply defined. Yet the relative importance of TVEs decreased in the face of this reform, presenting a second puzzle. TVEs remain an important part of the Chinese economy, but it is unclear whether they are a transitional form that will fade over time or a lasting innovation.

EARLY TVE SUCCESS

The term *township and village enterprise* covers a variety of organizational and legal types. Classically, a TVE was a business association that is owned, controlled, or in some way closely tied to the local government at the township or village level. In some cases, government officials themselves initiate and control the business. In other cases, an entrepreneurial individual or family starts and runs the business, but the local government is given a share as a way of protecting the business from further government interference. The 1996 Law on Township Enterprises also includes enterprises owned by farmers as TVEs (see Articles 2 and 10 of Law). Thus, some TVEs are really private enterprises. The typical

TVE is small, with an average of a little over six employees in 2005. (In 2005 there were 22,495,902 TVEs, which employed 142,723,584 persons, an average of 6.3 employees per TVE. *See* China TVE Yearbook 2006, p. 155.)

TVEs did not start out as part of a centralized, well-thought-out innovation. Rather, they were an outgrowth of limited economic liberalization and China's decentralized government. Liberalization allowed the creation of product markets, with individual businesses able to set the prices of their goods and services, up to a point. Decentralized government required local governments to provide a wide range of social services for their residents, and local governments needed money to pay for those services. The opening of markets allowed local governments to set up or sponsor businesses, capturing much of the revenue from those businesses to pay for social services.

The results were dramatic. At the beginning of the reform era, state-owned enterprises (SOEs) employed over twice as many people as TVEs, including a large majority of all workers in urban areas. SOEs are medium to large businesses owned and run by government agencies at the national or provincial level (although most SOEs have now been turned into corporations, with some of their shares sold to private persons or entities). As reform took hold, SOEs became relatively less important, and by 1993 TVEs employed more persons than SOEs. By 2005, TVEs employed more than twice as many persons as SOEs (see Table 1).

Employed persons in China, rural areas, township and village enterprises (TVEs), and state-owned enterprises (SOEs)

(figures in 10,000s)

Year	China total	Rural total	TVEs	SOEs	TVEs as % of China	TVEs as % of rural	SOEs as % of China
1978	40,152	30,638	2,827	7,451	7.0	9.2	18.5
1980	42,361	31,836	3,000	8,019	7.1	9.4	18.9
1985	49,873	37,065	6,979	8,990	14.0	18.8	18.0
1989	55,329	40,939	9,367	10,108	16.9	22.9	18.3
1990	64,749	47,708	9,265	10,346	14.3	19.4	16.0
1991	65,491	48,026	9,609	10,664	14.7	20.0	16.3
1992	66,152	48,291	10,625	10,889	16.1	22.0	16.5
1993	66,808	48,546	12,345	10,920	18.5	25.4	16.3
1994	67,455	48,802	12,017	11,214	17.8	24.6	16.6
1995	68,065	49,025	12,862	11,261	18.9	26.2	16.5
1996	68,950	49,028	13,508	11,244	19.6	27.5	16.3
1997	69,820	49,039	13,050	11,044	18.7	26.6	15.8
1998	70,637	49,021	12,537	9,058	17.7	25.5	12.8
1999	71,394	48,982	12,704	8,572	17.8	25.9	12.0
2000	72,085	48,934	12,820	8,102	17.8	26.2	11.2
2001	73,025	49,085	13,086	7,640	17.9	26.6	10.5
2002	73,740	48,960	13,288	7,163	18.0	27.1	9.7
2003	74,432	48,793	13,573	6,876	18.2	27.8	9.2
2004	75,200	48,724	13,866	6,710	18.4	28.4	8.9
2005	75,825	48,494	14,272	6,488	18.8	29.4	8.5

SOURCE: *China Statistical Yearbook* (2006), pp. 128–129.

Table 1

Consider two examples of TVEs that illustrate some of the complexity and variety of organizations lumped together under the term. The Liuyue Fabric Factory is a large enterprise with 222 employees. Doumen Township established the factory in 1980, under the township's direct control. Since 1994, the market manager (who won this right through bidding) has leased the factory from the township (Chen 2000, pp. 98–99). In contrast, the Jieshan County Colloidal Products Factory was founded in 1980 by a farmer. He gave legal control to the township because a private person could not use land or open a bank account. The business later relocated to a township with a better business environment. It pays 1 percent of its gross sales to the township (Byrd and Lin 1990, pp. 146–147).

PUZZLES OF TVE SUCCESS

The success of TVEs poses a puzzle for standard economic theory, according to which clearly defined rights over who makes decisions and who receives the surplus a business generates are key to success. Yet property rights were murky during the early period of TVE formation. The nominal owners of TVEs were the local residents collectively, but in fact local government officials had the true legal authority. The government officials were dependent on the local Communist Party. Both local government and party in turn needed to report to governmental or party officials at higher levels. Within the enterprises themselves, government officials rarely actively ran the businesses—the managers of the businesses did that. In larger enterprises, managers had to delegate some decisions to lower-level employees. Thus, control lines were complicated, and often not clearly spelled out. As for income shares, in early TVEs there were often no clear rules for determining what managers would receive, and even where there were rules, they were not necessarily followed (Chen 2000; Weitzman and Xu 1994).

In short, according to economic theory, early TVEs should have failed. Yet many of them succeeded in generating jobs and wealth. How could that be? First, the TVEs were superior to both private enterprises and SOEs. Government predation was still an omnipresent threat for private businesses in China, but the TVEs' ties to local government sheltered them from such predation (Chang and Wang 1994; Che and Qian 1998). TVEs were superior to SOEs because they were smaller and thus did not suffer the problems of corporate governance that come with bigger businesses. In addition, competition among the many local governments was crucial to the success of TVEs. Because there were many competing businesses, an enterprise that was run inefficiently would be unable to sell its goods at a price that generated revenues for its governmental sponsor. Also, the soft-budget constraint was much less of a problem

for TVEs. Sponsoring agencies and large banks controlled by the central government would typically prop up poorly run SOEs. TVEs, in contrast, lacked deep pockets that could keep them operating—TVEs had to either sink or swim (Che and Qian 1998).

The resulting economic pressure forced TVEs to improve their internal governance to provide better results. Over time, they evolved to give managers stronger incentives to run businesses efficiently. Early on, the managers of most TVEs received a fixed wage, which did not rise when the business was successful or fall when it was unsuccessful. Later, many enterprises shifted to forms of profit sharing, where the manager received a fraction of the profit the business generated. Later still, some shifted to a fixed-payment system, where the manager made a fixed payment to the local government and was then entitled to all of the profit the business generated. These changes gave managers progressively stronger incentives to run their businesses efficiently, and evidence suggests that they responded to those incentives (Chen 2000).

TVE SLOWDOWN

Beginning in the early 1990s, the absolute and relative growth of TVEs slowed. Table 1 traces the growth of employment in TVEs. In both absolute numbers and as a percentage of the total labor force, the number of TVE employees grew quickly from 1978 into the mid-1990s, rising from 7 percent of the labor force to a peak of 19.6 percent in 1996. However, between 1996 and 2005 the absolute number of TVE employees remained more or less constant—indeed, the number fell slightly from the 1996 peak and reached that same level again only in 2003. Between 1992 and 2005, TVE employees as a percentage of the total labor force fluctuated between 17 and 19 percent.

Why did this slowdown occur? There are many possible reasons. TVEs are, in a sense, being squeezed from two sides. On the one hand, SOEs continue to have preferred access to finance on a large scale. Major banks and the stock markets are much more open to SOEs than to TVEs. On the other hand, private and foreign enterprises have become more important in China. Where once individual entrepreneurs needed the shelter of governmental protection that TVEs provided, entrepreneurs are increasingly willingly to set up their own businesses.

Another possible explanation for the TVE slowdown is that there is a limit to the effective size and appropriate industrial setting of most TVEs. The property-rights problem mentioned above may have been easier to overcome with small-scale businesses engaged in relatively simple production, but the issue became more severe when TVEs grew larger and more complex. Perhaps, then, TVEs grew rapidly to fill an appropriate niche, but have found it difficult to expand beyond that niche.

Sector	Total TVE employees, 2005	Percent of TVE employees, 2005	Percent of all employees, 2002	Percent of all non-farm employees, 2002
Farming, forestry, animal husbandry, fishery	2,852,069	2.0	44.0	—
Mining	6,037,725	4.2	0.8	1.3
Manufacturing	78,482,840	55.0	11.3	20.1
Construction	13,627,502	9.5	5.3	9.4
Transport, storage	8,468,626	5.9	2.8	5.0
Wholesale, retail, food, lodging	26,385,784	18.5	6.7	12.0
Social services	4,192,331	2.9	1.5	2.6
Other	2,676,707	1.9	—	—

Employed persons by sector for township and village enterprises (TVEs), China overall

SOURCE: *China TVE Yearbook* (zhong guo xiang zhen qiye nian jian) (2006), p. 155; *China Statistical Yearbook* (2006), p. 130.

Table 2

Yet another explanation is that TVEs have stagnated as China's rural population stagnated, with millions of people moving from rural to urban areas. Table 1 indicates that the number of TVE employees has continued to rise slowly as a percentage of the rural labor force. But this growth in importance within rural areas has been balanced by the decreasing percentage of employees located in rural areas, so the number of TVE employees as a percentage of China's total labor force has leveled off.

Despite signs of slowing down, TVEs do not yet seem likely to disappear. The number of TVE enterprises and employees has stabilized, but not dropped substantially. Indeed, in the 1990s, the central government became aware of the importance of TVEs for rural economic development, and cast about for ways to reinforce them.

PROPERTY REFORMS

China enacted a variety of legal reforms in the 1990s that had an impact on TVEs: these include the Company Law (1993), the Law on Township Enterprises (1996), and a Securities Law (1998). Under these laws and other regulations, many TVEs were turned into companies with limited liability. Share ownership took a variety of forms—local governments remained the sole owners of some TVEs, others were transferred to solely private hands (recall that farmer-owned enterprises are still classified as TVEs), and others had a mix of both types of ownership. Companies classified as TVEs thus now take a variety of forms.

The move to share ownership was intended to address problems arising from China's ambiguous property rights. There is some evidence that these changes in the legal form of TVEs have in fact led to stronger economic performance (Chang and Wang 1994). It remains unclear why the growth of TVEs began to lag just when these reforms were being implemented. One reason may be that although the performance of TVEs improved, the relative attractiveness

of private enterprises increased even more during this time, and thus the comparative advantage of TVEs declined. Even among enterprises characterized as TVEs, there has been a trend toward more businesses that are privately owned. (Chen 2000, p. 8)

MARKET SECTORS AND REGIONAL VARIATIONS

Table 2 lists the types of products and services that TVEs provide. TVEs are concentrated in manufacturing—slightly over half of all TVE employees worked for manufacturing firms in 2005. This is a much greater concentration than for the Chinese labor force generally. In 2002 only 11.3 percent of all employed persons in China were engaged in manufacturing, and even if farming (which includes few TVEs) is eliminated from the calculation, only 20.1 percent of all Chinese workers were employed in manufacturing. Other than that, the sectoral distribution of TVEs is not much different from that of the Chinese economy generally. The next most common sectors for TVE employment are wholesale and retail sales, construction, and the food and lodging industry.

There is much regional variation in the TVE sector. In some areas most TVEs are collectively owned, while elsewhere more are private. They also differ as to the proportion of enterprises at the township versus village level. Some areas have many successful and relatively large enterprises, whereas others are in earlier stages of development (Byrd and Lin 1990, pp. 7–9).

A TRANSITIONAL FORM?

The long-term future for TVEs remains unclear. Although they may resume their growth in relative importance, that development appears unlikely. Other organizational forms have become stronger competitors, and there is little reason to expect that to change. TVEs remain an attractive option for local governments, however, and for that reason they may more or less retain their current relative position within the Chinese economy. Local governments need tax revenues, as well as productive jobs for the residents of rural and underdeveloped areas. The availability of attractive jobs in rural areas will help slow migration to urban areas, helping to solve a major social problem. TVEs offer a proven means of promoting those goals.

In an alternative scenario, TVEs may gradually fade away. On this theory, TVEs provided a useful but temporary transitional form at a time when China was not ready to open the floodgates to private entrepreneurship. TVEs provided a venue for entrepreneurial activity and enterprise formation, while protecting businesses from governmental expropriation. The form had many problems, but it presented opportunities for ambitious persons with few alternatives, causing TVEs to flourish. However, as the Chinese law and economy have opened up and provided more protection and structure for private business, the relative attractiveness of, and need for, TVEs has gradually eroded.

SEE ALSO *Economic Reform since 1978; Labor; Rural Development since 1978; Socialist Market Economy; State-Owned Enterprises.*

BIBLIOGRAPHY

Byrd, William, and Lin Qingsong, eds. *China's Rural Industry: Structure, Development, and Reform.* Oxford and New York: Oxford University Press, 1990.

Chang Chun and Wang Yijiang. The Nature of the Township-Village Enterprise. *Journal of Comparative Economics* 19, 3 (1994): 434–452.

Chang Chun, Brian McCall, and Wang Yijiang. Incentive Contracting versus Ownership Reforms: Evidence from China's Township and Village Enterprises. *Journal of Comparative Economics* 31, 3 (2003): 414–428.

Che Jiahua and Qian Yingyi. Institutional Environment, Community Government, and Corporate Governance: Understanding China's Township-Village Enterprises. *Journal of Law, Economics, and Organization* 14, 1 (1998): 1–23.

Chen Hongyi. *The Institutional Transition of China's Township and Village Enterprises: Market Liberalization, Contractual Form Innovation, and Privatization.* Brookfield, VT: Ashgate, 2000.

China Statistical Yearbook. Beijing: State Statistical Bureau, 2006.

China TVE Yearbook [*Zhong guo xiang zhen qiye nian jian*]. Beijing: China Agricultural Press, 2006.

Weitzman, Martin L., and Xu Chenggong. Chinese Township-Village Enterprises as Vaguely Defined Cooperatives. *Journal of Comparative Economics* 18, 2 (1994): 121–145.

Brett H. McDonnell

TRADEMARKS

SEE *Brands.*

TRANSITION ECONOMY

Following the fall of Communist governments in Eastern Europe in late 1989, the term *transition economy* came to refer to the economies of countries reinstating capitalist market institutions after a generation or more under communism. In the economies of communist countries, prices were set by government planners who directed resource allocation according to physical output targets rather than price signals. Though much decision making was done at provincial and lower levels, China before 1979 nonetheless conformed to the planned-economy mold, at times even suppressing market forces more rigorously than most Communist regimes. With the ascent of Deng Xiaoping after the death of Mao Zedong in 1976, China reversed course, gradually reintroducing market forces and opening up to international trade.

Until 1992, China's economic system remained more akin to a mixed form of state socialism, like that of the Soviet Union in the 1920s or Hungary in the 1970s and 1980s, than like the economies of Central and Eastern European countries in full-fledged transition to capitalism after 1989. The commanding heights of the economy (i.e., the banking system, heavy industry, and most medium- and large-scale enterprises) remained firmly under government control. But state-enterprise managers began to be judged by their enterprises' financial performance, earned bonuses from retained profits, and were expected to respond to market forces once quantity targets, gradually declining in importance, were met. And consumer-goods markets were enlivened by abundant agricultural produce and new light manufactures being produced by small-scale rural and urban collective enterprises responding to market demand.

FROM DECOLLECTIVIZATION
TO STATE ENTERPRISE REFORM

China's early reforms were at their most radical in the countryside. By 1983 the collective farming system (in place in various forms since 1956) had been abandoned in favor of a system of household-based farming on land contracted out by the former production teams and brigades (after 1984, by village governments). The change in the farm production unit was accompanied by freedom to sell surplus output on the market and an across-the-board relaxation of constraints on rural production, all of which led to rapid growth in nonstaple-crop production, animal husbandry, handicrafts, building, and trade activities. Former commune and brigade enterprises were reborn as township and village enterprises, with a far wider range of products and mushrooming output and employment. Since rural dwellers comprised some 80 percent of China's population, changes in the countryside had a profound effect.

Although popular jitters about inflation and resentment over the unequal gains of the officially connected contributed to unrest and temporary backtracking on reforms at the end of the 1980s, by 1992 the early reform era could be called a success. China's gross domestic product had sustained growth at a pace at least 50 percent faster than in the Mao era (1949–1976), average levels of consumption were growing substantially faster, and several hundred million rural poor had been brought out of the most grinding poverty to a standard of minimal subsistence or better. A hundred million jobs had been created in rural nonfarm enterprises. Urban state-owned enterprises had been gradually exposed to market forces, with nearly 100 percent of their inputs obtained, and outputs sold, outside of the state plan and at market or negotiated prices. While the share of state-owned enterprise in industrial output had declined from over three-quarters in 1978 to only a third in the mid-1990s, its labor force continued growing, from 32 million workers in 1979 to 45 million in 1992, and state-owned enterprises absorbed the lion's share of investment funds loaned out by the state banks. Yet competition from township and village enterprises, other nonstate firms, and even other state-owned enterprises steadily drove down profit rates. As a result, total profits of state-owned enterprises fell from 14 percent of the gross domestic product in 1979 to 2 percent in 1992, and government revenues (derived mainly from taxes on state-owned enterprises) declined from over 30 percent of the gross domestic product in 1979 to less than 15 percent in 1992 and only 11 percent in 1996. At least 20 percent of the debt on the books of the state banking system was nonperforming, most of it money loaned to state-owned enterprises.

The government having gradually reformed China's economy for a dozen years while leaving the formal urban workforce largely unscathed, the post-Tiananmen Communist Party leadership, now including many who had reached senior positions in the post-Mao era, was ready to begin "breaking the iron rice bowl" of secure state employment in earnest. Local governments were freed to close down, privatize, or merge smaller state-owned enterprises, and rural cadres and managers were also encouraged to convert township- and village-owned enterprises to shareholding or privately owned firms. Larger state-owned enterprises were converted into joint stock corporations, most of which had publicly traded shares but remained predominantly owned by public bodies. More than 30 million workers in state-owned enterprises were laid off.

CHINA'S GRADUALISM

The decision to reform and the gradualism of reform and transition were not brought about by economic factors alone. Though in 1978 the Soviet bloc was still under the heel of the neo-Stalinist regime of Leonid Brezhnev, the Chinese Communist Party was a fully independent actor. By 1978 advocates of more pragmatic, incentive-harnessing policies had been vying with Mao's ultraleftist approach for decades. Their influence was constrained in the early period after the Great Leap Forward (1958–1960) and in the early 1970s, but Mao's death in 1976 and his mixed legacy to China's economy and polity created an opening for their return. And comparison of the economic transformations of South Korea, Taiwan, and Hong Kong with the less dynamic economic growth of China since the 1950s probably induced Deng and his associates to move even further to the right than had been their inclination when the pragmatist-leftist clash first began.

The gradualism of China's reforms owed much to the reformers' need to compromise, in the early years, with more orthodox Communists, then still in the Communist Party leadership. These included Chen Yun, whose discomfort with Maoism did not translate into love of markets. So reform proceeded in a step-by-step fashion, and care was taken to benefit as many Chinese as possible so that the tide of change could not easily be rolled back.

Deng's openness to markets and the profit motive in the economic sphere had no counterpart in the political sphere, and when Mikhail Gorbachev's experiment with political openness led to the collapse of the East European satellites, followed by that of the Soviet Union itself, the leaders of the Chinese Communist Party took pains to prevent economic reform from threatening their party's monopoly on power. From late 1989 to 1991, the government under Li Peng seemed unsure that this could be done without holding economic reform itself in check. Deng insisted that there was no other way forward, and as his final intervention, he launched a new wave of reforms in 1992. China's reforms entered a new stage that would ultimately end the sharp contrast between its gradualism and Eastern Europe's rapid postcommunist transitions.

Both politically and economically the acceleration of reform paid off, for rapid economic growth, especially in the urban coastal regions, seemed by the early 2000s to have produced a new generation too excited by the prospect of material success to identify with the students of the 1989 prodemocracy movement. This success was all the more remarkable because in the late 1990s some 30 million state-sector workers were laid off. Meanwhile, China witnessed the resumption and dwarfing of the previous decade's foreign-investment boom, further growth and technical upgrading of its export-oriented manufacturing sector, and unprecedented construction and real-estate booms in its cities.

Another reason that China's early reforms were gradual was that communist parties had fallen from power before the East European and Soviet transitions, while the Chinese Communist Party had every intention of retaining power when it began economic reforms in 1979. China was more like Hungary in the 1970s than Poland or Russia in the 1990s. Whereas postcommunist governments were prepared to risk bursts of inflation and job loss in view of the promise of a better system in the making, communist governments like those of Hungary in the 1970s and China in the 1980s felt compelled to keep workers employed and prices of basic commodities in check. In China, this meant that the state-owned enterprises were maintained through the early 1990s as islands of security for the urban labor elite while the most radical changes were occurring outside the state sector. Reform *with* losers, a process more like the postcommunist transitions, began in China only after considerable nonstate employment had grown up and when many who had entered state employment in the Mao years were nearing retirement.

THE FUTURE

Shutting down and privatizing smaller state-owned enterprises and converting larger state-owned enterprises into corporations would not be the final steps of China's transition. In the early 2000s, government entities remained the dominant owners of nontraded shares of many listed companies, ordinary shareholders had little or no influence over management, stock and bond markets were still minor sources of funds in comparison with bank financing, bank reforms were still an ongoing affair, and the opening of financial-services markets to foreign competition was in its infancy. Business connections with government officials remained important, and a new hybrid elite consisting of both officials and newly wealthy Chinese businessmen, many of them former officials or state-enterprise managers, was still in the process of emerging. In an interesting development, forward-thinking members of this elite evinced concern about sharing the benefits of China's growth with broader segments of Chinese society, as signaled by the new rhetoric about building a "harmonious society."

BIBLIOGRAPHY

Lin, Justin Yifu, Fang Cai, and Zhou Li. *The China Miracle: Development Strategy and Economic Reform.* Hong Kong: Chinese University Press, 1996.

Naughton, Barry. *Growing Out of the Plan: Chinese Economic Reform, 1978–1993.* New York: Cambridge University Press, 1995.

Naughton, Barry. *The Chinese Economy: Transitions and Growth.* Cambridge, MA: MIT Press, 2007.

Wu, Jinglian. *Understanding and Interpreting Chinese Economic Reform.* Singapore: Thomson, 2005.

Louis Putterman

TRANSLATION OF FOREIGN LITERATURE

The first boom in the translation of foreign literature in modern China occurred in the last years of the Qing dynasty (1644–1912). It was heralded in by the immense success of Lin Shu's translation of Alexandre Dumas's *La dame aux camélias* in 1899. Together with Sherlock Holmes, the Lady of Camellias was one of the most popular figures in the Chinese imagination of the West in the early twentieth century. Although Lin Shu himself did not know Western languages and collaborated with others who did, it was his elegant literary Chinese that initially endowed his translations with a sufficient measure of respectability and made it possible for them to reach a traditionally educated readership. In the following decade, some four hundred Western novels and plays were translated. Lin himself went on to translate 160 titles, including such influential and controversial works as Harriet Beecher Stowe's *Uncle Tom's Cabin* and Rider Haggard's *Joan Haste*.

THE MAY FOURTH ERA

During the May Fourth era (1915–1925), translated literature played a major role in the New Culture movement and in the construction of the modern Chinese vernacular. In June 1918, the influential journal *Xin qingnian* (New youth) published a special issue on Henrik Ibsen that included essays about the Norwegian writer as well as translations of his plays. Prominently featured was Ibsen's *A Doll's House*, translated by Luo Jialun and Hu Shi, both proponents of the New Culture movement. Ibsen's Nora became synonymous with the New Woman. Its popular reception gave rise to nine retranslations, multiple literary imitations, and wave after wave of debates on the modern individual, women's liberation, and family and society. In the 1920s, literary periodicals not specifically devoted to translation frequently published significant quantities of translated literature: *Xiaoshuo yuekan* (Fiction monthly) had special issues on Lord Byron, Rabindranath Tagore, and Romain Rolland; *Chuangzao yuekan* (Creation monthly) introduced Percy Bysshe Shelley, Heinrich Heine, John Keats, Oscar Wilde, Victor Hugo, and Walt Whitman. A major landmark was Johann Wolfgang von Goethe's *Sorrows of Young Werther*, translated by Guo Moruo in 1922. This work was highly influential in the conception of the Romantic hero and is largely responsible for the highly introspective, often epistolary explorations of the inner self frequently seen in the literature of this period. Contributing further to the increasingly popular genre of autobiographical fiction was a translation of Jean-Jacques Rousseau's *Confessions*, the earliest complete translation by Zhang Jingsheng appearing in 1928. The influence of Rousseau can be detected in the works of many prominent writers, Guo Moruo, Yu Dafu, and Lu Xun—especially in

Lu Xun's self-dissection and his critique of the Chinese national character.

THE 1930s AND 1940s

Despite the political upheaval and social chaos caused by the Second Sino-Japanese War and then the civil war between the Nationalists and Communists, this period saw the publication of large translation projects, such as a nearly complete rendering of William Shakespeare, a large portion of Honoré de Balzac's *La comédie humaine*, and a great many translations from Russian and Eastern European literature.

Zhu Shenghao (1912–1944) began his translation of Shakespeare with the publication of *The Tempest* in 1936. Himself a poet, Zhu's translation is known for its elegant lyricism and contributed to the establishment of modern Chinese poetry. Despite wartime dislocation, temporary loss of jobs, and loss of manuscripts, Zhu finished thirty-one of Shakespeare's plays before his own untimely death.

Fu Lei (1908–1966) first made a name for himself with his 1937–1941 translation of Rolland's four-volume *Jean-Christophe*, a work influential in China for several generations. His fame largely rests on his highly readable translation of more than a dozen of Balzac's novels, including *Le père Goriot* (1944), *Eugénie Grandet* (1948), *Le cousin Pons* (1952), and *Le colonel Chabert* (1954).

The translation of Russian and Eastern European literature may be traced to the early days of the May Fourth era and *Xiaoshuo yuekan*'s 1921 special issue on literature from oppressed nationalities, which featured works by Polish, Czech, Bulgarian, Syrian, Ukrainian, and Finnish writers. In the 1930s this trend was greatly enhanced by the League of Left-Wing Writers, which championed works by such Russian and Soviet writers as Fyodor Dostoyevsky (*Notes from the Underground* and *The Idiot*, translated by Geng Jizhi), Alexander Fadeyev (*Destruction*, by Lu Xun), Nikolai Gogol (*Dead Souls*, by Lu Xun), Maxim Gorky (*Mother*, by Xia Yan), Alexander Pushkin (*Onegin*, by Lü Ying), Ivan Turgenev (*Fathers and Sons* and *Virgin Soil*, by Ba Jin), and Leo Tolstoy (*Anna Karenina*, by Gao Zhi; *War and Peace*, by Gao Zhi and Guo Moruo). The introduction of critical realism, and later socialist realism, had a significant impact on works by Chinese writers.

The one Soviet Russian novel that would have the greatest influence in the 1950s and 1960s is *How the Steel Was Tempered*, an autobiographical work by the paralyzed and blind Ukrainian writer Nikolai Ostrovsky (1904–1936). It was first translated in 1937 from Japanese, and retranslated in 1942 from English by Mei Yi, a task given to him by his then underground Communist Party contact. The story of an authentic revolutionary hero in the approved style of socialist realism made it an ideal textbook for young readers of the early Communist era.

Children behind a display of "Harry Potter" books, Beijing, December 9, 2007. *After the Cultural Revolution, translations of notable works in Western literature began to reach new readers in China. This trend has continued into the twenty-first century as many publishers look to reach new audiences with bestsellers of the Western market.* **AP IMAGES**

THE COMMUNIST ERA

The period from the mid-1950s to early 1960s saw a brief flourishing in the field of translation. Sanctioned and often commissioned by the Communist Party, a range of translations of non-Western literature appeared, including works by the Bengali poet Rabindranath Tagore, the north Korean writers Cho Kich'on and Yi Kiyŏng, and the Japanese proletarian writers Kobayashi Takiji and Miyamoto Yuriko. While Socialist Realism represented by Gorky and Vladimir Mayakovsky was most readily endorsed by the party, pre-Soviet Russian writers such as Pushkin, Turgenev, Mikhail Lermontov, and Tolstoy continued to be translated.

During the ten years of the Cultural Revolution (1966–1976), there was a hiatus in literary translation, as in nearly all areas of cultural production. Soon after it ended, there was another major translation boom in the 1980s and 1990s. What characterizes this period is the simultaneous translation (and often retranslation) of European and American classics and a strong fascination with modernist masters. The first major work to appear was Yang Jiang's translation of *Don Quixote* in 1978, a project started in the 1950s. This was followed by Li Wenjun's translation of Franz Kafka's *Metamorphosis* in 1979 and Tang Yongkuan's translation of Kafka's *The Castle* in 1980. The most influential translations to appear next were those of Gabriel García Márquez's *One Hundred Years of Solitude* in 1984 by Huang Jinyan and others, of James Joyce's *Ulysses* in 1994 by Xiao Qian and Wen Jieruo, and of William Faulkner's *The Sound and the Fury* in 1996 and *Go Down, Moses* in 1997 by Li Wenjun. A generation of experimental Chinese writers—authors such as Can Xue, Ge Fei, and Ma Yuan—may be said to have grown up on a concentrated diet of Kafka, Faulkner, and magic realism.

SEE ALSO *Ba Jin; Gao Xingjian; Guo Moruo; May Fourth Movement; Plays (huaju); Socialist Realism in Art; Xiao Qian (Xiao Bingqian).*

BIBLIOGRAPHY

Chan Sin-wai, and David E. Pollard, eds. *An Encyclopaedia of Translation: Chinese-English, English-Chinese.* Hong Kong: Chinese University Press, 1995.

Ma Zuyi. *Zhongguo fanyi shi* [A history of translation in China]. Vol. 1. Wuhan: Hubei Jiaoyu Chubanshe, 1999.

Pollard, David, ed. *Translation and Creation: Readings of Western Literature in Early Modern China, 1840–1918.* Philadelphia: John Benjamins, 1998.

Zou Zhenhuan. *Yingxiang Zhongguo jindai shehui de yibaiben yizuo* [One hundred translated works that influenced modern Chinese society]. Beijing: Zhongguo Duiwai Fanyi Chuban Gongsi, 1994.

Hu Ying

TRANSNATIONALISM

SEE *Chinese Overseas: Emigration and Globalization.*

TRANSPORT INFRASTRUCTURE

This entry contains the following:

OVERVIEW
Claude Comtois

PORTS
Daniel Todd

SHIPPING SINCE 1949
Paul T. W. Lee (Li TaiYú)

RAILWAYS SINCE 1876
Ralph W. Huenemann

AIR TRANSPORT
Claude Comtois

ROAD NETWORK
Claude Comtois

POSTAL AND TELECOMMUNICATION SERVICES
Becky P. Y. Loo

OVERVIEW

In 1949 the new Chinese regime inherited an underdeveloped and greatly damaged transportation network with a particularly marked dichotomy between the coastal regions of continuous accessibility and the vast hinterland areas of limited accessibility. Transport planning and policy were formulated by the Chinese Communist Party and the Central Committee through five-year plans. The central government concentrated on major infrastructural projects, while operations of transport infrastructures were managed by provincial and local authorities.

From the early 1950s to the late 1970s, the central government undertook serious and sustained efforts to reduce the domination of coastal regions in terms of accessibility. To this end, the Chinese developed the road and rail network of the interior—notably the frontier regions of the northeast and the southwest—and placed much emphasis on dredging and renovation of navigation routes on river transport with the Yangzi (Chang) River as the key artery, followed by the southern and northern sections of the Grand Canal. The importance of these efforts arose from seven considerations: (1) to facilitate central government control over the entire country; (2) to reduce regional disparities within the country by reaching out to areas populated by minority nationalities; (3) to improve the defense support system; (4) to facilitate the exploitation of minerals, mostly combustible, located in the interior; (5) to transport grain, coal, and wood; (6) to increase the regional exchanges of goods; and (7) to disperse the industrial base of the country in order to promote regional economic development.

With the adoption of the open-door policy in 1978, the Chinese government gave priority to transport facilities related to energy production, foreign trade, and the tourist industry. Extensive work was devoted to upgrading railway lines in North and East China, and investments were granted for the western extension of railways. Selected railway arteries have been double-tracked and electrified to accommodate the increasing demand for personal mobility between the developed coastal metropolises. Construction emphasis has shifted to improving the quality of existing roads, especially access routes to industrialized coastal cities. In addition, noticeable improvements have been made in the mechanization of Chinese ports, the construction of new ports, and the development of containerization. All provincial capitals have new or expanded airport facilities, both for passenger and freight services, and the number of international, regional, and domestic air routes has increased.

The introduction of market-based reforms led to massive restructuring of the transportation system. More flexibility has been introduced into what had become a rigid and bureaucratic system. A decentralization process took place, where more autonomy and responsibilities were granted to local authorities, leading to increased fragmentation of transport institutional structure. State-owned enterprises have been separated from the ministries to increase their effectiveness in the marketplace. Operations were streamlined, and responsibilities for the various core businesses were assigned to specialized entities. Chinese transport companies have adopted a development strategy mirroring those of the world's most important carriers and terminal operators. Their operations are indistinguishable from the activities of their privately owned foreign competitors.

BIBLIOGRAPHY

Comtois, Claude. Transport and Territorial Development in China, 1949–1985. *Modern Asian Studies* 24, 4 (1990): 777–818.

Rimmer, Peter J., and Claude Comtois. China's Transport and Communications Firms: Transforming National Champions into Global Players. *Asia Pacific Viewpoint* 43, 1 (2002): 93–114.

Claude Comtois

PORTS

China's ports can be classified as either *general* or *special*, with the former dealing in merchandise of every kind and the latter used primarily for commodities handled in bulk. General ports are container ports, whereas special ports mostly handle energy minerals and the ores vital to heavy industry. General ports, such as Guangzhou and Quanzhou, which in precontainer days primarily dispensed break-bulk cargoes, have had a long history in China. They appeared in large numbers in the 1840s in the guise of treaty ports. They and their successors aspired to emulate the long-standing success of Guangzhou. Special ports, Qinhuangdao chief among them, did not arise until the 1900s and the exploitation of the Kaiping coalfield.

Whether measured in terms of the volume of cargo passing over their berths or in the provision of facilities to handle this volume, late twentieth- and early twenty-first-century developments in ports of both types have been remarkable. The handful of embryonic "international" ports (those licensed to trade with other countries) in existence in the 1980s had been transformed by the early

2000s into a vast assemblage of vibrant ports, all contributing to the globalization that simultaneously underpins world trade while facilitating China's emergence as an industrial giant. Aggregate figures attest to this change: China's port throughput between 1985 and 2005 climbed more than eightfold, from 312 million tons to 2,928 million tons. Coal, shifted coastwise to furnish China's energy needs, alone amounted to 400 million tons in 2006. These feats could not have been achieved without radical additions to port infrastructure at existing harbors and at sites newly sprung up from creeks and mudflats.

Frantic port development can be seen to good advantage at the regional level, where new ports have been responsible for instilling growth in communities the length and breadth of China. Three coastal regions stand out in this respect: the Bohai, the Changjiang (Yangtze River) Delta, and the Zhujiang (Pearl River) estuary, with the latter two accessing the great rivers of the interior.

While centered on Tianjin—registering a throughput in 2005 of 241 million tons, more than twelve times its 1985 volume (see Table 1)—the Bohai embraces ports stretching from Dalian (171 million tons) to Qingdao (187 million tons) and an accompanying scatter fronting the Yellow Sea. Besides these major general ports, the region boasts such big-bulk ports as Rizhao (84 million tons), Lianyungang (60 million tons), and Qinhuangdao (169 million tons), the largest coal handler in the world. A newer port—Caofeidian—promises to eclipse Qinhuangdao as a bulk handler, importing both hydrocarbons for energy markets and the ore and coal required by a steel complex.

The Changjiang Delta has Shanghai, the city that rose to prominence in treaty port days, as its cornerstone. Shanghai once again acts as the chief interface between China and the world, its port rising to the top of the list of major global ports. In 2005 Shanghai handled 443 million tons of cargo, much of it containerized. In 2006, fueled by surging exports and the inauguration of the massive terminal at Yangshan (whose first phase alone cost $2.8 billion), Shanghai surpassed Singapore as the world's foremost container port. Shanghai is supplemented by a string of sizeable ports along the coast and in the lower reaches of the Changjiang. Ningbo (269 million tons), Zhoushan (91 million tons), Nantong (83 million tons), and Nanjing (107 million tons) are notable examples, with Ningbo's Beilun Harbor transshipping ore to Shanghai's huge Baoshan steel complex.

The Zhujiang estuary contains two ports emblematic of China's long-standing deep-sea trading links: Guangzhou (250 million tons) and Hong Kong (the latter only lately conceding container supremacy to Shanghai). Complementing them in the mouth of the Zhujiang are the upstarts of Shenzhen (154 million tons) and Zhuhai (36 million tons), with Zhanjiang (47 million tons) lying a little farther afield.

China's chief ports

Port	Location	Throughput (million tons) 2005	Growth 1985–2005 1985	(% change)
Shanghai	Changjiang Delta	443	113	292
Ningbo	Changjiang Delta	269	10	2485
Guangzhou	Zhujiang Outfall	250	18	1313
Tianjin	Bohai	241	19	1197
Qingdao	Yellow Sea	187	26	615
Dalian	Bohai	171	44	290
Qinhuangdao	Bohai	169	44	282
Shenzhen	Zhujiang Outfall	154	—	—*
Nanjing	Changjiang	107	—	—**
Zhoushan	Changjiang Delta	91	—	—**
Rizhao	Yellow Sea	84	—	—*
Nantong	Changjiang	83	—	—**
Yingkou	Bohai	75	1	7590
Fuzhou	East China Sea	74	—	—**
Huanghua	Bohai	68	—	—*
Lianyungang	Yellow Sea	60	1	6589
Zhenjiang	Changjiang	59	—	—**
Hangzhou	Changjiang	51	—	—**
Wuhan	Changjiang	49	—	—**
Xiamen	Taiwan Strait	48	—	—**
Zhanjiang	South China Sea	46	12	277
Yantai	Bohai	45	7	554
Quanzhou	East China Sea	41	—	—**
Zhuhai	Zhujiang Outfall	36	—	—*

*Port created after 1985
**Data incomplete

SOURCE: China Statistical Yearbook, 2006.

Table 1

This last group has benefited enormously from outside investment, initially sparked by the special economic zone policy that induced Hong Kong container handlers to expand into Shenzhen. Outside investment subsequently has spread throughout China's port system, bearing much fruit in the form of container terminals. A few examples attest to the scale of this activity. Guangzhou Port, together with Denmark's APM Terminals and the domestic shipping firm Cosco Pacific, inaugurated in 2006 the Nansha container terminal. These two firms operate joint ventures with Tianjin and Shanghai ports as well, while Cosco has forged an agreement with Singapore's PSA to create Taicang Port in the Changjiang Delta. PSA, fired with enthusiasm for joint ventures with port authorities, has additional terminals in Guangzhou, Hong Kong, Fuzhou, Tianjin, and Dalian, to say nothing of its 30 percent stake in the third phase of Yangshan. Not to be outdone, Dubai Ports World has adopted a similar strategy, operating terminals in Hong Kong, Qingdao, and Fangcheng (Guanxi Province).

All told, domestic and outside investment is expected to boost China's annual port-handling capacity from 80 million containers in 2007 to 140 million in 2011. While provincial and municipal governments assume responsibility for implementing these numerous projects, oversight remains within the grasp of the central government's Ministry of Communications. Beijing hopes to lend unity to national port planning, thereby avoiding the twin evils of wasteful spending and excess capacity that attend uncoordinated development.

SEE ALSO *Special Economic Zones; Treaty Ports.*

BIBLIOGRAPHY

Ministry of Communications. *China's Principal Ports for Foreign Trade.* Beijing: People's Communications Publishing House, 1990.

National Bureau of Statistics of P.R. China, *China Statistical Yearbook 2006.* Beijing: China Statistical Press, 2006.

Shen Weicheng. Development and Problems of China's Seaports. In *China's Spatial Economy: Recent Developments and Reforms,* eds. G. J. R. Linge and D. K. Forbes. Hong Kong and New York: Oxford University Press, 1990: 96–108.

Todd, Daniel. China's Energy Needs, Coal Transfers, and the Ports Sector. *Geoforum* 28, 1 (1997): 39–53.

Daniel Todd

SHIPPING SINCE 1949

In 1961 the People's Republic of China established its own international shipping company, China Ocean Shipping (Group) Company, COSCO, the first of its kind in China. Since the implementation of reform and the open policy from 1978 and further development, particularly in the transition from a planned to a market economy, China has reformed the state-owned shipping enterprises that undertake international marine transport. This reform can be divided into five stages: delegating power and making the enterprises more profitable (1978–1984); reforming the system from profit to taxation (1984–1986); changing the system of job responsibility through operation by contract (1987–1991); transforming the operational system (1991–1995); and experimenting in establishing a modern enterprise system (1995 onward).

CHINA'S SHIPPING INDUSTRY

After a series of government actions, the China Shipping (Group) Company (CSG) was founded in Shanghai China in 1997. CSG is the parent company of two smaller companies operating in North America: China Shipping (North America) Holding Co., Ltd. (CSNA Holding), and China Shipping (North America) Agency, Inc. (CSNA Agency). CSNA makes use of the services of China Shipping Container Lines (CSCL), established in 1997, which is a division of China Shipping Group (China Shipping) and provides storage, transshipment, customs clearance, and other related declaration services.

When China entered the World Trade Organization in 2002, the speed of its restructuring and reform in response to the demands of the international shipping market was further accelerated. As a result, by 2006 China was a major participant in the world shipping industry, controlling 3,184 cargo ships with 70.4 million deadweight tons and 84 percent of the exported goods from China sent abroad via ship.

China has a long coastline along the Bohai, Yellow, and East China seas in the east and the South China Sea in the south, as well as extensive and deep harbors, such as those in Shanghai, Tianjin, Guangzhou, Yantai, Qingdao, Qinhuangdao, Dalian, Beihai, and Hong Kong. Therefore, passenger and cargo liner shipping has developed on China's coast, along with routes to neighboring countries and islands: companies include the Sino-Japanese International Ferry Company between Shanghai and Japan's Kobe, Osaka, and Yokohama; Jinshen Steamboat Company between Tianjin and Kobe; Dalian Daren Steamboat Company between Dalian and Inchon in South Korea; and Weihaiwei Eastern Shipping Company between Weihai and Qingdao to Inchon.

The mainland of China is also crisscrossed by a total of 226,800 kilometers of rivers, including 136,000 kilometers of inland waterways. The Shanghai-Chongqing line along the Yangzi River extends for 2,399 kilometers. River cruise ships, luxury tourist boats, and river freight ships with barges are deployed for inland water transportation. Chinese ports (including those in Taiwan and Hong Kong) accounted for 118.6 million TEUs ("twenty-foot equivalent unit," a standard-size shipping container) in 2006, representing some 25.5 percent of the world's container port throughput.

As globalization accelerates, Asia, especially China, has grown into the world's largest importer of raw materials and largest exporter of finished products. China has become the most dynamic shipping region in the world. China's foreign trade has been growing dramatically, producing a huge demand for shipping services. Since 2003, the robustness of the shipping market has largely been due to the driving force of the "China factor," which has continued to power the shipping demand. China's foreign trade cargo totaled over one billion tons in 2006, and by 2008 Shanghai led the world in tonnage of cargo handled. Mainland China accounts for over 60 percent of the market share of the total container trades from Asia to North America and Europe. China had 256 container ships with a capacity of 777,522 TEU in 2006.

CARGO

In the dry-bulk business, China has been responsible for a structural change to the world shipping industry. China continues to be the main destination for world iron-ore shipments, with 326.3 million tons unloaded in Chinese ports in 2006—an increase of 18.4 percent over 2005 and a world share increase to 45.6 percent. In fact, China has contributed 50 percent of the world's net demand increase in dry-cargo shipping since 1999.

World grain shipments are estimated to have grown at a modest rate and to have reached 281 million tons in 2006. Soybeans are another bulk good imported into China. China's imports of soybean meal in 2005 and 2006 were estimated to have increased thirteenfold (69,000 metric tons to 900,000 metric tons) from 2004 and 2005. This resulted in China becoming a net importer of soybean meal for the first time in five years.

Oil China started importing oil in 1983, and by the late 1980s was a net oil importer. Its net export volume then rose, and reached 35.4 million tons in 1985. In 1993 China again became a net oil importer, with the net import volume growing steadily from 10 million tons in 1993 to 10.95 million tons in 1995, and 70.2 million tons in 2000. China imported 91 million tons of crude oil in 2003, or about 1.87 million barrels per day, up from 69 million tons a year earlier. Because of its high rate of economic growth, Chinese oil imports are expected to

China's oil imports and exports

Year	Import	Export
1983	9.05 m tons	
1985		35.4 m tons
1993	10.0 m tons	
1995	10.95 m tons	4.148 m tons (oil products)
1999	36.614 m tons (crude oil); 20.82 m tons (oil products)	7.17 m tons (crude oil); 6.451 m tons (oil products)
2000	70.265 m tons (crude oil); 18.047 m tons (oil products)	8.2712 m tons (oil products)
2001	60.256 m tons (crude oil); 21.377 m tons (oil products)	7.551 m tons (crude oil); 9.139 m (oil products)
2002	69.406 m tons (crude oil); 20.338 m tons (oil products)	7.208 m (crude oil); 10.684 m tons (oil products)
2003	91.02 m tons (crude oil); 28.236 m tons (oil products)	8.133 m tons (crude oil); 13.823 m tons (oil products)
2004	122.724 m tons (crude oil); 37.876 m tons (oil products)	5.492 m tons (crude oil); 11.463 m tons (oil products)
2005	130 m tons (crude oil;) 31.46 m tons (oil products)	7.069 m tons (crude oil); 14.01 m (oil products)
2006	145.8 m (crude oil); 45.9 m tons (oil products)	9.6 m tons (crude oil); 13.5 m tons (oil products)
2007	163.17 m tons (crude oil); 33.8 m tons (oil products)	38.85 m tons (crude oil); 15.51 m tons (oil products)

Note: m = million

Table 1

China's coal imports and exports

Year	Import	Export
1980	1.95 m tons	
1985	2.31 m tons	
1990	2 m tons	
1993	1.429 m tons	
1994	1.221 m tons	
1995	1.64 m tons	
1996	3.2 m tons	
1997	2 m tons	
1998	1.58 m tons	32 m tons
1999	1.68 m tons	39.26 m tons
2000	2.18 m tons	22.07 m tons
2001	2.66 m tons	90.12 m tons
2002	11.26 m tons	83.9 m tons
2003	10.76 m tons	93.88 m tons
2004	18.61 m tons	85.93 m tons
2005	26.17 m tons	71.72 m tons
2006	38.25 m tons	61.92 m tons
2007	51.02 m tons	53.17 m tons

Note: m = million

SOURCE: Data filed by Flynn Consulting Ltd., 2008.

Table 2

steadily increase. The Middle East and Africa are China's two major suppliers, while Southeast Asia and the Americas also export oil to China.

China started to export crude oil, to the Philippines, in 1974. According to a long-term trade agreement signed between Japan and China in 1978, China would export the following amounts of crude oil annually to Japan from 1978 to 1982: 7 million tons, 7.6 million tons, 8 million tons, 9.5 million tons, and 15 million tons. The agreement also established the amount of coal that China should export to Japan, while Japan agreed to export technology, equipment, and construction facilities to China on the basis of mutual benefit. The agreement also required China to gradually increase its exports of coal and crude oil to Japan from 1982 on.

In 1981 Japan and China reviewed the implementation of this agreement, and made modifications. The two parties agreed that China should supply 8.3 million tons of crude oil in both 1981 and 1982. Thus, from 1978 to 1985, China exported about 50 million tons of crude oil to Japan. After China became a net oil importer in 1993, the two parties signed another agreement in late 2000 which stipulated that China should export 3 to 4 million tons of crude oil every year from 2001 to 2003. In late 2003, Japan and China faced a serious dispute over the export volumes for 2004 and 2005, and China stopped exporting crude oil to Japan.

In the 1980s, China exported about one-fourth of its output of crude oil because the country faced a serious shortage of foreign currency. Deng Xiaoping even commented that the country was "changing foreign currency with petroleum." Petroleum was the most important source to obtain foreign currency before 1993.

Industrial and Food Products In 2005 China imported 280 million tons of iron-ore sand with a yearly increase of 32.3 percent; 130 million tons of crude oil with a yearly increase of 3.3 percent; 6.21 million tons of edible vegetable oil with a decrease of 8.1 percent; 7.59 million tons of paper pulp with an increase of 3.7 percent; and 26.59 million tons of soybeans with an increase of 31.4 percent.

In 2005 China imported $512.41 billion of finished industrial products with a yearly increase of 15.4 percent, including $174.84 billion of electric and electronic products with a yearly increase of 22.9 percent, $96.37 billion of machinery equipment with an increase of 5.2 percent, $17.09 billion nonferrous metal, $77.74 billion of chemical and related products, 163,000 automobiles with a decrease of 7.3 percent, and 25.82 million tons of steel products with a decrease of 11.9 percent.

Coal China started exporting coal in 1949, and exported 286.75 million tons of coal and imported 59.84 million tons from 1949 to 1995. Since 2003 China has adopted strict quota policies for coal exports, and only a small amount of the country's output can be exported. There are also restrictions on coal imports as China adopts a policy of automatic permits for coal imports. It is expected that the net imports of coal to China will reach 200 million tons in 2010.

Due to trade cost reasons, China's partners in the coal trade are mostly clustered in the Asia-Pacific region. Vietnam, Australia, South Korea, Mongolia, and Indonesia are the major coal exporters to China, while Japan, South Korea, Taiwan, India, and Belgium are the major coal importers from China.

SEE ALSO *Energy: Coal; Energy: Oil and Natural Gas.*

BIBLIOGRAPHY

Tae Wo Lee et al., eds. *Shipping in China.* Burlington, VT: Ashgate, 2002.

Paul T. W. Lee (Lî TaìYù)

RAILWAYS SINCE 1876

Prior to 1895, a fierce debate raged in intellectual and political circles in China about whether railways should be built. Railway advocates argued that only by adopting modern industrial technology (railways, steel mills, gunboats, and so on) could China hope to thwart the imperialist ambitions of foreigners. This school of thought was known as the Self-strengthening movement, and included some of the most powerful officials in the land—men like Li Hongzhang, Zhang Zhidong, and Liu Mingchuan. The opposition to railways came from conservatives like Woren, Liu Xihong, and Yu Lianyuan. The conservatives voiced worries on a number of fronts: Railways might facilitate invasion by foreign armies, railways might cause massive unemployment among traditional transport workers, railways might be unprofitable (and thereby create a drain on state finances), and so forth.

While this debate raged, a few short, isolated rail lines were built. The first was a 10-mile, narrow-gauge line from Shanghai to Wusong, built in 1876 by British interests, without Chinese approval. This line was dismantled the next year by the Chinese authorities—an action that the British expatriates interpreted as mindless opposition to modern technology, but which Qing officialdom saw as a necessary and appropriate assertion of Chinese sovereignty.

China's first permanent railway was built under Li Hongzhang's aegis to serve the coal mines at Tangshan. The first six miles were opened to traffic in 1881, and the line was gradually extended; by 1894 it stretched about 235 miles from Tianjin toward Manchuria, where Russian and Japanese territorial ambitions were becoming increasingly worrisome. Also during this period, Zhang Zhidong

built a 19-mile line to serve his Hanyeping steel mill in Hubei, and Liu Mingchuan built a 66-mile line in Taiwan. Taken together, these Self-strengthening railways totaled about 320 route miles (the United States at the same point in time had about 175,000 route miles in its rail system).

THE SCRAMBLE FOR CONCESSIONS AND THE NATIONALISTIC REACTION

Japan's stunning victory in the Sino-Japanese War (1894–1895) revealed China's great military and diplomatic weakness, and foreign railway proposals came pouring in from promoters of every stripe. Generally speaking, these proposals came from investment banks and other private interests, but as everyone—including the Chinese—understood all too well, aggressively expansionist governments often stood at the promoters' elbows and encouraged their activities. In the colorful phrase of the day, the foreign powers were keen to "carve up the melon," and before long China was forced to grant railway concessions to Russia in northern Manchuria, to Japan in southern Manchuria, to Germany in Shandong, to Belgium in central China, to France in the southern provinces bordering Indochina, and to Great Britain in a number of locations. A spurt of construction followed, and by 1911 China had about 5,780 miles of railways—though this was anything but an integrated system. The mileage was much too limited to cover a country the size of China, but even in regions where rail lines were contiguous, interchange of traffic was hampered by multiple gauges, diversity of rolling stock, and jealous rivalry over control of revenues.

In the face of these foreign railway concessions, the newly emerging voice of Chinese nationalism began to demand a revival of the Self-strengthening approach. Such slogans as *shouhui liquan* ("recover sovereign rights"), *bao lu* ("protect the railways"), and *ziban tielu* ("self-built railways") echoed through the land. The central government sympathized with these antiforeign slogans but with its limited resources could build only a few railways, of which the most famous was the 125-mile line from Beijing to Kalgan (Zhangjiakou), which was completed in 1909. This line was designed by a Yale-educated engineer named Zhan Tianyou (known to foreigners as Jeme Tien Yow). Because of the weakness of Qing finances, the government also granted charters to at least nineteen local companies to build railways in their respective regions—with their own money. However, these local efforts encountered many difficulties: inadequate funding, factional infighting, corruption, and so on, and in 1911 the Qing rulers made the fateful decision to rescind the charters. The locals were outraged. In Sichuan, on September 7, 1911, several thousand protestors gathered outside the viceroy's yamen, and about forty people were killed when the viceroy's troops fired on the crowd. Protests spread through the land, and on October 10, 1911, a group of conspirators at Wuchang launched the uprising that toppled the Qing dynasty and established the Republic of China, with Sun Yat-sen (Sun Yixian or Sun Zhongshan) as its nominal leader.

WARLORDS AND RAILWAYS

Sun Yat-sen was a great railway enthusiast who envisioned a grandiose network of 100,000 miles to be built in a decade. However, the political reality was that Republican China was fragmented into many separate fiefdoms, some controlled by foreign powers and some by local warlords, and Sun never controlled either the territory or the finances to implement his scheme. After Sun's death in 1925, his successor Chiang Kai-shek (Jiang Jieshi) struggled to suppress the warlords but succeeded in establishing only the semblance of a unified national government. To warlord recalcitrance was added Japanese aggression, which became overt in Manchuria in 1931 and evolved into open warfare in 1937. In principle, the Nationalist government, the warlords, and the Japanese were all keen to modernize China (which meant, among other things, building railways), but in practice all sides were often preoccupied with military confrontation. The result was that between 1911 and 1937 China's rail network was expanded from 5,780 to about 13,500 miles, but control of this network remained fragmented and traffic was often disrupted. Unsurprisingly, no significant additions to the network were built during the war years from 1937 to 1949.

EVALUATING THE ARGUMENTS OVER IMPERIALISM

No one disputes that both the traffic patterns and the profitability of China's railways were hampered by the fragmentation of the system and by military disruptions. But many authors, both Chinese and foreign, have asserted that—even in periods when the foreign-financed railways could operate normally—they made no economic contribution to China, or even caused economic harm. For example, Wu Chengming has written that capitalist investments in countries like China constitute "a powerful tool for the enslavement and robbery of their peoples" (Wu Chengming 1956, p. 2), an argument that echoes V. I. Lenin's famous accusation that foreign financiers "plunder the whole world simply by clipping coupons" (Lenin [1916] 1943, Vol. 5, p. 12). This same attitude motivated the Maoist economic policy of "self-reliance" (*zili gengsheng*), under which foreign trade was minimized and foreign investment was rejected altogether. However, even Lenin himself—Lenin of the New Economic Policy, to be sure, but Lenin nonetheless—was willing to entertain the possibility that foreign trade, foreign investment, and for-

eign expertise from capitalist countries might all be beneficial and that only "sentimental socialists" despise these things (Lenin [1921] 1943). And Deng Xiaoping's famous aphorism that any cat, black or white, is a good cat as long as it catches mice was enunciated as a justification for the 1978 reforms—reforms that overturned Maoist isolationism and welcomed foreign trade and foreign capital. Thus, even among left-wing thinkers, the question of imperialism's economic impact—as distinct from its political rapaciousness—remains a controversial issue (Huenemann 1984).

GROWTH OF ROUTES AND TRAFFIC AFTER 1949

After 1949, all of China's railways came under the control of the central Ministry of Railways, which remains to this day one of the largest and most influential ministries in the Chinese government, with about 1.6 million employees and total operating revenues of 236.4 billion yuan in 2006. For many years, the Ministry of Railways and the Ministry of Communications (which is responsible for highways and ports) shared an office building in Beijing, to facilitate coordination between traffic modes, and indeed in some periods they were combined into a single ministry. But this attempted integration was never entirely successful, and now that the Ministry of Communications has its own office building—and more important now that highway traffic is largely a private-sector activity—it seems clear that the two ministries will remain independent of each other. To a small degree, the Ministry of Railways has experimented with decentralization, with the building of a few local lines, but in reality the system is still controlled almost entirely from the ministry.

After 1949, China's rail network experienced significant integration, expansion, and intensification. Integration involved unifying the gauge of all lines to a uniform 4 feet, 8.5 inches, and standardizing the types of rolling stock. (At China's borders, where, for example, China's standard gauge meets lines of meter gauge in Vietnam and broad gauge in Mongolia and Russia, unification of gauge is impractical, and through shipments require transshipment or the physical exchange of axles on the rolling stock.)

Expansion has involved the building of new lines away from the coast into more-isolated interior and border provinces, often over extremely difficult terrain. Examples include the Chengdu-Kunming line (completed in 1970), which has about 250 miles of bridges and tunnels on its 674-mile route, and the Xiangfan-Chongqing line (1978), with bridges and tunnels on 45 percent of its 560-mile route. The most recent example of such difficult engineering challenges is the line to Tibet, carried as far as Golmud by 1980 but completed to Lhasa only in 2006. At the end

A train traveling along the Qinghai-Tibet Railway, Damxung County, Tibet Autonomous Region, October 25, 2006. After achieving victory in 1949, the People's Republic of China established the Ministry of Railways, charging the department with developing a national railroad system to reach every province in the country. With the 2006 completion of the Qinghai-Tibet Railway pictured above, China's national train network became a reality, over fifty-seven years in the making. © CHOGO/XINHUA PRESS/CORBIS

of 2006, the network totaled about 47,900 miles, or about half of Sun Yat-sen's original dream of 100,000 miles. The Ministry of Railways has announced plans to expand the network to about 75,000 miles by 2015. However, the geographical coverage of the system is now reasonably complete (in the sense that it reaches all of China's provinces), and further expansion of freight and passenger traffic on feeder routes might often be better served by motor vehicles than by additional rail lines.

The intensification of China's rail traffic can be demonstrated with a simple pair of comparisons: for freight, average density of traffic on the system grew from about 0.83 million tons per mile of route in 1949 to about 28.47 million tons in 2006, while the corresponding figures for passenger traffic are 0.60 million passengers in 1949 and 8.59 million passengers in 2006. Such heavy traffic densities (equaled by few other railways in the world) have been made possible only by heavy investments in right-of-way (double tracking and electrification have both been important) and in tractive power (all locomotives were steam in 1949; by 1985 45 percent of the fleet was diesel or electric; and by 2006 only ninety-one steam locomotives—less than 1 percent of the fleet—remained in service).

THE ENERGY ISSUE

Although China's steam locomotives have virtually disappeared, coal remains an essential element of the railway story—both as an input and an output. On the input side, despite the development of hydro and nuclear power, additional electricity in China comes predominantly from thermal plants burning coal, so electric locomotives are just as dependent on coal for fuel as steam locomotives were. On the output side, coal remains overwhelmingly the dominant category of freight on the railways (in 2006, coal and coke accounted for 49.5 percent of all the tonnage moved). Weaning China's railways (and its economy overall) from coal is going to be a long, slow, difficult process.

UNRESOLVED POLICY QUESTIONS

In addition to the energy question, China's railways face several other major policy dilemmas. On the passenger side, the proposed shift to high-speed trains (like the bullet trains of Japan and the French TGV) will be enormously expensive. For example, it is estimated that building such a line from Beijing to Shanghai with steel-wheel technology will cost about $30 billion, and utilizing Maglev (magnetic levitation) technology, like that used on the demonstration line that serves the Pudong airport in Shanghai, would cost substantially more. Also on the passenger side, modernization of the passenger-ticketing system is long overdue. On the freight side, upgrading of rolling stock to accommodate containerized freight has been slow, which is one of the reasons that factories in the coastal region continue to dominate China's export production.

In sum, China's experience with railways since 1949 must be considered a success story, but substantial problems remain to be solved.

BIBLIOGRAPHY

China's Infrastructure Splurge: Rushing on by Road, Rail, and Air. *Economist* (February 16, 2008): 30–32.

Guo Tingyi et al., eds. *Haifang dang* [Files on maritime defense]. Sec. 5: *Tielu* [Railways]. Taibei: Academia Sinica, 1957.

Huenemann, Ralph W. *The Dragon and the Iron Horse: The Economics of Railroads in China, 1876–1937.* Cambridge, MA: Harvard University Press, 1984.

Huenemann, Ralph W. Modernizing China's Transport System. In *China's Economic Dilemmas in the 1990s: The Problems of Reforms, Modernization, and Interdependence*, ed. Joint Economic Committee, U.S. Congress, 455–468. Washington, DC: U.S. Government Printing Office, 1991.

Lenin, V. I. *Imperialism, the Highest Stage of Capitalism.* 1916. In *V. I. Lenin: Selected Works*, Vol. 5, 3–119. New York: International Publishers, 1943.

Lenin, V. I. The Political Activities of the Central Committee: Report Delivered at the Tenth Congress of the R.C.P.(B.) (speech given March 6, 1921) and The Tax in Kind (speech given March 15, 1921). In *V. I. Lenin: Selected Works*, Vol. 9, 83–122. New York: International Publishers, 1943.

National Bureau of Statistics of China. *China Statistical Yearbook.* Beijing: China Statistics Press, various years.

Wu Chengming. *Diguo zhuyi zai jiu Zhongguo de touzi* [Imperialism's investments in old China]. Beijing: 1956.

Ralph W. Huenemann

AIR TRANSPORT

China's airline industry was established in 1954 as an instrument for government administration, trade, and tourism under the Civil Aviation Administration of China. Between 1958 and 1978 the Civil Aviation Administration pioneered several routes with friendly communist countries, often operating at financial losses. International routes were strictly regulated and based on bilateral agreements with other countries. The framework of these agreements was limited to third and fourth freedom rights, namely the freedom to carry traffic from China to another country and the freedom to pick up traffic from another country bound to China. These agreements were defined in terms of market shares rather than capacity. When the airline seats of participating foreign carriers sold out, the passenger had no option but to use the Chinese carrier.

The Civil Aviation Administration granted rights to fly these international routes and to use China's air space only to participating airline carriers. This restrictive policy reflected the Chinese airline industry's limited business experience in the international market and was designed to protect the country's uncompetitive carrier. Until 1978 the Civil Aviation Administration was a department of the air force, with 6 regional offices (Beijing, Shanghai, Guangzhou, Shenyang, Xi'an, and Wuhan), 23 provincial offices, and 78 civil aviation stations. The Civil Aviation Administration's function in the industry was to provide all air-transport services (flight operations, airport management, and navigation aids) and to regulate aviation.

Since 1978 the Civil Aviation Administration has undergone three rounds of reforms. The 1979 reform injected a business element into air transport by separating civil aviation from the air force. All the regional and provincial offices were made responsible for profits and losses. The 1987 reform ended the Civil Aviation Administration's monopoly by separating airport and airline operations, and thus encouraged market and route entry by carriers that were not part of the Civil Aviation Administration. This led to the emergence of independent state-owned airlines, many of which were unprofitable, had poor safety records, and were characterized by frequent delays. In 1993, acknowledging the need to improve the performance and efficiency of its airlines and to expand airport handling capacity, the Chinese government introduced a third round of reforms so that the country's airlines could meet domestic demand and become globally competitive. These reforms involved price deregulation, divestiture of airport development to local authorities, establishment of foreign joint ventures in airport and airline operations, and partial privatization of airport-terminal operations. These reforms triggered a process of consolidation focused on three carriers: Air China, China Eastern, and China Southern.

These Chinese carriers were allowed discretionary powers over buying and leasing aircraft, raising money through stock markets, making managerial appointments, setting tariffs, and hiring overseas staffing. Air China, China Eastern, and China Southern have been involved in the development of their respective hubs at Beijing Capital Airport, Shanghai Pudong Airport, and Guangzhou Baiyun International Airport. Anticipating an upsurge in international travel, the three Chinese airlines and several foreign airlines have negotiated code-sharing arrangements for specific routes, under which one carrier's flights are marketed by other carriers. The government has also called for increased consolidation among national carriers. By 2000 China's three main carriers controlled 80 percent of the domestic air-freight and passenger market.

The implementation of these reforms and the competitive advantage of the three Chinese airlines have led to dramatic changes in the geography of China's air-transport services. There is a distinct bias in the Chinese carriers' capacity and services along the East-West trades. As of 2005, these carriers have intensified their services toward North America, with over 110 flights per week on more than 25 routes. Anchorage has been established as a transit hub to shorten global transit time to Chicago and New York. The Chinese carriers are offering more than 130 flights per week across the Eurasian continent. They have ceased their operations on several connections with eastern Europe and are allocating these resources along 25 routes to western Europe and along 4 routes to Russia. Beijing and Shanghai have been strengthened as national hubs, and trunk-line connections have been established between China's airport hubs and Los Angeles on the trans-Pacific routes and with Frankfurt and Paris on the Eurasian routes. The feeder North-South network has similarly been restructured and augmented. China and Australia are linked by 30 long-distance flights per week to Sydney with stopovers in Melbourne. The Chinese air carriers have abandoned services to Africa and have eliminated connections to the Middle East, shifting these resources to Central and South Asia, a move that has permitted the emergence of Ürümqi as a new airport hub. In the intra-Asia service configuration, China's air-industry reforms have led to major service gains to Northeast and Southeast Asia. With over 500 flights per week on 153 routes, Chinese airlines have developed an urban circuit in air transport that knits together East Asia's major metropolitan areas. In Northeast Asia, weekly flights are most numerous between Shanghai and Tokyo and between Beijing and Seoul, each route having over 3 flights per day. In the service configuration to Southeast Asia, Bangkok and Singapore serve as hub airports. There are linkages with Rangoon, Kuala Lumpur, and Manila, emerging connections with Vietnam, Laos, and Cambodia, and a link between Guangzhou and Jakarta. Chinese airlines have established direct links between airports in Japan, South Korea, and Southeast Asia and airports in the Chinese hinterland. Domestically, they have increased service between the coastal areas and the interior. This process has confirmed Beijing, Shanghai, Guangzhou, and Hong Kong as national hubs for each of the three domestic aviation groups.

As of 2008, trajectories in China's air transport industry head in several directions. First, the increasing need for air-transport services has led to a convergence in air policies between China and Taiwan. The evolving strategies of airline carriers have produced similar responses from the Ministry of Communications in Beijing and the Ministry of Transport and Communications in Taibei (Taipei). Changes in air connections between China and Taiwan closely mirror the increasing integration of the mainland and island economies within global transport networks. The air carriers of China and Taiwan have broadened the exposure of Chinese and Taiwanese airports to the interna-

tional network of airline routes. Cross-strait strategic alliances in the air-transport sector is expected to result in expanded air-freight and passenger traffic. Second, the integration of China into the world market has led to increased imports and exports of products depending on air transport. Chinese air freight, estimated at 2 million tons, should grow at 7 percent annually. China intends to purchase cargo airplanes with capacities of 80 tons. China Air Cargo has already invested US$150 million for a load center in Shanghai. Third, China is developing its fleet of aircrafts. China could spend over US$100 billion in the next 15 years to purchase over 1,500 passenger aircrafts. The country plans to develop an indigenous aeronautic industry to cater to aircraft maintenance, repair, and construction. Fourth, meeting the challenges of developing its air-transportation infrastructure will require enormous capital investment. Private capital and ownership are accepted as part of the solution. Further consolidation of Chinese carriers may be required to obtain economies of scale. Already China indirectly controls Hong Kong's airline industry through its ownership of Dragonair, Air Macau, and Cathay Pacific. China will play a key role in shaping the geography of air transport in the region.

BIBLIOGRAPHY

Oum, Tae Hoon, and Yeong Heok Lee. The Northeast Asian Air Transport Network: Is There a Possibility of Creating Open Skies in the Region? *Journal of Air Transport Management* 8 (2002): 325–337.

Rimmer, P. J., and Claude Comtois. China's Transport and Communication Firms: Transforming National Champions into Global Players. *Pacific Viewpoint* 43, 1 (2002): 93–114.

Zhang, Anming, and Hongmin Chen. Evolution of China's Air Transport Development and Policy towards International Liberalization. *Transportation Journal* 42, 3 (2003): 31–49.

Claude Comtois

ROAD NETWORK

Since 1978, road transport has been labeled a priority by the central government. Plans were approved to equip China with a national trunk system comprising five north-south highways and seven east-west highways. Road corridors link major economic centers and connect the eastern seaboard to China's border regions. Other goals include linking ports and airports, relieving railway congestion, and improving access to tourist areas. In 2005 the length of the highway network totaled 1,199,584 miles (1,930,543 kilometers), with the national expressway network amounting to 25,478 miles (41,003 kilometers). Overcoming China's topography has required 336,648 bridges spanning 9,163 miles (14,747 kilometers) in total length. Highway construction still remains high on the government's agenda, especially in rural areas. Roads with slow speeds of under 25 miles per hour (40 kilometers per hour), carriage widths of 11.5 feet (3.5 meters), and poor surface conditions still account for 65 percent of China's total highway length.

Highway planning is the responsibility of the central government, but the national trunk highway system has been largely financed by provincial governments borrowing against long-term revenues to be earned from projected toll income. The remainder comes from fuel taxes, road-maintenance fees, and vehicle sales taxes imposed by the central government. In light of the debt-servicing obligations of local governments, foreign investments are regarded as crucial for helping China to realize development plans for its road network. Moreover, commercial road building is accepted in transportation projects. In 2005 Beijing announced a new plan for its national expressway network that shifts priorities to reducing the national disparity in prosperity through rural highway construction in Western China and to eradicating bottlenecks in Central China.

The adoption of market-based reforms since 1978 has accelerated the development of the light-industrial and service sectors, dictating that more freight be moved by truck over longer distances. Rising disposable income and the freedom to acquire motor vehicles has led to increased demand for personal mobility between the most developed of China's northern, central, and southern metropolises. These factors have combined to increase pressure on China's highway system. In 2005, 10 million trucks carried 14.8 billion short tons (13.4 billion metric tons) of freight, while 21 million passenger vehicles carried 1.6 billion people.

From 1990 to 2005, the length of urban road networks increased from 59,000 miles to 155,000 miles (or from 95,000 kilometers to 250,000 kilometers), at an average annual growth rate of 6.5 percent. Driven by rapid urbanization, network architecture has sought to relieve pressure on the roads in city centers and reroute traffic through suburban areas. Transit roads are being constructed around cities to lessen inner-city traffic. Crossovers, bridges, and underground tunnels are being built to improve urban traffic flows. The improvement in urban road capacity has nurtured the development of taxi services and increased the geographic coverage of buses and trolleybuses, which supplement urban subway and light-rail systems. On the negative side, the motorization of such cities as Beijing, Shanghai, and Guangzhou is crowding out bicycle usage, limiting walking facilities, and threatening pedestrian safety.

BIBLIOGRAPHY

Sit, Victor F. S., and Weidong Liu. Restructuring and Spatial Change of China's Auto Industry under Institutional Reform and Globalization. *Annals of the Association of American Geographers* 90, 4 (2000): 653–673.

Claude Comtois

POSTAL AND TELECOMMUNICATION SERVICES

While a domestic government postal service (*youyi*) existed in traditional China, major foreign post offices and the first telephone service were found in China only after the Opium War (1839–1842). Until World War II, both the postal and telephone services remained means of communications mainly for government officials and the wealthy. In general though, postal services were more accessible than the telephone among the general public. Postal services were provided through various official and nonofficial local providers until such services were declared a state monopoly in 1934.

Since the establishment of the People's Republic of China in 1949, a primary goal of the government has been to build a postal network and a fixed-line-telephone network throughout the vast territory of the country. Yet because of the political importance of information flows, market liberalization did not come immediately after the introduction of the Reform and Opening Policy in 1978. Prior to 1994, postal and telecommunications development was tightly controlled by the state via the monopoly of the Ministry of Posts and Telecommunications. Foreign investors were forbidden to operate telecommunications services. The advanced telecommunications infrastructure, particularly the Internet, was developed by the state (the Golden Bridge Project) and by the academic community (under the Chinese Academy of Sciences).

In preparation for China's accession to the World Trade Organization, beginning in 1994 the telecommunications industry began to undergo some reforms. In particular, China Unicom (Zhongguo Liantong) was established to compete with China Telecom (Zhongguo Dianxin) in the provision of mobile-phone services. Jitong Communications was established to focus on national network building and network integration. In 1997 the National Information Infrastructure Steering Committee was set up to coordinate and regulate the telecommunications industry, and the China National Network Information Center was established to oversee Internet development. Nonetheless, China Telecom remained the sole provider of fixed-line telephone service and commercial Internet service in China. In 1997 China Unicom accounted for less than 2 percent of the domestic mobile-telephone market (Loo 2004).

Because of the slow pace of change and mounting pressure from World Trade Organization negotiations, the central government took the more drastic step of establishing the Ministry of Information Industry by merging the Ministry of Posts and Telecommunications and the Ministry of Electronics Industry in March 1998. In this restructuring, the State Post Bureau was also established. The monopoly of China Telecom was further challenged by transferring one of its profitable arms, Guoxin Paging, to China Unicom. The latter also obtained a license to offer Internet telephone service in 1999. Furthermore, in the same year China Netcom (Zhongguo Wangtong) was established to provide broadband Internet services.

The liberalization of the telecommunication industry gathered momentum from 2000, when the State Council issued the Telecommunications Regulations of the People's Republic of China (*Zhonghua Renmin Gongheguo dianxin tiaoli*, degree no. 291). The regulations allowed foreign investment up to a maximum of 49 percent in basic telecommunications services. Many profitable value-added services, including Internet data centers and virtual private networks, were opened to foreign investment, and their charges were subject to less stringent state control. Most notably, China Telecom lost its monopoly power in the fixed-line telephone market, and fixed-line and other telecommunications services in ten major provinces/municipalities in the north were transferred to China Netcom. China Netcom also took over Jitong and offered mobile telecommunications services through Xiao Ling Tong. Currently, China Telecom, China Mobile, and China Netcom are the three major players in the domestic telecommunications market.

For telecommunications equipment, China still relied heavily on foreign imports in the early 2000s. Yet some breakthroughs were achieved by Huawei Technologies and Zhongxing Telecommunication Equipment. Huawei Technologies started off in 1988 as a major provider of network equipment (especially high-end routers). Its strong focus on research and development has proved highly successful. In 2008 Huawei Technologies is the world's number one provider of softswitch products, and it obtained a license to produce and sell mobile phones to consumers in China in 2005. Zhongxing is also a global supplier of telecommunications equipment and network solutions. Another successful telecommunication manufacturing company is Datang Telecom Technology & Industry Group. In 2000 Datang's technology for TD-SCDMA (time division-synchronous code division multiple access) was accepted as an international standard for third-generation mobile telecommunication. The technology has been used in major Chinese cities. With mobile telephone users already at over 450 million in 2006, the Chinese market for mobile-telephone services and equipment is enormous.

In comparison, major reforms of postal services began only in the mid-2000s. In late 2006 China Post was formally separated from the State Post Bureau to operate the commercial arms of the bureau. This change was a major milestone in China's separation of political and business functions (*zhengqi fenli*). By the end of 2006, China Post's business comprised three core areas: postal business, logistics business (particularly its express mail service, EMS), and banking business (which takes advantage of its extensive network of postal offices, especially in rural China).

SEE ALSO *Internet.*

BIBLIOGRAPHY

Loo, Becky P. Y. Telecommunications Reforms in China: Towards an Analytical Framework. *Telecommunications Policy* 28 (2004): 697–714.

Zeng Jianqiu. *Dianxin chanye fazhan gailun* [Overview of telecommunications development]. Beijing: Beijing Youdian Daxue Chubanshe, 2001.

Zhongguo Tongxin Qiye Xiehui. *2006 Zhongguo tongxinye fazhan fenxi baogao* [An analytical report on the development of China's communications industry, 2006]. Beijing: Renmin Youdian Chubanshe, 2007.

Zhongguo Youzheng (China Post). http://www.chinapost.cn/

Becky P. Y. Loo

TRANSSEXUALITY AND SEX-CHANGE OPERATIONS

Reflecting its yin-yang philosophy, the Chinese have long recognized that gender is an integral part of nature and that strict adherence to gender roles is essential for building a harmonious society. However, the Chinese also recognize that gender represents two ends of a continuum, and there is always a bit of the male in the female and vice versa (Ng Man-Lun and Lau Man-Pang 1990). Hence, ambiguous gender manifestations, though considered abnormal and unwelcome, have been accommodated or at least tolerated throughout Chinese history. Eunuchs held high positions in the imperial courts of nearly every dynasty, and since mixed-sex opera troupes were not allowed until the end of the last dynasty, actors who could play opposite-sex characters, some of whom were actually transvestites, were highly admired (van Gulik 1961). One of the most popular Chinese traditional gods, Guanyin, is said to be able to transcend gender, appearing in whatever sex the worshipper or the condition requires (Blofeld 1977).

The first documented case of sex-reassignment surgery on a Chinese person was performed on a male-to-female transsexual in Hong Kong in 1981. In 1986 a gender-identity team comprising a psychiatrist, a clinical psychologist, a gynecologist, an endocrinologist, a urologist, a medical social worker, and a lawyer was established in the Sex Clinic of Queen Mary Hospital in Hong Kong to cater to the needs of transsexuals (Ko Sik-Nin 2003). The team undertook about fifty cases between 1986 and 2005.

In mainland China, the first documented sex-reassignment surgery was performed in 1983 on a male-to-female transsexual, Zhang Kesha, in the Third Hospital of Peking (Beijing) Medical University. In her 2003 autobiography, Zhang described how she was blackmailed for her gender secret for fourteen years after she underwent the operation.

As of 2008, the youngest person in China to have undergone gender reassignment was seventeen at the time of the operation. The oldest was fifty. The most well-known case concerned the male-to-female dancer Jing Xing. Widely admired in China, Jing Xing has received numerous international dancing awards and performed for British prime minister Tony Blair during his visit to Beijing in 1998.

The first sex-change surgery in Taiwan took place in 1988 at Taipei Veterans General Hospital. By 2009, there were twelve hospitals (six private and six public) in Taiwan that offered comprehensive assessment, management, and surgery for transsexuals (Gao Xu-Kuan 2007). It is estimated that by 2005 about sixty male-to-female and 120 female-to-male reassignment operations had been completed in Taiwan. One prominent Taiwanese transsexual is the entertainer Li Ching.

The exact number of transsexuals in China's population is unknown. Based on sex-clinic data, it has been estimated to be one in every 200,000 Chinese, with a slight predominance of the male-to-female, a proportion that is similar to most international figures. It has been estimated that about one thousand sex-change operations had been performed in China by 2006, and about 400,000 transsexuals were awaiting operations.

Generally, the Chinese in mainland China are accepting of transsexuals. A 2005 Internet survey showed 38.8 percent of respondents accepted the presence of Internet advertisements from transsexuals seeking marital partners. Transsexuals have also been accepted under their reassigned sex as candidates in beauty contests, including the national competition to choose China's entrant in the Miss Universe Pageant.

Marriage laws in mainland China permit marriage of transsexuals under their reassigned sex. China's first documented marriage of a transsexual occurred in 2004, when a male-to-female in Sichuan married a man. Married transsexuals are also allowed to adopt children, as long as they satisfy the usual conditions for adoption.

Transsexuals in Taiwan and Hong Kong have faced greater difficulties than those in mainland China, due in part to the influence of Western laws and culture in these regions. Since the governments of Hong Kong and Taiwan recognize only one's chromosomal sex ("born sex") irrespective of whether a person has undergone sex-reassignment surgery, and since marriage is limited to unions between a man and a woman, marriages of transsexuals to persons with

Transgender patient prepping for sex-reassignment surgery, Changchun, Jilin province, March 6, 2004.
Since the nation's first sex-change operation in 1983, China has generally been accepting of transsexual citizens, allowing them the right to marry, adopt children, and even compete in beauty contests under their new gender. **CHINA PHOTOS/GETTY IMAGES**

the same chromosomal sex are not permitted. For legal purposes and documentation, a person's "born sex" applies. This situation results in social disadvantages for transsexuals, especially in signing contracts, buying insurance, finding a job, reporting crimes such as rape, or simply using public toilets (Ng Man-Lun 2001).

Transsexual groups have been formed in all three regions of China. They function as mutual support groups to fight for the welfare and rights of transsexuals. Cases of transsexuals attempting suicide have occasionally been reported by the media of all three regions, showing that the life of Chinese transsexuals is far from satisfactory.

SEE ALSO *Gender Relations; Identification and Belonging; Sexual Dysfunction.*

BIBLIOGRAPHY

Blofeld, John Eaton. *Bodhisattva of Compassion: The Mystical Tradition of Kuan Yin*. Boston: Shambhala, 1977.

Gao Xu-Kuan. *Bian Xing Pinggu: Taiwan De Yiyuan Yishi Ji Heermeng Zhiliao Shoufei Fenxi* [Sex change assessment: Fee analysis on medical and hormonal charges in Taiwan hospitals]. Center for the Study of Sexualities, National Central University, Taiwan. 2007. http://intermargins.net/repression/deviant/transgender/tgpamphlet/charge.htm.

Ko Sik-Nin. A Descriptive Study of Sexual Dysfunction and Gender Identity Clinic in the University of Hong Kong Psychiatric Unit, 1991–2001. Fellowship thesis, Hong Kong College of Psychiatrists, 2003. http://web.hku.hk/sjwinter/TransgenderASIA/paper_qmh_evaluation.htm (excerpt).

Ng Man-Lun Medico-legal Issues of Transsexualism in Hong Kong. *Journal of Asian Sexology* 2 (2001): 59–61.

Ng Man-Lun, and Lau Man-Pang. Sexual Attitudes in the Chinese. *Archives of Sexual Behavior* 19, 4 (1990): 273–388.

van Gulik, Robert Hans. *Sexual Life in Ancient China: A Preliminary Survey of Chinese Sex and Society from ca. 1500 B.C. till 1644 A. D*. Leiden, Netherlands: Brill, 1961.

Ng Man-Lun

TREATY PORTS

The treaty ports were commercial centers where non-Chinese had special permission to reside and conduct business according to a series of agreements between China and eighteen other states. Between 1842 and 1914, ninety-two towns in all were formally designated as treaty ports. Foreigners representing official, business, and Christian interests established residence in about half these centers. First established in treaties imposed on China through military force, the treaty ports were protected by foreign gunboats and other displays of power throughout the century of their existence. Although China gave up no territory in these places, recognition of extraterritorial status for the nationals of the so-called treaty powers amounted to a cession of Chinese authority over the foreign and Chinese inhabitants of the treaty ports. Both the opening of ports and the provisions for extraterritoriality were unilateral; China received no reciprocal privileges in the territories of the other signatory states.

Most of the major treaty ports were established in the nineteenth century. The Treaty of Nanjing (1842) designated Guangzhou, Xiamen, Fuzhou, Ningbo, and Shanghai as ports open to foreign residence and trade. In the Treaty of Tianjin (1858), not enforced until the 1860s, ten more ports were "opened": Niuzhuang, Dezhou, Zhenjiang, Nanjing, Hankou, Jiujiang, Danshui, Gaoxiong, Shantou, and Qiongzhou. Tianjin itself became a treaty port in the Convention of Beijing (1860).

Another set of centers, including Shashi and Suzhou, were designated as treaty ports when Japan became a treaty power with the Treaty of Shimonoseki in 1895.

The eighteen "treaty powers" that claimed privileges in China between 1842 and 1911 were: Britain, the United States, France, Norway, Sweden, Russia, Portugal, the Netherlands, Denmark, Spain, Belgium, Austria-Hungary, Italy, Peru, Germany, Japan, Brazil, and Mexico. Most of these nations had very few residents in China, and sometimes had to appoint businessmen from other countries as their consular representatives in the important treaty ports.

FOREIGN PRIVILEGES

The provision of extraterritoriality, intended to protect nationals from Chinese juridical authority and from irregular taxation, is key to the history of the treaty ports. Recognition of the foreigners' right of access to their own consular courts made it impractical for them to reside wherever they pleased throughout China. Their exemption from Chinese taxation, moreover, sharply distinguished the foreigners from their Chinese neighbors. An insular way of life became characteristic of the foreign treaty-port communities, which were separated by their distinct legal status as well as by language and culture from the vast majority of those who surrounded them. This was the case even though foreigners were numerically a tiny group in the treaty-port populations. In 1871, for instance, the proportion of British residents in Shanghai peaked at 1 percent of the city's population.

British residents dominated treaty-port affairs. The foreign population of the treaty ports was predominantly British before 1914. Thereafter, the number of Japanese residents grew to surpass the totals of all other groups combined. In Shanghai, for instance, about twenty thousand Japanese residents composed 70 percent of the city's total foreign population in 1931. Cultural differences, European racism, and the modest means of most members of the Japanese communities in China kept them separate from the Westerners, however, and the British thus continued to dominate treaty-port affairs into the 1940s.

Following a British Foreign Office decision to post a consul in each of the treaty ports, Britain's consular contingent in China expanded to become its largest worldwide. British consulates were established in each of the ports where the Imperial Maritime Customs (IMC) posted a commissioner. Created by the Qing government in the 1860s, the IMC also dominated treaty-port affairs. Staffed at the upper levels by foreigners, predominantly British nationals, the IMC functioned like a proxy government in the treaty ports, managing trade and remitting a large proportion of China's central revenue. Customs commissioners were agents of the Chinese government, and therefore were the social equals of the British consuls and

Shanghai Harbor, early 1900s. *British success in the Opium Wars forced the Chinese to open specific port cities, such as Shanghai, to Western business interests. Additional privileges accorded to Western residents of treaty ports, such as exemption from local laws and taxes, reinforced resentment among many citizens that China had become a colony for imperialist powers.* © **HULTON-DEUTSCH COLLECTION/ CORBIS**

consuls-general with whom they shared leadership in the various ports.

In a few of the treaty ports, "concessions" were established in agreements between foreign states and Chinese authorities. A concession was an area leased from the Chinese government to a foreign government. The foreign state then assumed responsibility for administration of the district and offered subleases of property within the concession area. In other cases, areas were set aside for foreign settlement by agreement between a group of foreigners and local or higher-level Chinese authorities. In the settlements, foreigners leased land directly from Chinese landholders. Over the years, these concessions and settlements tended to expand in size, usually following the resolution of an international dispute or a Chinese defeat at war.

SHANGHAI AND OTHER PORTS

In Shanghai, by far the most important of the treaty ports, there were no concessions in the strict sense. Originally separate, the British and American settlements were combined in 1863 into an International Settlement, which expanded to cover an area of 8.3 square miles by the 1930s. In 1900 British owners held long-term leases on about 90 percent of the land within the International Settlement area, and still held 78 percent of its land in 1930. Residents of the International Settlement paid rates to support services such as running water, a police force, and the maintenance of a public garden, which became notorious for refusing admission to the Chinese inhabitants of Shanghai (Bickers and Wasserstrom 1995). Meanwhile, the adjacent French Settlement of Shanghai, popularly known as a "concession," grew to cover an area of 3.9 square miles.

As formal privileges were extended through local practices, the major treaty ports became zones where foreigners enjoyed not only autonomy but also considerable authority over their Chinese neighbors. In Shanghai, the two foreign settlements each maintained autonomous courts as well as a police force. The Shanghai Municipal Council

(SMC), which administered the International Settlement, was like the oligarchic leadership of a small state. Its nine members were elected by about a hundred foreign rate-payers. During the 1920s, Chinese residents of the International Settlement protested against what they called "taxation without representation." Although well over 90 percent of the district's residents were Chinese, they were not represented in the SMC. Eventually, the SMC agreed to accept five Chinese representatives in an expanded council of fourteen members. Shanghai's French Settlement was a mini-monarchy; in that realm of 3.9 square miles, the French consul-general presided over a council of municipal affairs and was the chief judge in the district's court.

Shanghai, home base to more than half the foreigners resident in China, dominated the "treaty-port system" of Sino-foreign economic and political interaction (Fairbank 1953). As Shanghai developed into one of the world's most modern cities, it became an alluring model of efficient modernity and bourgeois ease to foreigners in the other treaty ports and also to the Chinese population. With the rise of popular Chinese nationalism after World War I (1914–1918), however, obstinate members of Shanghai's foreign communities reacted by exaggerating the legal and moral foundations of their privileges in China (Clifford 1991). Their attitude exacerbated the nationalists' resentment of foreign pretensions.

Tianjin was second in importance to Shanghai. In the multilateral agreement following the suppression of the Boxer movement in 1900, the nations that had sent armed forces against the uprising gained the right to post permanent garrisons in North China. Barracks were built in Tianjin to house thousands of foreign troops. By 1914, Britain, France, Japan, Italy, Russia, Austria, and Belgium had leased concession areas in Tianjin. The British concession of 1,000 acres was the most important of these, and British owners privately held a further 2,000 acres of land in other parts of the city.

Guangzhou (Canton) and Hankou (Hankow) were also major treaty ports. Proximity to Hong Kong strongly affected the economy of Guangzhou and was a consolation to foreign residents who were conscious of the slow pace of life in comparison to Shanghai. Westerners clustered in Shamian, a riverfront area separated from the city by a small canal. In the Yangzi (Chang) River port of Hankou, a series of foreign concessions stretched for three miles along its riverfront, and behind these zones a district with amenities such as a golf club and a racecourse was jointly managed by the foreign communities.

The other treaty ports were viewed as "outports" (Elder 1999). Consular and customs posts in these centers were staffed by junior and less-successful personnel, and steamship schedules were a major topic of conversation in

small communities of foreign residents. Chinese and foreign steamship companies connected the treaty ports, providing regular delivery of foreign-language newspapers published in Shanghai, and conveying passengers and mail between the outports and Shanghai, hub of the treaty-port system.

HISTORICAL SIGNIFICANCE

A few historians have sought to understand China's treaty ports as spaces where boundaries were blurred by migration and intercultural contact (Bickers and Henriot 2000). Nonetheless, the hierarchical nature of the treaty-port society should be stressed. Nationality was a key determinant of status. This is illustrated well by Japan's participation in the treaty-port system. In the eyes of both Chinese and Westerners, Japanese residents lacked the status of Europeans, despite the commensurate force of arms with which their country had earned treaty-power status. Priding themselves on superiority to the Chinese, the Japanese residents tended to resent this disregard. They also began to feel physically insecure as anti-Japanese sentiment swept China during the 1920s and 1930s. Tensions were exacerbated by the presence in the treaty ports of tens of thousands of Chinese and Koreans who were Japanese imperial subjects thanks to Japan's possession of Taiwan (1895) and annexation of Korea (1910). Either as sojourners in major centers or natives of ports such as Xiamen in Fujian, these Japanese subjects operated tax-exempt businesses and sometimes engaged in illicit activities under the protection of their extraterritorial status (Brooks 2000).

Although similar settlements existed elsewhere in Asia and beyond, none had precisely the same status as China's treaty ports. The treaty ports were an important aspect of a system of de facto colonial rule imposed on China by the treaty powers. As Chinese nationalism developed, particularly after World War I, nationalists viewed the treaty ports with resentment as sites of foreign privilege vis-à-vis the Chinese population and as symbols of external constraints on China's sovereignty.

The treaty ports may also be viewed in more positive ways. Their business and consular communities promoted technological innovation, such as the adoption of the telegraph during the 1870s, along with institutional changes in areas such as education, finance, and jurisprudence. The modernizing agency of the treaty ports was explicitly recognized in official statements in 1984, when China's central government granted special privileges in foreign trade and investment to fourteen coastal cities, all former treaty ports, as part of its program of economic reform and opening to the world. Despite the confined social life typically experienced by the foreign residents of the treaty ports, the larger centers offered broadened intellectual horizons to many Chinese. Shanghai in particular has been described as a cradle for the development of a modern Chinese civil society. Free from censorship and arrest in the foreign-administered districts of Shanghai, political dissidents could discuss and disseminate their ideas (Wagner 1995). Thus Shanghai became a center for militant radicalism, exemplified by the founding of the Chinese Communist Party in a member's house located in the French Settlement. Strong and ambivalent views about the nature of the treaty ports indicate that Chinese responses to their existence profoundly shaped the ideology and institutions of the modern Chinese nation-state.

THE END OF THE TREATY PORTS

A trend to dismantle the treaty-port system began with World War I, accelerating during the 1920s. After China joined the alliance against Germany, German and Austrian privileges in China were canceled and were not renewed following the war. In 1924 the newly established Soviet Union repudiated all czarist agreements and privileges in China. In February 1927 Britain relinquished its concessions in Nanjing, Hankou, and Jiujiang under pressure from the forces of the National Revolutionary Army. In January troops had besieged the British consulate in Nanjing, demanding the retrocession of "imperialist" privileges in China. Later in the year, the British-dominated Mixed Court of Shanghai's International settlement, where cases involving both Chinese and foreign residents had been tried since 1864, was dismantled. In 1928 the reestablished Republic of China in Nanjing announced that expired concessions to foreign governments would not be renewed and that all others would be either abolished or renegotiated. In response, the treaty powers agreed in principle that consular jurisdiction could not be above or separate from Chinese law. In 1930 Britain voluntarily gave up its concessions in Weihaiwei and Xiamen, and Belgium renounced its concession at Tianjin in 1931. Also in 1931, the French Consul-General in Shanghai announced rendition of the Mixed Court where he and his predecessors had judged cases involving Chinese residents of the French Settlement since 1869.

The treaty ports effectively lost their privileged status when the Pacific War began in December 1941. In that month, the Japanese extended their military occupation of China to the foreign settlement areas of Shanghai and other major ports, areas that had been neutral territory since the Sino-Japanese War began in 1937. The formal existence of the treaty ports ended in 1943, when Britain and the United States, in deference to China's status among the Allied Powers, notified China that they relinquished all privileges based on the "unequal treaties."

SEE ALSO *Extraterritoriality; Foreign Concessions, Settlements, and Leased Territories; Imperialism; Shanghai Mixed Court; Urban China: Cities and Urbanization, 1800–1949; Urban China: Organizing Principles of Cities; Urban China: Urban Planning since 1978.*

BIBLIOGRAPHY

Bickers, Robert, and Christian Henriot, eds. *New Frontiers: Imperialism's New Communities in East Asia, 1842–1953.* Manchester, U.K.: Manchester University Press, 2000.

Bickers, Robert, and Jeffrey N. Wasserstrom. Shanghai's "Dogs and Chinese Not Admitted" Sign: Legend, History, and Contemporary Symbol. *China Quarterly* 142 (1995): 444–466.

Brooks, Barbara. Japanese Colonial Citizenship in Treaty Port China: The Location of Koreans and Japanese in the Imperial Order. In *New Frontiers: Imperialism's New Communities in East Asia, 1842–1953,* eds. Robert Bickers and Christian Henriot, 109–124. Manchester, U.K.: Manchester University Press, 2000.

Clifford, Nicholas R. *Spoilt Children of Empire: Westerners in Shanghai and the Chinese Revolution of the 1920s.* Hanover, NH: University Press of New England, 1991.

Elder, Chris, ed. *China's Treaty Ports: Half Love and Half Hate.* New York: Oxford University Press, 1999.

Fairbank, John K. *Trade and Diplomacy on the China Coast: The Opening of the Treaty Ports, 1842–1854.* Cambridge, MA: Harvard University Press, 1953.

Feuerwerker, Albert. The Foreign Presence in China. In *The Cambridge History of China,* Vol. 12: *Republican China, 1912–1949,* Pt. 1, 129–208. Cambridge: Cambridge University Press, 1983.

Horowitz, Richard S. International Law and State Transformation in China, Siam, and the Ottoman Empire during the Nineteenth Century. *Journal of World History* 13, 4 (2005): 445–486.

Osterhammel, Jürgen. Semi-colonialism and Informal Empire in 20th-Century China. In *Imperialism and After: Continuities and Discontinuities,* eds. Wolfgang J. Mommsen and Jürgen Osterhammel, 290–341. London: Allen and Unwin, 1986.

Osterhammel, Jürgen. Britain and China, 1842–1914. In *The Oxford History of the British Empire,* Vol. 3: *The Nineteenth Century,* ed. Andrew Porter, 146–169. New York: Oxford University Press, 1999.

Peattie, Mark. Japanese Treaty Port Settlements in China, 1895–1937. In *Japanese Informal Empire in China, 1895–1937,* eds. Peter Duus, Ramon Myers, and Mark Peattie, chap. 6, 166–209. Stanford, CA: Stanford University Press, 1989.

Tyau Min-ch'ien Tuk Zung. (Diao Minqian) The Legal Obligations Arising Out of Treaty Relations between China and Other States. Ph.D. diss., University of London, 1917. Taibei: Cheng-wen, 1966.

Wagner, Rudolf G. The Role of the Foreign Community in the Chinese Public Sphere. *China Quarterly* 142 (1995): 423–443.

Emily M. Hill

TROTSKYISM

Of the dozens of Trotskyist organizations formed outside Russia after 1927, when Leon Trotsky (1879–1940) drafted his Programme of the United Opposition in the

Soviet Union, the Chinese Left Opposition was among the largest. Trotskyism emerged in Russia after 1923, when Trotsky confronted Joseph Stalin (1879–1953) by calling for party democracy and industrialization in the Soviet Union, an end to the Soviet alliance with conservative trade union leaders in Britain, and the withdrawal of the Chinese Communist Party (CCP) from the Guomindang (Nationalist Party). Communists everywhere were shocked by the Guomindang's brutal repression of the CCP in 1927 and were susceptible to Trotsky's criticism of Stalin's China policy. In China itself, the defeat alienated hundreds from the CCP's pro-Stalin leadership.

While Trotsky argued that the Chinese Revolution had been defeated, Stalin insisted that victory was within sight. Chen Duxiu (1879–1942), principal founder of the CCP, agreed instinctively with Trotsky. Some of his supporters, including Peng Shuzhi (1896–1983), Yin Kuan (1897–1967), and Zheng Chaolin (1901–1998), became Trotskyists. By mid-1928, at least 200 of the Chinese studying in Moscow were also Trotskyists. In late 1929, scores were imprisoned or deported.

Chinese Trotskyists who returned from Moscow in 1928 initially distrusted Chen Duxiu, whom they associated with the 1927 defeat. In any case, neither Chen nor his followers were ripe for an approach until early 1929, when Trotskyist documents first reached them. The documents appealed to Chen (1) because they blamed the 1927 defeat on Stalin, and (2) because they supported Chen's belief that the revolution was in a trough. In a sense, Chen's Trotskyist conversion was less a transfer of allegiance to yet another foreign ideology than an assertion of national independence. In 1922 Chen had worried not only about entering the Guomindang but even about joining the Comintern, for he thought the Chinese should make their own revolution.

Chen's followers accepted Trotsky's argument that the best way to revive the revolution was by campaigning for a constituent assembly. Observers were surprised at this turn, for Trotskyism was considered an extremist form of communism. However, it was above all Trotsky's advocacy of democratic slogans for China after 1927 that attracted Chen, who remained a radical democrat at heart.

In November 1929, Chen and his supporters were expelled from the CCP and declared themselves Trotskyists. Other secret Oppositionists began trickling back into China. In January 1931 Trotsky wrote urging them to join forces. In May, four groups (claiming 483 members) united under Chen and founded the journal *Huahuo* (Spark). However, within weeks most were in prison, where Chen joined them in 1932.

In 1934 the South African Frank Glass (1901–1987) helped restore Trotskyist organization in Shanghai, and in 1935 Wang Fanxi (1907–2002) was freed from jail and revived the Central Committee. (However, Chen Duxiu stayed aloof.) In 1941 the Trotskyists split, into a group around Wang that opposed supporting the Pacific War, and another around Peng Shuzhi that backed the Guomindang's participation in it. Some Trotskyists set up guerrilla bases but were destroyed by the CCP or the Japanese.

In late 1948, on the eve of Mao's victory, Peng Shuzhi's group went abroad, while Zheng Chaolin and others stayed on to organize a workers' movement. In 1952 around 1,000 Trotskyists were imprisoned, some until 1979. Those who had slipped abroad tried to keep the movement going, but they lacked credibility, resources, and even an audience. Later, however, interest in Trotskyism revived in Hong Kong and the diaspora. Trotskyist publications included *Shiyue pinglun* (October Review), *Zhanxun* (Combat Bulletin), and *Xinmiao* (New Sprouts).

The Trotskyists' early impact on the CCP was not negligible. Their supporters included Chen Duxiu, the CCP's main founder and general secretary, a score of senior veterans, and a third or more of the CCP's Moscow students. In 1931 an even bigger conversion seemed possible with the CCP in political disarray. However, their campaign to supplant the pro-Stalin leadership failed because of the CCP's disciplinary measures against them, their own lack of resources, and the anti-Trotskyist prejudice imported to China by Wang Ming (1904–1974), Stalin's main supporter in the CCP, whose group dominated the party from 1931 to 1934.

The Trotskyists shared the Marxist view that peasants play no independent role in politics. However, China's urban proletariat was not only tiny but disabled after 1937 by war and occupation. White terror confronted the Trotskyists in the cities, Red terror in the villages. They were tested more in jail than in struggle. By 1945, when the workers' movement revived, the political focus had switched to the villages and the battlefield.

Through their democratic critique of Stalinism and their antibureaucratic views, the Trotskyists became metaphors incarnate for unresolved problems of Chinese society and politics. For a while, Wang Fanxi and Peng Shuzhi were able to comment from exile on developments, but their last important writings preceded Mao's death. Even so, people interested in reform in the 1980s valued Chen Duxiu's tradition of openness, while such dissidents as Wang Xizhe, Chen Fu, and Shi Huasheng were attracted by Trotskyist theses on socialist democracy.

Chinese Trotskyism is best known today for its literary associations. Whereas many early CCP writers died or left the party, the Trotskyists continued to support Shanghai's cultural movement. After Chen Duxiu, their best-known writers were Wang Duqing (1898–1940) and Wang Shiwei (1906–1947), who though never actually members of any Trotskyist organization were very close to the Trotskyists on many questions and completely agreed with Trotsky's polemic against the idea of "proletarian literature." Until 1931 the Trotskyists published far more Marxist literature than the official party. It was mainly through their endeavor that Marxism in its classical form reached China in the 1930s.

In the 1980s, mainland scholars started to lift the curtain on Chinese Trotskyism, revealing a complex, original political experiment. However, the Trotskyists have not been formally rehabilitated.

SEE ALSO *Chen Duxiu; Chinese Marxism: Overview; Wang Shiwei.*

BIBLIOGRAPHY

Benton, Gregor. *China's Urban Revolutionaries: Explorations in the History of Chinese Trotskyism, 1921–1952.* Atlantic Highlands, NJ, and London: Humanities Press, 1996.

Kagan, Richard. The Chinese Trotskyist Movement and Ch'en Tu-hsiu: Culture, Revolution, and Polity. Ph.D. diss., University of Pennsylvania, Philadelphia, 1969.

Peng Shuzhi. *L'envol du communisme en Chine: Mémoires de Peng Shuzhi.* Ed. Claude Cadart and Cheng Yingxiang. Paris: Gallimard, 1983.

Tang Baolin. *Zhongguo Tuopai shi* [A history of Chinese Trotskyism]. Taibei: Dongda Tushu Gongsi, 1994.

Wang Fanxi (Wang Fan-hsi). *Memoirs of a Chinese Revolutionary.* Trans. Gregor Benton. New York: Columbia University Press, 1991. Rev. ed. of *Chinese Revolutionary, Memoirs, 1919–1949.* Oxford: Oxford University Press, 1980.

Zheng Chaolin. *An Oppositionist for Life: Memoirs of the Chinese Revolutionary Zheng Chaolin.* Ed. and trans. Gregor Benton. Atlantic Highlands, NJ: Humanities Press, 1997.

Gregor Benton

TUNG CHEE-HWA

SEE *Hong Kong: Government and Politics since 1997.*

THE TUNGAN REBELLION, 1862–1878

SEE *Muslim Uprisings.*

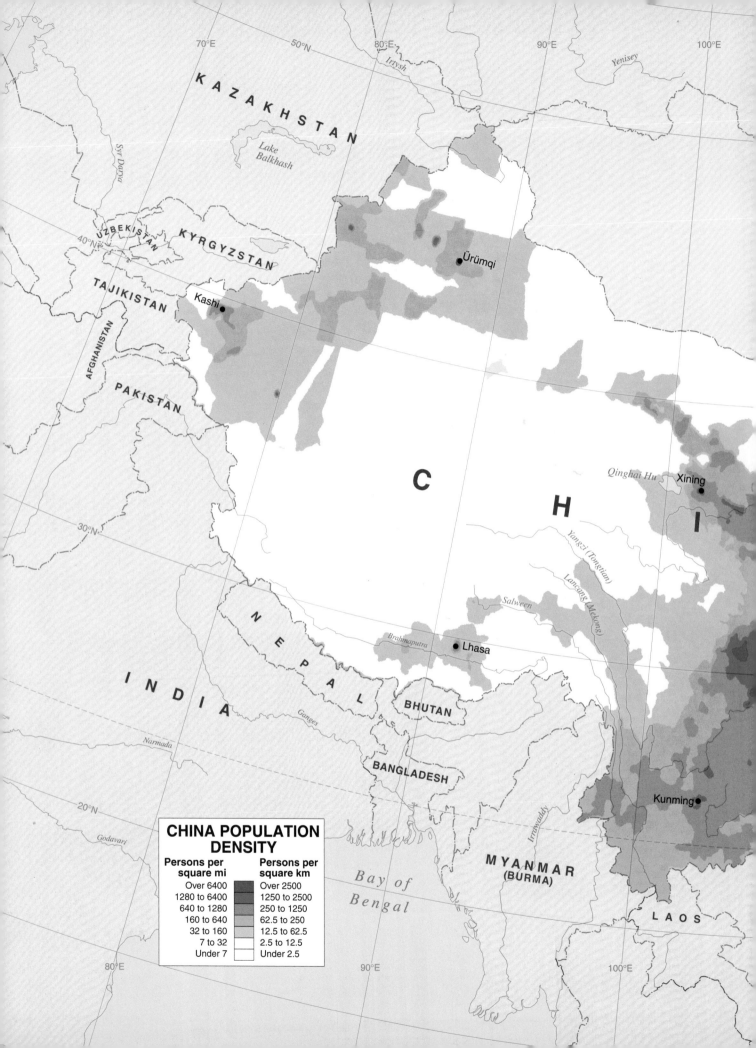

KAZAKHSTAN

Irtysh

Yenisey

*Lake
Balkhash*

UZBEKISTAN

KYRGYZSTAN

Syr Darya

40°N

TAJIKISTAN

Ürümqi

Kashi

AFGHANISTAN

PAKISTAN

C

H

I

Qinghai Hu

Xining

30°N

Yangzi (Tongtian)

Lancang (Mekong)

Salween

N E P A L

Brahmaputra

Lhasa

Ganges

I N D I A

BHUTAN

Narmada

BANGLADESH

Godavari

M Y A N M A R
(BURMA)

20°N

Irrawaddy

CHINA POPULATION DENSITY

Persons per square mi	Persons per square km
Over 6400	Over 2500
1280 to 6400	1250 to 2500
640 to 1280	250 to 1250
160 to 640	62.5 to 250
32 to 160	12.5 to 62.5
7 to 32	2.5 to 12.5
Under 7	Under 2.5

*Bay of
Bengal*

L A O S

Kunming

80°E

90°E

100°E